Ipswich Town
The Modern Era
– A Complete Record –

Ipswich Town: The Modern Era – A Complete Record	1-874287-43-0
Stoke City: The Modern Era – A Complete Record	1-874287-39-2
Stoke City: 101 Golden Greats	1-874287-46-5
Plymouth Argyle: 101 Golden Greats	1-874287-47-3
West Ham: The Elite Era – A Complete Record	1-874287-31-7
Bristol City: The Modern Era – A Complete Record	1-874287-28-7
Colchester Utd: Graham to Whitton – A Complete Record	1-874287-27-9
Halifax Town: From Ball to Lillis – A Complete Record	1-874287-26-0
Portsmouth: From Tindall to Ball – A Complete Record	1-874287-25-2
Portsmouth: Champions of England – 1948-49 & 1949-50	1-874287-38-4
Coventry City: The Elite Era – A Complete Record	1-874287-51-1
Coventry City: An Illustrated History	1-874287-36-8
Luton Town: The Modern Era – A Complete Record	1-874287-05-8
Luton Town: An Illustrated History	1-874287-37-6
Watford: An Illustrated History	1-874287-49-X
Hereford United: The League Era – A Complete Record	1-874287-18-X
Cambridge United: The League Era – A Complete Record	1-874287-32-5
Peterborough United: The Modern Era – A Complete Record	1-874287-33-3
Peterborough United: A Who's Who	1-874287-48-1
Wimbledon: From Southern League to Premiership	1-874287-09-0
Wimbledon: From Wembley to Selhurst	1-874287-20-1
Wimbledon: The Premiership Years	1-874287-40-6
Aberdeen: The European Era – A Complete Record	1-874287-11-2
The Story of the Rangers 1873-1923	1-874287-16-3
The Story of the Celtic 1888-1938	1-874287-15-5
History of the Everton Football Club 1878-1928	1-874287-14-7
The Romance of the Wednesday 1867-1926	1-874287-17-1
Red Dragons in Europe – A Complete Record	1-874287-01-5
The Book of Football: A History to 1905-06	1-874287-13-9
England: The Quest for the World Cup – A Complete Record	1-897850-40-9
Scotland: The Quest for the World Cup – A Complete Record	1-897850-50-6
Ireland: The Quest for the World Cup – A Complete Record	1-897850-80-8

Ipswich Town

THE MODERN ERA
— A Complete Record —

Series Editor: Clive Leatherdale

Rob Hadgraft

DESERT ISLAND BOOKS

First Published in 2001

DESERT ISLAND BOOKS LIMITED
89 Park Street, Westcliff-on-Sea, Essex SS0 7PD
United Kingdom
www.desertislandbooks.com

British Library Cataloguing-in-Publication Data
A catalogue record for this book is available from the British Library

ISBN   1-874287-43-0

Printed in Great Britain
by
The Bath Press

Photographs in this book are reproduced by kind permission of:
The East Anglian Daily Times, Roger Wash, Jim Brown

Contents

Preface

It is a great privilege for me to be the Chairman of Ipswich Town Football Club. As I delved into this fascinating book to recall so many glorious moments in the past it only underlined for me what a unique club we have. The achievements have been extraordinary, considering our size and limited resources, and yet under Sir Alf Ramsey, Bobby Robson, Bobby Ferguson, John Lyall and now George Burley, the Club has still thrived at the highest level of football in this country. This book, *Ipswich Town – The Modern Era* provides a nostalgic journey through the decades for all Ipswich Town fans as memories come flooding back of favourite moments, players and goals.

My own first game as a spectator at Portman Road was in April 1965 when we beat Leyton Orient 3-2. I remember not quite understanding why others around me were so intrigued to see Andy Nelson, our former Championship-winning captain, playing for the opposition! Nevertheless, we won and I was hooked. A fan for life!

Today we have a new team who have all played their part in our exhilarating return to the top flight of English football, delivering in the last twelve months one of the brightest times in the Club's history. It is a very special time for all who are associated with and love Ipswich Town: in my time the pride and passion, which goes with our badge, has never been stronger.

In 1995, after the misery of relegation, we clearly defined our objectives and saw promotion by the year 2000 as being realistically achievable. Everything we have done since has been geared towards the Premiership and continuous improvement in all aspects of the club, both on and off the pitch.

We have an excellent manager in George Burley, deservedly awarded Manager of the Year by his peers as well as the prestigious Carling Premiership Manager of the Year. It has been 30 years since George Burley first joined Ipswich Town and the combination of his determination and love for this club has been instrumental in elevating Ipswich Town back to the Premiership. Who will ever forget that most magical of days at Wembley in May 2000.

It has been twenty years since the club lifted the UEFA Cup and I am thrilled for our supporters that we are back in Europe, something that was felt by many to be an impossible dream only a few years ago.

Our strategy has so far delivered excellent progress on virtually all fronts, in particular our team of multi-talented players, many of whom are now regulars for international call-ups (like the old days). Our record for discipline has been unparalleled, with the team taking the Fair Play League in their first year back in the Premiership. Awards continued off the pitch, amongst which our head groundsman Alan Ferguson was awarded the Premier League Pitch of the Season.

While not always so popular, firm financial management has also been a cornerstone of our strong revival. Our policy has been to commit every single penny that we can reasonably budget towards achieving our objective of establishing Ipswich Town as one of the best clubs in the Premiership. The decision to invest in our Academy, when finances were tight in the First Division, has also paid dividends, as our future is the talent that flourishes beneath the first team.

All in all, it has been a phenomenal team effort and I am fortunate to be surrounded by such talented and committed staff. I hope you enjoy your trip down 'memory lane' as much as I did when I read this excellent book.

With best wishes
DAVID SHEEPSHANKS
Chairman
Ipswich Town FC

Author's Note

The remarkable recent history of Ipswich Town demanded to be set out in detail and I was delighted to embark on the task of adding another volume to the Desert Island Soccer History series.

The first half of this book tells how Town emerged from the shadows in 1972 to enjoy ten years as one of the nation's leading sides, only to slide back into obscurity when the manager left to take charge of England. It was the second time this had happened to the club in twenty years!

The latter section of the book is statistical, featuring a complete record of the last 30 seasons and incorporating 50-word summaries of every Town match (around 1,500 in all) played during that period. The book runs to at least 175,000 words in total and I trust it will jog memories, settle a few arguments and, hopefully, provide many readers with fresh information.

Although my memory provided some of the colour and anecdotal material, most of the hard facts had to be obtained through hours of research. In this respect, I often referred to the words of local journalists Tony Garnett, Dave Allard, Neal Manning and Mel Henderson. The work of this quartet was of invaluable assistance and its integrity is underpinned by a combined experience of around 120 years of writing about Ipswich Town!

I also consulted books such as *The Men Who Made The Town* and *In Quest of Glory* (both by John Eastwood and Tony Moyes), *Suffolk Punch* (Tony Moyes), *The Beat* (Kevin Beattie), *Time on the Grass* (Bobby Robson) and *Images of Sport: Ipswich Town* (Tony Garnett).

I am grateful for the assistance of staff at the Newspaper Library in Colindale, to Sharon Boswell and editor Terry Hunt at the *East Anglian Daily Times*, and Paul Browes, who provided an expert read-through of my draft manuscript. The support, guidance and advice of publisher Clive Leatherdale – including his words of warning at the outset – brought into focus the need to strive for excellence in a project such as this. Although I have run several marathons, they were nothing compared to the stamina required to prepare this book!

In addition to an agreement with the *East Anglian Daily Times* regarding use of photos, I was also fortunate to be able to plunder the picture collections of fellow-authors Jim Brown and Roger Wash. Finally, grateful thanks to my wife Katie, for providing unstinting encouragement and, occasionally, technical support too!

ROB HADGRAFT

Introduction

For many years the development of Ipswich Town FC was stifled by the stubborn refusal of its administrators to follow the example of others and turn professional.

The club's roots can be traced back to 1878 when a group of enthusiasts formed Ipswich Association Football Club. There was huge interest and potential in those early days, yet it took almost 60 years for the club to throw off the shackles of amateurism and make genuine progress.

The intervention of charismatic former Scots Guards captain John 'Ivan' Cobbold in the mid-1930s finally forced the issue and persuaded the idealists to emerge from the shadows. Once that big step was taken, a reservoir of energy was released and the club surged forward in leaps and bounds. Just nineteen full seasons after turning professional, Town had won the championships of the Southern League, Division Three (South), Division Two, and, unbelievably, Division One. Arguably, only the more recent rise of Wimbledon FC could compare with such an achievement.

The round-ball lovers of Ipswich had started their organised games on the Broom Hill fields beside Norwich Road in 1878. Less than a year later they amalgamated with Ipswich Football Club, a rugby outfit who used the Portman Road ground. In 1893 the rugby section folded, leaving Ipswich Town concentrating solely on soccer. But when the Southern League was formed shortly afterwards, the club spurned an invitation to join, steadfastly sticking to its 'play for fun' ideals.

After war broke out in 1914, the War Office commandeered Portman Road, as a result of which the footballing affairs of the club were put on hold until the ground was relinquished by the authorities in 1920.

As the 1920s drew to a close, professionalism was still being resisted, although the club did hire Edwin Dutton from South Shields as a professional trainer. Town's first supporters club was formed in 1930 amid mounting pressure on the football club to seek a higher standard of football after several comfortable Southern Amateur League title wins.

The turning point came in 1935 when Capt Cobbold – whose sons Johnny and Patrick would later become club chairmen – took over as president. While he was away in Canada, a meeting in the town decided professional football should be introduced via the formation of a new club, Ipswich United FC. The new organisation invited discussions on the subject with Ipswich Town FC.

But the proud men of Ipswich Town, after their own meeting at the Town Hall the following week, decided to remain a separate organisation and stick to amateurism. On his return, Capt Cobbold was asked his views. Unlike his committee colleagues, he strongly supported the idea of professionalism and quickly instigated further talks which led to the original decision to remain amateur being scrapped. At the end of this rather shambolic episode, Ipswich Town Football Club Limited was formed from the Town and United organisations and the area was soon buzzing with football fever.

Capt Cobbold became chairman and ex-Irish international Mick O'Brien was named manager. The club was welcomed into the Southern League for 1936-37, major improvement work began on the ground, and O'Brien began recruiting players.

Town cruised to the title at the first attempt but lost their manager due to family problems and replaced him with Manchester United's Scott Duncan. In 1938, with a first and third place in the Southern League to their credit, Town applied for Football League status.

Capt Cobbold wagered with his manager that Town would not succeed, but Duncan won the bet when it was announced that Town had gained 36 votes, beating re-election candidates Walsall (34) and Gillingham (28).

The big League baptism came in August 1938, when visitors Southend were despatched from Portman Road with a 4-2 beating, the opening goal coming after less than two minutes. That first season saw the club finish a creditable seventh in Division Three (South), but further progress was halted when the outbreak of World War II suspended League football for seven years.

The break didn't dim enthusiasm in Suffolk and resumption of normal service saw Town improve to sixth place in 1946-47. The following season witnessed a new record crowd of 24,361 for the visit of QPR and an impressive fourth place in the table.

After several unremarkable years, Town raced to the Third Division (South) championship of 1953-54 but found themselves ill-equipped for the rigours of the Second Division. The club's first relegation was confirmed in April 1955 and shortly afterwards Scott Duncan quit as manager.

His place was taken by former Spurs and England full-back Alf Ramsey, 35, a man whose demeanour as a thoughtful and intelligent footballer had long marked him out as manager material. In Ramsey's first season Town narrowly missed promotion back to Division Two, scoring 106 goals. However, twelve months later, in a thrilling finish, the club won the Third Division (South) title in May 1957, pipping Torquay on goal-average, with neighbours Colchester just a point behind. Suffolk-born Ted Phillips was a revelation, his cannonball shooting making him the League's leading scorer with 46, including five hat-tricks.

John Cobbold, 29, succeeded cousin Alistair as chairman and oversaw consolidation in the Second Division over the following three seasons. Ramsey discovered another key part of his jigsaw in centre-half Andy Nelson and then, prior to the silver jubilee season of 1960-61, recruited Roy Stephenson for the key role of supplying ammunition to strikers Phillips and Ray Crawford.

Town hit their stride early and powered to the championship, with their two front-men hitting 70 goals between them. Promotion was clinched in style with a 4-0 mauling of Sunderland, and East Anglia made the First Division for the first time.

Gloomy pundits tipped Town for a quick return, but manager Ramsey was happy with his squad, even though they took a while to adjust. The football world started taking notice when five games were won in succession, including a 6-2 thrashing of cultured Burnley. A genuine title challenge didn't really seem likely, even though the club slowly crept up to become part of a five-horse race for the championship by March.

With six games to go, Town found themselves on top – only for a 0-5 hammering at Old Trafford to follow. Such a calamity seemed to confirm that the upstarts from Suffolk would not hold their nerve over the final weeks. But once it became a two-horse race with Burnley, it was their Lancashire rivals who cracked, and Town nervelessly won three and drew two in a hectic closing spell of five games in fifteen days.

On the final day, 28,932 squeezed into Portman Road to see Town beat Aston Villa 2-0. After the final whistle news filtered through that Burnley had only drawn – the impossible had happened and Town were English champions.

They had become the first club in the twentieth century to win the title at the first attempt. Five of the squad had won championship medals for three different divisions, and this friendly little outpost would now represent England in the European Cup!

The element of surprise had definitely helped get results, as had an absence of injuries. Opponents were baffled by Ramsey's innovative deeper role for wingers, and old-fashioned defences were simply not equipped or flexible enough to cope. Ramsey, of course, would later develop this style to create the 'wingless wonders' who won the 1966 World Cup.

The first team to successfully thwart Town's unique style were Tottenham, who pulled their full-backs infield to outnumber Crawford and Phillips, while their wing-halves stifled the supply line from Town's 'wingers'. Spurs won the 1962 Charity Shield 5-1 – and the rest of Division One looked on and took careful note.

During 1962-63 the decline set in, with Town only recording five home wins all season. They slid ingloriously down the table, suffered a glut of injuries and went perilously close to relegation. The European Cup adventure featured a 10-0 win over Maltese side Floriana, but ended at the hands of AC Milan, who won the trophy.

During the course of that unhappy season Ramsey was named successor to Walter Winterbottom as England boss and the search for a replacement at Portman Road brought in Geordie folk-hero Jackie Milburn. Inheriting an ageing squad, Milburn's first season was a disaster. Town finished bottom, conceding 121 goals. The defensive calamities included ten conceded at Fulham, nine at Stoke, seven at home to Manchester United and six at Bolton, Arsenal, Liverpool and Spurs.

The pressure took its toll on Milburn and he resigned after the new season in Division Two opened with four further defeats and a draw. With Town now at the bottom of the Second Division, the situation clearly needed someone with a firm and more ruthless approach. Disciplinarian Bill McGarry was summoned to stop the rot. He introduced a new training regime, turned the club upside down, and results soon changed for the better, despite his military-style approach leading to disquiet among some players. Popular Ray Crawford returned to the club in 1966 and was a key figure as Town took the Second Division title two years later, pipping QPR by a point after an exciting run-in.

McGarry then shocked the club by deciding that Ipswich could never fulfil his long-term ambitions, and moved to Wolves just four months after the return to Division One. The board offered the vacant manager's job to Frank O'Farrell, who turned it down. Rumours that Bob Stokoe and Jimmy Scoular were next in line came to nothing. Interviews were lined up for Billy Bingham and Bobby Robson, but when the former withdrew, the recently-sacked Fulham boss Robson was the last name on the short-list.

So began a new era at Portman Road as Robson, still under 40 and working without a contract, threw himself into the task with great enthusiasm and determination.

He manfully overcame dissent in the playing ranks and on the terraces, and managed to sustain the club in the top flight despite a real struggle in his first two full seasons. The board remained patient and kept faith, providing Robson with the time and freedom to build a squad and a youth system that would provide firm foundations for the years ahead.

Chapter One

Heading for the Summit
1971-1977

LEAGUE DIVISION 1   **1971-72**
Division 1   13th
League Cup   2nd Round
FA Cup   4th Round

After two seasons spent hovering close to the Division One trap-door, the summer of 1971 saw renewed optimism at Portman Road. This was due to a transformation of the stadium, and also the signing of a highly rated international winger from 'foreign' shores.

In less than fifteen weeks, all told, construction of the huge Portman Stand transformed a homely ground into an arena befitting a top-flight team and raised the capacity by nearly 20% to 37,000. The new edifice replaced a quaint wooden stand often referred to as the 'chicken run', parts of which were more than 60 years old. It was given another lease of life by being transported across town to Foxhall Stadium to house spectators at Ipswich Speedway.

The new stand was officially opened on the first day of the 1971-72 season by England manager Sir Alf Ramsey, who had led the club to their 1962 League championship success and who still lived in the town. Also unveiled that day was new boy Bryan Hamilton, recruited after impressive displays in a Northern Ireland shirt in recent Home Internationals. Manager Bobby Robson paid Irish part-timers Linfield a reported £30,000 for a young man who until then had been an electronics engineer with the Ministry of Defence.

Hamilton's arrival took on extra significance due to the fact that he was the first import since Jimmy Robertson and Frank Clarke had arrived in March 1970, seventeen months earlier. The consensus was that Hamilton might need time to settle, however, and that further new signings would probably be necessary if the club was to harbour serious hopes of avoiding another weary winter of scrapping clear of the lower placings in Division One.

Those new signings arrived in the shape of another Northern Ireland international, centre-half Allan Hunter of Oldham, four weeks into the season, and former Leeds striker Rod Belfitt for £50,000 in early November. The latter's instant impact was a shot in the arm for a febrile attack, but it was the capture of Hunter that was to prove one of Robson's shrewdest ever deals at £80,000.

Four goalless draws in the opening six games represented a solid but unspectacular start to the campaign and it was no real surprise when restless home fans began to barrack Robson, especially after he'd substituted a leg-weary Mick Hill in a League Cup-tie with Manchester United. The unrest outraged chairman John Cobbold, although apparently did not faze the young manager.

Cobbold's dismay was born of an old-fashioned sense of fair play and was typical of his stoical approach to football matters. His often-repeated words 'the only crisis at this club will be when the wine in the boardroom runs out' may have been a throwaway line to amuse reporters, but summed up beautifully his perceived outlook on life. At the time, however, it hid considerable anger that his hard-working lieutenant should come in for ill-conceived criticism.

Some observers felt that Cobbold and his board stuck with Robson largely through inertia and a dislike for change (he was only Town's sixth manager since they turned professional in 1936). With hindsight, this view becomes discredited as the time and patience Robson was afforded ultimately made it possible for him to create something really special at Portman Road.

After nightmare experiences in charge at Vancouver Royals and Fulham, Robson must have felt Mr Cobbold's attitude and words of encouragement were like manna from heaven. After the Manchester United game, the board coughed up the money for Hunter, but the barrackers were not appeased by the new man, nor by Robson's dropping of David Best, Geoff Hammond and Peter Morris, even though the changes did spark a slight improvement in October.

Pre-Christmas victories proved hard to come by. Typical of Town's luck was the bizarre goal conceded at Arsenal when diminutive 20-year-old keeper Laurie Sivell dropped a straightforward header from John Radford, and then flailed about trying to recover, only to knock the ball into his own net past a horrified Ian Collard on the goal-line. It was a comic own-goal, and one of several high-profile mistakes by the young custodian, who to his credit often gamely cancelled out his blunders by pulling off remarkable saves.

Belfitt's arrival temporarily brought the smiles back to Portman Road. He galvanised the club on his debut by helping fashion an equaliser and then scoring the winner after Wolves had sneaked ahead through wily Derek Dougan. A week later Belfitt scored a fine goal at Crystal Palace to prove it had been no flash in the pan.

A defence that looked solid, particularly after Hunter settled down, then crumbled spectacularly at Bramall Lane when much-improved Sheffield United coasted to a 7-0 win. Nevertheless, Robson stayed loyal to his new-look line-up and they rewarded him by holding championship-chasers Liverpool to a goalless draw.

Poor Sivell promptly had another nightmare afternoon in a 0-4 drubbing at Manchester City and had no complaints about being taken out of the firing line, openly admitting that he'd lost some of his confidence. The more experienced David Best was recalled and kept a clean sheet when Manchester United were back in town.

Despite the short-term boost of Belfitt's arrival, goals failed to come. Nowhere was this more evident than at Stamford Bridge, when Town couldn't muster a goal against the grinning figure of Chelsea's David Webb, who played the entire 90 minutes as an emergency keeper, due to Bonetti, Phillips and Sherwood all being unavailable. It was Town's fifth game in a row without scoring.

Robson doggedly persevered with basically the same line-up, even after a two-goal lead against bottom club West Brom was tossed away on New Year's Day. He was rewarded by a run of four unbeaten games, which came to an abrupt end with a somewhat predictable exit from the FA Cup at the hands of Second Division Birmingham.

League form improved in the early weeks of the New Year and after sharing six goals in a muddy thriller at Stoke, there was further excitement in the home clash with Arsenal when twenty players were involved in a brawl after feisty midfielder Colin Viljoen challenged visiting keeper Bob Wilson. Mild-mannered winger Mick Lambert was the only outfield player not to get involved.

By the start of March, Town were picking up enough points to be reasonably confident about preserving their top-flight status for another year. However, any complacency after the somewhat comfortable win at lowly Nottingham Forest was misplaced, because a run of four games without victory soon saw the worry beads out again. That man David Webb returned to haunt the club, turning out at Portman Road this time as an emergency striker and bagging two early goals for Chelsea.

In this season of infuriating inconsistency, the tide finally turned in Town's favour in April when four wins and a draw ensured safety by some distance. Young Trevor Whymark, born deep in rural East Anglia, was called into action and looked a fine prospect over the closing weeks. He scored four crucial goals, including one against Manchester City, which wrecked their championship hopes.

A finishing position of thirteenth could be considered a highly satisfactory outcome after the struggles of the previous two campaigns, and the optimism of August returned in April, this time fortified by the knowledge that there was considerable talent emerging from the junior ranks. Indeed, the youth development side of the club looked stronger than ever before and Robson's early groundwork was about to bear fruit.

Match of the Season 1971-72
Ipswich 2 Manchester City 1

Division 1, 18 April 1972

Manchester City's title dream was wrecked by a superb Ipswich display, arguably their best since returning to the top flight in 1968. City went into the game one point off the top, but having to win as they had fewer games left than their rivals. They ultimately failed to win five of their eight-game run-in, having earlier looked favourites for the title. Fingers were pointing at coach Malcolm Allison, who'd tinkered with a winning side in order to accommodate expensive signing Rodney Marsh. Hence it was a nervous outfit that came to Portman Road to face a Town side now free from relegation fears.

Although a work-to-rule on the railways affected the size of the crowd, there was still an above-average turnout and a cup-tie atmosphere under the Portman Road floodlights. Even City's elder statesman, Joe Mercer, marvelled afterwards at the passion shown for a match that meant relatively little to the Suffolk side.

Town played without inhibition and more than matched the celebrated opposition. The breakthrough came after 31 minutes. Mick Lambert on the left, retrieved a cross-shot from flying Scot Jimmy Robertson on the right and fed the ball to Peter Morris, who teed up Trevor Whymark. With his back to goal, the youngster controlled the ball, swivelled, and smashed it high past Ron Healy.

A desperate Allison made tactical switches, but when he advanced to the touchline he was rebuked by referee Homewood, for Allison had recently incurred a lifetime touchline ban. Just before half-time Town enjoyed a slice of luck when Summerbee's shot was diverted over the crossbar by Colin Viljoen's hand. The ref ignored penalty appeals and gave the home side a free-kick instead.

City finally profited from a howler by Laurie Sivell. The smallest keeper in the League leaped to catch Tony Book's corner under pressure, but let the ball slip and Summerbee chested it over the line.

Roared on by their fans, Ipswich conjured a winning goal through an unlikely source. Full-back Colin Harper sent Lambert down the left and steamed forward looking for the return. Lambert sent over a perfect cross which Harper headed home off a post. It was only the second goal of his career and Harper milked the moment, racing to the Ipswich fans and pretending to fling his shirt at them – a reference to a match three days earlier when he'd torn his shirt off in disgust after being sent off against Sheffield United.

For City, with just one game left, the title had gone. Even victory over Derby proved insufficient. Derby beat Liverpool to pip them.

LEAGUE DIVISION 1	**1972-73**
Division 1	4th
League Cup	3rd Round
FA Cup	4th Round
Texaco Cup	Winners

Team changes, some enforced and others tactical, saw Ipswich make a bright start to the new campaign and then maintain a level of consistency throughout the subsequent eight months. From mid-October onwards, Town were never out of the top ten, and for much of that time, firmly established in the top four.

The most notable summer departure was Jimmy Robertson, who left for Stoke saying he needed a change. Robson hoped to replace him with Blackpool's Micky Burns, but when an offer of £100,000 was rejected it was left to home-grown Mick Lambert to assume Robertson's mantle. With Frank Clarke injured, there was a golden opportunity for the promising Trevor Whymark to stake a claim for a regular spot. But the two most instantly productive moves by the manager were the introduction of teenager Kevin Beattie for his debut on the opening day and the conversion of Ulster raider Bryan Hamilton into a probing midfielder.

Early results delighted Robson, particularly the opening-day win at Manchester United, where Beattie replaced the suspended Colin Harper and made a debut of rare quality and assurance for one so raw. The side showed they were made of the right stuff at Leeds, coming back from a goal down no fewer than three times and they sat proudly in second place by mid-September.

A couple of stuttering performances – at Chelsea and at home to Leicester were to follow – but after defensive hard-man Derek Jefferson departed for Wolves, the line-up slowly began to blend. Reigning champions Derby were given a roasting in October, sadly in front of Portman Road's lowest crowd of the season.

Jefferson, bespectacled and mild-mannered off the field, had been East Anglia's version of Norman Hunter for five seasons and he left to link up again with former manager Bill McGarry. Robson fretted over whether to replace him from inside or outside the club, and saw a big cash offer for Middlesbrough's Willie Maddren come to nothing. However, as the weeks passed it became clear the club was already adequately served in central defence by Hunter and Beattie, with John Peddelty waiting in the wings.

Robson swooped into the transfer market in early November, however, surprising everyone by swapping six-goal leading scorer Belfitt for Everton's little-known David Johnson. Sceptics were soon won over by Johnson's blinding pace and boundless enthusiasm.

DID YOU KNOW?

After Bobby Robson dropped out-of-form defender Steve Stacey, the player's wife
contacted the local press to accuse Robson of racial prejudice.

Sporting a new-look club crest, featuring a handsome Suffolk
Punch, Town's young team certainly didn't look like carthorses as
they embarked on a nine-match unbeaten run. This saw them soar
into fourth spot by the beginning of December, a position they
hung on to right until the final day of the campaign.

Strike partners Johnson and Whymark complemented each other
perfectly, recalling the halcyon days of Crawford and Phillips from
ten years earlier. Likewise, Beattie and Hunter formed a formidable
centre-back pairing, flanked by the consistent Mills and Harper.

A big factor in that successful run was the pace Town possessed
in key areas. Winger Lambert and the thrusting Hamilton often left
defences flat-footed and gave the maturing Viljoen plenty of options
for his cleverly considered passing.

With the new Pioneer Stand having boosted the ground capacity,
the stadium record was smashed twice and 30,000 was exceeded on
three occasions. The club's pride in its smart surroundings was
somewhat punctured, however, when a floodlight failure brought
the Coventry match to a sudden and premature end. The opposition
were leading at the time, but it was Town who won the re-match.

Wins and clean sheets over Tottenham and Newcastle, plus a 4-1
trouncing of Tommy Docherty's Manchester United, were the
League highlights of early 1973. Town had to look anxiously over
their shoulders in the closing weeks, but their place in the following
season's UEFA Cup was secured before the final game, which
brought their heaviest defeat on the heaviest pitch – Derby's mud-
clogged Baseball Ground.

Town's attacking prowess and ability to beat anyone on their day
gave them the look of a good cup side. It was therefore a major
disappointment when they again failed to impose themselves in
both FA and League Cups. This aberration was forgotten come
May, when silverware was captured in the unexpected shape of the
Texaco Cup. This competition was in its third year and involved
sixteen clubs – nine English and seven Scottish – with Town only
invited to compete following the withdrawal of four Northern Irish
sides on account of 'the troubles'.

The chance to face Scottish League opposition was the main
carrot for the English sides, but Dundee, Dundee United, St Johnstone, Kilmarnock and Ayr all fell at the first stage. In the quarter-
finals this left Hearts and Motherwell, who were paired together.

However, to the delight of fans from both sides of another border – Norfolk-Suffolk – it was Ipswich and Norwich who marched to the final. With Town securing their coveted UEFA Cup place and City avoiding relegation to Division Two with a late rally, both clubs were in buoyant mood as the final loomed – directly after the close of the League season. Local rivalry ensured that the two-legged final pulled in a combined attendance of more than 65,000 and delighted the sponsors. The two clubs earned a combined sum of £80,000 from the competition, a major reward by 1973 standards.

Town had logged two-legged victories over St Johnstone (4-2 at home, 2-0 away), Wolves (2-1 and 1-0), and Newcastle (1-0 and 1-1), whereas The Canaries overcame Dundee, Leicester and Motherwell.

The fierce shooting of Peter Morris saw Town power into a two-goal lead in the first leg at Portman Road, but after five men were booked in a niggly contest, full-back Clive Payne scrambled a late goal to put the contest back on a knife edge. At Carrow Road, City and their big crowd suffered a night of anti-climax as goals from the Norfolk-born pair, Trevor Whymark and Clive Woods, led to a Town aggregate win of 4-2.

Town fans swarmed onto the pitch and after lifting the trophy skywards skipper Mills promised them this would be the first of many such occasions. Indeed, with hindsight, that rainy May evening was a milestone for the club, for it would launch Ipswich into an established place among the League's elite. Although this relatively young club had already experienced an astonishing rise to prominence between 1957 and 1962, the 1972-73 season effectively heralded the start of ten glorious years as a real footballing force.

Almost as significant as the Texaco triumph were the success stories from lower down in the club, where the reserve side won the Football Combination by a six-point margin. Following the pre-season departure of coach Roy McCrohan to Luton, youth coach Bobby Ferguson had been promoted to take command of the reserves and under his stewardship they lost just five of 40 games, scoring more and conceding fewer than any other side.

Meanwhile, Bob Houghton, later to steer Malmo to the European Cup final, had taken control of Town's youth team in the summer of 1972. He launched the youngsters off on a fine campaign, but subsequently emigrated to be replaced by former player Charlie Woods. Ipswich Town's youngsters captured the FA Youth Cup by beating Bristol City in a two-legged final. They also reached the final of the Southern Junior Floodlight Cup and were third in the South East Counties League.

For the second season in succession, everything ended on a high note.

Match of the Season 1972-73

Leeds 3 Ipswich 3

Division 1, 23 August 1972

This drama-packed encounter was hailed by an entranced media as Ipswich's most exhilarating performance since the arrival of manager Robson three and a half-years earlier. More significantly, it can be viewed with hindsight as the night Ipswich Town really arrived and gave notice they were a force to be reckoned with, no longer also-rans who could be easily brushed aside.

Town's refusal to buckle in this match represented a real coming of age for proud Robson's young charges. Three times mighty Leeds went ahead, but three times the determined boys in blue bounced back to equalise. Don Revie's team were not used to such resistance; they were a powerful force held in awe, and taking a point at Elland Road was a rare achievement for any side, let alone scoring three times in front of that fiercely partisan Yorkshire crowd. The new season was less than two weeks old. Leeds had ended the previous campaign as FA Cup winners and League runners-up. Anything less than a victory at Fortress Elland Road was regarded as a major slip by the men in white, and few teams relished the prospect of visiting there during the early to mid-1970s.

Town's willingness to attack seemed to catch the home side by surprise and Colin Viljoen and Ian Collard's enterprise in midfield was crucial to Town's one-point reward.

Leeds took the lead after an incident in which Mick Jones forced the ball home Nat Lofthouse-style, heading in and simultaneously colliding in mid-air with keeper David Best, knocking the Ipswich man unconscious in the process. With Cyril Lea administering the smelling salts, captain Mick Mills was booked for protesting about the challenge, but referee Burns stood firm and the goal stood.

Town hit back when Bryan Hamilton – revelling in his role as an attacking midfielder – cut in at speed and beat David Harvey with a low drive. Leeds were stung into a quick response and regained the lead when Derek Jefferson clattered into Allan Clarke to concede a penalty, Johnny Giles sending his kick high past David Best.

Young Beattie ventured forward to hit a second equaliser after a goalmouth scramble, before Johnny Giles knocked a free-kick to Joe Jordan who fired home at the far post. To the disbelief of many, Town hit back yet again and it was former Leeds striker Belfitt who headed home after Jefferson had made a rare foray down the left.

Both sides went close in a heated finale, but the draw was a fair result and a fine reward for the visitors' mature display.

LEAGUE DIVISION 1   **1973-74**
Division 1   4th
League Cup   4th Round
FA Cup   5th Round
UEFA Cup   3rd Round

Encouraged by the steady progress of recent seasons, the board of directors chose to invest more money on the stadium, installing new floodlights and an indoor training area during the summer of 1973. There was little activity on the transfer front, the only significant news being the sale of Frank Clarke to Carlisle for £35,000.

The new campaign heralded the start of the three up and three down system between the top three divisions, expanding the number of clubs involved in the relegation dogfight. The need to get off to a good start was paramount, therefore, but Ipswich found themselves stuttering badly in the early weeks. After seven League games they were nineteenth and it needed another of manager Robson's shake-ups to get things moving in the right direction.

Best, Morris and Hunter were all axed for the visit of Manchester United and the first victory of the campaign was duly recorded, but the three absent men were soon back, playing vital parts in a season where 24 players were ultimately used because of a severe crop of injuries. The turning point was perhaps a horrendous own-goal by striker David Johnson at Newcastle. Back to help his beleaguered colleagues in defence, he somehow steered the ball past Sivell to seal a second win over Ipswich by the Geordies in just eight days.

Things could only get better from that point and, to his credit, Johnson picked himself up to score a brilliant goal at the correct end just minutes later — and suddenly things were looking up again. Town promptly embarked on a nine-match unbeaten run which saw them soar into the top six.

The League Cup gave Robson the opportunity to return for the first time to Fulham, scene of his humiliating sacking in November 1968. The Cottagers put up a real fight, but it must have been very satisfying for the Town boss to see his side ease past them into round three.

The fuel crisis affected football badly around this time, largely via a ban on the use of floodlights. Some clubs borrowed generators and found ways around the problem, but a number of matches had to be played during the afternoon in midweek. This led to a fall in attendances even though some fans were free to attend because of the three-day working week imposed by the Tory Government.

From mid-November onwards, despite the distractions of European competition and the persistent injury worries, Town would mostly remain a top-six side for the rest of the campaign. After the poor start it turned into a heartening season, particularly in view of the way untried youngsters rose to the occasion when called upon to replace injury-hit senior players.

Indeed, the youth development system was beginning to bear fruit in a big way. No fewer than five home-grown youngsters made their First Division debuts this season, following in the footsteps of Robson's 'diamond' Kevin Beattie, who at nineteen was by now an established star. In fact, Beattie would win the PFA Young Player of the Year award in the spring, adding a first call-up to the full England squad and a second successive Player of the Year award at club level.

Of the five youngsters introduced, George Burley, Roger Osborne, Brian Talbot and Eric Gates instantly looked the part and went on to enjoy long careers. The unlucky fifth was Canadian full-back Bruce Twamley, who had the heartbreak of sustaining a nasty knee injury on his debut against Wolves. Not even the bizarre sight of referee Brian Daniels being knocked senseless by a corner-kick can have cheered up poor Twamley.

The emerging young talent within the club meant Robson had no need to raid the transfer market. The only new import to appear in 1973-4 was goalkeeper Paul Cooper, who arrived on loan in the spring as cover for Laurie Sivell, following the sale of David Best to Portsmouth for £30,000. In fact, no transfer fees were paid out between David Johnson's arrival in November 1972 and the summer of 1974, when £30,000 was handed to Birmingham for the permanent services of Cooper.

The finances were further improved by income from no fewer than *fifteen* cup-ties, eight of them in the UEFA Cup. Apart from four ties in 1962, this was Town's first taste of European action and what an adventure it was.

Although admittedly not at their peak, Real Madrid represented one of the biggest names in world football, and when the Spanish giants arrived in Suffolk for the first round tie in September they became the first foreign opposition to sample the newly built facilities at Portman Road. Real were fancied to win the trophy and their star-studded side included West Germany's midfield maestro Gunter Netzer. After Mick Mills' deflected shot gave Town a 1-0 first-leg lead, the last thing the Bernabeu Stadium expected for the return was the sight of a little-known English team coming out to attack their Spanish hosts. But cavalier Town took the game to their opponents with style and silenced a crowd of 80,000. Despite this positive approach, the game ended goalless, but the experience was another huge step for Robson's fast-maturing squad.

DID YOU KNOW?

When Laurie Sivell babysat for manager Bill McGarry and his wife, the Town goal-keeper was too afraid of his strict boss even to eat the chocolates left out for him!

The next stage of the European adventure saw Town overcome Lazio of Rome, with both legs proving to be drama-packed occasions and covered in full later in this chapter. After licking their wounds following a rough ride against the Italians, the draw for the third round provided the club with a whole new challenge in the shape of the skilful Dutchmen of Twente Enschede.

For the third time, Town went into a tie as underdogs. The experts doubted their chances when they went into the second leg in Holland having beaten Dutch international keeper Piet Schrijvers just once in a first leg played on snow-covered Portman Road. But once again the Suffolk side proved how resolute and calm under pressure they could be, chalking up a stylish 2-1 win and gaining many admirers in Holland in the process.

Star turn in the Enschede line-up was Frans Thijssen, whose polished link-up play and uncanny ability to go past opponents impressed Robson to such an extent that he kept close tabs on the player and would subsequently bring him to Suffolk.

Both Enschede ties were followed by League defeats, but after the second leg there was a twelve-week gap before the quarter-finals, meaning Town could get back to the business of their League duties. Leeds and Liverpool were threatening to open a gap at the top, leaving the other clubs to be scrapping to finish as best of the rest. Town's League form was indifferent over this period, although exciting FA Cup victories over Sheffield United and Manchester United at Old Trafford sustained interest for the fans.

A 0-5 thrashing at Leicester took the wind out of the team's sails, but in the following League match they made amends by humbling Southampton 7-0, Town's best win by far in the top flight.

Defeat in the FA Cup at Anfield was followed by three dull 1-1 League draws before the East Germans of Lokomotiv Leipzig arrived in Suffolk for UEFA Cup action. The fifth European tie at Portman Road saw Town maintain their 100% record.

Local boy Brian Talbot, a newcomer to the side, made his European bow in this game and set up Beattie's winning goal four minutes from time. The slim lead gave Town a fighting chance and, after the obligatory tour of nearby Colditz Castle, they took the East Germans to a penalty shoot-out, having held them to 1-0 over 120 minutes. For most of that time Town were down to ten men, with Mills sent off for retaliating after a blow in the face.

Penalty shoot-outs were not commonplace in those days and it took nerves of steel to step up in front of 57,000 partisan fans in what was Ipswich's very first attempt at this controversial way of settling a game. Young Talbot coolly tucked away the first but his more experienced colleague Morris missed. Whymark and Beattie were on target but Johnson and the fifth German taker both missed. That meant sudden death and the pressure fell on the shoulders of Allan Hunter. Werner Friese made a sharp save and the game was over for plucky Town. It wouldn't be the last time Bobby Robson would experience the death of a dream in this fashion.

UEFA Cup elimination left eight remaining League games in which to secure a place in Europe the following campaign. The task was duly achieved, although losing the final two, against Leeds and Sheffield United, tossed away the opportunity to finish third in the table. Town had to wait and hope that runners-up Liverpool would lift the FA Cup and thus qualify for the Cup-Winners' Cup, vacating their UEFA place to Ipswich.

The Cup final result went in Town's favour and they celebrated with a jaunt to warmer climes, where they beat a Bermuda FA side 5-0. Robson could reflect on an enjoyable and eventful campaign and he appeared to have no regrets about turning down the overtures of bigger clubs Everton and Derby, who had both sought his services as manager.

Match of the Season 1973-74
Ipswich 4 Lazio 0

UEFA Cup, 2nd round, 1st leg, 24 October 1973.

After overcoming mighty Real Madrid, Town were paired with a Lazio side renowned for its strong defence and notorious for episodes of indiscipline. Three years earlier a brawl involving several Lazio players at Arsenal had seen the club banned from European competition.

Town were far from intimidated by the Italians' reputation or by their brilliant defensive record in their domestic league. For this first leg, Lazio employed a man-for-man marking system with a sweeper patrolling at the back, but they seemed ill-prepared for Town's speedy attacks, which involved heavy use of raiding full-backs Harper and Mills.

After just one goal over two legs against Real Madrid, Town fans could have been forgiven for expecting a grim struggle, but the breakthrough came after just seventeen minutes. Lambert fired in a cross and Whymark rose to head home.

Just before the interval Harper swung the ball in and Whymark's low shot bobbled over the dive of keeper Pulici. Shortly after half-time Whymark completed his hat-trick, pouncing on a ball from Lambert, who had forced his way into the crowded box.

The Italians' bewilderment turned to anger and frustration when things got even better for Town, Viljoen's shot being charged down and Whymark shooting home for 4-0. Whymark appeared to use his hand to control the ball and Lazio went berserk. Thereafter they abandoned their defensive strategy and pushed two attackers out wide. It was too little too late, and the match deteriorated, turning into a physical battle.

Johnson and Lambert had buzzed around making a nuisance of themselves, and the Italians decided it was time to take the law into their own hands, exacting punishment on Johnson in particular. Having survived an elbow in the face and a blow to the stomach, Johnson clashed with Oddi and was the victim of an assault that saw him injured in the groin area. He needed stitches and surgery and the extent of his wounds horrified those who treated him and got a close-up view.

The Swedish referee seemed ill-equipped to cope with the brutality and booked just two players, Town's Geoff Hammond for a late tackle, and Oddi for a shirt pull, probably the least of his crimes.

Town headed for Rome a fortnight later expecting a rough ride on the pitch, although they were delighted to be loaned a luxury team bus for the duration of their stay by Lazio officials.

Lazio scored in the first minute and again before half-time to give themselves a real chance of recovery. Town bravely rode the storm and with the Italians becoming increasingly frustrated, the award of an Ipswich penalty on 73 minutes ignited the tie. Viljoen scored, but all hell was let loose and two home goals by Georgi Chinaglia, both controversial, meant the aggregate score was now just 5-4 in Town's favour with two minutes remaining. Cometh the hour, cometh the man, and Town introduced substitute Johnson for his first action since recovering from Lazio's first-leg attentions. Within a matter of seconds the ebullient Scouser had scored a stunning goal to settle the tie.

Town players were pursued down the tunnel and attacked by Lazio players and fans alike. The team remained locked in their dressing room for two hours until the caribiniere deemed it safe for them to emerge. Lazio were condemned in the Italian press for the episode and even the club's own officials expected more than the £1,500 fine and one-year European ban ultimately imposed.

LEAGUE DIVISION 1   **1974-75**
Division 1   3rd
League Cup   5th Round
FA Cup   Semi-final
UEFA Cup   1st Round

After successive top-four finishes and with valuable experience in Europe, all seemed set fair for even greater Town triumphs. The club received a boost when Bobby Robson resisted an approach by managerless Leeds, who were looking to replace the new England supremo Don Revie. They settled instead for Brian Clough.

Town enjoyed a terrific start with four wins and four clean sheets, including a demolition of Arsenal that had Robson purring with delight. He seemed happy with the blend of his largely home-grown squad and had felt able to offload four players and sign just one – young goalkeeper Paul Cooper from Birmingham for £30,000. All four departures – Peter Morris, Johnny Miller, Glenn Keeley and Geoff Hammond – would play against Town this season.

Work continued off the field to improve the already swish stadium, with a new club shop, office accommodation and squash court built under the Portman Stand. A young Scottish journalist, Mel Henderson, had been appointed as the club's first public relations officer, combining commercial and sponsorship matters.

The early burst of League success underlined Town's potential as title contenders. Before the trip to Newcastle in late September they had won nine out of ten games. The only blip came at Sheffield United where the run of four successive clean-sheets was halted by Mick Mills' own-goal. It took an autumn drought – five League games without a goal – to dislodge Town from the top of the table, though injuries affected the front two, Johnson and Whymark.

The home form in the first half of the campaign was spectacular: it was away from Portman Road that Town's title credentials looked shaky. The autumn heralded seven successive away losses, but fortunately this sort of inconsistency was also evident elsewhere so that the leadership constantly changed hands. Only a handful of points separated the top ten for many months.

Ipswich-born winger Miller had left Town for Second Division Norwich but returned within weeks to score the two goals that knocked Town out of the League Cup at the quarter-final stage. Defeat was harder to swallow by being at Norwich's hands.

Portman Road's growing reputation as a League fortress was tarnished on Boxing Day when bottom-of-the-table Luton performed a smash-and-grab victory with an injury-time winner. By this time Town had exited the UEFA Cup at the first stage on the away goal rule. The only consolation was to be beaten by skilful and attractive Twente Enschede, and not muscled aside by the likes of Lazio.

By the turn of the year the title was there for the taking, with no team able to break clear. Town could hide behind the injuries excuse, particularly given the small size of the squad. Happily, Allan Hunter rejected a move to Leicester after the clubs had agreed a £200,000 fee. Robson was pleased by the Northern Ireland international's decision, which illustrated that after six years as a 'poor relation' in Division One, Town now had genuine potential.

Hunter was one of many key players to miss games through injury and only the fast-maturing Mick Mills was an ever present. The crisis peaked when five men missed the trip to Birmingham, where, ironically, a side that cost nothing in transfer fees recorded a victory to return Town to the top of the table. Town may have thought they were unlucky with injuries, but Stoke, who clung on in the top six for most of the season, suffered five broken legs during the campaign, two occurring against Ipswich!

Exit from the UEFA and League Cups was compensated by a thrilling run in the FA Cup that featured nine ties, two of which went to extra-time. Against Wolves and Aston Villa, Town overturned deficits, while home ties with Liverpool and Leeds saw the stadium crowd record smashed on both occasions. More than 38,000 crammed into Portman Road to see Jimmy Armfield's Leeds, the capacity having been raised by extensions to the Portman Stand.

The celebrations were long and loud after the two-goal deficit at home to Villa was pulled back. Sub Bryan Hamilton pounced twice in the closing stages to take Town into the last eight for the first time. Fears that the cup run would hamper the chase for the League title were magnified by the battle with Leeds for a place in the semi-finals. Four games were necessary, two requiring extra-time.

The goal that put Town into their first major semi-final was a curler from distance by winger Clive Woods, later voted BBC's Goal of the Month. Like fellow-flanker Mick Lambert, Woods had been at the club several years but had never established himself until now. He featured in 49 of the season's 58 games (seventeen as substitute).

Three youngsters made their debuts this season, most notably 17-year-old John Wark, who was plunged into the fray in place of the injured Beattie at Filbert Street for the third replay with Leeds. Dale Roberts and John Peddelty were ahead of him in the pecking order, but both were injured, so Wark had to be plucked from the youth squad heading for Germany to pit his wits against the likes of Allan Clarke and Joe Jordan. He coped manfully in central defence.

Alan Taylor's semi-final double-strike for West Ham at Stamford Bridge meant Town could now focus on League matters and the exhausted and injury-hit squad fought gamely in the closing weeks, only being defeated once in the final ten games.

Dave Mackay's Derby took the title by a two-point margin, having hit the top for the first time in the final fortnight of the season. Six wins and three draws from their final nine games was good enough to finish top, with runners-up Liverpool ruing a run of seven games without a win in February and March. Town were left to reflect that they had probably blown their chances in February when conceding eight goals in successive matches at Liverpool and Coventry. The 2-5 mauling at Anfield was a wonderful advert for football, with the home side in rampant form and hell-bent on revenge after Town had beaten them twice earlier in the campaign at Portman Road, by late scrambled goals on both occasions.

Despite going close to winning all three major domestic trophies, Town's season did not end in complete disappointment. The first team rounded things off with a highly-entertaining 4-1 trouncing of West Ham in front of the biggest League gate for more than a year; the reserves finished runners up in the Football Combination; and the youth team won the South East Counties League. Perhaps best of all, the FA Youth Cup was won by Ipswich's kids in emphatic style, with more than 16,000 witnessing the Portman Road leg of the final against West Ham.

Further national recognition was achieved when Beattie was voted by his peers into the PFA's Division One team of the season, and Bobby Robson was heralded manager of the year by readers of the *Sun*, also winning the Bell's Whisky Manager of the Month award for March.

Indeed, for Beattie it had been a particularly eventful season. He was selected for the England Under-23 squad to play Scotland on 18 December and duly headed north by train. But instead of joining up with the England party in Glasgow, the young defender made an impromptu decision to get off at his home-town Carlisle to visit family and friends instead. With Christmas looming and his new baby daughter keeping him awake at nights, Beattie admitted he had been exhausted at the time, so that when the train pulled in at Carlisle he had simply succumbed to an overwhelming temptation to get off and momentarily turn his back on all the pressures crowding in on him.

Fortunately, both Robson and England boss Don Revie took a lenient view. Beattie was soon back in the Ipswich team and selected again for the England Under-23s against Wales less than four weeks later. Inevitably, the episode delighted the press: the saga of the missing footballer made headlines, accompanied by photos of Beattie contentedly playing dominoes in a Carlisle pub.

Match of the Season 1974-75
Ipswich 1 West Ham 2

FA Cup, semi-final replay, 9 April 1975

West Ham and Ipswich ended goalless in the first semi-final, with Robson's men delighted to get a second bite, having been hampered by injuries in that first Villa Park encounter. With striker Johnson already definitely out, four more players received knocks during the first game and of this quartet Hunter would not recover in time. The replay at Stamford Bridge was war-weary Town's twelfth game in 40 days and provided another chance for 17-year-old Wark to impress.

This was the closest the club had ever been to Wembley and they set about the task with a vengeance. After seven minutes Hammers' young keeper Mervyn Day blocked Mills' shot, but the rebound was returned into the net by Hamilton. Although the linesman, who was better-placed, seemed happy, referee Clive Thomas whistled for offside. TV replays later proved the goal should have stood. Supporters were quick to recall the injustice on this same ground some years earlier when Chelsea had been awarded a goal after a shot had hit Town's side-netting. Had the jinx struck again?

It appeared so, for despite dominating for much of the first half, Town fell behind in virtually West Ham's first real attack. The scorer, Alan Taylor, 21, had begun the season with Fourth Division Rochdale and had just seven First Division games to his name. Town pressed on, and it appeared their luck might be changing when just before the interval Lambert's corner was sliced into his own net by Billy Jennings, back supposedly to help his defence.

The second period saw more Town pressure and on 63 minutes Mr Thomas ruled out another Town effort for offside. This time Woods had converted a Lambert cross, but the decision was correct. Lambert almost made the breakthrough with a fine shot in the 74th minute, but Day, the reigning PFA Young Player of the Year, pulled off a spectacular diving save. As the minutes ticked away, a header by young Wark fell at the feet of Taylor, who hammered a drive into the Ipswich net off a post. It was a sickening blow for Town.

Various West Ham personnel were honest enough to publicly admit they'd been fortunate. Bobby Robson was so irate he refused to speak to the press throughout the following day. However, when the dust settled he uttered philosophical words about character being bred from despair. His weary men were left to resume their chase for the League title. For the injured Hunter and Johnson, the tension at Stamford Bridge had been so great that they couldn't bear to watch and had left the ground for the solace of a nearby pub.

LEAGUE DIVISION 1   **1975-76**
Division 1   6th
League Cup   2nd Round
FA Cup   4th Round
UEFA Cup   2nd Round

After three seasons rubbing shoulders with the elite at the top of the table, Ipswich were no longer regarded as country cousins who could safely be written off as serious championship challengers.

The squad, albeit small, featured a useful blend of youth and international experience and on paper there appeared no reason why a top-four place should not be achieved again. Town prepared for the big kick-off with five games inside a week in Norway and Holland, including tough opponents like Anderlecht and fellow tourists Spartak Trnava. It was a busy schedule that required thirteen flights in a week, but Robson pronounced the trip a success and good for team spirit.

Town fans responded to the relative success of recent years by buying up season tickets in record numbers. But those who expected a smooth start were in for a rude awakening. Newcastle and new manager Gordon Lee came to Suffolk on the opening day and dished out a hammering. Malcolm MacDonald took up where he left off the previous season and blasted two fine goals.

The side failed to perform in the opening four games, leaving Robson unhappy with the commitment and attitude of his men. After a clear-the-air meeting, the players improved against Burnley, then savaged Birmingham, who found themselves four goals down before half-time.

Town had been rock bottom when the first league tables were published in August, but by the end of that month had begun a steady climb that continued through the season. The team reached the top six for the first time in April and managed to stay there.

As in the previous campaign, injuries played a major role and successive games with an unchanged line-up were rare. Brian Talbot broke his leg for a third time in the League Cup-tie at Leeds, while Kevin Beattie, Colin Viljoen, David Johnson and Mick Lambert were all plagued by fitness problems.

Viljoen, who had recently won full England caps at a relatively late age, suffered a thigh strain and then Achilles trouble and, after leaving the field during the Bruges debacle in November, would not pull on a first-team shirt for another two years. Johnson's nagging hamstring problem seemed to rob him of some of his pace. He ended the season disgruntled after being left out of the final game, and this hugely popular character never played for Town again.

DID YOU KNOW?

Bobby Robson's dropping of Billy Baxter and Tommy Carroll provoked a fist-fight. Defender Geoff Hammond and coach Cyril Lea came to Robson's aid.

For Beattie, 1975-76 marked the beginning of injury trouble that would never completely disappear and which subsequently curtailed his top-class career before the age of 30. There were no half measures with 'The Beat' and his amazing strength and buccaneering style put plenty of stress on his joints. His eagerness to play, and the desperation of the management to include him, often meant he was patched up and given pain-killers when a longer rest would surely have been more beneficial.

A surprising departure in November was that of Bryan Hamilton, who joined Everton, having racked up 199 first-team appearances and 56 goals for Town. Given that Robson had spent little lately and the club was reportedly in good shape financially, the fee of just £40,000 raised a few eyebrows.

With highly-capable defenders coming through from the youth ranks – the likes of John Wark, John Peddelty and Dale Roberts – Robson often chose to hand the No 3 shirt to Beattie, thus splitting his famed partnership with Allan Hunter. Mills' versatility also gave Robson options, the skipper able to slot into full-back and midfield roles when required.

The most horrifying of a catalogue of injuries came at Villa Park, where keeper Laurie Sivell had been recalled after more than six months in the reserves to replace Paul Cooper, who had had a poor game at QPR. Sivell made a brilliant stop from Chris Nicholl and when the ball ran free flung himself at the feet of big Andy Gray. A winning goal was prevented, but the damage to Sivell's face saw him carried off covered in blood and mud. He had a badly-gashed mouth, concussion, a black eye and was minus several teeth. He needed eleven stitches and the sports editor of the Ipswich local paper had to withdraw pictures of the incident for fear of upsetting readers over their Corn Flakes.

The constant team changes inevitably led to inconsistency, but the fans rarely had to wait long for an outstanding win to compensate for the disappointing league placing. Liverpool, and then the deadly enemy Norwich, were given a pounding at Portman Road, Arsenal were 'doubled' and Manchester United came to Suffolk chasing a League and Cup double but left with their hopes in tatters. Classy Feyenoord were also taken down a peg or two in both legs of the opening UEFA Cup encounter. FC Bruges were comfortably beaten in the first leg of the following round, but the subsequent surrender of the 3-0 lead in Belgium was a sickening blow to Ipswich.

In previous European excursions, Town had won praise for their resilience and defiant spirit, but in Belgium's beautiful historic city they caved in meekly to the horror of Robson and the thousands of supporters who had taken ferries across the North Sea. It was scant consolation that Bruges subsequently reached the final where they faced Liverpool.

Having participated in sixteen cup-ties the previous season, this season's total of eight left the fans feeling almost short-changed! The wounds inflicted by the UEFA Cup exit were not healed by an FA Cup run, with former Portman Road boss Bill McGarry and his Wolves side squeezing Town out after a replay.

With no new signings throughout the campaign, youngsters Keith Bertschin and Pat Sharkey made the greatest impact of four new faces introduced from within the ranks. Sharkey, whose career was later to be hampered by his social life, was given a run in the side and showed clever touches in midfield. The robust enthusiasm of big Bertschin exploded on the scene when he scored with a diving header at Highbury just 25 seconds into his debut – his first touch of the ball.

Robson was delighted with the lad's attitude and commitment and gave him a couple of outings at the end of the season. This was at the expense of new England cap David Johnson, who had been keen to play in the closing game with Derby and did not take kindly to the axe. Although he had the summer in which to cool down, Johnson would never play for the first team again, moving to Liverpool on the eve of the following campaign.

Mills enjoyed another splendid season, equally at home in both full-back berths and in midfield, and was the only man to appear in all 50 first-team games. He was rewarded by being recalled to the England squad in March 1976, winning seven more caps between then and the end of May.

Town's reserves narrowly won the Football Combination title and the youth team easily took the South East Counties League crown, two achievements that went some way towards compensating for the first team failing to get as close to a trophy as they had the previous year.

With Colin Harper, Ian Collard and Bryan Hamilton having played their final first-team games for Ipswich, the squad was now clearly a couple of players short of championship material, even though Town had proved capable of beating anyone on their day. The havoc wreaked by a few injuries had repeatedly driven that message home.

Match of the Season 1975-76

Ipswich 3 Manchester United 0

Division 1, 10 April 1976

Tommy Docherty's Man U came to Suffolk with serious hopes of capturing a League and FA Cup double in their first season back in the top flight. Seven days earlier they had beaten Derby in the semi-final and they were neck and neck for league honours with QPR, Liverpool and Derby. For Town, having beaten Manchester City three days earlier to finally reach the top six, the only remaining target was a place in Europe.

With Beattie out for the rest of the season, Mills moved to full-back allowing young Gates the chance to impress alongside Sharkey and Osborne in a relatively inexperienced midfield. Nearly 35,000 – one of the best crowds in Portman Road's history – squeezed in and were absorbed from start to finish by a fast and open game. Town took the lead on 33 minutes when Sharkey, brimful of confidence and doing his chances of a Northern Ireland call-up no harm, split the defence with a chip to Lambert, who had swapped flanks and angled a right-foot volley over Stepney into the far corner.

United attempted to get back on terms with Coppell twice going close, forcing Cooper into diving saves with a rising drive and then a neat header. Hunter gave an awesome display at the back, ably assisted by Burley and Mills, who restricted the threat of wingers Hill and Coppell. Victory was assured twelve minutes from time when Whymark produced a sweet header from Sharkey's free-kick, following a foul on Lambert by Sammy McIlroy. Alex Stepney got a hand to the ball couldn't keep it out.

That second goal sparked trouble among the away support, some of whom tried to scramble up a wall that housed the seated home fans. With their team heading for defeat, many United followers left early to cause trouble in surrounding streets. A police inspector was knocked unconscious and there were 37 arrests - only five of whom had local addresses.

Those inside the ground saw Town clinch the points in the 83rd minute when Woods chipped across the box and Johnson blasted a shot past Stepney. Defeat inflicted a mortal blow to United's title hopes, and they lost the Cup final to Second Division Southampton, too. Perhaps they were too complacent at Wembley, having read Mick Mills' programme notes: 'They might as well give [United] the FA Cup now for all the resistance I expect Southampton to offer.'

LEAGUE DIVISION 1   **1976-77**
Division 1   3rd
League Cup   2nd Round
FA Cup   4th Round

Although finishing sixth in 1976, Town had never been in the title race. That was about to change, although once again the side would only show its worth after shrugging off a shaky opening. Once they got the show on the road, Town would be in contention.

The main changes were the sale of popular striker David Johnson to Liverpool for £200,000; a change of Cobbold in the chairman's role, with 'Mr John' handing over to brother 'Mr Patrick'; and the introduction of goal-difference to replace goal-average.

Other important milestones arrived in October. After weeks of negotiations, Robson signed Johnson's replacement, Lancashire lad Paul Mariner, from Plymouth for a club record £220,000. The deal involved Terry Austin and John Peddelty (jointly valued at £100,000) going to Argyle. Red and yellow cards were introduced for referees. George Best saw an early red when performing for Fulham.

Mariner's arrival was a relief for Town fans, as Johnson's exit left the team with only one experienced striker – Trevor Whymark. Keith Bertschin and Robin Turner had been the main contenders for the No 9 shirt, but neither looked quite ready.

Tottenham, who had been beaten by Liverpool in the chase for Johnson's signature, were beaten on the opening day by two late goals. With new manager Keith Burkinshaw in charge, Spurs would finish bottom and suffer relegation for the first time in 42 years. That win was Town's only success, however, in their first eight league and cup encounters. It was not until late September that Robson would be able to field a side that looked capable of living up to the team's potential. Beattie returned to central defence after several games at full-back, Mills dropped back from midfield and young John Wark was given a midfield role for the first time. As for Brian Talbot, his surging runs and prodigious work-rate would see him picked for England.

Town embarked on an unbeaten run of sixteen games. Stretching into January, this pushed them from seventeenth to top. One of their victims was Bob Paisley's treble-chasing Liverpool, who were beaten 1-0 at Portman Road in December. The two points allowed Town to replace the Reds at the top and the two sides would jostle for supremacy until the closing weeks.

After a run of four straight wins, Robson finally landed Mariner in late October. The player and his schoolteacher wife had made it clear they preferred rural Suffolk to the urban attractions of fellow-

bidders West Brom and West Ham, but the deal had almost floun-
dered when the Plymouth chairman originally rejected the idea of a
player-exchange. Mariner went straight into the side at Old
Trafford, helping to earn a 1-0 win, and made his home debut a
week later. The cliché 'dream start' has rarely been more appropriate, for inspired by their energetic new target-man, Town ran riot
against West Brom and smashed in seven goals, six of them from
open play, three of which are still droolingly talked about.

Mariner headed a late winner in the tense clash with Liverpool,
in front of a huge crowd. That result underlined Town's title
credentials and capped an exciting period during which Robson
won the Bell's Manager of the Month, Talbot was the *Daily Mirror*
Player of the Month and Cooper took Granada TV's Save of the
Month accolade for foiling an effort by Liverpool's Steve Heighway.

The football world cast admiring eyes on the job Robson was
performing at this Suffolk outpost and he was approached by an
intermediary representing Everton. Robson recalls in his autobiog-
raphy, *Time On The Grass*, that he met the Everton chairman John
Moores and shook hands on a deal that would see him replace Billy
Bingham. But just as he was preparing to inform chairman Cobbold,
the story was leaked to the *Daily Express*.

'I couldn't believe it,' he wrote. 'I hadn't yet told the Ipswich
directors and here it was in a newspaper. I felt very bitter and very
angry. The contract hadn't been signed, yet they released the news.
They had let me down badly. In a few seconds my mind was made
up. I wouldn't go to Everton.'

As fate would have it, Town faced Everton at Portman Road a
few days after they fired Bingham. Without Robson on board, they
put coach Steve Burtenshaw in temporary charge. Town won
comfortably and Everton forward Duncan McKenzie hailed Town
the best side he'd seen all season. Several weeks later the vacant
post would go to Gordon Lee.

The second half of the league programme saw a crop of injuries
undermine the club's challenge. Operating with a first-team squad
of just thirteen or fourteen players inevitably meant that two or
three concurrent injuries could cause disruption. Few players
escaped altogether and, perhaps inevitably, the major sufferer was
Robson's 'diamond' Kevin Beattie. The defender's knee and back
continued to give him trouble. On Easter Sunday he also suffered a
nasty accident at home when trying to enliven a bonfire with petrol.
Beattie was hospitalised with serious burns to his upper body, in
particular the neck area, and would not play again this season.
Recalling the incident, Beattie reflected on how he didn't realise the
seriousness of his injuries at first. Originally all he could feel was a

stinging feeling on his nipples, but a fortnight later began suffering 'the worst pain of my life' due to nerve-ends being affected. The following week's tabloids ran stories suggesting the bonfire story was a fabrication and that Beattie's pregnant wife had thrown a chip-pan of oil over him, but this was strenuously denied.

At the time of the accident, Town were sitting on top of the League, but without Beattie in central defence they would win only two of their remaining seven games and finished five points behind champions Liverpool. Beattie's deputy, Dale Roberts, did a decent job, but Robson was left to reflect on another 'might have been'.

Another injury to have wider repercussions was that to Eric Gates' ankle at Bristol City. As trainer Cyril Lea attempted to treat the player, the referee – keen to get the game going again – started dragging Gates off the pitch by his ankles! Lea reacted furiously and was cautioned. The fact that Gates missed games because of the injury helped vindicate Lea and his booking was quashed.

Town's two cup exits at the hands of Second Division Brighton and Wolves had been frustrating but not disastrous, simply because they allowed Town to concentrate on Robson's major objective – the League. Without any European competition this time round, the directors were unhappy about the lack of cup revenue, although Mr Cobbold was able to announce a profit of £14,000 on the previous season's trading. Clearly, the £200,000 received for David Johnson was much needed, and of the fee splashed out on Mariner, almost half was the value of the two players in the swap arrangement.

There were no other transfers during the season. The only other new face for Ipswich was forward David Geddis, a former Carlisle schoolmate of Beattie, who was given his chance in the final two games. Geddis had actually made his League debut some weeks earlier on loan to Second Division Luton, where he looked lively, scoring four goals in fourteen appearances.

One man rarely seen this season was midfield ace Colin Viljoen, still rehabilitating after Achilles surgery. He saw some action in May, when playing for an hour in his own testimonial. This was in recognition of his ten years' service and saw Town beat the arch-enemy Norwich for the third time in the season.

Match of the Season 1976-77
Ipswich 7 West Brom 0

Division 1, 6 November 1976

Town fans waited ten weeks for a replacement for David Johnson, but soon realised it had been well worth the wait.

DID YOU KNOW?

When Bobby Robson arranged a 'secret' trial to watch starlet George Burley in action in Ayrshire, 500 spectators turned up to watch, including rival scouts!

Having debuted at Old Trafford, Paul Mariner now enticed an above-average home crowd a week later. Mid-table Albion were taken apart, the first goal arriving on nineteen minutes when Whymark stabbed the ball past John Osborne after Beattie had nodded Woods' corner to him. Talbot's deep cross was then headed down by Whymark into Wark's path and the Scot's drive was pushed on to a post and into the net by the hapless Osborne.

By half-time Albion did not look dead, and, prompted by player-manager Johnny Giles, still looked capable of getting back into the contest. These hopes took a knock on 55 minutes, when Beattie roared forward, burst past a couple of defenders and smashed the ball into the roof of the net from outside the area.

If the jubilant home fans thought this was a great goal, there was even better to come. Whymark, combining well with his new strike-partner, exchanged slick return passes with Mariner, collected the ball on the edge of the area and fired home, raising his eyes to the heavens in near disbelief at the sheer poetry of the goal. The crowd was in raptures, and Robson too, the manager later describing this as 'the goal of the decade, very nearly of the century!'

Town were on such a high it appeared everything they tried would come off and all it needed now was for the new boy to score. Just two minutes later this was duly achieved. Gathering the ball on the left, Mariner cut inside, brushing past three defenders and let go a cracking shot which gave Osborne no chance. In his own post-match interviews Mariner was to enthuse on similar lines to his manager, labelling this the best goal he'd ever scored. It earned him an ovation from the crowd that lasted more than a minute.

Although the excitement generated by purple patches can tend to exaggerate the quality of goals in the memory, reviewing on video the Beattie, Whymark and Mariner strikes in that eleven-minute spell confirms that these were indeed three of the finest and most spectacular goals of this or any other season.

Nor were Town finished for the day. Whymark completed a quartet of goals in the final two minutes, first collecting the ball from Roger Osborne, who had outrun two demoralised defenders, to knock in an easy effort. Then, close to the final whistle, he tried his luck from distance and produced a rueful smile as his rather under-hit pot-shot was deflected to leave poor Osborne stranded in no-man's land.

Burley, Sivell and Hunter fail to prevent Coventry scoring (February 1975)

Allan Hunter, an inspired signing by Bobby Robson

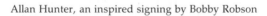

Bobby Robson, who had 13 wonderful years managing Ipswich Town

The squad of 1980-81, which lifted the UEFA Cup

Ipswich's glossy 2000-01 magazine won them 'Programme of the Year'

Brian Talbot forces home his second goal against Coventry (March 1974)

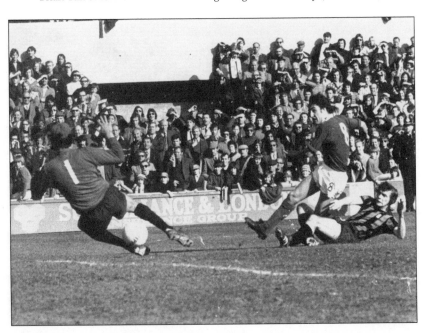

David Johnson heads in a Colin Viljoen cross (November 1974)

The new improved South Stand takes shape (April 2001)

Terry Butcher keeps an eye on Cyrille Regis (May 1985)

Russell Osman clears from close to the goal-line (January 1982)

## Chapter Two

The Glory Years
1977-1982

LEAGUE DIVISION 1	**1977-78**
Division 1	18th
League Cup	4th Round
FA Cup	Winners
UEFA Cup	3rd Round

With three players departed and another half-dozen injured, Town were delighted to start the new season by remaining unbeaten and not conceding a goal in their first four matches. Sadly, this sort of consistency was not maintained and the campaign turned into one where cup success by far outshone performances in Division One. Indeed, for some weeks, relegation became a genuine possibility, partly a consequence of what the club doctor called the worst injury situation for twenty years.

The summer of 1977 saw the club enjoy a roaring trade in season ticket sales and invest a large sum by way of major improvements to the popular Churchman's Stand. A smart new royal blue Adidas playing strip was introduced and the only clouds on the horizon were the poor results and injuries sustained on a pre-season tour.

The emergence of young David Geddis and the promise of untried Alan Brazil encouraged Robson to accept Birmingham's offer of £135,000 for striker Keith Bertschin, while injury-hit full-back Colin Harper and midfielder Pat Sharkey moved to Port Vale and Mansfield respectively. Once again there were no big-money summer arrivals, although Robson came close to obtaining the services of Tottenham's Pat Jennings, the keeper eventually opting for Arsenal when they offered him better terms.

Such was the injury glut that nobody could claim 'ever-present' status, something that had only happened twice in the previous twenty years. Kevin Beattie only featured in 21 of the 58 competitive games and Trevor Whymark in just 29. Despite this, Whymark still notched twenty goals, but was missing when things got underway in August. His replacement, Geddis, scored the winner at home to Arsenal, in a match memorable for the fact that the players had to leave the pitch for eleven minutes during a massive downpour.

The signs that this would be a year of struggle first became clear in October. Brian Clough's promoted Nottingham Forest tore Town apart 4-0 and the month ended with a home loss to struggling West Ham. Although not firing on all cylinders in the League, Ipswich were already making progress in the UEFA and League Cups. Whymark's haul included a foursome against Swedish part-timers Landskrona Bois, the third time a Town player had hit four in a European tie. Despite the best efforts of his flamboyant partner, Paul Mariner, Whymark looked set to become Town's leading scorer for a third successive season, but a Boxing Day challenge by Norwich's David Jones left him with damaged knee ligaments. He later absolved Jones of blame, but reappeared only sporadically over the next year and would never really be the same player again.

Well over 30,000 crammed inside Portman Road to see famous Barcelona, coached by Rinus Michels and starring none other than Johann Cruyff. The task of curbing the great man fell to unfussy Suffolk lad Roger Osborne, who carried out his man-marking task to perfection. With their creative genius stifled, the Catalan club had no answer to a sparkling Town performance. The 3-0 first-leg winning margin was more than Robson could have hoped for, but sadly it proved inadequate. In a wet and empty Nou Camp, Town were confronted by relentless home attacks that breached Paul Cooper's net three times. Unluckily, Town had two penalty claims brushed aside, Eric Gates and Colin Viljoen both hit the bar, and – as in Leipzig nearly four years earlier – it all came down to a penalty shoot-out. Mills tucked home his kick, but Talbot, Viljoen and Woods all failed. Goodbye Europe for another year.

Having exited the League Cup at the hands of Manchester City a week earlier, the Barcelona nightmare was quickly capped by a miserable defeat at lowly Bristol City in the League. This left Town marooned in mid-table, with their only realistic ambitions now centring on the FA Cup.

Skipper Mick Mills, playing the best football of his life at full-back or in midfield, wherever the need arose, broke the club's appearances record in the third round at Cardiff, which earned a dull win. This brought plucky Hartlepool to Portman Road in the fourth round and after some early resistance they were overcome to set up a tie at Second Division Bristol Rovers. Like Town, the Eastville side were not pulling up any trees in the League, but had already disposed of Sunderland and Southampton.

The referee surprised many by allowing the game to start, as the frozen Eastville pitch was covered by thick snow and tested Town's resolve to the full. After Robin Turner had scored his first goal for Town, the Pirates hit back with two from David Williams and a giant-killing looked on. Up popped Turner again with four minutes left to equalise, though many thought Osborne got the final touch.

A replay on Portman Road's green and pleasant land would surely be much less troublesome. Town were also buoyed by the knowledge that victory would bring a quarter-final against lowly Second Division Millwall. With Wembley's twin towers looming, almost 30,000 turned out on a bitter night for the replay, a clear indication that FA Cup fever was gripping the town again. Although Rovers looked sharp early on, Mills' first-half strike lifted the pressure and Town's win was capped by a magical goal from Clive Woods, who displayed skill, pace and shooting power in one rapier-like thrust.

No matter that Town were by now just a few points above the relegation zone – all of a sudden the FA Cup was the only thing on everyone's minds. Millwall's average home gate was almost trebled by a huge contingent of Town fans trekking to the inhospitable Cold Blow Lane. Not even Millwall's reputation could dampen the enthusiasm of the Suffolk folk, and demand for tickets beforehand far outweighed supply. With the pundits tipping Arsenal or Forest as likely FA Cup winners, skipper Mills said he was delighted Town were allowed to 'creep along the road to Wembley'.

Town's odds were quickly reduced after their performance at The Den, however, for they outclassed the home side, chalking up the biggest quarter-final away win since 1926. Although three of the goals came in the closing minutes when the Lions were whimpering rather than roaring, the five-goal margin did not flatter Robson's men. Sadly, however, the victory was overshadowed by appalling scenes of mayhem among the Millwall fans, who attacked Town's following and invaded the pitch. The players had to be led off for nearly twenty minutes in the first half. There was another stoppage later for the removal of missiles from the pitch.

Robson said afterwards he'd been shocked by the scenes and in the heat of the moment let slip an emotional demand that the perpetrators have flame-throwers turned on them. He later claimed this comment was intended to be off the record, but it was broadcast to all and sundry on BBC's Match of the Day. Although many folk actually agreed with him, and wrote to tell him so, the manager wisely took the opportunity the following day to appear on radio and give a more considered view.

Town were paired with Ron Atkinson's West Brom in the semi-finals, by which time there was a definite feeling this would be Town's year. The six League games between the quarter and semi-finals produced just one win, although the fans didn't complain because it just happened to be a 4-0 humbling of Norwich on Easter Monday. The Canaries enjoyed the rare luxury of perching higher than Town in the League, but were left with little to chirp about.

DID YOU KNOW?

Kevin Beattie once had a string of dead-end jobs, including 'chippie' for a cleaning firm. When asked to chip substances off old-folks' laundry, he quit after two hours!

The meeting with West Brom at Highbury produced exactly what a semi-final should – tension, drama, incident and goals – and both teams even spilled blood in their efforts to reach Wembley. Brian Talbot dived to head a dramatic opening goal, but in doing so clashed heads with big John Wile and both sustained serious cuts. Talbot was dazed and unable to continue beyond a further ten minutes. Mick Lambert was introduced and within two minutes he sent a corner-kick to Mills, who fired in No 2 off Cyrille Regis's legs.

Albion were forced onto the offensive, but time was running out before the noisy Town contingent had reason to feel anxious. Hunter, who'd had a sterling game, unaccountably handled a harmless loose ball and conceded a penalty. The big man admitted later he simply had no excuse and couldn't fathom why he'd done it. Tony Brown fired the kick home with fourteen minutes left and Town fans began biting their nails. The roar of relief when John Wark thumped home a header in the 89th minute told its own tale. Ipswich were at Wembley and the celebrations could begin.

Aside from the Wembley date with Arsenal, Town still had seven more League games to negotiate. Safety from relegation was by no means guaranteed. The first three games failed to produce a win, although the point gained at Anfield was precious and hard-earned. It took a single-goal triumph over Bristol City in late April to reach safety, after which the final three League games were lost.

Match of the Season 1977-78
Arsenal 0 Ipswich 1

FA Cup final, 6 May 1978

A week before the club's first FA Cup final, the side took the field at Aston Villa minus Cooper, Beattie, Osborne, Lambert and Mariner, and this weakened, reshuffled and less-than-fully commit-ted side were thrashed 6-1. It soon emerged that Robson had not been merely 'resting' players, but was in fact considering long-term injury victim Colin Viljoen for Wembley. If so, Talbot would be shunted into a new role to make way for the South African, and Osborne would be dropped.

It was a move regarded with horror by the players. Robson later admitted that they opposed his plan and sought to change it. He said he was aware Viljoen wasn't popular within the squad but had misjudged the depth of the resentment. It had been plain to see at Villa Park, however, for some players seemed reluctant to pass the ball to him.

Robson felt undermined and angry over this display of 'player power' but could hardly take disciplinary action just days before a Cup final. He realised he would have to revert to a midfield of Talbot, Wark and Osborne, and the unhappy Viljoen stepped down again, spilling his side of the story to a newspaper. Viljoen didn't travel with the team to their Hertfordshire hotel for Cup final week and shortly afterwards was transferred to Manchester City. He had been more than eleven years at Ipswich.

With this internal squabble resolved, Robson's only remaining worry was the fitness of first-choice central defenders Hunter and Beattie, who both had crocked knees. Hunter's fitness test was arranged for mid-morning on match-day, but the anxious player awoke early and used the hotel lawns to test the injury himself. With his team-mates peering from their windows, Hunter trotted around for a while and then gave the thumbs-up – to loud cheers from the others.

All manner of decorated vehicles streamed down the A12 for the 50th Wembley FA Cup final. The colour and noise generated inside the stadium was unprecedented for a small-town club. Osborne's large family from rural Suffolk made the trip in a special mini-bus and were delighted to see their boy mark Liam Brady out of the game, then score a glorious winner thirteen minutes from the end.

Osborne had nearly missed out altogether and it was astonishing to think he had only become a Town player after being invited to make up the numbers in a junior game while sitting in his car watching his kid brother. Now he pounced to score after a loose clearance by Willie Young, following a fine run down the right flank by Geddis. Osborne was already exhausted by heat and humidity and when the rest of the team swamped him in celebration, he almost passed out and had to be replaced.

Arsenal were frankly a disappointment, but Ipswich, quoted at an amazing 5-2 by some bookies, never let them into their stride and fully deserved the win. Mariner hit the bar in the early stages and later Wark twice hit the same post with shots from outside the box. Burley had a header well saved by Jennings and it had seemed a goal would never come when Osborne did his bit.

An unforgettable weekend was completed in traditional manner when the team toured Ipswich on an open-topped bus the following day, receiving heroes' welcomes on the balcony of the Town Hall.

LEAGUE DIVISION 1   **1978-79**
Division 1   6th
League Cup   2nd Round
FA Cup   Quarter-finals
European Cup-Winners' Cup   3rd Round

Every club suffers periods when injury incapacitates top players, but the mid-to-late-1970s seemed to be one long battle on this front for Ipswich. Bobby Robson had cause to complain long and loud about the club's misfortunes in this respect, and his gripes had become something of a mid-season tradition at Portman Road. However, 1978-79 was different: the injuries were evident right from the word 'go'.

Allan Hunter and Kevin Beattie both passed the summer of 1978 trying to shrug off knee problems, partly the legacy of playing in May's FA Cup final when not fully fit. They both underwent surgery and Beattie returned to play for thirteen minutes in the Willhire Cup pre-season tournament at Colchester before being carried off after jarring the knee on a rock-hard pitch. Wembley goal-scoring hero Roger Osborne also had knee problems that required surgery and this trio would all be unavailable for the opening weeks of the new campaign.

Indeed, Hunter would not return to the first team until October, while Osborne would become the forgotten man of Portman Road by missing the entire season. Terry Butcher fractured his cheekbone during pre-season, while David Geddis, Laurie Sivell and Brian Talbot all spent many sunny days on the treatment table.

With doubts about the availability of his keepers, Robson paid Bournemouth £20,000 for Kieron Baker, and spent considerable time and effort persuading Dutchman Arnold Muhren to join Town. The fee was £150,000. Robson had balanced the books by selling long-serving midfielder Colin Viljoen to Manchester City for £100,000 and defender John Stirk to Watford for £30,000, but getting former Ajax star Muhren to put pen to paper proved difficult.

Robson hired a small plane to Amsterdam for talks. He was desperate to get his man before the UEFA deadline so that Muhren would be available for Town's Cup-Winners' Cup fixtures. FC Twente and Muhren appeared happy after initial talks but after consulting his wife the player turned Town down. Robson dashed from his Amsterdam hotel to the Muhren home 30 minutes away and turned on the charm, persuading the couple to fly to Suffolk the next day to see the area. The Town boss conducted his guided tour of the countryside from the air and even persuaded the pilot to swoop low over the Portman Road training ground. Still Arnold politely declined, but then, just before the UEFA deadline, came a sudden change of mind.

Muhren was duly plunged into the fray at home to Liverpool in the opening home game, but hardly got a kick in a fast-moving encounter that saw Town hammered by an Anfield outfit hitting peak form. However, Town's style of play was altered to accommodate the new man and within weeks he'd settled down and was producing the goods.

The signing was an ambitious and inspired move and off the field the club also took forward-looking steps, spending £600,000 to create 24 executive boxes, an extension to the Centre Spot restaurant and the placing of 1,800 new seats on former terracing. The development reduced the ground's capacity to 32,000, but won the club an Institute of Marketing award and certainly increased its fund-raising potential.

As the season took shape the unsettled line-up showed flashes of top-drawer ability but results were inconsistent and a top-six place looked a distant dream. It seemed as if Cup adventures would outweigh League success for a second successive season, until the early weeks of 1979, when the new-look midfield really began turning on the style.

Although giving his usual all-action displays on the park, local lad Brian Talbot encountered personal problems off it, and decided he would be better off leaving Suffolk. He eventually signed for Arsenal for £450,000, a record fee for both clubs. Potentially his departure could have created a massive hole, but Robson looked again to Holland for a replacement and eventually captured a man he had long admired, the skilled Frans Thijssen. At this time, foreign players in English football were a rarity and Town's two signings created major interest with the inevitable 'Double Dutch' headline cropping up time and again.

Like Talbot, striker David Geddis would subsequently ask to leave Suffolk for non-footballing reasons. In his case he had been traumatised by a tragic late-night road accident on the A12 when his sports car went out of control. He and highly rated youth-team defender Peter Canavan were hurled clear and although Geddis landed on soft ground, his 17-year-old pal was killed.

The tragedy occurred during a hectic November, just days after Robson had to deal with four players breaking a late-night curfew during the trip to play SW Innsbruck. There was also a bizarre one-man walk-out by Eric Gates, who returned to his native north-east complaining about not getting a regular first-team place. Gates told the press he was spending his time potato-picking, but after a call from Robson and subsequent talks with the PFA, he was persuaded back and given a run in the side. Although his actions had seemed petulant and unnecessary, he responded well to being given a second chance and along with Muhren, Thijssen and the emerging Alan Brazil, produced some magical performances in the second half of the season.

Robson again fielded overtures from bigger clubs interested in his services, but his tenth anniversary at Portman Road came and went without his busy office becoming vacant. He turned down Barcelona before Christmas and then, in 1979, had serious discussions with Athletic Bilbao, who dangled a huge pay carrot. While Robson weighed up the pros and cons of such a move, Ipswich's compensation demands were firmly rejected by Bilbao and the move was called off anyway.

Results in the early weeks of the season were a strange mixture, with a handsome win over Manchester United a beacon of comfort in a sea of mediocrity. Defeat by a very ordinary Blackpool side in the League Cup was a bitter pill and home defeats by Aston Villa, Bristol City, Everton, West Brom and Leeds – all before Christmas – set the alarm bells ringing. However, by the time the League position reached its nadir – eighteenth place in mid-November – solid progress was being made in the club's first European Cup-Winners' Cup campaign.

AZ Alkmaar and SW Innsbruck were disposed of – the latter after a tense and physical extra-time – to set up the mouth-watering prospect of another crack at Barcelona after Christmas. Town would be out for revenge, following the events of December 1977, and were buoyed by the knowledge that this time they wouldn't have to face the maestro Johann Cruyff. On the minus side, they would be without the ineligible Frans Thijssen and the suspended Paul Mariner.

As it turned out, Mariner's stand-in, Gates, beat Spanish keeper Artola twice at Portman Road, but Esteban stunned Town by nabbing a vital away goal. The second leg, in front of 100,000, provided a mountainous task, but waves of home attacking were only rewarded by one first-half goal. That was how it stayed: Barca's away goal came back to haunt Town and decided the tie. It was scant consolation that in both two-legged meetings with the Catalonian giants, Town had avoided aggregate defeats.

League form picked up dramatically after Christmas, due in no small part to the excellent understanding that developed between the two Dutchmen and their brilliant link play with colleagues in defence and attack. Some of the football being played was sheer class and the division's strugglers, such as Chelsea, Wolves and QPR, simply had no answer to it.

> **DID YOU KNOW?**
>
> In his youth-team days George Burley once swallowed his false front teeth in a game. Later, in the dressing room, the club doctor told him to let nature take its course.

After the Liverpool Cup defeat, Robson announced that five first-team squad members – Lambert, Osborne, Tibbott and the keepers Sivell and Baker – were available for transfer. Les Tibbott was first to depart, attracting a £100,000 cheque from Sheffield United less than a fortnight later.

Between mid-December and the end of the campaign only two further League defeats were suffered and, as the points continued to accumulate, it became clear that Town were capable of reaching the top six and maybe claiming the final spot allocated for the following season's UEFA Cup. Seven wins and a draw in the run-in saw them salvage exactly that from a season that for many weeks had looked doomed to end in mid-table mediocrity at best.

Things were wrapped up in a typical end-of-season affair at Loftus Road, where fewer than 10,000 saw already relegated QPR hammered 4-0 by a Town side that never needed to engage top gear. Arnold Muhren deservedly won the Player of the Year award for his delightful contributions while the promising Steve McCall won the Peter Canavan Trophy, presented by the parents of the late Town youngster in conjunction with the Telford Oakengates Junior League, from where Canavan had been recruited. For Geddis, the man who survived the accident that killed Canavan, there were too many sad memories to remain in Suffolk. A sympathetic Robson subsequently engineered a welcome move to Aston Villa.

Match of the Season 1978-79

Ipswich 0 Liverpool 1

FA Cup, quarter-final, 10 March 1979

Having disposed of three sides from lower divisions, FA Cup holders Town saw their luck run out when the draw was made for the quarter-finals. They were paired with the toughest opponents possible in Bob Paisley's Liverpool, who had opened up a clear gap at the top of the League and would retain it all season.

Liverpool had won the earlier League match at Portman Road barely breaking sweat, and were one of six sides who had beaten Town on their own turf to that point. On the other hand, Town's unpredictable League form had been forgotten in cup competitions:

they had gone nine games unbeaten in the FA and Cup-Winners'
Cups. Barcelona had been beaten at Portman Road just three days
before the Liverpool tie and confidence was as high in the Suffolk
camp as it had been all season.

With the season's biggest home crowd roaring them on,
Robson's men powered forward in the first period, but found themselves up against a resolute defence, superbly marshalled by Alan
Hansen and Phil Thompson. Town quickly spotted a potential
weakness on Liverpool's left, however, where Emlyn Hughes
looked short of pace. The majority of Town's most threatening
moves came from that source, with Burley, Thijssen and Woods
linking well together.

Just before the half-hour mark, Muhren's cultured left foot nearly
broke the deadlock when he curled in a shot from distance, but Ray
Clemence flew across to tip the ball over one-handed. Despite the
home side's possession and purpose, this was a rare moment of
worry for the England keeper and the longer the game went without a Town goal, the more the tension increased.

Ipswich's worst fears were confirmed after 52 minutes when
Liverpool carved their first clear-cut chance and Kenny Dalglish
punished a rare error of judgement by goalkeeper Cooper. The Scot
controlled a Jimmy Case cross, swivelled and fired the ball home at
the near post from a tight angle. Everyone in the ground – including
Cooper – had expected a cross, and it was the sort of classic poaching that few other strikers of the time could have matched.

The effect of the goal was to strengthen Liverpool's resolve even
further and increase the frantic anxiety of Town, who continued to
pour forward, but now looked rather desperate instead of calm and
measured. A golden chance was wasted on 76 minutes, when
George Burley's drive was deflected into the side-netting and, from
the corner-kick by Muhren, Mariner volleyed wide after lunging
over-hastily at the ball.

As Town threw men forward in the dying minutes, their former
colleague David Johnson twice went close in Liverpool breakaway
raids. The final whistle saw Portman Road sink into depression,
Robson admitting later that the result had left him totally deflated.
Humble as always in victory, Bob Paisley conceded his side had
been lucky in the first period and he had words of sympathy for
Cooper, who had now been beaten three times by classic Dalglish
strikes in the short time since the ex-Celtic man had arrived in
English football. Town's misery was best summed up by young
defender Terry Butcher who had enjoyed a fine game. He said: 'Not
a word was spoken in the bath afterwards. That is our cup lost.'

LEAGUE DIVISION 1　　　　**1979-80**
Division 1　　　　　　　　　　3rd
League Cup　　　　　　　　　2nd Round
FA Cup　　　　　　　　　　　Quarter-finals
UEFA Cup　　　　　　　　　 2nd Round

With Town once again tipped for honours, Bobby Robson's eleventh full season in charge saw him appoint a new man as second-in-command. Reserve-team coach and former Newport County player-manager Bobby Ferguson was promoted to fill the vacancy left by long-serving Cyril Lea, who teamed up with Alan Durban at Stoke.

The new management team were frustrated by events in the opening weeks. A very moderate start was enlivened only by a good win at Arsenal, which featured a rare goal by Allan Hunter. Town fans who looked forward to a steady improvement through the autumn were in for a rude awakening, for results deteriorated alarmingly. Not counting the comfortable UEFA Cup wins against Norwegian part-timers Skeid Oslo, Town chalked up only four victories in their first fifteen games – a miserable run which included five successive League defeats. The inevitable consequence was an unhappy October fortnight spent at the very bottom of Division One table.

Clearly the talented squad was under-achieving and the Portman Road fans were not slow in expressing their anger, both vocally at games and via letters to the local press. Robson diplomatically appealed for calm and patience in his carefully-worded programme notes, but it was clear he was privately angry at the critics with 'short memories'.

Most fans knew better than to read too much into the ten goals (over two legs) fired past Scandinavian minnows Skeid Oslo, who battled gamely but were simply out of their class. Their one moment of glory had come in the opening minutes of the first leg when Svein Gunnar Rein cracked home a sensational shot from distance. In the second leg, poor goalkeeper Per Egil Nygaard was substituted after conceding a sixth goal, purely to save him further humiliation. He left the field with a big smile on his face, and his unfortunate replacement was promptly caught out by a 40-yard lob from teen-ager Steve McCall.

That goal-feast could not paper over the problems in the League, of course. Town's misfortunes in those early weeks were perhaps best summed up by the incredible own-goal that Hunter conjured up to help Liverpool on their way to victory at Portman Road. From out near the touchline he hoisted a massive lob towards his keeper, but poor Cooper was left flailing as it sailed into the net. The tide only slowly began to turn around the time of Robson's testimonial in November. The bumper crowd suggested the majority of fans did not hold him personally responsible for the poor results.

Town only put the bad start behind them after grinding out a couple of 1-0 wins, over Middlesbrough and Derby. It was perhaps no coincidence that the side that took the field at the Baseball Ground had a stronger and more balanced look, with nobody filling in for injured colleagues or playing out of position. A week later Southampton were taken apart on their own turf and confidence and optimism began to flood back into Portman Road.

A rapid climb up the table got underway in December, with Town only blotting their copybook once. Mick Ferguson – admired by Robson, but viewed as too expensive – hit four past Cooper at Coventry. Nothing more was heard of Town's interest in the big Geordie and, despite the fans' clamour for new signings, it would not be until January that a new face would arrive at Portman Road. This was the first purchase since Frans Thijssen nearly a year earlier and, at £250,000, Millwall's teenage winger Kevin O'Callaghan represented a record deal for both clubs. The outlay was, as usual, offset by money Robson garnered from sales. He pulled in £300,000 for striker David Geddis from Aston Villa, £50,000 from Hull for Dale Roberts, £40,000 from Peterborough for winger Mick Lambert, and £70,000 from Norwich for long-serving winger Clive Woods.

Woods and Geddis would both return to Portman Road during the season to face their old pals, as would Colin Viljoen, whose return with Manchester City was personally soured by a 4-0 drubbing and a hat-trick by the irrepressible Eric Gates. After a pulsating local derby on Boxing Day, Town continued their winning ways into the New Year and by the middle of January had stormed into Division One's top six – a remarkable feat considering they'd been rock bottom just ten weeks earlier.

The transformation had been astonishing and the new-found form continued throughout the second half of the season. Had their points tally in the first half of the campaign matched that of the second, Town would have won the title by a six-point margin. Although the defence must take much of the credit – only nine goals conceded in the last twenty League games – the source of the resurgence was undoubtedly the masterful displays turned in by the midfielders Muhren, Thijssen and Wark. This trio had skill, work-rate and strength and only Liverpool – with the likes of Souness and McDermott – could hold a candle to Town's engine room.

With Gates settling into a role just behind the main strikers, Town were fast becoming an outfit that was difficult to play and defend against. With Mariner now partnered by the dynamic figure of Alan Brazil, Town no longer missed the presence of Trevor Whymark. Indeed the new formation, built around the two Dutchmen, seemed to spell an end to out-and-out wingers. And with flankers Lambert and Woods having departed, it was hard to see exactly how the new boy O'Callaghan would fit in.

It was hard to believe Town could prosper having lost players of the calibre of Whymark and – for much of the time – Hunter and Beattie, who a year or two earlier had looked indispensable. Nevertheless, Russell Osman, the rugby-playing son of a former Derby player, had by now established himself as a regular. Young Osman was consistency personified and even on the rare occasions when Hunter and Beattie were fit to return, he could not be shifted from one of the central defensive berths. His partner for more than half of 1979-80 was another emerging star, Terry Butcher. This local lad with a towering physique filled in well at full-back when Mills was pushed into midfield, but was clearly a natural centre-half. Butcher and Osman were rewarded for their efforts with a senior England call-up for the centenary international in Australia after the end of the campaign.

Following his trip to Australia, Osman would head for Hungary, where he and six Town team-mates were invited to appear in the feature film *Escape to Victory*. Beattie and Cooper were recruited by director John Huston to act as stunt 'doubles' for Michael Caine and Sylvester Stallone, while Osman, Wark, O'Callaghan, Sivell and Turner all had minor roles. The story-line revolved around a football match between allied prisoners of war and a German team, and also featured Pele, Ossie Ardiles and Bobby Moore. The final cut of the film suggests superstar Stallone did not learn much about the art of goalkeeping from his expert 'consultant' from Ipswich, who had enjoyed a fine season at Portman Road.

Paul Cooper had won over any remaining sceptics among the fans, and boasted a superb record when facing penalties. During the season he faced a total of eight spot-kicks. He saved five of them, two were netted, and one was ballooned by former England skipper Gerry Francis. The six failed kicks raised the tally of misses to thirteen against Cooper in an Ipswich shirt, and his fast-growing reputation meant that takers faced him with mounting trepidation. He told the media he had a special routine for penalty situations, but would keep the details to himself, thank you!

Penalties were certainly a recurring theme at Town home games during the spring of 1980. Four successive home matches in a 36-day period yielded no fewer than nine penalties – with seven of them unconverted. In the memorable 6-0 thrashing of Manchester United, Town contrived to miss three times from the spot.

DID YOU KNOW?

During his early days at Ipswich, Bobby Robson went to watch Scunthorpe's Kevin Keegan four times. Robson decided the youngster wouldn't make the grade.

With spot-kick specialist Wark absent, due to a family funeral, Thijssen and Beattie both missed, the latter spurning a second chance when a re-take was ordered. Two weeks later, against Leeds, up stepped the returning Wark, only to see his effort saved by John Lukic. Wark was also invited to try again, but crashed the ball against the underside of the bar. The next visitors were Derby, who also managed to miss twice, Cooper saving from Powell and Daly. The sequence had a happy ending for Town when Wark stepped up to convert a couple more against Norwich on Easter Monday.

A penalty also provoked controversy at Anfield when Town travelled to meet the League leaders. After footage of the game was scrutinised it emerged that Thijssen had thrown a lump of mud at the ball just before McDermott stepped up to take a penalty – which was saved by Cooper. When asked, the referee said he didn't notice anything that interfered with the kick: hence play had continued. The scores ended level, but this did not prevent the Reds sailing to another championship victory. Town's final position of third, seven points behind, earned them a place in the following season's UEFA Cup and represented an extraordinary achievement considering the situation the previous autumn.

Town had to twice come from behind against less-fancied clubs in order to progress in the FA Cup, and were given a particularly tough time by little Chester in the fifth round. Town were strongly tipped to reach the semi-finals, even after being drawn away to Everton in the quarters. Goodison had earlier been the scene of one of the club's finest-ever away performances, a 4-0 destruction of Gordon Lee's men that featured brilliant creative play and was one of those afternoons when everything clicked perfectly. The cup-tie, just a month later, was a different kettle of fish, however, and Everton gained a measure of revenge.

Match of the Season 1979-80

Norwich 3 Ipswich 3

Division 1, 26 December 1979

Having won five of the six League games leading up to this Boxing Day local derby, Town had well and truly put their poor start behind them. With Norwich enjoying a prolonged spell in the top six – choosing this occasion to unveil their new £1 million River End stand and taking record gate receipts into the bargain – the stage was set for a contest to warm the Bank Holiday crowd.

With their four-man midfield in masterful form on a soft pitch, Town were raiding dangerously, channelling many attacks through Alan Brazil. Town opened the scoring after sixteen minutes. Mills sent in a curling cross, keeper Kevin Keelan flapped at it, and the loose ball was hooked in by Gates.

Norwich drew level when Martin Peters flicked on Greg Downs' cross and Peter Mendham headed firmly home. The see-saw contest turned City's way before the break when Muhren was dispossessed and Alan Taylor fooled Cooper into diving the wrong way, leaving the Norwich man to beat the back-tracking Burley with his shot.

Norwich were by now rampant, but after Muhren headed off the line to deny Peters, Town levelled after the interval against the run of play. Mills' cross was headed back by Gates, and after Muhren's first attempt was blocked by Peters, he made no mistake from the rebound. 2-2. The end-to-end thrills continued and Kevin Bond, son of the Norwich manager, executed a goal-line clearance to deny Gates, before City hit the woodwork twice in six minutes, first through a John Ryan drive and then a Keith Robson header.

Town rode the storm and eased 3-2 ahead when Muhren's precision cross was powered home by Wark's head for the best goal of the game. Ipswich looked to be finishing the game the stronger, roared on by their delighted travelling fans. However, Norwich threw on young substitute Justin Fashanu and were rewarded at the death when Robson deflected a wayward David Jones shot past Cooper for a dramatic leveller.

East Anglian derbies over the years have never been short of drama, but had never produced a contest quite like this. Many years later those present still referred to it as the most riveting ever clash between the two clubs. The two sides experienced vastly contrasting fortunes in the aftermath. Ipswich's winning ways carried them into third place, whereas Norwich only won one of their next thirteen games, sinking from fourth to fifteenth.

LEAGUE DIVISION 1	**1980-81**
Division 1	2nd
League Cup	4th Round
FA Cup	Semi-final
UEFA Cup	Winners

A season that extended for 40 weeks provided thrills, spills and huge drama. It ended with skipper Mick Mills hoisting silverware above his head, but with a lingering feeling that there could – and maybe should – have been more than just the UEFA Cup bound for Town's trophy cabinet.

By the time Christmas 1980 had come and gone, there was widespread recognition – expressed in the media and by rival managers and players – that Town were the best team in the country. A magnificent treble of League, FA Cup and UEFA Cup was a very real possibility – all it needed was for Town's key men to steer clear of injury and for a few lucky breaks to come their way.

The big prize was naturally the League championship, and Robson was desperate to get it. The imperious form of the two Dutch stars, plus the goalscoring flair of Scots Wark and Brazil, was a feature of the campaign and nobody could deny that this side had the credentials to take the title. Although success usually breeds success, there can be no doubt that the long FA and UEFA cup runs exerted heavy pressure on the business of winning League games. It is worthy of note that of nine League defeats suffered, seven occurred in the final ten fixtures – when the pressure really was on.

Town ploughed through the season with an average of one game every four days, with principal championship rivals Aston Villa generally having just one per week. And with virtually all Town's first-choice team having extra international duties to perform, the sheer toll of matches meant 21 different players were used. At Villa, on the other hand, only fourteen men made the first team, and seven of those were ever-present. This stability must have helped the Villa cause and although they could not match the flair and excitement of some of Town's victories, Ron Saunders certainly created a unit that was committed and difficult to beat.

Town had started so brightly, losing only twice in the first seven months of the League. With ten games left they were established at the top and looking well nigh impregnable. The early weeks saw much slick football and clinical finishing and by early November Town remained the only unbeaten side in the entire League. Everton were hammered 4-0, Liverpool were shackled on their own ground, and the fine run only ended when a side crippled by injury and suspension came undone at Brighton.

DID YOU KNOW?

When Trevor Whymark scored four goals against Lazio in the 1973-74 UEFA Cup, deadly rivals Roma presented him with a special commemorative plaque.

Although further points slipped away at Southampton and Tottenham, the overall pace was maintained by bumper performances in January. Birmingham boss Jim Smith saw his team crushed at Portman Road and pronounced Town the best side in Europe. This type of display was repeated shortly afterwards when Stoke and Coventry were also hammered by four-goal margins.

Town were hard to stop when in full flow. Keith Burkinshaw's Tottenham opted for physical intimidation when they arrived at Portman Road in March. However, despite the after-effects of three major cup-ties in seven days, Town showed great composure and disdain in the face of Spurs' provocation and won by three clear goals. Half a dozen players were crocked that day, with skipper Mills the most seriously affected – he left the field with a dislocated shoulder and would be forced to miss several crucial games.

With Burley already out for the rest of the season with damaged knee ligaments, Town were now without both senior full-backs. This meant Suffolk-born youngster Steggles had to be thrown in at the deep end and he gave a handful of mature performances in difficult circumstances. He would be the only player to make an Ipswich debut throughout the campaign. By coincidence, his League bow came at Old Trafford, just as fellow defenders Beattie and Burley did before him.

Having lost just two of the first 32 games, the grinding frequency of games during March seemed to catch up with the squad. Even so, they stayed top of the table throughout March and, having progressed to the last four of both the FA and UEFA Cups, there were genuine hopes of pulling off a remarkable treble. Then three successive League away defeats in a fortnight put the skids under the title challenge. This meant the trip to Aston Villa in mid-April boiled down in many people's eyes as a 'title decider'. Villa had taken over pole position and a win for them would virtually extinguish Town's hopes. Having played many fewer games than weary Town, Ron Saunders' men were favourites to triumph, particularly as Town had to pick themselves up after an unhappy FA Cup semi-final at the very same ground just three days earlier.

Ipswich rose to the challenge brilliantly and shocked Villa by forging a two-goal lead. In front of nearly 50,000, the tension rose when Gary Shaw pulled a goal back for Villa, but Town held on to open up the title race again. Delight turned to gloom the following week, however, when Town slipped up 0-2 at home to Arsenal and then 0-1 at Norwich.

By the penultimate Saturday, Town needed to win both their remaining fixtures to take the title – and then only if Villa lost their one remaining game, at Arsenal. Town's bright start at Middlesbrough, combined with news that Villa were losing at Highbury, brought excitement to fever pitch. The gloom returned when Boro's Bosko Jankovic scored twice after the break. Although Villa did lose at Arsenal, Town's defeat meant the title was bound for the Midlands. It was a bitter blow, but Robson and his men had to hide their pain and focus on the forthcoming UEFA Cup final. It was all that was left.

The quest for the FA Cup had ended at the semi-final stage just three days before that crunch League game with Villa. Town were beaten by Manchester City on a day when they enjoyed enough possession, but never quite got their normal game going. Only Beattie seemed to be unaffected by the stifling tension, and when he departed with a broken arm the writing was on the wall. Paul Power's winning goal in extra-time came was not unexpected.

Aston Villa, Shrewsbury and Charlton had been disposed of earlier in the competition, although the fourth round tie at Gay Meadow saw Ipswich survive a few scares after Burley sustained his long-term injury. The subsequent quarter-final thriller at Nottingham Forest saw the sides share six goals and England full-back Viv Anderson suffered a personal nightmare. His mistake led to Town's opening goal; he followed this with a horrendous own-goal; and then dislocated his shoulder. The replay three days later was a tense and nail-biting affair with just Muhren's volley separating the sides. The only distasteful aspect of this epic tie was when the club's new luxury Volvo team bus was vandalised at the City Ground.

The early rounds of the UEFA Cup gave Town little trouble, and also provided a Europe-wide stage for the goalscoring exploits of midfielder Wark. Aided by plenty of opportunities from the penalty spot, Wark went on a remarkable spree. His overall season's total of 36 was the club's highest since Ray Crawford in 1962.

First to be welcomed at Portman Road were Greek side Aris Salonika, whose crude tactics were not only unsavoury, but hugely unsuccessful as they lost 1-5. Gates was kicked every time he gained possession and Town ended up with three penalties – plus a numerical advantage when hatchet-man Firos was red-carded. The Greeks put the emphasis on skill in the second leg and gave Town a few anxious moments, but the four-goal deficit was insurmountable. The 200 Town fans who made the journey to Greece experienced problems from hostile home fans, but came home criticising the UK tabloid press, which had given the impression their trip had been one long nightmare.

Bohemians of Prague were also comfortably beaten at Portman Road, with Wark again on the scoresheet, and although the deficit was pegged back in the bone-chilling cold of the second leg, Town were deserved winners. The next visitors were Widzew Lodz from Poland, who were hammered 5-0 in a ruthless display, featuring another hat-trick from Wark, who by now had hit eight goals in the three home legs.

The much-fancied French outfit St Etienne were the quarter-final opponents and Robson was beaming with pride when his men overturned an early deficit to win 4-1 in France. It was perhaps the club's finest hour on foreign soil and the French sports paper *L'Equipe* remarked: 'Ipswich were better organised and complete in all aspects of the game. It was a classic performance.'

Ipswich were by now making headlines on all fronts, with the marvellous night in France followed by the PFA annual awards dinner at which Wark was named Player of the Year. Team-mates Thijssen and Mariner were second and third. As if this wasn't enough, Town also filled the first three places in the Football Writers' awards, with Thijssen first, followed by Mills and Wark.

St Etienne were comfortably seen off in the second leg. A two-legged semi-final against FC Cologne proved a much tighter affair. Wark (who else?) scored the solitary goal in the home leg, setting up a major battle in the second. Town repelled a side containing many German internationals and clinched their place in the final when the overworked Butcher headed the clincher.

After missing out in the League and FA Cup, the UEFA Cup final against the Dutchmen of AZ '67 Alkmaar had an 'all or nothing' atmosphere about it. But, when Wark slipped home his thirteenth and penultimate European goal in the first leg at Portman Road, Town fans sensed that this momentous season would have a happy ending. The newly crowned Dutch champions were skilled opponents, but Town's confidence after disposing of St Etienne and Cologne was sky high and they finished the first leg three goals up.

Match of the Season 1980-81

AZ '67 Alkmaar 4 Ipswich 2

UEFA Cup final, second leg, 20 May 1981

Town's 66th match of the season saw them head for the Olympic Stadium in Amsterdam with a three-goal cushion from the first leg and a full-strength side, apart from long-term injury-victim Burley.

Victory on this sultry night in Holland would go far towards easing the pain of losing out on the League title.

Despite the considerable advantage from the first leg, nothing could be taken for granted. Town had frittered away good leads in Europe before, and the home side had shown their true capabilities when clinching the Dutch championship a week or two earlier by thrashing Feyenoord 5-1 on their own ground. AZ, whose name comes from the 1967 amalgamation of Alkmaar and Zaanstraak, opted, for financial considerations, to play the final in the Olympic Stadium, twenty miles from their normal home. Although the 67,000-capacity ground was less than half full, the large contingent that made its way across the North Sea helped create a lively atmosphere on a muggy evening.

Town got off to a perfect start when Dutchman Thijssen volleyed in after less than four minutes. However, the home side responded positively and retrieved the deficit three minutes later, courtesy of skilful Austrian international Kurt Welzl. Further home attacks were rewarded midway through the first half when tall midfielder Johnny Metgod headed home a Jan Peters cross.

Town were stung into retaliation and Wark hooked home an equaliser that gave him his fourteen European goal, equalling the record set by AC Milan's Jose Altafini in 1963. Although Ipswich had restored their three-goal cushion, their ranks were pierced again before the break when Pier Tol scored at the far post after Jos Jonker knocked down Peters' cross. Alkmaar coach George Kessler threw caution to the wind in the second half and sent on sub Kees Kist for Tol. The barrage that Robson expected duly arrived and it was backs to the wall stuff for Town.

Just when it seemed Ipswich might weather the storm, the fate of the trophy was once more thrown into question as Jonker fired a free-kick around the Town wall and high into Cooper's net.

This left Town just one goal ahead on aggregate with seventeen minutes to hold out. But hold out they did. Mills lifted the huge UEFA trophy and all those fears of finishing a magnificent season empty-handed and broken-hearted were forgotten. Four days later the triumphant squad paraded the trophy to the townsfolk of Ipswich from an open-topped bus and were welcomed at a civic reception by Mayor Ann Smith.

LEAGUE DIVISION 1   **1981-82**
Division 1   2nd
League Cup   Semi-final
FA Cup   5th Round
UEFA Cup   1st Round

A season that introduced three points for a win, and the advent of the League's first artificial playing surface, got off to a promising start for Ipswich with pre-season friendly victories over Glasgow Rangers, Ajax and Standard Liege, plus the announcement of a major sponsorship deal involving Japanese hi-fi manufacturers Pioneer. The deal would be worth more than £400,000 over three years and would help fund a new stand for the west side of the stadium.

There were no new faces in the first-team squad when the new campaign kicked off, but there was new technology in the shape of a smart new electronic scoreboard and an 'electric blanket' for the Churchman's end of the pitch, which often tended to become frost-bound in winter. Season ticket sales were encouragingly high.

Sunderland nearly spoiled the opening-day party at Portman Road when they twice took a two-goal lead, but were eventually pegged back in a six-goal thriller. Despite missing long-term injury victim George Burley, the side had a settled look and got off to a brisk start, not tasting defeat until the ninth game. In fact, a rain-soaked victory over Leeds at the end of September saw Town take over at the top of the table – a position they held for three weeks until a ragged performance at Everton saw them slip back into the pack.

As UEFA Cup holders, the club were seeded in the draw for the first round, so somewhat easier opposition than Alex Ferguson's tigerish Aberdeen had been anticipated. Despite a fine goal by Thijssen in the home leg, the Dons gave two excellent displays – particularly in front of their fans at Pittodrie – and fully deserved to dump Town out of the competition.

The League Cup campaign did bear some fruit, however, and two good performances against a struggling Leeds outfit, who would ultimately be relegated under Allan Clarke, saw progress into the third round. Here, Fourth Division Bradford City proved a tougher nut to crack than their illustrious neighbours Leeds. They escaped from Portman Road with a draw and were only overcome at Valley Parade after a dramatic extra-time winner. Town's hero of the hour was the diving figure of Robin Turner, whose Town goals were few and far between, although he always seemed to come good in cup competitions.

DID YOU KNOW?

Eric Gates might have a humble northern background, but his full name is Eric
Lazenby-Gates, complete with hyphen. He was ribbed at school, so shortened it.

A fine win at Everton, followed by a hard-earned home victory
over Graham Taylor's up-and-coming young Watford, secured a
semi-final spot for the first time in this competition. Sadly Town
were off-colour in the first leg and a classy Liverpool performance
virtually decided the tie inside an hour. Just four days after exiting
the League Cup at Anfield came a humiliating FA Cup defeat at
Shrewsbury's Gay Meadow, a ground Town were asked to visit for
a second successive season.

This fifth round embarrassment came courtesy of two early and
well-crafted set-piece goals and undid all the good work in the
previous two rounds at Birmingham and Luton. A legacy of the 3-0
win at Kenilworth Road was a serious injury to Butcher, who,
despite being well over 6ft tall, took an accidental boot in the face
from Hatters' striker Brian Stein. Butcher bravely played on until
victory was assured, not realising that the blood streaming from his
nose was due to a cut artery and not merely a straightforward nose-
break, which is, of course, an occupational hazard of the central
defender.

When the flow of blood could not be stemmed in the dressing
rooms, Butcher was hospitalised. After eventually being allowed
home, the wound opened up again, to the horror of his pregnant
wife Rita, and he was whisked back for surgery. Ultimately the
amount of blood pumped into his body by way of transfusions left
him weak and unwell for a lengthy period. He would not return to
the side for ten weeks.

Although Kevin Steggles coped manfully in his place, Butcher's
absence placed considerable responsibility on the young shoulders
of Russell Osman. Following 133 consecutive appearances, Osman
himself missed a game in February, which meant an unexpected
recall for veteran Allan Hunter, who had been quietly seeing out his
testimonial season at Portman Road. Glasgow Celtic sent a side to
Suffolk for his big night and more than 15,000 turned out to pay
tribute to one of the most popular figures ever to pull on a Town
shirt. By the end of the season Hunter had been appointed player-
manager of neighbours Colchester United. He would quit after just
eight months in management, citing disillusionment with the nature
of the role.

By a strange twist of fate, the other half of the brilliant Hunter-
Beattie defensive partnership was also about to bid Town farewell,

and would also sign off with a well-attended testimonial match on an emotional night at Portman Road. Moscow Dynamo were the visitors for Kevin Beattie, whose battle to overcome a crippling knee injury was officially declared lost after five operations in four years. In his umpteenth comeback attempt in an October reserve match at Luton, Beattie appeared to get through the action reasonably well, but after unstrapping the knee in the dressing room he felt the joint collapse under him, leaving him in agony and in little doubt that the end was near.

Desperate not to turn his back on football, he would join Hunter at Colchester for a short period and after the U's physio, Charlie Simpson, worked a few miracles on the knee, actually played several more games. He then amazed all and sundry by moving to Middlesbrough, where Malcolm Allison made him skipper. Inevitably he could only manage a handful more games and a marvellous career was cut short before he reached 30.

Town's nine-match winning run, which began in November and extended to January, saw them regain top spot in the League for another three weeks. But a troubled six-week period of cup exits, injuries and loss of form meant they had slipped out of the top six by mid-March. At this point few would have anticipated the sort of recovery that would lead to a genuine title challenge – but that is precisely what happened. A 1-1 draw at Forest, which saw Steggles sent off and Sivell save a penalty, proved the turning point. From that afternoon on, Town recaptured their best form and steamed back up the table with a succession of well-deserved wins.

Robson was as pleased as punch. The only blot on the landscape was the post-Christmas form of Liverpool, who, remarkably, had started January back in twelfth position. The League leadership had been the property of a clutch of different sides, including Town, Manchester United, Swansea, West Ham, Manchester City and Southampton. None, in truth, looked genuine championship material, but by the time the Anfield juggernaut got into its stride there was an inevitability about the destination of the title. Bob Paisley's men turned in some awesome displays and chalked up twenty wins and three draws from their final 25 League games. Although they had huge ground to make up at the turn of the year, their progress was inexorable and by the closing weeks only Town looked capable of pipping them.

After the draw at Forest, Town won four League games in a row to reclaim second spot and moved into top gear themselves. But they clearly needed Liverpool to slip up badly if the championship was to come to Suffolk. Indeed, such was The Reds' consistency that Town couldn't even afford to draw if they hoped to keep pace.

When they took only a point at Maine Road – Brazil uncharacteristically missing a sitter and Wark blazing a penalty over the bar – the race was as good as over.

Liverpool subsequently took the title by four points, having avoided defeat in their final fifteen games. Town slipped up in their penultimate game, beaten by a virtuoso display by Forest's Peter Davenport – but even had they won, the championship would still have gone to Anfield.

It had been a fascinating season with plenty of highlights, not least the superb displays of Alan Brazil. The Scot really came of age in 1981-82, cracking home 28 goals, many of them involving clinical displays of the finisher's art. Brazil's speciality was the one-on-one cat and mouse with a goalkeeper, a situation from which he rarely missed. He single-handedly provided many Town fans with their season's personal highlight when he bulged Southampton's net no fewer than five times at Portman Road. The Saints were actually top of the table that night and Brazil was simply awesome. He equalled Ray Crawford's club record (notched against 'lesser' opposition – Floriana of Malta) and recorded the best top division tally in a single match for seven years.

Naturally Brazil, along with team-mates Wark and Burley, was a cert for Scotland's World Cup squad which travelled to Spain in the summer of 1982. Making the trip in the English party were Mills, Mariner and Butcher. Osman was omitted but had added to his international honours earlier in the season, while Gates found himself in manager Ron Greenwood's initial squad of 40.

When Greenwood intimated he would be quitting as England manager after the finals, speculation about his replacement centred on Town's manager. Bobby Robson had been at Portman Road for thirteen years and had turned down lucrative offers to go elsewhere, but this was one challenge he could surely not resist. He had already worked part-time with the England 'B' and Under-21 sides and as far as most observers were concerned it was not a question of if he would become England manager, it was when.

Match of the Season 1981-82

Ipswich 0 Liverpool 2

League Cup, semi-final, 1st leg, 2 February 1982

Town enjoyed their best run to date in their 21st League Cup campaign, reaching the last four along with West Brom and Tottenham, but were handed the toughest possible draw when paired with holders Liverpool – with the second leg at Anfield. After a club record nine successive wins, Town were beginning to buckle under the strain by the time Bob Paisley's men came to Portman Road. Butcher was missing, injured, and the run of wins had come to an abrupt halt at the hands of Notts County.

Liverpool were easing into top gear around this time and came into the tie off the back of five straight wins. Ipswich welcomed back Mariner, who missed the Notts County defeat, and Robson sprang a surprise by omitting Thijssen to make way for him. The Dutchman was not best pleased and his body language spoke volumes before kick-off when he trudged straight to the dug-outs and didn't bother to join the pre-match warm-up.

Liverpool looked well in control early on and by the interval the pressure was mounting on Town to get their noses ahead, to find a goal to defend in the second leg. Within seconds of the restart, however, the Merseysiders took the lead. Town disputed the goal, claiming they should have been given the throw-in that led to it. The throw was fed to Ian Rush who swept past Osman before firing a drive that Cooper could only parry into the path of McDermott, who netted his sixteenth goal of the season. With Town licking their wounds and grumbling at the referee, worse was to follow just two minutes later. Sammy Lee lobbed forward and Rush – looking marginally offside – burst clear. Even though he didn't need to, Cooper chose to race off his line and Rush knocked the ball past him, the shot evading Osman's attempt at a last-ditch clearance.

Defeat had turned to disaster in 90 seconds and Town's hopes of a third major cup final in four years looked in tatters. Although there was still more than 130 minutes to put things right, Liverpool looked so dominant that an atmosphere of gloom descended on Portman Road. Mariner and Brazil, so potent a week or two earlier, were completely shackled by Hansen and Lawrenson, and the only time Town threatened to reduce the deficit was when Grobbelaar made a super save from Wark, clinging acrobatically to his long-range effort.

The occasion had turned into a huge anti-climax and Robson admitted afterwards it had been 'a shocking night' for his men. He said they played poorly, didn't create chances and were thoroughly disjointed in their build-up. The goals had an element of controversy about them, but there was no question the better side had won. Although Town showed commendable fight in the second leg, digging out a 2-2 draw, Paisley's men headed for Wembley where they duly beat Tottenham 3-1 to retain the trophy.

Ipswich journalists take to the field. Your author is third from the right, back row

Ipswich and Barnsley prepare for battle at Wembley (May 2000)

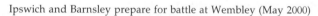

Laurie Sivell enjoys female attention during his testimonial year

Celebrations after the FA Cup semi-final win over West Brom (April 1978)

Ipswich Town's FA Cup-winning squad of 1978

Paul Mariner is beaten to the ball by the late Les Sealey (February 1981)

In his first full season, Brian Talbot took over penalty duties (November 1974)

George Burley puts Willie Young under pressure in the FA Cup final (May 1978)

Terry Butcher and Russell Osman block Luton's Ricky Hill (August 1984)

Brian Talbot and Kevin Beattie – home-grown talent in the Cup final (May 1978)

Chapter Three

After the Lord Mayor's Show 1982-1987

LEAGUE DIVISION 1	**1982-83**
Division 1	9th
Milk Cup	2nd Round
FA Cup	5th Round
UEFA Cup	1st Round

An era ended at Portman Road in the summer of 1982 when Bobby Robson finally relinquished the manager's chair for Lancaster Gate and the England job. Thirteen years and seven months earlier he'd arrived in Suffolk as the directors' third-choice candidate – and as an unemployed family man had been delighted to accept the job, even thought it initially came without a contract.

Within a few years he had proved his worth and was ensconced in the safest job in football, his signature at the end of a ten-year contract. He had become the longest-serving manager in the League, the only one to stay with one club throughout the 1970s, despite attempts to lure him to Derby, Leeds, Everton, Sunderland, Barcelona and Bilbao. Stepping into his shoes was an unenviable task, and it fell to the down-to-earth Geordie Bobby Ferguson, 44, who certainly knew what would be involved, because he had spent eleven years at Portman Road already. He'd risen from youth coach to first-team coach and knew the club almost as intimately as Robson.

Ferguson officially took up his duties nine days before the start of the season, knowing he was on a hiding to nothing. After ten years of great success he couldn't afford to let standards drop, and anything less than a top-six finish would surely be seen as failure. Only once in ten years had Town finished outside the top six and on that occasion they'd compensated by winning the FA Cup.

A no-nonsense character, Ferguson had cut his managerial teeth as the young player-boss of Newport County during their struggles at the bottom of Division Four. He knew all about pressure and had the stomach for a fight, but how would he follow an act like Robson? His first problem was how to replace midfield maestro Arnold Muhren, whose contract had expired and who had moved to Manchester United. Muhren's magical left foot had been a crucial weapon in Town's armoury over the previous four years and his link-up play with Mills and Brazil would be sorely missed.

DID YOU KNOW?

Mick Lambert was a substitute both in an FA Cup final and a Test Match. When on the Lord's groundstaff he once carried on drinks for England v West Indies.

Ferguson handed Muhren's No 8 shirt to reliable Steve McCall, but the campaign got off to a slow start. After an ordinary Stoke side came to Portman Road and made off with a 3-2 victory, Town were left winless and bottom of the table. Ferguson held his nerve, however, refused to make drastic changes, and was rewarded seven days later with a startling 6-0 victory at Notts County, the Meadow Lane club's worst home result in 94 years, as well as Town's best-ever away success.

That gave the side a fillip at just the right time, for a week later all-conquering Liverpool were in town, on an unbeaten run of 23 games and looking set to retain the League title they'd won a few months earlier. Despite the absence of main strikers Mariner and Brazil, Town rose to the occasion and won a tense match with a single goal from South African-born Mich D'Avray, whose glorious header was his first goal in eight months.

The climb back up the table was slow, steady, and remarkable, given that Mills, Brazil and Gates were all apparently on the verge of quitting Suffolk. Mills attracted interest from a variety of clubs and eventually left for Southampton in November for a cut-price £40,000. The 33-year-old, who had skippered England in the World Cup finals that summer, opted for The Dell after a late intervention by Saints manager Lawrie McMenemy. However, he had earlier pledged himself to Sunderland: the Rokerites had even arranged a press conference to unveil him. Manager Alan Durban was not best pleased by the late developments and described Mills' and Ipswich's behaviour as highly unethical.

As is often the way with these things, shortly after joining Southampton Mills had to face his former team-mates. Later in the season, on his first return to Portman Road, he was afforded the rare accolade of a 'guard of honour' of Town players, who applauded him on to the pitch. Having arrived at Ipswich as a kid when Portsmouth scrapped their youth team to cut costs, Mills had given wonderful service to Ipswich and broke the club appearances record into the bargain. He ultimately totalled 741 competitive matches, leaving him way ahead of anyone else on the list.

Gates and Brazil also spent time on the transfer list, although Brazil had reportedly signed an extension to his contract. With the expiry of Thijssen's contract looming, Town fans could see that the break-up of a great team was now well underway and there was concern that the club didn't appear keen to spend heavily to replace the departing stars. The new £1.4 million Pioneer Stand was erected in time for a February opening, which seemed to confirm that the directors' priorities lay off the field rather than on it. However, the cost of the stand was being funded, at least in part, by the Japanese hi-fi manufacturers Pioneer. This company's name also appeared on the players' shirts, provided TV cameras were not present. Overt sponsorship was still some years away.

Despite some players clearly feeling unsettled and a widespread feeling among fans that the abrasive Ferguson wasn't popular in the dressing room, Town's results improved as Christmas approached and an exciting 3-2 win at Sunderland saw them nudge up to seventh place.

A feature of Ipswich's performances around this time was the continued goalscoring exploits of John Wark, who was deadly around the edge of the box, grabbing many goals by expertly timing his runs from midfield. He scored what was surely the goal of the season when Manchester United were the visitors, lashing home a spectacular overhead kick in true Brazilian style. He had already bagged four goals against West Brom, the second time he had registered a foursome. His final tally of twenty League goals didn't include a single penalty – for the most basic of reasons. For the first time since Town joined the League they failed to be awarded a single spot-kick.

The traditional Christmas meeting with Norwich City brought disappointment with a 2-3 defeat Portman Road. The match was a thriller, however, and Martin O'Neill's late goal for the Canaries was worthy of winning any game. A chance for revenge came in the fifth round of the FA Cup, but Town old-boy Keith Bertschin scrambled in a scruffy early goal and Town couldn't get back on terms no matter how they tried.

The League fixture at Norwich in April was notable for the farewell display by Thijssen, who played brilliantly, took an ovation from Town fans, and then headed off to a new life in Canada. By the time of his departure Brazil had also gone, joining Tottenham in March and bagging half-a-dozen goals to help Keith Burkinshaw's team into a finishing place of fourth.

The League and UEFA Cups both saw exits at the first hurdle, although the opposition – Liverpool and AS Roma, respectively – was top class in both cases. European football would not return for the 1983-84 season as Town only won three of their final ten League games and ended the campaign ten points short of qualifying for a UEFA Cup place. Those fantastic European nights seemed to be a thing of the past.

Match of the Season 1982-83

Notts County 0   Ipswich 6

Division 1, 25 September 1982.

Having gone six League games and a UEFA Cup-tie without the taste of victory, Town's poor start to 1982-83 was well on the way to becoming a full-blown crisis in the eyes of fans who hadn't suffered such calamities in more than ten years. In addition to the poor results, skipper Mills and Gates looked set to follow Muhren out of Portman Road. Those who travelled up the M1 to Nottingham didn't exactly have a spring in their step.

However, six goals in 62 minutes, creating a club record away win, did much to dispel the gloom. Town fielded a team whose total cost was less than County's £600,000 winger John Chiedozie – a testament to Robson's careful husbandry and fine youth policy.

With Jimmy Sirrell having moved 'upstairs' at Meadow Lane, leaving Howard Wilkinson to oversee team affairs, County had been unpredictable since arriving in the top flight. Before this match, their defence had been quite miserly – conceding just three in five matches – but had spoiled things by going down 3-5 at Luton, in a game enjoyed by Anglia TV viewers three weeks earlier.

With a defence constructed around the imposing figure of Brian Kilcline, County were likely to be vulnerable to quick ground-based attacks, and so it proved. Although Town survived one worrying moment when Steve McCall cleared off the line from Goodwin, the rout commenced in the fifteenth minute, when Mariner swooped low to convert Gates' cross after the little man outpaced Kilcline.

Eight minutes later Brazil raced on to a long ball from McCall, checked inside Kilcline and fired past Raddy Avramovic to make it 2-0. Shortly afterwards the Scot had another effort disallowed, by which time Town were brimming with their old confidence. After the break Wark produced a precision header to convert Gates' cross, and within ten minutes it was four when Brazil burst through, sidestepped the advancing keeper, and allowed Mariner to apply the finishing touch.

Avramovic was beaten at his near post when Thijssen directed Brazil's pass low into the net, and two minutes later the effervescent Brazil sent McCall away down the left. McCall outwitted a defender before crashing home a spectacular sixth and final goal. The manner of the victory drew high praise from Jimmy Sirrell and the goal feast couldn't have come at a better time for Town, allowing them to move off the bottom place they'd occupied since losing to Stoke a week earlier.

LEAGUE DIVISION 1   **1983-84**
Canon Division 1   12th
Milk Cup   4th Round
FA Cup   4th Round

Bobby Ferguson's second season in charge began brightly enough — with four wins and a draw from the opening five League games — and a cash award from new League sponsors Canon for being the top scorers in September. But this was to prove a false dawn, and from the heady heights of second in the table, Town soon began an inexorable slide downwards to spend much of early 1984 in the lower reaches of Division One.

From New Year's Day onwards, a horrendous run of ten defeats in eleven games left the club staring relegation squarely in the face and it would need a dramatic recovery in the closing weeks to stave off the dreaded drop. The season featured plenty of off-field traumas too, and the break-up of the immortal 1978-81 glory team gathered momentum.

With no new faces on show when the season got underway, many fans were surprised at how Town raced out of the blocks and piled up thirteen points from their first five games. One disturbing feature, however, was the slide in attendances. In common with many clubs, Town's average gates slumped badly. Over the season as a whole, only five home matches would attract more than 20,000. The 12,900 who turned out for the visit of Birmingham was Portman Road's lowest League gate for over sixteen years.

The club was stunned in the autumn by the premature death of director and former chairman John Cobbold at the age of 56. This flamboyant old Etonian had been well liked throughout football and had played a major role in the development of the football club from mere 'country cousins' into a force in Europe. His death came days after Stoke were hammered 5-0 to put Town in second place, but was immediately followed by the first defeat of the season at Birmingham and a steady decline in fortunes thereafter.

Among other off-field problems that autumn was a pay dispute involving the side's two key men, Paul Mariner and John Wark. The pair demanded a substantial hike in wages or, failing that, a transfer. They were among the League's top performers at the time and it was clear that if the Ipswich board failed to appease their demands there would be no shortage of interest from more affluent big city clubs. What Mariner and Wark may not have bargained for, however, was the backlash from the ordinary man on the terraces. Although held in high esteem for their abilities on the field, the pair fell foul of fans who felt that their reputed annual earnings (Mariner

£50,000 and Wark £35,000) were more than generous by 1983 standards. Jeering from the terraces and letters fired off to the local press revealed just how deep the feelings went.

To their credit, Mariner and Wark never let their performances slip during this tense period and it was a shame such popular and talented performers should end lengthy stints at Portman Road on such a sour note. The goals continued to flow for both of them, but the directors refused to cave in to their demands, placing them on the transfer list with little hesitation. Mariner joined Arsenal in February for a bargain £150,000 and Wark signed for Liverpool a few weeks later for £450,000. By the time he left, Wark had established an Ipswich club record of 162 consecutive appearances and missed just four games in more than six years.

Given that both men had played well, right up to their departures, it was strange that once the door closed behind them the team immediately started winning. The slide down the table that had begun in the autumn reached its nadir in March, when a midweek defeat at Luton saw Town slip to twentieth. Four days later another reverse at Everton created a club record of seven successive defeats.

Although remedying the perilous league position was clearly the priority, nobody at the club was complacent about the humiliating FA Cup exit at mid-table Second Division Shrewsbury. It was, would you believe, Ipswich's third visit to Gay Meadow in four years in this competition, and their embarrassment at the 0-2 exit was heightened by the scrutiny provided by BBC's Match of the Day cameras.

Action was needed fast to halt the decline and the board released some funds from the Mariner and Wark sales to be spent on new faces. Ferguson signed midfielder Romeo Zondervan from West Brom, plus goalkeeper Mark Grew from Leicester to cover for Paul Cooper. Zondervan's neat touches and midfield industry were a real boost and he revitalised the side, along with fellow newcomer Alan Sunderland, on loan from Arsenal. After taking some weeks to settle, the experienced 30-year-old Sunderland notched several crucial goals and became a key part of the team. Also beginning to assert themselves were youngsters Mark Brennan, a composed midfielder, Canadian full-back Frank Yallop, and the skilful Jason Dozzell. The latter made headlines in February when he became the First Division's youngest goalscorer, coming on as a sub at the tender age of sixteen years and 57 days, and scoring the goal that sealed Town's only victory in a three-month barren spell. Dozzell had caught the eye with dazzling performances in the youth team and was plunged into the fray to the delight of Town fans, who liked nothing better than to see a local lad succeed. The rather bewildered teenager had to contend with press photographers in the playground when he returned to school the following Monday morning, and his life would never be quite the same again.

Victory over Luton on the last day of March, followed by a spirited 2-2 home draw with high-flying Nottingham Forest, provided real hope of a recovery. The optimism grew after a resounding victory at Wolves, although the Molineux side were at such a low ebb that even a Fourth Division side would probably have taken three points that day. With Wolves manager Graham Hawkins teetering on the verge of dismissal, the game attracted only 6,611 – Molineux's lowest crowd for 47 years. Town won 3-0.

The missing Town fans flocked back to Portman Road to see the enemy from Norfolk on Easter Monday and weren't disappointed as a revitalised side chalked up a comfortable 2-0 win and climbed out of the bottom three for the first time in more than five weeks. With light at the end of the tunnel at last, confidence soon flooded back and April ended with an unexpected point gained at Liverpool, who were a fortnight away from clinching their fifteenth League title. Ipswich fans were in fine voice a week later when Russell Osman's powerfully-headed winner meant three points against Sunderland and another huge step towards safety.

Any lingering fears of the drop were dispelled at Old Trafford on the first Bank Holiday in May, when title challengers Manchester United were overcome on their own ground – brave Town coming back from a goal down in the process. Victory over Aston Villa on the season's final day sparked a jubilant pitch invasion by fans not only relieved at the preservation of top division status, but rather amazed that a side so bereft of confidence and spirit had somehow recovered in the final few weeks to finish as high as twelfth in the table.

It had been another season when change was in the air, with the departures of Wark and Mariner followed by that of keeper Laurie Sivell, a one-club man whose debut had been fourteen years earlier. Although one of the smallest keepers ever to perform at senior level, Sivell had made up for his lack of inches with agile and courageous displays that left him battle-scarred. It was a persistent knee injury that forced him to call it a day. Long-serving Robin Turner, plus Tony Kinsella and David Barnes, also played their final games for the club in 1983-84. A testimonial match in recognition of George Burley's ten years in the first team saw Aberdeen beaten 3-0 at Portman Road at the beginning of the season, but Burley – along with Terry Butcher, Kevin O'Callaghan and Irvin Gernon – ended the campaign sidelined because of injury.

DID YOU KNOW?

Following the 1978 Cup final, Mrs Thatcher told BBC radio how impressed she was by Trevor Whymark. She did not know that he missed the game through injury.

Match of the Season 1983-84
Manchester United 1 Ipswich 2

Division 1, 7 May 1984

Town ensured survival from relegation and put paid to Manchester United's hopes of pipping Liverpool for the title by snatching a dramatic victory at Old Trafford in the penultimate match of the season. A month earlier Town had looked certainties for the drop, but, pepped by newcomers Zondervan and Sunderland, they were now just a point or two from safety. United, meanwhile, were a couple of points adrift of Liverpool at the other end of the table and still going flat out for the championship.

Inevitably Ron Atkinson's men piled forward in the first half and applied intense pressure, hitting Town's woodwork twice. After 25 minutes Town buckled. Ray Wilkins' cross was headed on by McGrath and Mark Hughes raced in to head past Cooper. However, spurred on by the tireless Trevor Putney in midfield, the visitors regrouped and keep United at bay for the remainder of the half.

The second period started brilliantly as Duxbury lost possession to Alan Sunderland on the left, and a perfectly weighted cross from the Arsenal loanee was headed home in classic fashion by D'Avray. It was a memorable goal and put Town in fine fettle for the battle that remained. Within minutes of the equaliser, Town lost the lively Zondervan with a back problem, but they stayed resilient, kept their shape, and dealt with everything the frustrated home side could throw at them.

With news filtering through that Liverpool were hammering Coventry at Anfield, United knew they simply had to take all three points and their late attacks were tinged with desperation. The baying Old Trafford fans were shocked into disbelief when, with four minutes left, young Brennan floated a free-kick for D'Avray to knock the ball into the path of Sunderland, who put Town in front. The three points were bound for Suffolk, safety was now a certainty and great were the scenes of jubilation among the away contingent as United fans streamed away from Old Trafford.

LEAGUE DIVISION 1   **1984-85**
Canon Division 1   17th
Milk Cup   Semi-final
FA Cup   Quarter-finals

Sporting a new strip identical to that of newly-crowned European nations champions, France, Ipswich seemed to lack a certain *je ne sais quoi* in attack during the opening weeks of the new season.

The skills of Romeo Zondervan and Brennan, and the industry of Trevor Putney, endowed them with a potent midfield, but much of the fine approach play came to nothing. Up to Christmas, D'Avray and Sunderland only mustered five League goals between them. Town's main offensive weapon continued to be the diminutive Gates, who weighed in with his usual supply of spectacular long-range goals, but was not the sort of poacher that was needed to snap up those 'scruffy' close-range bread-and-butter goals.

Defensively, Ipswich for the most part looked reasonably secure. Apart from one particular encounter with Luton's Mick Harford, Butcher had an excellent season, retaining his place in the England side and winning the club's Player of the Year award. Russell Osman also remained one of the League's leading defenders. In all, Town conceded more than two goals in a single match on only eight occasions throughout a 56-match campaign.

With the lucrative Pioneer sponsorship deal extended for another year, and manager Ferguson's contract extended for another two, Town kicked off the season with four draws. They plodded along in mid-table until the end of October, at which time a rot set in that saw them plummet to 21st place by the end of the year. A run of eleven League games yielded just one victory – and that was against a doomed Stoke side which was compiling the lowest points tally in Division One this century. Just four Ipswich victories in the League at the halfway stage of the season was clearly relegation form, the only redeeming factor being the solid progress made in the Milk Cup.

Most supporters were in no doubt that the major problem was the absence of anyone in the squad likely to get near twenty goals for the season. With the Sunderland-D'Avray partnership firing blanks, Ferguson tried his luck briefly with youngsters Dozzell and Cole, but the need for new blood only became more pronounced.

Major spending on the stadium had given the club a home to be proud of, but restricted Ferguson's ability to move into the transfer market – unless he sold somebody first. Winger Kevin O'Callaghan, frustrated at not being an automatic choice, asked for a move in October. His request was granted, giving Ferguson the means to generate the funds for another forward. O'Callaghan subsequently joined Portsmouth – initially on loan – for £100,000, and with full-back David Barnes headed for Wolves for £35,000, the money was raised to buy Derby's nippy little striker Kevin Wilson.

Wilson had made a great goalscoring start to the season for The Rams, and taken the eye in two lively displays against Town in the Milk Cup, but his season had been interrupted by a broken arm. Like Rod Belfitt and Paul Mariner before him, Wilson's arrival gave a real boost to Town's attack and enlivened the frustrated fans too. Wilson scored against Gillingham in the FA Cup on his debut, created another goal by sheer persistence, and in his early games generally made a nuisance of himself. In modern jargon, he 'made things happen' when Town went on the attack.

Frost-bound pitches and regular cup-ties meant Wilson's home League debut did not arrive until early March, when he inspired a win over Chelsea, opening the scoring with a goal that was down to sheer opportunism and speed off the mark. He later repeated the trick to spark a victory over West Brom that, with twelve matches to go, left Town with a reasonable chance of avoiding the drop. The long runs in both domestic cups, coupled with postponements due to the weather, produced fixture congestion for Ipswich and a situation where games came thick and fast. Town's season would ultimately stretch into the second half of May.

Despite a sweet League double over local rivals Norwich, Town's run in the Milk Cup came to a dramatic end in the dying minutes of the semi-final second leg at Carrow Road. With extra-time looming and Town still dreaming of their first final in this competition, a glorious late Norwich goal brought ecstasy to Norfolk and misery to Suffolk. The final whistle, moments later, left Town's players and fans stunned and bewildered, apart from big Terry Butcher who hurried for the dressing room with tears pouring down his face.

Battered and bruised, both physically and mentally, Town had to pick themselves up for the forthcoming relegation fight, and also for an FA Cup quarter-final at League leaders Everton just three days later. More misfortune would come their way on that day, too, for Town lost key defender Steve McCall at a crucial time. He was sent off for a tackle on Trevor Steven that would normally have merited a yellow card at most. Everton duly cancelled out Town's lead and the ten men had to settle for a Portman Road replay – the club's third massive cup-tie in just eight days. In a tense and delicately poised game, Town again had cause to question a refereeing deci-sion, with Everton's winner coming from a Graeme Sharp penalty, awarded when the ball smacked into the body of Osman, hitting his arm in the process.

DID YOU KNOW?

The 1979 film Yesterday's Hero was partly filmed at Portman Road. The fans, asked to get excited, winced as Ian McShane (Lovejoy) needed several takes before scoring.

So now there was only one thing to aim for – survival in the top flight. Although it was now mid-March, Town still had another seventeen fixtures to fulfil. Needing at least a week to recover from the draining experiences of Norwich and Everton, the players had to cope with just a three-day rest. Matches would now continue to come thick and fast, and although Town had games in hand on their rivals, they were stuck in twentieth place – beneath the trap-door – and could take nothing for granted.

Four games disappeared without a victory, following the Everton cup defeat, but by early April things were looking brighter. West Brom, Nottingham Forest and Norwich were all beaten in an eight-day period, and a stirring 3-2 win at high-flying Tottenham boosted morale further. By the time hapless Stoke were thrashed 5-1 at Portman Road – a hat-trick by Wilson – safety looked well within reach. A win at Roker Park over another doomed side, followed by a point against struggling Coventry, made things absolutely safe. Although a finishing position of seventeenth was the club's lowest for several years, the late rally and excitement generated by the fourteen cup-ties made up for this in most supporters' eyes.

The season featured two testimonials for long-serving players. Eric Gates' night was against an England Under-21 side, but the player's dispute with a local pressman meant the game received little pre-publicity and only 3,000 turned up. Goalkeeper Laurie Sivell, who had quit a year earlier after seventeen years at Portman Road, pulled in twice that number for a match involving Town's 1978 cup-winning players. Sivell deserved this happy send-off, as his last competitive game had been a miserable affair. He had been jeered by sections of the crowd, who may not have been aware that he was not fully mobile that night due to a knee problem.

Match of the Season 1984-85
Norwich 2 Ipswich 0

Milk Cup, semi-final, 2nd leg, 6 March 1985

Town travelled to Carrow Road with a slender one-goal advantage from the first leg, knowing that with a modicum of luck that margin might have been much greater. City boss Ken Brown admitted his side had got off lightly at Portman Road and coach Mel Machin said the Canaries could consider themselves very lucky to still be in with a chance of Wembley. These surprisingly generous views were given such prominence in the Norwich match programme that one wonders whether some sort of psychological ploy was being brought to bear.

Although Norwich would ultimately be relegated, they started this match ten places higher than Town in the Division One table. However, League form was an irrelevance on a night of drama that saw Town tackle their third big game in just five days.

With Norwich kicking off in arrears, an early onslaught was inevitable, but Town held firm for the first half-hour. During this period they suffered a blow when target-man Mich D'Avray left the field with concussion following a clash with Dave Watson. Referee Keith Hackett noticed the insensible South African was choking and apparently swallowing his tongue and was able to administer first aid. Although this collision had been accidental, the game featured many other flare-ups that trod a thin line between the legal and illegal. This was no arena for the faint-hearted.

Just as Town thought they had weathered the storm, City's Steve Bruce strode forward and headed against the bar on 33 minutes. Moments later the Norfolk side took the lead. Veteran Mick Channon fed skipper Deehan, whose shot took a wicked deflection off Cranson's knee to beat Paul Cooper.

Town came out after the break determined to regain their overall lead and went close when Sunderland got clear but rolled his shot wide of Woods' post. With Hartford continuing to impose himself physically on the midfield, Town struggled to get their game flowing and although the contest remained finely balanced, extra-time had a look of inevitability. The extra 30 minutes were moments away when Bruce again galloped forward. This time he powered a header under the crossbar to give Norwich fans a moment they will always treasure. To win a big match, reach Wembley and beat your deadly rivals – all in one split second – was almost too much ecstasy to cope with, and Carrow Road duly exploded into a frenzy. There was insufficient time for Town to save the day. After the final whistle there was no hiding place for the Suffolk hordes as they attempted to slip away into the dead of night.

LEAGUE DIVISION 1   **1985-86**
Canon Division 1   20th (relegated)
Milk Cup   Quarter-finals
FA Cup   4th Round

During the summer of 1985 two more senior pros from the Robson era departed, and another asked for a move. Gates joined Sunderland, Osman headed for Leicester and a few days before the curtain raiser Burley requested a transfer. Between them, the trio had totted up 1,200 competitive games for Town and many fans feared the loss of such battle-hardened campaigners would have dire consequences.

The starting line-up for the opening game at QPR featured just two remaining heroes from the glory days – Cooper and McCall. There was little or no cash available to Ferguson to strengthen his squad, which now looked as short on depth and experience as any since Town's arrival in the top flight eighteen years earlier.

With Gates gone, the main problem would soon emerge. Lack of firepower. Although he could count upon the aerial power of D'Avray, the speed and cunning of Wilson, and the know-how of Sunderland, Ferguson was unable to find a lethal combination. Not a single forward hit the target in the opening five League games, and after sixteen just a measly eight goals had been amassed by the entire team. Bizarrely, this drought was followed by a sudden goal-rush when three matches in ten days yielded no fewer than twelve.

However, this proved a false dawn and Town ultimately finished the campaign as the second-lowest scorers of all the 92 clubs. Accordingly, attendances continued to plummet and only one home game attracted more than 20,000. Just five seasons earlier every gate had exceeded 20,000 except one.

The opening weeks saw the defence looking reasonably secure despite Butcher's temporary absence, and, apart from trouncings by Liverpool and Villa, young Cranson pulled things together well. But five 0-1 defeats in the first ten games tells its own story, and by the end of September Town had slipped to 21st. The need for change was crystal clear. After an abject 0-3 home defeat by a moderate Villa, Burley signed for Sunderland, having completed exactly 500 senior appearances for Ipswich. Ferguson gave debuts the following week to midfielder Neill Rimmer, and the robust utility player Ian Atkins, both arriving from Everton, the latter initially on loan.

Atkins' work-rate and positive attitude undoubtedly helped a side riddled with anxiety but even he could not inspire a victory in the League until his 11th appearance. Progress was made in the Milk Cup, however, although the three clubs beaten – Darlington, Grimsby and Swindon – were all from lower divisions.

DID YOU KNOW?

Bobby Robson invited chubby 14-year-old Paul Gascoigne from Newcastle to Portman Road for trials. But Robson was not particularly impressed by what he saw.

Because of the legacy of the costly Pioneer Stand, the manager was forced to scratch around looking for bargain buys in the lower divisions. One gem he uncovered was midfielder Nigel Gleghorn, a fireman from the north-east who played his football for non-League Seaham Red Star. Possessor of a clever left foot, he was recruited for £5,000 and plunged into the fray in October at Arsenal. Gleghorn made a capable transition to First Division football and ended the season with more than twenty appearances to his credit.

After a depressing October, November came as a real shock to the system. A 2-1 half-time lead at defending champions Everton turned into a 3-4 defeat, and to general astonishment a similar thing happened at Oxford a week later – although this time a 3-0 lead was tossed away. The points had seemed in the bag until John Aldridge pulled one back and Town began to wobble. A revitalised home side took advantage to lash home another three goals. It was the first time any Town side had ever lost a senior game from 3-0 up. Young Jon Hallworth, making his debut in goal, accepted the blame for Oxford's equaliser, but other players came out of the game with less credit.

Hallworth's selection had been a surprise, considering that the more experienced Mark Grew was still on Town's books. Grew had become a forgotten man and clearly didn't see eye to eye with the manager. He requested a transfer and when asked by the local press why he'd not been called up for the Oxford game, wryly remarked that the club's laundry woman had a better chance of being picked than him.

Three days after the Oxford debacle, Swindon were hit for six in the Milk Cup, but what Ferguson and assistant Woods desperately needed were League points. Odd-goal victories over Sheffield Wednesday, QPR and Coventry gave cause for optimism, but then came a bizarre FA Cup-tie against Bradford City at Portman Road. The Second Division side hit four goals, taking the lead in the first half on no fewer than three occasions. Town struggled to match them, but put up a battling performance in the replay and won in extra-time, Brennan scoring the only goal of the 120 minutes. The victory meant Town became the first club ever to progress beyond the third round of the FA Cup on sixteen successive occasions.

After a second bout of knee surgery, Butcher had returned to the side in mid-November and although he made the defence stronger and better balanced, results continued to be erratic. January's fixture list was decimated by the severe wintry weather, but the return of League action in February warmed the cockles of Town hearts when Liverpool were sunk 2-1, thanks to a superb second-half recovery. If Town could reproduce this sort of display, surely safety could still be achieved. Sadly that win ended up as a rare highlight of early 1986. A four-game April run of three defeats and no goals left the club facing Second Division football.

The home match with Oxford took on massive importance. With the U's in similar difficulties, anything less than a win might prove fatal to Town. The game drew an above-average crowd, which whole-heartedly got behind the side, even after Town had fallen behind to that man Aldridge again. Excitement reached fever pitch when, out of the blue, Dozzell and Butcher netted to put Town ahead. But with heroic general Butcher off the pitch, having treatment to a cut head, the visitors drew level again.

In injury-time Town pushed forward and won themselves a fortunate indirect free-kick in a promising position. Atkins, adrenaline pumping and eyes ablaze, strode up as Brennan touched the ball aside and blasted it into the net. Just 30 seconds were left on the clock. Atkins fell to his knees, to be engulfed by team-mates and invading fans, amid joyous scenes unmatched at Portman Road for years. Three crucial points were in the bag – but would they be enough?

Relegation rivals were also picking up points, but the consensus was that three more points (from two away games) would probably see Town safe. First of these was at West Ham, still in with a chance of the championship and definitely not taking things easy. Sadly, John Lyall's Hammers repeated the job they did against Town in the FA Cup a few weeks earlier, although this time their winner was a hotly disputed penalty.

A blue army, many with radios pinned to their ears for news from other grounds, trekked to Hillsborough for the final game. A win was essential, although results elsewhere would have the final say. The occasion seemed too much for some players, and although there was no shortage of endeavour, the side looked ragged, tired and lacking cohesion. Brian Marwood grabbed a late winner for The Owls, leaving a grim-faced Town contingent pinning their hopes on news from elsewhere.

Leicester and Coventry had done enough to stay clear of trouble, meaning the last remaining relegation spot would go to Ipswich or Oxford. The latter had also been beaten but they had one game left. They now needed to beat Arsenal at The Manor 48 hours later to survive and send Ipswich down. A near-capacity crowd squeezed into the U's tiny ground for the Bank Holiday decider. Around 100 miles away Ferguson waited at home to learn of his team's fate, perhaps heartened by chairman Cobbold's message that no heads would roll, relegation or not. Arsenal, with little to play for, were no match for battling Oxford, and goals by Ray Houghton, John Aldridge and Billy Hamilton brought the curtain down on Ipswich's remarkable eighteen years of top-flight soccer in Suffolk.

Match of the Season 1985-86

Sheffield Wednesday 1 Ipswich 0

Division 1, 3 May 1986

With West Brom and Birmingham already relegated, four sides went into the final Saturday all needing a win to avoid accompanying them. With Butcher and Atkins leading by example, Town had plenty of fire and brimstone in their armoury, but they certainly had the hardest final fixture of the four.

Early on at Hillsborough a low shot by Brennan whistled past a post, and Wilson got clear, only to be foiled by the sprawling figure of Wednesday's player of the year, Martin Hodge. Dozzell and Atkins fired shots off target, but Town generally lacked fluency and sparkle and there was an over-riding feeling that Wednesday could step up a gear at any time and take control.

The game remained on a knife-edge into the final fifteen minutes as Town pushed forward in a do or die attempt to find a winner. News filtered through that Coventry and Leicester were both winning, meaning Town simply had to get the points. The gamble of leaving gaps at the back sadly failed on 81 minutes, when Carl Shutt burst past Butcher and whipped over a low cross that was buried by Marwood.

The match ended amid a peculiar atmosphere. Many of the blue army were convinced the club was definitely down, while others were not so sure. News that Oxford had lost meant all hope had not disappeared, but for Terry Butcher the game was up and he left the field in tears. He recovered some composure to accept a huge Teddy Bear, awarded to Town by Wednesday fans for having the 'Best Away Fans' of the season. It was a nice gesture but a comically insignificant consolation for the big man and his devoted followers. Division Two football duly became a reality 48 hours later when the final whistle sounded at the Manor Ground.

LEAGUE DIVISION 2   **1986-87**
Today Division 2   5th (play-offs)
Littlewoods Cup   3rd Round
FA Cup   3rd Round
Full Members' Cup   Semi-finals

The build up to Ipswich's first season outside the top flight in the lifetime of many younger supporters was boosted by news that the Football League was introducing a new play-off system to decide promotion and relegation issues. For Second Division teams, it meant the side finishing down in fifth would still be in with a shout of going up.

Other good news was Town's form during pre-season warm-ups. Eight friendlies produced eight victories, with a goals tally of 33 and just one conceded. Although the opposition on a Scandinavian tour was not of a high standard, it was good to see Town's forwards doing so well following the lack of goals in recent seasons.

Skipper Terry Butcher decamped for Glasgow Rangers in July for a Scottish record fee of £725,000. The sale was only partly down to financial considerations. With English clubs banned indefinitely from Europe following the carnage of Heysel – which saw 39 Juventus fans crushed to death before the 1985 European Cup final – the only prospect of European soccer competition was north of the border. Manager Graeme Souness's arrival at Ibrox sparked a change of policy, and Rangers now signed Englishmen and even Catholics! A week after Butcher's Rangers debut he was fined £1,000 by the English FA for bad-mouthing referee Gerald Ashby after Ipswich's defeat at West Ham at the tail-end of the previous season. Nor was Butcher the only major loss. Popular midfielder Trevor Putney joined Norwich City, of all people, while defender Kevin Steggles moved to Fulham on loan.

Once again the outgoings were not balanced immediately by a fresh intake, but considering the club had been relegated the exodus might have been a lot worse – particularly given Town's financial plight. Such were the difficulties in balancing the books that the players waived appearance money and bonuses for a September game against Plymouth in the newly introduced Full Members' Cup.

Some observers felt manager Bobby Ferguson had made a decent fist of things since taking over in 1982, particularly as he'd lost many big name players and had severe restrictions imposed on his spending. He was a very different character to predecessor Robson, and his bluff Geordie exterior hid an astute tactical brain – indeed, Atkins said in an interview that Ferguson was the best tactician he had worked with. However, Ferguson naturally had to carry the can for relegation and a sizeable number of supporters wanted to see a new man at the helm to halt the decline. An action group was formed in the summer of 1986 and was granted a meeting with club chairman Patrick Cobbold to put their views directly to him.

Several recent seasons had got off to a slow start and 1986-87 was no exception. The first four League games produced just one win and three goals scored. Perhaps inevitably, attendances continued to slide, but when fewer than 10,000 turned up for the visit of Shrewsbury in September it represented Portman Road's lowest League gate for more than twenty years.

Forward John 'Dixie' Deehan, signed from neighbours Norwich, failed to make a significant impact until his fifth appearance, shortly after his 29th birthday, when he starred in a bizarre game against his former club West Brom. As well as banging in a hat-trick, the genial Midlander hit the bar and had a penalty saved! It was the first of four Town hat-tricks during the season, three of which came away from Portman Road. Not since 1959-60 had Town players registered as many in a single season.

Unlike recent campaigns, goalscoring was not a serious problem in 1986-87. The ultimate away tally of 30 was the best in the top two divisions and Kevin 'Jocky' Wilson's impressive personal total was 21, plus another four in the Full Members' Cup. This competition was in its second season but it was Town's first inclusion. Although it dangled the carrot of a Wembley final, only about half the clubs from the top two divisions bothered to enter, and crowds were dismal until the latter stages. Town made it to the semi-finals where they lost 0-3 at Blackburn. Earlier they had beaten Plymouth 3-2 in front of 5,752 at Portman Road, with goals by Wilson, Gleghorn and Dozzell; then Reading at Elm Park in round two by 2-0, with Wilson and Deehan on target. First Division opposition was overcome in the third and fourth rounds to take Town to the semis. Aston Villa went down 1-0 at Portman Road in front of 8,224, with Wilson bagging the winner, and in the quarter-final Town beat Manchester City 3-2 at Maine Road with goals by Wilson, Tony Humes and Brennan from the penalty spot.

The FMC, if nothing else, kept cup interest alive at Portman Road following highly disappointing early exits in the two major competitions. Lively Cambridge dumped Town out of the League Cup (now sponsored by Littlewoods), thanks to David Crown's fine goal, and John Bond's Birmingham pinched an ill-tempered 1-0 win at Portman Road in the FA Cup. This meant that Town were out at the third round stage for the first time in seventeen years, although some measure of revenge over Birmingham was exacted with a 3-0 win a month later in the League.

DID YOU KNOW?

In Bobby Robson's 13 years at Ipswich he bought only 14 players (total outlay £1.03 million) but sold 45 players (earning the club £2.65 million).

After the topsy turvy start to the League campaign, Town moved smoothly upwards, reaching third spot by Christmas. Delight at this achievement was abruptly curtailed on Boxing Day when a muscular Millwall side recorded a single-goal win at the austere and poorly attended Cold Blow Lane. Things got back on song the following day, when Crystal Palace were brushed aside 3-0 in front of a bumper Portman Road crowd, and a fine win over Leeds on New Year's Day kept promotion hopes well and truly alive.

A feature of the season was the glut of penalties awarded both for and against Town. Three different Ipswich keepers faced a total of fourteen spot-kicks in competitive games. Paul Cooper faced eleven and saved six – a tremendous record that earned him much publicity and a reputation that seemed to intimidate some of those attempting to beat him from twelve yards. A seventh kick was off-target, which meant that Cooper was beaten just four times. Jon Hallworth faced two, both on target, while Cranson conceded one after replacing the injured Cooper in the last minute at Sunderland. All told, fourteen penalties was the most ever given against Town in a single season. Meanwhile, at the other end, five penalties were awarded to Town, but only one converted. Brennan scored one and missed two, with Wilson and Deehan missing one apiece. In total, Town's first-team games yielded nineteen penalties, only eight of which hit the net.

Solid home form formed the basis of Town's promotion challenge. For most of the spring they stayed in the top four, meaning a place in the new play-off system always looked likely, but a top-two automatic promotion spot was for the most part a distant dream. After defeats at Leeds and Barnsley, and a draw with Millwall – all in the space of eight days – Town, Crystal Palace and Plymouth emerged as the main contenders for the final play-off place. When Town beat Blackburn at Portman Road, while the other contenders lost, Ipswich cantered to a comfortable finish to the season proper, reaching the play-offs without any late scares or dramas.

In two-legged affairs, clubs generally prefer to be at home in the second match. It was therefore with trepidation that Town faced the play-off semi-final second leg at Charlton, having only drawn 0-0 in the first game. Although their support was smaller and less noisy than Town's, Charlton seemed more motivated and Jim Melrose headed two goals inside two minutes to leave Town in tatters.

Bouncing back into Division One at the first attempt would have been priceless, but it proved beyond Town. With the season ending on a losing note, change was felt to be in the air at Portman Road.

Match of the Season 1986-87
Charlton 2 Ipswich 1

Play-off, semi-final, 2nd leg, 17 May 1987

Nowadays, play-off places go to teams just missing promotion. In the first seasons after its introduction that was not the case. Three promotion hopefuls were pooled with the club that just escaped the drop. In 1987 that was Lennie Lawrence's Charlton. Nineteenth in Division One would face fifth in Division Two. The winner over two legs would play either Leeds or Oldham in a two-legged final.

Charlton had finished their season strongly, taking ten points from their final five games to avert automatic relegation. Their confidence was further boosted when they secured a goalless draw at Portman Road, a game they would have won had Colin Walsh's penalty not been saved by Cooper.

Charlton had abandoned The Valley for Selhurst Park, so it was there that 5,000 Ipswich fans congregated, making up nearly half the total crowd at The Addicks' temporary home. Sadly, things went awry in the early stages, and Town found themselves two down before the twenty-minute mark.

John Humphrey, a constant danger on the overlap, crossed from the right and Jim Melrose headed home. Ninety seconds later, with Town's defence seemingly in disarray, the Scot repeated the trick. Walsh's free-kick was headed back at the far post by Paul Miller and Melrose nodded his sixteenth goal of the season. As that goal ultimately kept Charlton in the top division, the ex-Manchester City striker had repaid his £30,000 transfer fee many times over.

Town lost top scorer Wilson at half-time with a thigh injury, following Walsh's fierce challenge, and with him went Town's last hopes. The stuffing had been knocked out of them and even a late goal by McCall had little effect. It came when Yallop crossed, D'Avray headed against a post and McCall netted via the woodwork.

Charlton boss Lawrence said he was relieved the game hadn't gone to extra-time as his men were more exhausted than Ipswich, although he did feel Charlton had coped better with the tension. If Town felt glum at the outcome, Oldham must have felt even worse. The Latics had finished third – seven points ahead of Leeds and eleven ahead of Town – but lost their play-off semi on away goals. Charlton went on to beat Leeds to stay in Division One.

Another save from Paul Cooper, a model of consistency (October 1978)

Trevor Whymark, a goalscoring legend in the 1970s

Tommy Parkin and George Burley admire another Paul Cooper save

Paul Cooper was Ipswich's last line of defence for 13 years

Forrest and Stockwell deny former colleague Gavin Johnson (October 1995)

Matchday programme for Wembley's 50th FA Cup final (May 1978)

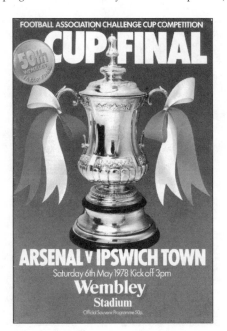

Martijn Reuser clinches victory over Barnsley in the play-off final (May 2000)

The UEFA Cup is paraded through Ipswich (May 1981)

Chapter Four

Marooned in Obscurity
1987-1990

LEAGUE DIVISION 2	1987-88
Barclays Division 2	8th
Littlewoods Cup	4th Round
FA Cup	3rd Round
Simod Cup	Quarter-final

English football enjoyed an upsurge in 1987-88, with an increase in attendances, commercial sponsorship innovations, exciting upsets in four different cup finals at Wembley and hooliganism apparently on the wane. It was all good news for the oldest league in the world, which, by coincidence, was celebrating its centenary.

But the atmosphere wasn't always so positive at Portman Road. Although Town now possessed a stadium to be proud of, come May the team would only finish eighth in Division Two, reasonable given financial restraints, but still the club's lowest position for 22 years.

Supporters bemoaning this fact could certainly not blame the directors for failing to make changes. The board had reacted quickly to the failure to secure promotion in 1986-87 by replacing manager Bobby Ferguson, who became the first manager in the club's history to be dismissed. Aged 49, Fergie had had five seasons in charge. Inheriting an all-star side that was breaking up, he was given little money to spend and when he failed to prevent relegation in 1986 there were mitigating circumstances. But failure to win immediate promotion meant his time was up.

Four weeks after his departure, his successor was appointed. The chief candidates had been Ferguson's assistant, Charlie Woods, Gillingham boss Keith Peacock, Chesterfield manager John Duncan, Stoke player-manager Mick Mills, and veteran Nottingham Forest midfielder Ian Bowyer. It emerged that Mills was not seriously in contention as he was still under contract at Stoke, while Woods was always an outsider. After the experience of Ferguson, the board was not keen on another internal appointment. That left a final short-list of just two. Duncan and Peacock were interviewed at length and the new man was unveiled at a press conference in mid-June: he was only Town's eighth manager since the club turned professional in 1936.

DID YOU KNOW?

The 1981 film Escape to Victory starred O'Callaghan, Osman and Wark as POWs, Sivell and Turner as guards, with Beattie and Cooper on stand-by as understudies.

Days before John Duncan's appointment, the board had sanctioned the sale of leading scorer Kevin Wilson to Chelsea for £300,000. Around the same time, goalkeeper Paul Cooper joined Leicester as an out-of-contract free agent. Cooper had been with Town for fourteen years and had become part of the furniture. He ended his Town days with a tally of nineteen penalty saves from 49 kicks faced. His farewell season had seen him save six from eleven, but his best year was 1979-80 when he kept out five out of seven. Another high-profile departure was dependable Steve McCall, after 257 League games, who tried his luck at Sheffield Wednesday.

Duncan, a former striker with Dundee, Tottenham and Derby, had a managerial knack of getting results on a limited budget at Chesterfield, Hartlepool and Scunthorpe. This had clearly helped him land his new job and he was quick to use his eye for a bargain, recruiting striker David Lowe from Wigan, full-back Graham Harbey from Derby, and forward Neil Woods from Glasgow Rangers.

He also signed Reading's Ron Fearon, who competed with Jon Hallworth for the keeper's jersey, and handed Simon Milton, a 24-year-old midfielder with Suffolk non-leaguers Bury Town, a late chance to make a career in the game. Andy Bernal, Australian-born, was introduced after a spell in Spanish football.

Lowe, Harbey and Woods debuted on the opening day of the season at home to Aston Villa. The Duncan era got off to an undistinguished start when rookie defender Chris O'Donnell fired an horrendous own-goal past Hallworth, but Nigel Gleghorn was quick to equalise and Town subsequently got through August unbeaten, albeit in unspectacular fashion. As the hard-working Lowe began to settle into his new surroundings, he became a very effective front-runner, unsettling the opposition and looking positive in the danger area. His goals beat both Leeds and Crystal Palace, and meant that September ended with Town on the fringe of the leading pack.

Not so promising was the way Town struggled to overcome Third Division Northampton in the Littlewoods Cup, nor the lacklustre displays against Barnsley and Hull, where entertainment was in short supply. Defeat at Middlesbrough, after Mich D'Avray had put Town ahead, was due in part to the loss of Frank Yallop, sent off for what looked a fairly minor offence.

Few away points were gathered during the autumn, but the team's consistency at home was impressive. Between 29 August and

19 December, no fewer than eleven successive League games were won, and these results were responsible for the top-six position first attained in October and not relinquished until the New Year.

Duncan had little money at his disposal for new players, so had to hunt high and low for bargains. In mid-season he borrowed Tom Carson, the Dundee goalkeeper, and Twente Enschede defender Ulrich Wilson. News that Duncan was pursuing former Town favourite John Wark, no longer assured of his place with Liverpool, was welcomed by everyone who recalled the Scot's amazing knack of conjuring up goals from midfield. After weeks of speculation, Wark arrived in mid-January for £100,000, shortly after the season's showpiece occasion – an FA Cup visit from Manchester United.

The Full Members knockout tournament was this year known as the Simod Cup. It earned the club much-needed revenue at the turnstiles thanks to three home ties pulling in higher-than-average gates for the competition. Middlesbrough were sent packing by a rare Neil Woods goal in the first round at Portman Road, and West Brom were beaten 2-1 in the second stage, thanks to Gleghorn and Zondervan strikes. Wark made his return to Portman Road in the third round tie with Watford and scored twice in a 5-2 win. He also missed a penalty, while Lowe, Deehan and D'Avray were the other scorers. Town went out in the quarter-finals, 0-2 at Coventry.

Manchester United's FA Cup visit diverted attention from the labours of the League. Once the dust had settled on this lively cup-tie, Town lost their way, embarking on five successive defeats. It dropped them to ninth and only a couple of moments of magic from Dalian Atkinson against Barnsley stopped the rot. The flying front-man scored two super goals in a 3-2 win, prompting Town fans to wonder why he couldn't do the business more often. They would have to wait until Middlesbrough's visit in April before Atkinson's next treats, by which time Town had slipped down ever further.

A 1-4 hammering at Sheffield United, destined for relegation, was particularly depressing. Not only did the Blades finish the game with ten men after Paul Williams' sending off, but they also hit the woodwork, and Richard Cadette, on a hat-trick, had a penalty saved by Fearon.

To balance the books, stalwarts Ian Cranson and Ian Atkins left in March for Sheffield Wednesday and Birmingham respectively, leaving Town lightweight at the back. By now it was evident Town would not be participating in the play-offs and even a flourish of five wins in the final five games came too late. The second of these was a thrilling 4-0 hammering of fourth-placed Middlesbrough, featuring a stunning hat-trick by Atkinson. Bruce Rioch's Boro had no answer to his blistering pace and shooting power, but they would recover their composure in the subsequent games and secure automatic promotion.

Town rounded off their season with a 3-2 win at Valley Parade. Jittery Bradford City needed the points to gain automatic promotion. The partisan home crowd had not seen such excitement for many a year, but the chance of elevation to the top flight must have caused altitude sickness, for Town won the day when home defender Lee Sinnott blundered, presenting Milton with a late winner.

Match of the Season 1987-88

Ipswich 1 Manchester United 2

FA Cup, 3rd round, 10 January 1988

After several seasons of tepid third round FA Cup draws, Town this year landed a plum. Alex Ferguson's side were in the championship race and among the favourites to win the Cup. In front of live TV cameras, a crowd of over 23,000 meant it was just like old times at Portman Road. This turned into a classic cup-tie, full of controversy and was not an occasion for the faint-hearted. United drew first blood when D'Avray diverted the ball past Hallworth, but the home side were undeterred and didn't take long to bounce back. Defender Humes, not tall but fearless in aerial battles, climbed above team-mate Cranson to head Brennan's corner goalwards. Humes was credited with the final touch, although Atkins and Lowe made desperate efforts to ensure the ball ended in the back of the net.

Town had their tails up and shortly after half-time thought they had won a penalty when Lowe chased Tony Brennan's lob into the area, leaving Steve Bruce in his wake. Chris Turner raced out and sent Lowe sprawling, but to Town's dismay Mr Stevens awarded a free-kick outside the area. The live TV cameras confirmed the offence was inside the box and United were lucky to escape.

The decision proved a turning point, for United began to impose themselves and Brian McClair forced Hallworth to save with his legs. The same player then shot against the post and knocked the rebound into the grateful keeper's arms. Shortly afterwards a melee in Town's goalmouth saw Harbey clear off the line before the ball was netted – only for an infringement to be spotted.

There was more despair in the Town ranks on 66 minutes when Colin Gibson's corner saw Viv Anderson rise with Hallworth and appear to bundle the ball from the keeper's hands and into the net. Hallworth claimed he had been impeded, but the goal stood. The pace never slackened and Town were denied an equaliser when Brennan's shot was turned aside by the diving Turner.

LEAGUE DIVISION 2   **1988-89**
Barclays Division 2   8th
Littlewoods Cup   4th Round
FA Cup   3rd Round
Simod Cup   Quarter-final

Remarkably, John Duncan's second season in charge at Portman Road turned into a carbon copy of his first. Not only did Town again finish eighth in the Second Division table; they also reached exactly the same stage in each of the three cup competitions as they had a year earlier. Punters would have got mighty good odds on all that happening.

Cynics said this succinctly proved the new boss was already in a rut and making no progress in his bid to restore the club to former glories. On the other hand, perhaps, he could be congratulated for well and truly stabilising things after the relentless decline of the five seasons before his arrival.

Whichever viewpoint was nearer the truth, the Scotsman certainly wasn't allowing stagnation in the playing staff. The 1988-89 season saw no fewer than eleven players make their Ipswich debuts – the highest figure for a single campaign since 1949-50. In addition, five men played their last games for the club, with a couple of others having departed before things kicked off in August. The playing turnover was high as Duncan sought to find the right combination to get Town moving in the right direction.

The directors allowed him to splash out a club record £300,000 for Shrewsbury central defender David Linighan in the summer, plus a further £90,000 for Scunthorpe midfielder David Hill, which was a record for the Humberside club. These two made their debuts on the opening day at Stoke, alongside another new boy, Canadian goalkeeper Craig Forrest. This giant of a man, whose arms were so long a local company came forward to offer tailor-made shirts, did well in the opening weeks and allowed the club to sell previous first choice Jon Hallworth to Oldham.

The annual pre-season tour of Scandinavia again threw up minor opposition, enabling Town to get plenty of shooting practice before the serious action commenced. Had Romeo Zondervan not missed a penalty at Stoke, a superb run of results over the opening five weeks might have been even better. A draw at the Victoria Ground was followed by four successive wins, including a 5-1 thrashing of Shrewsbury that featured a hat-trick by midfielder Simon Milton.

Shortly after the Gay Meadow walkover, West Brom were beaten on their own turf and Town rose to top spot in the division. This blistering pace could not be maintained once the colder weather arrived. The first real cracks appeared when a moderate Oxford side came to Portman Road, experimented with a sweeper system, and escaped with all three points. Poor Zondervan again failed from the spot and the defeat sparked a run of five successive losses which dropped Town back into mid-table.

Among the problems facing Duncan around this turbulent period were long-standing injuries to players like Neil Woods and Tony Humes. Yorkshire-born teenager Chris Kiwomya was plunged into senior action and showed bags of potential with some lively displays in attack. The midfield was strengthened with the arrival of £200,000 Ian Redford from Dundee United, just days after Town had beaten Swindon 3-2 in dramatic style, having been 0-2 down.

Ipswich's general inconsistency was amply illustrated by Redford's debut, which saw a defeat by lowly Brighton, Town having led 2-1 after an hour. Christmas 1988 came and went with Town floating around in mid-table again. Indeed, the only realistic chance of glory looked to be in the Simod Cup, where the club had progressed to the quarter-finals. This was achieved by way of a 3-2 victory at Oxford in the first round, courtesy of goals by Zondervan and David Lowe (two). This paved the way for an East Anglian derby with Norwich at Portman Road, which, astonishingly drew in a crowd of over 18,000. That figure was only bettered by two games in the entire competition – one of which was the final.

The Canaries were beaten by a single Milton goal in extra-time, whereupon Town overcame Blackburn in the third round by the same score, with Mick Stockwell on target. The run came to a halt when Nottingham Forest won 3-1 at Portman Road, Dozzell the Town scorer, in front of another bumper crowd of over 16,000. Forest also ended the club's FA Cup hopes at the first hurdle, while Littlewoods Cup aspirations were punctured by a 2-6 thrashing by Aston Villa, in which David Platt plundered four goals in a hectic eighteen-minute spell.

Three league wins in January renewed optimism. The third of these was a splendid 5-1 humbling of Stoke on a day when Portman Road witnessed history in the making. Defender Sergei Baltacha became the first Soviet to play in English football. He marked his arrival by scoring the first goal of the game shortly after half-time. But as the dust settled on this amazing afternoon, it became clear that the former Dynamo Kiev international, renowned in his homeland as a sweeper, was uncomfortable in the midfield roles given to him by manager Duncan.

The up-and-down nature of Town's results, following Baltacha's arrival, frustrated manager and fans alike. Nine goals and nine points were collected in a three-match spell in March, only for this to herald four straight defeats and twelve goals conceded. With hindsight, it is clear that the last chance of making the play-offs disappeared in an eleven-day nightmare, topped and tailed by 0-4 wallopings by Sunderland and Oldham, with defeats by Chelsea and Watford sandwiched in between. A late-season recovery – the final five games were all won – counted for little and only served to paper over the cracks.

Although two top-ten finishes doesn't look bad on paper, many Town fans were convinced Duncan was not the man to lead Town back to the promised land. An approachable and articulate man, he was undoubtedly hindered by the ghosts of the glorious Robson era. There was also a widespread perception that Town had become a more negative and physical side under his tenure. In the summer of 1989 it was clear that although Duncan had two years to run on his contract, he would be under immense pressure to get better performances from his team the following season.

Match of the Season 1988-89
Ipswich 5 Stoke 1

Division 2, 21 January 1989

The build-up to the visit of Stoke was dominated by the arrival of English football's first Soviet import. Sergei Baltacha had been pursued by John Duncan for months. He finally arrived in Suffolk in mid-January, accompanied by wife Olga, an ex-international pentathlete, and two children, one of whom would go on to play professional football in Scotland, the other becoming a tennis pro.

Via an interpreter, Sergei, 30, was introduced to team-mates in the dressing room at Walsall, presenting each with a Dynamo Kiev pennant and then sitting up in the stand to watch them beat The Saddlers 4-2 in front of a paltry crowd of 4,623. He witnessed Mick Stockwell breaking his leg, presumably unaware that a week later he would be asked to fill Stockwell's role in midfield.

Baltacha's arrival was a clear sign that Mikhail Gorbachev's 'perestroika' (reconstruction) had even reached Soviet soccer. A few years earlier it would have been unthinkable for a Soviet to join a foreign club. As Sergei himself explained, only people who had made a substantial contribution to Soviet sport, and were aged about 30, were now allowed to leave the country to pursue their careers. He was not the first Soviet player to be allowed to move abroad, following in the recent footsteps of Oleg Blokhin, who had signed for Vorwaerts Steyr in Austria, and Aleksandr Zavarov who had replaced Ian Rush at Juventus.

DID YOU KNOW?

Paul Mariner was not a typical footballer, being a keen collector of art and antiques. Known to team-mates as the 'mad hippy', he later moved to USA.

Sergei's arrival in Suffolk inevitably aroused huge media interest and a local car dealer was quick to present him with a sponsored Lada in which to explore the East Anglian countryside. With the rouble not convertible on world markets, the Soviet footballing authorities knew that transferring players abroad was one way of acquiring hard currency. It emerged that Sergei would not be paid by Ipswich Town: instead his salary would be paid directly to Sovintersport, the country's international sports committee, who would return a percentage to the player.

Everything was clearly very new to Baltacha, not least the fact that he would no longer have to wash his own kit. And he was no longer obliged to use the old, often-repaired, but very well cared-for football boots he had brought with him. In the early days the only player he could communicate properly with was Romeo Zondervan – for they shared an understanding of German.

Baltacha's debut against Stoke got off to a quiet start with a goalless first half, but burst into life a minute after half-time when Kiwomya zipped down the right and pulled the ball back. Baltacha seized possession, turned, and fired past keeper Fox and the lunging Berry. It was fairy-tale stuff and brought the house down. Not only that, it unleashed a goal bonanza with Town scoring four more over the next thirty minutes or so.

Redford's cross was guided home by Dozzell's head from twelve yards for the second goal. Shortly after the hour both Dozzell and Kiwomya looked offside when Redford played a through ball, but play was not halted and Kiwomya finished coolly. After Linighan and Wark collided, leaving the Scot with a neck injury, Stoke pulled a goal back through Bamber, from Parkin's free-kick.

Town extended their lead when Redford set up Yallop, who thundered home an eighteen-yard drive. The fifth and final goal saw Dozzell finish a neat move involving Redford and Kiwomya. It had been a magnificent start for Baltacha, but sadly there were not too many happy days to follow. He was rarely given the chance to play his natural role of sweeper and subsequently struggled to stay in the side.

LEAGUE DIVISION 2   **1989-90**
Barclays Division 2   9th
Littlewoods Cup   2nd Round
FA Cup   4th Round
ZDS Cup   Area Semi-final

Once again, Town got off to a promising start under John Duncan's leadership, only to fall off the pace once autumn descended. A handsome 4-0 win over Norwich in a pre-season contest attracted almost 8,000 to Portman Road and delighted the fans, as did seven goals and maximum points from the first two league encounters.

But things soon began to go pear-shaped. A home defeat by Wolves was swiftly followed by red faces all round when Third Division Tranmere came to town and snatched victory in the Littlewoods Cup. And once Stoke escaped with a 2-2 draw – Town's fourth successive home fixture without a win – it signalled that Portman Road was no longer the fortress it was once cracked up to be.

The second leg at Tranmere resulted in another defeat and quick exit from a cup competition. For John King's Merseysiders, victory over Ipswich sparked a cup bonanza that carried them to a fourth round replay in the Littlewoods Cup and victory in the final of the Leyland Daf Cup – not to mention a play-off final at Wembley and a 600 per cent increase in home attendances.

Having hardly troubled the Littlewoods Cup organisers, Town once again set off on a run in the much-maligned Full Members' competition, by now sponsored by Zenith Data Systems. Rookie midfielder David Gregory did his prospects no harm when Watford were the visitors in round two by netting a hat-trick in a 4-1 win in front of 5,078. More than 8,000 came along for the next stage when Wimbledon were seen off 3-1 in extra-time, the goals coming via a last-minute Neil Thompson penalty, Simon Milton and Gavin Johnson. The southern area semi-final, also at Portman Road, saw Town go down 2-3 to Chelsea in front of 13,365, with Louie Donowa and Gregory the marksmen. Town old boy Kevin Wilson was among the visitors' scorers.

There was little to get excited about in the League throughout the autumn, and following defeat by Bradford City the table showed Town just above the relegation places, their lowest resting spot since 1964. Duncan candidly admitted to the press that he knew he wasn't getting things right and that supporters had every right to feel disgruntled. To his credit, he turned things round at this point and the side embarked on an unbeaten run that extended to thirteen League games and the rest of 1989.

DID YOU KNOW?

Bobby Ferguson collected the opposing team-sheet at Man Utd and returned to the dressing room to pass comment. All went quiet. He was in United's dressing room!

This run was enough to hoist Town to fifth, and some of the criticism was quietened. Thompson, a full-back from Scarborough, had settled into the side and his cannonball shooting reminded older supporters of the legendary Ted Phillips. Other new recruits were Louie Donowa, a winger born and bred in Ipswich but who had made his name up at Norwich, and Glenn Pennyfather, a midfielder signed from Crystal Palace. Steve Palmer, a Cambridge graduate, put on hold a career in computers to play for Town, and made his senior debut at Oxford, of all places! Duncan also tried to obtain the services of Soviet goalkeeper Mikhailov, but ran up against red tape that could not be unravelled, even with the help of the local MP Michael Irvine.

An important factor in Town's overall inconsistency was the loss of injured striker David Lowe. Subsequently Lowe perhaps returned to the side too hastily and didn't appear fully fit until play-off hopes had already been dashed. The bite of injury-prone Tony Humes was also badly missed, but even after his return Duncan was not entirely happy with Town's defensive formation. To rectify this he invested a club record £330,000 in centre-back Brian Gayle of Manchester City. The former Wimbledon stopper thought long and hard about a move to Suffolk and his eventual agreement was said to have been influenced by encouraging words from City team-mate Paul Cooper, who'd enjoyed the best years of his career at Portman Road.

Gayle's arrival was certainly welcomed by those who witnessed the humiliating 0-5 New Year's Day defeat at Port Vale, a result that shattered the long unbeaten run and certainly wasn't the best way to welcome a new decade. Typical of Town's recent ways, the unbeaten run triggered a seven-game stint without a league victory. Being marooned in mid-table for the third year in a row prompted more terrace discontent, and what began as occasional and isolated chants of 'Duncan out' grew into a sustained campaign against the manager.

Angry letters flooded into the local press and noisy malcontents made their presence felt on the terraces in all nine home matches from March onwards, irrespective of whether Town were actually winning at the time. Beleaguered Duncan toiled away in dignified fashion, but must have felt inwardly dismayed by the criticism, considering that the club had never finished lower than eighth under his stewardship.

Around the time of Gayle's arrival in February, Town had been handily placed for a promotion push, but their away form let them down. The fans called for a new striker to be signed, but Duncan's moves in this direction were not hugely successful. He recruited on loan from Odense ex-Arsenal forward Raphael Meade, but he failed to provide any answers, and although Mark Stuart, borrowed from Plymouth, scored twice on his debut, he wasn't influential in the remaining games.

By the time Town had succumbed twice to struggling Hull, the knives were really out for Duncan. Although a top-ten finish was again on the cards, the local media were campaigning against Duncan, arguing that his time was up. The directors' hands looked likely to be forced by the sheer weight of the discontent. A club famous for never sacking managers was now under pressure to terminate a contract that still had one year to run. With a board meeting scheduled to follow the final game, at West Brom, the writing was on the wall.

Match of the Season 1989-90

West Brom 1 Ipswich 3

Division 2, 5 May 1990

Ominously, a higher than usual quota of Town directors attended the final game of the season at West Brom, and poor John Duncan must have known this would probably be his last game in charge of Ipswich Town.

However, he must have been cheered to find the first twenty minutes treated by his players as anything but an end-of-season stroll. Town raced into a 3-0 lead, which ironically sparked home supporters to start calling for their own manager's head!

Player-boss at the Hawthorns was none other than Brian Talbot, the former Ipswich stalwart, who – rather unwisely as it transpired – had chosen this game to be his swansong as a player. Having not played for ten weeks, Talbot picked himself to wear the No 4 shirt against his former club and made it clear this would be his farewell appearance on the field. With his side 0-3 down, the home fans began jeering his every touch. It was a nightmarish way for an excellent playing career to end. Not surprisingly Talbot substituted himself before the end.

Talbot at least had the minor consolation of seeing his team prevent the loss of further goals. However, like Duncan, he too must have wondered whether his days as manager were now numbered.

Town's stunning opening salvo began in the twelfth minute when Lowe, by now transfer listed, scored his sixth goal in four games. The ball was threaded through by Jason Dozzell and Lowe shook off Bradley's attentions to strike it past the advancing Naylor. Five minutes later Dozzell set up Simon Milton for the second and then snatched the third himself, heading in a cross from Lowe with just eighteen minutes on the clock.

Donowa and Lowe both miskicked when good chances went begging for a fourth goal, while for debutant Chris Neville in goal, it turned into a relatively untroubled afternoon's work. His hopes of keeping a clean sheet, however, were dashed near the end when Foster headed McNally's cross against the crossbar and Bannister snapped up the rebound.

John Duncan's departure was not long postponed. But the club surprised some fans by moving swiftly to install his successor. At a press conference just six days after the West Brom match, chairman Patrick Cobbold called for order and asked the new manager of Ipswich Town to join the meeting. As the assembled hacks held their collective breath, into the room strolled John Lyall.

Lyall, a respected figure with many contacts in the game, had been in charge of West Ham for fifteen years before his surprise sacking in 1989. His rapid appointment by Ipswich not only gave him the whole summer to prepare for the following season, it also ensured a boost in season ticket sales. The new man retained the club's existing coaching staff and for Town fans August could not come quickly enough.

Roger Osborne (7) receives attention after his Cup final winner (May 1978)

Titus Bramble, one of the new generation of local talent

The Ipswich Town squad of 1983-84

Clive Woods (centre) puts Ipswich ahead against Coventry (March 1978)

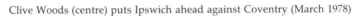

Jubilation as Ipswich celebrate the final whistle at Wembley (May 1978)

Ipswich score during the 4-1 demolition of Luton (September 1974)

Steve McCall admires the safe hands of Paul Cooper

Ipswich's 1985-86 squad, which suffered relegation from the top division

## Chapter Five

John Lyall's Yo-Yo Years 1990-1995

LEAGUE DIVISION 2	**1990-91**
Division Two	14th
Rumbelows Cup	2nd Round
FA Cup	3th Round
ZDS Cup	Southern Semi-final

Appointed the club's ninth manager since it turned professional, John Lyall quickly recruited assistance in the shape of Chelsea coach Mick McGiven – a former colleague at West Ham. The previous manager, John Duncan's, coaching team – Charlie Woods, Peter Trevivian and Bryan Klug – were also retained.

Fans hoping for new faces on the field were to be disappointed, for despite the departures of Baltacha, Wark, Donowa and D'Avray, the only new arrival between May and December 1990 was veteran goalkeeper Phil Parkes, recruited merely as cover for Craig Forrest.

A healthy crowd of over 17,000 assembled for the big kick-off at Portman Road, hoping Lyall could inspire something special from the players after the continuing frustrations of previous years. But Sheffield Wednesday spoiled the party atmosphere, going two goals up before half-time. There was no further scoring, and when Town went down by the only goal at Swindon three days later, the fans had their grumbling heads on again.

Early pressure on Lyall and McGiven was lifted in September when the players showed character to come back from deficits and win games against West Brom and Blackburn in the closing stages. Most fans knew the new management team couldn't be expected to bring about an overnight transformation, but the reluctance to invest in new players was worrying and seemed to illustrate a lack of real ambition.

On its day, the existing squad could play fine, flowing football and look as good as any in this division, but all too often they only performed in patches, and results were mixed, at best. At the end of September Colin Lee's bottom-club Watford came to Portman Road and were treated with too much respect. Watford took the lead and went agonisingly close to really embarrassing Town. Fortunately, a misjudgement by young keeper David James helped Town equalise and prevent a complete disaster.

DID YOU KNOW?

Kevin Wilson was given the match-ball after scoring a Milk Cup hat-trick at Darlington in 1985. But when he heard how hard up Darlo were, he gave it back.

Those who analysed the display against Watford and concluded that there was trouble ahead, were proved right. Three days later a dreadful first-half performance at Oakwell saw mid-table Barnsley storm into a 4-0 lead before the interval. Lyall refused to panic. The players recovered from the Barnsley hammering to lose only once in the next five encounters – a mini-run that saw the club rise to the heady heights of eighth – the best they would attain all season.

An incident-packed 3-3 draw at Hull in November set Town off on a sequence of seven successive league draws. This run of stalemates was halted on Boxing Day. Not only was the weather foul, but this normally exciting football date featured the lowest Portman Road 'Christmas crowd' since 1964. Even Middlesbrough's winning goal had an air of inevitability about it, Ian Baird's header being well and truly 'wind-assisted', to use athletics parlance.

So how would the experienced and down-to-earth Mr Lyall react to the gloom pervading Portman Road? Via the local press he urged supporters to be patient and said he was scouring the transfer market for the right people. There was unease on the terraces, for his record so far involved disposing of four experienced players and bringing in a reserve keeper. The only other significant movement, to cover for an injury to Phil Parkes, had been the introduction of teenage keeper Ian Walker, on loan from Tottenham, and the arrival of relative unknown, Dugald McCarron on loan from Celtic, who was never given a look-in anyway.

The news all Town fans wanted to hear came in early January – Lyall had bought a new centre-forward. The brief was to halt a run of fourteen games without victory, and the man to do it was Steve Whitton, a £150,000 purchase from Sheffield Wednesday reserves. Another former Hammer, Whitton had been unable to force his way into the Hillsborough team on account of the form of David Hirst, Paul Williams and Trevor Francis, and he grabbed the chance of a move with both hands.

Whitton was not exactly the household name the fans had been calling for, but they were shouting his name to the rafters after a magnificent debut at home to West Brom. Whitton played like a man possessed, working hard and showing a willingness to shoot on sight that had rarely been seen lately at Ipswich. In true comic-book style, Whitton cracked the wining goal in the second half and then repeated the trick in a 1-0 success at Blackburn a week later.

Rather like corporation buses in nearby Civic Drive, no new players came along for ages, then they all arrived at once. Whitton was swiftly followed into Portman Road by yet another ex-Hammer in Paul Goddard, a capable marksman who'd had an unhappy spell at Millwall. Then came the skilful but enigmatic Mark Burke on loan from Middlesbrough, followed a few weeks later by another loanee, Scott Houghton, an explosive left-sided Tottenham attacker who had a fine future ahead of him, by all accounts.

Goddard was first seen as a sub against his ex-Millwall team-mates. He hit his stride on his full debut, improving upon Whitton's achievement by scoring twice to bring victory over Hull. This game marked the end of the February big-freeze, which had caused many postponements and, in Ipswich's case, led to fourteen league games having to be played in eight weeks in March and April. These included a rare Thursday night game at Portman Road, something that clearly didn't impress the locals, as under 8,000 turned out for the contest with Barnsley – the lowest League crowd for 36 years.

Town huffed and puffed in mid-table between Christmas and the end of the season, climbing no higher than eleventh and slipping no lower than seventeenth. A disappointing run-in of just two wins from twelve games saw them finish fourteenth, their lowest resting place in a quarter of a century. More to the point, this was considerably lower than any of John Duncan's three seasons in charge.

The last kick of the season saw a dramatic winning goal by Dean Wilkins that put Brighton in the play-offs, leaving Town to traipse off the pitch with heads down, while their hosts celebrated wildly. The Cup had brought little cheer, with early exits to First Division Southampton in both the major competitions, both due in no small part to the genius of Matt Le Tissier. The Zenith Data Systems competition brought a flicker of excitement when Town reached the fourth round – labelled the 'Southern Semi-final' to generate a little extra excitement. Opponents were none other than the old enemy from Norfolk, but in front of 16,225 at Carrow Road, Town were ousted 0-2. It at least meant Town maintained their record of generating the biggest crowds in this competition. Only the Wembley final outnumbered the crowd at Carrow Road. For the record, earlier victories in this competition were 2-0 over Wimbledon in front of 1,787 at an eerily silent Plough Lane, when Redford and Kiwomya were on target. Oxford United were then seen off 2-1 by Milton and Dozzell goals in front of 7,456 at Portman Road.

Standing above the mediocrity around him, Jason Dozzell had a fine season and scored some cracking goals. The no-nonsense David Linighan was also a consistent figure in central defence, deserving his player of the year accolade.

Match of the Season 1990-91

Ipswich 4 Charlton 4

Division 2, 29 December 1990

Short on confidence, Town – on the back of a run of seven draws and two defeats – welcomed Lennie Lawrence's Charlton to Portman Road desperate for a victory. The Addicks were on the up, having earlier been rock bottom of the division. The improvement in their fortunes was down in no small part to the midfield work of new signing Alan Curbishley.

A see-saw thriller got off to a great start for Town when Neil Thompson's cross was swept home by Stockwell with just six minutes on the clock. Shortly afterwards Dozzell got to the by-line, pulled a clever ball back and Thompson powered home a typical pile-driver.

Charlton pulled one back in the vital couple of minutes before the interval, when Reid was fouled by Humes and Peake netted a fierce free-kick. An equaliser arrived after the break when Reid's cross caused panic in the Town penalty box and Mortimer fired into the net.

The home side raised its game at this point and regained the lead when Thompson's cross was headed down by Linighan and Dozzell shot past Bolder. Three minutes later the lead was extended to 4-2 as Yallop and Lowe combined to set up Milton. Town by this time were turning on probably their best football of the season and there seemed no way back for the Londoners.

However the seeds of doubt were sown in Town's minds when Dyer's hopeful shot was half-saved but somehow squirmed over the line. Now it was Charlton's turn to apply pressure and they were rewarded with three minutes remaining when the ball struck Redford's hand and Caton tucked home the penalty.

A relieved Lawrence was happy to heap praise on Town's attractive football, but for the home manager it was another furrowed brow and a case of two points tossed away again.

LEAGUE DIVISION 2   **1991-92**
Division Two   Champions
Rumbelows Cup   2nd Round
FA Cup   5th Round
ZDS Cup   3rd Round

After John Lyall's disappointing first season at Portman Road, Town fans were not sure what to expect. The club had a new man at the helm in chairman John Kerr, but with little action in the summer transfer market, there were few concrete reasons for optimism.

Events on the opening day, when a 3-0 lead at Bristol Rovers was frittered away in the final 24 minutes, did little to raise hopes. Nevertheless, those quick to say 'here we go again' were made to eat their words by the end of August, for three successive 2-1 wins left the club sitting proudly at the top of the table. Pride came before a fall, however, for Glenn Hoddle's Swindon then came to Portman Road and beat Town 4-1 to bring the top dogs crashing down to earth.

Town's fortunes were certainly unpredictable in the early weeks, with the team often hitting the heights with some neat football, but also occasionally looking vulnerable under pressure. The bookies offered generous odds against Town winning the title in May, but few fans were rushing to place their bets at this stage.

The club's financial position meant no big-money signings could be contemplated unless someone was sold first. This duly occurred in mid-September when solid centre-back Brian Gayle left for Sheffield United for £700,000, realising a profit of almost £400,000. A fortnight earlier midfielder David Hill, reduced to the fringes of the squad, went back to his former club Scunthorpe for £30,000.

Lyall didn't spend any of the Gayle cash until eight weeks later when he signed promising young defender Eddie Youds from Everton for £250,000. By the time of Youds' debut at Derby, Town had slipped out of the top six and clean sheets were a rarity. The defence clearly needed bolstering and hopes were high that Youds was the answer, but his debut turned into a nightmare. Damaging knee ligaments in a clash with winger Ted McMinn, Youds would not appear again for the first team this season.

Another defender, Darren Edmonds, a former Leeds trainee, had been recruited earlier on a free transfer but never looked the part. Fortunately, a familiar face lurking in the background could come to the rescue. John Wark, unhappy at Middlesbrough, had been training at Portman Road while a free agent and had turned out for Town reserves. By late September it appeared the popular Scot was not arousing interest elsewhere so Lyall signed him up. Wark's appearance at Grimsby as a sub heralded his third spell as a Town first-team player.

Town fans, encouraged by the flirtation with the top, looked down in the mouth during the autumn, particularly after John Beck's Cambridge upstarts made their first ever visit to Portman Road and pinched a cheeky 2-1 win with a late Steve Claridge goal. The game generated huge interest and the crowd of 20,000+ was more than doubled that for the Sunderland visit of four days earlier.

Despite frailties elsewhere in Town's rearguard, David Linighan had clearly been boosted by his new status as team captain and was enjoying a fine campaign. Nobody played a more vital role than he in keeping Town in the thick of the promotion race throughout the winter. Mick Stockwell was also in the forefront, working tirelessly in midfield, while livewire Chris Kiwomya continued where he left off in 1990-91, scoring regularly and proving a slippery customer for the archetypal big Second Division centre-backs.

After failing to score in early December at both Plymouth and Swindon, Town enjoyed two fine home triumphs against Charlton and Blackburn over Christmas and this proved to be something of a turning point. The team was firmly establishing itself in the top three and events on the field overshadowed bad news from the boardroom. Chairman Kerr announced a record loss of £747,246, adding the rider that he was confident about the future. The loss was largely due to a rise of 24 per cent in wages and salaries, which amounted to more than £350,000.

Cup runs can hold the key to boosting a club's finances, so Town welcomed an FA Cup challenge that only ended on a February evening at Anfield, when Graeme Souness' Liverpool were forced into extra-time before they squeezed home 3-2. Earlier FA Cup wins over Hartlepool and Bournemouth had been straightforward affairs, but the performance level against Liverpool over 210 minutes underlined Town's promotion credentials.

Ipswich had made a quick exit from the Rumbelows Cup at the hands of Derby. Then, in the Zenith Data Systems competition, Town succumbed to Chelsea after a penalty shoot-out, having earlier beaten Luton – also on penalties – on a night when the two sides combined to miss seven out of the ten spot-kicks taken.

In the league, Town saved their best for more polished opponents. They disposed of Kenny Dalglish's expensive Blackburn, but struggled to cope with 'scufflers' such as Plymouth and Cambridge. To gain promotion, grinding out a few 1-0 victories was clearly the order of the day – but this didn't seem to be Town's style early on. After Christmas stubborn opponents such as Bristol Rovers, Tranmere and Watford were all beaten by solitary second-half goals.

DID YOU KNOW?

When Ipswich physio Brian Owen raced on to attend to Mich D'Avray at Cambridge (during Keith Osgood's testimonial), he found the player had a bee stuck in his ear.

Lyall persisted with the same nucleus of players, although John Moncur was given a handful of games after arriving on loan from Tottenham. Injury-prone defender Tony Humes left for Wrexham for £40,000, and former leading scorer David Lowe moved to Port Vale on loan. Humes had broken his arm against Newcastle, adding this to his other catalogue of fractures – two legs, a jaw, a collar-bone, plus a host of other ailments.

A 5-2 thrashing of Portsmouth in early February saw Town move into second spot and – apart from a hiccup in mid-March – they would not drop into the chasing pack again. But failure to beat Leicester and Watford at home was the first of two bouts of jitters, which nearly knocked the promotion wagon off the rails.

After failing for a second time to beat battling Cambridge, things were put right with four successive wins – and the emergence of an unexpected star-turn from the reserves. Young Phil Whelan, a towering figure with film-star looks, was the grandson of a pre-war Town player. Phil had the girl fans swooning and the males roaring when he thundered two awesome headers in his first two matches. His first set Town up for a thrilling late win at Southend; he then repeated the trick at home to Wolves three days later.

Overturning a 1-2 deficit to beat Newcastle, Town had established a handsome lead at the top with just five games to go. Then came the second spell of the jitters. A 0-3 hammering by lowly Sunderland was followed by defeat at strugglers Bristol City. Three points at Ashton Gate would have made promotion a certainty, but a goal by Andy Cole sank Town.

More than 22,000 turned up at Portman Road a few days later to roar Town back into the top flight, but they endured a goalless draw with Grimsby in which Jason Dozzell stuck the woodwork in the final minute. The celebrations were thus delayed again, so Town headed for the cramped Manor Ground still needing another point to be certain of going up. Oxford may have been rooted at the bottom but Jim Magilton quickly shot them ahead. Town levelled almost instantly, and at the final whistle went Town fans streamed onto the pitch to acclaim the club's first promotion in 24 years. Coincidentally it was 30 years to the day that Alf Ramsey's wingless wonders had claimed the English championship. However, with Oxford police and club officials expressing concern about crowd safety, Lyall grabbed a microphone, and made a request of the noisy rabble. Sounding like Sergeant Wilson from *Dad's Army*, he asked if they 'wouldn't mind awfully' leaving the stadium in an orderly fashion and postponing the party until seven days later.

His wish was their command. Some 27,000 packed into Portman Road to acclaim the Division Two champions, showing little concern for the plight of opponents Brighton, who needed points to have a chance of staying up. A 3-1 Town win brought a memorable season to a close. It was the club's fifth promotion and each time it had been as divisional champions. As for Brighton, when news came through that Oxford had won at Tranmere, they were down.

The icing on the cake for Town was the divisional manager of the season award for Lyall, plus the realisation that the club would partake of the first FA Premier League the following August. And, apart from the prestige, there would also be a share of the huge cash sum to be paid out for TV rights of the new league.

Match of the Season 1991-92
Ipswich 2   Blackburn 1

Division 2, 28 December 1992

The first time in 1991-92 that Town really looked convincing title contenders was in this Christmas fixture with Kenny Dalglish's Rovers, who topped the division with Town sitting close behind in third. Mike Newell, who cost the Lancashire club £1 million, engineered a superb goal, pulling the ball back for Alan Wright to score with a first-time volley from the edge of the box.

Town pounded away at the Rovers defence in a bid for an equaliser but were repelled time and again until finally finding a way through just after the interval. Again it was a classic goal, with Steve Whitton's well-directed cross powered past Bobby Mimms by way of Gavin Johnson's spectacular diving header.

With referee Mr Hamer allowing the game to flow, the fans were treated to some see-saw action. Town's second goal came with only five minutes left when Whitton threaded a dangerous ball into the area for Kiwomya to touch back neatly to Dozzell, who swivelled, shrugged off his marker, and slid a low shot just inside the near-post from eight yards. The ground erupted, and the decibels remained high until the final whistle and beyond, as Town fought a desperate rearguard action to prevent an equaliser.

Whitton, Dozzell and Simon Milton had been outstanding, but it was a splendid team effort. Even the usually poker-faced Dalglish allowed himself a rare moment of magnanimity and credited Town with a deserved victory.

FA PREMIER LEAGUE   **1992-1993**
Premier League   16th
Coca Cola Cup   Quarter-finals
FA Cup   Quarter-finals

In addition to the boost of returning to the top flight after a six-year absence, Ipswich spent the summer of 1992 basking in the knowledge that they would be a pioneering member of the new FA Premier League and would reap big cash rewards thanks to the deal struck with the TV companies. The 22 founder member clubs would share out £37.5 million, with the exact amounts depending on appearances in 'live' games and finishing position in the table.

Shortly before the players returned from their summer break, a surprise announcement from Portman Road revealed that John Lyall would become 'club manager' and his right-hand man Mick McGiven elevated to 'first-team manager'. The following day a club record fee of £650,000 was paid for Derby midfielder Geraint Williams, a highly motivated 30-year-old Welshman with more than 400 games under his belt. Part of this fee was recouped when striker David Lowe departed for Leicester.

As well as a restructuring of the League, other innovations included green kit for referees, a choice from three substitutes (one a goalkeeper) and half-time breaks lasting fifteen minutes instead of ten. The Full Members Trophy was scrapped, a move generally welcomed although Town had usually done well in this competition and had pulled in good crowds.

In common with many newly promoted sides over the years, Town's winning momentum continued and they got off to a decent start, being the last Premier League side to relinquish its unbeaten tag. Half-a-dozen draws and two victories was the achievement of the first eight games, but this run came to a juddering halt at Boundary Park when an ultra-defensive approach backfired as Oldham smashed four goals past Craig Forrest.

Forrest made headlines the following week when he was sent off after just two minutes for clattering into Sheffield United's Adrian Littlejohn. The new rules allowed Town to bring on a sub keeper and poor Eddie Youds was hauled off the pitch to make way for him, not having touched the ball since the warm-up. The new keeper was Norfolk-born Clive Baker, a free-transfer from Coventry who subsequently kept his place in the side and had a fine season. Short for a keeper, he reminded some fans of Laurie Sivell, another good little 'un who had worn Town's green shirt with distinction.

The defeat at Oldham suggested the honeymoon period might be over, but Town kept plugging away and by Christmas were in the top six. By the time of a hard-won point at Highbury on Boxing Day, the side had only lost twice, but had drawn twelve of their 21 fixtures. On balance it was a pretty impressive record, but the fans couldn't allow themselves to gloat because up the road deadly rivals Norwich had shocked everyone by topping the table for a number of weeks. At one point, Mike Walker's men even established an eight-point gap over everyone else.

Moreover, while Norwich were being lauded for their attractive style, McGiven seemed to lean towards the over-cautious with some of his formations. Consolidation is not a word in many supporters' vocabulary, but McGiven showed he was not afraid of 'shutting up shop' when he felt the occasion demanded. As well as annoying some of the supporters, McGiven also found himself in trouble with magistrates when he was fined £1,500 for speeding and 'inconsiderate driving' on the A12.

In February, while fans ruminated on the suitability of McGiven, three former Town employees secured themselves managerial posts elsewhere. Terry Butcher, earlier sacked by Coventry, took the player-manager's role at Sunderland, Russell Osman became boss of Bristol City and John Duncan took over at Chesterfield. Within hours of his appointment at Ashton Gate, Osman sold Andy Cole to Newcastle and signed midfielder Glenn Pennyfather from Ipswich. Town's biggest mid-season swoop into the transfer market came in December when they captured two 'flair' players from Sporting Lisbon for a six-figure fee. At the time, Bobby Robson was at the helm of the Portuguese club and had a large quota of foreign players on his books. As regulations only permitted him to use four or five at one time, he was keen to offload some, so he phoned his old friends in Suffolk.

As a result, the Bulgarian Bontcho Guentchev and Vladimir Bozinoski, who was born in Macedonia but raised in Australia, arrived at Portman Road. With Bozinoski's wife being Portuguese, there were no problems in obtaining him a work permit, but as Guentchev was a non-EC citizen he presented more of a problem. Eventually the authorities relented when the President of the Bulgarian FA sent a letter stating Guentchev had scored six goals in twelve internationals for his country. A week or two later suspicious pressmen smelled a rat. Their investigations revealed Guentchev had in fact only gained one full cap and his other appearances were not at senior level. This ruffled the Professional Footballers' Association (PFA), who were wary about young UK players being deprived of opportunities in such circumstances. The row rumbled on for weeks, but eventually Guentchev was allowed to keep his permit as it was felt revoking it would cause more problems than it would solve. This saga would lead to a general re-think of the permit system a few weeks later.

Although his CV was widely questioned, likeable Bontcho showed on the field that he could do the business and he quickly won over the Town fans. In Continental fashion he had a tendency to fall over rather too easily in opponents' boxes, but his pace and clever touches made him a firm favourite. Interestingly, Guentchev would go on to settle permanently in his adopted country, unlike Bozinoski who had a much better command of the language. Guentchev seemed keen to establish a rapport with the fans, but his poor English meant he failed to respond to early chants of 'Bontcho, give us a wave'.

He made a major contribution to an FA Cup run that ended in the quarter-finals when Town were gunned down in a thrilling encounter at Portman Road which ended 2-4 to Arsenal. This season Guentchev hit five Cup goals, including a hat-trick to sink Grimsby in the fifth round. The FA Cup run was matched in the Coca-Cola Cup, which also reached the quarter-final stage. This time Town bowed out by a single goal at Hillsborough.

Back in the League, there was light relief amid the tension at Norwich's Carrow Road after Town's second goal went in. Believing the final whistle had sounded, scorer Jason Dozzell's half-brother Tony sprinted onto the pitch and planted a blue-and-white hat on his relative's head. Red-faced Jason ushered him off and Tony ended up answering to Norwich magistrates a few weeks later. The fine of a paltry £24 suggests the chairman of the bench was not a keen Canaries fan! There was more gleeful laughter when champions-elect Manchester United came to Portman Road. Their normally reliable keeper Peter Schmeichel dashed out of his goal to kick clear but comically missed the ball, conceding a goal for his sins and setting Town on the way to a surprise 2-1 win.

The cup heroics overshadowed league results for long spells and might well have played a part in the dip in form that saw a slump from fifth in the table in January, all the way down to seventeenth by early April. The possibility of relegation was banished in the local derby with Norwich and this result – along with victory on the final day over Nottingham Forest – did much to make the fans forget some of the poorer displays after Christmas.

The season's finale focused the eyes of the nation on Portman Road when Brian Clough bowed out of management on the same day that his Forest outfit slipped through the relegation trapdoor. Ipswich ensured a marvellous career was fully recognised, but the man himself insisted that a special presentation by Town directors was made behind closed doors.

DID YOU KNOW?

Ipswich fan Keith Deller used to be a ball-boy at Portman Road in the 1970s. He grew up to become Embassy World Darts champion in 1983.

Match of the Season 1992-93

Ipswich 3 Norwich 1

Premier League, 19 April 1993

Although Town had gone thirteen games without a league win, there was plenty to motivate them in the build-up to this local derby. A win would finally end any lingering fears of relegation and would also make sure Norwich could not sneak in and pip Manchester United for the title. The contest was staged before a national audience when BSkyB chose to cover it live.

With injury-plagued Milton back in the side and playing well, McGiven and Lyall decided to drop Guentchev and push Dozzell alongside Kiwomya in attack. The ploy worked a treat and with 21 minutes on the clock Dozzell hit the target. Williams and Whitton combined well, the former knocking a ball across the box. Keeper Bryan Gunn somehow missed it, allowing the Town man to joyfully net.

The match was played at breakneck speed and Norwich looked determined not to be 'doubled' by their old enemy. Five minutes before the interval Johnson fouled winger Fox and Crook curled a free-kick to the far post where Chris Sutton was on hand to head home an equaliser.

Town responded positively to this setback and the irrepressible Stockwell put them ahead on 54 minutes, regaining possession after his own shot was blocked and stabbing the ball past Gunn. Three minutes later there was more joy for the Blue Army as Dozzell cut inside Polston and let fly with a superb low shot that beat Gunn all ends up.

Although Robins and Culverhouse both struck the woodwork for City, Town had risen well to the occasion and were in no mood to surrender the two-goal cushion. Afterwards City boss Mike Walker had angry words about his defence, while a jubilant McGiven was keen to pay tribute to the absent John Lyall and the part he had played in the planning of this crucial win, despite being ill at home.

FA CARLING PREMIERSHIP   1993-1994

Premiership	19th
Coca-Cola Cup	3rd Round
FA Cup	5th Round

It had been clear for weeks that the influential figure of Jason Dozzell would be leaving Ipswich and, with the directors confident of netting around £2 million for their 'local boy made good', they cleared the way for Lyall and McGiven to go shopping.

Highly rated Paul Mason, a Liverpool-born midfielder previously with FC Groningen and Aberdeen, appeared to be good value for £400,000. Dozzell put pen to paper at Tottenham at the beginning of August, but the clubs wrangled over the fee. Eventually a tribunal ordered the London club to cough up £1.75 million.

A week after Dozzell waved goodbye to his home town, burly Ian Marshall was captured from Oldham for a club record £750,000. Able to play in central defence or as a target-man, Marshall made his debut five days later against his former club. A robust and direct player, he lacked the class of a Paul Mariner, but most observers agreed he would give the attack much-needed presence and vitality.

Marshall and Mason stepped straight into the side for the opening game in the renamed FA Carling Premiership at Boundary Park. Oldham fans were not best pleased to see their former hero Marshall lining up against them and he rubbed their noses in it when scoring just before half-time. Two excellent goals after the break gave Town a fine start and further goals by the enthusiastic Marshall beat Southampton and Chelsea the following week, to give the side a 100% record after three games with no goals conceded.

Inevitably this sort of pace couldn't be maintained, and failure to win any of the next eight games meant the fans feared another winter of discontent. Kevin Keegan's cavalier Newcastle side came to Suffolk and showed Town how to play positive football, and although the game ended all-square, the home fans jeered Town's miserly approach. McGiven's determination to frustrate opposing attacks brought a handful of away points, but occasionally failed miserably. At Arsenal, for example, Kevin Campbell and Ian Wright tore Town to pieces. Calls for changes were answered in October when the club splashed out another record fee of £800,000 for Celtic's Stuart Slater, who ironically hailed from nearby Sudbury.

Slater was tossed into the side at QPR, which ended in a 0-3 defeat, and this was followed by two drab home games with Leeds and Everton which failed to yield a Town goal. Things were coming to a head and the discontent in the stands spread to the dressing rooms. Skipper David Linighan was withdrawn at half-time in the

Everton game after a row with McGiven, but was reinstated a week later for the visit of Sheffield Wednesday, 24 hours after McGiven suffered minor injuries when his car overturned on the A12. Lyall, who had retained the trust of the fans, took over from his colleague in the dug-out, but saw the side crash to a 1-4 defeat. Wednesday's final goal was a solo effort by Carlton Palmer, of all people.

Most fans seemed to think the answer to Town's troubles was to re-install Lyall as team manager, and either get rid of McGiven or demote him to coach. Lyall was absent from many games, apparently on scouting duties, and the fans felt his influence was sorely missed. Although he probably didn't deserve all the criticism that came his way, McGiven certainly had a different set of priorities to the purists watching from the stands. His negative formations in away games didn't win Town many friends and criticism mounted in both the national and local press.

Relations were at an all-time low with the local media. Near the end of the campaign Dave Allard, a long-time football reporter with the *Evening Star*, hit out at the approach of the team management. He added: 'If my words cause offence, I make no apologies. I have suffered insults galore and a few more won't make a difference to me.' The national press also had their say about Town. One paper called them the most dull and uninspiring side in the land, who 'make George Graham's Arsenal look like Brazil.' Unsurprisingly, McGiven didn't enjoy post-match press conferences: there was usually tension in the air if Town hadn't won.

Amid all the discontent, a couple of Town forwards departed, seeking pastures new. Steve Whitton, after persistent interest from neighbouring Colchester, finally joined the Essex club for a cut-price £10,000 as player-coach. Promising youngster Neil Gregory headed on loan to Chesterfield.

League matches rarely gave Town fans much to enthuse about, but there was some excitement in the FA Cup. Swindon were luckily beaten in extra-time at Portman Road and then Tottenham were seen off 3-0 in the fourth round. These were mere distractions, however, from a slow but relentless slide down the table. The discontent reared its head in the dressing rooms before the home match with Coventry when striker Chris Kiwomya reacted badly to being dropped and stormed out of the ground. Reports suggested that team-mates disapproved of his over-reaction, but, like Linighan before him, the player was soon forgiven and reinstated.

The fans' protests reached a crescendo at the end of a miserable home defeat by a moderate QPR. At the whistle a crowd of dissenters assembled near the players' tunnel where they took root, angrily calling for McGiven's head. Chairman John Kerr urged them to disperse, and to 'pull together, don't pull us apart'. He said the side were fifteenth in the table and not twentieth, so the fans ought not to be so harsh. His words fell on deaf ears.

Although positioned around midway in mid-March, Town failed to win any of their final eleven league games and slid inexorably downwards. Relegation looked on the cards after a 0-5 hammering at Hillsborough. The display was labelled 'gutless' by the *Sunday Mirror* and left Town as one of six clubs in danger of accompanying Swindon through the relegation trapdoor.

The final home game saw a good performance against champions Manchester United, though not good enough to avert defeat, even though United keeper Schmeichel left the field injured. When you are near the bottom, luck seems to desert you – and poor Phil Whelan fell awkwardly and sustained a badly broken ankle. His crumpled leg was a distressing sight for all who saw it, and the horrified onlookers included his father Paddy.

And so arrived the climax to an unhappy season – a trip to high-flying Blackburn, where at least a point would be needed to stand any chance of survival. The congested nature of the lower end of the table meant six sides were still under threat and it turned into one of those afternoons where everybody had radios pinned to their ears, but no one really knew what was going on. As Town were holding Alan Shearer's men to a goalless draw, it became clear that some of the other results were going Town's way and others were not. A single goal at a number of grounds could change the whole picture in an instant. The drama and tension mounted and then, in the 90th minute at Stamford Bridge, Chelsea's Mark Stein hit the 105th league goal of his career. It was a routine strike for him, but the implications for others were huge.

Match of the Season 1993-94
Blackburn 0 Ipswich 0

Premiership, 7 May 1994

At kick-off time on the final Saturday, Ipswich and five other clubs were still fretting about relegation. There were many permutations, but Town travelled to Ewood Park knowing they would probably need a win to survive. A draw might be enough, but defeat would surely spell disaster.

The home side were secure in second place no matter what the outcome and had little to motivate them, with Manchester United having already secured the title. Rovers had several stars missing and there was a strange atmosphere at Ewood.

DID YOU KNOW?

Goalkeeper Jon Hallworth was nicknamed 'Boris' because he looked like Becker, and Mick Stockwell 'Stumper', for dismissing Bobby Robson in a charity cricket game.

The huge contingent of Town fans, however, did their best to whip up the noise levels. At times the game was surprisingly open and both sides missed chances. Town worked like demons and the deadly Shearer had few opportunities to add to his tally of 33 goals. As the game laboured towards its goalless conclusion the tension mounted grimly for the visitors.

Hearts were in mouths when a Rovers penalty appeal was turned down and then, just before the end, up popped Mick Stockwell to make a heroic goal-line clearance. Reports and rumours were coming in from other grounds, but no one could really say what the big picture was. Shortly after Stockwell's goal-line save came the final whistle. After a few moments of confusion – both on and off the field – Town's Steve Palmer, who had earlier been subbed, raced onto the pitch with arms held aloft.

Palmer had heard the news that Sheffield United had been beaten by Chelsea's last-minute goal. Being a university graduate, he'd done his maths and calculated that Town were safe. Other players followed his lead and began celebrating. The fans joined in. Mark Stein couldn't have imagined the joy his goal had brought to thousands of strangers, hundreds of miles away. Lyall ran on to hug his players, and, significantly, McGiven headed straight for the dressing rooms.

Within a day or two, chairman Kerr promised a re-think on the management structure. He subsequently announced that for next season Lyall would be reinstated as team manager, and McGiven would become football development manager.

A little of the gloss was taken off the celebrations when the verdicts of the media were published the day after the game. The *Sun* said Alan Shearer and his mates had betrayed the nation by not beating Town. The *Guardian* said Town deserved to be relegated and it would have been 'good riddance'. The *Daily Star* said Town were the most bland and negative waste of space in the Premiership. After such a season, things could surely only get better. Or could they?

FA CARLING PREMIERSHIP   1994-95

Premiership	22nd (relegated)
Coca-Cola Cup	2nd Round
FA Cup	3rd Round

Having twice flirted with relegation, Ipswich would find the 1994-95 campaign memorable – but, sadly, for all the wrong reasons. During the summer the board gave the fans what they craved – the return of John Lyall to a more hands-on role – and coughed up (in Ipswich Town terms) a large wedge of cash for team strengthening.

Lyall resumed his old role and reshuffled his 'cabinet', with the much-maligned Mick McGiven embarking on a slightly mysterious new role as football development officer. Loyal Charlie Woods was confirmed as assistant manager, Paul Goddard named as first-team coach, and John Wark player-coach. Also staying were reserve coach Bryan Klug, youth coach Peter Trevivian, and youth development officer Tony Dable. It was a big line-up for a big season. Would too many cooks spoil the broth, or was there safety in numbers?

In June a club record £1 million was paid to Tottenham for versatile Steve Sedgley and £250,000 to Aarhus for the Danish midfielder Claus Thomsen. A further five players arrived later. The debuts of Sedgley and Thomsen were delayed by injury, and by the time they got a taste of the action the squad had been augmented by two South Americans – the speedy Uruguayan forward Adrian Paz (£900,000 from Penarol) and left-sided Argentine defender Mauricio Taricco (£175,000 from Argentinos).

There was little to cheer early on, although Bontcho Guentchev bounced back into the side at QPR and, inspired by his summer appearances in the World Cup with Bulgaria, gave a lively display. Within a four-minute spell he upset the home defenders with another theatrical penalty-box fall, missed the spot-kick, but then whacked home a fine goal that turned out to be the winner.

This cameo aside, the new season didn't come to life until a thrilling 3-2 home win over Manchester United in late September. Three days earlier Town had embarrassingly lost at home to First Division Bolton in the Coca-Cola Cup – but against United Paul Mason banged in a couple before the interval and, undaunted by United levelling with two goals in three minutes, Town earned a standing ovation when new-boy Sedgley fired a late winner.

After the euphoria, things went downhill for both Sedgley and the team. He struggled to find his feet, perhaps intimidated by the size of his fee. At the same time, injuries and tactical reshuffles meant a lack of overall cohesion and consistency, and by the end of November Ipswich had sunk to the bottom.

A sweet goal by Thomsen stole a point at Newcastle, prompting frustrated home boss Kevin Keegan to lash out at Town's negative tactics. He likened Ipswich to 'hoofers' from non-League circles, and said the game had been 'a waste of a Saturday'. Having gained a valuable point, Town could laugh at these jibes, but events shortly afterwards suggested that the words of the ex-England skipper had been taken to heart within the Portman Road corridors of power. Was Keegan right? Had one of the most attractive and popular clubs in the land descended to the level of the primitive lower leagues?

The straw that broke the camel's back was the miserable first-half display at home to Manchester City. Town went in at the interval two goals down, bereft of confidence, inspiration and hope. On the Monday morning it was announced that Lyall had resigned 'by mutual agreement'. The former West Ham boss had been a hero when Town romped to the Second Division title in 1992, but now he was leaving behind a team in crisis, having spent £5.5 million on players that for the most part looked expensive flops. Relations with the local media and fans' morale were at an all-time low.

A change of manager before Christmas would perhaps give the club a reasonable stab of staving off relegation. Many names were put forward, ranging from ex-players like Mick Mills and Alan Brazil to more experienced candidates such as David Pleat and Graham Turner. Others touted included Mike Walker, Russell Osman and Steve Perryman, all of whom had recently lost their jobs at other clubs. Mills emerged as the favourite and the names on the shortlist were interviewed in the week before Christmas.

The focus of the gossip suddenly switched from Mills to his old full-back partner George Burley. Having made 500 appearances for Town, Burley was now boss of Third Division neighbours Colchester. He'd joined them that summer and although his managerial baptism had got off to a dreadful start, he'd pulled things round and the U's were climbing the table. The rumour mill said Town had been given permission by Colchester to speak to Burley; the young Scot had not been at his Layer Road desk for several days.

Apparently Turner, Mills, Perryman and Howard Kendall were all interviewed, Walker was telephoned, while Pleat was one of three men Town were not given permission to approach.

On Boxing Day the facts started to emerge. Colchester fans turned up for their match with Northampton to hear that Burley had walked out to join Ipswich. He had eighteen months of a two-year contract to run and there were conflicting reports over whether he'd been head-hunted or whether he'd put his own name forward. U's fans were not pleased: neither was the Colchester board, whose compensation demands exceeded what Town were prepared to pay.

The dispute turned into a protracted affair that had to be settled by a tribunal, souring relations between the two clubs.

Ipswich drew 1-1 at West Ham on Boxing Day, but Burley was still lying low. He was officially unveiled at the Arsenal home game two days later. Six goals conceded in defeats by the Gunners and then Everton gave Burley a baptism of fire and revealed the extent of the job in hand. Town were rock bottom and went into the New Year having won just one game from their last sixteen.

The new boss blooded young midfielder Adam Tanner for the home match with Leicester, and fans could immediately detect signs of hope. Tanner fired a superb debut goal in a 4-1 win over Town's relegation rivals. Next up was a trip to Fortress Anfield. Remarkably Tanner did the business again, cracking home a sensational winner. It was the club's first victory at Liverpool in 34 attempts.

These six points proved a false dawn as the old problems quickly resurfaced. But the directors backed their new boss's judgement by releasing funds to purchase extra fire-power in Alex Mathie from Newcastle for £500,000 and veteran Lee Chapman for £70,000 from West Ham. Both made an immediate impact, the latter just short of his 36th birthday and performing for his eleventh league club. Defender Chris Swailes, who'd been released several years earlier as an untried youngster, was recruited for £150,000 from hard-up Doncaster. His debut saw him head into his own net in the dying seconds to give Aston Villa victory at Portman Road.

Many observers felt the root of Town's problems were mistakes in the transfer market. Normally frugal and shrewd, Ipswich had recruited expensive players who'd generally flopped. A long injury list was also a key factor. Ian Marshall encountered head, hip and elbow injuries, Mick Stockwell missed much of the season with a knee problem, while Stuart Slater, Simon Milton and Paul Mason were all out for long periods. Skipper Geraint Williams missed three games and returned to find the captaincy was now the full-time job of Sedgley, as Burley changed things round.

Handing million-pound man Sedgley the black armband didn't have the desired result. His indifferent form continued and by mid-March he'd been axed for the duration of the season. Also off the scene were Chris Kiwomya, who went to Arsenal for £1.5 million, Eddie Youds, who left for Bradford City, and Phil Whelan who joined Middlesbrough for £300,000. Clearly the directors had to try and balance the books, but the big picture didn't change much.

A season of lows reached its nadir with the visit to Old Trafford in March. A nine-goal pounding left players and fans shell-shocked and saw Andy Cole net the same number of goals (five) in 65 minutes that Town's leading scorer would manage all season. That debacle was followed by another thrashing at Tottenham, after which Burley axed five players and gave youth its chance. In all, fifteen new faces appeared during the season, the most in a single campaign for nearly 50 years. Town used a total of 34 men in league games – a new club record. Only Frank Yallop, who missed just one game after a couple of years on the fringes, plus consistent keeper Craig Forrest could take satisfaction from this nightmarish season.

By February relegation looked certain. The only question was whether Town or Leicester would end up with the wooden spoon. After defeat at QPR, results elsewhere confirmed the worst – even though it was mid-April and Town still had half-a-dozen fixtures to fulfil. Only one of these was won and it was Leicester who won the 'race' to avoid the wooden spoon. A clear-out was necessary in the summer and Burley would need time to build his own squad.

Match of the Season 1994-95
Manchester United 9 Ipswich 0

Premiership, 4 March 1995

If a 0-4 reverse constitutes a hammering, what do you call 0-9? The media struggled for adjectives after this black day in Town's history, but seemed quite gleeful about the fate of a side who had often employed unpopular tactics in recent times. Perhaps attitudes were changing now that Burley was in charge, but for the time being results were not. The new boss described this as his worst day in football and refused to attend the post-match press conference. His newly appointed assistant, Dale Roberts, revealed that the team bus home was 'a horrible place to be'. United boss Alex Ferguson had sympathetic words for his fellow Scot, Burley, but naturally sang the praises of his own side. 'We were brilliant,' he crowed. 'I had a couple of 8-0 wins at Aberdeen, but never a nine!' Had it not been for Craig Forrest, Ferguson could have been celebrating double figures. As it was, it was United's biggest win for 103 years, and the nine-goal margin equalled Town's record defeat.

The avalanche began in the fifteenth minute when Keane buried a drive from Hughes' pass. Two more were netted by the electric Cole before the break. Three more goals arrived in a six-minute spell before the hour. Cole grabbed his fourth after Forrest had bravely blocked McClair. The flood continued, and two minutes from time Cole swivelled to lash his fifth and United's ninth. It was the second game of a run that saw Town lose seven games in a row, conceding 23 and scoring nil. Ferguson's smile was wiped from his face when United were pipped by Blackburn for the title.

Marcus Stewart, leading scorer in 2000-01

Bryan Hamilton had four very productive years with Ipswich Town

Gus Uhlenbeek challenges Luton's ex-Ipswich man Bontcho Guentchev (March 1996)

Phil Whelan gets ahead of Coventry's Mick Quinn (December 1992)

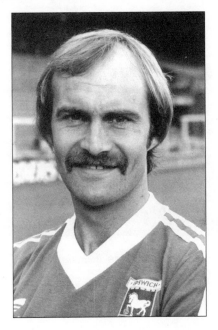

Mick Mills was on Ipswich's books for nearly 17 years

Geraint Williams jinks past Luton's Gary Waddock (October 1995)

Training facilities fit for the Premiership (April 2001)

Matt Holland (centre) and Jim Magilton meet the fans (April 2001)

Chapter Six

Return to the Top
1996-2001

LEAGUE DIVISION 1	1995-96
Division 1	7th
Coca-Cola Cup	2nd Round
FA Cup	5th Round

Things could only get better. Or could they? Swindon had recently departed the top flight in similar circumstances. Rather than climb back up, they had plummeted into the Second Division. However, three Ipswich wins in the opening weeks of the new campaign left most fans confident that Ipswich wouldn't be 'doing a Swindon'.

There was a new man at the top at Portman Road. David Sheepshanks, a director for several years, was installed as chairman in August. Like his predecessors, this young businessman was from strong Suffolk stock. His father, Captain Robin, was a well-known chairman of the county council, and David had been committed to the Town cause since being taken as a small boy to watch a game with Leyton Orient in 1965.

On the eve of the new campaign, wide-man Gus Uhlenbeek was purchased from Dutch side SV Tops for £100,000. He made a highly promising start, supplying ammunition for the 'M-men' strike duo. Alex Mathie started well, hitting six in the opening five league games, and continued to score regularly. After a slower start than his pal, Ian Marshall soon caught up and the pair engaged in friendly combat for the rest of the season, with a private wager of £50 resting on who would end up top scorer.

Argentine wing-back Mauricio Taricco, who looked superb going forward but occasionally suspect when defending, finally established himself as a regular more than a year after arriving from Latin America. Indeed by the time big central defender Tony Mowbray arrived from Celtic for £300,000 in October, it was clear Burley was constructing a side capable of mounting a serious promotion challenge. And, just as importantly, one that would play the type of football Ipswich fans had come to expect, thus banishing the dour image that had dogged the club in recent seasons.

Three subs could now be used for the first time and Town made use of the new allowance in the opening game, with third sub Milton coming on in place of second sub Yallop. In the clash with

Charlton, Burley paid the price for not having a keeper on his bench. Forrest collided with Kim Grant and sustained what at first seemed a serious neck injury. He was stretchered off and young striker Neil Gregory went in goal. Despite the usual heroics of a stand-in, Gregory was beaten four times in a 1-5 home defeat.

This result sparked an indifferent patch, despite the arrival of a new club skipper in Mowbray. Indeed, after a yawn-inducing home draw with Southend, Town found themselves entrenched in the lower half of the table and apparently going nowhere. For the next game Burley recalled Tanner, Marshall, Milton and the long-time absentee Thompson, and these changes paid immediate dividends. Portsmouth were beaten 3-2 thanks to a last-minute thunderbolt from Thompson's left boot. The side embarked on an eleven-match unbeaten run which included a fine win away to Charlton, a 5-1 hammering of Port Vale, and, best of all, a truly memorable night at Ewood Park when reigning Premiership champions Blackburn were dumped out of the FA Cup.

After a goalless draw at Portman Road in the third round, few gave Town much of a chance against Alan Shearer and company in the replay. However, the costly firepower purchased with Jack Walker's millions could find no way past a teenage goalkeeper with only six league games under his belt. Richard Wright, Ipswich-born and bred, stepped up for the most daunting task of his life and played a blinder. His display not only earned him the praise of stony-faced Shearer, it won him a regular place in the first team from that point on and effectively ended the Ipswich career of 'Giant Haystacks' Forrest. Everyone at Portman Road had known young Wright had talent, but was he ready for the first team? Now they knew the answer. Burley would no longer have to go hunting for loan keepers to replace Forrest – people like Andy Petterson and Fred Barber, who did stints at Portman Road before Christmas.

Wright's heroics and a stunning extra-time goal by Mason earned Town their win at Blackburn, launching a cup run that would end in the fifth round against Villa. According to the new chairman, that win put the club on the map and served notice that Ipswich Town had shrugged off the embarrassments and disappointments of recent times. The Blackburn replay was the highlight of eleven cup-ties fought out during the season. Least memorable had been the extra-time home defeat at the hands of David Jones' Stockport in the Coca-Cola Cup, when a certain Alun Armstrong did much of the damage. More would be heard of him in years to come.

The revived Anglo-Italian Cup gave the fans a diversion between early September and late January. Town progressed to the semi-finals, where they faced the less-than-glamorous Port Vale, but with a Wembley final beckoning, went down 2-4 at Portman Road with Tony Naylor grabbing a hat-trick. The tie pulled in less than 6,000 but the two earlier home clashes with Italian opposition attracted better gates and revived memories of the glory days in Europe some fifteen years earlier. A second-half revival saw Reggiana beaten 2-1, with goals from Mathie and Tanner in front of 10,000. Salernitana were beaten 2-0, with Mowbray and Gregory on target. Trips to Brescia and Foggia captured the imagination of a few fans who made midweek treks to Italy and were rewarded with a 2-2 draw at the former (Sedgley, Mason) and a 1-0 win at the latter (Mason).

A disappointing aspect of the 95-96 winter was the untypically poor state of the Portman Road pitch. Over the years the club had gained a reputation for providing a playing surface that was second to none, and often resembled a bowls green – but for the cup ties with Blackburn and Walsall, in particular, many of the older fans observed that it had never looked in a worse state. Thankfully, this was only a temporary state of affairs. By spring the team's form began to improve along with the pitch.

Four games in a three-week spell saw the side hit ten goals and show great spirit. At Watford, who were celebrating the return of prodigal son Graham Taylor, the Hornets took a two-goal lead, but Town hit back after the break and Uhlenbeek had a hand in all three Ipswich goals. Next up were fellow play-off contenders Leicester at home. Town cruised into a three-goal led within thirteen minutes, including a peach from veteran John Wark. Ten days later Town completed the double over the Foxes, but not before Ipswich had staged a grandstand finish at Barnsley, drawing 3-3 after Danny Wilson's men had led 3-0 with just five minutes remaining.

The momentum could not be sustained, otherwise automatic promotion might have been on the cards. As it was, home defeats by Tranmere and Reading, plus emphatic losses at Grimsby and Tranmere, meant Town entered the home straight not even certain of the play-offs. It all came down to the final day, when a win was required over lowly Millwall at Portman Road to pip Charlton or Leicester for the final play-off slot. But Millwall were playing for survival and the subsequent 0-0 draw was no good to either side.

Match of the Season 1995-96
Ipswich 0 Millwall 0

Division 1, 5 May 1996

A few weeks prior to this final-day showdown, Town had seemed a certainty for the play-offs, but a couple of surprise defeats left them

---

DID YOU KNOW?

Goalkeeper Paul Cooper had a knack of saving penalties. During his 13 years at Ipswich he faced 73 spot-kicks and saved 21. In 1979-80 he saved five out of seven!

---

needing all three points against a side teetering on the precipice at the other end of the table. Jimmy Nicholl's men needed at least a draw to survive the drop, probably more.

Charlton, hit by injury and suspension, could be overhauled by an Ipswich win, and Leicester too, if the Foxes lost at Watford. There were a number of possible permutations, but the bottom line was that three points would do the trick for both Town and Millwall. Which meant heartache for one or other, perhaps both.

Thanks to Millwall's reputation, the police presence at Portman Road was the largest ever seen. Sadly this didn't prevent outbreaks of trouble. There were fourteen arrests, six coaches on a special train were wrecked, and inside the stadium seats were broken and hurled in the direction of home fans.

On the pitch, the game was tense and tight, with Millwall having eyes on a draw and banking on lowly rivals Portsmouth failing to beat Huddersfield. That was a dangerous ploy, but it certainly stifled the creativity of a Town side who had scored more goals than any other club in the Endsleigh League and Premiership combined.

The nearest to a goal before the interval came on 40 minutes when a sharp save by Kasey Keller foiled Town's newly crowned 'player of the year' Simon Milton. There were more glum faces after the change-around when 39-year-old Wark limped off with a recurrence of an Achilles problem, and in the process brought down the curtain on a marvellous career.

With fifteen minutes left, tension increased further as James Scowcroft headed Milton's cross against a post and near the end Sedgley skied a decent chance over the bar. At the final whistle, with the deadlock unbroken, news filtered through that Leicester had won 1-0 at Vicarage Road. That result secured Leicester a play-off place and relegated Watford. Portsmouth had won at the McAlpine Stadium to save themselves and send Millwall down. Charlton's draw with Wolves left the Addicks sixth, with Town in seventh, two points adrift.

It was all a massive anti-climax and Burley confessed to being heart-broken at having missed out, considering the good football Town had played and the size of their goal tally.

LEAGUE DIVISION 1   **1996-97**
Division 1   4th (play-offs)
Coca-Cola Cup   Quarter-finals
FA Cup   3rd Round

George Burley, anxious to strengthen his squad before it returned for pre-season training, thought he'd found just the man to aid a promotion bid when Norwich midfielder Ian Crook agreed to come to Portman Road. The 33-year-old signed on the dotted line and was paraded before the media. Around the same time, Mike Walker returned to Carrow Road as manager, following a spell at Everton. Walker, assessing the squad he had inherited, expressed regret that Crook had been allowed to leave.

Exactly what happened next may never become fully clear, but the upshot was that Crook made a complete U-turn and resumed his Norwich career. Naturally, all at Portman Road were furious and legal advice was taken. Subsequently, Crook was allowed to honour his Norwich contract and cancel the Ipswich one, but was fined £250 for his actions, and Town received undisclosed compensation. Commenting later on this bizarre series of events, Crook said he hadn't intended to upset anyone, but Walker's return had changed the circumstances at Norwich and he no longer wanted to leave. The Crook affair left a sour taste south of the Norfolk-Suffolk border and Town fans began storing up the vitriol in readiness for the two derby games.

Burley turned his attentions elsewhere and signed 24-year-old ex-Burnley midfielder Danny Sonner, who'd spent the last three years plying his trade on the Continent. The other significant arrival was young Dutch forward Bobby Petta, a free transfer from Feyenoord. Petta showed up well in pre-season matches, particularly John Wark's testimonial against Arsenal, and won himself a place in the starting line-up for the opening league fixture. Wark, who had celebrated his 39th birthday before his testimonial, was appointed the club's Football in the Community coach, but kept himself fit and was retained in the first-team squad, despite apparently having retired a few months earlier. Sure enough, the old solider was called into action a couple of times during the season. More comebacks than Frank Sinatra!

The campaign got off to a moderate start, but the departure of popular striker Ian Marshall for £875,000 at the end of August didn't bode well in the eyes of many supporters. His replacement, local youngster James Scowcroft, was plunged into the fray, but the team looked far from promotion challengers over the early weeks. By mid-October, things had come to a head. With Town entrenched in the bottom half, leading scorer Alex Mathie damaged his shoulder against Crystal Palace in the Coca-Cola Cup, leaving Town short of attacking options without him. Gerry Creaney, struggling to live down his big transfer fee at Manchester City, was obtained on loan to temporarily fill the breach. Another contender emerged in the shape of enthusiastic youngster Richard Naylor, who revelled in the nickname 'Bam Bam' (after the Flintstones character) and delighted home fans with his robust and direct style.

When results failed to improve, Town swooped for Tottenham defender Jason Cundy, and after a delay due to red tape, he was introduced in early November. But no sooner had he had established himself in the side than his season was halted by a diagnosis of testicular cancer. Understandably, this was not widely publicised at the time, although after he had made a complete recovery the brave Cundy was happy to help raise awareness of the need for early detection of this disease.

Cundy's first goal came in the defeat at lowly Bradford City, a result which meant Town had only won four of eighteen league games to that point. Five days later the club's annual meeting was scheduled, and one wondered whether the grim results would make this a stormy affair. It was therefore, perhaps, rather timely that Town beat Swindon just 48 hours before the meeting. The earning of these three welcome points was watched by only 7,086 – the smallest league crowd at Portman Road since 1955. The win marked something of a turning point and within a month Town were moving slowly back up the table. A particular highlight came when a late Scowcroft goal beat leaders Bolton on their own turf. Further momentum was gained after the turn of the year with a ten-match unbeaten League run. With another ten matches still to go, victory at Stoke saw Town rise to sixth and remain as play-off contenders from thereon in.

More new faces emerged in the course of the campaign. West Indian-born forward Earl Jean was given his opportunity, Bobby Howe was borrowed for a time from Nottingham Forest, the highly promising local lad Kieron Dyer made his bow, and Swede Niklas Gudmundsson arrived on loan from Blackburn. Gudmundsson looked a very useful acquisition. Claus Thomsen was allowed to leave for Everton for a fee of £900,000, which represented a handsome profit on the player. With Jason Cundy absent, recovering from cancer surgery, the club faced a further unexpected blow when midfielder Adam Tanner failed a drugs test. Although the player apologised to all concerned and admitted he'd made a big mistake, he was inevitably withdrawn from the squad in the aftermath of this episode.

DID YOU KNOW?

After rejoining from Liverpool, John Wark won Ipswich's Player of the Year award four times. Curiously, he never won it during his long earlier stint with Town.

Chairman David Sheepshanks, 44, was elected by his peers to the post of Chairman of the Football League, a role that also carried a place on the FA Council. His mandate was to lead investigations into the whys and wherefores of changes to the League's structure. The new job did not require him to step down as Town's chief. Meanwhile, Pat Godbold, who had worked at Portman Road for 43 years, was preparing to vacate her role as manager's secretary/PA, having worked for nine different managers since 1954.

The team's recovery helped Town reach the Coca-Cola Cup quarter-finals, where they were beaten at home by Leicester. Earlier, the club had competed in the first round of this competition for the first time. A troublesome trip to Bournemouth saw many fans miss the first half due to traffic congestion. They could have made good use of the mountain bike that was later won by Scowcroft for being the Coke man-of-the-match!

Town's quick exit from the FA Cup at Forest was disappointing, but may well have assisted the surge up the league. Despite the loss of Marshall and Mathie, the goals flowed in early 1997. West Brom were hammered 5-0 while Oldham and Swindon were trounced 4-0. These scores put the side in confident frame of mind to tackle the local derby with Norwich. It was one of the most eagerly awaited Portman Road games in ages, due in no small part to the intensive build-up the game received in the local press. Naturally a certain Mr Crook got a hostile reception, but of greater importance was the securing of three points which boosted Town's chances of securing a play-off spot while extinguishing Norwich's.

Two odd-goal wins in the wake of the Norwich euphoria made it five wins in a row and clinched a top-six place. When the dust had settled, Town found themselves paired with Sheffield United in the play-offs, a side they headed in the final table and twice beaten by a two-goal margin.

Match of the Season 1996-97

Ipswich 2 Sheffield United 2

Division 1, play-off, semi-final, 2nd leg, 14 May 1997

Around 5,000 Town fans travelled to Bramall Lane for the first leg. They saw their side come away with a 1-1 draw that made them favourites to win a tension-packed second leg at Portman Road. Matters got off to a bad start, however, when the Belarussian Petr Katchouro collected Carl Tiler's long ball and fired in a shot which hit the underside of the bar and came down. The linesman signalled a goal and, despite the serious doubts of the partisan home fans, TV later proved he was right. Town levelled half an hour later when Scowcroft headed player-of-the-year Mauricio Taricco's cross beyond Alan Kelly.

There was no let up in the pace or tension and seven names were jotted into Mr Pearson's notebook. On 73 minutes Town got their noses ahead when Stockwell crossed from the right and Gudmundsson headed home. It had become clear that the Blades' keeper Kelly was hampered by injury and was struggling with crosses. However, manager Howard Kendall had no keepers on his bench and Kelly was forced to soldier on. With Town fans in full voice about reaching Wembley, the Blades bounced back within four minutes of falling behind. Mitch Ward headed back Dane White-house's cross for sub Andy Walker to convert. With extra-time looming, Kelly saved well from Scowcroft, and then Sedgley cracked a fierce free-kick against a post.

As extra-time began, Town knew they had to score because a 2-2 result after 120 minutes would hand United victory on away goals. They continued to pour forward and leading marksman Paul Mason went agonisingly close. When Blades defender Nicky Henry aimed his knee at the grounded Taricco, the red card was produced.

The final whistle heralded a Blades victory by the narrowest of margins. It was sheer heartbreak for Town, who had still not lost in four meetings with the South Yorkshire side. The apparent injustice of it all saw several players leave the field in tears. Taricco's obvious distress was doubly understandable for he had been taunted at close quarters by a jubilant Jan-Aage Fjortoft at the end. Howard Kendall was magnanimous, praising Ipswich's quality, while a disappointed David Sheepshanks promised that Town would be back for another crack in a year's time.

LEAGUE DIVISION 1   **1997-98**
Division 1   5th (play-offs)
Coca-Cola Cup   Quarter-finals
FA Cup   4th Round

Preparing for his third full season in charge, George Burley certainly made his presence felt in the summer transfer market, bringing in five new faces before the end of August and shipping out three. Manchester City paid £1.35 million for defender Tony Vaughan and Wolves agreed a £500,000 fee for Steve Sedgley. A further half-million was recouped when goalkeeper Craig Forrest left for West Ham. Some of this income was made available to strengthen the squad, and Burley recruited the hard-working young Bournemouth midfielder Matt Holland for £800,000. He also took the experienced and versatile Mark Venus from Wolves as part of the Sedgley deal, and signed keeper Lee Bracey for £40,000 from Bury as cover for Richard Wright. Former Tottenham defender David Kerslake came in on a free transfer, and the tiny but talented Chelsea striker Mark Stein arrived on loan.

Early on in the campaign the side was considerably hampered by injury problems, losing Gus Uhlenbeek and Paul Mason for most of the season, and others for shorter periods. Alex Mathie returned from an eleven-month injury absence, but while he was finding his feet the side struggled to recapture former glories. It all added up to a poor start to the season and a home defeat by Stoke in September saw Town drop into the dreaded bottom three. They stayed down among the dead men until December. There was little for the fans to cheer during the autumn and on an unhappy Friday night at Carrow Road, Town's woes increased when James Scowcroft and Matt Holland collided heavily, the former coming off worst and having to be stretchered off to hospital after a lengthy hold-up. The diagnosis was a temporarily paralysis following bruising and spasm of his spinal chord. A freak own-goal by Jason Cundy ultimately handed Norwich the three points in this, for Ipswich, local derby-to-forget.

As the injury crisis worsened, further loanees were introduced in the shape of David Whyte, a talented under-achiever, and wideman Andy Legg. Former local hero Jason Dozzell was welcomed back on a weekly contract after four years with Tottenham. Results, however, failed to improve as winter closed in and the season's black spot arrived in early November when Stockport pinched a 2-0 win at Portman Road in front of the season's lowest crowd. The fans shook their heads in dismay, and the under-strength Town side were jeered off the pitch at the end.

DID YOU KNOW?

At home to Everton in 1993, Town had three captains. Linighan had a half-time row and didn't reappear, Wark went off injured, so the black band passed to Stockwell.

After that gloomy night, things could only improve. With Mathie off colour and Scowcroft being rather harshly barracked by sections of the crowd, the need was clear for new blood in attack. Burley eventually got his man when £1.1 million-rated David Johnson put pen to paper in mid-November. Some of this outlay was offset by defender Chris Swailes going in part-exchange to Bury. Johnson, whose namesake from Merseyside had been a goalscoring hero of the 1970s, was an instant hit in Suffolk and the goals soon began to flow. Having hit eight for Bury before his arrival, he would ultimately end the season as the leading scorer at both Gigg Lane and Portman Road!

Johnson's arrival, around the same time as the return of former player Bryan Hamilton as coach, saw things begin to fall in place. A number of players departed, including Dozzell, who was said to have broken a club-imposed curfew, Stein, Whyte, Legg and Kerslake. Striker Neil Gregory was loaned to Peterborough and later joined neighbours Colchester for £50,000. By Christmas, Town were steadily moving upwards – in similar fashion to the previous season – and the final piece in Burley's jigsaw looked like being Jamie Clapham, a left-sided player who arrived from Tottenham, initially on loan, and later on a permanent basis in exchange for £300,000.

It took a while for the home form to catch up with the huge improvement in away results, but once this happened there was simply no stopping Ipswich's onwards march. In the second half of the campaign, they would only lose once – and that was at the home of champions-elect Nottingham Forest, whose attack was based on their mercurial Dutch star Pierre Van Hooijdonk. This run included seven successive home wins and a remarkable mini-series of three successive home matches when five goals were scored each time. How quickly things can change – there were no jeers to be heard now! The second of the nap-hand trio was a 'demolition derby' against neighbours Norwich, who were steamrollered aside. Mathie notched a first-half hat-trick, an achievement which seemed to signal an end to the eighteen months of problems he had experienced. However, a week or two later he was dropped to the bench and promptly gave the management an earful: 'I had a go and said my piece,' he told the Ipswich *Evening Star*.

Town again reached the last eight of the Coca-Cola Cup and only exited this competition by losing a penalty shoot-out with Chelsea at

Portman Road. The spot-kicks that Scowcroft and Taricco missed that night could be added to six other failures from twelve yards by various Town players over the course of the season. Highlight of the cup run was a comfortable win over Manchester United at Portman Road, although nobody was kidding themselves that the tie had any real significance for the opposition. Alex Ferguson picked a squad in which Andy Cole and Philip Neville were probably the only players who would have made the first-choice United side.

The post-Christmas league run saw Town ultimately gather an impressive total of 83 points. A year earlier that would have been enough for automatic promotion. As it was, they stormed into the play-offs in the sort of form that made them hot favourites to lift the trophy at Wembley. Sadly, the semi-final with Charlton got off to a bad start, got steadily worse, and became the biggest anti-climax in recent memory. The omens had not been good, for the night before the first leg the Town players' sleep was rudely interrupted by a fire alarm that went off in the early hours at their hotel on the edge of Ipswich. On a tense afternoon, a packed Portman Road watched grim-faced as Alan Curbishley's men employed uncharacteristic spoiling tactics that stifled the blue goal-machine. The Valiants, crucially, got the sort of start they could only have dreamed about, unlucky Clapham burying the ball into his own net. The rest of the game was dominated by over-physical challenges, scuffles and confrontations. Nine players were yellow-carded and Danny Mills was sent off for clashing with Taricco, a player whose antics meant he was not exactly the most popular in Division One circles. The bad feeling spilled over after the game, too, and Taricco emerged from the players' bar with a bloodied nose after reportedly clashing with one of the Charlton players.

The London side appeared a much more accomplished outfit in the second leg, and Town never looked like preventing them from reaching the final. And, unlike the first leg at Portman Road, Charlton and Sunderland produced a real classic in the Wembley final (won by Charlton in a penalty shoot-out), leaving Town to lick their wounds and prepare for yet another tilt the following year.

Match of the Season 1997-98

Ipswich 5 Norwich 0

Division 1, 21 February 1998

Unbeaten in eight league games, Town were shrugging off their poor pre-Christmas form and surging up the table by the time of Norwich's visit. The Canaries were certainly not in chirpy mood, however, having spent virtually all the season in the lower reaches of the table. They looked all set for a roasting at Portman Road, despite the fact that local derbies often defy the formbook.

The bookies offered 100-1 against a 5-0 win for Town, clearly not anticipating a dreadful performance by Norwich's back four, nor the first-half sharpness of Mathie. The pattern was set after only 64 seconds when Clapham's throw-in found Mathie, who rifled in the opener. Before the half-hour Uhlenbeek and Stockwell combined neatly to enable Mathie to burst through and shoot a second, with Norwich half-heartedly calling for offside.

Just before the interval the hat-trick was complete when Mathie's shot from a Stockwell cross crept over the line after being half-saved by Andy Marshall. Although Mathie didn't reappear after the break, on account of a calf problem, Town didn't take their foot off the throttle. On 56 minutes Cundy and Johnson combined to set up Bobby Petta, who sprinted into the box and netted a low drive.

City's Robert Fleck, enjoying a long record of mutual animosity with Town fans, made a hash of converting a gaping chance. Cue the inevitable mocking laughter (the little Scot would be back a few weeks later with his new club Reading, but things didn't improve for him that day either). Dutchman Petta showed him how it's done for a second time, seizing onto a pass from the irrepressible Holland. There was unconfined joy in the stands as home fans celebrated this, the third occasion that Town had hit five against the local enemy. Mathie became the sixth man to score a Town hat-trick in an East Anglian derby – following in the footsteps of Albert Day (1946), Jackie Brown (1949), Colin Viljoen (1968), Trevor Whymark (1976) and John Wark (1980). Whatever else he did at Portman Road, Mathie's lifetime hero-status was now assured.

LEAGUE DIVISION 1   **1998-99**
Division 1   3rd (play-offs)
Worthington Cup   2nd Round
FA Cup   4th Round

After successive top five finishes – promotion squandered on both occasions – George Burley was determined to go the extra mile in 1998-99 and take the club back to the top flight. If he was looking for lucky omens during the summer of 1998, he would not have been amused by news from the home of defender Jason Cundy. Showing a commendable desire to be fit for the start of pre-season training, Cundy got busy with the skipping rope. Top boxers look impressive when they whirl the rope, but maybe footballers should stick to other things: Cundy somehow tweaked an ankle. It was an injury that would need surgery and keep him out of the first team for nine months.

Unlucky Cundy could only watch from the fringes as new signings Sean Friars from Liverpool and Marco Holster from the Netherlands arrived at Portman Road, along with new coach Stewart Houston, the ex-Chelsea and Manchester United defender. The season got off to a quiet start, with Town failing to score in their first four games – three goalless draws plus a home defeat by Peter Reid's Sunderland, the team most pundits fancied for the title.

The goal drought ended in style when four successive league games registered three goals apiece. The back four looked solid, too, despite Cundy's absence. Tony Mowbray and Mark Venus performed manfully at the heart of the defence, until Mowbray's withdrawal at home to Bradford City. The big man was replaced by another huge frame, that of new singing Manu Thetis, a Frenchman on the books of Spanish club Seville. His robust style soon won the hearts of home fans, but earned him a series of yellow cards. Thetis proved a valuable asset in attack at set pieces, but sadly followed his finest goal – an overhead kick against West Brom – by being sent off later in the same game.

The club's finances were not healthy. In mid-October speculation about striker Alex Mathie's future was finally laid to rest when he departed for Dundee United for a sizable fee. The income eased the overdraft, but gave cause for concern about the strength in depth of the attack. In the same week that the Mathie deal was completed, Danny Sonner left for Sheffield Wednesday for a somewhat smaller fee, having a week or two earlier been disciplined by the club for off-field indiscretions.

Injuries prompted Burley to plunder the loan market. Over the season as a whole he would borrow half-a-dozen players, with only one of them – Jim Magilton – being retained on a more permanent basis. When the strike partnership of David Johnson and James Scowcroft was disrupted by injury, the inexperienced but eager youngsters Samassi Abou and Marlon Harewood were signed on loan to plug the gap – from West Ham and Nottingham Forest respectively. Young Richard Naylor was apparently not considered ready for regular first-team action. The deal that caused the biggest fuss, however, was the sale of popular Argentine Mauricio Taricco to Tottenham for £1,775,000. The manager and chairman were both quick to emphasise that they, like the fans, didn't want to see the player depart, but were forced to sell by the financial situation.

By the time of Taricco's exit, Town had got their act together following their indifferent start and had moved into second place in the table. Sunderland had already opened up a chasm at the top, however, and would not relinquish that position for the remainder of the campaign. The Wearsiders only lost three times all season, failed to score in just five games, and piled up 91 goals and 105 points. The race for the second automatic spot was less clear-cut. After Christmas it developed into a battle royal between Town and surprise packets Bradford City, under the stewardship of rookie manager Paul Jewell.

Town lost a Worthington Cup thriller in the dying seconds at Second Division Luton, and were also embarrassed by drawing with Third Division Exeter, but the team put these hiccups behind them with some consistent displays. The defence performed particularly well throughout the winter and by the time West Brom were beaten at Portman Road in March, a new club record of 22 clean sheets had been established. The future looked bright from a defensive point of view, too, for a 17-year-old colossus named Titus Bramble enjoyed an eye-catching debut in a live televised game with Sheffield United. He was clearly a star of the future.

In central midfield, Town fans watched with bewilderment as a series of players were plunged into the deep end – loanees Paolo Vernazza, Jonathan Hunt and Lee Hodges to name but three – to assist newly-appointed skipper Matt Holland in the engine room. The vacancy was not properly filled until the arrival from Sheffield Wednesday of Northern Ireland international Jim Magilton. His purchase consumed £682,500 of the money received for Taricco, and another slice was used to bring in Surinam-born Fabian Wilnis – a speedy defender and good crosser of the ball – from Dutch football.

Magilton's keen performances compensated for the temporary loss of talented youngster Kieron Dyer, who fractured his leg against Watford but unknowingly played on for a few minutes, even managing to score with the other leg during that time!

Fortunately, the break wasn't serious and Dyer missed just seven games, returning for the tense run-in in the spring.

Cundy, by this time keeping clear of skipping ropes, made a welcome return for the trip to Swindon. On a lively afternoon, the Robins never recovered from having a man sent off and Town romped to a 6-0 club record away win. As April unfolded it became clear Town would need nerves of steel to sustain their pace and pip Bradford City for the second automatic promotion place. However, things went pear-shaped and only two of the final six games were won. Particularly frustrating was a 1-2 home defeat by lowly Crewe, who ended the game with only ten men. Their impressive manager Dario Gradi must have thought Christmas had come eight months early as Town failed to match his skilful youngsters in front of a seething 20,000-plus crowd.

On the penultimate weekend of the league programme Bradford City slipped up, drawing with relegation-bound Oxford. However, Town failed to capitalise and were beaten at St Andrews, where Birmingham's Paul Furlong hit the only goal after fine work by Bryan Hughes. These results meant that on the final day Town had to beat Sheffield United at Portman Road and hope that Bradford City would lose at Wolves, who themselves would be going flat out for a play-off place. Ipswich did what was required, winning 4-1, but Jewell's boys rose to the occasion and won 3-2 at Molineux to condemn Town to another appearance in the dreaded play-offs.

In years gone by, third place would have guaranteed promotion, but the play-off system meant Town had three more hurdles to clear – including two games with Bolton, who had finished ten points below them. Play-offs certainly create a nail-biting climax and generate extra interest, but they're not a fun prospect when you've just finished third.

Another sad note clouded the end of the season. Sir Alf Ramsey, who had lived in Ipswich since leading Town to the league title in 1962, died of Alzheimer's disease at the age of 79. Concerns about his health had been voiced throughout the late 1990s, ever since he failed to attend a memorial service for Bobby Moore. Sir Alf had bought a modest house in Valley Road with his bonus for winning the 1966 World Cup and for many years lived just around the corner from Bobby Robson. He became private and withdrawn, and died in a nursing home, leaving a widow Lady Vickie. Plans were launched to erect a statue in his honour near the football ground.

During the season the club also announced the death after illness of director John Kerridge. The board was later supplemented by the arrival of Lord Ryder, formerly chief whip in John Major's government, and a long-time Town supporter.

Match of the Season 1998-99

Ipswich 4   Bolton 3

Play-off, semi-final, 2nd leg, 19 May 1999

Surely it wouldn't happen again? Nobody gets beaten in the play-offs three years in a row, do they?

Although Town had finished three places and ten points above Bolton, the two league encounters had seen them 'doubled' by Colin Todd's men. Nobody at Portman Road was underestimating the size of the task. Trailing 0-1 following the first leg in Lancashire, the Superblues had a fighting chance of winning through as 21,755 took their seats for the return, helping to whip up a marvellous atmosphere.

It was an astonishing game, the sort of contest where nobody could afford to takes their eyes off the pitch for a moment, let alone consider slipping out for a pie or coffee. The outcome hung in the balance for 120 minutes, plus stoppages, and the crowd was at fever pitch for most of that time.

The all-important early goal went Town's way. James Scowcroft fed Matt Holland, whose shot found the net via a post after just fourteen minutes. The aggregate scores remained level until shortly after half-time when Bolton's Ricardo Gardner crossed and Eidur Gudjohnsen fed Bob Taylor for an equaliser. Town's response was immediate. Kieron Dyer, the subject of recent transfer speculation, shot home from a tricky angle after being set up by Scowcroft.

In the play-offs, the away goals rule only takes effect after the completion of extra-time. With the extra period looming, Bolton reclaimed the lead when a Michael Johansen corner was converted by Per Frandsen. Then, with Town just 24 seconds from defeat, up popped Dyer again, getting on the end of a Fabian Wilnis cross to loop a header over keeper Steve Banks. Portman Road erupted and the final whistle blew to confirm a further 30 minutes of almost unbearable tension. Though the aggregate scores were level, Town had to score again or go out.

Six minutes into extra-time it was 'advantage Bolton' when Claus Jensen and Gudjohnsen combined to allow veteran Taylor to score expertly again. Town now needed two goals to reach the final, and had only 24 minutes to get them. With 116 minutes on the clock, skipper Holland set up a frantic finale by seizing onto Mark Fish's weak clearance to beat Banks. The 4-3 win seemed a superb achievement, but it wasn't enough because of the away goals rule. Referee Kirkby's final whistle sparked tearful scenes with Town players slumping to the turf for a third successive season.

Chairman David Sheepshanks confessed that the crushing disappointment at that moment was the lowest point of his chairmanship. Young Dyer, meanwhile, was quick to announce he would see out his contract and pledged to help make sure Town got promotion next time round. A few weeks later he did leave the club, but he clearly meant what he said at the time and his words struck the right note with thousands of crushed Town supporters.

The following day some of those disappointed fans vented their anger on the Football League and its policy that second-leg games be played in the evenings and not on a Saturday afternoon. The issue had surfaced because two Bolton fans were killed in a car crash on their way back north after the match. The accident occurred deep into the night as they made their weary way north from Suffolk following a game that finished well after 10pm.

LEAGUE DIVISION 1   **1999-2000**
Division 1   3rd (play-offs, promoted)
Worthington Cup   2nd Round
FA Cup   3rd Round

In terms of league success, Ipswich Town had been 'nearly men' for the best part of ten years under Bobby Robson. Now, with a Robson protege at the helm, they were again in danger of falling agonisingly short of the breakthrough the supporters craved. Three successive play-off failures was hard to stomach, though at least it was better than being a Norwich fan during the same period. Those deadly Norfolk rivals had finished thirteenth, fifteenth, and nineteenth.

Patience is said to be a virtue and there was plenty in evidence at Portman Road in the mid and late 1990s. Disappointment had had to be swallowed in triplicate and resolve hardened yet again in 1999 as another attempt was prepared to reach the gold-paved promised land of the Premiership.

George Burley, still a young man in managerial terms, by now knew the Division One scene inside out. If anyone knew what was needed to get promotion, he surely did. The squad he had rebuilt after the disasters of 1994-95 was maturing nicely and some of his excursions into the transfer market had proved astute. He wheeled and dealt again in the summer of 1999, aided by the £6 million raised from the club record sale of local product Kieron Dyer to Newcastle. Over the course of the season Burley would spend more than half that sum on four new players, all of whom would make a major impact. First arrival was Jermaine Wright from Dario Gradi's academy of talent at Crewe, ostensibly to fill the boots of Dyer. He cost £500,000 and would add a new dimension to a Town midfield strengthened a few months earlier by Jim Magilton's arrival. Wright had impressed Burley when playing against Town, and another in that category was John McGreal, a polished and unflappable defender, who in August was prised from Tranmere for £650,000.

Unlike the previous three ill-fated campaigns, Town roared out of the traps and by the end of August topped the table with four wins and a draw. David Johnson was red-hot, banging in seven goals in the five games, including a brace in a 6-1 spanking of Dave Bassett's Barnsley. It was the type of form that had international managers keeping tabs on Johnson's services. He played and scored for his country of birth, Jamaica, but expressed his preference for switching to one of the home nations. He accepted an invitation to join up with the Welsh squad, but injury kept him on the sidelines. Later he welcomed overtures from Craig Brown and Scotland, which apparently upset a few Jamaicans, who accused him of being a traitor and issued death threats. Johnson stuck to his guns, only to discover that he was ineligible for Scotland anyway. He would end the season with four full Jamaican caps, plus England schoolboy and 'B' honours to his name.

In attack, Johnson was often partnered by the robust Richard Naylor, who emerged from the shadows to 'put himself about' and give headaches to many an opposing defender. The introduction of Naylor allowed James Scowcroft to move back into midfield, an experiment that paid off for Burley, who wasn't afraid to tinker with the formation in the interests of improvement and consistency.

Burley won the Manager of the Month prize for August, but if the canny Scot thought the autumn would continue in similar vein he was mistaken. September yielded just one victory, a 2-1 win over Manchester City in which new signing Gary Croft bagged the winning goal. Croft, an England Under-21 cap who couldn't claim a regular spot at Blackburn, cost £800,000 and looked a useful acquisition. He blotted his copybook within days of signing, however, being arrested for motoring-related offences. Subsequently he found himself a guest of Her Majesty's hospitality. The club publicly deplored the actions which gave rise to this outcome, but stood behind him, as did the fans, who gave Croft a huge ovation when he returned to action later as a sub against Swindon. As he stepped out that afternoon he made League history by becoming the first player to wear an electronic security tag. Strapped to his left ankle, the device had been a condition of his early freedom.

Town lightened the wages bill and gave valuable experience to youngsters Neil Midgley and Titus Bramble by loaning them out to Luton and Colchester, respectively. Midgley returned to Portman Road to earn his Ipswich debut almost immediately. He responded by scoring the third goal in a win over a West Brom side that finished with only nine men after a flurry of red cards.

In addition to the Croft saga, midfielder Adam Tanner was also in trouble with the local constabulary and found himself released by the club. The beleaguered Burley was then faced with problems from big defender Manu Thetis. Reports from the dressing room before the Charlton home game suggested the fiery Frenchman had reacted badly to being omitted and landed a punch to his manager's jaw before storming out from the stadium. Burley later laughed off this rumour, suggesting that if the giant stopper really had whacked him, he, Burley, wouldn't have survived to tell the tale!

Fans campaigning for a permanent memorial for the late Sir Alf Ramsey were delighted when the council agreed to name a street after him, in addition to a statue to be erected beside the ground. A less well-known figure was also publicly applauded for his efforts for Ipswich Town. Versatile and tigerish midfielder Mick Stockwell chalked up his 600th first-team game, a rare achievement in an era when many fellow professionals change clubs simply for maximum financial gain.

Two goals in the final fifteen minutes at Blackburn saved Town a point in November and Tony Mowbray's last-gasp equaliser seemed to signal an end to an inconsistent patch. The side embarked on an unbeaten run lasting eighteen league games extending into March, by which time Town were looking a decent bet to fill one of the automatic promotion spots. The attack by now had been bolstered by the purchase of Marcus Stewart for a club record £2.5 million from cash-strapped promotion rivals Huddersfield. Slightly-built, but skilful and composed, Stewart was a great finisher with superb close control and at 27 had already bagged around 150 senior goals. Just to make matters worse at the disgruntled McAlpine Stadium, Stewart returned there to score Town's winner just eleven days after signing. Steve Bruce's outfit would never recover from the sale of their leading scorer and slid slowly out of the promotion race.

The promotion bid faltered in mid-March. Waves of attacks were launched on Blackburn at Portman Road, but Tony Parkes' men escaped with a goalless draw, a result that seemed to dent Town's confidence. Defeat at Wolves followed, and worse was to come when mid-table Norwich snatched a 2-0 win at Portman Road, helped by a dismal display by off-colour Town. The fans reacted angrily but the players bounced back with a stylish win at Tranmere that reclaimed second place and meant promotion was still within reach. However, that earlier hiccup had effectively put paid to any realistic chance of catching runaway leaders Charlton.

Chairman David Sheepshanks, who earlier had lost out narrowly to Geoffrey Thompson for the post of Chairman of the FA, was happy to extend Burley's contract. During the March 'wobble', many fans wondered whether Burley had taken the club as far as he could. The chairman's confidence in the Scot raised a few eyebrows and was a brave step. Sheepshanks then rubber-stamped Burley's request to bring on board flying Dutchman Martijn Reuser on loan. This exciting wide player was on the fringe of his national team and had experience at Ajax and Vitesse Arnhem. Like Stewart, Reuser bagged a goal on his debut – a last-minute winner over Fulham – and his arrival gave the squad a more balanced look. It now had genuine strength in depth and even the talented Reuser couldn't be guaranteed a regular place.

The 46-match league programme ended with a flourish – six wins out of the last seven – as Town vied with Manchester City for the runners-up spot. The only blip came in a 1-3 loss at QPR, where former Portman Road favourite Chris Kiwomya responded to abuse from Town fans by setting up one goal and scoring another. Town then party-pooped at The Valley, beating champions Charlton 3-1. It left Town to tackle the final game knowing that victory over Walsall would earn promotion, provided Manchester City lost at Blackburn.

Ray Graydon's Walsall needed the points to avoid the drop, so they wouldn't lie down. Town fans generated a terrific atmosphere and any nerves were dispelled by a second-half brace from deadly Johnson. With almost an hour gone everything was going according to plan: Town were winning, while at Ewood Park, Rovers were beating City 1-0 and had hit the woodwork four times. Once City equalised, however, everything went sour. City cruised to a 4-1 win, meaning Town had finished third once again and would again face sixth-placed Bolton in the play-offs.

After a spirited comeback to force a draw in the first leg at the Reebok Stadium, the home leg with Bolton was a momentous affair. A year earlier it had ended 4-3, so many pundits expected a goal-starved affair this time round. The odds against another goal feast must have been enormous, but the game ended 5-3 on a night of unprecedented drama. Sam Allardyce's men took the lead no fewer than three times and extra-time was only secured in the dying seconds when Jim Magilton completed the first hat-trick of his career, having already missed a penalty. Bolton were furious with the referee, particularly after two of their players – Mike Whitlow and Robbie Elliott – were red-carded and when Town won a second penalty in extra-time. Bolton's players and officials failed to contain their collective anger and would later face eight misconduct charges. On the pitch, with a two-man advantage, Town romped to victory, hitting the net twice in extra-time, the final whistle bringing an explosion of relief that must have been heard miles away.

Fourth time lucky? Now for Wembley!

Match of the Season 1999-2000

Barnsley 2 Ipswich 4

Play-off, final, Wembley, 29 May 2000

In the light of the Bolton come-back, there were fears that Town had used up their excitement quota for one season. But 37,000 Town fans, adorned with banners and balloons, headed for Wembley, sure that this would be their day. The cup fever of 1978 washed over Suffolk once more. Confidence was high: opponents Barnsley had already been beaten twice, with Town totting up eight goals.

DID YOU KNOW?

Five members of Ipswich's UEFA Cup-winning squad made a career on radio or TV –
Osman, Beattie, Butcher, Gates and Brazil all became media pundits.

With hardly any neutrals in the sun-bathed stadium, Wembley
on Bank Holiday Monday was a sea of Ipswich blue and Barnsley
red. Noise levels seemed to exceed even that historic day in 1978.
For James Scowcroft, however, the play-off final was tinged with
sadness. Town's newly crowned Player of the Year had to sit out
the game because of a hamstring injury.

After David Johnson had gone close in the opening seconds, it
was Dave Bassett's underdogs who drew first blood. With six
minutes on the clock, Craig Hignett let fly with a dipping shot from
distance which hit the underside of the bar and rebounded into the
net off Richard Wright's body. Composure and patience were called
for, and Town were rewarded when Jim Magilton sent over a cross
that was powerfully headed home by popular player-coach Tony
Mowbray.

Town started to look the better side, but just before the break
Barnsley's Hignett placed his body between ball and keeper and
Wright couldn't stop himself bringing him down. Had Wright been
reckless, or was it clever positioning by Hignett? Whatever the
cause, Wright redeemed the situation by diving to save Darren
Barnard's spot-kick.

After the break Town snatched a two-goal lead, Richard Naylor
stabbing home Stewart's flick and Marcus Stewart heading in Jamie
Clapham's curling cross. The songs of victory gained momentum
and continued even when Hignett tucked home a penalty after
Mowbray felled Geoff Thomas. It was left to substitute Martijn
'Rolls' Reuser to put the icing on the cake. The Dutchman streaked
clear to blast home a marvellous fourth goal and finally clinch
promotion.

The normally composed Burley danced with delight, alongside
assistant Dale Roberts on the touchline, while a distinctly tearful
Sheepshanks surveyed the joyful scenes from the Royal Box. Matt
Holland hoisted the trophy aloft and the celebrations continued into
the next day when thousands of supporters squeezed into Ipswich
town centre for the victory parade. Promotion at last, and within
days preparations for a new era began in earnest.

FA CARLING PREMIERSHIP   **2000-01**

Premiership	5th
Worthington Cup	Semi-finals
FA Cup	4th Round

Having finally cleared the promotion hurdle, the big question was whether Ipswich would be strong enough to hang on to their hard-earned place in the Premiership. The survival record of previous play-off winners was dismal and bookmakers quoted Town as odds-on for the drop. One writer tipped them to last three seasons – autumn, winter and spring. Wags at the Norwich local paper even introduced an Ipswich 'relegation countdown' feature.

What subsequently transpired not only made the doubters eat their words, it created shock waves at the elite clubs. To finish fifth and claim a place in the UEFA Cup – and come close to qualifying for the Champions' League – was a remarkable achievement. No wonder George Burley gathered no fewer than four Manager of the Year awards. He had spent frugally in the transfer market: nevertheless, the season was a triumph for enterprising attacking play, team spirit and discipline, tactical flexibility and self-belief.

Stylish Ipswich won the admiration of football followers everywhere. In the twelve months since winning the Wembley play-off, Town performed feats that fell not far short of the achievements of Alf Ramsey's unlikely lads of 1962. In those days, the club was saddled with a 'small town' image, but this time round the home fans had the last laugh on rivals who tried to apply a disparaging 'agricultural' label on the boys from Suffolk. Acknowledging the PR demands of the modern game, Town were eventually happy to acknowledge a new nickname – The Tractor Boys. Some at the club, including Burley himself, had initial doubts about a sobriquet that suggested no finesse or style. But most fans embraced it warmly and chanted it with glee at opposite numbers who used the well-worn farmyard noises as a weapon of abuse.

A losing start at Tottenham failed to deflate Burley and his troops, for what followed produced Suffolk smiles as broad as the Orwell Bridge. Stunning away wins at Leeds and Liverpool were just two of the headline-grabbing results achieved on the road. The manner in which the squad adapted to new surroundings, showing scant respect for the reputations of the big and mighty, surpassed even the dreams of even the most devout followers. Any lingering fears that Town would allow themselves to be brushed aside by the big boys quickly evaporated at the opening home game, when Ipswich had the better of a draw against defending champions Manchester United.

In all, Town recovered to win five matches in which they had trailed – no other side bettered this. They scored in all but three Premiership fixtures – again the best record in the League. They won the Fair Play award, after collecting the fewest yellow cards in the League (33). Town strikers were caught offside just 104 times, the lowest total in the top flight. Burley called upon 23 players over the season – no Premiership boss used fewer. Tottenham's highest gate of the season came on the opening day (36,148) and Derby's came on the final day (33,239) – both when Ipswich came to town. Life has rarely been dull for Ipswich fans during the club's relatively short history, and this season became the third in a row that a major prize was up for grabs on the final day. For the team finishing third, a place in the 2001-02 Champions League beckoned. That place was still there for the taking and although Town forced a draw at Derby, Liverpool's win at Charlton was sufficient to secure the prize.

In recent years many promoted clubs had dismantled the side that took them up and replaced key players from Nationwide League days with so-called stars from overseas. Ipswich, however, determinedly stuck with the core of their existing squad. Burley saw stability as a key factor. He had, crucially, been careful to sign players earlier who had genuine Premiership potential. His main summer signing was Wimbledon's Icelandic central defender Hermann Hreidarsson for a club record £4 million, rising to £4.5 million. Burley also closed a deal to keep Martijn Reuser, who had initially arrived on loan, for £1 million. This was followed as the season got under way by the astute capture of Alun Armstrong from Middlesbrough and Chris Makin from Sunderland.

Skipper Matt Holland, with a 100 per cent appearance record since arriving from Bournemouth in 1997, was a key performer. His work-rate and boundless enthusiasm rubbed off on others and he chipped in with some crucial goals, too. Goalkeeper Richard Wright was also a model of consistency on the big stage, and a defiant display at Arsenal underlined his England credentials. But it was striker Marcus Stewart who really stole the show. Arriving in the top flight at a relatively advanced stage of his career, Stewart showed poise, skill and confidence as the goals began to flow. He came close to finishing top of the Premiership's scoring charts, and his form was such that Town could afford to offload the previous season's hero – David Johnson – for a £3 million fee to Nottingham Forest.

After the dust had settled Chairman David Sheepshanks revealed that he and Burley had always thought the club was good enough to at least stay up. The directors budgeted to finish in seventeenth place although the actual target talked about in the boardroom was somewhere around mid-table. The chairman and manager had agreed the squad needed strengthening, but there was never any intention of breaking up what already existed. Following the relegation of 1995 with a meagre 27 points, Sheepshanks had given Burley a fairly generous (in modern football terms) five years to return the club to the top flight. He then set a target of taking the club into Europe within another three. The first goal was achieved bang on time, and the second two years early.

When the season's TV money was shared out, Town received £15.66 million (£5.38 million as a merit award for finishing fifth, £3.98 million in facility fees for TV appearances, plus the standard £6.30 million that all twenty clubs received). Another £30,000 arrived for winning the Fair Play League. Burley won four Manager of the Year awards – from Carling, the League Managers' Association, plus *FourFourTwo* and *Match* magazines. Marcus Stewart was the *Match* player of the year, Sheepshanks was voted top chairman by his peers, the club scooped awards for its match programme and Alan Ferguson was named Groundsman of the Year. With all these accolades pouring in, it was hardly surprising the Town fanzine 'Those Were The Days' renamed itself 'These Are The Days'!

Burley's recognition was richly deserved. His first six months at the helm back in 1995 were highly difficult for an inexperienced man, and he recalled 'having to be strong' to deal with the players who he felt were not 'with him'. Like Robson before him, Burley developed great enthusiasm for the job and said he enjoyed 99 per cent of it. He sets high standards, has the knack of spotting players who can be improved upon to fit into his formation, and has proved a good judge in the transfer market. In more than six years as manager to the end of August 2001, he spent around £25 million on players and sold others for £26.6 million. He had no choice but to sell, particularly in 1998, because of the club's financial position, but he never used this as an excuse for failing to secure promotion. Burley had to resolutely bounce back from repeated disappointment and heartbreak in the play-offs.

While the Carling manager's award may be the higher-profile prize, the LMA accolade is voted for by the managers themselves. In this, Burley edged out Rotherham's Ronnie Moore, who won a second successive promotion, and Sir Alex Ferguson, who guided Manchester United to a seventh Premiership crown in nine years. Humbly accepting the plaudits, Burley insisted that Ipswich will not prove to be a one-season wonder and he remains ambitious to improve still further. He realised expectations among supporters would now be sky-high, but he was not about to get carried away.

DID YOU KNOW?

Jim Magilton's wife was amazed by local soccer passions. Shopping at Sainsbury's, she overheard two old ladies discussing Richard Wright's contract dispute.

Overall, the year saw more progress at Portman Road than any other twelve-month period in the club's history. The Churchman's End has changed beyond recognition to accommodate the South Stand and rebuilding began on a vastly improved North Stand. A smart new training centre now sits at the edge of town. Every home fixture in 2000-01 was a virtual sell-out, but now the capacity has been increased to cope with increased demand. Burley signed an extended contract, new sponsors were in place, and new players were being recruited long before the start of 2001-02 season.

In January, Hassan Kachloul of Southampton rejected a move to Ipswich, but four months later announced he was now ready to sign. A few days later he angered the club by doing a 'U-turn' and opting for Aston Villa instead. Most fans were also disappointed to see Richard Wright go to Arsenal for £6 million and James Scowcroft join Leicester for £3 million in the summer of 2001. Norwich's Andy Marshall was quickly purchased to replace Wright and Burley also recruited Spanish Under-21 striker Pablo Counago from Celta Vigo and Tommy Miller from Hartlepool.

On the eve of the campaign, winger Finidi George arrived from Real Mallorca for £3.1 million, and the club outgoing record was smashed to buy keeper Matteo Sereni from Sampdoria for £5 million.

Bookmakers rarely make mistakes, but when they do, they are quick to learn lessons. At the start of 2000-01 season, Town had been quoted at 2,500-1 to win the Premiership, while 21-goal Stewart was available at 150-1 to be the top-flight's leading scorer! A year later the price against a Town title had gone down to 125-1 and Stewart was offered at 14-1.

Match of the Season 2000-01
Ipswich 1 Manchester U 1

Premiership, 22 August 2000

The first home match of the season generated an atmosphere rarely, if ever, experienced at Portman Road. The sheer noise was spine-chilling and prompted even Sir Alex Ferguson to praise the home fans. All that was needed to complete a perfect evening was for the players to come out and give the reigning champions one hell of a fright.

Within six minutes of the start the ground exploded as Fabian Wilnis ventured up the right flank, received the ball from David Johnson just inside the United box, and kept cool to drill a firm, low shot into the corner past Fabian Barthez. United were rocked and little was seen of them as an attacking force in the opening 30 minutes. For Ipswich, Jermaine Wright and Jim Magilton went close with long-range efforts.

The disappointing opening day defeat at Tottenham was forgotten as Town rose to the occasion, looking solid at the back, creative on the ball, and always likely to cause problems as they pushed forward. United were slow to settle into their stride and Paul Scholes had a shot well saved by Wright before both Jamie Clapham and Marcus Stewart missed the target with good opportunities.

Wright made a sharp save to deny Ryan Giggs after the Welshman accelerated into the box, but six minutes before the break he was beaten by a David Beckham free-kick 'special'. The England man whipped in a bender, team-mate Ronnie Wallwork lunged to make contact, and before Wright could react the ball dipped at high speed into the far corner. Magilton almost put Town ahead again with an ambitious attempt from the halfway line which the back-pedalling Barthez did well to claw away as he collided with his own goalpost. Ole Gunnar Solskjaer and Dwight Yorke, who both had quiet games, were off target early in the second period, and at the other end Stewart and Johnson both missed half-chances.

Wright saved an angled drive from Solskjaer as the excitement remained at fever pitch, and Barthez flung himself full-length to keep out Clapham. Wright clawed away another Beckham curler following a United short-corner routine, and Johnson forced another save from Barthez with a powerful header. Gary Neville volleyed narrowly off target for United, before sub James Scowcroft headed Town's last chance of the night over the bar.

The final whistle signalled a huge ovation from the home fans. Ipswich might not have won, but the performance proved that the players had been prepared for the challenges that lay ahead and would not be satisfied with merely making up the numbers. Ipswich Town were back in business!

Richard Wright gives his thoughts to the media (April 2001)

Celebrating the Play-Off victory at Wembley (May 2000)

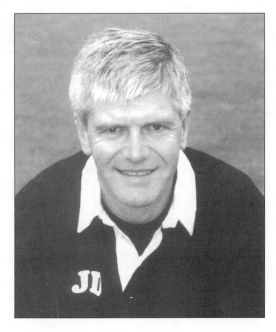

John Duncan, who managed Ipswich between 1987 and 1990

David Johnson heads in, watched by Trevor Whymark (March 1974)

Matt Holland chases Colchester's Steve McGavin (July 2000)

Kevin Beattie, whose career was cruelly cut short by injury

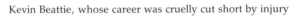

GUIDE TO SEASONAL SUMMARIES

Col 1: Match number (for league fixtures); Round (for cup-ties).
e.g. 2:1 means 'Second round; first leg.'
e.g. 4R means 'Fourth round replay.'

Col 2: Date of the fixture and whether Home (H), Away (A), or Neutral (N).

Col 3: Opposition.

Col 4: Attendances. Home gates appear in roman; Away gates in *italics*.
Figures in **bold** indicate the largest and smallest gates, at home and away.
Average home and away attendances appear after the final league match.
N.B. Home attendances are those registered with the Football League
and should be taken as accurate.

Col 5: Respective league positions of Ipswich and their opponents after the match.
Ipswich's position appears on the top line in roman.
Their opponents' position appears on the second line in *italics*.
For cup-ties, the division and position of opponents is provided.
e.g. *2:12* means the opposition are twelfth in Division 2.

Col 6: The top line shows the result: W(in), D(raw), or L(ose).
The second line shows Ipswich's cumulative points total.

Col 7: The match score, Ipswich's given first.
Scores in **bold** indicate Ipswich's biggest league win and heaviest defeat.

Col 8: The half-time score, Ipswich's given first.

Col 9: The top line shows Ipswich's scorers and times of goals in roman.
The second line shows opponents' scorers and times of goals in *italics*.
A 'p' after the time of a goal denotes a penalty; 'og' an own-goal.
The third line gives the name of the match referee.

Team line-ups: Ipswich line-ups appear on the top line, irrespective of whether
they are home or away. Opposition teams appear on the second line in *italics*.
Players of either side who are sent off are marked !
Ipswich players making their league debuts are displayed in **bold**.
In the era of squad numbers, players' names are positioned as far as
possible as if they were still wearing shirts 1 to 11.

Substitutes: Names of substitutes appear only if they actually took the field.
A player substituted is marked *
A second player substituted is marked ^
A third player substituted is marked "
These marks indicate the sequence of substitutions.

N.B. For clarity, all information appearing in *italics* relates to opposing teams.

LEAGUE DIVISION 1

Manager: Bobby Robson

SEASON 1971-72

No	Date	V	Club	Att	Pos	Pt	Res	F-A	H-T	Scorers, Times, and Referees	1	2	3	4	5	6	7	8	9	10	11	12 sub used
1	14/8	H	EVERTON	23,757		1	D	0-0	0-0	Ref: D Nippard	Best	Hammond	Harper	Morris	Bell	Jefferson	Robertson	Mills	Clarke	**Hamilton***	Miller	Whymark
			(Everton)								*West*	*Wright**	*Newton*	*Kendall*	*Labone*	*Scott*	*Husband*	*Ball*	*Royle*	*Hurst*	*Morrissey*	*Kenyon*
2	17/8	H	COVENTRY	19,269		3	W	3-1	2-1	Clarke 4, 49p, Hamilton 42; Carr 35; Ref: R Challis	Best	Hammond	Harper	Morris	Bell	Jefferson	Robertson	Mills	Clarke	Hamilton	Miller	Miller
			(Coventry)								*Glazier*	*Smith*	*Cattlin**	*Machin**	*Blockley*	*Barry*	*Mortimer*	*Carr*	*O'Rourke*	*Hunt*	*Parker*	*Coop*
3	21/8	A	SOUTHAMPTON	17,931	5	4	D	0-0	0-0	Ref: W Castle	Best	Hammond	Harper	Morris	Bell	Jefferson	Robertson	Mills	Clarke	Hamilton	Miller	
			(Southampton)		*10*						*Martin*	*Kirkup*	*Fry*	*Fisher*	*McGrath*	*Gabriel*	*Paine*	*Channon*	*Stokes*	*O'Neil*	*Jenkins*	
4	23/8	A	WEST HAM	25,714	5	5	D	0-0	0-0	Ref: D Pugh	Best	Carroll	Harper	Morris	Bell	Jefferson	Robertson	Mills	Clarke	Hamilton	Miller	Howe
			(West Ham)		*22*						*Ferguson*	*McDowell*	*Lampard*	*Bonds*	*Taylor*	*Moore*	*Ayris**	*Best*	*Hurst*	*Brooking*	*Robson*	
5	28/8	H	LEEDS	26,658	10	5	L	0-2	0-2	Lorimer 26, Belfitt 32; Ref: K Burns	Best	Hammond	Harper	Morris	Bell	Jefferson	Robertson	Mills	Clarke*	Hamilton	Hill	Hill
			(Leeds)		*8*						*Sprake*	*Reaney*	*Cooper*	*Bremner*	*Charlton*	*Hunter*	*Lorimer*	*Clarke*	*Belfitt**	*Bates*	*Madeley*	*Yorath*
6	31/8	H	DERBY	18,687	9	6	D	0-0	0-0	Ref: K Walker	Best	Hammond	Harper	Morris	Bell	Jefferson	Robertson	Mills	Clarke	Hamilton	Miller	Hill
			(Derby)		*2*						*Boulton*	*Todd*	*Robson*	*Hennessey*	*McFarland*	*McGovern*	*Gemmill*	*Durban*	*Wignall*	*Hector*	*Hinton*	
7	4/9	A	MANCHESTER U	44,852	14	6	L	0-1	0-1	Best 43; Ref: W Gow	Best	Hammond	Harper	Morris	Bell	Jefferson	Robertson	Mills	Clarke	Hamilton	Miller*	Collard
			(Manchester U)		*4*						*Stepney*	*O'Neil*	*Dunne*	*Gowling*	*James*	*Sadler*	*Morgan*	*Kidd*	*Charlton*	*Law**	*Best*	*Aston*
8	11/9	H	LEICESTER	18,483	17	6	L	1-2	0-2	Clarke 86p; Sammels 25, Kellard 30; Ref: R Crabb	Best	Hammond	Harper	Morris	Bell	Jefferson	Robertson	Mills	Clarke*	Hamilton	Miller*	Collard
			(Leicester)		*15*						*Shilton*	*Whitworth*	*Nish**	*Kellard*	*Sjoberg*	*Cross*	*Munro*	*Brown*	*Fern*	*Sammels*	*Glover*	*Partridge*
9	18/9	A	WEST BROM	18,885	13	8	W	2-1	2-0	Robertson 28, Clarke 44; Brown 53; Ref: H Williams	Sivell	Mills	Harper	Viljoen	Hunter	Jefferson	Robertson	Collard	Clarke*	Hamilton	Miller	Hamilton
			(West Brom)		*19*						*Cumbes*	*Hughes*	*Wilson*	*Cantello*	*Wile*	*Kaye*	*Suggett*	*Brown*	*Gould*	*Hartford*	*McVitie*	
10	25/9	H	NEWCASTLE	18,270	13	9	D	0-0	0-0	Ref: B Homewood	Sivell	Mills	Harper	Viljoen	**Hunter**	Jefferson	Robertson	Collard	Clarke	Hill	Miller	Hamilton
			(Newcastle)		*17*						*McFaul*	*Craig*	*Guthrie*	*Gibb*	*Howard*	*Clark*	*Barrowcl'gh Tudor*		*MacDonald*	*Nattrass*	*Hibbitt*	

Match notes

1. Town's third successive goalless opening day and their 12th game without defeat. With Viljoen absent due to a pay dispute, Hamilton steps in and shows some promise, but finds the pace at this level breathtakingly fast. Town lack punch in attack, despite having most of the possession.

2. The refs' new 'get tough' policy leads to three bookings for each side, while Machin breaks his leg and Best plays on with a bandaged arm in a game that was never really dirty. Clarke's early header and penalty after Cattlin's handball, plus Hamilton's neat shot, secures both the points.

3. Town defy periods of Saints' pressure in a drab affair where the clean-up campaign seems to have deterred the usual physical contact. Harper looks polished and Robertson very lively on the wing, but there is little real threat from Town's attack. Hamilton and Channon go the closest.

4. Ron Greenwood's off-form Hammers win their first point of the season. Morris goes closest with a long-range effort which thumps the post and Hamilton misses a sitter, while Morris clears off the line from Clyde Best. Transfer-listed Carroll steps in for his only game of the season.

5. Town's early promise sees Mills skim Sprake's crossbar with a 25-yarder before the defensive discipline of earlier games disappears and poor defending is punished with two quick strikes. Best is kept busy and prevents a real hammering with fine saves from Allan Clarke and Bremner.

6. The goal-starved home fans breathe a sigh of relief as Derby's dominance fails to pay off. A second-half Jefferson header goes agonisingly close completely against the run of play. With Hector in superb form, Wignall forces the ball past Best but the effort is disallowed for pushing.

7. The drought continues with several chances spurned and claims for a penalty refused after Sadler's heavy challenge on Hamilton. George Best wins the game by curling a flag-kick directly into goal. He claims later it was deliberate as he'd noticed his namesake standing at the near post.

8. An efficient debut by Hunter but Jimmy Bloomfield's City cruise ahead through shots by Suffolk-born Sammels and ex-Town player Kellard. A Robertson effort is disallowed before a second vociferous penalty appeal produces the consolation goal when Munro handles Morris's cross.

9. Pay-rebel Viljoen returns as Best, Hammond and Morris are all axed. In a scrappy affair, Robertson nips in to snatch a smart opener to end the away goals drought. Wile is pushed by Jefferson and the returning Sivell heroically blocks the spot-kick, but Brown forces home the rebound.

10. Hunter impresses again by keeping a tight rein on man-of-the-moment MacDonald and goes close himself with a header. The hectic opening spell of 20 minutes is replaced by a dour affair featuring two uninspired sets of attackers. Hill's narrow miss with a header is a rare highlight.

11 · A · TOTTENHAM · (Pos 16) · L 1-2 (HT 1-0) · Att 33,562 · Opp pos 7 · Pts 9
Collard 17 / Chivers 58, Peters 75
Ref: D Turner
Town: Sivell, Mills, Harper, Viljoen, Hunter, Jefferson, Robertson, Collard, Hamilton, Hill, Miller*, Morris
Tottenham: Jennings, Kinnear, Knowles, Mullery, England, Beal, Coates, Perryman, Chivers, Peters, Gilzean
Collard's neat side-footed goal gives hope, but a horrendous misunderstanding between Sivell and Jefferson allows an equaliser against the run of play. Bill Nicholson's side take both points after Mr Turner waves aside Town appeals for a foul by Gilzean in the build-up to the winner.

12 · H · NOTT'M FOREST · (Pos 13) · D 1-1 (HT 0-1) · Att 16,285 · Opp pos 21 · Pts 10
Harper 89 / Moore 14
Ref: H New
Town: Sivell, Mills, Harper, Viljoen, Hunter, Jefferson, Robertson, Collard, Clarke*, Hill, Miller, Hamilton
Nott'm Forest: Barron, Hindley, Winfield, Chapman*, O'Kane, Richardson, Lyons, McKenzie, Martin, Jackson, Moore, White
Unmarked Moore converts a smartly-taken goal from Lyons' cross, then Forest are forced to sit back and take a pounding for long periods. Just when all seemed lost, Harper strides forward in the dying moments to head home the equaliser from Miller's cross – his first goal for the club.

13 · A · EVERTON · (Pos 14) · D 1-1 (HT 0-1) · Att 31,590 · Opp pos 19 · Pts 11
Hill 48 / Royle 29
Ref: D Corbett
Town: Sivell, Mills, Harper, Viljoen, Hunter, Jefferson, Robertson, Collard, Clarke, Hill, Miller
Everton: West, Scott, Newton K, Newton H, Kenyon, Kendall, Royle, Husband, Johnson, Hurst, Whittle*, Morrissey
The Town party flies north from RAF Wattisham for this encounter with a subdued home side. Johnson's drive strikes a post and Royle knocks home the rebound into an empty net. Robertson's floated free-kick is pushed out by West straight to Hill, who whips home a deserved leveller.

14 · H · STOKE · (Pos 13) · W 2-1 (HT 2-1) · Att 17,677 · Opp pos 10 · Pts 13
Hill 27, 36 / Bernard 32
Ref: R Raby
Town: Sivell, Mills, Harper, Viljoen, Hunter, Jefferson, Robertson, Collard*, Clarke, Hill, Miller, Lambert
Stoke: Banks, Marsh, Pejic, Bernard, Bloor, Stevenson, Haslegrave, Conroy, Mahoney, Dobing, Jump
Hill celebrates his call-up by Wales for the European Championship game with Czechoslovakia by converting two fine headers. The first from a corner and the second a pinpoint cross, both supplied by winger Robertson. Banks prevents the hat-trick by saving an effort at close range.

15 · A · ARSENAL · (Pos 14) · L 1-2 (HT 0-0) · Att 39,065 · Opp pos 6 · Pts 13
Hill 80 / Sivell 72 (og), George 84
Ref: J Yates
Town: Sivell, Mills, Harper, Viljoen, Hunter, Jefferson, Robertson, Collard, Clarke, Hill, Miller
Arsenal: Wilson, Rice, Nelson, Storey, Roberts, McLintock, Armstrong, George, Radford, Kennedy, Graham
The game turns on a tragic own-goal by Sivell who drops Radford's gentle header and then knocks the ball into his own net in attempting to retrieve it. Collard, defending on the line for both goals, takes the blame for the second when George's shot bobbles in through a crowded area.

16 · H · WOLVERHAMPTON · (Pos 13) · W 2-1 (HT 0-1) · Att 21,938 · Opp pos 14 · Pts 15
Hill 49, Belfitt 71 / Dougan 35
Ref: J Hunting
Town: Sivell, Mills, Harper, Viljoen, Hunter, Jefferson, Robertson, Collard, Belfitt, Hill, Miller
Wolverhampton: Parkes, Taylor, Parkin, Bailey, Munro, McAlle, McCalliog, Hibbitt, Dougan, Curran*, Wagstaffe, Richards
New signing Belfitt becomes an instant hero, heading on a Robertson flag-kick for Hill to equalise with a spectacular overhead kick and later scrambling home the winner himself. Wolves are torn to shreds in the second period as Miller hits the bar and Jefferson's effort is disallowed.

17 · A · CRYSTAL PALACE · (Pos 14) · D 1-1 (HT 1-1) · Att 18,462 · Opp pos 22 · Pts 16
Belfitt 4 / Wallace 25
Ref: H Davey
Town: Sivell, Mills, Harper, Viljoen, Hunter, Jefferson, Robertson, Collard, Belfitt, Hill, Miller
Crystal Palace: Jackson, Payne, Taylor, Craven, Bell, Blyth, Tambling, Queen, Hughes, Kellard, Wallace
Belfitt's powerful drive from distance puts Town ahead and Miller thinks he's doubled the lead but it is ruled out with two players in an offside position. In a rather physical match, a powerful drive by Hughes is parried by Sivell straight to the feet of Wallace who converts the equaliser.

18 · H · HUDDERSFIELD · (Pos 12) · W 1-0 (HT 1-0) · Att 16,168 · Opp pos 18 · Pts 18
Hill 14
Ref: K Sweet
Town: Sivell, Mills, Harper, Viljoen, Hunter, Jefferson, Robertson, Collard, Belfitt, Hill, Miller
Huddersfield: Lawson D, Hutt, Clarke, Jones, Ellam, Cherry, Smith D, Smith S, Worthington*, Lawson J, Chapman, Dolan
Ian Greaves' struggling side puts up a brave display on a snow-covered pitch, but lack the necessary punch in attack. The decisive early goal is made by Miller, who comes from deep on a long run and feeds Hill, who takes the ball forward and powers a drive past the exposed Lawson.

19 · A · SHEFFIELD UTD · (Pos 12) · L 0-7 (HT 0-4) · Att 26,233 · Opp pos 4 · Pts 18
— / Woodward 9, 31p, 59, 86, Badger 36, Dearden 51, Reece 34
Ref: K Burns
Town: Sivell, Hammond, Harper, Viljoen, Hunter, Jefferson, Robertson, Collard, Belfitt, Hill*, Miller, Clarke
Sheffield Utd: Hope, Badger, Hemsley, Flynn, Colquhoun, Hockey, Woodward, Salmons, Dearden, Currie, Reece
Town's tidy defensive record thus far is shattered. A mis-hit shot by Woodward bobbles past Sivell for the first and, after Hunter fouls Salmons, Woodward's spot-kick opens up the floodgates. Reece's bullet header and Woodward's long-range drive for his third are the pick of the goals.

20 · H · LIVERPOOL · (Pos 12) · D 0-0 (HT 0-0) · Att 21,362 · Opp pos 6 · Pts 19
Ref: W Castle
Town: Sivell, Hammond, Harper, Viljoen, Hunter, Jefferson, Robertson, Collard, Belfitt, Hill, Miller
Liverpool: Clemence, Lawler, Lindsay, Smith, Ross, Hughes, Keegan, Boersma, Heighway, Whitham, Callaghan
Boersma misses a sitter and Whitham hits the bar, but managers Robson and Shankly are full of praise for young Clemence who keeps Ipswich at bay with a fine display. He foils Hill twice, turning aside a header from Viljoen's cross and then blocking a full-blooded shot from six yards.

21 · A · MANCHESTER C · (Pos 13) · L 0-4 (HT 0-3) · Att 26,900 · Opp pos 2 · Pts 19
— / Davies 5, Mellor 24, Bell 41, Lee 48
Ref: E Wallace
Town: Sivell, Hammond, Harper, Viljoen, Hunter, Jefferson, Robertson, Collard*, Hill, Miller, Morris
Manchester C: Corrigan, Book, Donachie, Doyle, Booth, Oakes, Summerbee, Bell, Davies, Lee, Mellor
Honest Sivell admits he's having a crisis of confidence and accepts the blame for three of City's goals. A tame display by Town, who have no answer to Davies' aerial dominance. Davies sets up the second and third goals with his head and City are able to stroll through the final stages.

LEAGUE DIVISION 1

Manager: Bobby Robson

SEASON 1971-72

No	Date	Venue	Opponent	Att	Town Pos	Opp Pos	Pt	Res	F-A	H-T	Scorers, Times	Ref
22	18/12	H	MANCHESTER U	29,213	12	1	20	D	0-0	0-0	—	C Nicholls
23	27/12	A	CHELSEA	43,896	15	10	20	L	0-2	0-0	Kember 63, Garland 73	A Oliver
24	1/1	H	WEST BROM	16,883	15	22	20	L	2-3	1-0	Hill 38, Belfitt 50; Brown 61, Gould 72, McVitie 82	M Kerkhof
25	8/1	A	LEEDS	32,194	16	3	21	D	2-2	1-0	Hunter 35, Clarke 60; Bremner 62, Clarke 83	J Taylor
26	22/1	A	COVENTRY	18,183	17	15	22	D	1-1	0-1	Hunter 66; Blockley 4p	F Nicholson
27	29/1	H	WEST HAM	22,757	14	13	24	W	1-0	0-0	Morris 89	H Williams
28	12/2	A	STOKE	20,244	14	11	25	D	3-3	1-0	Lambert 14, 63, Miller 66; Ritchie 55, Greenhoff 77p, Smith 88	H Hackney
29	19/2	H	ARSENAL	28,657	16	4	25	L	0-1	0-1	George 6	J Thacker
30	26/2	A	WOLVERHAMPTON	19,349	13	6	26	D	2-2	2-1	Belfitt 26, 29; Hibbitt 4, McCalliog 89p	C Howell
31	4/3	H	CRYSTAL PALACE	17,221	15	19	26	L	0-2	0-2	Wallace 28, Tambling 44	R Tinkler

Line-ups

No	Team	1	2	3	4	5	6	7	8	9	10	11	12 sub used
22	Town	Best	Hammond	Harper	Morris	Hunter*	Jefferson	Robertson	Viljoen	Belfitt	Hill	Miller	Clarke
22	Manchester U	Stepney	Dunne	Burns	Gowling	James	Sadler	Morgan	Kidd	Charlton	Law	Best	
23	Town	Best	Hammond	Harper	Morris	Hunter	Jefferson	Robertson	Woods	Belfitt	Hill*	Miller	Clarke
23	Chelsea	Webb	Harris	Houseman	Hollins	Dempsey	Mulligan	Garland	Kember	Osgood	Hudson	Baldwin*	Cooke
24	Town	Best	Hammond	Harper	Morris	Hunter	Jefferson	Robertson	Viljoen	Belfitt*	Hill	Miller	Woods
24	West Brom	Smith	Wilson	Nisbet	Cantello	Wile	Robertson	McVitie	Brown	Gould	Suggett	Hartford	
25	Town	Best	Hammond	Harper	Morris	Hunter	Jefferson	Robertson	Viljoen	Clarke*	Hill	McNeil	Miller
25	Leeds	Sprake	Madeley	Cooper	Bremner	Charlton*	Hunter	Lorimer	Clarke	Jones	Giles	Gray	Reaney
26	Town	Best	Mills	Harper	Morris	Hunter	Jefferson	Robertson	Viljoen	Belfitt*	Hill	Miller*	Woods
26	Coventry	Glazier	Smith	Cattlin	Machin	Blockley	Parker	Young	Carr	Chilton	Rafferty	Mortimer	
27	Town	Best	Mills	Harper	Morris	Hunter	Jefferson	Robertson	Viljoen	Belfitt	Hill	Miller	Miller
27	West Ham	Grotier	McDowell	Lampard	Bonds	Taylor	Moore	Redknapp	Best	Hurst	Brooking	Robson	
28	Town	Best	Mills	Harper	Morris	Hunter	Jefferson	Miller*	Viljoen	Belfitt	Clarke	Lambert	Woods
28	Stoke	Banks	Marsh	Skeels	Bernard*	Smith	Bloor	Conroy	Greenhoff	Ritchie	Dobing	Mahoney	Jackson
29	Town	Best	Mills	Harper	Morris	Hunter	Jefferson	Robertson	Viljoen	Belfitt	Clarke*	Lambert	Woods
29	Arsenal	Wilson	Rice	Nelson	Kelly	McLintock	Simpson	Armstrong	Ball	George	Kennedy	Graham	
30	Town	Best	Mills	Harper	Morris	Hunter	Jefferson	Robertson	Viljoen	Belfitt	Clarke*	Lambert	Whymark
30	Wolverhampton	Parkes	Shaw	Parkin*	Taylor	Munro	McAlle	McCalliog	Hibbitt	Richards	Dougan	Wagstaffe	Sunderland
31	Town	Best	Mills	Harper	Morris	Hunter	Jefferson	Robertson	Viljoen*	Wallace	Whymark	Lambert	Hamilton
31	Crystal Palace	Jackson	Payne	Goodwin	Kellard	McCormick	Blyth	Craven	Queen	Wallace	Taylor	Tambling	

22 — Manchester U: Inevitably Sivell is withdrawn, while Morris is also recalled to add steel against the League leaders. Town look much-improved and go close to victory. Town are angry when the ref allows Hill's goal but then changes his mind, and later ignores a linesman flagging for a home penalty.

23 — Chelsea: With Bonetti and Phillips injured and Sherwood unable to reach London in time for kick-off, Chelsea put defender Webb in goal. He makes a good save early on from Hill, but is largely untroubled. Kember converts Cooke's corner and Garland benefits from superb work by Osgood.

24 — West Brom: Hill scores after Belfitt's header hits the post, then Belfitt increases the lead with a text-book header from Robertson's cross. Smith's saves keep the score down and he aids a superb fightback by setting up Gould's equaliser when venturing well out of his area to retrieve a loose ball.

25 — Leeds: Seven games without a win despite a two-goal lead forged through headers by Hunter and Clarke. The referee was content that Allan Clarke's equaliser did cross the line before being cleared, but Town were not so sure. However, luck was with them when Leeds hit the bar three times.

26 — Coventry: Blockley converts a spot-kick after Jefferson is adjudged to have handled when a powerful shot strikes him. Any injustice here is cancelled out when Town gain a suspicious-looking corner and Hunter heads it firmly home. Best performs well in a match that provides poor entertainment.

27 — West Ham: Transfer-listed Morris, making his 150th appearance, volleys home a spectacular winner after seizing on to Moore's headed clearance just 32 seconds before the final whistle. Jefferson's shin wound is so horrific he almost passes out, but he returns to the fray after having stitches.

28 — Stoke: Recalled Lambert is the star of the show, causing havoc with his pacy runs. Miller puts Town 3-1 ahead after a stunning solo run is capped by a thunderous shot. Stoke roar back to win a controversial penalty. Sub Woods enters the action to be cautioned before even touching the ball.

29 — Arsenal: Another ill-tempered affair shrouded in controversy with Town convinced George's goal was offside. The heroic Simpson and Wilson do most to preserve Arsenal's unbeaten run. Twenty players join an ugly melee after Arsenal object to Viljoen's challenge on their floored goalkeeper.

30 — Wolverhampton: Belfitt stoops to head home Viljoen's flick and then dives to head in Robertson's corner. Bill McGarry's side salvages a late point as Dougan causes havoc in the Town area, leading to Mills handling Shaw's shot on the goal-line. McCalliog nets the penalty kick, but only after a re-take.

31 — Crystal Palace: Defensive errors by both Morris and Harper allow Wallace to score and the lead is extended when Tambling sweeps home Taylor's fine cross. The off-colour home side are second best throughout and fade even more after Viljoen fails to re-appear, having passed blood during half-time.

#		Date	Opponent	Pos	Res			Att	Scorers
32	A	11/3	NOTT'M FOREST	13	W	2.0	2-0	9,872	Vijoen 30, Whymark 35
				22		28			Ref: K Burns

Best Mills Harper Morris Hunter Jefferson Miller Vijoen Belfitt Whymark* Hamilton
Barron Gemmill Winfield Chapman Cottam Fraser Lyons O'Neill Cormack Richardson McKenzie Macintosh*

Matt Gillies' Forest lack confidence and bite in front of their lowest attendance in 17 years. Recovered from his bruised kidneys, Vijoen hits a fine opener, and then Whymark's shot from Miller's cross goes in off a post. Robertson is rested due to transfer speculation involving Wolves.

| 33 | H | 18/3 | SOUTHAMPTON | 13 | D | 1-1 | 0-1 | 15,528 | Whymark 66 |
| | | | | 19 | | 29 | | | Stokes 31 · Ref: A Hart |

Best Mills Harper Morris Hunter Jefferson Robertson Vijoen Belfitt Whymark Lambert
Martin Kirkup Hollywood Steele McGrath Gabriel Stokes O'Neil Channon O'Brien Paine!

Stokes races through and rounds Best to score, but Town hit back when Whymark scrambles home a Robertson corner. Paine is sent off for a head-butt on Mills, Steele is booked and Kirkup later hospitalized. Unlucky Belfitt has one header cleared off the line and another hit the bar.

| 34 | A | 22/3 | DERBY | 15 | L | 0-1 | 0-1 | 26,738 | Hector 15 |
| | | | | 2 | | 29 | | | Ref: E Wallace |

Best Hammond Harper Morris Hunter Jefferson Robertson Mills Belfitt* Whymark Lambert
Boulton Webster Robson Durban MFarland Todd McGovern Gemmill O'Hare Hector Walker*

Boulton's long kick bounces awkwardly, deceives Jefferson and Hunter on the bumpy surface and Hector nips in to take advantage. Ipswich look impotent without the influential Vijoen, who is absent with a foot injury, which occurred when he dropped his bag of golf clubs on it!

| 35 | A | 25/3 | LEICESTER | 16 | L | 0-1 | 0-1 | 19,769 | Tomlin 2 |
| | | | | 13 | | 29 | | | Ref: J Williams |

Best Mills Harper Morris Hunter Jefferson Robertson Vijoen Belfitt Whymark Lambert
Shilton Whitworth Nish Cross Manley Woollett Weller Sammels Birchenall Tomlin Glover

Weller creates panic in the Town defence by producing a long throw that is converted by Tomlin. Ipswich create enough chances to take the points comfortably, but Lambert is guilty of spurning three good opportunities. Shilton is in top form, saving superbly from Vijoen and Belfitt.

| 36 | H | 1/4 | CHELSEA | 16 | L | 1-2 | 1-2 | 24,319 | Vijoen 45p |
| | | | | 9 | | 29 | | | Webb 3, 9 · Ref: R Kirkpatrick |

Best Mills Harper Morris Hunter Jefferson Robertson Vijoen Belfitt Whymark* Hamilton
Bonetti Mulligan Boyle Hollins Dempsey Harris Kember Webb Osgood Hudson Cooke

From makeshift keeper to stand-in winger, Webb returns to haunt Ipswich yet again. This time he delights manager Dave Sexton with two early opportunist efforts. His opener sees him profit from an ill-advised back-heel by the normally safe Mills. Bonetti held firm as Town rallied late.

| 37 | H | 3/4 | TOTTENHAM | 16 | W | 2-1 | 0-0 | 24,302 | Want 59 (og), Belfitt 77 |
| | | | | 5 | | 31 | | | Chivers 62 · Ref: P Walters |

Best Mills Harper Morris Hunter Jefferson Robertson Vijoen Belfitt Whymark Lambert
Jennings Evans Want Coates Collins Naylor Pearce Perryman Chivers Pratt Morgan Kinnear*

Relegation fears are all but banished as Want heads Whymark's cross into his own net past Jennings under heavy pressure from Lambert. After Chivers' 39th goal of the season, Mills' cross finds Whymark and he heads into the path of Belfitt who finds the space to ram home the winner.

| 38 | A | 5/4 | NEWCASTLE | 14 | W | 1-0 | 0-0 | 22,979 | Whymark 87 |
| | | | | 11 | | 33 | | | Ref: G Hill |

Best Mills Harper Morris Hunter Jefferson Robertson Vijoen Belfitt Whymark Lambert
McFaul Craig Clark Reid Howard Moncur Barrowc'gh Green MacDonald Tudor Cassidy

Joe Harvey's Newcastle are furious as MacDonald's headed goal is mysteriously ruled out, but they merely second best in a drab game. Morris runs the show in midfield but picks up a booking. Whymark grabs a dramatic late winner, being knocked out as he dives to head home.

| 39 | A | 8/4 | HUDDERSFIELD | 13 | W | 3-1 | 1-0 | 12,139 | Belfitt 11, Morris 48, Robertson 71 |
| | | | | 21 | | 35 | | | Hunter 53 (og) · Ref: C Howell |

Best Mills Harper Morris Hunter Jefferson Robertson Vijoen Belfitt Whymark Lambert
Pierce Clarke Hutt Smith Ellam Cherry Hoy Dolan Krzywicki Lawson Chapman Barry*

Best keeps Ian Greaves' side at bay in a lively opening, but once Morris capitalises on good work by Robertson the game is effectively over. Hunter lobs a crazy own-goal over the head of Best, but Robertson seals the points, tucking home the rebound when Lambert's drive is parried.

| 40 | H | 15/4 | SHEFFIELD UTD | 12 | D | 0-0 | 0-0 | 17,052 | |
| | | | | 9 | | 36 | | | Ref: G Kew |

Best Mills Harper Morris Hunter Jefferson Robertson Vijoen Belfitt Whymark* Hamilton
Sivell McAlister Badger Hemsley MacKenzie Colquhoun Flynn Scullion Dearden Currie Salmons

A drab affair enlivened only by events late in the second half when United win a penalty following a collision between Hunter and Dearden. Jefferson is booked for dissent as Dearden's kick is brilliantly saved. Harper continues to argue and is sent off after grabbing the referee's arm.

| 41 | H | 18/4 | MANCHESTER C | 12 | W | 2-1 | 1-0 | 24,464 | Whymark 31, Harper 61 |
| | | | | 9 | | 38 | | | Summerbee 53 · Ref: B Homewood |

Best Mills Harper Morris Hunter Jefferson Robertson Vijoen Belfitt Whymark* Hamilton
Sivell Book Donachie Doyle Booth Lee Summerbee Bell Davies Marsh Towers Oakes*

City's title hopes are dashed as Whymark takes Morris's pass and swivels to fire a fine goal. City are denied a penalty after a clear Vijoen handball, but equalise when Summerbee fastens on to a Sivell error. Harper powers home a thrilling headed winner from Lambert's neat cross.

| 42 | A | 22/4 | LIVERPOOL | 13 | L | 0-2 | 0-1 | 54,316 | Toshack 40, 67 |
| | | | | 2 | | 38 | | | Ref: R Tinkler |

Best Mills Harper Morris Hunter Jefferson Robertson Vijoen Belfitt Whymark Lambert*
Clemence Lawler Lindsay Smith Lloyd Hughes Keegan Hall Highway Toshack Callaghan Hamilton

Anfield's one-millionth paying customer of the season sees The Reds in full command. Toshack heads home Keegan's flick-on after a probing Heighway cross. The Welshman then deflects Hughes' pile-driver past Best. Clemence is rarely troubled as Town soak up massive pressure.

Home 20,923 · Away 26,803 · Average

LEAGUE DIVISION 1 (CUP-TIES)

Manager: Bobby Robson

League Cup

	Att	F-A	H-T	Scorers, Times, and Referees	1	2	3	4	5	6	7	8	9	10	11	12 sub used
2 H MANCHESTER U 14	28,143 *1:4*	1-3	1-3	Robertson 8 / *Morgan 29p, Best 37, 43* / Ref: A Hart	Best	Hammond	Harper	Morris	Bell	Jefferson	Robertson	Mills	Clarke	Hill*	Miller	Hamilton
7/9					*Stepney*	*O'Neil*	*Dunne*	*Gowling*	*James*	*Sadler*	*Morgan*	*Kidd*	*Charlton*	*Best*	*Aston*	

Harper brings down Kidd to concede a penalty equaliser and then George Best takes over. He scores a typical cheeky goal while lying on the floor, knocking in the rebound after his header comes back off the bar. Robson substitutes Hill, provoking home fans to chant for his dismissal.

FA Cup

	Att	F-A	H-T	Scorers, Times, and Referees	1	2	3	4	5	6	7	8	9	10	11	12 sub used
3 A PETERBOROUGH 16	16,973 *4:15*	2-0	1-0	Viljoen 37, Hill 75 / Ref: G Kew	Best	Mills	Harper	Morris	Hunter	Jefferson	Robertson	Viljoen	Belfitt	Hill	Miller	Miller
15/1					*Drewery*	*Carmichael*	*Brookes*	*Oakes*	*Turner*	*Wright*	*Moss**	*Price*	*Barker*	*Conny*	*Robson*	*Darrell*

Posh manager Jim Iley gets steamed up as loud penalty appeals are ignored when Price is grounded by Hunter's muscular challenge. After this Ipswich hardly break sweat as Mills and Hill combine to set up Viljoen's opener. Hill makes absolutely sure of progress with a powerful drive.

	Att	F-A	H-T	Scorers, Times, and Referees	1	2	3	4	5	6	7	8	9	10	11	12 sub used
4 A BIRMINGHAM 14	40,709 *2:4*	0-1	0-1	*Latchford 2* / Ref: G Hartley	Best	Mills	Harper	Morris	Hunter	Jefferson	Robertson	Viljoen	Belfitt	Hill	McNeil*	Miller
5/2					*Cooper*	*Carroll*	*Pendrey*	*Page*	*Hynd*	*Harland*	*Campbell*	*Francis*	*Latchford*	*Hatton*	*Taylor*	

Ex-England cap McNeil is recalled from the reserves as an extra defender, but the plan backfires as his clearance after just 80 seconds falls for Hatton who sets up Latchford's goal. City's third-choice keeper Cooper,18, performs well against the club he will later make his name with.

		P	W	D	L	F	A	W	D	L	F	A	Pts
				Home					**Away**				
1	Derby	42	16	4	1	43	10	8	6	7	26	23	58
2	Leeds	42	17	4	0	54	10	7	5	9	19	21	57
3	Liverpool	42	17	3	1	48	16	7	6	8	16	14	57
4	Manchester C	42	16	3	2	48	15	7	8	6	29	30	57
5	Arsenal	42	15	2	4	36	13	7	6	8	22	27	52
6	Tottenham	42	16	3	2	45	13	6	5	10	18	29	51
7	Chelsea	42	12	7	2	41	20	6	5	10	17	29	48
8	Manchester U	42	13	2	6	39	26	6	8	7	30	35	48
9	Wolves	42	10	7	4	35	23	8	4	9	30	34	47
10	Sheffield Utd	42	10	8	3	39	26	7	4	10	22	34	46
11	Newcastle	42	10	6	5	30	18	5	5	11	19	34	41
12	Leicester	42	9	6	6	18	11	4	7	10	23	35	39
13	IPSWICH	42	7	8	6	19	19	4	8	9	20	34	38
14	West Ham	42	10	6	5	31	19	2	6	13	16	32	36
15	Everton	42	8	9	4	28	17	1	9	11	9	31	36
16	West Brom	42	6	7	8	22	23	6	4	11	20	31	35
17	Stoke	42	6	10	5	26	25	4	5	12	13	31	35
18	Coventry	42	7	10	4	27	23	2	5	14	17	44	33
19	Southampton	42	8	5	8	31	28	4	2	15	21	52	31
20	Crys Palace	42	4	8	9	26	31	5	5	12	13	34	29
21	Nott'm Forest	42	6	4	11	25	29	2	5	14	22	52	25
22	Huddersfield	42	4	7	10	12	22	2	6	13	15	37	25
		924	227	129	106	723	437	106	129	227	437	723	924

Odds & ends

Double wins: (1) Huddersfield.

Double losses: (3) Leicester, Arsenal, Chelsea.

Won from behind: (1) Wolves (h).

Lost from in front: (3) Manchester U (LC) (h), Tottenham (a), West Brom (a).

High spots: Successful swoops into transfer market (Hamilton, Hunter, Belfitt).

Senior players Best and Morris return to form after being dropped for two months.

Excellent form in April ensures relegation is avoided.

Low spots: The seven-goal hammering at Sheffield Utd.

A shortage of goals (17 in 24 games before end of 1971).

The 20-man brawl in the Arsenal home game.

The barracking of manager Robson after a mediocre start.

Harper's sending off v Sheffield Utd for continuing dissent and man-handling of the referee.

Ever-presents: (2) Colin Harper, Derek Jefferson.

Hat-tricks: (0).

Opposing hat-tricks: (1) Woodward (Sheffield Utd).

Leading scorer: (8) Mick Hill.

		Appearances						**Goals**			
		Lge	Sub	LC	Sub	FAC	Sub	Lge	LC	FAC	Tot
Belfitt, Rod		26				2		7			7
Bell, Bobby		7		1							
Best, David		27		1		2					
Carroll, Tommy		1									
Clarke, Frank		18	3	1				5			5
Collard, Ian		13	1					1			1
Hamilton, Bryan		8	8								
Hammond, Geoff		15				1		1			1
Harper, Colin		42		1		2		2			2
Hill, Mick		20	1	1		2		7		1	8
Hunter, Allan		35		1		2		2			2
Jefferson, Derek		42				2					
Lambert, Mick		14	2				2	2			2
McNeil, Mick		1									
Miller, John		29	1	1		1	1	1			1
Mills, Mick		35		1		2					
Morris, Peter		29	2	1		2		2			2
Robertson, Jimmy		40				2		2		1	3
Sivell, Laurie		15									
Viljoen, Colin		32				2		2	1		3
Whymark, Trevor		12	2					4			4
Woods, Clive		1	4					1			1
(own-goals)											1
22 players used		462	24	11	1	22	1	39	1	2	42

LEAGUE DIVISION 1

Manager: Bobby Robson

SEASON 1972-73

No	Date		Att	Pos	Pt	F-A	H-T	Scorers, Times, and Referees	1	2	3	4	5	6	7	8	9	10	11	12 sub used
1	A 12/8	MANCHESTER U	51,459		2	W 2-1	1-0	Whymark 8, Hamilton 84 / Law 88 / Ref: E Wallace	Best / *Stepney*	Mills / *O'Neil*	**Beattie** / *Dunne*	Collard / *Morgan*	Hunter / *James*	Jefferson / *Buchan*	Hamilton / *Best*	Viljoen / *Kidd*	Belfitt / *Charlton**	Whymark / *Law*	Lambert* / *Moore*	Hammond / *McIlroy*
2	H 15/8	NORWICH	29,544		2	L 1-2	1-1	Hamilton 24 / Anderson 13, Bone 72 / Ref: R Kirkpatrick	Best / *Keelan*	Mills / *Payne*	Beattie / *Butler*	Collard / *Stringer*	Hunter / *Forbes*	Jefferson / *Briggs*	Hamilton / *Livermore*	Viljoen / *Bone*	Belfitt / *Cross*	Whymark / *Paddon*	Lambert / *Anderson*	
3	H 19/8	BIRMINGHAM	17,775	6 / 13	4	W 2-0	1-0	Miller 7, Whymark 67 / Ref: W Gow	Best / *Cooper*	Hammond / *Carroll*	Mills / *Want*	Collard / *Campbell*	Hunter / *Hynd*	Jefferson / *harland*	Hamilton / *Pendrey*	Viljoen / *Francis**	Belfitt* / *Latchford*	Whymark / *Hatton*	Miller / *Taylor*	Morris / *Page*
4	A 23/8	LEEDS	32,461	6 / 8	5	D 3-3	2-2	Hamilton 30, Beattie 43, Belfitt 68 / Jordan 17, 52, Giles 37p / Ref: K Burns	Best / *Harvey*	Mills / *Reaney**	Beattie / *Madeley*	Collard / *Bremner*	Hunter / *Charlton*	Jefferson / *Hunter*	Hamilton / *Lorimer*	Viljoen / *Clarke*	Belfitt / *Jordan*	Whymark / *Giles*	Miller / *Gray*	*Cherry*
5	A 26/8	NEWCASTLE	24,601	6 / 10	7	W 2-1	2-0	Lambert 23, Viljoen 36 / MacDonald 81 / Ref: A Jones	Best / *McFaul*	Mills / *Craig*	Beattie / *Clark*	Collard / *Cowan*	Hunter / *Howard*	Jefferson / *Young*	Hamilton / *Smith*	Viljoen / *Reid**	Belfitt / *MacDonald*	Whymark* / *Tudor*	Lambert / *Hibbitt*	Miller / *Cassidy*
6	A 29/8	SHEFFIELD UTD	23,522	4 / 10	8	D 0-0	0-0	Ref: V Batty	Best / *McAlister*	Mills / *Goulding*	Harper / *Hemsley*	Collard* / *Flynn*	Hunter / *Colquhoun*	Beattie / *Hockey*	Hamilton / *Woodward*	Viljoen / *Salmons*	Belfitt / *Cammack*	Whymark / *Currie*	Lambert / *Reece*	Miller
7	H 2/9	TOTTENHAM	23,140	7 / 3	9	D 1-1	0-0	Viljoen 52 / Peters 64p / Ref: J Yates	Best / *Jennings*	Mills / *Kinnear*	Beattie / *Knowles*	Collard / *Pratt*	Hunter / *England*	Jefferson / *Beal*	Hamilton / *Gilzean*	Viljoen / *Perryman*	Belfitt* / *Chivers*	Whymark / *Peters*	Lambert / *Pearce*	Miller
8	A 9/9	SOUTHAMPTON	13,919	5 / 15	11	W 2-1	0-0	Hamilton 55, Belfitt 58 / Channon 71p / Ref: J Taylor	Best / *Martin*	Mills / *McCarthy*	Beattie / *Burns*	Collard / *Fisher*	Hunter / *McGrath*	Jefferson / *Steele*	Hamilton / *Paine*	Viljoen / *Channon*	Belfitt / *Davies*	Whymark / *Byrne*	Lambert / *Stokes**	*Gilchrist*
9	H 16/9	STOKE	17,754	2 / 20	13	W 2-0	1-0	Belfitt 24, 54 / Ref: K Sweet	Best / *Banks*	Mills / *Marsh*	Harper / *Pejic*	Collard / *Mahoney**	Hunter / *Smith*	Jefferson / *Bloor*	Hamilton / *Robertson*	Morris / *Greenhoff*	Belfitt / *Ritchie*	Whymark / *Hurst !*	Lambert / *Conroy*	*Skeels*
10	A 23/9	CHELSEA	29,647	4 / 8	13	L 0-2	0-0	Osgood 50, Feely 59 / Ref: E Jolly	Best / *Bonetti*	Mills / *Mulligan*	Harper / *McCreadie*	Collard* / *Hollins*	Hunter / *Droy*	Jefferson / *Harris*	Hamilton / *Garland*	Morris / *Kember*	Belfitt / *Osgood*	Whymark / *Feely*	Lambert / *Cooke*	Beattie

Match commentaries

1. Teenager Beattie enjoys a magnificent debut, subduing George Best, having a hand in both Ipswich goals and almost scoring himself with a remarkable header from distance. Whymark takes advantage of defensive hesitancy for the first and Hamilton's neat volley clinches the points.

2. The first East Anglian derby in the top division is a tense and physical affair. The points go City's way as Bone tucks home Cross's return pass. Paddon's superb through-ball sets up Anderson to lob the exposed Best for the first. Hamilton volleys home after Forbes' misplaced clearance.

3. Tireless and enterprising, Collard produces a fine display in midfield. He finds Miller's head with a free-kick for the first. His long-throw is flicked on by Belfitt for Whymark to head home the clinching goal. City's talented attack is snuffed out and Best enjoys a quiet afternoon.

4. An evening of thrills and spills sees Town emerge with enormous credit after pegging Leeds back three times. Best is knocked unconscious for the first goal but resumes to aid a five-star team effort. Pick of the goals is by the irrepressible Hamilton, who cuts in to blast home a low drive.

5. Lambert intercepts Hibbitt's careless back-pass to open the scoring and Mills' cross enables Viljoen to power home a fine drive. Belfitt's early strike is disallowed and Howard hits his own bar with a back-pass. McDonald's close-range consolation effort flatters the well-beaten visitors.

6. The unbeaten away run continues but Town look less convincing than of late. Reece and Whymark hit the crossbar. Jefferson, who is out injured, is reportedly a transfer target of Wolves, for whom Beattie takes his place in central defence, a position he will fill for many years to come.

7. Viljoen's well-taken goal is cancelled out by Peters' spot-kick after he collides with Beattie. Town get heated over the award and also with Gilzean, who lunges into Best with an upraised leg. Gilzean also has a goal disallowed for offside and then hits the goal-post in a lively spell.

8. Saints miss several first-half chances and are sunk when Hamilton stabs home the loose ball after Martin only parries Viljoen's shot. Collard's corner is powerfully headed home by Belfitt. Beattie and Channon tangle and a penalty is given, the striker only scoring after a second attempt.

9. Hamilton's chip puts Belfitt through and he lobs Banks. The second is a magnificent drive from the edge of the box after Lambert's precision pull-back. Town's midfield controls the game and Hurst is sent off for the first time after he is booked twice for dissent in the final 20 minutes.

10. The Chelsea jinx strikes again, but Robson is angry at the defensive blunders which gift the points to the Londoners. Osgood's header breaks the deadlock and is followed by a weak Feely shot which is somehow deflected past defenders on the goal-line. Collard picks up a groin injury.

11 — LEICESTER (H) 30/9 — 8 L 0-2 — 17,811 — 17 13

1	2	3	4	5	6	7	8	9	10	11	12
Best	Mills	Harper	Morris	Hunter	Beattie	Hamilton*	Viljoen	Woods	Whymark	Lambert	Miller
Shilton	*Whitworth*	*Rofe*	*Sammels*	*Sjoberg*	*Cross*	*Farrington*	*Birchenall*	*Weller*	*Worthington*	*Glover*	

Glover 19, Worthington 76
Ref: G Hartley

Jefferson joins Bill McGarry at Wolves and Belfitt and Collard are missing but as Town come a cropper on a windy day. Beattie's error sets up Glover whose fierce shot flies in from an angle. Shilton performs heroics before Suffolk-born Sammels supplies the cross for the second.

12 — WEST HAM (H) 7/10 — 9 D 1-1 — 22,218 — 10 14

1	2	3	4	5	6	7	8	9	10	11
Best	Mills	Harper	Collard	Hunter	Beattie	Hamilton	Viljoen	Belfitt	Whymark	Lambert
Grotier	*Lampard*	*Charles*	*Bonds*	*Taylor*	*Moore*	*Tyler*	*Best*	*Holland*	*Brooking*	*Robson*

Hamilton 82
Best 65
Ref: K Wynn

Best keeps Town on terms with a breathtaking save from a Hunter deflection. Hamilton, revelling in his new attacking midfield role, produces a late header to bring the scores level.

13 — ARSENAL (A) 14/10 — 11 L 0-1 — 34,196 — 2 14

1	2	3	4	5	6	7	8	9	10	11	12
Best	Mills	Harper	Collard*	Hunter	Beattie	Hamilton	Viljoen	Belfitt	Whymark	Lambert	Morris
Barnett	*Rice*	*McNab*	*Storey*	*McLintock*	*Blockley*	*Marinello*	*Ball*	*Radford*	*George*	*Graham*	

Graham 63
Ref: I Smith

The unproductive run continues despite an even contest. Hamilton has a goalbound shot cleared off the line by McNab and other chances are spurned. Graham is perfectly placed to punish the visitors as he drills home a rasping 30-yarder as the ball is cleared straight to him by Beattie.

14 — DERBY (H) 21/10 — 8 W 3-1 — 16,948 — 16 16

1	2	3	4	5	6	7	8	9	10	11
Best	Mills	Harper	Morris	Hunter	Beattie	Hamilton	Viljoen	Belfitt	Whymark	Lambert
Boulton	*Robson*	*Nish*	*Hennessey*	*McFarland*	*Todd*	*McGovern*	*Powell*	*Hinton*	*Durban*	

Belfitt 27, Beattie 39, Whymark 87
Hinton 59p
Ref: R Crabb

Brian Clough's reigning champions look lacklustre in the first half and can thank Todd for keeping the score down. Belfitt heads in Lambert's corner to set the ball rolling. Beattie doubles the lead, firing home Hennessey's clearance. Town receive a standing ovation at the final whistle.

15 — EVERTON (A) 28/10 — 9 D 2-2 — 30,185 — 5 17

1	2	3	4	5	6	7	8	9	10	11
Best	Mills	Harper	Morris	Hunter	Beattie	Hamilton	Viljoen	Belfitt	Whymark	Lambert
Lawson	*Scott*	*Newton*	*Kendall*	*Kenyon*	*Hurst*	*Whittle*	*Buckley*	*Johnson*	*Harvey*	*Connolly*

Lambert 64, Belfitt 71
Kenyon 26, Whittle 45
Ref: T Reynolds

Everton dominate early on and Best's heroics restrict them to two by the break. Town re-organise and storm back into contention as Lambert pounces on a loose ball dropped by Lawson. Belfitt rescues a lucky point, looking suspiciously offside when he drives his shot past Lawson.

16 — LEEDS (H) 4/11 — 8 D 2-2 — 27,547 — 2 18

1	2	3	4	5	6	7	8	9	10	11	12
Best	Mills	Harper	Morris	Hunter	Beattie	Hamilton	Viljoen	Johnson	Whymark*	Lambert	Hill
Harvey	*Madeley*	*Cherry*	*Bremner*	*Charlton*	*Hunter*	*Lorimer*	*Clarke*	*Jones*	*Bates*	*Gray*	

Madeley 18 (og), Whymark 27
Charlton 10, Lorimer 60
Ref: D Turner

Robson shocks the fans by swapping crowd-favourite Belfitt for Everton's Johnson, but the new man has a lively debut. Charlton scores a rare goal with his feet but Madeley diverts Hamilton's pass past the stranded Harvey. Lorimer's powerfully-hit equaliser is his 100th League goal.

17 — NORWICH (A) 11/11 — 7 D 0-0 — 34,640 — 8 19

1	2	3	4	5	6	7	8	9	10	11
Best	Mills	Harper	Morris	Hunter	Beattie	Hamilton	Viljoen	Johnson	Whymark	Lambert
Keelan	*Butler*	*Black*	*Stringer*	*Forbes*	*Briggs*	*Livermore*	*Bone*	*Cross*	*Paddon*	*Anderson*

Ref: H Hackney

The local derby tension spoils the game as a spectacle. Town have most of the possession, but are not ruthless in front of goal. Johnson's pace and enthusiasm seems to be winning the fans over. Keelan is in fine form but when Beattie finally beats him, Butler is on the line to kick clear.

18 — WOLVERHAMPTON (A) 18/11 — 5 W 1-0 — 14,888 — 14 21

1	2	3	4	5	6	7	8	9	10	11	12
Best	Mills	Harper	Morris	Hunter	Beattie	Hamilton	Viljoen	Johnson	Whymark	Lambert	
Parkes	*Shaw*	*Taylor*	*Bailey*	*Munro*	*McAlle*	*McCalliog*	*Hibbitt**	*Richards*	*Dougan*	*Wagstaffe*	*Kindon*

Whymark 53
Ref: D Nippard

Bill McGarry's Wolves have their lowest crowd for eight years as Ipswich dominate on a snow-covered pitch. Whymark gets on the end of Johnson's cross to slide home the winner. A 30-yard free-kick by Mills smashes against the post and Parkes survives several nasty moments.

19 — MANCHESTER C (A) 2/12 — 6 D 1-1 — 27,838 — 14 22

1	2	3	4	5	6	7	8	9	10	11	12
Best	Mills	Harper	Morris	Hunter	Beattie	Hamilton	Viljoen	Johnson	Whymark	Lambert	
Corrigan	*Book*	*Donachie*	*Doyle*	*Barrett*	*Jeffries*	*Carrodus**	*Bell*	*Marsh*	*Lee*	*Towers*	*Hill*

Johnson 61
Lee 15
Ref: R Kirkpatrick

After the Coventry home game is abandoned due to floodlight failure while losing 0-1, Town set out on yet another away trip. Johnson curls a left-foot shot past Corrigan for his first goal for the club and nearly wins the game when his late effort is blocked by the big keeper's knees.

20 — COVENTRY (H) 5/12 — 5 W 2-0 — 17,786 — 9 24

1	2	3	4	5	6	7	8	9	10	11	12
Best	Mills	Harper	Morris	Hunter	Beattie	Hamilton	Viljoen	Johnson	Whymark	Lambert	
Ramsbottom	*Coop*	*Cattlin*	*Smith*	*Barry**	*Parker*	*Mortimer*	*Alderson*	*Stein*	*Carr*	*Hutchison*	*Dugdale*

Johnson 43, Whymark 70
Ref: N Burtenshaw

This re-arranged game never looks like being a repeat of the earlier proceedings. Key defender Barry is hospitalised with a hip injury after a collision with Hunter. Gordon Milne's side succumb to Johnson's header from a Beattie knock-on and Whymark's clever overhead kick.

21 — CRYSTAL PALACE (H) 9/12 — 4 W 2-1 — 18,079 — 22 26

1	2	3	4	5	6	7	8	9	10	11
Best	Mills	Harper	Morris	Hunter	Beattie	Hamilton	Viljoen	Johnson	Whymark	Lambert
Jackson	*Mulligan*	*Taylor*	*Phillip*	*Bell*	*Blyth*	*Hughes*	*Payne*	*Craven**	*Rogers*	*Kellard*

Johnson 12, 46
Hughes 6
Ref: H Davey

Bert Head's expensively assembled team has gone four games without defeat but are still bottom of the table. They take a shock early lead, but have to return to London pointless as Johnson's electric form continues. His winner sees him sweep the ball home after great work by Lambert.

No	Date	Venue	Att	Pos	W/D/L	Pt	F-A	H-T	1	2	3	4	5	6	7	8	9	10	11	12 sub used	Scorers, Times, and Referees
22	16/12	H LIVERPOOL	25,990	4	D	27	1-1	0-1	Best	Mills	Harper	Morris	Hunter	Beattie	Hamilton	Viljoen	Johnson	Whymark	Lambert		Lambert 53; Heighway 24; Ref: P Walters
				1					*Clemence*	*Lawler*	*Lindsay*	*Thompson*	*Lloyd*	*Hughes*	*Keegan*	*Cormack*	*Heighway**	*Boersma*	*Callaghan*	*Hall*	
23	23/12	A WEST BROM	12,147	4	L	27	0-2	0-1	Best	Mills	Harper	Morris	Hunter	Beattie	Hamilton	Viljoen	Johnson	Whymark*	Lambert	Woods	Glover 37, Hartford 50; Ref: R Raby
				17					*Latchford*	*Wilson*	*Nisbet*	*Cantello*	*Wile*	*Merrick*	*Brown A*	*Brown T*	*Glover*	*Hartford*	*Johnston*		
24	26/12	H CHELSEA	26,229	4	W	29	3-0	2-0	Phillips	Mills	Harper	Morris	Hunter	Beattie	Hamilton*	Viljoen	Johnson	Whymark*	Lambert	Woods	B'tie 35, Whymark 41, Hollins 66 (og); Ref: R Challis
				16					*Harris*	*Wilkins G*	*Hollins*	*Dempsey*	*Webb*	*Baldwin*	*Hudson*	*Osgood*	*Boyle**	*Garland*	*Hinton*		
25	30/12	A BIRMINGHAM	32,705	4	W	31	2-1	2-0	Best	Mills	Harper	Morris	Hunter	Beattie	Hamilton	Viljoen	Johnson*	Whymark*	Lambert	Hammond	Johnson 5, Hamilton 19; Hatton 67; Ref: M Sinclair
				19					*Latchford D*	*Bowker*	*Want*	*Pendrey*	*Hynd*	*Harland*	*Smith*	*Hope*	*Latchford R*	*Phillips**	*Taylor*	*Hatton*	
26	6/1	H NEWCASTLE	19,609	4	W	33	1-0	1-0	Best	Mills	Harper	Morris	Hunter	Beattie	Hamilton*	Viljoen	Johnson	Whymark	Lambert	Clarke	Whymark 22; Ref: J Taylor
				6					*McFaul*	*Craig*	*Clark*	*Nattrass*	*Howard*	*Moncur*	*Barraclough*	*Smith*	*MacDonald*	*Tudor*	*Hibbitt*		
27	20/1	A TOTTENHAM	33,014	4	W	35	1-0	0-0	Best	Mills	Harper	Morris	Hunter	Beattie	Hamilton	Viljoen	Johnson	Whymark	Lambert		Hamilton 69; Ref: D Smith
				9					*Jennings*	*Evans*	*Knowles*	*Pratt*	*England*	*Naylor*	*Gilzean*	*Pearce*	*Chivers*	*Peters*	*Coates*		
28	27/1	H SOUTHAMPTON	19,629	4	D	36	2-2	1-1	Best	Mills	Harper	Morris	Hunter	Beattie	Hamilton	Viljoen	Johnson	Whymark*	Lambert		Viljoen 40p, Hamilton 55; Davies 15, Channon 58; Ref: J Hunting
				9					*Martin*	*McCarthy*	*Kirkup*	*Fisher*	*Bennett*	*Walker*	*Paine*	*Channon*	*Davies*	*O'Neil*	*O'Brien*		
29	17/2	H MANCHESTER U	31,587	4	W	38	4-1	2-0	Best	Mills	Harper	Morris*	Keeley	Beattie	Hamilton	Viljoen	Johnson	Whymark	Lambert	Collard	Hamilton 3, 53, Harper 29, Viljoen 74p; Macari 59; Ref: R Toseland
				21					*Stepney*	*Forsyth*	*Dunne*	*Graham*	*Holton*	*Buchan*	*Martin*	*McDougall*	*Charlton*	*Macari*	*Kidd*		
30	24/2	A LIVERPOOL	43,875	4	L	38	1-2	0-0	Best	Mills	Harper	Morris	Hunter	Peddelty	Hamilton	Viljoen	Johnson	Whymark	Lambert		Johnson 67; Heighway 64, Keegan 80; Ref: P Baldwin
				1					*Clemence*	*Lawler*	*Lindsay*	*Smith*	*Lloyd*	*Hughes*	*Keegan*	*Toshack**	*Boersma*	*Heighway*	*Callaghan*	*Thompson*	
31	2/3	A WEST HAM	37,004	4	W	40	1-0	0-0	Sivell	Mills	Harper	Morris	Hunter	Beattie	Hamilton	Viljoen	Johnson	Whymark	Lambert		Johnson 51; Ref: H New
				7					*Ferguson*	*McDowell*	*Lampard*	*Bonds*	*Taylor*	*Moore*	*Tyler*	*Best*	*Holland*	*Brooking*	*Robson*		

Match reports

22 — Liverpool: Town mount a long series of attacks after the break and deservedly draw level when Lambert pounces on Johnson's overhead kick to score. Lambert earlier hit the bar, while Mills headed Boersma's effort off the line. Robson praises the fans for creating a marvellous atmosphere.

23 — West Brom: Don Howe's struggling team take the points in a generally drab affair. Best believes he had prevented Glover's shot from crossing the line and chases the referee to protest, only to earn himself a booking. This incident livens things up, but the home side stays on top.

24 — Chelsea: Town's first win in more than ten years over Chelsea as Beattie nods home Lambert's miscued shot. Whymark heads home Morris's free-kick and Hamilton's probing cross is turned past his own keeper by unlucky Hollins. Earlier, Mills rocked the crossbar with an effort from 30 yards.

25 — Birmingham: Freddie Goodwin's side offers little resistance even though Best is hobbling for 85 minutes after a collision. Johnson heads home Lambert's early cross. Dave Latchford casually attempts to tip over a Viljoen shot, only for it to hit the bar and fall conveniently for Hamilton to convert.

26 — Newcastle: In the first half Town run the Geordies ragged but only score once when Whymark seems to hang in the air above the defence to steer home Viljoen's cross. Hunter keeps a tight hold on MacDonald, although Newcastle end up netting three times with all of them ruled out by the ref.

27 — Tottenham: A long-awaited win in London after Viljoen and Johnson combine to set up Hamilton who shoots home from the edge of the area. A linesman controversially rules out a Spurs effort for a foul on Best. Bad feeling spills over after the final whistle with Johnson and Knowles scuffling.

28 — Southampton: Davies stabs Ted Bates' side ahead from Paine's corner-kick. Viljoen levels after Whymark is brought down by McCarthy. Hamilton converts the rebound after Johnson's header hits a post, but Saints are level when Channon gets clean through and dances round the advancing keeper.

29 — Manchester U: A record crowd sees Town's teenage centre-halves cope admirably. Hamilton pounces to score after just 150 seconds when Lambert's header comes back off the bar. Harper nets with a flying header and Hamilton's clincher is a disaster for Stepney who helps it into the back of the net.

30 — Liverpool: Toshack hits the bar and Heighway scrambles the ball home. Merseysider Johnson is overjoyed to score the ball past Clemence after a fine through-ball by Viljoen. Keegan produces a fierce shot to take Bill Shankly's side back to first place. Best is again hampered by an injury.

31 — West Ham: Johnson hits the bar after a fine solo run. Whymark attempts to burst clear but is pulled back by McDowell, who is booked. Johnson hits the target with a precision header from Lambert's cross. Ferguson produces a handful of fine saves, and at the other end Clyde Best misses a sitter.

Match record (matches 32–42)

No	Venue	Date	Opponent	Div	Score	Result	Pts	Attendance	Pos
32	H	10/3	ARSENAL	4	1-2	L	40	**34,636**	2
33	H	17/3	WEST BROM	4	2-0	W	42	17,614	22
34	H	24/3	EVERTON	4	0-1	L	42	20,580	15
35	A	31/3	COVENTRY	4	1-2	L	42	17,130	10
36	A	4/4	STOKE	4	0-1	L	42	18,419	16
37	H	7/4	MANCHESTER C	4	1-1	D	43	19,107	13
38	A	14/4	CRYSTAL PALACE	4	1-1	D	44	29,214	21
39	H	21/4	WOLVERHAMPTON	4	2-1	W	46	23,932	7
40	A	24/4	LEICESTER	4	1-1	D	47	20,373	18
41	H	28/4	SHEFFIELD UTD	4	1-1	D	48	19,271	15
42	A	30/4	DERBY	4	0-3	L	48	20,374	7

Home Average 22,228   Away 27,696

---

32 — ARSENAL (H) 1-2
Whymark 43, Harper 44 (og), Ball 66p   Ref: J Williams

Ipswich: Sivell, Mills, Harper, Morris, Hunter, Beattie, Hamilton, Viljoen, Johnson, Whymark, Lambert
Arsenal: Wilson, Rice, McNab, Storey, McLintock, Simpson, Armstrong, Ball, Radford, Kennedy, Kelly

Another record crowd watches Whymark take Lambert's cross on his chest once more space before shooting past Wilson. Seconds later Bertie Mee's team are level when Harper scoops Radford's header past his own keeper. Hunter falls onto the ball to concede the decisive penalty.

33 — WEST BROM (H) 2-0
Beattie 24, Viljoen 83p   Ref: J Thacker

Ipswich: Best, Mills, Harper, Morris, Hunter, Beattie, Hamilton, Viljoen, Johnson, Whymark, Lambert
West Brom: Osborne, Nisbet, Wilson, Cantello, Wile, Robertson, McLean*, Brown, Astle, Shaw, Johnston, (Merrick)

In a poor quality encounter, Beattie produces a fine header and Town never look back. Albion look certain for the drop and their gloom is deepened further when Town win a highly debatable penalty. Johnson's full-blooded shot hits the unlucky Wilson and Viljoen does the rest.

34 — EVERTON (H) 0-1
Harper 76   Ref: D Nippard

Ipswich: Best, Mills, Harper, Morris, Hunter, Beattie, Hamilton*, Viljoen, Johnson, Whymark, Lambert, (Miller)
Everton: Lawson, Wright, Scott, Hurst, Kenyon, Newton*, Darracott, Kendall, Lyons, Harper, Connolly, (Styles)

Harry Catterick's side put out a defensive formation, hoping for breakaways, and get their reward when Joe Harper capitalises on a misplaced header by his Ipswich namesake. Town look off-colour and squander chances. Everton are delighted with their first away win for five months.

35 — COVENTRY (A) 1-2
Beattie 53 | Alderson 36, Stein 86   Ref: A Hart

Ipswich: Best, Mills, Harper, Morris, Hunter, Beattie, Hamilton, Viljoen, Johnson, Whymark, Lambert
Coventry: Ramsbottom, Coop, Cattlin, McGuire*, Barry, Dugdale, Mortimer, Alderson, Stein, Carr, Hutchison, (Smith)

Alderson meets Hutchison's cross and his effort is deflected past Best by Beattie. The Ipswich defender makes up for it as he drives home an equaliser from Morris's free-kick. Stein gets away from his markers to nod home Cattlin's free-kick to give the Sky Blues a deserved victory.

36 — STOKE (A) 0-1
Ritchie 13   Ref: D Smith

Ipswich: Best, Mills, Harper, Morris, Hunter, Beattie, Hamilton*, Viljoen, Johnson, Whymark, Lambert
Stoke: Farmer, Marsh, Pejic, Mahoney, Smith, Bloor, Haslegrave, Greenhoff, Ritchie, Hurst, Conroy, (Woods)

Town's European hopes are put in jeopardy as Tony Waddington's side squeeze home. Haslegrave's long-range effort looks bound for the arms of Best, but the ball strikes Richie and deflects past him. Beattie goes close to an equaliser. Winger Lambert chalks up his 100th appearance.

37 — MANCHESTER C (H) 1-1
Lambert 45 | Oakes 32   Ref: I Jones

Ipswich: Best, Mills, Harper, Morris, Hunter*, Beattie, Hamilton, Viljoen, Johnson, Whymark, Lambert
Manchester C: Healey, Book, Donachie, Doyle, Booth, Oakes, Summerbee, Bell, Lee, Jeffries, Towers, (Woods)

City, under caretaker-boss Johnny Hart, take the lead when Donachie's through-ball sends Oakes through to score a rare goal. Hunter collides with keeper Healey and is off the field with concussion when Lambert hooks home Hamilton's corner seconds before the half-time whistle.

38 — CRYSTAL PALACE (A) 1-1
Hamilton 62 | Rogers 52p   Ref: D Biddle

Ipswich: Best, Mills, Harper, Morris, Hunter, Peddelty, Hamilton, Viljoen, Johnson*, Whymark, Lambert
Crystal Palace: Jackson, Mulligan, Taylor, Roffey, Blyth, Wall, Possee, Payne, Whittle, Cooke, Rogers, (Collard)

Amid speculation that Everton will appoint Robson as their manager, Rogers puts Town behind from the spot when Hunter is controversially adjudged to have handled. Lambert's shot is blocked and the rebound steered in by Hamilton. Lambert calls one Jackson save the best he's ever seen.

39 — WOLVERHAMPTON (H) 2-1
Morris 59, Whymark 71 | Richards 31   Ref: G Kew

Ipswich: Best, Mills, Harper, Morris, Hunter, Beattie, Hamilton, Viljoen!, Johnson, Whymark, Lambert
Wolverhampton: Parkes, Taylor, Parkin, Bailey, Munro!, McAlle, Powell, McCalling*, Richards, Dougan, Wagstaffe, (Kindon)

A poor back-pass by Hamilton is collected by Richards who opens the scoring. Viljoen is obstructed by Munro and the pair begin brawling and are sent off. Morris levels with a typical low drive. Whymark then settles a highly entertaining and stormy game with a splendid diving header.

40 — LEICESTER (A) 1-1
Lambert 18 | Cross 86   Ref: K Burns

Ipswich: Best, Mills, Harper, Morris, Hunter, Beattie, Hamilton, Viljoen, Johnson, Whymark, Lambert
Leicester: Shilton, Whitworth, Rofe, Woollett, Munro, Cross, Tomlin, Lee, Weller, Worthington, Glover*, (Stringfellow)

Lambert volleys home after a knock-out, from a corner. Shilton's alertness and agility foils Johnson and Beattie. Leicester come to life in the closing stages after introducing Stringfellow and when Worthington is tripped, the free-kick is hoisted to Cross who heads home.

41 — SHEFFIELD UTD (H) 1-1
Whymark 2 | Woodward 62p   Ref: D Turner

Ipswich: Best, Mills, Harper, Morris, Hunter, Beattie, Hamilton*, Viljoen, Johnson, Whymark, Lambert
Sheffield Utd: McAlister, Badger, Hensley, Mackenzie, Faulkner, Eddy*, Scullion, Salmons, Dearden, Currie, Woodward, (Speight)

After 85 seconds a long Best clearance is misjudged by Faulkner and McAlister and Whymark steps in to take advantage. John Harris's side fight back and when Scullion is sent tumbling, Woodward produces a fierce spot-kick. Town are left to worry about missing out on Europe.

42 — DERBY (A) 0-3
Davies 36, Hector 46, 67   Ref: G Hartley

Ipswich: Best, Mills, Harper, Morris, Hunter, Beattie, Hamilton, Viljoen, Johnson, Clarke, Lambert
Derby: Boulton, Webster, Nish, O'Hare, McFarland, Todd, McGovern, Gemmill, Davies, Hector, Hinton

Results elsewhere have ensured next season's UEFA Cup place is secure and Town fail to reach the heights at a muddy Baseball Ground. Davies flicks the ball home after a corner and then Hector heads home Hinton's free-kick. Defensive dithering is exploited by the alert Hector.

LEAGUE DIVISION 1 (CUP-TIES) Manager: Bobby Robson SEASON 1972-73

League Cup		Att		W	F-A	H-T	Scorers, Times, and Referees	1	2	3	4	5	6	7	8	9	10	11	12 sub used
2	A NEWPORT	9,516	7 4:14	W	3-0	1-0	Lambert 31, Collard 67, Miller 87 Ref: B Homewood	Best	Mills	Harper	Collard*	Hunter	Beattie	Hamilton	Viljoen	Belfitt	Whymark	Lambert	Miller
								Macey	*Williams*	*Sprague*	*Screen*	*Aizlewood*	*Coldrick*	*Thomas*	*Hill*	*Brown*	*Hawkins*	*White*	

Lambert sprints into acres of space to lob home the first. Moments later White stretches and goes agonisingly close to an equaliser. Billy Lucas's team cannot contain the First Division side and they rarely pose a serious threat. Miller puts the icing on the cake with a rasping drive.

		Att			F-A	H-T	Scorers, Times, and Referees	1	2	3	4	5	6	7	8	9	10	11	12
3	H STOKE	14,387	8 20	L	1-2	1-0	Viljoen 38 Hurst 64, Ritchie 88 Ref: R Tinkler	Best	Mills	Harper	Collard	Hunter	Beattie	Hamilton	Viljoen	Hill	Whymark	Lambert	Conroy
								Banks	*Marsh*	*Pejic*	*Skeels*	*Smith*	*Bloor*	*Robertson**	*Greenhoff*	*Ritchie*	*Hurst*	*Mahoney*	

Viljoen's shot hits Skeels and spins away from Banks and into the net. A linesman flags for a foul by Ritchie on Harper, but is ignored by Mr Tinkler and Hurst collects the pass and equalises. Salt is rubbed into Town's wounds when Ritchie grabs the winner against the run of play.

FA Cup

		Att			F-A	H-T	Scorers, Times, and Referees	1	2	3	4	5	6	7	8	9	10	11	12
3	A CHELMSFORD	15,557	4 SL	W	3-1	2-0	Harper 9, Johnson 35, Hamilton 75 Woolcott 89 Ref: I Jones	Best	Mills	Harper	Morris	Hunter	Peddelty	Hamilton	Viljoen	Johnson	Whymark	Lambert	Thornley
								Taylor	*Coakley*	*Gomersall*	*Delea*	*Loughton*	*Tomkins*	*Lewis*	*Price**	*Woolcott*	*Peterson*	*Dilsworth*	

Dave Bumpstead's Southern League part-timers fall behind when Harper rockets home a pull-back from Morris. Johnson flicks a Morris corner past the besieged Taylor. Hamilton rounds the keeper to score with ease. Teenager Peddelty has a largely trouble-free debut in place of Beattie.

		Att			F-A	H-T	Scorers, Times, and Referees	1	2	3	4	5	6	7	8	9	10	11	12
4	A CHELSEA	36,491	4 13	L	0-2	0-1	Garner 38, 46 Ref: G Hill	Best	Mills	Harper	Morris	Hunter	Beattie	Hamilton	Viljoen	Johnson	Whymark	Lambert	Hinton
								Phillips	*Locke*	*Harris*	*Hollins*	*Dempsey*	*Webb**	*Garner*	*Hudson*	*Osgood*	*Kember*	*Houseman*	

Fatal hesitation in defence allows Garner the time to lob over Best's head. The same player then sees his drive deflected into goal off the body of Beattie. Town fail to convert a host of chances and their injury-hit opponents are relieved to make it through. They go on to face Sheff Wed.

Football League Division One — Final Table

Pos	Team	P	Home W	Home D	Home L	Home F	Home A	Away W	Away D	Away L	Away F	Away A	Pts
1	Liverpool	42	17	3	1	45	19	8	7	6	27	23	60
2	Arsenal	42	14	5	2	31	14	9	6	6	26	29	57
3	Leeds	42	15	4	2	45	13	6	7	8	26	32	53
4	IPSWICH	42	10	7	4	34	20	7	7	7	21	25	48
5	Wolves	42	13	3	5	43	23	5	8	8	23	31	47
6	West Ham	42	12	5	4	45	25	5	7	9	22	28	46
7	Derby	42	15	3	3	43	18	4	5	12	13	36	46
8	Tottenham	42	10	5	6	33	23	6	8	7	25	25	45
9	Newcastle	42	12	6	3	35	19	4	7	10	25	32	45
10	Birmingham	42	11	7	3	39	22	4	5	12	14	32	42
11	Manchester C	42	12	4	5	36	20	3	7	11	21	40	41
12	Chelsea	42	9	6	6	26	17	4	8	9	19	29	40
13	Southampton	42	8	11	2	28	18	3	7	11	21	35	40
14	Sheffield Utd	42	11	4	6	28	18	4	6	11	23	41	40
15	Stoke	42	11	8	2	38	17	3	2	16	23	39	38
16	Leicester	42	7	9	5	23	18	4	6	11	17	28	37
17	Everton	42	9	5	7	27	21	4	6	11	14	28	37
18	Manchester U	42	9	5	7	24	19	3	6	12	20	41	37
19	Coventry	42	9	5	7	27	24	4	4	13	13	31	35
20	Norwich	42	7	9	5	22	19	4	1	16	14	44	32
21	Crys Palace	42	7	7	7	25	21	2	5	14	16	37	30
22	West Brom	42	8	7	6	25	24	1	3	17	13	38	28
		924	236	130	96	724	436	96	130	236	436	724	924

Appearances and Goals

Player	App Lge	Sub	LC	Sub	FAC	Sub	Goals Lge	LC	FAC	Tot
Beattie, Kevin	37	1	2		1		5			5
Belfitt, Rod	14	1	1				6			6
Best, David	40		2		2					
Clarke, Frank	1	1								
Collard, Ian	12	3	2		2			1		1
Hamilton, Bryan	42		2		2		11	1		12
Hammond, Geoff	1	2								
Harper, Colin	35		2		2		1		1	2
Hill, Mick		1	1							
Hunter, Allan	41		2		2					
Jefferson, Derek	9									
Johnson, David	27		2		2		7		1	8
Keeley, Glenn	1									
Lambert, Mick	40		2		2		5	1		6
Miller, John	3	5		1			1	1		2
Mills, Mick	42		2		2					
Morris, Peter	31	2	2	0	2		1			1
Peddelty, John	2				1					
Sivell, Laurie	2									
Viljoen, Colin	40		2		2		5		1	6
Whymark, Trevor	41		2		2		11			11
Woods, Clive	1	4					2			2
(own-goals)							2			2
22 players used	462	19	22	1	22		55	4	3	62

Odds & ends

Double wins: (4) Manchester U, Birmingham, Newcastle, Wolves.
Double losses: (1) Arsenal.

Won from behind: (2) Crystal Palace (h), Wolves (h).
Lost from in front: (2) Arsenal (h), Stoke (h) (LC).

High spots: Qualified for Europe.
Second-best league position in club's history.
Home attendance record broken twice (Man U, Arsenal).
Victory in Texaco Cup competition.
The emergence of Kevin Beattie.
First England cap for Mick Mills.

Low spots: Home defeat by Norwich in opening week.
Disappointing exits from both cups.
Average crowd increase relatively low, despite much-improved performances.
Only two victories over the bottom ten clubs.

Player of the Year: Kevin Beattie.
Ever-presents: (2) Mick Mills, Bryan Hamilton.
Hat-tricks: (0).
Opposing hat-tricks: (0).
Leading scorer: (12) Bryan Hamilton.

LEAGUE DIVISION 1 — Manager: Bobby Robson — SEASON 1973-74

Each match lists the Ipswich Town line-up (top row) and the opponents (bottom row, italic). Positions given as Ipswich / Opponent.

---

1 · H LEICESTER — 25/8
Att 20,116 · Pt D 1 · F-A 1-1 · H-T 1-0
Scorers: Munro 7 (og); Sammels 55 · Ref: G Kew

1	2	3	4	5	6	7	8	9	10	11	12 sub used
Best	Mills	Harper	Morris	Hunter	Beattie	Hamilton	Collard	Johnson*	Whymark	Lambert	Hammond
Shilton	*Whitworth*	*Rofe*	*Stringfellow*	*Munro*	*Cross*	*Weller*	*Sammels*	*Worthington*	*Birchenall*	*Glover*	

Collard's low drive is deflected past Shilton by Munro early on, but the England keeper stands firm after that and makes a series of tremendous saves. Dominant Ipswich simply can't beat him. Best fails to hold Glover's shot and a melee results, with Sammels forcing the ball into goal.

---

2 · A WEST HAM — 27/8
Att 23,335 · Pt D 2 · F-A 3-3 · H-T 1-2
Scorers: Whymark 12, Johnson 64, 71; Bonds 4, Brooking 6, Best 81 · Ref: D Biddle

1	2	3	4	5	6	7	8	9	10	11	12 sub used
Best	Mills	Harper	Morris	Keeley	Beattie	Hamilton	Viljoen	Johnson	Whymark	Lambert	
Day	*Lampard*	*Lock*	*Bonds*	*Taylor*	*Moore*	*Best*	*Holland*	*McDougall*	*Brooking*	*Robson*	

Bonds nets the rebound after Robson's header strikes wood, then Brooking converts Robson's through-ball. Whymark pounces to score from Harper's free-kick. Johnson turns the game on its head with two opportunist goals before Clyde Best's chip completes the day's entertainment.

---

3 · A EVERTON — 1/9
Att 32,469 · Pos 17/10 · Pt L 2 · F-A 0-3 · H-T 0-2
Scorers: Connolly 7, Hurst 27, Harper 88 · Ref: H Hackney

1	2	3	4	5	6	7	8	9	10	11	12 sub used
Best	Mills	Harper	Morris*	Hunter	Beattie	Hamilton	Viljoen	Johnson	Whymark	Lambert	Collard
Lawson	*Darracott*	*Newton*	*Kendall*	*Kenyon*	*Hurst*	*Harvey**	*Lyons*	*Royle*	*Harper*	*Connolly*	*Bernard*

A poor display by Ipswich, who are brushed aside by Billy Bingham's men. Connolly blasts home Royle's flick from a Joe Harper corner-kick. Defender Hurst heads home a rare goal to mark his 300th appearance for Everton and Harper wraps it up by heading home Connolly's cross.

---

4 · H NEWCASTLE — 4/9
Att 21,766 · Pos 17/8 · Pt L 2 · F-A 1-3 · H-T 1-2
Scorers: Whymark 10; Cassidy 24, Robson 40, Smith 52 · Ref: M Sinclair

1	2	3	4	5	6	7	8	9	10	11	12 sub used
Best	Mills	Harper	Morris	Hunter	Beattie	Hamilton	Viljoen	Johnson	Whymark	Lambert	
McFaul	*Nattrass*	*Clark*	*McDermott*	*Howard*	*Moncur*	*Barrowclough*	*Smith*	*Cassidy*	*Robson*	*Hibbitt*	

Real Madrid spies see another off-colour display by Town. Whymark heads in Beattie's cross, but Cassidy cancels this out as he makes the most of Beattie and Hunter's indecision. Robson rounds Best to score from McDermott's pass and Smith tucks home an all too easy third goal.

---

5 · H MANCHESTER U — 8/9
Att 22,005 · Pos 14/16 · Pt W 4 · F-A 2-1 · H-T 2-1
Scorers: Lambert 6, Johnson 42; Anderson 85 · Ref: G Hill

1	2	3	4	5	6	7	8	9	10	11	12 sub used
Sivell	Mills	Harper	Collard	Peddelty	Beattie	Hamilton	Viljoen	Johnson	Whymark	Lambert*	Miller
Stepney	*Young*	*Buchan*	*Daley*	*Sadler*	*Greenhoff*	*Morgan*	*Anderson*	*Kidd**	*Graham*	*McIlroy*	*Macari*

Robson makes major changes and the result is a huge improvement and the season's first win. Beattie's long ball sets Lambert free and he scores in style. Johnson is allowed space to head home from Mills' free-kick. Stepney is kept busy before Anderson heads a late consolation.

---

6 · A NEWCASTLE — 12/9
Att 30,604 · Pos 19/6 · Pt L 4 · F-A 1-3 · H-T 0-2
Scorers: Johnson 75; MacDonald 24, 28, Johnson 66 (og) · Ref: V James

1	2	3	4	5	6	7	8	9	10	11	12 sub used
Sivell	Mills	Harper	Collard	Peddelty	Beattie	Hamilton	Viljoen	Johnson*	Whymark*	Lambert	Woods
McFaul	*Nattrass*	*Clark*	*McDermott*	*Howard*	*Moncur*	*Cassidy*	*Smith*	*MacDonald*	*Robson*	*Hibbitt*	

Joe Harvey's side repeat their win of eight days earlier, with Smith in fine form. MacDonald heads in Cassidy's pass and converts a driven cross by Nattrass. Johnson races to stop Nattrass reaching a long ball but helps it past Sivell. His diving header at the other end is academic.

---

7 · A STOKE — 15/9
Att 17,103 · Pos 19/16 · Pt D 5 · F-A 1-1 · H-T 0-0
Scorers: Woods 48; Hurst 72 · Ref: A Jones

1	2	3	4	5	6	7	8	9	10	11	12 sub used
Best	Mills	Harper	Collard	Peddelty	Beattie	Hamilton	Viljoen	Johnson	Woods	Lambert	
Farmer	*Marsh*	*Pejic*	*Mahoney*	*Smith*	*Bloor*	*Robertson**	*Greenhoff*	*Hurst*	*Conroy*	*Haslegrave*	*Ritchie*

Ex-Town winger Robertson hits the post after a superb solo run. Woods' weak-looking shot is deflected past Farmer by the unlucky Smith. Long periods of Stoke pressure inevitably produce an equaliser when Hurst steps in and crashes home a fierce drive. Best is kept very busy.

---

8 · H BURNLEY — 22/9
Att 19,126 · Pos 14/6 · Pt W 7 · F-A 3-2 · H-T 2-1
Scorers: Hamilton 28, 34, Harper 60; James 44, Collins 77 · Ref: R Challis

1	2	3	4	5	6	7	8	9	10	11	12 sub used
Best	Mills	Harper	Collard	Hunter	Beattie	Hamilton	Viljoen	Johnson	Whymark	Lambert	
Stevenson	*Noble*	*Newton*	*Dobson*	*Waldron*	*Thomson*	*Nulty*	*Hankin*	*Fletcher*	*Collins*	*James*	

Top-class entertainment as Hamilton fires home Lambert's cross then produces a spectacular diving header for the second, again with Lambert assisting. The winger does it again on the hour mark, finding Harper who heads home. Burnley battle in vain to preserve their unbeaten run.

---

9 · A BIRMINGHAM — 29/9
Att 26,919 · Pos 13/22 · Pt W 9 · F-A 3-0 · H-T 0-0
Scorers: Lambert 70, Hamilton 76, Harper 90 · Ref: K Styles

1	2	3	4	5	6	7	8	9	10	11	12 sub used
Best	Mills	Harper	Collard	Hunter	Beattie	Hamilton	Viljoen	Johnson	Whymark	Lambert	
Latchford D	*Clarke*	*Want*	*Burns*	*Hynd*	*Roberts*	*Calderwood*	*Hope**	*Latchford R*	*Hatton*	*Taylor*	*Campbell*

Whymark and Bob Latchford hit the post before three late goals settle it. Lambert heads in Viljoen's cross. Hamilton nips in to convert another Viljoen pass. With the last kick of the match Harper tries his luck from 35 yards, the ball flying into the roof of the net for a goal in a million.

---

10 · H TOTTENHAM — 6/10
Att 23,903 · Pos 13/18 · Pt D 10 · F-A 0-0 · H-T 0-0
Ref: H Davey

1	2	3	4	5	6	7	8	9	10	11	12 sub used
Best	Mills	Harper	Collard	Hunter	Beattie	Hamilton	Viljoen	Johnson	Whymark	Lambert	
Daines	*Evans*	*Knowles*	*Pratt*	*England*	*Beal*	*Gilzean*	*Perryman*	*Chivers*	*Peters*	*Coates*	

Ipswich look fresh despite their recent return from Madrid, but Bill Nicholson's team put on a rugged defensive display. Daines has a match to remember, defying everything and is grateful when Johnson's shot strikes a post. Coates almost nicks it late on, but Best is alert to the danger.

---

11 · A CHELSEA — 13/10
Att 25,111 · Pos 10/16 · Pt W 12 · F-A 3-2 · H-T 2-1
Scorers: Hamilton 9, Johnson 15, 82; Baldwin 13, Hollins 88 · Ref: P Walters

1	2	3	4	5	6	7	8	9	10	11	12 sub used
Best	Mills	Harper	Morris	Hunter	Beattie	Hamilton	Viljoen	Johnson*	Whymark	Lambert	Miller
Bonetti	*Lock**	*Harris*	*Hollins*	*Droy*	*Webb*	*Britton*	*Baldwin*	*Garland*	*Kember*	*Houseman*	*McCreadie*

Town's first win at Stamford Bridge comes courtesy of three deflected goals. Hamilton's effort goes in off Lambert's elbow and Johnson's first loops over Bonetti after hitting Droy. Best makes a fine save from Hollins' penalty-kick, but the Chelsea man converts the rebound.

12 | A | 20/10 | ARSENAL | 28,344 | 11 D | 14 13 | 1-1 | 0-0
Lambert 61 / *Simpson 82*
Ref: K Burns

Town: Best, Mills, Harper, Morris, Hunter, Beattie, Hamilton, Viljoen, Johnson, Whymark, Lambert
Arsenal: *Wilson, Rice, McNab, Stoney, Simpson, Kelly, Armstrong, George, Batson, Kennedy, Price*

Simpson surprises Town by nodding home a late equaliser from a corner-kick, but the biggest shock for the club comes with the the news that Derby have formally offered Robson the chance to replace Brian Clough as manager. He subsequently says no and Dave Mackay is appointed.

---

13 | H | 27/10 | WOLVERHAMPTON | 20,882 | 9 W | 19 15 | 2-0 | 1-0
Morris 34, Hamilton 88
Ref: B Daniels

Town: Best, Mills, Harper, Morris, Hunter, Beattie, Hamilton, Osborne*, Woods, Whymark, Lambert* — Gates
Wolverhampton: *Parkes, Palmer, Parkin, Hegan*, Munro, McAlle, McCalling, Hibbitt, Richards, Dougan, Wagstaffe, Sunderland*

Morris blasts the side's first penalty of the season high over the bar, but atones just six minutes later with a rasping drive from the edge of the area past Parkes. Gates replaces fellow debutant Osborne and sets up Hamilton for the late clincher. Injury-hit Town are grateful for the points.

---

14 | A | 3/11 | COVENTRY | 18,733 | 7 W | 10 17 | 1-0 | 0-0
Whymark 68
Ref: R Lee

Town: Best, Mills, Harper, Morris, Hunter, Beattie, Hamilton, Viljoen, Woods, Whymark, Lambert* — Gates
Coventry: *Glazier, Coop, Holmes, Mortimer, Philpotts, Dugdale, Cartwright, Alderson, Stein, McGuire, Hutchison*

The club's unbeaten run in all competitions is stretched to 13 games. Town are comfortably the better side for long periods and Whymark climbs high above his marker to head home Woods' cross. The only real scare comes when Best has to make a fine save to keep McGuire out.

---

15 | H | 10/11 | DERBY | 23,551 | 6 W | 8 19 | 3-0 | 0-0
Lambert 53, 75, Beattie 69
Ref: A Hart

Town: Best, Mills, Harper, Morris, Hunter, Beattie, Hamilton, Viljoen, Johnson*, Whymark, Lambert — Woods
Derby: *Boulton, Webster, Nish, Newton, McFarland, Todd, McGovern, Gemmill, O'Hare, Hector, Hinton*

For the second season in succession Derby are hammered at Portman Road. After a quiet first half, Lambert combines with Johnson and fires home a superb goal. Beattie shrugs off the attentions of three defenders before blasting a shot past Boulton and Lambert flicks in a header.

---

16 | A | 17/11 | LIVERPOOL | 37,420 | 6 L | 3 19 | 2-4 | 1-3
Johnson 35, Hamilton 68
Keegan 17, 22, 90p, Cormack 45
Ref: P Baldwin

Town: Best, Mills, Harper, Morris, Hunter, Beattie, Hamilton, Viljoen, Johnson, Whymark, Miller* — Woods
Liverpool: *Clemence, Lawler, Lindsay, Thompson, Lloyd, Hughes, Keegan, Cormack, Heighway, Toshack, Callaghan*

Keegan's first hat-trick is the highlight, but Town play their part in a fine game. Keegan heads in Toshack's cross and then pounces to punish Mills' poor clearance. Johnson and Hamilton score with marvellous headers, but Hammond trips Heighway and Keegan converts the penalty.

---

17 | H | 24/11 | MANCHESTER C | 19,210 | 6 W | 15 21 | 2-1 | 1-0
Whymark 11, 64
Leman 46
Ref: H Williams

Town: Best, Mills, Harper, Morris, Hunter, Beattie, Hamilton, Viljoen, Johnson, Whymark, Lambert* — Woods
Manchester C: *MacRae, Pardoe, Donachie, Doyle, Booth, Towers, Barrett, Bell, Summerbee, Leman, Marsh*

In strong winds, Whymark heads home Morris's free-kick, only for City to equalise 90 seconds after the break. Leman stabs the ball home after Summerbee's run, with Town calling in vain for offside. The complaints are forgotten as Whymark dives in to head home from a Viljoen cross.

---

18 | H | 8/12 | LEEDS | 27,313 | 7 L | 1 21 | 0-3 | 0-0
Yorath 51, Jones 58, Clarke 87
Ref: J Taylor

Town: Best, Hammond, Mills, Morris*, Hunter, Beattie, Collard, Viljoen, Johnson, Whymark, Lambert* — Hamilton
Leeds: *Harvey, Reaney, Cherry, Bremner, McQueen, Hunter, Lorimer, Clarke*, Jones, Yorath, Madeley, Jordan*

Leeds produce one of their best-ever displays, according to manager Revie. They equal the record of remaining unbeaten for their 19 opening League games. Yorath fires a shot home off Hunter, Jones nods in Yorath's cross and Clarke tucks away a beauty after jinking past defenders.

---

19 | A | 15/12 | SOUTHAMPTON | 14,633 | 11 L | 5 21 | 0-2 | 0-0
Channon 75p, Gilchrist 90
Ref: D Smith

Town: Best, Hammond, Mills, Morris, Hunter, Beattie, Hamilton, Viljoen, Johnson, Whymark*, Woods* — Gates
Southampton: *Martin, McCarthy, Mills, Fisher, Steele, Hunter, Paine, Channon, O'Neil, Stokes, Gilchrist*

Looking jaded after their UEFA Cup-tie in Holland, Town fail to create many chances. Beattie and Channon tangle in the box and Saints are grateful for the penalty award. Channon tucks the kick home and in the last minute Gilchrist scores after Best and Channon clash in mid-air.

---

20 | H | 22/12 | BIRMINGHAM | 15,457 | 8 W | 20 23 | 3-0 | 1-0
Lambert 35, 89, Hammond 66
Ref: H Hackney

Town: Best, Hammond, Mills, Morris, Hunter, Beattie, Hamilton, Viljoen, Johnson*, Whymark, Lambert* — Woods
Birmingham: *Latchford D, Martin, Gallagher, Pendrey, Hynd, Burns, Campbell, Francis, Latchford R, Hatton, Hendrie*, Roberts*

The return of Lambert after injury peps Town's attack and he chips home coolly from Whymark's pass. After Lambert is fouled, Morris's free-kick finds Hammond who produces a rare headed goal. Viljoen's pin-point pass allows Lambert to slip through and knock home the third goal.

---

21 | A | 26/12 | NORWICH | 29,637 | 6 W | 22 25 | 2-1 | 0-1
Johnson 63p, Lambert 78
McDougall 26
Ref: V James

Town: Best, Hammond*, Mills, Morris, Hunter, Beattie, Hamilton, Osborne, Johnson, Whymark, Lambert* — Woods
Norwich: *Keelan, Butler, Prophett, Stringer, Forbes, Steel, Grapes, McDougall, Suggett, Briggs, Howard*

Lowly Norwich take the lead when Best's punch is seized on by Steel who hits the bar. McDougall tucks home the rebound. Town step up a gear after the break and Forbes holds back Johnson, who scores from the resulting penalty. Johnson sets up Lambert to flick home the winner.

---

22 | A | 29/12 | MANCHESTER U | 36,365 | 7 L | 19 25 | 0-2 | 0-0
McIlroy 77, Macari 79
Ref: J Yates

Town: Best, Mills, Burley, Morris, Hunter, Beattie, Hamilton, Viljoen, Johnson, Whymark*, Lambert* — Woods
Manchester U: *Stepney, Young, Griffiths, Buchan, Holton, Greenhoff, Morgan, Macari, McIlroy, Graham, Best*

Only two players could take satisfaction from this mediocre Town display. One is 17-year-old debutant Burley, who looked composed against George Best, and the other is keeper David Best who performed heroics. Macari clinched the points with a far-post header from a short corner.

---

23 | H | 1/1 | EVERTON | 23,444 | 6 W | 5 27 | 3-0 | 1-0
Hamilton 15, 84, Woods 88
Ref: R Kirkpatrick

Town: Best, Burley, Mills, Morris, Hunter, Beattie, Hamilton, Viljoen, Johnson, Whymark, Woods* — Harper
Everton: *Lawson, Darracott, Styles, Clements, Kenyon, Hurst, Bernard, Buckley, Royle, Lyons, Telfer*, Harper*

Johnson's flick wrong-foots the Everton defence and Hamilton shoots home. A drab hour's play ensues, until Hurst's clearance unluckily hits Clements and falls for Hamilton who makes the most of his good fortune. Woods is even luckier as his intended cross squeezes past Lawson.

LEAGUE DIVISION 1 — Manager: Bobby Robson — SEASON 1973-74

No	Date	Att	Pos	Pt	F-A	H-T	Scorers, Times, and Referees	1	2	3	4	5	6	7	8	9	10	11	12 sub used
24	H 12/1	18,583	6	28	1-1 D	0-0	Johnson 63 / Hurst 70 / Ref: R Toseland	Best	Burley	Mills	Morris	Keeley	Beattie	Hamilton	Viljoen	Johnson	Whymark*	Lambert	Woods
								Farmer	Marsh	Pejic	Skeels	Smith	Bloor	Robertson	Greenhoff	Hurst	Dodd	Mahoney	
25	A 19/1	24,280	8	28	0-5 L	0-2	Worthington 36p, 54p, 80, Munro 45 / [Beattie 81 (og)] / Ref: R Crabb	Sivell	Burley	Mills	Morris	Keeley	Beattie	Hamilton	Viljoen	Johnson	Whymark	Lambert	Woods
								Shilton	Whitworth	Rofe	Earle	Munro	Cross	Weller	Sammels	Worthington	Birchenall	Tomlin	
26	H 2/2	20,046	7	30	7-0 W	2-0	L'bert 6, Whym'k 29, 63, H'ton 55, 75 / [Beattie 60, Mills 83] / Ref: K Styles	Sivell	Burley	Mills	Morris	Keeley	Beattie	Hamilton	Viljoen	Johnson	Whymark	Lambert*	Woods
								Martin	McCarthy	Peach	Fisher	Bennett	Steele	Paine	Channon	Stokes	Byrne*	O'Brien	Spinner
27	H 5/2	25,734	7	30	1-3 L	0-2	Hamilton 69 / [Mills 32 (og), McDowell 37, Best 71] / Ref: P Reeves	Sivell	Burley	Mills	Morris	Hunter	Beattie	Hamilton	Viljoen*	Johnson	Whymark	Lambert	Gates
								Day	Coleman	Lampard	Bonds	Taylor	McGiven	Holland	Paddon	McDowell	Brooking	Best	
28	A 9/2	15,497	3	32	1-0 W	1-0	Morris 39 / Ref: J Williams	Sivell	Burley	Mills	Morris	Peddelty	Beattie	Hamilton	Talbot	Johnson*	Whymark	Lambert	Osborne
								Stevenson	Noble	Newton	Dobson	Waldron	Thomson	Nulty*	Hankin	Fletcher	Collins	Ingham	Casper
29	A 23/2	26,289	4	33	1-1 D	1-0	Whymark 25 / Pratt 55 / Ref: T Reynolds	Sivell	Burley	Mills	Morris	Hunter	Beattie	Hamilton	Talbot	Johnson	Whymark	Lambert	Osborne
								Jennings	Evans	Naylor	Pratt	England	Beal	McGrath	Perryman	Chivers	Peters	Coates	
30	H 26/2	22,414	4	34	1-1 D	0-1	Mills 47 / Garland 29 / Ref: J Hunting	Sivell	Burley	Mills	Morris	Hunter	Beattie	Hamilton*	Talbot	Johnson	Whymark	Lambert	Osborne
								Phillips	Lock	Harris	Hollins	Dray	Webb	Britton	Garland	Kembre	Garner	Cooke	
31	H 2/3	24,988	5	35	1-1 D	0-0	Hamilton 49 / Boyer 81 / Ref: A Hart	Sivell	Burley	Mills	Morris	Hunter	Beattie	Hamilton	Talbot	Johnson	Whymark	Woods	
								Keelan	Machin	Benson*	Stringer	Forbes	Howard	Prophett	McDougall	Suggett	Boyer	Sissons	Kellock
32	A 9/3	23,984	6	35	1-3 L	0-1	Woods 73 / [Sunderland 26, Withe 61, Dougan 85] / Ref: A Jones	Sivell	Mills	Twamley	Morris	Hunter	Beattie	Hamilton	Talbot	Johnson*	Whymark	Woods	Gates
								Pierce	Palmer	Parkin	Bailey	Munro	McAlle	Hibbitt	Sunderland	Withe	Dougan	Daley	
33	A 12/3	10,832	4	37	3-0 W	1-0	Johnson 9, Morris 60, Hamilton 66 / Ref: H New	Sivell	Burley	Mills	Morris	Hunter	Beattie	Hamilton	Talbot	Johnson*	Whymark	Woods	Osborne
								Hope	Badger	Hemsley	Flynn*	Colquhoun	Eddy	Woodward	Garbett	Franks	Currie	Salmon	Nichol
34	H 16/3	22,275	4	38	2-2 D	2-1	Whymark 28, Hamilton 42 / [Kennedy 6, Simpson 78] / Ref: D Nippard	Sivell	Burley	Mills	Morris	Hunter	Beattie	Hamilton	Talbot	Johnson*	Whymark	Woods	Miller
								Wilson	McNab	Nelson	Storey	Simpson	Kelly	George	Brady	Radford	Kennedy	Armstrong	

24 — Johnson heads home from Lambert's cross, but Town are made to pay for not punishing Tony Waddington's side further. Inevitably it is the ex-Portman Road favourite Robertson who plays a part, silencing his barrackers by heading against a post for Hurst to force home the rebound.

25 — Leicester do their bit for the UK fuel crisis by paying for a generator to power their floodlights. Best is dropped but replacement Sivell is not to blame for this result. Morris's handball and Beattie's foul concede penalties and the latter deflects Sammels' pass past Sivell for an own-goal.

26 — The Leicester debacle is forgotten as McMenemy's side are crushed. This time a borrowed generator is used and Lambert turns on the power with a fierce 20-yard opener. Everything they try comes off and the club's record First Division win is sealed by Mills' bizarre dipping shot.

27 — Bonds' long throw in the heavy rain causes panic and Mills can only hook the ball high into his own net. McDowell scores with a long-range screamer before Hunter has a goal disallowed and Hamilton hits a post. Clyde Best quells the mini-revival when he squeezes in a delicate shot.

28 — With an average age of under 23, this is Town's youngest-ever line-up and they battle well in the Turf Moor mud. Morris hits the only goal as his powerful low drive beats Stevenson. Sivell's clearance hits Hankin, who nets the loose ball, but after long deliberations, handball is given.

29 — Improving Spurs hold Town as Pratt capitalises on a Chivers' long throw, hurled high into the danger area. Town have 22 shots on goal, the only success coming when Whymark wins the race to a Morris cross and shoots firmly home. Jennings is kept very active in the first period.

30 — Garland's downward header beats Sivell and Chelsea attempt to sit on their lead. Mills cuts in from the left and lets fly with a great drive to break their resistance. Town are reduced to ten men when Lambert is hospitalized with a fractured skull after an accidental clash with Lock.

31 — Winger Woods plays his usual starring role against his home-town club, but Town are frustrated by John Bond's men. Suggett's late cross is converted by Boyer for his first goal since arriving from Bournemouth for £145,000. Johnson and Morris set up Hamilton's neat opening goal.

32 — More injury worries as debutant Twamley is carried off after Palmer's tackle, shortly after Johnson departs. Sunderland's brilliant overhead kick is followed by Withe netting from close range. Woods gives Town hope with a rising drive, but Sivell is always the busier of the keepers.

33 — A midweek afternoon kick-off to save power results in a small crowd as Town coast to victory in muddy conditions. Johnson heads Town in front from a Mills cross, but later skies a penalty-kick over after Woods is flattened by Badger. Morris cracks home another 25-yard rocket.

34 — Sivell keeps his place as young Cooper is recruited on loan from Birmingham. Kennedy's back-header from Kelly's cross is cancelled out as Whymark holds off Simpson to rifle the ball home. Arsenal save a point when George's overhead kick falls for Simpson to score from close in.

League

#		Opponent	Date	Att.	Pos		Res	Res	HT
35	A	DERBY	23/3	23,860	5	3	L	0-2	0-0
36	H	COVENTRY	30/3	17,404	4	14	W	3-0	1-0
37	A	MANCHESTER C	6/4	22,269	4	11	W	3-1	1-0
38	A	QP RANGERS	12/4	27,567	3	5	W	1-0	0-0
39	H	LIVERPOOL	13/4	33,292	3	2	D	1-1	1-0
40	A	QP RANGERS	15/4	26,093	3	6	W	1-0	0-0
41	A	LEEDS	20/4	44,055	3	1	L	2-3	1-2
42	H	SHEFFIELD UTD	27/4	22,391	4	12	L	0-1	0-1

Home 22,380 Away 25,681 Average 22,380

35 Sivell, Burley, Mills, Morris, Hunter, Beattie*, Hamilton, Talbot, Johnson, Woods, Miller — Osborne
Boulton, Thomas, Nish, Rioch, McFarland, Todd, Powell, Gemmill, Davies, Hector, Bourne
Rioch 51p, Hector 65
Ref: A Morrissey
Shortly after returning from Leipzig, Town fail to impress at Derby. The home side look dominant but Mills feels a penalty is unjust when Hector wilts under his challenge. Rioch slots it home and Hector rubs salt in the wounds by scoring the clincher despite looking clearly offside.

36 Sivell, Burley, Mills, Peddelty, Hunter, Beattie, Hamilton, Talbot, Johnson, Whymark, Woods
Ramsbottom, Smith, Holmes, Mortimer, Craven, Hindley, Cartwright, Alderson, Cross, Carr, Hutchison
Johnson 32, Talbot 72, 83
Ref: E Wallace
Beattie celebrates a call-up to the full England squad by keeping a close eye on Cross and assisting this easy win. Johnson scores after his first effort hits Ramsbottom. Talbot gets the first goal of his career when a mistake lets him through on goal. A second follows from Woods' cross.

37 Sivell, Burley, Mills, Morris, Hunter, Beattie, Hamilton*, Talbot, Johnson, Whymark, Woods — Gates
MacRae, Pardoe, Donachie, Doyle, Barrett, Horswill, Summerbee, Bell, Carrodus, Oakes, Tueart
Johnson 7, Hamilton 68, Morris 79 — Summerbee 65
Ref: H Williams
A first win at Maine Road is prompted by Johnson's glorious volley at the end of a fine move. Hamilton's 20-yarder is his 18th of the season but his first from outside the box! Ron Saunders' men could have been even worse off had Whymark's header not rebounded off the post.

38 Sivell, Burley, Mills, Morris, Hunter, Beattie, Hamilton, Talbot, Johnson, Whymark, Woods
Parkes, Clement, Gillard, Beck, Mancini, Hazell, Thomas, Francis, Leach, Bowles, Givens
Whymark 47
Ref: R Challis
Mr Challis upsets both sides, ruling a Givens goal offside and denying Town a penalty when Woods is manhandled by Clement. The only goal of a lively tussle with Gordon Jago's side comes when Whymark dives to head home the rebound after a Woods effort hits the crossbar.

39 Sivell, Clemence... Burley, Mills, Morris, Hunter, Beattie, Hamilton, Talbot, Johnson, Whymark, Woods
Clemence, Smith, Lindsay, Thompson, Cormack, Hughes, Keegan, Hall, Heighway, Boersma, Callaghan
Whymark 24 — Hughes 63
Ref: H Davey
Town damage Bill Shankly's title hopes, as they dominate the first half. Whymark climbs high above Lindsay to head home but later misses an easier opportunity to wrap things up by shooting over. Liverpool rally and Hughes rescues them a point with a stunning drive from long-range.

40 Sivell, Burley, Mills, Morris, Hunter, Beattie, Hamilton, Talbot, Johnson, Whymark*, Woods — Abbott
Parkes, Clement, Gillard, Venables, Mancini, Hazell, Thomas, Francis, Leach, Bowles, Givens*
Johnson 47
Ref: D Turner
Johnson sustains a nasty head wound that needs stitches, but stays on the pitch after strike partner Whymark picks up an ankle injury. The bloodied hero bursts through to shoot past Parkes for the winner. Francis and Givens go close in the later stages but Town maintain third place.

41 Cooper, Burley, Mills, Morris, Hunter, Beattie, Hamilton, Talbot, Johnson, Osborne, Woods — Gray
Harvey, Reaney, Cherry, Bremner, McQueen, Hunter, Lorimer, Clarke, Jones, Madeley, Gray
Talbot 27, Hamilton 55 — Lorimer 15, Bremner 22, Clarke 69
Ref: K Baker
Champions-elect Leeds race ahead with Lorimer's thunderbolt and Bremner's header. Town bounce back well and Osborne sets up Hamilton's smartly-taken and deserved equaliser. Town get nothing for their endeavours after Clarke appears to use an arm as he collects the winning goal.

42 Sivell, Burley, Mills, Morris, Hunter, Beattie, Hamilton, Talbot, Johnson, Whymark, Woods — Field
Brown, Badger, Hemsley, Eddy, Franks, Flynn, Woodward, Salmons, Cammack, Nicholl, Field
Woodward 32
Ref: T Spencer
After Hunter's careless ball, Cammack beats Mills in the air to set up Woodward who rifles home a winner for Ken Furphy's side. Town need a win to be sure of a UEFA Cup place, but this loss means they slip a place and must rely on Newcastle losing the FA Cup final to Liverpool.

League Cup

#		Opponent	Date	Att.	Pos		Res	Res	HT
2	H	LEEDS	8/10	26,279	13	1	W	2-0	1-0
3	A	FULHAM	31/10	8,964	9	2:13	D	2-2	1-2
3R	H	FULHAM	14/11	21,355	6	2:15	W	2-1	0-1

2 Best, Mills, Harper, Collard*, Hunter, Beattie, Hamilton, Vijoen, Johnson, Whymark, Lambert — Morris
Harvey, Reaney, Cherry, Bremner, Ellam, Hunter, Liddell, Yorath, Jones, Madeley, Gray F* — O'Neill
Johnson 25, Hamilton 77
Ref: J Bent
Leeds are not at full strength for this tie and Town always look to have the upper hand. Beattie's square ball finds Johnson, who powers the ball home from outside the box. Victory is assured when Hamilton seizes on to Lambert's flick and finds the target from a difficult angle.

3 Best, Mills, Harper, Morris, Hunter, Beattie, Hamilton, Vijoen, Woods, Whymark, Lambert — Moreline
Webster, Cutbush, Slough, Mullery, Went, Lacy, Conway Jn, Busby, Mitchell, Lloyd, Barrett*
Whymark 12, Woods 81 — Mullery 24, Barrett 37
Ref: J Hunting
Alec Stock's side put up a real fight and Woods saves the day late when he steers Vijoen's pass wide of Webster. Whymark nets the first with a glorious header, but Mullery levels with a left-foot drive. Barrett heads the Londoners in front from Mullery's pass and later strikes the post.

3R Best, Hammond, Mills, Morris, Hunter, Beattie, Hamilton, Vijoen, Johnson, Whymark, Lambert* — Woods
Webster, Cutbush, Slough, Mullery, Went, Dunne, Conway Jn, Earle, Mitchell, Lloyd, Barrett — Woods
Vijoen 72, Mills 82 — Earle 23
Ref: J Hunting
Conway's effort is blocked by Best and Earle shoots Fulham ahead. After a long wait Vijoen levels, heading home off the underside of the bar. Mitchell misses a sitter and seconds later lucky Town break to the other end and feed the advancing Mills who fires home from 30 yards.

LEAGUE DIVISION 1 (CUP-TIES) Manager: Bobby Robson SEASON 1973-74

League Cup (continued)

4 H BIRMINGHAM 21/11 — Att 12,228 · 22 · L · 6 · F-A 1-3 · H-T 1-0
Scorers/Times: Miller 28; Latchford 46, 61, 74. Ref: B Homewood

	1	2	3	4	5	6	7	8	9	10	11	12 sub used
Town	Best	Hammond	Mills	Morris	Hunter	Beattie	Hamilton	Viljoen	Johnson	Whymark	Miller*	Woods
Opp.	*Sprake*	*Clarke*	*Want*	*Pendrey*	*Hynd*	*Burns*	*Campbell**	*Francis*	*Latchford*	*Hatton*	*Hendrie*	*Phillips*

The fuel crisis means a midweek afternoon kick-off and a low crowd. Miller clips a shot over Sprake and in off the bar. Freddie Goodwin's side forget their lowly league status after the break as Latchford runs riot and collects a real poacher's hat-trick. Sprake has a quiet afternoon.

FA Cup

3 H SHEFFIELD UTD 5/1 — Att 17,929 · 13 · W · 6 · F-A 3-2 · H-T 3-2
Scorers/Times: Hamilton 21, Beattie 44, 45; Salmons 26, Currie 38. Ref: J Bent

	1	2	3	4	5	6	7	8	9	10	11	12 sub used
Town	Best	Burley	Mills	Morris	Hunter	Beattie	Hamilton	Viljoen	Johnson	Whymark	Lambert	
Opp.	*Connaughton*	*Badger*	*Hemsley*	*Flynn*	*Colquhoun*	*Speight*	*Woodward*	*Eddy*	*Dearden*	*Currie*	*Salmons*	

Hamilton fires home Lambert's pass, but the Blades hit back via Salmons' header and Currie's 30-yard gem. In 90 hectic seconds before half-time, Beattie levels with a towering header and then nods in Morris's free-kick. In the last minute Best saves well to prevent a Beattie own-goal.

4 A MANCHESTER U 26/1 — Att 37,177 · 21 · W · 8 · F-A 1-0 · H-T 1-0
Scorers/Times: Beattie 8. Ref: G Hill

	1	2	3	4	5	6	7	8	9	10	11	12 sub used
Town	Sivell	Burley	Mills	Morris	Hunter	Beattie	Hamilton	Viljoen	Johnson	Whymark	Lambert*	Viljoen
Opp.	*Stepney*	*Buchan*	*Forsyth*	*Greenhoff*	*Holton*	*James*	*Morgan*	*Macari*	*McIlroy*	*Young*	*Martin**	*Kidd*

A great start for Town as Johnson heads on Morris's corner and Beattie converts. Forsyth saves on the line from Lambert and penalty appeals are turned down when Holton clatters into Hamilton. United's best attempt at an equaliser sees Morris clear Holton's header off the goal-line.

5 A LIVERPOOL 16/2 — Att 45,340 · 2 · L · 3 · F-A 0-2 · H-T 0-1
Scorers/Times: Hall 33, Keegan 55. Ref: J Hunting

	1	2	3	4	5	6	7	8	9	10	11	12 sub used
Town	Sivell		Mills	Morris	Hunter	Beattie	Hamilton	Talbot	Johnson	Whymark	Lambert*	Viljoen
Opp.	*Clemence*	*Smith*	*Lindsay*	*Thompson*	*Cormack*	*Hughes*	*Keegan*	*Hall*	*Boersma*	*Waddle*	*Callaghan*	

Hall is put through by Callaghan and scores with a fine shot. Keegan makes the tie safe by scoring from close range after Waddle's cross. Bill Shankly's side are in top form and never look in any real danger. Sivell makes a series of fine saves to earn the man-of-the-match accolades.

UEFA Cup

1:1 H REAL MADRID (Spain) 19/9 — Att 25,280 · W · 19 · F-A 1-0 · H-T 0-0
Scorers/Times: Rubinan 52 (og). Ref: S Eksztajn (Poland)

	1	2	3	4	5	6	7	8	9	10	11	12 sub used
Town	Best	Mills	Harper	Collard	Hunter	Beattie	Hamilton	Viljoen	Johnson	Whymark	Lambert*	Miller
Opp.	*Remon*	*Jose Luis*	*Rubinan*	*Pirri*	*Benito*	*Tourino*	*Amancio**	*Grosso*	*Planelles^*	*Netzer*	*Mas*	*Aguilar/Maranon*

Remon's superb save denies Johnson in the opening seconds. Town press confidently but without success until Mills' shot is deflected in by Rubinan. Aguilar shoots home but is given offside. Viljoen keeps a tight rein on Gunter Netzer and Town are delighted to keep a clean sheet.

1:2 A REAL MADRID 3/10 — Att 80,000 · D · 13 · F-A 0-0 · H-T 0-0
Ref: R Vigliani (France) · (Town win 1-0 on aggregate)

	1	2	3	4	5	6	7	8	9	10	11	12 sub used
Town	Best	Mills	Harper	Collard	Hunter	Beattie	Hamilton	Viljoen	Johnson	Whymark	Lambert	Morris
Opp.	*Remon*	*Jose Luis*	*Tourino*	*Pirri**	*Benito*	*Zoco*	*Aquilar*	*Grosso*	*Planelles*	*del Bosque*	*Mas*	*Maranon*

The biggest crowd to witness any Town game fails to intimidate them and Madrid are taken aback by their willingness to attack. Harper's shot hits the underside of the bar and Town create several good chances. Madrid press strongly in the latter stages and Best saves well from Aquilar.

2:1 H LAZIO (Italy) 24/10 — Att 26,433 · W · 11 · F-A 4-0 · H-T 2-0
Scorers/Times: Whymark 17, 43, 47, 62. Ref: B Loow (Sweden)

	1	2	3	4	5	6	7	8	9	10	11	12 sub used
Town	Best	Mills	Harper	Morris	Hunter	Beattie*	Hamilton	Viljoen	Johnson^	Whymark	Lambert	Hammond/Woods
Opp.	*Pulici*	*Facco*	*Martini*	*Wilson*	*Oddi*	*Nanni^*	*Garlaschelli^*	*Re Cecconi*	*Chinaglia*	*Frustalupi*	*Petrelli*	*Manservisi/D'Amico*

Lazio's much-vaunted defence is torn to shreds by deadly Whymark. The Italians lose all discipline after this fourth, which they hotly dispute. The tie becomes a battleground, Beattie and Johnson are taken off injured but, amazingly, there is just one Lazio booking – for shirt-pulling!

2:2 A LAZIO 7/11 — Att 20,000 · L · 7 · F-A 2-4 · H-T 0-2
Scorers/Times: Viljoen 73p, Johnson 89; Garlaschelli 1, Chinaglia 28, 85p, 88. Ref: L Van der Kroft (Holland) · (Town win 6-4 on aggregate)

	1	2	3	4	5	6	7	8	9	10	11	12 sub used
Town	Best	Mills	Harper*	Morris	Hunter	Beattie	Hamilton	Viljoen	Woods*	Whymark	Miller	Hammond/Johnson
Opp.	*Pulici*	*Facco*	*Martini*	*Wilson*	*Oddi*	*Nanni*	*Garlaschelli*	*Re Cecconi*	*Chinaglia*	*Frustalupi*	*D'Amico*	

The first-leg brutality seems small fry compared to the disgraceful scenes here. After Woods is fouled, Town's penalty award sparks a riot, the pitch is invaded and Frustalupi aims flying kicks at Viljoen. Town players race off at the end but are attacked by Lazio players and their fans.

3:1 H TWENTE ENSCHEDE (Holland) 28/11 — Att 18,918 · W · 6 · F-A 1-0 · H-T 0-0
Scorers/Times: Whymark 80. Ref: I Jursa (Czechoslovakia)

	1	2	3	4	5	6	7	8	9	10	11	12 sub used
Town	Sivell	Hammond	Mills	Morris	Keeley	Beattie	Hamilton	Viljoen^	Johnson	Whymark	Achterberg^	Woods
Opp.	*Schrijvers*	*Notten*	*De Vries*	*Van Ierssel*	*Oranen*	*Thijssen*	*Van der Vall^*	*Achterberg*	*Schwemmle*	*Zuidema*	*Pahplatz*	*Gates/Collard*

On a snow-covered pitch, injury-hit Town are foiled by their clever football, particularly Frans Thijssen, of whom Town fans will soon be seeing a lot more. The Dutchmen impress with their clever football, particularly Frans Thijssen. Time is running out when Whymark nets after Woods again hits the frame.

3:2 A TWENTE ENSCHEDE 12/12 — Att 18,000 · W · 7 · F-A 2-1 · H-T 0-0
Scorers/Times: Morris 57, Hamilton 71; Streuer 82. Ref: R Scheurer (Switzerland) · (Town win 3-1 on aggregate)

	1	2	3	4	5	6	7	8	9	10	11	12 sub used
Town	Best	Hammond	Mills	Morris	Hunter	Beattie	Hamilton	Viljoen^	Johnson	Whymark	Achterberg^	Woods
Opp.	*Schrijvers*	*Notten*	*De Vries*	*Van Ierssel*	*Oranen*	*Thijssen*	*Van der Vall^*	*Achterberg*	*Schwemmle*	*Zuidema*	*Pahplatz*	*Brinks/Streuer*

Morris completes a neat move with an emphatic finish. Hamilton clinches victory as he fires home Viljoen's pull-back. Sub Streuer pulls one back with a fine drive and then Town survive a scare as Morris clears Thijssen's effort off the line. Town looked generally superior in the rain.

OF				W				
1	H 6/3	LOKOMOTIV LEIPZIG 26,466 (E Germany)	5	W	1-0	0-0	Beattie 86	Ref: L Somlai (Hungary)
OF				L				
2	A 20/3	LOKOMOTIV LEIPZIG 57,000	4	L	0-1	0-0	Giessner 49	Ref: F Martinez (Spain) (Town lose on penalties)

Match line-ups (Town / Leipzig):

Sivell	Burley	Mills	Hunter	Morris	Beattie	Hamilton	Talbot	Johnson	Whymark	Woods
Friese	Sekora	Grobner	Fritsche	Giessner	Attmann	Hammer	Frenzel	Lisewicz	Matoul	Loewe / Osborne
Sivell	Burley	Mills !	Hunter	Morris	Beattie	Hamilton	Talbot	Johnson	Whymark	Woods*
Friese	Sekora	Grobner	Fritsche	Giessner	Attmann^	Hammer	Frenzel	Lisewicz*	Matoul	Loewe / Woods* / Geisler/Moldt

Town miss the injured Viljoen and Lambert as they toil to break down a tough defence. Mills hits the bar early on. Leipzig are finally broken when Talbot's pass finds Beattie and he steers a left-foot shot home. Four days earlier he was voted the PFA's Young Player of the Year.

Mills is sent off for retaliating against Loewe, but Town almost win as Talbot's late shot hits the bar. After extra-time it is goalless, Town lose a penalty shoot-out when their sixth effort, by Hunter, is saved. During the tense finale, Hunter is spotted having a drag on a borrowed cigarette!

			Home					Away					
		P	W	D	L	F	A	W	D	L	F	A	Pts
1	Leeds	42	12	8	1	38	18	12	6	3	28	13	62
2	Liverpool	42	18	2	1	34	11	4	11	6	18	20	57
3	Derby	42	13	7	1	40	16	4	7	10	12	26	48
4	IPSWICH	42	10	7	4	38	21	8	4	9	29	37	47
5	Stoke	42	13	6	2	39	15	2	10	9	15	27	46
6	Burnley	42	10	9	2	29	16	4	5	10	27	37	46
7	Everton	42	12	7	2	29	14	4	5	12	21	34	44
8	QP Rangers	42	8	10	3	30	17	5	7	9	26	35	43
9	Leicester	42	10	7	4	35	17	3	9	9	16	24	42
10	Arsenal	42	9	7	5	23	16	5	7	9	26	35	42
11	Tottenham	42	9	4	8	26	27	5	10	6	19	23	42
12	Wolves	42	11	6	4	30	18	2	9	10	19	31	41
13	Sheffield Utd	42	7	7	7	25	22	7	5	9	19	27	40
14	Manchester C	42	10	7	4	25	17	4	5	12	14	29	40
15	Newcastle	42	9	6	6	28	21	4	6	11	21	27	38
16	Coventry	42	10	5	6	25	18	4	5	12	18	36	38
17	Chelsea	42	9	4	8	36	29	3	9	9	20	31	37
18	West Ham	42	7	7	7	36	32	4	8	9	19	28	37
19	Birmingham	42	10	7	4	30	21	2	6	13	22	43	37
20	Southampton	42	8	10	3	30	20	3	4	14	17	48	36
21	Manchester U	42	7	7	7	23	20	3	5	13	15	28	32
22	Norwich	42	6	9	6	25	27	1	6	14	12	35	29
		924	218	149	95	674	433	95	149	218	433	674	924

	Appearances								Goals					
	Lge	Sub	LC	Sub	FAC	Sub	Eur	Sub	Lge	Sub	LC	FAC	Eur	Tot
Beattie, Kevin	42		4		3		8		2			3	1	6
Best, David	22		4				5							
Burley, George	20				3		2							
Collard, Ian	8	1	1				2							
Cooper, Paul	1						2						1	
Gates, Eric		6						1						
Hamilton, Bryan	41	1	4		3		8		16		1	1	1	19
Hammond, Geoff	7	1	2				2		1					1
Harper, Colin	14		2				4		2					2
Hunter, Allan	34		2		3		7							
Johnson, David	40		3		3		7		13		1	1		15
Keeley, Glenn	3						1							
Lambert, Mick	26	3	3		3		3		9					9
Miller, John	2	3	1				1						1	1
Mills, Mick	42		4		3		8		2		1			3
Morris, Peter	36		3	1			6		4			1		5
Osborne, Roger	3	6					1						1	
Peddelty, John	5													
Sivell, Laurie	19		2				3							
Talbot, Brian	15		1		2		2		3					3
Twamley, Bruce	1													
Viljoen, Colin	24		4		2		6				1	1		2
Whymark, Trevor	39		4		3		8		11		3	1		17
Woods, Clive	18	9	1	2			5		3			1		4
(own-goals)									1				1	2
24 players used	462	27	44	3	33	1	88	9	67		7	4	11	89

Odds & ends

Double wins: (5) Birmingham, Burnley, Coventry, QPR, Manchester C.

Double losses: (2) Newcastle, Leeds.

Won from behind: (3) Fulham (LC) (h), Sheffield U (FAC) (h), Norwich (a).

Lost from in front: (2) Birmingham (LC) (h), Newcastle (h).

High spots: Qualifying for Europe again.

The seven-goal drubbing of Southampton.

Good displays in all eight European ties.

First-ever victories at Chelsea and Manchester C.

Beattie's England call-up and PFA Young Player award.

Low spots: The disgraceful scenes during the final stages of both Lazio ties.

A long run of injuries preventing a settled side.

Defeat in a penalty shoot-out in Leipzig.

The 5-0 hammering at Leicester.

Player of the Year: Kevin Beattie.

Ever-presents: (2) Kevin Beattie, Mick Mills.

Hat-tricks: (1) Trevor Whymark (4 goals v Lazio).

Opposing hat-tricks: (4) Kevin Keegan, Bob Latchford (LC), Frank Worthington, Giorgio Chinaglia (UEFA).

Leading scorer: (19) Bryan Hamilton.

LEAGUE DIVISION 1 — Manager: Bobby Robson — SEASON 1974-75

No	Date	Att	Pos	Pt	F-A	H-T	Scorers, Times, and Referees	1	2	3	4	5	6	7	8	9	10	11	12 sub used
1	A TOTTENHAM 17/8	26,344		2	W 1-0	0-0	Johnson 68 Ref: G Hill	Sivell	Burley	Mills	Talbot	Hunter	Beattie	Hamilton	Viljoen	Johnson	Whymark	Lambert	
								Jennings	Evans	Naylor	England	Osgood	Coates	McGrath	Perryman	Peters	Peters	Neighbour	
2	A ARSENAL 20/8	31,027		4	W 1-0	0-0	Lambert 86 Ref: D Turner	Sivell	Burley	Mills	Talbot	Hunter	Beattie	Hamilton	Viljoen	Johnson	Whymark	Lambert*	Gates
								Rimmer	Storey	Nelson	Kelly	Simpson	Matthews	Armstrong	Hornsby	Radford	Kidd	Brady	
3	H BURNLEY 24/8	22,324	2	6	W 2-0	1-0	Talbot 35p, Whymark 57 Ref: R Challis	Cooper	Burley	Mills	Talbot	Hunter	Beattie	Hamilton	Viljoen	Johnson	Whymark	Lambert*	Woods
								Stevenson	Noble	Newton	Dobson	Waldron	Rodaway	Nulty	Hankin	Fletcher	Collins	James	
4	H ARSENAL 27/8	28,035	1	8	W 3-0	3-0	Lambert 5, 32, Beattie 9 Ref: T Spencer	Sivell	Burley	Mills	Talbot	Hunter	Beattie	Hamilton	Viljoen	Johnson*	Whymark	Lambert	Woods
								Rimmer	Rice	Nelson	Kelly	Simpson	Matthews	Brady	George	Radford	Kidd	Storey	
5	A SHEFFIELD UTD 31/8	17,963	9	8	L 1-3	0-2	Lambert 79; Mills 34 (og), Field 35, 59 Ref: J Hunting	Sivell	Burley	Mills	Talbot	Hunter	Beattie	Hamilton*	Viljoen	Johnson	Whymark	Lambert	Woods
								Brown	Badger	Hemsley	Eddy	Colquhoun	Franks*	Woodward	Speight	Dearden	Currie	Field	France
6	H EVERTON 7/9	23,386	5	10	W 1-0	1-0	Woods 29 Ref: M Sinclair	Sivell	Burley	Mills	Talbot	Hunter	Beattie	Hamilton	Viljoen	Johnson*	Whymark	Lambert	Woods
								Lawson	Darracott	Seargeant	Clements	Kenyon	Lyons	Buckley*	Dobson	Royle	Latchford	Connolly	Pearson
7	A LUTON 14/9	17,577	20	12	W 4-1	2-0	Talbot 9, 60p, Hamilton 30, [Whymark 80] Alston 67 Ref: T Reynolds	Sivell	Burley	Mills	Talbot	Hunter	Beattie	Hamilton	Viljoen	Woods	Whymark	Lambert*	Gates
								Barber	Shanks	Thomson	Anderson	Faulkner	Ryan	Hindson	Husband	Butlin	West	Alston	
8	H CHELSEA 21/9	23,121	14	14	W 2-0	1-0	Talbot 4, Johnson 51 Ref: H New	Sivell	Burley	Mills	Talbot	Hunter	Beattie	Hamilton	Viljoen	Johnson	Whymark*	Lambert	Osborne
								Phillips	Locke	Houseman	Hollins	Dempsey	Harris	Hay	Garland	Cooke	Hutchinson	Sissons	
9	H STOKE 24/9	24,470	11	16	W 3-1	0-0	Viljoen 60, Hamilton 71, Whymark 76 Salmons 90 Ref: B Daniels	Sivell	Burley	Mills	Talbot	Hunter	Beattie	Hamilton	Viljoen	Johnson	Whymark	Lambert*	Gates
								Farmer	Marsh	Pejic	Mahoney	Smith	Dodd !	Hasletgrave	Hudson	Ritchie*	Greenhoff	Salmons	Robertson
10	A NEWCASTLE 28/9	43,520	6	16	L 0-1	0-0	Howard 61 Ref: W Johnson	Sivell	Burley	Mills	Talbot	Hunter	Beattie	Hamilton	Viljoen	Johnson*	Whymark	Lambert	Gates
								McFaul	Nattrass	Clark	McDermott	Keeley	Howard	Burns	Gibb	MacDonald	Tudor	Hibbitt	

1. A TOTTENHAM — Bill Nicholson is coming to the end of his reign as Spurs boss and there is discontent on the terraces as his side disappoints in a strangely drab opener. Morris has left for Norwich, but there are no new faces in Town's line-up as Johnson's neat winner caps a competent performance.

2. A ARSENAL — Town make it an impressive North London double when Lambert pounces in the dying minutes, but moments later the winger is assisted off with concussion after an accidental clash of heads. A less-than-thrilling game sees Town create most of the genuine scoring opportunities.

3. H BURNLEY — Lambert is hauled down by a desperate Nulty challenge to give Talbot his first success as the club's new penalty taker. Town never look in trouble after this and Hamilton and Whymark both have efforts cleared off the line. Jimmy Adamson's side soon wilt on a hot and sunny day.

4. H ARSENAL — The in-form Lambert tears Bertie Mee's side to shreds with his lightning pace and crisp shooting as Town batter Arsenal in a sensational first half of relentless attacking. Robson says it's the best display he's witnessed and only Rimmer's second-half heroics prevent a bigger scoreline.

5. A SHEFFIELD UTD — The run of clean sheets ends unluckily when Woodward's shot hits the post and bounces over the line off Mills' body. Field's second goal clinches the win as he curls home a real beauty after a long solo run. Lambert grabs a consolation goal after Viljoen feeds him from a free-kick.

6. H EVERTON — A piledriver from Beattie is flicked home by substitute Woods just nine minutes after his early arrival. The match is spoiled by gale-force winds and previously unbeaten Billy Bingham's Everton adopt a robust approach. There are four bookings as Johnson and Mills both pick up injuries.

7. A LUTON — The First Division newcomers are demolished after Town arrive in a smart new £30,000 luxury bus. Talbot's low shot starts the scoring and victory is assured after Ryan holds Gates back and Talbot scores from the spot. Aussie international Alston and Whymark net superb headers.

8. H CHELSEA — Hunter is booked for the third successive game as Town cruise to a comfortable win. The in-form Viljoen creates both goals, finding Talbot in acres of space to shoot home the first and later crossing for Johnson to head firmly home. Johnson and Hamilton both strike the woodwork.

9. H STOKE — Town clinch victory after Dodd handles in midfield and is sent off, having previously been booked. A few minutes earlier Stoke lost Ritchie with a broken leg after Beattie's tackle. Five names go into Mr Daniels' book. Viljoen opens the scoring with a crisp shot in his 300th game.

10. A NEWCASTLE — Burns' free-kick lands at Howard's feet and he blasts home the winner from close range. Keeley looks strong against his former team and the home side deserves its win, only Sivell's saves preventing further Town misery. Full-back Hammond is sold to Manchester City for £40,000.

11 A QP RANGERS 5/10 — 1 L 17 16 — 0-0 — 19,494
Francis 56
Ref: I Jones

Town	QPR
Sivell	Parkes
Mills	Clement
Harper	Gillard
Talbot	Beck
Hunter	Mancini
Beattie	Hazell
Hamilton	Thomas
Viljoen	Francis
Johnson	Leach*
Woods	Bowles
Lambert	Givens
	Rogers

Town look jaded after their midweek trip to Enschede and are sunk by Francis' mis-hit shot which bobbles into the net with Mancini and Sivell both stretching but missing it. Johnson is bundled over by Francis' challenge from behind in the closing minutes but no penalty is awarded.

---

12 H LEEDS 12/10 — 1 D 17 17 — 0-0 — 29,815
Ref: A Hart

Town	Leeds
Sivell	Harvey
Mills	Reaney
Harper	Cherry
Talbot	Yorath
Hunter	McQueen
Beattie	Hunter
Woods	Lorimer
Viljoen	Clarke
Johnson	Jordan
Whymark	Giles
Lambert	Cooper

The reigning champions and the current leaders are locked together in a titanic struggle. Jimmy Armfield's side count themselves lucky to get away with a point after a fine game which sees Talbot and Beattie both hit the woodwork and keeper Harvey make a series of superb saves.

---

13 A BURNLEY 15/10 — 2 L 10 17 — 0-1 — 17,711
Fletcher 44
Ref: P Reeves

Town	Burnley
Sivell	Stevenson
Mills	Newton
Harper	Brennan
Talbot	Flynn
Hunter	Waldron
Beattie	Rodaway
Woods	Noble
Viljoen	Hankin
Johnson*	Fletcher
Whymark	Collins
Lambert	James
Hamilton	

A third successive single-goal away defeat after Fletcher is left unmarked to score at the far post. Stevenson and Sivell are both in good form with the latter making a brilliant save from James in the closing minutes. Mills' shot goes narrowly wide and Lambert's effort thumps the post.

---

14 A WEST HAM 19/10 — 3 L 10 17 — 0-1 — 33,543
Jennings 34
Ref: R Perkin

Town	West Ham
Sivell	Day
Mills	Coleman
Harper	Lampard
Talbot	Bonds
Hunter	Taylor
Beattie	Lock
Hamilton	Jennings
Collard	Paddon
Johnson	Gould
Woods	Brooking
Lambert*	Robson
Gates	

The team bus gets stuck in traffic and manager Robson runs to the ground with his team-sheet to beat the deadline. Jennings jinks past several challenges to fire in after good work by Bryan Robson. Town's best effort sees Talbot's powerful shot smash against the underside of the bar.

---

15 H MANCHESTER C 26/10 — 3 D 2 18 — 1-1 — 25,177
Hamilton 16
Bell 66
Ref: R Toseland

Town	Manchester C
Sivell	McRae
Mills	Hammond
Harper	Donachie
Talbot	Doyle
Hunter	Clarke
Beattie	Oakes
Hamilton	Summerbee
Collard	Bell
Johnson	Marsh
Whymark	Henson
Lambert	Barrett
Woods*	

The League goal-drought ends as Hamilton fires in off the bar. Beattie and Sivell misjudge a cross by Henson and Bell scores an easy leveller. Hammond is booked on his return to Portman Road for a tackle on Woods. Miller is the latest departure, joining Norwich for a £42,500 fee.

---

16 H LIVERPOOL 2/11 — 2 W 1 20 — 1-0 — 30,575
Talbot 84
Ref: J Bent

Town	Liverpool
Sivell	Clemence
Mills	Smith
Harper	Lindsay
Talbot	Lawler
Hunter	Boersma*
Beattie	Hughes
Hamilton*	Keegan
Viljoen	Hall
Johnson	Heighway
Woods	Kennedy
Lambert	Callaghan
	Cormack

A deserved victory in a hectic game is sealed when Talbot brushes off a challenge and toe-pokes the ball past Clemence. Town are angry not to get a penalty when Callaghan diverts Lambert's shot past the post with his hands. Woods gives veteran Smith a torrid time on the right flank.

---

17 A WOLVERHAMPTON 9/11 — 4 L 12 20 — 1-2 — 20,123
Woods 31
Hibbit 5, Munro 63
Ref: A Jones

Town	Wolverhampton
Sivell	Parkes
Mills	Palmer
Harper	Parkin
Talbot	Bailey
Hunter	Munro
Beattie	McAlle
Hamilton	Hibbit
Viljoen	Powell
Woods	Richards
Whymark	Sunderland
Lambert*	Farley

Hamilton strikes the post after three minutes but Town promptly fall behind to Hibbit's fine solo effort. Woods equalises with a deflected shot. Richards hits the post from a tight angle, but Bill McGarry's side sneak ahead when Munro heads in from close range after Town's best spell.

---

18 H COVENTRY 16/11 — 1 W 16 22 — 4-0 — 21,176
Johnson 46, 60, 72, Talbot 63p
Ref: P Walters

Town	Coventry
Sivell	Glazier
Mills	Smith
Harper	Cattlin
Talbot	Mortimer
Hunter	Lloyd
Beattie	Hindley
Hamilton*	Holmes
Viljoen	Carr
Johnson	Stein
Whymark	Cross
Lambert	Hutchison
Lee	

Johnson registers the first Town League hat-trick for nearly seven years. The best goal sees Harper feed Viljoen wide on the left and his cross is headed powerfully home by Johnson. Gordon Milne's skilful side are saved in the first half by Glazier's heroics, but crumble after the break.

---

19 A DERBY 23/11 — 3 L 5 22 — 0-2 — 24,341
Hector 8, Rioch 28
Ref: B Homewood

Town	Derby
Sivell	Boulton
Burley	Webster
Harper	Nish
Talbot	Rioch
Peddelty	Daniel
Mills	Todd
Hamilton	Newton
Viljoen*	Gemmill
Johnson	Davies
Whymark	Hector
Woods	Lee
	Osborne

Rioch's short-corner routine sees Hector net with a looping header. With the defence all at sea, Rioch fires home off the post. With Hunter suspended and Beattie injured, things get worse as Viljoen and Johnson complain of feeling unwell and Mills is limping with an ankle injury.

---

20 H CARLISLE 30/11 — 2 W 21 24 — 3-1 — 20,122
Hamilton 3, Johnson 19, Lambert 82
O'Neill 54
Ref: T Spencer

Town	Carlisle
Sivell	Ross
Mills	Carr
Harper	Gorman
Talbot	O'Neill
Peddelty	Green
Beattie	Parker
Hamilton	Martin
Viljoen	Train*
Johnson	Clarke
Whymark*	Prudham
Lambert	Laidlaw
	Barry

Woods has a first-minute effort mysteriously ruled out, but Hamilton converts after being set up by Viljoen and Johnson. O'Neill gives Alan Ashman's outfit a glimmer of hope with a long-range swerving shot, but they are foiled by Lambert's clinching goal which looks well offside.

---

21 A MIDDLESBROUGH 7/12 — 5 L 8 24 — 0-3 — 23,735
Souness 23, 25, Foggon 49
Ref: M Lowe

Town	Middlesbrough
Sivell	Platt
Burley	Spraggon
Mills	McAndrew
Talbot*	Souness
Hunter	Boam
Beattie	Madden*
Hamilton	Brine
Viljoen	Hickton
Johnson	Willey
Whymark	Foggon
Lambert	Armstrong
	Smith

The dreadful run of away results continues. Souness rockets home a drive through Town's defensive wall, then fires in another after Hickton miskicks Willey's cross. Injury-hit 'Boro' clinch the win from their only corner of the day when Foggon volleys home from Brine's flag-kick.

LEAGUE DIVISION 1

Manager: Bobby Robson

SEASON 1974-75

No	Date	V	Opponent	Att	Pos	Pt	F-A	H-T	Scorers, Times, and Referees	1	2	3	4	5	6	7	8	9	10	11	12 sub used
22	14/12	H	TOTTENHAM	20,812	5	26	W 4-0	2-0	Viljoen 13, Beattie 27, Lambert 53, [Osborn 80] — Ref: D Turner	Sivell	Burley	Mills	Talbot	Hunter	Beattie	Osborne	Viljoen	Johnson*	Whymark	Lambert	Collard
			Tottenham		*16*					*Jennings*	*Beal*	*Knowles*	*McNab**	*England*	*Naylor*	*Coates*	*Perryman*	*McGrath*	*Peters*	*Duncan*	*Pratt*
23	20/12	A	LEICESTER	18,636	1	28	W 1-0	1-0	Whymark 23 — Ref: J Rice	Sivell	Burley	Mills	Talbot	Hunter*	Peddelty	Osborne	Viljoen	Johnson	Whymark	Lambert	Hamilton
			Leicester		*20*					*Jayes*	*Whitworth*	*Yates*	*Earle*	*Munro*	*Cross*	*Weller**	*Waters*	*Worthington*	*Birchenall*	*Glover*	*Stringfellow*
24	26/12	H	LUTON	23,406	3	28	L 0-1	0-0	Futcher R 90 — Ref: D Nippard	Sivell	Burley	Mills	Talbot	Peddelty	Beattie	Osborne	Hamilton	Johnson	Whymark	Lambert	
			Luton		*22*					*Horn*	*John Ryan*	*Buckley*	*Anderson*	*Faulkner*	*Futcher P*	*Jim Ryan*	*Husband*	*Futcher R*	*West*	*Aston*	
25	28/12	A	BIRMINGHAM	30,266	1	30	W 1-0	1-0	Osborne 2 — Ref: J Williams	Sivell	Burley	Mills	Talbot	Peddelty	Roberts	Osborne	Viljoen	Woods	Whymark	Lambert*	Collard
			Birmingham		*16*					*Latchford*	*Page*	*Styles*	*Kendall*	*Gallagher*	*Pendrey*	*Campbell**	*Taylor*	*Burns*	*Hatton*	*Calderwood*	*Hendrie*
26	11/1	H	MIDDLESBROUGH	24,720	1	32	W 2-0	1-0	Osborne 24, Johnson 90 — Ref: R Tinkler	Sivell	Burley	Mills	Talbot	Peddelty	Beattie	Osborne	Viljoen	Johnson	Whymark*	Lambert	Woods
			Middlesbrough		*3*					*Platt*	*Craggs*	*Spraggon*	*Souness*	*Boam*	*Madden*	*Murdoch*	*Mills*	*Hickton*	*Foggon**	*Armstrong*	*Willey*
27	18/1	A	CARLISLE	13,054	2	32	L 1-2	1-1	Whymark 35 / Clarke 25, Laidlaw 50 — Ref: D Richardson	Sivell	Burley	Mills	Talbot	Hunter	Beattie	Osborne*	Viljoen	Johnson	Whymark	Lambert	Woods
			Carlisle		*19*					*Ross*	*Spearritt*	*Gorman*	*O'Neill*	*Green*	*Parker*	*Martin*	*Train*	*Owen*	*Laidlaw*	*Clarke*	
28	1/2	H	WOLVERHAMPTON	22,184	2	34	W 2-0	2-0	Beattie 22, Viljoen 27 — Ref: L Hayes	Sivell	Burley	Mills	Talbot	Hunter	Beattie	Collard	Viljoen	Johnson*	Whymark	Lambert	Woods
			Wolverhampton		*16*					*Parkes*	*Williams*	*Parkin*	*Bailey*	*Jefferson*	*McAlle*	*Hibbitt**	*Powell*	*Richards*	*Kindon*	*Daley*	*Withe*
29	8/2	A	LIVERPOOL	47,421	4	34	L 2-5	1-3	Beattie 27, Whymark 68 / Hall 5, Tck 9, 65, L'lsay 40, C'm'k 88 — Ref: P Partridge	Sivell	Burley	Mills	Talbot	Hunter	Beattie	Collard*	Viljoen	Johnson	Whymark	Lambert	Woods
			Liverpool		*5*					*Clemence*	*Neal*	*Lindsay*	*Thompson*	*Cormack*	*Hughes*	*Keegan*	*Hall*	*Heighway*	*Toshack**	*Callaghan*	*McDermott*
30	22/2	A	COVENTRY	16,973	6	34	L 1-3	0-0	Hunter 86 / Ferguson 73, Green 84, 90 — Ref: P Willis	Sivell	Burley	Mills	Talbot	Hunter	Beattie	Hamilton	Viljoen	Johnson*	Whymark	Lambert	Woods
			Coventry		*15*					*Ramsbottom*	*Oakey*	*Cattlin*	*Cartwright*	*Lloyd*	*Dugdale*	*Carr*	*Alderson*	*Ferguson*	*Green*	*Hutchison*	
31	25/2	H	DERBY	23,132	4	36	W 3-0	2-0	Johnson 12, Hamilton 42, Beattie 66 — Ref: R Perkin	Sivell	Burley	Mills	Talbot	Hunter	Beattie	Hamilton	Viljoen	Johnson*	Whymark	Lambert	Woods
			Derby		*7*					*Boulton*	*Thomas*	*Nish*	*Rioch*	*Daniel*	*Todd*	*Newton*	*Gemmill*	*Bourne*	*Hector*	*Lee**	*Powell*

22 — Tottenham: Already missing two regulars, Town go down to ten men as Johnson and Whymark go off for treatment but just seconds later take the lead! Lambert's corner is headed home by Beattie and victory is assured when Lambert volleys home. Osborne neatly rounds Jennings for the fourth.

23 — Leicester: The 'shattered' Beattie is axed following the much-publicised episode in which he got off a train to visit his family home in Carlisle instead of completing a journey to join the England U-23 party. Whymark fires home Johnson's cross then performs heroically as a stand-in defender.

24 — Luton: Desperate for a point, Harry Haslam's Luton frustrate leaders Town with their tactics and then cause a real shock by grabbing an injury-time winner. Ron Futcher, making his debut at the age of 17, rises to head home a fine goal from Aston's right-wing cross after 92 minutes' play.

25 — Birmingham: Town's injury crisis gets worse. This line-up cost nothing in transfer fees and featured teenage debutant Roberts. Osborne scores early after Lambert's corner sees Mills' header blocked on the line. Sivell protects the points, saving superbly from Kendall's fierce shot from distance.

26 — Middlesbrough: Town never look in trouble in this top-of-the-table clash. Osborne tucks home the vital breakthrough goal and Lambert and Viljoen both hit the woodwork before the late clincher. A delighted Robson sticks his neck out and suggests his team are now looking like genuine title contenders.

27 — Carlisle: Carlisle cling on for victory despite missing a twice-taken penalty. Parker's first effort is saved, but Sivell moved early, O'Neill then shoots wide. Town old boys Spearritt and Clarke inspire the home side to a well-earned win and are relieved to see a fine shot by Lambert hit the post.

28 — Wolverhampton: Ex-Town defender Jefferson gives away a series of free-kicks with robust challenges, two of which are taken by Viljoen and converted into goals. Williams appears to foul Collard inside the area but no penalty is given. Everton's 1-0 win over Tottenham keeps Town off the top spot.

29 — Liverpool: Liverpool, hungry for revenge, race into an early lead and are outstanding in an entertaining game. Town's last hope of salvaging something vanishes when Mills, attempting an equaliser, sees his shot hit a post and rebound to Clemence, who clears upfield to set up Lindsay's clincher.

30 — Coventry: Hutchison ties Town in knots as the poor away run continues. He strikes the bar in the early stages and helps end the stalemate in the final 20 minutes by creating both of City's opening goals. Town look uninspired in attack and lose Johnson at half-time with a badly swollen ankle.

31 — Derby: Robson rallies his troops after the Coventry 'disaster' and Town respond with a fine display. Lambert's corner produces a glorious Johnson headed goal, then Johnson's cross is chested down by Lambert for Hamilton to score. Lively but fragile Johnson is withdrawn to save his legs.

Season match-by-match record (Ipswich Town)

32 — SHEFFIELD UTD (H) 1/3
- Attendance: 21,813 — Pos: 4 L 12 36
- Result: 0-1 (HT 0-0)
- Ipswich: Sivell, Burley, Mills, Talbot, Hunter, Beattie, Hamilton, Viljoen, Johnson, Whymark*, Lambert, Woods
- Sheffield Utd: *Brown, Badger, Hensley, Eddy, Colquhoun, Flym, Woodward, Speight, Dearden, Currie, Field*
- Scorers: Woodward 65
- Ref: G Kew

Ken Furphy's squad defend well and break effectively when a flagging linesman is overruled in the build-up to Woodward's well-taken goal. Mr Kew incurs further wrath by disallowing a Mills effort in the dying moments. Robson admits he is perplexed by his side's inconsistency.

33 — NEWCASTLE (H) 15/3
- Attendance: 23,070 — Pos: 4 W 13 38
- Result: 5-4 (HT 2-3)
- Ipswich: Sivell, Burley, Mills, Talbot, Hunter, Beattie, Hamilton, Viljoen, Johnson, Whymark, Lambert, Woods
- Newcastle: *McFaul, Craig D, Barker, Smith, McCaffery, Nattrass*, Barrow'gh, Tudor, MacDonald, Gibb, Craig T*
- Scorers: Ham'ton 4, 54, 64, H'ter 34, J'son 51; MacDonald 7, 84, Tudor 21, 41
- Ref: K Styles

A remarkable match played on a muddy pitch produces several magnificent goals. MacDonald's brace features powerful shooting with both feet and Town's fifth sees Hamilton convert a breathtaking effort. Town's defence takes an unexpected pounding from Joe Harvey's team.

34 — STOKE (A) 18/3
- Attendance: 28,585 — Pos: 2 W 5 40
- Result: 2-1 (HT 0-0)
- Ipswich: Sivell, Burley, Mills, Talbot, Hunter, Beattie, Hamilton, Osborne, Johnson, Whymark*, Lambert*, Woods
- Stoke: *Shilton, Marsh*, Lewis, Mahoney, Smith, Dood, Skeels, Greenhoff, Moores, Hudson, Salmons, Hurst*
- Scorers: Whymark 56, Mills 66; Greenhoff 61
- Ref: W Gow

Bad feeling from previous encounters rises to the surface and the foul count exceeds 40. In hauling down Lambert, Smith breaks his own leg, but only departs after several minutes of hobbling around. Mills forces home his first goal for over a year to win a very bad-tempered affair.

35 — EVERTON (A) 22/3
- Attendance: 46,269 — Pos: 2 D 1 41
- Result: 1-1 (HT 1-0)
- Ipswich: Sivell, Burley, Mills, Talbot, Hunter, Beattie, Hamilton, Viljoen, Johnson, Whymark*, Lambert, Woods
- Everton: *Davies, Scott, Seargeant, Clements, Kenyon, Hurst, Buckley, Pearson, Lyons, Latchford, Jones*
- Scorers: Whymark 1; Lyons 60
- Ref: J Hunting

Whymark pops up to shock Everton after 66 seconds. Johnson nearly doubles the lead only to hesitate when in the clear and Davies races out and handles the ball to prevent a goal and is booked for his trouble. The relieved leaders save a point via Joe Royle's temporary replacement.

36 — LEICESTER (H) 29/3
- Attendance: 28,745 — Pos: 3 W 20 43
- Result: 2-1 (HT 0-1)
- Ipswich: Sivell, Twamley, Mills, Talbot, Hunter, Wark, Hamilton, Viljoen, Austin, Whymark*, Lambert, Woods
- Leicester: *Wallington, Whitworth, Rofe, Lee, Blockley, Cross, Weller, Sammels, Worthington, Birchenall*, Garland, Glover*
- Scorers: Woods 47, Viljoen 68; Worthington 27
- Ref: D Biddle

Jimmy Bloomfield's in-form Leicester succumb to a patched-up Town side which rallies superbly after the break, thanks partly to great support from the fans. With five men missing, Town were easily second-best in the first half and relieved to see City defied twice by the woodwork.

37 — CHELSEA (A) 31/3
- Attendance: 35,005 — Pos: 4 D 18 44
- Result: 0-0 (HT 0-0)
- Ipswich: Sivell, Burley, Mills, Osborne, Hunter, Wark, Hamilton, Viljoen, Austin*, Whymark, Lambert, Woods
- Chelsea: *Phillips, Locke, Harris, Hollins, Wicks, Hinton, Kember, Hay, Langley, Britton, Cooke, Gates*
- Ref: K Baker

Ron Suart's Chelsea are defiantly battling to avoid relegation and scoring chances are rare in a scrappy encounter on Easter Monday. Robson is grateful for a point and counts his walking wounded for the Birmingham game just 24 hours later – the club's 25th fixture in just ten days.

38 — BIRMINGHAM (H) 1/4
- Attendance: 27,417 — Pos: 4 W 17 46
- Result: 3-2 (HT 1-1)
- Ipswich: Cooper, Mills, Collard, Talbot, Hunter, Beattie, Hamilton, Viljoen, Woods, Whymark, Lambert*, Gates
- Birmingham: *Kelly, Calderwood, Bryant, Page, Gallagher, Pendrey, Hendrie, Morton, Burns, Hatton, Emmanuel*
- Scorers: Collard 44, Woods 55, Lambert 66; Burns 21, Hatton 76
- Ref: H Davey

Cooper's second game of the season is against his old team-mates, who like Ipswich have just achieved a rare place in the FA Cup semi-finals. A full-blooded encounter sees Town bounce back to the top of the League, Lambert returning from injury to strike home the decisive goal.

39 — QP RANGERS (H) 12/4
- Attendance: 28,684 — Pos: 4 W 11 48
- Result: 2-1 (HT 0-0)
- Ipswich: Sivell, Burley, Mills, Talbot, Wark, Beattie, Hamilton, Viljoen, Johnson*, Whymark*, Lambert, Woods
- QP Rangers: *Parkes, Shanks, Pritchett, Masson, McLintock*, Gillard, Thomas, Francis, Beck, Bowles, Givens, Abbott*
- Scorers: Hamilton 72, Whymark 75; Gillard 90
- Ref: K Burns

Dave Sexton's side are looking for a European place and give Town a tough time, particularly on the heels of the nightmare FA Cup semi-final experience. Resilient Parkes, in superb form, is finally beaten when two fine strikes in a three-minute spell.

40 — LEEDS (A) 19/4
- Attendance: 30,174 — Pos: 4 L 8 48
- Result: 1-2 (HT 1-1)
- Ipswich: Sivell, Burley, Mills, Talbot, Hunter, Beattie, Hamilton, Osborne, Johnson*, Whymark, Lambert, Woods
- Leeds: *Letheren, Reaney, Cherry, Bremner, McQueen, Hunter, Lorimer, Madeley, Yorath, Giles*, Gray E, Harris*
- Scorers: Talbot 26; Cherry 39, Harris 62
- Ref: R Lee

Championship hopes are virtually buried as Jimmy Armfield's side come back from a goal down to win when debutant Harris nets after Sivell can only parry Bremner's effort to him. Leeds levelled rather luckily when Cherry's long-range pot-shot deflected past Sivell off Hamilton.

41 — MANCHESTER C (A) 23/4
- Attendance: 29,391 — Pos: 4 D 10 49
- Result: 1-1 (HT 0-1)
- Ipswich: Sivell, Burley, Mills, Talbot, Hunter, Beattie, Hamilton, Osborne, Johnson*, Whymark, Lambert, Woods
- Manchester C: *Corrigan, Hammond, Donachie, Doyle, Booth, Oakes, Hartford, Bell, Marsh, Daniels, Tueart*
- Scorers: Hamilton 66; Bell 4
- Ref: K Styles

Penalty claims are turned aside as Hamilton crashes over in the City box, but City break upfield to score through Bell. A spectacular Marsh overhead kick is disallowed for offside before Daniels... – but a point is not enough to prevent Derby claiming the championship crown.

42 — WEST HAM (H) 26/4
- Attendance: 31,592 — Pos: 3 W 13 51
- Result: 4-1 (HT 1-1)
- Ipswich: Sivell, Burley, Mills, Talbot, Hunter, Beattie, Hamilton, Viljoen, Woods, Whymark, Lambert
- West Ham: *Day, Coleman, Lampard, Holland, McDowell, Lock, Jennings, Best, Taylor A, Brooking, Gould*
- Scorers: Talbot 28, Whymark 62, Beattie 87, [Hunter 90]; Holland 37
- Ref: D Turner

No title, but Town are roared to a UEFA place by an enthusiastic crowd. Scrambling home two late goals provides a flattering scoreline, with mid-table West Ham nearly spoiling the party, having had decent claims for a penalty turned down just before Town's third killed the contest.

Average — Home 24,924 — Away 27,121

LEAGUE DIVISION 1 — Manager: Bobby Robson — SEASON 1974-75

League Cup

Rnd			Att			F-A	H-T	1	2	3	4	5	6	7	8	9	10	11	12 sub used
2	A COVENTRY 10/9	13,211	2 / 20	W	2-1	0-1		Sivell	Burley	Mills	Talbot	Peddelty	Beattie	Hamilton	Viljoen	Woods	Whymark	Lambert	Craven
								Glazier	*Oakey*	*Cattlin*	*Mortimer*	*Lloyd*	*Dugdale*	*McGuire**	*Alderson*	*Stein*	*Carr*	*Hutchison*	*Craven*
3	H HEREFORD 8/10	16,337	1 / 3:15	W	4-1	3-0		Sivell	Mills	Harper	Talbot	Hunter	Beattie*	Woods	Viljoen	Johnson	Whymark	Lambert	Osborne
								Hughes	*Emery*	*Byrne*	*Moran*	*Layton*	*Rudge*	*Tyler*	*Paine*	*Redrobe**	*McNeil*	*Evans*	*Lee*
4	H STOKE 12/11	20,661	4 / 8	W	2-1	0-0		Sivell	Mills	Harper	Talbot	Hunter	Beattie	Hamilton	Viljoen	Johnson	Whymark	Woods	Lambert
								Farmer	*Lewis*	*Pejic*	*Mahoney*	*Smith*	*Dodd*	*Robertson*	*Hudson*	*Moores*	*Greenhoff*	*Salmons*	
5	A NORWICH 4/12	34,731	2 / 2:3	D	1-1	1-1		Sivell	Mills	Harper	Talbot	Hunter	Beattie	Hamilton	Viljoen	Johnson*	Whymark	Woods	Lambert
								Keelan	*Machin*	*Sullivan*	*Morris*	*Forbes*	*Stringer*	*Miller**	*MacDougall*	*Boyer*	*Suggett*	*Powell*	*Grapes*
5R	H NORWICH 10/12	29,228	6 / 2:3	L	1-2	1-1		Sivell	Burley	Mills	Talbot	Hunter	Beattie	Hamilton*	Viljoen	Johnson	Whymark	Woods	Lambert
								Keelan	*Machin*	*Sullivan*	*Morris*	*Forbes*	*Stringer*	*Miller*	*MacDougall*	*Boyer*	*Suggett*	*Powell*	*Lambert*

Scorers, Times, and Referees

- **2 COVENTRY:** Whymark 58, Hamilton 67 / Stein 17. Ref: R Matthewson. Hunter is missing due to transfer talks with Leicester which break down. City deservedly take the lead through Stein's powerful header from Mortimer's cross. Whymark heads in Viljoen's free-kick. Viljoen creates the winner, feeding Beattie who chests down for Hamilton to score.
- **3 HEREFORD:** Johnson 2, Talbot 14, Hunter 39, Evans 58 [Whymark 54]. Ref: R Tinkler. Lambert's early corner is headed home by Johnson and Town never look real threat from these renowned giant-killers. Best goal of the night arrives when Hunter climbs high to head home the third. Talbot, the side's new penalty-taker, fires wide with his 24th-minute attempt.
- **4 STOKE:** Hamilton 59, Johnson 72 / Robertson 90. Ref: R Challis. Town have a let-off just before the interval as Greenhoff hits the woodwork. Hamilton is left unmarked to head the first goal and Johnson bursts clear to seize Harper's through-ball and hit the second. Ex-Town favourite Robertson manages a last-minute consolation with a header.
- **5 NORWICH:** Whymark 40 / Suggett 17. Ref: J Taylor. Town apply pressure in the early stages but against the run of play City forge ahead. Whymark's header is scooped away by the agile Keelan, but Mr Taylor rules it had already crossed the line. Moments later Hamilton nearly makes it two, but hits the post. A draw is a fair outcome.
- **5R NORWICH:** Johnson 30 / Miller 34, 47. Ref: J Taylor. Miller, who joined City from Ipswich just six weeks earlier, has a night to remember, gliding home MacDougall's cross to equalise, then ramming the winner high into the net after taking Boyer's pass and rounding Sivell. Johnson had put Town ahead after a goalmouth scramble.

FA Cup

Rnd			Att			F-A	H-T	1	2	3	4	5	6	7	8	9	10	11	12 sub used
3	A WOLVERHAMPTON 4/1	28,542	1 / 12	W	2-1	1-1		Sivell	Burley	Mills	Talbot	Peddelty	Beattie	Osborne	Viljoen	Johnson	Woods	Lambert	
								Parkes	*Palmer*	*Parkin*	*Bailey*	*Munro*	*McAlle*	*Hibbitt*	*Powell*	*Richards*	*Kindon*	*Farley*	*Woods*
4	H LIVERPOOL 25/1	34,709	2 / 4	W	1-0	0-0		Sivell	Burley	Mills	Talbot*	Hunter	Beattie	Collard	Viljoen	Johnson	Woods	Lambert	Woods
								Clemence	*Neal*	*Lindsay*	*Thompson*	*Cormack*	*Hughes*	*Keegan*	*Hall*	*Heighway*	*Toshack*	*Callaghan*	
5	H ASTON VILLA 15/2	31,297	6 / 2:4	W	3-2	0-1		Sivell	Burley	Mills	Talbot	Hunter	Beattie	Woods*	Viljoen	Johnson	Whymark	Lambert	Hamilton
								Cumbes	*Robson*	*Aitken*	*Ross*	*Rioch*	*McDonald*	*Graydon*	*Evans*	*Leonard*	*Hamilton*	*Carrodus*	
QF	H LEEDS 8/3	38,010	4 / 6	D	0-0	0-0		Sivell	Burley	Mills	Talbot	Hunter	Beattie	Hamilton	Viljoen	Johnson	Whymark	Lambert	
								Stewart	*Madeley*	*Gray F*	*Bremner*	*McQueen*	*Hunter*	*Yorath*	*Clarke*	*Jordan*	*Giles*	*Gray E*	
QF R	A LEEDS 11/3	50,074	4 / 6	D	1-1 aet	1-0		Sivell	Burley	Mills	Talbot	Hunter	Beattie	Hamilton	Viljoen	Johnson	Whymark	Lambert*	
								Stewart	*Reaney**	*Gray F*	*Bremner*	*Madeley*	*Hunter*	*Lorimer*	*Clarke*	*Jordan*	*Giles*	*Yorath*	*Woods*
2R	N LEEDS 25/3 (At Filbert Street)	35,195	2 / 11	D	0-0 aet	0-0		Sivell	Burley	Mills	Talbot	Hunter	Beattie	Hamilton	Viljoen	Johnson	Whymark	Woods*	Osborne
								Stewart	*Reaney*	*Gray F*	*Bremner*	*Madeley*	*Hunter*	*Lorimer**	*Clarke*	*Jordan*	*Giles*	*Yorath*	*MacKenzie*

Scorers, Times, and Referees

- **3 WOLVERHAMPTON:** Viljoen 44, Johnson 85 / Richards 14. Ref: W Gow. A rip-roaring cup-tie in which Town produce a battling performance to pinch victory from a Wolves side who had more of the ball and created more clear-cut chances. Town fans are ecstatic as the patched-up Beattie heads back Lambert's corner for Johnson to head in the late winner.
- **4 LIVERPOOL:** Mills 86. Ref: P Partridge. The Portman Road crowd record is broken and they witness a thrilling battle in the mud. Honours are even in the first period, with Toshack's lob hitting the bar. Town apply constant pressure after the break and win it late when Burley heads down Beattie's cross and Mills stabs it in.
- **5 ASTON VILLA:** Johnson 63, Hamilton 77, 85 / McDonald 11, Evans 49. Ref: B Homewood. Attempting to reach their second cup final of the season, Second Division Villa storm into a deserved two-goal lead. Johnson pulls one back, but the FA Cup dream looks dead until Hamilton's arrival transforms Town. The fans are jubilant as the last eight is reached for the first time.
- **QF LEEDS:** Ref: E Wallace. The ground record is smashed again and the gates are closed nearly an hour before kick-off. Despite the rain and mud, the match flows well and Johnson goes agonisingly close when a neat chip hits the bar and rebounds on to Stewart. McQueen's shot is pushed on to the post by Sivell.
- **QF R LEEDS:** Mills 17 / McKenzie 90. Ref: E Wallace. A fine header subdues a huge crowd, but Leeds pile on late pressure and Lorimer's last-minute shot is blocked by Beattie but falls to McKenzie who volleys home. It's backs-to-the-wall stuff in extra-time for Town, and an own-goal by Allan Hunter is ruled out for pushing.
- **2R LEEDS:** Ref: J Taylor. A second replay takes the teams to Leicester's Filbert Street. Another hectic encounter remains deadlocked with both keepers making crucial saves. Sivell foils Jordan twice and Stewart rises to the occasion after the interval. The stalemate means real fixture congestion for both sides.

FA Cup

3R	2/3	(At Filbert Street)	19,5?0 11		Clarke 33, Giles 13		Ref: J Taylor

Stewart · Reaney* · Gray F · Bremner · Madeley · Hunter · Gray E · Clarke · Jordan · Giles · Yorath · McKenzie

Back to Filbert Street and after more than 400 minutes' play, a tremendous curling shot from the edge of the box by Woods settles a real epic tie. Beattie's injury gives 17-year-old Wark a pressure-cooker debut. An unforgettable night for the fans who managed another day off work!

SF	N 5/4	WEST HAM	58,000 12	(At Villa Park)	4 D	0-0	0-0	Ref: C Thomas

Sivell · Burley · Mills · Talbot · Hunter · Beattie · Hamilton · Woods · Whymark · Viljoen* · Lambert · Gould* · Osborne · Holland
Day · McDowell · Lampard · Bonds · Taylor T · Lock · Jennings · Paddon · Taylor A · Brooking

With Johnson already out, Town's big day is spoiled by an injury crisis. Beattie is hurt in the opening minutes but returns as a limping forward, with Whymark dropping back as an emergency defender. Hunter goes off after a clash with Gould and Burley and Hamilton are also injured.

SF R	N 9/4	WEST HAM	45,344 12	(At Stamford Bridge)	4 L 12	1-2	1-1	Jennings 44 (og) / Taylor A 28, 82 · Ref: C Thomas

Sivell · Burley · Mills · Talbot · Hunter · Beattie · Hamilton · Woods · Whymark · Viljoen* · Lambert · Gould · Holland
Day · McDowell · Lampard · Bonds · Taylor T · Lock · Jennings* · Paddon · Taylor A · Brooking

Day blocks a Mills shot, but Hamilton nets the rebound. The linesman indicates a goal but to Town's fury, Mr Thomas overrules him and gives offside. John Lyall's side go ahead, but Jennings slices Lambert's corner into his own net to level matters. Taylor's 20-yard drive is decisive.

UEFA Cup

1:1	H	TWENTE ENSCHEDE	28,047	(Holland)	1 D	2-2	2-1	Hamilton 33, Talbot 38 / Zuidema 22, Pahlplatz 84 · Ref: H Weyland

Sivell · Burley · Mills · Talbot · Hunter · Beattie · Hamilton · Woods · Viljoen* · Whymark · Lambert · Gates/Collard · Woods · Gates/Collard
Ardesch · Van Ierssel · Drost · De Vries · Oranen · Thijssen* · Harper · Bos · Zuidema · Pahlplatz · Notten · Overweg/Jeuring

Zuidema produces a delightful finish to Pahlplatz's pass, but Hamilton heads home Whymark's knock-down. Town forge ahead when Talbot side-foots home Burley's low cross. An entertaining match ends all square after casual defending lets in Pahlplatz in a breakaway Dutch raid.

1:2	A	TWENTE ENSCHEDE	18,000		1 D	1-1	1-1	Hamilton 14 / Bos 7 · Ref: P Schiller

(Town lose on away goals)

Sivell · Burley · Harper · Talbot · Hunter · Beattie · Hamilton · Woods · Johnson* · Whymark · Lambert · Gates · Woods · Gates
Ardesch · Van Ierssel · Drost · De Vries · Oranen · Thijssen · Van der Vall · Bos* · Zuidema · Pahlplatz · Notten · Jeuring*/Overweg

A sweet half-volley from Whymark's pass brings Hamilton an equaliser. Skilful Twente are severely hampered by losing their goalscorer Bos to an early injury and then his replacement Jeuring suffers the same fate. Ardesch's superb save keeps a Talbot shot out in the 87th minute.

Appearances and Goals

	Appearances								Goals				
	Lge	Sub	FAC	Sub	LC	Sub	Eur	Sub	Lge	LC	FAC	Eur	Tot
Austin, Terry	2												
Beattie, Kevin	37		5		8		2		6				6
Burley, George	31		2		9		2						
Collard, Ian	5	2	1		1				1				1
Cooper, Paul	2												
Gates, Eric		2						6				2	2
Hamilton, Bryan	33	2	4		6	1	2		10	2	3	2	17
Harper, Colin	10	3			2		2						
Hunter, Allan	36		4		7		2		3		1		4
Johnson, David	35		4		7		2		9	3	3		15
Lambert, Mick	31	5	2	2	7		7		7				7
Mills, Mick	42		9		5				2				2
Osborne, Roger	10	2	1	1	1		3		3				3
Peddelty, John	6	1			1								
Roberts, Dale	1												
Sivell, Laurie	40		5		9		2						
Talbot, Brian	40		5		9		2		8		1	1	10
Twamley, Bruce	1												
Viljoen, Colin	37		5		9		2		4		1		5
Wark, John	3		2										
Whymark, Trevor	40		5		8		2		10	3	1		14
Woods, Clive	20	16	5		6	2	2		4			1	5
(own-goals)									1				1
22 players used	**462**	**33**	**55**	**3**	**99**	**6**	**22**	**3**	**66**	**10**	**11**	**3**	**90**

Odds & ends

Double wins: (5) Tottenham, Arsenal, Stoke, Leicester, Birmingham.

Double losses: (1) Sheffield Utd.

Won from behind: (6) Newcastle (h), Leicester (h), Birmingham (h). Coventry (a) (LC), Wolves (a) (FAC), Aston Villa (h) (FAC).

Lost from in front: (2) Leeds (a), Norwich (h) (LC).

High spots: The best home record in Division One. Qualification for Europe again. An increase in average home attendances. Long runs in both domestic cups. Overcoming Leeds after a four-match FA Cup marathon.

Low spots: Missing out on an FA Cup final place in controversial circumstances. Seven successive League away defeats in the autumn. The early exit from the UEFA Cup. The shock League Cup defeat by local rivals Norwich.

Player of the Year: Colin Viljoen.

Ever-presents: (1) Mick Mills (League only).

Hat-tricks: (2) David Johnson, Bryan Hamilton.

Opposing hat-tricks: (0).

Leading scorer: (17) Bryan Hamilton.

League Table

		P	W	D	L	F	A	W	D	L	F	A	Pts
			Home					Away					
1	Derby	42	14	4	3	41	18	7	7	7	26	31	53
2	Liverpool	42	14	5	2	44	17	7	7	7	16	22	51
3	IPSWICH	42	17	2	2	47	14	6	3	12	19	30	51
4	Everton	42	10	9	2	33	19	6	9	6	23	23	50
5	Stoke	42	12	7	2	40	18	5	8	8	24	30	49
6	Sheffield Utd	42	12	7	2	35	20	6	6	9	23	31	49
7	Middlesbro	42	11	7	3	33	14	7	5	9	21	26	48
8	Manchester C	42	16	3	2	40	15	2	7	12	14	39	46
9	Leeds	42	10	8	3	34	20	6	5	10	23	29	45
10	Burnley	42	11	6	4	40	29	6	6	9	28	38	45
11	QP Rangers	42	10	4	7	25	17	6	6	10	29	37	42
12	Wolves	42	12	5	4	43	21	2	6	13	14	33	39
13	West Ham	42	10	6	5	38	22	3	7	11	20	37	39
14	Coventry	42	8	9	4	31	27	4	6	11	20	35	39
15	Newcastle	42	12	4	5	39	23	3	5	13	20	49	39
16	Arsenal	42	10	6	5	31	16	3	5	13	16	33	37
17	Birmingham	42	10	4	7	34	28	4	5	12	19	33	37
18	Leicester	42	8	7	6	25	17	4	5	12	21	43	36
19	Tottenham	42	8	4	9	29	27	5	4	12	23	36	34
20	Luton	42	8	6	7	22	26	3	5	13	20	39	33
21	Chelsea	42	4	9	8	22	31	5	6	10	20	41	33
22	Carlisle	42	8	2	11	22	21	4	3	14	21	38	29
		924	235	124	103	753	460	103	124	235	460	753	924

LEAGUE DIVISION 1

Manager: Bobby Robson — SEASON 1975-76

Results

No	Date	Venue	Opponent (opp. pos.)	Att	Pos	Pt	Res	F-A	H-T	Scorers, Times, and Referees
1	16/8	H	NEWCASTLE	27,680		0	L	0-3	0-2	MacDonald 27, 68, Craig 43p; Ref: K Styles
2	20/8	A	TOTTENHAM (5)	28,311		1	D	1-1	0-0	Viljoen 52, Duncan 72; Ref: T Spencer
3	23/8	A	LEEDS (5)	30,912	22	1	L	0-1	0-0	Lorimer 57; Ref: E Wallace
4	26/8	H	BURNLEY (13)	23,579	20	2	D	0-0	0-0	Ref: R Toseland
5	30/8	H	BIRMINGHAM (21)	22,659	17	4	W	4-2	4-0	Johnson 7, Whymark 34, 43p, [Hamilton 35] Hatton 75, 77; Ref: G Kew
6	6/9	A	COVENTRY (6)	17,622	15	5	D	0-0	0-0	Ref: R Tinkler
7	13/9	H	LIVERPOOL (7)	28,151	12	7	W	2-0	1-0	Johnson 5, Austin 80; Ref: J Taylor
8	20/9	A	MANCHESTER U (1)	50,513	15	7	L	0-1	0-1	Houston 28; Ref: M Lowe
9	23/9	H	NORWICH (10)	35,077	15	9	W	2-0	0-0	Beattie 55, Hamilton 65; Ref: K Baker
10	27/9	H	MIDDLESBROUGH (5)	22,321	16	9	L	0-3	0-1	Foggon 3, Armstrong 74, Hickton 87p; Ref: R Challis

Line-ups

No	Team	1	2	3	4	5	6	7	8	9	10	11	12 sub used
1	Town	Sivell	Burley	Mills	Talbot	Wark	Beattie	Hamilton	Viljoen	Johnson	Whymark*	Lambert	Osborne
1	Newcastle	Mahoney	Nattrass	Kennedy	Nulty	Howard	Hibbitt	Burns	Bruce	MacDonald	Gowling	Craig	
2	Town	Cooper	Burley	Mills	Talbot	Hunter	Beattie	Hamilton	Viljoen	Austin	Osborne	Lambert*	Lambert
2	Tottenham	Jennings	Naylor*	Knowles	Pratt	Osgood	McAllister	McNab	Perryman	Chivers	Jones	Neighbour	Duncan
3	Town	Cooper	Burley	Mills	Talbot	Hunter	Beattie	Hamilton	Viljoen	Johnson	Whymark*	Lambert	Osborne
3	Leeds	Harvey	Reaney	Gray F	Hunter	McQueen	Cherry	Lorimer	Clarke	McKenzie	Yorath	Gray E	
4	Town	Cooper	Burley	Mills	Talbot	Hunter	Beattie	Hamilton	Osborne	Johnson	Whymark	Lambert*	Austin
4	Burnley	Stevenson	Docherty	Newton	Noble	Waldron	Thomson	Flynn	Hankin	Summerbee	Collins	James	
5	Town	Cooper	Burley	Mills	Talbot	Hunter	Beattie	Hamilton	Osborne	Johnson	Whymark	Lambert*	Austin
5	Birmingham	Latchford	Martin	Bryant	Kendall	Gallagher	Burns	Hope	Francis	Withe	Hatton	Pendrey	
6	Town	Cooper	Burley	Mills	Talbot	Hunter	Beattie	Hamilton	Osborne	Johnson	Whymark*	Lambert	Woods
6	Coventry	King	Oakey	Brogan	Craven	Dugdale	Holmes	Coop	Mortimer	Cross	Green	Hutchison	
7	Town	Cooper	Burley	Mills	Osborne	Hunter	Peddelty	Hamilton	Viljoen	Johnson*	Whymark	Woods	Austin
7	Liverpool	Clemence	Neal	Jones	Smith	Cormack	Hughes	Keegan	McDermott	Heighway	Kennedy	Callaghan	
8	Town	Cooper	Burley	Mills	Osborne	Hunter	Beattie	Hamilton*	Viljoen	Johnson	Whymark	Woods	Lambert
8	Manchester U	Stepney	Nicholl	Houston	McCreery	Greenhoff	Buchan	Coppell	McIlroy	Pearson	Macari	Daly	
9	Town	Cooper	Burley	Mills	Osborne	Hunter	Beattie*	Hamilton	Viljoen	Lambert	Whymark	Woods	Austin
9	Norwich	Keelan	Machin	Butler	Morris	Forbes	Powell	McGuire	MacDougall*	Boyer	Suggett	Peters	Stringer
10	Town	Cooper	Burley	Mills	Osborne	Hunter	Beattie	Hamilton	Viljoen	Lambert*	Whymark	Woods	Gates
10	Middlesbrough	Platt	Craggs	Cooper	Souness	Boam	Maddren	Brine	Mills	Hickton	Foggon	Armstrong	

Match notes

1 — Newcastle. The battle of the England centre-forwards is emphatically won by MacDonald who cracks home two goals and is tripped by Sivell for Craig's penalty. Well-beaten Town go closest through two shots by Mills, one of which hits a post. It is the club's first opening-day defeat in 16 years.

2 — Tottenham. Hunter's return stabilises the defence and Town look much sharper all round. Viljoen, left out of the England squad, nets with a deflected shot, but Town's future manager equalises soon after arriving as sub. Osborne scores in the dying moments but a linesman spotted an infringement.

3 — Leeds. Robson hits out at the criticism and pressure being put on Town's two goalkeepers. Cooper looks at fault when Lorimer's shot gets past him, but redeems himself by keeping Leeds at bay after this. Town again look harder off-colour and are not helped by an injury worry over Viljoen.

4 — Burnley. Robson calls for more effort and enthusiasm in a 'clear-the-air' team talk and this leads to a much-improved display. Burnley are put on the back foot for much of the game and Hamilton and Johnson go agonisingly close, the latter hitting the side-netting with only Stevenson to beat.

5 — Birmingham. Over three hours of home action without a goal ends when Johnson sends in a cracking low drive through a crowded area. The floodgates open and the game is won by the interval, but Freddie Goodwin's men salvage some pride in a late rally. Robson is angry with his side for easing up.

6 — Coventry. Mortimer's long-range effort produces a good save by Cooper as the defence gives a sound display. Chances are limited but Hamilton and Johnson both have shots cleared off the goal-line. Lambert, playing on with a foot injury, goes to ground but penalty appeals are waved away.

7 — Liverpool. Brushing aside a growing injury crisis, Woods sets up Johnson who rises above Jones to head the vital early breakthrough. Johnson is carried off with a rib injury and his replacement knocks home the clincher from close range. Bob Paisley's men are mostly on top but short of bite.

8 — Manchester U. After the fine win at Feyenoord, Town fail to get going in the first half and Tommy Docherty's table-toppers scramble a close-range goal from Houston after a corner-kick. A burst of attacking after the break by Town sees Mills go closest when his effort strikes Stepney's woodwork.

9 — Norwich. Portman Road's second-biggest ever crowd roars Town to the first home League win over the old enemy in ten years. Powell makes a brilliant goal-line clearance from Woods, who along with Hunter, has a phenomenal game. Lively Beattie scores, gets booked and then goes off injured.

10 — Middlesbrough. Town's highly-praised 'bacon and eggs' duo of Beattie are at fault with all three goals. Jack Charlton's direct style destroys Town. On a slippery pitch, Hunter drags back David Mills for the penalty. Perhaps some players are conscious of the big night in Europe looming?

11 A DERBY 4/10
26,056 — 16 / 5 / 9 — L 0-1 0-1
Lee 64
Ref: P Partridge

Town: Cooper · Burley · Mills · Osborne* · Hunter · Hamilton · Gates · Johnson · Whymark · Woods · Turner
Derby: Boulton · Thomas · Nish · Rioch · McFarland · Powell · Gemmill · Lee · Hector · George

Both teams had barely recovered from fine midweek European victories and this showed in a dour first half. Lee is felled by Mills, but penalty appeals are ignored. Moments later Lee exacts revenge. Town's defence appears to cope well without Beattie, who has a nagging back injury.

---

12 A STOKE 11/10
21,975 — 15 / 11 / 11 — W 1-0 1-0
Hamilton 30
Ref: J Hunting

Town: Cooper · Burley · Mills · Osborne · Hunter · Hamilton · Viljoen · Johnson · Whymark · Woods* · Austin
Stoke: Shilton · Dodd · Pejic · Mahoney · Smith · Bloor · Haslegrave · Greenhoff · Moores · Hudson · Salmons* · Marsh

Hunter and Beattie, whose tackles the previous season broke the legs of Ritchie and Smith, are jeered continually and coins are thrown. After the game Hunter has to use his size to dispel a threatening mob of home fans. Robson praises his players' resolve in the face of such pressures.

---

13 H LEICESTER 18/10
23,418 — 14 / 20 / 12 — D 1-1 1-1
Whymark 29 · Lee 44
Ref: M Taylor

Town: Cooper · Burley · Mills · Osborne · Hunter · Hamilton · Viljoen · Johnson · Whymark · Woods
Leicester: Wallington · Whitworth · Rofe · Woollett · Blockley · Kember · Weller · Sammels · Worthington · Alderson · Lee

Jimmy Bloomfield's struggling Leicester are allowed off the hook as Town dominate the first half. Johnson gets clean through but fails to convert and Wallington saves well from scorer Whymark. A poor second half suggests Town's thoughts are on another looming European tie.

---

14 A MANCHESTER C 25/10
30,644 — 14 / 9 / 13 — D 1-1 1-1
Hamilton 18 · Bell 40
Ref: E Wallace

Town: Cooper · Beattie* · Mills · Osborne · Hunter · Hamilton · Mills · Austin · Whymark · Woods · Sharkey
Manchester C: Corrigan · Clements · Donachie · Doyle · Booth · Oakes · Barnes · Watson · Hartford · Tueart

Hamilton scores a wonderful goal, jinking past three defenders before thundering a shot past Corrigan. This comes shortly after a glaring miss. Bell levels with a classic diving header, but injury-hit Town hold on. Robson says that 48 hours after the match ten men were having treatment.

---

15 H ASTON VILLA 1/11
24,687 — 12 / 15 / 15 — W 3-0 1-0
Peddelty 44 · Whymark 56 · Hamilton 63
Ref: M Sinclair

Town: Cooper · Burley · Mills · Osborne · Hunter · Hamilton · Gates · Austin* · Whymark · Woods · Johnson
Aston Villa: Burridge · Gidman · Aitken · Ross · Nicholl · Phillips* · Graydon · Gray · Deehan · Carrodus · McDonald

A typical Whymark goal, a towering header as he climbs above Nicholl, clinches the points. Ron Saunders' side looked full of fight earlier on, pulling men behind the ball whenever possession was lost. A set-piece routine ends with Hamilton sliding home a sweet third goal for Town.

---

16 A WOLVERHAMPTON 8/11
16,191 — 12 / 20 / 15 — L 0-1 0-0
Daley 90
Ref: A Robinson

Town: Cooper · Burley · Beattie · Osborne · Hunter · Hamilton · Mills · Johnson · Whymark* · Woods · Austin
Wolverhampton: Pierce · Palmer · Parkin · Daley · Munro · McAlle · Hibbitt · Carr · Richards · Sunderland · Farley*

Bill McGarry's relegation-bound side are jubilant with a last-minute winner from man-of-the-match Daley. The game was a shocker and a real hangover from the UEFA Cup nightmare of three days earlier. After the promise of recent years this season seems in danger of falling apart.

---

17 H QP RANGERS 15/11
25,543 — 11 / 4 / 16 — D 1-1 1-0
Peddelty 38 · Givens 53
Ref: T Reynolds

Town: Cooper · Burley · Beattie · Osborne · Hunter · Hamilton · Mills · Johnson · Whymark · Woods · Austin
QP Rangers: Parkes · Clement · Gillard · Leach · McLintock · Webb · Thomas · Francis · Masson · Hollins · Givens

Dave Sexton's surprise title-challengers are rejuvenated after the break and deserve their point. Town dominate the opening period, as skipper Mills runs the show in midfield on this 400th appearance for the first team. He will be rewarded with a testimonial at the end of the campaign.

---

18 A LEICESTER 22/11
20,115 — 12 / 17 / 17 — D 0-0 0-0
Ref: R Lee

Town: Cooper · Burley · Beattie · Osborne · Hunter · Hamilton · Mills · Johnson · Whymark · Woods
Leicester: Wallington · Whitworth · Rofe · Kember · Blockley · Weller · Woollett · Garland · Alderson · Worthington

Cooper looks in fine form and Jimmy Bloomfield's side are foiled by a quartet of world-class saves. Many are surprised when Town sell their prolific scorer Hamilton to Everton for a fee of only £40,000, particularly as the club had made a record profit of £165,000 the previous year.

---

19 H SHEFFIELD UTD 29/11
20,802 — 12 / 22 / 18 — D 1-1 0-1
Whymark 83 · Peddelty 39 (og)
Ref: B Homewood

Town: Cooper · Burley · Beattie* · Osborne · Hunter · Hamilton · Woods · Johnson · Whymark · Lambert · Austin
Sheffield Utd: Brown · Badger · Garner · Eddy · Colquhoun · Franks · Cammack* · Johnstone · Guthrie · Bradford · Woodward · Dearden

Before the game optimistic Mills has a flutter on Town to win the title at 100-1, but those odds lengthen when Jimmy Sirrell's bottom-of-the-table team steals a point. Ex-Celtic winger Johnstone sends in a teasing cross and Peddelty deflects it into goal. Keeper Brown plays a blinder.

---

20 A EVERTON 6/12
24,601 — 12 / 10 / 19 — D 3-3 1-2
Lambert 39 · Johnson 83 · Woods 86
Dobson 5, 60 · Latchford 28
Ref: A Hamil

Town: Cooper · Burley · Beattie · Osborne · Talbot* · Hunter · Mills · Johnson · Whymark · Lambert · Gates
Everton: Lawson · Darracott · Clements · Bernard · Kenyon · Hamilton* · Lyons · Dobson · Latchford · Telfer · Jones · Pearson

Hamilton has a fine home debut against his old team, helping create both Dobson goals. For the first, Latchford seems to impede Cooper and Town fury increases as Darracott's handball is ignored. Lambert volleys in after a bad back-pass and Woods' deflected shot evens matters up.

---

21 H LEEDS 13/12
26,855 — 11 / 6 / 21 — W 2-1 0-0
Lambert 69 · Peddelty 75 · McKenzie 82
Ref: J Bent

Town: Cooper · Beattie · Talbot · Osborne · Hunter · Peddelty · Woods · Johnson · Whymark · Woods · Lambert
Leeds: Harvey · Reaney · Gray F · Bremner · Madeley · Cherry · Lorimer · Clarke · McKenzie · Yorath · Gray E

With Talbot back from his broken leg, Town look strong going forward. In a fine match Whymark lays on two goals in six minutes to upset Jimmy Armfield's side. Bremner's drive is pushed onto the crossbar by Cooper and Reaney is in place to head off the line from Whymark.

In each match the Town line-up is given on the first row and the opponents' line-up (in italics) on the second row. The italic number in the Pos column is the opponents' position.

No	Date		Att	Pos	Pt	F-A	H-T	Scorers, Times, and Referees	1	2	3	4	5	6	7	8	9	10	11	12 sub used
22	A 20/12	NEWCASTLE	25,098	11 / *13*	22	D 1-1	1-0	Talbot 34; Nulty 46; Ref: R Matthewson	Cooper	Burley	Beattie	Talbot	Hunter	Roberts	Woods	Mills	Johnson	Whymark	Lambert	
									Mahoney	*Nattrass*	*Kennedy*	*Nulty*	*Craig D*	*Howard*	*Burns*	*Barrowcl'gh*	*MacDonald*	*Gowling*	*Craig T*	
23	H 26/12	ARSENAL	28,476	11 / *18*	24	W 2-0	1-0	Woods 6, Hunter 77; Ref: K Baker	Cooper	Burley	Beattie	Talbot	Hunter	Peddelty	Woods	Mills*	Johnson	Whymark	Lambert	Osborne
									Rimmer	*Rice*	*Kelly*	*Storey*	*O'Leary*	*Powling*	*Armstrong*	*Ball*	*Radford*	*Kidd*	*Brady*	
24	A 27/12	WEST HAM	32,741	11 / *6*	26	W 2-1	0-0	Lambert 49, Peddelty 84; Taylor T 75p; Ref: T Spencer	Cooper	Burley	Beattie	Talbot	Hunter	Peddelty	Woods	Mills	Austin	Whymark	Lambert	
									Day	*Coleman**	*McDowell*	*Holland*	*Taylor T*	*Lock*	*Taylor A*	*Paddon*	*Brooking*	*Jennings*	*Robson !*	*Curbishley*
25	A 10/1	LIVERPOOL	40,547	9 / *3*	27	D 3-3	1-2	Whymark 30, 83, Gates 65; Keegan 13, 33, Case 78; Ref: D Civil	Cooper	Burley	Beattie	Talbot*	Hunter	Peddelty	Osborne	Mills	Johnson	Whymark	Gates	Woods
									Clemence	*Smith*	*Neal*	*Thompson*	*Kennedy*	*Hughes*	*Keegan*	*Case*	*Heighway*	*Toshack*	*Callaghan*	
26	H 17/1	COVENTRY	23,543	10 / *14*	28	D 1-1	1-1	Osborne 13; Murphy 12; Ref: L Hayes	Cooper	Burley	Tibbott	Talbot	Hunter	Beattie	Osborne	Mills	Johnson	Whymark	Lambert*	Gates
									Blyth	*Coop*	*Brogan*	*Craven*	*Dugdale*	*Holmes*	*Powell**	*Green*	*Cross*	*Murphy*	*Hutchison*	*Oakey*
27	H 31/1	TOTTENHAM	24,049	10 / *14*	28	L 1-2	0-1	Johnson 86; Coates 2, Osgood 83p; Ref: R Challis	Cooper	Burley	Mills	Talbot*	Hunter	Beattie	Woods	Osborne	Johnson	Whymark	Lambert	Gates
									Jennings	*Walford*	*McAllister*	*Pratt*	*Young*	*Osgood*	*Coates*	*Perryman*	*Duncan*	*Jones*	*Neighbour*	
28	A 7/2	BURNLEY	17,307	8 / *21*	30	W 1-0	0-0	Beattie 57p; Ref: T Bosi	Cooper	Burley	Beattie	Mills	Hunter	Wark	Woods	Osborne	Johnson	Austin	Lambert	
									Peyton	*Newton*	*Scott*	*Ingham*	*Waldron*	*Thomson*	*Morley*	*Flynn*	*Summerbee*	*Fletcher*	*Noble*	
29	H 17/2	WOLVERHAMPTON	19,301	8 / *20*	32	W 3-0	2-0	Beattie 4, 28, Whymark 76; Ref: M Sinclair	Cooper	Burley	Beattie	Mills	Hunter	Peddelty	Woods*	Osborne	Austin	Whymark	Lambert	Gates
									Parkes	*Palmer*	*Parkin*	*Hibbitt**	*McAlle*	*Carr*	*O'Hara*	*Jefferson*	*Daley*	*Gould*	*Richards*	*Bell*
30	A 21/2	QP RANGERS	22,593	8 / *2*	32	L 1-3	0-0	Lambert 81; Wark 68 (og), Webb 86, Thomas 89; Parkes; Ref: H Davey	Cooper	Burley	Beattie*	Mills	Wark	Peddelty	Woods	Osborne	Austin	Whymark	Lambert	Johnson
									Parkes	*Clement*	*Gillard*	*Leach**	*Hollins*	*Webb*	*Thomas*	*Francis*	*Masson*	*Bowles*	*Givens*	*McLintock*
31	A 6/3	ASTON VILLA	32,477	8 / *14*	33	D 0-0	0-0	Ref: A Lees	Sivell*	Burley	Mills	Sharkey	Hunter	Peddelty	Woods	Osborne	Johnson	Whymark	Lambert	Austin
									Burridge	*Gidman*	*Robson*	*Ross*	*Nicholl*	*Phillips*	*Graydon*	*Little**	*Gray*	*Mortimer*	*Carrodus*	*McDonald*

Match reports

22 — Newcastle: Town looked set to avenge their opening-day hammering, but settle for a point after long periods of dominance. Their luck is out as Hunter's effort thuds against the post. The unbeaten run goes on and there's good news as long-term injury victim Viljoen gets the all-clear after x-rays.

23 — Arsenal: One-way traffic on Boxing Day as Town completely dominate. Cooper has just one save to make, foiling an Armstrong effort. With better finishing it could have been a hammering. Peddelty, proving a useful auxiliary attacker, hits the bar as Bertie Mee's side back-pedal furiously.

24 — West Ham: Robson is booked for an ugly tackle on Woods and later retaliates on Burley, landing a punch on the full-back. After his exit, Paddon crashes to the ground and earns a penalty to level the scores. He admits later he'd dived, but the future policeman Peddelty ensures justice is done.

25 — Liverpool: Town bounce back three times to knock the Reds off top spot. Gates shines in his new role behind the two main strikers. Whymark's vintage header provides the first. Gates, fed by Osborne, nets with a smart angled drive and Whymark bulldozes the ball into the net from close range.

26 — Coventry: In a bruising encounter, Cooper is motionless as Murphy cracks home a superb half-volley. Osborne bravely levels and is injured in the process as he slides the ball past the on-rushing Blyth. Ex-Town winger Frank Brogan pays a visit to see old friends and watch brother Jim in action.

27 — Tottenham: A first home defeat for 18 weeks on a rock-hard pitch and in an icy wind. Spurs deserve the win after Coates slips past Beattie and fires home a rising drive. Jones is bundled over by Cooper for Osgood's penalty. Johnson nods in a late consolation after Jennings blocks Lambert's effort.

28 — Burnley: Thomson climbs over Austin and a controversial penalty is awarded, Beattie converting his first spot-kick for the club. Joe Brown's side could have few complaints because more clear-cut awards were turned down earlier when Lambert was tripped and Newton appeared to handle.

29 — Wolverhampton: Revenge for the cup defeat puts Wolves in serious relegation danger and lifts Town into the top six for the first time this season. Beattie lashes in a left-foot drive, then a towering header, and looks set for a remarkable hat-trick but steers the easiest of his three chances wide of the post.

30 — QP Rangers: Town look set for a point at title-chasing Rangers, until Wark blasts home a spectacular own-goal when trying to clear a Francis cross. Lambert nips in to level as defenders dither. Mills' clearance hits Webb and ricochets past stranded Cooper, who is also at fault with Thomas' late third.

31 — Aston Villa: Cooper is dropped, but replacement Sivell's comeback is clouded by dreadful facial injuries incurred when he dives to save at the feet of Gray in the closing minutes. He is carried off covered in blood and will need 11 stitches in the mouth area, has lost several teeth and has a black eye.

Match-by-match results

---

32 — H STOKE — 13/3
Position/Result/Pts: 9 D 34 · Att 22,860 · 10 · HT 0-0 · FT 1-1
Scorers: Osborne 83 / Smith 53 — Ref: D Biddle

Town: Cooper, Burley, Mills, Sharkey, Hunter, Peddelty, Woods*, Osborne, Johnson, Whymark, Lambert (Austin)
Stoke (italic): Shilton, Marsh, Pejic, Mahoney, Smith, Dodd, Haslegrave, Greenhoff, Moores, Hudson, Salmons

Yet another bruising battle with the Potters ends all square with Town really only coming to life in the later stages. Shilton makes a great reflex save from Whymark's header and this sparks the revival that brings Osborne's leveller. Pejic clears off the line to save Stoke a point.

---

33 — A SHEFFIELD UTD — 20/3
Position/Result/Pts: 7 W 36 · Att 15,220 · 22 · 2-1
Scorers: Johnson 2, Mills 31 / Colquhoun 18 — Ref: P Partridge

Town: Cooper, Burley, Beattie*, Sharkey, Hunter, Peddelty, Woods*, Osborne, Johnson, Whymark, Lambert (Woods)
Sheffield Utd (italic): Brown, Goulding, Garner, Franks, Colquhoun*, Flynn, Woodward, Johnstone, Guthrie, Currie, Edwards, Speight

The Blades bounce back from a nightmare start as Colquhoun heads home a corner, but his effort is parried by Brown. It falls for Mills to inflict the home side's tenth home defeat.

---

34 — H EVERTON — 27/3
Position/Result/Pts: 7 W 38 · Att 22,370 · 16 · 1-0
Scorers: Whymark 33p — Ref: A Turvey

Town: Cooper, Burley, Mills, Sharkey, Hunter, Peddelty, Osborne, Talbot, Johnson*, Whymark, Lambert (Woods)
Everton (italic): Lawson, Bernard, Jones, Lyons, McNaught, Buckley, Hamilton, Dobson, Telfer, Pearson, Connolly

A dreary encounter is won and lost when Town old boy Hamilton is penalised for alleged handball – he claims the ball hit his hip – and Whymark tucks the kick home. Billy Bingham's side look in a bad way, while Town now have an outside chance of the last UEFA Cup spot.

---

35 — A NORWICH — 31/3
Position/Result/Pts: 7 L 38 · Att 31,021 · 12 · 0-1
Scorers: Peters 39 — Ref: J Taylor

Town: Cooper, Burley, Mills, Sharkey, Hunter, Peddelty, Osborne, Talbot, Johnson, Whymark, Lambert (Woods)
Norwich (italic): Keelan, Morris, Sullivan, McGuire, Davids, Powell, Miller, MacDougall*, Boyer, Suggett, Peters, Steele

Town can have few complaints about this local derby defeat. John Bond's Canaries look chirpy as MacDougall forces a breathtaking save from Cooper and Boyer strikes the post. Peddelty is dispossessed by Peters who strides forward and fires past Cooper to win both points.

---

36 — A MIDDLESBROUGH — 3/4
Position/Result/Pts: 10 L 38 · Att 15,000 · 9 · 0-1
Scorers: Mills 24, Armstrong 81 — Ref: K McNally

Town: Cooper, Burley, Tibbott, Sharkey, Hunter, Peddelty, Johnson, Talbot, Austin, Whymark*, Lambert (Gates)
Middlesbrough (italic): Cuff, Craggs, Cooper, Souness, Boam, McAndrew, Brine, Mills, Woof, Smith, Armstrong

Town are doubled by a side missing several of its regulars. Young Sharkey, being given a run in the side, hits the Boro' woodwork, but they respond immediately through Mills and Town never get another look-in. The UEFA Cup place for next season is now looking out of reach.

---

37 — H MANCHESTER C — 7/4
Position/Result/Pts: 6 W 40 · Att 21,290 · 7 · 2-1 · HT 1-0
Scorers: Lambert 40, Whymark 58 / Keegan 47 — Ref: R Tinkler

Town: Cooper, Burley, Beattie, Sharkey, Hunter, Peddelty, Osborne, Johnson, Whymark, Lambert, Woods
Manchester C (italic): Corrigan, Hammond, Donachie, Doyle, Booth, Barnes, Power, Barnes, Keegan, Royle, Hartford, Tueart

Lambert powers home a fine header from Johnson's cross, but is hurt in the process. Royle hits the underside of the bar, the rebound falling to Barnes and his shot is blocked, Keegan following up to score. Whymark collects Beattie's pass to outpace Doyle and fire home superbly.

---

38 — A MANCHESTER U — 10/4
Position/Result/Pts: 6 W 42 · Att 34,889 · 3 · 3-0
Scorers: Lambert 33, Whymark 78, Johnson 83 — Ref: D Lloyd

Town: Cooper, Burley, Mills, Sharkey, Hunter, Peddelty, Gates*, Osborne, Johnson, Whymark, Lambert (Woods)
Manchester U (italic): Stepney, Forsyth, Houston, Daly, Greenhoff, Buchan, Coppell, McIlroy, Pearson, Macari, Hill

Crowd trouble mars a fine Town victory over the League and Cup double seekers. Lambert lashes home a fine volley from Sharkey's cool chip. Sharkey's free kick is headed sweetly home by Whymark and Johnson takes advantage of hesitancy to fire home Woods' chipped pass.

---

39 — A BIRMINGHAM — 13/4
Position/Result/Pts: 6 L 42 · Att 20,497 · 20 · 0-3
Scorers: Francis 8p, Hibbitt 60, Burns 87 — Ref: I Smith

Town: Cooper, Burley, Mills, Sharkey, Hunter, Peddelty, Gates, Osborne, Johnson, Whymark, Lambert (Woods)
Birmingham (italic): Latchford, Calderwood, Styles, Page, Gallagher, Want, Emmanuel, Francis, Burns, Withe, Hibbitt

In slippery conditions Town often look uncomfortable and Willie Bell's side seem more hungry for the points as they battle to avoid the drop. Burns bursts through and shoots wide before falling under the challenge of Peddelty and Burley. To Town's horror a penalty is given.

---

40 — A ARSENAL — 17/4
Position/Result/Pts: 6 W 44 · Att 26,937 · 15 · 2-1
Scorers: Bertschin 72, Sharkey 87 / Stapleton 6 — Ref: D Turner

Town: Cooper, Burley, Mills, Sharkey, Hunter, Peddelty, Gates*, Osborne, Johnson, Whymark, Lambert (Bertschin)
Arsenal (italic): Rimmer, Rice, Nelson, Ross, O'Leary, Powling, Rostron, Ball, Stapleton, Brady, Cropley

Town go down to ten men for a long period as Mills has stitches in a facial wound. Bertschin's sensational diving header is his very first touch and Sharkey fires the winner after an error by Ball.

---

41 — H WEST HAM — 19/4
Position/Result/Pts: 6 W 46 · Att 28,217 · 18 · 4-0
Scorers: Bertschin 23, Talbot 44, Whymark 70, [Peddelty 90] — Ref: K Styles

Town: Cooper, Burley, Mills, Sharkey, Hunter, Peddelty, Talbot, Osborne, Johnson, Whymark, Lambert (Johnson)
West Ham (italic): Day, Bonds, McGiven, Curbishley, Taylor, McDowell, Ayris, Paddon, Orhan*, Brooking, Robson, Pike

With a European final looming, John Lyall's side have little to play for. Bertschin, preferred to the disgruntled Johnson, shoots home from Lambert's pass. Talbot fires in after a scramble and Whymark nets after Bertschin's shot is blocked. Peddelty heads home Sharkey's cross.

---

42 — H DERBY — 26/4
Position/Result/Pts: 6 L 46 · Att 26,971 · 4 · 2-3
Scorers: Lambert 14, Whymark 20 / Hector 8, 54, Rioch 11p, 15, Lee 88, 90 — Ref: P Walters

Town: Cooper, Burley, Mills, Sharkey, Hunter, Peddelty, Osborne*, Talbot, Bertschin, Whymark, Lambert (Johnson)
Derby (italic): Moseley, Webster, Newton, Rioch, McFarland*, Todd, Powell, Gemmill, Lee, Hector, King, Davies

Town's last hopes of a point vanish when Whymark's penalty hits the post at 2-3. Former England ace Lee has announced his retirement and Town's casual defence seem content to allow him a scoring farewell during a sloppy finale. It is the club's worst home defeat for 12 seasons.

Home Average 25,366
Away Average 26,067

LEAGUE DIVISION 1 (CUP-TIES)　　Manager: Bobby Robson　　SEASON 1975-76

League Cup

					Att		F-A	H-T	Scorers, Times, and Referees
2	A	LEEDS	9/9		15,318	15 / 3	L 2-3	1-3	Johnson 28, Hunter 78 · McKenzie 17, Lorimer 20, Clarke 42 · Ref: R Matthewson

1	2	3	4	5	6	7	8	9	10	11	12 sub used
Cooper	Burley	Mills	Talbot*	Hunter	Beattie	Hamilton	Viljoen	Johnson	Whymark	Lambert	Woods
Harvey	*Cherry*	*Gray F*	*Bremner*	*Madeley*	*Hunter*	*Lorimer*	*Clarke*	*McKenzie*	*Yorath*	*Gray E*	

Talbot breaks his leg for the third time after catching his studs in the turf with nobody near him. Lorimer doubles Leeds' advantage when he lashes home the rebound after Cooper saves his spot-kick. Talbot looks offside for the crucial third and Town battle in vain to stay in the cup.

FA Cup

					Att		F-A	H-T	Scorers, Times, and Referees
3	H	HALIFAX	3/1		23,426 / 3:16	11	W 3-1	3-1	Lambert 2, 12, 30 · McHale 23p · Ref: M Sinclair

1	2	3	4	5	6	7	8	9	10	11	12 sub used
Cooper	Burley	Beattie	Talbot	Hunter	Peddelty	Woods	Mills	Johnson*	Whymark	Lambert	Austin
Gennoe	*Smith*	*Collins*	*McHale*	*Veitch*	*Phelan*	*Jones*	*Blair*	*Bell**	*Gwyther*	*Pugh*	*Downes*

After non-League Stafford in Round Two, relegation-bound Halifax find Town far too powerful and Lambert's classy hat-trick buries them early. He shoots the first on 88 seconds, but sees John Quinn's side pull one back when Beattie catches the ball, thinking he'd heard a whistle.

					Att		F-A	H-T	Scorers, Times, and Referees
4	H	WOLVERHAMPTON	24/1		30,110 / 20	10	D 0-0	0-0	Ref: M Lowe

1	2	3	4	5	6	7	8	9	10	11	12 sub used
Cooper	Burley	Tibbott	Talbot	Hunter	Beattie	Woods	Mills	Johnson	Whymark	Lambert	
Parkes	*Sunderland*	*Parkin*	*Bailey*	*McAlle*	*Carr*	*Hibbitt*	*Munro*	*Bell*	*Gould*	*Richards*	

Ex-Town boss Bill McGarry winds his old club up by promising his side will win, but it needs Parkes to make a series of fine saves to keep Town at bay. Johnson tucks the ball home, but offside is given. Town have their eyes on the cup, especially as few top division sides are left in.

					Att		F-A	H-T	Scorers, Times, and Referees
4R	A	WOLVERHAMPTON	27/1		31,333 / 20	10	L 0-1	0-1	Gould 37 · Ref: M Lowe

1	2	3	4	5	6	7	8	9	10	11	12 sub used
Cooper	Burley	Mills	Talbot	Wark	Beattie	Woods	Osborne	Johnson*	Austin	Lambert	Gates
Parkes	*Sunderland*	*Parkin*	*Bailey*	*McAlle*	*Carr*	*O'Hara*	*Munro*	*Bell*	*Gould**	*Richards*	*Kindon*

A nightmare for Cooper as he allows a speculative cross from Gould on the left wing to slip from his grasp and over the line. Town force 11 corners to Wolves' three and have more possession, but are foiled by Parkes' finger-tip save from a Burley shot while Austin hits the crossbar.

UEFA Cup

					Att		F-A	H-T	Scorers, Times, and Referees
1:1	A	FEYENOORD (Holland)	17/9		30,000	12	W 2-1	1-0	Whymark 32, Johnson 77 · De Jong 69 · Ref: A Rudnev (USSR)

1	2	3	4	5	6	7	8	9	10	11	12 sub used
Cooper	Burley	Mills	Osborne	Hunter	Beattie	Hamilton	Viljoen	Johnson*	Whymark^	Woods	Lambert/Austin
Treytel	*Schneider*	*Everse*	*Ramljak*	*Van Daele*	*Jansen*	*Rijsbergen**	*De Jong^*	*Vreijsen*	*Kreuz*	*Kristensen*	*Olsen/Wegerle*

Dutch League leaders and UEFA Cup favourites, the home side are humbled by fine Town finishing as the nimble Woods sets up both goals. An early storm is weathered, including Kreuz hitting a Town post. Near the end Austin feeds Lambert who nets, but has the effort ruled out.

					Att		F-A	H-T	Scorers, Times, and Referees
1:2	H	FEYENOORD	1/10		30,411	16	W 2-0	2-0	Woods 6, Whymark 40 · Ref: E Linemayr (Austria) · (Town win 4-1 on aggregate)

1	2	3	4	5	6	7	8	9	10	11	12 sub used
Cooper	Burley	Mills	Osborne^	Hunter	Beattie	Hamilton	Viljoen	Johnson*	Whymark	Woods	Lambert/Gates
Treytel	*Schneider*	*Everse**	*Ramljak*	*Van Daele*	*Jansen*	*Van Hanegem*	*Wegerle*	*Vreijsen*	*Kreuz*	*Vos*	

The Dutch badly need an early goal and Vreijsen misses a great chance from close in. Just moments later Woods conjures up a brilliant volley to increase the advantage. The home side sits back and Jansen hits the post, only for Cooper to make a superb save from Wegerle's follow-up.

					Att		F-A	H-T	Scorers, Times, and Referees
2:1	H	FC BRUGES (Belgium)	22/10		28,719	14	W 3-0	1-0	Gates 21, Peddelty 55, Austin 65 · Ref: A Prokop (E Germany)

1	2	3	4	5	6	7	8	9	10	11	12 sub used
Cooper	Burley	Beattie	Osborne	Hunter	Peddelty	Hamilton	Gates^	Johnson*	Whymark	Woods	Austin/Lambert
Jensen	*Bastijns*	*Krieger*	*Leekens*	*Volders*	*Cools*	*V der Eycken Van Gool*		*R Lambert**	*De Cubber*	*Le Fevre*	*Sanders*

Town chalk up a memorable win over Ernst Happel's men, with three stand-ins hitting the goals. Town forget injury worries and inconsistent League form, as Gates and Austin both lash home awesome shots from outside the area. Raoul Lambert hits the post for a subdued Bruges.

					Att		F-A	H-T	Scorers, Times, and Referees
2:2	A	FC BRUGES	5/11		30,000	12	L 0-4	0-3	L'bert 12p, De Cubber 25, Le Fvre 42, [Van der Eycken 88] · Ref: M Correia (Portugal) · (Town lose 3-4 on aggregate)

1	2	3	4	5	6	7	8	9	10	11	12 sub used
Cooper	Burley	Mills	Osborne	Hunter	Peddelty	Hamilton	Viljoen*	Johnson	Whymark	Woods	Gates
Jensen	*Bastijns*	*Krieger*	*Leekens*	*Volders**	*Cools*	*V der Eycken Van Gool*		*Lambert*	*De Cubber*	*Le Fevre*	*Denaeghel*

An astonishing comeback against the odds takes the Belgians through. Town are put under heavy pressure right from the start and Bruges pull back the three-goal deficit before the interval. At 2-0 down, Johnson's effort hits the crossbar and falls into the arms of the grateful Jensen.

Home / Away League Table

	P	W	D	L	F	A	W	D	L	F	A	Pts
1 Liverpool	42	14	5	2	41	21	9	9	3	25	10	60
2 QP Rangers	42	17	4	0	42	13	7	7	7	25	20	59
3 Manchester U	42	16	4	1	40	13	7	6	8	28	29	56
4 Derby	42	15	3	3	45	30	6	7	8	30	28	53
5 Leeds	42	13	3	5	37	19	8	6	7	28	27	51
6 IPSWICH	42	11	6	4	36	23	5	8	8	18	25	46
7 Leicester	42	9	9	3	29	24	4	10	7	19	27	45
8 Manchester C	42	14	5	2	46	18	2	6	13	18	28	43
9 Tottenham	42	6	10	5	33	32	8	5	8	30	31	43
10 Norwich	42	10	5	6	33	26	6	5	10	25	32	42
11 Everton	42	10	7	4	37	24	5	5	11	23	42	42
12 Stoke	42	8	5	8	25	24	7	6	8	23	26	41
13 Middlesbro	42	9	7	5	23	11	6	3	12	23	34	40
14 Coventry	42	6	9	6	22	22	7	5	9	25	35	40
15 Newcastle	42	11	4	6	51	26	4	5	12	20	36	39
16 Aston Villa	42	11	8	2	32	17	0	9	12	19	42	39
17 Arsenal	42	11	4	6	33	19	2	6	13	14	34	36
18 West Ham	42	10	5	6	26	23	3	5	13	22	48	36
19 Birmingham	42	11	5	5	36	26	2	2	17	21	49	33
20 Wolves	42	7	6	8	27	25	3	4	14	24	43	30
21 Burnley	42	6	6	9	23	26	3	4	14	20	40	28
22 Sheffield Utd	42	4	7	10	19	32	2	3	16	14	50	22
	924	229	127	106	736	494	106	127	229	494	736	924

Odds & ends

Double wins: (2) Arsenal, West Ham.
Double losses: (2) Derby, Middlesbrough.

Won from behind: (1) Arsenal (a).
Lost from in front: (0).

High spots: The memorable double triumph over Feyenoord.
Bertschin's fine goal within 30 seconds of his debut.
Another rise in average home attendances.
A fine 3-0 win to damage Manchester Utd's double hopes.

Low spots: Losing a three-goal lead in Bruges.
The poor start – one win in the opening seven games.
Emphatic home defeats by Newcastle, Middlesbrough and Derby.
The nasty facial injuries suffered by Sivell at Aston Villa.
The start of Beattie's long battle with injuries.

Player of the Year: Allan Hunter.
Ever-presents: (1) Mills, Burley (League only).
Hat-tricks: (1) Lambert (LC).
Opposing hat-tricks: (0).
Leading scorer: (15) Trevor Whymark.

Appearances / Goals

	Appearances								Goals					
	Lge	Sub	LC	Sub	FAC	Sub	Eur	Sub	Lge	Sub	LC	FAC	Eur	Tot
Austin, Terry	8	9						1	1				1	2
Beattie, Kevin	29		1		3		3		2					2
Bertschin, Keith	2	1									2			2
Burley, George	42		1		3		3		2					2
Cooper, Paul	40		1		3		4							
Gates, Eric	7	6		1	1	1	2		2					2
Hamilton, Bryan	18		1				4		5					5
Hunter, Allan	40				2		4	1	2					2
Johnson, David	32	3	1		3		4		6			1	1	8
Lambert, Mick	30	1			3		4		7				3	10
Mills, Mick	42				3		4		1					1
Osborne, Roger	33	3	1		1		4		2					2
Peddelty, John	27		1		1		2		5				1	6
Roberts, Dale	1													
Sharkey, Pat	12	1			1				1					1
Sivell, Laurie	2													
Talbott, Brian	19				3				2					2
Tibbott, Les	2		1											
Turner, Robin		1												
Viljoen, Colin	9		1		3		3		1					1
Wark, John	3				1									
Whymark, Trevor	40		1		2		4		13			2		15
Woods, Clive	24	7	1		3	0	4		2				1	3
(own-goals)														
23 players used	462	32	11	1	33	2	44	7	54	7	2	3	7	66

LEAGUE DIVISION 1 — Manager: Bobby Robson — SEASON 1976-77

No	Date		Opponent	Att	Pos	Pt	Res	F-A	H-T	Scorers, Times, and Referees
1	21/8	H	TOTTENHAM	28,859	2	2	W	3-1	0-1	Lambert 52, 90, Bertschin 88 / Jones 41 / Ref: J Sewell
2	24/8	A	EVERTON	33,070		3	D	1-1	0-0	Beattie 75 / Telfer 73 / Ref: P Willis
3	28/8	H	QP RANGERS	24,491	2	4	D	2-2	1-0	Abbott 4 (og), Beattie 51p / Givens 48, Masson 54 / Ref: R Toseland
4	4/9	A	ASTON VILLA	36,916	14	4	L	2-5	1-1	Wark 17, Bertschin 76 / Little 5, Gray 58, 63, 77, Graydon 88 / Ref: K Ridden
5	11/9	H	LEICESTER	19,636	12	5	D	0-0	0-0	Ref: R Challis
6	18/9	A	STOKE	20,171	17	5	L	1-2	0-2	Whymark 55 / Tudor 3, 18 / Ref: G Flint
7	25/9	H	ARSENAL	25,505	13	7	W	3-1	1-0	Osborne 39, Gates 49, Beattie 82p / Hunter 78 (og) / Ref: H Robinson
8	2/10	A	BRISTOL CITY	21,114	8	9	W	2-1	1-0	Whymark 37, Osborne 73 / Tainton 54 / Ref: T Spencer
9	16/10	A	WEST HAM	24,534	7	11	W	2-0	1-0	Woods 10, 87 / Ref: J Bent
10	23/10	H	MANCHESTER C	25,041	5	13	W	1-0	0-0	Whymark 52 / Ref: R Lewis

Line-ups (1–11, 12 sub used) — Town (roman) / Opposition (italic)

No	Team	1	2	3	4	5	6	7	8	9	10	11	12 sub used
1	Town	Cooper	Burley	Beattie	Talbot	Wark*	Peddelty	Mills	Sharkey	Bertschin	Whymark	Lambert	Woods
1	Tottenham	*Daines*	*Naylor*	*McAllister*	*Pratt*	*Young*	*Osgood*	*Coates*	*Perryman*	*Armstrong*	*Jones*	*Neighbour*	
2	Town	Cooper	Burley	Beattie	Talbot	Wark	Peddelty	Mills	Sharkey*	Bertschin	Whymark	Lambert	Woods
2	Everton	*Davies*	*Bernard*	*Seargeant*	*Lyons*	*McNaught*	*Kenyon*	*King*	*Dobson*	*Latchford*	*Pearson*	*Telfer*	
3	Town	Cooper	Burley	Beattie	Talbot	Hunter	Wark	Mills	Sharkey	Bertschin	Whymark	Lambert*	Woods
3	QP Rangers	*Parkes*	*Clement*	*Gillard*	*Hollins*	*McLintock*	*Abbott*	*Thomas*	*Leach*	*Masson*	*Bowles*	*Givens*	
4	Town	Cooper	Burley	Beattie	Talbot	Hunter	Wark	Mills	Sharkey*	Bertschin	Woods	Lambert	Turner
4	Aston Villa	*Burridge*	*Gidman*	*Smith*	*Phillips*	*Nicholl*	*Mortimer*	*Graydon*	*Little*	*Gray*	*Robson*	*Carrodus*	
5	Town	Sivell	Burley	Beattie	Talbot	Hunter	Peddelty	Turner*	Mills	Woods	Whymark	Lambert	Bertschin
5	Leicester	*Wallington*	*Whitworth*	*Rofe*	*Kember*	*Blockley*	*Woollett*	*Weller*	*Alderson**	*Worthington*	*Birchenall*	*Garland*	*Lee*
6	Town	Sivell	Burley	Mills	Talbot	Hunter	Peddelty	Turner*	Gates	Bertschin	Whymark	Lambert	Tibbott
6	Stoke	*Shilton*	*Marsh*	*Pejic*	*Greenhoff*	*Dodd*	*Bloor*	*Salmons*	*Tudor*	*Conroy*	*Hudson*	*Crooks*	
7	Town	Cooper	Burley	Mills	Talbot	Hunter	Beattie	Osborne	Gates	Bertschin	Whymark	Woods	
7	Arsenal	*Rimmer*	*Rice*	*Nelson*	*Ross*	*O'Leary*	*Howard*	*Ball*	*Brady*	*MacDonald*	*Stapleton*	*Armstrong*	
8	Town	Cooper	Burley	Mills	Talbot	Hunter	Beattie	Osborne	Gates*	Bertschin	Whymark	Lambert	Woods
8	Bristol City	*Cashley*	*Sweeney*	*Drysdale*	*Gow*	*Collier*	*Merrick*	*Tainton*	*Ritchie*	*Mann*	*Gillies**	*Whitehead*	*Fear*
9	Town	Cooper	Burley	Mills	Talbot	Hunter	Beattie	Osborne	Wark	Bertschin*	Whymark	Lambert	
9	West Ham	*Day*	*Coleman*	*Lock*	*Bonds*	*Green*	*Taylor T*	*Jennings*	*Paddon*	*Taylor A**	*Brooking*	*Robson*	*Ayris*
10	Town	Cooper	Burley	Mills	Talbot	Hunter	Beattie	Osborne	Wark	Bertschin	Whymark	Woods	
10	Manchester C	*Corrigan*	*Clements*	*Donachie*	*Doyle*	*Watson*	*Power*	*Owen*	*Kidd*	*Royle*	*Hartford*	*Tueart*	

Match reports

1. Tottenham (H): Led by new boss Keith Burkinshaw, Spurs subdue Town for long periods but a tentative start without striker Johnson is forgotten as Lambert collects a loose ball to fire a leveller. With time running out, Bertschin forces the ball in from close range after Daines blocks his initial effort.

2. Everton (A): Cooper has his best game to date, pulling off several superb saves to keep Billy Bingham's men at bay. It takes a magnificent long-range shot by Telfer to beat him after Bernard's free-kick. Two minutes later Beattie curls in a picture goal from 25 yards after picking up Talbot's throw.

3. QP Rangers (H): Abbott chests a bouncing ball into his own net under pressure from Bertschin. Givens hits back with a fine volley from Masson's free-kick, but then handles to give Beattie the chance to power home from the spot. Rangers refuse to cave in and Masson nets a fine shot from a Leach pass.

4. Aston Villa (A): Smith's long-throw is blasted home by Little. Wark levels with a drive from outside the box, but Villa regain the lead when Gray produces a fine header from Little's cross. The Scot completes a 19-minute hat-trick, squeezing two shots inside the post and Town tumble down the table.

5. Leicester (H): Robson's tetchy programme notes betray the pressure he feels after a poor start, but reports have suggested he could be close to recruiting the Plymouth striker Mariner to replace the departed Johnson. Jimmy Bloomfield's side defend in depth and bring about yet more frustration.

6. Stoke (A): Tudor, on loan from Newcastle, pounces after Salmons' drive rebounds to him off Sivell. He extends the lead with a header from Pejic's cross. In a second-half transformation Whymark converts Lambert's pass, Turner misses from close-in and a Dodd own-goal is ruled out for offside.

7. Arsenal (H): Four players return with instant effect. Osborne dives to head in Mills' cross and restores confidence. Gates produces a clever chipped goal from a narrow angle. Nelson's drive is deflected past Cooper by Hunter, but Ross fouls Whymark and Beattie fires home from the penalty spot.

8. Bristol City (A): Bertschin puts Whymark clear and he shoots in off a post. Tainton levels with a sizzling drive after a short free-kick, but unmarked Osborne heads the winner from Woods' cross. Trainer Lea is cautioned after complaining when the referee attempts to drag injured Gates off the pitch.

9. West Ham (A): Wark plays in midfield for the first time and Town are well on top. After a clever Whymark dummy Woods fires the opener. A Talbot effort is cleared off the line and a Wark drive goes just over. Day's superb save prevents a Woods hat-trick.

10. Manchester C (H): Whymark ends the resistance of the overworked Corrigan as he picks up a Mills pass, controls the ball and shoots low into the net with his right foot despite being surrounded by defenders. Three days later Mariner finally joins Town in a record deal, spurning West Ham and WBA.

11. A MANCHESTER U — 30/10 · Ipswich pos 3 · W · 15 pts · Att 57,416 · Man U pos 11 · 1-0 (HT 1-0) · Woods 2 · Ref: J Taylor
Ipswich: Cooper, Burley, Mills, Talbot, Hunter, Beattie, Osborne, Wark, Mariner, Whymark, Woods
Manchester U: Stepney, Nicholl, Albiston, Daly, Greenhoff, Houston, Coppell, McIlroy, Pearson, Marcari*, Hill — sub McCreery
Mariner's debut and Talbot's England call-up give the club a boost. Town get off to a great start when Woods collects Burley's cross and sees his low shot squirm under Stepney in the early stages. Mariner's big day is almost capped by a goal, but Houston gets back to head off the line.

12. H WEST BROM — 6/11 · Ipswich pos 2 · W · 17 pts · Att 26,706 · West Brom pos 12 · 7-0 (HT 2-0) · Whymark 19, 63, 88, 90, Wark 44, [Beattie 55, Mariner 65] · Ref: A Grey
Ipswich: Sivell, Burley, Mills, Talbot, Hunter, Beattie, Osborne, Wark, Mariner*, Whymark, Woods — sub Bertschin
West Brom: Osborne, Mulligan, Cantello, Brown T, Wile, Robertson, Martin, Treacy, Brown A, Giles, Trewick
Player-manager Johnny Giles has no answer to a rampant Town performance. Four-goal Whymark concedes some of the limelight due to the spectacular nature of the Mariner and Beattie strikes. However, his sweet second goal is described by jubilant Robson as 'goal of the decade.'

13. H LEEDS — 20/11 · Ipswich pos 2 · D · 18 pts · Att 30,096 · Leeds pos 8 · 1-1 (HT 0-0) · Talbot 75 · McQueen 51 · Ref: M Sinclair
Ipswich: Cooper, Burley, Mills*, Talbot, Hunter, Beattie, Osborne, Wark, Mariner, Whymark, Woods — sub Bertschin
Leeds: Harvey, Reaney, Hampton, Cherry, McQueen, Gray F, Lorimer, Hankin, Jordan, Currie, Gray E
After beating Celtic in a Parkhead friendly, Town fall behind to Jimmy Armfield's side when McQueen heads Eddie Gray's cross home. With Mills off injured and Hunter and Osborne struggling after knocks, Talbot thunders into the Leeds box to meet Whymark's cross and fire home.

14. H SUNDERLAND — 23/11 · Ipswich pos 2 · W · 20 pts · Att 24,605 · Sunderland pos 21 · 3-1 (HT 3-1) · Whymark 6, Beattie 10, Burley 25 · Hughes 26p · Ref: A Turvey
Ipswich: Cooper, Burley, Tibbott, Talbot, Hunter, Beattie, Osborne, Wark, Mariner, Whymark, Woods
Sunderland: Siddall, Henderson, Bolton, Rowell, Clarke, Holton, Kerr, Hughes, Lee, Train, Greenwood* — sub Gibb
Injured Mills misses his first domestic game for almost five years. His stand-in Tibbott sets up Whymark for the first goal and after Siddall takes too many steps, the free-kick is touched to Beattie who powers home. Burley's 20-yard thunderbolt is his first goal in 134 appearances.

15. A MIDDLESBROUGH — 27/11 · Ipswich pos 2 · W · 22 pts · Att 20,000 · Middlesbrough pos 14 · 2-0 (HT 1-0) · Mariner 42, Talbot 71 · Ref: W Johnson
Ipswich: Cooper, Burley, Tibbott, Talbot, Hunter, Beattie, Osborne, Wark, Mariner, Whymark, Woods
Middlesbrough: Platt, Craggs, Cooper, Souness, Boam, Maddren, McAndrew, Cummins*, Hickton, Armstrong, Mills
Mariner heads home Woods' in-swinging corner. Wark does a great job subduing the prompting of Souness, and Town win much praise for an all-round team performance of skill and maturity. The well-deserved points are made safe as Woods cuts in and lays on an easy goal for Talbot.

16. H LIVERPOOL — 4/12 · Ipswich pos 2 · W · 24 pts · Att 35,082 · Liverpool pos 1 · 1-0 (HT 0-0) · Mariner 75 · Ref: C White
Ipswich: Cooper, Burley, Mills, Talbot, Hunter, Beattie, Osborne, Wark, Mariner, Whymark, Woods
Liverpool: Clemence, Neal, Jones*, Thompson, Kennedy, Hughes, Keegan, McDermott, Heighway, Toshack, Callaghan — sub Fairclough
The top two sides are deadlocked for most of this tense affair, played in freezing conditions. Mariner produces a fine far-post header to win the points after Town manfully soak up intense pressure late in the game. Bob Paisley's men now have only a one-point lead at the top of the table.

17. A BIRMINGHAM — 7/12 · Ipswich pos 1 · W · 26 pts · Att 31,161 · Birmingham pos 8 · 4-2 (HT 1-2) · Mariner 10, Wark 50, Talbot 75, 77 · Connolly 13, Burns 25 · Ref: F Garner
Ipswich: Cooper, Burley, Mills, Talbot, Hunter, Beattie, Osborne, Wark, Mariner*, Whymark, Woods
Birmingham: Latchford, Page, Styles, Pendrey*, Gallagher, Want, Emmanuel, Francis, Burns, Connolly, Rathbone
Mariner holds off two defenders to convert the first, but Connolly soon equalises with a cracking drive. Town attack in numbers after half-time and overwhelm City. Wark picks up Want's clearance and lashes home a sweet volley. Talbot surges into the box from deep to score two more.

18. H DERBY — 18/12 · Ipswich pos 1 · D · 27 pts · Att 23,256 · Derby pos 16 · 0-0 (HT 0-0) · Ref: B Homewood
Ipswich: Cooper, Burley, Mills, Talbot, Hunter, Beattie, Osborne, Wark, Mariner*, Whymark, Woods
Derby: Boulton, Thomas, Newton, Macken, McFarland, Todd, Powell, Gemmill, Hales, George, James
After the game at Newcastle is abandoned due to a frozen pitch, this dull affair fails to warm the fans. McFarland and Todd look impregnable, although Town go closest to a goal. It emerges later that Robson was being approached over this period to take the manager's job at Everton.

19. A COVENTRY — 27/12 · Ipswich pos 2 · D · 28 pts · Att 28,269 · Coventry pos 11 · 1-1 (HT 1-1) · Bertschin 31 · Green 20 · Ref: W Gow
Ipswich: Cooper, Burley, Mills, Talbot, Roberts, Beattie, Osborne, Wark, Bertschin, Whymark, Woods
Coventry: Blyth, Coop, McDonald, Yorath, Dugdale, Holmes, Beck*, Green, Murphy, Powell, Hutchison — sub Cartwright
With both teams missing a couple of star names, Gordon Milne's team takes the lead when Green gets clear of his marker to head Coop's cross powerfully past the helpless Cooper. Burley's pass then splits the defence and Bertschin produces a superb low drive from the edge of the area.

20. H MANCHESTER U — 3/1 · Ipswich pos 2 · W · 30 pts · Att 30,164 · Man U pos 13 · 2-1 (HT 0-1) · Greenhoff B 79 (og), Woods 84 · Pearson 1 · Ref: B Daniels
Ipswich: Cooper, Burley, Mills, Talbot, Roberts, Beattie, Osborne*, Wark, Bertschin, Whymark, Woods
Manchester U: Stepney, Nicholl, Albiston, McIlroy, Greenhoff B, Buchan, McCreery, Greenhoff J, Pearson*, Macari, Hill — sub McGrath
A dreadful start as Wark is robbed by Macari, who feeds Pearson. He skates across the frozen pitch to shoot past Cooper with just 23 seconds on the clock. But there's a thrilling finale as Greenhoff heads Woods' cross into his own net and Woods scrambles home a free-kick by Mills.

21. H EVERTON — 15/1 · Ipswich pos 2 · W · 32 pts · Att 25,578 · Everton pos 15 · 2-0 (HT 1-0) · Whymark 34, Wark 49 · Ref: T Bune
Ipswich: Cooper, Burley, Mills, Talbot, Roberts, Beattie, Osborne, Wark, Mariner, Whymark*, Woods — sub Bertschin
Everton: Lawson, Seargeant, Jones, Lyons, McNaught, Rioch, King, Dobson, Latchford, McKenzie, Hamilton
Everton sack Billy Bingham and offer his job to Town boss Robson, but their plan is leaked to the press and he stays put. Ironically the teams come face to face and Duncan McKenzie says Town are the best side he's seen. Whymark's header and a rasping Wark drive wins the points.

LEAGUE DIVISION 1 — Manager: Bobby Robson — SEASON 1976-77

No	Date	Opponent	Att	Pos	Res	Opp Pos	Pt	F-A	H-T	Scorers, Times, and Referees
22	22/1	A TOTTENHAM	35,126	2	L	19	32	0-1	0-0	Taylor 68 · Ref: C Maskell
23	12/2	H ASTON VILLA	29,750	2	W	4	34	1-0	1-0	Woods 45 · Ref: T Spencer
24	15/2	H NORWICH	34,735	2	W	12	36	5-0	2-0	Wark 12p, Whymark 39, 75, 84, [Mariner 68] · Ref: R Capey
25	19/2	A LEICESTER	21,134	2	L	7	36	0-1	0-0	Earle 78 · Ref: J Bent
26	26/2	H STOKE	25,865	2	L	15	36	0-1	0-1	Goodwin 38 · Ref: D Reeves
27	5/3	A ARSENAL	34,688	2	W	10	38	4-1	0-0	Talbot 49, Bertschin 59, Wark 60p, MacDonald 84p, [Mariner 85] · Ref: P Reeves
28	9/3	A NEWCASTLE	31,790	2	D	7	39	1-1	0-1	Wark 89, Nattrass 44 · Ref: E Garner
29	12/3	H BRISTOL CITY	24,547	2	W	22	41	1-0	0-0	Wark 59p · Ref: K Baker
30	16/3	A WEST BROM	22,659	2	L	7	41	0-4	0-0	Robson 69, 70, 89, Cunningham 82 · Ref: R Crabb
31	19/3	A SUNDERLAND	35,376	2	L	19	41	0-1	0-0	Waldron 71 · Ref: A Morrissey

Line-ups

No	Team	1	2	3	4	5	6	7	8	9	10	11	12 sub used
22	Ipswich	Cooper	Burley	Mills	Talbot	Roberts	Beattie*	Osborne	Wark	Mariner	Whymark	Woods	Bertschin
22	Tottenham	Jennings	Naylor	Gorman	Hoddle	Keeley	Osgood	Jones	Perryman	Duncan	McNab	Taylor	
23	Ipswich	Sivell	Mills	Tibbott	Talbot	Hunter	Beattie	Osborne	Wark	Mariner	Whymark	Woods	
23	Aston Villa	Burridge	Gidman	Robson	Phillips	Nicholl	Mortimer	Deehan	Little	Cowans	Cropley	Carrodus	
24	Ipswich	Cooper	Burley	Mills	Talbot	Hunter	Beattie	Osborne	Wark*	Mariner*	Whymark	Woods	Gates
24	Norwich	Keelan	Ryan	Sullivan	Machin*	Forbes	Powell	Neighbour	Reeves	Gibbins	Steele	Peters	Evans
25	Ipswich	Cooper	Burley	Mills	Talbot	Hunter	Beattie	Osborne	Wark	Mariner	Whymark	Woods*	Bertschin
25	Leicester	Wallington	Whitworth	Rofe	Kember	Woollett	Sims	Weller	Sammels	Worthington	Alderson	Earle	
26	Ipswich	Sivell	Burley	Mills	Talbot	Hunter	Beattie	Osborne	Wark	Mariner	Whymark	Woods*	Bertschin
26	Stoke	Shilton	Dodd	Bowers	Johnson	Smith	Bloor	Robertson	Tudor	Goodwin	Conroy	Salmons	
27	Ipswich	Sivell	Burley	Mills	Talbot	Hunter	Beattie	Osborne	Wark	Mariner	Whymark*	Woods*	Bertschin
27	Arsenal	Rimmer	Rice	Young	Ross	Howard	Powling	Brady	Matthews*	MacDonald	Stapleton	Armstrong	Nelson
28	Ipswich	Sivell	Mahoney	Tibbott	Talbot	Hunter	Beattie	Osborne*	Wark	Mariner	Whymark*	Woods	Gates
28	Newcastle	Mahoney	Kennedy	Nattrass	Blackhall	McCaffery	Nulty	Barrowc'gh	Oates	Burns	Gowling	Craig	
29	Ipswich	Cooper	Burley	Mills	Talbot	Hunter	Tibbott	Osborne	Wark*	Mariner	Whymark*	Woods	Gates
29	Bristol City	Shaw	Gillies	Merrick	Sweeney	Collier	Hunter	Ritchie	Mann	Garland	Cormack	Whitehead	
30	Ipswich	Sivell	Burley	Tibbott	Talbot	Hunter	Wark*	Osborne	Gates	Mariner	Whymark*	Woods	Roberts
30	West Brom	Godden	Mulligan	Statham	Brown T*	Wile	Robertson	Robson	Cunningham	Cross	Giles	Johnston	Brown A
31	Ipswich	Cooper	Burley	Tibbott	Talbot	Hunter	Roberts	Osborne	Gates	Mariner	Bertschin*	Woods	Beattie
31	Sunderland	Siddall	Docherty	Bolton	Arnott	Waldron	Ashurst	Kerr	Elliott	Holden	Lee	Rowell	

Match reports

22 — Tottenham (A): Town weather some early Spurs pressure and look set to win as they move into a higher gear. Jennings foils Beattie with two great saves, and three goalbound efforts are cleared off the line. Then Taylor pops up to net a cracking left-foot drive and the 16-match unbeaten run is ended.

23 — Aston Villa (H): Whymark is hauled down by Nicholl, but Beattie shoots the spot-kick wide. Moments before the interval Town pressure is rewarded as Beattie heads Talbot's free-kick into Woods' path and he nets past Burridge. Talbot and Osborne's industry in the muddy midfield proves decisive.

24 — Norwich (H): One for the fans to treasure as the local rivals are buried without trace. The breakthrough penalty is lucky as Peters' foul on Woods seems to be outside the area. Whymark sweeps home Burley's cross and swoops to poach two late efforts with the Canaries' defensive feathers in disarray.

25 — Leicester (A): Mariner's shot is parried by Wallington but as Whymark follows up to net, Mr Bent blows for a foul. Jimmy Bloomfield's men generally have the upper hand in a drab game and Sims has a goal disallowed for pushing. Earle wins the points, diving to head home Worthington's cross.

26 — Stoke (H): With Hudson sold to Arsenal, Stoke seem to be less of a threat, but Town are unable to pierce a defence well marshalled by Smith and Bloor. Shilton makes a fine save from Mariner's header, but a careless Beattie pass sees Conroy fly past Hunter and tee up Goodwin for the winner.

27 — Arsenal (A): After a break in the Kuwaiti sunshine, Town are refreshed and three goals in 11 minutes sinks the Gunners. Talbot powers through to blast the first, Bertschin converts a handsome lob after Mariner's flick-on and Wark converts a spot-kick after Young brings down the lively Talbot.

28 — Newcastle (A): The original game was abandoned due to an icy pitch and this encounter sees a floodlight failure, but the ref plays on in reduced light. Nattrass' 30-yard free-kick sails in and Town don't respond until the dying seconds. Woods robs Oates and feeds Wark who blasts home a real beauty.

29 — Bristol City (H): Top versus bottom is not a pretty sight as Alan Dicks' side pack their defence and hope for the best. Mariner looks the most likely to cause them problems and sure enough he goes on a run and tempts Hunter to bring him crashing to the floor. The penalty is tucked home by Wark.

30 — West Brom (A): With four key men out, things get even worse as Sivell and Wark pick up knocks. Hunter takes over in goal for ten minutes and battered Town hold on until the final 21 minutes when starlet Bryan Robson sweeps them aside with a hat-trick. His tally is now seven goals in just 22 days.

31 — Sunderland (A): The injury crisis is now of 'mammoth proportions' reports the local press as Town get stuck in during a match of fearsome tackling and rugged defending. Waldron, on loan from Manchester United, drives home the winner past the limping Cooper after a Kerr corner is partially cleared.

Match results grid

No	V	Date	Opponent	Pos	Res	Score	HT	Att	OppPos	Pts
32	H	22/3	WEST HAM	2	W	4-1	0-0	27,315	22	43
33	A	2/4	MANCHESTER C	2	L	1-2	0-1	42,780	3	43
34	H	5/4	COVENTRY	1	W	2-1	1-1	23,635	17	45
35	A	9/4	NORWICH	1	W	1-0	1-0	31,088	13	47
36	H	11/4	BIRMINGHAM	1	W	1-0	1-0	29,025	12	49
37	A	16/4	LEEDS	2	L	1-2	1-2	28,578	9	49
38	H	23/4	MIDDLESBROUGH	3	L	0-1	0-0	23,342	11	49
39	A	30/4	LIVERPOOL	3	L	1-2	0-0	56,044	1	49
40	H	7/5	NEWCASTLE	3	W	2-0	0-0	24,760	4	51
41	A	14/5	DERBY	3	D	0-0	0-0	24,491	15	52
42	A	16/5	QP RANGERS	3	L	0-1	0-1	19,171	14	52

Home Average 26,668 — Away 33,197 — Average 33,197

Scorers and referees

- **32:** Taylor T 57 (og), Mariner 69, 73, 73, 82 / Robson 86p / Ref: B Martin
- **33:** Whymark 55 / Kidd 34 Watson 86 / Ref: J Taylor
- **34:** Mariner 12, Burley 46 / Ferguson 41 / Ref: T Bune
- **35:** Whymark 24 / Ref: K Styles
- **36:** Bertschin 12 / Ref: C Maskell
- **37:** Bertschin 22 / McGhie 20, Clarke 35p / Ref: K McNally
- **38:** Armstrong 83 / Ref: R Challis
- **39:** Wark 86p / Kennedy 69, Keegan 73 / Ref: P Willis
- **40:** Osborne 53, Wark 72 / Ref: B Daniels
- **41:** Ref: D Richardson
- **42:** Givens 15 / Ref: P Reeves

Line-ups (Town player — opponent)

32 WEST HAM: Cooper–Day, Burley–Bonds, Mills–Lampard, Talbot–Otulakowski Taylor, Hunter–Taylor, Roberts–Lock, Osborne–Pike, Wark–Robson, Mariner–Devonshire, Whymark*–Brooking, Woods–Jennings, Bertschin

33 MANCHESTER C: Cooper–Corrigan, Burley–Clements, Mills–Donachie, Talbot–Booth, Hunter–Watson, Beattie–Keegan, Lambert–Barnes, Wark*–Kidd, Mariner–Royle, Whymark–Hartford, Woods–Owen*, Tibbott–Henry

34 COVENTRY: Cooper–Blyth, Burley–Roberts, Tibbott–McDonald, Talbot–Yorath, Hunter–Gooding, Beattie–Coop, Lambert–Beck, Mills–Wallace, Mariner*–Ferguson, Whymark–Powell, Woods–Hutchison, Bertschin

35 NORWICH: Cooper–Keelan, Burley–Ryan, Mills–Sullivan, Talbot–Machin*, Hunter–Jones, Beattie–Powell, Osborne–Neighbour, Wark–Reeves, Mariner*–Gibbins, Whymark–Steele, Woods–Peters, Lambert–Boyer

36 BIRMINGHAM: Cooper–Montgomery Rathbone, Burley–Pendrey, Mills–Kendall, Talbot, Hunter–Stragia, Tibbott–Want, Osborne–Jones, Wark*–Francis*, Bertschin–Burns, Whymark–Hibbitt, Woods–Connolly, Lambert–Emmanuel

37 LEEDS: Cooper–Stewart, Burley–Reaney, Tibbott–Gray, Talbot–Cherry, Hunter–McQueen, Roberts–Madeley, Osborne–Harris, Mills–Clarke, Bertschin–Jordan*, Whymark–Currie, Woods–McGhie, Lorimer

38 MIDDLESBROUGH: Cooper–Platt, Burley–Craggs, Tibbott–Cooper, Talbot–Souness, Hunter–Boam, Roberts–Madren, Osborne*–McAndrew, Sharkey–Mills, Mariner–Wood, Whymark–Brine, Woods–Armstrong, Bertschin

39 LIVERPOOL: Cooper–Clemence, Burley–Neal, Mills–Jones, Talbot–Smith, Hunter–Kennedy, Roberts–Hughes, Osborne–Keegan, Wark–Case, Mariner–Heighway*, Whymark*–Johnson, Woods–McDermott, Fairclough

40 NEWCASTLE: Cooper–Mahoney, Burley–Blackhall, Mills–Kennedy, Talbot–Cassidy, Hunter–McCaffery, Roberts–Nulty, Osborne–Barrowcl'gh Cannell, Wark–Burns, Mariner–Craig, Whymark–Oates, Woods, Geddis

41 DERBY: Cooper–Boulton, Burley–Langan, Mills–Daniel, Talbot–Daly, Hunter–McFarland, Roberts–Todd, Osborne–Powell, Wark!–Gemmill, Mariner–Hector, Whymark–George!, Bertschin*–King, Geddis

42 QP RANGERS: Cooper–Parkes, Burley–Hollins, Mills–Gillard, Talbot–Kelly, Hunter–McLintock, Roberts–Webb, Osborne–Thomas, Gates–Francis*, Mariner–Masson, Whymark–Eastoe, Bertschin*–Givens, Geddis–Leach

Match notes

32: John Lyall's lowly Hammers cave in after Taylor heads Talbot's free-kick into his own net under no real pressure. Mariner marks his England call-up by sweeping home Osborne's pass, then dives to head home after Mills hits the bar. A clinical finish clinches his first Town hat-trick.

33: Booth heads on Hartford's free-kick for Kidd to pounce and score. Whymark levels matters by rounding Corrigan after a through-ball from Mills. Barnes' corner-kick finds Watson unmarked and he heads in. Talbot bungles a late chance to equalise, firing well over from close range.

34: Mariner's goal is disputed by City, whose offside shout is ignored, as are later penalty claims by Gooding. Ferguson's equaliser inspires Town to hit back straight after the interval and within 37 seconds of the re-start Burley fires home, his shot taking a crucial deflection off Yorath.

35: City open in lively fashion following a recent win over Manchester United, but their fire is extinguished when Talbot's free-kick is nodded down by Beattie and Whymark swoops in ahead of Machin and Keelan to shoot home. Mariner and Lambert both suffer hamstring injuries.

36: Beattie is in hospital with serious burns to his chest, neck and face after a bonfire accident in his back garden and may miss the remainder of the season. Mariner's replacement, Bertschin, clips a superb drive past Montgomery from 15 yards. City rarely threaten after Francis limps off.

37: Jordan challenges Cooper and the ball breaks for McGhie to net a debut goal. Bertschin smashes home Woods' corner on the volley. Jordan is brought down by Roberts and Clarke nets from the spot. Town's title chances have been dented but they are still only one point off the lead.

38: Jack Charlton announces his impending resignation as Boro' boss and his team responds by ruining a title dream. Craggs finds the unmarked Wood, but he mis-hits his shot and Armstrong swoops to net. 'If my lads play cards one of them will break a wrist,' reflects injury-hit Robson.

39: It's all or nothing at Anfield and the commitment cannot be faulted in a first half of real tension with five bookings and missiles on the pitch. Kennedy heads home Case's cross and then Keegan does likewise from Johnson's pass. Wark's penalty for a handball is just too little, too late.

40: A win will ensure UEFA Cup qualification and a fine contest ensues. Woods' corner-kick is flicked on by Hunter and then Mariner to allow Osborne to score. A lightning-quick break out of defence sees Woods set up Wark for the clincher. Both keepers make a series of fine saves.

41: Town beat Norwich in a testimonial for long-term injury victim Colin Viljoen. Five days later Derby get the single point they need to avoid relegation, but the game is marred by an ugly confrontation between George and Wark which sees both sent off - rather harshly in Wark's case.

42: Town, with little to play for, succumb to a neat passing move between Kelly and Eastoe, which sees Givens send a cracking drive past Cooper. Mariner has a goal ruled out and a penalty claim turned down, but Cooper is busiest of the two keepers, making two great saves from Eastoe.

LEAGUE DIVISION 1 (CUP-TIES) Manager: Bobby Robson SEASON 1976-77

League Cup

Round	Venue	Opponent	Date	Att		F-A	H-T	Scorers, Times, and Referees	1	2	3	4	5	6	7	8	9	10	11	12 sub used
2	H	BRIGHTON	31/8	16,027	2 *2:3*	D 0-0	0-0	Ref: C White	Cooper	Burley	Beattie	Talbot	Hunter	Wark	Mills	Sharkey	Bertschin	Whymark	Lambert*	Woods
									Grummitt	*Cattlin*	*Wilson*	*Burnett*	*Rollings*	*Cross*	*Towner*	*Ward*	*Binney**	*Piper*	*O'Sullivan*	*Mellor*
2R	A	BRIGHTON	7/9	26,748	14 *2:1*	L 1-2	0-0	Lambert 56 / Binney 60, Cross 88 Ref: M Taylor	Sivell	Burley	Beattie	Talbot	Hunter	Wark	Turner	Mills	Woods	Whymark	Lambert	Mellor
									Grummitt	*Beal*	*Wilson*	*Horton*	*Cross*	*Burnett*	*Towner**	*Ward*	*Binney*	*Piper*	*O'Sullivan*	*Mellor*

Alan Mullery's side keep Town at bay during a one-sided opening period. The Seagulls then settle down and Grummitt is given little to do as the game wears on. The closest Town come is when Beattie sees a pot-shot tipped over by the 34-year-old veteran keeper, now in his last year.

Brighton are caught on the break as Woods feeds Lambert who nets the first goal in two-and-a-half-hours of this tie. After Binney levels, the contest seems set for extra-time until Cross sends the Goldstone crazy as he scrambles the ball in after Sivell fails to hold a Binney header.

FA Cup

Round	Venue	Opponent	Date	Att		F-A	H-T	Scorers, Times, and Referees	1	2	3	4	5	6	7	8	9	10	11	12 sub used
3	H	BRISTOL CITY	8/1	25,157	2 *19*	W 4-1	3-0	Mariner 16, 36, Whymark 41, Gates 82 / Fear 66 Ref: J Hunting	Cooper	Burley	Mills	Talbot	Roberts	Beattie	Osborne	Wark	Mariner	Whymark*	Woods	Gates
									Shaw	*Gillies*	*Merrick*	*Sweeney*	*Collier*	*Hunter*	*Tainton*	*Ritchie*	*Fear*	*Cormack*	*Whitehead*	
4	H	WOLVERHAMPTON	29/1	32,996	2 *2:5*	D 2-2	0-1	Mariner 75, Burley 90 / Richards 31, 87 Ref: D Richardson	Cooper	Burley	Mills	Talbot	Hunter	Roberts	Osborne	Wark	Mariner	Whymark	Woods	Kindon
									Pierce	*Palmer*	*Parkin*	*Daley*	*Munro**	*McAlle*	*Hibbitt*	*Richards*	*Sunderland*	*Patching*	*Carr*	*Kindon*
4R	A	WOLVERHAMPTON	2/2	33,686	2 *2:5*	L 0-1	0-1	Richards 20 Ref: D Richardson	Cooper	Burley	Mills	Talbot	Hunter	Roberts	Osborne*	Wark	Mariner	Whymark	Woods	Gates
									Pierce	*Palmer*	*Parkin*	*Daley*	*Brazier*	*McAlle*	*Hibbitt*	*Richards*	*Sunderland*	*Patching*	*Carr*	

Mariner flicks in a close-range header and then turns to fire home off the underside of the bar. Whymark makes the tie safe as he stabs in a Mills cross. Fear pulls one back from Tainton's cross, but the last word goes to sub Gates, who hooks the ball home through a crowded area.

Richards converts the rebound after Cooper saves from Sunderland. Munro comes off with chest pains and Town level as Mariner nets after an Osborne miskick. Richards coolly slots in Kindon's pass, but Burley saves the day with a dramatic last-ditch strike from an 'impossible' angle.

Sammy Chung's side are up for it again and Town fall behind as the ever-dangerous Richards nets a superb header from Sunderland's cross. Cooper hauls down Richards but Hibbitt wastes a chance to settle the tie, firing his penalty against a post. Wolves hang on and and deserve the win.

League Table

	Team	P	Home					Away					Pts
			W	D	L	F	A	W	D	L	F	A	
1	Liverpool	42	18	3	0	47	11	5	8	8	15	22	57
2	Manchester C	42	15	5	1	38	13	6	9	6	22	21	56
3	IPSWICH	42	15	4	2	41	11	7	4	10	25	28	52
4	Aston Villa	42	17	3	1	55	17	5	4	12	21	33	51
5	Newcastle	42	14	6	1	40	15	4	7	10	24	34	49
6	Manchester U	42	12	6	3	41	22	6	5	10	30	40	47
7	West Brom	42	10	6	5	38	22	6	7	8	24	34	45
8	Arsenal	42	11	6	4	37	20	5	5	11	27	39	43
9	Everton	42	9	7	5	35	24	5	5	7	27	40	42
10	Leeds	42	8	8	5	28	26	7	4	10	20	25	42
11	Leicester	42	8	9	4	30	28	4	9	8	17	32	42
12	Middlestbro	42	11	6	4	25	14	3	7	11	15	31	41
13	Birmingham	42	10	6	5	28	25	3	6	12	25	36	38
14	QP Rangers	42	10	7	4	31	21	3	5	13	16	31	38
15	Derby	42	9	9	3	36	18	0	10	11	14	37	37
16	Norwich	42	12	4	5	30	23	2	5	14	17	41	37
17	West Ham	42	9	6	6	28	23	2	8	11	18	42	36
18	Bristol City	42	8	7	6	25	19	3	6	12	13	29	35
19	Coventry	42	7	9	5	34	26	3	6	12	14	33	35
20	Sunderland	42	9	5	7	29	16	2	7	12	17	38	34
21	Stoke	42	9	4	8	21	16	1	6	14	7	35	34
22	Tottenham	42	9	7	5	26	20	3	2	16	22	52	33
		924	240	137	85	753	430	85	137	240	430	753	924

Odds & ends

Double wins: (6) Arsenal, Birmingham, Bristol City, Manchester U, Norwich, West Ham.

Double losses: (1) Stoke.

Won from behind: (3) Tottenham (h), Manchester U (h), Birmingham (a).

Lost from in front: (1) Brighton (a) (LC).

High spots: The 7-0 mauling of West Brom.

The immediate impact made by record signing Mariner.

A 16-match unbeaten run from 25 September.

Increase in average home attendances for seventh successive season.

Two wins and clean sheets against local rivals Norwich.

Bobby Robson turning down the chance to join Everton.

Low spots: Another heavy crop of injuries to key players.

Only one win from last six games – ending championship hopes.

Defeat by Second Division clubs in both cups.

Player of the Year: George Burley.

Ever-presents: (1) Brian Talbot.

Hat-tricks: Trevor Whymark (2), Paul Mariner (1).

Opposing hat-tricks: (2) Andy Gray, Bryan Robson.

Leading scorer: (15) Trevor Whymark.

Appearances and Goals

Player	Appearances						Goals			
	Lge	Sub	LC	Sub	FAC	Sub	Lge	LC	FAC	Tot
Beattie, Kevin	30	1	2				5			5
Bertschin, Keith	17	12	2				6			6
Burley, George	40		2		3		2		1	3
Cooper, Paul	34		2		3					
Gates, Eric	6	6				2	1		1	2
Geddis, David		6								
Hunter, Allan	36		2		3					
Lambert, Mick	8	3		1			2	1		3
Mariner, Paul	28				3		10		3	13
Mills, Mick	37		2		3		3			3
Osborne, Roger	34		2		3					
Peddelty, John	4									
Roberts, Dale	12	1			3					
Sharkey, Pat	5									
Sivell, Laurie	8									
Talbot, Brian	42		2		3		5			5
Tibbott, Les	11	2								
Turner, Robin	3									
Wark, John	33		2		3		10			10
Whymark, Trevor	36		2		3		14		1	15
Woods, Clive	38		2		3		5			5
(own-goals)							3			3
21 players used	462	31	22	1	33	2	66	1	6	73

LEAGUE DIVISION 1 — Manager: Bobby Robson — SEASON 1977-78

Results

No	Venue	Date	Opponent	Att	Res	Pos	Pt	F-A	H-T	Scorers, Times, and Referees
1	H	20/8	ARSENAL	30,173	W		2	1-0	1-0	Geddis 43 — Ref: R Kirkpatrick
2	A	24/8	DERBY	19,809	D	3	3	0-0	0-0	Ref: K Styles
3	A	27/8	MANCHESTER U	57,904	D	3	4	0-0	0-0	Ref: W Johnson
4	H	3/9	CHELSEA	20,835	W	19	6	1-0	1-0	Talbot 37 — Ref: J Sewell
5	A	10/9	LEEDS	24,280	L	6	6	1-2	0-0	Mariner 50, Hankin 52, 80 — Ref: K McNally
6	H	17/9	LIVERPOOL	29,658	D	2	7	1-1	0-1	Whymark 69, Dalglish 22 — Ref: A Grey
7	A	24/9	MIDDLESBROUGH	19,843	D	16	8	1-1	1-0	Mariner 25, Mills 50 — Ref: D Richardson
8	H	1/10	NEWCASTLE	21,797	W	22	10	2-1	1-1	Mills 28, Gates 61, McCaffery 17 — Ref: R Challis
9	A	4/10	NOTT'M FOREST	26,845	L	1	10	0-4	0-1	Withe 42, 59, 88, 89 — Ref: J Worrall
10	A	8/10	WEST BROM	22,918	L	4	10	0-1	0-0	Robson 60 — Ref: W Gow
11	H	15/10	BIRMINGHAM	21,250	W	16	12	5-2	2-1	Mariner 3, Mills 42, Woods 46, Whymark 75p, 88; Francis 1, 64 — Ref: A Turvey

Line-ups (Ipswich / opponent in italic) — columns 1–12 sub used

No	1	2	3	4	5	6	7	8	9	10	11	12 sub used
1	Cooper	Burley	Tibbott	Talbot	Hunter	Beattie	Osborne	Gates	Mariner	Geddis	Woods	
	Jennings	*Rice*	*Nelson*	*Ross*	*Young*	*O'Leary*	*Powling*	*Brady**	*MacDonald*	*Stapleton*	*Rix*	*Price*
2	Cooper	Burley	Tibbott	Talbot	Hunter	Beattie	Osborne	Gates	Mariner	Geddis	Woods	
	Boulton	*Langan*	*Nish**	*Daly*	*McFarland*	*Todd*	*O'Riordan*	*Gemmill*	*Hales*	*Hector*	*Hughes*	*Webster*
3	Cooper	Burley	Tibbott	Talbot	Hunter	Beattie	Osborne*	Gates	Mariner	Geddis	Woods	
	Stepney	*Nichol**	*Albiston*	*McIlroy**	*Greenhoff*	*Buchan*	*McGrath*	*McCreery*	*Coppell*	*Macari*	*Hill*	*Grimes*
4	Cooper	Burley	Tibbott	Talbot	Hunter	Osman	Osborne	Gates	Mariner	Whymark	Woods	
	Phillips	*Harris*	*Wilkins G*	*Britton*	*Droy*	*Wicks*	*Stanley*	*Wilkins R*	*Finnieston**	*Swain*	*Langley*	*Garner*
5	Cooper	Burley	Tibbott	Talbot	Hunter	Osman	Osborne	Gates	Mariner	Whymark*	Woods	Turner
	Stewart	*Cherry**	*Gray F*	*Lorimer*	*McQueen*	*Madeley*	*Gray E*	*Hankin*	*Jordan*	*Currie*	*Graham*	*Stevenson*
6	Cooper	Burley	Tibbott	Talbot	Hunter	Beattie	Osborne*	Gates	Mariner	Whymark	Woods	Geddis
	Clemence	*Neal*	*Jones*	*Smith*	*Kennedy*	*Hughes*	*Dalglish*	*Case*	*Heighway**	*McDermott*	*Callaghan*	*Fairclough*
7	Cooper	Burley	Tibbott	Talbot	Hunter	Beattie	Osborne	Gates	Mariner	Whymark	Woods	Geddis
	Platt	*Craggs**	*Bailey*	*Souness*	*Boam*	*Ramage*	*Mahoney*	*Mills*	*Ashcroft*	*McAndrew*	*Armstrong*	*Willey*
8	Cooper	Burley	Tibbott	Talbot	Hunter	Beattie	Mills	Gates	Mariner	Whymark*	Woods	Lambert
	Mahoney	*Craig D**	*Kennedy*	*Callachan*	*McCaffery*	*Nattrass*	*Barrowcl'gh*	*McLean*	*Burns*	*Gowling*	*Craig T*	*Oates*
9	Shilton	Burley	Tibbott	Talbot*	Hunter	Beattie	Mills	Gates	Mariner	Withe	Woods	Lambert
	Shilton	*Anderson*	*Barrett*	*McGovern*	*Lloyd*	*Burns*	*O'Neill*	*Bowyer*	*Withe*	*Woodcock*	*Robertson*	*Lambert*
10	Cooper	Burley	Tibbott	Talbot	Hunter	Beattie	Mills	Gates	Mariner*	Whymark	Woods	Geddis
	Godden	*Mulligan*	*Statham*	*Brown*	*Wile*	*Robertson*	*Cantello*	*Cunningham*	*Regis*	*Robson*	*Johnston*	*Geddis*
11	Cooper	Burley	Tibbott	Talbot	Hunter	Osman	Mills	Gates	Mariner*	Whymark*	Woods	Turner
	Montgomery	*Calderwood*	*Pendrey*	*Page*	*Howard*	*Went*	*Towers*	*Francis*	*Bertschin*	*Hibbitt*	*Emmanuel*	*Turner*

Match notes

1. v ARSENAL. Jennings, who nearly joined Town in the summer, makes a brilliant one-handed stop from Mariner's shot, but Geddis pounces for his first goal at this level. Rain stops play in the second half when a torrential downpour floods the pitch. The teams are led off for 11 minutes until it eases.

2. v DERBY. Cooper makes a series of fine saves as Colin Murphy's Derby dominate the second period without managing a breakthrough. Town fail to score for the eighth successive visit to the rain-soaked Baseball Ground. Derby have just launched an innovative sponsorship deal with Saab.

3. v MANCHESTER U. With Bertschin sold to Birmingham for £135,000 and Whymark on the treatment table, Town are lacking potency in attack and are unable to convert early superiority into goals. Coppell's drive hits the Town bar and rebounds to McCreery but he steers his header over the open goal.

4. v CHELSEA. Osman is called up for the injured Beattie, who had just been recalled by Greenwood for the England squad. Ken Shellito's side are beaten when Talbot forces the ball home after Droy blocks Mariner's shot and Phillips can only half-save Whymark's attempt from the rebound.

5. v LEEDS. Gates' miskick falls conveniently for Mariner to put Town ahead, but two minutes later Hankin dives to head Graham's deep cross beyond a despairing Cooper. Eddie Gray has a fine game in midfield and from his cross McQueen nods the ball on for Hankin to force home the winner.

6. v LIVERPOOL. Dalglish conjures up a superb chip after spotting Cooper a short way off his line, but later misses an easier chance. The arrival of Geddis sees a switch involving Woods and the game is transformed. Beattie soars high to meet Talbot's corner and finds Whymark who flicks in a header.

7. v MIDDLESBROUGH. Whymark flicks the ball up and is about to shoot when Mariner nips in and helps himself to a goal! Souness puts Mills through and he tucks the ball past the advancing Cooper. Good football is at a premium in windy conditions, and John Neal's Middlesbrough go closest to a winner.

8. v NEWCASTLE. Richard Dinnis' bottom-of-the-table side take a surprise lead, but Mills tucks home his first goal in 18 months to level. Town are well on top after this and a smart drive by Gates wins the points. Two days later Woods and Whymark get their first call-ups to the England senior squad.

9. v NOTT'M FOREST. Brian Clough's newly-promoted side continue their superb start. Winger Robertson is a constant menace and helps create all four goals for big Withe. His first was a fine header and the second sees him stab home a low cross. Lloyd has a piledriver from distance disallowed for offside.

10. v WEST BROM. Town are proud to have five men reporting for senior England duty this weekend, but fail to sparkle against Ronnie Allen's men after being under much pressure in the first half. Having apparently ridden the storm, Cantello shoots against Hunter and it rebounds for Robson to score.

11. v BIRMINGHAM. An unhappy return to Ipswich for Sir Alf Ramsey, in temporary charge of City, although Francis shows dazzling skill to shoot them ahead in just 63 seconds. Mariner levels with a fine header and Town take control. Whymark makes the points safe from the spot after Page's handball.

#		Opponent	Date	Att	Pos	Res	HT	Scorers / Referee
12	A	COVENTRY	22/10	20,014	10 6 13	D	1-1	0-0 — Mariner 48, Hutchison 59 — Ref: R Lewis
13	H	WEST HAM	29/10	27,308	10 19 13	L	0-2	0-1 — Hales 25, 82 — Ref: M Sinclair
14	H	MANCHESTER C	5/11	23,636	10 6 15	W	1-0	1-0 — Mariner 4 — Ref: D Richardson
15	A	LEICESTER	12/11	13,779	11 21 15	L	1-2	1-2 — Talbot 20, Williams 25, Salmons 27 — Ref: A McDonald
16	H	EVERTON	19/11	22,795	11 2 16	D	3-3	0-0 — Mariner 64, Whymark 71p, 82, Lyons 75, Pearson 81, Buckley 90 — Ref: K Salmon
17	A	WOLVERHAMPTON	26/11	18,468	11 12 17	D	0-0	0-0 — Ref: B Martin
18	H	ASTON VILLA	3/12	20,917	10 11 19	W	2-0	2-0 — Whymark 6, Gates 37 — Ref: C Downey
19	A	BRISTOL CITY	10/12	24,701	11 14 19	L	0-2	0-1 — Tainton 5, Gillies 85 — Ref: D Reeves
20	H	LEICESTER	17/12	16,905	10 22 21	W	1-0	1-0 — Whymark 19 — Ref: B Homewood
21	A	NORWICH	26/12	27,887	7 - 21	L	0-1	0-1 — Ryan 17 — Ref: P Reeves
22	H	QP RANGERS	27/12	22,317	10 19 23	W	3-2	1-0 — Geddis 3, 70, Mills 63, Bowles 50p, McGee 84 — Ref: C Maskell
23	H	DERBY	31/12	20,816	11 12 23	L	1-2	1-2 — Mariner 17, Ryan 41, George 43 — Ref: T Bune

12 — COVENTRY
Ipswich: Cooper, Burley*, Roberts, Talbot, Mills, Osman, Hunter, Tibbott, Gates, Mariner, Whymark, Osborne, Geddis
Coventry: Blyth, Oakey, McDonald, Yorath*, Nardiello, Coop, Dugdale, Wallace, Ferguson, Powell, Hutchison, Graydon
Annoyed by the poor away results, Robson switches to a five-man defence with Hunter sweeping behind Roberts and Osman. It works well and Town could have had more than Mariner's second-half header. Gordon Milne's side save a point with Hutchison's first goal of the season.

13 — WEST HAM
Ipswich: Cooper, Mills, Tibbott, Talbot, Osborne*, Osman, Hunter, Gates*, Mariner, Whymark, Woods, Geddis
West Ham: Day, Lampard, Brush, Bonds, Devonshire, Pike, Taylor, Robson, Radford, Brooking, Hales
Town lack ideas and are deservedly beaten by John Lyall's spirited side. Pike's cross is knocked into space by Radford and Hales swoops to flash a volley home. He clinches the win late on as he outpaces Tibbott to reach a Radford through-ball and lobs neatly over Cooper's head.

14 — MANCHESTER C
Ipswich: Cooper, Stirk, Talbot, Mills, Osman, Hunter, Gates*, Mariner, Whymark, Woods, Turner
Manchester City: Corrigan, Clements, Donachie, Doyle, Watson, Owen, Barnes, Channon, Kidd, Hartford, Power
An early start due to the threat of power cuts and Mariner catches City asleep as he nets twice in the first five minutes, but the second effort is ruled out for a push on Doyle. Injury-hit Town have to battle to keep the lead with only one established defender, Hunter, fit enough to play.

15 — LEICESTER
Ipswich: Cooper, Stirk, Talbot, Mills, Osman, Hunter, Gates, Mariner, Whymark, Woods*, Williams
Leicester: Wallington, Whitworth, Rofe, Kember, Blockley, Webb, Sammels, Weller, Waddle, Williams, Salmons
Bottom-of-the-table Leicester are jubilant to snatch their first away win for eight months and only their second win of the season. Williams and Salmons, who made their City debuts in a two-minute spell to cancel out Talbot's effort.

16 — EVERTON
Ipswich: Cooper, Stirk, Talbot, Mills, Osman, Roberts, Gates, Mariner, Whymark, Woods, Ross
Everton: Wood, Jones, Pejic*, Lyons, Higgins, Buckley, King, Dobson, Latchford, Pearson, Thomas
An inexperienced Ipswich defence is let off the hook by in-form Everton, who might have won had they attacked in numbers earlier. Gordon Lee's side extend their unbeaten run to 17 matches with three goals in the last 15 minutes after man-of-the-match Mills nearly fashions a win.

17 — WOLVERHAMPTON
Ipswich: Cooper, Stirk, Talbot, Mills, Osman, Hunter, Gates, Mariner, Whymark, Woods
Wolverhampton: Bradshaw, Palmer, Parkin, Patching, Hibbitt, McAlle, Carr, Richards, Eves, Kelly, Daley
After the Barcelona euphoria, this is a tame affair with the incident-free first period improving only slightly after the break as both keepers are called into action, Bradshaw foiling Mariner and Cooper saving from Richards. Beattie returns in the reserves just 25 days after knee surgery.

18 — ASTON VILLA
Ipswich: Cooper, Stirk, Mills, Talbot, Osman, Hunter, Tibbott, Viljoen, Gates, Mariner, Whymark, Woods
Aston Villa: Rimmer, Gidman, Smith, Phillips, McNaught, Mortimer, Cowans, Little, Gray, Gregory, Carradus
England's two UEFA Cup sides meet and Viljoen returns to start a game for the first time in over two years. The in-form Whymark strikes again but Ron Saunders' team are a shade unfortunate to come away pointless and goalless. Gray's first-half strike is disallowed for offside.

19 — BRISTOL CITY
Ipswich: Cooper, Mills, Talbot, Osman, Hunter, Tibbott*, Viljoen, Gates, Mariner, Whymark, Woods
Bristol City: Shaw, Sweeney, Merrick, Gow, Collier, Tainton, Ritchie, Royle*, Gillies, Whitehead, Mabbutt
Alan Dicks' side fly off the starting blocks with bemused Town pinned back for 20 minutes. Cooper keeps Town in the contest in the ninth minute with an excellent save from Sweeney's penalty after Gates handles Ritchie's header. Town get back into it, but fail to create chances.

20 — LEICESTER
Ipswich: Cooper, Stirk, Tibbott*, Talbot, Mills, Osman, Hunter, Gates, Mariner, Whymark, Woods, Gates
Leicester: Wallington, Williams, Rofe, Goodwin, Sims, Woollett, Weller, Davies, Farmer*, Kelly, White, Sammels
A 25-yard blast from Mariner hits the underside of the bar and is headed home by Whymark. Wallington is responsible for keeping Frank McLintock's side in the contest with a number of good saves. Christmas, plus indifferent form, leads to the lowest League gate for four years.

21 — NORWICH
Ipswich: Cooper, Burley, Mills, Talbot, Osman, Hunter, Tibbott, Gates, Mariner, Whymark, Woods, Gates
Norwich: Keelan, Bond, Sullivan, Ryan, Powell, Jones, Neighbour, Suggett, Gibbins, Paddon*, Peters, Reeves
Osman's handball gives Ryan a penalty and he nets the rebound after Cooper pushes his first attempt against the crossbar. Town claims for a spot-kick near the end are ignored after Gibbins appears to handle. Whymark collides with Jones and picks up a serious knee ligament injury.

22 — QP RANGERS
Ipswich: Cooper, Burley, Tibbott, Talbot, Mills, Osman, Hunter, Viljoen*, Gates, Mariner, Geddis, Bowles, Turner
QP Rangers: Richardson, Shanks, Gillard, Hollins, Howe, Cunningham, James, Francis, Givens, Bowles, Eastoe*, McGee
An entertaining contest is highlighted by Mills' brilliant second-half strike. He takes Tibbott's pass on his chest, turns and fires home shortly after Town are angered by a disputed penalty award. Hunter looks to have chested the ball, but Mr Maskell begs to differ and Bowles scores.

23 — DERBY
Ipswich: Cooper, Burley, Tibbott, Talbot, Mills, Osman, Hunter, Viljoen, Gates, Mariner, Geddis, Ryan*, Gates
Derby: Middleton, Langan, Daniel, Daly, Hunt, Todd, Curran, Powell, Masson, George, Ryan*, Chesters
After recent penalty controversies, Town now have more reason to be angry. After Talbot fouls Ryan, the referee is heard to whistle and play comes to a halt. But, after George bangs the loose ball into the net a goal is given! Geddis, Hunter and Mariner all hit Derby's woodwork, too.

LEAGUE DIVISION 1

SEASON 1977-78 — Manager: Bobby Robson

No 24 — A ARSENAL — 2/1 — Att 43,705 — Pos 12 — Pt 23 — F-A 0-1 (H-T 0-1) — L
Scorers: Price 37. Ref: M Taylor

Team	1	2	3	4	5	6	7	8	9	10	11	12 sub used
Town	Cooper	Burley	Tibbott	Talbot	Hunter	Osman	Mills	Viljoen	Mariner	Geddis	Turner*	Osborne
Arsenal	*Jennings*	*Rice*	*Nelson*	*Price*	*O'Leary*	*Young*	*Brady*	*Sunderland*	*MacDonald*	*Heeley**	*Rix*	*Simpson*

The woodwork foils Town again as Burley's second-half shot somehow stays out. Town have more of the play but are missing Whymark. In a rare raid Sunderland clips the post for Terry Neill's side. Town are boosted by news that Wark, Lambert and Beattie are nearly ready to return.

No 25 — H MANCHESTER U — 14/1 — Att 22,654 — Pos 13 — Pt 23 — F-A 1-2 (H-T 1-2) — L
Scorers: Mariner 32; McIlroy 11, Pearson 29. Ref: J Hunting

Team	1	2	3	4	5	6	7	8	9	10	11	12 sub used
Town	Cooper	Mills	Tibbott	Talbot	Hunter	Osman	Wark	Viljoen	Mariner*	Geddis	Gates	**Brazil**
Manchester U	*Roche*	*Nicholl*	*Albiston*	*McIlroy*	*Houston*	*Buchan*	*Coppell*	*Greenhoff*	*Pearson*	*Macari*	*Hill*	

Dave Sexton's men put on a slick first-half performance and Town never recover despite working hard. The in-form Mills, now moved back to full-back, is presented with a silver salver by Tommy Parker for breaking his club appearances record, which has stood for more than 20 years.

No 26 — A CHELSEA — 21/1 — Att 26,044 — Pos 16 — Pt 23 — F-A 3-5 (H-T 2-1) — L
Scorers: Osb' 14, Wrk 29, Mam't 81 (Lang' 90); Swain 27, 67, Finn' 74, Wicks 84. Ref: S Bates

Team	1	2	3	4	5	6	7	8	9	10	11	12 sub used
Town	Sivell	Mills	Tibbott	Talbot	Hunter	Osman	Osborne	Wark	Mariner*	Geddis	Woods	Brazil
Chelsea	*Bonetti*	*Locke*	*Harris*	*Britton*	*Droy*	*Wicks*	*Garner**	*Wilkins*	*Langley*	*Swain*	*Walker*	*Finnieston*

'At times like these we need your support more than ever,' says Robson, as fans moan about the fourth successive League loss. Prompted by the lively Gates, Town are on top until Swain equalises in the second half, looking well offside. The injury crisis shows few signs of easing up.

No 27 — H LEEDS — 4/2 — Att 24,023 — Pos 16 — Pt 23 — F-A 0-1 (H-T 0-0) — L
Scorers: Gray E 79. Ref: J Bent

Team	1	2	3	4	5	6	7	8	9	10	11	12 sub used
Town	Cooper	Burley	Mills	Talbot	Hunter	Roberts	Wark	Viljoen	Geddis	Turner	Woods	Osborne
Leeds	*Harvey*	*Cherry*	*Gray F*	*Lorimer*	*Parkinson*	*Madeley*	*Gray E*	*Hankin*	*Currie*	*Flynn*	*Graham*	

A fifth League defeat in a row thanks to Eddie Gray's scrambled late effort. Robson urges patience, denying reports that Mariner and Beattie will move, but also insists Town has no funds to splash out on any expensive new players. The gloom is only lifted by progress in the FA Cup.

No 28 — A NEWCASTLE — 25/2 — Att 22,521 — Pos 15 — Pt 25 — F-A 1-0 (H-T 0-0) — W
Scorers: Woods 62. Ref: C Seel

Team	1	2	3	4	5	6	7	8	9	10	11	12 sub used
Town	Cooper	Burley	Mills	Talbot	Hunter	Osman	Wark	Viljoen	Mariner	Turner	Woods*	Osborne*
Newcastle	*Mahoney*	*Nattrass*	*Barker*	*Cassidy*	*Bird*	*Blackley*	*Barrowc'gh*	*Burns*	*Larnach*	*Kennedy*	*Gowling*	

A rare headed goal by Woods lifts fears of plunging into the relegation mire, but it was poor fare against Bill McGarry's troubled side. 'We simply had to win that one,' reflects Robson, who has just been put in charge of England 'B' for the first time, working alongside Don Howe.

No 29 — H WEST BROM — 4/3 — Att 22,084 — Pos 16 — Pt 26 — F-A 2-2 (H-T 1-0) — D
Scorers: Mills 39, Wark 51; Brown T 55p, 90. Ref: D Smith

Team	1	2	3	4	5	6	7	8	9	10	11	12 sub used
Town	Cooper	Burley	Mills*	Talbot	Hunter	Osman	Osborne	Wark	Mariner	Turner	Woods	
West Brom	*Godden*	*Batson*	*Statham*	*Brown T*	*Wile*	*Robertson*	*Martin**	*Brown A*	*Regis*	*Trewick*	*Johnston*	*Cunningham*

Town dominate the first half and Wark seems to have clinched the first home League win since December. Albion fight back well, aided by an injury to the influential Mills. With Woods screaming for a penalty after a Statham challenge, Albion break to the other end and Brown levels.

No 30 — H COVENTRY — 18/3 — Att 21,110 — Pos 17 — Pt 27 — F-A 1-1 (H-T 0-0) — D
Scorers: Woods 62; Osgood 67. Ref: D Reeves

Team	1	2	3	4	5	6	7	8	9	10	11	12 sub used
Town	Cooper	Burley	Mills	Talbot	Hunter	Beattie	Osborne	Wark	Mariner*	Turner	Woods	Lambert
Coventry	*Blyth*	*Roberts*	*McDonald*	*Yorath*	*Holton*	*Coop*	*Nardiello**	*Osgood*	*Wallace*	*Powell*	*Hutchison*	*Beck*

Chances go astray and Woods strikes a post with a superb volley. He hits the target later on from Turner's cross, just as Nardiello is being helped off with a broken collar-bone. City respond when Osgood fires home a powerful shot after Powell back-heels a free-kick into his path.

No 31 — H MIDDLESBROUGH — 21/3 — Att 17,789 — Pos 17 — Pt 28 — F-A 1-1 (H-T 0-0) — D
Scorers: Wark 51p; Ashcroft 84. Ref: A Gunn

Team	1	2	3	4	5	6	7	8	9	10	11	12 sub used
Town	Cooper	Burley	Mills	Talbot	Hunter	Beattie	Osborne	Wark	Mariner	Turner	Woods	Lambert
Middlesbrough	*Platt*	*Craggs*	*Bailey*	*Mahoney*	*Baam*	*Ramage*	*Johnston**	*Cummins*	*Ashcroft*	*McAndrew*	*Armstrong*	*Hickton*

Another disappointing display and the sixth home League match without a win. Mills says he cannot recall a Town side giving the ball away as often as they did on this night against John Neal's moderate side. Craggs hauls down Woods to give Wark the chance to convert from the spot.

No 32 — A WEST HAM — 24/3 — Att 23,687 — Pos 17 — Pt 28 — F-A 0-3 (H-T 0-0) — L
Scorers: Cross 50, 55, 58. Ref: H Robinson

Team	1	2	3	4	5	6	7	8	9	10	11	12 sub used
Town	Cooper	Mills	Tibbott	Talbot	Hunter	Beattie	Osborne*	Wark	Mariner	Turner	Woods	Lambert
West Ham	*Ferguson*	*Bonds*	*Lampard*	*Curbishley*	*Taylor*	*Green*	*Pike*	*Holland*	*Cross*	*Brooking*	*Hales*	

Cross, signed by John Lyall to lift the Hammers out of the relegation zone, boosts their chances with a quick-fire second-half hat-trick. Town, with games coming thick and fast in advance of the cup semi-final, look dejected and lifeless and goalkeeper Ferguson is largely unemployed.

No 33 — A QP RANGERS — 25/3 — Att 15,563 — Pos 16 — Pt 29 — F-A 3-3 (H-T 1-2) — D
Scorers: Wark 28, Burley 57, Mariner 61; James 30, McGee 44, 46. Ref: B Stevens

Team	1	2	3	4	5	6	7	8	9	10	11	12 sub used
Town	Cooper	Burley	Mills	Talbot	Hunter	Beattie	Osborne	Wark	Mariner	Geddis	Woods	
QP Rangers	*Parkes*	*Clement*	*Gillard*	*Hollins*	*Howe*	*Cunningham*	*Shanks*	*Busby*	*James*	*Bowles*	*Givens**	*McGee*

After the West Ham debacle, Town show much more fight in dreadful conditions. Nearby, the University boat race ends in farce when a crew sinks, but Town stay afloat despite going two behind. Young Irish substitute McGee strikes twice, his only other goal having been at Ipswich.

No 34 — H NORWICH — 27/3 — Att 29,930 — Pos 16 — Pt 31 — F-A 4-0 (H-T 2-0) — W
Scorers: Talbot 12, 32, Geddis 62, Mills 79. Ref: K Styles

Team	1	2	3	4	5	6	7	8	9	10	11	12 sub used
Town	Cooper	Burley	Mills	Talbot	Hunter	Beattie	Osborne*	Wark	Mariner	Geddis	Woods	Lambert
Norwich	*Hansbury*	*Ryan*	*Sullivan*	*McGuire**	*Jones*	*Powell*	*Neighbour*	*Downs*	*Paddon*	*Reeves*	*Robson*	*Suggett*

The improvement continues and never-say-die local lad Talbot delights Town fans by sending the old enemy reeling in the first period. Mariner plays a starring role in a comfortable win and is unlucky when his drive hits the bar. Having been top-six, City are sinking down the table fast.

Football season records — League matches 35–42 and League Cup rounds 2–4. Each entry: Ipswich Town line-up (roman) / opponents (italic), with scorers and referee, followed by a match report.

35. A — 1/4 — MANCHESTER C — 34,975 — 16 · 4 · 31 — L 1-2 (0-1)
- Cooper, Burley, Mills, Talbot, Hunter, Osman, Osborne*, Wark, Mariner, Geddis, Woods, *Lambert*
- *Corrigan, Clements, Donachie, Doyle, Watson, Owen, Channon, Booth, Palmer, Hartford, Barnes*
- Mariner 84 — Palmer 41, Channon 81
- Ref: J Butcher

With the semi-final looming, FA Cup fever has a firm grip on the club and the town and defeat is not unexpected in this sixth League match in a 14-day period. Mariner's late consolation was one of several chances that went begging, as City advance their claims for a UEFA Cup place.

36. A — 11/4 — BIRMINGHAM — 19,289 — 16 · 12 · 32 — D 0-0 (0-0)
- Cooper, Tibbott, Mills, Osman, Beattie, Osborne, Wark, Mariner, Geddis*, Woods, *Lambert*
- *Montgomery, Calderwood, Towers, Gallagher, Howard, Page, Francis, Bertschin, Hibbitt*, Fox, Connolly*
- Ref: A Challinor

After the dust settles on the semi-final victory, more radical team changes are forced upon Robson. Patched-up Town fight hard for this very handy point, with Osman having a fine game to keep Francis quiet after the England man had scored in all his previous seven League games.

37. A — 15/4 — EVERTON — 33,402 — 16 · 2 · 32 — L 0-1 (0-0)
- Cooper, Burley, Tibbott, Mills, Osman, Butcher, Osborne, Wark, Geddis, Turner*, Woods, *Lambert*
- *Wood, Jones, Pejic, Lyons, Robinson, Buckley, King, Dobson, Latchford, McKenzie, Thomas*
- Latchford 62p
- Ref: K Hackett

The central-defensive partnership of teenagers Butcher and Osman makes its debut and copes well until the latter climbs all over Dobson to concede the winning penalty. Dobson hits the Town crossbar in a very one-sided affair and Wood remains a spectator for most of the match.

38. A — 18/4 — LIVERPOOL — 40,044 — 16 · 4 · 33 — D 2-2 (1-0)
- Cooper, Burley, Mills, Talbot, Hunter, Osman, Osborne, Wark, Whymark*, Geddis, Woods, *Lambert*
- *Clemence, Neal, Smith, Thompson, Hughes, Fairclough, Dalglish, Case, Heighway*, McDermott, Souness, Lee*
- Whymark 45, Lambert 80 — Dalglish 58, Souness 62
- Ref: T Mills

On the night Forest emulate Town's 1962 achievement of winning the title at the first attempt, a much-improved display wins a precious point to edge Town nearer safety. Clemence keeps the home side on terms until Whymark, back after 16 weeks out, scores on the stroke of half-time.

39. H — 22/4 — BRISTOL CITY — 22,535 — 15 · 16 · 35 — W 1-0 (1-0)
- Cooper, Burley, Mills, Talbot, Hunter, Osman, Osborne, Wark, Whymark, Geddis, Woods, *Lambert*
- *Shaw, Sweeney, Merrick, Gow !, Rodgers, Hunter, Tainton, Ritchie, Royle, Cormack*, Mann, Mabbutt*
- Mills 64
- Ref: B Daniels

Mills is presented with the Player of the Year award and celebrates by firing a goal which guarantees safety from relegation. Royle hits the post and Woods has a spectacular goal ruled out for offside. Osman fouls Gow and a free-kick is given but the City man lashes out and is sent off.

40. H — 25/4 — NOTT'M FOREST — 30,062 — 16 · 1 · 35 — L 0-2 (0-0)
- Cooper, Burley, Mills, Talbot, Hunter, Osman, Osborne*, Wark, Mariner, Whymark, Woods, *Lambert*
- *Shilton, Anderson, Barrett, O'Hare, Needham, Burns, O'Neill, Bowyer, Withe*, Gemmill, Robertson, Clark*
- Mariner 73 (og), Clark 78
- Ref: K Salmon

Safe from the drop and playing forward to Wembley, Town fans are in benevolent mood and give Brian Clough a warm ovation for the title success. Mariner, equally generous, flicks Robertson's corner over his own net. Clark swoops to become Forest's 14th scorer of the season.

41. A — 29/4 — ASTON VILLA — 30,955 — 16 · 8 · 35 — L 1-6 (0-4)
- Overton, Burley, Mills, Talbot, Hunter, Osman, Vijoen, Wark, Geddis, Whymark, Woods, *Lambert*
- *Rimmer, Gidman, Smith, Evans, McNaught, Mortimer, Deehan, Little, Gray, Cowans, Carrodus, Clark*
- Whymark 89 [Carr 53, Cowans 68] — Deehan 14, 44, Gray 17, Little 24, [Carr 53, Cowans 68]
- Ref: G Owen

Overton becomes the youngest first-teamer in the club's history at 17 years, 11 days. A week before the cup final, with a midfield re-shuffle and a clear lack of commitment, Ron Saunders' side are allowed to run riot. The exposed young keeper makes fine saves and is not to blame.

42. H — 9/5 — WOLVERHAMPTON — 25,904 — 18 · 15 · 35 — L 1-2 (0-2)
- Cooper, Bradshaw, Mills, Talbot, Hunter, Osman, Osborne*, Butcher, Wark, Mariner, Geddis, Woods, *Parkin*
- *Palmer, Parkin, Daley, Hazell, McAlle, Patching, Berry, Richards, Eves*, Rafferty, Clarke*
- Wark 82 — Rafferty 2, 16
- Ref: R Lewis

If ever an end-of-season game was meaningless, this was it. The excesses of the cup celebrations seem to be taking a toll as Rafferty poaches two early goals and later debutant Clark strikes the post. Town wake up in the final quarter and apply pressure, but it was all a little too late.

Home 23,552
Away 26,981
Average 25,904

League Cup

2. H — 30/8 — NORTHAMPTON — 15,276 — 9 · 4:9 — W 5-0 (2-0)
- Cooper, Burley, Mills, Talbot, Hunter, Beattie*, Osborne, Gates, Whymark, Mariner, Woods, *Lambert*
- *Garnham, Tucker, Bryant, Liddle, Robertson, Best, Farrington, Williams, Martin*, Reilly, Christie, Mead*
- Whymark 11p, 54, Gates 40, [Woods 86, Mariner 87]
- Ref: B Homewood

After a long hold-up while an injured linesman is replaced in the opening minutes, Robertson trips Mariner for a penalty and John Petts' side are on their way out. Best goal of the night sees Woods set off down the right and beat three men before crashing home from a very tight angle.

3. A — 25/10 — BURNLEY — 9,607 — 10 · 2:22 — W 2-1 (2-1)
- Cooper, Burley, Roberts, Talbot, Osman, Mills, Osborne, Gates, Mariner, Whymark, Woods, *Geddis*
- *Stevenson, Newton, Brennan, Noble, Rodaway, Thomson, Cochrane, Smith, Fletcher, Morley, Flynn*
- Whymark 16, 18 — Fletcher 5
- Ref: K Hackett

Town's defence dithers as Morley crosses and Fletcher swoops to score. Whymark levels by heading in Gates' cross and two minutes later accepts an easy chance after Mariner's header causes a mix-up in Harry Potts' side's defence. Stevenson later does well to prevent a hat-trick.

4. H — 29/11 — MANCHESTER C — 22,120 — 11 · 6 — L 1-2 (1-1)
- Cooper, Stirk, Mills, Talbot, Hunter, Beattie*, Osborne, Gates, Whymark, Mariner, Woods, *Lambert*
- *Corrigan, Clements, Donachie, Booth, Watson, Power, Barnes, Channon, Kidd, Hartford, Tueart*
- Whymark 44p — Kidd 34, Tueart 58
- Ref: R Toseland

Tony Book's men are worthy winners but when Stirk stretches to prevent Kidd's effort from crossing the line, Mr Toseland gives a goal and sparks furious arguments. Justice seems to be done before the break when he gives Town a penalty after a rather innocuous challenge on Osman.

LEAGUE DIVISION 1 (CUP-TIES)

Manager: Bobby Robson **SEASON 1977-78**

FA Cup

3 — A CARDIFF, 7/1 — Att 13,584 2:19 — W 2-0 (H-T 0-0)
Scorers, Times, and Referees: Mariner 49, 73 — Ref: J Bent

1	2	3	4	5	6	7	8	9	10	11	12 sub used
Cooper	Mills	Tibbott	Talbot	Hunter	Osman	Wark	Viljoen	Mariner	Geddis*	Gates	Parkin
Healey	Dwyer	Pethard	Campbell	Pontin	Larmour	Giles	Sayer	Went	Bishop	Attley*	Grapes

Mills breaks the club record of 493 first-team appearances and returns to full-back with Wark coming into midfield for his first game of the season. Jimmy Andrews' strugglers never look likely giant-killers and Mariner's lethal touch is the difference between the sides in a dull affair.

4 — H HARTLEPOOL, 28/1 — Att 24,207 4:23 — W 4-1 (H-T 2-1)
Scorers, Times, and Referees: Viljoen 6p, 66, Mariner 27, Talbot 49; Downing 40 — Ref: B Homewood

1	2	3	4	5	6	7	8	9	10	11	12 sub used
Cooper	Burley*	Mills	Talbot	Hunter	Beattie	Lambert	Viljoen	Mariner	Turner	Woods	Wark
Edgar	Malone	Downing	Gibb	Ayre	Smith	Creamer	McMordie*	Newton	Paskett	Bieby	Linacre

91st in the League, but Billy Horner's side are full of fight and look rather hard-done-by when Downing's challenge on Mariner is deemed worthy of a penalty. Downing pulls a goal back with a powerful shot from the edge of the box, but Town are rarely troubled in this routine win.

5 — A BRISTOL ROV, 18/2 — Att 23,453 2:11 — D 2-2 (H-T 1-0)
Scorers, Times, and Referees: Turner 27, 86; Williams 58, 64 — Ref: B Daniels

1	2	3	4	5	6	7	8	9	10	11	12 sub used
Cooper	Burley	Mills	Talbot	Hunter	Osman	Wark	Viljoen*	Mariner	Turner	Woods	Osborne
Thomas	Aitken	Bater	Day	Taylor	Prince	Barry	Pulis	Gould	Williams	Randall	

The game gets the go-ahead despite a real skating rink of a pitch. Special footwear is called for, but doesn't prevent a lot of farcical skidding around by some players. Gould nearly ends the cup run but has his effort disallowed. Turner is credited with the late goal that wins a replay.

5R — H BRISTOL ROV, 28/2 — Att 29,090 2:11 — W 3-0 (H-T 1-0)
Scorers, Times, and Referees: Mills 27, Mariner 57, Woods 78 — Ref: B Daniels

1	2	3	4	5	6	7	8	9	10	11	12 sub used
Cooper	Burley	Mills	Talbot	Hunter	Osman	Wark	Viljoen	Mariner	Turner*	Woods	Brazil
Thomas	Aitken	Bater	Day	Taylor	Prince	Barry	Pulis	Gould	Staniforth*	Randall	Williams

Rovers are not overawed and carve a few opportunities, but once Town edge ahead they seem to have the measure of Bobby Campbell's side and cruise into the quarter-finals. Woods lights up the night with a magnificent goal, cutting in after a run and firing home an unstoppable shot.

6 — A MILLWALL, 11/3 — Att 23,082 2:20 — W 6-1 (H-T 1-0)
Scorers, Times, and Referees: Burley 10, Mariner 52, 72, 89, Mehmet 84 [Wark 87, Talbot 88] — Ref: W Gow

1	2	3	4	5	6	7	8	9	10	11	12 sub used
Cooper	Burley	Mills	Talbot	Hunter	Osman	Osborne*	Wark	Mariner	Turner	Woods	Lambert
Johns	Donaldson	Moore	Walker	Kitchener	Hazell	Pearson	Chambers	Hamilton	Lee	Cross*	Mehmet

Burley paves the way for a semi-final date with a long-range special past helpless Johns. The biggest quarter-final away win for over 50 years doesn't flatter Town, who are way ahead of George Petchey's men. Sadly, violence by home fans requires two stoppages, one of 18 minutes.

SF — N WEST BROM, 8/4 — Att 50,922 8 — W 3-1 (H-T 2-0)
Scorers, Times, and Referees: Talbot 8, Mills 20, Wark 89; Brown T 76p — Ref: C Thomas

1	2	3	4	5	6	7	8	9	10	11	12 sub used
Cooper	Burley	Mills	Talbot*	Hunter	Beattie	Osborne	Wark	Mariner	Turner	Woods	Lambert
Godden	Mulligan	Statham	Brown T	Wile*	Robertson	Martin !	Brown A	Regis	Trewick	Johnston	Cunningham

Talbot dives to head a fine goal but a nasty clash of heads with Wile leaves both bloodied and unable to complete the game. Mills scrambles a second and Town seem safe until Hunter's handball gives Albion a lifeline. Martin gets a second booking before Wark's fine header seals it.

F — N ARSENAL, 6/5 — Att 100,000 4 — W 1-0 (H-T 0-0)
Scorers, Times, and Referees: Osborne 77 — Ref: D Nippard

1	2	3	4	5	6	7	8	9	10	11	12 sub used
Cooper	Burley	Mills	Talbot	Hunter	Beattie	Osborne*	Wark	Mariner	Geddis	Woods	Lambert
Jennings	Rice	Nelson	Price	O'Leary	Young	Brady*	Sunderland	MacDonald	Stapleton	Hudson	Rix

On a wet pitch, Beattie and Hunter pass late tests and Town get better as the game goes on. Mariner hits the bar, Wark twice hits the post and Jennings makes a great save from Burley. When it seems a goal will never come, Young diverts Geddis's cross to Osborne and he fires home.

UEFA Cup

1:1 — A LANDSKRONA BOIS (Sweden), 14/9 — Att 7,156 — W 8-0 (H-T 1-0)
Scorers, Times, and Referees: Whymark 44 — Ref: N Rolles (Luxembourg)

1	2	3	4	5	6	7	8	9	10	11	12 sub used
Cooper	Burley	Tibbott	Talbot	Hunter	Beattie	Osborne	Gates	Mariner^	Whymark*	Woods	Geddis/Turner
Sorensson	Nilsson	Martensson	Cronquist	Augustsson B	Augustsson J	Theander	Sjoberg*	Petersson	Johansson	Aronsson	Elgstrom

Led by the Finn Willy Sorensen, the part-time Swedish outfit benefits from the blustery winds but Town keep their composure and Cooper's goal is rarely threatened. Mariner's lay-off finds Whymark who coolly fires home. Town's Swedish-based fan club make their presence felt.

1:2 — H LANDSKRONA BOIS (Sweden), 28/9 — Att 18,741 — W 5-0 (H-T 4-0)
Scorers, Times, and Referees: Whymark 15, 33, 39, 52p, Mariner 38 — Ref: I Neilsen (Denmark) (Town win 6-0 on aggregate)

1	2	3	4	5	6	7	8	9	10	11	12 sub used
Cooper	Burley	Tibbott	Talbot	Hunter*	Beattie	Mills	Gates	Mariner	Whymark	Woods*	L'Ibert/Osman
Sorensson	Nilsson	Elgstrom	Gustavsson	Augustsson B	Augustsson J	Theander	Sjoberg	Petersson	Johansson	Aronsson	

The injury-hit Landskrona defence has no answer to Whymark's all-round expertise and he snatches a hat-trick of headers. He matches his foursome against Lazio with a penalty, given for pushing. Mariner adds to the Swedes' woes by scoring with a well-executed overhead kick.

2:1 — H LAS PALMAS (Spain), 19/10 — Att 22,195 — W 1-0 (H-T 1-0)
Scorers, Times, and Referees: Gates 24 — Ref: J Dubasch (Switzerland)

1	2	3	4	5	6	7	8	9	10	11	12 sub used
Cooper	Burley*	Tibbott	Talbot	Hunter	Osman	Osborne	Gates	Mariner	Whymark^	Woods	Osb'ne/Geddis
Carnevali	Estevez	Paez	Roque	Filipe	Maciel	Brindisi	Felix	Morete	Jorge	Juani*	Gerardo

Gates caps a bright opening period as he heads home neatly from Talbot's cross. Town take their foot off the pedal, but get a chance to open up a good lead when Estevez handles. With first-choice penalty-taker Whymark substituted, Woods steps up but Carnevali makes a diving save.

European matches

2:2 A LAS PALMAS — 2/11 — 25,000 — 10 — D — 3:3 — 2-1

Mariner 12, 74, Tibbott 28
Morete 23, 55, Fernandez 76
Ref: H Verbeke (France)
(Town win 4-3 on aggregate)

Town: Cooper, Mills, Tibbott, Talbot, Hunter, Osman, Osborne, Gates, Mariner, Whymark*, Woods^ — subs Geddis/Roberts
Las Palmas: Carnevali, Estevez, Paez, Roque, Filipe^, Felix, Maciel, Brindisi, Morete, Jorge, Juan* — Fern'z/Hern'z

Town again start well with Talbot's score ruled out before Mariner pounces for the lead. Las Palmas hit the post, then level after a disputed throw. Even the partisan home fans applaud Town as a fine game ends level, the best goal from Tibbott, whose 25-yarder goes in off the bar.

3:1 H BARCELONA (Spain) — 23/11 — 33,663 — 11 — W — 3-0 — 1-0

Gates 16, Whymark 61, Talbot 77
Ref: A Prokop (East Germany)

Town: Cooper, Mills, Tibbott, Talbot, Hunter, Osman, Osborne, Gates*, Mariner, Whymark, Woods — subs Viljoen
Barcelona: Artola, Macizo^, Migueli, Olmo, De la Cruz, Neeskens, Sanchez, Heredia^, Cruyff, Asensi, Zuviria — Rexach/Clares

The slippery Gates shoots home after Woods' fine flank play and Town never let the momentum drop. Rinus Michel's side look unhappy all night long and Osborne wins praise for subduing Johann Cruyff. Woods looks sharp and creates further goals for Whymark and Talbot.

3:2 A BARCELONA — 7/12 — 24,000 — 10 — L — 0:3 — 0-1 aet

Cruyff 21, 46, Rexach 87p
Ref: M Linemayr (Austria)
(Town lose 1-3 on penalties)

Town: Cooper, Mills, Tibbott, Talbot, Hunter, Osman, Osborne, Gates^, Mariner, Whymark*, Woods — subs Geddis/Viljoen
Barcelona: Artola, Macizo^, Migueli, Olmo, Rexach, Neeskens, Sanchez*, Fortes, Cruyff, Asensi, Zuviria^ — Amarillo/Clares

Cruyff puts Town under the cosh in the rain-soaked Nou Camp. Osborne fouls Clares for the equalising penalty after Gates had hit the bar and Mariner had a goal ruled out. In the penalty shoot-out Mills scores, but Talbot, Viljoen and Woods all miss; Barca miss just one and Town exit.

Appearances and Goals

	Appearances								Goals				
	Lge	Sub	LC	Sub	FAC	Sub	Eur	Sub	Lge	LC	FAC	Eur	Tot
Beattie, Kevin	14		1		3		3						
Brazil, Alan		2											
Burley, George	31	2			6		1						2
Butcher, Terry	3												
Cooper, Paul	40		3		7		6						
Gates, Eric	23	1	3	1	6				2	1		2	5
Geddis, David	20	6			4	2					4		4
Hunter, Allan	37		3		7		6						
Lambert, Mick	1	9				3	1				1		1
Mariner, Paul	37		3		7		6		11	1	7	3	22
Mills, Mick	34		2		7		5		6		2		8
Osborne, Roger	24	2	3	1	4	1			1		1		2
Osman, Russell	28	2			4		3		1				1
Overton, Paul	1												
Parkin, Tommy		1						1					
Roberts, Dale	3				1								
Sivell, Laurie	6						1						
Stirk, John	6												
Talbot, Brian	40		3		7		6		4		3	1	8
Tibbott, Les	28	2			5		5				1		1
Turner, Robin	9	5			1				2				2
Viljoen, Colin	10	4			2		2						
Wark, John	18				6	1					5	2	7
Whymark, Trevor	19	1	3		6				9		5	6	20
Woods, Clive	36		2		6		6		3	1	1		5
25 players used	462	27	33	2	77	7	66	11	47	8	21	13	89

Odds & ends

Double wins: (1) Newcastle.
Double losses: (3) Leeds, Nott'm Forest, West Ham.
Won from behind: (3) Newcastle (h), Birmingham (h), Burnley (h) (LC).
Lost from in front: (4) Leeds (a), Leicester (a), Derby (h), Chelsea (a).
High spots: The euphoria of a first FA Cup final victory.
Scoring 42 goals in 16 Cup-ties.
The 3-0 hammering of star-studded Barcelona.
The six-goal response to yob intimidation at Millwall.
The emerging potential of defenders Osman and Butcher.
No fewer than five Town players being called up for an England World Cup qualifying match.
Low spots: The lowest League placing for seven years.
Only one away win in the League.
Whymark's serious injury and Beattie's recurring problems.
Loss of a three-goal lead at Barcelona's Nou Camp.
The violence suffered by Town fans and the stoppages to play in the Millwall Cup-tie.
Player of the Year: Mick Mills.
Ever-presents: (0).
Hat-tricks: (2) Whymark (Eur), Mariner (FAC).
Opposing hat-tricks:(2) Withe (Nott'm Forest), Cross (West Ham).
Leading scorer: (22) Paul Mariner.

League table

		P	Home					Away					Pts
			W	D	L	F	A	W	D	L	F	A	
1	Nott'm Forest	42	15	6	0	37	8	10	8	3	32	16	64
2	Liverpool	42	15	4	2	37	11	9	5	7	28	23	57
3	Everton	42	14	4	3	47	22	6	8	7	29	23	55
4	Manchester C	42	14	4	3	46	21	6	8	7	28	30	52
5	Arsenal	42	14	5	2	38	12	7	5	9	22	25	52
6	West Brom	42	13	5	3	35	18	6	9	7	27	35	50
7	Coventry	42	13	5	3	48	23	5	5	11	27	39	48
8	Aston Villa	42	11	4	6	33	18	7	6	8	24	24	46
9	Leeds	42	12	4	5	39	21	6	6	9	24	32	46
10	Manchester U	42	9	6	6	32	23	7	4	10	35	40	42
11	Birmingham	42	8	5	8	32	30	6	5	10	23	30	41
12	Derby	42	10	7	4	37	24	4	6	11	17	35	41
13	Norwich	42	10	8	3	28	20	1	10	10	24	46	40
14	Middlesbro	42	8	8	5	25	19	4	7	10	17	35	39
15	Wolves	42	7	4	10	30	27	5	4	12	21	37	36
16	Chelsea	42	7	11	3	28	20	4	3	14	18	49	36
17	Bristol City	42	9	6	6	37	26	2	7	12	12	27	35
18	IPSWICH	42	10	5	6	32	24	1	8	12	15	37	35
19	QP Rangers	42	8	8	5	27	26	1	7	13	20	38	33
20	West Ham	42	8	6	7	31	28	4	2	15	21	41	32
21	Newcastle	42	4	6	11	26	37	2	4	15	16	41	22
22	Leicester	42	4	7	10	16	32	1	5	15	10	38	22
		924	223	132	107	741	490	107	132	223	490	741	924

LEAGUE DIVISION 1

Manager: Bobby Robson

SEASON 1978-79

No	Date	Att	Pos	Pt	F-A	H-T		1	2	3	4	5	6	7	8	9	10	11	12 sub used
1 A WEST BROM	19/8	21,700	–	0	1-2	1-1	Town	Cooper	Burley	Mills	Talbot*	Osman	Wark	Parkin	Gates	Mariner	Whymark*	Woods	Lambert
							Opp	Godden	Batson	Statham	Brown T	Wile	Robertson	Robson	Brown A	Regis	Cantello	Cunningham	

Scorers: Woods 15 / Brown A 1, Regis 62. Ref: E Read

After the Charity Shield horror show a week earlier, Town regain some composure and nearly save a point. Under-strength Town concede the fastest goal of the new season as Ally Brown fires home on 22 seconds, when Mariner heads Woods' flag-kick against a post.

No	Date	Att	Pos	Pt	F-A	H-T		1	2	3	4	5	6	7	8	9	10	11	12 sub used
2 H LIVERPOOL	22/8	28,114	–	0	0-3	0-2	Town	Cooper	Burley	Mills	Talbot*	Osman	Wark	Parkin	Muhren	Mariner	Whymark	Woods	Gates
							Opp	Clemence	Neal	Kennedy A	Thompson	Kennedy R	Hughes	Dalglish	Case	Highway	McDermott	Souness	

Scorers: Souness 19, Dalglish 23, 73. Ref: C Maskell

New executive boxes are opened and £150,000 Dutchman Muhren makes his debut, but the pace of the game is clearly new to him and he sees little of the ball. With four men still out, Town are roared on in a cup-tie atmosphere but Bob Paisley's side's all-round strength is awesome.

No	Date	Att	Pos	Pt	F-A	H-T		1	2	3	4	5	6	7	8	9	10	11	12 sub used
3 H MANCHESTER U	26/8	21,894	14	2	3-0	1-0	Town	Cooper	Burley	Mills	Talbot	Osman	Beattie	Wark	Muhren	Mariner	Whymark	Woods	
							Opp	Roche	Greenhoff B	Albiston	McIlroy	McQueen	Buchan	Coppell	Greenhoff J	Jordan	Macari	McCreery*	McGrath

Scorers: Mariner 16, 67, Talbot 68. Ref: D Reeves

Beattie's return sees Wark back in midfield and Town look a better proposition, with Woods and Muhren working well down the left. After Mariner's first, Burley makes a fine goal-line save from Jimmy Greenhoff. Talbot caps a good display by slipping the ball under Roche's dive.

No	Date	Att	Pos	Pt	F-A	H-T		1	2	3	4	5	6	7	8	9	10	11	12 sub used
4 A MIDDLESBROUGH	2/9	14,427	14	3	0-0	0-0	Town	Cooper	Burley	Mills	Talbot	Osman	Beattie	Wark	Muhren	Mariner	Lambert	Woods	Whymark
							Opp	Stewart	Craggs	Bailey	Mahoney	Boam	Ramage	Proctor	Mills	Ashcroft	Woof	Armstrong	

Ref: K Hackett

Town are clearly the better side, but allow a host of chances to go astray. Lambert nets after the break, a goal is signalled but then the ref spots a raised flag. Stewart is the hero for John Neal's side with a series of saves. In the reserves, Hunter and Butcher are now on the comeback trail.

No	Date	Att	Pos	Pt	F-A	H-T		1	2	3	4	5	6	7	8	9	10	11	12 sub used
5 H ASTON VILLA	9/9	22,166	17	3	0-2	0-1	Town	Cooper	Burley	Mills	Talbot	Osman	Beattie	Wark	Muhren	Mariner	Gates*	Woods	Whymark
							Opp	Rimmer	Gidman*	Smith	Evans	McNaught	Mortimer	Craig	Little	Gray	Cowans	Gregory	Jenkins

Scorers: Gregory 17, Gray 90p. Ref: T Bune

Town fire blanks again, but were angry not to get a penalty when Gregory appeared to tug Wark off the ball, shortly before popping up at the other end to score himself. A bright early spell is not built upon and despite Muhren now looking far more at home, Town fail to beat Rimmer.

No	Date	Att	Pos	Pt	F-A	H-T		1	2	3	4	5	6	7	8	9	10	11	12 sub used
6 A WOLVERHAMPTON	16/9	16,409	15	5	3-1	2-1	Town	Cooper	Burley	Mills	Talbot	Osman	Beattie	Wark	Muhren	Mariner	Whymark	Woods*	Brazil
							Opp	Bradshaw	Palmer	Parkin	Daniel*	Hazell	McAlle	Patching	Carr	Clarke	Bell	Daley	Rafferty

Scorers: Mariner 41, Muhren 44, Whymark 71 / Beattie 15 (og). Ref: G Owen

Beattie tries to hack Daley's cross clear but can only fire it past a shocked Cooper. Mariner levels after Bradshaw drops the ball, then Muhren fires a fine goal through a tight opening at the near post. A goalmouth scramble ends with Whymark clinching the second win in nine games.

No	Date	Att	Pos	Pt	F-A	H-T		1	2	3	4	5	6	7	8	9	10	11	12 sub used
7 H BRISTOL CITY	23/9	20,168	18	5	0-1	0-0	Town	Cooper	Burley	Mills	Talbot	Osman	Beattie	Wark	Muhren	Mariner	Whymark*	Woods	Brazil
							Opp	Shaw	Sweeney	Gillies	Gow	Rodgers	Hunter	Tainton	Ritchie	Royle	Mann	Mabbutt	

Scorers: Ritchie 67p. Ref: B Daniels

A Swedish film crew train their cameras and microphones on Cooper throughout the game for a special feature. He is beaten twice, once by Ritchie's spot-kick after Beattie holds Mabbutt back and then by Mabbutt's spectacular long-range effort, which comes back off a post.

No	Date	Att	Pos	Pt	F-A	H-T		1	2	3	4	5	6	7	8	9	10	11	12 sub used
8 A SOUTHAMPTON	30/9	21,264	13	7	2-1	2-0	Town	Cooper	Burley	Mills	Talbot	Osman	Beattie	Wark	Muhren	Mariner	Mills	Woods	
							Opp	Gennoe	Golac	Peach	Williams	Pickering	Waldron	Ball	Boyer	McDougall	Holmes	Curran	

Scorers: Mariner 5, 19 / McDougall 67. Ref: C Thomas

Town's shaky League form is temporarily forgotten as all-action Mariner nets twice. Pickering and Gennoe dither to allow him to pounce for the first and then he tucks home a superb solo effort. Cooper saves Peach's penalty, then Saints strike wood twice and have a goal disallowed.

No	Date	Att	Pos	Pt	F-A	H-T		1	2	3	4	5	6	7	8	9	10	11	12 sub used
9 A COVENTRY	7/10	21,859	14	8	2-2	2-0	Town	Cooper	Burley	Hunter	Talbot	Osman	Beattie	Wark	Muhren	Mariner	Mills	Woods	
							Opp	Sealey	Coop	McDonald	Yorath	Holton	Hagan	Hutchison	Wallace	Thompson	Powell*	Hunt	Green

Scorers: Osman 35, Woods 44 / Green 67, Thompson 70. Ref: A Challinor

Missing since the FA Cup final with knee trouble, Hunter returns as a sweeper. Town cruise ahead with Osman's first ever goal, but Gordon Milne's side turn on the heat after the break. They pile men forward and cancel out the two-goal deficit and Town end up grateful for a point.

No	Date	Att	Pos	Pt	F-A	H-T		1	2	3	4	5	6	7	8	9	10	11	12 sub used
10 H EVERTON	14/10	22,676	15	8	0-1	0-1	Town	Cooper	Burley	Mills	Talbot*	Osman	Hunter	Wark	Muhren	Mariner	Whymark	Woods	Brazil
							Opp	Wood	Todd	Pejic	Lyons	Wright	Ross	King	Dobson	Latchford	Walsh	Thomas*	Nulty

Scorers: Latchford 44. Ref: R Toseland

More than 10,000 Town fans flock to the club's first Open Day and photographer Owen Hines takes 600 shots of fans posing with the FA Cup, but the big smiles are not evident during this game as home goals remain mysteriously hard to come by. Latchford's classic header is decisive.

#	Venue & Opponent	Date	Att	Pos	Res		Pts	FT	HT	Scorers	Ref
11	A NOTT'M FOREST	21/10	28,911	18	L	3	8	0-1	0-1	O'Neill 13	D Shaw
12	H QP RANGERS	28/10	20,428	15	W	16	10	2-1	0-0	Gates 49, Mariner 53; Francis 61	A Grey
13	A ARSENAL	4/11	35,269	17	L	5	10	1-4	1-3	Mariner 11; Stapleton 18, 29, 48, Nelson 43	J Hunting
14	H WEST BROM	11/11	20,914	18	L	3	10	0-1	0-1	Brown A 22	C Downey
15	A MANCHESTER U	18/11	4,109	18	L	6	10	0-2	0-1	Coppell 7, Greenhoff J 85	K Styles
16	H MIDDLESBROUGH	21/11	17,570	17	W	15	12	2-1	1-1	Burley 33, Woods 73; Armstrong 35	K Salmon
17	A MANCHESTER C	25/11	38,256	15	W	12	14	2-1	0-0	Gates 54, Talbot 75; Hartford 76	C Seel
18	H LEEDS	2/12	22,526	16	L	9	14	2-3	1-2	Beattie 29, Wark 79p; Hankin 1, Harris 36, Cherry 75	J Bray
19	A TOTTENHAM	9/12	33,882	16	L	8	14	0-1	0-0	Pratt 53	A Robinson
20	H BOLTON	16/12	16,593	16	W	19	16	3-0	1-0	Mariner 10, Gates 72, Talbot 77	B Homewood
21	H NORWICH	26/12	26,336	16	D	14	17	1-1	0-1	Mills 46; Davies 25	M Taylor

Line-ups (Ipswich in roman, opponents in *italics*):

11 — Nott'm Forest
Cooper, Burley, Mills*, Talbot, Osman, Butcher, Wark, Brazil, Muhren, Woods, Whymark
Shilton, Anderson, Clark, McGovern, Needham, Burns, O'Neill, Bowyer, Birtles, Woodcock, Robertson
Town slip further down the table, as Cooper puts on a heroic display to keep the champions down to just O'Neill's strike. At the other end Shilton has a quiet day. Brian Clough's men are unlucky not to get a second-half penalty when Osman clatters into Anderson inside the box.

12 — QP Rangers
Cooper, Burley, Mills, Talbot, Osman, Butcher, Wark, Mariner, Muhren, Gates, Woods
Parkes, Shanks, Gillard, Hollins, Howe, Busby, Eatoe, Francis, Harkouk, Bowles, Cunningham, McGee*
Town are foiled in the first half by several fine Parkes saves, one from a powerful long-range effort by Mills. Town fans celebrate the first home League goals since August as Gates and Mariner both net superb strikes after the break. Francis hits his first League goal for over a year.

13 — Arsenal
Cooper, Burley, Tibbott, Talbot, Osman, Butcher, Wark, Mariner, Muhren, Geddis*, Woods, Whymark
Jennings, Rice, Nelson, Price, O'Leary, Young, Brady, Sunderland, Stapleton, Gatting, Rix
With four senior players fined £200 for breaking a curfew in Innsbruck and Gates unhappy over being dropped, Town look dispirited as Frank Stapleton bags the first senior hat-trick of his career. Mariner plays well, and another minor consolation is when Cooper saves Brady's penalty.

14 — West Brom
Cooper, Mills, Tibbott, Talbot, Osman, Beattie, Wark, Mariner, Muhren, Geddis, Woods*, Brazil
Godden, Batson, Trewick, Brown T, Wile, Robertson, Robson, Brown A, Regis, Cantello, Cunningham
Unhappy Gates walks out and returns to his native North East. He spends a few days potato picking, asks for a move, but Robson suspends and fines him. After talks with the PFA he returns. Town see more of the ball, but Ally Brown's early strike wins the day for Ron Atkinson's men.

15 — Manchester U
Cooper, Bailey, Mills, Talbot, Osman, Beattie, Wark, Mariner, Muhren*, Gates, Woods, Geddis
Bailey, Albiston, Houston, Greenhoff B, McQueen, Buchan, Coppell, Greenhoff J, Jordan, Sloan, McIlroy, McGrath*
Former Town trialist Gary Bailey, son of the club's ex-keeper Roy, has a superb debut for United, handling well in rainy conditions. Gates is back in the side and Town work hard, but again fail to get any of the breaks. United get back to winning ways after a thrashing at Birmingham.

16 — Middlesbrough
Cooper, Burley, Mills, Talbot, Osman, Beattie, Wark, Mariner, Muhren, Gates, Woods
Stewart, Craggs, Bailey, Mahoney, Boam, McAndrew, Mills, Ashcroft, Burns, Armstrong, Procter*
At last the fans have something to shout about as Woods wins two important points. He conjures up a brilliant solo goal to beat Stewart after John Neal's side looked like absorbing all Town's pressure. The visitors are dangerous on the break and the game is a lively affair throughout.

17 — Manchester C
Cooper, Burley, Mills, Talbot, Osman, Beattie, Wark, Mariner, Muhren, Gates, Woods
Corrigan, Clements, Donachie, Booth, Watson, Power, Owen, Deyna, Kidd, Hartford, Barnes, Palmer*
The players wear black armbands following the death of Town youth international Peter Canavan in a car crash, in which David Geddis was injured. Gates is superb and deserves his goal, followed by a strike from the unsettled Talbot. Clements breaks his leg after a Beattie tackle.

18 — Leeds
Cooper, Burley, Mills, Talbot, Osman, Beattie, Wark, Mariner, Muhren, Gates, Woods
Harvey, Cherry, Gray F, Flynn, Hart, Madeley, Gray E, Hankin, Hawley, Currie, Harris
New Leeds boss Jimmy Adamson sees his side create two chances in the opening 90 seconds, Hankin accepting the second. Beattie's free-kick near halfway is floated into the box and the ball swirls freakishly in the wind over Harvey into the goal. Town's late rally is not quite enough.

19 — Tottenham
Cooper, Burley, Mills, Talbot, Osman, Butcher, Wark, Mariner, Muhren, Brazil*, Woods, Whymark
Kendall, McAllister, Gorman, Holmes, Lacy, Perryman, Pratt, Ardiles, Lee, Hoddle, Taylor
Robson is full of praise for the 'man-sized job' being done in defence by teenage deputies Osman and Butcher. The duo help restrict Spurs to just one goal, a lucky one for John Pratt, whose shot deflects past Cooper off Wark. Home boss Keith Burkinshaw admits they had all the luck.

20 — Bolton
Cooper, Burley, Mills*, Talbot, Osman, Butcher, Wark, Mariner, Muhren, Gates, Woods, Parkin
McDonagh, Nicholson, Dunne, Greaves, Jones, Walsh, Morgan, Reid, Gowling, Worthington, McNab
Town look far more confident than of late and respond to good terrace support with a display of constant attacking, Ian Greaves' side is totally outclassed and the goal tally could have been higher. Man-of-the-match Muhren is outstanding in midfield and he helps create all three goals.

21 — Norwich
Cooper, Burley, Mills, Talbot, Osman, Butcher, Wark, Mariner, Muhren, Gates, Woods
Keelan, Bond, Davies, Ryan, Hadley, Powell, McGuire, Reeves, Chivers, Robson, Symonds, Neighbour*
A highly-entertaining local derby sees young full-back Ian Davies have his first career goal cancelled out by Mills' close-range header just 30 seconds after the break. City boss John Bond organises a man-for-man marking system that keeps Town at bay despite relentless pressure.

LEAGUE DIVISION 1 — Manager: Bobby Robson — SEASON 1978-79

No	Date	Venue / Opponent	Att	Pos	Pt	Res	F-A	H-T	Opp Pos
22	30/12	H CHELSEA	21,439	13	19	W	5-1	3-0	21
23	20/1	H WOLVERHAMPTON	17,965	12	21	W	3-1	2-1	20
24	3/2	A BRISTOL CITY	17,025	14	21	L	1-3	0-2	7
25	10/2	H SOUTHAMPTON	19,520	13	22	D	0-0	0-0	16
26	24/2	A EVERTON	29,031	13	24	W	1-0	1-0	3
27	28/2	A DERBY	15,935	12	26	W	1-0	0-0	16
28	3/3	H NOTT'M FOREST	27,198	12	27	D	1-1	0-1	6
29	13/3	H COVENTRY	16,095	11	28	D	1-1	1-0	10
30	17/3	H ARSENAL	26,407	9	30	W	2-0	1-0	4
31	24/3	A LIVERPOOL	43,243	12	30	L	0-2	0-1	1

22 — H CHELSEA (30/12)
Scorers: Osman 23, Muhren 25, 46, Wark 35, Langley 65 [Mariner 77]. Ref: B Martin

Ipswich (1–12): Cooper, Burley, Mills, Talbot*, Osman, Butcher, Wark, Muhren, Mariner, Gates, Woods, Geddis
Chelsea: Phillips, Harris, Stride, Nutton, Wicks, Bumstead, Stanley*, Lewington, Aylott, Langley, Britton, Walker

The tide is now turning and Muhren is again superb. Butcher hits the bar, before Muhren's free-kick finds Osman for the opener. Muhren's first Portman Road goal is lucky, as Wicks' clearance hits him and rebounds into the net. After this Danny Blanchflower's team crumbles.

23 — H WOLVERHAMPTON (20/1)
Scorers: Wark 24, 54p, Mariner 30, Berry 34. Ref: A Cox

Ipswich (1–12): Cooper, Burley, Tibbott, Mills, Osman, Beattie, Wark, Muhren, Mariner, Whymark, Woods, Geddis
Wolverhampton: Bradshaw, Palmer, Parkin, Daniel, Berry, McAlle, Hibbitt, Carr, Bell, Eves*, Daley, Patching

Unsettled Talbot gets his way and moves for £450,000 to Arsenal. Robson is working behind the scenes to replace him with another Dutchman in Frans Thijssen. Town terminate Wolves' brief comeback attempt when Woods is hauled down by Parkin and Wark scores from the spot.

24 — A BRISTOL CITY (3/2)
Scorers: Mariner 90, Whitehead 19, Tainton 25, Gow 90. Ref: C Newsome

Ipswich (1–12): Cooper, Mills, Tibbott, Parkin*, Osman, Butcher, Wark, Muhren, Mariner, Whymark, Woods, Geddis
Bristol City: Shaw, Sweeney, Cooper, Gow, Rodgers, Collier, Tainton, Mabbutt, Royle, Cormack, Whitehead

A rather subdued-looking Town let Alan Dicks' side dominate much of this game and Whitehead snatches his first goal for a year and Tainton his first of the season. The side is down to ten men when Mills departs after a clash with Mabbutt to have stitches in a gash on his forehead.

25 — H SOUTHAMPTON (10/2)
Ref: R Challis

Ipswich (1–12): Cooper, Burley, Tibbott, Mills, Butcher, Beattie, Wark, Muhren, Mariner, Brazil*, Woods, Geddis
Southampton: Gennoe, Golac, Peach*, Williams, Nicholl, Waldron, Ball, Boyer, Hebberd, Holmes, Curran, Baker

A chilly and forgettable afternoon is preceded by Whymark's departure for £150,000 to Vancouver Whitecaps in the same week that Town beat Norwich 2-1 in his testimonial match. On Valentine's day, Robson pays FC Twente £200,000 to capture the signature of Frans Thijssen.

26 — A EVERTON (24/2)
Scorers: Mariner 37. Ref: A McDonald

Ipswich (1–12): Cooper, Burley, Tibbott, Mills, Osman, Beattie, Wark, Muhren, Mariner, Brazil, Woods, Geddis
Everton: Wood, Todd, Lyons, Higgins, Wright, Heard, King, Dobson, Latchford, Telfer, Thomas*, Walsh

Town's first win in 16 attempts at Goodison is shaped from two crazy first-half minutes. Beattie is harshly adjudged to have fouled Lyons, but Wright steps up to shoot the spot-kick wide. Town break to the other end and Woods and Muhren engineer a fine move, finished by Mariner.

27 — A DERBY (28/2)
Scorers: Woods 67. Ref: G Courtney

Ipswich (1–12): Cooper, Mills, Tibbott, Thijssen, Osman, Butcher, Wark, Muhren, Mariner, Brazil*, Woods, Geddis
Derby: McKellar, Langan, Buckley, Daly, McFarland, Wicks, Carter, Powell, Caskey*, Rioch, Greenwood, Duncan

Recently humiliated in court over the Willie Morgan affair, Derby boss Tommy Docherty is verbally abused by home fans in the smallest Derby crowd for ten years. Town stroll to a comfortable win, but only net once, with Woods taking Mills' pass and hammering home a beauty.

28 — H NOTT'M FOREST (3/3)
Scorers: Brazil 54, Birtles 23. Ref: C White

Ipswich (1–12): Cooper, Burley, Tibbott, Thijssen, Osman, Butcher, Wark, Muhren, Mariner, Brazil*, Woods, Geddis
Nott'm Forest: Shilton, Anderson, Clark, McGovern, Lloyd, Needham, O'Neill, Gemmill, Birtles, Francis, Robertson

Shilton has an outstanding game and produces one incredible flying save to keep out a fierce long-range Wark effort. After a defensive error, Town fall behind to Birtles, but after the break the effervescent Brazil benefits from a rare Forest slip to fire his first League goal past Shilton.

29 — H COVENTRY (13/3)
Scorers: Muhren 36, Thompson 72. Ref: K Salmon

Ipswich (1–12): Cooper, Burley, Mills, Thijssen, Osman, Butcher, Wark, Muhren, Mariner, Brazil*, Woods, Gates
Coventry: Sealey, Coop, McDonald*, Yorath, Holton, Hagan, Roberts, Wallace, Thompson, Blair, Hutchison, Green

On a rainy night, Muhren's shot is deflected past Sealey, but after netting again with a beauty from a free-kick he is told the kick was indirect. City's defence is worked very hard, but then a Yorath through-ball is allowed to reach Thompson and he stretches to poke home an equaliser.

30 — H ARSENAL (17/3)
Scorers: Wark 32, Rix 87 (og). Ref: D Turner

Ipswich (1–12): Cooper, Burley, Mills, Thijssen, Osman, Butcher, Wark, Muhren, Mariner, Brazil*, Woods, Gates
Arsenal: Jennings, Rice, Nelson, Talbot, O'Leary, Walford, Brady, Sunderland, Stapleton, Price*, Rix, Gatting

An uncertain opening half-hour is forgotten as clever play by Thijssen sets up a splendid strike by Wark. Town visibly grow in confidence and never look in danger after this. The clincher was a real Rix farce, the midfielder passing back without noticing the completely unguarded goal!

31 — A LIVERPOOL (24/3)
Scorers: Dalglish 41, Johnson 81. Ref: A Saunders

Ipswich (1–12): Cooper, Mills, Tibbott*, Thijssen, Osman, Butcher, Wark, Muhren, Mariner, Gates, Woods, Brazil
Liverpool: Clemence, Neal, Hughes, Thompson, Kennedy, Hansen, Dalglish, Johnson, Case, McDermott, Souness

Just 16 hours after returning from Spain, Town set off for Liverpool and the prospect of a windswept Anfield and Bob Paisley's champions-elect. Typically neat finishing by Dalglish ends the resistance and the result is never in doubt. After the game Tibbott joins Sheffield United.

Match-by-match record (matches 32–42)

No	Date	V	Opponent	Att	Pos	Opp	Res	Score	Pts	Ipswich scorers	Opp scorers	Ref
32	31/3	H	MANCHESTER C	20,773	12	16	W	2-1	32	Geddis 23, Brazil 43	Silkman 64	M Taylor
33	3/4	A	BIRMINGHAM	12,499	12	21	D	1-1	33	Muhren 35	Gallagher 64	J Hough
34	7/4	A	LEEDS	24,153	10	5	D	1-1	34	Gates 78	Cherry 39	N Midgley
35	14/4	A	NORWICH	25,061	9	12	W	1-0	36	Thijssen 63		M Sinclair
36	16/4	H	DERBY	19,899	9	18	W	2-1	38	Mariner 12, Mills 16	Crawford 25	C Downey
37	17/4	H	BIRMINGHAM	17,676	7	21	W	3-0	40	Gates 23, Butcher 25, Brazil 79		A Gunn
38	21/4	A	BOLTON	20,073	7	17	W	3-2	42	Brazil 39, 63, Wark 44	Worthington 35, Allardyce 74	R Bridges
39	28/4	H	TOTTENHAM	28,179	7	15	W	2-1	44	Muhren 8, Brazil 15	Hoddle 90p	G Flint
40	2/5	A	ASTON VILLA	26,636	7	8	D	2-2	45	Muhren 35, 62	Swain 9, Deehan 14	R Lewis
41	5/5	A	CHELSEA	15,462	7	22	W	3-2	47	Brazil 9, 23, Woods 41	Langley 26, 44	P Reeves
42	11/5	A	QP RANGERS	9,819	6	20	W	4-0	49	Butcher 6, Brazil 41, Gates 58, 63		K Baker

Home Average 21,673   Away Average 24,451

Line-ups and reports

32 — MANCHESTER C (H)
Ipswich: Cooper, Burley, Mills, Thijssen, Beattie, Butcher, Wark, Muhren, Geddis*, Brazil, Woods, Lambert
Man C: Corrigan, Ranson, Power*, Reid, Watson, Henry, Channon, Owen, Silkman, Hartford, Barnes, Futcher R
Victory is sealed when Corrigan and Geddis tussle, the ball breaking to Woods who scores. With Corrigan racing back to his line, Muhren lays the ball to Brazil who scores. Silkman's consolation goal on his City debut is a brilliant solo run that ends with a classy chip.

33 — BIRMINGHAM (A)
Ipswich: Cooper, Burley, Mills, Thijssen, Beattie, Butcher, Wark, Muhren, Mariner, Brazil, Woods*, Geddis
Birmingham: Freeman, Page, Dennis, Towers, Gallagher, Tarantini, Ainscow, Buckley, Calderwood, Dillon, Barrowc'gh
Jim Smith's relegation-threatened side draw their lowest crowd thus far this term and fall behind when Muhren fires in a wonderful 20-yard volley. Gallagher's leveller signals a spell of Blues pressure, but Town defend well against a side including record-buy Tarantini of Argentina.

34 — LEEDS (A)
Ipswich: Cooper, Burley, Mills, Thijssen, Osman, Beattie, Wark, Muhren, Geddis, Gates*, Woods
Leeds: Harvey, Cherry, Gray F, Flynn, Hart, Madeley, Gray E, Hankin, Hawley, Currie*, Graham, Hird
Having engineered an outside chance of a UEFA place, Town fight well in a scrappy affair at Elland Road and deserve at least the point gained as Gates is on target after a free-kick. Cooper goes off for stitches to his hand after being trodden on by Beattie, Woods replacing him in goal.

35 — NORWICH (A)
Ipswich: Sivell, Burley, Mills, Thijssen, Osman, Beattie*, Wark, Muhren, Mariner, Gates, Woods, Geddis
Norwich: Hansbury, Bond*, Davies, McGuire, Hoadley, Powell, Symonds, Reeves, Robson, Paddon, Peters, Fashanu
The Canaries are livid as Town win via Thijssen's first goal in English football. Geddis had been kneeling tying his bootlaces in an offside position when Muhren and Gates set up Thijssen, but was deemed not to be interfering. Sivell plays well in his first game for nearly 15 months.

36 — DERBY (H)
Ipswich: Cooper, Burley, Mills, Thijssen, Osman, Butcher, Wark, Muhren, Mariner*, Geddis, Woods, Gates
Derby: McKellar, Langan, Buckley, Moreland, Webb, Wicks, Carter, Powell, Greenwood, Emson, Crawford
Derby are rocked by a fine opening spell which sees Muhren lob onto the bar, the rebound falling nicely for Mariner. Muhren makes a second for Mills and a big win seems certain. Crawford has other ideas and his 25-yarder is a cracking response. Emson goes close in the final minute.

37 — BIRMINGHAM (H)
Ipswich: Cooper, Burley, Mills, Thijssen, Osman, Butcher, Wark, Muhren*, Brazil, Gates, Woods, Geddis*
Birmingham: Freeman, Calderwood, Tarantini, Towers, Gallagher, V d Hauwe, Ainscow, Buckley*, Givens, Page, Barrowc'gh, Ivey
Three Easter wins out of three and the result is never in doubt after Butcher converts Muhren's first senior goal to put Town two up. Freeman is kept busy throughout and relegation now looks a certainty for City. It's the final away game for Tarantini, who is about to return to foreign shores.

38 — BOLTON (A)
Ipswich: Cooper, Burley, Mills, Thijssen, Osman, Butcher, Wark, Muhren, Brazil, Gates*, Woods, Geddis
Bolton: McDonagh, Nicholson, Walsh, McNab, Jones*, Allardyce, Morgan, Whatmore, Gowling, Worthington, Smith, Nowak
In the days before cameras attended every game, the TV people were glad they chose this one, for there were five brilliant goals and many near misses. The best is by Worthington who juggles the ball with his back to goal, flicks it up and turns between defenders to volley a great goal.

39 — TOTTENHAM (H)
Ipswich: Cooper, Burley, Mills, Thijssen, Osman, Butcher, Wark, Muhren, Brazil, Gates, Woods, Geddis
Tottenham: Aleksic, Lee, McAllister, Miller, Lacy, Perryman, Pratt, Ardiles, Jones, Hoddle, Villa
A fifth successive win looks a formality as newly-crowned Player of the Year Muhren and Brazil sweep Town ahead early. Spurs battle back into the game after the break and are encouraged as Aleksic saves Wark's penalty. Butcher hacks down Ardiles and Hoddle narrows the gap.

40 — ASTON VILLA (A)
Ipswich: Cooper, Burley, Mills, Thijssen, Osman, Butcher, Wark, Muhren, Brazil, Gates*, Woods, Geddis
Villa: Rimmer, Gidman, Gibson, Gregory, Evans, Mortimer, Cowans, Shelton, Deehan, Cropley, Swain
Villa have won four in a row and Town five and one of these sides should capture the final UEFA spot. It's a game of 'three thirds' as Villa roar into a two-goal lead only for the immaculate left foot of Muhren to peg them back. Cooper heroically keeps Villa at bay in the final third.

41 — CHELSEA (A)
Ipswich: Cooper, Burley, Mills, Thijssen, Osman, Butcher, Wark, Muhren, Brazil, Gates*, Woods*, Lambert
Chelsea: Bonetti, Wilkins G, Harris, Bannon, Dray, Chivers, Stanley, Wilkins R, Osgood, Langley, Filery*, Frost
Danny Blanchflower's side is already relegated, but put up a useful fight after the interval and almost share the spoils as Bannon nets with a great drive, but an offside flag goes up. Brazil underlines his potential with lethal early strikes that take Chelsea's goals against' tally to 89.

42 — QP RANGERS (A)
Ipswich: Cooper, Burley, Mills, Thijssen, Osman, Butcher, Wark, Muhren, Brazil, Gates, Woods*, Lambert
QP Rangers: Richardson, Clement, Gillard, Hollins, Roeder, Shanks, Busby, Francis, Walsh, Allen, Goddard, Beattie
Tommy Docherty is appointed Rangers' boss just hours before the game but this fails to inspire an already-relegated side. Gates thumps home two fine 20-yard drives but then fires over from close range when a hat-trick is there for the taking. These easy points confirm a UEFA place.

LEAGUE DIVISION 1 (CUP-TIES)   Manager: Bobby Robson   SEASON 1978-79

	1	2	3	4	5	6	7	8	9	10	11	12 sub used

Charity Shield

	Att	F-A	H-T	Scorers, Times, and Referees
N NOTT'M FOREST 12/8	68,000	L 0-5	0-2	O'Neill 11, 75, Withe 28, Lloyd 46, [Robertson 87] — Ref: P Reeves

1	2	3	4	5	6	7	8	9	10	11	12
Cooper	Burley	Mills	Talbot	Osman	Wark	Parkin	Gates	Mariner	Whymark*	Woods	Turner
Shilton	*Anderson*	*Barrett*	*McGovern*	*Lloyd*	*Burns*	*O'Neill*	*Gemmill*	*Withe*	*Woodcock*	*Robertson*	*Needham*

With five men injured, under-strength Town crumble to easily the biggest losing margin of any of the previous 66th major club matches at Wembley. The fans' support is good despite Forest's superiority being almost embarrassing. Shilton saves rare efforts by Parkin and Talbot.

League Cup

	Att		F-A	H-T	Scorers, Times, and Referees
2 A BLACKPOOL 30/8	10,029 3:19	14	L 0-2	0-1	Davidson 4, 86 — Ref: T Farley

1	2	3	4	5	6	7	8	9	10	11	12
Cooper	Burley	Mills	Talbot	Osman	Beattie	Parkin*	Wark	Mariner	Whymark	Woods	Lambert
Ward	*Gardner*	*Pashley*	*Thompson*	*Suddaby*	*McEwan*	*Hockaday*	*Ronson*	*Spence*	*Davidson*	*Chandler*	

Town see more of the ball but never pose a real threat in attack and Bob Stokoe's side gain huge encouragement from Davidson's early strike. With new play-maker Muhren back in Holland finalising his move to the UK, Town struggle to create chances and can have no complaints.

FA Cup

	Att		F-A	H-T	Scorers, Times, and Referees
3 H CARLISLE 10/1	17,660 3:6	13	W 3-2	2-1	Beattie 25, Muhren 37, Wark 80p; Tait 40, Kemp 50 — Ref: T Morris

1	2	3	4	5	6	7	8	9	10	11	12
Cooper	Burley	Tibbott	Mills	Osman	Beattie	Wark	Muhren	Mariner	Whymark*	Woods	
Swinburne	*Hoolickin*	*McCartney*	*MacDonald*	*Tait*	*Parker*	*McVitie*	*Bonnyman*	*Ludlam*	*Kemp*	*Hamilton*	

Mariner pulls the ball back for Beattie to crash home against his home-town club. At a snow-covered Portman Road, Town's early command is ended when Kemp swoops after the break. Woods, whose nimble footwork torments Hoolickin all evening, wins a penalty and Wark converts.

	Att		F-A	H-T	Scorers, Times, and Referees
4 H ORIENT 27/1	23,377 2:7	12	D 0-0	0-0	Ref: T Mills

1	2	3	4	5	6	7	8	9	10	11	12
Cooper	Burley	Tibbott	Mills	Osman	Beattie	Wark	Muhren	Mariner	Whymark	Woods	
Jackson	*Fisher*	*Roffey*	*Grealish*	*Gray*	*Went*	*Chiedozie*	*Moores*	*Mayo*	*Kitchen*	*Coates*	

Jimmy Bloomfield's side battle heroically to keep the scores level and big Jackson stonewalls all attempts that the cup holders get on target. Mariner and Whymark are closely attended by Went and Gray and on a snow-covered pitch the match fails to reaches any great heights.

	Att		F-A	H-T	Scorers, Times, and Referees
4R A ORIENT 30/1	13,672 2:7	12	W 2-0	0-0	Mariner 47, 74 — Ref: T Mills

1	2	3	4	5	6	7	8	9	10	11	12
Cooper	Burley	Tibbott	Mills	Osman	Roberts	Wark	Muhren	Mariner	Whymark	Woods	
Jackson	*Fisher*	*Roffey**	*Grealish*	*Gray*	*Went*	*Chiedozie*	*Moores*	*Mayo*	*Kitchen*	*Coates*	*Banjo*

Well over two hours of stalemate is spectacularly ended when Mariner latches on to the ball outside the box and thumps home a great volley which dips just under the bar. Town's defence is rarely troubled although Mayo gives The O's fans some rare excitement when he hits a post.

	Att		F-A	H-T	Scorers, Times, and Referees
5 H BRISTOL ROV 26/2	23,231 2:12	13	W 6-1	4-0	Brazil 8, 34, Mills 28, Muhren 44, White 84 [Geddis 81, Mariner 90] — Ref: A Robinson

1	2	3	4	5	6	7	8	9	10	11	12
Cooper	Burley*	Tibbott	Mills	Osman	Beattie	Wark	Muhren	Mariner	Brazil	Woods	Geddis
Thomas	*Jones*	*Bater*	*Harding*	*Taylor*	*Prince*	*Dennehy*	*Williams*	*White*	*Emmanuel*	*Hendrie**	*Staniforth*

Brazil's first senior goal is followed by Mills' emphatic header. This one-sided tie is all over by half-time as Brazil strikes again and Muhren brings the house down, dancing past several defenders and the keeper before netting the fourth. Mills and Muhren run the show completely.

	Att		F-A	H-T	Scorers, Times, and Referees
QF H LIVERPOOL 10/3	31,322 1	12	L 0-1	0-0	Dalglish 52 — Ref: R Challis

1	2	3	4	5	6	7	8	9	10	11	12
Cooper	Burley	Mills	Thijssen	Osman	Butcher	Wark	Muhren	Mariner	Gates*	Woods	Brazil
Clemence	*Neal*	*Hughes*	*Thompson*	*Kennedy*	*Hansen*	*Dalglish*	*Johnson*	*Case*	*McDermott*	*Souness*	

An intriguing and tense contest is on a knife-edge throughout. In the first serious raid on Cooper's goal, typically clinical finishing by Dalglish, from a difficult angle, breaks Ipswich hearts. Bob Paisley's team has to draw on all its experience and strength to keep the cup holders at bay.

Cup-Winners' Cup

	Att	F-A	H-T	Scorers, Times, and Referees
1:1 A AZ ALKMAAR 13/9 (Holland)	18,000	D 0-0	0-0	Ref: J Redells (West Germany)

1	2	3	4	5	6	7	8	9	10	11	12
Cooper	Burley	Tibbott	Talbot	Osman	Beattie	Mills	Wark	Mariner	Whymark*	Woods	Geddis
Mescovic	*Arntz*	*Spelbos*	*Metgod*	*V Rijnsoever^ Peters*		*Ressel*	*V Henegem*	*Kist*	*Nygaard**	*De Graaf /Hovenk js/Tol*	

Town begin the club's sixth European campaign by maintaining an unbeaten run on Dutch soil. They look strong against George Kessler's side and Mariner has a goal disallowed after he converts Burley's cross. The only scare is when Kees Kist tries a shot from distance and hits the bar.

	Att	F-A	H-T	Scorers, Times, and Referees
1:2 H AZ ALKMAAR 27/9	21,330	W 2-0	1-0	Mariner 3, Wark 90p — Ref: M van Langenhove (Belgium) (Town win 2-0 on aggregate)

1	2	3	4	5	6	7	8	9	10	11	12
Cooper	Burley	Tibbott	Talbot	Osman	Beattie	Mills	Wark	Mariner	Whymark*	Woods	Geddis
Vooys	*Arntz*	*Spelbos*	*Metgod*	*V Rijnsoever Peters*		*Ressel*	*V Henegem*	*Kist*	*Hovenkamp*	*De Graaf**	*Nygaard*

Keeper Vooys is beaten early but goes on to shine, keeping lively Town at bay. A dubious offside decision rules out a Wark goal, but perhaps justice is done when Spelbos' challenge on Mariner is deemed a penalty. Town recapture some of the verve currently missing in the League.

European matches

2:1 — H SW INNSBRUCK — 18/10 — 19,958 (Austria) — **W 1-0** (0-0)
Wark 54p
Ref: A Castillo (Spain)

Town: Cooper, Burley, Tibbott, Talbot, Hunter, Osman, Mills, Wark, Mariner*, Whymark, Woods, Geddis
SW Innsbruck: Koncilia F, Zanon, Auer, Sikic, Schwarz W*, Scharman, Hanschitz, Koncilia P, Oberacher, Hickersberger, Braschler^, G'tner/Sc'z Wg

Town again come up against a resolute defence and inspired keeper and the only breakthrough comes when Werner Schwarz handles and Wark tucks home the penalty. Osman tries a hopeful long-range shot which hits the inside of a post and rebounds into the arms of a grateful Koncilia.

2:2 — A SW INNSBRUCK — 1/11 — 18,000 — **D 1-1** (0-0) aet
Burley 100
Oberacher 75
Ref: M Jarguz (Poland)
(Town win 2-1 on aggregate)

Town: Cooper, Burley, Tibbott, Talbot, Hunter, Osman, Mills, Wark, Mariner!, Whymark, Woods, Geddis*
SW Innsbruck: Koncilia F, Zanon, Auer, Sikic*, Forstinger, Scharman, Hanschitz, Koncilia P, Oberacher^, Hickersberger, Braschler, Muller/Sc'z, Gates

A stormy tie follows the off-field curfew trouble at Town's hotel. Hanschitz's break sets up Oberacher and extra-time is needed. Burley regains the lead but is injured by a dreadful tackle by Peter Koncilia, who also hurts Cooper. Mariner's alleged time-wasting gets a second yellow card.

3:1 — H BARCELONA — 7/3 — 29,197 (Spain) — **W 2-1** (0-0)
Gates 51, 64
Esteban 53
Ref: K Palotai (Hungary)

Town: Cooper, Burley, Tibbott, Talbot, Hunter, Osman, Mills, Wark, Mariner*, Whymark, Woods, Geddis*
Barcelona: Artola, Zuviria, Migueli, Olmo, Mills, Butcher, Neeksens*, De la Cruz, Esteban^, Heredia, Krankl, Martinez, Costas/Alba^

Gates replaces the suspended Mariner and is a thorn in Barca's side for the second season running. Krankl crosses for Esteban to convert a crucial away goal. Lucien Muller's side adopt a rugged approach and this infuriates Town fans, who hurl cushions from the stands on to the pitch.

3:2 — A BARCELONA — 21/3 — 100,000 — **L 0-1** (0-1)
Migueli 38
Ref: E Azimzade (USSR)
(Town lose on away goals)

Town: Cooper, Burley, Tibbott, Beattie, Hunter, Osman, Mills, Wark^, Muhren, Brazil, Woods, Geddis/Parkin
Barcelona: Artola, Zuviria, Migueli, Olmo, Mills, Butcher, Albaladejo, Neeksens, Rexach, Heredia, Krankl, Asensi, Martinez

Town are faced with a huge crowd and overwhelming pressure, but somehow restrict the rampant home side to a single goal. Martinez floats across a corner-kick, Krankl heads it down and Migueli fires past Cooper, whose view is partly blocked. Despite its closeness, the result is fair.

Odds & ends

Double wins: (6) Bolton, Chelsea, Derby, Manchester C, QP Rangers, Wolves.

Double losses: (3) Bristol City, Liverpool, West Brom.

Won from behind: (2) Wolves (a), Bolton (a).

Lost from in front: (1) Arsenal (a).

High spots: Just two defeats after Christmas, rising from 16th to 6th. The successful double 'transfer swoop' in Holland. Playing in front of 100,000 in Barcelona's Nou Camp. Bobby Robson celebrates 10 years at the club by turning down several new further attempts to lure him away.

Low spots: The Charity Shield thrashing at Wembley. The League Cup exit at struggling Blackpool. Four players disciplined 'curfew-breaking' at Innsbruck. Eric Gates' walk-out, in protest at not playing regularly. The death of the highly-rated Peter Canavan in a car crash.

Player of the Year: Arnold Muhren.

Ever-presents: (2) Mick Mills, John Wark.

Hat-tricks: (0).

Opposing hat-tricks: (1) Frank Stapleton (Arsenal).

Leading scorer: (17) Paul Mariner.

League table

Pos	Team	P	W	D	L	F	A	W	D	L	F	A	Pts
			Home					Away					
1	Liverpool	42	19	2	0	51	4	11	6	4	34	12	68
2	Nott'm Forest	42	11	10	0	34	11	10	8	3	26	16	60
3	West Brom	42	13	5	3	38	15	11	6	4	34	20	59
4	Everton	42	12	7	2	32	17	5	10	6	20	23	51
5	Leeds	42	11	4	6	41	25	7	10	4	29	27	50
6	IPSWICH	42	11	4	6	34	21	9	5	7	29	28	49
7	Arsenal	42	11	8	2	37	18	6	6	9	24	30	48
8	Aston Villa	42	8	9	4	37	26	7	7	7	22	23	46
9	Manchester U	42	9	7	5	29	25	6	8	7	31	38	45
10	Coventry	42	11	7	3	41	29	3	9	9	17	39	44
11	Tottenham	42	7	8	6	19	25	6	7	8	29	36	41
12	Middlesbro	42	10	5	6	33	21	5	5	11	24	29	40
13	Bristol City	42	11	6	4	34	19	4	4	13	13	32	40
14	Southampton	42	9	10	2	35	20	3	6	12	12	33	40
15	Manchester C	42	9	6	6	34	28	4	7	10	24	28	39
16	Norwich	42	7	10	4	29	19	0	13	8	22	38	37
17	Bolton	42	10	5	6	36	28	2	6	13	18	47	35
18	Wolves	42	10	4	7	26	26	3	4	14	18	42	34
19	Derby	42	8	5	8	25	25	2	6	13	19	46	31
20	QP Rangers	42	5	8	8	24	33	1	5	15	23	40	25
21	Birmingham	42	5	9	7	24	25	1	1	19	13	39	22
22	Chelsea	42	3	5	13	23	42	2	5	14	21	50	20
		924	209	144	109	716	501	109	144	209	501	716	924

Appearances and Goals

Player	Lge	Sub	LC	Sub	FAC	Sub	Eur	Sub	Lge	Sub	LC	FAC	Eur	Tot
	Appearances								Goals					
Beattie, Kevin	19	1	1		3		3		1				1	2
Brazil, Alan	14	5			5		6		9				2	11
Burley, George	38		1		5		6		1				1	2
Butcher, Terry	21				1		2		2					2
Cooper, Paul	41		1		5		6							
Gates, Eric	20	2	1		5	1	7		8				1	9
Geddis, David	6	9		1			2	3	1				1	2
Hunter, Allan	4						2							
Lambert, Mick	1	3			1									
Mariner, Paul	33				5		4		13			3	1	17
Mills, Mick	42		1		5		6		1			2		3
Muhren, Arnold	41		1		5		2		8				2	10
Osman, Russell	39		1		5		6		2					2
Parkin, Tommy	3	1						1						
Roberts, Dale	1													
Sivell, Laurie	1													
Talbot, Brian	21		1		4		4		3					3
Thijssen, Frans	16						1					1		1
Tibbott, Les	11				4		5							
Wark, John	42		1		5		6		6				2	9
Whymark, Trevor	8	5			3		3	1	5					5
Woods, Clive	41		1		5		5		5					5
(own-goals)														1
22 players used	**462**	**26**	**11**	**1**	**55**	**2**	**66**	**7**	**63**			**6**	**11**	**80**

LEAGUE DIVISION 1   Manager: Bobby Robson   SEASON 1979-80

Match Results

No	Date	Venue	Opponent	Att	Pos	Pt	F-A	H-T	Scorers, Times, and Referees
1	8/8	H	NOTT'M FOREST	27,371		L 0	0-1	0-0	Woodcock 46 — Ref: R Challis
2	21/8	A	ARSENAL	33,245		W 2	2-0	1-0	Hunter 22, Muhren 63 — Ref: C Thomas
3	25/8	A	WOLVERHAMPTON	22,025	17	L 2	0-3	0-1	Carr 37, Daniel 53, Eves 86 — Ref: N Ashley
4	1/9	H	STOKE	17,539	12	W 4	3-1	2-1	Brazil 11, Mariner 45, Wark 90, Butcher 20 (og) — Ref: B Daniels
5	8/9	H	BRISTOL CITY	16,915	6	W 6	1-0	0-0	Woods 52 — Ref: K Salmon
6	15/9	A	BRIGHTON	23,608	12	L 6	0-2	0-1	Clark 18, Ryan 85 — Ref: C Downey
7	22/9	H	EVERTON	19,251	12	D 7	1-1	0-1	Wark 86 / Kidd 8 — Ref: R Toseland
8	29/9	A	CRYSTAL PALACE	29,885	14	L 7	1-4	1-3	Gates 44 [Francis 34p, Cannon 58] Swindlehurst 17, Hinshelwood 28 — Ref: A Glasson
9	6/10	A	LEEDS	19,342	16	L 7	1-2	1-0	Mariner 35 / Cherry 49, Hird 63p — Ref: R Chadwick
10	9/10	H	ARSENAL	21,527	16	L 7	1-2	0-1	Brazil 89 / Sunderland 26, Rix 71 — Ref: M Scott

Line-ups (Town player / opponent)

No	1	2	3	4	5	6	7	8	9	10	11	12 sub used
1	Sivell / *Shilton*	Mills / *Anderson*	Butcher / *Gray*	Thijssen / *McGovern*	Hunter* / *Lloyd*	Osman / *Needham*	Wark / *O'Neill*	Muhren / *Hartford*	Mariner / *Birtles*	Gates / *Woodcock*	Woods / *Robertson*	Brazil
2	Cooper / *Jennings*	Mills / *Rice*	Butcher / *Nelson*	Thijssen / *Talbot*	Hunter / *O'Leary*	Osman / *Young*	Wark / *Brady*	Muhren / *Sunderland*	Mariner / *Stapleton*	Gates / *Price**	Woods / *Rix*	Brazil / *Hollins*
3	Cooper / *Bradshaw*	Mills / *Parkin*	Butcher / *Palmer*	Thijssen / *Daniel*	Hunter / *Hughes*	Osman / *Berry*	Wark* / *Hibbitt*	Muhren / *Carr*	Mariner / *Rafferty*	Gates / *Clarke**	Woods / *Patching*	Brazil / *Eves*
4	Cooper / *Jones*	Burley / *Richardson*	Mills / *Scott*	Thijssen / *Irvine*	Osman / *Smith*	Butcher / *Doyle*	Wark / *Randall*	Muhren / *Heath*	Mariner / *O'Callaghan*	Brazil* / *Crooks*	Woods / *Ursem**	Gates / *Busby*
5	Cooper / *Shaw*	Burley / *Tainton*	Mills / *Whitehead*	Osborne / *Gow*	Osman / *Sweeney*	Butcher / *Merrick*	Wark / *Fitzpatrick*	Muhren / *Ritchie*	Mariner* / *Royle*	Brazil / *Jantunen**	Woods / *Mabbutt*	Gates / *Cormack*
6	Cooper / *Steele*	Burley / *Gregory*	Mills / *Williams*	Osborne / *Horton*	Osman / *Foster*	Butcher / *Stevens*	Wark / *Clark**	Muhren / *Ward*	Mariner / *Maybank*	Brazil / *Sayer*	Woods* / *O'Sullivan*	Gates / *Ryan*
7	Cooper / *Wood*	Burley / *Barton*	Mills / *Bailey*	Osborne / *Lyons*	Osman / *Higgins*	Butcher / *Ross*	Wark / *Hartford*	Muhren / *Wright*	Mariner / *Nulty*	Brazil / *Kidd*	McCall / *Eastoe*	Gates
8	Cooper / *Burridge*	Burley / *Hinshelwood*	Mills / *Sansom*	Thijssen / *Nicholas*	Osman / *Cannon*	Butcher / *Gilbert*	Wark / *Murphy*	Muhren / *Francis*	Mariner / *Swindlehurst*	Gates / *Flanagan*	McCall / *Hilaire*	Osborne / *Osborne*
9	Cooper / *Harvey*	Mills / *Hird*	Butcher / *Hampton*	Thijssen / *Flynn*	Hunter / *Greenhoff*	Osman / *Parkinson*	Wark / *Hamson*	Muhren* / *Cherry*	Mariner / *Hankin*	Turner / *Curtis*	McCall / *Graham*	Brazil
10	Cooper / *Jennings*	Mills / *Walford*	Butcher / *Nelson*	Thijssen / *Talbot*	Hunter / *O'Leary*	Osman / *Young*	Wark / *Brady*	Osborne* / *Sunderland*	Mariner / *Stapleton*	Brazil / *Hollins*	Woods / *Rix*	Turner

Match Reports

1. Shilton plays superbly to repel a determined Town's best efforts. Cooper is out with a painful mouth abscess and his deputy Sivell is beaten by Woodcock after parrying a Birtles effort. Woodcock had created the goal himself with a lengthy run from deep.

2. After surviving early pressure, Town pick up where they left off against Forest, and their positive outlook fully warrants both points against Terry Neill's side. Hunter knocks in his first goal for four years. He then sprays a fine cross-field ball to Woods who tees up Muhren's strike.

3. John Barnwell's side maintain a 100% start. They are inspired by recent signing Emlyn Hughes and the opening of a huge new £2.5 million grandstand. After Carr opens the scoring, Town never look capable of clawing back a point and their lethargic performance angers Robson.

4. O'Callaghan spurns early chances before Mariner's shot wrong-foots Jones and Brazil follows up to score. Butcher nods a cross back towards his own goal, but Cooper is off-guard and the ball goes in. Superb headed goals follow from Mariner, via Thijssen's cross, and a diving Wark.

5. City are overrun in the middle of the park, but for all Town's hard work Shaw is only beaten once. Woods produces a superb volley to win the points. Osborne does well in his first appearance since scoring the winner at Wembley 16 months ago. David Geddis joins Villa for £300,000.

6. The result turns on a three-minute spell in which Clark, in acres of space, gives Alan Mullery's side the lead and Woods is injured. No-frills Albion are driven forward by new men Steve Foster, John Gregory and ex-Town junior Gary Stevens on his debut. Ryan heads a late clincher.

7. Gordon Lee's men pack their defence and frustrate Town until Wark blasts a powerful last-gasp point-saver. Before this everything was going to plan for the visitors after Kidd's shot gave them the early breakaway lead they wanted. A fourth successive home gate falls short of 20,000.

8. After ending the Everton game on a high, Town slump after an explosive start by Venables' young side. Hilaire's cross is netted via a brilliant 'scissors-kick' by Swindlehurst. There's no way back for Town as Francis nets a re-taken penalty, the first effort having been ballooned over.

9. Mariner neatly beats a couple of defenders before firing past Harvey to boost Town's shaky confidence. But the bad luck continues as Muhren departs injured and then Cherry appears to handle before grabbing an equaliser. Hankin pressurises Hunter into conceding a penalty to win it.

10. Town's slide continues as Arsenal run the show from midfield. The ref gets in the way and unwittingly helps Hollins set up Sunderland for the opening goal. After Rix tucks home a deserved second, the crowd gets on Robson's back with cries of 'spend some money' and 'go to Bilbao!'

11 H LIVERPOOL 13/10 — 25,310 — Pos 22 — Pts 7 — **1-2 L**

Scorers: Mariner 70 / Hunter 18 (og), Johnson 54 — Ref: D Reeves

Ipswich: Cooper, Burley, Butcher, Thijssen, Hunter, Osman, Wark, Mills, Mariner, Brazil*, Woods, Turner
Liverpool: Clemence, Neal, Kennedy A, Thompson, Kennedy R, Hansen, Dalglish, Case, Johnson, Heighway, Souness

A bad day, as Town sink to the bottom of the table, is summed up by Hunter's astonishing own-goal. His huge lob from out near the touchline beats Cooper all ends up. Bob Paisley's side clinches a well-deserved first away win of the season as ex-Town man Johnson poaches a second.

---

12 A MANCHESTER U 20/10 — 50,816 — Pos 22 — Pts 7 — **0-1 L**

Scorers: — / Grimes 68 — Ref: B Martin

Ipswich: Cooper, Burley, Mills, Thijssen, Osman, Butcher, Wark, Turner*, Mariner, Gates, Woods, Brazil
Manchester U: Bailey, Nicholl, Albiston, McIlroy, McQueen, Buchan, Grimes, Wilkins, Coppell, Macari, Thomas

Town battle ferociously but concede a hotly disputed penalty. Cooper makes a fine diving save from Thomas's kick. Thijssen is then clearly obstructed by Macari, but there is no whistle and McIlroy advances to tee-up Grimes' winner. Nicholl nets a real cracker, but offside is given.

---

13 H MIDDLESBROUGH 27/10 — 17,593 — Pos 19 — Pts 9 — **1-0 W**

Scorers: Brazil 66 — Ref: A Cox

Ipswich: Cooper, Burley, Butcher, Thijssen, Osman, Beattie, Wark, Mills, Mariner*, Brazil, Gates, Turner
Middlesbrough: Platt, Craggs, Bailey, Johnston, Ashcroft, McAndrew, Cochrane*, Proctor, Hodgson, Burns, Armstrong, Jankovic

A drab affair short on atmosphere, but the result lifts Town off the bottom. John Neal's unambitious side look content to hold on for a point, but are foiled as Thijssen produces an exquisite through-ball and Brazil confidently thunders it past Platt with his left foot. Relief all round.

---

14 A NOTT'M FOREST 3/11 — 24,593 — Pos 20 — Pts 9 — **0-2 L**

Scorers: — / Francis 52, 87 — Ref: K Hackett

Ipswich: Cooper, Burley, Butcher, Thijssen, Osman, Beattie, Wark, Muhren*, Mariner, Mills, Gates, Turner
Nott'm Forest: Shilton, Anderson, Gray, McGovern, Lloyd, Burns, Francis, O'Hare, Birtles*, Woodcock, Robertson, Mills

Town are unlucky when Gates has the ball in the net, but an infringement on Shilton is signalled. Lloyd heads against a post and the ball falls conveniently for Francis to net the rebound from close range. His second is more difficult as he swivels to fire home a cross from Woodcock.

---

15 H ASTON VILLA 10/11 — 17,807 — Pos 20 — Pts 10 — **0-0 D**

Ref: C White

Ipswich: Cooper, Burley, Butcher, Thijssen, Osman, Beattie, Wark, Muhren, Mariner, Mills, Turner, Shaw
Aston Villa: Rimmer, Swain, Gibson, Evans, McNaught, Mortimer, Bremner, Little, Geddis, Cowans, Shaw

Geddis, Villa's new signing from Town, goes close to his first goal for Ron Saunders' side but Burley is in position to clear off the line. Osman clatters into Little, but no penalty is awarded. Muhren's fine ball gives Wark an opportunity, but his drive hits the post in the closing minutes.

---

16 A DERBY 17/11 — 16,699 — Pos 20 — Pts 12 — **1-0 W**

Scorers: Mariner 40 — Ref: D Webb

Ipswich: Cooper, Burley, Butcher, Thijssen, Osman, Beattie, Wark, Muhren, Mariner, Mills, Gates, Turner
Derby: McKellar, Langan, Buckley, Rioch*, McCaffery, Osgood, Emery, Powell, Duncan, Davies, Hill, Clark

Robson names a line-up that really appears to 'click'. Osgood is robbed by Gates and he feeds Wark, who crosses for Mariner to head home a fine winner. Four days earlier a bumper 23,284 turn out for Bobby Robson's testimonial, in which George Best is Town's number 11.

---

17 H SOUTHAMPTON 24/11 — 18,685 — Pos 20 — Pts 14 — **3-1 W**

Scorers: Gates 12, Wark 13, Brazil 31 / Williams 87 — Ref: B Hill

Ipswich: Cooper, Wells, Butcher, Mills, Osman, Beattie, Wark*, Muhren, Mariner, Brazil, Gates, D'Avray
Southampton: Wells, Golac*, Holmes, Williams, Watson, Waldron, Ball, Boyer, Channon, Nicholl, Hebberd, Andr'szewski

Wells stars for Town as Lawrie McMenemy's five-man defensive ploy is wrecked. Wark saves Saints from a much bigger defeat and in the closing stages Mariner blasts a penalty over the bar after he was fouled by Watson. Regular taker Wark had been subbed by debutant D'Avray.

---

18 A COVENTRY 1/12 — 16,439 — Pos 20 — Pts 14 — **1-4 L**

Scorers: Wark 67p / Ferguson 11, 50, 62, 79 — Ref: D Shaw

Ipswich: Cooper, Sealey, Butcher, Mills, Osman, Beattie, Wark, Muhren, Mariner, D'Avray, Gates, Hunt
Coventry: Sealey, Coop, McDonald, Gooding, Holton, Gillespie, Hutchison, Wallace, Ferguson, Blair, Hunt

Robson reportedly felt Mick Ferguson's £750,000 transfer valuation was inflated, but he has to eat his words as the big Geordie poaches four goals, despite limping with a knee problem. City deserve the win, but are slightly flattered by the margin. Wark nets after a foul on Mariner.

---

19 H MANCHESTER C 8/12 — 18,221 — Pos 19 — Pts 16 — **4-0 W**

Scorers: Mills 7, Gates 12, 14, 53 — Ref: J Martin

Ipswich: Cooper, Burley, Butcher, Thijssen, Osman, Beattie*, Wark, Muhren, Mariner, Gates, Mills, McCall
Manchester C: Corrigan, Ransom, Power, Bennett, Caton, Booth, Gooding, Daley, Robinson, Viljoen, Palmer

Town are lifted by a dramatic opening 15 minutes as livewire Gates sets up Mills and then fires home two goals himself. He flicks the ball past the advancing Corrigan to celebrate a superb hat-trick. Henry hits the bar from 30 yards but it's a miserable return to Suffolk for Colin Viljoen.

---

20 A BOLTON 15/12 — 10,929 — Pos 17 — Pts 18 — **1-0 W**

Scorers: Brazil 44 — Ref: K Redfern

Ipswich: Cooper, Burley, Butcher, Thijssen, Osman, Mills, Wark, Muhren, Mariner, Brazil, Gates
Bolton: McDonagh, Nicholson, Burke, Greaves, Jones, Walsh, Morgan*, Whatmore, Gowling, Cantello, Thompson, Carter

In the Burnden Park mud, Brazil conjures up a brilliant winner, cutting inside and firing a 25-yarder into the corner of the net. Brazil and Mills also hit the woodwork and Mariner has an effort cleared off the line. Cooper confidently deals with all threats by Ian Greaves' struggling outfit.

---

21 H TOTTENHAM 21/12 — 18,852 — Pos 15 — Pts 20 — **3-1 W**

Scorers: Mariner 33, Muhren 37, Gates 50 / McAllister 16 — Ref: J Hunting

Ipswich: Cooper, Burley, Butcher, Thijssen, Osman, Mills, Wark, Muhren, Mariner, Brazil, Gates, Villa
Tottenham: Daines, Hughton, Miller, Yorath, McAllister, Perryman, Ardiles, Jones, Lee, Hoddle, Villa

Town show they have turned the corner at last, digging in and grafting for the points after McAllister tucks home an opening goal. Gates and Mariner unsettle Keith Burkinshaw's defence constantly and the result is in no doubt, even though Cooper is kept on his toes in the late stages.

LEAGUE DIVISION 1

Manager: Bobby Robson

SEASON 1979-80

No	Date		Att	Pos		Pt	F-A	H-T	Scorers, Times, and Referees	1	2	3	4	5	6	7	8	9	10	11	12 sub used
22	26/12	A NORWICH	24,335	5	D	21	3-3	1-2	Gates 15, Muhren 54, Wark 71 / Mendham 23, Taylor 43, Robson 89 Keelan — Ref: D Hutchinson	Cooper	Burley	Butcher	Thijssen	Hunter	Osman	Wark	Muhren	Mills	Brazil	Gates	
										Keelan	Bond	Downs	Ryan*	Brown*	Jones	Mendham	Taylor	Robson	Paddon	Peters	Fashanu
23	29/12	H WOLVERHAMPTON	22,333	10	W	23	1-0	0-0	Butcher 56 — Ref: C Downey	Cooper	Burley	Mills	Thijssen	Osman	Butcher	Wark	Muhren	Mariner	Brazil	Gates	
										Bradshaw	Palmer*	Brazier	Daniel	McAlle	Berry	Hibbitt	Carr	Gray	Richards	Eves	Clarke
24	1/1	H WEST BROM	22,477	10	W	25	4-0	2-0	Mariner 8, Wark 10p, Osman 59, [Thijssen 67] Godden — Ref: M Bidmead	Cooper	Burley	Mills	Thijssen	Osman	Butcher	Wark	Muhren	Mariner	Brazil	Gates	
										Godden	Batson	Pendrey	Trewick	Wile	Robertson*	Robson*	Brown A	Deehan	Brown T	Barnes	Regis
25	12/1	A STOKE	15,253	7	W	27	1-0	1-0	Mariner 34 — Ref: G Napthine	Cooper	Burley	Mills	Thijssen	Osman	Butcher	Wark	Muhren	Mariner	Brazil*	Gates	McCall
										Fox	Pejic	Irvine	Johnson	Dodd	Doyle	Heath	Richardson	O'Callaghan	Randall*	Chapman	
26	19/1	A BRISTOL CITY	14,218	5	W	29	3-0	1-0	Gates 42, Brazil 73, Mariner 85 — Ref: J Warner	Cooper	Burley	Mills	Thijssen	Osman	Butcher	Wark	Muhren	Mariner	Brazil	Gates	
										Shaw	Tainton	Whitehead	Gow	Rodgers	Sweeney	Pritchard	Fitzpatrick	Royle	Jantunen	Garland	
27	2/2	H BRIGHTON	22,494	5	D	30	1-1	1-0	Wark 28p / Stevens 90 — Ref: J Bray	Cooper	Burley	Mills	Thijssen	Osman	Butcher	Wark	Muhren	Mariner	Brazil	Gates	
										Moseley	Gregory	Williams	Horton	Foster	Suddaby	Ryan*	Ward	Clarke	Lawrenson	O'Sullivan	Stevens
28	9/2	A EVERTON	31,218	5	W	32	4-0	1-0	Mariner 3, Brazil 54, 75, Gates 63 — Ref: A Hamil	Cooper	Burley	Beattie	Thijssen	Osman	Butcher	Wark*	Muhren	Mariner	Brazil	Gates	O'Callaghan
										Hodge	Bailey	Gidman	Wright	Lyons	O'Keefe	Megson	Eastoe	Latchford	Hartford	McBride	
29	19/2	H CRYSTAL PALACE	23,012	3	W	34	3-0	2-0	Gates 26, Wark 34, Brazil 62 — Ref: P Reeves	Cooper	Burley	Mills	Thijssen	Osman	Butcher	Wark	Muhren	Mariner	Brazil	Gates	
										Burridge	Hinshelwood	Sansom	Nicholas	Cannon	Gilbert	Murphy	Francis	Walsh	Flanagan	Hilaire	
30	23/2	A LIVERPOOL	47,566	3	D	35	1-1	0-1	Gates 84 / Fairclough 8 — Ref: C Newsome	Cooper	Burley	Mills	Thijssen	Osman	Butcher	Wark	Muhren	Mariner	Brazil*	Gates	McCall
										Clemence	Neal	Kennedy A	Thompson	Kennedy R	Hansen	Dalglish	Case	Fairclough	McDermott	Souness	
31	1/3	H MANCHESTER U	30,120	3	W	37	6-0	3-0	Brazil 2, 53, Mariner 23, 27, 86, [Thijssen 79] — Ref: A Robinson	Cooper	Burley*	Beattie	Thijssen	Osman	Butcher	Mills	Muhren	Mariner	Brazil	Gates	O'Callaghan
										Bailey	Nichol*	Houston	McIlroy	McQueen	Buchan	Coppell	Sloan	Jordan	Macari	Grimes	Jovanovic

22 A NORWICH: A real Boxing Day thriller and arguably the best East Anglian derby to date as City's new River End stand is opened. Both managers feel their side did enough to win a game packed with chances. In a breathtaking finish, big Keith Robson stuns Town as he deflects the ball past Cooper.

23 H WOLVERHAMPTON: Carr hits the crossbar and John Barnwell's men create early scares for Town. Butcher's first goal of the season wins the points with Muhren also rapping the woodwork. Gray nearly undoes all the good work when he picks up a bad back-pass, but Cooper is down quickly to smother.

24 H WEST BROM: After a presentation to Mills to mark his 600th first team game, Town strike early. Ron Atkinson's side is deflated as Wile is harshly penalised for a challenge on Gates leading to the penalty. Osman volleys home the game's best goal to take it easy on the frozen surface.

25 A STOKE: Several chances go begging in the first half, before Mariner pounces for the lead. Alan Durban's youngsters battle in vain to rescue a point and go agonisingly close as Crooks hits the bar from outside the area. Robson pays Millwall a club record £200,000 for winger Kevin O'Callaghan.

26 A BRISTOL CITY: Gates thunders a loose ball in after Mariner leaps bravely for Mills' cross. Brazil beats the offside trap to fire home the second. Mariner hits the bar, then races on to Wark's pass to fire through Shaw's legs. Angry home fans abuse boss Alan Dicks and police are called in to calm matters.

27 H BRIGHTON: Suffolk-born substitute Stevens produces a fine shot in the last minute to frustrate the club that recently released him. This forgettable game is littered with illegal challenges and there's little fluent play. Wark nets from the spot, but Alan Mullery's stubborn side simply refuse to cave in.

28 A EVERTON: One of Town's best displays of the era, as they ooze class and cruise to a comfortable win. Best goal of the day sees the impish Gates pull off a series of one-twos with Muhren, Brazil and Mariner before climaxing the move with a classic shot. The lively Brazil is inches from a hat-trick.

29 H CRYSTAL PALACE: Media reports that Town called in 'shrinks' to improve their fortunes are an exaggeration, claims Robson, but he confirms two psychologists have been working with his team. The side gives another polished display to subdue Palace, with Thijssen and Butcher especially outstanding.

30 A LIVERPOOL: Controversy rages as McDermott's penalty is saved by Cooper, with Thijssen accused of hurling mud at the ball just as he takes it. The ref says the mud didn't interfere, but The Reds are livid. An even affair ends level when in-form Gates pounces to power home Butcher's knock-down.

31 H MANCHESTER U: The unbeaten run goes on in an incredibly one-sided win. United simply cave in and can thank Bailey for keeping it down to six. Nicholl's dreadful pass gifts the first goal and the errors continue. Bailey saves three penalties – from Thijssen and Beattie, and then Beattie's re-take!

#	Date	V	Opponent	Att	Pos	Pts		Res	Score	HT	Scorers	Ref
32	11/3	A	MIDDLESBROUGH	18,713	8	38	3	D	1-1	1-0	Mariner 10 / Ashcroft 85	Ref: R Chadwick
33	14/3	H	LEEDS	23,140	11	40	3	W	1-0	0-0	Mariner 89	Ref: M Taylor
34	22/3	A	ASTON VILLA	22,386	9	41	3	D	1-1	1-0	Wark 15 / Morley 74	Ref: B Stevens
35	29/3	H	DERBY	19,718	19	42	3	D	1-1	0-0	Gates 83 / Swindlehurst 61	Ref: D Hedges
36	2/4	A	TOTTENHAM	26,423	12	44	3	W	2-0	1-0	Mariner 43, Osman 81	Ref: R Challis
37	5/4	H	NORWICH	28,968	15	46	3	W	4-2	1-0	Wark 21, 71p, 90p, Mariner 85 / Bond 82, Robson 90	Ref: R Lewis
38	7/4	A	WEST BROM	19,844	9	47	3	D	0-0	0-0		Ref: R Banks
39	12/4	H	COVENTRY	20,502	14	49	3	W	3-0	3-0	Butcher 11, Mariner 16, Brazil 29	Ref: A Gunn
40	19/4	A	SOUTHAMPTON	22,028	6	51	3	W	1-0	0-0	Muhren 87	Ref: L Shapter
41	26/4	H	BOLTON	21,447	22	53	3	W	1-0	0-0	Gates 64	Ref: C Maskell
42	3/5	A	MANCHESTER C	31,648	17	53	3	L	1-2	1-2	Hunter 7 / Reeves 4, Henry 12	Ref: G Courtney

Home 21,620 Away 24,853 Average 24,853

Lineups (Town in bold / opponents in italic):

32 Middlesbrough: Cooper / *Platt*, Burley / *Craggs*, Mills / *Johnson**, Beattie* / *Johnston*, Butcher / *McAndrew*, Osman / *Ramage*, Mills / *Cochrane*, Muhren / *Proctor*, Mariner / *Hodgson*, Brazil / *Hedley*, Gates / *Armstrong*, Wark / *Ashcroft*
John Neal's side is unable to dispossess Thijssen on a typical probing run and he sets up Mariner for the opening goal. Town absorb plenty of pressure, but are shocked by a late goal as Mills slips to allow Ashcroft in. Long-serving winger Woods moves to Norwich for a £70,000 fee.

33 Leeds: Cooper / *Lukic*, Burley / *Cherry*, Mills / *Parkinson*, Thijssen / *Flynn*, Butcher / *Madeley*, Osman / *Hart*, Wark / *Gray**, Muhren / *Hird*, Mariner / *Connor*, Brazil / *Parlane*, Gates / *Graham*, *Chandler*
A double penalty miss for the second home match running. After Thijssen is floored by Lukic, the keeper saves Wark's kick. A re-take is ordered, but Wark then hits the underside of the bar. A lively game is climaxed in the final minute as Burley's cross is headed in by Mariner.

34 Aston Villa: Cooper / *Rimmer*, Burley / *Linton*, Mills / *Gibson*, Thijssen / *Ormsby*, Butcher / *Bullivant*, Osman / *McNaught*, Wark / *Bremner*, Muhren / *Swain*, Mariner / *Evans*, Brazil / *Cowans*, Gates / *Morley*
Wark thumps home a fine goal to compensate for his Leeds penalty miss. Villa pour forward in numbers and create many chances, Cowans hitting the bar. They deserve their late equaliser from Morley. Butcher's kidney problem means a return for Hunter after a lengthy absence.

35 Derby: Cooper / *McKellar*, Burley / *Langan*, Mills / *Buckley*, Osborne* / *Powell S*, Butcher / *Osgood*, Osman / *McFarland*, Wark / *Daly*, Muhren / *Powell B*, Mariner / *Biley*, Brazil / *Swindlehurst*, Gates / *Emson**, O'Callaghan / *McCaffery*
Osborne returns after nearly six months out, but Gates, with a late equaliser, and Cooper, with two penalty saves, take the limelight. Cooper's save from Barry Powell was outstanding after Beattie's challenge on Biley and the second comes from Daly's effort after an Osman handball.

36 Tottenham: Cooper / *Daines*, Burley / *Naylor*, Mills / *Hughton*, Thijssen / *Yorath*, Butcher / *McDowell*, Osman / *McAllister*, Hunter* / *Ardiles*, Muhren / *Jones*, Mariner / *Pratt*, Brazil / *Hoddle*, Gates* / *Taylor*
Fresh from beating League-leaders Liverpool, Spurs are put in their place as Town cruise to victory with goals at the end of each half. Daines is by far the busiest of the keepers and with Thijssen back after one match out, Town rule the roost in midfield to maintain their unbeaten run.

37 Norwich: Cooper / *Hansbury*, Burley / *Bond*, Mills / *Symonds*, Thijssen / *McDowell*, Butcher / *Hoadley*, Osman / *Jones*, Wark / *Woods*, Muhren / *Robson*, Mariner / *Taylor*, Brazil / *Paddon*, Gates* / *Peters*
Wark's first hat-trick and two of them are penalties, slotted into either corner of Hansbury's net. There's now been nine spot-kicks in the last four home games – seven missed! A scruffy and physical game bursts into life in the last 20 minutes when five of the goals are scrambled in.

38 West Brom: Cooper / *Godden*, Burley / *Batson*, Butcher / *Cowdrill*, Thijssen / *Moses*, Hunter* / *Wile*, Osman / *Robertson*, Wark / *Robson*, Muhren / *Deehan**, Mariner / *Regis*, Brazil / *Owen*, O'Callaghan / *Barnes*, McCall / *Trewick*
Two sides on long unbeaten runs cancel each other out. Town's defence is rarely troubled although Regis gets clear but shoots a fine chance over. Good news awaits Town fans with Muhren and Robson both deciding to stay at Portman Road, the latter after an approach by Barcelona.

39 Coventry: Cooper / *Blyth*, Burley / *Coop*, Butcher / *McDonald*, Thijssen / *Roberts*, Hunter / *Dyson*, Osman / *Gillespie*, Wark / *Wallace**, Muhren / *English*, Mariner / *Thompson*, Brazil / *Hunt*, Gates / *Hutchison*, McCall / *Gooding*
Emphatic revenge for the away defeat by Gordon Milne's side. Butcher volleys home from close range, then Mariner drills a shot through a pack of players. Brazil heads the third in a one-sided first half, but poor finishing after that saves shell-shocked City from further punishment.

40 Southampton: Cooper / *Wells*, Burley / *Golac*, Butcher / *Andr szewski Williams*, Thijssen / *Williams*, Hunter / *Watson*, Osman / *Nicholl*, Wark / *Helberd**, Muhren / *Boyer*, Mariner / *Channon*, Brazil / *Holmes*, Gates / *Hayes*, McCall / *Rogers*
After considering issues such as his children's education, Muhren confirms he'll stay in Suffolk for another two years. Dutch teammate Thijssen is voted Town fans Player of the Year. He celebrates by ending the deadlock at The Dell by smashing home a fine volley to win the points.

41 Bolton: Cooper / *McDonagh*, Burley / *Bennett*, Mills / *Graham*, Thijssen / *Nicholson*, Butcher / *Jones*, Osman / *Walsh*, Wark / *Cantello*, Muhren / *Whatmore*, Mariner / *Carter*, Brazil / *Wilson*, Gates / *Gowling*, McCall / *Reeves*
The unbeaten run is now 23 games long and a UEFA Cup place looks certain. Stan Anderson's already-relegated side prevent the goal-feast Town fans hope for and their massed ranks are only pierced once. Town are on top throughout, but Whatmore goes close on a breakaway raid.

42 Manchester C: Cooper / *Corrigan*, Burley / *Reid*, Mills / *Power*, Thijssen / *Futcher P*, Butcher / *Caton*, Osman / *Henry**, Wark* / *McKenzie*, Muhren / *Daley*, Mariner / *Deyna*, Brazil / *Sugrue*, Gates / *Reeves*, McCall / *Bennett*
Malcolm Allison's inconsistent side look sharp early on, but can thank Corrigan for ending Town's run. Good football at a premium on a hard pitch and Town go down to ten men as Mills breaks his wrist. Arsenal lose 0-5 at Middlesbrough to ensure the UEFA Cup place is safe.

LEAGUE DIVISION 1 (CUP-TIES)

Manager: Bobby Robson SEASON 1979-80

League Cup

		Att	F-A	H-T	Scorers, Times, and Referees	1	2	3	4	5	6	7	8	9	10	11	12 sub used
2:1 H	COVENTRY 29/8	13,217	17 16	L 0-1	0-1	English 18 Ref: P Richardson	Cooper *Blyth*	Burley *Roberts*	Mills *McDonald*	Thijssen *Blair*	Osman *Holton*	Butcher *Gillespie*	Wark *Hutchison*	Muhren *English*	Mariner *Ferguson*	Brazil *Gooding**	Gates *Hunt*	*Coop*

Teenager English, formerly a star in Suffolk non-League circles, nets the only goal after shots by Hunt and Blair are blocked. English then has another effort ruled out for offside. Gordon Milne packs his defence to protect the lead, and Blyth saves superbly to foil Brazil and Osman.

		Att	F-A	H-T	Scorers, Times, and Referees	1	2	3	4	5	6	7	8	9	10	11	12
2:2 A	COVENTRY 4/9	16,705	12 10	D 0-0	0-0	Ref: J Sewell (Town lose 0-1 on aggregate)	Cooper *Sealey*	Burley *Roberts*	Mills *McDonald*	Thijssen *Blair*	Osman *Holton*	Butcher *Gillespie*	Wark *Hutchison*	Muhren *English*	Mariner *Ferguson*	Brazil* *Powell*	Woods *Hunt*	Gates

A scrappy and unimpressive display by both sides sees Coventry go through. Holton and Gillespie are dominant in the home defence allowing Town little chance to test Sealey, the third keeper City have used in three games. All this on a night when Arsenal and Palace each hit seven!

FA Cup

		Att	F-A	H-T	Scorers, Times, and Referees	1	2	3	4	5	6	7	8	9	10	11	12
3 A	PRESTON 5/1	16,986 2:10	10 W	W 3-0	0-0	Mariner 54, 76, Brazil 65 Ref: J Hough	Cooper *Tunks*	Burley *Taylor*	Mills *McAteer*	Thijssen *Doyle*	Osman *Baxter*	Butcher *O'Riordan*	Wark* *Bell*	Muhren *Haslegrave*	Mariner *Elliott*	Brazil *McGee*	Gates *Bruce*	Beattie

Town hang on rather luckily in a frenzied first half, but Nobby Stiles' men run out of steam after the break. Gates' slippery run sets up Mariner for the crucial breakthrough. Brazil fires a precision goal from Burley's cross and then flicks Muhren's cross to his partner Mariner for a third.

		Att	F-A	H-T	Scorers, Times, and Referees	1	2	3	4	5	6	7	8	9	10	11	12
4 A	BRISTOL CITY 26/1	19,608	5 20	W 2-1	1-1	Wark 45, Mariner 87 Whitehead 38 Ref: T Bune	Cooper *Shaw*	Burley *Tainton*	Mills *Whitehead*	Thijssen *Gow*	Osman *Rodgers*	Butcher *Merrick**	Wark *Pritchard*	Muhren *Fitzpatrick*	Mariner *Mabbutt*	Brazil *Sweeney*	Gates *Garland*	Doyle

After around 500 minutes without conceding, Town fall behind to full-back Whitehead. A typical blood-and-thunder tie sees Town unable to dictate as they did a week earlier against City. A replay looks likely until Shaw saves from Thijssen, but lets the ball slip and Mariner pounces.

		Att	F-A	H-T	Scorers, Times, and Referees	1	2	3	4	5	6	7	8	9	10	11	12
5 H	CHESTER 16/2	26,353 3:5	5 W	W 2-1	2-1	Burley 41, Wark 44 Jones 8 Ref: B Daniel	Cooper *Millington*	Burley *Jeffries*	Mills *Walker*	Thijssen *Storton*	Osman *Cottam*	Butcher *Oakes*	Wark *Sutcliffe*	Muhren *Jones*	Gates *Rush*	Brazil *Phillips*	Woods *Howat*	Beattie

Alan Oakes' side battle gamely in vain after Bryn Jones' shock early goal. Burley levels matters with a diving header, meaning all ten Town outfielders have scored at least once this season. Robson is named Manager of the Month and Woods plays his 267th and final Ipswich game.

		Att	F-A	H-T	Scorers, Times, and Referees	1	2	3	4	5	6	7	8	9	10	11	12
6 A	EVERTON 8/3	45,104 19	3 L	L 1-2	0-1	Beattie 89 Latchford 29, Kidd 76 Ref: J Hunting	Cooper *Wood*	Burley *Gidman*	Mills *Bailey*	Thijssen *Wright*	Osman *Lyons*	Butcher *Eastoe*	Wark* *Megson*	Muhren *King*	Mariner *Latchford*	Brazil *Kidd*	Beattie *McBride*	

A month after annihilating Everton 4-0 at Goodison, Town end up second best this time, despite looking very lively early on. Gidman floats over a cross for Latchford to head home and Kidd ends any serious hopes of progress. Beattie's amazing leap and header is a mere consolation.

UEFA Cup

		Att	F-A	H-T	Scorers, Times, and Referees	1	2	3	4	5	6	7	8	9	10	11	12
1:1 A	SKEID OSLO 19/9 (Norway)	3,190	12 W	W 3-1	2-1	Mills 9, Turner 36, Mariner 53 Rein 5 Ref: O Amundsen (Denmark)	Cooper *Nygaard*	Burley *Pettersen*	Butcher *Nielsen*	Mills *Vinje*	Hunter *Gronfor*	Osman *Dyrstad*	Parkin *Johansen*	Muhren* *Thue **	Mariner *Kristensen*	Turner *Skjønsberg*	McCall *Rein*	Parkinson *Skrettingland*

With seven first-teamers unfit, Town have to work hard against the Norwegian part-timers, surviving two major scares en route. Rein rockets home a short-free kick which Cooper calls the best shot that's ever gone past him. At 1-1, Cooper makes a great save from Johansen's penalty.

		Att	F-A	H-T	Scorers, Times, and Referees	1	2	3	4	5	6	7	8	9	10	11	12
1:2 H	SKEID OSLO 3/10	13,440	14 W	W 7-0	4-0	Wark 8, Muhren 19, 21, Thijssen 38, Mariner 57, McCall 62, 83) Ref: E Gudmundsson (Iceland) (Town win 10-1 on aggregate)	Cooper *Nygaard**	Burley^ *Pettersen*	Butcher *Nielsen*	Thijssen *Vinje*	Hunter *Amundsen*	Osman *Dyrstad*	Wark *Johansen*	Muhren *Thue^*	Mariner *Kristensen*	Brazil* *Skjønsberg*	Mills *Rein*	Turner/Parkinson *Hilland/Niltsen*

Wark fires in Butcher's cross from 25 yards, then Muhren lashes home two quick goals, assisted by Brazil and Butcher. McCall's first senior goal is a low drive to make it six. Nygaard is subbed to save him further misery, but McCall spots the sub off his line and nets from 40 yards.

		Att	F-A	H-T	Scorers, Times, and Referees	1	2	3	4	5	6	7	8	9	10	11	12
2:1 A	GRASSHOPPERS 24/10 (Zurich, Switz)	16,000	22 D	D 0-0	0-0	Ref: R Schoeters (Belgium)	Cooper *Berbig*	Burley *Inalbon*	Butcher *HermannHz*	Thijssen *Nafzger*	Osman *Meyer*	Beattie *Traber**	Wark *Pfister*	Mills *Wehrli*	Mariner *Sulser*	Brazil *Ponte*	Gates *Egli*	Hermann Ht *Herrmann Ht*

The closest to a breakthrough comes as Sulser hits Town's crossbar with Egli firing the rebound wide. Mariner and Wark nearly give Town a first-leg lead, but a draw looks good enough against a useful side containing seven Swiss internationals and leading its own domestic league.

		Att	F-A	H-T	Scorers, Times, and Referees	1	2	3	4	5	6	7	8	9	10	11	12
2:2 H	GRASSHOPPERS 7/11	19,574	20 D	D 1-1	1-0	Beattie 43 Sulser 69 Ref: K Scheuerll (East Germany) (Town lose on away goals)	Cooper *Berbig*	Burley *Inalbon*	Butcher *Hermann Hz*	Thijssen *Nafzger*	Osman *Meyer*	Beattie *H'rrmann Ht**	Wark* *Pfister*	Muhren *Wehrli*	Mariner *Sulser*	Brazil *Ponte*	Gates *Egli*	Brazil *Traber*

Town look in control, particularly after Beattie steers them ahead, but they fail to kill off Grasshoppers despite dominating midfield. The away goals rule means Sulser's breakaway goal changes the whole context of the tie. Mariner has a great chance near the end but his header is saved.

Ipswich Town — Season Record

League Table

Pos	Team	P	W (H)	D (H)	L (H)	F (H)	A (H)	W (A)	D (A)	L (A)	F (A)	A (A)	Pts
1	Liverpool	42	15	6	0	46	8	10	4	7	35	22	60
2	Manchester U	42	17	3	1	43	8	7	7	7	22	27	58
3	IPSWICH	42	14	4	3	43	13	8	5	8	25	26	53
4	Arsenal	42	10	10	3	24	12	10	6	5	28	24	52
5	Nott'm Forest	42	16	4	1	44	11	4	4	13	19	32	48
6	Wolves	42	9	6	6	29	20	10	3	8	29	27	47
7	Aston Villa	42	11	5	5	29	22	5	9	7	22	28	46
8	Southampton	42	14	2	5	53	24	4	7	10	12	29	45
9	Middlesbro	42	11	7	3	31	14	5	5	11	19	30	44
10	West Brom	42	9	8	4	37	23	2	11	8	17	27	41
11	Leeds	42	10	7	4	30	17	3	7	11	16	33	40
12	Norwich	42	10	8	3	38	30	3	6	12	20	36	40
13	Crys Palace	42	9	9	3	26	13	3	7	11	15	37	40
14	Tottenham	42	11	5	5	30	22	4	5	12	22	40	40
15	Coventry	42	12	2	7	34	24	4	5	12	22	42	39
16	Brighton	42	8	8	5	25	20	3	7	11	22	37	37
17	Manchester C	42	8	8	5	28	25	4	5	12	15	41	37
18	Stoke	42	9	4	8	27	26	4	6	11	17	32	36
19	Everton	42	7	7	7	28	25	2	10	9	15	26	35
20	Bristol City	42	6	6	9	22	30	3	7	11	15	36	31
21	Derby	42	9	4	8	36	29	2	4	15	11	38	30
22	Bolton	42	5	11	5	19	21	0	4	17	19	52	25
		924	228	134	100	722	437	100	134	228	437	722	924

Appearances and Goals

Player	Lge	Sub	LC	Sub	FAC	Sub	Eur	Sub	G Lge	Sub	G LC	G FAC	G Eur	Tot
Beattie, Kevin	10						2				1	1		2
Brazil, Alan	31	4	2		4		2	2	12	1	1			13
Burley, George	38		2		4		4					1		1
Butcher, Terry	36		2		4		4		2					2
Cooper, Paul	40		2		4		4							
D'Avray, Mich	1	1												
Gates, Eric	34	2		1	4		2		13					13
Hunter, Allan	16		2		3		2		2					2
Mariner, Paul	41		2		3		4		17		2	3		22
McCall, Steve	3	7					2							
Mills, Mick	37		2		4		3		1			1		2
Muhren, Arnold	37		2		3		3		4		1	1		6
O'Callaghan, Kevin	1	3						2						
Osborne, Roger	4	2												
Osman, Russell	42		2		4		4		2					2
Parkin, Tommy							1							
Parkinson, Noel										2				
Sivell, Laurie	2													
Thijssen, Frans	37		2		4		3		2			1		3
Turner, Robin	3	4		1				1		1		1		1
Wark, John	40	1	2		4		3		12		1	2		15
Woods, Clive	9		1		1				1					1
22 players used	462	24	22	1	44	2	44	3	68		8	11		87

Odds & ends

Double wins: (5) Bolton, Bristol City, Southampton, Stoke, Tottenham.

Double losses: (1) Nott'm Forest.

Won from behind: (4) Tottenham (h), Bristol City (a) (FAC), Chester (h) (FAC), Skeid Oslo (a) (Eur).

Lost from in front: (1) Leeds (a).

High spots: A remarkable 23-game unbeaten League run. Qualification for a seventh European campaign in eight seasons. The outstanding display at Everton in February. The 6-0 annihilation of second-placed Manchester U. The 3-3 local derby thriller at Norwich on Boxing Day. Paul Cooper saving five of the seven penalties he faced.

Low spots: Run of six autumn defeats, leaving Town bottom in October. Four-goal hammerings by Coventry and Crystal Palace. The end of the Hunter and Beattie defensive partnership. Town players missing six out of 11 penalty attempts.

Player of the Year: Frans Thijssen.

Ever-presents: (1) Russell Osman.

Hat-tricks: (3) Alan Brazil, Eric Gates, Paul Mariner.

Opposing hat-tricks: (1) Mick Ferguson (Coventry).

Leading scorer: (22) Paul Mariner.

LEAGUE DIVISION 1 — Manager: Bobby Robson — SEASON 1980-81

No	Date	Match	Att	Res	F-A	Pos	Pt	H-T	Scorers / Ref	1	2	3	4	5	6	7	8	9	10	11	12 sub used
1	16/8	A LEICESTER	21,640	W	1-0		2	0-0	Wark 88; Ref: A Read	Cooper	Burley	Mills	Thijssen	Osman	Butcher	Wark	McCall	Mariner	Gates	O'Callaghan	
										Wallington	*Williams*	*Gibson*	*Peake*	*May*	*O'Neill*	*Edmunds**	*Melrose*	*Young*	*Wilson*	*Smith*	*Henderson*
2	19/8	H BRIGHTON	21,568	W	2-0		4	1-0	Wark 36p, Gates 74; Ref: G Napthine	Cooper	Burley	Mills	Thijssen	Osman	Butcher	Wark	Muhren	Mariner	Gates	O'Callaghan	
										Mosley	*Gregory*	*Williams*	*Horton*	*Foster*	*Lawrenson*	*McHale*	*Ward*	*Robinson*	*Smith*	*McNab*	
3	23/8	A STOKE	10,722	D	2-2	2	5	2-1	Brazil 15, Gates 40; Ursem 8, Chapman 79; Ref: A Challinor	Cooper	Burley	Mills	Thijssen	Osman	Butcher	Wark	Muhren	Mariner	Brazil*	Gates	O'Callaghan
										Fox	*Evans*	*Hampton*	*Dodd*	*Thorley*	*Richardson*	*Ursem*	*Johnson**	*Chapman*	*Cook*	*Bracewell*	*Randall*
4	30/8	H EVERTON	20,879	W	4-0	1	7	2-0	Brazil 11, Wark 12, Butcher 80, Mariner 84; Ref: M Taylor	Cooper	Burley	Mills	Thijssen	Osman	Butcher	Wark	Muhren	Mariner	Brazil	Gates	
										McDonagh	*Gidman*	*Ratcliffe*	*Wright*	*Lyons*	*Stanley**	*McMahon*	*Hartford*	*Latchford*	*Eastoe*	*McBride*	*O'Keefe*
5	6/9	H ASTON VILLA	23,192	W	1-0	1	9	0-0	Thijssen 56; Ref: M Bidmead	Cooper	Burley	McCall	Thijssen	Osman	Butcher	Wark	Muhren	Mariner	Brazil	Gates	
										Rimmer	*Swain*	*Gibson*	*Evans*	*McNaught*	*Mortimer*	*Bremner*	*Shaw*	*Withe*	*Cowans*	*Morley*	
6	13/9	A CRYSTAL PALACE	24,282	W	2-1	1	11	1-0	Wark 27, Gates 85; Lovell 90; Ref: M Baker	Cooper	Burley	Mills	Thijssen	Osman	Beattie	Wark	Muhren	Mariner	Brazil*	Gates	O'Callaghan
										Barron	*Hinshelwood*	*Fenwick*	*Lovell*	*Cannon*	*Gilbert*	*Smillie*	*Francis*	*Allen*	*Flanagan*	*Hilaire**	*Sealy*
7	20/9	H COVENTRY	20,507	W	2-0	1	13	0-0	Wark 57, 63; Ref: D Letts	Cooper	Burley	Mills	Thijssen	Osman	Butcher	Wark	Muhren	Mariner	Brazil*	Gates	O'Callaghan
										Sealey	*Coop*	*Roberts*	*Blair*	*Dyson*	*Jacobs*	*Bodak**	*Daly*	*Hateley*	*Hutchison*	*Hunt*	*English*
8	27/9	A WOLVERHAMPTON	18,503	W	2-0	1	15	2-0	Brazil 29, Mariner 44; Ref: C Thomas	Cooper	Burley	Mills	Thijssen	Osman	Butcher	Wark	Muhren	Mariner	Brazil	Gates	
										Bradshaw	*Palmer*	*Parkin*	*Daniel*	*Hughes*	*Brazier*	*Villazan*	*Atkinson*	*Gray*	*Clarke**	*Eves*	*Richards*
9	4/10	H LEEDS	24,087	D	1-1	1	16	0-0	Wark 70; Sabella 47; Ref: T Bune	Cooper	Burley	Mills	Thijssen	Osman	Butcher	Wark	Muhren*	Mariner	Brazil	Gates	O'Callaghan
										Lukic	*Greenhoff*	*Gray*	*Flynn*	*Hart*	*Cherry*	*Harris*	*Curtis*	*Parlane*	*Sabella*	*Graham*	
10	11/10	A LIVERPOOL	48,084	D	1-1	3	17	1-1	Thijssen 28; McDermott 38p; Ref: A Hamil	Cooper	Burley	Mills	Thijssen	Osman	Butcher	Wark	Muhren	Mariner	Gates	McCall	
										Clemence	*Neal*	*Cohen*	*Thompson*	*Kennedy*	*Hansen*	*Dalglish*	*Lee*	*Johnson*	*McDermott*	*Souness*	

Match reports

1. Mariner strikes the post and Osman, McCall and Burley all go close to the season's first goal. In the nick of time Gates' cross finds Wark and he heads past Wallington to sink Jock Wallace's side. First choice players Brazil and Muhren both miss this opener with ankle problems.

2. Thijssen and Williams tangle inside the area and the ref points to the spot for Wark to step up and score. Town look smooth and efficient, and Wark and Mariner both hit the woodwork in the first half. Burley finds Gates, who produces a spectacular drive to ensure the points are safe.

3. Dutchman Ursem's first goal for City is almost cancelled out as Mariner lobs in, but is pulled up for dangerous play. Brazil nips in to fire past Fox and Town look well in command. A meagre crowd comes to life as Chapman converts the rebound after Cooper blocks Randall's drive.

4. Gates' cross is headed in by Brazil and before the cheers have died down, Mariner crosses from the right for Wark to lash home a spectacular volley as he falls. Muhren's corner is headed in at the near post by Butcher. Mariner combines neatly with Muhren for his first of the season.

5. End-to-end action is settled by a scruffy goal as Thijssen's scrambled shot is helped into the net by Evans' attempted clearance. Villa create many chances, but Shaw is out of luck. Burley clears one certain goal off the line. Bobby Robson receives the Manager of the Month whisky.

6. Brazil slips the ball to Wark, whose fierce shot rebounds off the sprawling Barron and loops into the air, Wark finishing off when it descends. Brazil and Mariner set up Gates for an emphatic finish. Three Town men are booked for dissent. Lovell fires a late consolation past Cooper.

7. Wark springs a creaky offside trap to maintain his spectacular scoring form. City bring back veteran Hutchison from the USA, but waste early chances. Bobby Robson's post-match remark that the quiet home fans were like 'zombies' leads to uproar when reported in the local press.

8. The excellent start in the League stretches to seven wins and a draw thanks to clinical finishing. Brazil volleys in Gates' cross and Thijssen's exquisite work is finished by Mariner. Gray hits Town's woodwork. Some fans react to Robson's remarks by wearing 'I'm a Zombie!' badges.

9. Negative Leeds are struggling under new boss Allan Clarke, with just one win from their opening ten games. They are thrown a lifeline when record signing Alex Sabella nets against the run of play. Teenage keeper Lukic keeps Town at bay until Wark converts a fine diving header.

10. An excellent contest, not for the faint-hearted. Town silence the Kop as Thijssen seizes on Kennedy's clearance and fires in. He later brings down lively Dalglish and McDermott nets from the spot. Young McCall has a fine game. Bob Paisley's men are unbeaten here for three years.

Ipswich Town — match-by-match record (games 11–21)

11 H MANCHESTER U — 18/10 — 28,451
1 D 1-1 · 7 · 18
Mariner 55 / *McIlroy 67p*
Ref: R Challis
Ipswich: Cooper, Burley, Mills, Thijssen*, Osman, Butcher, Wark, Muhren, Mariner, Brazil, Gates, McCall
Manchester U: *Bailey, Nicholl, Albiston, McIlroy, Jovanovic, Moran, Coppell, Duxbury, Jordan, Macari, Thomas*

Thijssen is helped off injured and an early re-shuffle is required. Mariner cracks home a spectacular effort from a difficult angle. Butcher's under-hit back-pass is intercepted by Coppell and he is brought crashing down by Cooper. McIlroy tucks home the penalty to save a point.

12 A SUNDERLAND — 25/10 — 32,368
2 W 2-0 · 9 · 20
Muhren 40, Brazil 67
Ref: D Webb
Ipswich: Cooper, Burley, Mills, Beattie, Osman, Butcher, McCall, Muhren*, Mariner*, Brazil, Gates, D'Avray
Sunderland: *Turner, Whitworth, Bolton, Allardyce, Elliott, Chisholm, Arnott, Rowell, Cooke, Brown, Cummins*

Ken Knighton's newly-promoted Rokerites give Town plenty to worry about in the first half and it needs a Muhren breakaway goal to stifle the home pressure. Mariner tears his calf muscle, but Town make the points safe when substitute D'Avray pulls the ball back for Brazil to score.

13 H WEST BROM — 1/11 — 23,043
2 D 0-0 · 6 · 21
Ref: A Grey
Ipswich: Cooper*, Burley, Mills, Thijssen*, Osman, Butcher, Wark, Muhren, Mariner, Brazil, Gates, Turner
West Brom: *Godden, Trewick, Statham*, Moses, Wile, Robertson, Robson, Brown, Regis, Mills, Monaghan, Benjamin*

The injury problems begin to stack up as Cooper is left hobbling after an early clash with Monaghan. Thijssen pulls a hamstring but cannot go off because of the Cooper situation. Eventually Osman goes in goal and is an instant hero, saving Wile's volley and several other tricky shots.

14 A SOUTHAMPTON — 8/11 — 21,261
2 D 3-3 · 15 · 22
Gates 19, Wark 23, Mariner 69 / *Williams 44, Boyer 48, Moran 75*
Ref: B Stevens
Ipswich: Sivell, Burley*, Mills, Beattie, Osman, Butcher!, Wark, Muhren, Mariner, Brazil, McCall, Gates
Southampton: *Katalinic, Golac, Holmes, Williams, Watson, Nicholl, Keegan, Channon, Boyer, Moran, Baker*

Lawrie McMenemy's side salvages a point from a real thriller when Moran pounces after an almighty goalmouth scramble. Butcher, booked for fouling Channon, brings down Williams and Town players get agitated when Keegan urges the ref to send him off – and gets his wish!

15 A BRIGHTON — 11/11 — 17,055
3 L 0-1 · 20 · 22
Robinson 83
Ref: A Robinson
Ipswich: Sivell, Burley*, Mills, Osman, Hunter, Turner, Wark, Muhren, Mariner, Brazil, Gates, D'Avray
Brighton: *Moseley, Gregory, Stevens, Foster, Horton, Lawrenson, McNab, Ritchie, Robinson, Smith, O'Sullivan*

Crippled by injury and suspension, it's backs-to-the-wall stuff as Ipswich preserve the League's only remaining unbeaten record. However, Burley's injury in the final ten minutes is the final straw and Robinson wins it for Alan Mullery's bottom-of-the-table strugglers.

16 H LEICESTER — 15/11 — 19,852
2 W 3-1 · 22 · 24
Gates 21, Williams 56 (og), D'Avray 85 / *Williams 89*
Ref: C Maskell
Ipswich: Sivell, Mills, McCall, Osman, Butcher, Hunter, Wark, Muhren, Mariner, Brazil, Gates*, D'Avray
Leicester: *Wallington, Carr, Scott, Peake, May, O'Neill, Hamill, Lineker*, Young, Wilson, Williams, Henderson*

Brazil's header sends Gates through to force the ball home. Young hits Town's bar before Brazil's driven cross is swept past his own keeper by Williams. D'Avray's first League goal is tucked home neatly after fine work by Mariner. Williams feels better after a volley at the correct end!

17 A NOTT'M FOREST — 22/11 — 24,423
2 W 2-1 · 8 · 26
Brazil 37, Wark 79p / *Wallace 76*
Ref: D Shaw
Ipswich: Sivell, Mills, McCall, Thijssen, Osman, Butcher, Wark, Muhren, Mariner, Brazil, Gates, D'Avray
Nott'm Forest: *Shilton, Anderson, Gray, McGovern, Lloyd, Burns, Mills, Ward, Bowyer, Wallace, Robertson*

Gates seizes on a mistake by Ward to set up Brazil, who beats Lloyd and Shilton in great style. Mills' cross is headed on by Lloyd and Wallace nets an overhead kick to silence his barrackers. Gray fouls Thijssen to concede the winning penalty. Brave Sivell plays a heroic role in goal.

18 A MANCHESTER C — 6/12 — 35,215
3 D 1-1 · 15 · 27
Muhren 12 / *Gow 75*
Ref: P Partridge
Ipswich: Cooper, Burley, Mills, Thijssen, Osman, Butcher, Wark, Muhren, Mariner, Brazil*, Gates, O'Callaghan
Manchester C: *Corrigan, Ransom, McDonald, Reid, Power, Booth, Hutchison, Gow, McKenzie, Tueart*, Reeves, Bayer*

After a dreadful start at Maine Road, John Bond has turned things round and is named Manager of the Month. However his team look second best in the first half and Town are well worth their lead. A goalmouth melee as Cooper breaks his nose and Gow equalises.

19 H LIVERPOOL — 13/12 — 32,274
3 D 1-1 · 2 · 28
Brazil 23 / *Case 62*
Ref: D Reeves
Ipswich: Cooper, Burley, Mills, Thijssen, Osman, Butcher, Wark, Muhren, Mariner, Brazil, Gates, O'Callaghan
Liverpool: *Clemence, Neal, Kennedy A, Irwin, Kennedy R, Hansen, Lee, Rush, Johnson*, McDermott, Souness, Case*

Town seem to have the measure of Bob Paisley's men, who are without Dalglish and lose Johnson early, meaning they have debutant Ian Rush partnered by makeshift striker Lee. But the final half-hour belongs to the Reds as Case's header ends up going in when Lee distracts Cooper.

20 A TOTTENHAM — 17/12 — 22,741
3 L 3-5 · 10 · 28
Mariner 42, 65, Gates 55 / *Cr'ks 10, H'ddle 45, P'man 60, Arc' 81* [Ardiles 88!]
Ref: J Martin
Ipswich: Cooper, Burley, Mills, Thijssen, Osman, Butcher, Wark, Muhren, Mariner, Brazil, Gates!, O'Callaghan
Tottenham: *Daines, McAllister, Hughton, Roberts, Lacy, Perryman, Ardiles, Archibald, Villa*, Hoddle, Crooks, Yorath*

Crooks converts Archibald's pass, then Mariner nets Muhren's free-kick. Hoddle chips a free-kick home before Gates' cross-shot is helped in by the wind. Perryman slides in a third, when Mariner levels with his head. Gates is sent off after tangling with Roberts and 10-man Town fade.

21 A BIRMINGHAM — 20/12 — 16,161
3 W 3-1 · 13 · 30
Mariner 42, Wark 52, Brazil 82 / *Ainscow 88*
Ref: G Owen
Ipswich: Cooper, Burley, Mills, Thijssen, Osman, Butcher, Wark, Muhren, Mariner, Brazil, Gates, O'Callaghan
Birmingham: *Wealands, Langan, Hawker, Curbishley, Gallagher, Todd, Ainscow, Bertschin, Worthington, Gemmill, Givens*, Dillon*

Mariner sprints in to bury Brazil's low cross. Wark heads home Muhren's cross and Town are cruising in the comfort zone. Wark drives forward and then backheels to Brazil, who hits a fabulous goal with a fierce drive from an 'impossible' angle. Ainscow fires in a consolation.

LEAGUE DIVISION 1

Manager: Bobby Robson — SEASON 1980-81

---

22. H NORWICH — 26/12

	Att	Pos	Pt	F-A	H-T
	27,890	3 (19)	W 32	2-0	1-0

Team	1	2	3	4	5	6	7	8	9	10	11	12 sub used
Town	Cooper	Burley	McCall	Thijssen	Osman	Butcher	Wark	Muhren	Mariner	Brazil	Gates*	O'Callaghan
Norwich	*Baker*	*Bond*	*Powell*	*McGuire**	*Hoadley*	*Watson*	*Mendham*	*Fashanu*	*Royle*	*Paddon*	*Goble*	*Woods*

Scorers, Times: Brazil 43, Wark 49. **Ref:** P Reeves

Two clinical finishes as Brazil jinks into the box past Bond and tricks Baker before firing into the corner of the net. Muhren crosses from the left and a first-timer by Wark leaves Baker helpless. There is concern over Thijssen's future – he remains locked in a dispute over his contract.

---

23. A ARSENAL — 27/12

	Att	Pos	Pt	F-A	H-T
	42,818	3 (4)	D 33	1-1	0-1

Team	1	2	3	4	5	6	7	8	9	10	11	12 sub used
Town	Cooper	Burley	McCall*	Thijssen	Osman	Butcher	Wark	Muhren	Mariner	Brazil	Gates	O'Callaghan
Arsenal	*Jennings*	*Devine*	*Sansom*	*Talbot*	*Walford*	*Young*	*Hollins*	*Sunderland*	*Stapleton*	*Gatting*	*Rix*	

Scorers, Times: Wark 77p. Sunderland 35. **Ref:** K Baker

Terry Neill's side go ahead as Sunderland converts Hollins' corner, with Town appealing it should have been a throw. Maybe justice is done as Gatting is rather unlucky to concede a penalty when challenging Mariner for a loose ball. The deadly Wark makes no mistake from the spot.

---

24. H NOTT'M FOREST — 10/1

	Att	Pos	Pt	F-A	H-T
	25,701	2 (7)	W 35	2-0	0-0

Team	1	2	3	4	5	6	7	8	9	10	11
Town	Cooper	Burley	Mills	Thijssen	Osman	Butcher	Wark	Muhren	Mariner	Brazil	O'Callaghan
Nott'm Forest	*Shilton*	*Anderson*	*Gray*	*McGovern*	*Needham*	*Burns*	*O'Neill*	*Ward*	*Francis*	*Bowyer*	*Robertson*

Scorers, Times: Mariner 53, Muhren 74. **Ref:** C White

Town subdue Brian Clough's side with a lively display and Brazil, after passing a late fitness test, is a constant menace. Shilton produces two superb saves to defy him, and Bowyer's last-ditch clearance off the line foils Mariner. The win is clinched by Muhren's close-range stab-in.

---

25. H BIRMINGHAM — 13/1

	Att	Pos	Pt	F-A	H-T
	21,158	1 (14)	W 37	5-1	3-1

Team	1	2	3	4	5	6	7	8	9	10	11	12 sub used
Town	Cooper	Burley	Mills	Thijssen	Osman	Butcher	Wark	Muhren	Mariner	Brazil	O'Callaghan	
Birmingham	*Wealands*	*Langan*	*Hawker*	*Curbishley*	*Gallagher*	*Todd*	*Ainscow*	*Bertschin*	*Worthington*	*Gemmill*	*Evans**	*Lynex*

Scorers, Times: Wark 9, Butcher 22, Mariner 40, Gates 85, Worth'gton 23 [Muhren 61, Brazil 67]. **Ref:** C Downey

Hazardous roads keep the crowd down, but Town look classy on the snow-covered pitch. City boss Jim Smith says Town are Europe's best team on current form. Neat moves and sharp finishing make a mockery of conditions – a great way for Robson to celebrate 12 years in charge.

---

26. A EVERTON — 17/1

	Att	Pos	Pt	F-A	H-T
	25,516	1 (10)	D 38	0-0	0-0

Team	1	2	3	4	5	6	7	8	9	10	11	12 sub used
Town	Cooper	Burley	Mills	Thijssen	Osman	Butcher	Wark	Muhren	Mariner	Brazil	O'Callaghan	
Everton	*McDonagh*	*Ratcliffe*	*Bailey*	*Wright*	*Lyons*	*Ross*	*McMahon*	*Eastoe*	*Varadi*	*Hartford*	*O'Keefe**	*McBride*

Ref: M Heath

The pitch is passed playable despite heavy downpours and the sides dominate a half each. Town are liveliest early on, but Gordon Lee's half-time pep talk seems to galvanise Everton, who are from then on a constant threat. Lyons goes closest; his long-range shot is superbly saved.

---

27. H STOKE — 31/1

	Att	Pos	Pt	F-A	H-T
	23,843	1 (13)	W 40	4-0	2-0

Team	1	2	3	4	5	6	7	8	9	10	11	12 sub used
Town	Cooper	Burley	McCall	Thijssen	Osman	Butcher	Wark	Muhren	Mariner*	Brazil	Gates	O'Callaghan
Stoke	*Fox*	*Doyle*	*Hampton*	*Dodd*	*O'Callaghan*	*Munro*	*Bracewell*	*Griffiths**	*Chapman*	*Heath*	*Maguire*	*Ursem*

Scorers, Times: Wark 30p, Brazil 44, 48, Gates 85. **Ref:** D Vickers

Town are in irresistible form and show no mercy to Alan Durban's men. Notice is served in the first 30 seconds as Brazil hits the post and Mariner's effort is hacked off the line. Munro brings down Gates and Wark converts the penalty. It's a stroll after Brazil poaches his second.

---

28. H CRYSTAL PALACE — 7/2

	Att	Pos	Pt	F-A	H-T
	25,036	1 (22)	W 42	3-2	0-1

Team	1	2	3	4	5	6	7	8	9	10	11
Town	Cooper	McCall	Beattie	Thijssen	Osman	Butcher	Wark	Muhren	Mariner	Brazil	Gates
Crystal Palace	*Barron*	*Lovell*	*Hinshelwood*	*Gilbert*	*Boyle*	*Brooks*	*Smillie*	*Nicholas*	*Allen*	*Murphy*	*Walsh*

Scorers, Times: Mariner 51, Wark 53p, Gilbert 58 (og), Walsh 41, Mariner 80 (og). **Ref:** D Richardson

Dario Gradi's side pack their defence and score on the break via Walsh. Mariner levels matters and is then hacked down for the penalty. He pressurises Gilbert into an own-goal and his busy day is complete as he glances Murphy's corner into his own net to give Palace late hope.

---

29. H MIDDLESBROUGH — 17/2

	Att	Pos	Pt	F-A	H-T
	24,781	1 (11)	W 44	1-0	1-0

Team	1	2	3	4	5	6	7	8	9	10	11	12 sub used
Town	Cooper	Mills	Beattie	Thijssen	Osman	Butcher	Wark	Muhren	Mariner*	Brazil	Gates	O'Callaghan
Middlesbrough	*Platt*	*Nattrass*	*Bailey*	*Johnston*	*Ashcroft*	*McAndrew*	*Craggs*	*Proctor*	*Hodgson*	*Shearer*	*Armstrong*	

Scorers, Times: Brazil 41. **Ref:** R Lewis

Brazil's header looks to be heading for Platt's safe hands, but a deflection off Nattrass sees it hit the net. John Neal's outfit look resilient for the rest of the game and Town miss the power of the injured Mariner in attack. Long-serving Roger Osborne leaves to join Colchester for £25,000.

---

30. H WOLVERHAMPTON — 21/2

	Att	Pos	Pt	F-A	H-T
	24,218	1 (18)	W 46	3-1	2-1

Team	1	2	3	4	5	6	7	8	9	10	11	12 sub used
Town	Cooper	Mills	Beattie	McCall	Osman	Butcher	Wark	Muhren	Mariner	Brazil	O'Callaghan	Gates
Wolverhampton	*Bradshaw*	*Palmer*	*Parkin*	*Daniel**	*McAlle*	*Berry*	*Hibbitt*	*Atkinson*	*Gray*	*Richards*	*Eves*	*Bell*

Scorers, Times: Wark 23, Gates 42, Beattie 66, Gray 3. **Ref:** D Hedges

Town survive an early shock as Gray swoops, but the Scot is kept in check after this by a determined Osman. John Barnwell's men spurn the chance to equalise when Beattie is harshly penalised for a challenge on Richards. His penalty is saved by Cooper and he hits the rebound over.

---

31. A COVENTRY — 28/2

	Att	Pos	Pt	F-A	H-T
	17,557	1 (16)	W 48	4-0	1-0

Team	1	2	3	4	5	6	7	8	9	10	11
Town	Cooper	Mills	Beattie	Thijssen	Osman	Butcher	McCall	Muhren	Mariner	Brazil	Gates
Coventry	*Sealey*	*Thomas*	*Roberts*	*Jacobs*	*Dyson*	*Gillespie*	*Bodak*	*Daly*	*Thompson*	*English*	*Hunt*

Scorers, Times: Brazil 32, Gates 47, McCall 77, [Osman 83]. **Ref:** T Spencer

On a very heavy pitch, Town survive an early scare when Gillespie's goal is ruled out. They move up a gear and turn on the power, but are never fully extended again. Thijssen is outstanding and the pick of the goals is McCall's first in the League, a thundering drive from 25 yards.

Ipswich Town — Match-by-Match Results

No	Date	Venue	Opponent	Attendance	Pos	Result	Opp Pos	Pts	Score	HT	Scorers / Referee
32	14/3	H	TOTTENHAM	32,052	1	W	8	50	3-0	2-0	Gates 8, Wark 45p, Brazil 67 — Ref: R Toseland
33	21/3	A	MANCHESTER U	46,685	1	L	9	50	1-2	1-1	Butcher 7 / Thomas 17, Nicholl 54 — Ref: T Morris
34	28/3	H	SUNDERLAND	25,450	1	W	16	52	4-1	1-1	Muhren 44, Mariner 62, 63, [Thijssen 90] / Rowell 18 — Ref: A Gunn
35	31/3	A	LEEDS	26,462	1	L	11	52	0-3	0-2	Hird 6p, Harris 15, Hart 84 — Ref: D Richardson
36	4/4	A	WEST BROM	22,216	2	L	3	52	1-3	1-2	Brazil 9 / Brown A 8, Batson 44, Barnes 54 — Ref: N Midgley
37	14/4	A	ASTON VILLA	47,495	2	W	1	54	2-1	1-0	Brazil 5, Gates 80 / Shaw 83 — Ref: B Hill
38	18/4	H	ARSENAL	30,935	2	L	5	54	0-2	0-1	Nicholas 17, Sansom 58 — Ref: B Martin
39	20/4	A	NORWICH	26,083	2	L	17	54	0-1	0-0	Fashanu 62 — Ref: R Challis
40	25/4	H	MANCHESTER C	22,684	2	W	12	56	1-0	0-0	Butcher 51 — Ref: K Salmon
41	2/5	A	MIDDLESBROUGH	15,503	2	L	14	56	1-2	1-0	Mariner 35 / Jankovic 56, 87 — Ref: A Porter
42	13/5	H	SOUTHAMPTON	19,504	2	L	6	56	2-3	2-3	Brazil 26, Wark 41 / Keegan 5, Moran 20, 21 — Ref: T Mills

Home Average 24,619   Away 26,780

Line-ups and match reports

32 — TOTTENHAM (H): Cooper, Mills*, McCall, Thijssen, Osman, Butcher, Wark, Muhren, Mariner, Brazil, Gates, O'Callaghan.
Spurs: Daines, Hughton, Miller, Roberts, McAllister, Perryman, Ardiles*, Archibald, Galvin, Hoddle, Crooks, Brooke.
After the rigours of three big cup-ties in seven days, Town could have done without Spurs' over-physical approach. Mills goes off with a dislocated shoulder and O'Callaghan is attacked off the ball behind the ref's back. A bad tackle on Mariner gives Wark his penalty opportunity.

33 — MANCHESTER U (A): Cooper, Steggles, McCall, Thijssen, Osman, Butcher, Wark, Muhren, Mariner, Brazil, Gates, O'Callaghan.
Man U: Bailey, Nicholl, Albiston, Moran, McQueen, Buchan, Coppell, Birtles, Jordan, Duxbury, Thomas.
Butcher gives Town a great start in muddy conditions, but Dave Sexton's outfit roar back into contention in a lively game. Nicholl fires home his first of the season to give them a deserved win. Championship rivals Villa also lose, so Town stay a point clear on top with a game in hand.

34 — SUNDERLAND (H): Cooper, Steggles, McCall, Thijssen, Osman, Butcher, Wark, Muhren*, Mariner, Brazil, Gates, O'Callaghan.
Sunderland: Siddall, Himigan !, Bolton, Hindmarch, Elliott, Buckley, Arnott, Brown, Ritchie, Bowyer, Cummins, Rowell.
Ken Knighton's side put up a good fight, but superior finishing tells. Muhren equalises with a brilliant free-kick, and then sends a precise corner to the head of Mariner who nets. Himigan is sent off for lashing out at O'Callaghan and the resulting free-kick leads to Thijssen's goal.

35 — LEEDS (A): Cooper, Mills, McCall*, Thijssen, Osman, Butcher, Wark, Muhren, Mariner, Brazil, Gates, O'Callaghan.
Leeds: Lukic, Greenhoff, Gray, Flynn, Hart, Cherry, Harris, Hird, Parlane, Stevenson, Graham.
Hird converts a penalty after Osman is penalised for an aerial challenge on Hart. Allan Clarke's side adds the killer second goal when Harris goes on a long run down the left, cuts in and curls a stunning goal past Cooper. Lukic defies Gates, but Town never look in serious contention.

36 — WEST BROM (A): Cooper, Steggles*, McCall, Mills, Osman, Butcher, Wark, Muhren, O'Callaghan, Brazil, Gates, Parkin.
West Brom: Godden, Batson, Statham, Moses, Wile, Robertson, Robson, Brown A, Regis, Owen, Barnes.
After a hectic March, Town look slightly off-colour against Ron Atkinson's side and lose the leadership to Villa. After the early flurry, an even contest ensues, but Town miss chances and are punished by the clinching third goal, when Barnes' drive takes a nasty deflection off Butcher.

37 — ASTON VILLA (A): Cooper, Mills, McCall, Thijssen, Osman, Butcher, Wark, Muhren, Mariner, Brazil, Gates, O'Callaghan.
Aston Villa: Rimmer, Swain, Gibson, Williams, McNaught, Mortimer, Bremner, Shaw, Withe, Cowans, Morley.
After the misery of the cup semi-final defeat at Villa Park, Town return just three days later and turn on the heat in brilliant fashion. Mariner dispossesses McNaught to set up Brazil for the first and later assists Gates for a breakaway second. Now the great title race is wide open again!

38 — ARSENAL (H): Cooper, Mills, McCall, O'Callaghan, Osman, Butcher, Wark, Muhren, Mariner, Brazil, Gates*, Parkin.
Arsenal: Jennings, Devine, Sansom, Talbot, O'Leary, Young, Hollins, Sunderland, Stapleton, Nicholas, Davis.
An 18-month unbeaten home run is ended and all the good work at Villa Park is undone. Nicholas scores while Town are down to ten men with Gates the latest injury victim. Mariner misses a chance to equalise, shortly before Sansom increases the lead. Thijssen is badly missed.

39 — NORWICH (A): Cooper, Mills, McCall, Parkin, Osman, Butcher, Wark, Muhren, Mariner, Brazil, Gates, D'Avray.
Norwich: Woods, Symonds, Downs, McGuire, Walford, Watson, O'Neill, Fashanu, Royle, Paddon, Barham*, Jack.
The title now looks bound for Villa after Fashanu wins a tense home derby when he fires home from distance, with Town's defenders expecting a cross. The points are vital to Ken Brown's men in their relegation battle. Town's best chance of a goal sees Turner fail with just Woods to beat.

40 — MANCHESTER C (H): Cooper, Steggles, McCall, Mills, Osman, Butcher, Wark, Muhren, Turner, Brazil, Gates*, O'Callaghan.
Man C: Corrigan, Ranson, Henry, Reid, Power, Booth, Bennett, Tueart, MacKenzie, Buckley*, Reeves, May.
Butcher, the hero of Colgone three days earlier, does it again by rising to head home Wark's cross. The points keep alive the title dream – but only just. Brazil rises above Henry to head against the crossbar and Wark also strikes the woodwork. Corrigan makes a series of good saves.

41 — MIDDLESBROUGH (A): Cooper, Steggles*, McCall, Mills, Osman, Butcher, Wark, Muhren, Mariner, Brazil, Gates, O'Callaghan.
Middlesbrough: Platt, Craggs, Bailey, Ross, Angus, McAndrew, Cochrane, Proctor, Shearer, Jankovic, Armstrong.
Town need to win the final two games and hope Villa lose at Arsenal. The latter goes to plan, but Town's title hopes go down the drain as the enigmatic Jankovic surprises his critics by converting two second-half headers. It's a devastating blow after Town's fine first-half performance.

42 — SOUTHAMPTON (H): Cooper, Mills, McCall, Parkin, Osman, Butcher, Wark, Muhren, D'Avray*, Brazil, Gates, O'Callaghan.
Southampton: Wells, Baker S, Holmes, McCartney, Watson, Nicholl, Keegan, Channon*, Baker G, Moran, Ball, Puckett.
Meaningless for Town, but Lawrie McMenemy's side need the points for a UEFA Cup place and roar into a big lead early on. Town fight back with two superb goals before the break and are unlucky not to equalise. Robson tells the fans that the best team didn't win the championship.

LEAGUE DIVISION 1 (CUP-TIES)

Manager: Bobby Robson

SEASON 1980-81

League Cup	Att	F-A	H-T	Scorers, Times, and Referees	1	2	3	4	5	6	7	8	9	10	11	12 sub used
2:1 A MIDDLESBROUGH 26/8	14,459	L 1-3	1-3	Wark 24 / *Shearer 21, 37, Proctor 45* / Ref: P Tyldesley	Cooper	Mills	McCall	Thijssen	Osman	Butcher	Wark	Muhren	Mariner	Gates	O'Callaghan	
					Platt	*Craggs*	*Bailey*	*Johnston**	*Ashcroft*	*Nattrass*	*Proctor*	*Hedley*	*Hodgson*	*Shearer*	*Armstrong*	*Jankovic*

Boro are well on top and Town's equaliser is against the run of play. Mariner's cross is completely missed by Thijssen but Wark is on hand to convert. John Neal's side force 18 corners and could have scored more. They have one disallowed and see Muhren clear off the goal-line.

League Cup	Att	F-A	H-T	Scorers, Times, and Referees	1	2	3	4	5	6	7	8	9	10	11	12 sub used
2:2 H MIDDLESBROUGH 2 2/9	14,780 20	W 3-0	2-0	Osman 33, Mariner 39, 52 / Ref: B Daniels / (Town win 4-3 on aggregate)	Cooper	Burley	Mills	Thijssen	Osman	Butcher	Wark	Muhren	Mariner	Brazil	Gates	
					Platt	*Craggs*	*Bailey*	*Angus*	*McAndrew*	*Nattrass**	*Proctor*	*Hedley*	*Hodgson*	*Shearer*	*Armstrong*	*Jankovic*

Gates, a Boro supporter as a boy, creates mayhem and spoils the visitors' plan to sit on their lead. The necessary goals are scored with nearly 40 minutes remaining and Town are rarely in any trouble. The nearest to a problem is when as McAndrew crashes a late header against the bar.

League Cup	Att	F-A	H-T	Scorers, Times, and Referees	1	2	3	4	5	6	7	8	9	10	11	12 sub used
3 H NORWICH 1 23/9	26,462 19	D 1-1	1-0	Osman 14 / *Fashanu 84* / Ref: P Richardson	Cooper	Burley	Mills	Thijssen	Osman	Butcher	Wark	Muhren	Mariner	Brazil*	Gates	O'Callaghan
					Hansbury	*Bond*	*Muzinic*	*Barham*	*Hoadley*	*Powell*	*Woods*	*Fashanu*	*Jack**	*Paddon*	*Goble*	*Royle*

Town fans respond to Robson's accusations of not making enough effort, to encourage the team in an entertaining contest. Osman powers home a great header to open the scoring. Relentless Town attacking is foiled by an inspired Hansbury before they are punished by a late equaliser.

League Cup	Att	F-A	H-T	Scorers, Times, and Referees	1	2	3	4	5	6	7	8	9	10	11	12 sub used
3R A NORWICH 1 8/10	24,523 19	W 3-1	1-0	Mariner 26, 79, Muhren 76 / *Powell 49* / Ref: P Richardson	Cooper	Burley	Mills	Thijssen	Osman	Butcher	Wark	Muhren	Mariner	Brazil	Gates	
					Hansbury	*Bond*	*Hoadley*	*Barham*	*Jack**	*Powell*	*Woods*	*Fashanu*	*Muzinic*	*Paddon*	*Goble*	*Symonds*

A close contest swings Town's way when the Dutchmen combine beautifully – Thijssen's superb run setting up his fellow countryman. Kevin Bond has a header cleared off the line, but Town run out deserved winners. Shortly afterwards City boss John Bond quits for Manchester City.

League Cup	Att	F-A	H-T	Scorers, Times, and Referees	1	2	3	4	5	6	7	8	9	10	11	12 sub used
4 A BIRMINGHAM 2 28/10	18,968 14	L 1-2	1-1	Wark 24p / *Worthington 29p, Ainscow 53* / Ref: K Walmsley	Cooper	Burley	Mills	McCall	Osman	Butcher	Wark	Muhren	D'Avray	Brazil	Gates	
					Wealands	*Dennis*	*Page*	*Curtishley*	*Gallagher*	*Todd*	*Ainscow*	*Bertschin*	*Worthington*	*Gemmill*	*Dillon*	

Gallagher pulls D'Avray back for the first penalty, converted by Wark. The second is not so clear-cut, as Mr Walmsley decides Butcher was pushing Bertschin when Cooper collects a cross. Mills clears Bertschin's header off the line, but the rebound falls to Ainscow, who hits the net.

FA Cup

No		Opponent	Date		Res	Score	HT	Att		Scorers	Ref
3	H	ASTON VILLA	3/1	3	W	1-0	1-0	27,721	1	Mariner 14	Ref: G Courtney
4	A	SHREWSBURY	24/1	1	D	0-0	0-0	18,000	2:18		Ref: C Downey
4R	H	SHREWSBURY	27/1	1	W	3-0	1-0	27,543	2:18	Gates 21, 51, Wark 71	Ref: C Downey
5	H	CHARLTON	14/2	1	W	2-0	0-0	30,221	3:2	Wark 57, Mariner 88	Ref: P Reeves
6	A	NOTT'M FOREST	7/3	1	D	3-3	2-2	34,796	5	Mariner 14, Ands'n 24 (og), Thijssen 81 / Francis 25, Walsh 42, Robertson 51p	Ref: C Thomas
6R	H	NOTT'M FOREST	10/3	1	W	1-0	0-0	31,060	5	Muhren 67	Ref: C Thomas
SF	N	MANCHESTER C	11/4	2	L	0-1	0-0	46,537	14	Power 100 (aet)	Ref: P Partridge

(SF at Villa Park)

3 — ASTON VILLA (H)

Town: Cooper, Burley, Mills, Thijssen, Osman, Butcher, Wark, Muhren, Mariner, Brazil, Gates

Villa: *Rimmer, Swain, Williams, Evans, McNaught, Mortimer, Bremner, Shaw, Withe, Cowans, Morley*, Geddis*

After Mariner's goal Town produced long spells of attacking but Villa prevent further damage. Withe and Shaw never get a look-in against the commanding Butcher. The Ipswich defender comes off with a ripped shirt and huge stud marks down his back, the result of a Withe challenge.

4 — SHREWSBURY (A)

Town: Cooper, Burley, Mills, Thijssen, Osman, Butcher, Wark, Muhren, Mariner, Brazil*, Gates, O'Callaghan

Shrewsbury: *Wardle, King, Leonard, Turner, Griffin, Keay, Tong, Atkins, Bates, Biggins, Cross, O'Callaghan*

Graham Turner's side raise their game in front of Gay Meadow's second biggest crowd of all time. Cooper is kept busy and Town are grateful to escape to Suffolk for a replay. Burley battles on gamely after a knee injury, which later turns out to be very serious damage to his ligaments.

4R — SHREWSBURY (H)

Town: Cooper, Wardle, McCall, Thijssen, Osman, Butcher, Wark, Muhren, Mariner, Brazil*, Gates, O'Callaghan

Shrewsbury: *King, Leonard, Turner, Griffin, Keay, Tong, Atkins, Bates, Biggins*, Cross, Dungworth*

Wardle keeps Town at bay with some fine early saves, but slips up when Gates' shot goes under his body and in off the post. The Taming of the Shrew is on at the local theatre and the goal seems to have that effect! Cooper deals confidently with the visitors' best efforts in response.

5 — CHARLTON (H)

Town: Cooper, McCall, Beattie, Thijssen, Osman, Butcher, Wark, Muhren, Mariner, Brazil, Gates

Charlton: *Johns, Naylor, Warman, Shaw, Berry*, Tydeman, Powell, Walsh, Hales, Robinson, Walker, Smith*

With a makeshift back four, Town look well short of top form. A typically tense cup-tie is only settled in the closing minutes as Mariner defies the tugging arms of Naylor to lift a shot over Johns. The keeper plays superbly and exercises the memory of conceding six to Town in 1978.

6 — NOTT'M FOREST (A)

Town: Cooper, Shilton*, McCall*, Thijssen, Osman, Butcher, Wark, Muhren, Mariner, Brazil, Gates, O'Callaghan

Forest: *Shilton, Anderson*, Gray F, Gray S, Burns, Gunn, Mills, Wallace, Francis, Walsh, Robertson, Ponte*

Anderson's weak back-pass is pounced upon by Mariner for the first and then Anderson heads Muhren's cross into his own net. A dislocated shoulder completes his misery. A thrilling tie against the European Cup holders ends level as Thijssen's drive is deflected by Gary Mills.

6R — NOTT'M FOREST (H)

Town: Cooper, Mills, McCall, Thijssen, Osman, Butcher, Wark, Muhren, Mariner, Brazil*, Gates, O'Callaghan

Forest: *Shilton, Gunn, Gray F, Gray S, Burns, Needham, Mills, Wallace, Francis*, Walsh, Robertson, Ponte*

Forest hold Town in check until the interval, when Town make a crucial tactical change, withdrawing Gates to a deeper role. They look more potent as a result. Mills, Thijssen and Mariner combine to forge a chance for Muhren – he buries it on the volley with his unfavoured right foot.

SF — MANCHESTER C (N, at Villa Park, aet)

Town: Cooper, Mills, Beattie*, Thijssen, Osman, Butcher, Wark, Muhren, Mariner, Brazil, Gates, McCall

Manchester C: *Corrigan, Ranson, McDonald, Reid, Power, Caton, Bennett, Gow, MacKenzie, Hutchison, Reeves*

Despite plenty of possession and pressure, Town don't quite look themselves. Early chances go begging in the tense atmosphere. Beattie is the side's major threat in attack until he breaks his arm in the closing minutes. Power breaks Town hearts with a curling 25-yard shot in extra-time.

LEAGUE DIVISION 1 (CUP-TIES)

Manager: Bobby Robson

SEASON 1980-81

UEFA Cup	Att		F-A	H-T	Scorers, Times and Referees
1:1 H ARIS SALONIKA 17/9 (Greece)	20,842	1 W	5-1	3-0	Wark 13p, 15, 29p, 79p, Mariner 61 / Pallas 48p / Ref: A Garrido (Portugal)
1:2 A ARIS SALONIKA 1/10	40,000	1 L	1-3	0-2	Gates 75 / Tsirimokos 4, Drambis 22, Zelidis 65 / Ref: A Jarguz (Poland) / (Town win 6-4 on aggregate)
2:1 H BOHEMIANS 22/10 (Prague, Czech)	17,163	1 W	3-0	0-0	Wark 48, 54, Beattie 85 / Ref: O Amundsen (Denmark)
2:2 A BOHEMIANS 5/11	16,000	2 L	0-2	0-1	Micinec 2, Panenka 52 / Ref: P Cesarin (Italy) / (Town win 3-2 on aggregate)
3:1 H WIDZEW LODZ 26/11 (Poland)	20,445	2 W	5-0	3-0	Wark 22, 44, 78, Brazil 41, Mariner 70 / R Wurtz (France)
3:2 A WIDZEW LODZ 10/12	9,000	3 L	0-1	0-0	Pieta 55 / Ref: J Redellas (West Germany) / (Town win 5-1 on aggregate)
QF 1 A ST ETIENNE 4/3 (France)	42,000	1 W	4-1	1-1	Mariner 28, 57, Muhren 47, Wark 76 / Rep 16 / Ref: M Rainea (Romania)
QF 2 H ST ETIENNE 18/3	30,141	1 W	3-1	0-0	Butcher 46, Wark 82p, Mariner 89 / Zimako 80 / Ref: E Linemayr (Austria) / (Town win 7-2 on aggregate)
SF 1 H FC COLOGNE 8/4 (W Germany)	24,780	2 W	1-0	1-0	Wark 34 / Ref: A Castillo (Spain)
SF 2 A FC COLOGNE 22/4	55,000	2 W	1-0	0-0	Butcher 64 / Ref: A Palotai (Hungary) / (Town win 2-0 on aggregate)

Line-ups (1–11) and subs used

Match	1	2	3	4	5	6	7	8	9	10	11	subs used
1:1 Town	Cooper	Burley	Mills	Thijssen	Osman	Butcher	Wark	Muhren*	Mariner	Brazil^	Gates	O'Callaghan/Beattie
1:1 Aris	Pantziaris	Mokalis	Pallas	Venos	Firos !	Kouis	Zindros	Balis	Tsirimokos*	Samertzidis	Zelidis	Drambis
1:2 Town	Cooper	Burley	Mills	Thijssen	Osman	Butcher	Wark	Muhren^	Mariner	Brazil*	Gates	McCall/Beattie
1:2 Aris	Pantziaris	Mokalis	Chatziari'u^	Venos	Michalitsos	Kouis	Drambis	Balis*	Tsirimokos	Samertzidis	Zelidis	Tzfi'Is/Zelidis
2:1 Town	Cooper	Burley	Mills	McCall	Osman	Butcher	Wark*	Muhren	Mariner	Brazil	Gates	Beattie
2:1 Bohemians	Hruska	Roubicek	Jakubec	Prokes	Ondra	Bicovsky	Nemec	Panenka	Cermac	Chaloupka	Koukal*	Kottba
2:2 Town	Sivell	Burley	Mills	Beattie	Osman	Butcher	Wark	Muhren	Gates	Brazil*	McCall	Turner
2:2 Bohemians	Postulka	Micinec	Jakubec	Prokes	Ondra	Bicovsky	Nemec	Panenka	Cermac	Chaloupka	Koukal*	Kottba
3:1 Town	Cooper	Mills^	McCall	Thijssen	Osman	Butcher	Wark	Muhren	Mariner	Brazil*	Gates	O'Callaghan/Beattie
3:1 Widzew	Mlynarcyk	Plich	Grebosz	Mazejko	Zmuda	Tlonkinski	Pieta*	Jezewski	Boniek	Razborski	Smolarek	Romke
3:2 Town	Cooper	Klepcynski	McCall	Thijssen	Osman	Butcher	Wark	Muhren*	Mariner^	Brazil	Gates	Beattie/O'Callaghan
3:2 Widzew	Mlynarcyk	Plich	Grebosz	Mazejko	Romke	Tlonkinski	Pieta*	Jezewski	Surfit	Razborski	Smolarek	Lisiak
QF 1 Town	Cooper	Mills	Beattie	Thijssen	Osman	Butcher	Wark	Muhren	Mariner	Brazil	Gates	
QF 1 St Etienne	Castaneda	Battiston	Zanon	Gardon	Lopez	Janvion	Paganelli	Larios	Roussey*	Platini	Rep	Zimako
QF 2 Town	Cooper	Steggles	McCall	Thijssen	Osman	Butcher	Wark	Muhren	Mariner	Brazil*	Gates^	O'Callaghan/D'Avray
QF 2 St Etienne	Castaneda	Battiston	Zanon	Gardon	Lopez	Janvion	Zimako	Larios	Roussey	Platini	Rep	
SF 1 Town	Cooper	Mills	McCall^	Thijssen	Osman	Butcher	Wark	Muhren	Mariner	Brazil*	Gates	O'Callaghan/Beattie
SF 1 Cologne	Schumacher	Prestin	Konopka	Strack*	Gerber	Cullmann	Littbarski	Botteron	Muller^	Engels	Woodcock	Kroth/Willmer
SF 2 Town	Cooper	Steggles	McCall	Thijssen	Osman	Butcher	Wark	Muhren	Mariner	Brazil*	Mills	Kroth
SF 2 Cologne	Schumacher	Prestin	Konopka	Zimmerm'nn*Bonhof	Cullmann	Littbarski	Botteron	Muller	Engels		Woodcock	

Match reports

1:1 Michel Vican's side employ crude, spoiling tactics which backfire badly. A series of dreadful tackles on Gates, the first after just 20 seconds, hands Town three penalty kicks – all despatched confidently by Wark. Firos is red-carded after half-an-hour of kicking anything that moves.

1:2 Aris look much better at their own ground and give Town a real scare. Two of their goals are disputed, after officials rule that Mills' clearances in both cases came after the ball crossed the line. After Gates' late clincher, the departing Town party is stoned by an angry mob of home fans.

2:1 Wark makes the important breakthrough as his drive deflects off Prokes past Hruska. Beattie comes on to replace a limping Wark and his first contribution is to fire home a powerful drive from Mills' free-kick. Chaloupka nearly nabs a vital away goal, hitting the bar in the final minute.

2:2 An injury-weakened Town side endures yet another second-leg struggle after conceding an early goal. In sub-zero temperatures Beattie is a real colossus in defence, defiantly sporting his trademark short-sleeved shirt. Turner misses a chance to ease the pressure when he hits a post.

3:1 The conquerors of Manchester United and Juventus are brushed aside with a fluent display that has Robson purring with delight. Wark poaches a hat-trick without the aid of penalties, but goal of the night is from Mariner, who launches a diving header into the net after a Muhren cross.

3:2 The sensitive political situation in Poland puts the match in jeopardy, but once underway Town turn in a professional display on a rock-hard frozen pitch. Uncharacteristic indecision in defence allows Pieta to pull one goal back, but the home side badly miss suspended star Boniek.

QF 1 Rep heads the cup favourites into the lead, but Town hit back brilliantly. Mariner heads home at the far post before Muhren powers in a beauty from distance. Butcher's shot is saved but Mariner nets the rebound and Wark completes a wonderful night by heading his 30th of the season.

QF 2 St Etienne's president Roger Rocher calls Town the best side they have ever faced, which may explain the apparent inferiority complex of this players in this leg! A big crowd sees Town go through to the semis in comfortable fashion and Suffolk-born Steggles is given his senior debut.

SF 1 A resilient Schumacher and well-organised defending restricts Town to just one goal. Tony Woodcock looks lively in Cologne's attack, but Town's only worrying moment is when Littbarski's shot is deflected by Butcher, and Cooper has to pull off an outstanding save to keep it out.

SF 2 Town's third game in just six days is a fairly even contest, but Cooper is mightily relieved to see Engels' header hit the post. Five minutes later Robson does a dance of delight as Butcher rises to head home Mills' centre. After recent FA Cup and League setbacks this win is a huge boost.

UEFA Cup Final

F1   H   AZ '67 ALKMAAR   2   W   3-0   1-0   Wark 28p, Thijssen 46, Mariner 56
6/5   27,532   (Netherlands)   Ref: A Prokop (East Germany)

Ipswich: Cooper, Mills, McCall, Thijssen, Osman, Butcher, Wark, Muhren, Mariner, Brazil, Gates
AZ '67: Treytel, V d Meer, Spelbos, Metgod, Hovenkamp, Peters, Jonker, Arntz, Kist, Nygaard*, Tol, Welzl

Gates' early challenge on Van der Meer might have given the Dutch a penalty, but after this Town are never in trouble. Hovenkamp handles to give Wark another penalty and Thijssen nods home seconds after the break. Mariner's flicked header brings the trophy closer to Town's grasp.

F2   A   AZ '67 ALKMAAR   2   L   2-4   2-3   Thijssen 4, Wark 31
20/5   28,500   Welzl 7, Metgod 24, Tol 39, Jonker 73
Ref: H Weschweiler (W Germany)
(Town win 5-4 on aggregate)

Ipswich: Cooper, Mills, McCall, Thijssen, Osman, Butcher, Wark, Muhren, Mariner, Brazil, Gates
AZ '67: Treytel, Reyders, Spelbos, Metgod, Hovenkamp, Peters, Jonker, Arntz, Welzl^, Nygaard^, Tol*, Kist/Talan

With June just around the corner, it's hot in Holland and Alkmaar turn up the heat further with a super display. Welzl, Metgod and Peters are dominant and Jonker's brilliant free-kick leaves Town just one ahead with 20 minutes left. Town hang on desperately in a tremendous finale.

League Table

			Home					Away					
	P	W	D	L	F	A	W	D	L	F	A	Pts
1 Aston Villa	42	16	3	2	40	13	10	5	6	32	27	60
2 IPSWICH	42	15	4	2	45	14	8	6	7	32	29	56
3 Arsenal	42	13	8	0	36	17	6	7	8	25	28	53
4 West Brom	42	15	4	2	40	15	5	8	8	20	27	52
5 Liverpool	42	13	5	3	38	15	4	12	5	24	27	51
6 Southampton	42	15	4	2	47	22	5	6	10	29	34	50
7 Nott'm Forest	42	15	3	3	44	20	4	9	8	18	24	50
8 Manchester U	42	9	11	1	30	14	6	7	8	21	22	48
9 Leeds	42	10	5	6	19	19	7	5	9	20	28	44
10 Tottenham	42	9	9	3	44	31	5	6	10	26	37	43
11 Stoke	42	8	9	4	31	23	4	9	8	20	37	42
12 Manchester C	42	10	7	4	35	25	4	13	4	21	34	39
13 Birmingham	42	11	5	5	32	23	2	7	12	18	38	38
14 Middlesbro	42	14	4	3	38	16	2	1	18	15	45	37
15 Everton	42	8	6	7	32	25	5	4	12	23	33	36
16 Coventry	42	9	6	6	31	30	4	4	13	17	38	36
17 Sunderland	42	10	4	6	32	19	4	3	14	20	34	35
18 Wolves	42	11	2	8	26	20	2	7	12	17	35	35
19 Brighton	42	10	3	8	30	26	4	4	13	24	41	35
20 Norwich	42	9	7	5	34	25	4	0	17	15	48	33
21 Leicester	42	7	5	9	20	23	6	1	14	20	44	32
22 Crys Palace	42	6	4	11	32	37	0	3	18	15	46	19
	924	243	118	101	756	472	101	118	243	472	756	924

Appearances and Goals

	Appearances								Goals				
	Lge	Sub	LC	Sub	FAC	Sub	Eur	Sub	Lge	LC	FAC	Eur	Tot
Beattie, Kevin	7						2						4
Brazil, Alan	35		7		2		12		17	1			18
Burley, George	23		7		2		5						
Butcher, Terry	40		7		5		12						
Cooper, Paul	38		5		7		11						
D'Avray, Mich		4		1			1		1				1
Gates, Eric	37		5		7		11		11	2	1		14
Hunter, Allan	1												
Mariner, Paul	36		4		7		11		13	4	3	6	26
McCall, Steve	30	1	2		4	1	9		1				1
Mills, Mick	33		5		6		10						
Muhren, Arnold	41		5		7		12		5	1	1	1	8
O'Callaghan, Kevin	11	13	1	1		4							
Osborne, Roger							5						
Osman, Russell	42		5		7		12		1		2		3
Parkin, Tommy	2	2											
Sivell, Laurie	4		1										
Steggles, Kevin	6		2										
Thijssen, Frans	31		4		7		10		3	1		2	6
Turner, Robin	3	1							1				
Wark, John	40		5		7		12		18	2	2	14	36
(own-goals)									2			1	3
21 players used	462	21	55	1	77	5	132	14	77	9	10	28	124

Odds & ends

Double wins: (8) Aston Villa, Birmingham, Coventry, Crystal Palace, Leicester, Nott'm Forest, Sunderland, Wolves.

Double losses: (0).

Won from behind: (4) Palace (h), Wolves (h), Sund' (h), St Etienne (Eur) (a).

Lost from in front: (4) Man U (a), M'boro (a), Birm' (LC) (a), Alkmaar (Eur) (a).

High spots: Winning the UEFA Cup.
Wark's amazing goalscoring exploits, 36 from midfield.
The sustained challenge in early 1981 for a 'treble'.
A near-15% increase in home League attendances.
A clean sweep in the PFA and Football Writer's awards, with a 1-2-3- in both (winners: Wark and Thijssen).
Five Town men picked for England: Mariner, Mills, Osman, Butcher, Gates
Finishing as Division One's top scorers with 77 goals.

Low spots: Missing out on the League title and FA Cup.
Two players sent off for the first time in a single season.

Player of the Year: Paul Cooper.

Ever-presents: (1) Russell Osman.

Hat-tricks: (2) John Wark.

Opposing hat-tricks: (0).

Leading scorer: (36) John Wark.

LEAGUE DIVISION 1 — Manager: Bobby Robson — SEASON 1981-82

Match summary

No	Date	Venue	Opponent	Att	Pos	Opp Pos	Res	Pt	F–A	H–T
1	29/8	H	SUNDERLAND	24,060			D	1	3-3	0-1
2	1/9	A	BIRMINGHAM	17,328			D	2	1-1	0-1
3	5/9	A	MANCHESTER U	45,645	7	21	W	5	2-1	2-1
4	12/9	H	LIVERPOOL	27,603	3	17	W	8	2-0	1-0
5	19/9	A	NOTTS CO	12,559	2	10	W	11	4-1	1-0
6	22/9	H	WEST BROM	20,524	2	19	W	14	1-0	0-0
7	26/9	H	LEEDS	22,319	1	22	W	17	2-1	0-1
8	3/10	A	SOUTHAMPTON	22,552	1	7	L	17	3-4	3-1
9	10/10	H	WOLVERHAMPTON	20,498	1	21	W	20	1-0	1-0
10	17/10	A	EVERTON	25,146	3	8	L	20	1-2	1-2

Line-ups (1–11, 12 = sub used)

No	Team	1	2	3	4	5	6	7	8	9	10	11	12 sub used
1	Ipswich	Cooper	Mills	McCall	Thijssen	Osman	Butcher	Wark	Muhren	Mariner	Brazil	Gates	
1	*Sunderland*	*Turner*	*Hinnigan*	*Munro*	*Buckley*	*Clarke*	*Hindmarch*	*Chisholm*	*Ritchie*	*Brown**	*Rowell*	*Pickering*	*McCoist*
2	Ipswich	Cooper	Mills	McCall	Thijssen	Osman	Butcher	Wark	Muhren	Mariner	Brazil	Gates	
2	*Birmingham*	*Wealands*	*Langan*	*Dennis*	*Dillon*	*Broadhurst*	*Todd*	*Brocken*	*Whatmore*	*Evans*	*Gemmill*	*Van Mierlo*	
3	Ipswich	Cooper	Bailey	McCall	Thijssen	Osman	Butcher	Wark	Muhren	Mariner	Brazil	Gates	
3	*Manchester U*	*Bailey*	*Gidman*	*Albiston*	*Wilkins*	*McQueen*	*Buchan*	*Coppell*	*Birtles*	*Stapleton*	*Macari*	*McIlroy**	*Duxbury*
4	Ipswich	Cooper	Mills	McCall	Thijssen	Osman	Butcher	Wark	Muhren	Mariner	Brazil	Gates	
4	*Liverpool*	*Grobbelaar*	*Neal*	*Kennedy A*	*Thompson*	*Kennedy R*	*Hansen*	*Dalglish*	*Lee*	*Johnson*	*McDermott**	*Souness*	*Johnston*
5	Ipswich	Cooper	Mills	McCall	Thijssen*	Osman	Butcher	Wark	Muhren	Mariner	Brazil	Gates	Turner
5	*Notts Co*	*Avramovic*	*Benjamin*	*O'Brien*	*Hunt*	*Kilcline*	*Richards*	*Chiedozie**	*Masson*	*Christie*	*McCulloch*	*Hooks*	*Lahtinen*
6	Ipswich	Cooper	Mills	McCall	Parkin*	Steggles	Butcher	Wark	Muhren	Mariner	Brazil	Gates	O'Callaghan
6	*West Brom*	*Godden*	*Batson*	*Statham*	*Brown*	*Wile*	*Robertson**	*Deehan*	*Mills*	*Regis*	*Cross*	*MacKenzie*	*Arthur*
7	Ipswich	Cooper	Mills	McCall	Parkin	Steggles	Butcher	Wark	Muhren	Mariner	O'Callaghan	Gates	
7	*Leeds*	*Lukic*	*Greenhoff**	*Gray*	*Flynn*	*Stevenson*	*Cherry*	*Harris*	*Graham*	*Thomas*	*Hird*	*Barnes*	*Arins*
8	Ipswich	Cooper	Steggles	McCall	Mills	Osman	Butcher	Wark	Muhren	Mariner	Parkin*	Gates	O'Callaghan
8	*Southampton*	*Wells*	*Golac*	*Holmes*	*Baker*	*Watson*	*Waldron*	*Keegan*	*Channon*	*Moran*	*Armstrong*	*Ball*	
9	Ipswich	Cooper	Mills	McCall	Thijssen	Osman	Butcher	Wark	Muhren	Mariner	O'Callaghan	Gates	
9	*Wolverhampton*	*Bradshaw*	*Palmer*	*Parkin*	*Atkinson*	*Gallagher*	*Villazan*	*Hibbitt*	*Clarke*	*Gray*	*Bell*	*Matthews**	*Brazier*
10	Ipswich	Cooper	Mills	McCall	Thijssen	Osman	Butcher	Wark	Muhren	Mariner	O'Callaghan	Gates	
10	*Everton*	*Southall*	*Stevens*	*Bailey*	*Walsh*	*Lyons*	*Thomas**	*McMahon*	*O'Keefe*	*Ferguson*	*Ross*	*McBride*	*Biley*

Scorers, times and referees

1. SUNDERLAND — Wark 55, Gates 64, 80 / Ritchie 41, Buckley 53, 63. Ref: C Downey.
Mariner heads on to the bar and then hits it again with the rebound. After Alan Durban's side go two up, Wark rises above Hindmarch to head home in a hectic 11-minute spell. Gates pounces twice, but is denied a dramatic late winner as Turner races out of his box to bring him down.

2. BIRMINGHAM — Brazil 64 / Evans 44. Ref: G Flint.
Jim Smith's team have an inspired first period and their new Dutchmen, Van Mierlo and Brocken, impress the crowd. City deserve their lead, but Town look much sharper after the break and are rewarded by Brazil's leveller. Dillon hits Cooper's post with a superb drive from 25 yards.

3. MANCHESTER U — Brazil 6, Wark 27 / Stapleton 14. Ref: B Martin.
Ron Atkinson's disappointing start as new United manager continues and Town get their first three-point haul. Stapleton's fine equaliser is cancelled out by another Wark header. Bailey, son of ex-Town keeper Roy, maintains his spot-kick record against Town by saving from Wark.

4. LIVERPOOL — Neal 15 (og), Wark 64p. Ref: R Lewis.
Thijssen's cross is headed into his own net by unlucky Neal. Thompson's poor pass is collected by Brazil, who is hauled down by Hansen and Wark fires home the penalty. Despite a groin injury, Cooper makes some excellent saves in this first win over Liverpool for nearly five years.

5. NOTTS CO — Brazil 7, 87, Wark 58, Muhren 65 / Osman 81 (og). Ref: D Lloyd.
Magnificent finishing by Town draws high praise from all quarters, including home boss Jimmy Sirrell. Pick of the goals is the third, which sees Muhren volley in a superb 40-yard pass from Thijssen. Town had arrived at Meadow Lane in taxis after their team bus was vandalised.

6. WEST BROM — Deehan 85 (og). Ref: A Gunn.
Osman's Meadow Lane injuries see him drop out after 133 consecutive appearances. An even contest looks to be heading for stalemate until Brazil's cross is headed into his own net by Deehan. Injury-hit Town are boosted by excellent displays from stand-ins Steggles and Parkin.

7. LEEDS — Butcher 64, Gates 76 / Barnes 27. Ref: M Dimblebee.
Allan Clarke's struggling side make Town work hard for the points that take them top. Butcher has a storming game in the rain and scores the equaliser and then lays on the winner. Meanwhile, Beattie — out for six months — reports a setback after his fifth knee operation in four years.

8. SOUTHAMPTON — Wark 1, 32p, Mariner 34 (Moran 56) / Keegan 23p, Armstrong 52, 62. Ref: C Thomas.
Robson calls this his worst result in 10 years as a 3-1 lead is lost. Wark scores after just 12 seconds after Baker's slip. Osman's handball and a Holmes foul provides two penalties. A poor clearance is punished by lively Moran, then Armstrong's mazy run ends with a dramatic winner.

9. WOLVERHAMPTON — O'Callaghan 8. Ref: A Ward.
O'Callaghan fires in a spectacular first goal for the club. After receiving a pass from Muhren and jinking past two defenders he crashes the ball in from a tight angle. After the interval John Barnwell's side roll their sleeves up and Town have to battle hard to maintain their advantage.

10. EVERTON — Gates 37 / Ferguson 2, Stevens 40. Ref: A Hamil.
Swansea take over the leadership after a sloppy Town display, which Robson criticises heavily. Gates beats the debut-making keeper Neville Southall, but Town badly miss the sparkle of the injured Brazil. After the game, Mills hits out angrily at the idea Town are in a false position.

Football results grid — Ipswich Town 1981–82 (matches 11–21)

#	V	Date	Att.		Res		Pts	FT	HT
11	H	24/10	24,362	2	W	17	23	2-1	1-0
12	A	31/10	32,652	2	W	12	26	1-0	1-0
13	H	7/11	24,190	2	L	3	26	2-3	0-1
14	A	21/11	13,802	3	L	12	26	0-2	0-0
15	H	28/11	20,476	3	W	9	29	2-0	0-0
16	A	5/12	13,577	2	W	21	32	1-0	1-0
17	H	5/1	19,188	1	W	19	35	3-2	2-0
18	A	16/1	11,719	1	W	16	38	4-2	1-1
19	H	30/1	21,570	3	L	13	38	1-3	0-1
20	A	6/2	41,316	6	L	3	38	0-4	0-3
21	H	16/2	20,264	6	W	1	41	5-2	3-1

---

11. H ARSENAL — 24/10
Scorers: Mariner 43, Mills 51; Sunderland 61
Ref: C Maskell
Ipswich: Cooper, Steggles, Thijssen, McCall, Mills, Osman, Butcher, Wark, Muhren, Mariner, Gates
Arsenal: Jennings, Hollins, Talbot, Sansom, O'Leary, Young, Davis, Sunderland, Meade, Nicholas, Rix
Mills puts on a superb midfield display to counter Terry Neill's side's rugged approach. He supplies a cross that gets the defence in a tangle, allowing Mariner to pounce for the opener. After the break he's on the spot to convert his first goal in 22 months to win a bad-tempered affair.

12. A ASTON VILLA — 31/10
Scorers: Osman 9
Ref: J Worrall
Ipswich: Cooper, Mills, Thijssen, McCall, Butcher, Osman, Wark, Muhren, Mariner, Brazil, Gates
Villa: Rimmer, Swain, Evans, Gibson, Mortimer, Ormsby, Bremner, Shaw, Withe, Cowans, Morley
Villa, unbeaten in 14 games, are sent reeling as Osman heads early. It's certainly no classic as Town stifle Ron Saunders' side's best moves and prevent any direct efforts on goal. Three days later 15,269 attend Allan Hunter's testimonial at Portman Road when Celtic beat Town 3-2.

13. H SWANSEA — 7/11
Scorers: Mariner 53, Muhren 81; Curtis 7, Latchford 62, Stanley 83
Ref: K Salmon
Ipswich: Cooper, Mills, Thijssen, McCall, Butcher, Osman, Wark, Muhren, Mariner, Brazil, Gates
Swansea: Davies, Robinson, Rajkovic, Stanley, Stevenson, Irwin, Curtis, James R, James L, Mahoney, Latchford
Curtis has the noisy visiting fans in raptures as he curls a beauty past Cooper. Mariner rises to head in Muhren's cross, but Wark is then caught in possession and Latchford finishes neatly. Gates swaps passes with Muhren to level, but Stanley hits a low 20-yarder past the diving Cooper.

14. A STOKE — 21/11
Scorers: Chapman 60, Maguire 89
Ref: H King
Ipswich: Cooper, Burley, Mills, McCall, Butcher, O'Callaghan, Wark, Muhren*, Mariner, Brazil, Gates
Stoke: Fox, Evans, Hampton, Dodd, Smith, Heath*, Griffiths, Chapman, Bracewell, Johnson, Maguire
Against the run of play, Chapman breaks the deadlock as he thunders home a splendid header. Richie Barker's side grows in confidence and Maguire makes the points safe. Mills is approached to join Sunderland as player/assistant-manager and he agrees to meet boss Alan Durban.

15. H MANCHESTER C — 28/11
Scorers: Wark 63p, D'Avray 70
Ref: M Taylor
Ipswich: Cooper, Burley, Mills, McCall, Butcher, Osman, Wark, Muhren, O'Callaghan, Brazil, Gates*
Manchester C: Corrigan, Ranson, McDonald, Reid, O'Neill, Bond, Tueart, Reeves, Francis, Hartford, Hutchison
After a dull hour's play, O'Callaghan is fouled by Ranson, and Wark fires home the penalty. Minutes later the winger crosses for D'Avray to score the clincher. He is then hurt in a bad tackle by McDonald, who is lucky to stay on the field having already been cautioned by Mr Taylor.

16. A MIDDLESBROUGH — 5/12
Scorers: D'Avray 26
Ref: D Owen
Ipswich: Cooper, Burley, Mills, McCall, Butcher, Osman, Wark, Muhren, D'Avray, Turner, Parkin
Middlesbrough: Platt, Nattrass, Bolton, Ross, Baxter, McAndrew, Cochrane, Otto, Woof*, Hodson, Thomson, Ashcroft
Town have five regulars missing, but overcome Bobby Murdoch's struggling outfit with a first-half goal. D'Avray exchanges passes with Parkin before tucking in the winner. He goes twice more and Wark misses from close range. Woof's shot is brilliantly saved by Cooper.

17. H BIRMINGHAM — 5/1
Scorers: Mariner 29, 40, Brazil 69; Van Mierlo 70, Broadhurst 76
Ref: A Grey
Ipswich: Cooper, Burley, Mills*, McCall, Butcher, Osman, Wark, Muhren, Mariner, Brazil, Gates, O'Callaghan
Birmingham: Coton, Langan, Dennis, V d Hauwe, Todd, Broadhurst, Dillon, Whatmore, Worthington, Gemmill, Van Mierlo
After four December games are called off because of the weather, Mariner makes a welcome return to goalscoring form with two expertly-taken efforts. Somehow City are allowed back into this game and Town are relieved to win, particularly after Mills goes off with back trouble.

18. A COVENTRY — 16/1
Scorers: Wark 20, Muhren 80, Mariner 84; Hunt 37, Daly 60 [Brazil 86]
Ref: J Hough
Ipswich: Cooper, Burley, Mills, McCall, Butcher, Osman, Wark, Muhren, Mariner, Brazil, Gates
Coventry: Blyth, Thomas, Francis*, Barnes, Dyson, Gillespie, Bodak, Daly, Hateley, Hendrie, Hunt, Harmantchuk
New loan signing Gerry Francis does a good job for City before limping off injured. Town fall behind to a remarkable goal when Daly juggles the ball before volleying in. Town keep going forward and are rewarded in a dramatic finale, beating Blyth three times in the final ten minutes.

19. H NOTTS CO — 30/1
Scorers: Thijssen 54; Mair 21, Kilcline 57, Hooks 80
Ref: B Daniels
Ipswich: Cooper, Burley, Mills, McCall, Steggles*, Osman, Thijssen, Wark, Muhren, Brazil, Gates
Notts Co: Avramovic, Benjamin, O'Brien, Goodwin, Kilcline, Richards, Chiedozie*, Masson, McCulloch, Hooks, Mair, Christie
Jimmy Sirrell's side conjure up a slick opening goal with a series of neat passes setting up Mair. Thijssen heads home McCall's cross to level, but the absent Mariner and the hospitalised Butcher are sorely missed. Kilcline heads in and Hooks nets at the second attempt to stun Ipswich.

20. A LIVERPOOL — 6/2
Scorers: [Whelan 58]; McDermott 15, Rush 18, Dalglish 44
Ref: A Saunders
Ipswich: Cooper, Burley, Mills, McCall, Steggles, Thijssen, Wark, Muhren, Mariner, Gates, Parkin*, O'Callaghan
Liverpool: Grobbelaar, Neal, Kennedy A, Lawrenson, Whelan, Hansen, Dalglish, Lee, Rush, McDermott, Souness
Town are hit by a double blow as McDermott nets a fierce shot and then McCall wins a tackle with Whelan but sees the ball fall to Rush who converts. Muhren hits a post but when Steggles fails to clear Dalglish picks his spot. Lee hits a post and later crosses for Whelan to head home.

21. H SOUTHAMPTON — 16/2
Scorers: Brazil 14, 17, 19, 69, 86; Puckett 43, Keegan 76
Ref: J Bray
Ipswich: Cooper, Burley, Mills, Steggles, Osman, Butcher, Wark, Muhren, D'Avray, Brazil, Gates
Southampton: Katalinic, Golac*, Holmes, Baker, Waldron, Nicholl, Puckett, Channon, Keegan, Armstrong, Ball, Lawrence
Lethal Brazil shatters the League leaders. He pounces after Katalinic misjudges a high ball and nips in again from Steggles' long ball. Assured finishing from a D'Avray nod-down and a Gates pass completes his nap hand. Meanwhile, Mills and Osman make crucial goal-line clearances.

LEAGUE DIVISION 1

Manager: Bobby Robson — SEASON 1981-82

Each match is shown with two player lines: the top (bold) line is Ipswich Town; the lower (italic) line is the opponents. In the Pos column the upper figure is Ipswich's position and the lower figure the opponents' position.

No	Venue/Opponent	Date	Att	Pos	Res	Pt	F-A	H-T	1	2	3	4	5	6	7	8	9	10	11	12 sub used
22	A LEEDS	20/2	20,287	5 / 19	W	44	2-0	0-0	Cooper	Burley	McCall	Mills	Osman	Steggles	Wark	Muhren	D'Avray	Brazil	Gates	O'Callaghan
									Lukic	Hird	Gray F	Stevenson	Hart	Aspin	Butterworth	Graham	Parlane	Gray E	Barnes	
23	A WOLVERHAMPTON	27/2	12,439	6 / 20	L	44	1-2	1-2	Cooper	Burley	McCall	Mills*	Osman	Steggles	Wark	Muhren	D'Avray	Brazil	Gates	O'Callaghan
									Bradshaw	Palmer	Parkin	Matthews	Gallagher	Coy	Hibbitt	Carr	Gray	Richards	Clarke	
24	A WEST HAM	2/3	24,846	6 / 12	L	44	0-2	0-1	Cooper	Burley	McCall	Mills	Osman	Steggles*	Wark	Muhren	D'Avray	Brazil	Gates	O'Callaghan
									Parkes	Stewart	Brush	Bonds	Orr	Devonshire	Allen	Goddard	Van der Elst	Brooking	Pike	
25	H EVERTON	6/3	19,360	4 / 11	W	47	3-0	1-0	Sivell	Burley	McCall	Mills	Osman	Steggles	Wark	Muhren	D'Avray	Brazil	Gates	
									Southall	Borrows	Bailey	Higgins	Wright	Richardson	Irvine	Heath	Sharp*	Biley*	Ross	McMahon
26	A ARSENAL	13/3	25,977	7 / 4	L	47	0-1	0-1	Sivell	Burley	McCall	Mills	Osman	Steggles	Wark	Muhren	D'Avray	Brazil	Gates	
									Wood	Hollins	Sansom	Talbot	O'Leary	Whyte	Gorman	Sunderland	Davis	Robson	Rix	
27	A NOTT'M FOREST	17/3	16,686	7 / 10	D	48	1-1	0-0	Sivell	Burley	Gernon	Mills*	Osman	Steggles !	Wark	Muhren	D'Avray	Brazil	Gates	O'Callaghan
									Shilton	Anderson	Bowyer	McGovern	Young	Gunn	Plummer	Proctor	Ward	Wallace	Roeber	
28	H ASTON VILLA	20/3	20,407	5 / 13	W	51	3-1	2-0	Sivell	Burley	Gernon	Mills	Osman	Steggles	Wark	Muhren	O'Callaghan	Brazil	Gates	
									Rimmer	Swain	Williams	Evans	McNaught	Bullivant	Blair*	Shaw	Donovan	Cowans	Morley	Heard
29	A SWANSEA	27/3	20,750	5 / 2	W	54	2-1	1-1	Sivell	Burley	Gernon	Mills	Osman	Steggles	Wark	Muhren	D'Avray	Brazil	Gates	
									Davies	Stanley	Marustik	Irwin	Kennedy	Stevenson	Curtis	James R	James L	Thompson	Mahoney	
30	H BRIGHTON	30/3	19,361	3 / 11	W	57	3-1	1-0	Sivell	Burley	McCall	Mills	Osman	Steggles	Wark	Muhren	D'Avray	Brazil	Gates	
									Digweed	Shanks	Nelson	Grealish*	Foster	Gatting	Stevens	Ritchie	Robinson	McNab	Thomas	Stille
31	H COVENTRY	3/4	20,411	2 / 18	W	60	1-0	1-0	Cooper	Burley	McCall	Mills	Osman	Gernon	Wark	Muhren	D'Avray	Brazil	Gates	
									Sealey	Thomas*	Roberts	Jacobs	Dyson	Gillespie	Whitton	Francis	Hateley	English	Butterworth	Thompson

Scorers, Times, and Referees

22 — Brazil 73, Mills 78. Ref: R Banks
The unbeaten home run of Allan Clarke's men ends when the irrepressible Brazil scores and lays on a second for Mills in the last 17 minutes. Unlucky D'Avray hits the woodwork three times and home winger Graham once. Burley tangles with Barnes but penalty claims are rejected.

23 — Gates 21 / Clarke 4, 20. Ref: N Midgley
Robson is livid about a lethargic first-half display. Ian Greaves' side haven't won for three months in the League, but Wayne Clarke swoops twice, his second a fine volley although he looks well offside. Gates converts a header to give Ipswich hope, but Bradshaw keeps them at bay.

24 — Devonshire 39, Van der Elst 64. Ref: B Hill
Parkes keeps out Brazil and D'Avray efforts before Devonshire's shot takes a crucial deflection off Steggles to beat Cooper. John Lyall's men are filled with confidence from this point and Belgian Van der Elst makes sure of the points with a fine goal that gives busy Cooper no chance.

25 — Wark 32, Brazil 48, Gates 63. Ref: J Moules
Richardson nets but Sharp, clearly not interfering, is flagged offside. Wark fires home through a crowd after a corner and Brazil hits a sizzling low drive past Southall. Set up by Mills, Gates nets with a fierce angled drive from 10 yards. Sivell has a quiet return after a 16-month absence.

26 — Robson 11. Ref: T Bune
Stewart Robson's first ever goal is the result of an early defensive mix-up. Rix forces Sivell into a magnificent save. Town create few chances. Three days earlier, Town and Moscow Dynamo drew 2-2 in a testimonial for Kevin Beattie, who has accepted his top-level career is now over.

27 — Wark 83p / Plummer 70. Ref: D Hutchinson
Debutant Gernon concedes a penalty by fouling Anderson, but Sivell dives to save Ward's spot-kick. Steggles is sent off moments later for his second bookable offence. Plummer's goal is cancelled out by 10-man Town when O'Callaghan is fouled by Bowyer and Wark steps up to net.

28 — Wark 25, McCall 44, Gates 69 / McNaught 77. Ref: A Robinson
Town look sharp in the opening period and Tony Barton's men are under the cosh. Rimmer is well beaten by Wark's glorious long-distance effort. On his 100th appearance, McCall boosts Town just before half-time and the points are safe as Brazil squares to Gates for a simple third.

29 — Brazil 20, Gates 88 / James R 32p. Ref: C Newsome
D'Avray causes havoc and a poor clearance by Thompson allows Brazil to score. The ball bounces against Wark's arm and to Town's dismay a spot-kick is given, James converting. The winner is a stunning late volley by Gates, but the unsung hero is Sivell, who pulls off great saves.

30 — Brazil 38, 71, Wark 84 / Robinson 77. Ref: J Deakin
Brazil seizes on to Mills' low cross and finds time and space to score. He cracks home a shot on the turn against the run of play, but Robinson hits back, steering a shot past Sivell after McNab's lob. A corner is partially cleared to Muhren, who turns it back for Wark to clinch the win.

31 — Wark 31. Ref: D Vickers
After doing well on his long-awaited return, unlucky Sivell has to drop out again with a knee problem, but Cooper returns to makes good saves from Thompson and Whitton. Brazil and D'Avray are kept tightly in check, but Wark finds space to nick the winner in a rather drab match.

No	H/A	Date	Opponent	Att	Pos	Result	HT	FT	Pts
32	A	7/4	SUNDERLAND	11,843	22	D	1-1	0-0	61
33	A	10/4	TOTTENHAM	45,215	7	L	0-1		61
34	H	13/4	WEST HAM	28,767	8	W	3-2	2-1	64
35	H	17/4	STOKE	20,309	21	W	2-0	1-0	67
36	H	20/4	MANCHESTER U	25,763	4	W	2-1	1-1	70
37	A	24/4	MANCHESTER C	30,329	10	D	1-1	1-0	71
38	H	1/5	MIDDLESBROUGH	17,980	22	W	3-1	2-1	74
39	A	5/5	WEST BROM	12,564	20	W	2-1	1-0	77
40	A	8/5	BRIGHTON	17,786	13	W	1-0	1-0	80
41	H	15/5	NOTT'M FOREST	19,937	11	L	1-3	0-0	80
42	H	17/5	TOTTENHAM	20,764	10	W	2-1	1-0	83

Home 21,925 Away 22,620 Average 21,925

32. A SUNDERLAND — Steggles 85 / West 64 — Ref: D Scott
Cooper, Burley, McCall, Mills*, Osman, Steggles, Wark, Muhren, D'Avray, Brazil, Gates, O'Callaghan
Turner, Hinnigan, Munro, Hindmarch, Chisholm, Elliott, Buckley, West, Rowell, Pickering, Cummins
Cooper fumbles a Hinnigan cross and West rams home his first goal for the Rokerites from close range. O'Callaghan does superbly out on the right to cross to Steggles, back from suspension, who heads a deserved late leveller. Roker Park's lowest crowd of the season is left deflated.

33. A TOTTENHAM — Hoddle 81 — Ref: A Gunn
Cooper, Burley, McCall, Mills, Osman, Steggles, Wark*, Muhren, D'Avray, Brazil, Gates, O'Callaghan
Clemence, Hughton, Miller, Roberts, Hazard, Perryman, Villa, Archibald*, Galvin, Hoddle, Crooks, Brooke
Roberts' poor back-pass is pounced on by Brazil and he wins a penalty when Clemence brings him down. The keeper saves Wark's effort with his knee and Spurs then seize the initiative. Cooper makes several fine saves, but is beaten as Hoddle's shot somehow bobbles out of his reach.

34. H WEST HAM — Brazil 15, Wark 26p, Osman 51 / Cross 42, 80 — Ref: M Taylor
Cooper, Burley, McCall, Mills, Osman, Butcher, Wark, Muhren, Mariner, Brazil, Gates
Parkes, Stewart, Allen, Orr, Martin, Devonshire, Van der Elst, Goddard, Cross, Brooking, Neighbour*, Cowie
A cracking evening's entertainment sees Butcher catch the Hammers square to set up Brazil. Stewart trips Brazil for a Wark penalty, but Cross pulls one back from Brooking's cross. Osman heads home Gates' cross and Cross nets a simple second after McCall is caught in possession.

35. H STOKE — Mariner 38, Wark 89 — Ref: A Ward
Cooper, Burley, McCall, Mills, Osman, Butcher, Wark, Muhren, Mariner, Brazil, Gates
Fox, Johnson, Hampton, Dodd, Watson, Biley, McIlroy, O'Callaghan, Chapman, Bracewell, Maguire
Chapman's goalbound effort hits Mills on the line and then a Mariner handball is not spotted. Lucky Town break to the other end and Mariner nets from Burley's cross. Fox makes some good saves to frustrate Town and the fans, but in the final minute Wark heads in from close range.

36. H MANCHESTER U — Wark 36, 76, Gidman 18 — Ref: C White
Jackson, Burley, McCall, Mills, Osman, Butcher, Wark, Muhren, Mariner, Brazil, Gates
Bailey, Gidman, Albiston, Wilkins*, Moran, McQueen, Robson, Stapleton, McGarvey, Grimes, Duxbury, Birtles
Emergency loan keeper John Jackson does well, saving at Birtles' feet, but can do nothing about Gidman's thundering drive which swerves past him. Gates' corner is nodded down by Osman and Wark scores from a rebound. He gets a second after being set up by Mariner's header.

37. A MANCHESTER C — Brazil 36 / Hartford 80 — Ref: R Bridges
Cooper, Burley, McCall, Mills*, Osman, Butcher, Wark, Muhren, Mariner, Brazil, Gates
Corrigan, Ranson*, McDonald, Power, Bond, Caton, Ryan, Reeves, Francis, Hartford, Kinsey, May
Brazil uncharacteristically misses with only Corrigan to beat when faced with the chance to put Town two up. Moments later Hartford heads in off a post. Corrigan brings down Gates, but Wark blazes the penalty over. It will now need a miracle for Town to overhaul Liverpool at the top.

38. H MIDDLESBROUGH — Wark 30, Muhren 37, Brazil 85 / Thomas 40 — Ref: D Axcell
Cooper, Burley, McCall, Mills, Osman, Butcher, Wark, Muhren, Mariner*, Brazil, Gates, O'Callaghan
Platt, Craggs, Bailey, Ross, Baxter, Nattrass, McAndrew, Otto, Hodgson, Shearer*, Thomas, Ashcroft
Gates' cross is superbly hooked back by the lunging Brazil and Wark volleys in. Muhren then bends in a truly memorable free-kick. Gates gets a touch on a Muhren cross, but it falls to Brazil who gives another lesson in finishing. Allan Hunter leaves Town to become Colchester's boss.

39. A WEST BROM — Gates 10, Brazil 86 / Owen 62 — Ref: A Robinson
Cooper, Burley, Gernon, Mills, Osman, Butcher, Wark, Muhren, McCall, Brazil, Gates*, O'Callaghan
Godden, Batson, Cowdrill, Bennett, Wile, Robertson, Zondervan, Brown, Regis, Owen, McKenzie*, Monaghan
Gates forces the ball home but sprains an ankle and will miss the closing games. An lucky bounce allows Owen to beat Cooper, but Brazil is on the spot to strike a late goal to win the points and keep alive the very slender title hopes. Ronnie Allen's side are in trouble at the other end.

40. A BRIGHTON — Mariner 26 — Ref: D Reeves
Sivell, Burley, Gernon, Mills, Osman, Butcher, Wark, Muhren, Mariner, Brazil, McCall
Moseley, Shanks, Nelson, Stevens, Foster, Gatting, Case, Ritchie, Robinson, McNab*, Thomas, Grealish
Town seem to have accepted that leaders Liverpool will not slip up at this late stage and there's little urgency or excitement at the Goldstone Ground. Mariner knocks in a simple goal after assistance from Muhren and Brazil. David Barnes, brought up in Suffolk, signs from Coventry.

41. H NOTT'M FOREST — Brazil 67 / Davenport 52, 64, 72 — Ref: K Salmon
Sivell, Burley, McCall, Mills*, Osman, Butcher, Wark, Muhren, Mariner, Brazil, O'Callaghan, Turner
Shilton, Anderson, Bowyer, Gunn, Young, Gray, Roeber, McGovern, Hodge*, Davenport, Robertson, Proctor
Debutant Hodge and the inexperienced Davenport have a day to remember, the latter scoring three superbly taken goals. Brazil hits Town's consolation after Mills punishes a McGovern error. A win would have been meaningless as Liverpool made sure of the title by beating Spurs.

42. H TOTTENHAM — Mills 35, Brazil 68 / Crooks 74 — Ref: P Richardson
Sivell, Burley, McCall, Mills, Osman, Butcher, Wark, Muhren, Mariner, Brazil, O'Callaghan
Parks, Hughton, Miller, Roberts, Hazard, Perryman, Brooke, Archibald, Villa, Hoddle*, Crooks, Price
Mariner's pull-back sets up Mills from 10 yards. Brazil bursts on to Muhren's through-ball for his 28th of the season, dribbling around Parks to score. Crooks nets a looping header for the cup finalists. Robson is now being widely tipped to take over as England boss during the summer.

LEAGUE DIVISION 1 (CUP-TIES)

Manager: Bobby Robson

SEASON 1981-82

League Cup

Round			Att		F-A	H-T	Scorers, Times, and Referees
2:1	A	LEEDS	16,994	1 W 22	1-0	0-0	Gates 71

1	2	3	4	5	6	7	8	9	10	11	12 sub used
Cooper	Steggles	McCall	Thijssen	Osman	Butcher	Wark	Muhren	Mariner	Mills	Gates	
Lukic	*Stevenson**	*Gray F*	*Hird*	*Hart*	*Cherry*	*Harris*	*Graham*	*Balcombe*	*Gray F*	*Barnes*	*Thomas*

Ref: M Peck

Mariner turns past Graham with great skill and feeds Gates, who goes past Hart and forces a shot past Lukic at his near post. Butcher misses a great chance when heading well wide after misjudging the flight of a cross. After a Muhren handball, Hird's free-kick is well saved by Cooper.

Round			Att		F-A	H-T	Scorers, Times, and Referees
2:2	H	LEEDS	16,464	2 W 18	3-0	3-0	Gates 6, Mariner 35, Steggles 41

1	2	3	4	5	6	7	8	9	10	11	12 sub used
Cooper	Steggles	McCall	Thijssen	Osman	Butcher	Wark	Muhren	Mariner*	Mills	Gates	
Lukic	*Greenhoff*	*Gray F*	*Hird**	*Hart*	*Cherry*	*Harris*	*Graham*	*Connor*	*Hamson*	*Barnes*	*Stevenson*

Ref: D Reeves
(Town win 4-0 on aggregate)

Town put on some exhibition stuff in the first half and look a class above the visitors. Gates heads in the first and when Hart fails to deal with Muhren's probing pass, Mariner pounces. Lukic parries a header by Mariner and Steggles pounces for the third. A quiet second period ensues.

Round			Att		F-A	H-T	Scorers, Times, and Referees
3	H	BRADFORD C	13,694	2 D 4:2	1-1	1-0	Watson 83 / Wark 21

1	2	3	4	5	6	7	8	9	10	11	12 sub used
Cooper	Burley	Mills	Thijssen	Osman	Butcher	Wark	Muhren	Mariner	Brazil	Gates	
Ramsbottom	*Podd*	*Watson*	*Ingham*	*Jackson*	*Wood*	*Gallagher*	*Black*	*Campbell*	*McNiven*	*Ellis*	

Ref: J Hunting

Roy McFarland's Fourth Division promotion-chasers pose a few problems although Town threaten to swamp them early. Wark has two efforts well saved after his goal. Burley returns after 10 months out injured, but lesser-known full-back Watson grabs the headlines with his equaliser.

Round			Att		F-A	H-T	Scorers, Times, and Referees
3R	A	BRADFORD C	13,518	3 W 4:5	3-2 aet	1-1	O'Cal'ghan 15, Muhren 97, Turner 115 / Ingham 44, Gallagher 99p

1	2	3	4	5	6	7	8	9	10	11	12 sub used
Cooper	Burley	McCall	Mills	Osman	Butcher	Wark	Muhren	O'Callaghan	Brazil*	D'Avray	Turner
Ramsbottom	*Podd*	*Watson*	*Ingham*	*Jackson*	*Wood*	*Gallagher*	*Staniforth*	*Campbell*	*McNiven*	*Ellis*	

Ref: D Owen

In an entertaining cup-tie O'Callaghan makes an early breakthrough, but Ramsbottom pulls off some great saves to keep City in it. They level against the run of play and extra-time is needed. The winner comes from a brave diving header by Turner after a Burley effort hits the crossbar.

Round			Att		F-A	H-T	Scorers, Times, and Referees
4	A	EVERTON	15,759	3 W 8	3-2	2-0	Gates 17, Brazil 33, Wark 68 / McMahon 46, 61

1	2	3	4	5	6	7	8	9	10	11	12 sub used
Cooper	Burley	McCall	Thijssen*	Osman	Butcher	Wark	Muhren	Mills	Brazil	Gates	O'Callaghan
Arnold	*Stevens*	*Ratcliffe*	*Walsh*	*Lyons*	*Kendall*	*McMahon*	*Ross*	*Sharp*	*Biley**	*O'Keefe*	*Ferguson*

Ref: K Baker

Just prior to recruiting Adrian Heath, manager Howard Kendall is forced to pick himself. Town dominate before the break, but McMahon pulls one back with a shot that deflects off McCall and then levels with a magnificent solo effort. A lively tie is settled by Wark's 23rd goal of 1981.

Round			Att		F-A	H-T	Scorers, Times, and Referees
5	H	WATFORD	20,817	1 W 2:3	2-1	0-0	Wark 52, Brazil 75 / Barnes 55

1	2	3	4	5	6	7	8	9	10	11	12 sub used
Cooper	Burley	McCall	Mills	Osman	Butcher	Wark	Muhren	Mariner	Brazil	Gates	
Sherwood	*Rice*	*Pritchett*	*Taylor*	*Terry*	*Bolton*	*Callaghan**	*Arm strong*	*Jenkins*	*Blissett*	*Barnes*	*Train*

Ref: A Seville

Town's first-half dominance comes to nothing, but when the breakthrough finally comes they seem to relax. They are punished by teenager John Barnes whose header is cleared by Muhren but had already crossed the line. Hornets hero Sherwood is beaten by Brazil's slick footwork.

Round			Att		F-A	H-T	Scorers, Times, and Referees
SF 1	H	LIVERPOOL	26,690	4 L 6	0-2	0-0	McDermott 47, Rush 49

1	2	3	4	5	6	7	8	9	10	11	12 sub used
Cooper	Burley	McCall	Mills	Osman*	Steggles	Wark	Muhren	Mariner	Brazil	McDermott	Thijssen
Grobbelaar	*Neal*	*Kennedy*	*Lawrenson*	*Whelan*	*Hansen*	*Dalglish*	*Lee*	*Rush*	*McDermott*	*Souness*	

Ref: B Stevens

The club's first appearance in a League Cup semi-final turns sour as Liverpool outplay them in all departments. Two goals in less than three minutes sees the tie swing out of Town's reach. McDermott taps in after a Rush shot is blocked and Rush nets as Cooper rashly leaves his line.

Round			Att		F-A	H-T	Scorers, Times, and Referees
SF 2	A	LIVERPOOL	34,933	6 D 3	2-2	0-1	Gates 75, Brazil 79 / Rush 26, Dalglish 47

1	2	3	4	5	6	7	8	9	10	11	12 sub used
Cooper	Burley	McCall	Mills	Hunter	Butcher*	Wark	Muhren	O'Callaghan	Brazil	Gates	Turner
Grobbelaar	*Neal*	*Kennedy*	*Lawrenson*	*Whelan*	*Hansen*	*Dalglish*	*Lee**	*Rush*	*McDermott*	*Souness*	*Johnson*

Ref: L Shapter
(Town lose 2-4 on aggregate)

With four centre-backs unfit, Town recall 35-year-old Hunter for his first game in 15 months. Town fight back well after falling 0-4 behind on aggregate. Brazil forces home a second goal to restore a little pride. More injuries pile up as Thijssen is taken off with a serious shin problem.

FA Cup

Round			Att		F-A	H-T	Scorers, Times, and Referees
3	A	BIRMINGHAM	17,236	1 W 19	3-2	1-1	Brazil 35, 77, Wark 72 / Worthington 43p, Curbishley 51

1	2	3	4	5	6	7	8	9	10	11	12 sub used
Cooper	Burley	McCall	Mills	Osman	Steggles	Wark	Muhren	Mariner	Brazil	Gates	
Coton	*Langan*	*Dennis*	*Curbishley**	*Broadhurst*	*Todd*	*Dillon*	*Worthington*	*Evans*	*Gemmill*	*Van Mierlo*	*Handysides*

Ref: R Lewis

Gates sets up Brazil to score, aided by a Mariner dummy, but Jim Smith's side hit back. Curbishley's shot somehow squeezes through the hands of a horrified Cooper. Wark volleys twice from a corner and then a thrilling tie is won as Brazil nets after great work by Gates.

Round			Att		F-A	H-T	Scorers, Times, and Referees
4	A	LUTON	20,188	1 W 2:1	3-0	0-0	Brazil 62, Gates 71, 86

1	2	3	4	5	6	7	8	9	10	11	12 sub used
Cooper	Burley	McCall	Mills	Osman	Butcher*	Wark	Muhren	Mariner	Brazil	Gates	O'Callaghan
Findlay	*Stephens*	*Aizlewood**	*Horton*	*Goodyear*	*Donaghy*	*Hill*	*Stein*	*White*	*Fuccillo*	*Moss*	*Antic*

Ref: C Thomas

Town chalk up a club record ninth successive win, punishing David Pleat's side with some slick finishing after the break. The only real scare is when a Hill shot hits the crossbar. Stein's boot catches Butcher in the face and he eventually departs when the flow of blood can't be stemmed.

Match 5

5 A SHREWSBURY 7 L 1-2 0-2 D'Avray 76
13/2 13,965 2:18 Cross 15, King 23
Ref: K Walmsley

Cooper, Burley, Mills*, McCall, Thijssen, Hunter, Osman, Wark, Muhren, O'Callaghan, Gates, D'Avray
Wardle, King, Johnson, Watson, Griffin, Keay, Tong, McNally, Atkins, Biggins*, Bates, Dungworth

A visit to Gay Meadow for a second successive year goes awry thanks to two clever set-piece moves. With Thijssen out, Town are permitted to field another import and S. African D'Avray gets a chance, coming on to score a fine goal. Graham Turner's men are good value for their win.

UEFA Cup

1:1 H ABERDEEN 3 D 1-1 1-0 Thijssen 43
16/9 18,535 Hewitt 51
(Scotland) Ref: G Menegali (Italy)

Cooper, Burley, Mills, McCall, Thijssen, Osman, Butcher, Wark, Muhren, O'Callaghan*, Brazil, Gates
Leighton, Kennedy, Rougvie, Watson, McLeish, Miller, Strachan, Cooper, McGhee, Hewitt, Simpson

A disappointingly tough draw considering Town are seeded, but Alex Ferguson's men provide interesting opposition for Town fans. Thijssen dances past defenders and lashes home a great goal. The Dons refuse to sit back and, prompted by Strachan, they conjure up a deserved draw.

1:2 A ABERDEEN 1 L 1-3 1-1 Wark 34p
30/9 24,000 Strachan 19p, Weir 55, 85
Ref: M Vautrot (France)
(Town lose 2-4 on aggregate)

Cooper, Burley, Mills, McCall, Thijssen*, Osman, Butcher, Wark, Muhren, O'Callaghan, Gates
Leighton, Kennedy, Rougvie, Watson, McLeish, Miller, Strachan, Cooper^, McGhee, Hewitt, Weir*, Bell/Simpson

The defence of the UEFA Cup ends in an electric atmosphere. Wark fouls Strachan for the opening penalty then Cooper brings down Gates to set up an equaliser from the spot. Record-signing Weir speeds in to fire two great goals. Cooper saves a re-taken last-minute Strachan penalty.

League Table

		P	Home					Away					Pts
			W	D	L	F	A	W	D	L	F	A	
1	Liverpool	42	14	3	4	39	14	12	6	3	41	18	87
2	IPSWICH	42	17	1	3	47	25	9	4	8	28	28	83
3	Manchester U	42	12	6	3	27	9	10	6	5	32	20	78
4	Tottenham	42	12	4	5	41	26	8	7	6	26	22	71
5	Arsenal	42	13	5	3	27	15	7	6	8	21	22	71
6	Swansea	42	13	3	5	34	16	8	3	10	24	35	69
7	Southampton	42	15	2	4	49	30	4	7	10	23	37	66
8	Everton	42	11	7	3	33	21	6	6	9	23	29	64
9	West Ham	42	9	10	2	29	21	6	6	9	24	28	58
10	Manchester C	42	9	7	5	32	23	6	6	9	17	27	58
11	Aston Villa	42	9	6	6	28	24	6	6	9	27	29	57
12	Nott'm Forest	42	7	7	7	19	20	8	5	8	23	28	57
13	Brighton	42	8	7	6	30	24	5	4	12	13	28	52
14	Coventry	42	9	4	8	31	24	4	7	10	25	38	50
15	Notts Co	42	8	5	8	32	33	5	3	13	29	36	47
16	Birmingham	42	8	6	7	29	25	2	8	11	24	36	44
17	West Brom	42	6	6	9	24	25	5	5	11	22	32	44
18	Stoke	42	9	2	10	27	28	3	6	12	17	35	44
19	Sunderland	42	6	5	10	19	26	5	6	10	19	32	44
20	Leeds	42	6	11	4	23	20	4	1	16	16	41	42
21	Wolves	42	8	5	8	19	20	2	5	14	13	43	40
22	Middlesbro	42	5	9	7	20	24	3	6	12	14	28	39
		924	214	121	127	672	501	127	121	214	501	672	1265

Appearances / Goals

	Appearances								Goals				
	Lge	Sub	LC	Sub	FAC	Sub	Eur	Sub	Lge	LC	FAC	Eur	Tot
Brazil, Alan	35		6	1	3		2		22	3	3		28
Burley, George	29		6		3		1						
Butcher, Terry	27		6		3		2					1	1
Cooper, Paul	32		8		3		2						
D'Avray, Mich	12	1	1				1		2	1			3
Gates, Eric	38		7		3		2		9	4	2		15
Gernon, Irvin	4												
Hunter, Allan						1							
Jackson, John	1												
Mariner, Paul	25		5		2		1		8		1		9
McCall, Steve	42		7		3		2		1				1
Mills, Mick	42		8		3		2		3				3
Muhren, Arnold	42		8		3		2		4		1		5
O'Callaghan, Kevin	7	12	2	1		1	1	1	2				2
Osman, Russell	39		7		3		2		2				2
Parkin, Tommy	5	1											
Sivell, Laurie	9												
Steggles, Kevin	18		3										
Thijssen, Frans	12		5		1		2		1			1	2
Turner, Robin	1	2							1				1
Wark, John	42		8		3		2		18	3	1	1	23
(own-goals)									2				2
21 players used	462	16	88	5	33	2	22	2	75	15	7	2	99

Odds & ends

Double wins: (7) Villa, Brighton, Coventry, Leeds, Man U, M'boro, WBA.
Double losses: (0).

Won from behind: (4) Coventry (a), Man U (h), Leeds (h), Birm' (FAC) (a).
Lost from in front: (1) Southampton (A).

High spots: A club record nine successive wins.
Maintaining a serious title challenge into May.
Brazil's brilliant five-goal salvo against Southampton.
Qualification for Europe for a ninth time in ten seasons.
Seven men in the England and Scotland World Cup squads.
The signing of a major sponsorship deal with Pioneer.

Low spots: Defeat by Shrewsbury Town in the FA Cup.
The end of the road for injury-plagued Kevin Beattie.
Being outclassed in the League Cup semi-final first-leg.
Serious injuries to Terry Butcher and Frans Thijssen.
The impending loss of Bobby Robson to the England job.

Player of the Year: Alan Brazil.
Ever-presents: (4) McCall (Lge only), Mills (Lge only), Muhren, Wark.
Hat-tricks: (1) Alan Brazil.
Opposing hat-tricks: (1) Peter Davenport.
Leading scorer: (28) Alan Brazil.

LEAGUE DIVISION 1

Manager: Bobby Ferguson

SEASON 1982-83

No	Date	Att	Pos	Pt	F-A	H-T	Scorers, Times, and Referees	1	2	3	4	5	6	7	8	9	10	11	12 sub used
1	A BRIGHTON 28/8	13,641	D	1	1-1	1-1	Gates 25, Ritchie 32. Ref: D Hedges	Cooper	Burley	Mills	Thijssen	Osman	Butcher	Wark	McCall	Mariner	O'Callaghan	Gates	
								Digweed	*Shanks*	*Pearce*	*Grealish*	*Stevens*	*Gatting*	*Smillie*	*Ritchie**	*Robinson*	*McNab*	*Smith*	*Ryan*
2	H TOTTENHAM 31/8	24,968	L	1	1-2	1-0	Brazil 32, Archibald 73, Crooks 78. Ref: A Grey	Cooper	Burley	Mills	Thijssen	Osman	Butcher	Wark	McCall	Mariner	Brazil	Gates*	O'Callaghan
								Clemence	*Hughton*	*Miller*	*Lacy*	*Brooke*	*Perryman*	*Mabbutt*	*Archibald*	*Galvin*	*Hoddle*	*Crooks*	
3	H COVENTRY 4/9	16,662	D	2	1-1	0-0	Mariner 72, Thomas 86. Ref: M James	Cooper	Burley	Mills	Thijssen	Osman	Butcher	Wark	McCall	Mariner	Brazil	Gates	
								Sealey	*Thomas*	*Roberts*	*Jacobs*	*Dyson*	*Gillespie*	*Hom'tschuk*	*Francis*	*Hateley*	*Thompson*	*Whitton*	
4	A WEST HAM 7/9	21,963	D	3	1-1	1-0	Wark 31, Lampard 60. Ref: K Barratt	Cooper	Burley	Mills	Thijssen	Osman	Butcher	Wark	McCall	Mariner	Brazil	Gates	D'Avray
								Parkes	*Stewart*	*Lampard*	*Bonds*	*Martin*	*Devonshire*	*Van der Elst*	*Goddard*	*Clark*	*Allen*	*Pike*	
5	A MANCHESTER U 11/9	43,140	L	3	1-3	1-1	Mariner 35, Whiteside 2, 85, Coppell 75. Ref: A Saunders	Cooper	Burley	Mills	Thijssen	Osman	Butcher	Wark	McCall*	Mariner	Brazil	Gates	D'Avray
								Bailey	*Duxbury*	*Albiston*	*Wilkins*	*Moran*	*McQueen*	*Robson*	*Muhren*	*Stapleton*	*Whiteside*	*Coppell*	
6	H STOKE 18/9	19,119	L	3	2-3	2-2	Brazil 27, Wark 39, Thomas 12, Maguire 19, 47p. Ref: M Taylor	Cooper	Burley	Mills	Thijssen	Osman*	Butcher	Wark	McCall	Mariner	Brazil	Gates	Parkin
								Fox	*Parkin*	*Hampton*	*Bracewell*	*Watson*	*Berry*	*Maguire*	*McIlroy*	*O'Callaghan*	*Thomas*	*Chamberlain*	
7	A NOTTS CO 25/9	8,454	W	6	6-0	2-0	Mariner 15, 67, Brazil 23, Wark 57, Thijssen 75, McCall 77. Ref: J Lovatt	Sivell	Burley	Mills	Thijssen	Osman	Butcher	Wark	McCall	Mariner	Brazil	Gates	O'Callaghan
								Avramovic	*Benjamin*	*Worthington*	*Hunt*	*Kitchine*	*Richards*	*Chiedozie*	*Harkouk*	*Christie*	*Goodwin*	*McCulloch*	
8	H LIVERPOOL 2/10	24,342	W	9	1-0	0-0	D'Avray 81. Ref: R Lewis	Sivell	Burley	Gernon	Thijssen*	Osman	Butcher	Wark	McCall	D'Avray	Mills	Gates	O'Callaghan
								Grobbelaar	*Neal*	*Kennedy*	*Thompson*	*Whelan*	*Hansen*	*Dalglish*	*Lee**	*Johnston*	*Lawrenson*	*Souness*	*Fairclough*
9	H ARSENAL 9/10	20,792	L	9	0-1	0-0	Woodcock 59. Ref: J Hunting	Sivell	Burley	Gernon*	Mills	Osman	Butcher	Wark	McCall	Mariner	Brazil	Gates	**Putney**
								Wood	*Hollins**	*Sansom*	*Talbot*	*O'Leary*	*Whyte*	*Davis*	*Sunderland*	*Robson*	*Woodcock*	*Rix*	*Hawley*
10	A LUTON 16/10	13,378	D	10	1-1	1-0	Brazil 12, Stein 59p. Ref: D Lloyd	Cooper	Burley	Gernon	Mills	Osman	Butcher	Wark	McCall	Mariner	Brazil	Gates	Moss
								Findlay	*Stephens*	*Money*	*Horton*	*Goodyear*	*Donaghy*	*Hill*	*Stein*	*Walsh*	*Fuccillo*	*Moss*	

1. BRIGHTON: After nearly 14 years, Town take to the field with no Bobby Robson in the dugout. The side gives a stuttering display, with Mills soldiering on in pain after three stitches in a head wound following a clash of heads with Smillie. Jimmy Melia's side give them a tough start to the new era.

2. TOTTENHAM: Hoddle is in scintillating form, spraying long balls around the field. Defensive errors cost Town dear in a lively game. Brazil returns to the side and is Town's best player, getting off to a spectacular start by giving Town the lead. He comes closest to an equaliser after Spurs bounce back.

3. COVENTRY: Les Sealey, returning after injury, keeps Town at bay with several outstanding saves until Mariner beats him, sweeping home a pinpoint cross by Gates. Full-back Thomas gets forward in a late spell of pressure by Dave Sexton's side, and crashes home a superb equaliser from 25 yards.

4. WEST HAM: Wark rattles in a fierce angled drive – marking his 101st goal, an incredible record for a player who has never played as a striker. Cooper saves Stewart's penalty after Osman fouls Van der Elst. Lampard's drive is blocked, but he nets the rebound.

5. MANCHESTER U: Coppell heads United ahead after Wark blocks Wilkins' shot and the ball deflects into his path. Town almost netted in the opening seconds but found themselves a goal down moments later. Transfer rumours surround Mills, who is surprisingly left out of Robson's first England squad.

6. STOKE: Thomas and Maguire sweep Richie Barker's side ahead, but Brazil waltzes around Fox for the first and Wark levels after the break. Bracewell is jostled from behind by Butcher, winning a debatable decisive penalty. Gates asks for a move, but Brazil agrees to sign a new two-year deal.

7. NOTTS CO: The winless run is ended in style, with sharp finishing and rapier-like breakaway attacks. Brazil also has one disallowed and Town have now hit ten in two visits to Meadow Lane. McCall rounds off the afternoon by cutting in from the flank and crashing home the sixth from an angle.

8. LIVERPOOL: D'Avray, only playing due to Mariner's throat infection and Brazil's flu, is the Town hero with a majestic header from O'Callaghan's cross. Town create more chances and deserve to win. It ends The Reds' 23-match unbeaten run, proving Bob Paisley's team is not invincible after all!

9. ARSENAL: Woodcock sweeps home from close range to win a game stifled by Terry Neill's side's negative tactics. Mariner hits the bar and Butcher and McCall both go close to an equaliser. Town's directors agree to Gates' transfer request, while Mills denies he is in line to be Derby's next boss.

10. LUTON: Brazil is stranded yards offside, but amazingly is waved on and shoots past Findlay. A TV inquest later reveals the referee thought he had been played on-side by Hill, but replays prove this incorrect. Stein hits the bar, before Mariner scythes down Stephens for Stein to net from the spot.

Ipswich Town — League match record (games 11–21)

No	V	Opponent	Date	Pos	Res	FT	HT		Pts	Att
11	A	BIRMINGHAM	23/10	18	D	0-0	0-0	22	11	12,051
12	H	WEST BROM	30/10	15	W	6-1	4-0	4	14	20,011
13	A	NOTT'M FOREST	6/11	18	L	1-2	1-0	5	14	17,461
14	H	MANCHESTER C	13/11	16	W	1-0	1-0	6	17	19,523
15	A	SOUTHAMPTON	20/11	12	W	1-0	0-0	19	20	18,449
16	A	COVENTRY	23/11	11	D	1-1	0-0	10	21	9,550
17	H	SWANSEA	27/11	8	W	3-1	2-0	16	24	17,849
18	A	SUNDERLAND	4/12	7	W	3-2	2-1	22	27	15,000
19	H	EVERTON	11/12	9	L	0-2	0-2	14	27	17,512
20	A	WATFORD	18/12	10	L	1-2	0-2	4	27	18,048
21	H	NORWICH	27/12	11	L	2-3	1-1	20	27	29,596

---

11 · A BIRMINGHAM · 23/10 · D 0-0

Town: Cooper, Burley, Mills, Thijssen, Osman, Butcher, Wark, McCall, Mariner!, Brazil, Gates
Birmingham: Blyth, Mumford, V d Hauwe, Stevenson, Blake, Broadhurst, Dillon, Bremner, Brazier, Curbishley, Handysides

Town put on a mediocre display, but are rarely troubled by Ron Saunders' men, and even spurn a couple of chances to win. Mariner is sent off near the end for retaliation. The club announces a trading loss of £173,395. Mills is linked with Chelsea and a group bidding to buy Reading.
Ref: N Ashley

12 · H WEST BROM · 30/10 · W 6-1 — Gates 5, Thijs'n 9, Wark 27, 29, 51, 68 / Regis 57

Town: Cooper, Burley, Gernon, Thijssen, Osman, Butcher, Wark, McCall, Mariner, Brazil*, Gates; sub O'Callaghan
West Brom: Godden, Batson*, Statham, Zondervan, Wile, Robertson, Jol, Brown, Regis, Owen, Whitehead; sub Cross

The second foursome of his career comes after Wark almost quits at half-time because of a painful knee. Gates fires in a smart shot on the turn and Thijssen's low drive becomes Town's 2,500th League goal. Wark's second is a slick creation that owes much to a clever dummy by Gates.
Ref: D Reeves

13 · A NOTT'M FOREST · 6/11 · L 1-2 — McCall 26 / Robertson 64p, Osman 82 (og)

Town: Cooper, Burley, Gernon, Thijssen*, Osman, Butcher, Wark, McCall, Mariner, Brazil, Gates; sub D'Avray
Forest: V Breukelen, Swain, Gunn, Todd, Young, Bowyer, Proctor, Wallace, Birtles, Hodge, Robertson

Osman challenges Hodge and a disputed penalty is given. The unlucky stand-in skipper hits the net when trying to head clear after a Wallace flick-on. Kevin Beattie joins Middlesbrough, infuriating Town who'd paid up his contract and staged a testimonial, believing he was quitting.
Ref: N Wilson

14 · H MANCHESTER C · 13/11 · W 1-0 — Wark 22

Town: Cooper, Burley, Mills, Thijssen, Osman, Butcher, Wark, McCall, O'Callaghan, Brazil, Gates
Manchester C: Corrigan, Ransom, MacDonald, Bond, Power, Caton, Tueart, Reeves, Cross, Hartford, Baker*; sub Reid

Brazil and Gates are in dazzling form, but the only success is when Butcher's through-ball is flicked to Wark by Gates. Sunderland accuse Town and Mick Mills of unethical behaviour after he chooses to join Southampton instead, after a last-minute approach by Lawrie McMenemy.
Ref: D Vickers

15 · A SOUTHAMPTON · 20/11 · W 1-0 — Thijssen 59

Town: Cooper, Burley, Gernon, Thijssen, Osman, Butcher, Wark, McCall, Mariner, Brazil, Gates
Southampton: Shilton, Agboola, Mills, Williams, Nicholl, Wright, Holmes, Moran, Cassells*, Armstrong, Wallace; sub Puckett

Thijssen goes on a typical solo run, and fires home a 25-yarder with his left foot past Shilton. Town put in a neat and tidy display against their ex-captain Mills. Both sides have penalty appeals turned down. Manchester United make an unsuccessful bid to re-unite Brazil with Muhren.
Ref: K Salmon

16 · A COVENTRY · 23/11 · D 1-1 — Brazil 75 / Thomas 69

Town: Cooper, Burley, Gernon, Thijssen, Osman, Butcher, Wark, McCall, Mariner, Brazil, Gates; sub D'Avray
Coventry: Sealey, Thomas, Roberts, Jacobs, Dyson, Gillespie, Whitton, Hunt, Hateley, Thompson, Hunt

City are generally on top and look the more likely winners throughout. A neat move involving Hunt, Roberts and Hateley sets up Thomas for a fine goal, his second of the season against Town. Against the run of play, Brazil quickly levels with Town's only real opening of the evening.
Ref: R Chadwick

17 · H SWANSEA · 27/11 · W 3-1 — Osman 22, Burley 34, Wark 65 / James L 83

Town: Cooper, Burley, Barnes, Thijssen, Osman, Butcher, Wark, McCall, Mariner, Brazil, Gates
Swansea: Davies, Stanley, Hadziabdic, Charles, Mahoney, Rajkovic, Loveridge, James R, James L, Stevenson, Latchford

Osman, who passed a late fitness test on a calf problem, climbs high to power a header past Davies. Wark gets in front of Stanley to flick home the goal that ensures the points. Barnes, raised in Suffolk but recruited from Coventry, makes a steady debut in place of the injured Gernon.
Ref: J Moules

18 · A SUNDERLAND · 4/12 · W 3-2 — Gates 38, Brazil 40, 67 / Atkins 25, Worthington 69

Town: Cooper, Burley, Barnes, Thijssen, Osman, Butcher, Wark, McCall, Mariner, Brazil, Gates
Sunderland: Turner, Nicholl, Munro, Atkins, Elliot, Hindmarch, Buckley, Rowell, Worthington, McCoist, Cummins

A magnificent 30-yarder by Atkins gives Alan Durban's men the lead. Brazil, now on the transfer list with Gates and reportedly a Stoke target, has a fine game and is unlucky not to get three. He shows Scotland they were wrong to axe him. Debutant Worthington ensures a frantic finale.
Ref: T Fitzharris

19 · H EVERTON · 11/12 · L 0-2 — Sheedy 60, Richardson 90

Town: Cooper, Burley*, Barnes, Thijssen, Osman, Butcher, Wark, McCall, Mariner, Brazil, Gates; sub O'Callaghan
Everton: Arnold, Stevens, Bailey, Ratcliffe, Higgins, McMahon, Curran, Heath, Johnson, Richardson, Sheedy

The mini-run of good results ends in gloom as Town turn in their worst display of the year. Their passing is poor and there is little penetration against Howard Kendall's side. Burley picks up another serious knee injury and the misery is compounded by Richardson's last-minute strike.
Ref: C Donney

20 · A WATFORD · 18/12 · L 1-2 — Mariner 81 / Jenkins 18, Taylor 27

Town: Cooper, Steggles*, Gernon, Thijssen, Osman, Butcher, Wark, McCall, Mariner, Brazil, Gates; sub O'Callaghan
Watford: Sherwood, Rostron, Rice, Taylor, Bolton, Sims, Callaghan, Barnes, Jenkins, Jackett, Jobson

Slack marking by Butcher allows Jenkins to swoop for the first goal, a diving header. Les Taylor grabs a second after Cooper fails to leave his line to collect a cross. Town, without a recognised full-back, rally after the break but Graham Taylor's team keep them at bay in a lively finish.
Ref: M Robinson

21 · H NORWICH · 27/12 · L 2-3 — Osman 39, Mariner 68 / Mendham 24, 65, O'Neill 88

Town: Cooper, McCall, Steggles, Thijssen, Osman, Butcher, Wark, O'Callaghan*, Mariner, Brazil, Gates; sub Putney
Norwich: Woods, Haylock, Hareide, Mendham, Walford, Watson, Barham, O'Neill, Channon, Bertschin, Van Wyk

A real thriller goes right to the wire. Mendham's header is cancelled out by Osman's powerful header off the bar. Watson's cross is fired in off the bar by Mendham from 12 yards, but Mariner levels from Gates' cross. O'Neill conjures up a superb winner with a 25-yard curling effort.
Ref: A Gunn

LEAGUE DIVISION 1

Manager: Bobby Ferguson — SEASON 1982-83

No	Date	1	2	3	4	5	6	7	8	9	10	11	12 sub used	Att	Pos	Pt	F-A	H-T	Scorers, Times, and Referees
22	A ASTON VILLA 29/12	Cooper / *Spink*	Steggles / *Williams**	Gernon / *Gibson*	Thijssen / *Evans*	Osman / *McNaught*	Butcher / *Mortimer*	Wark / *Bremner*	Putney* / *Shaw*	McCall / *Withe*	Brazil / *Cowans*	Gates / *Walters*	O'Callaghan / *Morley*	21,912	13 D / *7*	28	1-1	1-1	Wark 44 / Withe 20 / Ref: R Milford. — Courageous Cooper is Town's hero, pulling off fine saves despite breaking a rib in a 16th-minute collision. Withe beats him when his shot is deflected in by Butcher. Wark levels with a header from Gates' pass. Cooper keeps Villa at bay after repeated attention from physio Eggleston.
23	H SOUTHAMPTON 1/1	Sivell / *Shilton*	Steggles / *Agboola*	Gernon / *Mills*	Thijssen / *Williams*	Osman / *Nicholl*	Butcher / *Wright*	Wark / *Holmes*	McCall / *Moran*	Mariner / *Puckett*	Brazil / *Armstrong*	Gates / *Wallace*		18,866	10 W / *15*	31	2-1	1-0	Mariner 38, Osman 65 / Wright 72 / Ref: H Taylor. — The returning Mills comes on through a 'guard of honour' of Town players, in recognition of his 17 years at Ipswich. Osman shoots low past Shilton after a free-kick is squared to him. The points are in the balance when Wright tucks the ball home after Holmes beats Osman in the air.
24	H BRIGHTON 15/1	Sivell / *Moseley*	Steggles / *Ramsey*	Gernon / *Pearce*	Thijssen / *Grealish*	Osman / *Foster*	Butcher / *Gatting*	Wark / *Case*	McCall / *Ward**	Mariner* / *Robinson*	Brazil / *Ritchie*	Gates / *Smillie*	Putney / *Smith*	17,092	9 W / *21*	34	2-0	1-0	Wark 20, Brazil 72 / Ref: J Bray. — The relegation-threatened visitors struggle after Gates' corner-kick is headed home by Wark. Mariner goes off as a precautionary measure after a clash of heads, but immediately the transfer-listed Brazil ends his mini-goal famine by ramming a superb right-foot pile-driver past Moseley.
25	A STOKE 22/1	Sivell / *Fox*	Steggles* / *Parkin*	Gernon / *Hampton*	Thijssen / *Bracewell*	Osman / *Watson*	Butcher / *Berry*	Wark / *Maguire*	McCall / *McIlroy*	Mariner / *O'Callaghan*	Brazil / *Thorne*	Gates / *Painter**	O'Callaghan / *Bould*	14,026	11 L / *12*	34	0-1	0-0	Painter 59 / Ref: T Mills. — Prior to kick-off, City parade a camel around the pitch. Town get the hump after a Maguire corner, as the ball flicks off Butcher leaving Sivell stranded and Painter beats Gernon to head the winner. With Brendan O'Callaghan towering over Sivell, Town look vulnerable at set-pieces.
26	H MANCHESTER U 5/2	Sivell / *Bailey*	Putney / *Duxbury*	Gernon / *Albiston*	Thijssen / *Moses*	Osman / *Moran*	Butcher / *McQueen*	Wark* / *Robson*	McCall / *Muhren*	Mariner / *Stapleton*	Brazil / *Whiteside*	O'Callaghan / *Coppell*	D'Avray /	23,581	13 D / *2*	35	1-1	1-0	Wark 41 / Stapleton 47 / Ref: K Baker. — Portman Road's new £1.4 million Pioneer Stand is officially opened by Sports Minister Neil Macfarlane, a United fan. Muhren's return gets off to a bad start as Wark performs a magnificent overhead kick to net Mariner's flick-on. Town rule the roost early on, with Putney in good form.
27	A LIVERPOOL 12/2	Cooper / *Grobbelaar*	Putney* / *Neal*	Gernon / *Kennedy*	Thijssen / *Thompson*	Osman / *Johnston**	Butcher / *Hansen*	Wark / *Dalglish*	McCall / *Lee*	Mariner / *Rush*	Brazil / *Lawrenson*	O'Callaghan / *Souness*	D'Avray / *Whelan*	34,976	13 L / *1*	35	0-1	0-0	Dalglish 66 / Ref: G Tyson. — Town please Ferguson by fighting tooth and nail to give the champions and runaway leaders plenty to worry about. Ian Rush is well shackled by Osman, but after Gernon tangles with him a free-kick is conceded. Dalglish bends this neatly inside the post past Cooper's despairing dive.
28	H LUTON 26/2	Cooper / *Findlay*	Putney / *Stephens*	Gernon / *Turner*	Parkin / *Horton*	Osman / *Goodyear*	Butcher / *Donaghy*	Wark / *Hill**	McCall / *White*	Mariner / *Walsh*	Brazil / *Fuccillo*	O'Callaghan / *Moss*	/ *Kellock*	18,615	11 W / *18*	38	3-0	1-0	Brazil 2, Wark 46, Putney 56 / Ref: M Bodenham. — David Pleat's leaky defence looks anxious after Brazil's quick-fire opener and Town cruise to victory. White makes his First Division debut, but Luton lack punch and rarely trouble Cooper. Putney fires a fine goal after good work by Brazil and Pleat is happy to concede just the three.
29	H BIRMINGHAM 5/3	Cooper / *Coton*	Putney / *Hagan*	Gernon / *Dennis*	Parkin / *Stevenson*	Osman / *Blake*	Butcher / *Broadhurst*	Wark / *Gayle**	McCall / *Ferguson*	Mariner / *Harford*	Brazil / *Curbishley*	O'Callaghan / *Dillon*	/ *V d Hauwe*	16,436	8 W / *21*	42	3-1	0-0	Putney 46, Osman 54, Brazil 56 / Dennis 67 / Ref: D Letts. — Ron Wylie's side is in danger of being buried as Brazil hits the woodwork three times. Putney's left-foot drive is followed by a glorious Osman header and a solo effort by Brazil which goes in off a post. Ferguson misses several chances, but Dennis is on target from the edge of the area.
30	A WEST BROM 12/3	Cooper / *Barron*	Putney / *Webb*	Gernon / *Statham*	Parkin / *Zondervan*	Osman / *Wile*	Butcher / *Bennett*	Wark / *Whitehead*	McCall / *Thompson*	Mariner / *Regis**	Brazil / *Owen*	Gates / *Cross*	O'Callaghan / *Eastoe*	12,892	9 L / *6*	42	1-4	0-2	Wark 55 / Thompson 8, 82, Statham 33, [Gernon 77 (og)] / Ref: F Roberts. — Expensive new signing Thompson squeezes the ball home after a run by Cross and Statham's low drive puts Albion in command. Wark heads O'Callaghan's cross home, but defeat is assured when unlucky Osman dives to reach Regis' cross but can only direct the ball into his own net.
31	H NOTT'M FOREST 19/3	Cooper / *V Breukelen*	Burley / *Anderson*	Gernon / *Swain**	Putney / *Gunn*	Osman / *Fairclough*	Butcher / *Bowyer*	Wark / *Wilson*	McCall / *Hodge*	Mariner* / *Davenport*	D'Avray / *Walsh*	O'Callaghan / *Robertson*	Thijssen / *Smedley*	17,534	10 W / *6*	44	2-0	1-0	Mariner 25, 64 / Ref: A Robinson. — Brazil departs for Spurs for £470,000 and the resulting change of responsibilities in Town's attack means Mariner is now deployed to attack the near post. This tactic bears fruit immediately with his excellent headers beating Van Breukelen. Cooper stops Robertson's 56th-minute penalty.

Ipswich Town — Season results (matches 32–42)

No		Fixture	Date	Att	Pos	b	Pts	Res	FT	HT
32	A	ARSENAL	22/3	17,639	8	14	45	D	2-2	0-2
33	A	MANCHESTER C	26/3	21,845	6	17	48	W	1-0	0-0
34	H	ASTON VILLA	2/4	19,912	8	4	48	L	1-2	1-1
35	A	NORWICH	4/4	23,476	8	19	49	D	0-0	0-0
36	H	NOTTS CO	9/4	15,924	11	14	50	D	0-0	0-0
37	A	TOTTENHAM	16/4	30,557	11	8	50	L	1-3	0-2
38	H	SUNDERLAND	23/4	16,193	11	17	53	W	4-1	2-0
39	A	SWANSEA	30/4	8,568	11	22	54	D	1-1	0-0
40	H	WEST HAM	3/5	18,690	11	10	54	L	1-2	1-1
41	H	WATFORD	7/5	19,921	9	2	57	W	3-1	2-0
42	A	EVERTON	14/5	17,420	9	7	58	D	1-1	0-0

32 A ARSENAL 22/3 — D 2-2 (0-2)
Wark 69, Putney 87 | Rix 20, Whyte 42 | Ref: J Deakin
Ipswich: Cooper, Burley, Gernon, Putney, Osman, Butcher, Wark, McCall, D'Avray, Thijssen*, O'Callaghan, Parkin
Arsenal: Wood, Hollins, Sansom, Talbot, Devine, Whyte, Davis, Sunderland, Nicholas, Woodcock, Rix
Rix's stinging drive squeezes under Cooper's body for the opening goal and then defender Whyte seizes on to a Germon mistake to fire past Cooper. Town stage an excellent second-half comeback, Wark firing past Wood before Putney produces a stunning drive in the dying minutes.

33 A MANCHESTER C 26/3 — W 1-0 (0-0)
Wark 56 | Ref: K Hackett
Ipswich: Cooper, Burley, Gernon, Putney, Osman, Butcher, Wark, McCall, D'Avray, O'Callaghan
Man City: Williams, Ransom, Bond, Reid, Caton, Power, Reeves, Baker, Hartford, Cross, Tueart
Town's outside hopes of gaining a UEFA Cup place are boosted as hard-working D'Avray crosses to Wark, who scores via Bond's boot. It's enough to win a game desperately short on entertainment. City keeper Joe Corrigan bids an emotional farewell after 17 years at Maine Road.

34 H ASTON VILLA 2/4 — L 1-2 (1-1)
McCall 2 | Shaw 45, Withe 64 | Ref: E Scales
Ipswich: Cooper, Burley, Gernon, Putney, Osman, Butcher, Wark, McCall, D'Avray, O'Callaghan, Thijssen
Aston Villa: Spink, Williams, Gibson, Evans, McNaught, Mortimer, Bremner, Shaw, Withe, Cowans, Walters
McNaught's clearance cannons in off the on-rushing McCall to give Town a great start. Things go wrong after injuries to Putney and D'Avray. Germon, picked for England U-21 in midweek, is dispossessed in the build-up to Shaw's goal, and is then caught out of position as Withe nets.

35 A NORWICH 4/4 — D 0-0 (0-0)
Ref: B Hill
Ipswich: Cooper, Burley, Gernon, Thijssen, Osman, Butcher, Wark, McCall, D'Avray, Kinsella, O'Callaghan
Norwich: Woods, Haylock, Downs, Mendham, Walford, Watson, Channon, O'Neill, Deehan, Bertschin, Van Wyk*, Barham
A very physical affair with relegation-haunted City showing the greater hunger to win. Kinsella, a £60,000 buy from Tampa Bay Rowdies, has a reasonable debut in difficult circumstances. Thijssen is given a huge ovation on his farewell appearance before joining Vancouver Whitecaps.

36 H NOTTS CO 9/4 — D 0-0 (0-0)
Ref: T Ward
Ipswich: Cooper, Burley, Barnes, Putney, Osman, Butcher, Wark, McCall, D'Avray, O'Callaghan*, Kinsella
Notts Co: Avramovic, Benjamin, Worthington, Hunt, Kilcline, Richards, Chiedozie, Lahtinen, Christie, Goodwin*, McCulloch, McParland
The smallest League crowd for almost ten years is given poor entertainment, with County boss Howard Wilkinson having to shoulder much of the blame for his negative tactics. New skipper Mariner leads the line well, but Gates – confined to bed with a back problem – is sorely missed.

37 A TOTTENHAM 16/4 — L 1-3 (0-2)
Mariner 78 | Brazil 15, 27, Mabbutt 89 | Ref: T Spencer
Ipswich: Cooper, Burley*, Barnes*, Putney*, Steggles, Butcher, Wark, McCall, D'Avray, Kinsella, Turner
Tottenham: Clemence, Hughton, O'Reilly*, Roberts, Miller, Perryman, Mabbutt, Archibald, Galvin, Brazil, Hoddle, Falco
Brazil nets twice against his old mates, the second a bizarre and scrappy effort after he and Cooper seem to freeze in a one-on-one situation. Mariner wrong-foots Clemence to reduce the arrears, but in the last minute Mabbutt is teed up by sub Hoddle and cracks home a real beauty.

38 H SUNDERLAND 23/4 — W 4-1 (2-0)
Wark 35, 76, Mariner 44, Turner 89 | Pickering 68 | Ref: M Dimblebee
Ipswich: Cooper, Burley, McCall, Putney*, Steggles, Butcher, Wark, Kinsella, Mariner, O'Callaghan, Turner
Sunderland: Prudhoe, Venison, Munro, Atkins, Hindmarch, Chisholm, Cooke, West, Worthington*, Pickering, James, McCoist
Skilful O'Callaghan sets up the first two goals with fine wing-play. Highlight of the day is a superb long-range goal by popular Turner, his first in the League after ten years at Ipswich! He had been loaned to Maastricht for the season, but returned when that club had financial problems.

39 A SWANSEA 30/4 — D 1-1 (0-0)
Mariner 54 | Rajkovic 77 | Ref: V Callow
Ipswich: Cooper, Burley, McCall, Steggles*, Steggles*, Butcher, Wark, Gernon, Mariner, O'Callaghan, Turner
Swansea: Sander, Marustik, Richards, Charles, Lewis, Rajkovic, Loveridge*, Gale, James R, Kennedy, Latchford, Pascoe
John Toshack's men look doomed after five games without a win. Their lowest crowd of the season sees youngsters Gale, Pascoe and Sander thrown into the fray as they fight to stay in the top flight. A draw does neither side any good. Yugoslav Rajkovic nets his first goal of the year.

40 H WEST HAM 3/5 — L 1-2 (1-1)
D'Avray 33 | Goddard 9, Stewart 80p | Ref: G Napthine
Ipswich: Cooper, Burley, Barnes, Parkin*, Gernon, Butcher, Wark, McCall, Mariner, O'Callaghan, Turner
West Ham: Parkes, Stewart, Lampard, Bonds, Martin, Devonshire, Van der Elst, Goddard, Swindlehurst, Dickens, Pike
Lingering hopes of a UEFA Cup place are ended as Germon brings down Goddard and Stewart nets from the penalty spot. Earlier Cooper gets caught off his line and Goddard's header loops over him. D'Avray's equaliser is a gem. He juggles the ball and swivels to volley home sweetly.

41 H WATFORD 7/5 — W 3-1 (2-0)
McCall 2, Wark 35, 72 | Rostron 62 | Ref: D Axcell
Ipswich: Cooper, Burley, Gernon, Putney*, Osman, Butcher, Wark, McCall, Mariner, O'Callaghan, Turner
Watford: Sherwood, Rice, Rostron, Callaghan, Sims, Jackett, Sterling, Barnes, Blissett, Lohman, Armstrong
In an entertaining final home game, McCall nets early after an Osman cross. Wark scores with a close-range header and later has an easy job as Sherwood fails to hold O'Callaghan's shot. The Hornets finish second in the table, but boss Graham Taylor agrees they are second best today.

42 A EVERTON 14/5 — D 1-1 (0-0)
Mariner 53 | Wark 80 (og) | Ref: G Courtney
Ipswich: Cooper, Burley, Gernon, Putney, Osman, Butcher, Wark, McCall, Mariner, O'Callaghan, Turner
Everton: Southall, Stevens, Bailey, Ratcliffe, Higgins, Richardson*, Ainscow, Johnson, Sharp, Heath, Irvine, Sheedy
There is no end-of-season atmosphere to this lively contest. Town look on course for victory after Southall gets a hand to Mariner's effort but can't keep it out. Cooper pulls off a fine diving save from Sharp's penalty, but two minutes later Irvine's corner flies past him off Wark's head.

Home 19,676
Away 18,783
Average 18,783

LEAGUE DIVISION 1 (CUP-TIES)　　Manager: Bobby Ferguson　　SEASON 1982-83

Milk Cup

	Att	F-A	H-T	1	2	3	4	5	6	7	8	9	10	11	12 sub used	Scorers, Times, and Referees
2:1 H LIVERPOOL 5/10	16 19,329 1	L 1:2	0:1	Sivell *Grobbelaar*	Burley *Neal*	Gernon *Kennedy*	Mills *Thompson*	Osman *Whelan*	Butcher *Hansen*	Wark *Dalglish*	McCall *Lee*	D'Avray *Rush*	Brazil *Lawrenson*	O'Callaghan *Souness*	O'Callaghan *Hodgson*	Wark 67 *Rush 18, 64* Ref: B Daniels
2:2 A LIVERPOOL 26/10	18 17,698 4	L 0:2	0:2	Sivell *Grobbelaar*	Burley *Neal*	Gernon *Kennedy*	Mills *Thompson*	Osman *Whelan*	Butcher *Hansen*	Wark* *Dalglish* *	McCall *Lee*	D'Avray *Rush*	Brazil *Lawrenson*	Gates *Souness*	O'Callaghan *Hodgson*	*Whelan 7, Lawrenson 43* Ref: A Challinor (Town lose 1-4 on aggregate)

After uncharacteristic hesitation by Butcher, the deadly Ian Rush nips in to shoot home. He grabs a second when Dalglish's header is palmed out by Sivell after Lee's cross, leaving him an easy task. Wark then powers home a glorious header after an Osman cross to give Town hope.

Whelan's sweet volley is followed by Lawrenson hooking a shot over Cooper. Town never look like getting back into the tie and after a depressing evening, the team returns to its hotel to stage a team meeting which apparently features a lot of 'straight talking' about recent form.

FA Cup

	Att	F-A	H-T	1	2	3	4	5	6	7	8	9	10	11	12 sub used	Scorers, Times, and Referees
3 A CHARLTON 8/1	10 16,699 2:19	W 3:2	2:2	Sivell *Jones*	Steggles *Gritt*	Gernon *Aizlewood*	Thijssen *McAllister*	Osman *Eliott*	Butcher *Berry*	Wark *Simonsen*	McCall *Harris*	Mariner *Hales*	Brazil *Bullivant*	Gates *Robinson*		Thijssen 40, Wark 44p, 89 *Robinson 12, Hales 15* Ref: A Robinson
4 H GRIMSBY 29/1	12 21,455 2:8	W 2:0	1:0	Cooper *Batch*	Steggles *Moore D*	Gernon *Crombie*	Thijssen *Waters*	Osman *Cooper*	Butcher *Moore K*	Wark *Ford*	McCall *Whymark* *	Mariner *Drinkell*	Brazil *Bonnyman*	O'Callaghan *Speight*	Wilkinson	Osman 43, McCall 86 Ref: M Heath
5 A NORWICH 19/2	13 28,001 21	L 0:1	0:1	Cooper *Woods*	Putney *Haylock*	Gernon *Hareide*	Thijssen *Mendham*	Osman *Walford*	Butcher *Watson*	Wark *Barham*	McCall* *Van Wyk*	Mariner *Deehan*	Brazil *Bertschin*	O'Callaghan *Downs*	Turner	*Bertschin 6* Ref: R Lewis

Robinson cuts in to net a deflected shot, and then Hales converts after Simonsen's shot is parried by Sivell. Thijssen's text-book volley and a controversial penalty brings Town level. Lennie Lawrence's men can't believe their bad luck as Wark steals victory from a last-minute corner.

The return of Trevor Whymark lasts just two minutes as the big striker is stretched off with serious knee ligament damage. David Booth's side succumb after a 20-yard pile-driver from Osman following a free-kick and a late drive by McCall, who was set up by Mariner's neat pass.

Keith Bertschin strikes early against his former teammates after Butcher rashly dives into a tackle and the striker's shot bobbles agonisingly through Cooper's legs. Brazil hits the crossbar and Butcher has a goalbound effort blocked on the line as Town battle in vain to save the day.

UEFA Cup

	Att	F-A	H-T	1	2	3	4	5	6	7	8	9	10	11	12 sub used	Scorers, Times, and Referees
1:1 A AS ROMA 15/9 (Italy)	21 60,334	L 0:3	0:2	Cooper *Tancredi*	Burley *Nappi*	Mills *Nella*	Thijssen *Vierchowod*	Osman *Falcao*	Butcher *Maldera*	Wark *Valigi*	McCall* *Prohaska*	Mariner *Pruzzo*	Brazil *Di Barth'l'mei Iorio*	O'Callaghan		Osman 9 (og), Pruzzo 34, 68 Ref: M Tokat (Turkey)
1:2 H AS ROMA 29/9	19 17,751	W 3:1	1:0	Sivell *Tancredi 71]*	Burley *Nappi*	Mills	Thijssen *Vierchowod*	Osman *Falcao*	Butcher *Maldera*	Wark *Valigi*	McCall* *Projhaska*	Mariner *Pruzzo*	Brazil *Di Barth'l'mei Conti* *	Gates *Di Barth'l'mei Conti* *	Linford *Chierico*	Gates 41, McCall 54, Maldera 64 [Butcher 71] Ref: V Christov (Czech'vakia) (Town lose 3-4 on aggregate)

Errors by Cooper give Roma a two-goal lead. Mariner gets in front of Vierchowodo to volley in, but the ref blows up for a handling offence. Brazilian Falcao, not fully fit, gives a classy display. Iorio, deputising for Bruno Conti, gives Mills a hard time, working tirelessly on the flank.

Gates nets before the break with a spectacular dipping shot. Town's hopes are boosted further when McCall's drive is deflected into the net by Vierchowod. Maldera then administers the killer blow, heading home when unmarked. Emergency striker Butcher heads in to give late hope.

League Table

		P	Home					Away					Pts
			W	D	L	F	A	W	D	L	F	A	
1	Liverpool	42	16	4	1	55	16	8	6	7	32	21	82
2	Watford	42	16	2	3	49	20	6	3	12	25	37	71
3	Manchester U	42	14	7	0	39	10	6	6	10	17	28	70
4	Tottenham	42	15	4	2	50	15	5	5	11	15	35	69
5	Nott'm Forest	42	12	5	4	34	18	8	4	9	28	32	69
6	Aston Villa	42	17	2	2	47	15	4	3	14	15	35	68
7	Everton	42	13	6	2	43	19	5	4	12	23	29	64
8	West Ham	42	13	3	5	41	23	7	1	13	27	39	64
9	IPSWICH	42	11	3	7	39	23	4	10	7	25	27	58
10	Arsenal	42	11	6	4	36	19	5	4	12	22	37	58
11	West Brom	42	11	5	5	35	20	4	7	10	16	29	57
12	Southampton	42	11	5	5	36	22	4	7	10	18	36	57
13	Stoke	42	13	4	4	34	21	3	5	13	19	43	57
14	Norwich	42	10	6	5	30	18	4	6	11	22	40	54
15	Notts Co	42	12	4	5	37	25	3	3	15	18	46	52
16	Sunderland	42	7	10	4	30	22	5	4	12	18	39	50
17	Birmingham	42	9	7	5	29	24	3	7	11	11	31	50
18	Luton	42	7	7	7	34	33	5	6	10	31	51	49
19	Coventry	42	10	5	6	29	17	3	4	14	19	42	48
20	Manchester C	42	9	5	7	26	23	4	3	14	21	47	47
21	Swansea	42	10	4	7	32	29	0	7	14	19	40	41
22	Brighton	42	8	7	6	25	22	1	6	14	13	46	40
		924	255	111	96	810	454	96	111	255	454	810	1275

Odds & ends

Double wins: (3) Manchester C, Southampton, Sunderland.

Double losses: (2) Newcastle, Tottenham.

Won from behind: (2) Sunderland (a), Charlton (FAC) (a).

Lost from in front: (3) Spurs (h), A.Villa (h), Nott'm F (a).

High spots: A club record 6-0 away win at Notts Co.

The 6-1 hammering of West Brom.

The top-ten finish, after a bad start and loss of key players.

Low spots: The season's bad start (no wins in seven).

The departures of Muhren, Mills, Thijssen and Brazil.

The air of discontent in the squad after Robson's departure.

The lowest average attendances for 15 seasons.

Exits at the first hurdle in the UEFA and Milk Cups.

No penalty-kicks won in 42 League games – a club 'first'.

Failure to beat local rivals Norwich in three attempts.

Player of the Year: Paul Mariner.

Ever-presents: (3) Terry Butcher, Steve McCall, John Wark.

Hat-tricks: (1) John Wark.

Opposing hat-tricks: (0).

Leading scorer: (23) John Wark.

Appearances and Goals

Name	Appearances								Goals					
	Lge	Sub	LC	Sub	FAC	Sub	Eur	Sub	Lge	Sub	LC	FAC	Eur	Tot
Barnes, David	6													
Brazil, Alan	28		2		3		2		10					10
Burley, George	31		2		2		2		1					1
Butcher, Terry	42		2		3		2						1	1
Cooper, Paul	35		1		2		1							
D'Avray, Mich	13	4			1		1		2					2
Gates, Eric	24		1		1				3			1		4
Gernon, Irvin	26		1				2							
Kinsella, Tony	3	1					3							
Linford, John							1							
Mariner, Paul	37		1		3		1		13					13
McCall, Steve	42		2		3		2		4			2		6
Mills, Mick	11		2				2							
O'Callaghan, Kevin	20	8	1	1	2			1		1				
Osman, Russell	38		2		3		2		4			1		5
Parkin, Tommy	4	2					1							
Putney, Trevor	17	3	1				1		3					3
Sivell, Laurie	7		1				1							
Steggles, Kevin	9		2		1		1							
Thijssen, Frans	27	2	1		3		2		3			1		4
Turner, Robin		5						1	1					1
Wark, John	42		2		3		2		20		1		2	23
22 players used	462	25	22	1	33	1	22	2	64	2	1	5	3	73

CANON DIVISION 1

Manager: Bobby Ferguson   **SEASON 1983-84**

Results

No	Date	V	Opponent	Att	Res	Pos	Pt	F–A	H–T	Scorers, Times, and Referees
1	27/8	H	**TOTTENHAM**	26,185	W		3	3-1	1-0	Gates 36, 50, Mariner 89. Archibald 55. Ref: M Scott
2	30/8	A	**WATFORD**	15,388	D		4	2-2	2-2	O'Callaghan 17, Gates 45. Lohman 29, Callaghan 42. Ref: B Stevens
3	3/9	A	**NOTTS CO**	9,023	W	2	7	2-0	0-0	Fashanu 48 (og), Mariner 63. Ref: D Allison
4	6/9	H	**EVERTON**	16,543	W	2	10	3-0	0-0	Mariner 53, Wark 66, Turner 89. Ref: T Ward
5	10/9	H	**STOKE**	16,315	W	2	13	5-0	3-0	Burley 2, Gates 17, Wark 42, 90p, [Mariner 48]. Ref: K Salmon
6	17/9	A	**BIRMINGHAM**	13,159	L	4	13	0-1	0-0	Gayle 62. Ref: A Robinson
7	24/9	H	**WEST BROM**	16,611	L	5	13	3-4	2-2	Wark 40p, Gates 42, Mariner 71. Zondervan 13, Regis 44, Perry 87, [Thompson 90p]. Ref: J Moules
8	1/10	A	**COVENTRY**	10,492	W	3	16	2-1	2-0	Mariner 33, O'Callaghan 35. Gibson 63. Ref: N Glover
9	15/10	H	**QP RANGERS**	17,959	L	6	16	0-2	0-1	Stainrod 29, Gregory 87. Ref: K Barrett
10	22/10	H	**LEICESTER**	14,994	D	5	17	0-0	0-0	Ref: D Letts

Line-ups (Town above; opponents in italic)

No	Team	1	2	3	4	5	6	7	8	9	10	11	12 sub used
1	Town	Cooper	Burley	Gernon	Parkin*	Osman	Butcher	Wark	McCall	Mariner	Gates	Putney	O'Callaghan
1	*Tottenham*	*Clemence*	*Thomas*	*Mabbutt*	*Roberts*	*Stevens*	*Perryman**	*Hazard**	*Archibald*	*Galvin*	*Hoddle*	*Brazil*	*Falco*
2	Town	Cooper	Burley	Gernon	Putney	Osman	Butcher	Wark	McCall*	Mariner	Gates	O'Callaghan	Parkin
2	*Watford*	*Sherwood*	*Rice*	*Rostron*	*Taylor*	*Bolton*	*Franklin*	*Callaghan*	*Barnes*	*Reilly*	*Lohman*	*Sterling*	
3	Town	Cooper	Burley	Gernon	Putney*	Osman	Butcher	Wark	McCall	Mariner	Gates	O'Callaghan	Parkin
3	*Notts Co*	*McDonagh*	*Lahtinen*	*Worthington*	*Goodwin**	*Kilcline*	*Hunt*	*Chiedozie*	*Fashanu*	*McCulloch*	*Harkouk*	*O'Neill*	*Christie*
4	Town	Cooper	Burley	Gernon	Parkin	Osman	Butcher	Wark	McCall	Mariner	Gates*	O'Callaghan	Turner
4	*Everton*	*Arnold*	*Harper*	*Bailey**	*Ratcliffe*	*Higgins*	*Richardson*	*Curran*	*Steven*	*Sharp*	*Johnson*	*Sheedy*	*Reid*
5	Town	Cooper	Burley	Gernon	Parkin*	Osman	Butcher	Wark	McCall	Mariner	Gates	Putney	O'Callaghan
5	*Stoke*	*Fox*	*Chamberl'n N*	*Hampton*	*James*	*Dyson*	*Berry*	*Painter*	*McIlroy**	*Maguire*	*Thomas*	*Ch'mberl'n M*	*O'Callaghan*
6	Town	Cooper	Burley	Gernon*	Parkin	Osman	Butcher	Wark	McCall	Mariner	Gates	Putney	O'Callaghan
6	*Birmingham*	*Coton*	*Mumford*	*V d Hauwe*	*Blake*	*Wright*	*Broadhurst*	*Gayle*	*Phillips*	*Harford*	*Halsall**	*Rees*	*Stevenson*
7	Town	Cooper	Parkin	Gernon	Putney	Osman	Butcher	Wark	McCall	Mariner	Gates	O'Callaghan	
7	*West Brom*	*Barron*	*Whitehead*	*Cowdrill*	*Zondervan*	*McNaught*	*Bennett*	*Lewis*	*Thompson*	*Regis*	*Robson**	*Cross*	*Perry*
8	Town	Cooper	Burley	Gernon	Putney	Osman	Butcher	Wark	McCall	Mariner*	Gates	O'Callaghan	D'Avray
8	*Coventry*	*Avramovic*	*Harm'tsch'k**	*Roberts*	*Grimes*	*Peake*	*Allardyce*	*Withey*	*Daly*	*Platnauer*	*Gibson*	*Bennett*	*Hendrie*
9	Town	Cooper	Burley	Gernon	Putney*	Osman	Butcher	Wark	McCall	Mariner	Gates	O'Callaghan	D'Avray
9	*QPR*	*Hucker*	*Neill**	*Dawes*	*Waddock*	*McDonald*	*Fenwick*	*Micklewhite*	*Stewart*	*Allen*	*Stainrod*	*Gregory*	*Fereday*
10	Town	Cooper	Burley	Gernon	Parkin	Osman	Butcher	Wark	McCall	Mariner	Gates	O'Callaghan*	Turner
10	*Leicester*	*Wallington*	*Williams*	*Wilson*	*MacDonald*	*Hazell*	*Banks*	*Lynex*	*Lineker**	*Eastoe*	*Ramsey*	*Rennie*	*Smith A*

Match reports

1. Mariner's effort is blocked by Clemence, but Gates pounces on the rebound to hammer home. Galvin's bad back-pass allows in Mariner and he squares the ball for Gates to net. Archibald chips the best goal of the day after Hoddle's superb pass. Putney's late cross is drilled in by Mariner.

2. Gates' cross is firmly despatched by O'Callaghan, but Graham Taylor's side level as Lohman capitalises on Butcher's slip. Cooper saves from Barnes but moments later is beaten by Callaghan's drive. On the stroke of half-time Gates goes clear, falls, but recovers to slot past Sherwood.

3. Justin Fashanu unwittingly breaks the deadlock as he rises and heads O'Callaghan's corner into his own net. Larry Lloyd's side is demoralised further when unlucky Fashanu manages to chest down a Gates free-kick straight into the path of Mariner, and he picks his spot from ten yards.

4. Howard Kendall gives debuts to Peter Reid and Terry Curran and his side holds out until Bailey's awful error provides Mariner with a gift goal. A stunning volley by Wark puts Town in the driving seat and then in the final minute Wark's cross is slotted home by substitute Robin Turner.

5. Burley's cross is helped in off a post by Berry. Gates slots home after an unselfish lay-off by O'Callaghan. The winger sends over a corner for Wark to fire home and then crosses for Mariner to rifle in the fourth. Wark converts the penalty after Berry hauls him down in the final minute.

6. A minute's silence is held and black armbands worn following the death of ex-chairman John Cobbold four days earlier. Gernon lets Gayle get free and he lashes in a powerful drive from just inside the box. Cooper, on his 400th outing, had no chance. Late Town pressure is to no avail.

7. Thompson's cross is converted by Zondervan. Mariner is pushed by Bennett, Wark netting from the spot. Gates converts Putney's cross, but Regis levels with a shot on the turn. Mariner's fine shot is cancelled out by Perry's header. Butcher fouls Regis for the dramatic penalty winner.

8. Mariner heads Town ahead, sweet revenge for a wild tackle on him by Allardyce earlier. Hormantschuk slips to allow O'Callaghan to increase the lead shortly afterwards. Withey hits Town's bar then Gibson nets. Bobby Gould's side are stronger after the interval, but Town hold firm.

9. Stainrod rams in Allen's low cross. The points are made safe when Stainrod rounds O'Callaghan and crosses to allow the unmarked Gregory an easy goal. Town look ragged by the end following injuries to Putney and Gates. They paid the penalty for some wasteful finishing earlier on.

10. Town's lowest League crowd for nearly 20 years expresses its anger at missed chances and also at Wark and Mariner who have threatened to leave if not given pay rises. Cooper makes a superb save from Banks' free-kick. In midweek Town draw 2-2 in an exhibition match in Israel.

No.	Venue	Opponent	Date	Pos	Result	Score	Opp Pos	Pts	Attendance
11	A	SOUTHAMPTON	29/10	9	L	2-3	5	17	18,515
12	A	WEST HAM	5/11	13	L	1-2	3	17	20,682
13	H	ARSENAL	12/11	10	W	1-0	13	20	21,652
14	A	NOTT'M FOREST	19/11	12	L	1-2	8	20	14,979
15	H	LIVERPOOL	26/11	12	D	1-1	1	21	23,826
16	A	SUNDERLAND	3/12	13	D	1-1	14	22	15,555
17	H	MANCHESTER U	10/12	13	L	0-2	3	22	19,779
18	A	ASTON VILLA	17/12	14	L	0-4	7	22	16,548
19	H	WOLVERHAMPTON	26/12	13	W	3-1	22	25	14,477
20	A	NORWICH	27/12	14	D	0-0	10	26	25,679
21	H	NOTTS CO	31/12	14	W	1-0	20	29	14,146

11 — A SOUTHAMPTON (29/10)
Scorers: Mariner 18, 28; Williams 58, Holmes 58, Moran 88
Ref: M Robinson
Team (Ipswich): Cooper, Burley, Gernon, Parkin, Osman !, Butcher, Wark, McCall, Mariner, Kinsella, O'Callaghan
Opponents: Shilton, Whitlock, Baker, Williams, Armstrong K Wright*, Holmes, Foyle, Worthington Armstrong D Wallace, Moran, Turner
Report: Town are in charge until Holmes fires home against the run of play. Ten minutes later skipper Osman is unluckily sent off. Booked for fouling Foyle earlier, he is shocked to be red-carded after Williams falls when bursting past him. Moran slots home Wallace's cross for a late winner.

12 — A WEST HAM (5/11)
Scorers: Osman 38; Swindlehurst 25, 40
Ref: T Bune
Opponents: Parkes, Stewart, Walford, Bonds*, Martin, Devonshire, Orr, Cottee, Swindlehurst, Dickens, Pike, Lampard
Report: Stewart's free-kick is powerfully headed in by Swindlehurst. Wark, now officially transfer-listed alongside fellow pay rebel Mariner, has a goal disallowed. Osman steams in to head home the equaliser from O'Callaghan's corner. Swindlehurst heads the winner from a Devonshire centre.

13 — H ARSENAL (12/11)
Scorer: Gates 53
Ref: K Baker
Opponents: Jennings, Robson, Sansom, Whyte, O'Leary, Hill, Sunderland* Davis, Woodcock, Nicholas, Rix, Gorman
Report: Terry Neill's side are aggrieved at not getting a penalty on 29 minutes when Burley launches a lunging challenge on Nicholas, but Mr Baker is not impressed as the Scotsman hits the deck. O'Leary's poorly-hit back-pass falls short and Gates nips in to flick the ball past keeper Jennings.

14 — A NOTT'M FOREST (19/11)
Scorers: Butcher 58; Birtles 70, Swain 71
Ref: A Saunders
Opponents: Sutton, Anderson, Swain, Fairclough, Hart, Bowyer, Wigley, Davenport, Birtles, Thijssen*, Hodge, Walsh
Report: Butcher nets O'Callaghan's cross but the lead disappears as Cooper's mistimed punch allows Davenport to head across goal for Birtles to net. Steggles' challenge on Davenport inside the box is harshly deemed illegal and after Walsh's spot-kick hits a post, Swain follows up and scores.

15 — H LIVERPOOL (26/11)
Scorers: Wark 60; Dalglish 62
Ref: M Bodenham
Opponents: Grobbelaar, Neal, Kennedy, Lawrenson, Nicol, Hansen, Dalglish, Lee, Rush, Whelan, Souness
Report: Town take the lead in an entertaining contest as neat touches by O'Callaghan and Mariner allow Wark to burst through and score. Joe Fagan's side responds quickly with Dalglish's 100th goal for the club. He picks up Lee's short-corner and fires an angled drive high into Cooper's net.

16 — A SUNDERLAND (3/12)
Scorers: Gates 14; Rowell 44
Ref: K Hackett
Opponents: Turner, Venison, Pickering, Atkins, Chisholm, Elliott, Bracewell, Rowell, West, Proctor, James
Report: Ferguson wields the axe and Putney, Brennan and O'Callaghan are missing from the side beaten in the Milk Cup in midweek. Mariner beats Chisholm and squares to Gates, who cleverly beats Turner from 20 yards. James' free-kick goes in off the shoulder of the unmarked Rowell.

17 — H MANCHESTER U (10/12)
Scorers: Graham 11, Crooks 52
Ref: B Hill
Opponents: Bailey, Duxbury, Albiston, Wilkins, Moran, McQueen, Robson, Moses, Stapleton, Crooks, Graham
Report: Cooper misjudges Wilkins' corner and Graham drops to his knees to head home. Stapleton turns Barnes inside out, his cross is poorly dealt with by Steggles and Crooks swoops to score. Only one win in nine League games now and the home fans begin calling for Ferguson's head.

18 — A ASTON VILLA (17/12)
Scorers: Mariner 4 (og), Rideout 56, [McMahon 68, Evans 77pl]
Ref: D Scott
Opponents: Spink, Williams, Deacy, Evans, Ormsby, Mortimer, Curbishley, Rideout, Withe, McMahon, Walters
Report: Cooper cannot get to a cross as his foot is trodden on, and Mariner heads an attempted clearance into his own net. Cooper is left with a broken toe and ligament damage, but bravely continues. The misery is complete as O'Callaghan barges into Walters and Evans converts from the spot.

19 — H WOLVERHAMPTON (26/12)
Scorers: Mariner 10, O'Callaghan 49, McCall 64; Clarke 61p
Ref: D Reeves
Opponents: Burridge, Daniel, Palmer, Blair, Pender, Dodd, Troughton* Clarke, Cartwright, Eves, Crainie, Towner
Report: Town's smallest Boxing Day crowd since 1956 have three fine goals to cheer. Burley feeds Mariner who lashes in a venomous shot. A free-kick is tapped to O'Callaghan who nets from 25 yards. Mariner tees up McCall for another long-ranger. Clarke concedes a penalty by fouling Blair.

20 — A NORWICH (27/12)
Ref: J Hunting
Opponents: Woods, Haylock, Downs, Mendham*, Deehan, Watson, Donowa, Channon, Devine, Bertschin, Van Wyk, Hareide
Report: The 50th East Anglian local derby ends in stalemate, despite Town outplaying the home side for long spells. Ken Brown's men are thankful for a series of fine saves by Woods. A hard-fought game produces 43 free-kicks and Mariner is booked for a hefty challenge on the heroic Woods.

21 — H NOTTS CO (31/12)
Scorer: Mariner 2
Ref: C Downey
Opponents: McDonagh, Goodwin, Worthington Richards, Kilcline, Hunt, O'Neill, Fashanu*, Christie, Harkouk, Chiedozie, Clarke
Report: A win, but little else for the fans to enjoy in a spluttering display by Town. The winner comes early as Mariner heads in O'Callaghan's free-kick. With time ticking away, keeper McDonagh is lectured by police after shouting angrily at a ball-boy who seems slow in returning the ball.

CANON DIVISION 1

Manager: Bobby Ferguson — SEASON 1983-84

No	Date	V	Opponents	Att	Pos	Pt	F-A	H-T	Scorers, Times, and Referees
22	2/1	A	WEST BROM	11,199	14 / 15	L 29	1-2	1-1	Gates 9 / Owen 16, Thompson 56 / Ref: J Lovett
23	14/1	A	TOTTENHAM	25,832	15 / 12	L 29	0-2	0-2	Roberts 41, Falco 45 / Ref: C Thomas
24	21/1	H	BIRMINGHAM	12,900	17 / 19	L 29	1-2	1-1	D'Avray 17 / Harford 19, Butcher 54 (og) / Ref: M Dimblebee
25	4/2	H	COVENTRY	13,406	15 / 8	W 32	3-1	2-0	Mariner 13, Brennan 16, Dozzell 89 / Gibson 71 / Ref: K Salmon
26	11/2	A	STOKE	10,315	15 / 20	L 32	0-1	0-0	Painter 86 / Ref: J Worrell
27	21/2	H	SOUTHAMPTON	14,934	16 / 6	L 32	0-3	0-3	Worthington 10, Moran 33, (Armstrong D 36) / Ref: D Axcell
28	25/2	A	LEICESTER	11,399	17 / 18	L 32	0-2	0-1	Smith A 44, O'Neill 86 / Ref: D Vickers
29	3/3	H	WEST HAM	17,297	19 / 4	L 32	0-3	0-1	Hilton 4, Butcher 49 (og), Cottee 56 / Ref: J Bray
30	10/3	A	ARSENAL	24,000	19 / 8	L 32	1-4	0-1	Gates 62 / Mariner 38, 57, Talbot 52, (Woodcock 61) / Ref: A Robinson
31	13/3	A	LUTON	8,776	19 / 8	L 32	1-2	0-1	Putney 83 / Aylott 39p, 53 / Ref: H Taylor

Line-ups (1–11 and 12 sub used)

No	Team	1	2	3	4	5	6	7	8	9	10	11	12 sub used
22	Ipswich	Sivell	Parkin	Gernon	Putney*	Osman	Butcher	Wark	McCall	Mariner	Gates	O'Callaghan	D'Avray
22	West Brom	Barron	Whitehead	Cowdrill	Zondervan*	McNaught	Bennett	Lewis	Thompson	Regis	Owen	Morley	Cross
23	Ipswich	Sivell	Parks	Gernon	Parkin	Osman	Butcher	Wark	McCall	Mariner	Gates	Putney*	O'Callaghan
23	Tottenham	Parks	Stevens	Bowen	Roberts	Miller	Perryman	Cooke	Archibald	Falco	Hoddle*	Galvin	Crooks
24	Ipswich	Cooper	Burley	Gernon	Parkin	Osman	Butcher	Wark	McCall	Mariner	Gates*	O'Callaghan	Turner
24	Birmingham	Coton	McCarrick	V d Hauwe	Blake	Wright	Broadhurst	Gayle	Kuhl	Harford	Halsall	Hopkins*	Rees
25	Ipswich	Cooper	Burley	McCall	Putney	Osman	Butcher	Wark	Brennan	Mariner	Gates*	Parkin*	Dozzell
25	Coventry	Avramovic	Hom'tsch'k*	Roberts	Grimes	Peake	Allardyce	Withey	Daly	Platnauer	Gibson	Bennett	Hendrie
26	Ipswich	Cooper	Bould?/Burley	Gernon*	Putney*	Osman	Butcher	Wark	Brennan	D'Avray	Turner	Ch'berl'n M*	Painter
26	Stoke	Fox	Bould	Hampton	James	Dyson	O'Callaghan	Maskery	McIlroy	Maguire	Hudson	Painter	Painter
27	Ipswich	Cooper	Burley	McCall	Burley/Putney	Osman	Butcher	Wark	Brennan	D'Avray	Armstrong	Sunderland Parkin	Turner
27	Southampton	Shilton	Mills	Dennis	Williams	Agboola	Wright	Holmes	Moran	Worthington	Armstrong	Wallace D Wallace	—
28	Ipswich	Cooper	Smith R?/Burley	McCall	Putney	Osman	Butcher	Wark	Brennan	D'Avray	Sunderland	O'Callaghan	O'Callaghan
28	Leicester	Wallington	Smith R	Wilson	MacDonald	Hazell	O'Neill	Lynex	Lineker	Smith A	Ramsey	Peake	Peake
29	Ipswich	Cooper	Parkin	McCall	Putney	Osman	Butcher	Wark	Brennan*	D'Avray	Sunderland	Gates	Dozzell
29	West Ham	Parkes	Stewart	Lampard	Bonds	Walford	Hilton	Orr	Cottee	Swindlehurst	Brooking	Allen	Dozzell
30	Ipswich	Cooper	Burley	Barnes	Putney	Osman	Butcher	Wark	McCall	Turner	Sunderland	Gates	Gates
30	Arsenal	Jennings	Hill	Sansom	Talbot	O'Leary	Caton	Nicholas	Davis	Mariner	Woodcock	Rix*	Allinson
31	Ipswich	Cooper	Burley	Barnes	Putney	Osman	Butcher	Wark	McCall	Turner*	Sunderland	Gates	Dozzell
31	Luton	Sealey	Stephens	Thomas	Antic	Elliott	Goodyear	Donaghy	Stein	Walsh	Aylott	Bunn	Dozzell

Match notes

22 — Gates produces a lovely chip from 20 yards after O'Callaghan touches a free-kick to him. In appalling weather, defensive hesitancy allows Owen to flick home McNaught's free-kick. The limping Sivell fails to come out for Bennett's long ball and Thompson nips in for the winner.

23 — Sivell fails to get hold of a swirling corner and Roberts steams in to head the ball home. A superb ball by Hoddle reaches Falco, who heads a magnificent goal on the stroke of half-time. Peter Shreeve's men could have had more, but Hoddle and Archibald are foiled by the woodwork.

24 — The lowest League crowd at Portman Road since 1967 sees Town go ahead when Gernon's forceful run allows D'Avray to fire home. Harford heads in unchallenged to bring Ron Saunders' men level. Butcher gets in an uncharacteristic tangle and misjudges a header into his own goal.

25 — The gloom is lifted by goals from two teenagers. Brennan puts Town two up, as the side adapts well after injuries to Gates and Mariner. Local schoolboy Dozzell (16 yrs, 57 days), whose inclusion put several hundred on the gate, fires in to become Division One's youngest ever scorer.

26 — Chamberlain is left visibly upset after a collision results in Gernon breaking his leg. Butcher fails to clear properly and Painter bends home a great shot to boost Bill Asprey's lowly side. Pay rebel Mariner joins Arsenal and Town travel to beat Malta 2-1 in a midweek exhibition match.

27 — Alan Sunderland arrives on loan, but this is Town's most depressing display in years. The defence is all at sea and it's a tragic way for popular Sivell to make his farewell appearance. Worthington's chip opens the scoring, unmarked Moran heads in, and Armstrong nets a diving header.

28 — City boss Gordon Milne sympathetically says he thinks Town will survive the drop, but another defeat increases the concern at Portman Road. Lineker looks offside as he crosses for Smith to slot home. MacDonald is given acres of space to find O'Neill, who clinches it with a header.

29 — Brooking chips a free-kick into the danger area and Hilton heads home. Brooking's centre deflects off Cottee and then off Butcher into Town's net for a crazy own-goal that virtually kills Town off straight after the interval. Cottee bursts past the unfortunate Butcher to chip over Cooper.

30 — Old boys Mariner and Talbot rub salt into Town's current wounds. Talbot's free-kick is headed in by Mariner. Rix's cross is smartly converted by Talbot and then Mariner produces a superb header from Sansom's cross. Woodcock taps in after Mariner beats two men and tees him up.

31 — Bunn is fouled by Osman and Aylott slots home the penalty. On a snow-covered pitch, Aylott chips in a brilliant second and Town heads drop. Putney's simple tap-in comes too late. Bad weather keeps the crowd low and David Pleat's side are relieved with their second win in 12 games.

No		Date	Opponent	Pos	Result	Pts	Attendance	Scorers	Score	HT	Referee
32	A	17/3	EVERTON	20	L	14	32	18,013	Mountfield 5	0-1	0-1	Ref: A Seville
33	H	24/3	WATFORD	20	D	7	33	14,956	—	0-0	0-0	Ref: M James
34	H	31/3	LUTON	20	W	11	36	14,570	Gates 48, Putney 62, D'Avray 75	3-0	3-0	Ref: R Lewis
35	A	7/4	QP RANGERS	20	L	4	36	12,251	Allen 55	0-1	0-0	Ref: J Deakin
36	H	14/4	NOTT'M FOREST	20	D	3	37	15,429	Zondervan 78, D'Avray 87 / Wigley 1, Davenport 81	2-2	0-1	Ref: A Gunn
37	A	21/4	WOLVERHAMPTON	20	W	22	40	6,611	D'Avray 30, Osman 39, Sunderland 88	3-0	2-0	Ref: R Guy
38	H	23/4	NORWICH	19	W	12	43	22,135	Zondervan 27, Sunderland 74	2-0	1-0	Ref: A Challinor
39	A	28/4	LIVERPOOL	19	D	1	44	32,069	Gates 19, 57 / Kennedy 31, Rush 37	2-2	1-2	Ref: T Mills
40	H	5/5	SUNDERLAND	16	W	15	47	17,657	Osman 35	1-0	0-0	Ref: T Ward
41	A	7/5	MANCHESTER U	15	W	2	50	44,257	D'Avray 47, Sunderland 86 / Hughes 25	2-1	0-1	Ref: G Tyson
42	H	12/5	ASTON VILLA	12	W	9	53	20,043	Gates 23, D'Avray 75 / Withe 28	2-1	1-1	Ref: M Bodenham

Home 17,464   Away 17,368   Average

Line-ups (Town player / opponent in italics)

32 Everton: Cooper / *Southall*, Yallop / *Stevens*, Barnes / *Harper*, Putney* / *Ratcliffe*, Osman / *Mountfield*, Butcher / *Reid*, Wark / *Irvine*, McCall / *Heath*, D'Avray / *Sharp*, Sunderland / *Gray**, Brennan / *Richardson*, Dozzell / *Steven*

Everton, much changed since the earlier meeting with Town, go ahead when Derek Mountfield converts a Gary Stevens free-kick. Brennan hits a post and the ball runs along the line to strike the other upright! Unlucky Sunderland continues to miss the chances that come his way.

33 Watford: Cooper / *Sherwood Bardsley*, Yallop / *Rostron*, Barnes / *Taylor*, Zondervan / *Terry*, Osman / *Sinnott*, Butcher / *Callaghan*, Putney / *Johnston*, McCall / *Gilligan*, Gates / *Jackett*, Sunderland / *Barnes*, Brennan

Pay rebel Wark leaves for Liverpool after creating a club record of 162 consecutive games at Everton. Zondervan replaces him and the run of defeats ends. A week or two earlier Watford played in four games featuring 27 goals, and this bore is their first goalless match of the season.

34 Luton: Cooper / *Sealey*, Burley / *Stephens*, McCall / *Thomas*, Zondervan* / *Horton*, Osman / *Antic*, Butcher / *Goodyear*, Putney / *Donaghy*, Brennan / *Stein*, D'Avray / *Walsh*, Sunderland / *Moss**, Gates / *Bunn*, Barnes / *Breacker*

Only the second win since New Year's Day comes courtesy of much second-half pressure. Gates' penalty is pushed out by Sealey, but he pounces to net the rebound. Luton, with Tim Breacker making his debut, fade badly and Zondervan stamps some authority on the midfield.

35 QP Rangers: Cooper / *Hucker*, Burley / *Neill*, Barnes / *Dawes*, McCall / *Waddock*, Osman / *Wicks*, Cranson / *Fenwick*, Putney / *Micklewhite*, Brennan* / *Fillery*, D'Avray / *Allen*, Sunderland / *Stainrod*, Gates / *Fereday*, Kinsella

On the Loftus Road plastic, stand-in skipper Gates fluffs two chances. D'Avray appears to be fouled by Fenwick, but no penalty is given. Rangers, with an outside chance of the title, net via Allen's close-range chance. Their manager Terry Venables is being sought by Barcelona.

36 Nott'm Forest: Cooper / *V Br'kelen Anderson*, Burley* / *Swain*, Barnes / *Walker*, Zondervan / *Hart*, Osman / *Bowyer*, Butcher / *Wigley*, Putney / *Davenport*, Brennan / *Mills*, D'Avray / *Walsh*, McCall / *Hodge*, Gates, Turner

Wigley nets after just 49 seconds with a powerful shot off the bar. Zondervan levels with a clinical low shot, but Davenport converts a cross by Wigley to restore the lead for Brian Clough's men. Town refuse to give up and D'Avray heads over Van Breukelen after Brennan's error.

37 Wolverhampton: Cooper / *Burridge*, Putney / *Buckland*, Barnes / *Palmer**, Zondervan / *Bayly*, Osman / *Rodger*, Cranson / *Dodd*, Sunderland / *Hibbitt*, Brennan / *McGarvey*, D'Avray / *Livingstone*, McCall / *Towner*, Gates / *Crainie*, Rudge

Things are desperate at Molineux where the lowest gate for 47 years sees Town crush Graham Hawkins' hapless side. Gates' pass is fired in by D'Avray, who earlier hit the bar. Osman swoops to head in a corner and Sunderland's close-range header seals the first away win in 15.

38 Norwich: Cooper / *Woods*, Putney / *Haylock*, Barnes / *Downs*, Zondervan / *Van Wyk**, Osman / *Hareide*, Cranson / *Watson*, Sunderland / *Devine*, Brennan / *Bertschin*, D'Avray / *Deehan*, McCall / *Rosario*, Gates / *Donowa*, Clayton

In a lively derby match, Town show the spirit needed to avoid the drop. Zondervan fires in after McCall's cross and Sunderland nets after Osman sweeps in a cross. Gates misses his second penalty since taking over from Wark, Woods saving superbly after Deehan had handled.

39 Liverpool: Cooper / *Grobbelaar Neal*, McCall / *Kennedy*, Zondervan / *Lawrenson**, Putney / *Whelan*, Osman / *Hansen*, Cranson / *Dalglish*, Sunderland / *Lee*, Brennan / *Rush*, D'Avray / *Wark*, Gates / *Souness*, Nicol

Brennan rolls a free-kick to Gates who nets a low shot. Rush gives Joe Fagan's side the lead as Wark dummies over Lee's cross. Joy for Town as Gates fires in a brilliant shot from D'Avray's pass.

40 Sunderland: Cooper / *Turner*, Yallop / *Venison*, McCall / *Pickering*, Zondervan / *Atkins*, Osman / *Hindmarch*, Cranson / *Elliott*, Putney / *Bracewell*, Brennan / *Robson*, D'Avray / *West*, Sunderland / *Chisholm**, Gates / *James*, Proctor

The home fans respond to the recent recovery by enthusiastically roaring Town to another victory. Osman powers home the winning goal with his head from Brennan's free-kick. Len Ashurst's side is beaten by a team of boys who are doing men's jobs, says a delighted Ferguson.

41 Manchester U: Cooper / *Bailey*, Yallop / *Duxbury*, McCall / *Albiston*, Zondervan* / *Wilkins*, Osman / *Moran*, Cranson / *McGrath*, Putney / *Robson*, Brennan / *Moses*, D'Avray / *Stapleton*, Sunderland / *Hughes*, Gates / *Graham*, Parkin

Survival is assured and Ron Atkinson's men have title hopes wrecked from Sunderland's cross. Wilkins' cross is headed in by Hughes, but D'Avray responds with a magnificent header from Sunderland's cross. The two combine again for Sunderland to bundle home a winner.

42 Aston Villa: Cooper / *Day*, Yallop / *Williams*, McCall / *Deacy*, Parkin / *Ormsby*, Osman / *Foster*, Cranson / *Mortimer*, Putney / *Blair*, Brennan / *Birch*, D'Avray / *Withe*, Sunderland / *Walters**, Gates / *McMahon*, Dorigo

Gates pokes the ball under Day's dive, but Villa quickly level after Withe dispossesses McCall. Tony Barton's last game as Villa comes as D'Avray heads in Parkin's cross. The final whistle sparks a pitch invasion by the joyful fans. Tony Dorigo's League debut — ends in defeat as D'Avray heads in Parkin's cross.

CANON DIVISION 1 (CUP-TIES)

Manager: Bobby Ferguson — SEASON 1983-84

Milk Cup

2:1 H BLACKBURN 3 W 4-3 H-T 0-2 — Att 11,478 2:15 — 5/10
Scorers, Times: Mariner 46, Wark 58p, 78, 81; *Garner 21, 40, Miller 66* — Ref: D Vickers

1	2	3	4	5	6	7	8	9	10	11	12 sub used
Cooper	Burley	Gernon*	Putney	Osman	Butcher	Wark	McCall	Mariner	Gates	O'Callaghan*	D'Avray
Gennoe	*Branagan*	*Hamilton*	*Randell*	*Keeley*	*Fazackerley*	*Miller*	*Lowey*	*Thompson*	*Garner*	*Brotherston*	

Bobby Saxton's men go two up as Thompson twice sets up the lively Garner. Mariner nets after Hamilton's bad back-pass, and Wark levels after his own cross is handled. Miller bundles the ball in, but Wark completes his sixth Town hat-trick with two well-taken efforts near the end.

2:2 A BLACKBURN 5 W 2-1 H-T 2-1 — Att 8,990 2:9 — 26/10
Scorers, Times: Hamilton 21 (og), Wark 32; *Garner 41* — Ref: R Bridges (Town win 6-4 on aggregate)

1	2	3	4	5	6	7	8	9	10	11	12 sub used
Cooper	Burley	Gernon	Parkin	Osman	Butcher	Wark	McCall	Mariner	Kinsella	O'Callaghan	D'Avray
Gennoe	*Branagan*	*Hamilton*	*Randell*	*Keeley**	*Fazackerley*	*Lowey*	*Thompson*	*Garner*	*Brotherston*	*Mail*	

Under pressure from Wark, Hamilton crashes Mariner's cross past Gennoe and into his own net. Wark nets with a majestic shot after Mariner headed the ball down to him. Garner makes the most of uncharacteristically lax play by Osman to bring Rovers back into it before the interval.

3 H QP RANGERS 13 W 3-2 H-T 1-1 — Att 12,343 6 — 9/11
Scorers, Times: Wark 36p, 90, Mariner 77; *Stewart 33, Gregory 89* — Ref: J Martin

1	2	3	4	5	6	7	8	9	10	11	12 sub used
Cooper	Burley	Gernon*	Putney	Osman	Butcher	Wark	McCall	Mariner	Gates	O'Callaghan	Brennan
Hucker	*Dawes*	*Neill*	*Waddock*	*McDonald*	*Fenwick*	*Micklewhite*	*Stewart*	*Allen**	*Stainrod*	*Gregory*	*Fillery*

Gernon 's badly gashed shin gives Brennan his debut. Stewart scores with a fine rising drive, but Town level from the spot when McDonald fouls Gates. Mariner tucks in Wark's pass, but Gregory levels from Stewart's cross. In the dying seconds Wark shoots in while looking offside.

4 H NORWICH 12 L 0-1 H-T 0-0 — Att 25,570 11 — 30/11
Scorers, Times: *Channon 54* — Ref: M Taylor

1	2	3	4	5	6	7	8	9	10	11	12 sub used
Cooper	Woods	McCall	Putney	Steggles	Butcher	Wark	Brennan*	Mariner	Gates	O'Callaghan	D'Avray
Woods	*Haylock*	*Downs*	*Mendham*	*Deehan*	*Watson*	*Donowa*	*Channon*	*Van Wyk*	*Bertschin*	*Barham*	

Two days after his 35th birthday, veteran Mick Channon scores a simple winner as Donowa heads back Barham's cross to him. Bertschin hits the post for Ken Brown's side. Town are very disappointing and lack sparkle. 'Our worst display of the season so far', says angry Ferguson.

FA Cup

3 A CARDIFF 14 W 3-0 H-T 1-0 — Att 10,188 2:15 — 7/1
Scorers, Times: Gates 37, 48, 67 — Ref: A Ward

1	2	3	4	5	6	7	8	9	10	11	12 sub used
Sivell	Burley	Gernon	Parkin	Osman	Butcher	Wark	McCall	Mariner	Gates	O'Callaghan*	D'Avray
Dibble	*Elsey*	*Bodin*	*Dwyer*	*Bennett*	*Tong*	*Owen*	*Gibbins*	*Evans*	*Vaughan*	*Burke*	

Owen hits the bar for Len Ashurst's team, but generally Town are well on top. Gates turns and fires home from a pass by Gernon. His second is a tremendous shot from 25 yards that goes in off the post. His first hat-trick since 1979 is completed when he slides in to net a McCall cross.

4 A SHREWSBURY 17 L 0-2 H-T 0-0 — Att 11,110 2:10 — 28/1
Scorers, Times: *Hackett 71, Robinson 88* — Ref: N Ashley

1	2	3	4	5	6	7	8	9	10	11	12 sub used
Cooper	Burley	McCall	Parkin	Osman	Butcher	Wark	Kinsella*	D'Avray	Gates	O'Callaghan	Gernon
Ogrizovic	*Williams*	*Cross*	*MacLaren*	*Pearson*	*Griffin*	*McNally*	*Petts*	*Stevens*	*Brown**	*Hackett*	*Robinson*

Red-faced Town fail to win at Gay Meadow for a third time in four years. Hackett nips inside Burley to fire a tremendous goal. It's all over as Robinson hooks McNally's cross over Cooper. Chairman Patrick Cobbold's verdict: 'When it's time to panic, that's the time you mustn't panic!'

League Table

	P	W	D	L	F	A	W	D	L	F	A	Pts
			Home						**Away**			
1 Liverpool	42	14	5	2	50	12	8	9	4	23	20	80
2 Southampton	42	15	4	2	44	17	7	7	7	22	21	77
3 Nott'm Forest	42	14	4	3	47	17	8	4	9	29	28	74
4 Manchester U	42	14	4	3	43	18	6	11	4	28	23	74
5 QP Rangers	42	14	4	3	37	12	8	3	10	30	25	73
6 Arsenal	42	10	5	6	41	29	8	4	9	33	31	63
7 Everton	42	9	9	3	41	21	7	5	9	23	30	62
8 Tottenham	42	11	4	6	31	24	6	6	9	33	41	61
9 West Ham	42	10	4	7	39	24	7	5	9	21	31	60
10 Aston Villa	42	14	3	4	34	22	3	6	12	25	39	60
11 Watford	42	9	7	5	36	31	6	2	13	32	46	57
12 IPSWICH	42	11	4	6	34	23	8	4	9	21	34	53
13 Sunderland	42	8	9	4	26	18	5	5	11	16	35	52
14 Norwich	42	9	8	4	34	20	3	7	11	14	29	51
15 Leicester	42	11	5	5	40	30	2	7	12	25	38	51
16 Luton	42	7	5	9	30	30	4	10	7	23	33	51
17 West Brom	42	10	4	7	30	25	4	5	12	18	37	51
18 Stoke	42	11	4	6	30	23	2	7	12	14	40	50
19 Coventry	42	8	5	8	33	33	5	6	10	24	44	50
20 Birmingham	42	7	7	7	19	18	5	5	11	20	32	48
21 Notts Co	42	6	7	8	31	36	4	4	13	19	36	41
22 Wolves	42	4	8	9	15	28	2	3	16	12	52	29
	924	226	118	118	745	505	118	118	226	505	745	1268

Appearances & Goals

			Appearances					Goals		
	Lge	Sub	LC	Sub	FAC	Sub	Lge	LC	FAC	Tot
Barnes, David	10	1								
Brennan, Mark	19		1		1		1			1
Burley, George	28		4		2		1			1
Butcher, Terry	34		4		2		1			1
Cooper, Paul	36		4		2					
Cranson, Ian	8									
D'Avray, Mich	17	6		2		1	6			6
Dozzell, Jason		5				1	1			1
Gates, Eric	37		3		2		13		3	16
Gernon, Irvin	19		3		1					
Kinsella, Tony	4	1	1		1					
Mariner, Paul	23		4		1		11	2		13
McCall, Steve	42		4		2		1			1
O'Callaghan, Kevin	23	2	4		2		3			3
Osman, Russell	37		3		2		3			3
Parkin, Tommy	18	3	1		2					
Putney, Trevor	32	3	3	1			2			2
Sivell, Laurie	6									
Steggles, Kevin	5		1							
Sunderland, Alan	15						3			3
Turner, Robin	3	7					1			1
Wark, John	32		4		2		5	6		11
Yallop, Frank	6						1	1		2
Zondervan, Romeo	8						2			2
(own-goals)							2			2
24 players used	462	28	44	3	22	2	55	9	3	67

Odds & ends

Double wins: (3) Coventry, Notts Co, Wolves.

Double losses: (5) Birmingham, QP Rangers, Southampton, West Brom, West Ham.

Won from behind: (3) Blackburn (LC) (a), Manchester U (a), QP Rangers (LC) (h).

Lost from in front: (5) Birmingham (h), Nott'm Forest (a). Southampton (a), West Brom (a), West Brom (h).

High spots: The late-season rally that prevented relegation. The superb win at Old Trafford in May. The excellent five-match start to the season. The battling displays of Trevor Putney. The spectacular debut of schoolboy Jason Dozzell.

Low spots: The mid-season run of 10 defeats and a draw. The exit of Paul Mariner and John Wark after a pay dispute. The death of Mr John Cobbold. The substantial drop in attendance figures. The FA Cup fourth round defeat at Shrewsbury Town.

Player of the Year: Trevor Putney.

Ever-presents: (1) Steve McCall.

Hat-tricks: (2) Wark (Blackburn, LC), Gates (Cardiff, FAC).

Opposing hat-tricks: (0).

Leading scorer: (16) Eric Gates.

CANON DIVISION 1

Manager: Bobby Ferguson

No	Date	Att	Pos	Pt	F-A	H-T	Scorers, Times, and Referees	1	2	3	4	5	6	7	8	9	10	11	12 sub used
1	A WEST HAM 25/8	19,032		1	0-0	0-0	D — Ref: H Taylor	Cooper	Burley	McCall	Zondervan	Osman	Butcher	Putney	Brennan	D'Avray	Sunderland*	Gates	O'Callaghan
								McAlister	Stewart	Walford	Allen	Martin	Gale	Whitton*	Cottee	Gaddard	Dickens	Pike	Hilton
2	H LUTON 28/8	15,331		2	1-1	1-0	D — Gates 2; Moss 80; Ref: M Bodenham	Cooper	Burley	McCall	Zondervan	Osman	Butcher	Putney	Brennan	D'Avray	O'Callaghan	Gates	
								Dibble	Thomas	Grimes	Breacker	North	Donaghy	Hill	Stein	Elliott S	Bunn*	Moss	Nwajiobi
3	H MANCHESTER U 1/9	20,434	15	3	1-1	0-1	D — Sunderland 73; Hughes 33; Ref: A Buksh	Grew	Burley	McCall	Zondervan	Osman	Butcher	Putney	Brennan	D'Avray	O'Callaghan*	Gates	Sunderland
								Bailey	Duxbury	Albiston	Moses	Moran	Hogg	Robson	Strachan	Hughes	Brazil*	Olsen	Whiteside
4	A EVERTON 4/9	22,314	14	4	1-1	0-0	D — Gates 64; Heath 72; Ref: D Hutchinson	Grew	Burley	McCall	Zondervan	Osman	Butcher	Putney	Brennan	D'Avray	Sunderland	Gates	O'Callaghan
								Southall	Stevens	Bailey	Ratcliffe	Mountfield	Reid	Steven	Heath	Sharp	Bracewell	Richardson*	Curran
5	A LEICESTER 8/9	10,737	15	4	1-2	0-0	L — Gates 73; Lineker 49, Lynex 90; Ref: J Lovatt	Grew	Burley	McCall	Zondervan	Osman	Butcher	Putney	Brennan	D'Avray	Sunderland*	Gates	O'Callaghan
								Wallington	Smith R	Wilson	McDonald	Hazell	O'Neill	Lynex	Lineker	Smith A*	Ramsey	Peake	Bright
6	H ARSENAL 15/9	**24,508**	4	7	2-1	2-0	W — Osman 14, Zondervan 29; Nicholas 58; Ref: J Bray	Grew	Burley	Butcher	Zondervan	Osman	Cranson*	Putney	McCall	D'Avray	O'Callaghan*	Gates	Brennan
								Jennings	Anderson	Sansom	Talbot	O'Leary	Caton		Rix	Mariner	Woodcock	Nicholas	
7	A SHEFFIELD WED 22/9	25,558	5	8	2-2	1-0	D — Gates 41, 81; Marwood 76, Chapman 78; Ref: N Ashley	Grew	Burley	McCall	Zondervan	Osman	Butcher	Putney	Brennan	D'Avray	O'Callaghan	Gates	
								Hodge	Sterland	Shirtliff	Smith*	Lyons	Worthington	Marwood	Blair	Varadi	Chapman	Heard	Pearson
8	A ASTON VILLA 29/9	15,630	13	11	3-0	1-0	W — Sunderland 11, Osman 58, Gates 80; Ref: D Letts	Cooper	Burley	McCall	Zondervan	Osman	Butcher	Putney*	Brennan	Sunderland	O'Callaghan	Gates	D'Avray
								Day	Williams	Gibson !	Evans	Ormsby	Mortimer	Birch	Rideout	Withe !	Cowans	Walters*	Kerr
9	A NEWCASTLE 6/10	25,094	7	11	0-3	0-2	L — Burley 1 (og), Waddle 36, Heard 50; Ref: N Midgley	Cooper	Burley	Butcher	Zondervan	Osman	Cranson*	Putney	McCall	Sunderland	O'Callaghan	Gates	D'Avray
								Carr	Brown	Saunders	Heard	Anderson	Roeder	McDonald	Wharton	Waddle	Beardsley	McCreery	
10	H QP RANGERS 13/10	15,733	14	12	1-1	1-0	D — Gates 41p; Gregory 74; Ref: J Ashworth	Cooper	Burley	Butcher	Zondervan	Osman	Cranson*	Putney	McCall	Sunderland	O'Callaghan	Gates	D'Avray
								Hucker	Neill	Dawes	Fereday	McDonald	Fenwick	Micklewhite	Fillery	Bannister	Stainrod	Gregory	

Match reports

1. A satisfactory opening, although the hard work and skilful approach play could have yielded a goal or two with a bit more poise in attack. John Lyall's side give a debut to summer purchase Tony Gale. Town have no new faces, although Sunderland has now signed on a permanent basis.

2. After Gates' early breakthrough, Dibble produces a string of excellent saves to keep Town at bay. Luton's woodwork is also struck and later David Pleat's side punish Town for failing to get that killer second goal. North's throw finds Moss, who cuts in and fires in a clever equaliser.

3. Hughes guides a header past Grew. Ex-Town hero Brazil is jeered by home fans and battered by the defence and doesn't reappear after the break. Ferguson's gamble on a Sunderland ankle problem pays off handsomely when the striker nets a scorching header from Putney's centre.

4. Grew makes two excellent early saves from Sharp. Town take the lead with a superbly executed goal by Gates from a fast breakaway raid. Sub Curran sets up Heath for the equaliser. Everton are livid near the end when a clear handball inside the area by Osman is missed by the referee.

5. After exchanging passes with Alan Smith, Gary Lineker holds off Burley's challenge to score. Gates produces a typical cracking drive to level matters. In the final minute, Lineker shields the ball well before slipping it to Lynex, who wins all three points for Gordon Milne's outfit.

6. On his 350th appearance, Osman chests down a Gates corner and pokes the ball home. From another flag-kick, Zondervan extends the lead with a neat header. A Rix free-kick which appears to be going wide is parried by Grew and falls for Nicholas, who fires home from an angle.

7. O'Callaghan touches aside a free-kick and Gates rockets home a magnificent shot. Town are hit by a double blast as Marwood dives to head in Varadi's pass and then Chapman outpaces Osman to scoop a shot past Grew. Town re-group well and Gates sweeps in a cross by Zondervan.

8. Sunderland converts the rebound after Gates hits a post. Rideout gesticulates at a linesman and after discussions Mr Letts sends off Withe in a clear case of mistaken identity. Gibson follows for two bookable offences. Osman heads in a corner and Gates nets after McCall's through ball.

9. A hopeful punt forward by McDonald after just 20 seconds is scooped disastrously past his own keeper by Burley. Waddle looks offside as he runs clear to add a second. Town's misery is complete when Jack Charlton's new signing Heard fires his first goal from Wharton's pass.

10. Gregory's handball gives Gates the opportunity to score from the spot. He gets another go on 58 minutes, but this time Hucker makes a great save. Rangers boss Alan Mullery says players should never take a second penalty in one game. Gregory fires home a fierce drive after a corner

#	V	Date	Opponent	Pos	W/L/D	OppPos	Pts	Attendance	FT	HT
11	H	20/10	WEST BROM	10	W	15	15	14,154	2-0	1-0
12	A	27/10	CHELSEA	12	L	11	15	19,213	0-2	0-0
13	H	3/11	WATFORD	15	D	21	16	15,680	3-3	1-2
14	A	10/11	COVENTRY	16	L	17	16	8,790	0-1	0-0
15	H	17/11	TOTTENHAM	17	L	4	16	21,894	0-3	0-0
16	A	24/11	LIVERPOOL	18	L	8	16	34,918	0-2	0-1
17	H	1/12	SOUTHAMPTON	20	L	5	16	14,113	0-1	0-0
18	A	8/12	STOKE	19	W	24	19	7,925	2-0	0-0
19	H	15/12	SUNDERLAND	20	L	13	19	12,493	0-2	0-0
20	A	22/12	MANCHESTER U	20	L	2	19	35,168	0-3	0-1
21	A	26/12	NOTT'M FOREST	21	L	7	19	17,123	0-2	0-2

11. H WEST BROM 20/10
Cooper, Burley, Butcher, Zondervan, Osman, Cranson, Putney*, McCall, D'Avray, Sunderland, Gates, O'Callaghan
Godden, Whitehead, Statham, Hunt, Bennett, Robertson, Grealish, Thompson, Cross, McKenzie, Valentine*, Robson
Sunderland 6, Gates 53 — Ref: A Gunn
In a game affected by swirling winds, Sunderland gives Town a great start by steering a neat shot past Godden. Gates rifles a low free-kick into the corner to finish off Johnny Giles' team. Town winger O'Callaghan, unhappy at being in and out of the team, has a transfer request granted.

12. A CHELSEA 27/10
Cooper, Burley, Butcher, Zondervan, Osman*, Cranson, Putney, McCall, D'Avray, Sunderland, Gates, O'Callaghan
Niedzwiecki, Wood, Rougvie, Pates, McLaughlin, Bumstead, Nevin, Spackman*, Dixon, Speedie, Canoville, Jones K
Dixon 60, 83 — Ref: R Milford
Newly-promoted Chelsea kill off Town in the second half when Canoville crosses and Dixon has room to head in a comfortable goal. Deadly Dixon gets goalside of Cranson and races clear to slip a shot past the exposed Cooper. Full-back Wood makes his debut for John Neal's outfit.

13. H WATFORD 3/11
Cooper, Bardsley, Butcher, Brennan, Osman, Cranson, O'Callaghan, McCall, D'Avray, Sunderland, Gates
Coton, Bardsley, Jackett, Taylor, Terry, Sinnott, Callaghan, Blissett, Reilly, Rostron, Barnes
D'Avray 13, Butcher 64, Brennan 75; Blissett 3, 19, Barnes 88 — Ref: J Moules
Blissett holds off Burley to fire home. D'Avray levels with a diving header from O'Callaghan's cross. Blissett regains the lead, firing in from ten yards. Butcher nets after a corner and Brennan puts Town ahead with a fine 25-yard drive. Barnes levels with a stunning dipping free-kick.

14. A COVENTRY 10/11
Cooper, Burley, McCall, Zondervan, Osman, Cranson, O'Callaghan, Brennan, Putney*, Sunderland, Gates, Dozzell
Ogrizovic, Stephens, Adams, Hibbitt, Butterworth, Peake, Bennett, Gynn, Latchford, Gibson, Jol
Adams 72 — Ref: R Guy
Bobby Gould's team bounce back from a 2-6 hammering at Chelsea with a gritty performance. Watched by their lowest crowd of the season, City are missing the fire-power of Regis and Barnes. Lacklustre Town are sunk when defender Adams gets forward to rifle in a fierce drive.

15. H TOTTENHAM 17/11
Cooper, Burley, McCall, Zondervan, Osman, Butcher, O'Callaghan*, Brennan, D'Avray, Sunderland, Gates, Cranson
Clemence, Stevens, Mabbutt, Roberts, Miller, Perryman, Chiedozie, Falco, Allen, Hoddle, Hazard
Mabbutt 68, Hoddle 76, Allen 88 — Ref: G Napthine
Sunderland hits the bar, then Town go behind when O'Callaghan's casual backheel falls for Chiedozie, who sets up Mabbutt. Hoddle nets with a wonderful curling shot from distance. Town's miserable day is capped when Allen breaks clear near the end and drives the ball past Cooper.

16. A LIVERPOOL 24/11
Cooper, Burley, McCall, Zondervan, Osman, Butcher, Putney, Brennan, D'Avray, Sunderland*, Gates, Parkin
Grobbelaar, Neal, Kennedy, Lawrenson, Nicol, Hansen, Dalglish, Molby, Rush*, Johnston, Wark, Whelan
Wark 41, 53 — Ref: J Hough
Ipswich's 27th visit to Anfield and still not a single victory recorded! Inevitably ex-Town star Wark does the damage. Brennan's error allows Wark to regain possession and shoot home before the interval. The crucial second comes as Dalglish chips into the box and Wark heads home.

17. H SOUTHAMPTON 1/12
Cooper, Burley, McCall, Zondervan*, Osman, Butcher, Putney, Brennan, D'Avray, Sunderland, Gates, O'Callaghan
Shilton, Mills, Dennis, Moran, Whitlock, Bond, Holmes, Curtis, Jordan, Armstrong, Wallace*, Puckett
Armstrong 46 — Ref: M Scott
A largely uneventful contest is decided when Armstrong strides forward and bends in a tremendous shot from outside the box. It happens so soon after the break that many are still not back in their seats.

18. A STOKE 8/12
Cooper, Burley, McCall, Zondervan, Osman, Butcher, Putney, Brennan, D'Avray, Sunderland*, Gates, Cole
Roberts, Bould, Spearing, Maskery, Dyson, Berry, Painter, McIlroy, Heath, Bertschin*, Chamberlain, Saunders
Putney 80, D'Avray 83 — Ref: D Allison
Transfer speculation surrounds Stoke. Town leave it late to inflict a tenth successive defeat on Bill Asprey's struggling Stoke. Putney's powerful effort flies into the roof of the net from 25 yards to end the stalemate. McCall's shot is deflected by D'Avray over unlucky 17-year-old Stuart Roberts, making his debut in goal.

19. H SUNDERLAND 15/12
Cooper, Burley, McCall, Zondervan, Osman, Butcher, Putney, Brennan, D'Avray, Sunderland*, Gates, Dozzell
Turner, Venison, Pickering, Berry, Bennett, Elliott, Chisholm, Gayle, West, Proctor, Walker
Bennett 65, Walker 87 — Ref: E Scales
After another home defeat, Ferguson pleads for patience and says he doesn't have the big money to spend on a striker. Decent approach play again fails to produce goals. A corner is nodded on by Berry and Bennett is there to finish. Defeat is assured when Walker adds a late second.

20. A MANCHESTER U 22/12
Cooper, Yallop, McCall, Zondervan, Osman, Butcher, Putney, Brennan, D'Avray, Sunderland*, Gates, Cole
Bailey, Gidman, Albiston, Moses, McQueen, Duxbury, Robson, Strachan, Hughes, Stapleton, Olsen
Strachan 31p, Robson 63, Gidman 87 — Ref: A Seville
Town create many chances, particularly in an early spell, but fail to take any of them. A strong penalty appeal is turned down and Putney and Gates both hit a post. After Olsen falls over Cooper, Strachan nets the penalty. Robson powers home a crisp shot and Gidman slides in a third.

21. A NOTT'M FOREST 26/12
Cooper, Yallop, Butcher, Zondervan, Osman, Cranson, Putney*, Brennan, D'Avray, Sunderland*, McCall, Gates, Cole
Segers, McInally, Swain, Fairclough, Hart, Bowyer, Wigley, Metgod, Clough, Davenport, Hodge
Hodge 53, Metgod 55 — Ref: T Holbrook
Brian Clough gives teenage son Nigel his debut, but new signing Hans Segers steals the show with some great saves to frustrate Town. Hodge puts Forest ahead with a close-range header and Metgod doubles the lead shortly afterwards with a shot that squeezes under the diving Cooper.

CANON DIVISION 1 — Manager: Bobby Ferguson — SEASON 1984-85

Results

No	Venue	Opponents	Date	Att	Opp Pos	Pos	Res	Pt	F-A	H-T	Scorers, Times, and Referees
22	H	EVERTON	29/12	16,045	2	21	L	19	0-2	0-0	Sharp 60, 86 — Ref: D Vickers
23	H	NORWICH	1/1	21,710	11	20	W	22	2-0	1-0	Gates 3, Dozzell 65 — Ref: T Bune
24	A	ASTON VILLA	2/2	15,051	12	21	L	22	1-2	0-1	Osman 87 / Cowans 38, Gibson 80 — Ref: R Gifford
25	H	CHELSEA	2/3	17,735	9	20	W	25	2-0	1-0	Wilson 39, Cranson 83 — Ref: J Key
26	A	QP RANGERS	16/3	9,518	14	21	L	25	0-3	0-2	Fereday 12, 13, Bannister 57 — Ref: K Barrett
27	A	ARSENAL	19/3	18,365	6	21	D	26	1-1	0-0	Dozzell 60 / Meade 72 — Ref: L Burden
28	H	NEWCASTLE	23/3	14,366	15	20	D	27	1-1	0-0	Gates 80 / McDonald 55 — Ref: T Ward
29	A	LUTON	30/3	12,640	20	21	L	27	1-3	1-2	Gates 18 / Harford 30, 66, Nwajiobi 43 — Ref: D Letts
30	A	WEST BROM	3/4	8,112	12	21	W	30	2-1	2-0	Wilson 12, D'Avray 16 / Hunt 77 — Ref: R Groves
31	H	NOTT'M FOREST	6/4	16,296	8	20	W	33	1-0	1-0	Sunderland 31 — Ref: A Buksh

Ipswich Town line-ups

No	1	2	3	4	5	6	7	8	9	10	11	12 sub used
22	Cooper	Yallop	Butcher	Zondervan	Osman	Cranson	O'Callaghan	Brennan*	Dozzell	McCall	Gates	Parkin
23	Cooper	Yallop	Butcher	Zondervan	Osman	Cranson	Putney	Brennan	Dozzell	McCall	Gates	Gordon
24	Cooper	Burley	Butcher	Zondervan	Osman	Putney	McCall	Brennan	Wilson	Dozzell	D'Avray*	Parkin
25	Cooper	Burley	McCall	Zondervan	Cranson	Butcher	Putney	Brennan	D'Avray*	Wilson	Gates	Sunderland
26	Grew	Yallop	Butcher	Zondervan	Osman*	Cranson	Parkin	McCall	Sunderland	Wilson	Gates	Dozzell
27	Cooper	Burley	Gernon	Zondervan	Osman	Butcher	Brennan	McCall	Dozzell	Wilson*	Gates	Parkin
28	Cooper	Burley	Gernon	Zondervan	Osman	Butcher	Putney	Brennan	Dozzell	Wilson*	Gates	D'Avray
29	Cooper	Burley	Gernon	Zondervan	Osman	Butcher	Putney*	Brennan	D'Avray	Wilson	Gates	Dozzell
30	Cooper	Burley	Cranson	Zondervan	Osman	Butcher	McCall	Brennan	Wilson	D'Avray	Gates	Dozzell
31	Cooper	Burley	Gernon	Zondervan	Osman*	Butcher	McCall	Brennan	D'Avray	Wilson	Gates	Sunderland

Opponents' line-ups

No	1	2	3	4	5	6	7	8	9	10	11	12 sub used
22	Southall	V d Hauwe	Bailey	Ratcliffe	Mountfield	Reid	Steven	Curran	Sharp	Bracewell	Sheedy	
23	Woods	Haylock	Downs	Bruce	Mendham	Watson	Devine	Channon	Deehan	Farrington*	Donowa	
24	Day	Williams	Gibson	Evans	Ormsby	Mortimer	Birch	Rideout	Withe	Cowans	Walters*	Kerr
25	Niedzwiecki	Jones J*	Rougvie	Bumstead	Jasper	Thomas	Nevin	Spackman	Dixon	Speedie	Canoville	Dublin
26	Hucker	Chivers	Dawes	Waddock	Wicks	Fenwick	Robinson*	Fillery	Bannister	Fereday	Gregory	Byrne
27	Lukic	Anderson	Sansom	Williams	Adams	Caton	Robson	Davis*	Mariner	Meade	Nicholas	Talbot
28	Thomas	Brown	Anderson	McCreery	Clarke	Roeder	McDonald	Cunningham	Reilly*	Beardsley	Heard	Waddle
29	Sealey	Breacker	Thomas	Nicholas	Foster	Donaghy	Hill	Stein	Harford	Nwajiobi	Preece	Daniel
30	Godden	Whitehead	Statham	Hunt	Forsyth	Robertson	Owen	Thompson	Robson	Cross*	Valentine	Grealish
31	Segers	McInally	Swain	Fairclough	Hart	Bowyer	Wigley	Metgod	Birtles*	Davenport	Hodge	Mills

Match reports

22 — Everton: Town's plight gets worse as the year ends and goals continue to be a rarity. 'This was our most disappointing display of the season,' says an upset Ferguson afterwards. Sharp scores on the hour, heading in Sheedy's cross, then turns Yallop and fires out of Cooper's reach near the end.

23 — Norwich: Delight for home fans after 558 minutes without a home League goal. Gates swoops after being set up by Butcher and Dozzell. The points are safe midway through the second half when Putney's cross is nodded by Zondervan to Dozzell and the youngster fires in a neat shot on the turn.

24 — Aston Villa: Gibson's shot rebounds off Cooper and Cowans pounces to score. Unlucky Town have two penalty appeals turned down and Wilson hits the woodwork. Cowans chips to Gibson, who fires past Cooper. Osman gives Town late hope with a powerful header from Brennan's corner-kick.

25 — Chelsea: Unpredictable Jasper underhits a back-pass to Niedzwiecki and Wilson shows an astonishing turn of speed to nip in between them and convert the opportunity. Gates floats over a corner-kick and Butcher heads across to Cranson who finishes it off for the first senior goal of his career.

26 — QP Rangers: Cranson miskicks and Fereday pounces to loop a shot past Grew. Seconds later another defensive calamity sees Osman robbed by Dawes and he finds Fereday, whose shot goes in off a post. Subdued Town are finished off when the unmarked Bannister cuts in to fire a shot past Grew.

27 — Arsenal: McCall clears off the line from Anderson before Town take a surprise lead through Dozzell. He swaps passes with Gates to shoot home a very well taken goal. Don Howe's men draw level when a Sansom free-kick reaches Caton, who knocks it down for Meade to fire in from 12 yards.

28 — Newcastle: McDonald's long-range shot skims past the diving Cooper to give Jack Charlton's men the lead. Town leave it late to equalise and Gates, born in nearby Ferryhill, is delighted to be the man responsible. He lobs home a clever goal after Burley's cross is only partially-cleared by Roeder.

29 — Luton: Gates whips in a fine 20-yarder and several other early chances come and go. Once level, fellow relegation-battlers Luton dominate the match and the in-form Harford gives Town a torrid time with his aerial power. Skilful Nwajiobi squeezes home and Town never look like recovering.

30 — West Brom: Wilson's speed and anticipation sees him seize onto Robertson's back-pass to give Town a real early tonic. D'Avray increases the lead when he flicks home Wilson's low cross. Brennan hits the bar, but the home side launch a late revival when Forsyth's cross is headed home by Hunt.

31 — Nott'm Forest: One of the best displays of the season revives hopes of achieving safety. Sunderland's all-important goal is a diving header as he meets Gates' corner to send the ball beyond Segers. Zondervan has a fine match, prompting from midfield, while Gates is unlucky not to win a penalty-kick.

#	Venue	Date	Opponent	Attendance	Pos	W/L/D	Score	Pts
32	A	8/4	NORWICH	18,227	18	W	2-0	11	36
33	H	13/4	SHEFFIELD WED	16,268	20	L	1-2	5	36
34	A	16/4	WATFORD	16,074	20	L	1-3	13	36
35	A	20/4	TOTTENHAM	20,348	20	W	3-2	4	39
36	H	23/4	LEICESTER	13,666	17	W	2-0	18	42
37	H	27/4	LIVERPOOL	24,484	19	D	0-0	4	43
38	A	4/5	SOUTHAMPTON	16,156	19	L	0-3	5	43
39	H	6/5	STOKE	14,150	17	W	5-1	22	46
40	A	11/5	SUNDERLAND	9,389	17	W	2-1	21	49
41	H	14/5	COVENTRY	14,038	18	D	0-0	20	50
42	H	17/5	WEST HAM	19,326	17	L	0-1	14	50

Home 17,050 Away 17,607 Average 17,607

---

32 — NORWICH (A) 8/4 — 2-0
Butcher 5, D'Avray 47
Ref: C Downey
Town: Cooper, Burley, Gernon, Zondervan, Sunderland, Butcher, McCall, Brennan, D'Avray, Wilson, Gates
Norwich: Woods, Haylock, Van Wyk, Bruce, Devine, Watson, Barham, Channon, Deehan, Hartford!, Donowa

In a physical encounter, Hartford is sent off after a foul on Brennan, beginning a slow slide towards relegation, are sunk as D'Avray shows neat control to convert a McCall free-kick. Ken Brown's men, after six bookings. Butcher roars in to power home Gates' lofted free-kick.

33 — SHEFFIELD WED (H) 13/4 — 1-2
D'Avray 55; Marwood 20p, Cooper 69 (og)
Ref: R Lewis
Town: Cooper, Burley, McCall*, Zondervan, Gernon, Butcher, Sunderland, Brennan, D'Avray, Wilson, Gates
Sheffield Wed: Hodge, Shirtliff, Morris, Smith, Lyons, Worthington, Marwood*, Blair, Varadi, Chapman, Shelton, Stainrod

Marwood is brought down by Gernon and gets up to convert the penalty. Town level against the run of play as D'Avray heads home a corner. Howard Wilkinson's men get a lucky winner as Gernon clears off the line only to see the ball cannon off Zondervan and Cooper into the net.

34 — WATFORD (A) 16/4 — 1-3
Sunderland 62; West 17, Rostron 54, Barnes 90
Ref: E Read
Town: Cooper, Burley, Steggles, Zondervan, Butcher, Gernon, Sunderland, Brennan, D'Avray, Wilson*, Gates
Watford: Coton, Gibbs, Rostron, Taylor, Terry, McClelland, Callaghan, Blissett, West, Jackett, Barnes

Graham Taylor's side dump Town back in the mire. West opens the scoring after a defensive mix-up and Rostron gets forward to net a diving header. Sunderland reduces the deficit with an opportunist effort after a slick move. A typical Watford long-ball move sees Barnes blast home.

35 — TOTTENHAM (A) 20/4 — 3-2
Sunderland 5, Brennan 76, Gates 89p; Leworthy 64, 90
Ref: K Cooper
Town: Cooper, Burley, Gernon, Zondervan, Steggles, Butcher, Sunderland, Brennan, D'Avray, Parkin, Gates
Tottenham: Clemence, Thomas, Bowen, Roberts, Miller*, Perryman, Ardiles, Falco, Leworthy, Hoddle, Galvin, Chiedozie

Sunderland's fierce left-footer gives Town a perfect start. Leworthy, a new recruit from non-League, levels but Brennan regains the lead, some fine skills preceding his ten-yard shot. Gates sends Clemence the wrong way from the spot after Perryman fouls Zondervan to clinch the win.

36 — LEICESTER (H) 23/4 — 2-0
Sunderland 4, D'Avray 39
Ref: N Butler
Town: Cooper, Burley, Gernon, Zondervan, Steggles, Butcher, Sunderland, Brennan, D'Avray, Parkin, Gates
Leicester: Andrews, Feeley, Wilson, Smith R, Williams, O'Neill, Lynex, Lineker, Smith A, Peake*, Banks, Ramsey

Brennan's free-kick finds its way to Sunderland, who fires past Andrews. The win gives Town a great chance of escaping the drop, but the gate is disappointingly low. A late effort by Sunderland skims the bar.

37 — LIVERPOOL (H) 27/4 — 0-0
Ref: B Hill
Town: Cooper, Burley, Gernon, Zondervan, Steggles, Butcher, Sunderland, Brennan, D'Avray, Parkin, Gates*
Liverpool: Grobbelaar, Neal, Beglin, Lawrenson, Nicol, Hansen, Dalglish, Whelan, Walsh, Gillespie, Wilson, Wark

High winds and a rock-hard pitch spoil the contest. The conditions don't suit key men Gates and Wilson, who have gone off the boil recently. Cooper is kept busy but a draw is a fair outcome. Town are denied two penalties, one when Parkin is blatantly hauled down by Gary Gillespie.

38 — SOUTHAMPTON (A) 4/5 — 0-3
Moran 54, 61, 77p
Ref: D Brazier
Town: Cooper, Burley, Gernon, Zondervan, Steggles*, Butcher, Brennan, Sunderland, D'Avray, Parkin, Gates
Southampton: Shilton, Mills, Townsend, Case, Wright, Bond, Holmes, Moran, Jordan, Armstrong, Lawrence, Wilson

Shilton is rarely troubled and Moran's second-half trio flattens Town. Steggles goes off with concussion after being barged off the pitch and into the crowd by Jordan. Moran nets after Jordan hits the woodwork, then a cross-shot sails over Cooper. Butcher fouls Jordan for the penalty.

39 — STOKE (H) 6/5 — 5-1
Wilson 12, 26, 52, Putney 40, Bertschin 68 [Gates 76]
Ref: D Reeves
Town: Cooper, Burley, Gernon, Zondervan*, Steggles, Butcher, Putney, Brennan, D'Avray, Wilson, Gates
Stoke: Siddall, Bould, Maskery, Dodd, Dyson, Berry, Callaghan*, McIlroy, Bertschin, Saunders, Heath, Hemming

Stoke's awful season continues and their goals-against tally goes into the 80s. Wilson races through alone for the first and nets two from Gates set-pieces. Putney fires in Siddall's near post and Gates converts Wilson's cross. Ex-Town man Bertschin's consolation goes in off Cooper.

40 — SUNDERLAND (A) 11/5 — 2-1
Wilson 17, 88; Wallace 17
Ref: D Richardson
Town: Cooper, Burley, Gernon*, Zondervan, Cranson, Butcher, Putney, Brennan, D'Avray, Wilson, Gates*
Sunderland: Turner, Cornforth, Pickering, Bennett*, Armstrong, Berry, Cooke, Wallace, Hodgson, Lemon, Atkinson, Elliott

Wilson accelerates, leaving Bennett for dead and fires past Turner. Len Ashurst, in his last game as manager, sees his side level when Wallace lobs over Cooper after being set up by Hodgson. After a series of brilliant saves by Turner, Wilson beats him with a shot in off the woodwork.

41 — COVENTRY (H) 14/5 — 0-0
Ref: M Bodenham
Town: Cooper, Burley, Yallop, Zondervan, Cranson, Butcher, Parkin, Brennan, Dozzell, Wilson, Gates
Coventry: Ogrizovic, Butterworth, Pearce, Hibbitt*, Kilcline, Peake, Bennett, Gynn, Regis, Gibson, Adams, McGrath

With safety now assured Town can relax, but there's no such luxury for new City boss Don Mackay whose side are still in peril. Kilcline hits the bar as rain lashes down. Cooper makes fine saves from Pearce and Bennett. The Sky Blues must now win their last three games to survive.

42 — WEST HAM (H) 17/5 — 0-1
Cottee 10
Ref: V Callow
Town: Cooper, Burley, Yallop, Zondervan, Osman, Steggles*, Putney, Brennan, Dozzell, Wilson, Gates
West Ham: Parkes, Stewart, Brush, Walford, Martin, Hilton, Barnes, Bonds, Goddard, Cottee, Pike, Parkin

Depleted Town have nothing to play for and there's little to entertain an above-average crowd after Cottee beats Osman in the air to score early on. John Lyall's men celebrate a win that clinches their own safety from the drop. Pioneer announce an end to the four-year sponsorship deal.

CANON DIVISION 1 (CUP-TIES) — SEASON 1984-85

Manager: Bobby Ferguson

Milk Cup

Rnd		Opponent	Date	Att		Res	F-A	H-T	Scorers, Times, and Referees
2:1	H	DERBY	25/9	10,809 3:12		W	4-2	4-1	Gates 9, Osman 11, Sunderland 36, Putney 38 / Wilson 23, 87 / Ref: C Downey
2:2	A	DERBY	10/10	14,374 3:14		D	1-1	1-0	D'Avray 34 / Buckley 55p / Ref: D Shaw / (Town win 5-3 on aggregate)
3	H	NEWCASTLE	30/10	15,084		D	1-1	0-1	Gates 58 / McDonald 20 / Ref: B Hill
3R	A	NEWCASTLE	7/11	22,982		W	2-1	1-1	D'Avray 11, Gates 70 / Waddle 41 / Ref: K Hackett
4	H	OXFORD	20/11	18,879		W	2-1	1-1	D'Avray 28, Zondervan 66 / Brock 31 / Ref: D Axcell
5	H	QP RANGERS	23/1	16,143		D	0-0	0-0	Ref: J Bray
5R	A	QP RANGERS	28/1	14,563		W	2-1	2-1	D'Avray 26, Zondervan 31 / Bannister 39 / Ref: J Worrall
SF 1	H	NORWICH	23/2	27,404		W	1-0	1-0	D'Avray 6 / Ref: D Hutchinson
SF 2	A	NORWICH	6/3	23,545		L	0-2	0-1	Deehan 35, Bruce 87 / Ref: G Courtney / (Town lose 1-2 on aggregate)

Line-ups (Town in roman, opponents in italic)

	1	2	3	4	5	6	7	8	9	10	11	12 sub used
2:1	Cooper	Burley	McCall	Zondervan	Osman	Butcher	Putney	Brennan	Sunderland	O'Callaghan	Gates	
	Burridge	*Palmer*	*Buckley*	*Powell*	*Streete*	*Burns*	*Taylor*	*Wilson*	*Davison*	*Hooks*	*Robertson*	
2:2	Cooper	Burley	Butcher	Zondervan	Osman	Cranson	Putney	McCall	Sunderland	D'Avray	Gates	O'Callaghan
	Burridge	*Palmer*	*Buckley*	*Powell*	*Streete*	*Burns*	*Taylor*	*Wilson*	*Davison*	*Hooks*	*Robertson*	
3	Cooper	Burley	McCall	Zondervan*	Osman	Butcher	Putney	Brennan	Sunderland	D'Avray	Gates	O'Callaghan
	Carr	*Brown*	*Saunders*	*Carney*	*Anderson*	*Roeder*	*McDonald*	*Wharton*	*Waddle*	*Beardsley*	*McCreery*	
3R	Cooper	Burley*	McCall	Putney	Cranson	Butcher	O'Callaghan	Brennan	Sunderland	D'Avray	Gates	Parkin
	Carr	*Brown*	*Saunders*	*Carney**	*Anderson*	*Hedworth*	*McDonald*	*Wharton*	*Waddle*	*Beardsley*	*McCreery*	*Ferris*
4	Cooper	Burley	McCall	Zondervan	Osman	Butcher	Putney	Brennan	Sunderland	D'Avray	Gates	
	Hardwick	*Langan*	*McDonald*	*Trewick*	*Briggs*	*Shotton*	*R'des-Br'wn**	*Aldridge*	*Hamilton*	*Hebberd*	*Brock*	*Phillips*
5	Cooper	Burley	Butcher	Zondervan	Osman	Cranson	Putney	Brennan	Dozzell	McCall	Gates	
	Hucker	*Neill*	*Dawes*	*Waddock*	*Chivers*	*Fenwick*	*Wicks*	*Fillery*	*Bannister*	*Stainrod*	*Micklewhite*	
5R	Cooper	Burley	Butcher	Zondervan	Osman!	Cranson	Putney	Brennan	Dozzell	McCall	D'Avray*	Gates
	Hucker	*Micklewhite*	*Dawes*	*Waddock*	*Chivers*	*Fenwick*	*Wicks*	*Fillery**	*Bannister*	*Stainrod!*	*Gregory*	*Fereday*
SF 1	Cooper	Burley	McCall	Zondervan	Osman	Butcher	Putney	Brennan	Sunderland	D'Avray	Gates	
	Woods	*Devine*	*Van Wyk*	*Bruce*	*Mendham*	*Watson*	*Barham*	*Channon*	*Deehan*	*Hartford*	*Clayton*	
SF 2	Cooper	Burley	McCall	Zondervan	Osman	Butcher	Putney	Brennan	Sunderland	D'Avray*	Gates	
	Woods	*Haylock*	*Van Wyk*	*Bruce*	*Mendham*	*Watson*	*Barham*	*Channon*	*Deehan*	*Hartford*	*Donowa*	*Sunderland*

Match notes

2:1 — Gates' rasping drive is followed by a free-kick being touched aside for Osman to hammer in. Butcher's clearance goes in off Wilson at the other end. Sunderland lobs Burridge and then Putney hammers home after a free-kick routine. Wilson bursts clear near the end to shoot home.

2:2 — Cooper makes a series of excellent early saves as Derby set off at a lively pace. Putney's cross is smashed home by D'Avray to extend Town's aggregate lead. Arthur Cox's men draw level when Cranson pulls back Wilson and the penalty is smashed home powerfully by full-back Buckley.

3 — Beardsley squares for McDonald from 20 yards. McCall's fine cross is headed out by Brown, but goes straight to Gates who flashes home a marvellous half-volley past a stunned Carr. Jack Charlton's men work hard to keep the home side at bay and earn a replay.

3R — Town get off to a great start as Burley's free-kick finds D'Avray and he fires home. Carney's effort is blocked by Cooper, but Waddle is on hand to knock in the equaliser. With the Geordies striving for a winner, Sunderland engineers a breakaway raid expertly finished by Gates.

4 — Sunderland heads the ball across to partner D'Avray, who heads past Hardwick. The lead is quickly cancelled out by Brock, who thunders home a spectacular goal. On a slippery surface, the tie is won by Zondervan who keeps his feet and finishes smartly after an impressive move.

5 — Five cup-ties are cancelled in the bad weather, but frosty Portman Road is deemed playable. Town dominate this quarter-final tie but Alan Mullery's men fight an impressive rearguard action and keep them at bay. With several regulars missing, Rangers are pleased to force a replay.

5R — All the game's major incidents occur during a 15-minute spell. Stainrod and Osman are sent off after exchanging blows. Moments later D'Avray nets a header from Brennan's free-kick. Zondervan half-volleys in from a corner. Cooper fumbles a cross and Bannister gets one back.

SF 1 — Town take a step towards their first League Cup final with an early goal in this highly-charged affair. Van Wyk is pulled up for a foul, Burley floats the free-kick to unmarked D'Avray, who heads in. City are relieved to escape as a Zondervan shot is ruled not to have crossed the line.

SF 2 — Brave and battered Town tackle their third big game in five days on a night of high emotion and tension. Deehan levels on aggregate when his shot cannons in off Cranson's knee. Sunderland rolls a great chance wide. Bruce heads a glorious winner near the end to break Town hearts.

FA Cup

Rnd		Opponent	Date	Att		Res	F-A	H-T	Scorers, Times, and Referees
3	A	BRISTOL ROV	5/1	12,123 3:5		W	2-1	1-0	Dozzell 31, Brennan 89 / Holloway 52 / Ref: L Shapter

	1	2	3	4	5	6	7	8	9	10	11	12 sub used
3	Cooper	Yallop	Williams B	Zondervan	Osman	Cranson	Putney	Brennan	Dozzell	McCall	Gates	
	Cashley	*Williams G*	*Williams D*	*Bater*	*Parkin*	*McCaffery*	*Holloway*	*Williams D*	*Randall*	*Stephens*	*O'Connor*	

3 — Dozzell fires home a left-foot shot from Putney's cross to put Town ahead. Holloway volleys in a fine equaliser for David Williams' side. With a replay looking likely, Brennan pops up in the dying minutes with a 35-yarder which hits the bar and then Cashley before ending up in the net.

4 — H GILLINGHAM

4	H GILLINGHAM	18	W	3:3	3-2	1-0
26/1	16,547					

Wilson 42, Sage 52 (og), Dozzell 74
Leslie 56, Sage 63
Ref: H Taylor

Cooper · Butcher · Zondervan · Cranson · Osman · McCall · Brennan · Wilson · Dozzell · D'Avray
Hillyard · Hinnigan · Oakes · Shaw · Musker · Cochrane · Shinners* · Robinson · Leslie · Weatherly · Sharpe

Wilson heads in a corner on his debut. Cranson lofts the ball forward and Sage, under pressure from Wilson, heads into his own net. Leslie nets Weatherly's cross and then Sage scores from Musker's long ball to delight 4,000 away fans. Shaw fails to clear and Dozzell fires in the winner.

5 — H SHEFFIELD WED

5	H SHEFFIELD WED	20	W	4	3-2	0-1
4/3	17,459					

Zondervan 49, Burley 70, S'land 88
Varadi 24, Lyons 88
Ref: K Baker

Cooper · Butcher · Zondervan · Cranson · Osman · McCall · Burley · Wilson · D'Avray · Gates · Sunderland
Hodge · Sterland · Madden · Worthington · Marwood · Smith · Lyons · Varadi · Pearson · Shelton · Shirtliff

Zondervan levels after Varadi's first-half shock, but Lyons responds quickly with a glorious header to restore the lead. A scintillating move ends with Burley slotting an equaliser. Wednesday players remonstrate angrily after Sunderland shoots home with D'Avray looking offside.

QF — A EVERTON

QF	A EVERTON	20	D	1	2-2	2-1
9/3	36,468					

Wilson 15, Zondervan 32
Sheedy 4, Mountfield 85
Ref: A Robinson

Cooper · Butcher · Zondervan · Cranson · Osman · McCall · Burley · Wilson · Dozzell · Brennan† · Gates
Southall · Stevens · V d Hauwe · Ratcliffe · Mountfield · Reid · Steven · Curran · Bracewell · Sheedy

Cooper handles outside the box and Sheedy bends in a free-kick, repeating the trick when a re-take is ordered. After a great recovery, Unlucky Town are stunned as McCall is sent off for a challenge on Steven. Ex-Everton manager Harry Catterick collapses and dies at the final whistle.

QF R — H EVERTON

QF R	H EVERTON	20	L	1	0-1	0-0
13/3	27,737					

Sharp 76p
Ref: A Robinson

Grew · Yallop · Zondervan · Cranson · Butcher · McCall · Burley · Sunderland · Wilson · Gates · Osman
Southall · Stevens · V d Hauwe · Ratcliffe · Mountfield · Reid · Steven · Gray · Bracewell · Sharp

In a pulsating quarter-final replay, McCall's long-range effort hits the post and Steven fires against the underside of Town's bar. Sharp breaks the deadlock from the penalty spot after his own cross hits unlucky Osman on the arm. Howard Kendall's side are now unbeaten in 13 games.

Odds & ends

Double wins: (3) Norwich, Stoke, West Brom.
Double losses: (1) Southampton.
Won from behind: (1) Sheffield Wed (FAC) (h).
Lost from in front: (1) Luton (a).
High spots: Long runs in both cup competitions.
An improvement in late-season form to avoid the drop.
A series of magnificent goals by Eric Gates.
An outstanding display on the QP Rangers 'plastic' in January.
Low spots: Long spells in the division's bottom three.
The last-gasp defeat in an epic Milk Cup semi-final.
The controversial exit from the FA Cup quarter-finals.
Another substantial drop in average attendances.
McCall's record run of games ended by an unlucky red card.
Player of the Year: Terry Butcher.
Ever-presents: (0).
Hat-tricks: (1) Kevin Wilson.
Opposing hat-tricks: (1) Steve Moran (Southampton).
Leading scorer: (16) Eric Gates.

League table

		P	W	D	L	F	A	W	D	L	F	A	Pts
1	Everton	42	16	3	2	58	17	12	3	6	30	26	90
2	Liverpool	42	12	4	5	36	19	10	7	4	32	20	77
3	Tottenham	42	11	7	3	46	31	11	2	5	32	20	77
4	Manchester U	42	13	6	2	47	13	9	4	8	30	34	76
5	Southampton	42	13	4	4	29	18	6	7	8	27	29	68
6	Chelsea	42	13	3	5	38	20	5	9	7	25	28	66
7	Arsenal	42	14	5	2	37	14	5	4	12	24	35	66
8	Sheffield Wed	42	12	7	2	39	21	5	7	9	19	24	65
9	Nott'm Forest	42	13	4	4	35	18	6	3	12	21	30	64
10	Aston Villa	42	10	7	4	34	20	5	4	12	26	40	56
11	Watford	42	10	5	6	48	30	4	8	9	33	41	55
12	West Brom	42	11	4	6	36	23	5	4	13	22	39	55
13	Luton	42	12	5	4	40	22	3	3	14	17	39	54
14	Newcastle	42	11	4	6	33	26	2	9	10	22	44	52
15	Leicester	42	10	4	7	39	25	5	2	14	26	48	51
16	West Ham	42	7	8	6	27	23	6	4	11	24	45	51
17	IPSWICH	42	8	7	6	27	20	5	4	12	19	37	50
18	Coventry	42	11	3	7	29	22	4	2	15	18	42	50
19	QP Rangers	42	11	6	4	41	30	2	5	14	12	42	50
20	Norwich	42	9	6	6	28	24	4	4	13	20	40	49
21	Sunderland	42	7	6	8	20	26	3	4	14	20	36	40
22	Stoke	42	3	3	15	18	41	0	5	16	6	50	17
		924	237	107	118	785	503	118	107	237	503	785	1279

Appearances / Goals

	Lge	Sub	LC	Sub	FAC	Sub	Lge	LC	FAC	Tot
Brennan, Mark	35	1	8		5		2	1		3
Burley, George	37		9		3			1		1
Butcher, Terry	41		9		5		2			2
Cole, Michael		2								
Cooper, Paul	36		9		4					
Cranson, Ian	19	1	6		5		1			1
D'Avray, Mich	30	3	7	1	2		6	5		11
Dozzell, Jason	9	5	5		2		2		2	4
Gates, Eric	41		8		4		13	3		16
Gernon, Irvin	13									
Grew, Mark	6		1							
McCall, Steve	31		9		5					
O'Callaghan, Kevin	10	5	2	1						
Osman, Russell	29		6		2		3		1	4
Parkin, Tommy	6	5		1						
Putney, Trevor	27		9		4		2		1	3
Steggles, Kevin	6									
Sunderland, Alan	23	3	5	1	2	1	7	1	1	9
Wilson, Kevin	15	2	2		4		7		2	9
Yallop, Frank	7	3			2					
Zondervan, Romeo	41		8		5		1	2	2	5
(own-goals)									1	1
21 players used	462	30	99	4	55	3	46	13	10	69

CANON DIVISION 1

Manager: Bobby Ferguson

SEASON 1985-86

Match summary

No	Date	Opponent	Att	Pos	Pt	Res	F-A	H-T	Scorers, Times, and Referees
1	A 17/8	QP RANGERS	12,755		0	L	0-1	0-0	Byrne 71. Ref: H King
2	H 20/8	MANCHESTER U	18,777		0	L	0-1	0-0	Robson 63. Ref: D Vickers
3	H 24/8	TOTTENHAM	17,758		3	W	1-0	0-0	Zondervan 64. Ref: H Taylor
4	A 26/8	LIVERPOOL	29,383	15 (8)	3	L	0-5	0-3	[Johnston 90/] Nicol 15, Rush 23, 67, Molby 27. Ref: T Holbrook
5	H 31/8	SOUTHAMPTON	11,588	19 (20)	4	D	1-1	1-0	Cranson 17. Armstrong 85p. Ref: J Moules
6	A 7/9	WEST BROM	7,763	16 (22)	7	W	2-1	2-0	Putney 19, Sunderland 30. Crooks 84. Ref: D Allison
7	H 14/9	BIRMINGHAM	11,616	18 (10)	7	L	0-1	0-0	Geddis 74. Ref: E Scales
8	H 21/9	ASTON VILLA	11,598	19 (11)	7	L	0-3	0-2	Walters 13, Hodge 45, Birch 47. Ref: K Miller
9	A 28/9	LEICESTER	7,290	21 (19)	7	L	0-1	0-0	Smith A 70. Ref: R Gifford
10	A 1/10	LUTON	8,533	21 (14)	7	L	0-1	0-0	Nwajiobi 61. Ref: M Cotton

Line-ups

No	Team	1	2	3	4	5	6	7	8	9	10	11	12 sub used
1	Ipswich	Cooper	Yallop	Putney	Zondervan	Cranson	Gernon	Sunderland	Brennan	D'Avray	Wilson*	McCall	Dozzell
1	QP Rangers	Hucker	Chivers	Dawes	Waddock	McDonald	Fenwick	James*	Robinson	Bannister	Fereday	Gregory	Byrne
2	Ipswich	Cooper	Yallop	Putney	Zondervan	McCall*	Gernon	Dozzell	Brennan	Sunderland	Wilson	D'Avray	Putney
2	Manchester U	Bailey	Gidman*	Albiston	Whiteside	McGrath	Hogg	Robson	Strachan	Hughes	Stapleton	Olsen	Duxbury
3	Ipswich	Cooper	Burley	Yallop	Zondervan	Cranson	Gernon	Putney	Brennan	Sunderland	D'Avray	Dozzell	
3	Tottenham	Clemence	Thomas	Hughton	Allen P	Miller	Roberts	Ardiles	Falco	Waddle	Hazard	Galvin*	
4	Ipswich	Cooper	Burley	Yallop	Zondervan	Cranson	Gernon	Parkin*	Brennan	Sunderland	D'Avray	Dozzell	Cole
4	Liverpool	Grobbelaar	Neal*	Kennedy	Lawrenson	Whelan	Hansen	Johnston	Nicol	Rush	Molby	Lee	Walsh
5	Ipswich	Cooper	Burley	Yallop	Zondervan	Cranson	Gernon	Putney	Brennan	D'Avray	Sunderland	Dozzell	
5	Southampton	Shilton	Golac	Dennis	Case	Wright	Bond	Townsend	Puckett	Curtis	Armstrong	Wallace	
6	Ipswich	Cooper	Burley	Yallop	Zondervan	Cranson	Butcher	Putney	Brennan	Sunderland	D'Avray*	Dozzell	Wilson
6	West Brom	Godden	Nicholl	Statham	Robson*	Armstrong	Forsyth	Crooks	Varadi	Grealish	MacKenzie	Anderson	Valentine
7	Ipswich	Cooper	Burley	Yallop	Zondervan	Cranson	Gernon	Putney	Brennan	Sunderland*	D'Avray	Dozzell	Wilson
7	Birmingham	Seaman	Ranson	Jones	Wright	Hagan*	Kuhl	Dicks	Roberts	Kennedy	Geddis	Hopkins	Platnauer
8	Ipswich	Cooper	Burley	Yallop	Zondervan	Cranson	Gernon*	Putney	Brennan	Wilson	Sunderland	Dozzell	Cole
8	Aston Villa	Spink	Williams	Dorigo	Evans	Ormsby	Gibson	Birch	Walters	Gray*	Hodge	Daley	Bradley
9	Ipswich	Cooper	Yallop	Gernon	Zondervan	Cranson	Steggles	Rimmer	Brennan	Wilson*	Sunderland	Dozzell	Atkins
9	Leicester	Andrews	Ramsey	Rennie	McAllister	Williams	O'Neill	Lynex	Sealy*	Bright	Mauchlen	Wilson	Smith A
10	Ipswich	Cooper	Yallop	Gernon	Zondervan	Cranson	Steggles*	Putney	Brennan	Sunderland	Wilson	Atkins	Dozzell
10	Luton	Sealey	Breacker	Thomas	Nicholas	Foster	Donaghy	Hill	Stein B	Harford	Nwajiobi	Preece	

Match reports

1. With Osman now departed and Butcher recovering from knee surgery, Town look fragile at the back. After nine minutes Putney and Gernon collide and both receive nasty head wounds. Half-time sub Byrne receives Fereday's pass and crashes home a powerful drive to win the points.

2. In the closing seconds of the first half a Brennan piledriver hits the foot of Bailey's post. Strachan pulls the ball back and Robson powers his shot home. McCall departs with a suspected broken toe. Twelve minutes from the end a good chances goes to waste as Sunderland heads over.

3. In the opening minutes Clemence dives to save at Burley's feet and sends him tumbling. The keeper is enraged when a penalty is given, but recovers his composure to save Brennan's kick. Cranson earns a throw, takes it himself and from D'Avray's flick, Zondervan drills the ball in.

4. Three neat goals in 12 minutes shatter Town's hopes. Whelan's clever passes set up goals for Rush and Molby in the first half-hour. A slick move ends with Rush grabbing his second. In the final minute the hammering is completed when Johnston dives to head home Hansen's cross.

5. The lowest league crowd at Ipswich for over 21 years is cheered by Cranson's opening goal. He nets with a low drive after Dozzell tees him up from a Brennan flag-kick. Close to the end Putney's fierce tackle on Bond is controversially deemed a penalty and Armstrong levels the scores.

6. Johnny Giles' struggling team are repelled by fine saves from Cooper in the early stages. Putney blasts home and Sunderland doubles the lead with a close-range header. With the home crowd calling for Albion's directors to resign, Crooks grabs a late consolation goal with a fine strike.

7. A depressing afternoon as Town press forward but look less than sharp in attack. Ron Saunders' men haven't won away for several months, but take the lead when Kennedy's header finds Town old boy Geddis and he turns to fire home. A late goal by sub Wilson is disallowed for hands.

8. An emphatic defeat and the small crowd chants for Ferguson to go. Chairman Cobbold responds with the dreaded vote of confidence. Hodge nets the crucial goal after Gernon is caught in possession. A reshuffle at the interval fails to improve things and Birch lashes in a dipping drive.

9. After 500 matches George Burley departs for Sunderland and Ferguson gives debuts to Rimmer and Atkins. A 20-yard piledriver by Yallop is tipped over by Andrews. In the lush Filbert Street turf Cranson's back-pass fails to reach Cooper and Smith nips in to take the ball round him.

10. Putney returns in place of Rimmer and Dozzell is dropped, but Town again struggle to impose themselves. David Pleat's side always look likely winners and Nwajiobi converts Stein's cross. Johnny Giles quits as boss of fellow strugglers West Brom.

11 A NOTT'M FOREST   21 L 1-3 0-3   12,120 15 7
Atkins 47
Pearce 7, Bowyer 12, 27   Ref: T Jones

| Cooper | McCall | Gernon* | Zondervan | Cranson | Dozzell | Putney | Brennan | Sunderland* | Wilson | Atkins | Steggles |
| Sutton | McInally | Pearce | Butterworth | Walker | Bowyer | Metgod | Campbell* | Clough | Davenport | Robertson | Birtles |

A free-kick is touched to Pearce who rockets the ball home. Bowyer makes it two from Davenport's cross after McCall's misdirected header. Town are dead and buried when Bowyer fires home a third. Atkins, Town's liveliest performer, refuses to slacken and fires home a consolation.

---

12 H NEWCASTLE   21 D 2-2   8 8   12,536
Cole 29, Zondervan 39
Beardsley 43, McDonald 54   Ref: N Butler

| Cooper | Yallop | Gernon* | Zondervan | Cranson | Steggles | Atkins | Cole | Brennan | Wilson | Dozzell | Sunderland |
| Thomas | Anderson | Davies | Clarke | Roeder | McDonald | Reilly | Beardsley | Stewart | | | |

Cole nets a fine curling shot and the lead is extended when Zondervan's fierce drive beats Thomas. Willie McFaul's men fight back well and things begin to go their way when Beardsley's shot is deflected past Cooper before the break. A flying header by McDonald wins them a point.

---

13 A ARSENAL   21 L 0-1 0-1   19,522 4 8
Davis 4   Ref: R Milford

| Cooper | Yallop | Zondervan | Cranson | Steggles* | Atkins | Cole | Brennan | Wilson | Dozzell | Gleghorn | |
| Lukic | Anderson | Sansom | Davis | O'Leary | Caton | Whyte | Allinson | Nicholas* | Woodcock | Rix | Rocastle |

Town get off to a bad start when Davis' long-range effort is helped into the net by the flailing Cooper. Fresh from non-league circles, Gleghorn comes on to make an impressive debut. Dozzell gets a chance to level but instead of shooting tries to take the ball round Lukic and is stopped.

---

14 H WEST HAM   21 L 0-1 0-1   16,849 7 8
Cottee 26   Ref: M Scott

| Cooper | Yallop | Zondervan | Cranson | Gleghorn* | Atkins | Cole | Brennan | Wilson | Dozzell | D'Avray | |
| Parkes | Parris | Gale | Martin | Devonshire* | Ward | McAvennie | Dickens | Cottee | Orr | Potts | |

Quicksilver Cottee nips in to head over the advancing Cooper for his tenth goal of the season. A spirited display by Town brings no reward as they go close in a late rally. It's now one point from a possible 12 and the shortage of goals being scored is giving major cause for concern.

---

15 H CHELSEA   21 L 0-2 0-2   15,324 4 8
Dixon 2, Speedie 10   Ref: B Hill

| Cooper | Yallop | Zondervan | Cranson | Putney* | Atkins | Cole | Brennan | Wilson | Dozzell | D'Avray | |
| Niedwiecki | Isaac | Dublin | Pates | McLaughlin | Nevin | Spackman | Dixon | McAllister | Rimmer | | |

Goal-shy Town are given a lesson in cool finishing by Dixon and Speedie. Isaac crosses and Dixon produces a superb volley from 12 yards and minutes later Speedie picks his spot after being fed by Dixon. Two weeks after further knee surgery, Butcher offers to play but is told to wait.

---

16 A MANCHESTER C   21 D 1-1 1-1   20,853 20 9
Gleghorn 14
Lillis 44p   Ref: K Hackett

| Cooper | Yallop | McCall | Gleghorn | Cranson | Steggles* | Atkins | Cole | Brennan | Wilson | D'Avray | Dozzell |
| Nixon | Reid | May | Clements | McCarthy | Phillips | Lillis | Power | McNab | Simpson | | |

Gleghorn heads his first goal in senior football to give Town an early lead. Gordon Davies sprints clear but is stopped in his tracks as Cooper throws himself at his feet to push the ball away. Davies tumbles over the keeper and to Town's dismay a penalty is given, despatched by Lillis.

---

17 H EVERTON   21 L 3-4 2-1   13,910 6 9
D'Avray 6, Wilson 31, Butcher 72
Hth 34, Sharp 49, Sh'dy 58, Stv'n 78p   Ref: D Axcell

| Cooper | Yallop | McCall | Putney | Cranson | Butcher | Atkins | Dozzell | Brennan | Wilson | D'Avray | |
| Southall | V d Hauwe | Ratcliffe | Stevens | Heath | Steven | Lineker | Sharp | Bracewell | Sheedy | | |

Boosted by Butcher's return, Town shock the reigning champions by taking a 2-0 lead through Wilson's curling shot. Headers by Heath and Sharp pull it back. Butcher heads an equaliser after Sheedy's rare right-footed goal. Cooper hauls down Lineker for the penalty-kick winner.

---

18 A OXFORD   21 L 3-4 2-0   9,387 18 9
Wilson 24, Brennan 43p, Dozzell 53
Aldridge 55, 56, 62, Slatter 80   Ref: M Dimblebee

| Hallworth | Yallop | McCall | Putney | Cranson | Butcher | Atkins | Dozzell | Brennan | Wilson | D'Avray* | Gleghorn |
| Hardwick | Langan | Slatter | Trewick | Hebberd | Shotton | Houghton | Aldridge | Thomas | Phillips | Rh'des-Br'wn | |

Town are cruising after Hebberd fouls Wilson and Brennan converts the penalty. Dozzell makes it three, but Town then crumble to Aldridge's stunning hat-trick. Debutant Hallworth is at fault with the third. Slatter's winner means Town lose after being 3-0 ahead for the first time ever??

---

19 H SHEFFIELD WED   21 W 2-1 1-1   12,918 5 12
D'Avray 24, 74
Yallop 16 (og)   Ref: T Ward

| Cooper | Yallop | McCall | Parkin | Cranson | Butcher | Atkins* | Dozzell | Brennan | Wilson | D'Avray | Gleghorn |
| Hodge | Sterland | Madden | Morris | Hart | Marwood | Blair* | Chapman | Thompson | Shelton | Jonsson | |

After 12 goals in three games, Town look more confident in attack but are still conceding bad goals. Yallop slices his second own-goal in five days after a Marwood corner is deflected to him. D'Avray wins the day with a superb header and later a neat shot after two fine Wilson crosses.

---

20 A MANCHESTER U   21 L 0-1 0-1   37,981 1 12
Stapleton 34   Ref: P Vanes

| Hallworth | Yallop | McCall | Parkin | Cranson | Butcher | Atkins | Dozzell | Brennan | Wilson | D'Avray* | Sunderland |
| Bailey | Gidman | Gibson C | Whiteside | McGrath | Hogg | Strachan | Hughes* | Stapleton | Olsen | Brazil | |

A dream come true for ex-Manchester schoolboy Hallworth, but his big day at Old Trafford is somewhat spoiled when Stapleton beats him with a great finish after Cranson fails to clear Olsen's cross. D'Avray is bundled over at the other end but loud penalty claims are waved aside.

---

21 H QP RANGERS   21 W 1-0 1-0   12,032 13 15
Wilson 3   Ref: J Moules

| Cooper | Yallop | McCall | Zondervan* | Cranson | Butcher | Atkins | Dozzell | Brennan | Wilson | Sunderland | Parkin |
| Barron | Chivers | Dawes | Robinson | McDonald | Wicks | James | Fillery | Allen | Byrne | Fereday | |

Jim Smith's side lose a third successive game thanks to an early strike by Wilson. He is left unmarked and heads sweetly home after Zondervan collects a throw and crosses to him. Wilson is unlucky to not to register a second when his cracking 89th-minute piledriver rebounds off a post.

CANON DIVISION 1 — SEASON 1985-86

Manager: Bobby Ferguson

The lower (italic) line in each match is the opponents' line-up. In the *Pos* column the first figure is Ipswich Town's League position, the figure in brackets the opponents'.

No	Date	Match	Att	Pos	Pt	F-A	H-T	1	2	3	4	5	6	7	8	9	10	11	12 sub used
22	A 21/12	TOTTENHAM	18,845	21 (10)	L 15	0-2	0-1	Cooper	Yallop	McCall	Zondervan	Cranson	Butcher	Atkins*	Brennan	Sunderland	Wilson	Dozzell	Gleghorn
		Tottenham						*Clemence*	*Thomas*	*Hughton*	*Stevens*	*Mabbutt*	*Perrymans*	*Ardiles*	*Falco*	*Allen C*	*Hoddle**	*Waddle*	*Allen P*
23	A 26/12	COVENTRY	9,356	20 (17)	W 18	1-0	0-0	Cooper	Yallop	McCall	Gleghorn	Cranson	Butcher	Stockwell*	Brennan	D'Avray	Wilson	Dozzell	Sunderland
		Coventry						*Ogrizovic*	*Burrows*	*Downs*	*Bowyer*	*Kilcline*	*Rodger*	*Adams*	*Turner**	*Regis*	*Gibson*	*McGrath*	*Bennett*
24	H 28/12	LUTON	16,155	20 (8)	D 19	1-1	1-0	Cooper	Yallop	McCall	Gleghorn	Cranson*	Butcher	Stockwell	Brennan	D'Avray	Wilson	Dozzell	Sunderland
		Luton						*Sealey*	*Breacker*	*Thomas*	*Nicholas*	*North S*	*Donaghy*	*Hill*	*Stein B*	*Harford*	*North M*	*Preece*	
25	H 1/1	WATFORD	15,922	20 (12)	D 20	0-0	0-0	Cooper	Yallop	McCall	Gleghorn	Cranson	Butcher	Stockwell	Brennan	D'Avray	Wilson	Dozzell	Callaghan
		Watford						*Coton*	*Gibbs*	*Rostron*	*Talbot*	*Terry*	*McClelland*	*Sterling*	*Allen**	*West*	*Jackett*	*Barnes*	
26	A 11/1	BIRMINGHAM	6,856	20 (21)	W 23	1-0	1-0	Cooper	Yallop	McCall	Zondervan*	Cranson	Butcher	Gleghorn	Brennan	D'Avray	Wilson	Dozzell	Putney
		Birmingham						*Seaman*	*Ranson*	*Dicks*	*Hagan*	*Armstrong*	*Kuhl*	*Bremner*	*Platnauer*	*Kennedy*	*Jones**	*Hopkins*	*Russell*
27	A 18/1	SOUTHAMPTON	13,164	20 (14)	L 23	0-1	0-0	Cooper	Yallop	McCall	Zondervan*	Cranson	Butcher	Gleghorn*	Brennan	D'Avray	Wilson	Dozzell	Stockwell
		Southampton						*Shilton*	*Forrest*	*Dennis*	*Case*	*Wright*	*Bond*	*Holmes*	*Cockerill*	*Puckett*	*Armstrong*	*Wallace*	*Wallace*
28	H 1/2	LIVERPOOL	20,551	18 (4)	W 26	2-1	0-1	Cooper	Yallop*	McCall	Zondervan	Cranson	Butcher	Putney	Brennan	D'Avray	Wilson	Dozzell	Cole
		Liverpool						*Grobbelaar*	*Nicol*	*Beglin*	*Lawrenson*	*Whelan*	*Hansen*	*Walsh*	*Johnston**	*Lee*	*Molby*	*Gillespie*	*Wark*
29	H 8/3	NOTT'M FOREST	12,658	19 (9)	W 29	1-0	0-0	Cooper	Yallop	McCall	Zondervan	Cranson	Butcher	Putney	Brennan	Cole	Wilson	Dozzell	
		Forest						*Sutton*	*Fleming*	*Williams*	*Walker*	*Metgod*	*Bowyer*	*Carr*	*Webb*	*Clough*	*Davenport*	*Rice**	*Campbell*
30	H 11/3	ARSENAL	13,967	19 (7)	L 29	1-2	1-1	Cooper	Yallop*	McCall	Zondervan	Cranson	Butcher	Putney	Brennan	D'Avray	Wilson	Dozzell	Cole
		Arsenal						*Wilmot*	*Anderson*	*Sansom*	*Williams*	*O'Leary**	*Keown*	*Hayes*	*Rocastle*	*Nicholas*	*Woodcock*	*Rix*	*Mariner*
31	A 15/3	NEWCASTLE	18,851	19 (9)	L 29	1-3	1-0	Cooper	Yallop	McCall	Zondervan	Cranson	Butcher	Putney!	Brennan	Parkin	Wilson	Dozzell	**Atkinson**
		Newcastle						*McKellar*	*Anderson*	*Bailey*	*McCreery*	*Clarke*	*Roeder*	*Stephenson*	*Gascoigne*	*Whitehurst*	*Beardsley*	*McDonald**	*Cunningham*

Scorers, Times, and Referees — with match reports

22 — Allen C 21, Hoddle 60; Ref: R Groves
New signing Allen opens the scoring for David Pleat's attractive attack-minded side when he lobs over the exposed Cooper after being set up by Hoddle. Wilson goes close after a Stevens error, hitting a post. Cooper saves Falco's header, but Hoddle is on hand to convert the rebound.

23 — D'Avray 88; Ref: N Midgley
Don Mackay's side haven't won at home since October and both teams struggle to string passes together on a muddy pitch. With time running out a dull goalless draw seems inevitable until D'Avray musters a fine shot that goes in off the bar. City fans jeer their players off the field.

24 — Gleghorn 10, North M 82; Ref: A Gunn
Gleghorn scores from an unmarked position after a twice-taken free-kick, to give Town an early boost. Well marshalled by Foster, Luton's defence restricts further chances and Luton win a point when Preece's neat chip is stabbed in by Marc North – a recently-converted goalkeeper.

25 — Ref: A Seville
Many matches fall victim to the weather over this period but this one goes ahead on a tricky icy pitch. Defences are generally on top and a first Watford goalless draw of the season is no real surprise. Teenager Malcolm Allen fluffs the best chance of the match for Graham Taylor's side.

26 — Wilson 34; Ref: J Worrall
The lowest gate at St Andrews since the war watches in horror as Seaman miskicks into the wind and the ball fails to go above shoulder height. Hagan fails to deal with it and Wilson nips in to chip over Seaman, who otherwise played well. Ron Saunders' men have not won for 16 weeks.

27 — Wallace 50; Ref: D Reeves
Danny Wallace conjures up a stunning right-foot shot which flies past Cooper. The keeper later calls it the best shot he's had to face all season. Shilton shows magnificent reflexes to fling himself and block a powerful shot by Wilson. Town are a shade unlucky not to get at least a point.

28 — D'Avray 53, Wilson 80; Whelan 36; Ref: V Callow
A superb second-half performance gives Town a memorable victory. Whelan gives Kenny Dalglish's team the lead with a looping header from Molby's free-kick. D'Avray beats Grobbelaar in the air to head in Brennan's cross. Jubilant Wilson volleys the winner from a Zondervan cross.

29 — Butcher 52; Ref: D Reeves
A welcome return to action after a long league lay-off due to bad weather, but the pitch still has some frosty areas. Yallop's free-kick is nodded down by Butcher, Cole challenges Fleming and the ball falls for Butcher to crack in with his left foot. Survival hopes now look much brighter.

30 — Dozzell 40; Nicholas 15, Woodcock 49; Ref: D Axcell
Nicholas is left unmarked and he heads in a corner taken by Rix. Dozzell equalises after the ball is flicked to him by Wilson. Hoping for a third successive home victory, bad marking is again Town's undoing after the interval when Woodcock is left free to convert a Hayes centre.

31 — Wilson 14; Beardsley 69, Whitehurst 84, (Gascoigne 89); Ref: K Walmsley
McKellar, an ex-Town player on loan from Hibs, is beaten by a smartly-taken Wilson goal. Beardsley seizes on a Putney error and fires past Cooper. Whitehurst's first goal for United sees him convert Cunningham's cross. Teenager Paul Gascoigne scores a clever goal under pressure.

Ipswich Town — match-by-match results and line-ups (matches 32–42)

No	Venue	Opponent	Date	Pos	Res	FT	HT	Att	OppPos	Pts
32	H	WEST BROM	22/3	19	W	1-0	0-0	12,100	22	32
33	A	WATFORD	29/3	19	D	0-0	0-0	14,988	12	33
34	H	COVENTRY	31/3	17	W	1-0	0-0	13,485	16	36
35	A	CHELSEA	5/4	16	D	1-1	1-1	13,072	4	37
36	H	LEICESTER	8/4	18	L	0-2	0-2	11,718	16	37
37	H	MANCHESTER C	12/4	18	D	0-0	0-0	13,986	14	38
38	A	ASTON VILLA	16/4	18	L	0-1	0-1	13,611	17	38
39	A	EVERTON	19/4	19	L	0-1	0-1	39,055	2	38
40	H	OXFORD	26/4	17	W	3-2	0-1	17,827	20	41
41	A	WEST HAM	30/4	19	L	1-2	0-0	31,121	2	41
42	A	SHEFFIELD WED	3/5	19	L	0-1	0-0	22,369	5	41

Home 14,468 · Away 17,470 · Average 17,470

32 — H WEST BROM
Ipswich: Cooper, Yallop*, McCall, Zondervan, Cranson, Butcher, Putney, Parkin, D'Avray, Wilson, Dozzell, Cole
West Brom: Naylor, Whitehead, Statham, Palmer, Dickinson, Dyson, Thompson, Madden, Reilly, MacKenzie, Bradley*, Robson
Butcher 67. Ref: M James
New Albion boss Ron Saunders is still searching for his first win and gives a debut to striker Madden. The deadlock is broken when Butcher lets fly out of the blue from 25 yards and the ball flies into Naylor's net. Ferguson scoffs at speculation that Butcher is to join Manchester Utd.

33 — A WATFORD
Ipswich: Hallworth, Parkin, McCall, Zondervan, Cranson, Butcher, Gleghorn, Brennan, Cole, Wilson, Dozzell, Stockwell
Watford: Coton, Gibbs, Rostron, Atkins*, Terry, McClelland, Sterling, Callaghan, Roberts, Jackett, Barnes*, Bardsley
Ref: J Lovatt
A dull Easter Saturday affair and the second goalless draw between these sides this season. Ferguson believes it's the youngest side he's ever selected and is content with a point. Two patched up outfits work hard but fail to sparkle. Graham Taylor gives a debut to the teenager Roberts.

34 — H COVENTRY
Ipswich: Hallworth, Parkin, McCall, Atkins, Cranson, Butcher, Gleghorn, Brennan, Cole, Wilson, Dozzell*, D'Avray
Coventry: Ogrizovic, Borrows, Downs, McGrath, Kilcline, Peake, McNally*, Brazil, Regis, Pickering, Hibbitt, Bennett
Brennan 78. Ref: J Key
Alan Brazil returns again in new colours and is jeered throughout. In a drab affair, City stretch their run without a goal to over 750 minutes. Brennan crashes home a fine shot from well outside the area to secure all three points. Ferguson is delighted with an Easter haul of four points.

35 — A CHELSEA
Ipswich: Hallworth, Zondervan, McCall, Atkins*, Cranson, Butcher, Gleghorn, Brennan, Cole, Wilson, Dozzell, Putney
Chelsea: Godden, Howard, Dublin, Pates, McLaughlin, Bumstead, Nevin, Spackman, Dixon, Speedie, Murphy
Brennan 39, Speedie 5. Ref: J Martin
John Hollins' high-flying side takes an early lead when Speedie makes the most of being unmarked and heads home with Town's defence in disarray. A stroke of luck for Town when keeper Godden infringes the new 'steps' rule and from Atkins' indirect free-kick Brennan fires home.

36 — H LEICESTER
Ipswich: Hallworth, Parkin, McCall, Zondervan, Cranson, Butcher, Gleghorn, Brennan, Cole, Wilson, Putney*, Stockwell
Leicester: Andrews, Smith R, Morgan, McAllister, Osman, O'Neill, Lynex, Sealy, Smith A, Mauchlen, Banks
McAllister 12, Smith A 16. Ref: R Lewis
Two quick goals settle this dour battle between two relegation-threatened sides. McAllister goes past Cranson before shooting past Hallworth. Before Town can respond, Lynex's corner is headed on by O'Neill and Smith converts a sweet left-foot shot. Cranson hits the City woodwork.

37 — H MANCHESTER C
Ipswich: Cooper, Parkin, McCall, Zondervan, Cranson, Butcher, Gleghorn*, Brennan, D'Avray, Wilson, Dozzell, Stockwell
Manchester C: Siddall, Reid, Power, Redmond, McCarthy, Baker, Lillis, May, Beckford, McNab, Wilson
Ref: I Hemley
Billy McNeill's men employ negative tactics and Town toil without success to break them down. Ferguson is still under pressure from some fans and news filters through that ex-Town coach Cyril Lea has been sacked by neighbours Colchester, while Coventry's Don Mackay has quit.

38 — A ASTON VILLA
Ipswich: Cooper, Parkin, McCall, Zondervan, Cranson, Butcher, Gleghorn*, Brennan, D'Avray, Wilson, Dozzell, Stockwell
Aston Villa: Poole, Norton, Dorigo, Evans, Elliott, Hunt, Blair, Stainrod, Gray, Hodge, Walters*, Daley
Hodge 62. Ref: K Breen
This relegation six-pointer is an entertaining affair but Town again fail in front of goal. Hodge grabs the winner when a rebound falls to him and he nets from a tight angle after Cooper blocks a powerful shot by sub Daley. Graham Turner's men now look a good bet to avoid the drop.

39 — A EVERTON
Ipswich: Cooper, Atkins, McCall, Zondervan*, Cranson*, Butcher, Gleghorn, Brennan, D'Avray, Wilson, Dozzell, Stockwell
Everton: Mimms, Stevens, V d Hauwe, Ratcliffe, Mountfield, Reid, Steven, Heath, Sharp, Bracewell, Richardson
Sharp 64. Ref: A Saunders
Desperate for points, Town battle gamely against Howard Kendall's men but go down to an eleventh 0-1 defeat of the season. Sharp soars to head in from Richardson's cross. Town have now gone almost seven hours without a goal and clearly a win over Oxford is crucial for survival.

40 — H OXFORD
Ipswich: Cooper, Yallop, McCall, Atkins, Cranson, Butcher, Gleghorn, Brennan, D'Avray, Wilson, Dozzell, Cole
Oxford: Judge, Langan, Phillips, Trewick, Briggs, Shotton, Houghton, Aldridge, Charles*, Hebberd, Perryman, Brock
Dozzell 53, Butcher 55, Atkins 90; Aldridge 30, Phillips 62. Ref: T Holbrook
A tense day bursts into life when Town cancel out Aldridge's goal and quickly take the lead, only for Phillips to volley Maurice Evans' side back level again. Atkins nets a dramatic winner in the dying seconds after an indirect free-kick, sparking amazing scenes and a pitch invasion.

41 — A WEST HAM
Ipswich: Cooper, Parkin, McCall, Atkins*, Cranson, Butcher, Gleghorn, Brennan, Cole, Wilson, Dozzell
West Ham: Parkes, Stewart, Parris, Gale, Martin, Devonshire, Ward, McAvennie, Dickens, Cottee, Orr*, Goddard
Wilson 63; Dickens 72, Stewart 86p. Ref: G Ashby
Both sides are desperate for points with John Lyall's men still in the title race. In a tense atmosphere, Wilson races onto Brennan's pass and beats Parkes at the second attempt. Dickens levels with a fine shot, then Gleghorn is penalised for a tackle on Ward. Stewart nets from the spot.

42 — A SHEFFIELD WED
Ipswich: Cooper, Parkin, McCall, Atkins*, Cranson, Butcher, Gleghorn, Brennan, Cole, Wilson, Dozzell, Yallop
Sheffield Wed: Hodge, Sterland, Snodin, Shirtliff, Shelton, Hart, Marwood, Megson, Shutt, Thompson*, Knight, Chamberlain
Marwood 81. Ref: D Allison
Many Town fans head north for D-Day at Hillsborough. Although results elsewhere are crucial, Town know they must win. Heads drop when Marwood converting Shutt's cross late in the day. Oxford beat Arsenal two days later and Town are relegated.

CANON DIVISION 1 (CUP-TIES)　　Manager: Bobby Ferguson　　SEASON 1985-86

Milk Cup

Milk Cup	Att	F-A	H-T	Scorers, Times, and Referees
2:1 H DARLINGTON 24/9	19 W	3-1	1-1	Wilson 45, 90, Yallop 75 / Poskett 4 — Ref: D Reeves
	7,667 3:17			
2:2 A DARLINGTON 8/10	21 W	4-1	2-1	Wilson 22, 44, 50, Dozzell 65 / MacDonald 6 (Town win 7-2 on aggregate) — Ref: N Wilson
	3,321 3:18			
3 A GRIMSBY 29/10	21 W	2-0	2-0	Cole 1, Wilson 24 — Ref: J Key
	6,700 2:15			
4 H SWINDON 26/11	21 W	6-1	2-0	Brennan 8, Wilson 35, Butcher 68, 75, Yallop 70 (og) [Cole 78, 81] — Ref: C Downey
	12,083 3:4			
QF A LIVERPOOL 21/1	20 L	0-3	0-2	Walsh 17, Whelan 28, Rush 65 — Ref: J Deakin
	19,762 3			

Line-ups (Town / Opponent)

Match	1	2	3	4	5	6	7	8	9	10	11	12 sub used
2:1 Town	Cooper	Yallop	Gernon	Zondervan	Cranson	Steggles	Putney	Brennan	Wilson	Sunderland	Dozzell	Cole
2:1 Darlington	Barber	Aldred	Moran	Tupling	Woodcock	Carney	Haire*	Poskett	Airey	MacDonald	McLean	Wright
2:2 Town	Cooper	Yallop	Gernon	Atkins	Cranson	Steggles	Putney	Brennan	Wilson	McCall*	Dozzell	Cole
2:2 Darlington	Barber	Aldred	Nattress	Tupling	Huntley	Carney	Woodcock	Poskett	Airey	MacDonald	McLean*	Haire
3 Town	Cooper	Yallop	McCall	Zondervan	Cranson	Atkins	D'Avray	Brennan	Wilson	Cole	Dozzell	Stockwell
3 Grimsby	Batch	Barrett	Crombie	Moore A	Moore K	Ford	Peake	Bonnyman	Emson	Gilligan*	Hobson	Lund
4 Town	Cooper	Yallop	McCall*	Parkin	Cranson	Butcher	Atkins	Brennan	Cole	Wilson	Dozzell	Gleghorn
4 Swindon	Key	Coleman	Ramsey	Barnard	Cole	Calderwood*	Bamber	Henry	Gordon	Wade	Hockaday	Rowlands
QF Town	Cooper	Yallop	McCall	Putney	Cranson	Butcher	Atkins*	Brennan	D'Avray	Wilson	Dozzell	Stockwell
QF Liverpool	Grobbelaar	Nicol	Beglin	Lawrenson	Whelan	Hansen	Walsh	Johnston	Rush	Molby	Gillespie*	Wark

2:1 An early shock as Cranson gives the ball away and Poskett beats Cooper with a clinical curling shot. Cyril Knowles' side are pegged back when Putney's effort is parried by Barber and Wilson swoops to score. Zondervan's cross is headed firmly in by Yallop for his first senior goal.

2:2 Depleted and beaten 0-7 at York a few days earlier, Darlington nevertheless make a good start through MacDonald's volley. But Wilson's clinical hat-trick finishes them off, his second a clever chip over Barber. A classy goal by Dozzell is the icing on the cake for untroubled Town.

3 A perfect start for Town as youngster Cole fires a shot goalwards after 45 seconds and a deflection sends it well out of Batch's reach. A superb pass by Dozzell enables Wilson to extend the lead. David Booth's final match in charge of Grimsby is a scrappy affair with a spate of bookings.

4 Brennan slides in the first goal and the floodlights open. Butcher's headed goal is quickly followed by Yallop chesting the ball past his own keeper. Butcher produces another powerful header to extinguish any fightback and Cole adds two more as Lou Macari's side falls apart badly.

QF Butcher and Cooper get in a dreadful tangle and Walsh nips in to poke the ball home. Butcher slips up again, being caught in possession and Whelan completes Town's misery. Atkins returns after injury but limps off at the break with a toe problem.

FA Cup

FA Cup	Att	F-A	H-T	Scorers, Times, and Referees
3 H BRADFORD C 4/1	20 D	4-4	3-3	Ev' 12 (og), Wil' 18, Bren' 29, D'Av' 73 / G'dman 9, Abb'tt 13, 79p, Hendrie 27 — Ref: R Lewis
	13,003 2:11			
3R A BRADFORD C 13/1	20 W	1-0	0-0 aet	Brennan 100 — Ref: N Wilson
	10,108 2:11			
4 A WEST HAM 25/1	20 D	0-0	0-0	Ref: J Martin
	25,035 5			
4R H WEST HAM 4/2	18 D	1-1	0-0 aet	Dozzell 94 / Cottee 106 — Ref: J Martin
	25,384 5			
4R 2 H WEST HAM 6/2	18 L	0-1	0-0 aet	Cottee 111 — Ref: K Baker
	14,515 5			

Line-ups (Town / Opponent)

Match	1	2	3	4	5	6	7	8	9	10	11	12 sub used
3 Town	Cooper	Yallop	McCall	Zondervan	Cranson	Butcher	Gleghorn	Brennan	D'Avray	Wilson	Dozzell	
3 Bradford C	Litchfield	Oliver	Withe	Abbott	Jackson	Evans	Hendrie	Goodman*	Campbell	Singleton	Graham	Ellis
3R Town	Cooper	Yallop	McCall	Putney*	Cranson	Butcher	Gleghorn	Brennan	D'Avray	Wilson	Dozzell	Stockwell
3R Bradford C	Litchfield	Oliver	Withe	Abbott	Jackson	Evans	Hendrie	Ellis	Campbell	Singleton*	Graham	Goodman
4 Town	Cooper	Yallop	McCall	Stockwell*	Cranson	Butcher	Putney	Brennan	D'Avray	Wilson	Dozzell	Zondervan
4 West Ham	Parkes	Stewart	Walford*	Gale	Martin	Devonshire	Ward	McAvennie	Dickens	Cottee	Parris	Goddard
4R Town	Cooper	Yallop	McCall	Zondervan	Cranson	Butcher	Putney*	Brennan	D'Avray	Wilson	Dozzell	Cole
4R West Ham	Parkes	Parris	Walford*	Gale	Martin	Devonshire	Ward	McAvennie	Dickens	Cottee	Pike	Orr
4R 2 Town	Cooper	Yallop	McCall	Zondervan	Cranson	Butcher	Putney*	Brennan	D'Avray	Wilson	Dozzell	Stockwell
4R 2 West Ham	Parkes	Parris	Stewart	Gale	Martin	Orr	Ward	McAvennie	Dickens	Cottee	Pike	

3 An amazing opening half-hour sees Town equalise three times. Evans lofts a huge back-pass over his own keeper, Wilson heads neatly in and Brennan produces a crisp low drive. D'Avray heads Town in front for the first time, but Butcher concedes a spot-kick, hauling Hendrie down.

3R Town survive two major scares when Abbott hits the post and Withe rocks the crossbar on 87 minutes. The match goes into extra-time and Trevor Cherry's side are finally broken when Brennan latches onto McCall's through ball and fires in a fierce drive which goes in off a post.

4 On the coach journey to Upton Park the Town players are shown a video of the club's 1978 FA Cup win to inspire them. They produce a solid defensive display which frustrates the home side. Putney nearly grabs a surprise winner 20 minutes from time but he passes up a good chance.

4R A much more lively 90 minutes again ends goalless, sending the tie into extra-time. Dozzell draws first blood, steering a crisp left-foot shot past Parkes after Wilson and Cole combine on the right flank. Cole loses possession and Parris feeds the ball to Cottee, who brings things level.

4R 2 Ferguson calls 'heads' and wins the toss to stage the second replay at home. The pitch is snowbound and the dangerous state of some roads helps keep the crowd down. A 330-minute tie is settled in extra-time when Cottee pounces on a loose ball after Brennan fails to clear properly.

League Table

	Team	P	W	D	L	F	A	W	D	L	F	A	Pts
				Home					**Away**				
1	Liverpool	42	16	4	1	58	14	10	6	5	31	23	88
2	Everton	42	16	3	2	54	18	10	5	6	33	23	86
3	West Ham	42	17	2	2	48	16	9	4	8	26	24	84
4	Manchester U	42	12	5	4	35	12	10	5	6	35	24	76
5	Sheffield Wed	42	13	6	2	36	23	8	4	9	27	31	73
6	Chelsea	42	12	4	5	32	27	8	7	6	25	29	71
7	Arsenal	42	13	5	3	29	15	7	4	10	20	32	69
8	Nott'm Forest	42	11	5	5	38	25	8	6	7	31	28	68
9	Luton	42	12	6	3	37	15	6	6	9	24	29	66
10	Tottenham	42	12	2	7	47	25	7	6	8	27	27	65
11	Newcastle	42	12	5	4	46	31	5	7	9	21	41	63
12	Watford	42	11	6	4	40	22	5	5	11	29	40	59
13	QP Rangers	42	12	3	6	33	20	4	5	12	20	44	52
14	Southampton	42	10	6	5	32	18	2	4	15	19	44	46
15	Manchester C	42	7	7	7	25	26	4	5	12	18	31	45
16	Aston Villa	42	7	6	8	27	28	3	8	10	24	39	44
17	Coventry	42	6	5	10	31	35	5	5	11	17	36	43
18	Oxford	42	7	7	7	34	27	3	5	13	28	53	42
19	Leicester	42	7	8	6	35	35	3	4	14	19	41	42
20	IPSWICH	42	8	5	8	20	24	3	3	15	12	31	41
21	Birmingham	42	5	2	14	13	25	3	3	15	17	48	29
22	West Brom	42	3	8	10	21	36	1	4	16	14	53	24
		924	229	110	123	771	517	123	110	229	517	771	1276

Appearances and Goals

Player	Lge	Sub	LC	Sub	FAC	Sub	Lge	LC	FAC	Tot
Atkins, Ian	20	1	4				2			2
Atkinson, Dalian		1								1
Brennan, Mark	40		5		5		3	1	2	6
Burley, George	6									
Butler, Terry	27		2		5		4	2		6
Cole, Michael	12	6	2	1		1	1	3		4
Cooper, Paul	36		5		5					
Cranson, Ian	42		5		5		1			1
D'Avray, Mich	24	2	2		5		5	1		6
Dozzell, Jason	38	3	5		5		3	1	1	5
Gernon, Irvin	11		2							
Gleghorn, Nigel	17	4		1	2		2			2
Hallworth, Jon	6									
McCall, Steve	33		4		5					
Parkin, Tommy	13	1	1							
Putney, Trevor	18	3	3		4		1			1
Rimmer, Neill	1	1								
Steggles, Kevin	5	1	2							
Stockwell, Mick	3	5	1	1	1	2				
Sunderland, Alan	13	4	1				1			1
Wilson, Kevin	37	2	5		5		7	7	1	15
Yallop, Frank	32	2	5		5				1	1
Zondervan, Romeo	28		2		3	1	2			2
(own-goals)									1	1
23 players used	462	36	55	3	55	4	32	15	6	53

Odds & ends

Double wins: (2) Coventry, West Brom.

Double losses: (6) Arsenal, Aston Villa, Everton, Leicester, Manchester U, West Ham.

Won from behind: (5) Darlington (h & a) (LC), Sheffield W (h). Liverpool (h), Oxford (h).

Lost from in front: (4) Everton (h), Newcastle (a), Oxford (a), West Ham (a).

High spots: Going beyond the third round of the FA Cup for a record 16th successive time.

The 6-1 thrashing of Swindon Town.

Young Cranson successfully replacing Osman.

The second-half comeback to beat Liverpool.

Low spots: Relegation after 18 years at the top.

The collapse after going 3-0 ahead at Oxford.

The departure of Gates, Osman and Burley.

Only one home League crowd of over 20,000.

Losing Terry Butcher with knee problems.

Player of the Year: Terry Butcher.

Ever-presents: (1) Ian Cranson.

Hat-tricks: (1) Kevin Wilson (League Cup).

Opposing hat-tricks: (1) John Aldridge.

Leading scorer: (15) Kevin Wilson.

TODAY DIVISION 2 — Manager: Bobby Ferguson — SEASON 1986-87

No	Date		Att	Pos	Pt	F-A	H-T	Scorers, Times, and Referees	1	2	3	4	5	6	7	8	9	10	11	subs used
1	H	GRIMSBY			D	1-1	1-0	Wilson 37	Cooper	Zondervan	McCall	Atkins	Dozzell	Cranson	Gleghorn	Brennan	D'Avray*	**Deehan**	Wilson	Cole
	23/8		12,455		1			*Walsh 88*	*Batch*	*Burgess*	*Cumming*	*Peake*	*Lyons*	*Moore K*	*Robinson*	*Walsh*	*Hobson*	*O'Riordan*	*Turner*	
								Ref: K Barrett	Town's first game out of the top division in 18 years sees Wilson head home after Batch flaps at a cross. Mick Lyons' side, featuring four new signings, keeps plugging away and is rewarded two minutes from time when Walsh turns and fires in after O'Riordan's effort is charged down.											
2	A	PORTSMOUTH		12	D	1-1	0-0	Brennan 56	Cooper	Zondervan	McCall	Atkins	Dozzell	Cranson*	Gleghorn	Brennan	Cole	Deehan	Wilson	D'Avray
	30/8		*11,849*	*15*	2			*O'Callaghan 73*	*Knight*	*Swain*	*Hardyman*	*Dillon*	*Blake*	*Gilbert*	*Tait*	*O'Callaghan*	*Mariner*	*Quinn**	*Hilaire*	*Wood*
								Ref: G Ashby	Brennan nets a sweet left-foot shot after Dozzell sets up the chance with a clever backheel. A free-kick bitterly disputed by Town defenders is fired into Cooper's net by ex-Ipswich winger O'Callaghan. Cooper denies Alan Ball's men by turning Dillon's long-range effort over the bar.											
3	H	OLDHAM		12	L	0-1	0-1		Cooper	Zondervan	McCall	Atkins	Dozzell	Gernon	Gleghorn*	Brennan	Cole	Deehan	Wilson	D'Avray
	2/9		10,316	*1*	2			*Futcher 25p*	*Goram*	*Irwin*	*Donachie*	*Jones*	*Linighan*	*Barlow*	*Palmer*	*Henry*	*McDon'gh**	*Futcher*	*Milligan !*	*McGuire*
								Ref: M James	Veteran Ron Futcher repeats his Portman Road winner of 1974 in Luton colours, this time from the spot. McCall has a fracas with Milligan and the Latics man is sent off. Futcher misses with only Cooper to beat and seconds later Wilson hits the post after Goram blocks Atkins' shot.											
4	H	SHREWSBURY		14	W	1-0	1-0	D'Avray 37	Cooper	Yallop	McCall	Atkins	Dozzell	Gernon	Gleghorn	Zondervan	D'Avray	Deehan	Wilson	
	6/9		**9,339**	*20*	5				*Perks*	*Williams*	*Johnson*	*Hughes*	*Pearson*	*Griffin**	*McNally*	*Hackett*	*Waller*	*Robinson*	*Daly*	*Leonard*
								Ref: C Downey	Atkins' free-kick is headed on by Deehan and when keeper Perks and Pearson get in each other's way, D'Avray swoops to prod the ball home. Chic Bates' men's best effort comes when veteran Gerry Daly fires in a rasping drive from 30 yards that beats Cooper but hits the woodwork.											
5	A	WEST BROM		9	W	4-3	1-2	Deehan 40, 59, 78, Wilson 79	Cooper	Cranson	McCall	Atkins	Dozzell	Gernon*	Gleghorn	Zondervan	D'Avray	Deehan	Wilson	Yallop
	13/9		*9,031*	*10*	8			*Williamson 2, Bull 20, 54*	*Naylor*	*Whitehead*	*Burrows*	*Bennett*	*Dyson*	*Dickinson*	*Palmer*	*Bull*	*MacKenzie*	*Williamson*	*Cowdrill**	*Madden*
								Ref: M King	Ex-West Brom man 'Dixie' Deehan has a penalty saved and hits the bar as well as netting a hat-trick. He curls a shot in and sweeps in a pass from Dozzell to keep Town in the game. He levels by deliberately deflecting home an Atkins free-kick, then Wilson heads in Gleghorn's cross.											
6	H	SUNDERLAND		10	D	1-1	0-0	D'Avray 64	Cooper	**O'Donnell**	McCall	Atkins	Dozzell	Cranson	Gleghorn	Brennan	D'Avray	Deehan*	Wilson	Stockwell
	20/9		12,824	*15*	9			*Corner 57*	*Hesford*	*Burley*	*Kennedy*	*Armstrong*	*Corner*	*Agboola*	*Lemon*	*Doyle*	*Swindlehurst*	*Gray**	*Buchanan*	*Atkinson*
								Ref: A Buksh	Cooper attempts to punch clear but the ball falls conveniently for Corner to score from close range. Ipswich equalise when Wilson's shot is parried by Hesford and D'Avray is on hand to convert the rebound. New signing Steve Doyle has a fine game for Lawrie McMenemy's outfit.											
7	A	BIRMINGHAM		11	D	2-2	1-0	Brennan 45, Wilson 65	Cooper	Stockwell	McCall*	Atkins	Dozzell	O'Donnell !	Gleghorn	Brennan	Zondervan	Deehan	Wilson	Parkin
	27/9		*7,227*	*12*	10			*Clarke 55, 81*	*Hansbury*	*Roberts**	*Dicks*	*Hagan*	*Overson*	*Kuhl*	*Bremner*	*Clarke*	*Whitton*	*Mortimer*	*Cooke*	*Rees*
								Ref: M Cotton	The ref shocks Town on 19 minutes, sending off young O'Donnell for a foul on Clarke. Cooper saves Whitton's penalty. Brennan fires a free-kick through a forest of legs, but Clarke scrambles in an equaliser. Wilson curls a neat shot home, then hits the bar, but Clarke heads a leveller.											
8	A	HULL		16	L	1-2	0-1	Deehan 90	Cooper	Stockwell	Cranson	Atkins	Dozzell	O'Donnell*	Gleghorn	Brennan	Zondervan	Deehan	Wilson	Parkin
	4/10		*6,872*	*8*	10			*Saville 6, 89*	*Norman*	*Williams*	*Ablett*	*Heard*	*Skipper*	*McEwan*	*Parker*	*Saville*	*Flounders*	*Horton*	*Roberts*	
								Ref: N Midgley	After Parker's through ball, a jostling Cranson and Saville chase the ball into the net, with the latter claiming credit for the goal. Saville makes the points safe by heading home Parker's cross. Seconds before the final whistle, Deehan produces a smart half-volley from a pass by Wilson.											
9	H	BRIGHTON		9	W	1-0	0-0	D'Avray 62	Cooper	Parkin*	Zondervan	Atkins	Dozzell	Cranson	Gleghorn	Brennan	D'Avray	Atkinson	Wilson	Stockwell
	11/10		11,215	*8*	13				*Keeley*	*Berry*	*Hutchings*	*Wilson*	*Gatting*	*O'Regan*	*Penny*	*Saunders*	*Hughes**	*Connor*	*Jasper*	*Armstrong*
								Ref: A Seville	With Deehan missing after gashing his foot on his running-shoe spikes, Atkinson has a lively game, delighting the crowd with his amazing turn of speed. D'Avray breaks the deadlock with a stylish header from Atkins' free-kick. Alan Mullery's men play their part in a spirited encounter.											
10	A	BRADFORD C		7	W	4-3	2-3	Gleghorn 2, 48, 77, Dozzell 21	Cooper	Yallop	Zondervan	Atkins	Dozzell	Cranson	Gleghorn	Brennan	D'Avray	Deehan	Wilson*	Atkinson
	18/10		*5,348*	*16*	16			*Singleton 15, Abbott 35p, 43p*	*Litchfield*	*Oliver*	*Withe*	*Abbott*	*Jackson*	*Evans*	*Hendrie*	*Goodman*	*Leonard*	*Singleton*	*Ellis*	
								Ref: V Callow	Exactly a year after his debut, Gleghorn drills in three shots for a slick hat-trick. Cranson concedes two penalties in eight minutes with a push and a handball, to leave Town trailing at the break. Then Gleghorn steps in to shock a home crowd now temporarily housed at Odsal Stadium.											

Ipswich Town match record (matches 11–21)

Column order for each line-up (left→right): Cooper · Yallop · Zondervan · Atkins · Dozzell · Cranson · Gleghorn · Brennan · D'Avray · Deehan · Wilson · Stockwell

---

11 A PLYMOUTH 21/10 — 8 L 0-2 · 4 · 16 · Att 12,569

Town: Cooper, Yallop, Zondervan, Atkins, Dozzell, Cranson, Gleghorn, Brennan, D'Avray, Deehan, Wilson, Stockwell
Plymouth: Crudgington, Nisbet, Cooper L, Goodyear, McElhinney, Matthews, Hodges, Coughlin, Summerfield, Tynan, Cooper S

Coughlin 55p, Summerfield 80
Ref: R Hamer

In heavy rain and fierce winds, Town rarely trouble Crudgington. Cranson fouls Tynan after a bad Dozzell pass and Coughlin nets from the spot. His first effort has to be re-taken when Cooper moves before saving. Brennan's sloppy pass allows Summerfield to lash home a second.

---

12 H STOKE 25/10 — 6 W 2-0 · 20 · 19 · Att 11,054

Town: Cooper, Yallop, Zondervan, Atkins, Dozzell, Cranson, Gleghorn, Brennan, Cole, Deehan*, Wilson, Stockwell, Atkinson
Stoke: Fox, Dixon*, Parkin, Talbot, Bould, Berry, Ford, Kelly, Shaw, Bertschin, Heath, Saunders

Wilson 42, 50
Ref: M Reed

Mick Mills returns to Portman Road as a manager, but his side labour in vain to score. Razor-sharp Wilson shows them how it's done with deadly close-range poaching either side of the break. Heath hits a post and Berry and Saunders headers ensure that Cooper keeps on his toes.

---

13 H HUDDERSFIELD 1/11 — 5 W 3-0 · 19 · 22 · Att 10,211

Town: Cooper, Yallop, Zondervan, Atkins, Dozzell, Cranson, Gleghorn, Brennan, Stockwell, Deehan, Wilson
Huddersfield: Cox, Brown, Wilson Paul* / Banks, Mitchell, Jones, Rayner, Winter, Shearer, McDermott / Cowling, Cork

Atkins 19, Deehan 39, 89
Ref: R Wiseman

Atkins' 15-yard drive is deflected past Cox. Deehan extends the lead with a header from a Brennan corner. Yallop fouls Cork to concede a penalty, but Banks thunders his kick against the underside of the bar. Deehan's volley from a Wilson cross finishes off Mick Buxton's outfit.

---

14 A DERBY 8/11 — 7 L 1-2 · 6 · 22 · Att 14,145

Town: Cooper, Yallop, Zondervan, Atkins, Dozzell, Cranson, Gleghorn, Brennan, Stockwell, Deehan, Wilson
Derby: Wallington, Sage, Forsyth, Williams, Hindmarch, McLaren, Micklewhite, Gee, Davison, Harbey

Stockwell 29, Micklewhite 11, Davison 90
Ref: T Simpson

Stockwell scores his first senior goal, guiding the ball home after Wallington had only partially cleared an attack. With the scores level, Cooper produces a brilliant save to deny John Gregory from the penalty spot. Davison wins the points in the final minute, forcing home Sage's cross.

---

15 A CRYSTAL PALACE 15/11 — 8 D 3-3 · 13 · 23 · Att 7,138

Town: Cooper, Yallop, Zondervan*, Atkins, Dozzell, Cranson, Gleghorn, Brennan, Stockwell, Deehan, Wilson, Atkinson
Palace: Wood, Stebbing, Finnigan*, Taylor, Nebbeling, Cannon, Irvine*, Ketteridge, Bright, Wright, Otukdakowski / Sparrow

Wilson 17, 40, 75, Bright 45, Taylor 76, Wright 90
Ref: J Bray

Mark Bright scores on his Palace debut but Wilson takes centre-stage with a poacher's hat-trick. Then Town relax and fritter away their lead, Peter Taylor rifling in from 25 yards before Nebbeling heads into the path of Ian Wright during injury-time, and he blasts home an equaliser.

---

16 H BARNSLEY 22/11 — 5 W 1-0 · 22 · 26 · Att 10,150

Town: Cooper, Yallop, Zondervan, Atkins, Dozzell, Cranson, Gleghorn, Brennan, Stockwell, Deehan, Wilson
Barnsley: Baker, Ogley, Cross, Thomas, May, Duggan, Lowndes, Dobbin*, Foreman, Gray, Beresford / Ferry

Wilson 82
Ref: D Reeves

Allan Clarke's men look set to take a point as both keepers produce fine saves. Cooper makes three saves in one incident when Foreman, Ferry and Thomas all attempt to force the ball in. Baker blocks Atkins' effort from 30 yards. Relief comes when Wilson converts Stockwell's cross.

---

17 A BLACKBURN 29/11 — 6 D 0-0 · 20 · 27 · Att 4,951

Town: Cooper, Yallop, Zondervan, Atkins, Dozzell, Cranson, Gleghorn, Brennan, Stockwell*, Deehan, Wilson, Humes
Blackburn: Gennoe, Price, Rathbone, Barker, Keeley, Mail, Miller, Branagan, Quinn, Garner, Brotherston

Ref: G Napthine

Town create the three clearest scoring opportunities, but uncharacteristically Wilson spurns them all. Don Mackay's side fire on all cylinders early on, Brotherston hitting the woodwork, but the threat diminishes as the game goes on. Twenty-year-old Humes makes his senior debut.

---

18 H SHEFFIELD UTD 6/12 — 6 D 2-2 · 8 · 28 · Att 11,022

Town: Cooper, Yallop, Zondervan, Atkins, Dozzell, Cranson, Gleghorn, Brennan, Stockwell*, Deehan, Wilson, D'Avray
Sheffield Utd: Burridge, Barnsley, Pike, Arnott, Stancliffe, Eckhardt, Morris, Wigley, Daws, Walshaw, Beagrie* / Foley

Wilson 34, Gleghorn 85, Beagrie 2, Stancliffe 18
Ref: A Buksh

In an entertaining contest, Billy McEwan's side take an early two-goal lead through Beagrie and Stancliffe's far-post headers. Wilson brings Town back into it, stabbing home from close range. A point is saved as Gleghorn heads in Wilson's cross with United appealing for handball.

---

19 A READING 13/12 — 5 W 4-1 · 18 · 31 · Att 6,936

Town: Cooper, Yallop, Zondervan, Atkins, Dozzell, Cranson, Gleghorn, Brennan, D'Avray*, Deehan, Wilson, Stockwell, O'Donnell
Reading: Westwood, Richardson, Crombie, Beavon, Hazell, Wood, Williams, Taylor, Senior, Bremner, Smillie

Wilson 1, 54, Brennan 13, 61, Hazell 56
Ref: K Burge

Ex-Town reserve Westwood is beaten after 28 seconds when Wilson fires in from Cooper's long punt. A magnificent 25-yarder by Brennan makes it two. Hazell pulls one back but Wilson nets from a tight angle and Brennan skilfully lofts a clever shot over the advancing Westwood.

---

20 H PLYMOUTH 19/12 — 3 W 3-0 · 5 · 34 · Att 11,538

Town: Cooper, Yallop, Zondervan, Atkins, Dozzell, Cranson, Gleghorn, Brennan, Cole, Deehan, Wilson, Stockwell
Plymouth: Cherry, Nisbet, Cooper L, Goodyear, Burrows, Matthews* / Hodges, Coughlin, Tynan, Clayton, Nelson, Summerfield

Wilson 11, Brennan 47, 75
Ref: R Lewis

After persuasion by Atkins, Wilson puts himself forward for selection by N. Ireland – and his eligibility is confirmed. He celebrates by netting Stockwell's cross from 10 yards. Brennan beats Cherry at his near post with a fierce shot and rounds off good work by Dozzell and Deehan.

---

21 A MILLWALL 26/12 — 4 L 0-1 · 11 · 34 · Att 4,737

Town: Cooper, Yallop, Zondervan, Atkins, Dozzell, Cranson, Gleghorn, Brennan, Stockwell*, Deehan, Wilson, Cole
Millwall: Horne, Stevens, Coleman, N Briley, Walker, McLeary, Byrne, Salman, Morgan, Sheringham, Marks

Salman 46
Ref: M Bailey

John Docherty's men adopt a physical approach and benefit from lenient refereeing. Cooper makes his fourth penalty save of the season from Teddy Sheringham's effort. Salman, lucky to escape after scything down Stockwell, nets a deflected shot that just eludes McCall on the line.

TODAY DIVISION 2

Manager: Bobby Ferguson

SEASON 1986-87

Each match shows the Ipswich Town line-up (roman) above the opposition line-up (*italic*).

No	Date	Team	Att	Pos	Pt	F-A	H-T	Scorers, Times, and Referees	1	2	3	4	5	6	7	8	9	10	11	subs used
22	27/12	H CRYSTAL PALACE	15,007	4 / *10*	W 37	3-0	1-0	Cole 13, Deehan 78, Wilson 89 — Ref: M Scott	Cooper	Yallop*	Zondervan	Atkins	Dozzell	O'Donnell	Cole	Brennan	McCall	Deehan	Wilson	Gleghorn
									Wood	*Stebbing*	*Finnigan*	*Taylor*	*Nebbeling*	*Cannon*	*Irvine*	*Gray*	*Bright*	*Wright*	*Barber**	*Ketteridge*
23	1/1	H LEEDS	14,125	4 / *7*	W 40	2-0	1-0	Zondervan 45, Gleghorn 64 — Ref: N Butler	Hallworth	Yallop	McCall	Atkins	Dozzell	Humes	Gleghorn	Brennan	Zondervan	Wilson	Cole	
									Day	*Aspin*	*Stiles*	*Snodin*	*Ashurst*	*Ormsby*	*Buckley**	*Sheridan!*	*Ritchie*	*Baird*	*Rennie*	*Edwards*
24	3/1	A SHREWSBURY	4,783	4 / *14*	L 40	1-2	1-1	Dozzell 38; Pearson 45, McNally 78p — Ref: J Lovatt	Hallworth	Yallop	McCall	Atkins*	Dozzell	Humes	Gleghorn	Brennan	Zondervan	Wilson	Cole	Stockwell
									Perks	*Williams*	*Johnson*	*Leonard*	*Pearson*	*Linighan*	*McNally*	*Hackett*	*Brown*	*Robinson*	*Daly*	
25	24/1	A GRIMSBY	4,981	4 / *12*	D 41	1-1	1-1	Deehan 22; Robinson 26 — Ref: G Courtney	Cooper	Yallop*	McCall	Atkins	Dozzell	Cranson	Humes	Brennan	Zondervan	Wilson	Deehan	Gleghorn
									Batch	*Burgess*	*Agnew*	*Turner*	*Lyons*	*Moore K*	*Robinson*	*Walsh*	*Bonnyman*	*O'Riordan**	*Henshaw*	*Rawcliffe*
26	7/2	H PORTSMOUTH	18,670	5 / *1*	L 41	0-1	0-1	Tait 17 — Ref: C Downey	Cooper	Yallop*	McCall	Atkins	Dozzell	Cranson	Humes	Brennan	Zondervan	Wilson	Cole	Stockwell
									Knight	*Swain*	*Hardyman*	*Dillon*	*Blake*	*Daish*	*Tait*	*O'Callaghan*	*Mariner*	*Quinn**	*Hilaire*	*Wood*
27	14/2	A OLDHAM	5,584	5 / *3*	L 41	1-2	0-1	Wilson 46; Barlow 11, 86 — Ref: D Hutchinson	Cooper	Stockwell	McCall*	Atkins	Dozzell	Cranson	Humes	Brennan	Zondervan	Wilson	Deehan	Cole
									Goram	*Irwin*	*Donachie*	*Hoolickin*	*Linighan*	*Barlow*	*Palmer*	*Henry*	*Moore*	*Wright*	*Milligan**	*Williams*
28	21/2	H BIRMINGHAM	10,005	4 / *9*	W 44	3-0	0-0	Deehan 63, Cole 68, Cranson 74 — Ref: D Phillips	Cooper	Zondervan	O'Donnell	Atkins	Dozzell	Cranson	Stockwell	Humes	Deehan	Wilson	Cole	Atkinson
									Hansbury	*Roberts*	*Ranson*	*Hagan*	*Williams*	*Mortimer*	*Bremner*	*Kennedy*	*Whitton*	*Handysides*	*Kuhl*	
29	28/2	A SUNDERLAND	11,781	5 / *14*	L 44	0-1	0-0	Proctor 90p — Ref: N Midgley	Cooper*	Zondervan	O'Donnell	Atkins	Dozzell	Cranson	Stockwell	Humes	Deehan	Wilson	Cole	Atkinson
									Hesford	*Burley*	*Gray*	*Armstrong*	*Corner*	*Bennett*	*Lemon**	*Doyle*	*Curran*	*Agboola*	*Gates*	*Proctor*
30	3/3	H WEST BROM	9,704	4 / *11*	W 47	1-0	1-0	Brennan 22 — Ref: J Moules	Hallworth	Zondervan	McCall	Atkins	Dozzell	Cranson	Humes	Brennan	Deehan	Wilson	Cole	Atkinson
									Naylor	*Whitehead*	*Statham*	*Steggles*	*Dyson*	*Bradbury*	*Hopkins*	*Dickinson*	*Robson*	*Cowdrill**	*Crooks!*	*Palmer*
31	14/3	H BRADFORD C	10,330	4 / *21*	W 50	1-0	1-0	Deehan 21 — Ref: M James	Hallworth	Zondervan	McCall	Atkins	Dozzell	Cranson	Humes	Brennan	Deehan	Wilson	Cole	Atkinson
									Litchfield	*Mitchell*	*Goddard*	*McCall*	*Oliver*	*Evans**	*Hendrie*	*Goodman*	*Leonard*	*Clegg*	*Abbott*	*Thorpe*

Match reports

22. A long clearance by Cooper eludes Nebbeling and Cole streaks clear of the defence to shoot past the exposed Wood. The win is assured when Deehan heads in Gleghorn's cross. In the closing stages another Gleghorn cross reaches Wilson, who jubilantly volleys into the roof of the net.

23. After seeing in the new year, boisterous Leeds fans break into Portman Road at breakfast time, one of them cycling across the pitch! A lively match sees seven bookings and Sheridan sent off for a second bookable foul. Zondervan's shot is deflected in and Gleghorn nets from a corner.

24. Atkins' shot hits Wilson and falls conveniently for Dozzell who scores. Pearson picks his spot in oceans of space as Town appeal in vain for an offside whistle. Williams tumbles over in the box and despite vehement appeals that he dived, a penalty is given and McNally bags the winner.

25. Keeper Batch, just returned from an injury absence, is left floundering when Deehan's cross sails over him and into the net. Robinson equalises with his first goal for the Mariners since signing from Swansea, firing hard and low through a crowded Town area and beyond Cooper's reach.

26. A bruising encounter with Alan Ball's table-topping side is decided by an early goal by Tait. He heads powerfully home after a free-kick from ex-Town man O'Callaghan. Young Pompey debutant Liam Daish is picked for N. Ireland's match in Israel.

27. Wright's low driven cross is diverted past Cooper by Barlow. Wilson goes on a jinking run and brings Town level. Keeper Goram keeps Joe Royle's side level with some fine saves. Barlow looks to have lost control of the ball, but recovers to toe-poke the winning goal near the end.

28. After an hour of stalemate there is an 11-minute goal rush completely out of the blue. Deehan, who suffered a break-in and family illness in the week, sees his luck change as a 25-yard pot-shot dips into the net. Cole turns in Dozzell's cross and Cranson stoops to head in Deehan's pass.

29. Town look to have a point in the bag until an astonishing penalty decision in the final minute. Zondervan beats Curran to the ball and chests it back to Cooper. A linesman flags and the unsighted ref points to the spot. The injured Cooper is replaced in goal by Cranson and Proctor nets.

30. Brennan returns from a two-match suspension and scores the best goal of his career to date. His left-foot volley from outside the penalty area gives Naylor no chance. PFA official Garth Crooks blots his copybook by raising an arm in anger at Atkins and is dismissed by Mr Moules.

31. Cole heads on a cross from Cranson and Deehan swoops to score with a tremendous shot. Hallworth pulls off a series of excellent saves to keep Terry Dolan's relegation-threatened side at bay. The clean sheet means Town have conceded the fewest goals at home in Division Two.

Match-by-match records (games 32–42)

No	Venue	Date	Pos	Attendance	Opp Pos	Res	Score	Pts
32	A BRIGHTON	21/3	4	8,393	22	W	2-1	53
33	A STOKE	25/3	4	11,805	7	D	0-0	54
34	H HULL	28/3	4	10,240	20	D	0-0	55
35	H DERBY	4/4	4	16,533	1	L	0-2	55
36	A HUDDERSFIELD	11/4	4	5,888	20	W	2-1	58
37	A LEEDS	18/4	4	24,839	5	L	2-3	58
38	H MILLWALL	21/4	5	10,957	10	D	0-0	59
39	A BARNSLEY	25/4	6	5,536	12	L	1-2	59
40	H BLACKBURN	2/5	4	10,567	11	W	3-1	62
41	A SHEFFIELD UTD	4/5	5	8,324	9	D	0-0	63
42	H READING	9/5	5	16,036	13	D	1-1	64

Home — | Away 8,701 | Average 12,123

---

32 — A BRIGHTON, 21/3 — W 2-1
Town: Hallworth, Zondervan, McCall, Atkins, Dozzell, Cranson, Humes, Yallop*, Deehan, Wilson, Brennan, D'Avray
Brighton: Digweed, Brown*, Hutchings, Wilson, Isaac, Young, Crumplin, Gatting, Tiltman, Connor, Jasper, Campbell
Scorers: Wilson 70, D'Avray 90; Gatting 16
Ref: D Hedges

Crumplin, on his debut after signing from Bognor, crosses for Gatting to head the Seagulls in front. Barry Lloyd's strugglers are finally broken when Brennan lets fly and hits a post and Wilson snaps up the rebound. Zondervan then pulls a cross back for D'Avray's dramatic late winner.

33 — A STOKE, 25/3 — D 0-0
Town: Cooper, Yallop, McCall, Atkins, Dozzell, Cranson, D'Avray, Brennan, Deehan, Wilson, Zondervan, D'Avray
Stoke: Fox, Dixon, Parkin, Talbot, Hemming, Berry, Ford, Kelly, Morgan, Saunders*, Heath, Maskery
Ref: K Hackett

Mick Mills' side are saved when Parkin clears one effort off the line while Brennan is foiled by Fox's save. Cooper has to make crucial saves from Morgan and Ford. Old regional rivalry is recalled when the FA today fines John Bond for criticism of England manager Bobby Robson.

34 — H HULL, 28/3 — D 0-0
Town: Cooper, Yallop, McCall, Atkins, Dozzell, Cranson, Humes, D'Avray*, Brennan, Deehan, Wilson, Zondervan, Gleghorn
Hull: Norman, Palmer, Heard, Jobson, Skipper, Dyer, Parker, Bunn, Saville, Askew, Roberts
Ref: A Seville

Brian Horton's men are fighting to stay clear of the drop zone and give Town a tough time. Both keepers shine, but the visitors go closest when a Roberts shot hits Cooper's legs. A penalty is denied when Roberts tangles with McCall. Town's hopes of automatic promotion take a knock.

35 — H DERBY, 4/4 — L 0-2
Town: Cooper, Yallop, McCall, Humes, Dozzell, Cranson, D'Avray, Brennan, Gleghorn*, Wilson, Zondervan, Cole
Derby: Wallington, Blades, Forsyth, Williams, Hindmarch, McLaren, Micklewhite, Gee, Davison, Gregory, Callaghan
Scorers: Callaghan 50, Davison 59
Ref: A Gunn

The divisional leaders are relieved when Brennan makes a mess of a 40th-minute penalty, slicing it horribly wide. Callaghan puts The Rams ahead with a 25-yard curling shot. Micklewhite sets off on a mazy run and supplies a perfect cross for Davison to head in the clinching goal.

36 — A HUDDERSFIELD, 11/4 — W 2-1
Town: Hallworth, Yallop, McCall, Humes, Dozzell, Cranson, D'Avray, Brennan, Gleghorn, Wilson, Zondervan, Trevitt
Huddersfield: Dibble, Brown, Bray, Banks, Webster, Jones, Ward, Cork, Shearer, Wilson, Phil Cowling*
Scorers: Gleghorn 29, 66; McCall 22 (og)
Ref: P Tilsey

Cowling's drive is pushed aside by the excellent Hallworth, but the ball flies into the net off McCall's knee. Gleghorn equalises when Yallop's free-kick is parried to him by Dibble, on loan from Luton. Gleghorn snaps up a fine second by holding off two challenges and chipping Dibble.

37 — A LEEDS, 18/4 — L 2-3
Town: Cooper, Yallop, McCall, Atkins, Dozzell, Cranson, Humes, Brennan, Gleghorn*, Wilson, Zondervan, O'Donnell
Leeds: Day, Aspin, McDonald, Aizlewood, Ashurst, Ormsby, Ritchie, Sheridan, Baird, Pearson, Adams
Scorers: Humes 40, 77; McDonald 18, Sheridan 34, Ormsby 60
Ref: J Worrall

A rising drive by McDonald beats Cooper and Sheridan finishes off a free-kick move. Humes pulls one back after Cranson's effort is blocked and falls to him. Adams' shot is charged down but Ormsby is on hand to score. Humes bags another with a powerful header from a flag-kick.

38 — H MILLWALL, 21/4 — D 0-0
Town: Cooper, Yallop, McCall*, Atkins, Dozzell, Cranson, Humes, Brennan, O'Donnell, Wilson, Stockwell, Rimmer
Millwall: Horne, Stevens, Coleman N, Hurlock, Walker, McLeary, Briley, Byrne, Marks, Sheringham, Carter
Ref: I Hemley

Town throw everything at Millwall, but endure a frustrating evening. The Lions' spoiling tactics win them a point and several bookings. Town physio Brian Owen is booked for coming on without permission. McCall goes off concussed and can recall nothing of the game the next day.

39 — A BARNSLEY, 25/4 — L 1-2
Town: Cooper, Yallop, O'Donnell, Atkins, Dozzell, Cranson, Gleghorn, Brennan, D'Avray*, Wilson, Stockwell, Atkinson
Barnsley: Baker, Joyce, Hedworth*, Thomas, Gray, Futcher, Wylde, Dobbin, Agnew, McDonald, Clarke, Beresford
Scorers: Cranson 27; Thomas 74, Wylde 75
Ref: H Taylor

Brennan's corner causes chaos and Cranson nets. Wilson hits a post and Futcher the bar before Allan Clarke's men level as Thomas's shot goes in off Cooper. Seconds later Cranson hears a whistle in the crowd and handles – from the free-kick Wylde nets. Cooper saves a late penalty.

40 — H BLACKBURN, 2/5 — W 3-1
Town: Cooper, Yallop, McCall, Atkins, Dozzell, Cranson, Zondervan, Brennan, Humes, Wilson, Gleghorn, Sellars
Blackburn: O'Keefe, Price, Sulley, Barker, Keeley, Mail, Miller*, Ainscow, Hendry, Garner, Patterson
Scorers: Wilson 2, 26, 49; Hendry 42
Ref: P Vanes

A win is vital in the race for a play-off place and Wilson heads an early goal from Zondervan's cross. Under pressure, he hooks home a second and Town are cruising. His hat-trick is completed as he nips through a square defence for a fine solo goal. Hendry nets a cracking consolation.

41 — A SHEFFIELD UTD, 4/5 — D 0-0
Town: Cooper, Yallop, McCall, Atkins, Dozzell, Cranson, Zondervan, Brennan, Humes, Wilson, Gleghorn*, D'Avray
Sheffield Utd: Burridge, Barnsley, Pike, Kuhl, Frain, Eckhardt, Morris, Foley, Kennedy*, Dempsey, Beagrie, Mendonca
Ref: L Dilkes

The brilliant eccentric veteran Burridge defies Town with a vintage display. His highlight is a penalty save, touching Wilson's kick onto a post, following a handball offence. With superior goal difference, Town need only a point against Reading to win a place in the very first play-offs.

42 — H READING, 9/5 — D 1-1
Town: Cooper, Yallop, McCall, Atkins, Dozzell, Cranson*, Zondervan, Brennan, Humes, Wilson, Gleghorn, D'Avray
Reading: Francis, Richardson, Bailie, Beavon, Wood, Peters, Harris, Taylor, Senior, Bremner, Smillie
Scorers: Wilson 62; Richardson 73
Ref: D Axcell

In a lively atmosphere, Humes punts forward, Wood fails to cut the ball out and Wilson swoops. Covered in blood from a cut, Bremner pulls a cross back to Richardson who equalises out of the blue. With Palace and Plymouth both losing, the play-off place is comfortably achieved.

TODAY DIVISION 2 (CUP-TIES)   Manager: Bobby Ferguson   SEASON 1986-87

Play-offs

		Att	F-A	H-T	Scorers, Times, and Referees	1	2	3	4	5	6	7	8	9	10	11	subs used
SF 1	H CHARLTON 14/5	18,465 1:19	5 D 0-0	0-0	Ref: D Hedges	Cooper	Yallop	McCall	Atkins	Dozzell	O'Donnell	Zondervan	Brennan	Humes*	Wilson	Gleghorn	D'Avray
						Bolder	*Gritt*	*Reid*	*Peake*	*Thompson*	*Miller*	*Shipley*	*Stuart*	*Melrose**	*Walsh*	*Crooks*	*Milne*

A partisan crowd does its bit, but Town are repelled by Lennie Lawrence's troops in a lively game. Charlton go closest when Crooks goes down under Atkins' challenge and a penalty is given. Specialist Cooper dives to his right to keep out Walsh's kick. A draw is a fair outcome.

		Att	F-A	H-T	Scorers, Times, and Referees	1	2	3	4	5	6	7	8	9	10	11	subs used
SF 2	A CHARLTON 17/5	11,234 1:19	5 L 1-2	0-2	McCall 85 / Melrose 17, 19 Ref: L Shapter (Town lose 1-2 on aggregate)	Cooper	Yallop	McCall	Atkins	Dozzell	O'Donnell	Zondervan	Brennan	Humes	Wilson*	Gleghorn	D'Avray
						Bolder	*Humphrey*	*Reid*	*Peake*	*Thompson*	*Miller*	*Gritt*	*Stuart*	*Melrose*	*Walsh**	*Crooks*	*Leaburn*

A dreadful opening 20 minutes puts paid to Town's hopes of escaping Division Two at the first attempt. Melrose produces two headed goals to make it a miserable day for 5,000 travelling fans. Wilson goes off injured at the interval, and McCall scrambles home a late consolation goal.

Littlewoods Cup

		Att	F-A	H-T	Scorers, Times, and Referees	1	2	3	4	5	6	7	8	9	10	11	subs used
2:1	A SCUNTHORPE 23/9	3,919 4:18	10 W 2-1	2-0	Dozzell 6, Deehan 10 / Broddle 65 Ref: I Hendrick	Cooper	Stockwell	McCall	Atkins	Dozzell	O'Donnell	Gleghorn	Brennan	Gernon*	Deehan	Wilson	Parkin
						Green	*Russell**	*Longden*	*Money*	*Lister*	*Whitehead*	*Birch*	*McLean*	*Johnson*	*Broddle*	*Hill*	*Atkins*

Town start well as Green fumbles a cross-shot and collides with a post, allowing Deehan to set up scorer Dozzell. Deehan and Wilson efforts are blocked by Green before Deehan volleys in. Atkins trips Broddle, but Birch's penalty is saved by Cooper. Broddle nets a superb 20-yarder.

		Att	F-A	H-T	Scorers, Times, and Referees	1	2	3	4	5	6	7	8	9	10	11	subs used
2:2	H SCUNTHORPE 7/10	6,587 4:18	16 W 2-0	1-0	Brennan 41, Wilson 50 Ref: D Axcell (Town win 4-1 on aggregate)	Cooper	Parkin	Zondervan	Atkins	Dozzell	O'Donnell	Gleghorn	Brennan	Atkinson	Deehan*	Wilson	D'Avray
						Green	*Russell*	*Longden*	*Nicol*	*Lister*	*Whitehead*	*Birch**	*Atkins*	*Money*	*Broddle*	*Hill*	*Ferry*

Town make heavy weather of Frank Barlow's side. Dozzell heads down Zondervan's cross and Brennan blasts the first goal. A Brennan corner reaches Wilson and he pokes in the goal that finishes off the tie. Longden fouls D'Avray, but Green makes a great penalty save from Brennan.

		Att	F-A	H-T	Scorers, Times, and Referees	1	2	3	4	5	6	7	8	9	10	11	subs used
3	A CAMBRIDGE 28/10	8,893 4:14	6 L 0-1	0-1	Crown 45 Ref: B Hill	Cooper	Yallop^	Zondervan	Atkins	Dozzell	Cranson	Gleghorn	Brennan	Cole*	Deehan	Wilson	Stockwell/Atkinson
						Branagan	*Measham*	*Kimble A*	*Beattie*	*Smith*	*Littlejohns**	*Kimble G*	*Spriggs*	*Cooper*	*Crown*	*Flanagan*	*Rayment*

The Town team and supporters arrive late after a major hold-up on the A45. A near-capacity crowd roars the U's forward and on the stroke of half-time Crown produces a cracking left-foot shot on the run that beats Cooper. Dozzell misses a great chance to level ten minutes from time.

FA Cup

		Att	F-A	H-T	Scorers, Times, and Referees	1	2	3	4	5	6	7	8	9	10	11	subs used
3	H BIRMINGHAM 10/1	11,616 11	4 L 0-1	0-0	Mortimer 54 Ref: C Downey	Cooper	Yallop	McCall	Atkins	Dozzell	Humes	Gleghorn^	Brennan*	Deehan	Wilson	Zondervan	Cole/Cranson
						Hansbury	*Ransom*	*Roberts*	*Williams*	*Dicks*	*Bremner*	*Mortimer*	*Handysides*	*Whitton*	*Rees*	*Kuhl*	

After tangling with Handysides, Brennan is carried off with a knee injury in the second minute. Steve Whitton hits the Town bar, but John Bond's side go ahead when Mortimer's shot is deflected past Cooper by Cranson. Town exit the cup at this stage for the first time in 17 years.

League Table

		P	Home					Away					Pts
			W	D	L	F	A	W	D	L	F	A	
1	Derby	42	14	6	1	42	18	11	3	7	22	20	84
2	Portsmouth	42	17	2	2	37	11	6	7	8	16	17	78
3	Oldham	42	13	6	2	36	16	9	3	9	29	28	75
4	Leeds	42	15	4	2	43	16	4	7	10	15	28	68
5	IPSWICH	42	12	6	3	29	10	5	7	9	30	33	64
6	Crys Palace	42	12	4	5	35	20	7	1	13	16	33	62
7	Plymouth	42	12	6	3	40	23	4	7	10	22	34	61
8	Stoke	42	11	5	5	40	21	5	5	11	23	32	58
9	Sheffield Utd	42	10	8	3	31	19	5	5	11	19	30	58
10	Bradford C	42	10	5	6	36	27	5	5	11	26	35	55
11	Barnsley	42	8	7	6	26	23	6	6	9	23	29	55
12	Blackburn	42	11	4	6	30	22	4	7	11	15	33	55
13	Reading	42	11	4	6	33	23	4	6	11	19	36	53
14	Hull	42	10	6	5	25	22	3	8	10	16	33	53
15	West Brom	42	8	6	7	29	22	5	6	10	22	27	51
16	Millwall	42	10	5	6	27	16	4	4	13	12	29	51
17	Huddersfield	42	9	6	6	38	30	4	6	11	16	31	51
18	Shrewsbury	42	11	3	7	24	14	4	3	14	17	39	51
19	Birmingham	42	8	9	4	27	21	3	8	10	20	38	50
20	Sunderland *	42	8	6	7	25	23	4	6	11	24	36	48
21	Grimsby	42	5	8	8	18	21	5	6	10	21	38	44
22	Brighton	42	7	6	8	22	20	2	6	13	15	34	39
		924	232	122	108	693	438	108	122	232	438	693	1264

* Relegated after play-offs

Odds & ends

Double wins: (4) Bradford C, Brighton, Huddersfield, West Brom.
Double losses: (2) Derby, Oldham.

Won from behind: (4) Bradford C (a), Brighton (a), Huddersfield (a), West Brom (a).
Lost from in front: (2) Barnsley (a), Shrewsbury (a).

High spots: The best away goals tally in Division Two.
The consistency of Wilson, Dozzell and Zondervan.
Six penalty saves by Paul Cooper.

Low spots: A season's work being undone in the first 20 minutes at Charlton.
The pre-season departure of Terry Butcher.
Defeats by controversial late penalties at Shrewsbury and Sunderland.
The loss of a 3-1 lead at Crystal Palace.

Player of the Year: Romeo Zondervan.
Ever-presents: (2) Jason Dozzell, Kevin Wilson.
Hat-tricks: (4) Kevin Wilson (2), John Deehan, Nigel Gleghorn.
Opposing hat-tricks: (0).
Leading scorer: (21) Kevin Wilson.

Appearances and Goals

	Appearances								Goals					
	Lge	Sub	LC	Sub	FAC	Sub	PO	Sub	Lge	Sub	LC	FAC	PO	Tot
Atkins, Ian	40		3		1		2		1					1
Atkinson, Dalian	3	5	1			1								1
Brennan, Mark	37	3	1	1	2				7			1		8
Cole, Michael	11	5	1				2		2					2
Cooper, Paul	36		3		3		2							
Cranson, Ian	32		1				2		2					2
D'Avray, Mich	14	5	1	1	1		2		2	2				4
Deehan, John	29	3	3		1				10			1		11
Dozzell, Jason	42		3		1		2		2			1		3
Gernon, Irvin	3	1												
Gleghorn, Nigel	26	3	3		1		2		7					7
Hallworth, Jon	6													
Humes, Tony	21	1	1				2		2					2
McCall, Steve	26		1		1		2							
O'Donnell, Chris	8	2					2	2						
Parkin, Tommy	1	2	1		1		1						1	1
Rimmer, Neill		1												
Stockwell, Mick	16	5	1		1		1		1					1
Wilson, Kevin	42		3		1		2		20			1		21
Yallop, Frank	30	1	1		1		2							
Zondervan, Romeo	39	2	1		1		2		1					1
21 players used	462	30	33	4	11	2	22	2	59	2		4	1	64

BARCLAYS DIVISION 2　　Manager: John Duncan　　SEASON 1987-88

No	V	Date	Opponent	Att	Pos	Pt	F-A	H-T	Scorers, Times, and Referees	1	2	3	4	5	6	7	8	9	10	11	subs used
1	H	15/8	ASTON VILLA	14,580	–	1	1-1	1-1	Gleghorn 38; O'Donnell 29 (og); Ref: R Lewis	Hallworth	Yallop	**Harbey**	O'Donnell*	Dozzell	Cranson	**Lowe**	Brennan	**Woods**	Zondervan	Gleghorn	Stockwell
										Spink	*Gage*	*Gallacher*	*Cooper*	*Sims*	*Keown*	*Birch*	*Aspinall*	*Stainrod*	*Hunt D*	*Walters*	
2	A	18/8	PLYMOUTH	11,901	–	2	0-0	0-0	Ref: R Gifford	Hallworth	Stockwell	Harbey	Yallop	Dozzell	Cranson	Lowe	Brennan	Woods	Zondervan	Gleghorn	*Rowbotham/Clayton*
										Cherry	*Brimacombe*	*Cooper L*	*Law*	*Smith*	*Matthews*	*Cooper S**	*Summerfield*	*Tynan*	*Evans*	*Furphy^*	
3	A	22/8	SHREWSBURY	3,610	14	3	0-0	0-0	Ref: T Mills	Hallworth	Stockwell	Harbey	Yallop	Dozzell	Cranson	Lowe	Brennan	Woods*	Zondervan	Gleghorn	D'Avray
										Perks	*Williams W*	*Williams B*	*Narbett*	*Pearson*	*Linighan*	*Steele*	*McNally*	*Brown*	*Robinson*	*Tester*	
4	H	29/8	STOKE	11,149	6	6	2-0	1-0	Hemming 18 (og), Lowe 82; Ref: C Downey	Hallworth	Stockwell	Harbey	Yallop	Dozzell	Cranson	Lowe	Brennan	D'Avray	Zondervan	Gleghorn	Heath
										Fox	*Dixon*	*Carr*	*Talbot*	*Hemming*	*Berry*	*Ford*	*Parkin*	*Morgan*	*Saunders*	*Allinson**	
5	A	1/9	BLACKBURN	6,074	12	6	0-1	0-0	Hendry 65; Ref: D Phillips	Hallworth	Stockwell	Harbey	Yallop	Dozzell	Cranson	Lowe	Brennan	D'Avray^	Rimmer	Gleghorn*	Atkins/Humes
										*O'Keefe^*	*Price*	*Sulley*	*Parker*	*Hendry*	*Dawson*	*Gayle*	*Reid*	*Curry*	*Garner*	*Patterson**	*Sellars/Ainscow*
6	H	5/9	LEEDS	11,163	7	9	1-0	0-0	Lowe 79; Ref: D Hedges	Hallworth	Stockwell	Harbey	Yallop*	Dozzell	Cranson	Lowe	Brennan	D'Avray	Rimmer	Humes	Atkins
										Day	*Aspin*	*Adams*	*Aizlewood*	*Ashurst*	*Rennie*	*Williams*	*Sheridan*	*Edwards*	*Taylor**	*Haddock*	*Pearson*
7	A	12/9	MILLWALL	6,356	11	9	1-2	0-1	Brennan 52; Walker 32, O'Callaghan 81p; Ref: A Seville	Hallworth	Stockwell	Atkins*	Dozzell	Zondervan	Cranson	Brennan	Sheringham	Atkinson	Humes		Rimmer/Woods
										Horne	*Stevens*	*Sparham*	*Hurlock*	*Walker*	*O'Callaghan*	*Byrne*	*Briley*	*Cascarino*	*Salman*		
8	H	19/9	SWINDON	10,460	10	12	3-2	3-1	Yallop 6p, Brennan 12, D'Avray 34; Barnard 25, Quinn 61; Ref: D Elleray	Hallworth	Yallop	Humes	Rimmer	Dozzell	Cranson	Atkinson	Brennan	D'Avray	Zondervan	Stockwell	Kelly I
										Digby	*Hockaday*	*King*	*Kamara*	*Parkin*	*Calderwood*	*Bamber*	*O'Regan**	*Quinn*	*Foley*	*Barnard*	
9	A	26/9	CRYSTAL PALACE	10,828	7	15	2-1	0-0	Cranson 55, Lowe 71; Nebbeling 66; Ref: B Hill	Hallworth	Yallop	Harbey	Rimmer	Dozzell	Cranson	Lowe	Brennan	D'Avray	Zondervan	Stockwell	
										Wood	*O'Doherty*	*Shaw*	*Gray*	*Nebbeling*	*Taylor*	*Redfearn*	*Thomas*	*Bright*	*Wright*	*Salako*	
10	A	30/9	LEICESTER	11,533	7	16	1-1	1-1	Woods 31; Moran 10; Ref: T Simpson	Hallworth	Yallop	Harbey	Humes	Dozzell	Cranson	Lowe	Brennan	Woods	Zondervan	Stockwell	Brien
										Cooper	*Morgan*	*James*	*Osman*	*Horne**	*Ramsey*	*McAllister*	*Newell*	*Rantanen*	*Mauchlen*	*Moran*	
11	H	3/10	BARNSLEY	10,213	3	19	1-0	1-0	Lowe 11; Ref: A Buksh	Hallworth	Yallop	Harbey	Humes	Dozzell*	Cranson	Lowe	Brennan	D'Avray	Zondervan^	Stockwell	Woods/Atkins
										Baker	*Joyce*	*Cross*	*Thomas*	*Gray*	*Futcher*	*Wylde**	*Agnew*	*Lowndes*	*MacDonald^*	*Broddle*	*Beresford*

1. ASTON VILLA — A new membership scheme causes delays at turnstiles and some miss the big kick-off. Gage sends over a low driven cross and O'Donnell drills it into his own net. It's the first opposition goal at the North Stand end for over a year. Gleghorn shows good control in a tight spot to equalise.

2. PLYMOUTH — Hallworth makes some excellent saves and Cranson is also outstanding in a battling Town display at Home Park. Dave Smith's men look lively and Summerfield hits the Town bar in the second period. Cherry's most worrying moment comes when Woods' effort skims the bar.

3. SHREWSBURY — 'Boris' Hallworth enhances his reputation further with three magnificent saves to keep Chic Bates' side at bay. Perks also wins praise for two saves when Lowe gets clean through. Brown makes his debut for the Shrews, who go close when McNally hits the post ten minutes from time.

4. STOKE — John Duncan's first victory stems from a lucky breakthrough when Hemming over-hits his back-pass to Fox and the ball sails into the net. For the most part City match Town, but Lowe curls a fine shot past Fox to ensure a win. Hemming goes close to cancelling out his earlier blunder.

5. BLACKBURN — Town lack killer instinct and fall behind when sub Sellars' corner is only half-cleared and returns to the danger zone for Hendry to head home. Rimmer is recalled for his first game in nearly a year and does well. Shortly afterwards he wins a Barclay's Young Eagle of the month award.

6. LEEDS — Town overcome Billy Bremner's men with a late goal. Stockwell's cross is headed down by D'Avray and Lowe shoots in left-footed on the turn. Rimmer was on hand if he hadn't accepted the chance. Town sign Ron Fearon, 26, after the keeper completes a two-month trial period.

7. MILLWALL — O'Callaghan is now back in Millwall colours and continues to torment his old team. His corner is headed in by Walker. Town level as Atkins' free-kick is touched to Brennan, who fires home. Sheringham hits the bar before Humes brings down O'Callaghan for the decisive penalty.

8. SWINDON — Brennan is pulled down by Foley and Yallop nets from the spot. Brennan, the club's youngest ever captain, scores a magnificent goal when volleying home a D'Avray nod down. D'Avray is on hand to make the most of Atkinson's long throw. Sub Kelly is red-carded at the whistle.

9. CRYSTAL PALACE — Lowe fires in a rasping drive from Rimmer's corner and the ball bounces off Wood for Cranson to net. Nebbeling equalises, heading in a fine cross from O'Doherty. Good work by Dozzell puts Lowe clear and he rounds Wood to net the winner. Steve Coppell praises Town's display.

10. LEICESTER — Sub O'Brien knocks down McAllister's free-kick and Moran produces a spectacular overhead kick to open the scoring. A tremendous run and pull-back by Stockwell gives Woods the chance to equalise. Lowe and Dozzell both get clean through, but Paul Cooper comes out to smother.

11. BARNSLEY — Yallop sends a long ball out of defence and Brennan feeds Stockwell, whose precision cross is headed neatly home by Lowe. It was a rare moment of skill and Town struggle to keep their noses ahead. It proves a dour struggle against Allan Clarke's outfit as five are yellow-carded.

Match 12 — A HULL, 10/10

Att 6,962	Pos 7 2 19	L	0-1	HT 0-0	Thompson 58 — Ref: J Key

Ipswich: Hallworth, Yallop, Harbey, Humes*, Rimmer^, Cranson, Lowe, Brennan, D'Avray, Atkins, Stockwell, O'Donnell/Woods
Hull: Norman, Palmer, Heard, Jolson, Skipper, Parker, Roberts, Thompson, Saville, Askew, Williams

Moments after Williams hits the post, 18-year-old Les Thompson heads home Saville's corner. Brennan goes close with a 20-yarder that brings a fine save from Norman. The keeper is called up by Wales after the game. Brian Horton's men are flying high, but troubled times are ahead.

Match 13 — H MANCHESTER C, 17/10

Att 12,711	Pos 4 11 22	W	3-0	HT 2-0	Rimmer 14, 56, Harbey 30 — Ref: D Hedges

Ipswich: Hallworth, Yallop, Harbey, Rimmer, Dozzell, Cranson, Lowe, Brennan, D'Avray*, Zondervan, Stockwell, Woods
Man City: Nixon, White, Hinchcliffe, Clements, Brightwell, Redmond, McNab, Stewart, Lake, Simpson, Seagraves*/Varadi

City are on a long winless run away from home and without a win at Ipswich for 26 years. Rimmer beats White and cracks home a 25-yarder. Cranson lays the ball off to Harbey who lofts a shot over Nixon from distance. Another Harbey shot hits Redmond and is netted by Rimmer.

Match 14 — A MIDDLESBROUGH, 20/10

Att 10,491	Pos 6 2 22	L	1-3	HT 1-0	D'Avray 39; Pallister 55, Slaven 61, Kernaghan 82 — Ref: G Alpin

Ipswich: Hallworth, Yallop !, Harbey, Rimmer, Dozzell, Cranson, Lowe, Brennan, D'Avray*, Zondervan, Stockwell, Humes
Middlesbrough: Pears, Glover, Cooper, Mowbray, Parkinson, Pallister, Slaven, Kernaghan, Hamilton, Kerr, Laws

D'Avray heads in Harbey's chip. Kernaghan is held back by Yallop who is surprisingly sent off. Two minutes later Pallister forces in Glover's corner to equalise. Slaven's power header, followed by Kernaghan from a Hamilton cross, win the points for Bruce Rioch's confident outfit.

Match 15 — H SHEFFIELD UTD, 24/10

Att 11,949	Pos 5 12 25	W	1-0	HT 0-0	Lowe 90 — Ref: J Martin

Ipswich: Hallworth, Yallop, Harbey, Rimmer*, Dozzell, Cranson, Lowe, Brennan, D'Avray*, Zondervan, Stockwell, Gleghorn
Sheffield Utd: Hansbury, Wilder, Pike, Kuhl, Stancliffe, Barnsley*, Morris, Phillskirk, Beagrie, Dempsey, Frain*/Marsden/Mendonca

Heroics by borrowed keeper Roger Hansbury keep Ipswich at bay until the final minute. Gleghorn comes on for Rimmer and provides the cross that is guided home by a jubilant Lowe. Hansbury's best save of the day sees him leap to turn over a header by fellow defender Stancliffe.

Match 16 — A BOURNEMOUTH, 31/10

Att 8,105	Pos 5 18 26	D	1-1	HT 1-0	Brennan 20; Brooks 51 — Ref: K Burge

Ipswich: Hallworth, Yallop, Harbey, Rimmer^, Dozzell, Cranson, Lowe, Brennan, D'Avray^, Zondervan, Stockwell, Gleghorn/Humes
Bournemouth: Peyton, Heffernan, Morrell, Brooks, Williams, Whitlock, O'Driscoll, May, Aylott, Richards*, O'Connor/Shearer

Good work by Rimmer sets up Brennan, who arrows a fine shot into the corner. The Cherries equalise when Brooks' volley from 20 yards flies through a crowd of players past Hallworth. Bobby Robson omits Brennan and Dozzell from his England Under-21 squad for curfew breaking.

Match 17 — H HUDDERSFIELD, 3/11

Att 9,984	Pos 5 23 29	W	3-0	HT 2-0	Woods 10, Lowe 17, Brennan 87 — Ref: D Axcell

Ipswich: Hallworth, Humes*, Harbey, Rimmer, Dozzell, Cranson, Lowe, Brennan, Woods, Zondervan, Stockwell, Richardson/Peters
Huddersfield: Cox, Ward*, Bray, Banks, Webster, Walford*, Barham, Shearer, Winter, Cork, McStay/Tucker

Early goals deflate Malcolm MacDonald's side. Woods fires in a pass from Lowe after Harbey's cross from the left. The crowd grows restless after the break, but are appeased by Brennan's angled drive. Ex-Ipswich favourite Allan Hunter is sacked as coach of neighbours Colchester.

Match 18 — H READING, 7/11

Att 11,508	Pos 4 22 32	W	2-1	HT 2-1	Lowe 56, 78; Gordon 42 — Ref: T Ward

Ipswich: Hallworth, Humes, Harbey, Rimmer, Dozzell, Cranson, Lowe, Brennan, Woods, Zondervan, Stockwell, Deehan
Reading: Westwood, Jones, Gilkes, Tait^, Hicks, Curle, Williams, Taylor, White, Gordon, Horrix*/Deehan

A smart break by Reading sees Williams' cross netted by Gordon for his tenth of the season. Town equalise after a sweet move when Lowe heads in a measured cross from Gleghorn. Reading appeal in vain for offside as Brennan's shot is deflected by Lowe for the winning goal.

Match 19 — A WEST BROM, 14/11

Att 8,457	Pos 6 17 33	D	2-2	HT 2-2	Rimmer 5, Lowe 48; Gray 53, Goodman 72 — Ref: F Roberts

Ipswich: Hallworth, Yallop, Harbey, Rimmer, Dozzell, Cranson, Lowe, Brennan, Woods*, Zondervan, Stockwell, Deehan
West Brom: Naylor, Steggles, Burrows, Hogg, Palmer, Kelly, Lynex, Gray, Anderson, Morley, Goodman

From Yallop's long ball, Rimmer shoots carefully past Naylor. Brennan's shot is blocked, but Lowe nets the rebound. Gray's magnificent volley turns the tide and his goalbound header is helped in by Goodman. Town pull all 11 back on the goal-line to thwart an indirect free-kick.

Match 20 — H OLDHAM, 21/11

Att 11,007	Pos 4 21 36	W	2-0	HT 1-0	Brennan 20, Lowe 74 — Ref: M Bodenham

Ipswich: Hallworth, Yallop, Harbey*, Rimmer, Dozzell, Cranson, Lowe, Brennan, D'Avray*, Zondervan, Stockwell, Deehan/Humes
Oldham: Gorton, Irwin, Callaghan, Flynn, Linighan, Milligan*, Palmer, Kelly, Henry T, Wright, Williams/Cecere

Palmer has an effort well saved by Hallworth after he gets clean through. Brennan fires home after Zondervan's cross finds him unmarked. Deehan has penalty claims turned down. Joe Royle's side are down and out after Lowe hooks the ball home following a goalmouth scramble.

Match 21 — A BIRMINGHAM, 28/11

Att 6,718	Pos 6 9 36	L	0-1	HT 0-0	Frain 78 — Ref: J Rushton

Ipswich: Hallworth, Yallop, Harbey^, Rimmer, Dozzell, Humes, Lowe, Brennan, Deehan*, Zondervan, Stockwell, D'Avray/**Bernal**
Birmingham: Godden, Ranson, Trewick*, Roberts, Williams, Frain, Bremner, Childs, Whitton, Kennedy, Wigley/Handysides

A spectacular overhead attempt by Humes cracks against the City bar on 30 minutes. Harbey trips Wigley after the break but Kennedy hits the post with his penalty-kick. Hallworth appears to be impeded by Kennedy, but there is no whistle and Frain nets the loose ball to win the points.

Match 22 — H BRADFORD C, 5/12

Att 13,707	Pos 5 2 39	W	4-0	HT 1-0	Stockwell 36, Zondervan 47p, 83p, [Gleghorn 77] — Ref: D Vickers

Ipswich: Hallworth, Yallop, Harbey*, Atkins, Gleghorn, Humes, Woods, Brennan, Deehan*, Zondervan, Stockwell, Cole
Bradford: Tomlinson, Mitchell, Staunton^, Oliver, McCall, Evans*, Hendrie, Simnott, Palin, Leonard, Futcher/Abbott/Ellis

Terry Dolan's side, having their best season in living memory, go behind when Woods' close-range effort is blocked and Stockwell nets. After fouls on Gleghorn and Woods, Zondervan bags two penalties, sending Tomlinson the wrong way both times. Gleghorn heads in a corner-kick.

Match 23 — H SHREWSBURY, 19/12

Att 9,930	Pos 5 22 42	W	2-0	HT 0-0	Zondervan 50p, D'Avray 74 — Ref: M Bailey

Ipswich: Hallworth, Yallop, Harbey, Atkins, Gleghorn, Humes, Lowe, Brennan, D'Avray, Zondervan, Stockwell, Narbett/Leonard
Shrewsbury: Perks, Green, Williams B, Priest^, Moyes, Linighan, Steele, McNally, Brown, Robinson, Tester^

Cranson is fit again after injury and is shocked to be left out of the side. Town chalk up their 11th successive home win as Zondervan nets from the spot after Linighan's challenge on Lowe. D'Avray smashes home Lowe's cross. Alex Ferguson watches in preparation for the FA Cup-tie.

BARCLAYS DIVISION 2 — Manager: John Duncan — SEASON 1987-88

No	Date	Venue/Opponent	Att	Pos (opp)	Result/Pt	F-A	H-T	Scorers, Times, and Referees
24	26/12	H CRYSTAL PALACE	17,200	5 (2)	L / 42	2-3	1-1	Lowe 4, 89 / Redfearn 39p, Wright 48, 77 — Ref: P Foakes
25	28/12	A SWINDON	12,429	6 (11)	L / 42	2-4	0-2	Lowe 47, Brennan 62 / Cranson 33 (og), Quinn 42, King 75, [Bamber 86] — Ref: J Carter
26	1/1	A STOKE	9,976	6 (15)	W / 45	2-1	1-1	Lowe 40, D'Avray 52 / Morgan 8 — Ref: D Scott
27	2/1	H MILLWALL	13,710	8 (4)	D / 46	1-1	0-0	D'Avray 75 / Cascarino 90 — Ref: T Simpson
28	16/1	A ASTON VILLA	20,201	8 (1)	L / 46	0-1	0-1	Keown 5 — Ref: K Breen
29	30/1	H BLACKBURN	12,604	8 (5)	L / 46	0-2	0-2	Sellars 4, Ainscow 20 — Ref: P Don
30	6/2	A LEEDS	19,564	9 (7)	L / 46	0-1	0-1	Pearson 14 — Ref: G Aplin
31	13/2	H PLYMOUTH	10,476	9 (15)	L / 46	1-2	0-1	Deehan 24 / Law 49, Summerfield 63 — Ref: R Lewis
32	20/2	H LEICESTER	11,084	9 (17)	L / 46	0-2	0-1	Reid 40, Newell 76 — Ref: D Reeves
33	27/2	A BARNSLEY	6,482	8 (15)	W / 49	3-2	2-1	Atkinson 9, 19, Atkins 67p / Currie 29, 65 — Ref: G Tyson
34	5/3	A MANCHESTER C	17,402	8 (11)	L / 49	0-2	0-1	Morley 12, Varadi 80 — Ref: D Kirk

Line-ups, substitutes and reports

24 — H Crystal Palace
Town (1–11): Hallworth, Yallop, Harbey, Cranson, Gleghorn, Humes*, Lowe, Brennan, Deehan^, Dozzell, Stockwell. Subs: Bernal/Atkinson.
Palace: Wood, Stebbing, Burke, Penyfather, Nebbeling, Cannon, Redfearn*, Thomas, Barber, Wright, Salaka. Sub: Pardew.
Lowe sprints through to beat a hesitant defence and open the scoring. Cranson tackles Wright from behind to concede the equalising penalty. Lowe nets from close range to briefly raise the tempo near the end.

25 — A Swindon
Town: Hallworth, Yallop, Harbey*, Milton^, Gleghorn, Cranson, Lowe, Brennan, Cole, Dozzell, Stockwell. Subs: Wilson/Atkinson.
Swindon: Digby, Hockaday, King, Kamara, Parkin, Calderwood, Bamber, O'Regan*, Quinn, Foley, Barnard. Sub: Kelly.
Kamara's cross is headed powerfully past his own keeper by Cranson. Town pull back a two-goal deficit when Lowe converts Cranson's pass and sub Atkinson sets up Brennan's powerful drive. Swindon hit back well and ensure the points when Bamber thunders home a picture goal.

26 — A Stoke
Town: Hallworth, Yallop, Harbey, Atkins, Humes, Cranson, Lowe, Brennan, D'Avray*, Dozzell, Stockwell.
Stoke: Barrett, Dixon, Carr, Parkin, Bould, Berry, Ford, Henry*, Morgan, Stainrod^, Shaw. Subs: Talbot/Daly.
Berry flicks the ball on to Morgan who gives Mick Mills' side an early lead. Town bounce back well and Humes' header is knocked by Lowe, who later has another ruled out. D'Avray fires a winner from close range. City give a debut to Simon Stainrod, a new recruit from Villa.

27 — H Millwall
Town: Hallworth, Yallop, Harbey, Atkins, Humes, Cranson, Lowe, Brennan, D'Avray, Dozzell, Stockwell. Sub: Carter.
Millwall: Horne, Stevens, Salman, Coleman, Thompson, Morgan, Byrne, Briley, Sheringham, Cascarino, Carter.
Cranson drives forward and D'Avray powers through to crack home a fine goal. In the final minute, Hallworth dashes out and boots the ball into touch. From the throw-in, Byrne crosses and Cascarino's effort is deflected by Humes past Hallworth, who had the original effort covered.

28 — A Aston Villa
Town: Hallworth, Yallop, Harbey*, Atkins, Cranson, Humes*, Lowe, Brennan, D'Avray, Wark, Stockwell. Sub: Dozzell.
Villa: Spink, Gage, Gallacher, Gray A, Evans, Keown, Birch, Lillis, Thompson, Shaw, McInally.
Delight for Town fans as popular John Wark returns from Liverpool for £100,000. He replaces Dozzell and a compact display at the home of Graham Taylor's table-toppers probably deserved at least a point. Keown's early looping header from Gray's lofted free-kick proves decisive.

29 — H Blackburn
Town: Hallworth, Yallop, Harbey*, Atkins, Rimmer*, Cranson, Lowe, Brennan, D'Avray, Wark, Stockwell^. Subs: Atkinson/Gleghorn.
Blackburn: Gennoe, Price, Sulley, Ainscow, Hendry, Mail, Miller, Reid, Archibald, Garner, Sellars.
Stockwell's weak back-pass allows Sellars to slip the ball past Hallworth. Town waste two clear chances when Cranson and D'Avray both send headers straight at Gennoe. An unhappy home-coming – for Wark.

30 — A Leeds
Town: Hallworth, Yallop, Harbey*, Atkins, Dozzell*, Humes, Lowe, Brennan, Deehan, Wark, Stockwell. Subs: Gleghorn/Dozzell.
Leeds: Day, Aspin, Adams, Williams, Ashurst, Rennie, Haddock, Sheridan, Pearson, Davison, Snodin.
Atkins clears only as far as Haddock and he feeds Adams, who sends in a curling cross which is netted by the diving figure of Pearson. Billy Bremner's men defend resolutely and Town miss several half-chances. Cranson pulls a hamstring and Dozzell is forced to help out in defence.

31 — H Plymouth
Town: Hallworth, Yallop, Harbey, Atkins, Humes*, Cranson, Lowe, Gleghorn, Deehan, Stockwell. Subs: Brennan/Woods.
Plymouth: Cherry, Burrows, Cooper L, Law, Marker, McElhinney, Hodges, Matthews, Tynan, Evans, Summerfield.
Brennan is dropped as Duncan makes more changes in a bid to halt the poor run. Deehan heads Town ahead, but Law levels with a fortunate goal when his cross is caught by the wind and swirls in under the bar. Summerfield beats several men on a solo run to squeeze home a winner.

32 — H Leicester
Town: Carson, Yallop, Stockwell, Atkins, Humes, Cranson, Lowe, Brennan, Deehan*, Atkinson, Rimmer^. Subs: Woods/Harbey.
Leicester: Cooper, Morgan, Mauchlen, Osman, Walsh, Ramsey, McAllister, Cross, Newell, Reid, Weir.
More misery as Reid is given time and space to shoot past debutant Carson. Newell, in acres of space, is fed by Cross and shoots low into the net. David Pleat's men have inflicted Town's fifth successive defeat but chairman Cobbold says he hasn't thrown in the promotion towel yet.

33 — A Barnsley
Town: Hallworth, Yallop, Wark, Atkins, Cranson, Humes, Lowe*, Brennan, Deehan, Atkinson, Rimmer. Sub: Dozzell.
Barnsley: Baker, Joyce, Cross, Thomas, McGugan, Futcher !, Currie, Dobbin*, Lowndes, MacDonald, Beresford. Sub: Broddle.
Transfer-listed Atkinson weaves his magic to end the dismal run. He outstrips the defence to fire home in typical style and then lobs Baker from fully 30 yards. Currie pulls it back, but McGugan fouls Atkinson for the winning penalty. Paul Futcher is red-carded at the final whistle.

34 — A Manchester C
Town: Stowell, Yallop, Hinchcliffe, Atkins, Stockwell, Cranson, White, Brennan*, Deehan^, Atkinson, Rimmer. Subs: Dozzell/Bernal.
Manchester C: Lake, Clements, Brightwell, Redmond, White, Morley, Varadi, Scott*, Simpson. Sub: Moulden.
Trevor Morley's first goal for City sees him head in White's overhead kick after Humes and Hallworth get in a tangle. Cranson half-clears and Varadi drives home the second goal. Town look rather pedestrian and the introduction of a more physical approach is clearly not working well.

Match 35

H · 12/3 · HULL · 9,728 · 8 · 9 · 52 · W · 2-0 · 1-0
Woods 18, Lowe 78
Ref: R Wiseman

Town: Fearon, Yallop, Zondervan, Harbey, D'Avray, Lowe, Bernal, Dozzell, Woods, Atkinson, Stockwell*, Deehan
Hull: Norman, Williams, Jobson, Daniel, Skipper, Roberts, Brown*, Dyer^, Saville, DeMange, Barnes, Payton/Thompson

Another reshuffle and all-action Andy Bernal, the first Australian to play for Town, hits the post with a 30-yarder. Atkinson's cross is headed in by Woods. More powerful running by Atkinson on the break allows Lowe to convert the second. It's the first home victory since December.

Match 36

H · 19/3 · BOURNEMOUTH · 10,208 · 10 · 20 · 52 · L · 1-2 · 0-2
Woods 57 / Aylott 8, Close 36
Ref: I Hemley

Town: Fearon, Yallop, Zondervan, Harbey, D'Avray, Lowe, Bernal*, Dozzell, Woods^, Atkinson, Stockwell, Deehan
Bournemouth: Peyton, Langan, Brooks, Morrell, Williams, Newson, O'Connor, Pulis, Aylott, Cooke, Close, Gleghorn/Deehan

O'Connor's cross deflects off Stockwell to Aylott, who beats Fearon. Harry Redknapp's lowly-placed side increase their lead when Close nips in to score after Williams heads a free-kick to him. Woods pulls one back after the hard-working Lowe gets on the end of a Yallop free-kick.

Match 37

A · 26/3 · SHEFFIELD UTD · 8,753 · 10 · 19 · 52 · L · 1-4 · 1-2
Zondervan 25p / Cadette 15, 35, Webster 74, Downes 79
Ref: R Nixon

Town: Fearon, Yallop, Zondervan, Harbey, Humes*, Lowe, Bernal, Dozzell, Woods^, Deehan, Stockwell, Brennan/D'Avray
Sheffield Utd: Benstead 79, Barnsley, Todd, Pike, Webster, Hetherston, Smith, Williams !, Cadette, Downes, Beagrie

Town are hammered by a side reduced to ten men when Williams is sent off for a retaliatory elbow on Humes. The Town man goes off with a broken nose and from the free-kick Downes curls in the fourth. It could have been worse, for Fearon saves a Cadette penalty and his post is hit.

Match 38

A · 2/4 · READING · 9,953 · 10 · 22 · 53 · D · 1-1 · 0-0
Lowe 69 / Whitehurst 48
Ref: D Elleray

Town: Fearon, Yallop, Zondervan, Harbey, D'Avray, Lowe, Bernal, Dozzell, Woods^, Deehan, Stockwell, Atkinson/Milton
Reading: Francis, Baillie, Beavon, Richardson, Hicks, Jones*, Curle, Tait, Whitehurst, Smillie, Gilkes, Taylor

Fearon frustrates his former club with some good saves, but cannot prevent Whitehurst heading home after a fine run and cross by the lively Gilkes. Lowe equalises with his 18th goal of the season, heading in Zondervan's free-kick. Francis got his hand to it, but couldn't keep it out.

Match 39

H · 4/4 · WEST BROM · 10,665 · 10 · 19 · 54 · D · 1-1 · 0-1
Yallop 66 / Phillips 33
Ref: K Miller

Town: Fearon, Yallop, Zondervan, Wilson, D'Avray, Lowe, Milton, Dozzell, Deehan, Atkinson, Stockwell
West Brom: Naylor, Hobson, Talbot, Cowdrill, North, Hopkins, Dyson, Gray, Anderson, Palmer*, Phillips, Robson

Frank Yallop, on his 24th birthday, strolls through the game in his new role of sweeper. He caps the display with a 25-yard rocket of a shot which livens up a windswept Portman Road crowd and saves Town a point. Phillips had hooked Albion ahead after assistance from Palmer.

Match 40

A · 8/4 · HUDDERSFIELD · 4,023 · 10 · 23 · 57 · W · 2-1 · 0-1
Atkinson 53, 71, Banks 4
Ref: K Warmsley

Town: Fearon, Yallop, Zondervan, Wilson, D'Avray, Lowe, Milton, Dozzell, Deehan, Atkinson, Stockwell
Huddersfield: Martin, Trevitt, Mitchell, Brown, Tucker, Ward*, Shotton, Hutchings, Shearer, Banks, Madrick, France

Amid flurries of snow, sleet and rain, Town make hard work of beating the doomed Terriers in front of their lowest gate of the season. Wilson, on loan from Twente Enschede, has a solid game. Atkinson wins it with a stunning solo goal, having earlier cancelled out Banks' early shock.

Match 41

H · 23/4 · MIDDLESBROUGH · 12,773 · 9 · 4 · 60 · W · 4-0 · 3-0
Atkinson 4, 30, 56, D'Avray 35
Ref: A Buksh

Town: Fearon, Yallop, Zondervan, Wilson, Dozzell, Lowe, Deehan, Milton, D'Avray^, Atkinson, Stockwell*, Bernal
Middlesbrough: Pears, Glover*, Mowbray, Cooper, Laws, Slaven, Pallister, Ripley, Senior, Kerr, Burke, Kernaghan

A memorable trio by Atkinson rouses the fans after weeks of dull fare. He whacks home a blistering shot after Milton's through ball early on. After rounding Mowbray he fires in a stunning second. D'Avray nets in his 200th game but Atkinson has the last word after Lowe hits a post.

Match 42

A · 30/4 · OLDHAM · 5,018 · 11 · 9 · 60 · L · 1-3 · 1-1
Lowe 28 / Ritchie 7, Palmer 52, Bernal 75 (og)
Ref: J Key

Town: Fearon, Yallop, Zondervan, Wilson*, Dozzell, Lowe, Deehan, Milton, D'Avray^, Atkinson, Stockwell*, Bernal/Woods
Oldham: Rhodes, Irwin, Flynn, Barrett, Marshall, Palmer, Milligan, Donachie, Barlow, Wright, Ritchie

A D'Avray effort looks like it has crossed the line, but Lowe makes sure and is credited with the equaliser. Palmer puts the Latics ahead with a fierce shot. A point is put out of Town's reach when, under pressure from Donachie, Bernal can only head Wright's cross past his own keeper.

Match 43

H · 2/5 · BIRMINGHAM · 11,067 · 8 · 19 · 63 · W · 1-0 · 0-0
Atkinson 68
Ref: D Axcell

Town: Fearon, Yallop, Zondervan, Humes*, Dozzell, Lowe, Deehan, Milton*, D'Avray^, Atkinson, Stockwell, Wark
Birmingham: Hansbury, Ranson, Bird, Roberts, Overson, Trewick, Atkins, Yates*, Russell, Handysides, Wigley, Kennedy/Childs

A rather forgettable contest is enlivened by a memorable goal by the mercurial Atkinson. Lowe feeds Stockwell and his cross is backheeled into the net in cheeky fashion. It was an exquisite touch, out of keeping with the game, and proves Atkinson is not just about pace and power.

Match 44

A · 7/5 · BRADFORD C · 16,017 · 8 · 4 · 66 · W · 3-2 · 2-2
D'Avray 18, Dozzell 25, Milton 71 / Abbott 12, McCall 32
Ref: P Tyldesley

Town: Fearon, Yallop, Zondervan, Humes, Dozzell, Lowe, Deehan, Milton, D'Avray^, Atkinson, Stockwell*, Wark
Bradford C: Tomlinson, Abbott, Goddard, McCall, Oliver, Leonard, Evans^, Sinnott, Ormondroyd, Kennedy, Futcher*, Palin/Leonard

Promotion hopefuls City are desperate for a win, but Town are keen to end the campaign in style. D'Avray produces a clinical finish to cancel out Abbott's opener. Impressive Dozzell heads home, but McCall hits back with a solo effort. Milton wins it after Sinnott's dreadful back-pass.

Home 11,722
Away 10,039
Average 11,722

BARCLAYS DIVISION 2 (CUP-TIES) Manager: John Duncan SEASON 1987-88

Littlewoods Cup

			Att	F-A	H-T	Scorers, Times, and Referees	1	2	3	4	5	6	7	8	9	10	11	subs used
2:1	H	NORTHAMPTON 10	8,645 3:1	1-1 D	1-0	Zondervan 38 / Gilbert 54p / Ref: D Reeves	Hallworth	Yallop	Harbey	Rimmer	Dozzell	Humes	Atkinson	Brennan	D'Avray	Zondervan	Stockwell	Bruce/Scott
							Gleasure	*Reed*	*Logan*	*Chard^*	*Wilcox*	*McPherson*	*Longhurst **	*Benjamin*	*Gilbert*	*Morley*	*McGoldrick*	

After Stockwell is impeded but no penalty is awarded, Town go ahead with a delightful move. Rimmer feeds Atkinson and the cross is rolled into scorer Zondervan's path by D'Avray. Yallop handles unnecessarily and Gilbert levels from the spot to maintain his 100 per cent record.

			Att	F-A	H-T	Scorers, Times, and Referees	1	2	3	4	5	6	7	8	9	10	11	subs used
2:2	A	NORTHAMPTON 3	8,316 3:1	4-2 W aet	0-1	Harbey 65, D'Avray 93, 95, Lowe 100 / Morley 4, Donegal 119 / Ref: H King / (Town win 5-3 on aggregate)	Hallworth	Yallop	Harbey	Cranson	Dozzell	Humes	Lowe	Brennan*	D'Avray	Atkins	Stockwell	Woods
							Gleasure	*Reed*	*Logan*	*Chard*	*Wilcox*	*McPherson*	*Bunce **	*Benjamin^*	*Gilbert*	*Morley*	*McGoldrick*	*Senior/Donegal*

On a slippery surface, Morley rounds Hallworth to give Town an early shock. With only Gleasure to beat, Harbey forces extra-time with a fine left-foot drive. Town run riot with three goals in seven minutes including a neat D'Avray volley and then a header after Brennan hits the post.

			Att	F-A	H-T	Scorers, Times, and Referees	1	2	3	4	5	6	7	8	9	10	11	subs used
3	H	SOUTHEND 5	13,444 3:23	1-0 W	1-0	Harbey 45 / Ref: M Taylor	Hallworth	Yallop	Harbey	Rimmer*	Dozzell	Cranson	Lowe	Brennan	D'Avray	Zondervan	Stockwell	Gleghorn
							Steele	*Ramsey*	*Johnson*	*Ling*	*Martin*	*Hall*	*Clark*	*Pennyfather*	*Robinson **	*McDonough*	*Rogers*	*Westley*

Hall handles during a melee and Yallop squares the free-kick to Harbey, whose powerful shot beats the wall and takes a wicked deflection to beat the diving Steele. Town make hard work of keeping the Shrimpers at bay. It is reported that Duncan is trying to bring back John Wark.

			Att	F-A	H-T	Scorers, Times, and Referees	1	2	3	4	5	6	7	8	9	10	11	subs used
4	H	LUTON 6	15,643 1:12	0-1 L	0-1	Stein B 4 / Ref: T Mills	Hallworth	Stockwell	Harbey	Yallop	Dozzell	Cranson	Rimmer	Brennan	D'Avray	Lowe	Zondervan	Deehan
							Sealey	*Breacker*	*Harvey*	*McDonough*	*Foster*	*Donaghy*	*Wilson D**	*Stein B*	*Nwajiobi*	*Johnson^*	*Stein M*	*Black/Oldfield*

Missing several first-choice men, Ray Harford's side take an early lead with a superb piece of finishing by Brian Stein. Put in by brother Mark, he skips past Hallworth to slide in. Town work hard, but are repelled by Foster and Donaghy. Penalty claims are denied as Lowe crashes over.

FA Cup

			Att	F-A	H-T	Scorers, Times, and Referees	1	2	3	4	5	6	7	8	9	10	11	subs used
3	H	MANCHESTER U 8	23,012 1:4	1-2 L	1-1	Humes 44 / D'Avray 29 (og), Anderson 66 / Ref: B Stevens	Hallworth	Yallop	Harbey	Atkins	Cranson	Humes*	Lowe	Brennan	D'Avray	Zondervan^	Dozzell*	Stockwell/Gleghorn
							Turner	*Anderson*	*Duxbury*	*Bruce*	*Moran*	*Moses^*	*Robson*	*Strachan*	*McClair*	*Whiteside*	*Gibson^*	*Olsen/Davenport*

Town pose Alex Ferguson's men plenty of problems in a red-blooded cup-tie. After D'Avray unluckily concedes the lead, Humes powers in a dramatic equaliser, climbing high to head in. Town have a penalty appeal turned down before Anderson heads a winner from Gibson's corner.

			Home					Away						Odds & ends
		P	W	D	L	F	A	W	D	L	F	A	Pts	
1	Millwall	44	15	3	4	45	23	10	4	8	27	29	82	Double wins: (4) Barnsley, Bradford C, Huddersfield, Stoke.
2	Aston Villa	44	9	7	6	31	21	13	5	4	37	20	78	Double losses: (1) Blackburn.
3	Middlesbro *	44	15	4	3	44	16	7	8	7	19	20	78	
4	Bradford C	44	14	3	5	49	26	8	8	6	25	28	77	Won from behind: (5) Hudd'fr'd (a), Reading (h), Stoke (a), Bradford C(a).
5	Blackburn	44	12	8	2	38	22	9	6	7	30	30	77	Northampton (a) (LC).
6	Crys Palace	44	16	3	3	50	21	6	6	10	36	38	75	Lost from in front: (3) Middlesbrough (a), Crystal Palace (h).
7	Leeds	44	14	4	4	37	18	5	8	9	24	33	69	Plymouth (h).
8	IPSWICH	44	14	3	5	38	17	5	6	11	23	35	66	
9	Manchester C	44	11	4	7	50	28	8	4	10	30	32	65	High spots: Eleven home League wins in a row.
10	Oldham	44	13	4	5	43	27	5	7	10	29	37	65	The return of popular John Wark.
11	Stoke	44	12	6	4	34	22	5	5	12	16	35	62	Dalian Atkinson's spectacular hat-trick v Middlesbrough.
12	Swindon	44	10	7	5	43	25	6	4	12	30	35	59	David Lowe's outstanding work-rate and consistency.
13	Leicester	44	11	5	5	35	20	4	6	12	27	41	59	The win at promotion-challenging Bradford City.
14	Barnsley	44	11	4	7	42	32	4	5	13	19	30	57	
15	Hull	44	10	8	4	32	22	4	7	11	22	38	57	Low spots: Ten defeats in a 14-game run after Christmas which
16	Plymouth	44	12	4	6	44	26	4	4	14	21	41	56	wrecked promotion hopes.
17	Bournemouth	44	7	7	8	36	30	6	3	13	20	38	49	The 1-4 hammering at relegated Sheffield Utd.
18	Shrewsbury	44	7	8	7	23	22	4	8	10	19	32	49	The unlucky FA Cup defeat by Manchester U.
19	Birmingham	44	7	9	6	20	24	4	6	12	21	42	48	
20	West Brom	44	8	7	7	29	26	4	4	14	21	43	47	
21	Sheffield U**	44	8	6	8	27	28	5	1	16	18	46	46	
22	Reading	44	5	7	10	20	25	5	5	12	24	45	42	
23	Huddersfield	44	4	6	12	20	38	2	4	16	21	62	28	Player of the Year: Frank Yallop.
		1012	246	127	133	830	559	133	127	246	559	830	1391	

* promoted
after play-offs
** relegated
after play-offs

Ever-presents: (0).
Hat-tricks: (1) Dalian Atkinson.
Opposing hat-tricks: (0).
Leading scorer: (18) David Lowe.

	Appearances						Goals			
	Lge	Sub	LC	Sub	FAC	Sub	Lge	LC	FAC	Tot
Atkins, Ian	13	3	1		1		1			1
Atkinson, Dalian	13	4	1		1		8			8
Bernal, Andy	4	5								
Brennan, Mark	34	2	4		1		6			6
Carson, Tom	1									
Cole, Michael	1	1								
Cranson, Ian	29		3		1		1			1
D'Avray, Mich	26	3	4		1		7	2		9
Deehan, John	16	4		1			1			1
Dozzell, Jason	35	4	4		1		1			1
Fearon, Ron	10									
Gleghorn, Nigel	11	5		1	1		2			2
Hallworth, Jon	33		4		1					
Harbey, Graham	34	1	4		1		1	2		3
Humes, Tony	23	4	2		1		1			1
Lowe, David	41	3	3		1		17	1		18
Milton, Simon	7	1		2			1			1
O'Donnell, Chris		1								
Rimmer, Neil	18	1	3				3			3
Stockwell, Mick	42	1	4		1	1	1			1
Wark, John	5	2								
Wilson, Ulrich	5	1								
Woods, Neil	12	7								
Yallop, Frank	41		4		1		4			4
Zondervan, Romeo	29		3		1		2	1		3
(own-goals)							4		1	5
25 players used	484	50	44	4	11	2	61	6	1	68

No		Date	Att	Pos	Pt	F-A	H-T	1	2	3	4	5	6	7	8	9	10	11	subs used	Scorers, Times, and Referees
1	A	27/8 **STOKE**	8,639		D 1	1-1	0-1	Forrest	Yallop	Hill	Zondervan	Humes	Linighan	Lowe	Dozzell	D'Avray*	Atkinson	Wark	Milton	Humes 80
								Fox	*Gidman*	*Parkin*	*Kamara*	*Beeston*	*Henry*	*Hackett**	*Ford*	*Shaw*	*Saunders*	*Beagrie*	*Morgan*	Kamara 43 Ref: A Seville
2	H	3/9 **SUNDERLAND**	12,835	8	W 4	2-0	1-0	Forrest	Yallop	Hill	Zondervan	Humes*	Linighan	Lowe	Dozzell	D'Avray	Atkinson	Wark	Milton	Atkinson 3, Dozzell 46
								Hesford	*Kay*	*Agboola*	*Bennett*	*McPhail**	*Doyle*	*Lemon^*	*Armstrong*	*Gates*	*Gabbiadini*	*Pascoe*	*Ord/Gray*	Ref: D Reeves
3	A	10/9 **LEICESTER**	10,816	7	W 7	1-0	1-0	Forrest	Yallop	Hill	Zondervan	Humes	Linighan	Lowe	Dozzell	D'Avray	Atkinson	Wark	Milton	Atkinson 43
								Cooper	*Mauchlen**	*Spearing*	*Ramsey*	*Walsh*	*Brown*	*Reid^*	*Cross*	*Newell*	*McAllister*	*Quinn*	*Turner/Weir*	Ref: P Tyldesley
4	H	17/9 **WATFORD**	14,644	4	W 10	3-2	1-1	Forrest	Yallop	Hill	Zondervan	Humes	Linighan	Lowe	Dozzell	D'Avray*	Atkinson	Milton	Stockwell	Milton 13, Atkinson 88, Lowe 72
								Coton	*Gibbs*	*Falconer*	*Jackett*	*Holdsworth*	*Da McClelland*	*Roberts**	*Wilkinson*	*Bamber*	*Porter*	*Holden*	*Thomas*	Roberts 28, 47 Ref: J Moules
5	A	20/9 **SHREWSBURY**	4,154^	3	W 13	5-1	3-1	Forrest	Yallop	Hill	Stockwell	Humes	Linighan	Lowe	Dozzell	Milton	Atkinson	Wark	Melrose/Steele	Dozzell 7, Milton 33, 43, 64, Yallop 50
								Perks	*Williams W*	*Green*	*Bell^*	*Rougvie*	*Finley*	*Brown*	*McNally*	*Irvine*	*Thomas^*	*Kasule*	*Melrose/Steele*	Rougvie 8 Ref: K Cooper
6	H	24/9 **BRADFORD C**	13,074	3	D 14	1-1	0-0	Forrest	Yallop	Hill	Stockwell	Humes*	Harbey	Lowe	Dozzell	D'Avray	Atkinson	Milton	Woods^/Kiwomya	Atkinson 90
								Tomlinson	*Mitchell*	*Jackson*	*Banks*	*Oliver*	*Evans D*	*Thomas*	*Sinnott*	*Ormondroyd*	*Abbott**	*Leonard*	*Palin*	Mitchell 51 Ref: A Buksh
7	A	1/10 **WEST BROM**	9,357	1	W 17	2-1	1-0	Forrest	Yallop	Hill	Zondervan	Humes	D'Avray	Lowe	Dozzell	Milton	Atkinson	Wark		Lowe 41, Dozzell 78
								Naylor	*Alliston*	*Burrows*	*Talbot*	*Whyte*	*North*	*Hopkins*	*Goodman*	*Phillips*	*Palmer*	*Anderson*		Whyte 72 Ref: P Harrison
8	A	4/10 **CRYSTAL PALACE**	10,325	3	L 17	0-2	0-2	Forrest	Yallop	Hill	Zondervan	Humes*	D'Avray	Lowe	Dozzell	Milton	Atkinson	Wark	Linighan	
								Parkin	*Hone*	*Burke*	*Pardew*	*Hopkins*	*O'Reilly*	*Redfearn*	*Thomas*	*Bright*	*Wright**	*Barber*	*Salako*	Bright 8, Wright 14 Ref: R Milford
9	H	8/10 **MANCHESTER C**	15,521	3	W 20	1-0	1-0	Forrest	Yallop	Hill	Zondervan	Humes	D'Avray	Lowe	Dozzell	Milton	Atkinson	Wark	Linighan!	Dozzell 30
								Dibble	*Seagrave**	*Hinchcliffe*	*Gayle*	*Morley*	*Redmond*	*White*	*Lake*	*Moulden*	*McNab*	*Biggins*	*Williams*	Ref: P Danson
10	H	15/10 **OXFORD**	13,039	3	L 20	1-2	0-2	Forrest	Yallop	Hill	Zondervan	Humes	Linighan	Lowe	Dozzell	Milton*	Atkinson	Stockwell	Kiwomya	Dozzell 61
								Judge	*Bardsley*	*Phillips J*	*Phillips L*	*Briggs**	*Greenall*	*Reck*	*Foyle*	*Saunders*	*Mustoe*	*Slatter*	*Hill*	Foyle 7, Phillips J 25 Ref: M James
11	A	22/10 **BARNSLEY**	6,325	4	L 20	0-2	0-2	Forrest	Yallop	Hill	Zondervan	Stockwell	Linighan	Lowe	Dozzell	Milton*	Atkinson	Kiwomya*	D'Avray/Harbey	
								Baker	*Joyce*	*Beresford*	*Thomas*	*Shotton^*	*Futcher*	*Rees^*	*Dobbin*	*Cooper*	*Currie*	*Broddle*	*Lowndes/Agnew*	Cooper 22, 41 Ref: D Allison

Match reports

1. Each side fields three debutants and one of them, Chris Kamara, heads City ahead. Town have an effort cleared off the line and D'Avray has a goal disallowed. Saunders fouls Atkinson, but Zondervan's spot-kick is saved by Fox. Relief finally comes as Humes rises to head in a corner.

2. Town celebrate 50 years as a league club with a dream start as Atkinson heads in. Humes goes off early suffering from concussion. A game of fits and starts comes to life briefly when Dozzell's 20-yarder hits the net shortly after the break. Eric Gates has a quiet return to Portman Road.

3. City have most of the play but find Forrest in fine form. Town shock home fans as unmarked Atkinson fires past ex-Town keeper Cooper. City boss David Pleat politely describes Town's tactics as 'effective'. The club hosts a centenary fun day for fans at Portman Road on 11 September.

4. An exciting see-saw contest sees Milton flash home a 20-yarder against the run of play. Roberts knocks in two close-range efforts to give Steve Harrison's men the lead. A change of formation by Duncan sees Atkinson drive in a leveller and Dozzell feeds Lowe to fire home the winner.

5. Dozzell's header is cancelled out by a close-range Rougvie volley. With the home side beset by injuries, Milton turns on the style. He cracks home two loose balls and, after being booked, nets a crisp shot for his hat-trick. Yallop adds to the fun, firing a 30-yarder through Perks' legs.

6. Abbott's cross is converted by Mitchell. Humes goes off with a damaged knee and then sub Woods picks up a serious ankle injury just six minutes after coming on. Teenager Chris Kiwomya makes his debut. Atkinson flicks the equaliser home after four minutes of injury-time.

7. A powerful shot by Atkinson rebounds off Naylor and Lowe puts Town ahead. Whyte equalises for Ron Atkinson's side from close range, with Town complaining Forrest was fouled. Zondervan's cross is nodded on by D'Avray and Dozzell heads the winner to put Town top of the table.

8. Redfearn crosses for Bright to head home an early goal. It gets even worse minutes later as Redfearn again does the damage, sending Wright scampering through for the second. Steve Coppell's side remain in control and Town's fine unbeaten start is brought to a halt.

9. Dozzell's fierce tackle sees Seagrave carried off with a gashed leg. Linighan's free-kick is smartly converted by Dozzell. Linighan is red-carded after lashing out when Morley brings him down. Mel Machin's team have now failed to score in over nine hours of league football at Ipswich.

10. Neat finishing by Foyle and then Phillips, after a melee, puts Oxford the lead after 20 away games without a win. Boss Mark Lawrenson tries a sweeper system for the first time. Bardsley fouls Linighan but Zondervan fails from the spot again. Dozzell nets Lowe's cross to give late hope.

11. Town concede two soft goals before the interval. Steve Cooper turns and fires home a long ball from Paul Futcher and then heads in a free-kick by Beresford. Both looked preventable. Several chances are missed at the other end and generally it was a nightmarish 90 minutes for Ipswich.

12	H PORTSMOUTH	7	L	0-1	0-0												
25/10	14,796	4	20														

Town: Forrest, Yallop, Hill, Zondervan, D'Avray, Stockwell, Lowe, Dozzell, Wark, Atkinson, Kiwomya*, Milton
Portsmouth: Knight, Neil, Sandford, Kuhl, Hogg, Chamberlain, Horne, Aspinall, Quinn, Kelly, Ball
Horne 54
Ref: B Hill

Town fail to impress in a bruising game that does Pompey little credit. From a throw, Quinn assists Horne to punish slack defending. Quinn is lucky not to be sent off after kicking D'Avray. John Duncan, reportedly chasing two Russian players, fails in a bid for West Ham's Paul Hilton.

13	A BOURNEMOUTH	9	L	0-1	0-0
29/10	6,648	18	20		

Town: Forrest, Yallop, Hill, Zondervan, D'Avray, Stockwell, Lowe, Dozzell, Wark, Atkinson*, Milton^ — Kiwomya/Harbey
Bournemouth: Payton, Newson, Coleman, Bond, Williams, Pulis, O'Connor, O'Driscoll, Aylott, Bishop, Close
Bishop 70
Ref: P Don

Town's impressive build-up work continually fizzles out before they reach the danger area. They fall behind when a curling free-kick from Bishop is fumbled over the line by Forrest. The unlucky Canadian otherwise has an excellent game, keeping Harry Redknapp's team at bay.

14	H LEEDS	11	L	0-1	0-1
5/11	11,755	20	20		

Town: Forrest, Yallop, Harbey, Zondervan, Humes*, Linighan, Lowe, Dozzell, Wark, D'Avray, Stockwell* — Milton/Atkinson
Leeds: Day, Aspin, Snodin, Aizlewood, Blake, Rennie, Batty, Sheridan*, Baird, Davison, Hilaire^ — Pearson/Stiles
Sheridan 38p
Ref: A Gunn

The poor run of results continues against Howard Wilkinson's men. Forrest and Baird collide when going for a low cross from Davison and Mr Gunn shocks Town by awarding a penalty. Sheridan tucks the kick home, and a negative Leeds side ride their luck for the rest of the contest.

15	H WALSALL	6	W	3-1	1-0
8/11	9,067	21	23		

Town: Forrest, Yallop, Harbey, Zondervan, Humes, Linighan^, Lowe*, Dozzell, Wark, Atkinson, Stockwell^ — Kiwomya
Walsall: Barber, Taylor M, Mower, Shakespeare, Forbes, Hart, Marsh*, Jones P, Christie, Banton, Naughton^ — Pritchard/Bertschin
Wark 14p, 71p, Stockwell 84; Christie 90p
Ref: D Vickers

Forbes fouls Dozzell to give Wark his first goal of the season from the spot. He repeats the trick when Hart trips Lowe, whose elaborate swallow dive looked rather unnecessary! Barber performs heroics in goal to keep the score down, but Town are relieved to end their lean run.

16	A SWINDON	6	W	3-2	0-1
12/11	7,246	18	26		

Town: Forrest, Yallop, Harbey, Zondervan, Humes*, Linighan, Lowe, Dozzell, Wark, Atkinson, Stockwell^ — Milton/Kiwomya
Swindon: Digby, Hockaday, King, Jones, Parkin, Gittens, Foley, MacLaren, Henry, White, Barnes
Atkinson 67, Dozzell 87, Zondervan 89; Gittens 25, Henry 59
Ref: J Martin

Gittens shoots home after a free-kick and Henry surges through to double the lead. An Atkinson header then sparks an amazing comeback. MacLaren handles a through ball, but only helps direct it to Dozzell who levels. Unmarked Zondervan calmly strokes home an unlikely winner.

17	H BRIGHTON	8	L	2-3	2-1
19/11	12,386	22	26		

Town: Forrest, Yallop, Harbey, Zondervan, Milton*, Linighan^, Lowe, Dozzell, Wark, Atkinson, Stockwell^ — Redford/O'Donnell
Brighton: Keeley, Chivers, Dublin, Wilkins, May, Gatting, Nelson, Curbishley, Bremner, Owers, Penney
Lowe 28, Stockwell 32; Curbishley 31, May 59, Bremner 88
Ref: R Pawley

Ian Redford signs for £200,000 from Dundee United but can't help Town turn the tide in a below-par second-half display. May powers home a header to level for the Seagulls. Under pressure from Yallop, Bremner muscles in to crash home a glorious winner shortly before the whistle.

18	A BIRMINGHAM	9	L	0-1	0-1
26/11	5,932	24	26		

Town: Forrest, O'Donnell, Harbey, Wark, Dozzell, Milton, Redford, Linighan, Atkinson, Stockwell
Birmingham: Hansbury, Ranson, Roberts, Atkins, Overson, Langley, Brenner, Childs*, Whitton, Richards^, Wigley — Peer/Tait
Whitton 25
Ref: P Wright

A dour battle provides little entertainment for the small crowd. Harbey makes a hash of a back-pass and Steve Whitton gets clean through on goal. Forrest forces him wide, but he manages to hit the net despite the efforts of two defenders who have dashed back towards their own line.

19	H PLYMOUTH	7	D	2-2	1-2
3/12	9,929	16	27		

Town: Forrest, Yallop, Hill, Zondervan, Redford*, Linighan, Lowe, Dozzell, Wark, Atkinson, Stockwell — D'Avray/Milton
Plymouth: Miller, Brown, Uzzell, Burrows, Brimacombe, Summerfield, Plummer*, Hodges, Tynan, Campbell G, Stuart — Marker
Lowe 18, D'Avray 75; Campbell 3, Stuart 45
Ref: J Ashworth

Forrest comes out and misses a cross, allowing Campbell to score. Lowe levels with a nicely-taken goal, but Ken Brown's side regain the lead on the stroke of half-time. Claiming a penalty, they are given a free-kick which Stuart curls home. Town deservedly level via D'Avray's volley.

20	A BLACKBURN	13	L	0-1	0-1
10/12	7,258	2	27		

Town: Forrest, Yallop, Hill, Zondervan, Redford^, Linighan*, Lowe, Dozzell, Wark, Atkinson, Stockwell — D'Avray/Milton
Blackburn: Gennoe, Atkins, Dawson, Reid, Hendry, Mail, Gayle, Hildersley, Kennedy, Garner, Sellars
Gayle 36p
Ref: P Vanes

Sellars hits the post early on. To his dismay, Wark is judged to have fouled Atkins back and Gayle converts the penalty. Town's best attempt is a clever Redford chip which flies just wide. Sergei Baltacha of Dynamo Kiev arrives to join Town for £200,000, but will not arrive until January.

21	H OLDHAM	13	W	2-1	0-1
16/12	8,982	20	30		

Town: Forrest, Yallop, Hill, Zondervan, Redford^, Linighan, Lowe, Dozzell, Wark, Kiwomya*, Stockwell — D'Avray/Milton
Oldham: Rhodes, Irwin, Barrett, Skipper, Marshall, Milligan, Palmer, Kelly J, Ritchie, Barlow, Wright
Dozzell 53, Wark 78; Kelly 21
Ref: J Carter

Under the Portman Road floodlights, Town are jeered off at the interval and Duncan later admits they deserved all the cat-calls. Two superb goals after the break get the fans smiling again. Dozzell drives in a left-foot shot and then Wark wins the points, powering home Yallop's cross.

22	A CHELSEA	13	L	0-3	0-2
26/12	17,621	1	30		

Town: Forrest, Yallop, Harbey, Zondervan, Redford, Linighan, Lowe, Dozzell, Wark, Milton*, Stockwell — Kiwomya/Gregory
Chelsea: Freestone, Hall, Dorigo^, Roberts, McLaughlin, Wood, McAllister, Wilson K, Lee*, Durie, Wilson C — McAllister/Bumstead
Durie 27, Lee 40, Dixon 78
Ref: J Moules

Forrest is at fault for Chelsea's first two goals and Duncan is furious at how his players' heads drop after these clangers. Durie's weak effort squeezes in at the near post and Forrest juggles a Dixon header for Lee to poke the ball in. Looking offside, Dixon runs through to net the third.

23	A HULL	14	D	1-1	0-1
31/12	7,800	19	31		

Town: Fearon, Yallop, Harbey, Zondervan, Redford, Linighan, Lowe, Dozzell, Wark, Milton, Stockwell — DeMange
Hull: Hesford, Palmer, Daniel, Warren, Jobson, Buckley, Payton, Roberts, Whitehurst, DeMange, Smith* — Saville
Redford 77; Whitehurst 35
Ref: A Simmons

Whitehurst, built like a brick outhouse and starting his second spell at Boothferry Park, charges in Nat Lofthouse-style to head home Roberts' corner-kick. Lowe's cross finds Redford who produces a clinical finish to level matters. Fearon has a fine game in place of the 'rested' Forrest.

BARCLAYS DIVISION 2 — Manager: John Duncan — SEASON 1988-89

Key: stats line shows Att (attendance), Pos (Town position / opponent position), Pt (points), Res, F-A, H-T. In each team table the first (roman) row is Town, the second (italic) row is the opponents.

---

24 — H LEICESTER — 2/1
Att 14,037 · Pos 12 / 15 · Pt 34 · W · 2-0 · H-T 1-0

Team	1	2	3	4	5	6	7	8	9	10	11	subs used
Town	Fearon	Yallop	Harbey	Zondervan	Redford	Linighan	Kiwomya	Dozzell	Wark	Hill	Milton	
Leicester	*Cooper*	*Mauchlen*	*Spearing*	*Ramsey**	*Paris*	*Morgan^*	*Reid*	*Cross*	*Newell*	*McAllister*	*Turner*	*Quinn/Groves*

Scorers, Times, and Referees: Linighan 11, Milton 48. Ref: M Bailey

Linighan bags his first Town goal from close range after Kiwomya's effort is charged down. The crucial second arrives when Milton's diving header is palmed onto the post and in by the diving Paul Cooper. Ron Fearon bravely soldiers on with a head wound that later requires stitches.

---

25 — A WALSALL — 14/1
Att 4,623 · Pos 8 / 24 · Pt 37 · W · 4-2 · H-T 0-0

Team	1	2	3	4	5	6	7	8	9	10	11	subs used
Town	Fearon	Yallop	Harbey*	Zondervan	Redford	Linighan	Kiwomya	Dozzell	Wark	Hill	Stockwell^	D'Avray/Gregory
Walsall	*Barber*	*Dornan*	*Mower*	*Taylor M*	*Forbes*	*Hart*	*Pritchard*	*Goodwin*	*Bertschin*	*Christie**	*Marsh^*	*Rees/Goldsmith*

Scorers, Times, and Referees: Wark 52p, Dozzell 53, Kiwomya 56, Taylor M 54, Pritchard 87 [Redford 65]. Ref: P Don

New signing Baltacha watches from the stand and sees five goals in a crazy 13-minute spell. Kiwomya's pace creates the first two goals, Dozzell side-footing the second. Taylor's thundering shot is followed by Kiwomya fooling Mower and Barber to net a cheeky first career goal.

---

26 — H STOKE — 21/1
Att 14,692 · Pos 7 / 13 · Pt 40 · W · 5-1 · H-T 0-0

Team	1	2	3	4	5	6	7	8	9	10	11	subs used
Town	Fearon	Yallop	Harbey	Zondervan	Redford	Linighan	Kiwomya	Dozzell	Wark*	Hill	Battacha	D'Avray
Stoke	*Fox*	*Butler*	*Parkin*	*Kamara*	*Higgins*	*Berry*	*Ford*	*Henry*	*Bamber*	*Saunders**	*Beagrie*	*Hackett*

Scorers, Times, and Referees: Baltacha 46, Dozzell 50, 79, Kiwomya 63, Bamber 74 [Yallop 78]. Ref: A Ward

The much-heralded debut of the first Soviet in English soccer and Baltacha obliges by breaking the deadlock with a firm shot from Kiwomya's cross. It brings the house down and opens the floodgates for the biggest victory of the season. Fox saves Stoke from an even worse hammering.

---

27 — H CRYSTAL PALACE — 4/2
Att 14,568 · Pos 9 / 6 · Pt 40 · L · 1-2 · H-T 1-2

Team	1	2	3	4	5	6	7	8	9	10	11	subs used
Town	Fearon	Yallop	Harbey*	Zondervan	Redford*	Linighan	Kiwomya	Dozzell	Wark	Hill	Battacha	Milton
Crystal Palace	*Suckling*	*Pemberton*	*Burke*	*Pennyfather*	*Hopkins !*	*O'Reilly*	*McGoldrick*	*Pardew*	*Bright*	*Wright*	*Barber*	

Scorers, Times, and Referees: Wark 39, Wright 23p, 25. Ref: J Penrose

Bright falls on Wark who angrily pushes him away, conceding a penalty. Ian Wright nets his second from Pemberton's pass before Wark pulls one back with a header. Hopkins is surprisingly sent off for pulling back Kiwomya. Duncan is criticised for playing Baltacha out of position.

---

28 — A MANCHESTER C — 11/2
Att 22,145 · Pos 12 / 2 · Pt 40 · L · 0-4 · H-T 0-2

Team	1	2	3	4	5	6	7	8	9	10	11	subs used
Town	Fearon	Yallop	Harbey	Hill	Redford	Linighan	Kiwomya	Dozzell	Wark	Atkinson	Battacha*	**Juryeff**
Manchester C	*Dibble*	*Lake*	*Taggart*	*Gayle*	*Megson*	*Redmond*	*White*	*Morley*	*Gleghorn*	*McNab*	*Biggins*	

Scorers, Times, and Referees: Gayle 16, Biggins 34, 86, Morley 88. Ref: S Lodge

Atkinson is fined £500 for a 'play-me-or-transfer-me' ultimatum, but he is picked. Gayle beats Fearon in the air to head the first. Biggins nets a rebound after the bar is struck. Two runs by White yield further goals. Baltacha, normally a defender, again looks ill-at-ease in a midfield role.

---

29 — H BARNSLEY — 21/2
Att 9,995 · Pos 9 / 10 · Pt 43 · W · 2-0 · H-T 1-0

Team	1	2	3	4	5	6	7	8	9	10	11	subs used
Town	Fearon	Yallop	Johnson	Hill	Redford	Linighan	Milton	Dozzell*	Wark	Atkinson^	Battacha	Juryeff/Kiwomya
Barnsley	*Baker*	*Joyce*	*Beresford*	*Dobbin*	*McGugan **	*Futcher*	*Lowndes^*	*Agnew*	*Cooper*	*Currie*	*McDonald*	*Shotton/Broddle*

Scorers, Times, and Referees: Dozzell 5, Milton 67. Ref: P Jones

Allan Clarke's side are beaten as team changes by Duncan pay dividends. Baltacha is now playing at the back, but the game is a really dour affair. Paul McGugan breaks his leg in a challenge with Atkinson. Milton converts Hill's first-time cross to keep the promotion dream alive.

---

30 — A OXFORD — 25/2
Att 6,086 · Pos 9 / 19 · Pt 44 · D · 1-1 · H-T 0-1

Team	1	2	3	4	5	6	7	8	9	10	11	subs used
Town	Fearon	Yallop	Johnson	Hill	Redford	Linighan	Milton	D'Avray	Wark	Atkinson	Battacha	Baltacha
Oxford	*Hucker*	*Smart*	*Phillips L*	*Phillips J*	*Lewis*	*Slatter*	*Bardsley*	*Foyle*	*Durnin*	*Ford^*	*Shelton*	*Shelton*

Scorers, Times, and Referees: Linighan 46, Hill 27. Ref: J Rushton

Bardsley's free-kick is headed home by Richard Hill. Linighan, being watched by scouts from Spurs, heads a timely equaliser from Redford's corner-kick. John Duncan gets in trouble with the ref after some over-enthusiastic coaching. He says he thinks he was 'sent off' – but isn't sure!

---

31 — A PORTSMOUTH — 28/2
Att 7,145 · Pos 6 / 14 · Pt 47 · W · 1-0 · H-T 0-0

Team	1	2	3	4	5	6	7	8	9	10	11	subs used
Town	Fearon	Yallop	Johnson*	Hill	Redford	Linighan	Milton	D'Avray	Wark	Atkinson	Battacha	Harbey
Portsmouth	*Gosney*	*Neill*	*Whitehead*	*Dillon*	*Hogg*	*Maguire*	*Horne*	*Chamberlain*	*Powell**	*Connor*	*Sandford*	*Kelly*

Scorers, Times, and Referees: Milton 49. Ref: M Bodenham

Dour Pompey attract their smallest league crowd for seven years. Town move up the table thanks to a smartly-taken goal by Milton, who turns in Hill's cross. This comes shortly after a superb solo run from defence by Baltacha. Keeper Hallworth joins Oldham after a loan spell there.

---

32 — H SWINDON — 4/3
Att 11,542 · Pos 9 / 8 · Pt 47 · L · 1-2 · H-T 0-0

Team	1	2	3	4	5	6	7	8	9	10	11	subs used
Town	Fearon	Yallop	Johnson*	Hill	Redford	Linighan	Milton	D'Avray	Wark	Atkinson	Battacha	Baltacha
Swindon	*Digby*	*Hockaday*	*Bodin*	*Jones*	*Parkin*	*Calderwood*	*Foley*	*MacLaren*	*McLoughlin **	*White*	*Shearer*	*King*

Scorers, Times, and Referees: Milton 61, White 71, 89. Ref: P Don

Atkinson's thundering drive bounces off the chest of keeper Digby and Milton swoops to net the rebound. A fumble by Fearon permits Steve White to equalise. The same player benefits from another blunder to back-head the winner past Fearon. This time the culprit is Frank Yallop.

---

33 — A LEEDS — 11/3
Att 19,639 · Pos 9 / 12 · Pt 50 · W · 4-2 · H-T 1-0

Team	1	2	3	4	5	6	7	8	9	10	11	subs used
Town	Fearon	Yallop	Johnson*	Zondervan	Battacha*	Linighan	Milton	D'Avray	Wark	Atkinson	Hill	Kiwomya
Leeds	*Day*	*Williams G*	*Snodin*	*Aizlewood*	*Blake*	*Rennie^*	*Batty*	*Sheridan*	*Baird*	*Davison**	*Hilaire*	*Pearson/Whitlow*

Scorers, Times, and Referees: Atkinson 45, Milton 49, Wark 58, 85p, Hilaire 64, Blake 75. Ref: K Redfern

Town cruise into a surprise 3-0 lead via speedy breaks from the back after absorbing pressure. Atkinson nets after Wark's effort is blocked, then Milton sweeps in a miskick by Atkinson. Wark's header is followed by a fierce Leeds bombardment, but Wark's penalty clinches the win.

---

34 — H BOURNEMOUTH — 14/3
Att 10,747 · Pos 7 / 6 · Pt 53 · W · 3-1 · H-T 3-0

Team	1	2	3	4	5	6	7	8	9	10	11	subs used
Town	Fearon	Yallop	Johnson*	Zondervan	D'Avray	Linighan	Milton	Kiwomya	Wark	Atkinson	Hill	
Bournemouth	*Payton*	*Newson*	*Morrell**	*Teale*	*Williams*	*O'Driscoll*	*Cooke^*	*O'Connor*	*Aylott*	*Bishop*	*Blissett*	*Close/Coleman*

Scorers, Times, and Referees: Wark 14, Atkinson 28, 31, Blissett 75. Ref: R Wiseman

Wark heads Town ahead from a corner amid dreadful conditions due to wind and rain. Atkinson stuns the Cherries by firing home Kiwomya's pass. Three minutes later it's all over when irrepressible Atkinson blasts home a superb 25-yard shot. Blissett's consolation is too little, too late.

Matches 35–46

35. SHREWSBURY — H — 18/3
Att: 10,913 · Pos: 5 · Opp pos: 22 · Pts: 56 · Result: **W 2-0** (HT 0-0)
Scorers: Atkinson 72, 82
Ref: G Tyson
Town: Fearon, Humes, Yallop*, Zondervan, Linighan, Milton, Kiwomya, Wark, Atkinson, Hill, Baltacha
Shrewsbury: Perks, Priest, Williams B, Kelly, Finley, Brown, McNally, McGinley, Irvine*, Thomas^, Griffiths/Moyes

With the transfer deadline looming, Sheff Wed and Newcastle both show interest in Atkinson, who hammers in two great goals. After a free-kick is ordered to be re-taken, he fires it in with the wall unprepared. Ten minutes later he strikes a glorious second from Milton's superb pass.

36. SUNDERLAND — A — 25/3
Att: 13,859 · Pos: 5 · Opp pos: 13 · Pts: 56 · Result: **L 0-4** (HT 0-1)
Scorers: Gabbiadini 35p, 87, 90, Owers 54
Ref: D Allison
Town: Fearon, Humes, Baltacha, Zondervan, Linighan, Milton*, Kiwomya, Wark, Atkinson, Hill, Lowe
Sunderland: Norman, Bennett, Gray, Hay^, Ord, Owers, Armstrong, Hauser*, Gabbiadini / Pascoe, Gates/Lemon

Gabbiadini scores three, misses a penalty and is sent off! His first follows a tangle with Linighan and the second is a fierce angled drive. In the last minute he's pulled down by Fearon but sees his penalty saved. In netting the rebound he tangles with Humes, elbows him and is sent off.

37. CHELSEA — H — 28/3
Att: 22,950 · Pos: 5 · Opp pos: 1 · Pts: 56 · Result: **L 0-1** (HT 0-0)
Scorers: Durie 82
Ref: D Axcell
Town: Fearon, Humes, Yallop, Zondervan, Baltacha*, Linighan, Milton, Kiwomya, Wark, Atkinson, Hill
Chelsea: Beasant, Clarke, Dorigo, Roberts, McLaughlin, Wood, Wilson K, Dixon, Durie, Nicholas, McAllister

A rousing display by Town earns them a standing ovation at the end, but Chelsea sneak the points and go seven points clear at the top of Division 2. Durie's spectacular long-range shot dips under Fearon to win it. Visiting boss Bobby Campbell is ecstatic over Beasant's display.

38. WATFORD — A — 1/4
Att: 12,054 · Pos: 7 · Opp pos: 5 · Pts: 56 · Result: **L 2-3** (HT 0-2)
Scorers: Milton 48, Wark 57 · Wilkinson 11, Porter 36, Hodges 75
Ref: D Hutchinson
Town: Fearon, Humes*, Yallop, Zondervan, Baltacha, Linighan, Milton, Kiwomya, Wark, Atkinson, Hill
Watford: Coton, Gibbs, Jackett, Richardson, Miller, McClelland, Thomas, Wilkinson, Holdsw'th Dn Porter, Hodges, D'Avray/Lowe

With Dean Holdsworth making his full league debut, Watford cruise into a two-goal lead. Milton's low drive goes in off a post and then Wark heads in Yallop's curling free-kick. This great comeback counts for nothing when Zondervan's disastrous back-pass lets in the skilful Hodges.

39. OLDHAM — A — 4/4
Att: 5,182 · Pos: 8 · Opp pos: 19 · Pts: 56 · Result: **L 0-4** (HT 0-2)
Scorers: Ritchie 32, Palmer 42, 67, Milligan 52
Ref: W Burns
Town: Fearon, Humes, Yallop, Zondervan, Baltacha*, Linighan, Lowe, Kiwomya, Wark, Atkinson, Hill^
Oldham: Hallworth, Irwin, Barrett, Skipper, Marshall, Henry, Palmer, Milligan, Ritchie, Bunn, Wright, D'Avray/Redford

In a game affected by a howling gale and flurries of snow, veteran striker Roger Palmer creates a new Oldham goalscoring record. His first beats the previous tally of 110 for the club. His second is a fine long-range drive. In a very one-sided affair, Town put on a shabby display.

40. HULL — H — 8/4
Att: 10,191 · Pos: 8 · Opp pos: 21 · Pts: 57 · Result: **D 1-1** (HT 1-0)
Scorers: Swan 12 (og), Whitehurst 80
Ref: J Carter
Town: Fearon, Humes, Redford, Zondervan, Baltacha, Linighan, Lowe, Kiwomya, Wark, Atkinson*, Harbey
Hull: Hesford, Brown, Jacobs, Swan^, Jobson, Terry, McParland, Askew, Whitehurst, Edwards, Smith, Thompson

Hesford rushes out unexpectedly and a confused Swan heads Baltacha's cross into an unguarded net. The unlucky defender departs shortly afterwards with a hamstring problem. Ten minutes from time Fearon flaps at an Askew cross and Whitehurst steams in to head the equaliser.

41. BRADFORD C — A — 15/4
Att: 9,691 · Pos: 10 · Opp pos: 18 · Pts: 58 · Result: **D 2-2** (HT 1-2)
Scorers: D'Avray 45, Zondervan 74 · Oliver 17, Leonard 43
Ref: R Nixon
Town: Forrest, Humes, Baltacha*, Zondervan, D'Avray, Linighan, Lowe, Redford, Wark, Milton, Harbey^, Yallop
Bradford C: Tomlinson, Mitchell, Tinnion, Abbott, Oliver, Evans D, Campbell, Stinott, Leonard, Quinn, Jewell^, Ellis

Oliver, not properly marked, cracks the ball into the roof of Town's net. Leonard nets from close range after a scramble following a corner. Zondervan earns a point with an 18-yard scorcher to keep faint play-off hopes alive. D'Avray slips the ball past Tomlinson from Lowe's cross.

42. WEST BROM — H — 22/4
Att: 12,047 · Pos: 9 · Opp pos: 6 · Pts: 61 · Result: **W 2-1** (HT 0-0)
Scorers: Humes 47, Wark 61p · West 86
Ref: I Hemley
Town: Forrest, Humes, Baltacha, Zondervan, D'Avray, Linighan, Lowe, Redford, Wark*, Milton^, Harbey, Stockwell
West Brom: Naylor, Albiston, Ford, Banks, Whyte, North, Bartlett, Goodman*, West, Robson, Anderson, Paskin

Albion boss Brian Talbot, the ex-Town hero, says he is embarrassed by his team's display in front of his home-town crowd. North's mistake allows Humes to net a glancing header and Wark nets from the spot after Albiston's handball. There is a silent tribute to the Hillsborough dead.

43. BIRMINGHAM — H — 29/4
Att: 9,975 · Pos: 9 · Opp pos: 24 · Pts: 64 · Result: **W 4-0** (HT 2-0)
Scorers: Wark 3, Lowe 39, 87, Zondervan 76
Ref: B Hill
Town: Forrest, Humes, Baltacha, Zondervan, D'Avray, Linighan, Lowe, Redford, Wark*, Milton^, Harbey, Cheetham/Stockwell
Birmingham: Thomas, Clarkson, Frain, Peer, Overson, Roberts, Langley, Yates*, Whitton, Sturridge, Hopkins, Childs/Burton

An easy win against the bottom club. Cheetham, a Dutch-born former soldier, is given a debut. Wark heads in a corner early on. Lowe hooks home after a slick move. Zondervan finishes more good build-up play. Linighan hits the bar, but Lowe swoops on the rebound for the fourth.

44. PLYMOUTH — A — 1/5
Att: 6,484 · Pos: 9 · Opp pos: 20 · Pts: 67 · Result: **W 1-0** (HT 1-0)
Scorers: Humes 40
Ref: K Cooper
Town: Forrest, Humes, Baltacha, Zondervan*, D'Avray, Linighan, Lowe, Redford, Wark, Milton, Harbey, Yallop
Plymouth: Wilmot, Brown, Brimacombe Burrows, Marker, Smith, Byrne, McCarthy, Tynan, Hodges, Stuart

Town directors planning to fly to Devon for this game are left stranded when the flight is cancelled. They miss Humes shooting home from 12 yards after D'Avray touches on Redford's lofted pass. Wark has a great game in defence. An outside chance of reaching the play-offs remains.

45. BRIGHTON — A — 6/5
Att: 8,616 · Pos: 8 · Opp pos: 20 · Pts: 70 · Result: **W 1-0** (HT 1-0)
Scorers: D'Avray 20
Ref: R Groves
Town: Forrest, Humes^, Baltacha, Zondervan, D'Avray, Linighan, Kiwomya*, Lowe, Redford, Wark, Harbey, Cheetham/Milton
Brighton: Keeley, Chivers, Dublin, Wilkins, Bissett, Chapman, Nelson, Cadner, Bremner, Curdishley, Trusson

D'Avray hooks home a left-foot volley after a free-kick from Baltacha. The winning run has come too late, however, as Town's play-off rivals have gathered enough points to fend off the late challenge. Barry Lloyd's Brighton are now safe from relegation and have nothing to play for.

46. BLACKBURN — H — 13/5
Att: 10,861 · Pos: 8 · Opp pos: 5 · Pts: 73 · Result: **W 2-0** (HT 1-0)
Scorers: Wark 24p, 73p
Ref: R Lewis
Town: Forrest, Baltacha, Harbey, Zondervan*, D'Avray*, Linighan, Lowe, Redford, Wark, Milton, Hill/Milton
Blackburn: Collier, Atkins, Diamond*, Reid, Hendry, Mail, Gayle, Millar, Garner, Sellars, Ainscow

John Wark receives his Player of the Year award before kick-off and celebrates with two penalties to become joint-leading scorer for the year. In a fragmented game Town are a shade lucky to win by two. Zondervan is tripped and injured for the first kick and Cheetham for the second.

Home 12,565
Away 9,463
Average 12,565 / 9,463

BARCLAYS DIVISION 2 (CUP-TIES)

Manager: John Duncan

SEASON 1988-89

Littlewoods Cup	Att		F-A	H-T	Scorers, Times, and Referees	1	2	3	4	5	6	7	8	9	10	11	subs used
2:1 A PORT VALE 26/9	6,545	3 2:2 L	0-1	0-1	Sproson 44 Ref: J Lloyd	Forrest *Grew*	Yallop *Webb*	Hill *Hughes*	Stockwell *Walker**	D'Avray *Mills*	Harbey *Sproson*	Lowe *Ford*	Dozzell *Earle*	Milton *Futcher*	Atkinson *Beckford*	Wark *Riley*	 *Finney*
2:2 H PORT VALE 11/10	8,869	3 2:2 W	3-0	1-0	Lowe 24, Atkinson 50, 83 Ref: D Axcell (Town win 3-1 on aggregate)	Forrest *Grew*	Yallop *Webb*	Harbey *Hughes*	Zondervan *Walker*	Humes *Mills*	Linighan *Sproson*	Lowe *Ford*	Stockwell *Earle*	Milton *Futcher*	Atkinson *Beckford*	Kiwomya *Riley*	
3 H LEYTON ORIENT 1/11	9,751	9 3:16 W	2-0	0-0	Dozzell 48, Stockwell 57 Ref: D Hutchinson	Forrest *Wells*	Yallop *Howard*	Hill *Dickenson*	Zondervan *Hales*	Humes *Day*	Linighan *Sitton**	Lowe *Baker*	Dozzell *Ward*	D'Avray *Hull*	Stockwell *Juryeff*	Wark* *Comfort*	Harbey *Harvey*
4 A ASTON VILLA 30/11	16,284	9 1:14 L	2-6	0-2	Stockwell 83, Atkinson 90 McInally 11, 15, Platt 59, 61, 70, 77 Ref: K Cooper	Forrest *Spink*	O'Donnell *Price*	Harbey* *Gray S*	Redford *Gage*	Milton *Mountfield*	Linighan *Keown*	Lowe *Gray A**	Dozzell *Platt*	Atkinson *McInally*	Stockwell *Cowans*	Wark* *Daley*	Hill *Williams*

FA Cup

FA Cup	Att		F-A	H-T	Scorers, Times, and Referees	1	2	3	4	5	6	7	8	9	10	11	subs used
3 A NOTT'M FOREST 7/1	20,743	12 1:8 L	0-3	0-2	Yallop 3 (og), Gaynor 29, Chapman 62 Ref: L Shapter	Fearon *Sutton*	Yallop *Laws*	Harbey* *Pearce*	Zondervan *Walker*	Redford *Wilson*	Linighan *Hodge*	Kiwomya *Carr*	Dozzell *Webb*	Hill *Gaynor*	Stockwell* *Chapman*	Wark *Parker*	O'Donnell/Cheetham

2:1 A PORT VALE — Vale skipper Phil Sproson, who had been on Town's shopping list in the summer, fires home a spectacular 35-yard thunderbolt which wins the tie. Summer signing Ron Futcher gives a rather lacklustre Town side difficulties throughout and there are few complaints about the scoreline.

2:2 H PORT VALE — Missing several key men, Town level the tie on aggregate with a lucky goal when Humes' diagonal ball flies in off Lowe. Kiwomya, on his full debut, hits a post. Zondervan has a fine game in midfield and lays on the killer goal. Atkinson beats ex-Town man Grew again near the end.

3 H LEYTON ORIENT — Dozzell combines with D'Avray and his shot is pushed in off the post by Wells. Dozzell then goes close when his left-foot rocket cannons out off a post. The tie is effectively settled by Stockwell, who used to play for Orient juniors. He tucks in the rebound after Lowe's shot is blocked.

4 A ASTON VILLA — Town are murdered by David Platt and Alan McInally and could have let in ten. Andy Gray and McInally miss sitters, but there are plenty of examples of top-class finishing. Platt's remarkable quick-fire quartet includes a marvellous solo run and a bullet header past besieged Forrest.

FA Cup 3 A NOTT'M FOREST — Webb and Pearce combine and Yallop deflects the ball past Fearon. Carr rounds Linighan and crosses for Gaynor to sweep the ball home. It's curtains for Town when Parker breaks on the left and crosses for Chapman to convert. The board is glad it didn't budget for a cup run again!

			Home					Away					
		P	W	D	L	F	A	W	D	L	F	A	Pts
1	Chelsea	46	15	6	2	50	25	14	6	3	46	25	99
2	Manchester C	46	12	8	3	48	28	11	5	7	29	25	82
3	Crys Palace *	46	15	6	2	42	17	8	6	9	29	32	81
4	Watford	46	14	5	4	41	18	8	7	8	33	30	78
5	Blackburn	46	16	4	3	50	22	6	7	10	24	37	77
6	Swindon	46	13	8	2	35	15	7	8	8	33	38	76
7	Barnsley	46	12	8	3	37	21	8	6	9	29	37	74
8	IPSWICH	46	13	3	7	42	23	9	4	10	29	38	73
9	West Brom	46	13	7	3	43	18	5	11	7	22	23	72
10	Leeds	46	12	6	5	34	20	5	10	8	25	30	67
11	Sunderland	46	12	8	3	40	23	4	7	12	20	37	63
12	Bournemouth	46	13	3	7	32	20	5	5	13	21	42	62
13	Stoke	46	10	9	4	33	25	5	5	13	24	47	59
14	Bradford C	46	8	11	4	29	22	5	6	12	23	37	56
15	Leicester	46	11	6	6	31	20	5	2	10	25	43	55
16	Oldham	46	9	10	4	49	32	2	11	10	26	40	54
17	Oxford	46	11	6	6	40	34	3	6	14	22	36	54
18	Plymouth	46	11	4	8	35	22	3	8	12	20	44	54
19	Brighton	46	11	5	7	36	24	3	3	16	21	42	51
20	Portsmouth	46	10	6	7	33	21	3	6	14	20	41	51
21	Hull	46	7	9	7	31	25	4	5	14	21	43	47
22	Shrewsbury	46	4	11	8	25	31	4	7	12	15	36	42
23	Birmingham	46	6	4	13	21	33	2	7	14	10	43	35
24	Walsall	46	3	10	10	27	42	2	6	15	14	38	31
		1104	261	163	128	884	581	128	163	261	581	884	1493

* Promoted after play-offs

Odds & ends

Double wins: (4) Leicester, Shrewsbury, Walsall, West Brom.

Double losses: (2) Chelsea, Crystal Palace.

Won from behind: (3) Watford (h), Oldham (h), Swindon (a).

Lost from in front: (2) Brighton (h), Swindon (h).

High spots: Sergei Baltacha's goalscoring debut against Stoke.
Simon Milton's hat-trick at Shrewsbury.
Victory after being 0-2 down at Swindon.
A series of spectacular goals by Dalian Atkinson.

Low spots: A run of five defeats wiping out a great start to the season.
The unlucky home defeat by Chelsea in March.
Comprehensive defeats in both major cup competitions.
The dreadful display at Oldham in April.

Player of the Year: John Wark.

Ever-presents: (0).

Hat-tricks: (1) Simon Milton.

Opposing hat-tricks: (2) David Platt, Marco Gabbiadini.

Leading scorers: (13) John Wark (7 pens), Dalian Atkinson.

Appearances and Goals

Player	Lge	Sub	LC	Sub	FAC	Sub	Lge	LC	FAC	Tot
Atkinson, Dalian	33	1	3				10	3		13
Baltacha, Sergei	19	1					1			1
Cheetham, Michael	1	2				1				
D'Avray, Mich	24	8	2				3			3
Dozzell, Jason	29		3		1		11	1		12
Fearon, Ron	18				1					
Forrest, Craig	28		4							
Gregory, David		2								
Harbey, Graham	19	4	3		1	1				
Hill, David	35	1	2	1	1					
Humes, Tony	26		2		1		3			3
Johnson, Gavin	4									
Juryeff, Ian		2								
Kiwomya, Chris	16	10	1				2			2
Linighan, David	40		1	3	1		2			2
Lowe, David	30	2	4				6	1		7
Milton, Simon	25	10	3		1		10			10
O'Donnell, Chris	1	1	1							
Redford, Ian	22	2	1		1		2			2
Stockwell, Mick	20	3	4		1		2	2		4
Wark, John	41		3		1		13			13
Woods, Neil		1								
Yallop, Frank	38	2	3		1		2			2
Zondervan, Romeo	37		2				3			3
(own-goals)							1			1
24 players used	506	53	44	2	11	2	71	7		78

BARCLAYS DIVISION 2 — Manager: John Duncan — SEASON 1989-90

No	Date		Att	Pos	Pt	F-A	H-T	Scorers, Times, and Referees	1	2	3	4	5	6	7	8	9	10	11	subs used
1	19/8	H BARNSLEY	12,100		W 3	3-1	0-1	Woods 78, Humes 82, Lowe 90 / Lowndes 15 / Ref: D Hedges	Forrest	Yallop	Thompson	Zondervan	Redford*	Linighan	Lowe	Dozzell	Wark	Humes	Milton	Woods
									Baker	*Tiler*	*Braddle*	*Futcher*	*Shotton*	*Dobbin*	*Agnew*	*Lowndes*	*Gray*	*Cooper*	*Robinson*	
2	22/8	A SUNDERLAND	15,965	*3*	W 6	4-2	3-0	Lowe 7, 64, Milton 17, Dozzell 21 / Gates 50, Gabbiadini 68 / Ref: P Harrison	Forrest	Yallop	Thompson	Zondervan	Redford	Linighan	Lowe	Dozzell	Wark	Humes	Milton	
									Norman	*Agboola*	*Hardyman*	*Ord*	*McPhail*	*Owers*	*Cullen*	*Armstrong*	*Gates*	*Gabbiadini*	*Pascoe*	
3	26/8	A SHEFFIELD UTD	13,600	*3*	L 6	0-2	0-0	Deane 76, Morris 84 / Ref: I Hendrick	Forrest	Yallop	Thompson	Zondervan	Redford*	Linighan	Lowe	Dozzell	Wark	Humes	Milton	Woods
									Tracey	*Hill*	*Barnes*	*Booker*	*Stancliffe*	*Morris*	*Roberts*	*Gannon*	*Agana*	*Deane*	*Bryson*	
4	2/9	H BOURNEMOUTH	11,425	*11*	D 7	1-1	0-0	Dozzell 63 / Shearer 64 / Ref: A Buksh	Forrest	Yallop	Thompson	Zondervan	Redford*	Linighan	Lowe	Dozzell	Wark	Humes	Milton^	Woods/**Donowa**
									Peyton	*Newsom**	*Morrell*	*Teale*	*Miller*	*Peacock*	*Lawrence*	*Moulden*	*O'Driscoll*	*O'Connor*	*Blissett*	*Shearer*
5	9/9	A LEEDS	22,973	*10*	D 8	1-1	0-1	Milton 78 / Jones 13 / Ref: J Worrall	Forrest	Yallop	Thompson	Johnson	Woods	Linighan*	Lowe	Dozzell	Wark	Humes	Milton	Cheetham
									Day	*Sterland*	*Whitlow*	*Jones*	*Fairclough*	*Haddock*	*Strachan*	*Batty*	*Baird*	*Davison*	*Hendrie**	*Speed*
6	16/9	H WOLVERHAMPTON	14,506	*20*	L 8	1-3	0-1	Westley 82 (og) / Mutch 40, 77, Bellamy 53 / Ref: A Gunn	Forrest	Yallop	Thompson	Zondervan	Woods^	Johnson*	Lowe	Dozzell	Wark	Humes	Milton	Donowa /Baltacha
									Kendall	*Bellamy*	*Venus*	*Streete*	*Westley*	*Vaughan*	*Bennett*	*Gooding*	*Paskin*	*Mutch*	*Dennison*	
7	23/9	A OXFORD	5,131	*13*	D 9	2-2	0-1	Redford 82, Penney 86 (og) / Penney 25, Durnin 51 / Ref: J Martin	Forrest	Yallop	Thompson^	Zondervan	Redford	Linighan	Lowe	Dozzell	Wark	Hill*	Milton	Woods/**Palmer**
									Judge	*Smart*	*Phillips J*	*Lewis*	*Greenall*	*Slatter*	*Penney*	*Mustoe**	*Foyle*	*Durnin^*	*Simpson*	*Ford/Stein*
8	27/9	A BRIGHTON	9,770	*3*	L 9	0-1	0-0	Wilkins 88 / Ref: D Axcell	Forrest*	Humes	Palmer^	Zondervan	Redford	Linighan	Lowe	Dozzell	Wark	Woods*	Milton	Hill/Baltacha
									Keeley	*Chivers*	*Dublin*	*Curbishley*	*Bissett*	*Gatting*	*Nelson*	*Wood**	*Bremner*	*Codner*	*Wilkins*	*Owers*
9	30/9	H STOKE	10,389	*21*	D 10	2-2	2-0	D'Avray 11, Dozzell 23 / Palin 47p, Saunders 50 / Ref: D Elleray	Forrest	Humes	Palmer	Zondervan	Redford*	Linighan	Lowe	Dozzell	Wark^	D'Avray	Stockwell	Donowa/Thompson
									Fox	*Butler*	*Statham*	*Kamara*	*Cranson*	*Beeston*	*Hackett*	*Palin*	*Bamber*	*Saunders*	*Beagrie*	
10	7/10	H NEWCASTLE	13,679	*5*	W 13	2-1	2-0	Wark 13p, Lowe 37 / McGhee 82 / Ref: D Hutchinson	Forrest	Stockwell	Thompson	Zondervan	Humes	Linighan	Lowe	Dozzell	Wark	D'Avray	Donowa	
									Burridge	*Anderson*	*Stimson*	*Dillon*	*Scott*	*Thorn*	*Gallagher**	*Brown*	*Quinn*	*McGhee*	*Fereday*	*Brazil*
11	14/10	A SWINDON	8,039	*11*	L 13	0-3	0-2	Shearer 33, McLoughlin 41, Stockwell 50 (og) / Ref: M Bodenham	Forrest	Stockwell	Thompson	Palmer*	Humes	Linighan	Lowe	Dozzell	Zondervan	D'Avray	Donowa	Kiwomya/Harbey
									Digby	*Hockaday*	*King*	*McLoughlin*	*Calderwood*	*Parkin*	*Jones T*	*Shearer*	*White*	*McLaren*	*Badin**	*Cornwall*

Match notes

1. Lowndes shocks shaky Town early on, but forgotten man Woods comes on and sparks a late goal rush. He has had a nightmare time in Suffolk, but equalises and transforms the atmosphere. Ipswich then slip into top gear and Allan Clarke's outfit have no answer to the late onslaught.

2. One of the toughest tasks of the season looks like being a walkover as Town take up where they left off three days earlier. Roker is shocked by the three-goal salvo by Town's highly mobile attackers. Havoc is wreaked among Denis Smith's pedestrian-looking defence. It's a dream start.

3. Town are brought back to earth by Dave Bassett's purposeful side, who batter away with no reward until the final 15 minutes. Humes and Linighan keep the danger-men Deane and Agana in check, until Deane's joyously greeted breakthrough. The Blades look promotion material.

4. Lowe and Woods combine to set up Dozzell for a coolly-taken goal. The Cherries hit back within seconds, taking advantage of Town relaxing after the goal. Dozzell is blamed for not getting back to pick up Shearer, who is unmarked as he heads in. Ipswich-born Donowa gets a debut.

5. Big-spending Leeds go ahead when Strachan's corner is flicked on by Baird and Vinnie Jones heads his first goal for the club. Patient Ipswich are rewarded when Lowe's chip is headed against his own crossbar by Batty and Milton gets the final touch as the rebound is scrambled home.

6. Graham Turner tries a sweeper system for the first time. Mutch nets from close range and Bellamy scrambles another to increase the Town misery. It gets worse as Baltacha blunders, allowing Mutch to sweep past and tuck home a third. Westley fires a Lowe cross into his own net.

7. Brian Horton's men cruise into a two-goal lead, but panic late as Woods squares for Redford to fire in from 20 yards. A desperate chase for Dozzell's through-ball sees Penney slice the ball over his keeper Judge. It's an appropriate venue for the Cambridge graduate Palmer to debut.

8. Town look set to get at least a point until a sickening collision between Forrest, Wood and Palmer. The groggy keeper is taken to hospital with a back injury, and the other two come off soon after. Hill goes in goal and does well until he drops a late cross for Wilkins to scramble home.

9. After a misplaced Kamara pass, D'Avray heads in off the post. Dozzell thunders in a second, but frustratingly Town allow Mick Mills' side back into the game. Bamber is fouled for Palin's penalty, then Saunders levels with a cool finish. Bamber passes up a good chance to win it.

10. An Anderson handball gives Wark a spot-kick. He nets, but a re-take is ordered and again he beats Burridge, who is making his league debut for his eighth club. A fine shot by Lowe ensures the points, although McGhee causes a few flutters with a late headed goal from Scott's pass.

11. Jones squares for Shearer to net, with Forrest stranded out of position. Hockaday sends McLaughlin clear to take the ball round Forrest. White crosses and Stockwell, attempting a back pass, lofts it high over Forrest from 25 yards. Zondervan has a penalty saved after Donowa is fouled.

A season fixture log (Ipswich Town). Each entry: match number · venue (A/H) · opponents · date · result (F–A, half-time in brackets) · attendance · position · points · scorers · referee · line-ups (Ipswich, then opponents) · match report.

12 · A · BRADFORD C · 18/10 — L 0–1 (0–1)
Att 7,350 · Pos 17 · (18) · Pts 13
Scorers: Adcock 35. Ref: K Lupton
Ipswich: Forrest, Stockwell, Thompson, Kiwomya, Yallop, Linighan, Lowe, Dozzell, Zondervan, D'Avray, Donowa*, (sub) Redford
Bradford C: Tomlinson, Abbott, Tinnion, Oliver, Sinnott, Jackson, Megson*, Aizlewood, Adcock, Quinn, Jewell, (sub) Campbell

Tony Adcock's winner leaves Town in their worst league position since 1964. Manager Duncan admits he has not got things right and says the fans have every right to be upset. He moves into the transfer market and recruits Glenn Pennyfather from Crystal Palace for a fee of £80,000.

13 · H · PLYMOUTH · 21/10 — W 3–0 (2–0)
Att 10,362 · Pos 14 · (5) · Pts 16
Scorers: Kiwomya 20, 69, Milton 29. Ref: P Don
Ipswich: Forrest, Stockwell, Thompson, Kiwomya, Yallop, Linighan, Lowe, Dozzell, Zondervan, D'Avray, Milton, (sub) Redford
Plymouth: Wilmot, Brown, Brimacombe, Marker, Burrows, Morrison*, Hodges, Thomas, Tynan^, Campbell, Stuart, (subs) McCarthy/Whiston

Kiwomya scores a neat opener, side-stepping a challenge to ram the ball home after being set up by Milton and Lowe. Stockwell finds Milton and he sidefoots home from 12 yards. Town cruise along and after the interval Milton's cross is glanced past Wilmot by confident Kiwomya.

14 · A · PORTSMOUTH · 28/10 — W 3–2 (1–0)
Att 7,914 · Pos 12 · (22) · Pts 19
Scorers: Milton 28, 48, Dozzell 69; Neill 51, Kuhl 76. Ref: L Shapter
Ipswich: Forrest, Yallop, Thompson, Kiwomya, D'Avray, Linighan, Lowe, Dozzell, Zondervan*, Stockwell, Milton, (sub) Pennyfather
Portsmouth: Knight, Neill, Beresford, Sandford*, Hogg, Ball, Wigley, Kuhl, Whittingham, Gilligan, Black, (sub) Chamberlain

Milton beats Knight with a rasping drive, completely against the run of play. Good work by Lowe allows him to crack home a second. The players are led off for five minutes due to high winds and lashing rain. Town keep their noses ahead as Dozzell heads in from a Lowe corner.

15 · H · WATFORD · 31/10 — W 1–0 (0–0)
Att 12,587 · Pos 10 · (16) · Pts 22
Scorers: Thompson 78p. Ref: P Alcock
Ipswich: Forrest, Stockwell, Thompson, Pennyfather, Yallop, Linighan, Lowe, Dozzell, Wark, D'Avray, Milton
Watford: Coton, Gibbins, Drysdale, Jackett, Holdsworth, Roeder, Redfern, Wilkinson, Roberts, Porter, Hodges*, (sub) Thompson

Lukewarm Town end up rather fortunate to take all three points from Steve Harrison's struggling side. Wark has a penalty brilliantly saved by Coton and doesn't fancy another go when a chance arises. So up steps Thompson to crash home a rocket and maintain a fine spot-kick record.

16 · H · WEST BROM · 4/11 — W 3–1 (2–1)
Att 12,028 · Pos 7 · (16) · Pts 25
Scorers: Kiwomya 20, Lowe 15, Milton 70; Goodman 31. Ref: P Foakes
Ipswich: Forrest, Stockwell, Thompson, Zondervan, Yallop, Linighan, Lowe*, Dozzell, Wark, Kiwomya, Milton, (sub) D'Avray^
West Brom: Naylor, Burgess, Hadson, Talbot, Whyte, North, Barham*, Goodman, Bartlett, McNally, Ford, (subs) Thomas/Johnson

A great start as Kiwomya dribbles around Naylor and then Lowe smashes a second from close range. Ford's cross is cleared to Goodman who nets with a neat shot. Transfer-listed Yallop sets up Milton for a fine first-time shot for the third. Lowe is carried off with a serious knee injury.

17 · A · BLACKBURN · 11/11 — D 2–2 (1–0)
Att 7,913 · Pos 9 · (10) · Pts 26
Scorers: May 21 (og), Wark 61p; Johnrose 75, Atkins 90p. Ref: R Nixon
Ipswich: Forrest, Stockwell, Thompson, Zondervan, Yallop, Linighan, Donowa, Dozzell, Wark, Kiwomya, Milton, (subs) Johnrose/Finnican
Blackburn: Collier, Atkins, Oliver, Reid^, Hill, May, Irvine, Millar*, Stapleton, Garner, Sellars

May drills the ball into his own net from a Thompson cross. Oliver pulls down Kiwomya and Wark extends the lead from the spot. Substitute Johnrose pulls one back with a fine shot and Rovers apply heavy pressure. Milton impedes Atkins in the final minute and the penalty levels it.

18 · A · LEICESTER · 18/11 — W 1–0 (1–0)
Att 11,664 · Pos 7 · (22) · Pts 29
Scorers: Stockwell 27. Ref: N Midgley
Ipswich: Forrest, Stockwell, Thompson, Zondervan, Yallop, Linighan, Donowa*, Dozzell, Wark, Kiwomya, Milton, (sub) Gregory
Leicester: Hodge, Mauchlen, Morgan, Ramsey, Walsh, Paris, Reid*, Moran, Campbell, McAllister, Wright, (sub) Johnson

Mick Stockwell, back in form after major injury problems, nets his first goal of the season, firing home Kiwomya's low cross, against the run of play. Town hold out against David Pleat's outfit in a tense finale. Willie Kerr, an Ipswich board member for 18 years, dies at the age of 81.

19 · H · OLDHAM · 25/11 — D 1–1 (0–0)
Att 12,304 · Pos 8 · (5) · Pts 30
Scorers: Kiwomya 73; Yallop 68 (og). Ref: P Danson
Ipswich: Forrest, Stockwell, Thompson, Zondervan, Yallop, Linighan, Donowa*, Dozzell, Wark, Kiwomya, Milton, (sub) Gregory
Oldham: Rhodes, Irwin, Barlow, Henry, Barrett, Warhurst, Palmer, Ritchie, Marshall, Milligan, Holden R, (sub) Gregory

Chased by Warhurst, Donowa executes a swallow dive and wins a penalty. Justice is done as Rhodes touches Wark's kick around the post. Yallop heads Holden's cross the wrong way and a disputed goal is given.

20 · A · BARNSLEY · 2/12 — W 1–0 (1–0)
Att 6,097 · Pos 6 · (21) · Pts 33
Scorers: Humes 5. Ref: G Pooley
Ipswich: Forrest, Stockwell*, Thompson, Zondervan, Yallop, Linighan, Donowa, Dozzell, Humes, Kiwomya, Milton, (sub) Redford
Barnsley: Baker, Dobbin, Cross, Smith, Shotton, Lowndes*, Agnew, McCord, Gray, Cooper, Archdeacon, (sub) Foreman

The energetic Humes makes a welcome return from injury, firing home an early winner after Kiwomya's effort is cleared off the line. Ipswich MP Michael Irvine approaches the Home Office on Ipswich Town's behalf to plead for a work permit for the Soviet goalkeeper Mikhailov.

21 · H · SUNDERLAND · 9/12 — D 1–1 (0–1)
Att 13,833 · Pos 5 · (3) · Pts 34
Scorers: Wark 54; Owers 25. Ref: J Moules
Ipswich: Forrest, Humes, Thompson, Zondervan, Yallop, Linighan, D'Avray, Dozzell, Wark, Kiwomya, Milton, (sub) Redford
Sunderland: Carter, Agboola, Hardyman, Bennett, Rush, Owers, Atkinson, Armstrong, Gates, Gabbiadini, Pascoe

Duncan makes more team changes, recalling Mich D'Avray, who is now in his testimonial year. Owers powers home a header from a cross by Armstrong. Wark equalises, forcing home a corner. Gates works hard on his old stamping ground but finds Forrest in good shot-stopping form.

22 · H · WEST HAM · 26/12 — W 1–0 (1–0)
Att 25,326 · Pos 5 · (10) · Pts 37
Scorers: Stockwell 40. Ref: J Ashworth
Ipswich: Forrest, Stockwell, Thompson, Zondervan*, Yallop, Linighan, Donowa, Dozzell, Wark, Kiwomya^, Milton, (subs) Humes/D'Avray
West Ham: Suckling, Potts, Dicks, Strodder, Martin, Gale, Brady^, Slater*, Keen, Ward, Allen, (subs) Parris/Kelly D

A long period of inactivity after the Hull visit is called off due to a waterlogged pitch. Lou Macari's side succumb to a well-struck Stockwell shot. Suffolk lad Slater appears for the Hammers.

23 · H · MIDDLESBROUGH · 30/12 — W 3–0 (2–0)
Att 14,290 · Pos 5 · (18) · Pts 40
Scorers: Stockwell 18, Humes 38, Donowa 86. Ref: P Vanes
Ipswich: Forrest, Humes, Thompson, Stockwell, Yallop, Linighan, Donowa, Dozzell, Wark, Kiwomya^, Milton, (sub) D'Avray
Middlesbrough: Pears, Parkinson, Cooper, Mowbray, Coleman, Putney*, Slaven, Proctor, Kernaghan, Brennan, Davenport, (sub) Ripley

Division Two, unbeaten in six, Lou Macari's side succumb to a well-struck Stockwell shot. Pears blocks Milton's shot but Stockwell converts the rebound. Humes nets with a powerful drive after Stockwell's cross is headed to him by Cooper. Donowa flashes home a Kiwomya centre for his first Ipswich goal. Trevor Putney and Mark Brennan make a return to Portman Road.

BARCLAYS DIVISION 2 — Manager: John Duncan — SEASON 1989-90

No	Date	H/A	Opponent	Att	Opp Pos	Pos	Pt	Res	F-A	H-T
24	1/1	A	PORT VALE	8,617	14	6	40	L	0-5	0-3
25	13/1	H	SHEFFIELD UTD	16,787	2	6	41	D	1-1	0-1
26	20/1	A	BOURNEMOUTH	7,464	12	7	41	L	1-3	0-1
27	10/2	A	WOLVERHAMPTON	18,781	5	10	41	L	1-2	1-1
28	17/2	H	LEEDS	17,102	1	9	42	D	2-2	1-2
29	24/2	A	OLDHAM	10,193	4	11	42	L	1-4	0-2
30	3/3	H	LEICESTER	12,237	14	12	43	D	2-2	2-1
31	6/3	A	STOKE	10,815	24	11	44	D	0-0	0-0
32	10/3	H	BRIGHTON	10,886	16	9	47	W	2-1	1-1
33	13/3	H	OXFORD	10,380	12	8	50	W	1-0	0-0
34	17/3	A	NEWCASTLE	20,521	4	9	50	L	1-2	1-0

24 — PORT VALE (A), 1/1 — L 0-5 (0-3)

Scorers, Times: [Miller 87] / Beckford 19, 29, Earle 42, Cross 54. Ref: L Dilkes

1	2	3	4	5	6	7	8	9	10	11	subs used
Forrest	Stockwell	Thompson	Humes	Yallop	Linighan	Donowa*	Dozzell*	Wark	Kiwomya	Milton	D'Avray/Johnson
Grew	Mills	Hughes	Walker	Aspin	Glover	Porter^	Earle	Cross^	Beckford	Riley	Miller/Millar

Town heads drop after Beckford strikes early. The unbeaten run ends and coach Peter Trevivian is relieved his 'lucky' suit can now go to the cleaners! To cap it all, the weather is atrocious and the M6 blocked. Ex-Town men Mills and Chung take the reins at neighbouring Colchester.

25 — SHEFFIELD UTD (H), 13/1 — D 1-1 (0-1)

Scorers, Times: Lowe 87 / Deane 29. Ref: D Vickers

1	2	3	4	5	6	7	8	9	10	11	subs used
Forrest	Stockwell	Thompson	Humes	Yallop	Linighan	Donowa	Dozzell	Wark	Kiwomya*	Milton	Lowe
Tracey	Hill	Barnes	Lake^	Wilder	Morris	Francis^	Webster	Agana	Deane	Bryson	Rostron/Bradshaw

On the 21st anniversary of Bobby Robson joining Town, he attends as guest of honour. Lowe heads a late leveller after Deane earlier cashed in on a series of defensive mistakes. Lake breaks his leg in a collision with Humes. Ex-soldier Michael Cheetham joins Cambridge for £45,000.

26 — BOURNEMOUTH (A), 20/1 — L 1-3 (0-1)

Scorers, Times: Thompson 83p / Blissett 17, 47p, 63. Ref: R Wiseman

1	2	3	4	5	6	7	8	9	10	11	subs used
Forrest	Stockwell^	Thompson	Humes	Yallop	Linighan	Donowa*	Dozzell	Wark	Kiwomya	Milton	Lowe/Gregory
Peyton	Bond*	Morrell	Teale	Williams	Peacock	Lawrence	Moulden^	Shearer	Holmes	Blissett	Redknapp M/Newson

Luther Blissett's hat-trick features two spectacular strikes, plus a penalty after Newson is tripped. Milton is impeded for Town's consolation spot-kick. Brian Gayle signs from Man City for a Town record of £330,000, after a chat with Paul Cooper convinces him to come to Suffolk.

27 — WOLVERHAMPTON (A), 10/2 — L 1-2 (1-1)

Scorers, Times: Dozzell 17 / Bull 41, Linighan 46 (og). Ref: T Mills

1	2	3	4	5	6	7	8	9	10	11	subs used
Forrest	Stockwell	Pennyfather	Humes	Gayle	Linighan	Gregory*	Dozzell	Wark	Kiwomya	Milton	Donowa
Kendall	Bellamy	Venus	Downing	Westley	Streete	Jones	Cook	Bull	Mutch	Dennison	

Three weeks without a league game after Oxford's visit is cancelled. Dozzell unleashes a great shot from Milton's pass. Cook's corner-kick is headed in at close range by Bull to level matters. Straight after the break Linighan beats his own keeper, chesting Mark Venus' cross into goal.

28 — LEEDS (H), 17/2 — D 2-2 (1-2)

Scorers, Times: Kiwomya 42, Wark 48 / Chapman 21, 44. Ref: K Barratt

1	2	3	4	5	6	7	8	9	10	11	subs used
Forrest	Yallop	Thompson	Pennyfather	Gayle	Linighan	Stockwell*	Dozzell	Wark	Kiwomya	Milton	Lowe
Day	Kamara	Beglin	Jones	Fairclough	Haddock	Strachan	Batty	Chapman	Varadi	Hendrie^	Speed

Table-topping Leeds go ahead when expensive new signing Lee Chapman is left unmarked and converts Strachan's cross with ease. Kiwomya darts in to lift a shot over Day. A Strachan free-kick is headed in by Chapman just before the break. Wark levels from Pennyfather's corner.

29 — OLDHAM (A), 24/2 — L 1-4 (0-2)

Scorers, Times: Wark 52 / Marshall 38, 40, Palmer 49, Irwin 73. Ref: G Courtney

1	2	3	4	5	6	7	8	9	10	11	subs used
Forrest	Yallop	Thompson	Pennyfather	Gayle	Linighan	Stockwell*	Dozzell	Wark	Kiwomya^	Milton	Lowe/D'Avray
Hallworth	Irwin	Barlow	Henry	Barrett	Warhurst	Palmer	Adams	Marshall*	Milligan	Holden R	Blundell

On the Boundary Park plastic pitch, Joe Royle's outfit extend their unbeaten run to 34 matches. Ian Marshall nets with a shot and a header before the interval. Veteran Palmer lofts a shot over Forrest and Irwin combines well with Marshall before netting the fourth with a low drive.

30 — LEICESTER (H), 3/3 — D 2-2 (2-1)

Scorers, Times: Wark 10, Lowe 12 / Walsh 5, Oldfield 80. Ref: B Hill

1	2	3	4	5	6	7	8	9	10	11	subs used
Forrest	Zondervan	Thompson	Stockwell	Gayle	Linighan	Lowe*	Dozzell	Ramsey*	Kiwomya	Milton*	Donowa
Hodge	Mauchlen*	Paris	Mills	Walsh	James	Reid	Barham	Oldfield	McAllister	Wright	Russell/North

Walsh shocks Town as he rams home an early chance from Oldfield's cross. Makeshift striker Wark races on to a James error and shoots over Hodge. Back from injury, Lowe fires jubilant Town ahead moments later. After 62 minutes' stalemate, City's subs set up Oldfield's equaliser.

31 — STOKE (A), 6/3 — D 0-0 (0-0)

Ref: I Hemley

1	2	3	4	5	6	7	8	9	10	11	subs used
Forrest	Stockwell	Thompson	Zondervan	Gayle	Linighan	Lowe	Dozzell	Ellis	Pennyfather	Milton	Fowler
Fox	Butler	Sandford	Beeston	Blake	Berry*	Brooke	Kevan	Biggins	Palin		

Alan Ball has taken the reins at Stoke from Mick Mills, but they are still finding goals hard to come by. New signing Brooke misses a sitter after Forrest blocks Palin's effort. Town look little better than the bottom-placed club and fail to take the chance of a first win in the nineties.

32 — BRIGHTON (H), 10/3 — W 2-1 (1-1)

Scorers, Times: Wark 22, Milton 75 / Wilkins 26. Ref: D Hedges

1	2	3	4	5	6	7	8	9	10	11	subs used
Forrest	Stockwell	Thompson	Redford*	Gayle	Linighan	Lowe^	Dozzell	Wark	Pennyfather	Milton	Kiwomya/Baltacha
Digweed	Crumplin	Chapman	Curbishley^	Dublin	Gatting*	Gotsmanov	Barham	Bremner	Codner	Wilkins	Bissett/Nelson

Wark heads in after Pennyfather's corner is flicked on by Lowe. Gayle's bad back-pass leads to Bremner crossing for Wilkins to level. Town look disjointed and there are chants of 'Duncan out', which are temporarily silenced when Milton shoots under Digweed from Dozzell's pass.

33 — OXFORD (H), 13/3 — W 1-0 (0-0)

Scorers, Times: Pennyfather 90. Ref: A Seville

1	2	3	4	5	6	7	8	9	10	11	subs used
Forrest	Stockwell	Thompson	Redford	Gayle	Linighan	Lowe^	Dozzell	Wark	Pennyfather	Milton*	Baltacha/Kiwomya
Key	Smart	Phillips J	Lewis	Foster	Ford	Penney	Mustoe	Stein	Durnin	Simpson	

A rather forgettable evening's action, but Pennyfather snatches a last-gasp winner. Once again there is sustained chanting for John Duncan to be dismissed. Lowe is unhappy at being substituted, but he doesn't look his old self after his long injury lay-off and may not be fully match-fit.

34 — NEWCASTLE (A), 17/3 — L 1-2 (1-0)

Scorers, Times: Milton 24 / Quinn 51, 85. Ref: K Breen

1	2	3	4	5	6	7	8	9	10	11	subs used
Forrest	Stockwell	Thompson	Redford	Gayle	Linighan	Lowe*	Dozzell	Brown	Baltacha	Milton	Kiwomya
Wright	Bradshaw	Aitken	Sweeney	Anderson	Ranson	Dillon*	Quinn	McGhee	Gallagher^		Brazil/Robinson

Milton passes a late fitness test and opens the scoring by guiding a left-foot shot past Wright. A slip by Linighan leads to Gallagher crossing for Quinn to convert the equaliser. Town hang on until near the end when Quinn rises to power home a cross for his 30th goal of the campaign.

35 | H | 20/3 | SWINDON | 11,856 | 8 | 3 | W | 1-0 | 53 | 0-0 | Dozzell 70 | Ref: A Buskh

Forrest · Stockwell · Thompson · Redford · Gayle · Linighan · Lowe · Dozzell · Wark · Baltacha* · Milton
Digby · Kerslake · Bodin · McLoughlin · Calderwood Gittens · Jones T* · Shearer · White^ · McLaren · Simpson · Johnson · Hockaday/Close

Dozzell strikes in the final quarter, sealing Town's seventh 1-0 win of the seson. The fans are still disgruntled and call for new faces before the transfer deadline. There are no major imports, although Mark Stuart arrives on loan from Plymouth and Raphael Meade's loan is extended.

---

36 | H | 24/3 | BRADFORD C | 11,074 | 8 | 23 | W | 1-0 | 56 | 1-0 | Wark 15 | Ref: P Don

Forrest · Stockwell · Thompson · Redford · Gayle · Linighan · Lowe · Dozzell · Wark · Johnson* · Milton
Tomlinson · Mitchell · Tinnion · Morgan · Jackson · Davies · Aizlewood · Costello · White^ · McCall · Woods · Baltacha

Johnson is stretchered off with a nasty knee injury after five minutes. Lowe's corner is headed on by Gayle for Wark to score. The remaining 75 minutes produces little excitement and again sections of the crowd voice discontent. Neil Woods makes a quick return in his new colours.

---

37 | A | 31/3 | PLYMOUTH | 6,793 | 9 | 21 | L | 0-1 | 56 | 0-0 | Morrison 68 | Ref: B Stevens

Forrest · Stockwell · Thompson · Redford^ · Gayle · Linighan · Lowe · Dozzell · Wark · Baltacha* · Milton
Wilmot · Brown · Salmon · Marker · Burrows · Morrison · Byrne · McCarthy · Tynan* · Hodges · Flore · Pickard

Lowe gets clear on his own, but knocks his shot wide of the post as Wilmot advances. From Brown's cross, Morrison guides a header past Forrest. Lowe has a chance to level, but shoots straight at Wilmot. Debutant Meade goes agonisingly close near the final whistle with a header.

---

38 | A | 7/4 | WATFORD | 11,158 | 10 | 13 | D | 3-3 | 57 | 2-0 | Stuart 25, 68, Wark 29 / Hodges 55p, 72p, Penrice 76 | Ref: P Durkin

Forrest · Stockwell · Thompson · Zondervan* · Gayle · Linighan · Lowe^ · Dozzell · Wark · Stuart · Milton
Caton · Williams* · Drysdale · Harrison · Holdsworth Raeder · Thomas · Wilkinson · Penrice · Falconer · Hodges · Humes/Kiwomya · Ashby

Stuart nets after a quick free-kick. Wark heads in Stuart's corner, but Watford get one back when Linighan handles in the area. Penrice is fouled for another penalty and then levels himself. the eighth man to score twice on his Ipswich debut with a superb run and finish.

---

39 | H | 10/4 | PORTSMOUTH | 11,062 | 10 | 16 | L | 0-1 | 57 | 0-1 | Whittingham 11 | Ref: M Bailey

Forrest · Stockwell* · Thompson · Zondervan* · Gayle · Linighan · Lowe^ · Dozzell · Wark · Stuart · Milton
Knight · Neill · Stevens · Kuhl · Hogg · Maguire · Wigley · Chamberlain Whittingham Gilligan · Beresford ! · Humes/Kiwomya

Watched by England boss Robson, Town put in a dismal performance and never recover from Whittingham's early strike. Beresford gets a red card on 79 minutes but John Gregory's side hang on for the win. Broken leg victim David Hill breaks his foot in his comeback for the reserves.

---

40 | H | 14/4 | PORT VALE | 10,509 | 10 | 11 | W | 3-2 | 60 | 1-1 | Wark 45, Dozzell 51, Thompson 57p / Earle 13, Cross 69p | Ref: T Ward

Forrest · Yallop · Thompson · Zondervan · Gayle · Linighan · Lowe^ · Dozzell · Wark · Stuart · Milton
Grew · Parkin · Hughes · Walker · Aspin · Glover · Porter* · Earle · Cross^ · Beckford · Miller/Millar

Beckford puts Robbie Earle through for the first goal. Wark bundles in an equaliser and Dozzell heads in Gayle's cross. Thompson fires in after Zondervan is brought down in the area. Having missed a penalty earlier, Glover steps aside for Cross to convert Vale's second award.

---

41 | A | 17/4 | WEST HAM | 25,178 | 10 | 7 | L | 0-2 | 60 | 0-2 | Allen 27, Keen 36 | Ref: K Burge

Forrest · Yallop · Thompson · Zondervan* · Gayle · Linighan^ · Kiwomya* · Dozzell · Wark · Stuart* · Milton^
Miklosko · Slater · Dicks · Parris · Foster · Gale · Brady* · Quinn · Keen · Morley* · Allen · McAvennie/Potts

Town still harbour outside hopes of a play-off place, but two goals in nine minutes extends the improving Hammers' unbeaten run. Results and crowds have improved at Upton Park since Billy Bonds recently replaced Lou Macari as the manager, and Ipswich have to play second fiddle.

---

42 | H | 21/4 | HULL | 9,380 | 10 | 17 | L | 0-1 | 60 | 0-0 | Gayle 70 (og) | Ref: M James

Forrest · Yallop · Thompson · Zondervan · Gayle · Linighan^ · Donowa · Dozzell · Wark · Stuart* · Milton
Hesford · Brown · Jacobs · Jobson · Doyle · Brady · Roberts · Swan · Bamber · Palin · Thomas · Kiwomya/Humes

A thoroughly depressing afternoon as Town fail to break down stuggling Hull. With 20 minutes left, Palin crosses and as Bamber and Gayle stretch for the ball, it deflects off the Town man into the net. Police cordon off the director's box as angry Town fans express their discontent.

---

43 | A | 25/4 | MIDDLESBROUGH | 15,233 | 10 | 22 | W | 2-1 | 63 | 0-1 | Lowe 56, Milton 63 / Baird 11 | Ref: W Burns

Forrest · Yallop · Thompson · Zondervan · Gayle · Linighan · Lowe · Dozzell · Wark · Lowe · Milton
Pears · Parkinson · Phillips · Kernaghan · Coleman · Ripley · Slaven* · Proctor · Baird · Brennan · Davenport · Kerr

Town players seem happy to get away from the angry atmosphere and slow-handclapping of home games. They bounce back from a goal down to overcome Colin Todd's nervous side and plunge them further into the relegation mire. David Lowe scores his first goal in 13 matches.

---

44 | H | 28/4 | BLACKBURN | 11,007 | 9 | 5 | W | 3-1 | 66 | 2-1 | Milton 10, Lowe 16, 69 / Mail 20p | Ref: R Lewis

Forrest · Yallop · Thompson · Zondervan* · Gayle · Linighan · Lowe · Dozzell · Wark · Lowe · Milton
Gennoe · Atkins · Dawson · Reid · Moran · Mail · Kennedy* · Millar · Finnican · Garner^ · Sellars · Gayle/Irvine

Milton nets a fine shot after bursting into the area. Lowe turns and fires in a beauty from Gayle's free-kick. Mail tucks in a penalty after a push by Wark. Victory is assured as Lowe wins in a Donowa corner. The fans continue their protests, however, watched by a huge police presence.

---

45 | A | 1/5 | HULL | 5,306 | 10 | 14 | L | 3-4 | 66 | 0-1 | Lowe 68, 70, Redford 87 [Payton 89] / Swan 2, Shotton 56, Atkinson 58 | Ref: A Flood

Forrest · Yallop · Humes · Hesford · Atkinson · Jacobs · Jobson · Swan · Bamber · Payton · Thomas · Kiwomya/Redford

An inconsequential end-of-season affair provides entertainment galore for a small crowd. Andy Payton misses a penalty, but has the last laugh by grabbing the winner in the dying moments. The Tigers roar into a 3-0 lead but, led by energetic Lowe, Town unexpectedly claw back level.

---

46 | A | 5/5 | WEST BROM | 11,567 | 9 | 20 | W | 3-1 | 69 | 3-0 | Lowe 12, Milton 17, Dozzell 18 / Bannister 79 | Ref: D Elleray

Neville · Zondervan · Thompson · Humes · Gayle · Linighan · Lowe · Dozzell · Wark^ · Lowe · Milton
Naylor · Bradley* · Harbey · Talbot* · Whyte · Burgess · Ford · Goodman · Swan · Bannister · Shakespeare McNally · Hackett/Foster

The final game of a thoroughly unsatisfactory season in many fans' eyes. Duncan is widely thought to be on his way out, despite another top-ten finish. He seems to be going out with a bang as slick finishing secures an early 3-0 lead. Young keeper Neville has a relatively quiet debut.

Home 12,381 · Away 11,685 · Average

BARCLAYS DIVISION 2 (CUP-TIES)   Manager: John Duncan   SEASON 1989-90

Littlewoods Cup

			Att		F-A	H-T	Scorers, Times, and Referees	1	2	3	4	5	6	7	8	9	10	11	subs used
2:1	H	TRANMERE 19/9	7,757	12 L 3:8	0-1	0-1	Muir 22 Ref: I Hemley	Forrest *Nixon*	Baltaacha *Higgins*	Thompson *McCarrick*	Zondervan *Martindale*	Redford *Hughes*	Palmer^ *Garnett^*	Lowe *Morrissey**	Dozzell *Harvey*	Wark *Malkin*	Humes* *Muir*	Milton *Thomas*	Yallop/Donowa *Bishop/Steel*

On a night of cup shocks, Town toil away to no effect against John King's determined outfit. Martindale's shot pole-axes Wark and falls nicely for Morrissey, who crosses for Muir to head home. After the interval Ipswich exert more pressure but find keeper Eric Nixon in excellent form.

			Att		F-A	H-T	Scorers, Times, and Referees	1	2	3	4	5	6	7	8	9	10	11	subs used
2:2	A	TRANMERE 3/10	10,050	16 L 3:1	0-1	0-1	Malkin 9 Ref: J Kirkby (Town lose 0-2 on aggregate)	Forrest *Nixon*	Stockwell *Higgins*	Thompson *McCarrick*	Zondervan *Martindale^*	Humes *Hughes*	Linighan *Vickers*	Lowe *Morrissey**	Dozzell *Harvey*	D'Avray *Malkin*	Palmer* *Muir*	Hill^ *Thomas*	Donowa/Johnson *Steel/Bishop*

Malkin's early strike gives Town a mountain to climb in front of a partisan crowd. David Hill plays 70 minutes but Duncan puts him in the reserves the next day to get more match practice – only for the midfielder's leg to be broken by a dreadful tackle by Norwich's Theodosiou.

FA Cup

			Att		F-A	H-T	Scorers, Times, and Referees	1	2	3	4	5	6	7	8	9	10	11	subs used
3	A	LEEDS 6/1	26,766	6 W 1	1-0	0-0	Dozzell 54 Ref: G Courtney	Forrest *Day*	Stockwell *Sterland*	Thompson *Kerr*	Yallop *Jones*	Humes *Fairclough*	Linighan *Haddock*	Donowa *Strachan*	Dozzell *Batty*	Wark *Baird**	Kwomya *Shutt^*	Milton *Hendrie*	Pearson/Snodin

After three successive 3rd round losses, Town seize a notable scalp at the home of the table-toppers. Thompson, a Leeds supporter as a boy, whips over a great cross and Dozzell escapes the attentions of his marker Jones to head past Day. The joy is tempered by the 4th round draw.

			Att		F-A	H-T	Scorers, Times, and Referees	1	2	3	4	5	6	7	8	9	10	11	subs used
4	A	BARNSLEY 27/1	14,440	7 L 23	0-2	0-2	Taggart 8, Cooper 34 Ref: D Hedges	Forrest *Baker*	Stockwell* *Dobbin*	Thompson *Taggart*	Yallop *Futcher*	Gregory^ *Shotton*	Linighan *Lowndes*	Lowe *Agnew*	Dozzell *Glover*	Wark *Gray**	Donowa *Cooper*	Milton *Smith*	Yallop/Gayle *Tiler*

Defender Taggart gets forward to head a fine goal from Dobbin's cross. Town slip a step nearer the cup's exit door when Glover, on loan from Forest, weaves through the defence to set up Cooper, who fires past Forrest. After the interval Town fail to convert a handful of half-chances.

League table

		P	W	D	L	F	A	W	D	L	F	A	Pts
				Home						**Away**			
1	Leeds	46	16	6	1	46	18	8	7	8	33	34	85
2	Sheffield Utd	46	14	5	4	43	27	10	8	5	35	31	85
3	Newcastle	46	17	4	2	51	26	5	10	8	29	29	80
4	Swindon	46	12	6	5	49	29	8	8	7	30	30	74
5	Blackburn	46	10	9	4	43	30	9	8	6	31	29	74
6	Sunderland *	46	10	8	5	41	32	6	10	7	29	32	74
7	West Ham	46	14	5	4	50	22	6	7	10	30	35	72
8	Oldham	46	15	7	1	50	23	4	7	12	20	34	71
9	IPSWICH	46	13	7	3	38	22	6	5	12	29	44	69
10	Wolves	46	12	5	6	37	20	6	9	8	30	40	67
11	Port Vale	46	11	9	3	37	20	4	7	12	25	37	61
12	Portsmouth	46	9	8	6	40	34	6	8	9	22	31	61
13	Leicester	46	10	8	5	34	29	5	6	12	33	50	59
14	Hull	46	7	8	8	27	31	7	8	8	31	34	58
15	Watford	46	11	6	6	41	28	3	9	11	17	32	57
16	Plymouth	46	9	8	6	30	23	5	5	13	28	40	55
17	Oxford	46	8	7	8	35	31	7	2	14	22	35	54
18	Brighton	46	10	6	7	28	27	5	3	15	28	45	54
19	Barnsley	46	7	9	7	22	23	6	6	11	27	48	54
20	West Brom	46	6	9	8	35	37	7	1	15	32	34	51
21	Middlesbro	46	10	3	10	33	29	3	8	12	19	34	50
22	Bournemouth	46	8	6	9	30	31	4	6	13	27	45	48
23	Bradford C	46	9	6	8	26	24	0	8	15	18	44	41
24	Stoke	46	4	11	8	20	24	4	8	13	15	39	37
		1104	252	165	135	886	640	135	165	252	640	886	1491

* promoted after play-offs

Appearances and Goals

	Appearances						**Goals**			
	Lge	Sub	LC	Sub	FAC	Sub	Lge	LC	FAC	Tot
Baltacha, Sergei	3	5								
Cheetham, Michael		1					1			1
D'Avray, Mich	8	4	1				1			1
Donowa, Louie	17	6	2		2		1			1
Dozzell, Jason	46		2		2		8		1	9
Forrest, Craig	45		2		2					
Gayle, Brian	20									
Gregory, David	1	3		1						
Harbey, Graham		1								
Hill, David		1								
Humes, Tony	17	7	2		2		3			3
Johnson, Gavin	3	3		1						
Kiwomya, Chris	19	10	1		2		5			5
Linighan, David	41		1		2					
Lowe, David	31	3	2			1	13			13
Meade, Raphael		1								
Milton, Simon	41		1		2		11			11
Neville, Chris	1									
Palmer, Steve	3	2	2							
Pennyfather, Glenn	7	1	1							
Redford, Ian	14	4	1				1			1
Stockwell, Mick	34	1			2		3			3
Stuart, Mark	5						2			2
Thompson, Neil	44		2		2		3			3
Wark, John	41	1	1				10			10
Woods, Neil	3	4					1			1
Yallop, Frank	31		1	1	1	1				
Zondervan, Romeo	30		2							
28 players used	506	57	22	4	22	2	67		1	68

Odds & ends

Double wins: (3) Barnsley, Middlesbro, West Brom.

Double losses: (2) Wolverhampton, Hull.

Won from behind: (3) Barnsley (H), Middlesbro (A), Port Vale (H).

Lost from in front: (2) Newcastle (A), Wolverhampton (A).

High spots: A 13-match unbeaten run from mid-October.

The win at Newcastle, which ended a poor run of results.

The FA Cup victory at table-topping Leeds.

Low spots: A third successive failure to reach the play-offs.

Crowd demos against John Duncan.

Serious injuries to Hill, Lowe, Stockwell, Humes, Johnson.

Sinking to 17th place after a poor display at Bradford City.

Two cup defeats by Third Division Tranmere Rovers.

A 5-0 drubbing at Vale Park on the first day of the new decade.

Player of the Year: John Wark.

Ever-presents: (1) Jason Dozzell.

Hat-tricks: (0) (David Gregory in ZDS Cup).

Opposing hat-tricks: (1) Luther Blissett (Bournemouth).

Leading scorer: (13) David Lowe.

BARCLAYS DIVISION 2

Manager: John Lyall

SEASON 1990-91

Column key (shirt numbers 1–11): Ipswich Town line-up given first, opponents' line-up in *italics*.

No 1 — H — 25/8 — SHEFFIELD WED · Att 17,284 · F-A 0-2 · L, 0 pts · H-T 0-2
Scorers, Times: *Williams 28, Shirtliff 44* · Ref: D Elleray

1	2	3	4	5	6	7	8	9	10	11	subs used
Forrest	Yallop	Thompson*	Stockwell	Gayle	Linighan	Lowe	Humes	Redford	Kiwomya	Zondervan	Dozzell
Pressman	*Nilsson*	*King*	*Palmer*	*Shirtliff*	*Pearson*	*Wilson*	*Sheridan*	*Hirst*	*Williams*	*Worthington*	

New boss Lyall says he want fans to see 'something worthwhile', but Town are outclassed. £700,000 new signing Williams fires the first from Hirst's cross. Four minutes later Linighan's foul gives Hirst a penalty, but his kick hits the bar. Poor marking at a corner leads to a second.

No 2 — A — 28/8 — SWINDON · Att 10,817 · F-A 0-1 · L, 0 pts · H-T 0-0
Scorers, Times: *Shearer 77* · Ref: K Cooper

1	2	3	4	5	6	7	8	9	10	11	subs used
Forrest	Yallop	Thompson^	Stockwell	Gayle	Linighan	Lowe	Humes	Redford*	Kiwomya	Zondervan	Gregory/Palmer
Digby	*Kerslake*	*Bodin*	*Simpson*	*Calderwood*	*Gittens*	*Jones**	*Shearer*	*Close*	*MacLaren*	*Foley*	*McLoughlin*

More gloom as a late winning goal provides an ideal 28th birthday present for Duncan Shearer. Town's best attempt sees Thompson's fierce free-kick strike the crossbar. Redford departs with a badly cut leg. Forrest makes several fine saves to limit dangerman Shearer to just one goal.

No 3 — A — 1/9 — WEST BROM · Att 10,318 · Pos 15/21 · F-A 2-1 · W, 3 pts · H-T 0-1
Scorers, Times: Humes 84, Thompson 90 / *Bannister 41* · Ref: P Danson

1	2	3	4	5	6	7	8	9	10	11	subs used
Forrest	Yallop	Thompson	Stockwell	Gayle	Linighan	Lowe^	Humes	Redford*	Gregory*	Zondervan	Milton/Palmer
Naylor	*Hodson*	*Harbey*	*Robson*	*Brugess*	*Strodder*	*Ford*	*West*	*Bannister*	*Bradley*	*Shakespeare**	*Hackett*

A woeful first half display ends with a Gayle misjudgement which allows Bannister to nip through and score. Sub Milton swings over a late cross and Humes gets on the end of it to level. In injury time Thompson's corner dips and swings into the net, catching a deflection off West.

No 4 — H — 8/9 — BLACKBURN · Att 10,953 · Pos 10/18 · F-A 2-1 · W, 6 pts · H-T 0-1
Scorers, Times: Gregory 61, Stockwell 78 / *Richardson 36* · Ref: A Gunn

1	2	3	4	5	6	7	8	9	10	11	subs used
Forrest	Yallop	Thompson	Stockwell	Gayle	Linighan	Milton	Humes^	Kiwomya	Gregory	Zondervan*	Hill/Palmer
Collier	*Atkins*	*Sulley*	*Reid*	*Hill*	*Stapleton*	*Gayle**	*Millar*	*Starbuck*	*Richardson*	*Wilcox*	*Johnrose*

Major problems for Town as Zondervan goes off with back trouble and Humes departs with a broken jaw. Richardson nets after Gayle's header is parried. After the break Milton's header is pushed high into the air and Gregory bundles it home. Stockwell pounces to fire a winner.

No 5 — A — 15/9 — MILLWALL · Att 12,604 · Pos 12/3 · F-A 1-1 · D, 7 pts · H-T 1-1
Scorers, Times: Kiwomya 33 / *Rae 2* · Ref: G Singh

1	2	3	4	5	6	7	8	9	10	11	subs used
Forrest	Yallop	Hill	Stockwell	Gayle	Linighan	Milton	Kiwomya	Redford	Gregory	Zondervan	
Horne	*Stevens*	*Dawes*	*Morgan*	*Wood*	*McLeary*	*Carter*	*Allen*	*Sheringham*	*Rae*	*Briley*	

A smart move involving Teddy Sheringham sees Alex Rae fire Bruce Rioch's high-flying side ahead after just 81 seconds. A sharp breakaway move sees Hill play a nice ball through to Kiwomya who sprints clear and finishes expertly. Definitely a point gained at the inhospitable Den.

No 6 — A — 19/9 — WEST HAM · Att 18,764 · Pos 12/3 · F-A 1-3 · L, 7 pts · H-T 1-0
Scorers, Times: Milton 11 / *Bishop 62, Quinn 82, Morley 90* · Ref: G Ashby

1	2	3	4	5	6	7	8	9	10	11	subs used
Forrest	Yallop	Hill	Stockwell	Gayle	Linighan*	Milton	Kiwomya	Redford*	Gregory	Zondervan	Thompson!
Miklosko	*Potts^*	*Dicks*	*Foster*	*Martin*	*Keen*	*Bishop*	*McAvennie**	*Slater*	*Allen*	*Morley*	*Quinn/Parris*

Milton's effort is a dream start at Upton Park, but Bishop equalises with a 20-yard drive. Thompson brings down Morley on 79 minutes and is sent off under the new 'professional foul' clampdown. Moments later Quinn buries a diving header and Morley strikes in the last minute.

No 7 — H — 22/9 — BRISTOL ROV · Att 11,084 · Pos 12/18 · F-A 2-1 · W, 10 pts · H-T 0-0
Scorers, Times: Gayle 60, Kiwomya 64 / *Saunders 81* · Ref: A Smith

1	2	3	4	5	6	7	8	9	10	11	subs used
Forrest	Yallop	Hill	Stockwell	Gayle	Linighan	Milton	Kiwomya	Redford*	Gregory	Zondervan	Thompson
Parkin	*Hazel*	*Twentyman*	*Yates*	*Mehew*	*Jones*	*Holloway*	*Reece**	*White*	*Saunders*	*Pounder*	*Nixon*

Carl Saunders, whose confidence is low after 23 games without a goal, misses several chances to let Town off the hook. Gayle punishes a defensive mix-up, and then a curling shot by Kiwomya extends the lead. Gerry Francis' side hit back when Saunders ends his barren spell.

No 8 — H — 29/9 — WATFORD · Att 11,351 · Pos 11/24 · F-A 1-1 · D, 11 pts · H-T 0-0
Scorers, Times: Gayle 69 / *Wilkinson 47* · Ref: M James

1	2	3	4	5	6	7	8	9	10	11	subs used
Forrest	Yallop	Hill	Stockwell	Gayle	Linighan	Milton	Wilkinson	Redford	Gregory*	Zondervan	Thompson
James	*Dublin*	*Drysdale*	*Roeder*	*McLaughlin*	*Holdsworth*	*Williams*	*Inglethorpe**	*Falconer*	*Porter*	*Penrice*	*Pentice*

Town survive first-half near-things when Roeder hits the bar and Falconer has an effort disallowed. Colin Lee is in his final few weeks as Hornets' boss and sees Wilkinson convert a 'route one' attack. Thompson drills in a corner and Gayle beats David James in the air to level.

No 9 — A — 2/10 — BARNSLEY · Att 6,930 · Pos 13/10 · F-A 1-5 · L, 11 pts · H-T 0-4
Scorers, Times: Thompson 59p [*Agnew 44, Saville 90*] / *Taggart 18, Archdeacon 21, Rammell 28, Taggart 28* · Ref: J Rushton

1	2	3	4	5	6	7	8	9	10	11	subs used
Forrest	Yallop	Thompson	Stockwell	Gayle	Linighan	Milton	Kiwomya	Redford	Hill	Gregory*	Zondervan
Baker	*Banks*	*Taggart*	*McCord*	*Smith*	*Tiler*	*O'Connell*	*Rammell*	*Saville*	*Agnew*	*Archdeacon**	*Robinson*

A nightmare first half sees Town swamped. Taggart, Archdeacon and Agnew net with headers and Rammell fires in a 20-yarder. Ipswich improve after the break and pull one back when Kiwomya is tripped in the area. Saville hits an unguarded net after a Gayle-Forrest mix-up.

No 10 — A — 6/10 — PLYMOUTH · Att 5,935 · Pos 13/15 · F-A 0-0 · D, 12 pts · H-T 0-0
Scorers, Times: — · Ref: R Lewis

1	2	3	4	5	6	7	8	9	10	11	subs used
Forrest	Yallop	Zondervan	Stockwell	Gayle	Linighan	Milton	Kiwomya	Redford	Gregory	Hill	Thompson
Wilmot	*Brown*	*Morgan*	*Marker*	*Burrows*	*Hodges*	*Byrne**	*Fiore*	*Turner*	*Thomas*	*Salman*	*King*

After the Barnsley debacle, Town batten down the hatches at Home Park and escape with a point against David Kemp's side. Red faces for the home side as sub King comes on wearing a No 8 shirt. He is 'sent off' by the referee and returns in a No 14, although he is listed as the No 12!

No 11 — H — 13/10 — PORT VALE · Att 10,369 · Pos 12/15 · F-A 3-0 · W, 15 pts · H-T 1-0
Scorers, Times: Milton 1, 48, Stockwell 68 · Ref: K Hackett

1	2	3	4	5	6	7	8	9	10	11	subs used
Forrest	Yallop	Zondervan	Stockwell	Gayle	Linighan	Milton	Kiwomya^	Redford	Gregory	Hill	Johnson
Wood	*Mills*	*Hughes*	*Walker*	*Aspin*	*Glover*	*Ford*	*Porter*	*Jepson**	*Beckford*	*Jeffers^*	*Cross/Gibson*

A rising drive by Milton in the first minute catches Wood cold. Early in the second half Milton's header is saved but he converts the rebound. Stockwell bursts through to tuck home a neat third goal. Vale boss John Rudge is furious at how his team 'gifted' goals early in each half.

Match 12 — H NEWCASTLE, 20/10 — W 2-1 (15,567)

Gayle 27, Milton 35 | Quinn 49p
Ref: R Wiseman · Positions: 9 / 10 / 18

Forrest	Yallop	Zondervan	Stockwell	Gayle	Linighan	Milton	Kiwomya	Redford^	Gregory*	Hill	Johnson/Palmer
Burridge	Scott	Sweeney	Aitken	Anderson	Bradshaw^	Fereday	Brock	Quinn	Kristensen! O'Brien*	Hill	Sloan/Ranson

A healthy crowd sees Gayle head Town ahead from a Hill corner. Milton increases the lead with a confident finish. Jim Smith's men pull one back from the spot when Forrest hauls down sub Sloan. Forrest is lucky not to be sent off, but Kristensen does see red near the end for dissent.

Match 13 — A OLDHAM, 23/10 — L 0-2 (13,170)

Moulden 61, Currie 82
Ref: A Seville · Positions: 9 / 1 / 18

Forrest	Yallop	Zondervan	Stockwell	Gayle	Linighan	Milton	Kiwomya	Redford	Gregory*	Hill	Thompson
Hallworth	Warhurst	Barlow	Henry	Barrett	Jobson	Adams^	Currie	Marshall*	Redfearn	Holden R	Moulden/Donachie

Joe Royle's side are the unbeaten divisional leaders and stern opponents on their plastic pitch. Town start brightly and prospects of a point look good. Then Moulden scores a crucial opener when he skilfully beats Forrest following Barlow's fierce drive. Currie sweeps home the second.

Match 14 — A LEICESTER, 27/10 — W 2-1 (11,053)

Stockwell 4, 40 | Kelly 49p
Ref: P Don · Positions: 8 / 20 / 21

Forrest	Yallop	Zondervan	Stockwell	Gayle	Linighan	Milton	Lowe*	Redford	Gregory	Hill	Dozzell
Hooper	Mauchlen	North^	Hill	Walsh	Fenwick	Wright	Reid!	Oldfield*	Mills	Kelly	Kitson/Ramsey

Manager David Pleat is under verbal fire from unhappy home fans. Makeshift striker Stockwell increases the pressure by converting a chip by Gregory. The same man sets up Stockwell for a neat second. Hill handles to give City a penalty. Reid is unlucky to pick up two yellow cards.

Match 15 — H BRIGHTON, 3/11 — L 1-3 (11,437)

Stockwell 74 | Byrne 2, Small 5, 70p
Ref: J Ashworth · Positions: 10 / 9 / 21

Forrest	Yallop	Zondervan	Stockwell	Gayle	Linighan	Milton	Kiwomya	Redford	Gregory^	Hill*	Thompson/Dozzell
Digweed	Crumplin	Chapman	Wilkins	Gatting	Chivers	Barham	Byrne	Small	Codner	Walker	

A woeful performance by Town. With Forrest off his line Byrne lobs the first. It gets worse in the fifth minute when hesitancy by Linighan and Gayle allows Small to bustle in and score. Town steady the ship for a while, but then Gayle pulls down Byrne for the clinching penalty kick.

Match 16 — A HULL, 10/11 — D 3-3 (5,294)

Dozzell 52, Redford 66, Kiwomya 80 | Payton 40, 54, McParland 83
Ref: E Parker · Positions: 10 / 21 / 22

Forrest	Yallop	Zondervan	Stockwell	Gayle	Linighan	Dozzell	Kiwomya	Redford	Gregory*	Hill	Thompson
Hesford	Hockaday	Jacobs	Mail	Shotton	Doyle	Finnigan*	Payton	Bamber	Palin	Swan	McParland

Payton runs through to beat Forrest, but Dozzell's glancing header levels it. Payton hits back with a diving header only for Redford to squeeze home a shot. Kiwomya gleefully puts Ipswich ahead, assisted by Zondervan. The final blast in this thriller sees McParland blast in a free-kick.

Match 17 — H NOTTS CO, 17/11 — D 0-0 (10,778)

Ref: T Ward · Positions: 11 / 7 / 23

Forrest	Yallop	Zondervan	Stockwell	Gayle	Linighan	Dozzell	Kiwomya	Redford	Gregory	Hill	Thompson
Cherry	Palmer	Harding	Short Cr	Yates	O'Riordan	Thomas	Turner	Bartlett	Regis	Draper	

The familiar cry from Town fans for new faces in the forward line returns after this drab affair. Without Forrest's ultra-sharp reflexes this may have ended in defeat. County also miss a great chance near the end. Spurs' young keeper Ian Walker signs on loan as cover for injured Parkes.

Match 18 — H BRISTOL CITY, 24/11 — D 1-1 (10,037)

Dozzell 19 | Taylor 88
Ref: J Kirkby · Positions: 12 / 11 / 24

Forrest	Yallop	Humes	Stockwell	Gayle	Linighan	Dozzell	Kiwomya	Redford	Gregory	Hill	Thompson
Sinclair	Llewellyn	Aizlewood	May	Shelton	Rennie	Bent	Newman	Allison^	Morgan	Smith	Taylor

Another unhappy afternoon as victory is tossed away. Dozzell diverts Humes' shot in to give some early joy. Aizlewood fists away Kiwomya's shot but Thompson puts the penalty into the Churchman's Stand. Town pay for this miss when the lively Bent crosses for Taylor to equalise.

Match 19 — A WOLVERHAMPTON, 1/12 — D 2-2 (15,803)

Dozzell 41, Redford 45 | Bull 4, 78
Ref: J Lloyd · Positions: 11 / 5 / 25

Forrest	Yallop	Humes	Stockwell	Johnson	Linighan	Dozzell	Kiwomya*	Redford	Gregory*	Hill	Milton
Stowell	Roberts	Thompson	Bellamy	Stancliffe	Bennett	Steele*	Cook	Bull	Dennison	Taylor	Paskin

Bull's low drive from the edge of the box gets Town off to a bad start. Dozzell levels with an unfussy volley from Hill's cross. Redford nets off a post just before the break. Bull levels for Graham Turner's men and they nearly win it via a late piledriver, but Forrest saves superbly.

Match 20 — H SWINDON, 8/12 — D 1-1 (9,358)

Redford 47p | Shearer 69
Ref: P Vanes · Positions: 9 / 15 / 26

Forrest	Yallop	Humes	Stockwell^	Johnson	Linighan	Dozzell	Kiwomya	Redford*	Gregory	Hill	Milton/Lowe
Hammond	Kerslake	Bodin	McLoughlin	Viveash	Gittens	Jones	Shearer	White*	MacLaren	Foley	Simpson

Stockwell handles, but MacLaren sees his penalty saved by Forrest's legs. After Viveash fouls Gregory, stand-in taker Redford shows Swindon how it's done. A glorious pass by Foley sets up Shearer and he nets the equaliser. Another victory is snatched away and Town are jeered off.

Match 21 — A SHEFFIELD WED, 15/12 — D 2-2 (19,333)

Milton 12, Redford 21 | Francis 35, Pearson 68
Ref: A Dawson · Positions: 11 / 3 / 27

Forrest	Yallop	Thompson	Stockwell	Palmer	Linighan	Dozzell	Lowe	Redford	Gregory	Hill*	Milton
Pressman	Harkes	King*	Palmer	Shirtliff	Pearson	Wilson	Sheridan	Hirst	Williams	Worthington	Francis

Town thrive in the more exciting atmosphere and cruise to a 2-0 lead via Redford's header. Ron Atkinson reacts by bringing on 36-year-old sub Trevor Francis and transforms the contest. Francis curls in a beauty to upset Town's rhythm and Pearson levels after an error by Dozzell.

Match 22 — A PORTSMOUTH, 21/12 — D 1-1 (7,010)

Palmer 6 | Clarke 62
Ref: J Moules · Positions: 11 / 21 / 28

Forrest	Yallop	Thompson	Stockwell	Palmer*	Linighan	Dozzell	Lowe	Redford	Gregory	Hill	Milton
Knight	Neill	Beresford	Kuhl	Butters	Awford	Anderton	Stevens^	Whittingham	Aspinall	Chamberlain	Clarke

Cambridge blue Palmer crashes home a fine dipping volley for his first League goal. Town cling on to the lead for nearly an hour, but then succumb and have to settle for a seventh successive draw. The equaliser comes from the right boot of former Town reserve striker Colin Clarke.

Match 23 — H MIDDLESBROUGH, 26/12 — L 0-1 (12,508)

Baird 55
Ref: B Hill · Positions: 13 / 3 / 28

Forrest	Yallop	Thompson	Stockwell	Palmer*	Linighan	Dozzell	Lowe	Redford	Humes	Hill*	Gregory
Pears	Cooper	Phillips	Mowbray	Coleman	Proctor	Slaven	Wark	Baird*	Kerr	Hendrie	Ripley

Dugald McCarrison arrives on loan from Celtic, but is held in reserve. Dreadful weather and Town's lack of form means the lowest Boxing Day crowd since 1964. Baird's wind-assisted header clinches the points. The fans continue the call for new faces and Lyall says he is looking.

BARCLAYS DIVISION 2

Manager: John Lyall

SEASON 1990-91

No	Date	Att	Pos	Pt	F-A	H-T	Scorers, Times, and Referees	1	2	3	4	5	6	7	8	9	10	11	subs used
24	H CHARLTON 29/2	11,719	13 17	D 29	4-4	2-1	Stock'll 6, Thomps 20, Dozz 65, Milton 68 / *Peake 44, Mort 62, Dyer 76, Caton 87p* / Ref: J Martin	Forrest *Bolder*	Yallop *Pitcher*	Thompson *Reid*	Stockwell* *Peake*	Palmer *Webster*	Linighan *Caton*	Dozzell *Lee*	Lowe *Curtishley**	Redford *Dyer*	Humes *Minto*	Milton *Mortimer*	Gregory *Leaburn*
25	A OXFORD 1/1	5,103	14 17	L 29	1-2	0-1	Thompson 82 / *Magilton 30p, Durnin 52* / Ref: R Lewis	Forrest *Veysey*	Yallop *Robinson*	Thompson *Smart*	Stockwell *McLaren*	Palmer *Foster*	Linighan^ *Melville*	Dozzell *Magilton*	Lowe *Phillips*	Redford *Durnin*	Humes *Nogan*	Milton* *Simpson*	Gregory/Hill
26	H WEST BROM 12/1	11,036	13 18	W 32	1-0	0-0	Whitton 56 / Ref: R Bigger	Forrest *Rees*	Yallop *Shakespeare*	Thompson *Anderson*	Stockwell *Robson*	Palmer *Raven*	Linighan *Strodder*	Dozzell *Ford*	Lowe* *West*	Whitton *Bannister*	Zondervan^ *McInally*	Kiwomya *Palmer**	Redford/Hill *West*
27	A BLACKBURN 19/1	8,256	11 21	W 35	1-0	0-0	Whitton 81 / Ref: J Brandwood	Forrest *Mimms*	Yallop *Atkins*	Thompson *Sulley**	Stockwell *Reid*	Palmer *May*	Johnson *Dobson*	Dozzell *Gayle*	Lowe* *Richardson*	Whitton *Livingstone*	Zondervan *Garner*	Milton *Sellars*	Hill *Skinner*
28	H MILLWALL 2/2	13,338	14 7	L 35	0-3	0-2	*Sheringham 34, Goodman 37, Rae 72* / Ref: A Seville	Forrest *Horne*	Yallop *Cunningham*	Thompson *Dawes*	Stockwell *Waddock*	Palmer* *Thompson*	Linighan *McLeary*	Dozzell *Stephenson*	Lowe* *Goodman*	Whitton *Sheringham*	Zondervan *Rae*	Milton *McGlashan*	Goddard/Kiwomya
29	H HULL 23/2	9,900	12 24	W 38	2-0	1-0	Goddard 26, 76 / Ref: D Phillips	Forrest *Wright*	Yallop *Norton*	Thompson *Jacobs*	Stockwell* *Wilcox*	Humes *Shotton*	Linighan *Buckley*	Dozzell *Smith**	Goddard *Payton*	Whitton *Swan*	Zondervan *Warren*	Milton* *Atkinson^*	Palmer *De Mange/Hunter*
30	H WOLVERHAMPTON 2/3	13,350	13 8	D 39	0-0	0-0	Ref: L Shapter	Forrest *Stowell*	Yallop *Bennett*	Thompson *Thompson*	Stockwell *Hindmarch*	Palmer *Stancliffe*	Linighan *Birch*	Dozzell *Steele*	Goddard *Cook**	Whitton *Bull*	Zondervan *Mutch*	Milton* *Dennison*	Kiwomya *Taylor*
31	A BRISTOL CITY 9/3	11,474	15 5	L 39	2-4	1-2	Dozzell 18, Goddard 75 / *Taylor 26, 40, Shelton 49, Morgan 70* / Ref: H King	Forrest *Sinclair*	Yallop* *Llewellyn*	Thompson *Aizlewood*	Stockwell *May**	Palmer *Shelton*	Linighan *Scott*	Dozzell *Bryant*	Goddard *Newman*	Whitton *Taylor*	Zondervan *Morgan*	Milton *Donowa*	Hill *Smith*
32	A WATFORD 16/3	7,732	17 24	D 40	1-1	1-0	Linighan 23 / *Palmer 60 (og)* / Ref: R Groves	Forrest *James*	Yallop *Gibbs*	Thompson *Drysdale*	Stockwell *Falconer*	Gayle *Roeder*	Linighan *Dublin*	Dozzell *Byrne*	Goddard *Wilkinson*	Whitton *Callaghan*	Kiwomya *Nicholas*	Palmer *Porter*	
33	A PORT VALE 18/3	5,820	16 16	W 43	2-1	1-0	Glover 30 (og), Thompson 77 / *Van der Laan 79* / Ref: T Fitzharris	Forrest *Grew*	Yallop *Mills*	Thompson *Agboola*	Stockwell *Walker*	Gayle *Aspin*	Linighan *Glover*	Dozzell *Earle*	Goddard *Porter*	Whitton *Millar*	Kiwomya* *Parkin*	Palmer* *Ford**	Redford *Van der Laan*
34	H PLYMOUTH 22/3	9,842	15 18	W 46	3-1	1-0	Morgan 19 (og), Goddard 69, 87 / *Fiore 70* / Ref: J Carter	Forrest *Wilmot*	Yallop *Brown*	Thompson *Morgan*	Stockwell *Marker*	Gayle *Burrows*	Linighan *Salman*	Dozzell *Barlow**	Goddard *Fiore*	Whitton *Turner*	Kiwomya *Morrison*	Palmer *Hodges^*	Hill *Damerel/Clement*

A feast of goals for the fans, but a nightmare for the managers. Lennie Lawrence describes some of Ipswich's play as the best he's seen all season. However, John Lyall is upset how all the good work is cancelled out when a 4-2 lead disappears and how by the end it was a lottery.

It's an awful long time since Town have won, but Lyall says there's no need to panic. Linighan pulls down Durnin for Magilton to score from the spot. Durnin volleys a second to give Town a mountain to climb. Thompson's late cross swerves straight into the net for a consolation.

A new signing at last as Steve Whitton arrives for £150k from Sheffield Wed. He has a magnificent all-action debut and could have had a hat-trick. His shoot-on-sight policy pays off when he controls Dozzell's pull-back and fires home. Reports suggest Paul Goddard will also sign.

Whitton does it again, but leaves it late. He cracks home a fine shot after Lowe pulls the ball back to him from the left flank. Don Mackay's struggling outfit tumble to their fourth successive home defeat. Goddard – like Whitton, another ex-Hammer – arrives on a free from Millwall.

A poor display and the worst home loss in five years. Inevitably debutant Goddard is jeered by the visiting fans as Bruce Rioch's men cruise it. Lions sub O'Callaghan wants to stay over to socialise with ex-teammates afterwards, but Rioch says no, so the player storms off the team bus.

Town start in determined mood after last week's flop and Goddard both hit the post in the first 15 minutes. Goddard makes the breakthrough with a crisp drive after Linighan's knock-down. Victory is assured over lowly Hull as Goddard heads in Thompson's corner.

A fourth clean sheet in five games, with Yallop and Linighan both giving outstanding performances in defence. At the other end, late pressure nearly yields points as Whitton twice hits a post in the dying minutes. Mark Burke has joined on loan from Middlesbrough but is yet to feature.

City boss Jimmy Lumsden praises Town's open attacking play. His side comes back well after Dozzell's opening goal – an absolute cracker on the volley from 25 yards. Taylor's overhead kick levels matters and then the in-from Morgan plays a crucial role as City cruise into a 4-1 lead.

David James pushes Whitton's cross for a corner. He charges off his line for the flag-kick but Linighan gets there first and heads in. Under pressure from Falconer, Palmer misdirects a header into his own net. A draw is a frustrating outcome in the rain against the struggling Hornets.

Palmer chases Glover and the Vale man hooks the ball towards Grew, but can only lob over him from 30 yards. The lead is extended further as Thompson's drive spins under Grew in the wet. Town hang on to the points despite Linighan deflecting Van der Laan's cross past Forrest.

Friday night action at Portman Road sees Morgan deflect the ball past Wilmot after a scramble from a corner. Goddard drills home Stockwell's cross, but Fiore cuts in and scores a fine goal a minute later. A late goal removes any doubts when Dozzell sends Goddard through to convert.

Season match-by-match record (matches 35–46)

---

35. | A | 30/3 | MIDDLESBROUGH — D, HT 1-0, FT 1-1 | Att 15,140 | figures: 15 / 6 / 47
Scorers: Linighan 14; Mowbray 60 — Ref: P Harrison
Town: Forrest, Yallop, Thompson, Stockwell, Gayle, Linighan, Dozzell, Goddard, Whitton*, Kiwomya, Palmer, Redford
Boro: Dibble, Cooper, Phillips, Mowbray, Coleman, Putney^, Slaven, Walsh*, Baird, Mustoe, Ripley, Hendrie/Proctor

Skipper Linighan has an excellent game, and he opens the scoring with a superb left-foot volley. Forrest charges off his line after a Phillips free-kick and is left stranded as Mowbray loops a header into the net. With 12 minutes left Town go close to a winner as Linighan hits the post.

---

36. | H | 2/4 | PORTSMOUTH — D, HT 1-1, FT 2-2 | Att 11,314 | figures: 15 / 20 / 48
Scorers: Dozzell 44, Thompson 64p; Kuhl 24, 81p — Ref: J Ashworth
Town: Forrest, Yallop, Thompson, Stockwell, Gayle, Linighan, Dozzell, Goddard, Zondervan*, Kiwomya, Palmer, Houghton
Pompey: Knight, Russell, Daniel, Murray^, Butters, Maguire, Wigley, Kuhl, Whittingham, Clarke, Anderton*, Beresford/Black

Rugged Pompey look set for a fourth successive win at Portman Road when Kuhl thumps in a curling free-kick. Dozzell slides in the equaliser after a Kiwomya effort is charged down. Both sides convert a penalty in the second half, Town's coming when the lively Kiwomya is fouled.

---

37. | A | 6/4 | CHARLTON — D, HT 0-0, FT 1-1 | Att 6,443 | figures: 14 / 13 / 49
Scorers: Linighan 56; Lee 49 — Ref: K Cooper
Town: Forrest, Yallop, Thompson, Stockwell, Gayle, Linighan, Dozzell, Goddard, Houghton, Kiwomya*, Palmer, Zondervan
Charlton: Bolder, Pitcher, Minto, Curbishley, Webster, Balmer, Lee, Gorman, Wilson*, Bacon^, Mortimer, Leaburn/Salako

Town are outplayed early on and Gorman goes closest, hitting the bar. An error by Palmer lets in Lee for the opener. Minto heads Thompson's free-kick straight to Linighan and he makes no mistake. Houghton, loaned from Spurs, gets a full debut. Chris Swailes is sold to Peterborough.

---

38. | A | 10/4 | BRISTOL ROV — L, HT 0-1, FT 0-1 | Att 4,983 | figures: 16 / 12 / 49
Scorers: Sealy 42 — Ref: D Frampton
Town: Forrest, Yallop, Thompson, Stockwell, Gayle, Linighan, Dozzell, Goddard, Houghton, Zondervan, Humes^, Kiwomya
Rovers: Parkin, Alexander, Twentyman, Clark, Sealy*, Jones, Holloway, Reece, White, Saunders, Baily^, Jones/Pounder

Any lingering hopes of a late sprint towards the play-offs are finally wiped out in front of a tiny crowd. New winger Houghton proves a real handful for Rovers, however, and Town have the better of the second half. Sealy's first-half volley remains the difference between the sides.

---

39. | H | 13/4 | OXFORD — D, HT 1-1, FT 1-1 | Att 9,135 | figures: 16 / 10 / 50
Scorers: Kiwomya 26; Simpson 16 — Ref: B Hill
Town: Forrest, Yallop, Thompson, Stockwell, Gayle, Linighan, Dozzell, Goddard, Houghton, Zondervan, Kiwomya
Oxford: Veysey, Ford, Smart, Lewis, Foster^, Melville, Magilton*, Stein, Durnin, Nogan, Simpson, Gardner

Brian Horton's men go ahead when Simpson's free-kick bounces wickedly in front of Forrest and ends in the net. Kiwomya levels ten minutes later as he nods in Goddard's cross. Oxford battle gamely to stay level and skipper Foster is inspirational. Town loan David Hill to Scunthorpe.

---

40. | H | 17/4 | WEST HAM — L, HT 0-1, FT 0-1 | Att 20,290 | figures: 16 / 1 / 50
Scorers: Morley 29 — Ref: P Foakes
Town: Forrest, Humes^, Thompson, Stockwell, Gayle, Linighan, Dozzell, Goddard, Houghton, Zondervan, Kiwomya*, Milton/Yallop
West Ham: Miklosko, Potts, Parris, Foster^, Gale, Hughton, Dowie*, Bishop, Slater, Morley, Keen, McAvennie/Allen

Morley intercepts Humes' poor back pass and goes round Forrest for the winner. Billy Bonds' side outplays Town for much of the 90 minutes. Three days after an FA Cup semi-final hammering by Forest, the Hammers bounce back to win three points and go back to the top of the table.

---

41. | A | 20/4 | NEWCASTLE — D, HT 2-1, FT 2-2 | Att 17,638 | figures: 15 / 12 / 51
Scorers: Kiwomya 34, 44; Stimson 24, Quinn 73 — Ref: C Trussell
Town: Forrest, Humes^, Thompson, Stockwell, Gayle, Linighan, Dozzell, Goddard, Milton, Zondervan, Kiwomya
Newcastle: Srnicek, Watson S, Stimson, Roche^, Scott, Kristensen, Clark, Peacock, Quinn, Hunt*, Brock, Howey/O'Brien

Stimson opens the scoring for Ossie Ardiles' unpredictable side, but smart finishing by Kiwomya sees Town roar into a half-time lead. The Geordies snatch a point when Clark's effort is helped into the net by Quinn. Overall Town can be pleased with a much-improved display.

---

42. | H | 25/4 | BARNSLEY — W, HT 1-0, FT 2-0 | Att 7,379 | figures: 15 / 9 / 54
Scorers: Kiwomya 10, Goddard 80 — Ref: T Ward
Town: Forrest, Yallop, Thompson, Palmer, Gayle, Linighan, Dozzell, Milton, Zondervan, Kiwomya, Goddard
Barnsley: Baker, Fleming, Rimmer, Smith, Banks*, Tiler, O'Connell, Rammel^, Saville, Agnew, Archdeacon, Taggart/Dobbin

A Thursday evening game is a real rarity, and this re-arranged match attracts the lowest Portman Road crowd for 36 years. Fortunately the subdued atmosphere is enlivened early on when Kiwomya runs in a superb solo effort. Mel Machin's men are finally finished off near the end.

---

43. | H | 27/4 | OLDHAM — L, HT 0-1, FT 1-2 | Att 12,332 | figures: 15 / 2 / 54
Scorers: Kiwomya 80; Marshall 39, 67 — Ref: G Willard
Town: Forrest, Yallop, Thompson, Palmer^, Gayle, Linighan, Dozzell, Houghton, Milton, Zondervan*, Kiwomya, Gregory/Humes
Oldham: Hallworth, Halle, Barlow, Henry, Barrett, Jobson, Adams*, Warhurst, Marshall, Currie, Holden R, Redfearn

Joe Royle's outfit pick up the points that enable them to celebrate a return to the top flight for the first time in 68 years. Ian Marshall heads in Barlow's cross and then fastens on to Henry's through pass to beat Forrest. Goddard supplies the pass for Kiwomya to net a consolation goal.

---

44. | H | 4/5 | LEICESTER — W, HT 0-1, FT 3-2 | Att 11,347 | figures: 13 / 23 / 57
Scorers: Houghton 49, Gayle 60, Kiwomya 69; Reid 26, Mills 84p — Ref: A Buksh
Town: Parkes, Yallop, Thompson, Stockwell, Gayle, Linighan, Houghton, Goddard, Milton, Zondervan, Kiwomya, Humes
Leicester: Hodge, Spearing, North, Reid, Walsh, James, Wright, Kelly, Oldfield^, Mills, Russell, Gibson

Forrest has a hamstring injury so Phil Parkes, at 40, becomes Town's oldest debutant. Relegation-threatened City take the lead, but Town hit back and Gayle's diving header from Thompson's free-kick puts them ahead. Kiwomya heads in a Goddard cross to seal an entertaining win.

---

45. | A | 7/5 | NOTTS CO — L, HT 0-2, FT 1-3 | Att 6,902 | figures: 13 / 4 / 57
Scorers: Humes 80; Johnson 27, 62p, Regis 44 — Ref: M Bodenham
Town: Parkes, Yallop, Thompson, Stockwell, Gayle, Linighan, Houghton, Goddard, Humes, Johnson, Milton, Zondervan
Notts Co: Cherry, Palmer, Paris, Short Cr, Short Ch, O'Riordan, Turner, Thomas*, Johnson, Regis, Draper, Harding

In-form County chalk up a sixth successive win and Town look poor. Parkes saves them from a heavier loss. Linighan trips Harding for the clinching penalty kick. Town get a late consolation goal when Yallop's cross is headed out to Humes and he fires home an excellent volley.

---

46. | A | 11/5 | BRIGHTON — L, HT 0-1, FT 1-2 | Att 12,281 | figures: 14 / 6 / 57
Scorers: Kiwomya 83; Small 35p, Wilkins 90 — Ref: D Axcell
Town: Parkes, Humes, Johnson, Stockwell, Gayle, Linighan, Houghton, Goddard, Milton, Zondervan, Kiwomya
Brighton: Digweed, Crumplin, Gatting, Wilkins, Pates, Bissett^, Barham, Byrne*, Small, Codner, Walker, Wade/Chapman

Gayle's foul allows Small to convert a penalty. Barry Lloyd's side must win to make the play-offs. Houghton hits a post, then Crumplin trips Kiwomya, whose penalty is saved. He makes amends by jinking through to level. Then high drama as Albion win with a last-kick curling shot.

Average — Home 11,772 | Away 10,383

BARCLAYS DIVISION 2 (CUP-TIES)   Manager: John Lyall   SEASON 1990-91

Rumbelows Cup

			Att	F-A	H-T	Scorers, Times, and Referees
2:1	A	SHREWSBURY	12 3:22 2,764	D 1-1	1-1	Redford 8, Griffiths 21, Ref: J Worrall
2:2	H	SHREWSBURY	13 3:21 7,306	W 3-0	2-0	Redford 5, Kiwomya 18, Milton 82, Ref: R Pawley (Town win 4-1 on aggregate)
3	H	SOUTHAMPTON	8 1:14 15,573	L 0-2	0-1	Le Tissier 20, Wallace Ro 77, Ref: K Barrett

2:1 A SHREWSBURY — teams

1	2	3	4	5	6	7	8	9	10	11	subs used
Forrest	Yallop	Hill	Stockwell	Gayle	Linighan	Gregory	Redford	Zondervan*	Kiwomya*	Milton	Thompson
Perks	*Worsley*	*Gorman*	*Kelly*	*Heathcote*	*Blake*	*Moore*	*Coughlin*	*Spink*	*Brown*	*Griffiths*	

After an early corner-kick, Redford sends in a swerving drive shot from 20 yards to beat Perks. Asa Hartford's side level when Brown crosses for Griffiths to hook home. The tiny crowd gets some late excitement when Kelly's last-minute shot produces a stunning save from Forrest.

2:2 H SHREWSBURY — teams

1	2	3	4	5	6	7	8	9	10	11	subs used
Forrest	Yallop	Hill	Stockwell	Gayle	Linighan	Gregory	Redford	Zondervan	Kiwomya	Milton	Spink
Perks	*Worsley*	*Gorman*	*Kelly*	*Heathcote*	*Lynch*	*Moore*	*Summerfield*	*Shaw**	*Brown*	*Parrish*	

An inswinging corner by Hill is forced home by Redford. Town are really in the driving seat as Kiwomya nets a diving header from Hill's cross. A lengthy spell without a goal has the crowd dozing, but this ends with a bang with Milton's sizzling drive following a Yallop free-kick.

3 H SOUTHAMPTON — teams

1	2	3	4	5	6	7	8	9	10	11	subs used
Forrest	Yallop	Hill	Stockwell	Gayle	Linighan	Gregory*	Redford	Zondervan	Kiwomya	Milton	Dozzell
Flowers	*Dodd*	*Adams*	*Case*	*Ruddock*	*Moore*	*Le Tissier**	*Horne*	*Shearer*	*Rideout^*	*Wallace Ro*	*Cockerill/Benali*

Gayle loses possession and Le Tissier swoops to hammer in the vital first goal. After the interval Town look far more purposeful, but fail to beat Flowers. The tie is decided in the final stages when Rod Wallace links up with Cockerill and produces a clinical finish to beat Forrest.

FA Cup

			Att	F-A	H-T	Scorers, Times, and Referees
3	A	SOUTHAMPTON	14 1:15 15,101	L 2-3	1-2	Dozzell 11, 80, Shearer 35, Le Tissier 43, 59, Ref: T Ward

3 A SOUTHAMPTON — teams

1	2	3	4	5	6	7	8	9	10	11	subs used
Forrest	Yallop	Thompson	Stockwell	Palmer*	Linighan	Lowe	Redford	Dozzell	Kiwomya	Milton	Pennyfather
Flowers	*Cherednik*	*Adams*	*Cockerill*	*Ruddock*	*Moore*	*Le Tissier*	*Horne*	*Shearer*	*McLoughlin*	*Wallace Ro*	

Town pose the Saints problems early on and Dozzell looks very much at home alongside top-flight players, cracking home a fine opening goal. The home side slowly warm up and Alan Shearer's header levels it. Lethal Le Tissier chips in with two, but brave Town end the match on top.

League Table

		P	Home					Away					Pts
			W	D	L	F	A	W	D	L	F	A	
1	Oldham	46	17	5	1	55	21	8	8	7	28	32	88
2	West Ham	46	15	6	2	41	18	9	9	5	19	16	87
3	Sheffield Wed	46	12	10	1	43	23	10	6	7	37	28	82
4	Notts Co *	46	14	4	5	45	28	9	7	7	31	27	80
5	Millwall	46	11	6	6	43	28	9	6	8	27	23	73
6	Brighton	46	12	4	7	37	31	9	3	11	26	38	70
7	Middlesbro	46	12	4	7	36	17	8	5	10	30	30	69
8	Barnsley	46	13	7	3	39	16	6	5	12	24	32	69
9	Bristol City	46	14	5	4	44	28	6	2	15	24	43	67
10	Oxford	46	10	9	4	41	29	4	10	9	28	37	61
11	Newcastle	46	8	10	5	24	22	6	7	10	25	34	59
12	Wolves	46	11	6	6	45	35	2	13	8	18	28	58
13	Bristol Rov	46	11	7	5	29	20	4	6	13	27	39	58
14	IPSWICH	46	10	8	6	32	28	4	10	9	24	40	57
15	Port Vale	46	10	6	7	32	24	5	8	10	24	40	57
16	Charlton	46	8	7	8	27	25	5	10	8	30	36	56
17	Portsmouth	46	10	6	7	34	27	4	5	14	24	43	53
18	Plymouth	46	10	10	3	36	20	2	7	14	18	48	53
19	Blackburn	46	8	6	9	26	27	6	4	13	25	39	52
20	Watford	46	5	8	10	24	32	7	7	9	21	27	51
21	Swindon	46	8	6	9	31	30	4	8	11	34	43	50
22	Leicester	46	12	4	7	41	33	2	4	17	19	50	50
23	West Brom	46	7	11	5	26	21	3	7	13	26	40	48
24	Hull	46	6	10	7	35	32	4	5	14	22	53	45
		1104	253	163	136	866	615	136	163	253	615	866	1493

* promoted
after play-offs

Appearances and Goals

	Appearances						Goals			
	Lge	Sub	LC	Sub	FAC	Sub	Lge	LC	FAC	Tot
Dozzell, Jason	27	3		1		1	6	1	1	8
Forrest, Craig	43		3		1					
Gayle, Brian	33		3		1		4			4
Gregory, David	14	7		1			1			1
Goddard, Paul	18	1	3				6			6
Hill, David	18	5	3				1			1
Houghton, Scott	7	1								
Humes, Tony	15	1	1		1		2			2
Johnson, Gavin	5	2								
Kiwomya, Chris	34	3	3		1		10	1		11
Linighan, David	45		3		1		3			3
Lowe, David	12	1	1		1					
Milton, Simon	27	4	3		1		6	1		7
Palmer, Steve	18	5	3		1		1			1
Parkes, Phil	3									
Pennyfather, Glenn						1				
Redford, Ian	23	3	3		1		4	1	1	6
Stockwell, Mick	44		3		1		6			6
Thompson, Neil	33	5		1	1		6			6
Whitton, Steve	10				1		2			2
Yallop, Frank	44	1	3		1					
Zondervan, Romeo	33	1	3		1		2			2
(own-goals)										
22 players used	506	43	33	2	11	1	60	4	2	66

Odds & ends

Double wins: (4) Blackburn, Port Vale, Leicester, West Brom.
Double losses: (3) Brighton, Oldham, West Ham.

Won from behind: (3) Blackburn (H), West Brom (A), Leicester (H).
Lost from in front: (3) Southampton (FAC) (A), West Ham (A), Bristol City (A).

High spots: An eight-goal thriller at home to Charlton.
Excellent home debuts by Whitton and Goddard.
Dozzell's magnificent goal at Bristol City.

Low spots: Lowest finishing position since 1966.
Conceding four in the first-half at Barnsley.
A miserable home display against Millwall.
Portman Road's lowest league gate for 36 years – 7,379 v Barnsley.

Player of the Year: David Linighan.
Ever-presents: (0).
Hat-tricks: (0).
Opposing hat-tricks: (0).
Leading scorer: (11) Chris Kiwomya.

BARCLAYS DIVISION 2

Manager: John Lyall — SEASON 1991-92

No	Date	Att	Pos	Pt	F-A	H-T	Scorers, Times, and Referees	1	2	3	4	5	6	7	8	9	10	11	subs used
1	A BRISTOL ROV 17/8	6,444		D / 1	3-3	1-0	Dozzell 12, Goddard 55, Stockwell 65 / Stewart 66, White 73, 84. Ref: L. Shapter	Forrest	Yallop	Thompson	Zondervan	Gayle	Humes	Stockwell*	Goddard*	Johnson	Dozzell	Kiwomya	Lowe
								Parkin	*Alexander*	*Twentyman*	*Yates*	*Mehew*	*Boothroyd*	*Evans**	*Reece*	*White*	*Stewart*	*Pounder*	*Purnell*
2	H PORT VALE 20/8	8,937		W / 4	2-1	1-1	Walker 22, Thompson 50p / Walker 35p. Ref: G Willard	Forrest	Johnson	Thompson	Stockwell	Gayle	Humes	Zondervan	Goddard	Whitton	Dozzell	Kiwomya	Dozzell
								Grew	*Mills S*	*Hughes*	*Walker*	*Aspen*	*Glover*	*Jalink*	*Van der Laan*	*Houchen*	*Foyle*	*Kent**	*Swan*
3	H MIDDLESBROUGH [1] 24/8	9,822	17	W / 7	2-1	0-0	Dozzell 48, Goddard 66 / Wilkinson 81. Ref: M Brandwood	Forrest	Johnson	Thompson	Stockwell*	Gayle	Linighan	Zondervan	Goddard	Whitton	Dozzell	Kiwomya	Yallop/Lowe
								Pears	*Parkinson^*	*Phillips*	*Mowbray*	*Kernaghan*	*Falconer*	*Mustoe*	*Proctor**	*Wilkinson*	*Ripley*	*Hendrie*	*Slaven/Fleming*
4	A BLACKBURN [1] 31/8	8,898	21	W / 10	2-1	1-0	Kiwomya 30, Goddard 46 / Speedie 89. Ref: M Raymond	Forrest	Johnson	Thompson	Stockwell	Gayle	Linighan	Zondervan	Goddard	Whitton	Dozzell	Kiwomya	Kiwomya
								Mimms	*Atkins*	*Munro*	*Reid*	*May*	*Moran*	*Gayle*	*Richardson*	*Speedie*	*Sheepstone* Wilcox*	*Skinner*	*Skinner*
5	H SWINDON [3] 3/9	11,002	8	L / 10	1-4	1-2	Kiwomya 12 / White 2, Calderwood 43, Taylor 80 [Hazard 88]. Ref: P Danson	Forrest	Johnson	Thompson	Stockwell	Gayle	Linighan	Zondervan*	Goddard*	Whitton*	Dozzell	Kiwomya	Lowe/Yallop
								Digby	*Jones*	*Viveash*	*Hoddle*	*Calderwood*	*Taylor*	*Hazard*	*Shearer*	*Simpson*	*MacLaren*	*White**	*Ling*
6	H SOUTHEND [3] 7/9	12,732	15	W / 13	1-0	0-0	Thompson 48p. Ref: A Gunn	Forrest	Johnson	Thompson	Stockwell	Humes	Linighan	Zondervan	Goddard*	Whitton	Dozzell	Kiwomya	Kiwomya
								Sansome	*Austin*	*Powell*	*Martin**	*Scully*	*Prior*	*Ansah*	*Cornwall*	*Tilson**	*Benjamin*	*Angell*	*Sussex/O'Callaghan*
7	A BARNSLEY [4] 14/9	6,786	23	L / 13	0-1	0-0	Currie 81. Ref: P Wright	Forrest	Johnson*	Thompson	Stockwell	Humes	Linighan	Zondervan	Goddard	Whitton	Dozzell	Kiwomya	Lowe
								Butler	*Robinson*	*Fleming*	*Banks*	*Smith*	*Taggart*	*O'Connell*	*Redfearn*	*Saville**	*Currie*	*Archdeacon* Rammell*	
8	A NEWCASTLE [4] 17/9	16,336	20	D / 14	1-1	1-0	Kiwomya 36 / Quinn 68p. Ref: E Parker	Forrest	Johnson	Thompson	Stockwell	Humes*	Linighan	Zondervan	Goddard	Whitton	Dozzell	Kiwomya	Yallop
								Stnicek	*Peacock*	*Stimson*	*O'Brien*	*Scott*	*Bradshaw*	*Clark*	*Brock*	*Quinn*	*Carr**	*Hunt^*	*Roche/Howey*
9	H BRISTOL CITY [2] 21/9	9,692	10	W / 17	4-2	1-1	Thompson 37, Linighan 64, Kiwomya 86 [Goddard 88] / Allison 4, Smith 46. Ref: A Buskh	Forrest	Johnson^	Thompson	Stockwell*	Yallop	Linighan	Zondervan	Goddard	Whitton	Dozzell	Kiwomya	Lowe/Milton
								Welch	*Llewellyn*	*Scott*	*May*	*Bryant*	*Caesar*	*Shelton*	*Rennie*	*Allison*	*Connor*	*Smith*	
10	A GRIMSBY [2] 28/9	6,621	11	W / 20	2-1	1-1	Lowe 28, Johnson 55 / Gilbert 40. Ref: D Allison	Forrest	Johnson	Thompson	Stockwell*	Yallop	Linighan	Lowe	Zondervan	Whitton	Dozzell	Kiwomya	Wark
								Sherwood	*McDermott*	*Smith*	*Futcher*^*	*Lever*	*Cunnington*	*Childs*	*Gilbert*	*Jones**	*Dobbin*	*Woods*	*Hargreaves/Rees*
11	H OXFORD [2] 5/10	9,932	23	W / 23	2-1	2-0	Milton 28, Whitton 32 / Magilton 80. Ref: R Bigger	Forrest	Wark	Thompson	Stockwell	Yallop	Linighan	Lowe	Zondervan	Whitton	Milton	Kiwomya	Kiwomya
								Veysey	*Robinson*	*Smart*	*Lewis*	*Foster*	*Melville*	*Magilton*	*Penney**	*Aylott*	*Nogan*	*Simpson*	*Beauchamp*

Match reports

1. Town steam into a 3-0 lead as Dozzell's shot is deflected in; Goddard sweeps in Kiwomya's cross; then Stockwell blasts home. Alexander's spot-kick is saved but Rovers storm back. Marcus Stewart nets, then White heads in as Town crumble. White's superb curling volley equalises.

2. The lively Whitton supplies Kiwomya who beats ex-Town man Grew with a neat finish. Humes' challenge on Van der Laan gives Walker his penalty chance. Jalink brings Goddard crashing down and Thompson fires in the spot-kick winner. The crowd is well below recent averages.

3. Johnson hits a post and Dozzell grazes the bar as Town apply first-half pressure. After the break Dozzell nods in Thompson's corner. Goddard chases a through ball and slides it past Pears. An error by Yallop allows new signing Wilkinson to pull one back for Lennie Lawrence's side.

4. Kiwomya shakes off the physical attentions of Moran and toe-pokes the ball past Mimms. Goddard extends the lead, rattling the ball home after a slick move seconds after the restart. Struggling Rovers pull one back as Gayle hits the bar and Speedie nets the rebound from close in.

5. Steve White is back to torment Town, netting early after Hoddle's fine pass. Kiwomya levels after Digby's poor clearance. Shearer hits a post and Hoddle back-heads the ball for Calderwood to score. Swindon are flattered by Taylor's late header and Hazard nipping in to get a fourth.

6. A rare confrontation between these two sides turns into a grim battle. On his 100th League appearance for Town, Thompson nets the winner from the spot after Sansome pulls down Johnson when clear on goal. The ref's chosen card is yellow. Kiwomya is called up by England U-21s.

7. Stalemate until the final ten minutes when Linighan's weak back-pass allows Currie in to score in his first home match since returning to Oakwell. Town sell Brian Gayle to Sheffield U for £700k and David Hill to Scunthorpe for £30k. Darren Edmonds signs from Leeds on a free.

8. Injury-prone Humes breaks his arm in a 7th-minute collision. Dozzell feeds Kiwomya who fires home an angled shot. Zondervan tangles with Brock and a penalty is given. The Town man is booked for protesting on this 300th appearance for the club. Quinn shoots the spot-kick home.

9. Allison cracks home an early shock. Thompson levels after Whitton taps a free-kick to him. Town slip behind again, and Thompson has a spot-kick saved. Linighan's disputed header levels things. In the dying minutes Kiwomya coolly rounds Welch to net and Goddard fires a clincher.

10. Stockwell's cross is glanced home by the head of Lowe. Ex-Town forward Woods slips a pass to Gilbert and he shoots home under Forrest's body. After the interval Johnson sends in a driven cross which hits the post, rebounds directly to him and he finishes coolly to win the points.

11. Lowe crosses for Milton to blast the ball powerfully high into the net. Town's tails are up and Kiwomya robs Nogan, races down the left and crosses to Lowe. He slips it to Whitton who fires neatly in. Linighan lunges at Nogan's header and the ball falls nicely for Jim Magilton to net.

Match Results

#	H/A	Opponent	Date	Att	Pos	Opp Pos	Res	Pts	Score	HT
12	A	BRIGHTON	12/10	9,010	2	15	D	24	2-2	1-0
13	H	MILLWALL	19/10	11,175	3	15	D	25	0-0	0-0
14	A	PORTSMOUTH	26/10	8,007	5	12	D	26	1-1	1-1
15	A	CHARLTON	30/10	6,939	5	3	D	27	1-1	1-1
16	A	LEICESTER	2/11	11,331	5	6	D	28	2-2	0-0
17	H	SUNDERLAND	5/11	9,768	5	14	L	28	0-1	0-1
18	H	CAMBRIDGE	9/11	20,586	7	1	L	28	1-2	0-1
19	A	DERBY	16/11	12,493	9	3	L	28	0-1	0-0
20	A	WOLVERHAMPTON	23/11	11,915	6	21	W	31	2-1	0-1
21	H	TRANMERE	30/11	11,072	5	14	W	34	4-0	2-0
22	A	PLYMOUTH	7/12	4,986	6	23	L	34	0-1	0-1
23	A	SWINDON	20/12	7,404	6	8	D	35	0-0	0-0

Scorers / Referees

12 BRIGHTON — Milton 15, Dozzell 64 / Byrne 53, Chivers 69 — Ref: R Wiseman
13 MILLWALL — Ref: J Key
14 PORTSMOUTH — Milton 17 / Burns 44 — Ref: P Durkin
15 CHARLTON — Whitton 36 / Gatting 35 — Ref: P Jones
16 LEICESTER — Wark 47, Johnson 75 / Kitson 54, Oldfield 59 — Ref: P Vanes
17 SUNDERLAND — Armstrong 38 — Ref: M Bailey
18 CAMBRIDGE — Stockwell 79 / Rowett 36, Claridge 82 — Ref: G Pooley
19 DERBY — Davison 56 — Ref: R Milford
20 WOLVERHAMPTON — Linighan 54, Dozzell 61 / Birch 7 — Ref: R Groves
21 TRANMERE — Milton 4, Thompson 29, Linighan 70, [Wark 90p] — Ref: I Hemley
22 PLYMOUTH — Fiore 26 — Ref: D Frampton
23 SWINDON — Ref: M James

Line-ups

12 BRIGHTON
Town: Forrest, Wark, Thompson, Stockwell, Zondervan, Linighan, Lowe, Milton, Whitton, Dozzell, Kiwomya*; Gregory
Opp: Beeney, Crumplin, Chapman, Wilkins, Chivers, O'Reilly, Barham, Byrne, Meade, Codner, Robinson

13 MILLWALL
Town: Forrest, Yallop, Thompson, Stockwell, Zondervan, Linighan, Lowe, Milton*, Whitton, Dozzell, Kiwomya*; Edmonds
Opp: Davison, Stevens, Cooper, Bagie, Thompson, McLeary, Kerr, Colquhoun, Falco*, Rae, Stephenson^; Barber/Armstrong

14 PORTSMOUTH
Town: Forrest, Yallop, Thompson*, Stockwell, Wark, Linighan, Lowe^, Milton, Whitton, Dozzell, Kiwomya*; Johnson/Moncur
Opp: Knight, Awford, Beresford, Burns, Symons, Butters, Neill, Clarke*, Whittingham, Chamberlain^, Anderton; Aspinall/Hebberd

15 CHARLTON
Town: Forrest, Yallop, Thompson, Stockwell, Wark, Linighan, Johnson, Moncur, Whitton, Dozzell, Kiwomya*
Opp: Bolder, Pitcher, Minto, Peake, Webster, Gatting, Lee, Bumstead, Leaburn, Nelson, Walsh

16 LEICESTER
Town: Forrest, Yallop, Thompson, Stockwell, Wark, Linighan, Lowe*, Milton, Whitton, Dozzell, Kiwomya*; Johnson
Opp: Poole, Mills, Gibson, Smith, Walsh, Fitzpatrick, Oldfield, Thompson, Wright, Kitson, Gordon

17 SUNDERLAND
Town: Forrest, Yallop*, Thompson, Stockwell, Wark, Linighan, Milton^, Moncur, Whitton, Dozzell, Kiwomya*; Johnson/Edmonds
Opp: Norman, Kay, Rogan, Bennett, Ball, Davenport, Bracewell, Rush, Armstrong, Byrne, Pascoe

18 CAMBRIDGE
Town: Forrest, Johnson, Thompson, Stockwell, Wark, Linighan, Milton, Moncur, Whitton*, Dozzell, Kiwomya*; Yallop
Opp: Vaughan, Fensome, Kimble, Dennis, O'Shea, Daish, Rowett*, Baillie, Dublin, Claridge^, Philpott; Taylor/Heathcote

19 DERBY
Town: Forrest, Youds*, Thompson, Stockwell, Wark, Linighan, Lowe, Moncur, Johnson, Williams P, Kiwomya*; Yallop
Opp: Shilton, Sage*, Forsyth, Williams G, Coleman, Comyn, Micklewhite, Ormondroyd, Davison, McMinn, Hayward

20 WOLVERHAMPTON
Town: Forrest, Johnson, Thompson, Stockwell, Wark, Linighan, Moncur, Goddard, Whitton, Dozzell, Kiwomya*; Yallop
Opp: Stowell, Ashley, Venus, Bennett*, Clarke N, Downing, Birch, Mountfield, Bull, Mutch, Cook; Dennison

21 TRANMERE
Town: Forrest, Johnson, Thompson, Stockwell, Wark, Linighan, Milton, Palmer*, Whitton*, Dozzell, Kiwomya*; Lowe
Opp: Nixon, Higgins, Brannan, Irons, Hughes*, Vickers, Morrissey, Steel, Aldridge, Martindale^, Nolan; Malkin/Harvey

22 PLYMOUTH
Town: Forrest, Johnson, Thompson, Stockwell, Wark, Linighan, Moncur, Palmer*, Whitton*, Dozzell, Kiwomya*; Yallop
Opp: Wilmot, Spearing, Clement, Marker, Hopkins*, Morgan, Meaker, Marshall, Regis, Fiore, Turner; Morrison

23 SWINDON
Town: Forrest, Johnson, Thompson, Stockwell, Wark, Linighan, Milton, Palmer, Whitton, Dozzell, Kiwomya*; Yallop
Opp: Hammond, Jones, Kerslake, Foley, Calderwood, Taylor, Hazard, Shearer^, Simpson, MacLaren, White; Summerbee/Mitchell

Match Reports

12 BRIGHTON — A corner is half-cleared and Dozzell flicks it to Milton who scores a smart goal. Byrne brings it level when he breaks through and shoots in off the post. Milton's header is blocked, but Dozzell is on hand to convert the rebound. Chivers buries a firm header after a cross by Crumplin.

13 MILLWALL — After a short break on the Isle of Wight, under-strength Town struggle against Bruce Rioch's men. Wark, without a club and training at Town, has signed non-contract forms and now looks set to play a key role in this third spell at the club. John Moncur is recruited on loan from Spurs.

14 PORTSMOUTH — Moncur gets an early debut, coming on when Lowe gashes his head. Stockwell ventures into the Pompey area but is crowded out, the ball falling for Milton to fire past Knight. Shortly before the break Beresford crosses and Butters hits the bar, but Burns is on hand to do the rest.

15 CHARLTON — At Upton Park, Charlton's temporary home, the 'home' side goes ahead when Robert Lee's cross is headed in by Gatting. A minute later Town hit back in emphatic fashion as Whitton plays a sweet one-two and fires in a smart goal. Joint-manager Steve Gritt is full of praises for Town.

16 LEICESTER — On his 500th appearance for the club, Wark heads in an inswinging cross, but Kitson's angled drive brings it level. Brian Little's side take the lead when the reliable Oldfield pounces to head in Wright's cross. Yallop's centre is headed in by sub Johnson for Town's fifth draw in a row.

17 SUNDERLAND — The early-season promise is fading fast as Town sink to a disappointing defeat. They look second best to Denis Smith's side, who till now had the worst defensive away record in the division. Byrne bamboozles Wark out on the flank and crosses for Armstrong to net the winning goal.

18 CAMBRIDGE — The first local derby between these sides in the League draws a huge crowd. John Beck's men get on top after an injury to Whitton. Dublin flicks on for Rowett to score. Stockwell beats the U's offside trap to equalise, but Claridge puts his side top of the table after a late scramble.

19 DERBY — Eddie Youds signs from Everton for £250k but has a nightmare debut, damaging knee ligaments in a tackle with McMinn. While the damage is being assessed, Arthur Cox's newly-relegated side take advantage of the numerical supremacy. Ormondroyd crosses and Davison heads home.

20 WOLVERHAMPTON — Graham Turner's side take an early lead when Birch pounces on a chance to score from close-range. An inswinging corner by Thompson finds Linighan, who heads the equaliser. Town step up another gear and within minutes Dozzell dispossesses Clarke, jinks past two men and scores.

21 TRANMERE — The old confidence floods back as Milton flashes a scorching drive in off a post. Thompson exchanges passes with Kiwomya and drills home a second. Linighan heads in the third goal from a Thompson cross. After Steel's handball, Wark steps up to net his 50th penalty-kick for the club.

22 PLYMOUTH — Town's attempt to play a passing game is blown aside by the fitness and determination of David Kemp's men. Marshall knocks a ball forward and Fiore takes advantage of Stockwell's hesitancy to score. Whitton tangles with Turner and looks rather unlucky to get a second yellow card.

23 SWINDON — Whitton's clearance hits a teammate and falls conveniently for Shearer, but he spurns this fine chance. Other chances go begging in a lively first half. Palmer sends Kiwomya scampering clean through ten minutes from time, but his usual clinical finish is absent and Hammond saves.

BARCLAYS DIVISION 2 — SEASON 1991-92

Manager: John Lyall

No	Date	1	2	3	4	5	6	7	8	9	10	11	subs used
24	H CHARLTON 26/12	Forrest	Johnson	Thompson	Stockwell	Wark	Linighan	Pennyfather	Palmer	Milton	Dozzell	Kiwomya	Leaburn/Balmer
		Bolder	*Pitcher*	*Minto^*	*Wilder*	*Webster!*	*Gatting*	*Lee*	*Bumstead*	*Rosenior**	*Nelson*	*Walsh*	

Att 13,826 · **Pos** 6 · **W** · **Pt** 38 · **F-A** 2-0 · **H-T** 1-0 · Kiwomya 37, 57 · Ref: P Taylor

Kiwomya's speed and trickery is just too much for the side now managed jointly by Alan Curbishley and Steve Gritt. Thompson's cross is deflected into Kiwomya's path for the first and Milton sends him streaking though for the second. Simon Webster is red-carded near the end.

No	Date	1	2	3	4	5	6	7	8	9	10	11	subs used
25	H BLACKBURN 28/12	Forrest	Johnson	Thompson	Stockwell	Wark	Linighan	Milton	Palmer	Whitton	Dozzell	Kiwomya*	Pennyfather/Beardsmore
		Mimms	*Brown*	*Wright*	*Cowans*	*Hendrie*	*Moran*	*Wilcox*	*Atkins*	*Speedie*	*Newell*	*Hill**	

Att 17,675 · **Pos** 3 · **W** · **Pt** 41 · **F-A** 2-1 · **H-T** 0-1 · Johnson 48, Dozzell 85, Wright 11 · Ref: R Hamer

A top-of-the-table clash with a club rejuvenated by Kenny Dalglish's arrival and Jack Walker's cash. Newell sets up Wright for a splendid early volley. Johnson's diving header is a picture goal as Town hit back. The ground erupts as Dozzell converts Whitton's pass near the end.

No	Date	1	2	3	4	5	6	7	8	9	10	11	subs used
26	A PORT VALE 1/1	Forrest	Johnson	Thompson	Stockwell	Wark	Linighan	Milton	Palmer	Whitton	Dozzell	Kiwomya	Mills B
		Grew	*Mills*	*Hughes*	*Williams*	*Aspen*	*Glover*	*Jalink**	*Van derLaan*	*Houchen*	*Foyle*	*Jeffers*	

Att 8,075 · **Pos** 2 · **W** · **Pt** 44 · **F-A** 2-1 · **H-T** 1-0 · Kiwomya 41, 53, Hughes 55 · Ref: W Flood

A good contest in blustery conditions. Whitton sends Kiwomya through and he scores expertly past the advancing Grew. Kiwomya nips in to convert a Thompson corner. John Rudge's side hits back when Glover touches a free-kick to Hughes, who rifles in a fine shot from distance.

No	Date	1	2	3	4	5	6	7	8	9	10	11	subs used
27	A MIDDLESBROUGH 11/1	Forrest	Johnson	Pennyfather	Stockwell	Wark	Linighan	Milton	Palmer*	Whitton	Dozzell	Kiwomya	Yallop
		Pears	*Parkinson*	*Phillips*	*Mohan*	*Kernaghan*	*Falconer*	*Slaven*	*Pollock*	*Wilkinson*	*Ripley*	*Hendrie**	*Payton*

Att 15,104 · **Pos** 5 · **L** · **Pt** 44 · **F-A** 0-1 · **H-T** 0-0 · Payton 78 · Ref: T Fitzharris

Stout defending by Town keeps them on terms as Boro turn on the heat, particularly after the break. The breakthrough finally comes for the home side from their 13th corner. Ripley's kick is nodded down by Wilkinson and Payton forces the ball in after his first attempt is blocked.

No	Date	1	2	3	4	5	6	7	8	9	10	11	subs used
28	H BRISTOL ROV 18/1	Forrest	Johnson	Thompson	Stockwell	Wark*	Linighan	Milton	Palmer*	Whitton	Dozzell	Kiwomya	Zondervan
		Parkin	*Alexander*	*Moore*	*Yates*	*Maddison**	*Skinner*	*Cross*	*Reece*	*Browning*	*Stewart^*	*Saunders*	*Pounder/Bloomer*

Att 10,435 · **Pos** 3 · **W** · **Pt** 47 · **F-A** 1-0 · **H-T** 0-0 · Milton 54 · Ref: R Pawley

Denis Rofe's side put up a stubborn display, but he is unhappy at how few strikes on goal they have. Johnson and Linighan hit the woodwork. Yates' clearance falls into the path of Milton who flashes home a fine shot. It gives Town their 820th victory in exactly 2,000 League matches.

No	Date	1	2	3	4	5	6	7	8	9	10	11	subs used
29	A MILLWALL 1/2	Forrest	Johnson	Thompson	Stockwell	Wark*	Linighan	Milton	Palmer	Whitton	Dozzell	Kiwomya	Zondervan
		Davison	*Dawes*	*Cooper*	*Rae*	*Thompson*	*McLeary*	*Stephenson*	*Verveer*	*Bogie^*	*McGinlay*	*Falco**	*Kerr/Stevens*

Att 8,847 · **Pos** 3 · **W** · **Pt** 50 · **F-A** 3-2 · **H-T** 1-0 · Dozzell 33, Thompson 49, Kiwomya 62, Rae 67, Kerr 85p · Ref: K Lupton

Nearly a repeat of the Bristol Rov debacle in August. Town cruise to 3-0 and look set for a hatful. Bruce Rioch's men wake from their slumbers and Rae stabs in a free-kick. Kerr nets from the spot after being tripped. Town hang on grimly for a first League win at Millwall in 36 years.

No	Date	1	2	3	4	5	6	7	8	9	10	11	subs used
30	H PORTSMOUTH 8/2	Forrest	Johnson	Thompson	Stockwell	Wark*	Linighan	Milton	Palmer	Whitton	Dozzell	Kiwomya*	Goddard
		Knight	*Awford*	*Beresford*	*Powell*	*Symons*	*Butters**	*Neil^*	*Kuhl*	*Whittingham*	*Burns*	*Anderton*	*Clarke/Hendon*

Att 13,494 · **Pos** 2 · **W** · **Pt** 53 · **F-A** 5-2 · **H-T** 3-1 · Dozzell 3, 18, Kiwomya 6, 51, Anderton 8, Powell 53 [Awford 62 (og)] · Ref: V Callow

Pompey's run of success at Ipswich is ended in style. Slick finishing by Dozzell and a Kiwomya lob put Town 3-1 ahead early on. Kiwomya converts a rebound, but Powell's shot is deflected in by Linighan. Town have the final word when Milton's cross is deflected in by Awford.

No	Date	1	2	3	4	5	6	7	8	9	10	11	subs used
31	A TRANMERE 21/2	Forrest	Johnson	Thompson	Stockwell	Wark*	Linighan	Milton	Palmer	Whitton	Dozzell	Kiwomya*	Goddard
		Nixon	*Higgins*	*Nolan*	*Irons*	*Hughes**	*Vickers*	*Morrissey*	*Thomas*	*Aldridge*	*Martindale^*	*Muir*	*Malkin/Harvey*

Att 9,161 · **Pos** 2 · **W** · **Pt** 56 · **F-A** 1-0 · **H-T** 0-0 · Milton 63 · Ref: I Cruickshanks

Town complete the double over John King's side when Milton strikes after the interval with a stinging right-foot shot. The opening had been carved out by Thompson and Kiwomya. Seven victories from the last eight matches mean Town are very well-placed in the promotion race.

No	Date	1	2	3	4	5	6	7	8	9	10	11	subs used
32	H PLYMOUTH 29/2	Forrest	Johnson^	Thompson	Stockwell	Wark	Linighan	Milton	Palmer	Whitton	Dozzell*	Kiwomya	Goddard/Zondervan
		Wilmot	*Spearing*	*Morrison*	*Marker*	*Van Rossum*	*Morgan*	*Hodges K*	*Garner**	*Regis*	*Smith*	*Turner**	*Barlow/Clement*

Att 12,852 · **Pos** 2 · **W** · **Pt** 59 · **F-A** 2-0 · **H-T** 0-0 · Kiwomya 48, Whitton 88 · Ref: T Ward

Another vital win is partly overshadowed by a sickening injury to Turner. Trying to prevent Kiwomya's goal, Wilmot crashes into teammate Turner and it's clear his leg is broken. Even the home fans' goal celebrations are muted. Turner earlier broke two fingers and was booked!

No	Date	1	2	3	4	5	6	7	8	9	10	11	subs used
33	A WATFORD 7/3	Forrest	Johnson	Thompson	Stockwell	Wark	Linighan	Milton	Palmer	Whitton	Dozzell	Kiwomya	Goddard
		James	*Gibbs*	*Drysdale*	*Dublin*	*Holdsworth*	*Ashby*	*Porter*	*Nogan*	*Blissett*	*Butler*	*Soloman*	

Att 9,199 · **Pos** 2 · **W** · **Pt** 62 · **F-A** 1-0 · **H-T** 0-0 · Whitton 86 · Ref: J Rushton

Whitton has a nasty fall, toppling over some advertising boards and looks out of sorts for the rest of the game. However, he gets himself in position to flick home Thompson's cross for the late winner. Steve Perryman's lowly side are repelled time and again by the in-form Forrest.

No	Date	1	2	3	4	5	6	7	8	9	10	11	subs used
34	H LEICESTER 14/3	Forrest	Johnson	Thompson	Stockwell	Wark	Linighan	Milton	Palmer*	Whitton	Dozzell	Kiwomya	Goddard
		Poole	*Mills*	*Platnauer*	*Smith*	*Walsh*	*Grayson*	*Russell*	*Thompson*	*Wright*	*Gee*	*Ormondroyd*	

Att 16,174 · **Pos** 2 · **D** · **Pt** 63 · **F-A** 0-0 · **H-T** 0-0 · Ref: K Hackett

Town are a shade lucky to take a point. In a game that could have ended 3-3, both keepers give fine displays. Gee hits the bar for City. Lyall gets the Barclays Manager of the Month award before kick-off. Lowe goes on loan to Port Vale, and keeper Petterson is loaned from Luton.

Season fixture log (matches 35–46). Each entry: No. | Venue | Date | Opponent | HT | FT | League (Pos / Result / — / Pts) | Town scorers | Opponent scorers | Referee | Attendance, followed by the two line-ups (Town, then opponents in italics) and a match report.

#	V	Date	Opponent	HT	FT	Pos	Res	—	Pts	Att
35	H	17/3	WATFORD	0-0	1-2	3	L	17	63	12,484
36	A	21/3	CAMBRIDGE	0-0	1-1	3	D	2	64	9,766
37	H	28/3	DERBY	2-0	2-1	1	W	8	67	15,305
38	H	31/3	BARNSLEY	1-0	2-0	1	W	14	70	14,148
39	A	4/4	SOUTHEND	0-0	2-1	1	W	10	73	10,003
40	H	7/4	WOLVERHAMPTON	0-0	2-1	1	W	11	76	17,379
41	H	11/4	NEWCASTLE	1-2	3-2	1	W	19	79	20,673
42	A	14/4	SUNDERLAND	0-0	0-3	1	L	19	79	22,131
43	A	18/4	BRISTOL CITY	0-1	1-2	1	L	17	79	16,941
44	H	21/4	GRIMSBY	0-0	0-0	1	D	18	80	22,393
45	A	25/4	OXFORD	1-1	1-1	1	D	22	81	10,525
46	H	2/5	BRIGHTON	2-1	3-1	1	W	23	84	26,803

Home 14,274 Away 10,301 Average 10,301

35. H 17/3 WATFORD — Dozzell 87 / *Drysdale 69, 70* — Ref: A Gunn
Town: Forrest, Johnson, Thompson*, Milton, Linighan, Wark, Stockwell, Palmer, Whitton, Dozzell, Kiwomya, Goddard
Opp: *James, Gibbs, Drysdale, Hessenthaler, Ashby, Holdsworth, Dublin, Nogan*, Blissett, Butler, Soloman, Bazeley*
Drysdale blasts in a close-range shot to send Town towards their first loss in more than two months. A minute later the same player fires a free-kick past Forrest. After plenty of Town pressure, Dozzell heads in Goddard's pass to make the dying minutes interesting. The Hornets hang on.

36. A 21/3 CAMBRIDGE — Milton 52 / *Heathcote 55* — Ref: K Barrett
Town: Forrest, Zondervan, Thompson, Milton, Linighan, Wark, Stockwell, Goddard, Whitton, Dozzell, Kiwomya, Johnson
Opp: *Sheffield, Heathcote, Kimble, Wilkins, Daish, Chappell, Dennis, Leadbetter, Dublin, Claridge*, Heaney*, Norbury/Taylor*
Both clubs are flying high and there is much tension in this clash of contrasting playing styles. A fine Town moves is polished off by Milton's crisp shot. Battling Cambridge bounce straight back when Heathcote backs into Forrest and backheels the loose ball home amid Town protests.

37. H 28/3 DERBY — Dozzell 2, 14 / *Simpson 82* — Ref: P Alcock
Town: Forrest, Zondervan, Thompson, Milton*, Linighan, Wark, Stockwell, Goddard*, Whitton, Dozzell, Kiwomya, Johnson
Opp: *Sutton, Kavanagh, Forsyth, Johnson T, Comyn, Coleman, Williams G, Kitson, Gabbiadini, Simpson, McMinn*
Portman Road celebrates as Town hit top spot. Zondervan beats the offside trap to send Dozzell through for a dream start. Thompson causes more damage with his superb inswinging corners, Dozzell heading one in for the second goal. Simpson's late volley makes it a tense finish.

38. H 31/3 BARNSLEY — Kiwomya 34, 49 — Ref: P Danson
Town: Forrest, Zondervan, Thompson, Milton, Linighan^, Wark, Stockwell, Goddard, Whitton^, Dozzell, Kiwomya, Johnson/Palmer
Opp: *Butler, Robinson, Williams, O'Connell, Taggart^, Smith, Whitworth, Redfearn, Banks*, Rammell, Archdeacon, Currie/Fleming*
Kiwomya benefits from two simple opportunities, both created by Linighan. The first comes after a goalmouth melee. The second comes as Linighan's header is blocked but falls nicely for the grateful Kiwomya. Linighan sustains a serious knee injury.

39. A 4/4 SOUTHEND — Whelan 58, Thompson 89 / *Prior 79* — Ref: G Ashby
Town: Forrest, Zondervan, Thompson, Milton*, Linighan*, Wark, Stockwell, Goddard*, Whitton, Dozzell, Kiwomya, Johnson/Palmer
Opp: *Sansome, Austin, Powell, Ansah, Prior, Scully, Jones, Cornwell, Tilson, Benjamin*, Angell, O'Callaghan*
Deputising for Linighan, debutant Whelan nets a towering header to put Town ahead. After Dozzell is fouled Wark's penalty hits the bar. Prior's fierce header levels it, but near the whistle Thompson cuts in and fires a winner with the right foot normally only used for standing on!

40. H 7/4 WOLVERHAMPTON — Whelan 58, Whitton 89p / *Mutch 84* — Ref: D Axcell
Town: Forrest, Zondervan, Thompson, Milton*, Whelan, Wark, Stockwell, Goddard*, Whitton, Dozzell, Kiwomya, Johnson/Palmer
Opp: *Stowell, Ashley, Venus, Birch, Mountfield, Rankine, Rowell, Cook, Bull, Mutch, Downing*
Another magnificent header from young Whelan puts Town ahead. Graham Turner's side level with six minutes left via Mutch, who is injured doing so. Two points appear lost until Birch hauls down Kiwomya and Whitton successfully steps up to take over the spot-kick job from Wark.

41. H 11/4 NEWCASTLE — Whitton 30p, Wark 68, Kiwomya 72 / *Peacock 17, 42* — Ref: A Buskh
Town: Forrest, Zondervan, Thompson, Milton*, Whelan, Wark, Stockwell, Goddard*, Whitton, Dozzell, Kiwomya, Johnson/Palmer
Opp: *Wright, Ranson^, Stimson, Clark*, Howey, Scott, O'Brien, Peacock, Kelly, Sheedy, Brock, Quinn/Kristensen*
After this topsy-turvy thriller most observers agree this will surely be Town's year. Ranson's handball allows Whitton to cancel out Peacock's fine finish. Wark's header later does likewise. Palmer sets up Kiwomya for a tap-in and Kevin Keegan's battlers are finally put in their place.

42. A 14/4 SUNDERLAND — / *Goodman 53, 78, Rush 53* — Ref: P Harrison
Town: Forrest, Zondervan, Thompson, Johnson*, Whelan, Wark, Stockwell, Palmer, Whitton, Dozzell, Kiwomya, Milton
Opp: *Norman, Kay, Ragan, Goodman*, Mooney^, Hardyman, Bennett, Rush, Armstrong, Byrne, Atkinson, Davenport/Owers*
Battling against relegation, the Rokerites get their noses ahead through a spectacular solo goal. Rush finishes Town off with a rasping drive from outside the box. Town crumble badly as Goodman bursts through for a simple chance for record signing Goodman. In the closing stages Rush finishes Town off with a rasping drive from outside the box.

43. A 18/4 BRISTOL CITY — Whitton 83p / *Rosenior 37, Cole 53* — Ref: J Martin
Town: Forrest, Zondervan, Thompson, Milton*, Whelan, Wark*, Stockwell*, Goddard, Whitton, Dozzell, Kiwomya, Palmer/Johnson
Opp: *Welch, Atteveldt, Scott, Mellon, Osman, Bryant, Aizlewood, Dziekanowski, Cole, Rosenior, May*
Town are still five points clear at the top after this, but certainly seem to be getting the jitters. A win would have clinched promotion, but Rosenior has other ideas and neatly lobs Forrest. Andy Cole shows fine control to tuck in the second.

44. H 21/4 GRIMSBY — Ref: G Willard
Town: Forrest, Zondervan*, Thompson, Milton^, Whelan, Wark, Stockwell, Johnson^, Whitton, Dozzell, Kiwomya, Palmer/Goddard
Opp: *Reece, McDermott, Jobling, Watson, Cunnington, Futcher, Rodger, Gilbert, Smith, Agnew, Woods*
Nervous Town miss another chance to make certain of promotion and look very tense in the first half. Things get better after the break, but Alan Buckley's men cannot be broken down. Dozzell hits a post in the 90th minute, so the champagne goes on ice for at least four more days!

45. A 25/4 OXFORD — Johnson 9 / *Magilton 7* — Ref: J Worrall
Town: Forrest, Zondervan, Thompson, Milton, Whelan, Wark, Stockwell, Johnson, Whitton, Dozzell, Kiwomya, Goddard
Opp: *Key, Penney, Smart, Melville, Evans, Lewis, Beauchamp, Magilton, Durrin, Allen*, Bannister*
30 years to the day that Alf Ramsey's men won the title, Town need a point to go up. Magilton's low shot is an early shock, but Johnson hits back, heading in Whitton's free-kick. Lyall uses the PA system at the end to urge fans to leave the ground and have their party next Saturday.

46. H 2/5 BRIGHTON — Whitton 8p, 82, Johnson 44 / *Meade 45* — Ref: P Vanes
Town: Forrest, Zondervan^, Thompson^, Milton, Whelan, Wark, Stockwell*, Johnson, Whitton, Dozzell, Kiwomya, Palmer/Goddard
Opp: *Digweed, Munday, Gallacher, McCarthy, Barham^, Chivers, Chapman, Meade, Gall, Codner, Robinson, Crumplin/Funnell*
Top-of-the-table Town cannot be overtaken and it's party time at Portman Road. Whitton nets Town's 10th penalty of the season (three were missed) and there's no way back for Brighton. Barry Lloyd's men hear they have been relegated when news of an Oxford win comes through.

BARCLAYS DIVISION 2 (CUP-TIES)   Manager: John Lyall   SEASON 1991-92

	1	2	3	4	5	6	7	8	9	10	11	subs used

Rumbelows Cup

2:1 A DERBY 25/9 — Att 10,215 (11) — F-A 0-0 — H-T 0-0 — Ref: J Kirkby

Forrest	Johnson	Thompson	Stockwell	Yallop	Linighan	Zondervan	Goddard	Whitton	Dozzell	Kiwomya	
Shilton	*Sage*	*Forsyth*	*Williams G*	*Coleman*	*Comyn*	*Micklewhite**	*Ormondroyd*	*Gee^*	*Williams P*	*McMinn*	*Patterson/Hayward*

A good start to the cup campaign as Arthur Cox's side are held at the Baseball Ground. It's Town's first clean sheet in an away match this season. An excellent defensive display with Forrest taking paticular credit. John Wark is back in the squad, having signed non-contract forms.

2:2 H DERBY 8/10 — Att 8,982 (8) — F-A 0-2 — H-T 0-2 — Scorers: Gee 23, Williams P 29p — Ref: J Moules — (Derby win 2-0 on aggregate)

Forrest	Wark	Thompson	Stockwell	Yallop	Linighan	Zondervan	Lowe	Whitton	Milton*	Kiwomya	
Shilton	*Patterson*	*Forsyth*	*Williams G*	*Coleman*	*Comyn*	*Micklewhite*	*Ormondroyd*	*Gee*	*Williams P*	*McMinn*	*Gregory*

Derby begin where they left off in the first leg and press forward. From their sixth corner, Ormondroyd nods the ball on and Gee dives to head in. Forrest rushes out and crashes into Ormondroyd. He is booked and Williams tucks home the penalty. Shilton saves Thompson's spot-kick.

FA Cup

3 H HARTLEPOOL 4/1 — Att 12,502 (3:9) — F-A 1-1 — H-T 0-1 — D — Scorers: Dozzell 84 / Baker 38 — Ref: T West

Forrest	Johnson	Thompson	Stockwell^	Wark	Linighan	Milton	Palmer*	Whitton	Dozzell	Kiwomya	
Hodge	*Nobbs*	*McKinnon*	*McCreery*	*MacPhail*	*Tupling*	*Southall*	*Olsson*	*Baker*	*Tinker**	*Dalton*	*Pennyfather/Yallop Fletcher*

Tinkler and Olsson set up Baker to fire Alan Murray's team ahead. A shock looks on the cards but Town escape by the skin of their teeth. Pennyfather's pass allows Dozzell to equalise from close-range. Moments later Milton hits a post, but defeat would have been unjust for Pool.

3R A HARTLEPOOL 15/1 — Att 8,500 (3:7) — F-A 2-0 — H-T 1-0 — W — Scorers: Dozzell 40, Milton 79 — Ref: T West

Forrest	Johnson	Thompson	Stockwell	Wark	Linighan	Milton	Palmer*	Whitton	Dozzell	Kiwomya	
Hodge	*Nobbs*	*Fletcher*	*McCreery**	*MacPhail*	*Tupling*	*Honour*	*Olsson*	*Baker*	*Tinker*	*Dalton*	*Southall*

Playing in front of his home-town crowd, Linighan puts on a super display and marshals Town to victory. In misty conditions, Dozzell slots in Thompson's cross. Milton puts the result beyond serious doubt when he seizes onto Thompson's pass and clips home a fine long-range effort.

4 H BOURNEMOUTH 5/2 — Att 17,193 (3:12) — F-A 3-0 — H-T 2-0 — W — Scorers: Dozzell 18, Whitton 31, Kiwomya 59 — Ref: K Barrett

Forrest	Johnson	Thompson	Stockwell	Wark	Linighan	Milton	Palmer*	Whitton	Dozzell	Kiwomya	
Bartram	*Bond*	*Rowland*	*Morris*	*Mundee !*	*O'Driscoll*	*Brooks**	*Wood*	*Quinn*	*Case*	*Ekoku^*	*Morrell/Holmes*

Town have too much class for the Cherries and Dozzell knocks home a far-post header to open the scoring. Whitton's header goes in off the underside of the bar. Mundee is sent off for pulling down Kiwomya when he is clean through. A cheeky flick by Kiwomya ends the scoring.

5 H LIVERPOOL 16/2 — Att 26,140 (1:3) — F-A 0-0 — H-T 0-0 — D — Ref: A Buskh

Forrest	Johnson	Thompson	Stockwell	Wark	Linighan	Milton	Palmer	Whitton	Dozzell	Kiwomya	
Grobbelaar	*Jones R*	*Burrows*	*Nicol*	*Wright*	*Marsh*	*Saunders*	*Houghton*	*Rush*	*Redknapp**	*McManaman*	*Kozma*

Played on a Sunday to enable live TV coverage, Graeme Souness' outfit is saved by the woodwork. Wark's close-range header hits the bar just before the break, and later Houghton miscues a clearance against the post. Wright has the ball in Town's net but the ref spots some pushing.

5R A LIVERPOOL 26/2 — Att 27,355 (1:5) — F-A 2-3 — H-T 0-1 — L — aet — Scorers: Johnson 82, Dozzell 95 / Houghton 45, Molby 98, McManam'n 100 — Ref: K Leach

Forrest	Johnson	Thompson	Stockwell	Wark^	Linighan	Milton	Palmer*	Whitton	Dozzell	Kiwomya	
Grobbelaar	*Jones R*	*Harkness**	*Wright*	*Marsh*	*Saunders*	*Houghton*	*Walters^*	*Molby*	*McManaman Kozma/Rosenthal*	*Goddard/Zondervan*

The Reds are pushed all the way in a real cup thriller. Johnson's glorious header forces extra-time. Dozzell puts Town ahead after getting clean through, but Molby levels with a curling free-kick. A neat move between Rosenthal and McManaman sees the latter fire in the winning goal.

League table

Pos	Team	P	Home					Away					Pts
			W	D	L	F	A	W	D	L	F	A	
1	IPSWICH	46	16	3	4	42	22	8	9	6	28	28	84
2	Middlesbro	46	15	6	2	37	13	8	5	10	21	28	80
3	Derby	46	11	4	8	35	24	12	5	6	34	27	78
4	Leicester	46	14	4	5	41	24	9	4	10	21	31	77
5	Cambridge	46	10	9	4	34	19	9	8	6	31	28	74
6	Blackburn *	46	14	5	4	41	21	7	6	10	29	32	74
7	Charlton	46	9	7	7	25	23	11	4	8	29	25	71
8	Swindon	46	15	3	5	38	22	3	12	8	31	33	69
9	Portsmouth	46	15	6	2	41	12	4	6	13	24	39	69
10	Watford	46	9	5	9	25	23	9	6	8	26	25	65
11	Wolves	46	11	6	6	36	24	7	4	12	25	30	64
12	Southend	46	11	5	7	37	26	6	6	11	26	37	62
13	Bristol Rov	46	11	9	3	43	29	5	5	13	17	34	62
14	Tranmere	46	9	9	5	37	32	5	10	8	19	24	61
15	Millwall	46	10	4	9	32	32	7	6	10	32	39	61
16	Barnsley	46	11	4	8	27	25	5	7	11	19	32	59
17	Bristol City	46	10	8	5	30	24	3	7	13	25	47	54
18	Sunderland	46	10	8	5	36	23	4	3	16	25	42	53
19	Grimsby	46	7	5	11	25	28	7	6	10	22	34	53
20	Newcastle	46	9	8	6	38	30	4	5	14	28	54	52
21	Oxford	46	10	6	7	39	30	3	5	15	27	43	50
22	Plymouth	46	11	5	7	26	26	2	4	17	16	38	48
23	Brighton	46	7	7	9	36	37	5	4	14	20	40	47
24	Port Vale	46	7	8	8	23	25	3	7	13	19	34	45
		1104	262	144	146	824	594	146	144	262	594	824	1512

* promoted
after play-offs

Appearances and Goals

Player	Appearances						Goals			
	Lge	Sub	LC	Sub	FAC	Sub	Lge	LC	FAC	Tot
Dozzell, Jason	45		1		5		11		4	15
Edmonds, Darren		2								
Forrest, Craig	46		2		5					
Gayle, Brian	5									
Goddard, Paul	19	5	1			1	4			4
Gregory, David		1				1				
Humes, Tony	5									
Johnson, Gavin	33	9	1		5		5		1	6
Kiwomya, Chris	43	2	2		5		16		1	17
Linighan, David	36		2		5		3			3
Lowe, David	7	7	1		1		1			1
Milton, Simon	31	3	1		5		7		1	8
Moncur, John	5	1								
Palmer, Steve	16	7								
Pennyfather, Glenn	2	1		1						
Stockwell, Mick	46		2		5		2			2
Thompson, Neil	45		2		5		6			6
Wark, John	36	1	1		5		3			3
Whelan, Phil	8						2			2
Whitton, Steve	43		2		5		9		1	10
Yallop, Frank	9	8	2			1				
Youds, Eddie	1									
Zondervan, Romeo	25	3	2		5		1			1
23 players used	**506**	**48**	**22**	**1**	**55**	**3**	**70**		**8**	**78**

(own-goals)

Odds & ends

Double wins: (5) Blackburn, Port Vale, Southend, Tranmere, Wolves.

Double losses: (1) Sunderland.

Won from behind: (4) Bristol City (h), Blackburn (h), Newcastle (h), Wolverhampton (a).

Lost from in front: (1) Liverpool (FAC) (a).

High spots: The winning of a sixth championship title.

An increase in attendances of more than 20 per cent.

Excellent League form immediately after Christmas.

A settled side (8 men played 36 League games or more).

A fine display at Anfield in the FA Cup replay.

Three successive April games featuring dramatic late wins.

Low spots: A seven-day attack of the jitters in April, when three chances to clinch promotion were spurned.

Escaping with just a draw after being 3-0 up at Bristol Rov.

Expensive signing Eddie Youds seriously hurt on his debut.

Record losses of £747,246 announced by the directors.

Player of the Year: John Wark.

Ever presents: (2) Craig Forrest, Mick Stockwell.

Hat tricks: (0).

Opposing hat-tricks: (0).

Leading scorer: (17) Chris Kiwomya.

FA PREMIER LEAGUE

Manager: Mick McGiven

SEASON 1992-93

Column key: **No | Date | Att | Pos | Pt | F-A | H-T | Scorers, Times, and Referees** followed by playing positions **1–11** and **subs used**. Opponents' line-ups are shown in *italics*.

---

1 — H — 15/8 — ASTON VILLA
Att 16,818 · Pt 1 · D 1-1 · H-T 1-0
Scorers: Johnson 31 / *Atkinson 84* — Ref: A Buksh

1	2	3	4	5	6	7	8	9	10	11	subs used
Forrest	Whelan	Thompson	Stockwell*	Wark	Linighan	Williams	Goddard	Johnson	Dozzell^	Kiwomya	Milton/Youds
Spink	*Barrett*	*Staunton*	*Teale*	*McGrath*	*Richardson**	*Daley*	*Parker*	*Houghton*	*Atkinson*	*Froggatt*	*Regis*

The ground has been made 'all-seater' but the hoped-for 20,000 gate fails to materialise. New-boy Williams looks useful as Town roar ahead when Froggatt's misplaced pass is rocketed home by Johnson from 30 yards. Home debutant Youds miscues and Atkinson takes advantage.

---

2 — A — 18/8 — WIMBLEDON (21)
Att **4,594** · Pos 2 · Pt 4 · W 1-0 · H-T 1-0
Scorers: Johnson 37 — Ref: R Hart

1	2	3	4	5	6	7	8	9	10	11	subs used
Forrest	Whelan	Thompson	Stockwell	Wark	Linighan	Williams	Goddard	Johnson	Dozzell	Kiwomya*	Milton
Segers	*Joseph^*	*Elkins*	*Barton*	*Fitzgerald*	*Miller*	*Earle*	*Holdsworth*	*Sanchez*	*Berry**	*Blackwell*	*Clarke/Dobbs*

The first win back at top level comes courtesy of Johnson, who sweeps in a cross by Stockwell. Low on support, but high on spirit, Joe Kinnear's men dominate after the break but miss the aerial presence of Fashanu. McGiven is delighted at how Town hold firm in defence.

---

3 — A — 22/8 — MANCHESTER U (21)
Att 31,704 · Pos 9 · Pt 5 · D 1-1 · H-T 0-0
Scorers: Kiwomya 56 / *Irwin 58* — Ref: G Ashby

1	2	3	4	5	6	7	8	9	10	11	subs used
Forrest	Whelan^	Thompson	Stockwell	Wark	Linighan	Williams	Goddard	Johnson	Dozzell*	Kiwomya	Milton/Youds
Schmeichel	*Irwin*	*Blackmore^*	*Bruce*	*Ferguson*	*Pallister*	*Kanchelskis**	*McClair*	*Hughes*	*Giggs*	*Phelan*	*Dublin/Webb*

After a nervous start, Thompson's pass is flicked by Dozzell to Kiwomya, who nets. Irwin cuts in to fire a super goal. McGiven, by now promoted from coach to 'first team manager' under 'football manager' Lyall, opts for a packed defence and Wark, 35, is heroic as sweeper.

---

4 — H — 25/8 — LIVERPOOL (15)
Att 20,109 · Pos 10 · Pt 6 · D 2-2 · H-T 0-1
Scorers: Dozzell 56, Kiwomya 90 / *Walters 39, Molby 70p* — Ref: R Hamer

1	2	3	4	5	6	7	8	9	10	11	subs used
Forrest	Whelan	Thompson	Stockwell	Wark	Linighan	Williams	Goddard*	Johnson	Dozzell	Kiwomya	Milton
James	*Jones*	*Burrows*	*Harkness*	*Whelan*	*Wright*	*Saunders**	*Stewart*	*Rush*	*Molby*	*Walters*	*McManaman*

A thrilling game delights a big crowd. Walters nets against the run of play, but Dozzell levels from a Thompson cross. Town are furious as Whelan's fierce tackle on Saunders results in a penalty – Molby converts. Last-minute joy as Whelan's volley is nudged home by Kiwomya.

---

5 — H — 30/8 — TOTTENHAM (21)
Att 20,100 · Pos 8 · Pt 7 · D 1-1 · H-T 1-1
Scorers: Wark 45 / *Cundy 29* — Ref: K Hackett

1	2	3	4	5	6	7	8	9	10	11	subs used
Forrest	Whelan	Thompson	Stockwell	Wark	Linighan	Williams	Goddard*	Johnson	Dozzell	Kiwomya	Milton
Walker	*Austin*	*Edinburgh*	*Sedgley*	*Cundy*	*Ruddock*	*Anderton*	*Durie*	*Samways*	*Sheringham**	*Allen^*	*Gray*

A Sunday game to accommodate live TV cameras features a freak goal when Cundy hoofs the ball forward from 50 yards and the ball sails over Forrest. He later claims it was intentional, but no-one believes him! Williams and Dozzell set up Wark, who toe-pokes over Walker.

---

6 — A — 1/9 — MIDDLESBROUGH (9)
Att 14,255 · Pos 8 · Pt 8 · D 2-2 · H-T 1-0
Scorers: Wark 36, Goddard 60 / *Kernaghan 54, Wilkinson 83* — Ref: R Nixon

1	2	3	4	5	6	7	8	9	10	11	subs used
Forrest	Whelan	Thompson	Stockwell	Wark	Linighan	Williams	Goddard	Johnson	Dozzell	Youds	
*Ironside**	*Phillips*	*Parkinson*	*Kernaghan*	*Whyte*	*Peake*	*Slaven*	*Falconer*	*Wilkinson*	*Wright*	*Mustoe*	*Horne*

Wark fires in after Thompson's corner. Ironside goes off after injuring his back in saving his free-kick, but Kernaghan forces in a free-kick, but Goddard hits back after Linighan's long ball. Wilkinson evades Wark to fire an equaliser. He is then tripped, but Slaven misses the penalty.

---

7 — A — 5/9 — QP RANGERS (4)
Att 12,806 · Pos 13 · Pt 9 · D 0-0 · H-T 0-0
Ref: D Gallagher

1	2	3	4	5	6	7	8	9	10	11	subs used
Forrest	Whelan	Thompson	Stockwell	Wark	Linighan	Williams	Goddard^	Johnson	Dozzell	Youds*	Yallop/Pennyfather
Stejskal	*Bardsley*	*Wilkins*	*Peacock*	*McDonald*	*Impey*	*Barter*	*Ferdinand*	*Bailey**	*Sinton*	*Penrice*	

The highlight of a dull game at Loftus Road is a miraculous 76th-minute goal-line clearance by Youds, who injures his back and groin when stretching to block Ferdinand's header. Forrest makes three world-class saves. Whelan is boosted by being selected for England Under-21s.

---

8 — H — 12/9 — WIMBLEDON (20)
Att 13,333 · Pos 7 · Pt 12 · W 2-1 · H-T 1-1
Scorers: Stockwell 14, 48 / *Holdsworth 27* — Ref: S Lodge

1	2	3	4	5	6	7	8	9	10	11	subs used
Forrest	Whelan	Thompson	Stockwell	Wark	Linighan	Williams	Pennyfather	Johnson	Dozzell	Yallop	
Segers	*Joseph**	*Barton*	*Scales*	*Gibson^*	*Earle*	*Holdsworth*	*Fashanu*	*Clarke*	*Blackwell*		*Miller/Fitzgerald*

Town are without any recognised strikers for this early return with the Dons, but lively Stockwell's forays into the box pay off handsomely. Two wins against Kinnear's men plus six draws is now Town's record. Vinnie Jones enjoys his 'second debut', after returning from Chelsea.

---

9 — A — 19/9 — OLDHAM (11)
Att 11,150 · Pos 8 · Pt 12 · L 2-4 · H-T 0-1
Scorers: Wark 75, Thompson 88 / *Marshall 32, Sharp 53, Halle 56* *(Henry 82)* — Ref: J Key

1	2	3	4	5	6	7	8	9	10	11	subs used
Forrest	Whelan	Thompson	Stockwell	Wark	Linighan	Youds	Pennyfather	Johnson	Dozzell	Kiwomya	
Hallworth	*Redmond*	*Pointon*	*Henry*	*Jobson*	*Marshall*	*Halle*	*Sharp*	*Olney*	*Milligan*	*Bernard*	

Town look ultra-defensive early on, but the only remaining Premier League unbeaten run ends. Ian Marshall heads in the Latics' seventh corner. Whelan's weak header gifts Sharp a goal. Halle's header flies in off Wark and Henry finishes Town off, diving to head in Redmond's cross.

---

10 — H — 26/9 — SHEFFIELD UTD (20)
Att 16,353 · Pos 10 · Pt 13 · D 0-0 · H-T 0-0
Ref: R Groves

1	2	3	4	5	6	7	8	9	10	11	subs used
Forrest !	Whelan	Thompson	Stockwell	Wark	Linighan	Youds*	Williams	Johnson	Dozzell	Kiwomya	**Baker**
Kelly	*Gage*	*Cowen*	*Gannon*	*Gayle*	*Beasley*	*Bradshaw^*	*Rogers*	*Littlejohn*	*Deane*	*Whitehouse**	*Cork/Hartfield*

Littlejohn bursts clear in the second minute and is sent flying by Forrest. The keeper looks stunned to be sent off. Youds is subbed by Baker, who keeps a clean sheet on his debut. Man-of-the-match Williams delights the fans by accidentally bringing the referee crashing to the turf!

11 — H LEEDS — 3/10

Attendance 21,200 · Pos 8 (10) · HT 3-0 · **W** · FT 4-2 · Pts 16

Scorers: Kiwomya 25, Wark 36, 44p, Dozzell 70 — Chapman 55, Speed 64

Forrest	Whelan	Thompson	Stockwell	Wark	Linighan	Williams	Goddard	Johnson	Dozzell	Kiwomya
Lukic	*Sellars**	*Dorigo*	*Batty*	*Fairclough*	*White*	*Cantona*	*Chapman*	*McAllister*	*Speed*	*Rocastle*

Ref: D Elleray

Unmarked at a corner, Kiwomya heads Town ahead. Wark bends in a free-kick and then converts a spot-kick after Batty brings down Goddard. Chapman squeezes in a shot and Speed nets a diving header. A superb header by Dozzell eases any Town anxieties.

12 — A CHELSEA — 17/10

Attendance 16,707 · Pos 10 (11) · HT 0-2 · **L** · FT 1-2 · Pts 16

Scorers: Whitton 80 — Hall 27, Harford 29

Baker	Whelan^	Thompson	Stockwell	Wark	Linighan	Williams	Goddard*	Johnson	Dozzell	Whitton/Palmer
Hitchcock	*Hall*	*Sinclair*	*Townsend*	*Lee*	*Donaghy*	*Stuart**	*Fleck*	*Harford*	*Newton*	*Wise / LeSaux*

Ref: B Hill

Ian Porterfield's side take the lead in a breakaway raid when Hall cuts in and fires in. Just two minutes later Harford nets Fleck's flick after a Wise free-kick. Town look dead and buried until sub Whitton sparks a late rally, heading in on his first appearance since surgery on his knee.

13 — H CRYSTAL PALACE — 24/10

Attendance 17,861 · Pos 11 (18) · HT 0-0 · **D** · FT 2-2 · Pts 17

Scorers: Dozzell 72, 84 — Armstrong 60, Coleman 75

Baker	Johnson	Thompson	Stockwell	Wark	Linighan	Williams	Goddard*	Whitton	Dozzell	Kiwomya/Gregory
Martyn	*Shaw*	*Sinnott*	*Southgate*	*Young*	*Osborn*	*Williams*	*Coleman*	*Armstrong*	*Salako*	*McGoldrick*

Ref: G Ashby

Twice Town fall behind and Dozzell comes to the rescue. His first is a glorious header, the second after a well-timed run. Both sides miss from the spot, Southgate's going wide and Whitton's saved. Whelan is rested after hearing before the game that a family friend has been murdered.

14 — A NOTT'M FOREST — 31/10

Attendance 21,411 · Pos 8 (22) · HT 1-0 · **W** · FT 1-0 · Pts 20

Scorers: Dozzell 6

Baker	Whelan	Thompson	Stockwell	Wark	Linighan	Williams	Palmer	Johnson*	Dozzell	Gregory
Crossley	*Laws*	*Pearce*	*Keane*	*Tyler*	*Orlygsson**	*Crosby*	*Gemmill*	*Clough*	*Glover*	*Black / Bannister*

Ref: M Bodenham

McGiven goes for a five-man defence against Brian Clough's strugglers. Williams sends Stockwell streaking down the left and his cross is headed back by Palmer for Dozzell to score. Forest's best chance sees Orlygsson get clean through but Baker reacts quickly to save superbly.

15 — H SOUTHAMPTON — 7/11

Attendance 15,722 · Pos 9 (19) · HT 0-0 · **D** · FT 0-0 · Pts 21

Baker	Johnson	Thompson	Stockwell	Wark	Linighan	Williams	Palmer*	Whitton	Dozzell	Kiwomya/Goddard
Flowers	*Kenna*	*Adams*	*Hurlock*	*Hall*	*Monkou*	*LeTissier*	*Cockerill*	*Dowie*	*Maddison*	*Benali*

Ref: R Dilkes

Local lad Richard Hall, once rejected by Town, has a nervous game in front of many friends and family. Stockwell clears off the line from Dowie and Town go close as Goddard's late header rolls just wide. After the previous year's big loss, the Board announces a profit of £29,614.

16 — A SHEFFIELD WED — 21/11

Attendance 24,270 · Pos 10 (14) · HT 0-1 · **D** · FT 1-1 · Pts 22

Scorers: Kiwomya 74 — Thompson 16 (og)

Baker	Whelan	Thompson	Stockwell	Johnson	Linighan	Williams	Goddard	Palmer	Dozzell	Kiwomya
Woods	*Nilsson*	*Worthington*	*Palmer*	*Pearson*	*Warhurst**	*Wilson*	*Waddle*	*Hirst*	*Bright*	*Sheridan / Bart-Williams*

Ref: K Barrett

Trevor Francis's men go ahead when Worthington's free-kick is glanced into his own net by Thompson. Waddle looks threatening, but Town hit back when Kiwomya speeds clear, rounds Pearson and Woods and nets a cheeky goal. Concussed Williams loses a contact lens, but plays on.

17 — H EVERTON — 28/11

Attendance 18,034 · Pos 10 (19) · HT 0-0 · **W** · FT 1-0 · Pts 25

Scorers: Johnson 72

Baker	Whelan*	Thompson	Stockwell	Johnson	Linighan	Williams	Goddard	Whitton^	Dozzell	Kiwomya/Palmer
Southall	*Harper*	*Ablett*	*Snodin**	*Watson*	*Keown*	*Kenny*	*Beardsley*	*Barlow*	*Cottee^*	*Hinchcliffe / Rideout/Warzycha*

Ref: B Hill

Watched by the two new signings from Sporting Lisbon, Town allow Cottee and Barlow early chances which they spurn. Williams is tireless in midfield and earns man-of-the-match accolades. Town earn the points when Stockwell's cross is flicked on by Dozzell to scorer Johnson.

18 — A COVENTRY — 5/12

Attendance 11,294 · Pos 8 (11) · HT 1-1 · **D** · FT 2-2 · Pts 26

Scorers: Kiwomya 13, Whitton 70p — Gallagher 16, Quinn 51

Baker	Whelan*	Thompson	Stockwell	Wark	Linighan	Johnson	Goddard*	Whitton	Dozzell	**Kiwomya Youds/Bozinoski**
Ogrizovic	*Borrows*	*Babb*	*Atherton*	*Pearce^*	*Ndlovu*	*Robson**	*Hurst*	*Rosario*	*Quinn*	*Gallagher / Williams J/McGrath*

Ref: K Hackett

A lively contest with Bobby Gould's men gets off to a great start, but Quinn sets up Gallacher to quickly level. Quinn powers the Sky Blues ahead but Kiwomya wins a penalty, given after Mr Hackett consults a linesman. Macedonia-born Bozinoski is given a brief debut.

19 — H MANCHESTER C — 12/12

Attendance 16,833 · Pos 6 (11) · HT 0-1 · **W** · FT 3-1 · Pts 29

Scorers: Stockwell 58, Johnson 62, Goddard 88 — Flitcroft 37

Baker	Whelan	Thompson	Stockwell	Wark	Linighan	Johnson	Goddard*	Whitton^	Dozzell	**Guentchev*** Youds
Coton	*Brightwell*	*Phelan*	*McMahon*	*Curle*	*Hill**	*White*	*Reid*	*Quinn*	*Flitcroft*	*Holden / Sheron*

Ref: R Lewis

Williams is injured and Stockwell has flu, but Town hit back after falling behind. Coton parries Thompson's cross to Stockwell who heads in. Quinn heads off the line, but Johnson heads it straight back in from 18 yards. Whitton nods a cross down to Goddard who thrashes the clincher.

20 — A NORWICH — 21/12

Attendance 20,032 · Pos 6 (1) · HT 0-0 · **W** · FT 2-0 · Pts 32

Scorers: Kiwomya 52, Thompson 88

Baker	Johnson	Thompson	Stockwell	Wark	Linighan	Williams	Goddard*	Whitton	Dozzell	Kiwomya/Whelan
Gunn	*Culverhouse*	*Bowen*	*Butterworth*/Polston*	*Sutch*	*Megson*	*Beckford^*	*Robins*	*Fox*	*Phillips*	*Newman/Sutton*

Ref: D Elleray

Kiwomya nods in from close range after Thompson's corner. Dozzell and Whitton set up Thompson to score from a tight angle. Live cameras are present for a win Town fans have waited seven years for. After the second, Dozzell's half-brother Tony invades the pitch and is arrested!

21 — A ARSENAL — 26/12

Attendance 26,198 · Pos 6 (8) · HT 0-0 · **D** · FT 0-0 · Pts 33

Baker	Johnson	Thompson	Stockwell	Wark	Linighan D	Williams	Goddard*	Whitton^	Dozzell	Kiwomya/Whelan/Guentchev
Seaman	*Lydersen*	*Winterburn*	*Bould*	*Linighan A*	*Jensen^*	*Smith*	*Wright*	*Campbell**	*Flatts*	*Limpar/O'Leary*

Ref: R Milford

The PFA raises objections to new-boy Guentchev's work permit being granted, as they believe his claim of 12 full caps for Bulgaria is bogus. Bontcho then makes a few more enemies by falling theatrically under Winterburn's challenge. Baker is Town's hero in this one-sided affair.

FA PREMIER LEAGUE — SEASON 1992-93

Manager: Mick McGiven

Player cells are given as **Ipswich Town player / opponent player**. In the *Pos* column the first figure is Ipswich's league position and the figure in brackets is the opponents'.

No	Date	Fixture	Att	Pos	Res	F-A	H-T	Pt	Scorers, Times, and Referees
22	28/12	H BLACKBURN	21,431	5 (4)	W	2-1	0-0	36	Guentchev 80, Kiwomya 82 / Wegerle 73 · Ref: A Gunn
23	9/1	H OLDHAM	15,025	5 (18)	L	1-2	0-1	36	Kiwomya 60 / Brennan 16, Bernard 51 · Ref: K Redfern
24	16/1	A SHEFFIELD UTD	16,758	5 (19)	L	0-3	0-1	36	Deane 31, 72, 75 · Ref: D Allison
25	27/1	A TOTTENHAM	23,738	6 (15)	W	2-0	0-0	39	Yallop 47, Guentchev 80 · Ref: S Lodge
26	30/1	H MANCHESTER U	22,068	4 (2)	W	2-1	1-0	42	Kiwomya 21, Yallop 47 / McClair 84 · Ref: J Key
27	6/2	A ASTON VILLA	25,395	5 (2)	L	0-2	0-2	42	Yorke 33, Saunders 42 · Ref: P Durkin
28	9/2	H QP RANGERS	17,354	5 (8)	D	1-1	1-0	43	Thompson 40 / White 80 · Ref: R Milford
29	20/2	A LIVERPOOL	36,680	6 (15)	D	0-0	0-0	44	Ref: A Gunn
30	27/2	A LEEDS	28,848	7 (16)	L	0-1	0-0	44	Dorigo 71p · Ref: M Reed
31	2/3	H MIDDLESBROUGH	15,430	7 (20)	L	0-1	0-1	44	Wilkinson 35 · Ref: K Barett

Line-ups (Ipswich Town / opponent)

No	1	2	3	4	5	6	7	8	9	10	11	subs used
22	Baker / Mimms	Johnson / May	Thompson / Wright	Stockwell / Atkins	Wark / Hendry	Linighan / Marker	Williams / Sherwood	Guentchev / Cowans	Whitton / Wegerle	Dozzell / Newell	Kiwomya / Wilcox*	Ripley
23	Baker / Gerrard	Johnson / Halle	Thompson* / Barlow	Stockwell / Bernard	Wark / Jobson	Linighan / Fleming	Williams / Henry	Guentchev / Marshall^	Whitton / Olney	Dozzell / Milligan	Kiwomya / Brennan^	Goddard / Sharp/Redmond
24	Baker / Kelly	Johnson* / Gage	Thompson / Barnes	Stockwell^ / Hoyland	Wark / Gayle	Linighan / Beasley	Yallop / Kamara	Guentchev / Carr	Whitton / Cork*	Dozzell / Deane	Kiwomya / Hodges	Youds/Bozinoski / Bryson
25	Baker / Thorstvedt	Johnson / Austin	Thompson / Edinburgh	Williams / Samways	Whelan / Mabbutt	Linighan / Ruddock	Yallop / Nayim	Guentchev / Durie*	Bozinoski / Anderton	Dozzell / Sheringham	Kiwomya / Allen	Howells
26	Baker / Schmeichel	Johnson / Irwin	Thompson / Parker	Williams / Bruce	Whelan / Sharpe*	Linighan* / Pallister	Yallop / Cantona	Guentchev* / McClair	Bosinoski^ / Hughes	Dozzell / Giggs	Kiwomya / Ince	Stockwell/Wark / Kanchelskis
27	Baker / Bosnich	Whelan / Barrett	Thompson / Staunton	Stockwell / Teale	Wark / McGrath	Linighan* / Richardson	Williams / Yorke^	Guentchev / Parker	Whitton / Houghton	Dozzell / Saunders	Kiwomya* / Froggatt*	Johnson / Cox/Beinlich
28	Baker / Roberts	Johnson / Bardsley	Thompson / Brevett	Stockwell / Doyle^	Wark / Maddix	Linighan / McDonald	Williams / Wilson	Guentchev / Impey*	Whitton / Ferdinand	Dozzell / Allen B	Kiwomya* / Sinton	Bozinoski / Peacock/White
29	Baker / James	Johnson / Redknapp	Stockwell / Nicol	Wark / Bjornbye^	Linighan / Wright	Williams / Wright	— / McManaman	Guentchev / Hutchison*	Whitton / Rush	Dozzell / Barnes	Kiwomya / Stewart	Walters/Marsh
30	Baker / Lukic	Johnson / Newsome	Thompson / Dorigo	Stockwell / Batty	Wark / Fairclough	Linighan / Wetherall	Williams / Strachan	Guentchev* / Wallace Rod	Whitton / Strandli^	Dozzell / Wallace Ray	Kiwomya / Speed	Goddard / Chapman
31	Baker / Ironside	Yallop^ / Phillips	Thompson / Morris	Stockwell / Kernaghan	Wark / Whyte	Linighan / Peake	Williams / Hendrie	Guentchev / Kamara^	Whitton / Wilkinson	Bozinoski* / Wright	Kiwomya / Mustoe	Goddard/Whelan / Falconer

Match reports

22 Wegerle's excellent strike puts Rovers ahead but Town respond in a thrilling finale. Guentchev has won over the home fans with some neat touches and he conjures up a brilliant overhead kick to Kiwomya who lobs home a winner.

23 Inevitably former Town favourite Brennan gets on the scoresheet, netting the rebound after his fierce drive hits Baker's shoulder. Joe Royle's strugglers clinch a surprise first away victory – and Town's first home defeat – when Bernard nets. Their defence weathers a late Ipswich storm.

24 Town are hampered by a nasty knee injury to Stockwell. Dave Bassett's side are again grateful to Brian Deane who has ended a goal drought in style. After destroying Burnley in the cup, he sinks Town with his second hat-trick in five days, netting two headers and a low shot past Baker.

25 Stockwell's replacement Yallop nets his first goal in four years when his 30-yard drive rockets in off the underside of the bar. Ossie Ardiles' side look off-colour and their expensive forwards fire blanks. Guentchev's crisp shot, after a strong run and cross by Thompson, seals the win.

26 Kiwomya chases Guentchev's pass as Schmeichel gallops out but completely misses his kick, allowing an easy goal. Yallop crashes in his second rocket in four days. McClair nets from close range, then Baker denies Hughes with a wonder save. United are dislodged from top spot.

27 Town suffer a blow when Linighan departs early with a twisted ankle. Staunton goes on the overlap and crosses for Yorke to net a fine diving header. Saunders spots Baker off his line and belts in a magnificent shot from 30 yards. Villa finally beat Town at the fourth attempt this term.

28 Thompson blasts a typical pile-driver goalwards and the ball swerves and goes through poor Roberts' legs. Town relax after this and pay the price. Gerry Francis' outfit pinch a point when Bardsley's free kick is shipped to Devon White, who is unmarked as he forces it over the line.

29 No goals, no bookings and precious little entertainment at Anfield. Reds' boss Graeme Souness praises Town's stout defending. The clearest chance falls to Barnes, who steers the ball wide. Midfielder Glenn Pennyfather moves to Bristol C (now managed by Russell Osman) on loan.

30 On a bitterly cold day, both sides are in cautious mood and produce a sterile game. Stockwell brings down Batty with a reckless challenge and Dorigo tucks in the penalty, low to Baker's left. Leeds boss Howard Wilkinson says he hopes he can soon start employing less negative tactics.

31 Wright's free-kick to the far post sees Wilkinson escape his marker to head in. The only excitement for the home crowd comes when Yallop dispossesses the lively Hendrie in full flight and sets off on a 50-yard solo run, ultimately to no avail. Town are jeered off by the fed-up fans.

Ipswich Town — Match-by-match (games 32–42)

No	Venue	Opponent	Date	Attendance	Pos	Result	Score	Pts	H/T
32	H	SHEFFIELD WED	10/3	16,538	10	L	0-1	44	0-0
33	A	SOUTHAMPTON	13/3	15,428	11	L	3-4	44	2-1
34	H	COVENTRY	20/3	16,698	14	D	0-0	45	0-0
35	A	EVERTON	24/3	15,638	14	L	0-3	45	0-1
36	A	MANCHESTER C	3/4	20,680	16	L	1-3	45	1-0
37	H	CHELSEA	6/4	17,444	16	D	1-1	46	1-0
38	H	ARSENAL	10/4	20,358	17	L	1-2	46	1-1
39	A	BLACKBURN	12/4	14,071	17	L	1-2	46	0-2
40	H	NORWICH	19/4	21,081	16	W	3-1	49	1-1
41	A	CRYSTAL PALACE	1/5	18,881	17	L	1-3	49	1-2
42	H	NOTT'M FOREST	8/5	22,093	16	W	2-1	52	1-0

Home Average 18,223   Away 20,553

---

32 — SHEFFIELD WED (H) 0-1
Scorers: Hirst 55.   Ref: T Ward
Town: Baker, Johnson, Youds^, Stockwell, Wark, Linighan, Whelan*, Guentchev, Whitton, Dozzell, Kiwomya, Goddard/Pennyfath'r
Sheff Wed: Woods, King^, Worthington, Stewart, Watts, Anderson, Hyde, Jenson, Hirst*, Bright, Sheridan, Watson/Francis

A huge kick downfield by Woods finds Hirst on the right flank and he cuts in past Town to net a low drive. Woods has a fine game to keep Town at bay and player-boss Trevor Francis brings himself on to steady his ship. Another frustrating home defeat sees Town jeered off again.

33 — SOUTHAMPTON (A) 3-4
Scorers: Linighan 13, Goddard 35, Kiwomya 87 / Hall 18, LeTissier 65p, 89, Kenna 85.   Ref: D Elleray
Town: Baker, Johnson, Whelan, Stockwell, Wark, Linighan, Yallop, Guentchev, Goddard*, Dozzell, Kiwomya, Whitton
Southampton: Flowers, Kenna, Adams, Wild'gton*, Hall, Monkou, LeTissier, Banger, Dowie, Maddison, Dodd, Cockerill

More misery but a much better spectacle. Linighan beats the offside trap to net. Hall levels with a fine header. Goddard's persistence secures a second Town goal. Stockwell trips Maddison for a Saints penalty. Monkou hits the post and Le Tissier nets the rebound in a dramatic finale.

34 — COVENTRY (H) 0-0
Scorers: — .   Ref: J Worrall
Town: Baker, Johnson, Whelan, Stockwell, Wark, Linighan, Williams, Guentchev, Goddard*, Dozzell, Kiwomya, Whitton
Coventry: Ogrizovic, Borrows, Babb, Atherton, Busst, Williams J, Ndlovu, Rennie, Hurst, Quinn, Gallagher

Williams returns to stiffen the midfield, but two sides anxious not to get involved in the relegation battle provide dull fare. The losing run is ended, but this tedious game includes only rare moments of 'entertainment' – such as the ref's nose-bleed and Johnson shooting against a post.

35 — EVERTON (A) 0-3
Scorers: Barlow 18, Jackson 49, Cottee 66.   Ref: B Hill
Town: Baker, Johnson, Whelan*, Stockwell, Wark, Linighan, Williams, Guentchev, Goddard, Dozzell, Kiwomya, Youds
Everton: Southall, Holmes, Hinchcliffe, Snodin^, Watson, Jackson, Ward*, Beardsley, Ebrell, Cottee, Barlow, Rideout/Beagrie

Barlow lashes in a fierce drive to open the scoring. Ward's corner is flicked on to Jackson who shoots in from 10 yards. Cottee drives to head in a deep cross from Ward. Town are comprehensively beaten and a furious McGiven says the players let the fans down with this performance.

36 — MANCHESTER C (A) 1-3
Scorers: Johnson 2 / Quinn 55, Holden 66, Vonk 70.   Ref: R Gifford
Town: Baker, Whelan^, Johnson, Stockwell, Wark, Linighan, Williams, Guentchev, Milton*, Dozzell, Kiwomya, Goddard/Bozinski
Man City: Coton, Ranson, Phelan, Reid, Curle, Vonk, White*, Quinn, Sheron, Flitcroft, Holden, Ingebritsen

Johnson steers Kiwomya's pass past Coton to give Town a great start. Quinn levels after the break after a flick-on by Holden. Quinn returns the compliment, crossing for Holden to net from close-range. The points are out of Town's reach after Vonk converts a cross by the tricky Holden.

37 — CHELSEA (H) 1-1
Scorers: Guentchev 38 / Spencer 58.   Ref: J Lloyd
Town: Baker, Youds, Johnson, Stockwell, Wark, Linighan, Williams, Guentchev, Milton*, Dozzell, Kiwomya, Bozinski
Chelsea: Beasant, Clarke, Sinclair, Townsend, Johnson, Donaghy, Stuart, Spencer, Cascarino, Hall, Wise

Guentchev cracks in a rising drive after Dozzell's pass. Police speak to Chelsea boss David Webb at half-time after substitute Robert Fleck (a former foe from Norwich) gesticulates at Town fans while warming up behind the goal. Donaghy crosses and Spencer fires home the equaliser.

38 — ARSENAL (H) 1-2
Scorers: Wark 27p / Smith 2, Merson 87.   Ref: R Lewis
Town: Baker, Youds, Williams, Stockwell, Wark, Linighan D, Whitton, Guentchev, Milton, Dozzell, Kiwomya
Arsenal: Seaman, O'Leary*, Winterburn, Morrow, Keown, Linighan A, Jensen^, Merson, Smith, Campbell, Carter, Adams/Parlour

Winterburn's early cross is headed in off the bar by Smith. A questionable penalty allows Town to level. Keown hauls down Kiwomya for another spot-kick, but this time Seaman saves. A disputed late free-kick is curled in superbly by Merson and Town feel mightily aggrieved.

39 — BLACKBURN (A) 1-2
Scorers: Milton 68 / Ripley 6, Whelan 43 (og).   Ref: K Hackett
Town: Baker, Youds, Williams, Whelan, Linighan*, Whitton, Guentchev, Milton, Dozzell, Kiwomya, Bozinski
Blackburn: Mimms, May, LeSaux, Sherwood, Hendry, Moran, Ripley, Cowans, Gallacher, Newell, Wilcox

In front of live Sky viewers, Ripley heads firmly home from a Newell cross. Ripley drives the ball across Town's box and Whelan, attempting to hump it over the stand, blasts home a spectacular own-goal. Milton fires homes a superb 25-yarder. Intense Town pressure comes to nothing.

40 — NORWICH (H) 3-1
Scorers: Dozzell 21, 56, Stockwell 54 / Sutton 41.   Ref: R Milford
Town: Baker, Youds, Williams, Stockwell, Wark, Linighan, Whitton, Stockwell, Milton, Dozzell, Kiwomya
Norwich: Gunn, Culverhouse, Crook, Butterworth, Polston, Bowen, Goss, Robins, Sutton, Fox, Phillips

Town secure three points to ensure safety and extinguish City's outside hopes of the title in 90 joyous minutes! The first League win since January comes courtesy of two lethal finishes by Dozzell and the persistence of Stockwell. City hit the post twice as the 'Budgies' are silenced.

41 — CRYSTAL PALACE (A) 1-3
Scorers: Gregory 37 / Young 6, Armstrong 16, McG'drick 60.   Ref: P Don
Town: Baker, Gregory, Whelan, Stockwell, Wark, Linighan, Williams, Palmer^, Milton^, Dozzell, Kiwomya, Whitton/Guentchev
Crystal Palace: Martyn, Shaw, Coleman, Southgate, Young, Thorn, Humphrey, Thomas, Armstrong, Rodger, McGoldrick

Baker flaps at a corner and Young prods in the opening goal. Armstrong scores as he falls after a McGoldrick cross causes havoc. Gregory cracks a shot into the roof of Martyn's net. McGoldrick's first-time drive seals the points and gives Palace hope in the battle to avoid the drop.

42 — NOTT'M FOREST (H) 2-1
Scorers: Milton 40, Whitton 52p / Clough 64p.   Ref: M Reed
Town: Petterson, Youds, Johnson, Stockwell, Wark, Linighan, Williams, Whitton*, Milton, Dozzell, Kiwomya, Palmer
Nott'm Forest: Marriott, Laws, Williams, Keane, Tyler, Chettle, Woan, Gemmill, Clough, Glover, Black*, Orhgsson/Phillips

Petterson debuts due to Baker's wrist injury. Milton converts Dozzell's pass and Whitton nets from the spot after Kiwomya is pushed. Handball by Williams gives Clough Jnr a spot-kick. His father waves an emotional goodbye as his celebrated managerial career is brought to an end.

FA PREMIER LEAGUE (CUP-TIES)

Manager: Mick McGiven   SEASON 1992-93

Coca-Cola Cup

Rnd		Opp / Date	Att	F-A	H-T	1	2	3	4	5	6	7	8	9	10	11	subs used
2:1	A	WIGAN 22/9	2,684	D 2-2	1-0	Forrest	Whelan	Thompson	Stockwell	Wark	Linighan	Youds	Pennyfather	Johnson	Dozzell	Kiwomya	Worthington
		(Wigan)	*2:22*			*Adkins*	*Parkinson*	*Tankard*	*Johnson*	*Doolan*	*Langley**	*Jones*	*Robertson*	*Daley*	*Powell**	*Griffiths*	*Worthington*

2:1 Scorers: Johnson 1, Robertson 72 (og) / *Johnson 47, Worthington 90*. Ref: M Peck
A fine move puts Town ahead after 85 seconds. After this, Bryan Hamilton's men show more passion and Town's passing is poor. Johnson is left unmarked for the equaliser but Robertson slices the ball into his own net and Town are back ahead. Worthington nets Tankard's late cross.

Rnd		Opp / Date	Att	F-A	H-T	1	2	3	4	5	6	7	8	9	10	11	subs used
2:2	H	WIGAN 6/10	7,305	W 4-0	2-0	Forrest	Whelan*	Thompson	Stockwell	Wark	Linighan	Williams	Goddard	Johnson	Dozzell	Kiwomya	Worthington/Wilson Youds
		(Wigan)	*2:19*			*Adkins*	*Parkinson^*	*Tankard*	*Johnson*	*Doolan*	*Langley*	*Jones*	*Robertson*	*Daley*	*Powell**	*Griffiths*	*Griffiths*

2:2 Scorers: Johnson 6, Kiwomya 25, 71, 86. Ref: A Ward
(Town win 6-2 on aggregate)
A clinical destruction of the Second Division Latics, who are terrorised by the speedy Kiwomya. His first comes after Thompson's long-throw. Victory is assured with his second when he bursts clear and beats Adkins with a neat finish. He heads in Wark's pass for a first senior hat-trick.

Rnd		Opp / Date	Att	F-A	H-T	1	2	3	4	5	6	7	8	9	10	11	subs used
3	A	PORTSMOUTH 27/10	10,773	W 1-0	1-0	Baker	Johnson	Thompson	Stockwell	Wark	Linighan	Williams	Goddard*	Whitton	Dozzell	Kiwomya	Gregory
		(Portsmouth)	*1:9*			*Knight*	*Awford*	*Daniel*	*McLoughlin*	*Symons*	*Aspinall**	*Neill*	*Chamberlain*	*Clarke*	*Whittingham*	*Maguire*	*Walsh*

3 Scorers: Thompson 6. Ref: R Milford
Kiwomya is tripped by Symons and Thompson blasts home the free-kick from 30 yards. Town dominate for 20 minutes, but after this Pompey get into the game and besiege Baker's goal. Wark is a rock in his 550th Town game. The unbeaten Fratton Park run now stretches to 25 years.

Rnd		Opp / Date	Att	F-A	H-T	1	2	3	4	5	6	7	8	9	10	11	subs used
4	A	ASTON VILLA 2/12	21,545	D 2-2	0-0	Baker	Whelan	Thompson	Stockwell	Wark	Linighan	Johnson	Goddard*	Whitton	Dozzell	Kiwomya	Youds
		(Aston Villa)	*4*			*Spink*	*Barrett*	*Staunton*	*Ethiou*	*McGrath*	*Richardson*	*Houghton^*	*Parker**	*Saunders*	*Atkinson*	*Small*	*Cox/Regis*

4 Scorers: Kiwomya 74, 83 / *Atkinson 65, Saunders 77*. Ref: J Martin
After doing little for an hour, Town old boy Atkinson heads in the opener. Kiwomya fires in from 10 yards on his 23rd birthday. Atkinson's fine ball sets up Saunders. Town abandon their sweeper system and pour forward. Kiwomya volleys home a loose clearance from 25 yards.

Rnd		Opp / Date	Att	F-A	H-T	1	2	3	4	5	6	7	8	9	10	11	subs used
4R	H	ASTON VILLA 15/12	19,196	W 1-0	0-0	Baker	Whelan	Thompson	Stockwell	Wark	Linighan	Johnson	Goddard*	Whitton	Dozzell	Kiwomya	Williams
		(Aston Villa)	*2*			*Spink*	*Barrett*	*Staunton*	*Teale*	*McGrath*	*Richardson*	*Houghton*	*Parker**	*Saunders*	*Regis**	*Cox*	*Yorke/Beitkreutz*

4R Scorers: Kiwomya 57. Ref: M James
The sides are deadlocked until Thompson drives the ball into the Villa area and Dozzell heads on for Kiwomya to flick past Spink. Dangerman Atkinson is absent, but the visitors exert late pressure, finding Baker in fine form in goal. Villa slip to only their second defeat in 17 games.

Rnd		Opp / Date	Att	F-A	H-T	1	2	3	4	5	6	7	8	9	10	11	subs used
QF	H	SHEFFIELD WED 19/1	19,374	D 1-1	0-0	Baker	Johnson^	Thompson	Williams	Wark	Linighan	Yallop*	Guentchev	Whitton	Dozzell	Kiwomya	Whelan/Bozinoski
		(Sheffield Wed)	*10*			*Woods*	*Warhurst*	*Worthington*	*Harkes*	*Palmer*	*Shirtliff*	*Wilson*	*Waddle*	*Hirst**	*Bright*	*Sheridan*	*Bart-Williams*

QF Scorers: Whitton 83p / *Sheridan 49*. Ref: T Holbrook
Kiwomya is brought down but no penalty is given. Trevor Francis' side take the lead when Sheridan dives to head in at the far post. With time running out Town level after Guentchev is floored by Shirtliff. Mr Holbrook is unmoved by the visitors' accusations that the Bulgarian dived.

Rnd		Opp / Date	Att	F-A	H-T	1	2	3	4	5	6	7	8	9	10	11	subs used
QF R	A	SHEFFIELD WED 3/2	26,328	L 0-1	0-0	Baker	Woods	Thompson	Williams	Whelan	Linighan	Yallop	Guentchev*	Bozinoski^	Dozzell	Kiwomya	Stockwell/Wark
		(Sheffield Wed)	*9*			*Woods*	*Nilsson*	*Worthington*	*Harkes*	*Pearson*	*Shirtliff*	*Wilson*	*Waddle*	*Warhurst*	*B't-Will'ms**	*Sheridan*	*Pearson*

QF R Scorers: / *Warhurst 53*. Ref: V Callow
Town defend in depth in this tense replay, but fall behind after half-time. Nilsson's probing pass sees Warhurst burst through and tuck the ball past Baker. McGiven makes a double substituion and Town push forward in numbers. Wednesday survive the late pounding and Town are out.

FA Cup

Rnd		Opp / Date	Att	F-A	H-T	1	2	3	4	5	6	7	8	9	10	11	subs used
3	H	PLYMOUTH 12/1	12,803	W 3-1	1-1	Baker	Johnson	Thompson	Stockwell	Wark*	Whelan	Williams	Guentchev	Whitton	Dozzell	Kiwomya	Youds
		(Plymouth)	*2:14*			*Shilton*	*McCall*	*Morgan*	*Hill*	*Morrison*	*Joyce*	*Skinner**	*Castle*	*Nugent*	*Evans*	*Dalton*	*Marshall*

FAC 3 Scorers: Thompson 6, Dozzell 70, Whitton 86p / *Castle 32*. Ref: M Reed
A typical Thompson pile-driver gives Town an early lead, but Castle levels with a smart free-kick. Dozzell heads in Guentchev's cross. Whitton ensures victory with a penalty, sending player-manager Shilton the wrong way after former Town stalwart McCall trips lively Kiwomya.

Rnd		Opp / Date	Att	F-A	H-T	1	2	3	4	5	6	7	8	9	10	11	subs used
4	A	TRANMERE 23/1	13,683	W 2-1	0-1	Baker	Johnson	Thompson	Williams	Wark	Linighan	Yallop	Guentchev*	Whitton	Dozzell	Kiwomya	Whelan
		(Tranmere)	*1:2*			*Nixon*	*Higgins*	*Nolan*	*Irons*	*Mungall**	*Vickers*	*Morrissey*	*McNab*	*Makin*	*Muir^*	*Nevin*	*Hughes/Martindale*

FAC 4 Scorers: Dozzell 68, Guentchev 77 / *Nevin 17*. Ref: K Cooper
John King's promotion-chasers are quoted as favourites. Nevin caps a lively opening spell, firing home after Morrissey's header is deflected to him by Wark. Whitton sets up a fierce Dozzell drive for the equaliser. Kiwomya rounds Nixon, hits a post and Guentchev nets an easy winner.

5 H GRIMSBY^ — 13/2 — 17,894 — 1:7 — 5 W 5 — 4-0 — 1-0 — Guentchev 29, 73, 90, Wark 59 — Ref: V Callow

QF H ARSENAL — 6/3 — 22,054 — 12 — 7 L 12 — 2-4 — 1-1 — Kiwomya 16, G'chev 77 [Campbell 89], Wark 59
Adams 29, Wright 61p, Whelan 72 (og), Seaman — Ref: A Wilkie

Line-ups (top grid)

Match 5 (Grimsby):
Williams · Linighan · Wark · Thompson · Stockwell · Linighan · Johnson* · Guentchev · Dozzell · Goddard · Yallop/Bozinoski
Childs^ · Dobbin · Rodger · Futcher · Dickov · McDermott Agnew · Gilbert · Mendonca · Rees* · Croft/Smith

Match QF (Arsenal):
Baker · Williams · Carter* · Wark · Thompson* · Stockwell · Linighan · Johnson · Guentchev · Dozzell · Goddard · Kiwomya
Wilmot · Winterburn · Dixon · Linighan · Adams · Seaman · Wright · Smith^ · Merson · Morrow · Hillier/Campbell

Dozzell squares to Guentchev who nets a rising drive. Wark arrives late to head in a corner. Alan Buckley's men are finished as Goddard sets up Guentchev to slip the ball home from an angle. The Bulgarian completes his hat-trick as Thompson's shot rebounds to him off Wilmot's legs.
Kiwomya nets in a crowded goalmouth. Adams levels, heading in Merson's free-kick. Wark hauls down Wright, who nets the penalty. Wright and Whelan tussle and the latter toes the ball into his own net. Guentchev nets Stockwell's cross to give hope but Town are caught on the break.

	P	Home					Away					Pts
		W	D	L	F	A	W	D	L	F	A	
1 Manchester U	42	14	5	2	39	14	10	7	4	28	17	84
2 Aston Villa	42	13	5	3	36	16	8	6	7	21	24	74
3 Norwich	42	13	6	2	31	19	8	3	10	30	46	72
4 Blackburn	42	13	4	4	38	18	7	7	7	30	28	71
5 QP Rangers	42	11	5	5	41	32	6	7	8	22	23	63
6 Liverpool	42	13	4	4	41	18	3	7	11	21	37	59
7 Sheffield Wed	42	9	8	4	34	26	6	6	9	21	25	59
8 Tottenham	42	11	5	5	40	25	5	8	10	20	41	59
9 Manchester C	42	7	8	6	30	25	8	4	9	26	26	57
10 Arsenal	42	8	8	7	25	20	7	5	9	15	18	56
11 Chelsea	42	9	7	5	29	22	5	8	8	24	32	56
12 Wimbledon	42	9	4	8	32	23	5	5	11	24	34	54
13 Everton	42	7	6	8	26	27	8	4	9	27	28	53
14 Sheffield Utd	42	10	6	5	33	19	4	4	13	21	34	52
15 Coventry	42	7	4	10	29	28	6	9	6	23	29	52
16 IPSWICH	42	8	9	4	29	22	4	7	10	21	33	52
17 Leeds	42	12	8	1	40	17	0	7	14	17	45	51
18 Southampton	42	10	6	5	30	21	3	5	13	24	40	50
19 Oldham	42	10	6	5	43	30	3	4	14	20	44	49
20 Crys Palace	42	6	9	6	27	25	5	7	9	21	36	49
21 Middlesbro	42	8	5	8	33	27	3	6	12	21	48	44
22 Nott'm For	42	6	4	11	17	25	4	6	11	24	37	40
	924	214	132	118	723	499	118	132	214	499	723	1256

Appearances / Goals

	Appearances						Goals			
	Lge	Sub	LC	Sub	FAC	Sub	Lge	LC	FAC	Tot
Baker, Clive	30		5		4					
Bozinoski, Vlado	3	6	1	1		1				
Dozzell, Jason	41		7		4		7		2	9
Forrest, Craig	11		2							
Goddard, Paul	19	6	4		1	1	3			3
Gregory, David	1	2				1	1			1
Guentchev, Bontcho	19	2	2		4		3		5	8
Johnson, Gavin	39	1	7		4		5	2		7
Kiwomya, Chris	38		7		3		10	6	1	17
Linighan, David	42		7		3		1			1
Milton, Simon	7	5					2			2
Palmer, Steve	4	3								
Pennyfather, Glenn	2	2	1							
Petterson, Andy	1									
Stockwell, Mick	38	1	5	1	3		4			4
Thompson, Neil	31		7		4		3	1	1	5
Wark, John	36	1	6		4		6		1	7
Whelan, Phil	28	4	5	2	1	1				
Whitton, Steve	20	4	4		3		3	1	1	5
Williams, Geraint	37		4		4					
Yallop, Frank	5	1	2	1			2			2
Youds, Eddie	10	6	1		2	1	1			1
(own-goals)										
22 players used	462	45	77	8	44	5	50	11	11	72

Odds & ends

Double wins: (3) Norwich, Nott'm Forest, Wimbledon.
Double losses: (1) Oldham.
Won from behind: (3) Blackburn (h), Man City (h), Tranmere (FAC) (a).
Lost from in front: (3) Arsenal (h) (FAC), Man City (a), Southampton (a).
High spots: Helping launch new Premier League with eight unbeaten games.
Doing the 'double' over highly-placed local rivals Norwich.
Lengthy runs in both cup competitions.
Beating Norwich to end relegation fears and also end City's title hopes!
Two glorious goals in four days by Yallop – after four-year barren spell.
Toppling leaders Man Utd to end their long unbeaten run.
Low spots: The dreadful 10-week spell when Town slid from 4th to 17th.
Losing out in a thrilling FA Cup quarter-final with Arsenal.
Three awful home displays in March (v Boro, Coventry, Sheffield Wed).
Player of the Year: Mick Stockwell.
Ever-presents: (1) David Linighan (League only).
Hat-tricks: (2) Kiwomya (RC), Guentchev (FAC).
Opposing hat-tricks: (1) Deane (Sheff Utd) (a).
Leading scorer: (17) Chris Kiwomya.

FA CARLING PREMIERSHIP

Manager: Mick McGiven   SEASON 1993-94

No		Date	Att	Pos	Pt		F-A	H-T	Scorers, Times, and Referees
1	A OLDHAM	14/8	12,182	–	3	W	3-0	2-0	Marshall 41, Palmer 45, Mason 67 — Ref: K Barrett
2	H SOUTHAMPTON	17/8	14,958	–	6	W	1-0	0-0	Marshall 59 — Ref: A Wilkie
3	H CHELSEA	21/8	17,355	2	9	W	1-0	1-0	Marshall 33 — Ref: D Elleray
4	A NORWICH	25/8	18,976	5	9	L	0-1	0-1	Goss 30 — Ref: A Gunn
5	A SHEFFIELD UTD	28/8	17,932	6	10	D	1-1	0-1	Whitton 90 / Flo 26 — Ref: P Foakes
6	H NEWCASTLE	31/8	19,126	6	11	D	1-1	0-0	Kiwomya 78 / Cole 47 — Ref: D Gallagher
7	A ARSENAL	11/9	28,563	8	11	L	0-4	0-2	Wright 32, Campbell 40, 56, 64 — Ref: J Worrall
8	H ASTON VILLA	18/9	16,858	12	11	L	1-2	1-1	Marshall 10 / Saunders 19, Townsend 55 — Ref: R Dilkes
9	H TOTTENHAM	26/9	19,437	14	12	D	2-2	0-1	Milton 59, Marshall 69 / Sheringham 28, Dozzell 85 — Ref: G Ashby
10	A QP RANGERS	2/10	12,292	15	12	L	0-3	0-0	White 57, 62, Barker 65 — Ref: K Cooper

Squad numbers in use, subs used and match reports

1 — A OLDHAM
Town: Baker, Stockwell, Thompson, Mason, Wark, Linighan, Williams, Whelan, Palmer, Thompson*, Marshall. Sub used: Kiwomya
Oldham: Gerrard, Fleming, Pointon*, Henry, Jobson, Redmond, Halle, Ritchie^, Olney, Milligan, Bernard. Subs used: Adams/Sharp
A great start and the first time in 54 years two Town debutants have scored in the same game. Marshall – a record £750k buy from Oldham five days earlier – poaches a goal after Baker's huge kick. Palmer nets a stunning 20-yarder and new man Mason dribbles round Gerrard to score.

2 — H SOUTHAMPTON
Town: Baker, Stockwell, Thompson, Mason, Wark, Linighan, Williams, Whelan, Palmer, Thompson, Marshall. Sub used: Guentchev
Southampton: Flowers, Kenna, Adams, Widrington'n*, Hall, Monkou, Le Tissier, Cockerill, Dowie, Maddison, Benali. Subs used: Banger
Wark hits the post but minutes later Town surge ahead. Williams' volley is turned away for a corner by Flowers, and Thompson's flag-kick is headed in off the near post by Marshall. Baker makes an acrobatic late save from Banger. Delighted Town fans sing 'We are top of the league!'

3 — H CHELSEA
Town: Baker, Stockwell, Thompson, Mason^, Wark, Linighan, Williams, Fleck*, Palmer, Marshall^. Subs used: Guentchev/Whitton
Chelsea: Kharine, Clarke, Myers, Kjelberg, Johnsen, Donaghy^, Hoddle, Cascarino, Peacock, Wise. Subs used: Lee/Newton
A clash of heads leaves man-of-the-moment Marshall dazed, but he recovers and four minutes later scores. Palmer's pass finds him in space and he produces a confident finish. Kharine makes a brilliant save from Stockwell. Sub Guentchev goes close near the end with a fierce drive.

4 — A NORWICH
Town: Baker, Stockwell, Thompson, Whelan^, Wark, Linighan, Williams, Guentchev*/Whitton, Whitton, Palmer. Subs used: Milton/Yallop
Norwich: Gunn, Culverhouse, Bowen, Butterworth, Polston, Goss, Crook, Newman, Robins, Fox, Sutton.
300 minutes without conceding a goal is rudely interrupted when Robins goes on a run and sets up Goss, whose finish is clinical. Williams nets after the break, but the strike is disallowed for offside. Robins strikes Baker's crossbar and the ex-Norwich keeper makes several superb saves.

5 — A SHEFFIELD UTD
Town: Forrest, Stockwell, Thompson, Yallop^, Wark, Linighan, Williams, Palmer, Whitton, Whitton. Subs used: Guentchev/Milton
Sheffield Utd: Kelly, Gage^, Beesley, Falconer, Wirmola, Pemberton, Bradshaw, Kamara, Flo, Scott*. Subs used: Ward/Cork
Baker is surprisingly dropped for 'tactical reasons'. Scott's header is parried by Forrest and Flo squeezes the rebound in. Unlucky Whitton goes close to a leveller three times and hits the bar on 51 minutes. He finally succeeds in the last minute, heading in Milton's cross at the near post.

6 — H NEWCASTLE
Town: Forrest, Stockwell, Thompson, Palmer*, Wark, Linighan, Williams, Milton, Whitton, Goddard*. Subs used: Guentchev/Yallop
Newcastle: Srnicek, Venison, Bracewell, Beresford, Scott, Watson, Lee, Allen, Cole, Clark^. Subs used: Papavasi'u^/O'Brien/Neilson
Impatient Town fans jeer the side off the field after a goalless first half. Town fall behind when a fine move leads to Cole cracking home a sweet shot. Watson tackles Guentchev and the ball runs free to Kiwomya who levels. Town were generally outplayed, but look better late on.

7 — A ARSENAL
Town: Forrest, Stockwell, Thompson, Palmer, Wark, Linighan, Williams, Whelan, Whitton, Goddard. Subs used: Kiwomya
Arsenal: Seaman, Keown, Winterburn, Davis, Linighan, Adams, Jensen*, Wright, Campbell, Merson^. Subs used: McGoldrick/Hillier/Limpar
Wright guides home a beauty after Campbell's pass and the floodlights open. Wright chips against the bar and Campbell converts the rebound. Campbell heads the third from Winterburn's cross. Wright is tormenting Town and his clever play sends Campbell clean through for the fourth.

8 — H ASTON VILLA
Town: Forrest, Stockwell, Thompson, Mason^, Wark, Linighan, Williams, Whelan, Palmer*, Marshall. Subs used: Guentchev/Whitton
Aston Villa: Spink, Barrett, Staunton, Teale, McGrath, Richardson, Cowans, Townsend, Saunders, Atkinson^. Subs used: Whiting'm*/Houghton/Daley
Marshall is back from injury – and how! He smashes home early on after his first effort is blocked by Spink. It's downhill from here though, and Saunders lets fly with a fine shot after Staunton's pass. Marshall hits a post before Villa win it when Townsend crashes in a real beauty.

9 — H TOTTENHAM
Town: Forrest, Stockwell, Thompson, Mason, Wark, Linighan, Williams, Whitton, Whitton, Milton, Marshall. Subs used: Kiwomya
Tottenham: Thorstvedt, Carr*, Campbell, Samways, Calderw'd/Mabbutt, Sedgley, Durie, Dozzell, Sheringham^. Subs used: Sheringham/Anderton/Caskey
Sheringham deftly glances in Anderton's cross. Milton levels, sliding in to convert Stockwell's cross. Calderwood is red-carded on 65 minutes for two bookable offences. Milton sets up another Marshall goal, but ex-Town hero Dozzell pops up near the end to snatch the points away.

10 — A QP RANGERS
Town: Forrest, Stockwell, Thompson, Mason, Wark, Linighan, Williams, Slater, Milton, Marshall. Subs used: Kiwomya
QP Rangers: Stejskal, Bardsley, Wilson, Wilkins, Peacock, McDonald, Impey, Barker, Allen, White, Sinclair*. Subs used: Brevett
Born and raised in Suffolk, Stuart Slater arrives for a record £800,000 from Celtic. It's an unhappy debut as White whips in Allen's pin-point cross. White heads in Bardsley's cross after a fine eight-man move. The second-half hammering is completed as Barker heads in Wilkins' pass.

No		Fixture	Date	Att.				Res	Score	HT
11	H	LEEDS	17/10	17,532	16	*3*	13		0-0	0-0
12	A	WIMBLEDON	25/10	7,756	13	*10*	16	W	2-0	0-0
13	H	EVERTON	30/10	15,094	14	*11*	16	L	0-2	0-1
14	H	SHEFFIELD WED	6/11	14,767	14	*17*	16	L	1-4	0-1
15	A	SWINDON	20/11	13,860	15	*22*	17	D	2-2	1-1
16	A	MANCHESTER U	24/11	43,300	15	*1*	18	D	0-0	0-0
17	H	BLACKBURN	27/11	14,436	13	*5*	21	W	1-0	1-0
18	H	OLDHAM	4/12	11,789	16	*19*	22	D	0-0	0-0
19	A	SOUTHAMPTON	8/12	9,028	11	*21*	25	W	1-0	0-0
20	A	CHELSEA	11/12	13,208	12	*20*	26	D	1-1	0-1
21	H	NORWICH	18/12	19,571	10	*6*	29	W	2-1	1-1

11 — H LEEDS, 17/10

Ipswich: Forrest, Stockwell, Thompson, Mason, Wark, Linighan, Whelan, Slater, Palmer, Milton*, Kiwomya — *Whitton*

Leeds: *Beeney, Kelly, Wetherall, Dorigo, Fairclough, Newsome, Rocastle*, Wallace, Rod Deane, McAllister, Speed — Strandli*

Ref: M Bodenham

The fans are getting restless, but at least in-form Leeds are stopped in their tracks. Milton twice goes close, bringing a superb flying save from Beeney. The keeper also blocks a Whelan diving header. Midfielder Slater confesses afterwards he was surprised to be asked to play in attack.

12 — A WIMBLEDON, 25/10 — Mason 72, Stockwell 81

Ipswich: Forrest, Stockwell, Thompson, Mason, Wark, Linighan, Williams*, Slater, Marshall, Milton*, Kiwomya^ — *Palmer/Milton*

Wimbledon: *Segers, Fear, Fitzgerald, McAllister, Kimble, Ardley*, Earle, Sanchez, Jones, Blissett*, Holdsworth — Barton/Fashanu*

Ref: A Gunn

A third successive win over Joe Kinnear's side ends the winless run of eight league games. A rather uninspiring contest springs to life in the final 20 minutes. Paul Mason cracks home his first goal in League football and victory is assured when Stockwell bursts clear to beats Segers.

13 — H EVERTON, 30/10 — Barlow 13, Thompson 61(og)

Ipswich: Baker, Stockwell, Thompson, Mason, Wark*, Linighan*, Whitton^, Slater, Whitton, Milton*, Kiwomya — *Youds/Guentchev*

Everton: *Southall, Holmes, Hinchcliffe, Ebbrell, Watson, Abbett, Ward, Horne, Cottee, Barlow, Beagrie* — Snodin*

Ref: V Callow

Barlow seizes on Ward's pass and chips over Baker. Linighan fails to re-appear after a half-time dressing-room bust-up with the team manager. Beagrie's header is deflected in by Thompson. Before the match Kevin Beattie is awarded the Evening Star's best-ever ITFC player trophy.

14 — H SHEFFIELD WED, 6/11 — Marshall 84; Jemson 20, 50, Bright 54, Palmer 76

Ipswich: Baker, Stockwell, Thompson, Mason, Wark, Linighan, Whitton^, Slater, Marshall, Milton, Kiwomya — *Palmer/Youds*

Sheffield Wed: *Pressman, Nilsson, Worthington, Palmer, Pearce, Walker, Jones, Bright, Waddle, Jemson*, Snodin — Hyde*

Ref: V Callow

McGiven is absent following a car crash. Lyall makes a rare dug-out appearance and sees Town put in a dreadful display, and the home fans are not slow to let them know about it. Jemson scores for the first time in 22 months. Palmer bursts through to score a superb solo goal for 0-4.

15 — A SWINDON, 20/11 — Wark 17, 63p; Scott 45, Bodin 82p

Ipswich: Baker, Stockwell, Thompson, Youds, Wark, Linighan, Milton, Whelan, Palmer, Marshall, Kiwomya — *Kiwomya*

Swindon: *Digby, Summerbee*, Bodin, Nijholt, Whitbread, Taylor, Moncur, Mutch, Horlock, Scott, Fenwick — Ling*

Ref: R Dilkes

On his 600th appearance, Wark bangs home Milton's corner. Scott, making his Robins debut, heads in Fenwick's cross. Horlock brings down Kiwomya and Wark nets the spot-kick. John Gorman's strugglers save a point when Youds hauls down Ling and Bodin converts from the spot.

16 — A MANCHESTER U, 24/11

Ipswich: Forrest, Stockwell, Thompson, Mason*, Wark, Linighan, Youds, Whelan, Palmer, Marshall, Whelan — *Yallop*

Manchester U: *Schmeichel, Irwin, Parker, Bruce, Sharpe, Pallister, Cantona, Ince, Robson^, Hughes, Kanchelsk** — Giggs/Ferguson*

Ref: T Holbrook

A snowy night at Old Trafford sees Town battle hard to keep the leaders at bay. It's not a pretty sight, but coming away with a point is quite an achievement. Baker was unavailable due to flu and Forrest comes in to seize his opportunity, playing a blinder in the bitterly cold conditions.

17 — H BLACKBURN, 27/11 — Youds 40

Ipswich: Forrest, Stockwell, Thompson, Mason, Wark, Linighan, Youds, Slater, Palmer, Marshall, Kiwomya

Blackburn: *Flowers, May, Wright*, Batty, Hendry, Le Saux, Ripley, Sherwood, Shearer, Newell, Berg — Gallacher*

Ref: P Durkin

Flowers palms away a drive by Marshall but Youds steams in from distance to crash home the loose ball in great style. Batty fouls Slater near the end and Mason offers to take over spot-kick duties from Wark. The ex-Aberdeen man won't keep the job, though, as Flowers dives to save.

18 — H OLDHAM, 4/12

Ipswich: Forrest, Stockwell, Thompson^, Whelan, Wark, Linighan, Youds, Slater, Palmer*, Marshall, Whelan — *Whitton/Milton*

Oldham: *Walsh, Fleming, Pointon, Holden, Jobson, Redmond, Halle, McCarthy, Olney, Milligan, Bernard*

Ref: G Ashby

An uninspiring first half brings more jeers from the fans as the teams leave the pitch. Midway through the second half Youds clears off the line from Jobson's header. Crowd favourite Youds gets forward and goes close with a header. More boos at the end as Joe Royle's men take a point.

19 — A SOUTHAMPTON, 8/12 — Kiwomya 54

Ipswich: Forrest, Stockwell, Thompson, Whelan, Wark, Linighan, Youds, Slater, Palmer, Williams, Kiwomya* — *Goddard*

Southampton: *Beasant, Kenna, Adams, Charlton, Wood, Benali, Le Tissier, Hurlock*, Dodd, Maddison, Allen — Moody*

Ref: G Ashby

Beasant and Adams hesitate as Thompson lofts a ball forward, allowing Kiwomya to dart in and net. Late on, Beasant clatters into Kiwomya, who is currently public enemy No 1 in Ipswich! The Town man retaliates and both are booked. The victory takes a little pressure off McGiven.

20 — A CHELSEA, 11/12 — Kiwomya 57; Peacock 23

Ipswich: Forrest, Stockwell, Thompson, Williams, Wark, Linighan, Youds, Slater*, Palmer, Palmer, Kiwomya — *Guentchev*

Chelsea: *Kharine, Hall, Sinclair, Hopkin, Johnsen, Donaghy, Newton, Peacock, Stein, Cascarino, Wise* — Burley*

Ref: A Wilkie

Sinclair heads on a Wise corner-kick and Peacock dives to head Glenn Hoddle's side ahead. Their defence is at sixes and sevens when Slater pumps the ball goalwards and Kiwomya glances it into the net. Chelsea have now only won twice in 19 league games under new boss Hoddle.

21 — H NORWICH, 18/12 — Wark 7p, Megson 90(og); Bowen 40

Ipswich: Forrest, Stockwell, Thompson, Williams, Wark*, Linighan, Youds, Slater, Palmer, Whelan, Kiwomya — *Guentchev*

Norwich: *Gunn, Culverhouse, Bowen, Butterworth, Woodthorpe, Smith, Megson, Newman, Ekoku*, Fox, Sutton — Power!*

Ref: M Reed

Butterworth brings down Kiwomya and Wark converts the penalty. Forrest saves well from Sutton but is left helpless by Bowen's drive. Lee Power gets a second yellow card three minutes from time. High drama follows as Thompson's corner is headed into his own net by Megson.

FA CARLING PREMIERSHIP

Manager: Mick McGiven

SEASON 1993-94

No	Date	Venue & Opponent	Att	Pos	Pt	Res	F-A	H-T	Scorers (Town / Opp); Referee
22	27/12	H WEST HAM	20,988	12 (11)	30	D	1-1	1-0	Linighan 35 / Chapman 78 — Ref: G Poll
23	1/1	H LIVERPOOL	22,270	14 (7)	30	L	1-2	0-0	Marshall 75 / Ruddock 57, Rush 88 — Ref: A Gunn
24	15/1	A LEEDS	31,317	14 (4)	31	D	0-0	0-0	Ref: K Hackett
25	22/1	H WIMBLEDON	11,849	13 (12)	32	D	0-0	0-0	Ref: B Hill
26	2/2	A COVENTRY	11,244	13 (12)	32	L	0-1	0-1	Flynn 5 — Ref: D Allison
27	5/2	A MANCHESTER C	28,188	14 (18)	32	L	1-2	1-1	Marshall 16 / Griffiths 32, Flitcroft 71 — Ref: T Hart
28	12/2	A EVERTON	19,641	14 (15)	33	D	0-0	0-0	Ref: R Milford
29	22/2	H SHEFFIELD UTD	11,468	14 (21)	36	W	3-2	3-1	Linighan 2, Marshall 8, Slater 35 / Cork 23, Carr 49 — Ref: K Burge
30	5/3	H ARSENAL	18,803	15 (3)	36	L	1-5	0-3	Dixon 70 (og) / Wright 18, 41p, 86, Youds 24 (og), [Parlour 52] — Ref: K Barrett
31	12/3	A ASTON VILLA	23,732	12 (5)	39	W	1-0	1-0	Johnson 8 — Ref: A Wilkie

(Squad numbers in use — Town players roman, opponents italic. The figure in brackets in the Pos column is the opponents' league position.)

Match 22 — WEST HAM (H)

- **Town:** Forrest, Stockwell, Thompson, Youds, Wark*, Linighan, Williams, Slater, Palmer, Whelan, Kiwomya
- **West Ham:** *Mikosko, Breacker, Burrows, Potts, Gale, Bishop, Butler, Morley, Chapman, Marsh, Holmes^*
- **Subs used:** Marshall / *Rowland*

From a Thompson free-kick Linighan heads in off the bar. Chapman misses a sitter as Town cling on. Lyall and McGiven are desperate to beat their former club, but Billy Bonds' men deserve at least a point. Forrest fumbles a Burrows free-kick and Chapman stabs the ball into the net.

Match 23 — LIVERPOOL (H)

- **Town:** Forrest, Stockwell, Thompson, Youds*, Wark^, Linighan, Williams, Slater, Marshall, Whelan, Kiwomya
- **Liverpool:** *Grobbelaar, Jones, Harkness, Redknapp, Wright, Ruddock, Clough, Matteo^, Rush, McMana'n*, Fowler*
- **Subs used:** Guentchev, Yallop / *Barnes, Bjornbye*

Ruddock breaks the deadlock, heading in a Bjornbye cross. Redknapp rattles the bar ten minutes later. Sub Guentchev intercepts a Clough pass and sends Marshall through for the equaliser. Graeme Souness' side win the points late when Rush nods in after Fowler's header strikes the bar.

Match 24 — LEEDS (A)

- **Town:** Forrest, Stockwell, Thompson, Youds, Wark, Linighan, Williams, Guentchev, Palmer, Johnson^, Slater
- **Leeds:** *Beeney, Kelly, Dorigo, Hodge, Fairclough, Newsome, White^, Strachan, Deane, McAllister, Forrester*
- **Subs used:** Palmer / *Speed, Wetherall*

Leeds almost go ahead after just 15 seconds but Forrest is alert and dives to keep out Forrester's header. Town put on an ultra-defensive display and achieve their objective of a point, but win few friends at Elland Road. Wark has a fine game and versatile Stockwell has a stint at the back.

Match 25 — WIMBLEDON (H)

- **Town:** Forrest, Stockwell, Thompson, Youds*, Wark, Linighan, Williams, Guentchev, Marshall, Johnson, Slater*
- **Wimbledon:** *Segers, Barton, Fitzgerald, Scales, Elkins, Ardley, Earle, Sanchez, Joseph, Fashanu, Holdsw'th*
- **Subs used:** Kiwomya, Mason / *Blissett*

The Norwich win now seems like a distant memory as Town and the Dons serve up turgid fare. The rare highlights include Fashanu hitting the bar, Linighan clearing off the goalline and Forrest saving well at Holdsworth's feet. Segers does well to keep out a couple of Marshall headers.

Match 26 — COVENTRY (A)

- **Town:** Forrest, Stockwell, Thompson, Youds, Wark, Linighan, Williams, Guentchev^, Palmer, Johnson*, Slater
- **Coventry:** *Ogrizovic, Burrows, Morgan, Darby, Babb, Atherton, Flynn, Rennie, Williams J*, Ndlovu, Quinn*
- **Subs used:** Kiwomya, Palmer / *Quinn*

After the euphoria of the FA Cup win over Spurs, Town look poor at Highfield Road and fall behind to Flynn's fine early header. City boss Phil Neal has dropped Quinn, but after bringing him on for Williams, he steps up to take a spot-kick, only to see Forrest bring off a good save.

Match 27 — MANCHESTER CITY (A)

- **Town:** Forrest, Stockwell, Thompson, Youds, Wark, Linighan, Williams, Guentchev^, Marshall, Johnson, Slater*
- **Manchester City:** *Coton, Edghill, Lomas, Rocastle, Curle, Vonk, Shutt, Sheron, Griffiths, Flitcroft, Phelan*
- **Subs used:** Kiwomya, Palmer / *Phelan*

A poor back-pass by Flitcroft gifts an opener to Marshall. Rocastle's cross allows Griffiths to equalise. Curle's free-kick is headed down by Sheron and Flitcroft swoops to score, making amends for his earlier blunder. Brian Horton's men are jubilant with only their second win in 16.

Match 28 — EVERTON (A)

- **Town:** Forrest, Stockwell, Thompson, Youds, Wark^, Linighan, Williams, Slater*, Palmer, Marshall, Kiwomya
- **Everton:** *Southall, Jackson, Hinchcliffe, Ebbrell, Moore, Snodin, Radosavic^, Stuart, Rideout*, Angell, Beagrie*
- **Subs used:** Guentchev, Whelan / *Cottee, Watson*

Forrest has a great game to keep Everton at bay, to the frustration of new manager Mike Walker. Kiwomya hits the bar and a Youds header goes close in rare Town raids. A big talking point arrives when Ebbrell's shot hits the underside of the bar and bounces down, but no goal is given.

Match 29 — SHEFFIELD UTD (H)

- **Town:** Forrest, Stockwell, Thompson, Youds, Wark, Linighan, Williams, Slater, Palmer, Marshall, Kiwomya
- **Sheffield Utd:** *Kelly, Bradshaw, Nilsen^, Gannon, Tuttle, Gayle, Carr, Kamara, Littlejohn*, Hodges, Cork*
- **Subs used:** Guentchev, Mason / *Whitehouse, Blake*

In the snow, a Thompson corner is headed in powerfully by Linighan. Town are two up within eight minutes when another corner is stabbed in by Marshall. Cork's deft header gives the Blades hope, but Slater drills in a fine shot after a neat move. Carr's 25-yarder comes out of the blue.

Match 30 — ARSENAL (H)

- **Town:** Baker, Stockwell, Thompson, Youds, Wark, Linighan*, Williams, Slater, Palmer, Marshall, Kiwomya
- **Arsenal:** *Seaman, Dixon, Winterburn, Hillier^, Bould, Adams, Selley, Wright, Smith, Limpar*, Parlour*
- **Subs used:** Mason / *Merson, Keown*

A real horror show and the worst home defeat in 18 years. Wright is again the thorn in Town's side. Parlour heads in Hillier's cross and Town are 0-4 down with 40 minutes to go! Dixon slips up to head a cross high over his own keeper, but Wright has the last word after Adams' pass.

Match 31 — ASTON VILLA (A)

- **Town:** Baker, Stockwell, Johnson, Mason, Wark, Whelan, Williams, Slater, Palmer, Durrant, Kiwomya
- **Aston Villa:** *Bosnich, Barrett, Cox, Teale, Ehiogu, Richardson, Daley, Townsend^, Saunders, Atkinson, Parker^*
- **Subs used:** Kiwomya / *Yorke, Fenton*

20-year-old debutant Lee Durrant has a header on the edge of the box and the ball falls for Johnson who cracks in a great shot from 30 yards. Ex-Town favourite Atkinson has a very quiet game and manages to get barracked by both sets of supporters! Bosnich seemed to be unsighted.

Season match record (matches 32–42)

#	V	Date	Opponent	HT	Pos	Res	FT	Pts	Att	Opp Pos	Scorers	Ref
32	A	19/3	TOTTENHAM	1-0	12	D	1-1	40	26,653	17	Kiwomya 11; Barmby 56	G Ashby
33	A	23/3	NEWCASTLE	0-1	13	L	0-2	40	32,234	3	Sellars 37, Cole 75	K Cooper
34	H	26/3	QP RANGERS	0-0	13	L	1-3	40	14,653	7	Guentchev 90; Impey 65, 69, Ferdinand 71	B Hill
35	H	29/3	MANCHESTER C	1-1	13	D	2-2	41	12,871	19	Linighan 23, Guentchev 66p; Walsh 32, Rosler 52	P Don
36	A	2/4	WEST HAM	1-2	15	L	1-2	41	18,307	14	Mason 88; Rush 17, Morley 77	D Elleray
37	H	4/4	COVENTRY	0-2	15	L	0-2	41	12,782	12	Flynn 55, Ndlovu 66	R Gifford
38	A	9/4	LIVERPOOL	0-1	16	L	0-1	41	30,485	7	Dicks 74p	D Gallagher
39	H	16/4	SWINDON	1-1	16	D	1-1	42	14,760	22	Marshall 60; Fjortoft 15	V Callow
40	A	23/4	SHEFFIELD WED	0-2	17	L	**0-5**	42	23,854	6	Linighan 6 (og), Watson 15, Pearce 56, [Bart-Williams 69, Bright 90]	J Worrall
41	H	1/5	MANCHESTER U	0-1	19	L	1-2	42	22,478	1	Kiwomya 19; Cantona 36, Giggs 47	A Gunn
42	A	7/5	BLACKBURN	0-0	19	D	0-0	43	20,633	2		J Lloyd

Home 16,382   Away 21,114   Average 21,114

Line-ups (top line = Town, italic line = opponents)

32 – Tottenham
Town: Baker, Stockwell, Johnson, Mason, Wark, Whelan, Williams, Slater, Palmer, Marshall, Kiwomya
Spurs: *Walker, Austin*, Campbell, Sedgley, Scott, Mabbutt, Caskey, Barmby, Dozzell, Rosenthal, Anderton, Kerslake*
Johnson's pass finds Kiwomya unmarked and he picks his spot to beat Walker. Barmby shoots Ossie Ardiles' side level after Dozzell heads on a Rosenthal cross. Spurs exert heavy pressure and Baker has an excellent game, making some crucial stops to give Town a hard-earned point.

33 – Newcastle
Town: Baker, Stockwell, Johnson, Mason, Wark, Whelan, Williams, Slater, Palmer*, Marshall, Kiwomya, Durrant
Newcastle: *Srnicek, Venison, Beresford, Robinson, Elliott*, Watson^, Lee, Beardsley, Cole, Holland, Sellars, Mathie/Neilson*
Debutant Chris Holland crosses for Sellars to stroke home the first goal. Kevin Keegan's side are on a roll and a class above an uninspired Town side. It's a surprise the second goal is so long in coming. Holland is again the provider, setting up Andy Cole's 35th goal of the season.

34 – QP Rangers
Town: Baker, Stockwell, Thompson*, Mason, Whelan, Linighan, Williams, Slater, Johnson, Guentchev, Kiwomya, Durrant
QPR: *Stejskal, Ready, Wilkins, McCarthy, Yates, Impey, Holloway, White*, Ferdinand, Barker, Penrice*
Rangers hit three in five minutes to demoralise Town. Impey runs at the defence for the first, then heads in Wilkins' pass. Ferdinand's shot is deflected past Baker. Guentchev converts Mason's cross late on. A large crowd gathers near the tunnel at the end to call for McGiven's head.

35 – Manchester C
Town: Baker, Stockwell, Johnson, Williams, Whelan, Linighan, Durrant, Slater, Palmer, Guentchev, Kiwomya
Man City: *Dibble, Hill, Brightwell, McMahon, Curle, Vonk, Rocastle, Brightwell, Rosler, Walsh, Beagrie*
Linighan heads in Durrant's free-kick. New signing Beagrie hits a post and Walsh taps in the rebound. German loanee Rosler hits his first City goal, set up by Walsh. Vonk fouls Durrant and Guentchev converts the penalty. Chairman Kerr urges the depressed fans to get behind the side.

36 – West Ham
Town: Baker, Stockwell, Johnson, Williams, Whelan, Linighan, Durrant^, Slater, Palmer, Guentchev, Kiwomya*, Mason/Youds
West Ham: *Miklosko, Breacker, Rowland, Potts, Gale, Bishop, Butler, Rush*, Morley, Marsh, Brown*
Rush smacks home a 20-yard volley past Baker. An hour later Morley glides in a header to finally give the Hammers a degree of comfort. The Londoners deserve the victory and Town rarely look like scoring until substitute Mason heads in a consolation effort from Slater's late cross.

37 – Coventry
Town: Baker, Stockwell, Johnson, Mason, Whelan, Linighan, Williams, Youds*, Palmer, Guentchev, Slater, Durrant
Coventry: *Ogrizovic, Borrows, Morgan, Darby, Babb, Atherton, Boland, Rennie, Ndlovu, Flynn, Jenkinson*
Kiwomya storms out of the ground after being dropped, leading to speculation that he'll soon be transferred. City's Quinn is also angry at being dropped, but his side are too good for unhappy Town. Flynn fires a fine goal and Ndlovu clinches their first win in 17 visits.

38 – Liverpool
Town: Forrest, Stockwell, Johnson, Youds*, Wark, Whelan, Williams, Slater, Palmer, Kiwomya, Guentchev, Durrant
Liverpool: *James, Jones, Dicks, Redknapp, Nicol, Ruddock, McManaman, Whelan, Rush, Barnes, Fowler^, Hutchison*
Kiwomya is back in the line-up and misses a great opportunity on 55 minutes after a Johnson corner. On a snow-covered pitch, Whelan's tackle from behind on Hutchison is deemed a penalty and Dicks steps up to thrash in the only goal. Guentchev goes close with a last-minute header.

39 – Swindon
Town: Forrest, Stockwell, Johnson, Williams, Wark, Linighan, Milton*, Slater, Palmer^, Marshall, Kiwomya, Youds/Durrant
Swindon: *Hammond, Fenwick, Bodin, Horlock, Kilcline, Taylor, Moncur, Summerbee, Fjortoft, Scott, Sanchez*, Mutch/McAvennie*
Failure to beat the bottom club means relegation is now becoming a very real possibility for Town. The home fans respond to a call for support despite Fjortoft poaching an early goal. Johnson's pass finds Marshall in space and he picks his spot to salvage a little pride.

40 – Sheffield Wed
Town: Forrest, Stockwell, Johnson, Williams*, Wark, Linighan, Milton*, Slater, Palmer, Marshall, Kiwomya
Sheff Wed: *Pressman, Nilsson, Worthington, Palmer, Pearce, Walker, Jones*, Bright, B't-Williams, Watson, Sheridan^, Jemson/Hyde*
Many fans fear the worst after this fearful hammering. Linighan attempts to clear a Worthington cross but heads past Forrest. Watson cracks in a fine first-timer. Pearce and Bart-Williams net headers and, after Jemson hits the bar, Bright is on hand for the fifth. An abysmal performance.

41 – Manchester U
Town: Forrest, Stockwell, Johnson, Williams, Wark, Linighan, Milton, Whelan^, Palmer, Marshall, Kiwomya
Man U: *Schmeichel*, Irwin, Parker, Bruce, Kanchelskis, Pallister, Ince, Keane, Cantona, Hughes, Giggs, Walsh/Sharpe*
Town raise their game and battle hard. Schmeichel fails to hold Johnson's shot and Kiwomya is on hand. Man U's keeper goes off with an ankle injury. Whelan falls awkwardly and suffers an horrific-looking broken ankle. Cantona heads an equaliser and Giggs lashes home Keane's pass.

42 – Blackburn
Town: Forrest, Stockwell, Johnson, Mason, Wark, Linighan, Williams, Milton, Palmer*, Marshall, Kiwomya
Blackburn: *Flowers, May, Le Saux, Moran^, Hendry, Berg, Pearce*, Sherwood, Shearer, Atkins, Wilcox, Wright/Makel*
3pm on the final day and six clubs could still join Swindon in the relegation placings! A huge Town rally see listen closely to their 'trannies' for news of the others. Town earn a point as Stockwell clears off the line on. Then comes joyous news of Sheff U's late defeat at Chelsea.

FA CARLING PREM (CUP-TIES)

Manager: Mick McGiven — SEASON 1993-94

Coca-Cola Cup

Round	Date	Venue / Opponent	W/D/L	F-A	Att	H-T	Scorers, Times, and Referees
2:1	21/9	H CAMBRIDGE U	W	2-1	6 / 8,654 2:20	1-0	Milton 3, Whitton 65 / Claridge 89p — Ref: P Alcock
2:2	5/10	A CAMBRIDGE U	W	2-0	15 / 6,979 2:17	0-0	Marshall 50, Kiwomya 84 — Ref: M Pierce (Town win 4-1 on aggregate)
3	27/10	A LIVERPOOL	L	2-3	13 / 19,058 9	1-2	Marshall 22, Mason 77p / Rush 1, 16, 74 — Ref: J Lloyd

2:1 — H Cambridge United

Town: Forrest, Stockwell*, Thompson, Mason, Milton, Whitton, Williams, Linighan, Wark, Marshall — subs: Guentchev* Yallop/Goddard
Cambridge: *Filan, Fensome^, Barrick^, O'Shea, Claridge, Butler*, Fowler, Daish, Jeffrey, Clayton — Cheetham Nyamah/Danzey*

Filan comes out to block Marshall's path to goal, but the rebound falls for Milton, who nets from 20 yards. Whitton lets fly from distance to score the second after Claridge loses possession. Forrest brings down substitute Danzey near the end and Claridge despatches the penalty-kick.

2:2 — A Cambridge United

Town: Forrest, Stockwell, Thompson, Mason, Slater, Kiwomya, Williams, Linighan, Wark, Marshall — subs: Milton
Cambridge: *Filan, Rowett, Barrick^, O'Shea, Claridge, Clayton, Livett, Daish, Jeffrey, Dansey* — Nyamah/Fowler*

Hunter's slipshod clearance goes straight to the feet of Mason, who finds Stockwell, and he sets up Marshall to force in his sixth goal of the season. Mason and Marshall combine to set up unmarked Kiwomya, who makes the tie safe. Gary Johnson's men never posed a serious threat.

3 — A Liverpool

Town: Forrest, Stockwell, Thompson, Mason, Milton, Slater, Whelan, Williams^, Linighan, Wark, Marshall — subs: Guentchev* Whitton/Milton
Liverpool: *Grobbelaar, Jones, Dicks, Nicol, Harkness*, Rush, Stewart, Ruddock, Wright, Matteo — Fowler Hutchison*

Forrest can't hang on to a first-minute cross by Fowler and Rush does the rest. Rush robs dithering Linighan for the second. Grobbelaar's attempted clearance cannons into goal off Marshall. Rush completes his hat-trick before Wright handles a Slater cross to hand Town a second.

FA Cup

Round	Date	Venue / Opponent	W/D/L	F-A	Att	H-T	Scorers, Times, and Referees
3	8/1	A SWINDON	D	1-1	14 / 12,105 22	1-1	Marshall 28 / Mutch 45 — Ref: J Worrall
3R	18/1	H SWINDON	W	2-1	14 / 12,796 22	1-0	Stockwell 45, Marshall 107 / Fjortoft 75 — Ref: J Worrall (aet)
4	29/1	H TOTTENHAM	W	3-0	13 / 22,539 15	0-0	Marshall 53, Johnson 64, Thomp'n 85 — Ref: D Gallagher
5	19/2	A WOLVERHAMPTON	D	1-1	14 / 28,234 1:9	1-0	Wark 28 / Kelly 82 — Ref: S Lodge
5R	2/3	H WOLVERHAMPTON	L	1-2	14 / 19,385 1:9	0-2	Palmer 46 / Mills 8, Thompson 38 — Ref: S Lodge

3 — A Swindon

Town: Forrest, Stockwell, Thompson, Youds, Linighan, Williams, Johnson, Slater, Wark*, Marshall, Guentchev — subs: Palmer
Swindon: *Hammond, Summerbee, Bodin*, Hrlock, Taylor, Moncur, Mutch, Maskell^, Ling, Fenwick — Nijholt/Fjortoft*

Town fans release the traditional blue-and-white FA Cup balloons as the teams come out. Marshall scores a magnificent goal, shooting home after impressive inter-play between him and Slater. Bodin's cross from the left deflects off Wark, falling nicely for Mutch to secure a replay.

3R — H Swindon

Town: Forrest, Stockwell, Thompson, Youds, Linighan, Williams, Johnson, Slater, Wark^, Marshall, Guentchev — subs: Whitton/Palmer
Swindon: *Hammond, Summerbee, Bodin, Hrlock, Taylor, Nijholt, Mutch, Fjortoft*, Ling, Fenwick — Maskell*

Stockwell is on hand to net after Hammond blocks Johnson's effort. On-loan Fjortoft scores his first goal in England to force extra-time. Home fans jeer their side, who look second best. They are pacified when Marshall scores an easy goal after unlucky Hammond's horrendous miskick.

4 — H Tottenham

Town: Forrest, Stockwell, Thompson, Youds, Linighan, Williams, Johnson, Slater*, Wark, Marshall, Guentchev — subs: Palmer
Tottenham: *Walker, Austin, Edinburgh, Samways, Calderwood Sedgley, Caskey, Barmby, Anderton, Dozzell*, Nethercott Campbell*

Wark heads on Thompson's corner and Marshall nets a vicious volley. It gets better as Wark heads down Guentchev's corner and Johnson fires home. Ossie Ardiles is clearly not 'going to Wembley' this time, as Guentchev squares to Thompson who guides in the third goal from an angle.

5 — A Wolverhampton

Town: Forrest, Stockwell, Thompson, Youds, Linighan, Williams, Slater^, Palmer, Wark, Marshall — subs: Kiwomya/Mason
Wolverhampton: *Stowell, Rankine*, Thompson, Venus, Blades, Marsden, Ferguson, Regis, Kelly, Keen — Dennison*

Stockwell palms away Thompson's corner, but Wark is on hand to shoot home. Forrest makes a brilliant save from Thompson after the break. Wolves have a penalty shout that turned down with ten minutes left, but level moments later when Regis lays the ball to Kelly to net from an angle.

5R — H Wolverhampton

Town: Forrest, Stockwell*, Thompson, Youds*, Linighan, Williams^, Slater, Kiwomya, Palmer, Marshall — subs: Guentchev/Mason
Wolverhampton: *Stowell, Rankine, Thompson, Venus, Blades, Dennison, Ferguson*, Mills, Keen — Cook*

Hungry Wolves from the First Division devour Town and build a two-goal lead. Mills drives them ahead early on. Ferguson touches a free-kick aside to Thompson, who has plenty of time to shoot home. In his 100th game, Palmer brings Town back into the game after a scramble.

League Table

	Team	P	Home W	D	L	F	A	Away W	D	L	F	A	Pts
1	Manchester U	42	14	6	1	39	13	13	5	3	41	25	92
2	Blackburn	42	14	5	2	31	11	11	4	6	32	25	84
3	Newcastle	42	14	4	3	51	14	9	4	8	31	27	77
4	Arsenal	42	10	8	3	25	15	8	9	4	28	13	71
5	Leeds	42	13	6	2	37	18	5	10	6	28	21	70
6	Wimbledon	42	12	5	4	35	21	6	6	9	21	32	65
7	Sheffield Wed	42	10	7	4	48	24	6	9	6	28	30	64
8	Liverpool	42	12	4	5	33	23	5	5	11	26	32	60
9	QP Rangers	42	8	7	6	32	29	8	5	8	30	32	60
10	Aston Villa	42	8	5	8	23	18	7	7	7	23	32	57
11	Coventry	42	9	7	5	23	17	5	7	9	20	28	56
12	Norwich	42	4	9	8	26	29	8	8	5	39	32	53
13	West Ham	42	6	7	8	26	31	6	6	8	21	27	52
14	Chelsea	42	11	5	5	31	20	2	7	12	18	33	51
15	Tottenham	42	4	8	9	29	33	7	4	10	25	26	45
16	Manchester C	42	6	10	5	24	22	3	8	10	14	27	45
17	Everton	42	8	4	9	26	30	4	4	13	16	33	44
18	Southampton	42	9	2	10	30	31	3	5	13	19	35	43
19	IPSWICH	42	5	8	8	21	32	4	8	9	14	26	43
20	Sheffield Utd	42	6	10	5	24	23	2	8	11	18	37	42
21	Oldham	42	5	8	8	24	33	4	5	12	18	35	40
22	Swindon	42	4	7	10	25	45	1	8	12	22	55	30
		924	192	142	128	663	532	128	142	192	532	663	1244

Odds & ends

- Double wins: (1) Southampton.
- Double losses: (5) Arsenal, Coventry, Liverpool, QPR, Sheffield Wed.
- Won from behind: (0).
- Lost from in front: (3) Aston V (H), Man C (A), Man U (H).
- High spots: The fine start to 93-4 – especially Marshall's contribution.
- The magnificent goal by Marshall in the cup at Swindon.
- Gary Megson's last-minute own-goal, which beat Norwich.
- The news that a late goal had sent Sheffield Utd down instead of Town in the dying moments of the final day.
- Low spots: Widespread criticism for the many negative displays.
- The awful double thrashings by both Sheffield Wed and Arsenal.
- Failure to win any of the last 11 league matches of the season.
- Dressing-room 'bust-ups' involving Linighan and Kiwomya.
- Player of the Year: John Wark.
- Ever-presents: (1) Mick Stockwell.
- Hat-tricks: (0).
- Opposing hat-tricks:(3) I Wright, K Campbell, I Rush.
- Leading scorer: (15) Ian Marshall.

Appearances and Goals

	Appearances						Goals			
	Lge	Sub	LC	Sub	FAC	Sub	Lge	LC	FAC	Tot
Baker, Clive	15									
Durrant, Lee	3	4								
Forrest, Craig	27		3		5					
Goddard, Paul	3	1			1					
Guentchev, Bontcho	9	15	2	2	2	2	2			2
Johnson, Gavin	16		3				1		1	2
Kiwomya, Chris	34	3	1		2		5	1		6
Linighan, David	38		3		5		3			3
Mason, Paul	18	4	3		1	2	3	1		4
Marshall, Ian	28	1	3		5		10	2	3	15
Milton, Simon	11	4	2	1			1		1	2
Palmer, Steve	31	5	2		3		1		1	2
Slater, Stuart	28		2		5		1			1
Stockwell, Mick	42		3		5		1	1		2
Thompson, Neil	32		3		5					
Wark, John	38		3		5		3		1	4
Whelan, Phil	28	1	1		1					
Whitton, Steve	7	4	1	1	1	1	1	1		2
Williams, Geraint	34		3		5					
Yallop, Frank	2	5	1							
Youds, Eddie	18	5			5		1			1
(own-goals)							2			2
21 players used	462	52	33	4	55	8	35	6	8	49

FA CARLING PREMIERSHIP · SEASON 1994-95

Manager: John Lyall > George Burley

Results

No	Date		Opponent	Att	Pos	Pt	F-A	H-T	Scorers, Times, and Referees
1	H	20/8	NOTT'M FOREST	18,763	—	0	L 0-1	0-1	Roy 40 — Ref: S Lodge
2	A	23/8	WIMBLEDON	6,341	—	1	D 1-1	0-1	Milton 61 / Holdsworth 19 — Ref: J Worrall
3	A	27/8	QP RANGERS	12,456	9	4	W 2-1	1-0	Yates 19 (og), Guentchev 48 / Ferdinand 90 — Ref: P Danson
4	H	30/8	TOTTENHAM	22,430	12	4	L 1-3	0-3	Kiwomya 85 / Klinsmann 16, 38, Dumitrescu 28 — Ref: R Gifford
5	A	10/9	ASTON VILLA	22,241	16	4	L 0-2	0-1	Staunton 15, Saunders 85 — Ref: G Willard
6	H	19/9	NORWICH	17,406	16	4	L 1-2	1-1	Wark 45p / Newman 12, Bradshaw 53 — Ref: R Dilkes
7	H	24/9	MANCHESTER U	22,553	15	7	W 3-2	2-0	Mason 15, 43, Sedgley 80 / Cantona 70, Scholes 73 — Ref: P Jones
8	A	1/10	SOUTHAMPTON	13,266	16	7	L 1-3	0-0	Marshall 77 / Maddison 52, Ekelund 65, Dowie 89 — Ref: G Ashby
9	A	10/10	COVENTRY	9,509	18	7	L 0-2	0-1	Wark 45 (og), Cook 75p — Ref: R Hart
10	H	16/10	SHEFFIELD WED	12,825	21	7	L 1-2	0-1	Wark 52 / Bright 9, Hirst 90 — Ref: M Reed

Squad numbers in use / subs used

1 — Nott'm Forest (H)
Ipswich: Forrest, Stockwell, Yallop, Mason, Wark, Youds, Williams, Slater, Milton, Marshall, Kiwomya*
Forest: Crossley, Lyttle, Pearce, Cooper, Chettle, Stone, Phillips*, Gemmill, Lee, Woan, Ray^
Subs used: Guentchev | Bohinen/Rosario
Clough-less Forest are back after one year out of the top flight. Debutant Roy's curving shot wins the three points against a Town side lacking punch. The re-organised 'dug-out team' sees Lyall back as boss. Woods his assistant, Goddard and Wark are coaches and Klug is reserve coach.

2 — Wimbledon (A)
Ipswich: Forrest, Stockwell, Yallop, Mason, Wark, Youds, Williams, Slater, Milton, Marshall, Kiwomya
Wimbledon: Segers, Barton, Fitzgerald, Scales, Elkins, Ardley, Jones, Castledine, Gayle, Blissett*, Holdsworth
Subs used: — | Clarke
Dean Holdsworth puts Joe Kinnear's side ahead with a powerful shot and later misses several chances to extend the lead. On his 31st birthday, Simon Milton takes advantage of a Fitzgerald slip to crack in the equaliser. In five meetings between the clubs, Town have never been beaten.

3 — QP Rangers (A)
Ipswich: Forrest, Stockwell, Yallop, Mason, Wark, Youds, Williams, Slater, Milton, Guentchev, Kiwomya*
QPR: Roberts, Bardsley, Wilson, Barker, Yates, McDonald, Impey*, Holloway, Ferdinand, Gallen, Sinclair
Subs used: Marshall | Penrice
After Town survive an early onslaught, unlucky Yates slides Guentchev's cross into his own net. The Bulgarian crashes over in the box and after Rangers' protests, misses from the spot. Four minutes later he races clear to crack in a beauty. Ferdinand cashes in on Linighan's late slip.

4 — Tottenham (H)
Ipswich: Forrest, Stockwell, Yallop, Mason, Wark, Linighan, Williams, Slater, Milton, Marshall, Guentchev*
Tottenham: Walker, Kerslake, Edinburgh, Nethercott, Calderwood, Campbell, Anderton*, Barmby, Klinsmann, Sheringham, Dumitrescu
Subs used: Kiwomya | Mabbutt
Town are carved apart by Ossie Ardiles' side and new signing Jurgen Klinsmann opens the scoring. Dumitrescu heads in a deep cross. The killer third comes before the break as Klinsmann converts Anderton's corner. Williams sets up Kiwomya, who notches a late consolation goal.

5 — Aston Villa (A)
Ipswich: Forrest, Stockwell, Yallop, Mason, Wark, Linighan*, Williams, Slater, Milton, Guentchev, Kiwomya
Villa: Spink, Barrett, King, Ehiogu, McGrath, Richardson, Yorke, Fashanu^, Saunders, Townsend, Staunton
Subs used: Marshall | Atkinson
Saunders feeds Staunton and his trusty left foot produces a sweet drive that flies in off a post. For the next 70 minutes Ron Atkinson's side are held at bay. A powerful Townsend effort is touched onto the bar by Forrest. Sub Atkinson supplies Saunders, who nips round Forrest to score.

6 — Norwich (H)
Ipswich: Forrest, Johnson, Yallop, Sedgley, Wark, Linighan, Williams, Slater, Milton, Marshall, Guentchev*
Norwich: Gunn, Bradshaw, Bowen, Newsome, Polston, Newman, Crook, Goss, Adams, Sheron*, Milligan
Subs used: Kiwomya | Ekoku
Record £1m signing Sedgley is fit again to make a long-awaited debut. Makeshift striker Newman slides in to score. After Johnson skims the bar, Marshall is sent tumbling and Wark levels from the spot. Milton fouls Crook and Bradshaw nets after his spot-kick is parried back to him.

7 — Manchester U (H)
Ipswich: Forrest, Johnson, Yallop, Sedgley, Wark^, Mason, Thomsen, Williams, Slater*, Marshall, Paz*
Man U: Walsh, Irwin, Sharpe, Bruce, Pallister, Keane, Ince, McClair^, Kanchelskis**, Cantona, Giggs
Subs used: Milton/Guentchev | Scholes/Butt
After the Bolton cup debacle, Town are back with a vengeance. £900K Uruguayan Adrian Paz debuts. Mason scrambles in Thomsen's cross, then fires in Johnson's free-kick. Crosses by Keane set up Cantona and Scholes goals. Sedgley fires home Yallop's cross in a dramatic finale.

8 — Southampton (A)
Ipswich: Forrest, Johnson, Yallop, Sedgley, Wark^, Linighan, Williams, Thomsen, Mason*, Marshall, Guentchev
Southampton: Grobbelaar, Dodd, Charlton, Hall, Monkou, Magilton, Le Tissier*, Maddison, Dowie, Ekelund
Subs used: Marshall/Cotterell | Heaney
Le Tissier's cross is converted by Maddison. The Channel Islander hits the woodwork and Ekelund nets the rebound. Town respond through Marshall, who slots home a Thomsen pass. Alan Ball's men wrap up the points late when Dowie's effort is deflected past Forrest by Linighan.

9 — Coventry (A)
Ipswich: Forrest, Johnson, Yallop, Sedgley, Wark, Linighan, Williams, Palmer, Milton, Marshall, Guentchev
Coventry: Ogrizovic, Pickering, Morgan, Darby, Busst, Rennie, Flynn, Cook, Dublin, Wegerle*, Jones*
Subs used: Cotterell | Ndlovu
Another uninspired display and not exactly thrilling fare for the live Sky viewers. Phil Neal's side take a fortunate lead when Wark stretches to reach a cross and heads powerfully into his own net. The skilful Roy Wegerle is brought down by Linighan and Cook tucks home the penalty.

10 — Sheffield Wed (H)
Ipswich: Forrest, Johnson, Yallop, Sedgley, Wark, Williams, Palmer, Milton, Marshall, Guentchev, Thomsen*
Sheffield Wed: Pressman, Nolan, Atherton, Walker!, Pearce, Bright, Bt-Williams^, Hyde, Sheridan, Hirst, Bright
Subs used: Youds | Sinton/Taylor
Bright converts Hyde's low cross. Wark is left unmarked to head in Milton's cross and nets another beauty that is ruled out. Guentchev blazes a late penalty over the bar and then Hirst nets Taylor's last-minute pass. In the dying seconds Walker retaliates by butting Milton and is sent off.

11 — A CHELSEA, 23/10 — 0-2 L — Pos 21 — Att 15,068 (7 / 7)

Town: Forrest, Vaughan, Yallop, Sedgley, Youds, Milton, Williams*, Palmer, Guentchev, Paz^, Thomsen; subs Stockwell / Gregory D
Chelsea: Kharine, Hall, Barness, Kjelberg*, Johnsen, Newton, Rocastle, Shipperley, Furlong^, Peacock, Wise; subs Lee / Hopkin

Wise 74, Shipperley 86 — Ref: B Hill

With no Wark and Johnson, Youds is recalled along with youth product Vaughan who makes an excellent debut in defence. Guentchev hits the bar in the first-half with a header. Newton's long-range shot hits the bar but Wise taps in the rebound. Shipperley rounds Forrest for the second.

12 — H LIVERPOOL, 29/10 — 1-3 L — Pos 21 — Att 22,379 (5 / 7)

Town: Forrest, Vaughan, Stockwell, Sedgley, Youds, Johnson, Williams, Palmer*, Guentchev, Paz, Thomsen; sub Linighan
Liverpool: James, Jones, Bjornbye, Scales, Babb, Ruddock, McManaman / Redknapp, Rush, Fowler, Barnes

Paz 65 / Barnes 41, Fowler 58, 60 — Ref: P Durkin

Barnes cracks home a 25-yard stunner. Fowler swoops to score after Rush's shot is blocked and then converts Bjornbye's corner. Paz's angled drive is a mere consolation. The defeat means this is Town's worst sequence of results for 10 years and their worst start to a season in 31 years.

13 — H LEEDS, 1/11 — 2-0 W — Pos 20 — Att 15,354 (6 / 10)

Town: Forrest, Yallop, Stockwell, Sedgley, Youds, Linighan, Williams*, Whelan, Guentchev^, Paz, Thomsen; subs Milton / Kiwomya
Leeds: Lukic, Kelly, Worthington / Palmer, Wetherall, McAllister, White*, Wallace, Deane, Speed, Masinga

Sedgley 7, Williams 63 — Ref: D Gallagher

At last the slide is halted. Paz and Thomsen combine and Sedgley guides in the first. The all-important second is a rising shot by Williams – his first goal in 103 games. He celebrates in front of the Churchman's stand. 'People in the crowd must have nearly fainted!' he reflects afterwards.

14 — A CRYSTAL PALACE, 5/11 — 0-3 L — Pos 20 — Att 13,450 (11 / 10)

Town: Forrest, Yallop, Stockwell, Sedgley, Youds, Linighan, Williams, Whelan^, Guentchev^, Paz, Thomsen; subs Milton / Kiwomya
Crystal Palace: Martyn, Humphrey, Gordon, Southgate, Shaw, Coleman, Newman, Armstrong^, Preece, Salako

Newman 18, Armstrong 81, Salako 85 — Ref: A Wilkie

Newman's 25-yarder is deflected past unlucky Forrest. Alan Smith's men make the points safe in the closing stages. Armstrong nets at close-range after Preece's cross. Armstrong's centre is headed on by Preece and Salako nets. Lyall dishes out a 70-minute verbal lashing afterwards.

15 — H BLACKBURN, 19/11 — 1-3 L — Pos 20 — Att 17,607 (2 / 10)

Town: Forrest, Yallop, Mason, Sedgley, Youds, Linighan, Williams*, Whelan^, Guentchev^, Paz, Thomsen; sub Milton
Blackburn: Flowers, Warhurst, Le Saux, Sherwood, Gale, Ripley, Atkins, Shearer, Sutton, Slater

Thomsen 28 / Sutton 9, Sherwood 41, Shearer 70 — Ref: K Burge

Le Saux's cross is volleyed in by Sutton. Paz mishits a shot but it falls for Thomsen who equalises. Sherwood outpaces Youds to pick his spot. It's a poor display by Town and no surprise when Shearer nets the third for Kenny Dalglish's outfit, pouncing after Sutton's header is parried.

16 — A NEWCASTLE, 26/11 — 1-2 L — Pos 22 — Att 34,459 (3 / 11)

Town: Forrest, Yallop, Mason, Sedgley, Youds, Linighan, Williams, Whelan, Marshall^, Paz, Thomsen; sub Slater
Newcastle: Srnicek, Hottiger, Beresford, Venison, Albert*, Lee*, Beardsley, Cole, Fox, Watson; subs Mathie / Clark

Thomsen 90 / Cole 86 — Ref: K Cooper

Marshall goes off with a broken elbow after Albert's challenge. It's one-sided and Cole finally breaks through with a turn and shot. In the last minute Thomsen chips in a beauty. The home fans chant 'boring Ipswich' and boss Kevin Keegan angrily likens Town to 'non-League hoofers'.

17 — H MANCHESTER C, 3/12 — 1-2 L — Pos 22 — Att 13,754 (6 / 11)

Town: Forrest, Yallop, Mason, Sedgley, Youds, Linighan^, Williams, Whelan, Marshall*, Paz, Thomsen*; subs Slater / Johnson
Manchester City: Dibble, Edghill, Brightwell D / Flitcroft, Curle, Brightwell I* / Summerbee / Walsh^, Quinn, Rosler, Beagrie; subs Kernaghan / Simpson

Mason 74 / Flitcroft 21, Rosler 42 — Ref: S Lodge

Town lose thanks to a dreadful first-half display. Sedgley half-clears a cross and Flitcroft shoots home. Summerbee's cross produces a smart finish by Rosler. A cross by Paz finds Mason, who cracks in a consolation. Million-pound man Sedgley is looking like an expensive mistake.

18 — A NOTT'M FOREST, 10/12 — 1-4 L — Pos 22 — Att 21,340 (5 / 11)

Town: Forrest, Yallop, Mason, Sedgley, Johnson, Linighan^, Williams, Whelan, Guentchev, Paz*, Thomsen*; subs Slater / Milton
Nott'm Forest: Crossley, Lyttle, Pearce, Haaland, Chettle, Stone, Bohinen^, Gemmill, Woan, Roy*; subs Lee / McGregor

Thomsen 45 / Collymore 4, Gemmill 12, Haaland 28, (Pearce 44) — Ref: M Reed

Town lose to caretaker-boss when Lyall quits in the wake of the City defeat. Collymore nets twice before half-time. Collymore nets Haaland's punt forward, then engineers Gemmill and Haaland's strikes. Pearce nets a fierce free-kick.

19 — H WIMBLEDON, 16/12 — 2-2 D — Pos 22 — Att 11,367 (15 / 12)

Town: Forrest, Yallop, Mason, Sedgley, Johnson, Barton, Williams, Whelan, Gregory N*, Kiwomya, Milton, Thomsen, Paz
Wimbledon: Segers, Cunningham / Fitzgerald, Kimble, Thorn, Jones, Leonhard'n / Goodman, Ekoku, Holdsworth; subs Elkins / Harford

Milton 7, Sedgley 83 / Holdsworth 2, Goodman 62 — Ref: D Elleray

Names said to be on Town's shortlist include Graham Turner and David Pleat. Interviews are about to begin. Holdsworth nets a neat volley after 97 seconds for his first goal since August. Town hit back well and the under-fire Sedgley levels late. Neil Gregory makes his Town debut.

20 — A WEST HAM, 26/12 — 1-1 D — Pos 22 — Att 20,562 (18 / 13)

Town: Forrest, Yallop, Wark, Sedgley, Vaughan, Whelan, Williams*, Mason, Kiwomya, Milton, Thomsen; sub Slater
West Ham: Miklosko, Breacker, Dicks, Potts*, Martin, Bishop, Holmes, Rush, Cottee, Boere, Hughes; sub Rieper

Thomsen 70 / Cottee 17 — Ref: P Durkin

Rush sends Cottee through to finish expertly. Town keep Redknapp's men at bay after this and are rewarded when Thomsen nets a fine header from Kiwomya's cross. George Burley is rumoured to be Town's new boss, but a row with former club Colchester means it's not yet official.

21 — H ARSENAL, 28/12 — 0-2 L — Pos 22 — Att 22,047 (9 / 13)

Town: Forrest, Yallop, Wark, Sedgley, Vaughan, Whelan !, Williams*, Mason^, Kiwomya, Milton, Thomsen; subs Linighan / (Campbell^)
Arsenal: Bartram, Dixon, Schwarz, Winterburn / Bould, Keown !, Jensen, Wright, Smith*, Campbell^, Parlour; subs Guentchev / Palmer, Dickov

Wright 17, Campbell 79 — Ref: R Dilkes

Burley is officially unveiled to a near-full house. Wright forces home Schwarz's corner. Whelan is booked for a foul, then argues loudly and is shown a red card. Keown exits close to half-time for his second yellow. Milton hits the bar before Campbell's deflected shot settles matters.

FA CARLING PREMIERSHIP

Manager: John Lyall > George Burley **SEASON 1994-95**

No	Date	Venue / Opponent	Att	Pos	Pt	F-A	H-T	Scorers, Times, and Referees
22	31/12	A EVERTON	25,659	22 / 19	L 13	1-4	1-1	Sedgley 9 [Watson 90] Ferguson 27, Rideout 72, 76, Ref: R Dikes
23	2/1	H LEICESTER	15,803	21 / 22	W 16	4-1	1-0	Kiwomya 34, 62, Tanner 56, Yallop 73 / Roberts 53, Ref: T Holbrook
24	14/1	A LIVERPOOL	32,733	21 / 3	W 19	1-0	1-0	Tanner 30, Ref: R Gifford
25	21/1	H CHELSEA	17,296	21 / 12	D 20	2-2	0-0	Slater 74, Wark 81p / Stein 66, Burley 88, Ref: P.Don
26	28/1	A BLACKBURN	21,325	21 / 1	L 20	1-4	0-2	Wark 76p / Shearer 2, 28, 90p, Sherwood 49, Ref: G Poll
27	4/2	H CRYSTAL PALACE	15,570	21 / 16	L 20	0-2	0-0	Dowie 55, Gordon 87p, Ref: S Lodge
28	22/2	A MANCHESTER C	21,430	21 / 14	L 20	0-2	0-0	Quinn 67, Rosler 71, Ref: K Cooper
29	25/2	H SOUTHAMPTON	16,076	21 / 18	W 23	2-1	0-1	Mathie 70, Chapman 76 / Maddison 38, Ref: P Jones
30	28/2	H NEWCASTLE	18,639	21 / 3	L 23	0-2	0-2	Fox 12, Kitson 39, Ref: G Ashby
31	4/3	A MANCHESTER U	43,804	21 / 2	L 23	**0-9**	0-3	Keane 15, Cole 23, 37, 52, 65, 88, [Hughes 54, 72, Ince 58] Ref: G Poll

Squad Numbers In Use / Subs Used

22 — Everton
Town: Forrest, Yallop, Wark^, Vaughan, Linighan, Sedgley, Mason*, Palmer, Kiwomya, Guentchev, Thomsen — subs: Slater/Whelan
Opp: Southall, Jackson, Burrows, Watson, Unsworth, Ebbrell, Parkinson, Horne, Ferguson, Rideout, Hinchcliffe
Sedgley takes Kiwomya's pass and cracks in a firm shot. Ferguson levels when he hammers in Jackson's cross. After hitting the post, Rideout grabs two in four minutes, the second from Hinchcliffe's fine cross. Watson heads in at the far post. Burley sees the size of the task facing him.

23 — Leicester
Town: Forrest, Yallop, Whelan, Vaughan, Linighan, Sedgley, Mason*, Tanner*, Kiwomya, Slater, Thomsen — subs: Palmer/Gregory N
Opp: Poole, Grayson, Whitlow, Hill, Draper, Agnew, Thompson*, Roberts, Lewis, Lowe^ — subs: Philpott/Oldfield
Kiwomya's rising shot raises Town's morale. Grayson's cross is swept in by Roberts. A dream start for Adam Tanner as he fires homes from 25 yards. Kiwomya nips in to exploit a poor Thompson back-pass. Mark McGhee's outfit are finished off as Yallop heads in Kiwomya's centre.

24 — Liverpool
Town: Forrest, Yallop, Johnson, Vaughan, Linighan, Sedgley, Williams, Tanner, Paz, Slater, Thomsen — subs: Walters
Opp: James, Jones, Bjornbye*, Scales, Ruddock, McManaman, Redknapp, Rush, Fowler, Thomas
Kiwomya leaves for Arsenal for £1.55m. The new boss installs Sedgley as skipper. Tanner nets again, this one a powerful shot from just inside the box. Robust Liverpool challenges go unpunished, but Town stick to their task superbly and grind out their first win at Anfield in 34 visits.

25 — Chelsea
Town: Forrest, Yallop, Johnson, Vaughan, Linighan, Sedgley, Williams, Tanner, Paz*, Slater, Thomsen — subs: Chapman
Opp: Kharine, Minto, Sinclair, Kjeldbjerg, Johnsen, Newton, Spackman^, Spencer, Peacock*, Stein — subs: Hopkin/Burley
Chapman signs from West Ham for £70k, and Youds leaves for Bradford. Stein looks offside as he nets. Town hit back through Slater, and the same player is fouled by Kjelbjerg for Wark to convert the penalty. The manager's nephew Burley breaks Town hearts with a superb late drive.

26 — Blackburn
Town: Forrest, Yallop, Vaughan, Sedgley, Whelan, Wark, Williams*, Tanner, Chapman, Slater, Thomsen^ — subs: Johnson
Opp: Flowers, Warhurst*, Le Saux, Hendry, Pearce, Berg, Wilcox, Shearer, Sutton^, Sherwood — subs: Atkins/Newell
Shearer celebrates 100 games for Rovers by smashing in a fierce early shot. He follows this by cutting in and curling in a beauty. He then hits a post and Sherwood nets the rebound. Hendry brings down Chapman for Town's penalty. Whelan's challenge gives Shearer his hat-trick chance.

27 — Crystal Palace
Town: Forrest, Yallop, Vaughan, Sedgley, Linighan, Wark, Williams*, Tanner, Chapman, Slater, Thomsen^ — subs: Thomsen/Paz
Opp: Martyn, Patterson, Gordon, Southgate, Coleman, Dowie, Newman!, Armstrong*, Pitcher, Salako, Bowry
Thompson returns after a long absence and his cracking drive hits a post on 15 minutes. Newman is sent off after tangling with Tanner. Wark fouls Salako to concede a penalty.

28 — Manchester C
Town: Forrest, Yallop, Vaughan, Sedgley, Linighan, Wark, Williams, Thomsen, Chapman, Slater*, Paz — subs: Paz/Thompson
Opp: Coton, Summerbee, Phelan, Kernaghan, Curle, Brightwell, Gaudino, Walsh^, Flitcroft, Rosler, Beagrie — subs: Quinn/Simpson
Slater slides into pitch-side boards and damages knee ligaments. As the snow falls, Paz sends a header against a post. With Forrest well out of position Quinn squeezes in a header. Beagrie's shot is parried and Rosler rams in the loose ball. Burley pays Newcastle £500k for Alex Mathie.

29 — Southampton
Town: Forrest, Yallop, Thompson, Sedgley, Linighan, Tanner, Marshall*, Chapman*, Mathie, Slater*, Norfolk — subs: Johnson
Opp: Grobbelaar, Dodd, Charlton, Hall^, Magilton, Monkou, Le Tissier, Shipperley, Maddison, Allen*, Hughes — subs: Hughes/Tisdale
Shipperley hits the post before Maddison nets a looping header from Le Tissier's cross. With 20 minutes remaining, a Grobbelaar miskick allows debutant Mathie to fire an equaliser into the empty net. Fellow debutant Norfolk sends over a cross that is powered home by Chapman.

30 — Newcastle
Town: Forrest, Yallop, Thompson, Sedgley, Linighan, Norfolk, Tanner, Chapman, Mathie, Slater, Williams — subs: Mason
Opp: Srnicek, Hottiger, Beresford, Venison, Peacock, Howie, Lee, Beardsley, Kitson, Fox, Gillespie — subs: Marshall
Ipswich-born Fox cracks in a fine goal from 25 yards. Thompson hits a post and two minutes later Chapman hits the bar for unlucky Town. Keegan's side look safe when Kitson sidesteps Linighan and fires in a fierce shot before the interval. Wark makes his 650th Town appearance.

31 — Manchester U
Town: Forrest, Yallop, Thompson, Sedgley, Linighan, Wark, Tanner, Williams, Chapman*, Slater*, Mathie — subs: Mason
Opp: Schmeichel, Irwin, Keane, Bruce^, Pallister, Kanchelskis**, Cole, Ince, McClair, Hughes, Giggs — subs: Sharpe/Butt
Utter humiliation and arguably the worst day since ITFC turned pro in 1936. United's biggest top flight win in 103 years sees Cole poach five – although there's a half-hearted dispute over who got the Reds' fourth. Forrest makes some fine saves – it could easily have been double figures!

No		Date	Result	Pos		Score	Pts	Club	Attendance
32	A	8/3	L	21	6	0-2	23	TOTTENHAM	24,930

Klinsm'n 1, Barmby 14, Youds 82 (og)
Ref: B Hill

Forrest	Yallop	Thompson	Sedgley	Youds	Linighan	Williams	Tanner	Chapman	Paz^	Milton*	Thomsen/Marshall
Walker	Austin	Edinburgh	Howells	Calderwood	Mabbutt	Anderton*	Barmby	Klinsmann	Sheringham	Rosenthal	Caskey

Wholesale changes, but fit-again Marshall is upset at not being recalled. Another avalanche is on the cards as Klinsmann smashes in a corner in the opening minute. Barmby volleys home another corner, but then things calm a little. Youds' final act as an Ipswich player is an own-goal.

33	A	20/3	L	21	14	0-3	23	NORWICH	17,510

Cureton 53, Ward 58, Eadie 78
Ref: P Durkin

Forrest	Yallop	Thompson	Whelan	Thomsen	Wark !	Williams	Mathie	Marshall	Slater*	Milton	Chapman
Marshall	Ullathorne^	Bowen	Newsome	Polston	Adams	Crook	Milligan	Eadie	Ward^	Cureton	Newman/Sutch

Town are furious as Wark is sent off for hauling down Eadie just before the break. City, after 11 winless games, cruise home after Cureton skips round Forrest to end Town resistance. It's not happening for new skipper Sedgley – the £1m misfit gets dropped for the rest of the season.

34	H	1/4	L	21	13	0-1	23	ASTON VILLA	15,710

Swailes 90 (og)
Ref: J Worrall

Forrest	Yallop	Thompson	Swailes	Wark	Thomsen	Williams	Mathie	Marshall	Slater	Milton	Yorke/Fenton
Bosnich	Charles	Wright	Teale	McGrath	Ehiogu^	Atkinson^	Johnson	Saunders*	Townsend	Staunton	

Mathie hits the bar as Town bid to halt the slide. Defender Swailes, £150,000 from Doncaster, makes his debut, having left the club in 1991 without reaching first-team level. There's a tragic end to his big day when he glances Charles' last-minute cross into his own net. Unbelievable!

35	A	5/4	L	21	6	0-4	23	LEEDS	28,600

Yeboah 3, 35, 45, Speed 31
Ref: G Willard

Forrest	Yallop	Thompson	Swailes	Linighan	Thomsen	Williams	Mathie^	Chapman	Slater	Milton	Guentchev
Lukic	Kelly	Dorigo	Palmer	Wetherall	Pemberton	Yeboah	Wallace	Deane	McAllister	Speed	

Yeboah sidesteps Forrest to kick-start a hammering. Wallace feeds Speed who flicks in a neat but easy goal. Deane robs Swailes and sends Yeboah clear to bag the third. It's four before the break when Yeboah finishes superbly after Dorigo's run and cross. Elland Road is enraptured.

36	H	11/4	L	22	8	0-1	23	QP RANGERS	11,767

Sinclair 69
Ref: R Gifford

Forrest	Yallop	Thompson	Stockwell	Linighan	Palmer	Williams	Mathie*	Marshall	Slater	Thomsen	Chapman
Roberts	Brevett	Wilson	Barker*	Ready	McDonald	Impey	Holloway	Ferdinand	Gallen*	Sinclair	Penrice/Maddix

Stockwell makes a welcome return and Burley makes another batch of team changes, but to no avail. Shortly after Town reach ten hours without netting a single goal, Sinclair crosses and Ferdinand fires home the winner. Relegation is confirmed by results elsewhere on 14 April.

37	A	15/4	L	22	10	1-4	23	ARSENAL	36,818

Marshall 72
Merson 34, Wright 47, 50, 56
Ref: T Holbrook

Baker	Yallop	Ellis*	Stockwell	Linighan	Palmer	Williams	Mathie^	Marshall	Slater	Thomsen	Milton/Chapman
Seaman	Dixon	Winterburn*	Schwarz	Bould	Adams	Keown	Wright*	Hartson	Merson	Helder	Parlour/Kiwomya

Young Ellis gets a debut but it's another miserable day. Merson's fierce drive opens the floodgates and then Ian Wright runs rings round Town to notch a nine-minute hat-trick. Town's travelling fans cheer wildly when their side wins a corner! Marshall nips clear to slip in a consolation.

38	H	17/4	D	22	18	1-1	24	WEST HAM	19,099

Thomsen 11
Boere 90
Ref: M Bodenham

Baker	Yallop	Wark	Stockwell	Linighan	Milton*	Williams	Mathie	Marshall^	Slater	Thomsen	Mason/Chapman
Miklosko	Breacker	Dicks	Potts	Rieper	Allen*	Moncur	Bishop	Cottee	Boere	Holmes	Hutchison

A decent crowd in view of Town's plight. They are rewarded as Thomsen opens the scoring with a well-taken goal. In the 90th minute an ugly melee develops as Hutchison appears to kick Thomsen in the head, but only Dicks is booked. Deep into injury-time Boere nets Holmes' cross.

39	A	29/4	L	22	21	0-2	24	LEICESTER	15,248

Whitlow 68, Lowe 90
Ref: A Wilkie

Morgan	Yallop	Wark	Johnson	Linighan	Milton	Williams	Mathie	Marshall	Slater	Thomsen	Lawrence
Poole	Blake*	Whitlow	Hill	Willis	Carey	Draper	Parker	Roberts	Robins	Lowe	

Two relegated sides put on a sad spectacle. Young keeper Morgan gets a chance to show what he can do. Lawrence is hauled down by Johnson and Whitlow curls the free-kick home. To compound Town's misery, former striker David Lowe smashes a last-minute goal after a long throw.

40	H	6/5	W	22	27	2-0	27	COVENTRY	12,883

Marshall 52, Pressley 62 (og)
Ref: M Reed

Wright	Yallop	Wark	Tanner*	Linighan*	Milton	Williams^	Mathie	Marshall	Mason	Thomsen	Chapman/Norfolk
Gould	Borrows	Burrows	Richardson	Pressley*	Rennie	Strachan	Cook	Dublin	Hall	Ndlovu	Jones

Local lad Richard Wright debuts in goal – the 15th new face of the season! He has a superb game, showing maturity and confidence. After ten without a win, Town are able to punish defensive howlers by a City side now also in danger. New boss Ron Atkinson is 'disgusted' at his side.

41	H	9/5	L	22	15	0-1	27	EVERTON	14,951

Rideout 49
Ref: R Hart

Wright	Yallop*	Swailes	Milton	Linighan	Williams	Mathie	Marshall^	Mason	Thomsen		Johnson/Chapman
Southall	Barrett	Ablett	Ebbrell	Unsworth	Horne	Limpar*	Amokachi^	Rideout	Hinchcliffe	Waddle	Samways/Barlow !

Town put in a decent performance at last, but have no luck in front of goal. Shortly after the break a shot by the Nigerian Daniel Amokachi is beaten out by brave Wright, but falls conveniently for Rideout and he finds the net. Sub Barlow shows dissent and gets a second yellow card.

42	A	14/5	L	22	13	1-4	27	SHEFFIELD WED	30,213

Mathie 51
Whittingham 7, 59, Williams 55, [Bright 90]
Ref: G Poll

Wright	Yallop	Swailes	Milton	Linighan^	Williams	Mathie	Chapman	Mason	Thomsen*		Tanner/Gregory N
Woods	Nolan	Atherton	Walker !	Pearce	Sheridan*	Whittingham	Sinton	Hirst*	Williams	Waddle	Hyde/Bright

Whittingham's sweet shot sets the trend early. Thomsen is carried off with a serious-looking knee injury. Mathie levels from close range but Williams and Whittingham hit back via a quick double blast. An awful year ends in predictable fashion with a Bright goal in the dying seconds.

Home 16,818   Away 22,236   Average

FA CARLING PREM (CUP-TIES) Manager: John Lyall > George Burley SEASON 1994-95

Coca-Cola Cup

		Att	F-A	H-T	Scorers, Times, and Referees					subs used

2:1 H BOLTON 21/9 — Att 16 / 7,787 1:10 — F-A 0-3 L — H-T 0-1

McAteer 8, McGinley 84, Thompson 88
Ref: G Poll

Forrest	Yallop	Johnson	Taricco	Wark	Williams	Sedgley	Slater*	Mi_ton	Guentchev	Thomsen^
Branaghan	Lydiate	Phillips	McAteer	Thompson	Stubbs	Lee	Sneekes	Paatelainen* McGinlay^	Fisher	

subs used: Kiwomya/Linighan DeFreitas/Coyle

New foreign imports Thomsen and Taricco make their bow, but it's an awful night. McAteer sweeps in a loose ball. Lee's cross is whacked in by McGinlay and Thompson beats Taricco to build a big lead. Humiliated Town look bereft of ideas. The debutants look rather bewildered.

2:2 A BOLTON 5/10 — 16 / 8,212 1:8 — F-A 0-1 L — H-T 0-0

Sneekes 77
Ref: T Heilbron
(Town lose 0-4 on aggregate)

Forrest	Yallop	Johnson	Linighan	Wark*	Williams	Sedgley	Slater	Palmer	Guentchev	Thomsen
Branaghan	Lydiate	Phillips	McAteer	Thompson	Stubbs	Lee	Sneekes	Paatelainen* McGinlay^	Fisher	

subs used: Cotterell DeFreitas/Coyle

A very limp performance by Town, who never look like clawing back the deficit. The lively Adrian Paz is missed, and Steve Sedgley still seems to be having trouble settling. McGinlay provides a fine ball for Sneekes, who speeds clear and tucks home a nice goal. A night to forget.

FA Cup

3 A WREXHAM 7/1 — 21 / 8,324 2:11 — F-A 1-2 L — H-T 0-0

Linighan 86
Durkan 59, Bennett 88p
Ref: R Gifford

Baker	Yallop	Vaughan	Mason^	Whelan	Linighan	Sedgley	Slater*	Kiwomya	Thomsen	Tanner
Marriott	Jones	Hardy	Hughes	Hunter	Humes	Bennett	Owen	Connolly	Cross	Durkan

subs used: Paz/Johnson

Town are ripe fodder for a giant-killing. A stunning close-range volley from Durkan gives Brian Flynn's men the lead. Linighan levels, heading in Paz's corner. Two minutes from time Tanner fouls Connolly and the penalty is converted. Paz and Whelan hit the bar in the dying moments.

League table

	Team	P	Home W	D	L	F	A	Away W	D	L	F	A	Pts
1	Blackburn	42	17	2	2	54	21	10	6	5	26	18	89
2	Manchester U	42	16	4	1	42	4	10	6	5	35	24	88
3	Nott'm Forest	42	12	6	3	36	18	10	5	6	36	25	77
4	Liverpool	42	13	5	3	38	13	8	6	7	27	24	74
5	Leeds	42	13	5	3	35	15	7	8	6	24	23	73
6	Newcastle	42	14	6	1	46	20	6	6	9	21	27	72
7	Tottenham	42	10	5	6	32	25	6	9	6	34	33	62
8	QP Rangers	42	11	3	7	36	26	6	6	9	25	33	60
9	Wimbledon	42	9	5	7	26	26	6	6	9	22	39	56
10	Southampton	42	8	9	4	33	27	4	9	8	28	36	54
11	Chelsea	42	7	7	7	25	22	6	8	7	25	33	54
12	Arsenal	42	6	9	6	27	21	7	3	11	25	28	51
13	Sheffield Wed	42	7	7	7	26	26	6	5	10	23	31	51
14	West Ham	42	9	6	6	28	19	4	5	12	16	29	50
15	Everton	42	8	9	4	31	23	3	8	10	13	28	50
16	Coventry	42	7	7	7	23	25	5	7	9	21	37	50
17	Manchester C	42	7	7	7	37	28	4	6	11	16	36	49
18	Aston Villa	42	6	9	6	27	24	5	6	10	24	32	48
19	Crys Palace	42	6	6	9	16	23	5	5	11	18	26	45
20	Norwich	42	8	8	5	27	21	2	5	14	10	33	43
21	Leicester	42	5	6	10	28	37	1	5	15	17	43	29
22	IPSWICH	42	5	3	13	24	34	2	3	16	12	59	27
		924	205	134	123	697	498	123	134	205	498	697	1252

Odds & ends

Double wins: (0).

Double losses: (10) Arsenal, Aston Villa, Blackburn. C Palace, Everton, Man C, Norwich, Nott'm F, Sheff Wed, Tottenham.

Won from behind: (1) Southampton (H).

Lost from front: (1) Everton (A).

High spots: The arrival of Burley and the end of the Lyall-McGiven era. Goalscoring debuts by Alex Mathie and Adam Tanner. The club's first win at Anfield in 34 attempts. The thrilling 3-2 home victory over Manchester U. The highly-impressive debut of Richard Wright.

Low spots: Fewer wins and more losses than in any other season. Relegation confirmed with six games still remaining. The 0-9 humiliation at Old Trafford. Ten defeats in the first 13 games – the worst start in 31 seasons. Two defeats by First Division Bolton in the Coca-Cola Cup. Defeat at Second Division Wrexham in the FA Cup. The run of seven successive losses (goals for 0, against 23). Being compared to a non-League side by Kevin Keegan. The messy row with Colchester over Burley compensation. The death, aged 60, of ex-chairman Patrick Cobbold. The poor form of £1 million record purchase Steve Sedgley. The last-minute own-goal misery of debutant Chris Swailes.

Player of the Year: Craig Forrest.

Ever-presents: (0).

Hat-tricks: (0).

Opposing hat-tricks: (4) Andy Cole (Man U), Alan Shearer (Blackburn), Ian Wright (Arsenal), Tony Yeboah (Leeds).

Leading scorer: (5) Claus Thomsen.

Appearances & Goals

Player	Lge	Sub	LC	Sub	FAC	Sub	Gls Lge	LC	FAC	Tot
Baker, Clive	2									
Chapman, Lee	9	7				1			1	1
Cotterell, Leo	2	2				1				
Ellis, Kevin	1									
Forrest, Craig	36		2							
Gregory, David		1								
Gregory, Neil		2								
Guentchev, Bontcho	11	5	2				1			1
Johnson, Gavin	14	3	2			1				
Kiwomya, Chris	13	2	1		1		3			3
Linighan, David	31	1	1		1					
Marshall, Ian	14	4					3			3
Mason, Paul	19	2	1				3			3
Mathie, Alex	13						2			2
Milton, Simon	19	6	1				2			2
Morgan, Phil	1									
Norfolk, Lee	1	2								
Palmer, Steve	10	2	1							
Paz, Adrian	13	4		1			1			1
Sedgley, Steve	26	2	2		1		4			4
Slater, Stuart	22	5	2		1		1			1
Stockwell, Mick	14	1								
Swailes, Chris	4									
Tanner, Adam	9	1					2			2
Taricco, Mauricio		1								
Thomsen, Claus	31	2	2		1		5			5
Thompson, Neil	9	1								
Vaughan, Tony	10									
Wark, John	26	2					4			4
Whelan, Phil	12	1								
Williams, Geraint	38	2					1			1
Wright, Richard	3									
Yallop, Frank	41	2								
Youds, Eddie	9	1					2			2
(own-goals)							2			2
34 players used	462	55	22	3	11	2	36		1	37

ENDSLEIGH DIVISION 1 — Manager: George Burley — SEASON 1995-96

No	Date	Opponent	Att	Pos	Pt	F-A	H-T	Scorers, Times, and Referees	1	2	3	4	5	6	7	8	9	10	11	subs used
1	A 12/8	BIRMINGHAM	18,910		0	L 1-3	0-0	Marshall 47 · Ref: D Allison	Forrest	Stockwell	Thompson^	Vaughan	Wark^	Sedgley	Uhlenbeek	Williams	Mathie	Marshall	Thomsen	Chapman/Yallop"/Milton
								Tait 64, Otto 73, Bowen 85	Bennett	Poole	Frain	Ward	Edwards	Hunt	Daish^	Claridge	Muir"	Forsyth"	Tait	Donowa/Otto/Bowen
								Town look rather timid, despite the introduction of Dutch winger Uhlenbeek. Marshall's low shot is cancelled out as Tait takes an easy chance at the far post. Otto's solo run ends with a spectacular shot into the roof of the net. Barry Fry's men are safe as Bowen converts Donowa's pass.												
2	H 19/8	CRYSTAL PALACE	12,681	16	3	W 1-0	1-0	Mathie 38 · Ref: G Singh	Forrest	Stockwell	Vaughan	Sedgley	Wark	Williams	Uhlenbeek	Thomsen	Mathie	Marshall	Milton	Cox/Matthew
				11					Martyn	Edworthy	Gordon!	Hopkin*	Coleman	Shaw	Houghton	Pitcher	Dowie	Dyer	Ndah^	
								Martyn saves Vaughan's effort after a Sedgley corner, but Mathie pounces to slam the loose ball into the net. Dowie goes close to an equaliser, hitting the bar on the hour mark. Gordon pulls back Uhlenbeek as he races on to a through ball and is given the red card for a professional foul.												
3	A 26/8	WEST BROM	14,470	17	4	D 0-0	0-0	Ref: K Lynch	Forrest	Stockwell	Vaughan	Sedgley	Palmer	Williams	Uhlenbeek	Milton	Mathie*	Chapman	Slater^	Gregory/Tarico
				7					Naylor	Burgess	Edwards	Coldicott	Mardon	Raven	Donovan	Gilbert*	Taylor	Hunt	Hamilton	Ashcroft
								Stockwell makes a brilliant intervention to prevent a certain goal for Hamilton. Both sides fritter away a number of chances. Alan Buckley's side go closest as Ashcroft's big dipper hits the post. Sedgley has a good game and looks to have put last season's indifferent form behind him.												
4	H 30/8	STOKE	10,848	12	7	W 4-1	1-0	Slater 38, 62, Mathie 82, 86 · Ref: M Bailey	Forrest	Stockwell	Vaughan	Sedgley	Palmer	Williams*	Uhlenbeek	Milton^	Mathie	Chapman	Slater	Tarico/Tanner
				18				Peschisolido 83	Muggleton	Clarkson	Sandford	Sigurdsson	Overson	Orlygsson	Keen^	Wallace	Peschisolido	Scott	Gleghorn	Sturridge
								Lou Macari's men are flattened by some slick finishing. Slater picks his spot after Milton's pass. His second is a superb turn and shot. Mathie converts twice from corners. Chapman misses an open goal as Town cruise to the points. Peschisolido skips round Forrest for the consolation.												
5	H 2/9	SUNDERLAND	12,390	3	10	W 3-0	2-0	Mathie 36, 42, 55 · Ref: G Pooley	Forrest	Stockwell	Vaughan^	Sedgley	Palmer	Williams	Uhlenbeek	Milton^	Mathie	Marshall	Slater	Tarico/Tanner
				19					Chamberlain	Kubicki	Scott	Bracewell	Ball	Melville	Gray^	Stewart*	Howey	Smith	Russell^	Ord/Mullin/Aiston
								Marshall's shot is blocked by Ball, but Mathie fires home the rebound. Mathie snaps up another rebound after Chamberlain keeps out his first attempt. Marshall's through ball gives him his hat-trick. The scoreline flatters Ipswich, for Peter Reid's outfit were never three goals inferior.												
6	A 9/9	HUDDERSFIELD	12,057	7	10	L 1-2	0-2	Sedgley 81p · Ref: E Wolstenholme	Forrest	Stockwell	Tarico	Sedgley	Palmer!	Williams	Uhlenbeek	Tanner^	Mathie^	Marshall	Slater	Chapman/Thomsen
				10				Collins 33, Sedgley 44 (og)	Francis	Brown	Cowan^	Bullock	Scully	Sinnott	Dalton	Reid	Booth	Jepson	Collins	Baldry
								Both sides are amazed when a 50-50 challenge involving Palmer sees the Town man sent off after 25 minutes. Angry Town fall two behind as Bullock rounds Forrest and tees up Collins, then Booth's cross is bundled into his own net by Sedgley. Scully's foul gives Town a late penalty.												
7	A 12/9	OLDHAM	5,622	7	11	D 1-1	0-0	Marshall 47 · Ref: W Burns	Forrest	Stockwell	Tarico	Sedgley	Palmer	Williams	Uhlenbeek	Tanner^	Mathie*	Marshall	Slater^	Chapman/Vaughan
				11				McCarthy 78	Hallworth	McNiven	Makin	Henry	Jobson	Fleming	Halle	Bernard	McCarthy	Banger	Brennan^	Beresford
								Gregory steps up for his first start of the season in place of injured Mathie and Thomsen is recalled in place of Tanner. Latics old boy Marshall drills home Slater's cross shortly after the interval. Sean McCarthy celebrates his 30th birthday with the equaliser, heading in Beresford's cross.												
8	H 16/9	WATFORD	11,441	4	14	W 4-2	2-1	Gregory 5, 44, Thomsen 55, Uhlenbeek 85 · Ref: R Harris	Forrest	Stockwell	Tarico	Sedgley	Wark^	Williams	Uhlenbeek	Thomsen	Gregory^	Marshall	Slater^	Vaughan
				19				Phillips 9, Pitcher 82	Miller	Lavin	Johnson^	Foster	Holdsworth	Ramage	Bazeley	Payne	Mooney	Porter	Phillips	Pitcher
								Slater's shot is diverted in by Gregory for his first senior goal. Phillips quickly levels with a volley under Forrest. Gregory fires in from an Uhlenbeek back-heeled pass. Thomsen loops in a header. After sub Pitcher cracks home a fine effort, Uhlenbeek rifles in his first Town goal.												
9	H 23/9	CHARLTON	12,815	8	14	L 1-5	1-0	Thomsen 4 · Ref: G Barber	Forrest*	Tarico	Vaughan!	Sedgley	Wark^	Williams	Uhlenbeek	Thomsen	Mathie	Gregory	Slater	Chapman/Swailes
				4				Chapple 55, Leaburn 69, 70, 96p, [Linger 94]	Salmon	Humphrey	Stuart	Garland	Chapple	Balmer	Newton	Grant^	Robinson	Leaburn	Bowyer*	Robson/Linger
								Thomsen fires Town ahead early. After the break disaster strikes and the collapse begins. Forrest collides with Grant as he sets up the equaliser and is carried off with a neck injury. With no sub keeper on the bench, Gregory goes in and is beaten four times. Vaughan sees yellow twice.												
10	A 30/9	SHEFFIELD UTD	12,557	7	15	D 2-2	0-2	Marshall 61, 68 · Ref: P Richards	Wright	Tarico	Yallop	Sedgley	Swailes	Williams	Uhlenbeek	Thomsen	Mathie	Marshall	Milton	Slater
				17				Blake 10, Whitehouse 33p	Kelly	Blount	Nilsen	Rogers	Tuttle	Beard^	Flo^	Blake*	Hodges	Williams	Whitehouse/Scott/Holland/Veart	
								Blake combines with Flo for a neat goal. Swailes fouls Blake for the penalty. Whitehouse shoves Tarico to the ground and is sent off. After the interval Town hit back as Marshall guides in Slater's cross and then gets a second as his header bobbles over the line from Milton's cross.												
11	H 7/10	WOLVERHAMPTON	15,335	13	15	L 1-2	1-2	Sedgley 28p · Ref: M Pierce	Wright	Stockwell	Tarico^	Sedgley	Mowbray	Williams	Uhlenbeek	Thomsen	Mathie	Scowcroft	Slater	Yallop
				15				Goodman 35, Atkins 43	Stowell	Rankine	Thompson	Atkins	Young	Richards	Daley^	Goodman	Venus	Williams^	Ferguson	Cowans/Wright
								Tony Mowbray, signed from Celtic, makes his debut. After Scowcroft's back-heel hits the post, Young pulls down Sedgley for Town's penalty. Goodman outpaces Stockwell and powers in a stunning solo goal to level. New £1m signing Atkins gets the final touch for the winner.												

Match-by-match record (games 12–23)

No	V	Opponent	Date	Att	Pos	Res	FT	HT	Opp Pos	Pts	Scorers	Ref
12	A	DERBY	14/10	13,034	13	D	1-1	1-1	17	16	Sedgley 2 / Gabbiadini 27	N Barry
13	H	LUTON	22/10	9,123	14	L	0-1	0-1	21	16	— / Oldfield 24	T West
14	A	READING	28/10	10,281	11	W	4-1	1-0	18	19	Uhlenbeek 43, Mathie 67, Mason 85, Lovell 64 [Williams 89]	J Brandwood
15	H	GRIMSBY	4/11	10,250	13	D	2-2	2-0	12	20	Mason 17, 44 / Woods 62, Dobbin 69	G Pooley
16	A	MILLWALL	11/11	11,360	15	L	1-2	1-1	1	20	Mason 37 / Malkin 1, Witter 53	G Singh
17	A	NORWICH	19/11	17,862	15	L	1-2	0-1	6	20	Wark 82 / Newsome 9, Fleck 72	K Lynch
18	H	SOUTHEND	22/11	9,757	15	D	1-1	0-0	16	21	Uhlenbeek 48 / Regis 60	T Lunt
19	H	PORTSMOUTH	25/11	10,286	14	W	3-2	2-1	22	24	Milton 2, Marshall 26, Thompson 90 / Walsh 25, Allen 75	B Knight
20	A	WOLVERHAMPTON	3/12	20,867	15	D	2-2	1-0	21	25	Marshall 32, Mowbray 90 / Goodman 60, 71	G Cain
21	A	CHARLTON	9/12	10,316	13	W	2-0	0-0	9	28	Stockwell 49, Marshall 67	A D'Urso
22	H	SHEFFIELD UTD	16/12	9,630	14	D	1-1	0-0	23	29	Tuttle 60 (og) / Starbuck 65	J Rushton
23	H	BARNSLEY	22/12	11,791	14	D	2-2	1-0	15	30	Marshall 9, Mathie 66 / De Zeeuw 54, Liddell 61	D Orr

Line-ups and reports

12 — DERBY (A)
Town: Petterson, Stockwell, Yallop, Linighan", Mowbray, Williams^, Sedgley*, Uhlenbeek*, Mathie, Marshall, Slater — subs Milton/Gregory/Tanner
Derby: Hoult, Carsley, Nicholson, Preece, Yates, Rowett, Van der Laan, Wrack^, Willems, Gabbiadini, Powell* — subs Simpson/Sturridge
After an assist by Slater, Sedgley slots in a sweetly-taken early goal. Five minutes later Uhlenbeek is scythed down, but strong penalty appeals are waved aside. The unmarked Gabbiadini equalises for Jim Smith's side, heading in a cross from Preece. Petterson starts a second loan spell.

13 — LUTON (H)
Town: Forrest, Stockwell, Taricco, Linighan, Mowbray, Williams, Milton, Sedgley^, Mathie*, Marshall^, Slater — subs Gregory/Tanner
Luton: Feuer, Peake, Johnson M, Davis, Hughes, Vilstrup*, Alexander, Oakes, Oldfield, Marshall^, Harvey* — subs Wad'kJ'rson G/Guentchev
Town slump to a fourth successive home defeat in a dull game. Oldfield cuts in and buries a fine shot at Forrest's near post, his first since returning to Luton. Their boss Terry Westley has a happy return to Portman Road, and performs a David Pleat-style jig on the pitch at the end!

14 — READING (A)
Town: Forrest, Stockwell, Taricco, Vaughan, Mowbray^, Williams, Milton, Uhlenbeek*, Mathie, Marshall*, Mason — subs Slater/Gregory
Reading: Woods, Brown, Kerr, Codner^, Williams, Bernal, Glikes, Gooding, Dunn*, Lovell, Meaker* — subs Nogan/Morley/Lambert
Uhlenbeek converts Mason's cross to grab the lead. Lovell's left-footer levels, but Marshall's lofted ball puts Mathie through to quickly regain the lead. Transfer-listed Mason heads in and Town breathe easy. In the dying seconds Williams skips through to finish off mediocre Reading.

15 — GRIMSBY (H)
Town: Forrest, Stockwell, Taricco, Vaughan, Mowbray, Williams, Milton^, Uhlenbeek^, Mathie, Marshall^, Mason — subs Gregory/Tanner
Grimsby: Crichton, Laws, Croft, Handyside, Lever, Groves, Childs, Dobbin, Woods, Forrester^, Southall — subs Livingstone
A wall-pass with Marshall allows Mason to shoot home. His second comes after Crichton blocks his initial effort. Brian Laws' men roll their sleeves up and after Livingstone hits the bar. The Mariners level when unmarked Dobbin loops in a header.

16 — MILLWALL (A)
Town: Forrest, Stockwell, Taricco, Wark, Mowbray, Williams, Milton, Thomsen, Williams, Marshall, Mason — subs Gregory
Millwall: Keller, Newman, Thatcher, Bowry, Witter, Stevens, Taylor*, Rae, Ward, Malkin, Dixon^ — subs Savage/Fuchs
In the first minute Malkin heads Van Blerk's cross against a post and scrambles the rebound in. Town recover composure and Mason drills in a left-foot drive after Milton pulls the ball back to him. Mick McCathy's outfit win the points when Witter shoots home after a free-kick move.

17 — NORWICH (A)
Town: Forrest, Stockwell, Taricco, Wark, Mowbray, Williams, Thomsen, Williams, Mathie* Mathie, Marshall, Mason* — subs Gregory/Tanner
Norwich: Gunn, Bradshaw^, Ullathorne, Adams, Newsome, Prior, Bowen, Fleck, Ward, Milligan*, O'Neill — subs Akinbiyi/Sutch
Newsome beats Mowbray to head in O'Neill's free-kick. Fleck fastens onto Ward's header for the second. Town hit back as Ullathorne climbs all over Mathie. Mr Lynch then awards Town a second penalty, but there is pandemonium when he consults a linesman and changes his mind!

18 — SOUTHEND (H)
Town: Forrest, Stockwell, Taricco, Mowbray, Wark, Williams, Uhlenbeek, Thomsen, Mathie, Gregory^, Mason* — subs Tanner/Scowcroft
Southend: Royce, Dublin, Powell, Lapper, Bodley, Gridelet, Marsh, Byrne, Regis, Belsvik^, Hails — subs Jones
Town break through after the interval when Uhlenbeek drills a shot goalwards, which deflects in off Powell. Ronnie Whelan's side equalises when Regis flashes in a header from Byrne's curling cross. It's a poor display and there's discontent in the stands. Problem time for Burley.

19 — PORTSMOUTH (H)
Town: Forrest, Taricco, Thomson, Thomsen, Mowbray, Williams, Uhlenbeek*, Tanner, Mathie, Marshall, Milton — subs Scowcroft
Portsmouth: Knight, Pethick, Stimson, McLaughlin", Whitbread, Butters, Walsh, Allen, Durnin, Hall^, Carter* — subs Rees/Igoe/Griffiths
It's six home games without a win, but Milton boosts Town with an early strike. After Uhlenbeek loses possession, Walsh chips in. Marshall's shot beats Knight, but Allen deservedly levels with an angled drive. An open game is settled by Thompson's late 30-yard thunderbolt free-kick.

20 — WOLVERHAMPTON (A)
Town: Forrest, Taricco^, Thompson, Thompson, Sedgley, Mowbray, Thomsen*, Williams, Mathie, Marshall, Milton — subs Uhlenbeek/Mason
Wolverhampton: Stowell, Rankine, Thompson, Ferguson, Law, Richards, Venus, Goodman, Bull, Emblen*, Birch — subs Atkins
Debutant Barber makes a fine early save. Stowell slides out of his box and handles, the free-kick reaching Marshall, who nets. Goodman levels from close range and then takes Ferguson's pass to clip in a glorious goal. Town level in the last minute through Mowbray's powerful header.

21 — CHARLTON (A)
Town: Forrest, Taricco, Thompson, Humphrey*, Sedgley, Mowbray, Stockwell*, Williams, Mathie, Marshall, Milton — subs Uhlenbeek
Charlton: Barber, Stowell, Rankine, Stuart, Jones, Rufus, Balmer, Newton^, Grant", Robinson, White, Bowyer — subs Williams/Mortimer/Chandler
Mathie misses Milton's cross, but Stockwell is on hand behind him to pounce and score the opener. The points are safe after Marshall produces a stunning volley after good work on the flank by Milton. Town are now looking in better shape and hopes are restored of a rise up the table.

22 — SHEFFIELD UTD (H)
Town: Forrest, Taricco*, Thompson, Thomsen, Sedgley, Mowbray, Stockwell, Williams, Mathie, Marshall, Milton — subs Uhlenbeek
Sheffield Utd: Kelly, Rogers, Nilsen, Gannon, Fitzgerald, Tuttle, White, Veart^, Blake^, Ward, Holland — subs Hodges/Starbuck
The lowly Blades put up a grim fight, but are shattered when Marshall's cross is swept into his own net by the unfortunate Tuttle. Forrest is left stranded by White's pull-back and Starbuck guides the ball in. In the latter stages Marshall misses a good chance to win it when put through.

23 — BARNSLEY (H)
Town: Forrest, Taricco, Thomsen, Thomsen, Sedgley, Mowbray^, Williams, Mathie, Marshall, Milton — subs Milton
Barnsley: Watson, Eaden, Shirtliff, Sheridan, Moses, De Zeeuw, Liddell*, Redfearn, O'Connell, Rammell, Archdeacon — subs Payton/Appleby
Marshall nets a peach of a goal on the run. Danny Wilson's side play some attractive football and De Zeeuw levels from 15 yards after an Archdeacon cross. Eaden's cross is guided home by Liddell. Mathie saves a point when he seizes onto a long ball and pokes it past Watson.

24 — H, 1/1 — PORT VALE — Att 9,926 — Pos 12/19 — W, Pt 33 — F-A 5-1 — H-T 0-0

Scorers/Times: Milton 58, Sedgley 60, Marshall 73, Naylor 86 [Mathie 84, 90]
Ref: R Furnandiz

Pos	1	2	3	4	5	6	7	8	9	10	11	subs used
Town	Forrest	Stockwell	Yallop	Thomsen	Mowbray	Williams	Uhlenbeek*	Sedgley	Mathie	Marshall	Milton	Appleby
Opp	Musselwhite/Hill	Tankard	Bogie*	Griffiths	Glover	McCarthy	Porter	Foyle	Naylor	Guppy	Talbot	

They're a long time coming, but six goals in 32 minutes has the fans singing. Milton's shot is deflected in and Sedgley's low drive makes it two. Marshall's well-judged header is followed by Mathie ploughing through for the fourth. Forrest's long punt sets up Mathie for the final act.

25 — A, 13/1 — CRYSTAL PALACE — Att 14,097 — Pos 13/15 — D, Pt 34 — F-A 1-1 — H-T 0-1

Scorers/Times: Mathie 57, Davies 26
Ref: C Wilkes

Pos	1	2	3	4	5	6	7	8	9	10	11	subs used
Town	Wright	Stockwell	Taricco*	Thomsen	Mowbray	Williams	Mason	Sedgley	Mathie	Marshall	Milton	Wark
Opp	Martyn	Edworthy	Gordon	Hopkin	Roberts	Cundy	Houghton	Pitcher	Freedman*	Taylor^	Davies^	Dyer/Rodger/McKenzie

Teenager Wright replaces Forrest in goal and Mason is back in midfield to face Steve Coppell's men. A poor clearance falls to Houghton who launches a diagonal pass that loops into the net from the head of Davies. Sedgley's long pass is powered home by Mathie for the equaliser.

26 — H, 20/1 — BIRMINGHAM — Att 12,540 — Pos 11/10 — W, Pt 37 — F-A 2-0 — H-T 1-0

Scorers/Times: Milton 23, 57
Ref: I Hemley

Pos	1	2	3	4	5	6	7	8	9	10	11	subs used
Town	Wright	Uhlenbeek^	Vaughan	Thomsen	Mowbray	Williams	Mason^	Sedgley	Mathie	Gregory	Milton	Yallop/Scowcroft
Opp	Griemink	Briley^	Frain	Forsyth	Edwards	Hunt	Daish	Claridge	Francis	Bowen^	Johnson*	Tait/Finnan/Bull

The unbeaten run is extended to 11 games as Barry Fry's side are seen off without too much trouble. A free-kick is blocked but falls for Milton whose shot is deflected in past Griemink. Gregory holds the ball up well and feeds Milton who cracks in a great shot over the keeper's head.

27 — H, 3/2 — WEST BROM — Att 10,798 — Pos 6/23 — W, Pt 40 — F-A 2-1 — H-T 1-0

Scorers/Times: Marshall 45, Mowbray 84; Taylor 66
Ref: P Taylor

Pos	1	2	3	4	5	6	7	8	9	10	11	subs used
Town	Wright	Stockwell	Taricco	Thomsen	Mowbray	Williams	Mason^	Sedgley	Slater	Marshall	Milton	Stockwell/Scowcroft
Opp	Spink	Holmes	Smith	Cunnington*	Burgess	Raven	Donovan	Gilbert"	Rees^	Hunt	Darby	Coldicott/Taylor/Ashcroft

On the stroke of half-time, Slater catches Spink off his line and Marshall slides in to make sure the ball goes in. Hunt crosses to Taylor who smashes home from close range. Town look off-colour, but win the points thanks to man-of-the-match Mowbray heading in Taricco's cross.

28 — A, 10/2 — STOKE — Att 12,239 — Pos 9/7 — L, Pt 40 — F-A 1-3 — H-T 0-1

Scorers/Times: Scowcroft 54; Sheron 37, 75, Gleghorn 65
Ref: G Cain

Pos	1	2	3	4	5	6	7	8	9	10	11	subs used
Town	Wright	Uhlenbeek	Taricco	Thomsen	Mowbray	Williams	Mason^	Sedgley	Scowcroft	Marshall	Milton*	Stockwell/Slater
Opp	Prudhoe	Clarkson	Sandford	Sigurdsson	Cranson	Potter^	Beeston	Wallace	Sheron	Sturridge*	Gleghorn	Peschisolido/Dreyer

Sheron curls the ball round Wright after a pass to unlikely contract rebel Beeston. Scowcroft nets a fine header from Sedgley's free-kick. Ex-Town favourite Gleghorn, inevitably, is on target for Lou Macari's side with a rare header. Slick finishing by Sheron makes sure Town's run ends.

29 — A, 20/2 — SUNDERLAND — Att 14,052 — Pos 10/3 — L, Pt 40 — F-A 0-1 — H-T 0-1

Scorers/Times: Russell 38
Ref: W Burns

Pos	1	2	3	4	5	6	7	8	9	10	11	subs used
Town	Wright	Uhlenbeek	Taricco	Thomsen	Mowbray*	Stockwell	Mason	Sedgley	Scowcroft	Marshall^	Milton	Vaughan/Slater
Opp	Given	Kubicki	Hall	Bracewell	Ball	Melville	Gray	Russell	Howey	Cooke	Ord	

On a slippery, snow-covered Roker surface, Bracewell's long pass finds Russell, who controls the ball neatly and shoots past the advancing Wright. Town generally knocked the ball around very well in the tricky conditions and were highly unfortunate not to come away with a point.

30 — A, 24/2 — WATFORD — Att 11,872 — Pos 10/24 — W, Pt 43 — F-A 3-2 — H-T 0-2

Scorers/Times: Uhlenbeek 48, Mathie 66, 82; White 21, Palmer 44
Ref: P Richards

Pos	1	2	3	4	5	6	7	8	9	10	11	subs used
Town	Wright	Uhlenbeek	Taricco	Thomsen	Vaughan	Stockwell^	Mason	Sedgley	Mathie*	Marshall	Milton	Gregory/Scowcroft
Opp	Miller	Gibbs	Barnes	Hessenthaler	Holdsworth	Millen	Penrice^	Palmer	White	Mooney*	Phillips	Ramage/Bailey

The Hornets welcome Graham Taylor back to his spiritual home. Uhlenbeek begins the fightback with an angled shot. Mathie levels, heading in Uhlenbeek's cross. The wide-man again features in the winner, setting up Mathie's sweetly-taken goal.

31 — H, 3/3 — LEICESTER — Att 9,817 — Pos 7/8 — W, Pt 46 — F-A 4-2 — H-T 3-0

Scorers/Times: Wark 6, Milton 11, Marshall 13, 85; Roberts 55, 75
Ref: K Leach

Pos	1	2	3	4	5	6	7	8	9	10	11	subs used
Town	Wright	Uhlenbeek	Taricco	Thomsen	Wark	Williams	Mason*	Sedgley	Mathie	Marshall	Milton	Scowcroft
Opp	Poole	Grayson	Whitlow	Carey	Walsh	Parker	Lennon	Taylor*	Claridge	Roberts	Lewis^	Lawrence/Heskey

A free-kick routine sees Wark net a 20-yard screamer. Mason sets up Milton and then rampant Town go three up in 13 minutes when Marshall heads powerfully home. Two second-half goals by Roberts and a Wark penalty miss causes some concern, but then Marshall intervenes again.

32 — A, 9/3 — BARNSLEY — Att 7,705 — Pos 10/8 — D, Pt 47 — F-A 3-3 — H-T 0-2

Scorers/Times: Marshall 85, 87, Milton 89; Redfearn 24p, 47, Liddell 32
Ref: I Cruickshanks

Pos	1	2	3	4	5	6	7	8	9	10	11	subs used
Town	Wright	Uhlenbeek	Taricco	Thomsen	Wark*	Williams	Mason^	Sedgley	Mathie	Marshall	Milton	Vaughan/Scowcroft
Opp	Watson	Eaden	Shirtliff	Jones	Archdeacon	De Zeeuw	Liddell	Redfearn	O'Connell	Payton	Sheridan	

The dangerous Redfearn and Liddell power Danny Wilson's side into a handsome 3-0 lead. But with only five minutes remaining Town launch an astonishing comeback. Marshall takes advantage of a Watson error and then some hesitant defending. Milton equalises from a Mathie cross.

33 — A, 13/3 — LEICESTER — Att 17,783 — Pos 6/7 — W, Pt 50 — F-A 2-0 — H-T 0-0

Scorers/Times: Marshall 12, Mathie 36
Ref: K Leach

Pos	1	2	3	4	5	6	7	8	9	10	11	subs used
Town	Wright	Uhlenbeek	Taricco	Thomsen	Vaughan	Williams	Stockwell^	Sedgley	Mathie	Marshall	Milton	Scowcroft
Opp	Poole	Grayson	Rolling"	Willis	Walsh	Parker	Lennon	Lawrence	Claridge	Heskey	Lewis^	Robins/Lowe

This is a tense, all-ticket affair, and Town are now looking serious play-off contenders. Marshall nets a right-foot affair, and Town are now looking serious play-off contenders. Marshall nets a right-foot after chaos in the City area. Marshall knocks the ball down for Mathie to poke home the second. This duo have a private £50 bet over who will be leading marksman.

34 — H, 16/3 — TRANMERE — Att 11,759 — Pos 7/16 — L, Pt 50 — F-A 1-2 — H-T 1-0

Scorers/Times: Marshall 14; Aldridge 84, Bennett 85
Ref: S Baines

Pos	1	2	3	4	5	6	7	8	9	10	11	subs used
Town	Wright	Uhlenbeek	Taricco	Thomsen	Vaughan	Williams	Stockwell	Sedgley*	Mathie	Marshall*	Milton^	Mason/Scowcroft
Opp	Coyne	Stephens	Thomas	Rogers	Teale	Cook	Brannan	Aldridge	Moore	Nevin^	Branch*	Bennett/Irons

Williams hits the post and Marshall snaps up the rebound. Uhlenbeek blocks Bennett's shot as Town power forward. The vital second goal never comes, however, and with time running out Wright blocks Bennett's shot and Aldridge levels. Bennett then nets from Aldridge's cross.

Season record — matches 35–46

№		Opponent	Date	Att	Pos		Pts	Res	FT	HT	Scorers / Opponent scorers	Referee
35	H	OLDHAM	19/3	9,674	6	20	53	W	2-1	0-0	Mason 53, 85 / Richardson 72p	Ref: G Barber
36	A	PORT VALE	23/3	7,277	6	18	53	L	1-2	1-1	Marshall 38 / Bogie 41p, McCarthy 86	Ref: P Rejer
37	A	LUTON	30/3	9,151	5	23	56	W	2-1	1-0	Milton 5, 51 / Grant 49	Ref: G Singh
38	H	DERBY	2/4	16,210	5	2	59	W	1-0	1-0	Vaughan 34	Ref: G Pooley
39	H	READING	6/4	17,328	5	21	59	L	1-2	0-1	Mathie 71 / Bernal 22, Quinn 54	Ref: C Wilkes
40	A	GRIMSBY	8/4	5,904	5	13	59	L	1-3	0-0	Scowcroft 90 / Mendonca 69, 72, 88	Ref: M Bailey
41	H	NORWICH	14/4	**20,355**	6	15	62	W	2-1	1-0	Marshall 23, Ullathorne 86(og) / Cureton 62	Ref: J Rushton
42	A	TRANMERE	17/4	6,008	6	16	62	L	2-5	1-1	Mason 5, Marshall 73 / O'Brien 30, Irons 61, 63, Aldridge 81 (Morgan 88)	Ref: J Kirby
43	A	SOUTHEND	20/4	8,363	7	11	62	L	1-2	1-1	Milton 6 / Dublin 30, Marsh 90	Ref: T West
44	A	PORTSMOUTH	27/4	12,954	7	22	65	W	1-0	0-0	Mathie 80	Ref: M Riley
45	H	HUDDERSFIELD	1/5	17,473	6	8	68	W	2-1	1-1	Mathie 45, 84 / Thornley 25	Ref: M Pierce
46	H	MILLWALL	5/5	17,290	7	22	69	D	0-0	0-0		Ref: K Lynch

Home 12,604 — Away 11,930 — Average 12,604

Line-ups and match reports

35 OLDHAM
Town: Wright, Uhlenbeek, Taricco, Thomsen, Vaughan, Williams, Mason, Sedgley, Mathie, Scowcroft, Milton. Subs: Stockw'll / Gregory / Scowcroft
Oldham: Gerrard, Snodin, Serrant, Rickers*, Graham, Redmond, Halle, Richardson, McCarthy, Barlow, Gannon, Beresford
Mason's shot squirts under Gerrard's body to give Town the lead. Thomsen chases the lively Barlow and when they collide, the Dane looks rather unlucky to be penalised – Richardson fires in the penalty. Town smile again when Mason shoots in after the Latics fail to clear properly.

36 PORT VALE
Town: Wright, Uhlenbeek, Taricco, Thomsen, Vaughan^, Williams, Mason, Sedgley, Mathie, Scowcroft, Milton. Subs: Porter / Glover
Port Vale: Musselwhite, Hill, Stokes, Bogie, Griffiths, Aspin, McCarthy, Walker*, Foyle, Naylor*, Guppy
Milton sets up Marshall, who nets from the edge of the area. Town let the lead slip, but for the second game running this is down to a hotly disputed penalty. Uhlenbeek's illegal challenge sets up the goal. John Rudge's team triumph thanks to a brilliant curling shot by McCarthy.

37 LUTON
Town: Wright, Uhlenbeek, Taricco, Thomsen, Scowcroft, Williams, Stockwell, Mathie, Marshall, Milton*, Slater. Subs: Alex'der / Guent'v / Tomlinson
Luton: Feuer, James, Thomas, Davis, Waddock*, Patterson, Thorpe, Oakes", Oldfield^, Grant, Wilkinson
Milton powers home a stunning early volley. Debutant Kim Grant cracks home a fine equaliser for Lennie Lawrence's relegation threatened side. Defensive frailties prove Luton's undoing as James and Feuer misunderstand each other's intentions and Milton pounces for the winner.

38 DERBY
Town: Wright, Uhlenbeek, Taricco, Thomsen, Swailes, Williams, Sedgley, Mathie, Scowcroft, Vaughan, Milton. Subs: Simpson / Willems / Hodges
Derby: Hault, Wassell, Powell C", Powell D*, Yates, Flynn, Van der Laan, Sturridge, Ward", Carsley, Gabbiadini
Some of the missing thousands return for this tense occasion. After Wassell pulls Mathie, Sedgley sends his penalty high and wide. Town go ahead when Vaughan powers in a glorious header from Sedgley's cross. Jim Smith's promotion favourites are held at bay for three vital points.

39 READING
Town: Wright, Uhlenbeek, Taricco, Thomsen, Swailes*, Williams, Mason, Sedgley, Mathie, Scowcroft, Vaughan. Subs: Holsgrove / Lovell
Reading: Sheppard, Booty, Widowczyk, Caskey, Williams A*, Bernal, Gilkes, Gooding, Quinn, Williams M*, Parkinson
Ex-Town man Andy Bernal puts Reading ahead at the far post, having been left unmarked for Darren Caskey's free-kick. Things gets worse as Martin Williams' cross is netted neatly by Jimmy Quinn. Milton goes on a run and sets up Mathie to pull one back. Late pressure is all in vain.

40 GRIMSBY
Town: Wright, Uhlenbeek, Taricco, Thomsen, Vaughan!, Williams, Mason, Sedgley, Mathie, Scowcroft*, Milton. Subs: Liv'stone / Southall / Forrester
Grimsby: Crichton, Fickling, Gallimore, Smith", Handyside, Groves, Flatts, Shakesp're" Woods, Woods, Mendonca, Childs"
A first-half blow when Vaughan is sent off for pulling down Woods. Clive Mendonca punishes Town with a hat-trick inside a 19-minute spell. By the time Scowcroft heads in Uhlenbeek's cross, ten-man Town are a well-beaten side. The result is a serious blow for the promotion bid.

41 NORWICH
Town: Wright, Uhlenbeek, Taricco, Stockwell*, Wark*, Williams, Mason, Sedgley, Scowcroft, Marshall, Milton. Subs: Vaughan / Appleby
Norwich: Gunn, Bradshaw, Ullathorne, Crook, Polston, Newman, Adams, Fleck, Akinbiyi", Milligan", Eadie^, Prior / Johnson / Cureton
There's a 'win or bust' atmosphere about this derby. There's a dramatic and comical winner as Gunn tries to hack clear a back-pass but completely misses the ball! Returning hero Marshall nets after Wright's punt forward. Gary Megson's men level as Cureton fires in Eadie's pass.

42 TRANMERE
Town: Wright (Morgan 88), Uhlenbeek, Taricco*, Thomsen, Vaughan, Williams, Morrissey*, Sedgley, Scowcroft, Stockwell, Slater. Subs: Nevin / Morgan
Tranmere: Coyne, Stevens, McGreal, Rogers^, Higgins, Cook, Aldridge, Brannan, Morgan, O'Brien, Irons
Mason nets a fine shot early on, but O'Brien matches it with the equaliser. Town cave in to four second-half strikes. Irons grabs a couple of cracking goals inside two minutes, and ace marksman Aldridge inevitably gets in on the act. Town's consolation is a fine header by Marshall.

43 SOUTHEND
Town: Forrest, Swailes, Stockwell, Thomsen, Swailes, Williams, Mason, Mathie, Marshall, Marshall, Milton. Subs: Gregory
Southend: Royce, Hails, Stimson, McNally, Bodley, Tilson, Marsh, Byrne, Dublin, Willis, Turner
Williams robs Bodley and sets up Milton, who steadies himself and confidently beats Royce for a crucial early goal. Makeshift striker Dublin heads the equaliser from Turner's cross. The game is on a knife-edge as Mathie hits the post. Marsh wins it at the death with a 30-yard dipper.

44 PORTSMOUTH
Town: Wright, Stockwell, Taricco, Thomsen, Scowcroft, Scowcroft, Mason, Sedgley, Mathie, Marshall, Milton. Subs: Russell / Bradbury
Portsmouth: Knight, Igoe, Awford, McLoughlin, Thomson, Butters, Rees, Simpson, Burton, Hall, Carter*
Town probably need to win their last three games to secure a play-off place. Fratton Park is normally a lucky ground but the woodwork foils Sedgley and Mathie. Ten minutes from time Sedgley breaks forward and supplies Milton, whose perfect ball to Mathie is bent around Knight.

45 HUDDERSFIELD
Town: Wright, Stockwell, Taricco*, Thomsen, Wark, Scowcroft, Mason, Sedgley, Mathie, Marshall, Milton! Subs: Gregory / Baldry / Ward
Huddersfield: Francis, Jenkins, Cowan, Bullock, Scully, Gray, Collins*, Makel, Booth, Jepson, Thornley^
Thornley's drive beats Wright, who otherwise had a heroic game. Brian Horton's men look sharp, but after Milton misses his kick, Mathie is on hand to blast in. Milton is sent off for a second yellow on 66 minutes. A flowing move by the ten men ends with a brilliant Mathie finish.

46 MILLWALL
Town: Wright, Stockwell, Taricco, Thomsen, Wark*, Williams, Mason^, Sedgley, Mathie, Marshall, Milton. Subs: Vaughan / Scowcroft
Millwall: Keller, Newman, Thatcher, Bowry, Van Blerk, Stevens, Connor, Savage^, Doyle, Makin, Weir*, Witter / Neill
A crunch game. Town need a win to get in the play-offs, while Millwall – who have slipped down from top spot – need a win to avoid the drop. A draw is no good to either side. Scowcroft hits a post and Sedgley goes close but all the toil is in vain. Leicester win 1-0 to keep Town in 7th.

ENDSLEIGH DIVISION 1 (CUP-TIES)

Manager: George Burley

Coca-Cola Cup

2:1 A STOCKPORT — 19/9 — Att 4,865 2:8 — 4 — D — F-A 1:1 — H-T 1:1
Scorers: Sedgley 7 / Chalk 4 — Ref: U Rennie

1	2	3	4	5	6	7	8	9	10	11	subs used
Forrest	Stockwell	Taricco	Sedgley	Wark	Williams	Uhlenbeek	Thomsen	Gregory	Chapman	Slater*	Milton
Edwards	*Connolly*	*Todd*	*Bennett*	*Flynn*	*Gannon*	*Beaumont^*	*Ware**	*Helliwell*	*Armstrong*	*Chalk**	*Eckhardt/Allen*

Dave Jones' side take an early lead when Chalk nips in at the far post following a Flynn long-throw. Town hit back quickly and after Flynn trips Gregory, Sedgley hammers the quickly-taken free-kick into the top corner of Edwards' net. Both sides go close to forcing a winning goal.

2:2 H STOCKPORT — 3/10 — Att 8,250 2:5 — 7 — L — F-A 1:2 — aet — H-T 1:0
Scorers: Thomsen 25 / Armstrong 82, Gannon 106 — Ref: M Bailey
(Town lose 2-3 on aggregate)

1	2	3	4	5	6	7	8	9	10	11	subs used
Wright	Yallop	Taricco	Sedgley	Linighan	Williams^	Uhlenbeek	Thomsen	Gregory*	Mathie	Slater	Scowcroft/Milton
Edwards	*Connolly*	*Todd*	*Bennett**	*Flynn**	*Gannon*	*Beaumont^*	*Ware*	*Helliwell*^	*Armstrong*	*Eckhardt*	*Dinning/Oliver/Chalk*

Suffolk youngster Scowcroft debuts and both sides create a host of chances. Armstrong hits the bar and Uhlenbeek hits the post. Thomsen nets a fine goal from Mathie's pass to put Town on top. Armstrong forces extra-time with a late goal and then Gannon's half-volley puts Town out.

FA Cup

3 H BLACKBURN — 6/1 — Att 22,146 P:10 — 12 — D — F-A 0:0 — H-T 0:0
Ref: D Elleray

1	2	3	4	5	6	7	8	9	10	11	subs used
Forrest	Yallop*	Taricco	Sedgley	Mowbray	Williams	Stockwell	Thomsen	Marshall	Mathie	Milton	Uhlenbeek
Flowers	*Berg*	*Kenna*	*Sherwood*	*Hendry*	*Coleman*	*Ripley*	*McKinlay*	*Shearer*	*Newell*	*Gallacher*	

The reigning Premiership champions come to Portman Road and are put under considerable pressure. Sadly the traditionally handsome pitch is currently looking in a very bad way. Ray Harford's men survive all Town can throw at them, then go close themselves near the final whistle.

3R A BLACKBURN — 16/1 — Att 19,606 P:8 — 13 — W — F-A 1:0 — aet — H-T 0:0
Scorers: Mason 115 — Ref: D Elleray

1	2	3	4	5	6	7	8	9	10	11	subs used
Wright	Wark	Vaughan	Sedgley	Mowbray	Williams	Uhlenbeek	Thomsen	Marshall*	Mathie	Milton*	Mason/Gregory
Flowers	*Berg*	*Kenna*	*Batty^*	*Hendry*	*Coleman*	*Ripley*	*Bohinen*	*Shearer*	*Newell**	*Gallacher*	*McKinlay/Sherwood*

Teenager Wright has a sensational game. He makes half-a-dozen brilliant saves, the best of all to keep Shearer at bay. Town break clear twice but Mathie is stopped by Flowers both times. Deep into extra-time, Mathie's cross is knocked by Gregory to Mason, who nets a stunning shot.

4 H WALSALL — 13/2 — Att 18,489 2:15 — 9 — W — F-A 1:0 — H-T 1:0
Scorers: Mason 6 — Ref: D Gallagher

1	2	3	4	5	6	7	8	9	10	11	subs used
Wright	Wark	Taricco	Sedgley	Mowbray	Williams	Scowcroft	Stockwell*	Marshall	Mason	Milton	Uhlenbeek
Wood	*Ntamark^*	*Daniel*	*Viveash*	*Marsh*	*Roper*	*O'Connor*	*Bradley*	*Lightbourne* Wilson*	*Houghton^*		*Kerr/Butler/Evans*

Milton's superb through ball is struck home superbly by Mason from the edge of the area. Chris Nicholl's side toil valiantly, but cannot force an equaliser. Marshall nearly finishes them off after the break but his effort hits the underside of the bar. The pitch again looks in a bad way.

5 H ASTON VILLA — 17/2 — Att 20,748 P:4 — 9 — L — F-A 1:3 — H-T 0:2
Scorers: Mason 84 / Draper 10, Yorke 19, Taylor 55 — Ref: S Lodge

1	2	3	4	5	6	7	8	9	10	11	subs used
Wright	Stockwell*	Taricco	Sedgley	Mowbray	Williams	Thomsen	Scowcroft	Marshall	Mason	Milton	Uhlenbeek
Bosnich	*Charles*	*Wright*	*Southgate*	*Ehiogu*	*Staunton*	*Yorke*	*Draper**	*Milosevic*	*Johnson^*	*Townsend*	*McGrath/Taylor*

In-form Villa are too hot to handle. Draper conjures up a shot out of the blue and the lead is doubled by Yorke's header. Mason nets on the break, but sub Taylor seals it. Chairman Sheepshanks says the cup run has put us back on the map and the 'phoenix of Ipswich' is rising again.

Home / Away league table

#	Team	P	W	D	L	F	A	W	D	L	F	A	Pts
			Home					Away					
1	Sunderland	46	13	8	2	32	10	9	9	5	27	23	83
2	Derby	46	14	8	1	48	22	7	8	8	23	29	79
3	Crys Palace	46	9	9	5	34	26	11	6	6	33	26	75
4	Stoke	46	13	6	4	32	15	9	7	7	28	34	73
5	Leicester *	46	9	7	7	32	29	10	7	6	34	31	71
6	Charlton	46	8	11	4	28	23	9	9	5	29	22	71
7	IPSWICH	46	13	5	5	45	30	6	7	10	34	39	69
8	Huddersfield	46	14	4	5	42	23	3	8	12	19	35	63
9	Sheffield Utd	46	9	7	7	29	25	7	7	9	28	29	62
10	Barnsley	46	9	10	4	34	28	5	8	10	26	38	60
11	West Brom	46	11	5	7	34	29	5	7	11	26	39	60
12	Port Vale	46	10	5	8	30	29	5	10	8	29	37	60
13	Tranmere	46	9	9	5	42	29	5	8	10	22	31	59
14	Southend	46	11	8	4	30	22	4	6	13	22	39	59
15	Birmingham	46	11	7	5	37	23	4	6	13	24	41	58
16	Norwich	46	7	9	7	26	24	7	6	10	33	31	57
17	Grimsby	46	7	8	10	27	25	6	4	13	28	44	56
18	Oldham	46	10	7	6	33	20	4	7	12	21	30	56
19	Reading	46	8	7	8	28	30	5	10	8	26	33	56
20	Wolves	46	8	8	9	34	28	5	7	11	22	34	55
21	Portsmouth	46	8	6	9	34	32	5	7	11	27	37	52
22	Millwall	46	7	6	10	23	28	6	7	10	20	35	52
23	Watford	46	7	8	8	40	33	3	10	10	22	37	48
24	Luton	46	7	6	10	30	34	4	6	13	10	30	45
		1104	233	177	142	804	613	142	177	233	613	804	1479

* promoted
after play-offs

Odds & ends

Double wins: (3) Leicester, Portsmouth, Watford.
Double losses: (1) Tranmere.

Won from behind: (2) Huddersfield (h), Watford (a).
Lost from in front: (8) Birmingham (a), Charlton (h), Port Vale (a).
Southend (a), Tranmere (a&h), Wolverhampton (h), Stockport (LC) (h).

High spots: The FA Cup win at champions Blackburn.
Becoming leading scorers in all four divisions (79 goals).
The late fight-backs at Barnsley and Watford.
Last-minute winning goals versus Portsmouth and Wolves.
The emergence of young keeper Richard Wright.
37 goals from the Mathie-Marshall partnership.

Low spots: Failing to beat Millwall on the last day to miss the play-offs.
A 25 per cent drop in home attendances.
Four defeats in April, which scuppered the promotion bid.
The 1-5 hammering by Charlton after losing keeper Forrest.
The bizarre 'withdrawal' of a late penalty award at Norwich.
A run of poor home form in the autumn.

Player of the Year: Simon Milton.
Ever-presents: (0).
Hat-tricks: (1) Alex Mathie (v Sunderland).
Opposing hat-tricks: (2) C Leaburn (Charlton), C Mendonca (Grimsby).
Leading scorer: (19) Ian Marshall.

Appearances & Goals

Player	Appearances Lge	Sub	LC	Sub	FAC	Sub	Goals Lge	LC	FAC	Tot
Appleby, Richie		3								
Barber, Fred	1									
Chapman, Lee	2	4	1							
Forrest, Craig	21		2		1					
Gregory, Neil	5	12	2	1	1	1	2			2
Linighan, David	2		1							
Marshall, Ian	35				4		19			19
Mason, Paul	24	2	2		2		7		3	10
Mathie, Alex	39		1		4		18			18
Milton, Simon	34	3	2	2	4		9			9
Mowbray, Tony	19				3		2			2
Palmer, Steve	5									
Petterson, Andy	1									
Scowcroft, James	13	10	1		2		2			2
Sedgley, Steve	40		2		4		4	1		5
Slater, Stuart	11	6	2				2			2
Stockwell, Mick	33	4	1		3		1			1
Swailes, Chris	4	1								
Tanner, Adam	3	7								
Taricco, Mauricio	36	3	2		3					
Thompson, Neil	5		2		3		1			1
Thomsen, Claus	36	1	2		3		2	1		3
Uhlenbeek, Gus	37	3	2		1	3	4			4
Vaughan, Tony	19	6			1		1			1
Wark, John	13	1	1		2		2			2
Williams, Geraint	42	2	2		4		1			1
Wright, Richard	23		1		3					
Yallop, Frank	3	4	1		1					
(own-goals)							2			2
28 players used	506	70	22	3	44	5	79	2	3	84

NATIONWIDE DIVISION 1

Manager: George Burley — SEASON 1996-97

No	Date	V	Opponents	Att	Pos	Pt	Res	F–A	H–T	Scorers, Times	Referee
1	16/8	A	MANCHESTER C	29,126	–	0	L	0–1	0–1	Lomas 25	T Heilbron
2	24/8	H	READING	9,767	9	3	W	5–2	2–1	Vaughan 13, 69, Sedgley 45p, Tarico 72, [Scowcroft 87]; (Nogan 28, Hunter 62)	M Fletcher
3	27/8	H	GRIMSBY	9,762	11	4	D	1–1	1–1	Mason 22; Mendonca 10	B Knight
4	31/8	A	OLDHAM	5,339	20	5	D	3–3	2–2	Mathie 13, 75, Stockwell 23; Rickers 1, Redmond 29, Banger 70	F Stretton
5	7/9	H	HUDDERSFIELD	10,661	16	5	L	1–3	0–0	Mason 76; Payton 47, 57, Stewart 51	P Rejer
6	10/9	A	CRYSTAL PALACE	12,520	16	6	D	0–0	0–0	—	U Rennie
7	14/9	A	SHEFFIELD UTD	14,261	12	9	W	3–1	0–1	Sedgley 63, Scowcroft 77, 81; Ward 28p	E Lomas
8	20/9	H	CHARLTON	10,558	8	12	W	2–1	0–1	Sedgley 56, Mathie 72; Allen 34	G Singh
9	28/9	A	WEST BROM	15,606	8	13	D	0–0	0–0	—	J Kirkby
10	1/10	H	BARNSLEY	9,041	10	14	D	1–1	0–1	Mathie 63; Redfearn 26p	A D'Urso
11	11/10	A	NORWICH	20,256	12	14	L	1–3	0–2	Sonner 46; Johnson 19, 34, Polston 67	C Wilkes

Line-ups (Town / Opponents) and substitutes used

1. Manchester City
Town: Wright, Stockwell^, Tarico, Thomsen, Vaughan*, Sedgley, Uhlenbeek, Williams, Mason, Marshall, Petta — subs: Mathie/Tanner
Opp: Immel, Brightwell, Frontzeck, Lomas, Symons, Brown, Summerbee, Phillips*, Kavalashvili^, Kinkladze, Rosler — subs: Hiley/Creaney

2. Reading
Town: Wright, Stockwell, Tarico, Thomsen, Sedgley, Williams, Sonner, Vaughan, Mathie, Marshall*, Mason^ — subs: Petta/Scowcroft
Opp: Mikhailov!, Booty, Bodin*, Bernal, Hunter, Wdowczyk, Parkinson, Caskey^, Quinn, Nogan*, Gooding — subs: Gilkes/Lovell/Meaker

3. Grimsby
Town: Wright, Stockwell*, Tarico, Thomsen, Sedgley, Williams, Sonner, Vaughan, Mathie, Scowcroft, Mason — subs: Petta
Opp: Pearcey, McDermott, Gallimore, Shakespeare, Widdrington^, Handyside, Childs", Webb, Livingstone, Mendonca, Black" — subs: Southall/Walker/Fickling

4. Oldham
Town: Wright, Stockwell, Serrant, Tanner*, Sedgley, Williams, Sonner^, Vaughan, Mathie, Scowcroft, Mason — subs: Milton/Uhlenbeek
Opp: Hallworth, Halle, Henry, Fleming, Redmond, Orlygsson, Richardson, McCarthy, Banger, Rickers

5. Huddersfield
Town: Wright*, Stockwell, Tarico, Thomsen, Sedgley, Williams, Sonner, Mathie, Mathie^, Scowcroft, Mason — subs: Gregory/Milton
Opp: Francis, Jenkins", Cowan, Bullock, Morrison, Gray, Reid, Burnett, Stewart, Payton, Edwards — subs: Collins/Ryan

6. Crystal Palace
Town: Forrest, Uhlenbeek, Tarico*, Thomsen, Sedgley, Williams, Sonner, Mathie, Mathie, Scowcroft, Mason — subs: Vaughan
Opp: Day, Edworthy, Muscat, Roberts, Tuttle, Hopkin, Boxall, Houghton, Freedman, Dyer*, Veart^ — subs: Ndah/McKenzie

7. Sheffield United
Town: Forrest, Stockwell, Tarico, Thomsen, Sedgley, Williams, Uhlenbeek, Niven, Mathie*, Scowcroft, Milton — subs: Naylor
Opp: Kelly, Short, Sandford, Hutchison, Vonk!, Nilsen, Ward, Patterson, Taylor, Walker*, Whitehouse — subs: Katchouro^/White

8. Charlton
Town: Forrest, Stockwell, Vaughan, Thomsen, Sedgley, Niven^, Uhlenbeek, Swailes, Mathie*, Scowcroft, Milton — subs: Naylor/Sonner
Opp: Salmon, Barness, Stuart!, Brown^, Chapple, Balmer, Newton", Leaburn, Allen, Mortimer, Otto* — subs: White/Sturgess/Nicholls

9. West Brom
Town: Forrest, Stockwell, Vaughan, Thomsen, Sedgley, Williams, Uhlenbeek, Swailes, Mathie*, Scowcroft, Milton — subs: Mason
Opp: Crichton, Holmes, Nicholson, Sneekes, Mardon, Burgess, Hamilton, Gilbert*, Peschisolido, Hunt, Groves — subs: Darby

10. Barnsley
Town: Forrest, Stockwell, Vaughan, Thomsen, Sedgley, Williams, Sonner, Swailes, Mathie, Scowcroft, Milton^ — subs: Naylor/Mason
Opp: Watson, Eaden, Appleby, Shirtliff", Davis, De Zeeuw, V d Velden*, Wilkinson, Redfearn, Liddell, Thompson^ — subs: Bullock/Ten Heuvel/Hurst

11. Norwich
Town: Wright, Mills, Vaughan, Tarico, Mowbray, Sedgley, Stockwell, Swailes, Mathie, Scowcroft, Milton* — subs: Naylor
Opp: Gunn, Newman, Mills, Eadie, Polston, Sutch, Adams, Fleck, Milligan, Johnson^, O'Neill — subs: Crook/Akinbiyi

Match reports

1. Having been chosen for live Sky TV coverage, Town's season kicks off on a Friday evening. Bobby Petta, a 'free' from Feyenoord, debuts after impressing in friendlies. The 'retired' Wark is also in the squad. Alan Ball's men gain the upper hand when Lomas heads in Kinkladze's centre.

2. New signing Sonner debuts. Reading crumble after Mikhailov is sent off just before the break for bringing down Mathie. Bernal goes in goal and is beaten from the spot. Three fine headed goals by Vaughan and Tarico, plus Scowcroft's low shot, all add to the entertainment value.

3. Town are cut to ribbons by a fine move that ends with Mendonca's stinging shot beating Wright. Town's equaliser is almost as good, Mathie's fine cross producing a precision shot by Mason. Mendonca hits the post near the end. Marshall is left out as he is negotiating to join Leicester.

4. Rickers nets from an angle after just 17 seconds. When Hallworth spills Sonner's piledriver, Mathie levels. Stockwell flicks a fine goal on the run. Redmond nets a cracker and later Banger scores when unmarked. Mathie saves a point after Mason hits the bar. Home fans stage a demo.

5. After only 14 minutes Wright is carried off with a severe back spasm that needs hospital attention. Striker Gregory comes on to don the green jersey. He is left exposed after the break and the Terriers cruise home. Mason nets a consolation as he nips in to convert a Stockwell centre.

6. Forrest is recalled and has a fine game between the sticks. Town are put under heavy pressure by Dave Bassett's draw specialists, but ride their luck and come home with a well-earned point. Worryingly, the side is picking up a lot of injuries, latest sufferers being Tarico and Stockwell.

7. Only one win in six and Burley rings the changes, giving debuts to teenagers Stuart Niven and Richard Naylor. The turning point is Vonk's sending off for pulling back Scowcroft. Sedgley atones for conceding the penalty by going on a great run to equalise from Scowcroft's pass.

8. Three times in a ten-day period Town win after the opposition have a man sent off. Allen is left unattended to head the opener. Stuart is red-carded for bringing down Thomsen and Sedgley curls in the free-kick. Mathie rounds Salmon to win it, despite a rather subdued Town display.

9. Swailes has a fine game as a five-man defence keeps Alan Buckley's men at bay. Town miss a couple of chances after the break. The Ipswich press corps dig deep when Albion's bookies quote Thomsen at 40-1 to score first. International call-ups mean Town v Swindon is called off.

10. Van der Velden tumbles after rounding Forrest, the keeper is booked and Redfearn nets the penalty. Town have a poor first half. Mathie hits the bar after the break, but six minutes later fires a shot past Watson to equalise. The robust 'Bam Bam' Naylor gives his best display to date.

11. Williams and Sedgley get stuck in, but Mike Walker's men stay cool and Johnson does major damage, his first a tremendous shot. Sonner smashes in a fine drive to put Town back in the game. Crook, who signed for Town but then did a U-turn, is jeered mercilessly as he comes on.

No	V	Date	Opponent	Att	Pos	Opp Pos	Pts	Res	Score	HT
12	A	15/10	BIRMINGHAM	15,664	16	15	14	L	0-1	0-0
13	H	19/10	PORTSMOUTH	10,514	16	19	15	D	1-1	1-1
14	H	26/10	TRANMERE	11,003	19	6	15	L	0-2	0-1
15	A	30/10	QP RANGERS	10,562	17	11	18	W	1-0	0-0
16	A	2/11	OXFORD	7,903	18	10	18	L	1-3	1-3
17	H	9/11	SOUTHEND	10,146	17	16	19	D	1-1	1-0
18	A	16/11	BRADFORD C	10,504	19	22	19	L	1-2	1-1
19	H	19/11	SWINDON	7,086	16	7	22	W	3-2	1-0
20	H	23/11	PORT VALE	9,491	11	14	25	W	2-1	1-1
21	A	30/11	TRANMERE	10,127	13	5	25	L	0-3	0-1
22	H	7/12	WOLVERHAMPTON	12,048	16	5	26	D	0-0	0-0
23	A	14/12	BOLTON	13,314	14	1	29	W	2-1	1-0

12 — BIRMINGHAM (A)
Team: Wright, Stockwell^, Mowbray*, Sedgley, Vaughan, Uhlenbeck, Sonner, Naylor, Scowcroft, Swailes, Milton/Mason
Opposition: *Bennett, Finnan*, Bruce, Breen, Holland, Devlin^, Hunt^, Furlong, Horne, Legg, Poole/Bowen/Gabbiadini*
Bowen 50
Ref: K Lynch
Naylor has earned a full debut, but gets little change out of Steve Bruce. Town put on an improved performance after the local derby defeat.

13 — PORTSMOUTH (H)
Team: Wright, Taricco, Vaughan*, Mowbray, Sedgley, Uhlenbeck, Sonner, Mathie, Scowcroft, Mason, Milton/Naylor, Petta
Opposition: *Flahavan, Pethick, Russell, McLoughlin, Perrett", Awford, Carter^, Simpson, Durnin, Turner*, Hall/Igoe/Thomson*
Mason 34 / McLoughlin 40p
Ref: G Pooley
Tremendous saves by Wright keep Trevor Francis' side at bay until sub Bowen comes on and guides the ball home after impressive build-up. Mason nets a well-taken goal from Mathie's pass. Bradbury is sandwiched and McLoughlin nets the hotly-disputed penalty. Town don't look likely to create a winner and the crowd becomes very unhappy. The chant of 'sort it out Burley' suggests they have not lost all faith in the boss!

14 — TRANMERE (H)
Team: Wright, Uhlenbeck, Taricco, Mowbray, Sedgley, Williams, Vaughan*, Sonner, Creaney*, Scowcroft, Naylor/Stockwell
Opposition: *Coyne, Stevens, Thorn, Teale, O'Brien, Branman, Moore, Jones*, Cook, Mahon, Aldridge*
Branman 32, Vaughan 61(og)
Ref: N Parry
Gerry Creaney arrives on loan after Mathie is hurt in the Palace cup-tie. A stupendous 30-yarder from Branman starts the slide. Vaughan heads in at the wrong end trying to deal with Moore's cross. Jeers are directed at Burley, who later gets the chairman's dreaded vote of confidence.

15 — QP RANGERS (A)
Team: Wright, Stockwell*, Taricco, Mowbray*, Wark, Williams, Tanner, Sonner*, Creaney, Scowcroft, Mason/Uhlenbeck
Opposition: *Sommer, Graham, Brevett, Barker, McDonald, Ready, Brazier, Murray, Slade*, Sinclair, Impey*
Mason 66
Ref: S Bennett
Jason Cundy arrives from Spurs on loan and Wark comes out of semi-retirement to show there's life in the old dog yet. The latter plays a key part in a gritty display against Stewart Houston's side. Mason's half-volley flies past Sommer after Scowcroft knocks a Williams cross to him.

16 — OXFORD (A)
Team: Wright, Stockwell*, Taricco, Mowbray*, Ford, Williams, Tanner, Uhlenbeck*, Creaney, Scowcroft, Mason/Naylor
Opposition: *Whitehouse, Robinson, Smith, Elliott, Purse, Angel^, Gray, Aldridge*, Jemson^, Beauchamp, Rush/Moody/Massey*
Tanner 45 / Mowbray 13 (og), Jemson 40, Elliott 44
Ref: M Pearce
A first-half defensive nightmare. The first flies in off unlucky Mowbray's foot. Plagued by a groin injury, he later goes off feeling the effects of flu. Jemson slots in the second and then Elliott rises high to head a third for Denis Smith's outfit. Tanner's consolation is a well-struck effort.

17 — SOUTHEND (H)
Team: Wright, Stockwell*, Taricco, Cundy, Sedgley, Williams, Uhlenbeck, Tanner, Creaney*, Naylor, Mason/Milton
Opposition: *Royce, Harris, Dublin, McNally, Lapper, Nielsen, Gridelet, Hails, Rammell, Williams, Tilson*
Stockwell 7 / Rammell 60
Ref: P Taylor
Cundy is available at last for his debut. Creaney heads down for Stockwell to shoot an early goal. Town soon lose their impetus and Ronnie Whelan's side level when Rammell surges through and makes no mistake. Only 4 league wins out of 17 now, and the natives are very restless.

18 — BRADFORD C (A)
Team: Wright, Stockwell*, Taricco, Cundy, Sedgley, Williams, Milton, Tanner, Creaney*, Steiner, Mason/Naylor
Opposition: *Gould, Liburd, Kiwomya*, Cowans, Mohan, Sas, Waddle, Duxbury, Sundgot, Dreyer, Hamilton*
Cundy 37 / Sundgot 32, 75
Ref: D Laws
Wright saves well from Rob Steiner but Norwegian Ole Sundgot is on hand to convert the rebound. Town quickly get back on terms when Cundy fires home a sweetly-struck shot.

19 — SWINDON (H)
Team: Wright, Stockwell, Taricco, Cundy, Sedgley, Williams, Milton, Tanner, Creaney, Scowcroft*, Naylor/Uhlenbeck
Opposition: *Digby, Robinson, Gooden, Leitch, Seagraves^, Horlock, O'Sullivan", Darras, Finney*, Allison, Walters, Thorne/Cowel/Elkins*
Scowcroft 1, Creaney 52, Sedgley 61p / Thorne 75, Allison 90
Ref: T West
It's the club's lowest league crowd for 41 years, but confidence floods back when Scowcroft nets a stunning shot after just 22 seconds. Creaney flicks in his first Town goal and the Leitch's handball provides a penalty. The victory is very timely, coming two days before the club's AGM.

20 — PORT VALE (H)
Team: Wright, Stockwell, Taricco, Cundy, Sedgley, Williams, Milton, Tanner*, Creaney, Scowcroft*, Naylor R/Mason/Uhlenbeck
Opposition: *Musselwhite, Hill, Tankard, Jansson*, Griffiths, Glover, McCarthy, Porter, Talbot, Naylor T, Guppy, Mills*
Tanner 34, Mason 77 / Naylor 2
Ref: R Harris
The news that Mathie is out for the whole season because of a shoulder problem is a big blow, but stand-in Naylor is looking lively. The other Naylor puts John Rudge's side ahead on 66 seconds. Tanner pounces to level and Mason wins it with a clinical finish from Uhlenbeck's pass.

21 — TRANMERE (A)
Team: Wright, Stockwell, Taricco, Wark*, Williams, Uhlenbeck, Tanner*, Naylor, Scowcroft, Mason, Vaughan/Sonner
Opposition: *Nixon, Stevens, Rogers*, Higgins, Teale, O'Brien, Brannan, Moore^, Aldridge, Thomas, Irons/Nevin/Mahon*
Brannan 43, Aldridge 76, 80
Ref: E Wolstenholme
Brannan pounces after Wright parries a shot. Rovers' veteran player-manager John Aldridge shows how it's done with a late double strike, both headers. Stockwell has Town's best chance but pokes the ball wide. Wark plays what will become the final league game of a marvellous career.

22 — WOLVERHAMPTON (H)
Team: Wright, Stockwell*, Taricco, Cundy, Sedgley, Williams, Uhlenbeck, Sonner, Naylor, Scowcroft, Mason*/Tanner
Opposition: *Stowell, Thompson*, Dennison, Atkins, Venus, Emblen, Corica, Thomas, Bull, Roberts*, Smith/Goodman*
Ref: D Orr
Visiting keeper Stowell is man of the match as promotion-chasing Wolves keep Town at bay. Stockwell misses another glorious opportunity. Aussie Steve Corica also spuns a great chance. West Indian striker Earl Jean is signed on a free from União de Coimbra Felgueiras of Portugal.

23 — BOLTON (A)
Team: Wright, Stockwell, Taricco, Cundy, Sedgley, Williams, Uhlenbeck, Sonner, Naylor, Scowcroft, Mason*/Tanner
Opposition: *Branagan, Green, Phillips, Frandsen, Bergsson, Fairclough, Johansen, Sellars, Taylor, McGinlay, Pollock*, Lee*
Scowcroft 39, 88 / Bergsson 70
Ref: K Leach
Uhlenbeck leaves Phillips on his backside and crosses for Scowcroft to guide the ball in. Weakened by international call-ups, Colin Todd's league leaders are lucky to level when the ball cannons in off Bergsson's body. Cundy finds Scowcroft who chips home a surprise late winner.

NATIONWIDE DIVISION 1 — Manager: George Burley — SEASON 1996-97

No	Date		1	2	3	4	5	6	7	8	9	10	11	subs used	Att	Pos	Pt	F-A	H-T	Scorers, Times, and Referees
24	H 21/12 STOKE		Wright	Stockwell*	Taricco	Cundy	Sedgley	Williams	Uhlenbeek	Sonner	Naylor^	Scowcroft	Mason	Jean/Tanner	10,159	14 8	D 30	1-1	1-1	Mason 45 / Sheron 23; Ref: P Taylor
			Prudhoe	*Pickering*	*Griffin*	*Sigurdsson*	*Whittle*	*Forsyth*	*McMahon*	*Wallace*	*Stein**	*Sheron*	*Kavanagh^*	*Macari/MacKenzie*						

Lou Macari's men look lively early on and take the lead when Sheron nets a terrific volley. Town deservedly level when Mason scrambles the ball in just before the break. City go close when Stein blazes over and Wright saves from Sheron. New-boy Jean is given 35 minutes of action.

No	Date		1	2	3	4	5	6	7	8	9	10	11	subs used	Att	Pos	Pt	F-A	H-T	Scorers, Times, and Referees
25	H 26/12 CRYSTAL PALACE		Wright	Stockwell^	Taricco	Cundy	Sedgley*	Williams	Uhlenbeek	Sonner	Naylor	Scowcroft	Mason	Tanner/**Dyer**	16,020	11 4	W 33	3-1	1-0	Tanner 45p, Mason 52, Naylor 79 / Gordon 65p; Ref: G Singh
			Day	*Edworthy**	*Gordon*	*Roberts*	*Tuttle*	*Quinn**	*Muscat*	*Ndah*	*Shipperley*	*Dyer^*	*Veart*	*Hopkin/Freedman/McKenzie*						

Tanner strokes home from the spot after Tuttle handles. Mason nets a superb dipping shot from 30 yards. Young Kieron Dyer is introduced for his senior debut. Cundy fouls Shipperley and Palace pull one back from the spot. Naylor's rasping drive from 18 yards makes the points safe.

No	Date		1	2	3	4	5	6	7	8	9	10	11	subs used	Att	Pos	Pt	F-A	H-T	Scorers, Times, and Referees
26	A 28/12 HUDDERSFIELD		Wright	Stockwell^	Taricco	Cundy	Tanner	Williams	Uhlenbeek	Sonner	Naylor*	Scowcroft	Mason	Dyer/Thomsen	11,467	13 17	L 33	0-2	0-0	Lawson 50, Payton 85; Ref: A Wiley
			Norman	*Jenkins*	*Cowan*	*Bullock*	*Sinnott*	*Gray^*	*Makel**	*Collins"*	*Crosby*	*Payton*	*Edwards*	*Dyson/Burnett/Lawson*						

Town seem to have hit form at last, and are unlucky when Scowcroft rattles Norman's crossbar on 26 minutes. Teenage sub Ian Lawson comes on for the home side to score one and make one. Terriers' boss Brian Horton admits Town are unfortunate to be heading home empty-handed.

No	Date		1	2	3	4	5	6	7	8	9	10	11	subs used	Att	Pos	Pt	F-A	H-T	Scorers, Times, and Referees
27	A 1/1 CHARLTON		Wright	Stockwell	Taricco	Thomsen	Tanner	Cundy	Uhlenbeek	Sonner	Naylor"	Scowcroft	Mason	Jones/Lisbie/Robson	10,186	13 14	D 34	1-1	1-0	Tanner 43p / Robson 78; Ref: M Halsey
			Petterson	*Barness*	*O'Connell*	*Brown**	*Chapple*	*Scott*	*Newton^*	*Leaburn*	*Robinson"*	*Whyte*	*Kinsella*							

Uhlenbeek has now settled into the wing-back role and has a superb game. When Steve Brown brings down Sonner, Tanner knocks home the penalty. Alan Curbishley's side level when Derek Whyte feeds Mark Robson and he unleashes a fierce shot from 12 yards to beat Wright.

No	Date		1	2	3	4	5	6	7	8	9	10	11	subs used	Att	Pos	Pt	F-A	H-T	Scorers, Times, and Referees
28	A 18/1 BARNSLEY		Wright	Stockwell^	Vaughan	Cundy	Swailes	Williams	Uhlenbeek	Sonner	Howe^	Scowcroft	Mason	Naylor/Dyer	9,872	12 3	W 37	2-1	0-0	Mason 54, Cundy 67 / Liddell 82; Ref: G Laws
			Watson	*Eaden*	*Moses*	*Sheridan*	*Thompson^*	*De Zeeuw*	*Marcelle"*	*Wilkinson*	*Redfearn*	*Liddell*	*Bullock**	*Bosancic/Jones/Ten Heuvel*						

Bobby Howe, on loan from Forest, makes his bow. Mason bangs home Stockwell's cross, then Cundy knocks in Sonner's corner. Liddell's low shot produces a tense finish. Chairman David Sheepshanks becomes first chairman of a newly reconstituted nine-man Football League board.

No	Date		1	2	3	4	5	6	7	8	9	10	11	subs used	Att	Pos	Pt	F-A	H-T	Scorers, Times, and Referees
29	H 25/1 WEST BROM		Wright	Stockwell	Taricco	Cundy	Swailes	Williams"	Uhlenbeek	Sonner	Naylor	Scowcroft"	Mason^	Howe/Vaughan	9,381	10 18	W 40	5-0	4-0	Holmes 7(og), Scowcr'ft 32, St'kwell 36, [Naylor 45, Mason 69]; Ref: M Bailey
			Crichton	*Holmes"*	*Darby*	*Murphy*	*Mardon*	*Burgess*	*Raven*	*Coldicott*	*Taylor*	*Hunt**	*Hamilton*	*Peschisolido/Donovan*						

Holmes knocks Stockwell's whipped cross into his own net. Scowcroft converts Uhlenbeek's cross and Stockwell nets a fierce drive. Naylor converts Mason's pinpoint pass and it's four before the break! The best win in 14 years is sealed as Mason takes advantage of Crichton's error.

No	Date		1	2	3	4	5	6	7	8	9	10	11	subs used	Att	Pos	Pt	F-A	H-T	Scorers, Times, and Referees
30	A 1/2 SOUTHEND		Wright	Stockwell	Taricco	Sedgley	Swailes	Williams	Uhlenbeek	Sonner	Naylor	Scowcroft*	Mason	Mitton	7,232	12 22	D 41	0-0	0-0	Ref: J Kirkby
			Royce	*Harris*	*Hails*	*Dublin*	*Rogers*	*Marsh*	*Gridelet*	*Byrne*	*Rammell*	*Thomson^*	*Nielsen*	*Boere*						

Last week's lethal finishing is sadly absent. A drab game at Roots Hall leaves both managers expressing their disappointment. The nearest thing to a winning goal is when battling Phil Gridelet brings a super save out of Wright with a header. The Shrimpers look destined to drop.

No	Date		1	2	3	4	5	6	7	8	9	10	11	subs used	Att	Pos	Pt	F-A	H-T	Scorers, Times, and Referees
31	H 8/2 QP RANGERS		Wright	Stockwell	Taricco	Sedgley	Swailes	Williams	Uhlenbeek	Vaughan	Naylor	Howe^	Mason*	Mitton/Gregory	12,983	12 8	W 44	2-0	1-0	Naylor 6, Gregory 82; Ref: N Barry
			Sommer	*Graham*	*Brevett**	*Yates*	*McDonald*	*Ready*	*Spencer*	*Peacock*	*Hateley*	*Barker*	*Sinclair*	*Brazier*						

Sedgley's shot bobbles away from Jurgen Sommer and Naylor snaps the chance up. The American keeper goes on to have fine game as Town threaten to bag more. Uhlenbeek lays on the chance for sub Neil Gregory, who shows great composure before slotting in the clinching goal.

No	Date		1	2	3	4	5	6	7	8	9	10	11	subs used	Att	Pos	Pt	F-A	H-T	Scorers, Times, and Referees
32	A 15/2 PORT VALE		Wright	Stockwell	Taricco	Cundy	Swailes*	Williams	Uhlenbeek	Sedgley	Naylor	Scowcroft"	Mason^	Vaughan/Gregory/Mitton	6,115	8 10	D 45	2-2	1-2	Mason 9, Stockwell 69 / Mills 40, Porter 43p; Ref: T Jones
			Musselwhite	*Hill*	*Stokes*	*Bogie^*	*Aspin*	*Glover*	*McCarthy*	*Porter*	*Mills*	*Naylor^*	*Guppy"*	*Foyle/Talbot/Koordes*						

Mason goes on a long cross-field run and produces a marvellous curling shot to open the scoring. Lee Mills levels with a fine 20-yard free-kick. Andy Porter converts after Steve Guppy is brought down. Stockwell leans ahead of Paul Musselwhite to knock in a close-range leveller.

No	Date		1	2	3	4	5	6	7	8	9	10	11	subs used	Att	Pos	Pt	F-A	H-T	Scorers, Times, and Referees
33	H 22/2 OXFORD		Forrest	Stockwell	Taricco	Cundy	Swailes*	Williams^	Uhlenbeek	Sedgley	Naylor	Scowcroft"	Mason	Gregory/Vaughan/Milton	11,483	7 13	W 48	2-1	1-0	Naylor 45, Stockwell 89 / Gabbiadini 59; Ref: R Styles
			Whitehouse	*Robinson*	*Marsh*	*Smith*	*Purse*	*Gilchrist**	*Massey*	*Gray*	*Gabbiadini^*	*Jemson"*	*Ford*	*Beauchamp/Angel/Murphy*						

A drab first half comes to life when Naylor nets a controversial opening goal. He leaps to convert in true Maradona 'hand of God' style, but to Oxford's horror the officials are all apparently unsighted. Gabbiadini slides in to level, but in the nick of time Stockwell drills in a superb drive.

No	Date		1	2	3	4	5	6	7	8	9	10	11	subs used	Att	Pos	Pt	F-A	H-T	Scorers, Times, and Referees
34	A 1/3 WOLVERHAMPTON		Wright	Stockwell	Taricco	Vaughan	Swailes	Williams	Uhlenbeek	Sedgley	Naylor	Scowcroft"	Mason*	Milton/Gregory	26,700	8 2	D 49	0-0	0-0	Ref: C Wilkes
			Stowell	*Smith**	*Froggatt*	*Atkins"*	*Venus*	*Emblen*	*Corica*	*Curle*	*Bull**	*Roberts*	*Osburn*	*Thompson/Goodman/Thomas*						

With play-off talk in the air, Town frustrate high-flying Wolves with a dogged performance. Swailes has a fine game and dangerman Bull is kept so quiet he is eventually subbed – a rare event. The nearest to a goal is when a close-range drive by Roberts hits Wright full in the face.

Season match log (fixtures 35–46)

#	Venue / Date	Opponent	Att.	Pos.	Res.	Score	Pts	Ipswich scorers / Opp. scorers	Referee
35	H 4/3	BRADFORD C	9,367	21	W	3:2	52	Sedgley 18p, Sonner 87, Gregory 90 / Sundgot 64, 74	A D'Urso
36	A 8/3	STOKE	11,933	6 / 9	W	1:0	55	Taricco 7	E Wolstenholme
37	H 15/3	BOLTON	16,187	7 / 1	L	0:1	55	McGinlay 26	R Furmandiz
38	H 18/3	SHEFFIELD UTD	10,374		W	3:1	58	Gregory 1, 11, 37 / Fjortoft 21	T Heilbron
39	A 22/3	READING	10,058	16 / 6	L	0:1	58	Lovell 90	G Pooley
40	A 31/3	GRIMSBY	6,268	22 / 9	L	1:2	58	Mason 10 / Mendonca 14, Lee 74	P Richards
41	H 5/4	OLDHAM	11,730	23 / 7	W	4:0	61	Scowcroft 3, Williams 35, Stockwell 45, [Gregory 52]	J Brandwood
42	A 12/4	SWINDON	8,591	18 / 6	W	4:0	64	Swailes 38, Stockwell 49, Sedgley 70p, [Gudmundsson 86]	J Kirkby
43	H 18/4	NORWICH	22,397	5	W	2:0	67	Taricco 32, Mason 42	U Rennie
44	H 22/4	MANCHESTER C	15,824	15 / 4	W	1:0	70	Sedgley 41p	D Orr
45	A 25/4	PORTSMOUTH	12,101	8 / 3	W	1:0	73	Scowcroft 36	A Wiley
46	H 4/5	BIRMINGHAM	20,570	10 / 4	D	1:1	74	Gudmundsson 52 / Devlin 81	E Lomas

Home 11,953 Away 12,422 Average 11,953

35 — BRADFORD C
Ipswich: Wright, Stockwell*, Taricco, Vaughan, Swailes, Williams, Uhlenbeek^, Sedgley, Naylor, Scowcroft", Mason; subs: Milton/Sonner/Gregory
Bradford: Gould, Liburd, Pepper, Dreyer, Mohan, O'Brien*, Waddle, Duxbury, Edinho, Hamilton, Kiwomya*; subs: Murray/Sundgot

Kiwomya's handball gets Town off to a good start. First-half injuries cause disruption and after hitting the woodwork, City ease ahead with time running out. Drama near the end as Sonner levels with a cracking drive and then Milton heads on Mason's cross to the waiting Gregory.

36 — STOKE
Ipswich: Wright, Mowbray, Griffin, Vaughan, Swailes, Williams, Dyer, Sonner, Naylor*, Scowcroft, Mason^; subs: Gregory/Milton
Stoke: Muggleton, Pickering, Sigurdsson, Whittle, Rodger^, McMahon, Wallace, Macari, Sheron, Kavanagh; subs: Mackenzie/Nyamah

Uhlenbeek is replaced by Kieron Dyer, who starts a league game for the first time. Fans' favourite Taricco pounces to score after a free-kick causes havoc in the Stoke area. Scowcroft goes close with a diving header, well saved by Muggleton. Town are on top for most of the match.

37 — BOLTON
Ipswich: Wright, Stockwell, Taricco, Vaughan, Swailes, Williams, Uhlenbeek*, Mowbray^, Gregory, Scowcroft, Mason; subs: Dyer/Sonner
Bolton: Branagan, Bergsson*, Phillips, Pollock, Taggart, Fairclough, Frandsen, Blake, McGinlay, Thompson, Sheridan

Town are knocked out of the top six by the champions-elect. Blake crosses and McGinlay sends a screamer of a header past Wright. Town look better after the break but are held at bay. Bolton boss Colin Todd praises Ipswich. Taricco is booked for the eighth time and faces a ban.

38 — SHEFFIELD UTD
Ipswich: Wright, Stockwell, Taricco, Vaughan, Swailes, Williams, Uhlenbeek, Sedgley, Gregory, Scowcroft*, Mason^; subs: Dyer/Milton
Sheffield Utd: Tracy, Short, Nilsen, Hutchison, Spackman^, Holdsworth, Ward, Fjortoft, Henry, Katchouro^; subs: Whitehouse/White

In less than 20 seconds Mason's long ball finds Gregory, who calmly puts Town ahead. Scowcroft heads on Wright's long punt forward and Gregory is in again. After an unhappy recent loan spell at Torquay, it's dream time for Gregory as he completes a hat-trick from Mason's pass.

39 — READING
Ipswich: Wright, Stockwell, Taricco, Vaughan, Swailes, Williams, Uhlenbeek^, Sedgley, Gregory, Mason*; subs: Dyer/Petta
Reading: Mautone, Bernal, Holsgrove, Gooding, McPherson, Hopkins, Gilkes^, Lambert*, Morley, Lovell, Caskey; subs: Williams/Nogan/Parkinson

Swede Niklas Gudmundsson arrives on loan from Blackburn and gets a debut. His countryman Stuart Lovell nabs a shock late winner for Mick Gooding's side.

40 — GRIMSBY
Ipswich: Wright, Dyer, Taricco, Vaughan, Swailes, Williams^, Uhlenbeek, Sedgley, Gregory, Scowcroft↑, Mason*; subs: Gudmundsson/Sonner/Petta
Grimsby: Pearcey, Jobling, Gallimore, Rodger, Lever, Widdrington, Southall, Shakespeare, Livingstone*, Mendonca, Lester; subs: Childs/Lee

Dyer sends Mason clear and he picks his spot expertly. Clive Mendonca turns and fires in Jack Lester's pass. Ten minutes before the break Scowcroft is red-carded for an elbowing offence, which he maintains was accidental. Jason Lee wins it, heading in Craig Shakespeare's cross.

41 — OLDHAM
Ipswich: Wright, Stockwell, Taricco, Sedgley, Swailes, Williams, Uhlenbeek, Vaughan, Gregory, Scowcroft*, Mason^; subs: Dyer/Gudmundsson
Oldham: Kelly, Duxbury, Serrant, Snodin, Fleming, Ricters, Rush, Richardson^, Ritchie*, Barlow, Reid; subs: McCarthy/Hodgson

Scowcroft firmly heads in Mason's free-kick. Uhlenbeek hits a post, but Williams is on hand to net only his third goal in 223 games for Town. Stockwell powers through to beat Kelly. Gregory nets from an angle from Sedgley's pass. Neil Warnock is furious over his side's poor display.

42 — SWINDON
Ipswich: Wright, Stockwell, Taricco, Vaughan, Swailes, Williams^, Uhlenbeek, Sedgley, Gregory*, Scowcroft, Mason^; subs: Dyer/Gudmundsson/Sonner
Swindon: Digby, Robinson, King, Leitch, Coughlan, Darras^, Cowe*, Bullock, Thorne, Allison, Gooden; subs: Finney/Watson

Top quality stuff from an in-form side. Swailes converts Scowcroft's cross for a career-first goal. Stockwell converts after Mason's return pass. Mark Robinson fouls Scowcroft for Sedgley's fifth penalty success of the season. A scramble in the box leads to Gudmundsson netting the last.

43 — NORWICH
Ipswich: Wright, Stockwell, Taricco, Sedgley, Swailes, Williams, Uhlenbeek, Vaughan, Gregory, Scowcroft↑, Mason*; subs: Dyer
Norwich: Marshall, Jackson, Newman, Crook, Bradshaw*, Sutch, Adams, Fleck, Eadie, Mills, O'Neil*; subs: Polston/Simpson

Town are really up for this derby and Taricco takes Sedgley's pass and fires in a peach of a shot. An overhead kick by Williams finds Mason who nets off a post. The margin could have been wider. The local paper devotes ten pages to the win and front-page headline is a huge 'YES!'

44 — MANCHESTER C
Ipswich: Wright, Stockwell, Taricco, Sedgley, Swailes, Williams, Uhlenbeek, Vaughan, Gregory*, Scowcroft, Mason^; subs: Dyer/Gudmundsson
Man City: Margetson, Brightwell, Horlock, McGoldrick, Symons, Brannan, Summerbee, Atkinson, Heaney*, Kinkladze, Crooks; subs: Kavalashvili

Frank Clark, Man C's third boss this season, has guided them clear of the drop zone. This turns into a straightforward win for Town, who now look a good bet to reach the play-offs. Kit Symons hauls down Scowcroft for Sedgley's penalty winner. Dalian Atkinson heads against the bar.

45 — PORTSMOUTH
Ipswich: Wright, Stockwell^, Taricco, Sedgley, Swailes, Williams, Uhlenbeek, Vaughan, Gregory*, Scowcroft, Mason^; subs: Dyer/Milton/Gudmundsson
Portsmouth: Knight, Igoe, Thompson^, McLoughlin, Whitbread, McLoughlin, Awford, Hall, Simpson, Bradbury, Burton*; subs: Durnin/Waterman

Scowcroft leaps to head in Mason's corner. Alan Knight makes fine saves to restrict Town's lead. When Wright drops the ball, Swailes clears off the line to foil a desperate Pompey. The victory ensures a play-off spot, but the two 'automatic' promotion places are already out of reach.

46 — BIRMINGHAM
Ipswich: Wright, Stockwell, Taricco^, Sedgley, Swailes, Williams, Uhlenbeek^, Vaughan, Gregory*, Scowcroft, Mason^; subs: Gudmundsson/Tanner/Sonner
Birmingham: Bennett, Wassall, Grainger, Ablett, Johnson*, Devlin, Robinson, O'Connor, Hughes, Bowen^; subs: Legg/Francis

No pressure on either side and as a result this is a rather ordinary affair for the bumper crowd. Scowcroft and Stockwell set up Gudmundsson for his first Portman Road goal with a well-struck shot. Near the end big Kevin Francis rises high and Paul Devlin deflects his header home.

NATIONWIDE DIVISION 1 (CUP-TIES)   Manager: George Burley   SEASON 1996-97

Play-offs

SF 1 — 10/5 — A SHEFFIELD UTD — 22,312 (7) — 4 D — 1-1 — H-T 0-1
Scorers, Times, and Referees: Stockwell 78 / Fjortoft 41 / Ref: R Pearson

- Town: 1 Wright, 2 Stockwell, 3 Tarico, 4 Sedgley, 5 Swailes, 6 Williams, 7 Uhlenbeck, 8 Vaughan, 9 Gregory*, 10 Scowcroft*, 11 Dyer — subs used: Gudmundsson
- *Kelly, Ward, Nilsen, Hutchison, Tiler, Holdsworth, White^, Henry, Fjortoft, Katchouro*, Whitehouse — subs used: Taylor/Short*

Howard Kendall's side surge ahead when Jan-Aage Fjortoft turns sharply past Swailes and fires in a real beauty. Roared on by 5,000 noisy travelling fans, Town level when Stockwell nips round Kelly to score after getting on the end of a low ball into the danger area by Williams.

SF 2 — 14/5 — H SHEFFIELD UTD — 21,467 (7) — 4 D — 2-2 — H-T 2-1 (aet)
Scorers, Times, and Referees: Scowcroft 32, Gudmundsson 33 / Katchouro 9, Walker 77 / Ref: T Heilbron / (Town lose on away goals)

- Town: 1 Wright, 2 Stockwell, 3 Tarico, 4 Sedgley, 5 Swailes^, 6 Williams, 7 Uhlenbeck, 8 Vaughan, 9 Scowcroft, 10 Gudmund'n*, 11 Mason — subs used: Gregory/Dyer
- *Kelly, Short, Sandford, Henry!, Tiler, Holdsworth, White*, Ward, Fjortoft, Katchouro^, Whitehouse — subs used: Hutchison/Walker/Nilsen*

Katchuro's shot hits the bar and comes down over the line. Scowcroft and Gudmundsson convert crosses, but sub Andy Walker squeezes in an equaliser. Sedgley's late free-kick thumps a post. Nick Henry departs after assaulting Tarico in extra-time. It's heartbreak and tears for Town.

Coca-Cola Cup

1:1 — 20/8 — H BOURNEMOUTH — 6,163 — W 2-1 — H-T 1-0
Scorers, Times, and Referees: Marshall 41, Mason 71 / Fletcher 57 / Ref: M Pierce

- Town: 1 Wright, 2 Stockwell^, 3 Tarico, 4 Thomsen, 5 Sedgley, 6 Williams, 7 Mason, 8 Sonner, 9 Marshall, 10 Mathie, 11 Petta* — subs used: Uhlenbeck/Vaughan
- *Glass, Young, Beardsmore, Cull, Murray, Bailey, Holland, Cox, Gordon*, Fletcher, Brissett — subs used: O'Neill*

From Mason's cross, Marshall produces a wonderful overhead kick to open the scoring. Mel Machin's side are level as Steve Fletcher heads in Gordon's cross. Mason tries his luck from 18 yards and his shot deflects past Jimmy Glass. Petta is unable to recapture his pre-season form.

1:2 — 3/9 — A BOURNEMOUTH — 4,119 (2:10) — 11 W — 3-0 — H-T 1-0
Scorers, Times, and Referees: Scowcroft 12, Mathie 61, Stockwell 66 / Ref: J Brandwood / (Town win 5-0 on aggregate)

- Town: 1 Wright, 2 Stockwell, 3 Tarico, 4 Vaughan, 5 Sedgley, 6 Williams, 7 Vaughan, 8 Sonner, 9 Scowcroft, 10 Mathie, 11 Mason* — subs used: Uhlenbeck
- *Glass, Young, Beardsmore*, Cull, Murray, Bailey, Holland, Cox, Gordon*, Fletcher, Robinson — subs used: O'Neill/Vincent/Town*

Scowcroft nets an early opportunist effort to settle any nerves. Many visiting fans miss the first half due to severe traffic hold-ups. A slick move ends with Mathie netting a superb shot and Town are cruising. The tie is over when Stockwell scoops his shot over Jimmy Glass's head.

2:1 — 17/9 — A FULHAM — 6,947 (3:1) — 12 D — 1-1 — H-T 0-1
Scorers, Times, and Referees: Milton 78 / Morgan 4 / Ref: S Bennett

- Town: 1 Forrest, 2 Stockwell, 3 Tarico*, 4 Thomsen, 5 Sedgley, 6 Williams^, 7 Uhlenbeck^, 8 Wark, 9 Mathie, 10 Scowcroft, 11 Milton — subs used: Vaughan/Naylor/Gregory
- *Walton, Watson, Herrera, Cullip*, Cusack, Blake, Freeman, Cockerill, Conroy, Morgan, Angus — subs used: Scott*

A rare trip to the famous Cottage and Simon Morgan opens the scoring early, netting a fine left-foot volley from the edge of the area. Milton, playing close to his place of birth, is Town's saviour with a brilliant 30-yard drive. Mark Walton keeps Fulham in the tie with a series of saves.

2:2 — 24/9 — H FULHAM — 6,825 (3:1) — 8 W — 4-2 — H-T 1-1
Scorers, Times, and Referees: Sonner 28, Sedgley 50p, Mathie 63, 69 / Sedgley 31 (og), Brooker 72 / Ref: R Harris / (Town win 5-3 on aggregate)

- Town: 1 Forrest, 2 Stockwell, 3 Tarico, 4 Vaughan, 5 Sedgley, 6 Swailes, 7 Thomsen, 8 Mathie, 9 Scowcroft, 10 Milton, 11 Milton — subs used: Uhlenbeck
- *Walton, Watson^, Herrera, Cullip", Cusack, Blake!, Scott, Adams*, Conroy, Morgan, Angus — subs used: Mison/Marshall/Brooker*

A tremendous overhead kick by Sonner sparks the goal-rush. Sedgley deflects a cross by player-manager Micky Adams past Forrest. He makes amends after Brooker is fouled. Mark Blake is sent off for a foul on Mathie, whose goals settle the tie. He is denied a hat-trick by the bar.

3 — 22/10 — A CRYSTAL PALACE — 8,390 (4) — 16 W — 4-1 — H-T 2-1
Scorers, Times, and Referees: Mason 25, 76, Mathie 37, 68 / Veart 4 / Ref: E Wolstenholme

- Town: 1 Wright, 2 Uhlenbeck, 3 Tarico, 4 Mowbray, 5 Williams, 6 Sedgley, 7 Vaughan, 8 Sonner, 9 Mathie*, 10 Scowcroft, 11 Mason^ — subs used: Naylor/Stockwell
- *Day, Edworthy, Muscat, Roberts, Tuttle, Hopkin, Andersen^, McKenzie, Freedman*, Dyer, Veart — subs used: Harris/Quinn*

Town are stunned when Carl Veart finds space to pick his spot. The home side move up a gear; Mason and the deadly Mathie bag two apiece, each netting curling shots around Chris Day. Mathie goes off with a damaged shoulder, an injury that will keep him out for the rest of 1996-97.

4 — 26/11 — H GILLINGHAM — 13,537 (2:18) — 11 W — 1-0 — H-T 0-0
Scorers, Times, and Referees: Naylor 73 / Ref: J Brandwood

- Town: 1 Wright, 2 Stockwell, 3 Tarico, 4 Cundy*, 5 Williams, 6 Sedgley, 7 Milton*, 8 Tanner, 9 Naylor, 10 Scowcroft, 11 Mason — subs used: Sonner/Uhlenbeck
- *Marshall, Smith, Harris, Hessenthaler, Green, Pennock, O'Connor", Ratcliffe!, Armtrong, Butler, Bailey* — subs used: Puttnam/Piper*

Tony Pulis's stubborn Gillingham are finally put in their place when Naylor nets a gem of a goal from the edge of the area with time fast running out. The Gills get rattled and Stuart Ratcliffe is sent off for elbowing Tanner. Stuart Slater departs to join Leicester after a trial period.

QF — 21/1 — H LEICESTER — 20,793 (P:12) — 12 L — 0-1 — H-T 0-1
Scorers, Times, and Referees: Robins 42 / Ref: D Elleray

- Town: 1 Wright, 2 Stockwell, 3 Vaughan, 4 Cundy, 5 Williams, 6 Swailes, 7 Uhlenbeck, 8 Sonner^, 9 Howe^, 10 Scowcroft, 11 Mason — subs used: Naylor/Milton
- *Keller, Grayson*, Kamark, Parker, Watts, Prior, Lennon, Izzet, Claridge, Robins^, Heskey — subs used: Taylor/Hill*

A bumper gate as Town bid for the semis. New boss Martin O'Neill organises his troops and Town are not allowed to sparkle. Julian Watts and Steve Claridge set up Mark Robins for a clinical finish. Naylor's bad tackle sees Simon Grayson stretchered off, but only yellow is shown.

FA Cup

3 — 4/1 — A NOTTINGHAM F — 14,681 (P:19) — 13 L — 0-3 — H-T 0-2
Scorers, Times, and Referees: Saunders 19, 74, Allen 28 / Ref: M Bodenham

- Town: 1 Wright, 2 Stockwell, 3 Tarico, 4 Cundy, 5 Williams, 6 Tanner, 7 Uhlenbeck, 8 Sonner, 9 Thomsen, 10 Scowcroft, 11 Dyer* — subs used: Naylor
- *Crossley, Lyttle, Pearce, Cooper, Chettle, Phillips, Allen", Campbell^, Saunders, Haaland, Woan — subs used: Gemmill/Roy*

History repeats itself as Town go out to Forest at this stage by the same score as in 1989. Kieron Dyer looks lively on his full debut. Tanner plays his last game before a positive drugs test puts him out of the team. Dean Saunders is the main thorn in Town's side, clipping in a brace.

League table

#	Team	P	W	D	L	F	A	W	D	L	F	A	Pts
1	Bolton	46	18	4	1	60	20	10	10	3	40	33	98
2	Barnsley	46	14	4	5	43	19	8	10	5	33	36	80
3	Wolves	46	10	5	8	31	24	12	5	6	37	27	76
4	IPSWICH	46	10	7	3	44	23	5	7	9	24	27	74
5	Sheffield Utd	46	13	5	5	46	23	7	8	8	29	29	73
6	Crys Palace *	46	10	7	6	39	22	9	7	7	39	26	71
7	Portsmouth	46	12	4	7	32	24	8	4	11	27	29	68
8	Port Vale	46	9	9	5	36	25	8	7	8	22	27	67
9	QP Rangers	46	10	5	8	33	28	9	5	9	31	35	66
10	Birmingham	46	11	7	5	30	18	6	8	9	22	30	66
11	Tranmere	46	10	9	4	42	27	7	5	11	21	29	65
12	Stoke	46	15	3	5	28	22	3	7	13	17	35	64
13	Norwich	46	9	10	4	34	18	8	2	13	35	50	63
14	Manchester C	46	12	4	7	34	25	5	6	12	25	35	61
15	Charlton	46	11	8	4	36	28	5	3	15	16	38	59
16	West Brom	46	7	7	9	37	33	8	8	7	31	39	57
17	Oxford	46	14	3	6	44	26	2	6	15	20	42	57
18	Reading	46	13	7	3	37	24	2	5	16	21	43	57
19	Swindon	46	11	6	6	36	27	4	3	16	16	44	54
20	Huddersfield	46	10	7	6	28	20	3	8	12	20	41	54
21	Bradford C	46	10	5	8	29	32	2	7	14	18	40	48
22	Grimsby	46	7	7	9	31	34	4	6	13	29	47	46
23	Oldham	46	6	8	9	30	30	5	5	14	21	36	43
24	Southend	46	7	9	7	32	32	1	6	16	10	54	39
		1104	262	150	140	872	604	140	150	262	604	872	1506

* promoted after play-offs

Odds & ends

Double wins: (3) Sheffield Utd, QP Rangers, Swindon.
Double losses: (2) Tranmere, Huddersfield.

Won from behind: (5) Sheffield Utd (a), Charlton (h), Port Vale (h), Bradford C (h),Crystal Palace (h) (CCC).
Lost from in front: (1) Grimsby (a).

High spots: Post-Christmas form ensuring a play-off place.
A lengthy run in the Coca-Cola Cup.
The tense local derby win over Norwich in April.
Last-gasp victory at league leaders Bolton in December.
The excellent form of Mauricio Taricco.
A series of fine goals by Paul Mason.

Low spots: The heartbreak of the play-off semi-final defeat.
The bizarre on-off Ian Crook transfer saga.
The temporary depression that set in around mid-November.
The long-term loss of Alex Mathie and Jason Cundy.
Adam Tanner's positive drugs test.
The departure of popular Ian Marshall.

Player of the Year: Mauricio Taricco.
Ever-presents: (0).
Hat-tricks: (1) Neil Gregory (v Sheffield Utd).
Opposing hat-tricks: (0).
Leading scorer: (15) Paul Mason.

Appearances and Goals

Player	Lge	Sub	LC	Sub	FAC	Sub	PO	Sub	Lge	Sub	LC	FAC	PO	Tot
Creaney, Gerry	6										1			1
Cundy, Jason	13		2						2					2
Dyer, Kieron	2	11		1						1				
Forrest, Craig	6		2											
Gregory, Neil	10	7				1		1	6					6
Gudmundsson, Niklas	2	6						1	2			1		3
Howe, Bobby	2	1												
Jean, Earl		1												
Marshall, Ian	2		1						1					1
Mason, Paul	41	2	6		1				12		3			15
Mathie, Alex	11	1	5						4		5			9
Milton, Simon	8	15	3		2				1					1
Mowbray, Tony	8	1												
Naylor, Richard	19	8	1	3	1				4		1			5
Niven, Stuart	2		1											
Petta, Bobby	1	5												
Scowcroft, James	40	1	6		1		2		9		1	1		11
Sedgley, Steve	39		6				2		7		1			8
Sonner, Danny	22	7	5	1	1				2		1			3
Stockwell, Mick	42	1	6		2		2		7		1	1		9
Swailes, Chris	23	2	2						1					1
Tanner, Adam	10	6	1						4					4
Taricco, Mauricio	41		5	1	1		2		3					3
Thomsen, Claus	10	1	4	1	1									
Uhlenbeek, Gus	34	4	3	3	2		2		2					2
Vaughan, Tony	27	5	4	2	2		2		2					2
Wark, John	2	1												
Williams, Geraint	43		6	1	2		2		1					1
Wright, Richard	40		5	1	2		2							
(own-goals)														1
29 players used	506	82	77	13	11	1	22	3	68		15	3		86

NATIONWIDE DIVISION 1

Manager: George Burley

SEASON 1997-98

Key: roman = Ipswich player; *italic* = opponent player. Symbols as printed (`*` substituted, `^` substitute/booking, `!` sent off).

---

1 — A, QP RANGERS — 9/8
Att 17,614 · Pt 1 · F-A 0-0 · H-T 0-0
Scorers, Times: — · Ref: C Wilkes

Team	1	2	3	4	5	6	7	8	9	10	11	subs used
Ipswich	Wright	Stockwell	Taricco	Williams	Venus*	Cundy	Dyer	Holland	Petta^	Scowcroft^	Mason*	Gregory/Swailes/Milton
QPR	*Harper*	*Rose*	*Brevett*	*Barker*	*Maddix**	*Morrow*	*Spencer*	*Peacock*	*Brazier^*	*Gallen^*	*Murray*	*Perry/Sinclair/Slade*

Mark Venus from Wolves and Matt Holland from Bournemouth, two six-figure summer purchases, make their debuts. Stockwell misses a clear chance and Scowcroft has the ball in the net but is offside. Rangers exert heavy pressure in the final 20 minutes, but all attacks are repelled.

---

2 — A, BRADFORD C — 23/8
Att 13,913 · Pos 21 (*opp 5*) · Pt 1 · F-A 1-2 · H-T 0-1
Scorers, Times: Dyer 74 / *Steiner 10, Cundy 52 (og)* · Ref: T Jones

Team	1	2	3	4	5	6	7	8	9	10	11	subs used
Ipswich	Wright	Stockwell	Taricco	Williams	Cundy*	Dyer	Lawrence*	Holland	Stein	Scowcroft	Petta^	Milton/Kerslake
Bradford	*Prudhoe*	*Wilder*	*Jacobs*	*Beagrie*	*Youds*	*Dreyer*	*Pepper*	*—*	*Steiner^*	*Edinho*	*Murray*	*Blake/Sundgot*

Rob Steiner heads in Peter Beagrie's cross. Mark Prudhoe makes a great save from Mark Stein, on loan from Chelsea. Brazilian Edinho sees his cross diverted into his own net by Cundy. Dyer's goal sets up a tense finale but City hold on. Free-transfer signing David Kerslake debuts.

---

3 — H, WEST BROM — 30/8
Att 13,508 · Pos 22 (*opp 3*) · Pt 2 · F-A 1-1 · H-T 1-0
Scorers, Times: Stein 40 / *Sneekes 58* · Ref: M Halsey

Team	1	2	3	4	5	6	7	8	9	10	11	subs used
Ipswich	Wright	Stockwell	Taricco	Williams	Venus	Cundy	Dyer	Holland	Stein	Scowcroft	Milton^	Kerslake
WBA	*Miller*	*Holmes*	*Nicholson*	*Sneekes^*	*Mardon*	*Raven*	*Flynn*	*Butler*	*Taylor*	*Hunt^*	*Kilbane"*	*Hamilton/Caldicott/Smith*

Cundy heads back Milton's corner-kick and Stein nips in to convert from close range. Substitute David Smith's long ball sets Richard Sneekes free and he runs on to beat the advancing Wright and level. Town are generally the better side and are unlucky not to beat Ray Harford's men.

---

4 — H, SWINDON — 2/9
Att 11,246 · Pos 20 (*opp 4*) · Pt 5 · F-A 2-1 · H-T 1-1
Scorers, Times: Venus 36, Sonner 82 / *Allison 23* · Ref: P Taylor

Team	1	2	3	4	5	6	7	8	9	10	11	subs used
Ipswich	Wright	Stockwell	Taricco	Williams	Venus	Swailes	Dyer	Holland	Stein	Scowcroft*	Milton^	Mathie/Sonner
Swindon	*Digby*	*Darras*	*Drysdale*	*Leitch**	*Seagrave^*	*McDonald*	*Walters*	*Cuervo*	*Hay*	*Allison*	*Gooden*	*Bullock/Smith*

Mathie makes a welcome return after 11 months out with injury problems. Mark Walters' free-kick is nodded in by Wayne Allison. Venus levels by curling in a fine free-kick. Sonner's long-range shot is tipped on to the crossbar, but moments later he thumps in a 20-yard winner.

---

5 — A, HUDDERSFIELD — 13/9
Att 9,313 · Pos 20 (*opp 24*) · Pt 6 · F-A 2-2 · H-T 0-1
Scorers, Times: Edmondson 65 (og), Dyer 90 / *Jenkins 41, Dyer 88* · Ref: D Pugh

Team	1	2	3	4	5	6	7	8	9	10	11	subs used
Ipswich	Wright	Stockwell	Taricco	Williams	Venus	Swailes	Dyer	Holland	Stein	Mathie*	Sonner	Petta
Huddersfield	*Francis*	*Jenkins*	*Martin*	*Dyson*	*Morrison"*	*Beresford^*	*Baldry*	*Makel*	*Stewart*	*Facey*	*Burnett*	*Dyer/Edmondson/Dalton*

Steve Jenkins is left unmarked to head in a corner. Darren Edmondson completely misjudges a Sonner cross and heads the ball into his own net off a post. Substitute Alex Dyer races through to put Brian Horton's strugglers ahead, but Kieron Dyer chips a neat equaliser in the last minute.

---

6 — H, STOKE — 20/9
Att 10,665 · Pos 22 (*opp 14*) · Pt 6 · F-A 2-3 · H-T 0-2
Scorers, Times: Scowcroft 48, Holland 67 / *Thorne 13, 30, Stewart 55* · Ref: B Knight

Team	1	2	3	4	5	6	7	8	9	10	11	subs used
Ipswich	Wright	Stockwell	Taricco	Williams	Venus	Swailes!	Dyer	Holland	Stein	Scowcroft	Sonner*	Cundy
Stoke	*Muggelton*	*Pickering*	*Griffiths*	*Sigurdsson*	*Tweed*	*Keen*	*Forsyth*	*Wallace*	*Thorne*	*Stewart*	*Kavanagh*	

The defence looks static as Peter Thorne loops a header over Wright. Kevin Keen's corner falls for Thorne to make it two. Town make changes and Scowcroft dives to head in. Paul Stewart races clear to set up Stoke's first victory in Suffolk in 15 years. Swailes is sent off near the end.

---

7 — A, NORWICH — 26/9
Att 18,911 · Pos 22 (*opp 14*) · Pt 6 · F-A 1-2 · H-T 0-1
Scorers, Times: Stein 73 / *Eadie 8, Cundy 59 (og)* · Ref: J Brandwood

Team	1	2	3	4	5	6	7	8	9	10	11	subs used
Ipswich	Wright	Stockwell	Venus^	Williams	Mowbray	Cundy	Dyer	Holland	Stein	Scowcroft*	Petta	Mathie/Kerslake
Norwich	*Marshall*	*Fleming*	*Sutch*	*Grant*	*Scott*	*Adams*	*Jackson*	*Fleck*	*Eadie*	*Milligan^*	*Forbes^*	*Bellamy/Coote*

Scowcroft is stretchered off with a serious-looking neck injury. Craig Fleming splits the defence and Darren Eadie pounces. Mowbray heads Eadie's free-kick against Cundy's legs and the ball rolls slowly into the net. Kerslake's cross is headed in by Stein to set up a tight finish.

---

8 — H, MANCHESTER C — 4/10
Att 14,322 · Pos 22 (*opp 21*) · Pt 9 · F-A 1-0 · H-T 0-0
Scorers, Times: Mathie 63 · Ref: M Bailey

Team	1	2	3	4	5	6	7	8	9	10	11	subs used
Ipswich	Wright	Stockwell	Kerslake	Williams*	Mowbray	Dozzell	Dyer	Holland	Mathie	Gregory^	Petta	Milton/Tanner
Man City	*Margetson*	*Brightwell*	*Beesley*	*Wiekens*	*Symons^*	*Edghill*	*Dickov**	*Horlock*	*Bradbury*	*Kinkladze*	*Braman*	*Rosler/Scully*

Jason Dozzell is back from Spurs on a week-to-week contract. From Petta's pass, Mathie cracks in a low shot for his first goal for a year. Expensive signing Lee Bradbury misses several chances for Frank Clark's men. Georgi Kinkladze goes close to an equaliser near the whistle.

---

9 — A, OXFORD — 18/10
Att 7,594 · Pos 22 (*opp 18*) · Pt 9 · F-A 0-1 · H-T 0-0
Scorers, Times: *Smith 64* · Ref: A Wiley

Team	1	2	3	4	5	6	7	8	9	10	11	subs used
Ipswich	Wright	Stockwell	Taricco	Tanner	Mowbray^	Cundy	Dyer	Holland	Mathie	Dozzell	Petta*	Stein/Milton
Oxford	*Van Heusden*	*Remy*	*Angel*	*Robinson*	*Purse*	*Wilsterman*	*Ford*	*Smith*	*Banger^*	*Aldridge^*	*Beauchamp*	*Murphy/Folland*

Midfielder David Smith shoots home through a crowded goalmouth after Mike Ford's corner is not cleared. It's only his second league goal in eight years as a pro! Stockwell goes close to an equaliser. Denis Smith's outfit hold on and Town have still never won at the Manor Ground.

---

10 — A, CREWE — 21/10
Att 4,730 · Pos 22 (*opp 15*) · Pt 10 · F-A 0-0 · H-T 0-0
Scorers, Times: — · Ref: G Frankland

Team	1	2	3	4	5	6	7	8	9	10	11	subs used
Ipswich	Wright	Stockwell	Taricco	Tanner	Milton	Cundy	Dyer*	Holland	Mathie	Dozzell	Petta	Stein/Milton
Crewe	*Kearton*	*Smith*	*Bignot*	*Westwood*	*Unsworth*	*Charnock*	*Rivers**	*Lunt*	*Adebola*	*Johnson*	*Anthrobus*	*Little*

In their first ever visit to Gresty Road, Town do a fair share of the attacking. Jason Kearton is kept busy. Dyer has a fine game down the right flank. Stockwell shoots just wide when put in the clear. Dario Gradi's side are off the hook again when Holland's effort is cleared off the line.

---

11 — H, BURY — 25/10
Att 10,478 · Pos 20 (*opp 16*) · Pt 13 · F-A 2-0 · H-T 0-0
Scorers, Times: Tanner 80p, Dozzell 86 · Ref: A D'Urso

Team	1	2	3	4	5	6	7	8	9	10	11	subs used
Ipswich	Wright	Stockwell	Taricco	Williams	Tanner	Cundy	Dyer^	Holland	Mathie^	Dozzell	Petta	Milton/Gregory
Bury	*Kiely*	*Hughes!*	*Peake**	*Daws*	*Lucketti*	*Butler*	*Gray!*	*Johnson*	*Woodward*	*Battersby*	*Johnrose^*	*Randall/Rigby*

A dour game comes to life late as anxious Town win much-needed points. Stan Ternent's newly promoted side finally crack when Ian Hughes pulls down Holland to concede a penalty and gain a second yellow card. Birthday boy Tanner converts. Dozzell side-foots in Gregory's pass.

been struggling and are relieved to salvage a late point.

---

12 — A BIRMINGHAM, 28/10 · Att: 16,778 · 20 D 1-1 14 (13)
Holland 34 / Bruce 81 · Ref: M Bailey

Town: Wright, Stockwell*, Taricco, Williams, Tanner, Dyer, Holland, Mathie, Dozzell^, Petta", subs Milton/Gregory/Kerslake
Birmingham: Bennett, Bass, Grainger, Bruce, Ablett, Devlin, Robinson, Francis, McCarthy, Ndlovu*, Forster

From a cross by Stockwell, Holland cracks in a shot that goes past Ian Bennett via the post and Gary Ablett's body. The recalled Kevin Francis heads the ball on for Steve Bruce to score from close range.

---

13 — A CHARLTON, 1/11 · Att: 12,627 · 21 L 0-3 14 (3)
Mendonca 10, Chapple 34, Leaburn 90 · Ref: P Rever

Town: Wright, Stockwell, Taricco, Williams*, Kerslake, Dyer^, Holland, Gregory, Dozzell", Whyte, subs Milton/Mathie/Swailes
Charlton: Petterson, Brown, Bowen, Jones, Rufus, Newton^, Kinsella, Robinson, Mendonca, Leaburn, Holmes

David Whyte, seen by some as an expensive misfit, signs on a free from Reading. Town fall behind when Mendonca dribbles round Wright. Dozzell (virus) and Williams (hip injury) depart early. Chapple dives to head in Kinsella's corner. Leaburn heads home Robinson's late cross.

---

14 — H STOCKPORT, 4/11 · Att: 8,938 · 22 L 0-2 14 (10)
Angell 70, 81 · Ref: S Bennett

Town: Wright, Stockwell, Taricco*, Sonner, Tanner, Milton, Holland, Mathie^, Whyte, Legg, subs Gregory/Kerslake
Stockport: Nixon, Connelly, Woodthorpe*, Bennett, McIntosh, Gannon, Cook, Angell, Armstrong, Cooper, Searle

Attempting to halt the slide, Burley brings in another new face in loanee Andy Legg. Town have 11 men unavailable. Sonner is jeered as Brett Angell heads in two late goals, from crosses by Paul Cook and Kevin Cooper. On a depressing evening, Town are jeered off the line.

---

15 — H SHEFFIELD UTD, 9/11 · Att: 9,695 · 21 D 2-2 15 (4)
Legg 50, Gregory 87 / Taylor 9, Ward 79 · Ref: M Pierce

Town: Wright, Stockwell, Tanner^, Williams, Mowbray", Dyer, Holland, Mathie^, Dozzell, Legg^, subs Gregory/Sonner
Sheffield Utd: Tracey*, Borbokis, Hutchison, McGrath, Holdsworth, Patterson, Marker, Taylor, Deane, Whitehouse, Ward

Gareth Taylor steers in Brian Deane's cross, but Legg's diving header levels matters. Keeper Simon Tracey goes off with concussion after colliding with a post. Mitch Ward volleys in, but stand-in keeper Don Hutchison is beaten by sub Gregory, who then misses a chance to win it.

---

16 — A WOLVERHAMPTON, 15/11 · Att: 21,937 · 21 D 1-1 16 (9)
Johnson 44 / Keane 27 · Ref: J Kirkby

Town: Wright, Stockwell, Taricco, Williams*, Tanner, Dyer, Holland, Johnson*, Legg^, subs Gregory/Milton
Wolverhampton: Stowell, Atkins, Gilkes, Robinson, Williams, Curle, Ferguson^, Froggatt, Keane, Freedman, Paatalainen/Osborn

The new boy levels Robbie Keane's goal. Floundering near the foot, Town sign striker David Johnson from Bury for a club record £1.1 million, with Chris Swailes going the other way. Wolves are jeered by their fans.

---

17 — A READING, 22/11 · Att: 9,400 · 18 W 4-0 19 (21)
Holland 26, Johnson 30, Scowcroft 49, [Naylor 87] · Ref: T Leake

Town: Wright, Stockwell, Taricco, Williams", Mowbray, Cundy, Dyer, Holland, Johnson^, Scowcroft^, Legg, subs Mathie/Naylor
Reading: Hammond, Bernal", Swailes, Caskey^, McPherson, Primus, Parkinson, Houghton, Asaba, Morley, Williams, Booty/Hodge

Inspired by Johnson's arrival, Town rip into struggling Reading. Holland's shot is deflected home. Johnson shrugs off Keith McPherson to score and then robs the same player to set up Scowcroft. Sub Naylor adds icing on the cake and it's six wins out of seven visits to Elm Park.

---

18 — H NOTT'M FOREST, 29/11 · Att: 17,580 · 20 L 0-1 19 (1)
Campbell 65 · Ref: R Pearson

Town: Wright, Stockwell, Taricco, Williams, Mowbray, Cundy, Dyer, Holland, Johnson^, Scowcroft^, Legg, subs Naylor
Nott'm Forest: Beasant, Lyttle, Rogers, Cooper, Chettle, Hjelde, Stone, Gemmill, V Hooijdonk, Campbell, B't-Williams

The league leaders go ahead when Chris Bart-Williams sets up Kevin Campbell who nets a ten-yard drive. Pierre Van Hooijdonk hits the bar.

---

19 — H MIDDLESBROUGH, 2/12 · Att: 13,619 · 20 D 1-1 20 (2)
Johnson 90 / Merson 33 · Ref: M Fletcher

Town: Wright, Stockwell, Taricco, Milton", Mowbray", Cundy, Dyer, Holland, Johnson, Scowcroft!, Legg^, subs Mathie/Naylor/Tanner
Middlesbrough: Schwarzer, Fleming, Harrison!, Vickers, Pearson, Emerson, Hignett*, Summerbell, Beck, Merson*, Townsend, Ormerod/Whyte

Paul Merson pokes the ball in after being cut clear. Scowcroft and Craig Harrison are sent off for an off-the-ball scuffle. Townsend is initially red-carded, but after long discussions the true offender walks. In a last-minute scramble Taricco hits a post, before Johnson bundles the ball in.

---

20 — A TRANMERE, 6/12 · Att: 5,720 · 19 D 1-1 21 (17)
Johnson 27 / Jones L 73 · Ref: G Singh

Town: Wright, Stockwell, Taricco, Williams, Tanner, Dyer*, Holland, Johnson, Scowcroft, Petta, Milton
Tranmere: Simonsen, Stevens*, Morgan, McGreal, Challinor, Irons, Morrissey, Mellon, Kelly, O'Brien, Jones L^, Aldridge/Mahon

Johnson's close-range header puts Town ahead from a cross by the recalled Petta. Two minutes later Holland cracks a shot against the bar. Johnson looks to be brought down but no penalty is given. Lee Jones is injured as he grabs the equaliser after being set up by Dave Challinor.

---

21 — H PORTSMOUTH, 13/12 · Att: 11,641 · 16 W 2-0 24 (23)
Cundy 30, Johnson 68 · Ref: M Leach

Town: Wright, Stockwell, Taricco, Williams, Tanner, Cundy, Dyer^, Holland, Johnson, Scowcroft*, Petta*, subs Milton/Sonner
Portsmouth: Knight, Petrick, Thomson, McLoughlin, Whitbread, Awford", Hall, Simpson*, Durnin, Svensson, Hillier, Waterman/Igoe/Turner

Cundy heads in Petta's free-kick, the vital second, hitting the roof of the net from Holland's cross. Stockwell and Scowcroft both hit the woodwork. Terry Fenwick's days are numbered as Pompey boss. His side go close when Andy Turner's effort is knocked off the line.

---

22 — A PORT VALE, 20/12 · Att: 5,784 · 14 W 3-1 27 (17)
Mathie 10, 22, Johnson 43 / Foyle 50 · Ref: T Heilbron

Town: Wright, Stockwell*, Taricco, Williams, Tanner*, Cundy, Dyer^, Holland, Mathie, Johnson, Scowcroft, subs Mowbray/Kennedy/Keeble
Port Vale: Musselwhite, Stokes, Tankard", Bogie, Koordes^, Snijders*, Ainsworth, Talbot, Foyle, Naylor, Corden, Porter/Jansson/Eyre

Mathie, struggling to recapture form, celebrates his birthday in style on a foggy afternoon. Johnson nets after a horrendous mix-up. Gareth Ainsworth hits a post before Martin Foyle pulls one back for John Rudge's men. Young John 'Spider' Kennedy and Chris Keeble both debut.

---

23 — H BIRMINGHAM, 26/12 · Att: 17,549 · 16 L 0-1 27 (10)
McCarthy 83 · Ref: R Furnandiz

Town: Wright, Stockwell, Taricco, Williams, Tanner*, Cundy, Dyer, Holland, Mathie, Scowcroft, Mowbray
Birmingham: Bennett, Bass, Charlton, Bruce, Ablett, O'Connor, Forster, Robinson, Hughes*, McCarthy, Ndlovu^, Grainger/Francis

Trevor Francis' side are on top early, but Town improve slightly after half-time. Wright makes two particularly fine saves from Peter Ndlovu. A late corner-kick by Jon McCarthy sails over untouched and although Milton hacks it clear, it had already crossed the goalline. A bitter blow.

NATIONWIDE DIVISION 1   Manager: George Burley   SEASON 1997-98

No	Date		Att	Pos	Pt	F-A	H-T	Scorers, Times, and Referees	1	2	3	4	5	6	7	8	9	10	11	subs used
24	28/12	A SWINDON	10,609	13	30	2-0	0-0	Johnson 49p, Petta 79; Ref: D Orr	Wright	Stockwell	Taricco	Williams	Mowbray	Venus	Dyer*	Holland	Johnson	Sonner	Petta	Milton
				9					*Digby*	*Culverhouse*	*Robinson*	*Leitch^*	*Darras**	*McDonald*	*Walters**	*Thompson*	*Hay*	*Ndah*	*Gooden*	*Finney/Collins/Taylor*
25	10/1	H QP RANGERS	12,672	14	31	0-0	0-0	Ref: W Burns	Wright	Stockwell*	Taricco	Williams	Mowbray	Cundy	Clapham	Holland	Johnson	Scowcroft^	Petta	Milton/Mathie
				13					*Roberts*	*Yates*	*Brevett*	*Quashie*	*Maddix*	*Ready*	*Spencer**	*Peacock*	*Sinclair*	*Sheron*	*Murray*	*Gallen*
26	17/1	A MIDDLESBROUGH	30,081	15	32	1-1	0-0	Johnson 76; Pearson 63; Ref: M Dean	Wright	Stockwell	Taricco	Williams	Mowbray	Brown*	Tanner	Holland	Johnson	Mathie	Campbell*	Clapham*
				2					*Schwarzer*	*Maddison*	*Kinder*	*Festa!*	*Pearson*	*Mustoe*	*Hignett*	*Townsend*	*Beck*	*Merson*		*Vickers*
27	27/1	A WEST BROM	12,403	14	35	3-2	0-0	Holland 57, Scowcroft 75, Cundy 89; Murphy 70, Flynn 72; Ref: M Messias	Wright	Stockwell	Taricco	Dyer	Tanner	Cundy	Uhlenbeek	Holland	Johnson	Scowcroft	Clapham*	Sonner
				9					*Miller*	*Holmes*	*Nicholson*	*Sneekes*	*Murphy*	*Carbon*	*Flynn**	*Hamilton*	*Hughes*	*Hunt*	*Kilbane*	*Butler*
28	31/1	H BRADFORD C	11,864	13	38	2-1	0-0	Mathie 72, 86; Blake 56; Ref: R Styles	Wright	Stockwell	Taricco	Dyer	Tanner^	Cundy	Uhlenbeek*	Holland	Johnson	Scowcroft	Clapham*	Petta/Mathie/Mathie
				11					*Walsh*	*Wilder^*	*Jacobs*	*O'Brien*	*Youds!*	*Ramage"*	*Lawrence*	*Blake*	*Edinho*	*Murray*		*Steiner/Beagrie/Bolland*
29	7/2	A STOKE	11,416	13	39	1-1	0-1	Holland 78; Holsgrove 15; Ref: M Pike	Wright	Stockwell	Taricco!	Williams^	Clapham	Cundy	Uhlenbeek*	Holland	Mathie	Scowcroft	Dyer	Sonner/Johnson
				19					*Muggelton*	*Pickering*	*McKinlay*	*Sigurdsson*	*Whittle*	*Keen*	*Holsgrove*	*Wallace*	*McMahon^*	*Scully*	*Kavanagh**	*Macari/Gabbiadini*
30	14/2	H HUDDERSFIELD	10,509	12	42	5-1	1-1	Holland 42, Johnson 54, 61, Mathie 69, [Naylor 89]; Stewart 37; Ref: M Pierce	Wright	Stockwell	Taricco	Sonner*	Mowbray	Cundy	Clapham*	Holland	Johnson^	Mathie	Dyer	Petta/Naylor/Uhlenbeek
				19					*Harper*	*Jenkins*	*Edwards^*	*Watts*	*Phillips*	*Gray*	*Dalton**	*Horne*	*Stewart*	*Allison*	*Johnson*	*Barnes/Smith*
31	18/2	A MANCHESTER C	27,156	10	45	2-1	0-1	Petta 83, Dyer 90; Symons 5; Ref: G Frankland	Wright	Stockwell	Taricco	Dyer	Mowbray	Cundy	Uhlenbeek	Holland	Johnson^	Mathie^	Clapham*	Petta/Naylor
				22					*Wright*	*Edghill^*	*Tskhadadze*	*Sheila*	*Symons*	*Whitley Jim*	*Jeff Russell*	*Beardsley**	*Kinkladze*	*Rosler*		*Bradbury/Crooks?/Beesley*
32	21/2	H NORWICH	21,858	10	48	5-0	3-0	Mathie 2, 27, 42, Petta 56, 81; Ref: C Wilkes	Wright	Stockwell*	Clapham	Dyer	Mowbray	Cundy	Uhlenbeek	Holland	Johnson	Mathie*	Petta	Scowcroft/Sonner
				14					*Marshall*	*Segura^*	*Sutch*	*Grant*	*Fleming*	*Forbes**	*Jackson*	*Fleck**	*Eadie*	*Coote*	*Carey*	*Mills/Kenton/Llewellyn*
33	24/2	H OXFORD	11,824	7	51	5-2	3-1	Mathie 28, Jnson 35, 38, 85p, Holland 56; Francis 11, Donaldson 59p; Ref: P Danson	Wright	Stockwell*	Taricco	Dyer	Mowbray	Cundy	Clapham	Holland	Johnson	Mathie*	Petta*	Scowcroft/Sonner/Uhlenbeek
				16					*Whitehead*	*Robinson*	*Ford*	*Gray*	*Davis*	*Gilchrist*	*Powell**	*Smith*	*Francis*	*Donaldson^*	*Beauchamp*	*Cook/Weatherstone*
34	28/2	A SUNDERLAND	35,114	7	52	2-2	2-1	Petta 11, Dyer 28; Williams 13, Phillips 51; Ref: M Jones	Wright	Stockwell	Taricco	Dyer	Mowbray	Cundy	Clapham*	Holland	Johnson^	Mathie*	Petta*	Scowcroft/Sonner
				3					*Perez*	*Holloway*	*Gray*	*Clark*	*Craddock*	*Williams*	*Summ'rbee**	*Rae*	*Quinn*	*Phillips*	*Johnston*	*Ball*

24 — Swindon: The excellent away run continues. Petta is pushed and Johnson despatches the penalty. Alan McDonald has a header cleared off the line by Venus. Town break out after Swindon pressure and Petta goes on a 60-yard run that ends with his shot deflecting past despairing Fraser Digby.

25 — QP Rangers: Spurs loanee Jamie Clapham makes his debut. A typical mazy run by Petta ends with his shot going close. New QPR boss Ray Harford is pleased with the point.

26 — Middlesbrough: Wayne Brown gets a tough debut. Gianluca Festa is unlucky to see red after his challenge brings down Johnson on his way to goal. Wright makes three fine saves but Robbie Mustoe hits the bar. Nigel Pearson heads in Paul Merson's free-kick, but Johnson nets Stockwell's cross.

27 — West Brom: Holland shoots Town ahead after nearly an hour's deadlock. Denis Smith's men shock Town with two quickfire goals. Back come Town as Scowcroft accepts a simple tap-in to equalise. In the dying seconds Clapham chips a free-kick for Cundy to head decisively past Alan Miller.

28 — Bradford C: Robbie Blake cuts in and slips a shot past Wright. Fans' favourite Mathie comes on and fires the equaliser from Stockwell's cross. Eddie Youds is red carded after fouling Petta. Pepper bundles Mathie over for a second yellow card. Mathie nets his second from Stockwell's throw-in. Nigel

29 — Stoke: Stoke's new boss Chris Kamara is cheered by Paul Holsgrove's early success as he slides in to convert Tom McKinlay's cross. Lou Macari's son Paul makes a debut. After Clapham goes close, Holland nods in the equaliser. Taricco is sent off near the end after his second yellow card.

30 — Huddersfield: A marvellous solo run ends with Marcus Stewart on target for Peter Jackson's struggling side. Town respond via Holland's header. Johnson grabs two, the second into an empty net set up by Mathie. The Scot then converts Dyer's pass himself. Petta squares for Naylor to slot the fifth.

31 — Manchester C: City start on a high after welcoming new boss Joe Royle. Kit Symons heads in early from Craig Russell's cross. Sub Petta climbs off the bench and becomes the hero of the hour. First his cross skims the head of Mathie to elude Tommy Wright. Then his driven cross is forced in by Dyer.

32 — Norwich: A day the home fans will never forget. Mathie snaps up a joyous first-half hat-trick, the first after 64 seconds. He departs at half-time to protect a calf problem. After Robert Fleck's comical miss, Holland rolls the ball to Petta for the fourth goal. A run into the box leads to Petta's second.

33 — Oxford: A club record third successive 'nap hand' at home. Wright goes off for stitches and stand-in Holland is beaten by Kevin Francis. After Wright returns, Town rip into Oxford and Johnson poaches his very first hat-trick. He clinches it after Phil Gilchrist brings him down for the penalty.

34 — Sunderland: There's play-off talk in the air as confident Town go ahead when Petta fires in off a post. Darren Williams heads a leveller, but Mathie lays the ball back for Dyer to pick his spot. In a red-hot atmosphere in the new Stadium of Light, Kevin Phillips hooks in Niall Quinn's headed pass.

#									Team (starting XI + subs)				
35	A 3/3	SHEFFIELD UTD	14,120	6 / 5	W 55	1-0	1-0		Wright	Stockwell	Taricco	Dyer	Mowbray	Cundy	Clapham	Holland	Johnson	Mathie*	Petta^	Scowcroft/Sonner

35 — A 3/3 — SHEFFIELD UTD — 14,120 — 6 / 5 — W 55 — 1-0 — 1-0
Holland 18
Ref: A Wiley
Town: Wright, Stockwell, Taricco, Dyer, Mowbray, Cundy, Clapham, Holland, Johnson, Mathie*, Petta^, Scowcroft/Sonner
Opp: Kelly, Barbokis^, Short, Quinn, Derry*, Holdsworth, Ford, Marker, Taylor, Rush, Stuart, Marcello/Beard
The Blades, without a manager, go close when on-loan Ian Rush hits the bar. Town take the lead when Holland rises to head home Petta's free-kick. It's his tenth goal of the season and comes against the run of play. Petta strikes the bar as Town hang on for three very vital points.

36 — H 7/3 — CHARLTON — 19,831 — 5 / 4 — W 58 — 3-1 — 0-1
Stockwell 53, Cundy 76, Johnson 88
Mendonca 22
Ref: P Richards
Town: Wright, Stockwell, Taricco, Dyer, Mowbray, Cundy, Clapham, Holland, Johnson, Mathie*, Petta, Scowcroft
Opp: Ilic, Barness*, Bowen, Jones, Rufus, Balmer, Newton, Kinsella, Robinson, Mendonca, Bright, Lisbie
Clive Mendonca nips round Wright to punish a Cundy slip. Petta hits the bar again, but Stockwell levels with a superb volley from the edge of the box. Cundy makes amends, heading in Mathie's corner-kick. With Charlton pressing hard, Town break away and Johnson finishes coolly.

37 — A 14/3 — STOCKPORT — 8,939 — 5 / 9 — W 61 — 1-0 — 0-0
Johnson 55
Ref: J Kirkby
Town: Wright, Stockwell, Taricco, Dyer, Mowbray, Cundy, Clapham, Holland, Johnson, Mathie*, Petta, Scowcroft
Opp: Nixon, Connelly, Searle*, Phillips^, McIntosh, Flynn, Woodthorpe, Cook, Angell, Grant, Byrne, Nash/Travis
Johnson conjures up another cool finish as Holland finds him with a header. There's plenty of Stockport pressure to soak up, but Town look solid and the unbeaten run goes on. It's sweet revenge for the November home defeat. Clapham signs for £300,000 at the end of his loan spell.

38 — H 21/3 — WOLVERHAMPTON — 21,510 — 5 / 8 — W 64 — 3-0 — 1-0
Johnson 3, Holland 57, Scowcroft 74
Ref: B Knight
Town: Wright, Clapham, Taricco, Dyer^, Mowbray, Cundy, Uhlenbeek, Holland, Johnson, Mathie*, Petta*, Scowcroft/Sonner/Tanner
Opp: Segers, Wright, Naylor*, Richards^, Williams, Curle, Robinson, Froggatt, Bull, Paatalainen* Osborn !, Atkins/Keane/Freedman
A great start as Johnson beats Hans Segers in a race for the ball. Wolves are furious when the ref rules his effort has crossed the line. Petta's corner falls for Holland to fire in. Simon Osborn departs after two yellow cards. Scowcroft nets one of them.

39 — H 28/3 — READING — 19,075 — 5 / 24 — W 67 — 1-0 — 1-0
Scowcroft 39
Ref: B Coddington
Town: Wright, Stockwell, Taricco, Dyer^, Mowbray, Cundy, Clapham, Holland, Johnson, Scowcroft, Petta*, Mathie/Sonner
Opp: Howie, Berna !!, Legg !, Kelly, Caskey, Primus, Parkinson, Houghton*, Fleck, Gray, McIntyre^, Crawford/Brayson
Reading's new boss Tommy Burns picks five debutants. Hoping for a new dawn, 1,700 visiting fans make an almighty row, but Wright gets little to do. Scowcroft heads in Petta's cross. On 45 and 68 minutes, ex-Town men Andy Legg and Andy Bernal get their second yellow cards.

40 — A 5/4 — NOTT'M FOREST — 22,292 — 5 / 1 — L 67 — 1-2 — 0-0
Scowcroft 46
Cooper 53, Van Hooijdonk 58
Ref: W Burns
Town: Wright, Stockwell, Taricco, Dyer, Mowbray*, Cundy, Clapham, Holland, Johnson*, Scowcroft, Petta^, Mathie/Uhlenbeek
Opp: Beasant, Bonalair, Rogers, Cooper, Chettle, Johnson*, Stone, Gemmill, V Hooijdonk, Campbell, B't Williams Hjelde
The enigmatic Pierre Van Hooijdonk is almost anonymous in the first period. But shortly after Scowcroft opens the scoring, the Dutchman's amazing 35-yard free-kick is blocked by Wright, with the rebound netted by Colin Cooper. Van Hooijdonk wins it with an expertly-taken goal.

41 — H 11/4 — TRANMERE — 18,039 — 6 / 16 — D 68 — 0-0 — 0-0
Ref: M Bailey
Town: Wright, Stockwell, Taricco, Dyer^, Mowbray*, Cundy, Clapham, Holland, Johnson^, Scowcroft, Petta*, Venus/Mathie/Sonner
Opp: Simonsen, Kubicki, Thompson, McGreal, Challinor, Irons, Morrissey^, Mellon, Jones G*, O'Brien, Hill, Jones L/Morgan
John Aldridge's men have clearly come for a point and the first half is a real non-event. The run of seven home wins is at an end. Mark Venus returns after a broken toe. Mark Venus ... ecstatic at the final whistle, despite the jeers of the home fans.

42 — A 13/4 — PORTSMOUTH — 15,040 — 5 / 22 — W 71 — 1-0 — 1-0
Johnson 8
Ref: J Brandwood
Town: Wright, Stockwell, Taricco, Dyer, Mowbray*, Cundy, Clapham, Holland, Johnson, Mathie^, Petta, Venus/Scowcroft
Opp: Flahavan, Pethick, Robinson, Hillier, Whitbread, Awford, Vlachos, Simpson, Aloisi^, Durnin, Thomson*, Hall/Simpson
It's 31 years since Pompey beat Town at Fratton Park. Johnson slams in the rebound after his first effort is blocked. Then he misses a penalty after he'd been brought down by Andy Thomson. Aaron Flahavan is the busier of the two keepers and the win margin could have been bigger.

43 — H 18/4 — PORT VALE — 16,205 — 5 / 20 — W 74 — 5-1 — 3-0
Johnson 4, 58, Petta 27, 29, Mathie 56
Barnett 65
Ref: P Taylor
Town: Wright, Stockwell, Taricco, Dyer^, Mowbray, Cundy, Clapham, Holland, Johnson*, Mathie, Petta*, Scowcroft/Sonner/Tanner
Opp: Musselwhite, Carragher, Tankard, Bogie, Barnett, Glover, Ainsworth, Talbot, Mills, Naylor*, Jansson*, Porter/Foyle
Another goal bonanza on a rain-soaked pitch. Johnson is unmarked for the first, and Petta nets two cracking shots before the break. Mathie gets in on the act after Paul Musselwhite saves his first effort. Johnson nets the fifth from close-range before Dave Barnett heads in a consolation.

44 — A 25/4 — BURY — 7,830 — 5 / 19 — W 77 — 1-0 — 0-0
Stockwell 75
Ref: G Laws
Town: Wright, Stockwell, Taricco, Dyer, Venus, Cundy, Clapham, Holland, Johnson^, Mathie*, Petta*, Scowcroft/Sonner
Opp: Kiely, Woodward, Small*, Daws, Lucketti, Butler, Ellis, Matthews* Swan", Armstrong, Johnrose, Rigby/Swailes/Jemson
A big Town following (2,037) urges their side towards to clinch a play-off spot. On a dreadful playing surface, the home side are on top until Scowcroft comes on to supplement the front line. Stockwell nets a wonderful winner with a solo run and swerving shot.

45 — H 28/4 — SUNDERLAND — 20,902 — 5 / 3 — W 80 — 2-0 — 0-0
Holland 48, Mathie 61
Ref: K Leach
Town: Wright, Stockwell, Taricco, Dyer^, Venus, Cundy, Clapham, Holland, Johnson^, Mathie, Petta*, Scowcroft/Sonner/Tanner
Opp: Perez, Holloway^, Makin, Clark*, Craddock, Williams, Summerbee Ball, Quinn, Phillips, Johnston, Rae/Dichio
Joey Craddock upends Johnson, but Mathie sees his penalty saved by Lionel Perez's legs. A spectacular diving header by Holland puts Town ahead. Clapham swings over a cross and Mathie clinches the win with a volley. Sunderland's defeat means Nottingham Forest are promoted.

46 — H 3/5 — CREWE — 19,105 — 5 / 11 — W 83 — 3-2 — 1-1
Johnson 33, Stockwell 53, Mathie 55
Charnock 40, Garvey 60
Ref: R Furnandiz
Town: Wright, Stockwell*, Taricco", Dyer^, Venus, Cundy, Clapham, Holland, Johnson, Mathie*, Petta, Scowcroft/Sonner/Uhlenbeek
Opp: Bankole, Smith S, Bignot", Foran", Unsworth, Charnock, Garvey, Lunt, Smith P*, Johnson, Anthrobus, Rivers/Wright D/Wright J
Petta hits the bar after the prolific Johnson strikes. Peter Smith's through ball sets up Phil Charnock. Stockwell pounces at the far post, then Mathie nets with the outside of his boot. Steve Garvey rockets in a spectacular 30-yarder. Dyer is fouled and gets up to stroke the penalty wide.

Home 14,973
Away 14,753
Average 14,973

NATIONWIDE DIVISION 1 (CUP-TIES) Manager: George Burley SEASON 1997-98

Play-offs

SF 1 — H CHARLTON · 10/5 · Att 21,681 · L · F-A 0-1 · H-T 0-1
Scorers, Times: Clapham 12 (og). Ref: M Fletcher

1	2	3	4	5	6	7	8	9	10	11	subs used
Wright	Stockwell	Taricco	Dyer	Venus	Cundy	Clapham*	Holland	Johnson	Mathie	Petta^	Uhlenbeek/Scowcroft
Ilic	*Mills!*	*Bowen*	*Jones K"*	*Rufus*	*Youds*	*Newton*	*Kinsella*	*Bright^*	*Mendonca*	*Heaney^*	*Barness/Jones S/Brown*

A tense occasion gets off to a nightmare start as unlucky Clapham diverts Keith Jones' low cross into his own net. The visitors' physical approach is a surprise and it becomes a scrappy, ill-tempered affair. There are nine bookings and Danny Mills is sent off for a foul on Taricco.

SF 2 — A CHARLTON · 13/5 · Att 15,585 · L · F-A 0-1 · H-T 0-1
Scorers, Times: Newton 36. Ref: E Wolstenholme
(Town lose 0-2 on aggregate)

1	2	3	4	5	6	7	8	9	10	11	subs used
Wright	Stockwell^	Taricco	Dyer	Venus	Cundy	Uhlenbeek	Holland	Johnson	Mathie*	Petta	Scowcroft/Sonner
Ilic	*Barness*	*Bowen*	*Jones K*	*Rufus*	*Youds*	*Newton*	*Kinsella*	*Bright*	*Jones S**	*Heaney*	*Mortimer*

Missing injured Clive Mendonca, Charlton go ahead via a brilliant Shaun Newton goal after Venus concedes a free-kick. Bad feeling remains from the first leg, but Town have no complaints as Charlton are slicker and sharper in this game, and deserve to meet Sunderland at Wembley.

Coca-Cola Cup

1:1 — A CHARLTON · 13/8 · Att 6,598 · W · 1-0 · 1-0
Scorers, Times: Venus 15. Ref: D Orr

1	2	3	4	5	6	7	8	9	10	11	subs used
Wright	Stockwell	Taricco	Williams	Venus	Cundy	Dyer	Holland	Petta*	Scowcroft	Mason	Gregory
Petterson	*Barness*	*Brown^*	*Jones K*	*Rufus*	*Balmer*	*Newton*	*Kinsella*	*Robinson**	*Mendonca*	*Jones S*	*Bright/Nicholls*

Aussie keeper Andy Petterson is penalised for hanging on to the ball for more than six seconds. Mason touches the indirect free-kick to Venus who thunders home a powerful shot. Petterson saves well from Mason, while Scowcroft and Petta both miss decent chances to extend the lead.

1:2 — H CHARLTON · 26/8 · Att 10,989 · W · 3-1 · 2-0
Scorers, Times: Stein 31, Brown 45 (og), Scowcroft 61, Mendonca 89. Ref: S Bennett
(Town win 4-1 on aggregate)

1	2	3	4	5	6	7	8	9	10	11	subs used
Wright	Stockwell	Taricco	Williams	Venus	Cundy	Dyer	Holland	Stein^	Scowcroft	Milton*	Kerslake/Sonner
Petterson	*Konchesky**	*Brown^*	*Nicholl"*	*Chapple*	*Balmer*	*Newton*	*Kinsella*	*Robinson*	*Mendonca*	*Jones S**	*Bright/Lisbie/Stuart*

Mark Stein, on loan from Chelsea, nets his first Town goal with a left-foot drive. Dyer's cross is sliced into his own net by Steve Brown. The tie is well and truly over when man-of-the-match Scowcroft finds the target. Town knock the ball about confidently and look in good shape.

2:1 — H TORQUAY · 16/9 · Att 8,031 · D · 1-1 · 0-1
Scorers, Times: Holland 89, McFarlane 1. Ref: S Baines

1	2	3	4	5	6	7	8	9	10	11	subs used
Wright	Stockwell	Taricco	Williams	Venus	Swailes*	Dyer	Holland	Stein	Scowcroft	Sonner^	Petta/Mathie
Gregg	*Gurney*	*Gibbs*	*Robinson*	*Gittens*	*Watson^*	*Clayton*	*Hill*	*Jack*	*McFarlane*	*McCall**	*Thomas/Barrow*

Kevin Hodges' Gulls soar into an early lead when Andy McFarlane heads past Wright in the first minute. Paul Gibbs brings down Scowcroft, but Stein's penalty is saved by inexperienced young keeper Matthew Gregg. Stockwell saves off-colour Town's embarrassment late in the day.

2:2 — A TORQUAY · 23/9 · Att 3,598 · W · 3-0 · 1-0
Scorers, Times: Holland 21, 61, Dyer 90. Ref: A Wiley
(Town win 4-1 on aggregate)

1	2	3	4	5	6	7	8	9	10	11	subs used
Wright	Kerslake	Taricco	Williams	Mowbray	Cundy	Dyer	Holland	Stein*	Scowcroft	Petta	Mathie
Gregg	*Gurney*	*Gibbs*	*Robinson*	*Gittens*	*Watson*	*Clayton*	*Hill*	*Jack*	*McFarlane*	*Hapgood**	*Bedeau*

Ex-Spurs full-back David Kerslake, signed on a free from Charlton, makes his full debut. Around 800 Town fans make the long trek to the seaside. They are rewarded by a professional display which makes amends for the first leg. Holland takes his two goals well to ensure victory.

3 — H MANCHESTER U · 14/10 · Att 22,173 · W · 2-0 · 2-0
Scorers, Times: Mathie 13, Taricco 45. Ref: P Alcock

1	2	3	4	5	6	7	8	9	10	11	subs used
Wright	Stockwell	Taricco	Williams*	Mowbray	Cundy	Dyer	Holland	Mathie	Dozzell	Petta*	Milton/Stein
Van der Gouw	*Neville P*	*May*	*Johnsen"*	*Mulryne^*	*McClair*	*Cole*	*Crayff*	*Poborsky*	*Thornley^*		*Scholes/Nevland/Irwin*

Alex Ferguson's attitude to this competition is clear from the virtual reserve side he puts out. Nevertheless there are several internationals on view and it's an enjoyable night for Town fans. Jason Dozzell, back from Spurs on a weekly contract, inspires the win with a superb display.

4 — A OXFORD · 18/11 · Att 5,723 · W · 2-1 · 0-0 aet
Scorers, Times: Dozzell 63, Mowbray 93, Beauchamp 66. Ref: S Mathieson

1	2	3	4	5	6	7	8	9	10	11	subs used
Wright	Stockwell	Taricco	Williams	Mowbray	Cundy	Dyer	Holland	Mathie*	Dozzell	Legg	Gregory
Van Heusden Gray	*Ford M**	*Robinson*	*Purse*	*White*	*Gilchrist*	*Ford R*	*Smith*	*Banger^*	*Jemson*	*Beauchamp*	*Murphy/Powell*

Dozzell gets a breakthrough but Joey Beauchamp is quick to respond for Denis Smith's men, currently plagued by various off-field problems. Into extra-time and Mowbray nets a handsome diving header. He then tops this with an unbelievable clearance off the line from Beauchamp.

QF — H CHELSEA · 7/1 · Att 22,088 · D · 2-2 · 1-2 aet
Scorers, Times: Taricco 45, Mathie 62, Flo 32, Le Saux 45. Ref: P Durkin
(Chelsea win 4-1 on penalties)

1	2	3	4	5	6	7	8	9	10	11	subs used
Wright	Stockwell	Taricco	Williams	Mowbray	Venus^	Dyer	Holland	Mathie"	Scowcroft	Petta*	Petta/Tanner
De Goey	*Lambourde*	*Granville*	*Sinclair^*	*Leboeuf*	*Myers"*	*Wise*	*Matteo"*	*Flo*	*Zola*	*Le Saux*	*Gullit/Clarke/Hughes M*

A real thriller as Town come back from the dead, levelling via a fine Mathie goal. Petta hits a post in extra-time. The penalty shoot-out sees Frank Leboeuf, Gianfranco Zola, Roberto di Matteo and Mark Hughes all score. Tanner nets but Scowcroft and Taricco miss and Town go out.

FA Cup

3 — A BRISTOL ROV · 3/1 · Att 8,610 · D · 1-1 · 0-1
Scorers, Times: Stockwell 71, Beadle 36. Ref: M Halsey

1	2	3	4	5	6	7	8	9	10	11	subs used
Wright	Stockwell	Taricco	Williams	Mowbray	Venus	Dyer	Holland	Johnson^	Scowcroft	Petta*	Tanner/Mathie
Collett	*Pritchard*	*Lockwood*	*Penrice*	*White*	*Foster*	*Holloway*	*Ramasut"*	*Beadle*	*Cureton*	*Hayles*	*Bennett*

Jamie Cureton misses two great chances for Ian Holloway's men, before Peter Beadle blasts them ahead. With time running out, ever-reliable Stockwell keeps Town in the cup, blasting an angled drive in off the underside of the bar. Burley borrows Jamie Clapham from Tottenham.

Cup Matches

3R H BRISTOL ROV 14 W 1-0 Johnson 43
13/1 11,362 2:3
Ref: M Halsey

Wright Collett | Stockwell Pritchard* | Tarico Lockwood | Williams Penrice | Mowbray White | Cundy Foster | Tanner Holloway | Holland Ramasut* | Johnson Beadle | Scowcroft Cureton" | Petta Hayles | Hayfield/Perry/Bennett

The Pirates are up for this one and play well, making life difficult for Town. The only goal comes against the run of play. From a Petta cross, Stockwell is unable to make proper contact but the ball falls nicely for Johnson. He duly tucks home his eighth goal in 12 games since signing.

4 H SHEFFIELD UTD 15 D 1-1 Johnson 45
24/1 14,654 5 Saunders 82
Ref: A Wilkie

Wright Tracey | Stockwell Short ! | Tarico Sandford | Williams Ford* | Mowbray Beard | Cundy Holdsworth | Tanner Saunders | Holland Marker | Johnson Stuart | Scowcroft Marcello | Petta Katchouro Morris

Blades boss Nigel Spackman is without 13 players for this game. Johnson nets a peach of a header before the break. Chris Short is sent off for kicking Tarico. Two minutes later Petta's tackle on Marcello gives Dean Saunders a penalty. His first effort is saved, but he nets the rebound.

4R A SHEFFIELD UTD 13 L 0-1 Hutchison 13p
3/2 14,144 5 Ref: A Wilkie

Wright Tracey | Stockwell Short* | Tarico Sandford | Williams" Ford | Mowbray Nilsen | Cundy Holdsworth | Tanner* Saunders | Holland Marker | Johnson^ Stuart | Scowcroft Marcello^ | Petta/Mathie/Sonner Hutchison Quinn/Taylor

Tarico bundles over Marcello in the early stages and Don Hutchison nets the resultant penalty. Before this, United had missed four out of five spot-kicks. Town battle in vain to get back on level terms. Simon Tracey makes two excellent saves from Tarico and Dyer after the interval.

Appearances and Goals

	Appearances							Goals					
	Lge	Sub	LC	Sub	FAC	Sub	PO	Lge	Sub	LC	FAC	PO	Tot
Brown, Wayne	1												
Clapham, Jamie	22												
Cundy, Jason	40	1	6		3			3					3
Dozzell, Jason	8	1		2		2		1	1				2
Dyer, Kieron	41		7		2			4	1				5
Gregory, Neil	2	6		2		2		1					1
Holland, Matt	46		7		4		2	10	2				12
Johnson, David	30	1		4		2		20	2				22
Keeble, Chris	1		1										
Kennedy, John	1		1										
Kerslake, David	2	5	2	1						1			1
Legg, Andy	6	1	1										
Mason, Paul	1	1											
Mathie, Alex	25	12	2	2	3		2	13	2				15
Milton, Simon	7	13	1	1									
Mowbray, Tony	23	2	4		2						1		1
Naylor, Richard		5						2					2
Petta, Bobby	28	4	3	3	1	1		7					7
Scowcroft, James	19	12	6	4		2	2	6	1				7
Sonner, Danny	6	17	1	1	1	1		1	1			1	3
Stein, Mark	6	1		4				2	1				3
Stockwell, Mick	46		5		4		2	3		1	1		5
Swailes, Chris	3	2		1				1					1
Tanner, Adam	14	4	4	3	1	1		1					1
Tarico, Mauricio	41		5		4		2	2					2
Uhlenbeek, Gus	6	5	2	2				1				1	2
Venus, Mark	12	2	6	1		2		1				1	2
Whyte, David	2												
Williams, Geraint	23		7		4								
Wright, Richard	46		7		4		2						
(own-goals)								1		1			2
30 players used	506	94	77	10	44	5	22	4	77	14	3		94

Odds & ends

Double wins: (6) Reading, Port Vale, Man C, Swindon, Portsmouth, Bury.
Double losses: (1) Nott'm Forest.

Won from behind: (7) Swindon (h), Oxford (h), WBA (h), Brad C (h), Huddersfield (h), Man C (a), Charlton (h).
Lost from in front: (1) Nott'm Forest (a).

High spots: Reaching the play-offs again.
Only one league defeat after the season's halfway point.
Three 5-goal hauls in a row at home – including v Norwich.
The instant success of record purchase David Johnson.
A 25 per cent increase in league attendances.
The cup victory over (albeit understrength) Manchester U.
Seven successive home wins.
The emergence of talented local youngster Kieron Dyer.
Stockwell's superb winner at Bury to clinch a play-off spot.
The parade and re-union to mark 20 years since the 1978 FA Cup win, attended by thousands on the Cornhill.

Low spots: A second successive play-off semi-final defeat.
Eight missed penalties (Johnson 2, Mathie, Dyer, Tanner, Stein, Scowcroft and Tarico).
The unsavoury incident which left Tarico covered in blood in the players' bar after the first play-off game.
Farewell to long-serving favourites Milton and Williams.
The home defeat by Stockport in November, leaving Town in 22nd spot.

Player of the Year: Matt Holland.
Ever-presents: (3) Stockwell (Lge only), Holland, Wright.
Hat-tricks: (2) Mathie (v Norwich), Johnson (v Oxford).
Opposing hat-tricks: (0).
Leading scorer: (22) David Johnson.

League Table

	P	Home					Away					Pts
		W	D	L	F	A	W	D	L	F	A	
1 Nott'm Forest	46	18	2	3	52	20	14	7	2	30	22	94
2 Middlesbro	46	17	4	2	51	12	10	6	7	26	29	91
3 Sunderland	46	14	7	2	49	22	12	6	5	37	28	90
4 Charlton *	46	17	5	1	48	17	9	5	9	32	32	88
5 IPSWICH	46	14	5	4	47	20	9	9	5	30	23	83
6 Sheffield Utd	46	16	5	2	44	20	3	12	8	25	34	74
7 Birmingham	46	10	8	5	27	15	9	5	9	33	20	74
8 Stockport	46	14	6	3	46	21	5	2	16	25	48	65
9 Wolves	46	13	6	4	42	25	5	5	13	15	28	65
10 West Brom	46	9	8	6	27	26	7	5	11	23	30	61
11 Crewe	46	10	2	11	30	34	8	3	12	28	31	59
12 Oxford	46	12	6	5	36	23	4	4	15	24	44	58
13 Bradford C	46	10	9	4	26	23	5	6	13	20	36	57
14 Tranmere	46	9	8	6	34	26	5	5	12	20	31	56
15 Norwich	46	9	8	6	32	27	5	5	13	22	42	55
16 Huddersfield	46	9	5	9	28	28	6	6	12	22	44	53
17 Bury	46	7	10	6	22	22	4	9	10	20	36	52
18 Swindon	46	9	6	8	28	25	5	5	14	14	48	52
19 Port Vale	46	7	6	10	25	24	6	4	13	31	42	49
20 Portsmouth	46	8	8	9	28	30	5	4	14	23	33	49
21 QP Rangers	46	8	9	6	28	21	2	10	11	23	42	49
22 Manchester C	46	6	6	11	28	26	6	6	11	21	31	48
23 Stoke	46	8	5	10	30	40	3	8	12	14	34	46
24 Reading	46	8	4	11	27	31	3	5	15	12	47	42
	1104	262	146	144	835	575	144	146	262	575	835	1510

* promoted
after play-offs

NATIONWIDE DIVISION 1

Manager: George Burley

SEASON 1998-99

No	Date	Opponent	Att	Pos	Res	Pt	F-A	H-T
1	A 9/8	GRIMSBY	7,211		D	1	0-0	0-0
2	H 15/8	BURY	13,267	14	D	2	0-0	0-0
3	A 22/8	PORTSMOUTH	12,002	15	D	3	0-0	0-0
4	H 29/8	SUNDERLAND	15,813	18	L	3	0-2	0-2
5	A 31/8	PORT VALE	5,485	16	W	6	3-0	1-0
6	H 8/9	BRADFORD C	11,596	12	W	9	3-0	1-0
7	A 12/9	OXFORD	6,632	11	D	10	3-3	1-1
8	H 19/9	BRISTOL CITY	13,657	10	W	13	3-1	2-0
9	A 26/9	WATFORD	13,109	12	L	13	0-1	0-1
10	A 29/9	TRANMERE	5,072	8	W	16	2-0	1-0
11	H 3/10	CRYSTAL PALACE	16,837	5	W	19	3-0	1-0

Squad numbers in use (top line Ipswich, italic line opponent), scorers, subs used and referees:

1 — GRIMSBY — Ref: A Wiley
Wright, Stockwell, Taricco, Clapham, Mowbray, Venus, Dyer, Johnson, Holland, Holster*, Petta^
Davison, McDermott, Gallimore, Handyside, Smith R, Widdrington, Coldicott, Nogan, Black, Lester, Groves*
Subs used: Mathie^/Sonner*; *Smith D*
Town's 23rd Sunday game bursts into life when Wright brings down Lee Nogan after just 90 seconds, but Kingsley Black's penalty is saved. Wright saves superbly from Stacey Coldicott. On his debut, Dutch midfielder Marco Holster misses a great scoring chance and is withdrawn.

2 — BURY — Ref: P Robinson
Wright, Stockwell, Taricco, Clapham, Mowbray, Venus, Dyer, Johnson, Holland, Naylor*, Petta
Kiely, Woodward, Barrick, Daws, Lucketti, Redmond, Swailes, Patterson, D'Jaffo, Johnrose, Preece**
Subs used: Mathie^; *Ellis*
Dyer and Johnson both see good efforts narrowly clear the bar in the first period. Ex-Town defender Chris Swailes has a fine game for Neil Warnock's side against his old pals, and goes close to breaking the deadlock with a header. Town's second-half pressure fails to bring a goal.

3 — PORTSMOUTH — Ref: C Wilkes
Wright, Stockwell, Taricco, Clapham, Mowbray, Venus, Dyer, Johnson, Holland, Mathie^, Petta
Flahaven, Thomson, Simpson, McLoughlin, Whitbread, Awford^, Vlachos, Claridge, Aloisi, Durnin, Igoe*
Subs used: Naylor; *Kyzeridis/Robinson*
On Town's lucky ground, Stockwell chips onto the crossbar after 11 minutes. Before the half-hour mark, Venus shoots against a post and later sees an effort cleared off the goalline. The agile Aaron Flahaven keeps other efforts out. Alan Ball's outfit fails to survive with a point.

4 — SUNDERLAND — Scorers: Mullin 12, Phillips 36 — Ref: M Halsey
Wright, Stockwell, Taricco, Clapham, Mowbray, Venus, Dyer, Johnson, Holland, Mathie^, Petta
Sorensen, Williams, Gray, Ball, Melville, Butler^, Summerbee, Mullin, Dichio, Phillips, Johnston
Subs used: Holster/Scowcroft; *Craddock*
It's now six league games since the last Town goal – the club's second-worst run ever. Michael Gray's cross is cracked in by John Mullin. Mathie almost nets an equaliser but is foiled by the post. Kevin Phillips extends the visitors' lead, seizing onto the ball to dribble round Wright.

5 — PORT VALE — Scorers: Scowcroft 22, Johnson 57, Holland 90 — Ref: M Jones
Wright, Tanner, Taricco, Clapham, Mowbray, Venus, Dyer, Johnson, Holland, Scowcroft*, Petta^
Musselwhite, Carragher, Tankard, Bogie, Prewatchy^, Barnett, Ainsworth, Talbot, Walsh, Naylor, Clarke*
Subs used: Mathie/Holster; *Foyle/Corden*
A league goal at last! Scowcroft heads in a Dyer cross to end the barren spell. The points look safe when Johnson converts Petta's cross. Even safer when highly-rated Gareth Ainsworth gets clean through but misses badly. John Rudge's men are buried when Holland nets a late header.

6 — BRADFORD C — Scorers: Scowcroft 22, 83, Venus 65 — Ref: B Knight
Wright, Tanner, Taricco, Clapham, Mowbray, Venus, Dyer*, Johnson, Holland, Scowcroft, Petta
Walsh, Jacobs", Dreyer, McCall, Moore, O'Brien, Pepper, Rankin, Mills^, Whalley, Beagrie*
Subs used: Mathie/Sonner; *Wright/Grant/Ramage*
It's still early days for new City boss Paul Jewell and there's little sign of the great season his men have ahead of them. Scowcroft cuts in and fires in the crucial opening goal. A Petta corner reaches Venus, who heads home. Johnson is dispossessed but Scowcroft is on hand to convert.

7 — OXFORD — Scorers: Scowcroft 39, Johnson 64, Dyer 86 / Banger 21, Windass 50, Thomson 90 — Ref: E Lomas
Wright, Tanner*, Taricco, Clapham*, Mowbray, **Thetis**, Dyer, Johnson, Holland, Scowcroft, Petta
Whitehead, Robinson, Marsh, Gray, Whelan, Wilsterman, Powell, Smith, Banger*, Windass, Beauchamp*
Subs used: Stockwell/Sonner; *Thomson/Hill*
Defender Manu Thetis, £50,000 from Seville, makes his debut but can do nothing about Nicky Banger's header and Dean Windass's deflected free-kick. Scowcroft and Johnson headers keep Town level. Dyer's angled drive looks a winner, but Andy Thomson rockets in a late header.

8 — BRISTOL CITY — Scorers: Johnson 13, 90, Scowcroft 33 / Akinbiyi 88 — Ref: P Danson
Wright, Stockwell, Taricco, Clapham, Mowbray", **Thetis**, Dyer, Johnson, Holland, Scowcroft*, Petta^
Welch, Locke", Bell, Watts, Moore, Brennan, Carey, Hutchings^, Akinbiyi, Tinnion, Andersen*
Subs used: Holster/Sonner; *Edwards/Murray/Cramb*
Benny Lennartsson's side have gone eight league games without a win. Their heads drop after Johnson's early close-range header. Holland is foiled by the bar. Ade Akinbiyi's header is followed by Johnson's run and shot.

9 — WATFORD — Scorers: Kennedy 5p — Ref: G Singh
Wright, Stockwell^, Taricco, Clapham*, Mowbray, **Thetis**, Dyer, Johnson, Holland, Scowcroft, Petta
Chamberlain, Gibbs, Kennedy, Yates, Millen, Mooney, Smart, Hyde, Ngonge, Johnson, Wright*
Subs used: Clapham/Mathie; *Noel-Williams*
After his cup howler at Luton, Wright again blunders. Tanner's back-pass bounces off his knee and in the chase for the loose ball he brings down Nick Wright. Peter Kennedy nets from the spot. Town toil hard for an equaliser but Holland hits the bar and Kennedy clears off the line.

10 — TRANMERE — Scorers: Stockwell 43, Scowcroft 79 — Ref: A Butler
Wright, Stockwell*, Taricco, Tanner, Mowbray, **Thetis**, Dyer, Johnson, Holland, Scowcroft, Petta^
Achterberg, Allen, Thompson, McGreal, Challinor, Irons, Hill^, Santos^, Koumas", Mellon, Jones L
Subs used: Holster/Tanner; *Morrissey/Jones G/Mahon*
Eight league games without a win and John Aldridge's lowly Tranmere are there for the taking. Taricco's cracking drive hits a post and runs along the goalline before going to safety. Stockwell's shot is deflected in after a corner. A Clapham cross sets up Scowcroft, who heads home.

11 — CRYSTAL PALACE — Scorers: Venus 45p, Taricco 82, Mathie 90 — Ref: S Mathieson
Wright, Stockwell, Taricco, Clapham*, Mowbray, Venus, Dyer, Johnson, Holland, Scowcroft*, Petta^
Digby, Burton, Zhiyi, Curcic^, Tuttle, Foster^, Lombardo, Warhurst, Svensson, Rizzo, Mullins
Subs used: Mathie/Tanner; *Dyer/Thomson*
The turning point comes when a challenge by Paul Warhurst results in a rather lucky penalty for Venus. Terry Venables' side throw caution to the wind and Town exploit the gaps that result. Taricco goes on a solo run and cracks in a magnificent goal. Mathie blasts in a fine strike.

12 — H SWINDON 17/10 — 13,212 — 4 W 1-0 — 21/22 — Johnson 31 — Ref: J Brandwood

| Wright | Stockwell | Taricco | Clapham | Mowbray | Venus | Vernazza" | Holland | Johnson | Scowcroft^ | Petta* | Holster/Naylor/Tanner |
| Talia | Robinson | Hall | Leitch^ | Willis | Borrows | Walters | Ndah | Onoura* | Bullock" | Gooden | Hay/Davis/Watson |

Johnson races onto Scowcroft's header to bury his shot. Frank Talia makes a great save from man-of-the-match Mowbray. Popular Mathie, after much speculation, joins Sheffield Wed. Paolo Vernazza (£75k) joins Dundee U (£700k) and out-of-favour Sonner (£75k) is loaned from Arsenal.

13 — H NORWICH 20/10 — 22,079 — 4 L 0-1 — 9/22 — Bellamy 53 — Ref: J Kirkby

| Wright | Stockwell | Taricco | Clapham | Mowbray | Venus | Vernazza* | Holland | Johnson | Scowcroft | Petta | Hunt |
| Marshall A | Fugelstad | Kenton | Forbes* | Fleming | Segura^ | Marshall L | Roberts | Eadie | Brannan | | Sutch/Adams |

Bruce Rioch's outfit break the deadlock when Erik Fugelstad's cross is headed by Craig Bellamy. Scowcroft and Iwan Roberts both hit a post. Jonathan Hunt, on loan from Derby, debuts for Town. City fans cause extensive damage and trouble both inside and outside the stadium.

14 — A STOCKPORT 24/10 — 7,432 — 4 W 1-0 — 19/25 — Dyer 60 — Ref: K Lynch

| Wright | Stockwell* | Taricco | Clapham | Mowbray | Venus | Dyer | Holland | Johnson | Scowcroft | Hunt | Naylor |
| Nash | Connelly | Gannon | Cook | Flynn | McIntosh | Dinning | Cooper | Angell | Moore | Branch* | Wilbraham |

Wright produces three fine saves to keep Gary Megson's men at bay. The dangerous Brett Angell returns from injury, but is kept quiet. Dyer — the subject of transfer speculation — also returns from injury and nets the winner with a sweetly-taken goal after collecting a pass from Hunt.

15 — H WEST BROM 31/10 — 15,568 — 4 W 2-0 — 11/28 — Johnson 66, 74 — Ref: B Coddington

| Wright | Stockwell* | Taricco | Clapham | Mowbray | Venus | Dyer | Holland | Johnson | Scowcroft^ | Hunt" | Petta/Naylor/Thetis |
| Miller | McDermott^ | Van Blerk | Flynn | Murphy | Carbon | Quinn | Evans* | Bortolazzi | Hughes | Kilbane | De Freitas/Maresca |

Wright makes a great save when Lee Hughes breaks free. Dyer's cross is headed in by Johnson, who seals the win with a stunning shot from Clapham's pass. Thetis is lucky to get away with an assault on Jason Van Blerk. Baggies' boss Denis Smith says the scoreline flattered Town.

16 — H WOLVERHAMPTON 3/11 — 14,680 — 2 W 2-0 — 11/31 — Scowcroft 17, Stockwell 90 — Ref: R Furmandiz

| Wright | Stockwell* | Taricco^ | Clapham | Mowbray | Venus | Dyer | Holland | Johnson | Scowcroft* | Thetis | Naylor/Hunt |
| Stowell | Muscat | Gilkes | Emblen | Sedgley | Curle | Corica^ | Robinson* | Connolly | Whitingham | Osborn | Naylor/Foley |

Town win without clicking into top gear. Venus looks better value than Sedgley, the pair having swapped clubs in a deal 16 months earlier. Scowcroft fires through Mike Stowell's legs and Stockwell converts Naylor's late cross. Taricco is carried off after a Simon Osborn tackle.

17 — A HUDDERSFIELD 7/11 — 14,240 — 2 D 2-2 — 5/32 — Venus 25, Johnson 89 / Edwards 65, Allison 74 — Ref: A Hall

| Wright | Stockwell* | Thetis* | Clapham | Mowbray | Venus | Dyer | Holland | Johnson | Scowcroft | Petta | Tanner/Hunt |
| Vaesen | Jenkins | Edwards | Johnson | Jackson | Gray | Dalton* | Horne | Stewart | Allison | Beresford* | Phillips/Facey |

Venus's 30-yarder is matched by Rob Edwards' bending shot. Wayne Allinson's header narrowly crosses the line, but Johnson cuts in and levels at the death. The fans are angry as Taricco is sold to Spurs for £1.8 million, but the club says this was forced by the huge bank overdraft.

18 — A BARNSLEY 14/11 — 15,966 — 2 W 1-0 — 19/35 — Johnson 5 — Ref: M Fletcher

| Wright | Kennedy | Thetis | Clapham | Mowbray | Venus | Dyer | Holland | Johnson^ | Scowcroft* | Petta^ | Naylor/Hunt |
| Bullock T | Morgan | de Zeeuw! | Eaden | McClare" | Appleby | Bullock M* | Sheridan | Fjortoft^ | Dyer | Barnard | Moses/Hendrie/Moore |

With Stockwell injured, John Kennedy is told he's making his full debut shortly before kick-off. Johnson heads in Clapham's cross at the near post. Arjan de Zeeuw gets a second yellow card on 43 minutes. With all subs on, Barnsley go down to nine men when John Sheridan is injured.

19 — H BOLTON 21/11 — 17,225 — 3 L 0-1 — 10/35 — Taylor 90 — Ref: S Bennett

| Wright | Kennedy | Thetis | Clapham | Mowbray | Venus | Dyer | Holland | Johnson | Scowcroft* | Petta* | Hodges |
| Jaaskalainen | Cox | Whitlow | Frandsen | Fish | Newsome | Johansen | Jensen | Holdsworth* | Taylor | Sellars | Gunnlaugsson |

Town are out of luck as chances are missed and Holland hits a post. Near the end Arnie Gunnlaugsson's fine run sets up Bob Taylor's winner. In midweek 14,000 see Dyer play for England U-21 against the Czechs at Portman Road (0-1). Wright is called up for the full England squad.

20 — A CREWE 28/11 — 5,165 — 2 W 3-0 — 24/38 — Scowcroft 37, 57, 74p — Ref: T Heilbron

| Wright | Kennedy^ | Thetis | Clapham | Mowbray | Venus | Dyer | Holland | Johnson | Scowcroft* | Petta* | Naylor/Tanner/Hodges |
| Kaarten | Bignot | Smith | Unsworth | Macauley | Rivers^ | Wright J | Charnock | Jack | Little* | Anthrobus | Lunt/Street |

Scowcroft's first senior hat-trick comes when he's not fully fit due to a back problem! He shoots the first from 16 yards after Dyer hits a post. A firm shot off a post follows and he nets a penalty after Smith hauls down Dyer. Lee Hodges, borrowed from West Ham, gets another chance.

21 — A QP RANGERS 2/12 — 12,449 — 2 D 1-1 — 21/39 — Holland 90 / Gallen 57 — Ref: G Cain

| Wright | Tanner* | Thetis | Clapham | Mowbray^ | Venus | Dyer | Holland | Johnson | Scowcroft | Petta | Hodges/Kennedy |
| Miklosko | Heinola | Barraclough | Morrow | Ready | Maddix | Langley^ | Peacock* | Sheron" | Gallen | Murray | Rowland/Scully/Steiner |

Gerry Francis has returned to revive Rangers after a bad start. Mike Sheron sets up Kevin Gallen at the near post. Town battle back and in the last minute Dyer crosses, Scowcroft's shot is blocked, but Holland slides the ball in. Dyer has a fine game, watched by England boss Hoddle.

22 — H BIRMINGHAM 5/12 — 15,901 — 2 W 1-0 — 7/42 — Petta 16 — Ref: M Jones

| Wright | Tanner | Thetis | Clapham | Mowbray | Venus | Dyer | Holland | Abou | Scowcroft* | Petta* | Naylor |
| Poole | Rowett | Grainger | Robinson | Ablett | Johnson | McCarthy^ | O'Connor" | Forster | Holland" | Ndlovu | Furlong/Hughes/Bass |

With Johnson needing knee surgery, Burley signs Samassi Abou, a native of Ivory Coast, on loan from West Ham. He nearly has a dream start, going close with a great early shot. Venus's free-kick finds Petta, who powers home his first goal of the season. Naylor is cautioned for diving.

23 — H BARNSLEY 12/12 — 16,021 — 2 L 0-2 — 13/42 — McClare 69, Turner 90 — Ref: M Dean

| Wright | Bullock T | Thetis | Clapham | Mowbray | Venus | Dyer | Holland | Abou | Scowcroft* | Petta* | Naylor |
| Bullock T | Eaden | Moses | Jones | Appleby | Tinkler | McClare | Hignett | Burton* | Dyer | Barnard | Turner |

Injury worries increase as Scowcroft, already suffering from double vision, collides with Tony Bullock and breaks his collarbone. Debutant Michael Turner, fresh out of university, crosses for McClare to shoot home. A cross by man-of-the-match Craig Hignett is guided in by Turner.

NATIONWIDE DIVISION 1   Manager: George Burley   SEASON 1998-99

Column headers: No | Date | (Opponent) | Att | Pos | Pt | F-A | H-T | Scorers, Times, and Referees | SQUAD NUMBERS IN USE → Wright · Kennedy · Tanner · Clapham · Mowbray · Bramble · Dyer · Holland · Abou · Naylor · Petta | subs used

---

24 · A · SHEFFIELD UTD · 20/12 · Att 12,944 · Pos 2 · W · Pt 45 · F-A 2-1 · H-T 0-0
Scorers: Abou 49, Naylor 90; Devlin 78. Ref: R Styles

	Wright	Kennedy	Tanner	Clapham	Mowbray	Bramble	Dyer	Holland	Abou	Naylor	Petta	subs used
Town	Wright	Kennedy	Tanner^	Clapham	Mowbray	**Bramble**	Dyer	Holland	Abou*	Naylor	Petta	Hodges/Brown
Opp	*Kelly*	*Barbokis*	*Quinn*	*Ford*^	*Derry*	*O'Connor*	*Woodhouse*	*Marcelo*	*Marker*	*Hamilton^*	*Campbell^*	*Devlin/Morris*

A Sunday game, live on TV, sees local 17-year-old Titus Bramble make an assured debut in defence. Abou picks his spot after Petta's shot is deflected to him. Paul Devlin levels after Wright blocks Andy Campbell's effort. Jubilant Naylor, close to his birthplace, heads a late winner.

---

25 · H · PORTSMOUTH · 26/12 · Att 21,805 · Pos 2 · W · Pt 48 · F-A 3-0 · H-T 3-0
Scorers: Naylor 23, 25, Dyer 31. Ref: P Robinson

	Wright	Kennedy	Tanner	Clapham	Mowbray	Bramble	Dyer	Holland	Abou	Naylor	Petta	subs used
Town	Wright	Kennedy	Thetis	Clapham	Mowbray	Venus	Dyer"	Holland	Abou^	Naylor	Petta^	Johnson/Naylor/Bramble
Opp	*Petterson*	*Thøgarsen*^	*Robinson*	*Simpson*	*Hillier*	*Perrett*	*Thomson*	*Claridge^*	*Peron*	*Vlachos"*	*Igoe*	*Pethick/Night'gale/Andreasson*

Scowcroft's stand-in Naylor takes a return pass from Abou and shoots past Andy Petterson. Two minutes later he collects Venus's through ball and repeats the trick. Abou sets up Dyer for a big half-time lead. Pompey boss Alan Ball is livid and tells reporters his side were 'deplorable'.

---

26 · A · WOLVERHAMPTON · 28/12 · Att 24,636 · Pos 2 · L · Pt 48 · F-A 0-1 · H-T 0-0
Scorers: Muscat 88. Ref: M Halsey

	Wright	Kennedy	Tanner	Clapham	Mowbray	Bramble	Dyer	Holland	Abou	Naylor	Petta	subs used
Town	Wright	Kennedy^	Thetis	Clapham	Mowbray	Venus	Dyer*	Holland	Johnson	Naylor	Petta^	Holster/Logan
Opp	*Stowell*	*Muscat*	*Atkins*	*Richards*	*Sedgley"*	*Curle*	*Niestroj^*	*Robinson*	*Emblen*	*Whittingham Osborn^*		*Corica/Fernando/Gilkes*

Aussie international Kevin Muscat, known at Molineux as 'Psycho', is the hero and villain. After clattering into Dyer, who goes off injured, the makeshift full-back nets the winner with a 30-yard swerving shot. In the dying seconds Suffolk-born 16-year-old Richard Logan comes on.

---

27 · H · GRIMSBY · 9/1 · Att 15,575 · Pos 3 · L · Pt 48 · F-A 0-1 · H-T 0-1
Scorers: Handyside 14. Ref: L Cable

	Wright	Kennedy	Tanner	Clapham	Mowbray	Bramble	Dyer	Holland	Abou	Naylor	Petta	subs used
Town	Wright	Wilnis*	Thetis	Clapham	Mowbray	Venus	Dyer	Holland	Johnson	Naylor*	Petta^	Logan/Bramble
Opp	*Davison*	*McDermott Gallimore*	*Handyside*	*Smith R*	*Donovan*	*Coldicott*	*Smith D*	*Nogan*^	*Black^*	*Groves*		*Widdington/Clare*

Fabian Wilnis signs from De Graafschap of Holland for £200k. His foul leads to David Smith's free-kick being pushed out by Wright to Peter Handyside, who hooks the ball in. Clapham and Bramble both unleash rasping shots from long distance, which go close to levelling the game.

---

28 · A · SUNDERLAND · 17/1 · Att 39,835 · Pos 5 · L · Pt 48 · F-A 1-2 · H-T 1-2
Scorers: Holland 36; Quinn 27, 33. Ref: E Wolstenholme

	Wright	Kennedy	Tanner	Clapham	Mowbray	Bramble	Dyer	Holland	Abou	Naylor	Petta	subs used
Town	Wright	Wilnis	Thetis	Clapham	Bramble	Venus	Dyer	Holland	Johnson	Naylor	**Magilton**	Magilton
Opp	*Sørensen*	*Makin*	*Gray*	*Ball*	*Butler*	*Rae^*	*Clark*	*Quinn*	*Phillips*^	*Johnston*		*Dichio/Bridges*

N Ireland international Jim Magilton signs from Sheff Wed, initially on loan. He can't prevent Town losing further ground in the promotion race. Niall Quinn creates havoc with two goals in six minutes. Venus's cross is headed down by Naylor and lashed in off the bar by Holland.

---

29 · H · PORT VALE · 30/1 · Att 16,328 · Pos 5 · W · Pt 51 · F-A 1-0 · H-T 1-0
Scorers: Clapham 40. Ref: M Pierce

	Wright	Kennedy	Tanner	Clapham	Mowbray	Bramble	Dyer	Holland	Abou	Naylor	Petta	subs used
Town	Wright	Wilnis	Tanner	Clapham	Mowbray	Venus	Dyer	Holland	Johnson*	**Harewood**	Magilton	Naylor
Opp	*Musselwhite Talbot"*	*Tankard*	*Bogie*	*Aspen*	*Gardner*	*Rougier^*	*McGlinchey Bent*	*Foyle*	*Russell"*			*Beadle/Corden/Burns*

Marlon Harewood is recruited on loan from Forest to play alongside Johnson. Clapham cuts in and nets a fine 20-yard drive with his much less-favoured right foot. It's the first goal in a career spanning 64 league games. Harewood has a lively debut as Paul Musselwhite is kept busy.

---

30 · A · BURY · 6/2 · Att 4,750 · Pos 4 · W · Pt 54 · F-A 3-0 · H-T 0-0
Scorers: Venus 50p, Mowbray 70, Harewood 76. Ref: K Leach

	Wright	Kennedy	Tanner	Clapham	Mowbray	Bramble	Dyer	Holland	Abou	Naylor	Petta	subs used
Town	Wright	Wilnis*	Tanner	Clapham	Mowbray	Venus	Dyer	Holland	Johnson^	Harewood	Magilton	Stockwell/Naylor
Opp	*Kiely*	*Woodward Williams P*	*Daws*	*Billy*	*West*	*Swailes*	*Jemson*^	*James*	*Johnrose*	*Digby^*		*Preece/Forest*

Johnson is heavily challenged by Andy Woodward as he gets clear and Venus converts the penalty. The Shakers are furious, claiming their ex-team-mate dived. Johnson hits the bar and Mowbray nets from close in. Ex-Town man Chris Swailes' poor back-pass gifts Harewood a goal.

---

31 · A · BRADFORD C · 13/2 · Att 15,024 · Pos 4 · D · Pt 55 · F-A 0-0 · H-T 0-0
Ref: G Frankland

	Wright	Kennedy	Tanner	Clapham	Mowbray	Bramble	Dyer	Holland	Abou	Naylor	Petta	subs used
Town	Wright	Wilnis	Tanner	Clapham	Mowbray	Venus	Dyer	Holland	Johnson	Harewood*	Magilton	Naylor
Opp	*Walsh*	*Wright*	*Jacobs*	*McCall*	*Moore*	*Westwood*	*Lawrence*	*Blake*^	*Mills*	*Whalley*	*Beagrie*	*Rankin*

A top-of-the-table clash in which the meanest defence in the division visits the home of the most prolific attack. Mowbray is a real tower of strength in defence and Wright saves superbly from Stuart McCall. Last week's opposition will be interested to see Johnson booked for diving!

---

32 · H · OXFORD · 20/2 · Att 16,920 · Pos 4 · W · Pt 58 · F-A 2-1 · H-T 2-1
Scorers: Holland 6, Venus 8p; Remy 43. Ref: R Oliver

	Wright	Kennedy	Tanner	Clapham	Mowbray	Bramble	Dyer	Holland	Abou	Naylor	Petta	subs used
Town	Wright	Wilnis	Tanner	Clapham	Mowbray	Venus	Dyer	Holland	Johnson	Harewood*	Magilton	Naylor
Opp	*Gerrard*	*Robinson*	*Powell*	*Gray*	*Watson*	*Wilsterman Remy^*	*Murphy*^	*Francis*	*Windass*	*Beauchamp*		*Banger/Rose*

Harewood somehow hits a post from a yard out. Holland silences the groans, shooting in after Clapham's corner. Moments later Town are two ahead as Venus converts a penalty after Johnson is fouled by Brian Wilsterman. Christophe Remy cuts in from the flank to shoot past Wright.

---

33 · A · BRISTOL CITY · 27/2 · Att 14,065 · Pos 3 · W · Pt 61 · F-A 1-0 · H-T 0-0
Scorers: Naylor 56. Ref: B Knight

	Wright	Kennedy	Tanner	Clapham	Mowbray	Bramble	Dyer	Holland	Abou	Naylor	Petta	subs used
Town	Wright	Wilnis*	Thetis	Clapham	Mowbray	Venus	Dyer	Holland	Johnson	Naylor*	Magilton	Harewood*/Petta
Opp	*Phillips*	*Brennan*	*Sebok*	*Locke*	*Shail*	*Carey*	*Brown*	*Edwards*^	*Akinbiyi*	*Torpey*	*Andersen*	*Hill*

Deputising for suspended Johnson, Naylor is the hero of the hour, stroking home after the ball is squared by Dyer. Wright keeps struggling City at bay with fine saves. Coach Stewart Houston departs for Spurs and is given the 'Wimbledon treatment' of having his clothes vandalised!

---

34 · H · WATFORD · 2/3 · Att 18,818 · Pos 2 · W · Pt 64 · F-A 3-2 · H-T 2-0
Scorers: Dyer 17, Venus 27, Johnson 74; Smith 82, Mooney 84. Ref: T Heilbron

	Wright	Kennedy	Tanner	Clapham	Mowbray	Bramble	Dyer	Holland	Abou	Naylor	Petta	subs used
Town	Wright	Wilnis	Thetis*	Clapham	Mowbray	Venus	Dyer^	Holland	Naylor"	Magilton		Stockwell/Petta/Harewood
Opp	*Chamberlain Bazeley*	*Kennedy*	*Page*	*Palmer*	*Robinson*	*Daley^*	*Hyde*	*Smart"*	*Hazan*	*Easton"*		*Mooney/Iroha/Smith*

Burley takes the cheers for being named Manager of the Month. A tackle by Micah Hyde fractures Dyer's fibula, but he carries on and scores with his other leg, before collapsing in agony moments later. Venus nets a beauty and Johnson a neatly-taken goal before a late Hornets rally.

#		Date	Opponent	Att.	Div	Pos	Result		Pts	Scorers	Ref
35	H	6/3	TRANMERE	15,929	2	13	W	1-0	67	Thetis 76	Ref: P Walton
36	A	9/3	CRYSTAL PALACE	16,360	2	14	L	2-3	67	Johnson 10, Clapham 62; Mullins 45, Clapham 46, 70	Ref: C Foy
37	H	13/3	HUDDERSFIELD	17,170	2	10	W	3-0	70	Magilton 13, Johnson 45, Petta 83	Ref: F Stretton
38	A	20/3	WEST BROM	15,552	2	10	W	1-0	73	Thetis 15	Ref: P Laws
39	A	3/4	SWINDON	10,337	2	19	W	6-0	76	Venus 6p, Scowcroft 18, [Mowbray 22, Clapham 43, Wilnis 74]	Ref: P Rejer
40	H	5/4	QP RANGERS	22,162	2	19	W	3-1	79	Johnson 12, Scowcroft 65, Holland 75; Kiwomya 4	Ref: W Burns
41	A	11/4	NORWICH	19,511	2	11	D	0-0	80		Ref: P Taylor
42	A	17/4	BOLTON	19,894	3	5	L	0-2	80	Taylor 37, Gudjohnsen 69	Ref: K Lynch
43	H	20/4	STOCKPORT	17,056	3	14	W	1-0	83	Magilton 39	Ref: R Styles
44	H	24/4	CREWE	20,845	3	22	L	1-2	83	Venus 70p; Rivers 64, Macauley 84	Ref: C Wilkes
45	A	2/5	BIRMINGHAM	27,685	3	4	L	0-1	83	Furlong 60	Ref: R Pearson
46	H	9/5	SHEFFIELD UTD	21,689	3	8	W	4-1	86	Magilton 18, Scowcroft 32, Dyer 45, Donis 63, [Naylor 79]	Ref: P Taylor

Home Average 16,920 · Away Average 14,146

35 — TRANMERE: Town: Wright, Wilnis, Thetis, Clapham, Mowbray, Venus, Petta*, Holland, Johnson, Naylor^, Magilton, Stockwell/Scowcroft. Opp: Coyne, Allen, Thompson, McGreal, Parkinson, Irons, Hill^, Mahon, O'Brien^, Taylor, Jones L*, Kelly/Koumas/Challinor.
Lee Jones' goalbound shot hits Venus in the face and goes to safety. Wright is kept on his toes by John Aldridge's men. Liam O'Brien impedes Stockwell in the box, but Venus's penalty is turned round the post. However, from the subsequent corner Thetis pounces to force in the winner.

36 — CRYSTAL PALACE: Town: Wright, Wilnis^, Thetis, Clapham, Mowbray, Venus, Stockwell, Holland, Johnson, Naylor^, Magilton, Scowcroft*. Opp: Miller, Smith, Petric, Jihai*, Moore, Linghan, Thomson, Zhiyi, Bradbury, Morrison^, Mullins, Tuttle/McKenzie.
A Venus free-kick from deep in his own half bounces high leaving Kevin Miller stranded and Johnson heads in. Palace strike twice in a minute via Mullins and Morrison headers. Clapham nets a Johnson cross in a breakaway raid. Morrison punishes defensive chaos for the winning goal.

37 — HUDDERSFIELD: Town: Wright, Wilnis, Clapham, Mowbray, Venus, Stockwell*, Holland, Johnson, Scowcroft*, Magilton, Petta/Naylor/Tanner. Opp: Vaesen, Jenkins, Edwards, Johnson, Armstrong, Gray, Beech, Phillips, Stewart, Allison^, Thornley*, Facey/Baldry.
Johnson has a shot saved, but the rebound falls nicely for Magilton to convert. Scowcroft heads into the path of Johnson on the stroke of half-time and he nets from 12 yards. Stockwell and Scowcroft both hit the woodwork, before Petta's close-range goal seals a comfortable victory.

38 — WEST BROM: Town: Wright, Wilnis, Thetis!, Clapham, Mowbray, Venus, Stockwell, Holland, Johnson, Scowcroft, Magilton. Opp: Whitehead, Gabbidon, Potter*, Flynn!, Burgess, Carbon, Quinn^, Sneekes, De Freitas, Angel, Kilbane, Murphy/Maresca/Richards.
Thetis nets a brilliant overhead kick after a Clapham corner. After the break a Magilton rocket hits a post. Near the end Thetis and Sean Flynn are sent off after a flare-up. Thetis' has already been in big trouble with the FA. It's Town's 22nd clean sheet in the league – a new club record.

39 — SWINDON: Town: Wright, Wilnis, Tanner", Clapham, Mowbray, Venus, Stockwell*, Holland, Johnson, Scowcroft*, Magilton, Holster/Naylor/Cundy. Opp: Glass, Linton, Reeves, Taylor!, Hall, Borrows", Howe, Davis^, Onoura, Bradley*, Gooden, Walters/Hay/Hulbert.
Craig Taylor is sent off for handling Holland's shot and Venus converts the penalty. Scowcroft lobs a second and Mowbray heads in at the far post. Clapham's rising shot makes it four. Alan Reeves fouls Johnson for a second penalty. Wilnis' drive completes a club record away victory.

40 — QP RANGERS: Town: Wright, Cundy, Clapham, Mowbray, Venus, Stockwell, Holland, Johnson^, Scowcroft*, Magilton, Holster/Naylor. Opp: Miklosko, Breacker, Barraclough Morrow*, Ready^, Maddix, Murray, Peacock, Kulcsar, Jeanne, Kiwomya, Dowie/Linighan.
Cundy returns after his freak accident at home when he damaged an ankle while skipping. Paul Murray's free-kick is guided in by former Town favourite Chris Kiwomya. Johnson levels from Magilton's corner. Scowcroft powers in Venus's free-kick and Holland scrambles a third goal.

41 — NORWICH: Town: Wright, Tanner*, Clapham, Mowbray, Venus, Stockwell, Holland, Johnson, Scowcroft, Magilton, Cundy. Opp: Green, Fugelstad, Sutch, MacKay, Fleming, Jackson,*, Anselin, Bellamy, Carey, Mulryne, Dalglish^, Marshall L/Roberts.
Teenage keeper Robert Green is plunged into the local derby fray for a senior debut. He does well as Town fail to kill off the Canaries despite looking the better side. Johnson misses a sitter and Stockwell is unlucky when he gets clear, but the referee fails to apply the advantage rule.

42 — BOLTON: Town: Wright, Stockwell^, Thetis, Clapham, Mowbray, Venus, Petta*, Holland, Johnson, Scowcroft, Magilton, Dyer/Naylor. Opp: Banks, Cox, Phillips, Frandsen, Fish*, Bergsson, Johansen, Jensen, Gudjohns'n^ Taylor, Gardner, Warhurst/Hansen.
A Thetis header hits the post in the early stages. Eidur Gudjohnsen sets the Reebok Stadium alight with a brilliant solo run, which is halted by Wright, but Bob Taylor nets the rebound. Gudjohnsen is put clear after the break and he nets a low drive. Near the end Johnson hits the post.

43 — STOCKPORT: Town: Wright, Stockwell^, Thetis, Clapham, Mowbray, Venus, Dyer", Holland, Johnson^, Scowcroft, Magilton, Petta/Naylor/Cundy. Opp: Nash, Dinning, Gannon, Smith, Flynn, McIntosh, Bennett*, Woodthorpe Angell, Cooper*, Ellis, Moore/Matthews.
The battle with Bradford City for the second automatic promotion place hots up. Clapham sets up Magilton who nets a real blockbuster of a shot. Town are well on top and Gary Megson's County are lucky to get off this lightly. The 26th clean sheet in all games is a new club record.

44 — CREWE: Town: Wright, Stockwell*, Thetis*, Clapham, Mowbray, Venus, Petta*, Holland, Johnson, Scowcroft, Magilton, Naylor/Wilnis. Opp: Kearton, Wright D, Smith, Walton, Macauley, Charnock^, Wright J!, Johnson, Jack^, Murphy, Rivers, Little/Unsworth.
Fighting for survival, Dario Gradi's men take a shock lead when a fine run by Mark Rivers ends with a lethal shot. Dave Walton fouls Johnson and Venus nets from the spot. Jermaine Wright is sent off for a second yellow card and then Steve Macauley guides in a surprise winning goal.

45 — BIRMINGHAM: Town: Wright, Wilnis, Thetis", Clapham, Mowbray, Venus, Dyer", Holland, Johnson^, Scowcroft, Magilton, Stockwell. Opp: Poole, Rowett, Grainger, Hyde", Holdsworth Johnson, McCarthy, Robinson, Furlong^, Hughes, Bradbury*, Adebola/Ndlovu/Purse.
A minute's silence is observed following the recent death of Sir Alf Ramsey, who managed both sides. This tense occasion attracts a massive away following, but Town look nervous and off-colour. Bryan Hughes beats four men before pulling the ball back for Paul Furlong to score.

46 — SHEFFIELD UTD: Town: Wright, Wilnis, Clapham, Mowbray, Venus, Dyer, Holland, Johnson^, Scowcroft, Petta^, Stockwell/Naylor/Thetis. Opp: Kelly, Derry^, Kozluk!, Dellas, Jacobsen, Tebily^, Donis, Hunt, Marcelo, Devlin^, Morris, Quinn/Hamilton/Katchuro.
For automatic promotion, Town must win and hope Bradford City lose at play-off hopefuls Wolves. Magilton's shot, Scowcroft's header and Dyer's lob ensure the win. George Donis's rocket is followed by Rob Kozluk's second yellow card to keep Town third.

NATIONWIDE DIVISION 1 (CUP-TIES)

Manager: George Burley

SEASON 1998-99

Column headings: SQUAD NUMBERS IN USE | subs used
Left columns: (Round) | H/A | Opponent | Date | Att | | | F-A | | H-T | Scorers, Times, and Referees

---

Play-offs

SF 1 — A BOLTON — 16/5 — Att 18,295 — 3 6 — L — F-A 0-1 — H-T 0-0

Ipswich: Wright, Wilnis^, Clapham, Thetis, Mowbray, Venus, Dyer, Holland, Johnson*, Scowcroft, Magilton — subs used: Naylor
Bolton: Banks, Cox, Elliott, Frandsen, Todd, Fish", Johansen, Jensen, Gudjohns'n^, Taylor, Gardner* — subs used: Warhurst/Hansen/Bergson

Scorers: Johansen 84. Ref: M Halsey

Despite finishing ten points ahead, Town tackle Bolton on equal terms for a place in the final. Neil Cox hits the bar in one raid and Naylor is off target after getting clear of the defence. Bob Taylor chests the ball down to Michael Johansen, who fires a late winner from a narrow angle.

SF 2 — H BOLTON — 19/5 — Att 21,755 — 3 6 — W — F-A 4-3 aet — H-T 1-0

Ipswich: Wright, Wilnis^, Clapham, Magilton, Mowbray", Venus, Dyer, Holland, Johnson*, Scowcroft, Petta — subs used: Naylor/Stockwell/Thetis
Bolton: Banks, Cox, Elliott*, Frandsen, Todd, Fish, Johansen, Jensen, Gudjohns'n^, Taylor, Gardner* — subs used: Warhurst/Hansen/Bergson

Scorers: Holland 14, 116, Dyer 52, 90; Taylor 51, 96, Frandsen 84. Ref: J Kirkby
(Town lose on away-goals rule)

An enthralling contest ends with play-off heartbreak for a third successive season. Dyer loops a header over Steve Banks with just 24 seconds left to take the tie into extra-time. When Taylor nets, Town need another two to get through, but only manage one through the tireless Holland.

Worthington Cup

1:1 — A EXETER — 11/8 — Att 3,233 — 3: — D — F-A 1-1 — H-T 1-0

Ipswich: Wright, Stockwell, Clapham, Venus, Dyer*, Holland, Johnson, Naylor, Petta — subs used: Sonner
Exeter: Bayes, Gale, Curran, Gittens, Rowbotham, Rees, Crowe^, Clarke, Breslan* — subs used: Fry/Flack

Scorers: Holland 13; Richardson 90. Ref: P Rejer

Ashley Bayes hauls down Johnson after two minutes, but Venus misses from the spot. Holland heads home a Petta free-kick. Peter Fox's side battle on gamely and are rewarded in the last minute when Jason Rees' free-kick is headed on by Steve Flack and Jon Richardson does the rest.

1:2 — H EXETER — 18/8 — Att 7,952 — 3:18 — W — F-A 5-1 — H-T 3-1

Ipswich: Wright, Stockwell^, Clapham, Taricco, Mowbray, Venus, Dyer*, Holland, Johnson, Mathie, Petta^ — subs used: Naylor/Mason/Holster
Exeter: Bayes, Gale, Power^, Curran^, Richardson, Gittens, Rowbotham, Rees, Flack, Clarke, Breslan* — subs used: Fry/Holloway/Gardner

Scorers: Taricco 30, Holland 31, Stockwell 43, Richardson 44 (Mathie 80, Mason 87). Ref: F Stretton
(Town win 6-2 on aggregate)

Taricco nets a fine 25-yarder and moments later Holland sweeps home Johnson's pass. Stockwell is left unmarked for a rare headed goal. Jon Richardson nets after Wright parries a Darren Rowbotham effort. Mathie's cool finish and Mason's cracking volley see Town sign off in style.

2:1 — H LUTON — 15/9 — Att 9,032 — 2:3 — W — F-A 2-1 — H-T 0-0

Ipswich: Wright, Stockwell, Taricco, Clapham, Thetis, Venus*, Dyer*, Holland, Johnson, Scowcroft, Petta — subs used: —
Luton: Davis K, Alexander, McGowan, Spring, Johnson, Cox^, Evers, Douglas*, Gray, McIndoe, Tanner — subs used: Fotiadis/Bacque

Scorers: Scowcroft 48, Thetis 79; Douglas 60. Ref: A D'Urso

Lennie Lawrence fields a very young side and his kids respond well, pushing Town all the way. Scowcroft hooks in a Johnson cross, but Stuart Douglas swoops to pick his spot and equalise. Gavin McGowan's clearance hits Holland and falls nicely for home debutant Thetis to convert.

2:2 — A LUTON — 22/9 — Att 5,655 — 2:5 — L — F-A 2-4 aet — H-T 1-0

Ipswich: Wright, Stockwell*, Taricco", Tanner, Venus, Dyer, Holland, Johnson, Scowcroft, Petta^ — subs used: Mathie/Clapham/Sonner
Luton: Davis K, Alexander, McGowan, Spring, Davis S, Johnson, McKinnon", Evers, Douglas, Fotiadis*, Marshall^ — subs used: Bacque/Cox/White

Scorers: Johns'n 35, Davis S 118 (og); Fotiadis 52, Douglas 84, Davis S 98. Ref: P Taylor
(Town lose 4-5 on aggregate)

Johnson extends the aggregate lead, but Luton hit back twice to force extra-time. Bizarrely, skipper Steve Davis then nets at both ends to set up a thrilling finale. With the 120 minutes up and Town set to go through on away goals, Marvin Johnson heads a rare goal after a Wright fumble.

FA Cup

3 — A TRANMERE — 2/1 — Att 7,223 — 16 — W — F-A 1-0 — H-T 0-0

Ipswich: Wright, Kennedy, Thetis, Clapham, Mowbray, Venus, Dyer, Holland, Johnson, Naylor, Petta* — subs used: Holster
Tranmere: Coyne, Allen, Thompson", McGreal, Challinor, Irons, Mahan, Santos, Jones G, Mellon^, Taylor^ — subs used: Jones L/Parkinson/Morrissey

Scorers: McGreal 46 (og). Ref: D Crick

After a horrendous mix-up between Clapham and Wright, Scott Taylor can only hit the post with the empty goal gaping before him. Naylor puts John McGreal under pressure as a long throw from Johnson comes in and the defender accidentally heads the ball past his own keeper.

4 — A EVERTON — 23/1 — Att 28,854 — P:14 — L — F-A 0-1 — H-T 0-1

Ipswich: Wright, Wilnis, Thetis, Clapham, Mowbray, Venus, Dyer, Holland, Johnson, Stockwell*, Petta^ — subs used: Naylor/Tanner/Bramble
Everton: Myhre, Ward, Ball, Cleland", Materazzi !, Unsworth, Grant, Barmby, Cadamateri*, Oster, Hutchison — subs used: Branch/O'Kane

Scorers: Barmby 39. Ref: M Riley

A John Oster header hits a post, the rebound strikes Venus and falls for Nick Barmby to convert. Michael Ball misses a sitter just after the break. Marco Materazzi gets a second yellow card for fouling Johnson, who is booked for retaliating. A late Town effort is ruled out for a foul.

League Table

	Team	P	W	D	L	F	A	W	D	L	F	A	Pts
			Home					Away					
1	Sunderland	46	19	3	1	50	10	12	9	2	41	18	105
2	Bradford C	46	15	4	4	48	20	11	5	7	34	27	87
3	Ipswich	46	16	1	6	37	15	10	7	6	32	17	86
4	Birmingham	46	12	4	7	32	15	11	5	7	34	22	81
5	Watford *	46	12	8	3	30	19	9	6	8	35	37	77
6	Bolton	46	13	6	4	44	25	7	10	6	34	34	76
7	Wolves	46	11	10	2	37	19	8	6	9	27	24	73
8	Sheffield Utd	46	12	6	5	42	29	6	7	10	29	37	67
9	Norwich	46	7	12	4	34	28	5	10	8	28	33	62
10	Huddersfield	46	11	9	3	38	23	4	7	12	24	48	61
11	Grimsby	46	11	6	6	25	18	6	4	13	15	34	61
12	West Brom	46	12	4	7	43	33	4	7	12	26	43	59
13	Barnsley	46	13	7	3	35	30	7	8	8	24	26	59
14	Crystal Pal	46	11	10	2	43	26	3	6	14	15	45	58
15	Tranmere	46	8	7	8	37	30	4	13	6	26	31	56
16	Stockport	46	7	9	7	24	21	5	8	10	25	39	53
17	Swindon	46	7	8	8	40	44	6	3	14	19	37	50
18	Crewe	46	7	6	10	27	35	5	6	12	27	43	48
19	Portsmouth	46	10	5	8	34	26	1	9	13	23	47	47
20	QP Rangers	46	9	7	7	34	22	3	4	16	18	39	47
21	Port Vale	46	10	3	10	22	28	5	5	15	23	47	47
22	Bury	46	9	7	7	24	27	1	10	12	11	33	47
23	Oxford	46	7	8	8	31	30	3	6	14	17	41	44
24	Bristol City	46	7	8	8	35	36	2	7	14	22	44	42
		1104	250	163	139	846	609	139	163	250	609	846	1493

* Promoted after play-offs

Odds & ends

Double wins: (7) Bristol C, Port Vale, Sheffield U, Stockport, Swindon, Tranmere, West Brom.

Double losses: (2) Bolton, Sunderland.

Won from behind: (1) QPR (h).

Lost from in front: (2) Crystal Palace (a), Luton (a, LC).

High spots: The impressive points tally of 86.
A club record 25 'clean sheets' in league matches.
The 120-minute thriller with Bolton in the play-offs.
Mauricio Taricco's wonder goal at home to Crystal Palace.
The club record away win of 6-0 at Swindon.
Seven successive home wins from January 30.

Low spots: Another heartbreaking defeat in the play-offs.
Losing the battle with Bradford City for second place.
The departure of fans' favourites Mathie and Taricco.
The deaths of former manager Sir Alf Ramsey and director John Kerridge.
Home defeat by Norwich and vandalism by their fans.
Losing to 10-man Crewe in the penultimate home game.
Losing a 210-minute cup-tie to Second Division Luton.

Player of the Year: Jamie Clapham.
Ever-presents: (2) Matt Holland, Richard Wright.
Hat-tricks: (1) James Scowcroft (v Crewe).
Opposing hat-tricks: (0).
Leading scorers: (14) James Scowcroft and David Johnson.

Appearances and Goals

Player	Lge	Sub	LC	Sub	FAC	Sub	PO	Sub	Lge	LC	FAC	PO	Tot
	Appearances								Goals				
Abou, Samassi	5									1			1
Bramble, Titus	2	2				1							
Brown, Wayne	1												
Clapham, Jamie	45	1	3	1	2		2		3				3
Cundy, Jason	1	3											
Dyer, Kieron	36	1	4		2		2		5		2		7
Harewood, Marlon	5	1							1				1
Hodges, Lee		4											
Holland, Matt	46		4		2		2		5	2	2		9
Holster, Marco	1	9				1							
Hunt, Jonathan	2	4											
Johnson, David	41	1	4		2		2		13		1		14
Kennedy, John	6	1			1								
Logan, Richard		2											
Magilton, Jim	19						2		3				3
Mason, Paul		1				1					1		1
Mathie, Alex	2	6	1						1	1			2
Mowbray, Tony	40		2		2		2		2				2
Naylor, Richard	10	20	1	1	1	1		2	5				5
Petta, Bobby	26	6	4		2		1		2				2
Scowcroft, James	29	3	2		2		2		13		1		14
Sonner, Danny	23	7	4	2	1				2		1		3
Stockwell, Mick	13	6	1	1		1							
Tanner, Adam	16		4										
Taricco, Mauricio	29	2	2		2		1	1	1		2	1	2
Thetis, Manu	29	2	2	1	2		1	2	1		2	1	3
Venus, Mark	44		4		2		2		9				9
Vernazza, Paulo	2												
Wilnis, Fabian	17	1			1		2		1			1	1
Wright, Richard	46		4		2		2			1	1		2
(own-goals)													2
30 players used	506	85	44	8	22	4	22	4	69	10	10	1	84

Column headings: No · Date · Att · Pos · Pt · F-A · H-T · Scorers, Times, and Referees · SQUAD NUMBERS IN USE · subs used

---

1 · H · 7/8 · NOTT'M FOREST — Att 20,830 · Pos 2 *(23)* · Pt 3 · F-A 3-1 · H-T 2-0
Scorers: Naylor 19, Johnson 20, Scowcroft 71; *Bart-Williams 76p*; Ref: P Richards

											subs used
Wright R	Stockwell*	Wilnis	Thetis	Venus	Holland	McGreal	Wright J	Johnson^	Scowcroft	Naylor	Wilnis/Axeldal
Crossley	*Louis-Jean*	*Bonalair^*	*Mannini*	*Matecanu*	*B't-Williams*	*Scimeca*	*Quashie*	*Freedman*	*Petrachi~*	*Rodgers*	*Harewood/Allou*

Forest's David Platt has an unhappy managerial debut. Scowcroft tries a midfield role. Scowcroft's low drive is followed by a consolation after Thetis trips Marlon Harewood. Naylor produces a peach of a header from Venus's free-kick and Johnson's shot raises the roof moments later.

---

2 · A · 15/8 · SWINDON — Att *6,195* · Pos 1 *(22)* · W · Pt 6 · F-A 4-1 · H-T 1-1
Scorers: Johnson 44, 74, Naylor 55, 68; *Grazioli 16*; Ref: G Willard

											subs used
Wright R	Wilnis	Clapham	Thetis	Venus*	McGreal	Stockwell	Holland	Johnson"	Naylor	Scowcroft	Wright J/Brown
Talia	*Robinson^*	*Hall*	*Taylor*	*Hulbert**	*Williams*	*Howe*	*Ndah*	*Onuora"*	*Grazioli*	*McHugh*	*Walters/Willis/Hay*

Jimmy Quinn's side go ahead through Giuliano Grazioli's brilliant first-time drive. Great work by Venus sets up Johnson to coolly slot home from an angle. Naylor beats Frank Talia with a spinning volley and nips in to exploit slipshod defending. Johnson finishes off a slick move.

---

3 · H · 21/8 · BOLTON — Att 17,696 · Pos 1 *(12)* · W · Pt 9 · F-A 1-0 · H-T 0-0
Scorers: Johnson 69; Ref: R Furnandiz

											subs used
Wright R	Stockwell^	Clapham	Thetis!	Venus	Holland	McGreal	Wright J	Johnson^	Scowcroft	Naylor*	Wilnis/Axeldal/Magilton
Branagan	*Cox*	*Whitlow*	*Frandsen*	*Strong*	*Johansen*	*Todd*	*Jensen*	*Gudjohnsen*	*Taylor*	*Gardner*	

Town start brightly, but Bolton survive the storm. Keith Branagan pushes Wright's shot onto a post. An upfield punt finds Johnson, who picks his spot. Thetis is sent off for a second bookable foul on 81 minutes. A minute's silence is held for late supporters' club chief George Knights.

---

4 · A · 28/8 · SHEFFIELD UTD — Att 12,455 · Pos 1 *(23)* · D · Pt 10 · F-A 2-2 · H-T 2-0
Scorers: Scowcroft 3, Johnson 11; *Smith 54, Murphy 83*; Ref: C Foy

											subs used
Wright R	Wilnis	Clapham	Thetis*	Venus	Holland	McGreal	Magilton	Johnson	Scowcroft	Naylor	Stockwell/Mowbray
Tracey	*Kozluk*	*Quinn**	*Craddock*	*Murphy*	*Ford*	*Sandford*	*Derry*	*Marcelo*	*Smith*	*Woodhouse*	*Katchouro*

Town roar into a two-goal lead but go on to squander chances galore later. Adrian Heath's Blades launch a blistering revival as Martin Smith rams a shot in. Smith turned down a move to Town after a trial in the summer. Shaun Murphy scrambles a late equaliser after Smith's corner.

---

5 · H · 30/8 · BARNSLEY — Att 18,037 · Pos 1 *(10)* · W · Pt 13 · F-A 6-1 · H-T 3-0
Scorers: Johnson 14, 75, Venus 24, Naylor 45, *McClare 86*[Scowcroft 73, Magilton 90]; Ref: J Brandwood

											subs used
Wright R	Wilnis*	Clapham	Thetis	Venus"	Holland	McGreal	Wright J*	Johnson	Scowcroft	Naylor	Stockwell/Magilton/Brown
Miller	*Eaden*	*Appleby*	*Tuttle*	*Moses*	*Richardson"*	*Hignett*	*Jones*	*Sheran^*	*V der Laan**	*Barnard*	*Dyer/Hristov/McClare*

Town hit their stride early again, as Johnson heads in a Wilnis cross. After a scramble Venus fires home. With Dave Bassett's men appealing for offside, Naylor makes it three. It's party time in the stands near the end as Scowcroft, Johnson and Magilton score with near-arrogant ease.

---

6 · A · 11/9 · PORTSMOUTH — Att 16,034 · Pos 1 *(11)* · D · Pt 14 · F-A 1-1 · H-T 0-0
Scorers: Scowcroft 88; *Whittingham 46*; Ref: P Alcock

											subs used
Wright R	Wilnis"	Clapham	Brown	Venus	Holland	McGreal!	Wright J	Johnson*	Scowcroft	Naylor*	Stockwell/Axeldal/Magilton
Petterson	*Crowe^*	*Vlachos*	*Panopoulos*	*Whitbread*	*Cundy*	*Thogersen*	*Migliorazzi*	*Allen"*	*Whit'ngh'm^*	*Peron*	*McLoughlin/Igoe/Nightingale*

McGreal is red-carded for clattering into Guy Whittingham as he speeds goalwards. Mike Panopoulos' long ball sees Whittingham beat Wright in the air. Late pressure pays off when Stockwell robs Jeff Peron and his cross leaves Andy Petterson stranded, enabling Scowcroft to equalise.

---

7 · H · 18/9 · BIRMINGHAM — Att 19,758 · Pos 3 *(2)* · L · Pt 14 · F-A 0-1 · H-T 0-1
Scorers: *Furlong 10p*; Ref: B Knight

											subs used
Wright R	Wilnis"	Clapham	Thetis^	Venus	Holland	McGreal	Wright J*	Johnson	Scowcroft	Naylor*	Stockwell/Brown/Magilton
Poole	*Rowett*	*Lazaridis*	*Holdsworth*	*Purse*	*Johnson*	*McCarthy*	*O'Connor*	*Furlong^*	*Hyde*	*Ndlovu^*	*Hughes/Adebola*

Town are knocked off the top by Trevor Francis's outfit. Burley describes the Paul Furlong penalty as extremely harsh. Town hit back and create enough opportunities to win the game, but enjoy little luck. Scowcroft hits the woodwork and Johnson nets but has the effort disallowed.

---

8 · A · 26/9 · MANCHESTER C — Att 19,406 · Pos 2 *(3)* · W · Pt 17 · F-A 2-1 · H-T 1-0
Scorers: Johnson 43, Croft 67; *Goater 50*; Ref: A D'Urso

											subs used
Wright R	Wilnis"	Croft	Thetis	Venus	Holland	Stockwell"	Wright J*	Johnson	Magilton	Scowcroft	Clapham/Naylor/Brown
Weaver	*Crooks*	*Tiatto"*	*Wiekens*	*Jobson*	*Horlock*	*Kennedy*	*Whitley*	*Dickov*	*Goater*	*Bishop^*	*Granville/Cooke*

Johnson's bullet header is cancelled out by Shaun Goater's well-taken effort. Gary Croft, at £800,000 from Blackburn, debuts in place of the axed Clapham. Croft hits the winner with a deflected shot. A few days later he spends a night in police custody after serious motoring offences.

---

9 · A · 2/10 · GRIMSBY — Att 6,531 · Pos 5 *(9)* · L · Pt 17 · F-A 1-2 · H-T 0-1
Scorers: Magilton 54; *Donovan 39, Ashcroft 56*; Ref: M Warren

											subs used
Wright R	Stockwell	Clapham	Thetis*	Venus	Holland	McGreal	Magilton	Johnson	Scowcroft	Naylor	Wilnis
Coyne	*Butterfield*	*Gallimore*	*Burnett*	*Lever*	*Coldicott*	*Donovan*	*Ashcroft*	*Lester*	*Groves*	*Pouton*	

Hit by injuries to key players, Alan Buckley's side nevertheless look stronger and deserve the points. Magilton equalises Kevin Donovan's goal when he guides home a free-kick, but within minutes the Mariners are back in front. Lee Ashcroft profits from a McGreal misjudgement.

---

10 · H · 16/10 · QP RANGERS — Att 17,544 · Pos 6 *(10)* · L · Pt 17 · F-A 1-4 · H-T 1-1
Scorers: Holland 3; *Peacock 33, Wardley 65, Steiner 71, 82*; Ref: P Danson

											subs used
Wright R	Croft"	Clapham	Thetis	Venus	McGreal	Magilton!	Wright J*	Johnson	Stockwell*	Naylor	Stockwell/Naylor
Harper	*Breacker*	*Barraclough*	*Ready*	*Darlington*	*Maddix^*	*Langley*	*Steiner*	*Peacock^*	*Wardley*	*Kiwomya*	*Rowland/Gallen/Murray*

Holland nets from close range after Jermaine Darlington fails to deal with a Venus cross. Gavin Peacock chips home a real beauty to equalise. Magilton is sent off for kicking out at Peacock. Stuart Wardley coolly rounds Wright and then Rob Steiner is well positioned to bag two more.

---

11 · H · 19/10 · CHARLTON — Att 17,940 · Pos 4 *(1)* · W · Pt 20 · F-A 4-2 · H-T 2-2
Scorers: Scowcroft 4, Venus 29, Johnson 66, *Hunt 7, 11* [Stockwell 76]; Ref: P Dowd

											subs used
Wright R	Wilnis	Clapham	Thetis*	Mowbray	Holland	McGreal	Magilton	Johnson	Scowcroft	Stockwell	Wilnis
Kiely	*Shields*	*Powell"*	*Stuart^*	*Rufus*	*Youds*	*Newton*	*Kinsella*	*Hunt*	*Jones**	*Robinson*	*Brown/Salako/Barness*

Shenanigans in the dressing room as Thetis is axed, but Burley denies rumours the player landed a punch on him. Early slackness at the back keeps Alan Curbishley's side in contention, but Johnson's diving header and Stockwell's fine left-foot drive get Town back to winning ways.

12. A WALSALL — 23/10 — Att: 6,526 — Pos: 2 — W 1-0 — Pts: 23 — (23) — HT: 0-0 — Naylor 90 — Ref: M Jones

Wright R	Wilnis	Clapham	Venus	Mowbray	McGreal	Holland	Stockwell*	Johnson"	Scowcroft	Magilton^	Naylor/Wright J/Axeldal
Walker	*Marsh*	*Pointon*	*Viveash*	*Roper*	*Bukran*	*Wrack*	*Abou^*	*Rammell*	*Keates*	*Matias**	*Robins/Brissett*

In a largely tedious game, Stockwell is substituted after a clash of heads with McGreal. His replacement Naylor gets on the end of a Venus pass to send in a diving header which spins slowly past keeper James Walker as Town nick the net off a post. It's the side's first clean sheet since August.

13. A MANCHESTER C — 27/10 — Att: 32,799 — Pos: 2 — L 0-1 — Pts: 23 — (1) — HT: 0-0 — Horlock 58 — Ref: J Kirkby

Wright R	Wilnis	Clapham"	Venus	Mowbray	McGreal	Holland	Stockwell^	Johnson*	Scowcroft	Magilton^	Naylor/Axeldal/Croft
Weaver	*Edghill*	*Granville*	*Morrison*	*Jobson*	*Horlock*	*Kennedy"*	*Whitley*	*Dickov**	*Goater*	*Bishop^*	*Taylor/Crooks/Tiatto*

After surviving an early onslaught, Town are generally well on top. Stockwell sends in a good drive, but Johnson fails to convert a decent chance from the rebound. Kevin Horlock gives Wright no chance after a mistake by Mowbray. Axeldal brings a fine save out of Nicky Weaver.

14. H GRIMSBY — 30/10 — Att: 16,617 — Pos: 2 — W 2-0 — Pts: 26 — (14) — HT: 1-0 — Clapham 36, Naylor 60 — Ref: K Leach

Wright R	Wilnis	Clapham^	Venus	Mowbray	McGreal	Holland	Wright J	Johnson"	Stockwell	Naylor	Axeldal/Croft
Coyne	*Butterfield*	*Gallimore*	*Burnett**	*Lever*	*Coldicott*	*Pouton*	*Smith"*	*Allen**	*Lester*	*Groves*	*Black/Ashcroft/Buckley*

The Grimsby hoodoo is ended. Clapham sets up the win with a fine curling left-footer after a corner-kick routine. Wright sends over a corner which is miskicked by Mark Lever to Naylor who picks his spot from 10 yards. Danny Coyne saves superbly from Holland in the last minute.

15. A HUDDERSFIELD — 2/11 — Att: 12,093 — Pos: 4 — L 1-3 — Pts: 26 — (5) — HT: 1-1 — Holland 15 — Dyson 37 Beech 48, Stewart 57 — Ref: W Burns

Wright R	Wilnis	Clapham*	Venus	Thetis	McGreal	Holland	Wright J	Johnson*	Stockwell^	Naylor	Axeldal/Croft/Logan
Vaesen	*Jenkins**	*Vincent*	*Irons*	*Gray*	*Dyson*	*Baldry*	*Beech*	*Stewart*	*Thornley*	*Wijnhard*	*Edmondson*

Good work by Johnson allows Holland to celebrate his Eire call-up by firing home an unstoppable drive. Jon Dyson heads the Terriers level against a shaky looking defence. Chris Beech and Marcus Stewart convert Jamie Vincent crosses as Town are outplayed in the second half.

16. A BLACKBURN — 6/11 — Att: 18,512 — Pos: 5 — D 2-2 — Pts: 27 — (18) — HT: 0-1 — Holland 75, Mowbray 90 — Carsley 1, 67p — Ref: G Laws

Wright R	Wilnis	Clapham*	Venus	Mowbray	McGreal	Holland	Wright J	Johnson"	Stockwell	Naylor	Axeldal
Kelly	*Grayson*	*Harkness*	*Taylor*	*Dailly*	*Carsley*	*McAteer*	*Dunn^*	*Ward*	*Blake!*	*Duff"*	*Wilcox/Ostenstad*

Managerless Rovers get a dream start as skipper Lee Carsley heads in after 32 seconds. He doubles the lead from the spot after a Venus foul. Holland's screaming volley sets up a great finale and Mowbray wins a point with a fine shot. Nathan Blake departs after two cautionable fouls.

17. H TRANMERE — 12/11 — Att: 14,514 — Pos: 4 — D 0-0 — Pts: 28 — (13) — HT: 0-0 — Ref: M Messias

Wright R	Wilnis	Clapham*	Venus	Mowbray	McGreal	Holland	Wright J^	Johnson*	Stockwell	Naylor"	Scowcroft/Magilton/Axeldal
Murphy	*Allen*	*Hazell*	*Hill*	*Yates**	*Mahon*	*Parkinson^*	*Jones*	*Allison*	*Henry*		*Thompson/Taylor*

At the club's annual meeting the chairman announces cash is available for new players. Town look in need of a wide-man after firing blanks against John Aldridge's outfit. Steve Yates brings down Johnson on 22 minutes, but Venus's penalty-kick is well saved by young Joe Murphy.

18. A NORWICH — 21/11 — Att: 19,948 — Pos: 5 — D 0-0 — Pts: 29 — (12) — HT: 0-0 — Ref: T Heilbron

Wright R	Wilnis	Clapham	Thetis	Mowbray	Brown	Holland	Stockwell^	Johnson	Scowcroft	Magilton	Naylor
Marshall A	*Sutch*	*Kenton*	*De Blasis*	*Fleming*	*Jackson*	*Marshall L**	*Russell*	*Forbes*	*Milligan*	*Llewellyn^*	*Anselin/Dalglish*

City boss Bruce Rioch admits Town had more of the ball, but he was delighted with City's commitment. Thetis returns after McGreal pulls out with a virus. In a generally dull derby, Matt Jackson hits Town's bar. Johnson admits he faces being dropped after seven games without a goal.

19. H WOLVERHAMPTON — 24/11 — Att: 15,731 — Pos: 4 — W 1-0 — Pts: 32 — (11) — HT: 0-0 — Scowcroft 56 — Ref: G Cain

Wright R	Wilnis	Clapham	Venus	Mowbray	McGreal	Holland	Stockwell*	Johnson^	Scowcroft	Magilton	Wright J/Naylor
Stowell	*Bazeley*	*Muscat*	*Sedgley*	*Curle*	*Pollet*	*Robinson**	*Osborn*	*Akinbiyi*	*Taylor*	*Emblen*	*Flo/Sinton*

Man-of-the-match McGreal pumps the ball forward and Scowcroft beats Mike Stowell with a glorious header. Ake Akinbiyi and Neil Emblen swoop on a chance, but Wright is on hand to block and the ball eventually runs slowly wide. It's Colin Lee's team's first defeat in 11 games.

20. H CREWE — 27/11 — Att: 15,211 — Pos: 4 — W 2-1 — Pts: 35 — (23) — HT: 1-0 — Johnson 4, 76 — Rivers 75 — Ref: K Hill

Wright R	Croft	Clapham	Venus^	Mowbray	McGreal	Holland	Stockwell*	Johnson	Scowcroft	Magilton	Wright J/Friars
Kearton	*Wright D*	*Smith*	*Bignot*	*Macauley*	*Collins*	*Little*	*Lunt*	*Rivers*	*Tait*	*Sorvel*	

Johnson ends his drought, taking Stockwell's pass and outpacing defenders before firing home. A second goal won't come and Dario Gradi's side level as Mark Rivers races onto Paul Tait's flick to beat Wright. Just a minute later Johnson combines with Scowcroft to win the points.

21. A NOTT'M FOREST — 5/12 — Att: 15,724 — Pos: 4 — W 1-0 — Pts: 38 — (19) — HT: 0-0 — Holland 78 — Ref: R Styles

Wright R	Croft	Clapham	Brown	Mowbray	McGreal	Holland	Stockwell*	Johnson	Scowcroft	Magilton	Wright J
Beasant	*Doig*	*Brennan*	*Hjelde*	*Merino^*	*Scimeca*	*Prutton*	*Quashie*	*Beck**	*John*	*B't Williams*	*Freedman/Gray*

Town look much the better side and only Stern John from Trinidad give's any real threat, hitting a post with one effort. Johnson's flying header is saved by Dave Beasant and Holland wins the scramble to convert the rebound from close range. Scowcroft misses a sitter as Town dominate.

22. A CRYSTAL PALACE — 7/12 — Att: 13,176 — Pos: 4 — D 2-2 — Pts: 39 — (17) — HT: 2-1 — Holland 11, Johnson 34 — Svensson 5, Mowbray 61 (og) — Ref: S Baines

Wright R	Croft	Clapham	Brown	Mowbray	McGreal	Holland	Stockwell*	Johnson^	Scowcroft	Magilton	Wright J/Axeldal
Digby	*Austin*	*Frampton**	*Zhiyi*	*Foster*	*Linighan*	*Mullins*	*Rodger*	*Svensson*	*Martin^*	*McKenzie*	*Rizza/Woozley*

An early shock as big Matt Svensson muscles through to net. Holland heads Town level from a Johnson cross. Johnson then moves through to lash the ball in after a weak back-pass. Mowbray tries to clear, but on a tricky pitch the ball flies off his foot over the head of helpless Wright.

23. H WEST BROM — 18/12 — Att: 17,255 — Pos: 3 — W 3-1 — Pts: 42 — (15) — HT: 2-0 — Johnson 6, Scowcroft 27, Midgley 66 — De Freitas 77 — Ref: D Crick

Wright R	Stockwell*	Clapham	Brown	Mowbray	McGreal	Holland	Magilton	Johnson"	Scowcroft	Naylor"	Wright J/Axeldal/Midgley
Miller	*Gabbidon*	*Van Blerk*	*Raven*	*Sigurdsson/Carbon !*	*Quinn*	*Sneekes*	*Evans*	*Hughes"*	*Santos*	*De Freitas*	

Croft is absent, having been jailed for motoring offences. Alan Miller drops the ball and Scowcroft puts Town two ahead. Larus Sigurdsson is sent off after tangling with Johnson. Albion go down to 9 men on 51 minutes after Matt Carbon trips Naylor. Debutant Midgley heads the third.

NATIONWIDE DIVISION 1 — Manager: George Burley — SEASON 1999-2000

No	Date		Team	Att	Pos	Pt	Res	F-A	H-T	Scorers, Times, and Referees
24	26/12	A	FULHAM	17,255	4	43	D	0-0	0-0	Ref: A Hall
25	28/12	H	STOCKPORT	20,671	4	46	W	1-0	1-0	Scowcroft 34 — Ref: P Rejer
26	3/1	A	PORT VALE	6,908	3	49	W	2-1	1-0	Holland 43, Scowcroft 52 / Naylor 50 — Ref: M Pike
27	15/1	H	SWINDON	17,326	3	52	W	3-0	2-0	Stockwell 27, Naylor 37, 82 — Ref: P Walton
28	22/1	A	BOLTON	11,924	4	53	D	1-1	0-0	Holland 85 / Holdsworth 66 — Ref: G Frankland
29	29/1	H	SHEFFIELD UTD	17,350	4	54	D	1-1	1-0	Johnson 45p / Bent 54 — Ref: A Butler
30	5/2	A	BARNSLEY	17,601	3	57	W	2-0	0-0	Scowcroft 59, Stewart 60 — Ref: D Pugh
31	12/2	H	HUDDERSFIELD	21,233	3	60	W	2-1	1-0	Scowcroft 28, Stewart 73 / Gorre 56 — Ref: R Pearson
32	19/2	A	CREWE	6,393	2	63	W	2-1	0-0	Clapham 60, Wright J 89 / Tait 64 — Ref: K Lynch
33	27/2	H	BIRMINGHAM	20,493	2	64	D	1-1	1-1	Johnson 45 / Mowbray 17 (og) — Ref: A Leake
34	4/3	H	PORTSMOUTH	20,305	3	64	L	0-1	0-1	Claridge 26 — Ref: P Taylor

SQUAD NUMBERS IN USE / subs used

24 — A FULHAM
Town: Wright R, Wilnis, Clapham, Brown, Mowbray, McGreal, Holland, Magilton, Johnson*, Scowcroft, Naylor
Opponents: Taylor, Finnan, Uhlenbeek^, Melville, Symons, Morgan, Trollope, Clark, Hayles*, Ball, Collins
subs used: Midgley / Horsfield/Peschisolido
McGreal is again outstanding in a resolute Town defensive performance featuring three centre-backs. For Paul Bracewell's men, it's a fourth goalless league match in succession. Wilnis goes close to grabbing a late winner when his shot is deflected onto a post nine minutes from time.

25 — H STOCKPORT
Town: Wright R, Wilnis, Clapham, Venus, Mowbray, McGreal, Holland, Magilton^, Johnson^, Scowcroft, Naylor*
Opponents: Gray, Connelly, Nicholson, Dinning, Flynn, Gannon, Cooper*, Moore, D'Jaffo^, Fradin, Woodth'pe*
subs used: Stockwell/Wright J/Midgley / Wilbraham/Bailey/Allen
An open game full of missed chances. When flu-affected Holland pulls down Ian Moore, Wright goes full length to save Tony Dinning's spot-kick. Wright bounces up to smother the rebound, too. Eleven minutes later a Wilnis cross is headed down and Scowcroft nets a first-time shot.

26 — A PORT VALE
Town: Wright R, Wilnis, Clapham, Venus, Mowbray, McGreal, Holland, Wright J, Midgley^, Scowcroft, Naylor*
Opponents: Musselwhite, Tankard, Briscoe, Brammer, Carragher, Gardner, Rougier, Burns, Naylor, Minton*, Widdrington
subs used: Stockwell/Axeldal / Foyle
Vale are unlucky when McGreal clears off the line and Anthony Gardner hits the bar. A breathtaking right-foot volley from Holland breaks the deadlock. Tony Naylor equalises with a typical curling shot. Scowcroft responds almost instantly. Jonas Axeldal hits the underside of the bar.

27 — H SWINDON
Town: Wright R, Wilnis, Clapham, Venus, Mowbray, McGreal, Holland*, Magilton, Johnson*, Scowcroft, Naylor
Opponents: Talia, Robinson^, Hall, Leitch, Hulbert*, Reeves, Howe, Cowe*, Hay, Williams T, McHugh
subs used: Wright J/Axeldal/Croft / Williams J/Griffin/Campagna
Croft, released from prison early, comes on as sub to become the first league player to wear an electronic security tag in a game. Stockwell, in his 601st first-team match, nets clinically after a mistake by Bobby Howe. Naylor beats overworked Frank Talia with two well-taken strikes.

28 — A BOLTON
Town: Wright R, Wilnis^, Clapham, Venus, Mowbray, McGreal, Holland, Wright J, Johnson*, Scowcroft, Stockwell*
Opponents: Banks, Holden, Whitlow, Phillips, Bergson*, O'Kane*, Johansen, Jensen^, Gudjohnsen, Holdsworth, Passi
subs used: Axeldal/Croft / Gardner/Elliott
Sam Allardyce's men go ahead shortly after Steve Banks makes a superb save from Scowcroft's cracking shot. Claus Jensen crosses and Dean Holdsworth heads over Wright. Dean Holden stretches to keep out a Johnson effort. There is late reward as Holland drills home a crisp shot.

29 — H SHEFFIELD UTD
Town: Wright R, Croft, Clapham, Venus*, Mowbray, McGreal, Holland, Wright J, Johnson, Scowcroft, Naylor^
Opponents: Tracey, Kozluk, Quinn, Woodhouse, Murphy, Sandford, Brown, Devlin, Bent, Katchouro*, Ford
subs used: Stockwell/Axeldal / Ribeiro
Town are reportedly bidding to buy Huddersfield's Marcus Stewart. Michael Brown handles a Scowcroft cross and Johnson nets the penalty. A long ball forward by Simon Tracey is not dealt with by McGreal and Marcus Bent pounces to equalise. Unhappy home fans jeer the team off.

30 — A BARNSLEY
Town: Wright R, Croft*, Clapham^, Brown, Mowbray, McGreal, Holland, **Stewart**, Johnson*, Scowcroft, Magilton
Opponents: Miller, Curtis, Barker^, Morgan, Chettle, Van d'Laan*, Eaden, Hignett, Shipperley, Dyer*, Barnard
subs used: Naylor/Wilnis / Appleby/Sheron/Thomas
Stewart debuts after joining for a club record £2.5m. Barnsley begin to dominate after the break, but Scowcroft lets fly with a shot that beats Kevin Miller all ends up. Stewart makes it a dream start by beating two men on a dazzling run before rounding Miller to guide the ball home.

31 — H HUDDERSFIELD
Town: Wright R, Wilnis, Clapham^, Brown, Mowbray, McGreal, Holland, Magilton, Johnson*, Scowcroft, Stewart
Opponents: Vaesen, Jenkins, Edwards, Irons*, Armstrong, Dyson, Smith, Holland, Gorre, Sellars, Wijnhard
subs used: Naylor/Croft*/Stockwell / Thornley
Scowcroft strokes in a low shot after Holland's header hits the post. Johnson misses a penalty-kick after a foul on Scowcroft. Clyde Wijnhard flicks on Scott Sellars' pass for Dean Gorre to snatch a breakaway goal. Stewart upsets his old mates by letting fly to claim a glorious winner.

32 — A CREWE
Town: Wright R, **Clegg**, Wilnis, Clapham, Mowbray, McGreal, Holland, Magilton, Johnson, Scowcroft, Naylor*
Opponents: Kearton, Wright D, Boertien^, Bignot, Foran, Lightfoot, Jack*, Lunt, Rivers, Tait, Sorvel
subs used: Wright J / Little/Wright S
Michael Clegg arrives on loan from Man U. After McGreal misses a sitter, Clapham fires Town ahead with a fine shot from 25 yards. From a well-worked free-kick, Paul Tait is given room to equalise. Jermaine Wright rockets home the best goal of his career to sink his former team.

33 — H BIRMINGHAM
Town: Wright R, Clegg, Brown, Clapham, Mowbray, McGreal, Holland, Magilton, Johnson, Scowcroft, Stewart
Opponents: Bennett, Rowett, Charlton^, Hughes, Purse, Johnson, Holdsworth, Carrick*, Adebola, Rankin^, Grainger
subs used: Stewart / Lazaridis/Ndlovu/Gill
Live on Sky TV, the unbeaten run hits 18. Mowbray nets a powerful header at the wrong end, but Johnson equalises from close range on the stroke of half-time. After the break Town put together some good moves, but can't force a winner. McGreal ends the game with a knee injury.

34 — H PORTSMOUTH
Town: Wright R, Clegg, Brown, Clapham, Mowbray, Wilnis, Holland, Magilton, Johnson, Scowcroft*, Stewart
Opponents: Hoult, Crowe, Birmingh'm* Moore, Whitbread, Hiley, Thogersen, Claridge, Bradbury, Waterman, Fenton
subs used: Wright J / Igoe
Relegation-threatened Pompey shock Town by taking the lead when Steve Claridge powers home a bullet header from Sammy Igoe's centre. Russell Hoult has a fine game for Tony Pulis's side. Stewart and Johnson both spurn good chances and Holland goes close with a late header.

#		Date	Opponent	HT	FT				Pts	Att.	Scorers	Referee
35	H	7/3	BLACKBURN	0-0	0-0	2	D	10	65	18,871		Ref: M Fletcher
36	A	11/3	WOLVERHAMPTON	0-1	1-2	2	L	7	65	22,652	Scowcroft 75, Flo 4, 46	Ref: M Jones
37	H	19/3	NORWICH	0-2	0-2	3	L	13	65	21,760	Roberts 19, 45	Ref: R Styles
38	A	22/3	TRANMERE	1-0	2-0	2	W	14	68	6,933	Holland 18, Johnson 57	Ref: D Laws
39	H	25/3	FULHAM	0-0	0-0	2	W	10	71	20,168	Reuser 90	Ref: T Bates
40	A	4/4	WEST BROM	0-1	1-1	3	D	21	72	12,536	Holland 68, Hughes 43	Ref: C Wilkes
41	H	8/4	PORT VALE	3-0	2-0	3	W	23	75	19,663	Scowcroft 12, Johnson 39, Holland 83	Ref: C Wilkes
42	A	15/4	STOCKPORT	1-0	1-0	3	W	19	78	8,501	Johnson 44	Ref: T Heilbron
43	A	22/4	QP RANGERS	0-0	1-3	3	L	11	78	14,920	Magilton 79p, Peacock 46, Koejoe 58, Kiwomya 90	Ref: J Brandwood
44	H	25/4	CRYSTAL PALACE	1-0	1-0	3	W	18	81	18,798	Johnson 26	Ref: P Robinson
45	A	29/4	CHARLTON	3-1	3-1	3	W	1	84	20,043	Magilton 24, Johnson 56, Reuser 71, Hunt 81	Ref: P Richards
46	H	7/5	WALSALL	2-0	3-0	3	W	22	87	21,508	Johnson 49, 80	Ref: K Lynch

Home Average 18,524 — Away 14,180

---

35 — Blackburn (H)
Wright R, Wilnis, Clapham, Thetis, Mowbray, Brown, Holland, Wright J*, Johnson, Magilton, Stewart^, Stockwell/Naylor
Kelly, Grayson, Davidson, Broomes, Dailly, Flitcroft, Gillespie, Frandsen, Ward, Blake, Duff, Jansen*

A virtually non-stop first-half onslaught on Alan Kelly's goal fails to yield a goal but wins an ovation from impressed home fans at the break. After this, Rovers come back into the game a little. Well-known statistician and 'memory man' Ron Ellis – a Town fan for 65 years – has died.

36 — Wolverhampton (A)
Wright R, Wilnis, Clapham, Brown, Mowbray, McGreal, Holland, Wright J*, Johnson, Scowcroft, Magilton, Naylor
Oakes, Bazeley, Muscat, Sedgley, Curle, Pollet, Robinson, Flo, Branch, Sinton, Emblen

Stand-in striker Havard Flo turns and fires in Michael Branch's cross. Town are caught cold again after the interval and Flo nets an overhead kick. Unmarked Scowcroft pulls one back. Appeals for a penalty appeal are ignored and an angry Burley has to be restrained on the touchline.

37 — Norwich (H)
Wright R, Wilnis, Clapham, Thetis, Mowbray, Venus, Holland, Magilton, Johnson, Stewart^, Stockwell/Naylor
Marshall A, Sutch, Fugelstad, Marshall L, Fleming, Jackson, Russell, Dalglist, Roberts^, Milligan, Llewellyn, Anselin/Coote*

Injury-hit Town's worst display of the season and a massive disappointment for home fans. Ex-Town man Bryan Hamilton is ecstatic about his first game in charge of City. Stewart is less than fully fit and it shows. The attack rarely looks like responding to Iwan Roberts' double strike.

38 — Tranmere (A)
Wright R, Wilnis, Croft*, Clapham, Mowbray, Venus*, Holland, Wright J*, Johnson^, Scowcroft, Magilton, Stockwell/Naylor/Brown
Murphy, Challinor, Roberts, Hazell, Morgan, Yates*, Mahon, Parkinson^, Jones, Allison, Kelly, Koumas/Black*

After recent setbacks Town bounce back into second spot in style. Wright's shot is parried by both posts, but Johnson tucks the loose ball in. Rovers' only answer is to keep supplying Dave Challinor with a towel to aid his long throws. Scowcroft nets an overhead kick.

39 — Fulham (H)
Wright R, Croft, Clapham, Venus*, Mowbray, McGreal, Holland, Wright J", Johnson, Scowcroft^, Magilton, Stockwell/Naylor/Reuser
Taylor, Finnan, Phelan, Melville, Coleman, Morgan^, Hayward, Peschisolido Riedle, Stewart^, Ball*, Hayles, Davis/Goldhaek/Lewis*

Burley signs a new longer-term contract and recruits exciting Dutch talent Martijn Reuser on loan. He is the ninth debutant of the season and is hero of the hour when he takes Magilton's pass and slips the ball past Maik Taylor in the last minute. It came very late but was richly deserved.

40 — West Brom (A)
Wright R, Stockwell, Croft^, Venus, Mowbray, Clapham, Holland, Wright J, Johnson*, Scowcroft, Magilton, Stewart/Reuser
Jensen, Lyttle, Van Blerk, Flynn, Clement, Butler, Quinn, Sneekes, Taylor, Hughes, Santos, De Freitas*

Mowbray is dispossessed by Richard Sneekes who sets up Lee Hughes. When Johnson misses a great opportunity to equalise, Magilton gives him a ticking off, but gets shoved in the face for his trouble. Burley immediately withdraws Johnson. Clapham's pass is clipped in by Holland.

41 — Port Vale (H)
Wright R, Croft, Clapham, Venus", Mowbray, Brown, Holland, Magilton, Johnson^, Scowcroft, Stewart*, Wright J/Naylor/Reuser
Pilkington, Tankard, Carragher, Widdrington Snijders, Ready, Burton, O'Callagh'n Healy, Wijnen, Cummins, Rougier, Naylor*

Clapham's dummy wrong-foots several defenders before his shot is parried by Kevin Pilkington for Scowcroft to net the rebound. Johnson nets the second after a defensive mishap. Reuser twice goes close before setting up Holland, who blasts in the third goal off the inside of the post.

42 — Stockport (A)
Wright R, Croft, Clapham, Brown, Mowbray, McGreal*, Holland, Reuser", Johnson, Scowcroft, Magilton, Wilnis^/Stockwell/Wright J
Nash, Connelly, Nicholson, Dinning, Flynn, Gray, Cooper, Moore, Lawson, Fradin, Gibb, Ross*

After Scowcroft heads on a long Richard Wright punt, Johnson gets the better of skipper Mike Flynn to smash an unstoppable effort past Carlo Nash. Richard Wright – equalling Steve McCall's record of 175 successive games – makes a fine save from Ian Lawson's late headed effort.

43 — QP Rangers (A)
Wright R, Wilnis, Croft^, Brown, Mowbray, Clapham, Holland, Wright J*, Johnson, Scowcroft, Magilton, Naylor/Reuser
Harper, Perry, Barraclough Darlington, Ready, Bruce^, Langley, Peacock, Koejoe, Wardley, Kiwomya, Gallen/Kulcsar*

Gavin Peacock heads in after Wright blocks Richard Langley's effort. Chris Kiwomya pokes the ball past hesitant Mowbray and Sammy Koejoe hits his first Rangers goal. Magilton fouls Magilton, who gets up to net from the spot. Kiwomya shoots in to finish off his former club.

44 — Crystal Palace (H)
Wright R, Wilnis, Clapham, Thetis*, Mowbray, Brown, Holland, Reuser, Johnson, Scowcroft^, Magilton, Wright J/Naylor
Gregg, Smith, Cole, Austin, Carlisle, Linghan, Mullins, Foster, Morrison, Thomson, McKenzie

Town are assured of the play-offs, but could still make the top two. The club unveils a new £200,000 team bus. Marco Holster exits on a free transfer. Kick-off is delayed for Wright to change to a different colour shirt. A fine ball from Brown reaches Johnson, who cracks in a low shot.

45 — Charlton (A)
Wright R, Wilnis^, Croft, Venus*, Mowbray, Brown, Holland, Magilton, Johnson, Scowcroft^, Stewart*, Clapham/Thetis/Reuser
Kiely, Brown, Powell, Stuart, Rufus, Tiler, Newton, Kinsella, Hunt, Kitson^, Robinson, Parker/Svensson*

A carnival atmosphere at the home of the new divisional champions. Mark Kinsella fouls Johnson and Magilton sends a cracking free-kick past Dean Kiely. Johnson catches Charlton square for the second goal before Reuser cuts in to make it three. The pressure is now on Manchester C.

46 — Walsall (H)
Wright R, Wilnis^, Clapham, Thetis, Mowbray, Brown, Holland, Magilton, Johnson, Scowcroft*, Stewart", Naylor/Croft/Reuser
Walker, Marsh, Padula^, Viveash, Roper, Bennett, Hall, Fenton", Rammell^, Keates, Matias, Bukran/Wrack/Robins

To be promoted Town must win and hope Man City lose at Blackburn. Johnson relieves the tension, netting crosses by Mowbray and Clapham to relegate Ray Graydon's men. Blackburn go ahead and hit the woodwork four times but City bounce back to condemn Town to the play-offs.

Play-offs

		H	A	F-A	H-T	Att	Scorers, Times, and Referees
SF 1	A BOLTON		14/5	2-2	1-2	18,814	Stewart 36, 65 / Holdsworth 5, Gudjohnsen 26 — Ref: R Styles

Ipswich: Wright R, Wilnis", Clapham, Thetis, Mowbray*, Venus, Holland, Magilton, Johnson", Scowcroft, Stewart — subs used: Brown/Croft/Reuser
Bolton: Jaaskalainen, Bergsson, Whitlow, Warhurst, Fish, Ritchie", Johansen^, Jensen, Gudjohnsen*, Holdsworth*Johnston, Stewart — Hansen/Elliott/Phillips

Town finished even further ahead of Bolton than last year, but must face them again in the play-offs! Dean Holdsworth's header and an Eidur Gudjohnsen drive, plus Johnson's neck injury, put Town in trouble. Stewart responds with a superb volley and then dribbles round the keeper.

		H	A	F-A	H-T	Att	Scorers, Times, and Referees
SF 2	H BOLTON	17/5		5-3 aet	1-2	21,543	Magilton 18p, 49, 90, Clapham 94p / Holdsworth 6, 39, J'ston 50 [Reuser 109] — Ref: B Knight (Town win 7-5 on aggregate)

Ipswich: Wright R, Croft, Clapham, Brown^, Mowbray, Venus, Holland, Magilton, Johnson, Scowcroft*, Stewart — Naylor/Reuser
Bolton: Jaaskalainen, Whitlow /, Warhurst^, Fish, Ritchie, Johansen", Jensen, Elliott !, Holdsworth*Johnston — Hansen/Passi/Phillips

A marvellous night of tension and thrills. Three times Bolton take the lead before Magilton's drive forces extra-time in the dying seconds and completes his hat-trick. Mike Whitlow and Robbie Elliott both walk after second yellow cards. Reuser thunders home a wonderful clincher.

		H	A	F-A	H-T	Att	Scorers, Times, and Referees
F	N BARNSLEY (at Wembley)		29/5	4-2	1-1	73,427	Mowbray 28, Naylor 52, Stewart 58 / Wright R 6 (og), Hignett 78p [Reuser 90] — Ref: T Heilbron

Ipswich: Wright R, Croft, Clapham, Venus, Mowbray, McGreal, Holland, Magilton*, Johnson*, Stewart^, Naylor^ — Naylor^/Wilnis
Barnsley: Miller, Curtis^, Barnard, Morgan, Chettle, Brown, Appleby, Hignett, Shipperley, Dyer*, Tinkler" — Hristov/Eaden/Thomas

37,000 Town fans create an amazing atmosphere. Craig Hignett's shot hits the bar and goes in off Wright. Mowbray heads Town level. Wright hauls down Hignett but saves his penalty. Lethal finishing by Naylor and Stewart is followed by a thumping Reuser goal. The big party begins!

Worthington Cup

		H	A	F-A	H-T	Att	Scorers, Times, and Referees
1:1	A BRENTFORD		11/8	2-0	0-0	4,825 2:4	Johnson 64, Clapham 70 — Ref: P Rejer

Ipswich: Wright R, Stockwell, Clapham, Thetis, Venus, McGreal, Holland, Johnson", Scowcroft, Naylor^ — Axeldal/Wilnis
Brentford: Woodman, Boxall, Anderson, Quinn", Powell, Heidarsson, Evans, Owusu", Scott*, Partridge — Folan/Bryan/Rowlands

The Sky cameras come in search of an upset, but Town impose themselves well and make The Bees look very ordinary. After a poor free-kick by Andy Woodman, Naylor sets up Johnson to net with his right foot. Clapham curls a fine free-kick out of Woodman's reach for the second.

		H	A	F-A	H-T	Att	Scorers, Times, and Referees
1:2	H BRENTFORD	24/8		2-0	1-0	9,748 2:8	Scowcroft 41, Clapham 90 — Ref: W Jordan (Town win 4-0 on aggregate)

Ipswich: Wright R, Wilnis, Clapham, Brown, Venus, McGreal, Holland, Johnson*, Scowcroft*, Magilton — Naylor/Stockwell
Brentford: Pearcey, Boxall, Anderson, Rowlands, Powell", Heidarsson, Evans, Mahon, Bryan", Folan^, Partridge — Warner/Scott/Quinn

Ron Noades' outfit play some neat football but face an uphill task. Scott Partridge looks a lively customer. A neat Town move ends with Scowcroft having an easy tap-in for the opener. Clapham repeats his curling free-kick of the first leg with keeper Jason Pearcey flat-footed.

		H	A	F-A	H-T	Att	Scorers, Times, and Referees
2:1	A CREWE		14/9	1-2	1-0	4,759 19	Venus 30 / Rivers 66, Little 86 — Ref: M Pike

Ipswich: Wright R, Stockwell, Thetis, Venus, McGreal, Holland, Wright J, Johnson^, Magilton, Naylor^ — Axeldal/Scowcroft
Crewe: Kearton, Bignot", Smith S, Wright D, Macauley, Charnock^, Sorvel, Lunt, Jack", Cramb, Rivers — Street/Grant/Little

Venus comes forward as Town win a free-kick and orders team-mates to step aside before blasting Town ahead with a terrific shot. An error by Holland sees skilful Mark Rivers lob a fine equaliser. Wright makes a double save in a scramble before Colin Little forces home the winner.

		H	A	F-A	H-T	Att	Scorers, Times, and Referees
2:2	H CREWE	21/9		1-1	1-0	9,689 14	Scowcroft 38 / Rivers 86 — Ref: S Bennett (Town lose 2-3 on aggregate)

Ipswich: Wright R, Stockwell, Clapham, Brown, Venus, McGreal, Holland, Magilton, Johnson, Scowcroft, Naylor — Lightfoot
Crewe: Kearton, Unsworth, Smith S, Wright D, Macauley*, Charnock, Sorvel, Lunt, Little, Cramb, Rivers

Johnson and Naylor set up Clapham, who sends a sweet shot flying past Jason Kearton. The keeper turns it on after this, keeping out a series of goalbound efforts. A drive by Stockwell knocks Steve Macauley unconscious. Mark Rivers is left free to dance round Wright and win the tie.

FA Cup

		H	A	F-A	H-T	Att	Scorers, Times, and Referees
3	H SOUTHAMPTON	13/12		0-1	0-1	14,383 P:16	Richards 40 — Ref: G Barber

Ipswich: Wright R, Wilnis", Clapham, Brown, Mowbray, McGreal, Holland, Stockwell*, Johnson^, Scowcroft, Magilton — Naylor/Axeldal/Wright J
Southampton: Jones, Tessem, Bridge, Dodd, Lundekvam, Richards, Ripley, Softvedt, Pahars, Hughes M*Oakley — Beattie

Dean Richards joins the Saints attack to send a scorching header past Wright. David Jones' team had gone over 400 minutes without scoring prior to this. Johnson picks up a thigh injury. Town play some tidy football but lack thrust and Paul Jones has a relatively quiet evening in goal.

Final League Table — Division One

Pos	Team	P	Home W	D	L	F	A	Away W	D	L	F	A	Pts
1	Charlton	46	15	3	5	37	18	12	7	4	42	27	91
2	Manchester C	46	17	2	4	48	17	9	9	5	30	23	89
3	IPSWICH *	46	16	3	4	39	17	9	9	5	32	25	87
4	Barnsley	46	15	4	4	48	24	9	6	8	40	43	82
5	Birmingham	46	15	5	3	37	16	7	6	10	28	28	77
6	Bolton	46	14	5	4	43	26	7	8	8	26	24	76
7	Wolves	46	15	5	3	45	20	6	6	11	19	28	74
8	Huddersfield	46	14	5	4	43	21	7	6	10	19	28	74
9	Fulham	46	13	7	3	33	13	4	9	10	16	28	67
10	QP Rangers	46	9	12	2	30	20	7	6	10	32	33	66
11	Blackburn	46	10	9	4	33	20	5	8	10	22	31	62
12	Norwich	46	11	6	6	26	22	3	9	11	19	28	57
13	Tranmere	46	9	11	3	35	27	6	1	16	22	41	57
14	Nott'm Forest	46	10	8	5	29	18	4	6	13	24	37	56
15	Crystal Pal	46	7	11	5	33	26	6	4	13	24	41	54
16	Sheffield Utd	46	10	8	5	38	24	3	7	13	21	47	54
17	Stockport	46	8	8	7	33	31	6	4	13	22	36	51
18	Portsmouth	46	9	6	8	36	27	4	6	13	19	39	51
19	Crewe	46	9	5	9	27	31	6	1	16	19	36	51
20	Grimsby	46	10	8	5	27	25	3	4	16	14	42	49
21	West Brom	46	6	11	6	25	26	4	8	11	18	34	49
22	Walsall	46	7	6	10	26	34	4	7	12	14	39	46
23	Port Vale	46	6	11	6	27	30	1	4	18	21	39	36
24	Swindon	46	5	6	12	23	37	3	6	14	15	40	36
		1104	260	159	133	821	570	133	159	260	570	821	1497

* Promoted after play-offs

Odds & ends

Double wins: (8) Barnsley, Charlton, Crewe, Nott'm Forest, Port Vale, Stockport, Swindon, Walsall.

Double losses: (1) QPR.

Won from behind: (4) Barnsley (p/o), Bolton (H) (p/o), Charlton (h), Swindon (h).

Lost from in front: (3) Crewe (a, LC), Huddersfield (a), QPR (h).

High spots: Promotion at last – after an unforgettable day at Wembley. A breathtaking extra-time win over Bolton in the p/o semi-final. 16 goals and 13 points before the end of August. The six-goal romp at home to Barnsley. A series of polished displays by new recruit John McGreal. An 18-match unbeaten run from 6 November. Last-minute winners against Crewe, Fulham and Walsall.

Low spots: A dreadful display at home to Norwich. New signing Gary Croft imprisoned for motoring offences. The on-field flare-up between Magilton and Johnson. A 1-4 thrashing at home by QPR after Magilton is sent off.

Player of the Year: James Scowcroft.
Ever-presents: (2) Matt Holland, Richard Wright.
Hat-tricks: (1) Jim Magilton (v Bolton – p/o).
Opposing hat-tricks: (0).
Leading scorer: (23) David Johnson.

Appearances and Goals

Player	Lge	Sub	LC	Sub	FAC	Sub	PO	Sub	G Lge	G LC	G FAC	G PO	G Tot
Axeldal, Jonas	1	15				3							
Brown, Wayne	20	5	2					1	1				1
Clapham, Jamie	44	2	4	1			3		2				2
Clegg, Michael	3												
Croft, Gary	14	7					2		1				1
Friars, Sean		1											
Holland, Matt	46		4		1		3		10				10
Johnson, David	44		4		1		3		22		1		23
Logan, Richard		1											
McGreal, John	34		4		1		3						
Magilton, Jim	33	5	3				3		4			3	7
Midgley, Neil	1	3											
Mowbray, Tony	35		4		1		3		1			1	2
Naylor, Richard	19	17	3	1	1		2		8				9
Reuser, Martijn	2	6						3	2			2	4
Scowcroft, James	40	1	3	1	1		2		13			2	15
Stewart, Marcus	9	1					3		2				2
Stockwell, Mick	21	14	3	1	1		2		2				2
Thetis, Manu	15	1	3		1		1						
Venus, Mark	28		3		1		3		2		1		3
Wilnis, Fabian	30	5	1	1	1		1						
Wright, Jermaine	21	13	3	1	1	1	3		1				1
Wright, Richard	46		4		1		3						
23 players used	506	98	44	7	11	4	33	8	71		6	11	88

FA CARLING PREMIERSHIP

Manager: George Burley

No	Date		Att	Pos	Pt	F-A	H-T	Scorers, Times, and Referees
1	A	TOTTENHAM	36,148	L	0	1-3	1-2	Venus 9 — Anderton 30p, Carr 31, Ferdinand 82 — Ref: A Wiley
2	H	MANCHESTER U	22,007	D	1	1-1	1-1	Wilnis 6 — Beckham 39 — Ref: J Winter
3	H	SUNDERLAND	21,830	11 / 15	W / 4	1-0	0-0	Bramble 52 — Ref: G Poll
4	A	LEICESTER	19,598	14 / 3	L / 4	1-2	0-0	Magilton 89p — Akinbiyi 57, Elliott 73 — Ref: P Taylor
5	H	ASTON VILLA	22,065	16 / 13	L / 4	1-2	0-1	Stewart 88 — Hendrie 28, Dublin 54 — Ref: A D'Urso
6	A	LEEDS	35,552	11 / 9	W / 7	2-1	1-1	Scowcroft 12, J Wright 47 — Bowyer 3 — Ref: M Halsey
7	H	ARSENAL	22,030	11 / 3	D / 8	1-1	0-0	Stewart 49 — Bergkamp 84 — Ref: P Durkin
8	A	EVERTON	32,597	9 / 13	W / 11	3-0	1-0	McGreal 19, Stewart 49, 59 — Ref: J Winter
9	H	WEST HAM	22,243	7 / 20	D / 12	1-1	1-0	Stewart 5 — Di Canio 73 — Ref: N Barry
10	A	BRADFORD C	17,045	6 / 21	W / 15	2-0	1-0	Petrescu 34 (og), Clapham 88 — Ref: P Taylor

Squad numbers in use / subs used

1 — Tottenham (A)
Ipswich: Wright R, Croft, Clapham, Venus^, Magilton, Johnson, Holland, Bramble, Hreid'sson, Stewart, Scowcroft* — subs: Reuser/Brown
Tottenham: Sullivan, Carr, Thatcher^, Perry, Campbell, Sherwood, Freund, Leonhardsen, Rebrov, Anderton, Iversen* — subs: Ferdinand/Taricco

Venus' deflected free-kick flies in early, but Wright continues his bad habit of hauling down attackers, handing Spurs a spot-kick equaliser. Expensive debutant Rebrov creates the opening for Carr's drive 60 seconds later and Ferdinand wraps up the points with a thumping header.

2 — Manchester U (H)
Ipswich: Wright R, Wilnis, Clapham, Venus, Magilton, Johnson, Holland, Bramble, Heidarsson, Stewart, Wright J — subs: Reuser/Scowcroft
Manchester U: Barthez, Neville G, Neville P^, Wallwork, Scholes, Solskjaer*, Beckham, Stam, Keane, Yorke*, Giggs — subs: Cole/Silvestre/Sheringham

Beckham, G Neville and Yorke are booked for dissent as Town give the champions a torrid time in a red-hot atmosphere. Town lead through Wilnis' firm low drive, but Beckham swerves a free-kick through a crowd to level. Barthez produces a wonder save to deny Johnson's header.

3 — Sunderland (H)
Ipswich: Wright R, Wilnis, Clapham, Venus, Magilton, Johnson, Holland, Bramble, Heidarsson, Stewart*, Wright J — subs: Scowcroft
Sunderland: Macho, Makin, Gray, Hutchison, Butler P, Craddock, Thirlwell*, Holloway, Quinn, Phillips, Kilbane — subs: Oster

Just days after being picked for the England U-21 squad, teenager Bramble celebrates with his first senior goal after playing a one-two with Stewart. Johnson misses several chances, while the visitors' closest effort sees Clapham block on the line after Wright's punch goes astray.

4 — Leicester (A)
Ipswich: Wright R, Wilnis, Clapham, Scales, Magilton, Johnson, Holland, Bramble, Heidarsson, Stewart*, Wright J — subs: Scowcroft
Leicester: Flowers, Rowett, Guppy, Elliott, Izzet*, Akinbiyi, Oakes, Savage, Taggart, Eadie, Impey — subs: Collymore

Akinbiyi converts his first goal for Peter Taylor's men when the dangerous Eadie goes on a penetrating run and crosses. Elliott seals the win with a looping header from Guppy's corner which leaves Wright floundering. Magilton scores from the spot.

5 — Aston Villa (H)
Ipswich: Wright R, Wilnis, Clapham, Venus^, Magilton, Johnson, Holland, Bramble, Heidarsson, Scowcroft*, Wright J — subs: Reuser/McGreal/Stewart
Aston Villa: James, Alpay, Wright, Stone, Dublin, Boateng, Merson, Barry, Southgate^, Nilis*, Hendrie — subs: Vassell/Ehiogu/Ginola

Nilis breaks his leg when colliding with keeper Wright. Villa recover to lead when Hendrie curls the ball home after Merson's pass. Unmarked Dublin heads home a simple second against the run of play. Town waste several openings before sub Stewart's consolation from close range.

6 — Leeds (A)
Ipswich: Wright R, Wilnis, Clapham, McGreal, Magilton, Johnson, Holland, Bramble, Heidarsson, Scowcroft, Wright J — subs: Stewart
Leeds: Martyn, Kelly, Harte, Duberry, Smith, McPhail, Dacourt, Mills, Bowyer, Bridges, Huckerby

Injury-hit Leeds make a great start as Kelly's cross is converted by the unmarked Bowyer. Town hit straight back as Scowcroft dives to head home a miscued shot by Hreidarsson from Clapham's chip. Slick passing leads to Wright firing home after a neat interchange with Stewart.

7 — Arsenal (H)
Ipswich: Wright R, Wilnis, Clapham, McGreal, Magilton, Johnson, Holland, Bramble, Heidarsson, Scowcroft*, Wright J — subs: Naylor
Arsenal: Seaman, Luzhny, Silvinho, Keown, Grimandi*, Ljungberg, Parlour, Henry, Vivas, Bergkamp^, Wiltord* — subs: Vernazza/Kanu

Holland's header shaves the woodwork and Bramble's goalbound effort is blocked as Town pile on the pressure. Holland's flick is glanced over Seaman by Stewart and then Naylor's fizzing drive nearly doubles the lead. The recalled Bergkamp levels after Henry's shot is blocked.

8 — Everton (A)
Ipswich: Wright R, Wilnis, Clapham, McGreal, Magilton, Johnson, Holland, Bramble, Heidarsson, Stewart*, Naylor* — subs: Scowcroft/Johnson
Everton: Gerrard, Watson, Weir, Unsworth*, Gascoigne, Gemmill, Gravesen, Alex'rsson^, Nyarko, Campbell, Moore^ — subs: M Hughes/S Hughes/McL'd

A rare McGreal goal as he powers home Magilton's free-kick with his head. Naylor's pass is flicked home by Stewart and the contest is over as Stewart cleverly punishes Unsworth's sloppy back-pass. Gascoigne looks lively in midfield, but his lacklustre colleagues are in poor form.

9 — West Ham (H)
Ipswich: Wright R, Wilnis, Clapham, McGreal, Magilton, Johnson, Holland, Heidarsson, Venus, Stewart^, Naylor* — subs: Scowcroft/Johnson
West Ham: Hislop, Ferdinand, Stimac, Pearce, Sinclair, Winterburn*, Lomas, Lampard, Cole, Di Canio, Kanoute — subs: Moncur

Wilnis' cross is glanced in by the in-form Stewart and Magilton almost doubles the lead but hits the post. Di Canio produces a smart volley from Sinclair's cross to equalise. Town go in search of a winner and Hislop saves well from Naylor while Magilton misses a great opportunity.

10 — Bradford C (A)
Ipswich: Wright R, Wilnis, Clapham, McGreal, Magilton, Johnson, Holland, Heidarsson, Venus, Stewart^, Naylor* — subs: Wright J, Johnson/Scowcroft
Bradford C: Clarke, Nolan, McCall, Wetherall, Lawrence, Ward, Carbone, Windass, Beagrie, Atherton, Petrescu* — subs: Saunders

Holland's low, driven cross is turned past his own keeper by the unlucky Petrescu. Clarke produces a superb save to deny Johnson's header, but just seconds later Clapham is fouled and clinches the three points himself by curling a marvellous free-kick into the net from 20 yards.

#		Date	Att	Pos	Res	Score	Pld	Pts
11	H MIDDLESBROUGH	28/10	21,771	5	W	2-1	17	18

Naylor 25, Venus 28; Gordon 67 — Ref: N Barry

Wright R	Wilnis	Clapham	McGreal	Hreidarsson	Venus	Holland	Magilton^	Stewart*	Naylor*	Wright J	Johnson/Scowcroft
Crossley	Fleming	Gordon	Vickers	Festa	Karembeu	Deane^	Campbell^	Ricard^	Summerbell/Cooper	Whelan/Marinelli/Job

Crossley's mis-hits a first-time clearance towards Naylor and he shows composure by sending it straight back into the net. Cooper fouls Naylor and the free-kick is touched to Venus to fire home a great drive. After Whelan is tripped, Gordon's effort from a free-kick is deflected home.

| 12 | A NEWCASTLE | 4/11 | 50,922 | 6 | L | 1-2 | 5 | 18 |

Stewart 13; Shearer 22, 67p — Ref: A Wiley

Wright R	Wilnis	Clapham	McGreal^	Hreidarss'n"	Venus	Holland	Magilton	Stewart^	Naylor*	Wright J	Johnson/Scowcroft/Reuser
Given	Domi	Goma	Acuna^	Lee	Dyer	Speed	Solano	Shearer	Cordone*	Hughes	Lua Lua/Bassedas

Given blocks J Wright's shot and Stewart converts. Bobby Robson's men level as Goma's through-ball is controlled on his chest by Shearer and swept home. Venus' challenge on Shearer sees a disputed penalty given. It's the biggest crowd to watch a Town League game for 23 years.

| 13 | H CHARLTON | 11/11 | 22,263 | 6 | W | 2-0 | 9 | 21 |

Holland 80, Stewart 84 — Ref: S Bennett

Wright R	Wilnis*	Clapham	McGreal	Hreidarsson	Venus	Holland	Magilton	Stewart^	Scowcroft^	Wright J	Bramble/Naylor/Johnson
Kiely	Shields	Fish	Brown	Powell	Robinson*	Stuart	Jensen	Kinsella	Johansson	Svensson^	Salako/Bagheri

Confident Town leave it late as 'Mr Consistency' Holland blasts home a fine shot from 18 yards after turning Kinsella. Stewart then dances past Shields and fires home.

| 14 | A COVENTRY | 20/11 | 19,322 | 5 | W | 1-0 | 19 | 24 |

Wilnis 90 — Ref: D Elleray

Wright R	Wilnis	Clapham	McGreal^	Hreidarsson	Venus	Holland	Magilton	Stewart	Scowcroft	Wright J*	Reuser/Bramble
Kirkland	Telfer	Williams	Breen	Konjic	Edworthy	Thompson	Chippo	Hadji	Bellamy	Roussel*	Aloisi

Town struggle for their usual fluency. Wright keeps them in the game with stunning saves from Telfer and Thompson. Gordon Stachan's men are desperate to end a run of four defeats, but Wilnis, urged by his manager to get forward, heads an injury-time winner from a Reuser cross.

| 15 | A MANCHESTER C | 25/11 | 33,741 | 3 | W | 3-2 | 16 | 27 |

Stewart 9, 53, Hreidarsson 32; Wanchope 71, Howey 81 — Ref: M Dean

Wright R	Wilnis	Clapham	Scales	Hreidarsson	Venus	Holland	Magilton	Stewart	Scowcroft^	Wright J*	Johnson
Weaver	Haaland	Howey	Prior	Dunne^	Bishop	Charvet	Wr't-Phillips^	Goater^	Dickov^	Kennedy	Tiatto/Wanchope/Whitley

Stewarts nods in Clapham's cross and the lead is extended when unmarked Hreidarsson heads Wright's corner firmly home. Stewart walks the ball round Weaver with City in total disarray. Sub Wanchope's deflected shot and a Howey header give City late hope, but Town remain calm.

| 16 | H DERBY | 2/12 | 22,073 | 5 | L | 0-1 | 17 | 27 |

Delap 28 — Ref: M Halsey

Branagan	Wilnis*	Clapham	McGreal	Hreidarsson	Venus	Holland	Magilton	Stewart"	Johnson^	Wright J	Bramble/Scowcroft/Reuser
Poom	Carbonari	Powell	Delap	Burley	Johnston	Christie^	Martin"	Eranio^	Riggott	West	Morris/Burton/Higginboth

Tenacious Derby pose problems and Delap runs from halfway before cutting in to shoot home, aided by a deflection off Wright. Deputy keeper Branagan saves further Delap efforts. Scowcroft's arrival galvanises Town, who go all out to equalise. Venus and McGreal miss great chances.

| 17 | A LIVERPOOL | 10/12 | 43,509 | 3 | W | 1-0 | 5 | 30 |

Stewart 45 — Ref: A Wiley

Wright R	Wilnis	Clapham	McGreal^	Hreidarsson	Venus	Holland	Magilton	Stewart*	Scowcroft^	Wright J	Croft/Armstrong
Westerveld	Henchoz	Hyypia	Ziege"	Babbel	Carragher	Murphy	Barmby*	McAllister	Owen^	Fowler	Smicer/Heskey/Biscan

Fowler and Owen miss early chances. Anfield is stunned as Stewart dances past two defenders and to slot in a brilliant solo effort. Armstrong, an £800,000 buy from Middlesbrough, gets a taste of action. Liverpool apply much second-half pressure and Murphy clips the bar.

| 18 | H SOUTHAMPTON | 16/12 | 22,228 | 3 | W | 3-1 | 15 | 33 |

Scowcroft 48, Bridge 51(og), 90; Beattie 3 — Ref: B Knight

Wright R	Croft	Clapham*	Lundekvam Richards	Hreidarsson	Venus	Holland	Magilton	Stewart	Scowcroft^	Wright J*	Armstrong/Reuser
Jones	Dodd"			Bridge	Davies^	Tessem	Oakley*	El Khalej	Pahars	Beattie	Draper/Kachloul/Rosler

Pahars evades two challenges and crosses for Beattie to nod his eighth in seven games. Glen Hoddle's men miss other chances but Town move up a gear after the break. Scowcroft stabs in Magilton's cross. Sub Armstrong heads in Wayne Bridge and later converts a Magilton pass.

| 19 | A MANCHESTER U | 23/12 | 67,579 | 5 | L | 0-2 | 1 | 33 |

Solksjaer 20, 32 — Ref: S Bennett

Wright R	Wilnis^	Clapham*	McGreal	Hreidarsson	Venus	Holland	Magilton"	Scowcroft	Stewart	Wright J*	Armstrong/Hreid'sson/Reuser
Barthez	Neville G	Neville P	Brown	Silvestre	Beckham^	Keane"	Scholes	Giggs*	Solksjaer	Croft	Healey/Greening/Wallwork

United are unstoppable in the first half and the deadly Solksjaer gets clean through and skips around Wright to score. Beckham produces a trademark curling cross to set up Solksjaer for the second. Town look much livelier after the break and sub Armstrong goes close with a volley.

| 20 | H CHELSEA | 26/12 | 22,237 | 5 | D | 2-2 | 10 | 34 |

Scowcroft 43, Stewart 82; Gudjohnsen 8, 17 — Ref: J Winter

Wright R	Wilnis^	Clapham*	Hreidarsson	Bramble	Venus	Holland	Magilton"	Armstrong	Scowcroft	Wright J	Reuser/Croft
De Goey	Melchiot*	Leboeuf	Terry	Desailly	Wise	Dalla Bona	Morris	Gudjohnsen	Hasselbaink^	Zola"	Bogarde/Jokanovic/Harley

Claudio Ranieri's erratic outfit roar into a two-goal lead as Gudjohnsen sweeps home two similar goals from penetrating crosses, with Town's defence looking static. Wilnis' looping cross is headed in by Scowcroft and heavy pressure is rewarded as Stewart fires home under De Goey's body.

| 21 | H TOTTENHAM | 30/12 | 22,234 | 3 | W | 3-0 | 15 | 37 |

Stewart 9, Armstrong 62, Clapham 88 — Ref: M Messias

Wright R	Wilnis^	Venus	Hreidarsson	Bramble	Holland	Wright J	Scowcroft	Armstrong^	Stewart*	Croft	Johnson/McGreal/Clapham
Sullivan	Campbell	Perry	Thelwell	Sherwood^	Anderton	Karsten"	Leonhardsen	Clemence	King	Reuser	Doherty	Davies/Rebrov

Town cruise to the points thanks to Spurs' worst display for months. Stewart miskicks a cross and Sullivan is wrong-footed as it bobbles past him. Armstrong swoops in at close range for a second. Ex-Spurs man Clapham comes on to poke home the third with Johnson looking offside.

FA CARLING PREMIERSHIP

Manager: George Burley

SEASON 2000-01

22 — A 1/1 **SUNDERLAND** — Att 46,053 · Pos 4 · Pt 37 · F-A **1-4** · L · H-T 1-1
Stewart 5 [Schwarz 88] / Sorensen, Arca 25, Phillips 57, Dichio 63. Ref: N Barry

Wilnis	Venus	Heidarsson	Bramble	Clapham*	Wright R	Holland	Armstrong	Stewart	Scowcroft	**subs:** Reuser/McGreal
Sorensen	Makin	Thome	Craddock^	Gray	Rae	Hutchison	McCann*	Arca"	Phillips	Dichio — Williams/Varga/Schwarz

Holland finds Stewart unmarked and he flicks a shot over Sorensen. Venus fouls Dichio and Arca rockets home the free-kick. Dichio sets up the deadly Phillips to put Peter Reid's men ahead. Phillips outpaces Heidarsson to feed Dichio, who nets his first league goal for two seasons.

23 — H 14/1 **LEICESTER** — 22,002 · Pos 4 · Pt 40 · **2-0** · W · H-T 0-0
Stewart 80, Scowcroft 90. Ref: M Riley

Wright R	Wilnis	McGreal	Heidarsson	Bramble	Clapham^	Holland	Armstrong*	Stewart	Scowcroft	**subs:** Wright J/Reuser
Royce	Rowett	Davidson	Impey	Elliott	Jones"	Savage	Akinbiyi^	Benjamin^	Izzet	Guppy — Cres'i/Gilchrist/Gunlaugs'n

In front of new England boss Eriksson and the Sky cameras, Town toil hard to break dull but resolute Leicester in the closing stages. Rowett slips up to allow Heidarsson past and Armstrong fires the ball in for Stewart to convert. Scowcroft dives to head a well-worked clinching goal.

24 — A 20/1 **CHELSEA** — 34,948 · Pos 5 · Pt 40 · **1-4** · L · H-T 1-1
Stewart 23 / Poyet 45, 65, Wise 58, Hasselb'nk 73p. Ref: A D'Urso

Wright R	Wilnis	McGreal!	Heidarsson	Croft*	Clapham	Holland	Armstrong*	Stewart	Scowcroft	**subs:** Wright J/Brown
Cudicini	Babayaro	Desailly	Terry	Ferrer^	Wise	Poyet	Dalla Bona"	Zola	Gudjohns'n*	Hasselbaink — Melch'c/Jokan'ic/Gronkjaer

Stewart capitalises on lax defending, but Poyet's equalising header proves a turning point. Half-time tactical changes by Claudio Ranieri sees Town well beaten, although the margin is flattering. Wilnis' tackle on Dalla Bona is deemed a penalty, and McGreal is sent off for arguing.

25 — H 3/2 **LEEDS** — 22,015 · Pos 5 · Pt 40 · **1-2** · L · H-T 0-2
Venus 63 / Venus 28 (og), Keane 41. Ref: P Jones

Wright R	Venus	Heidarsson"	Croft*	Clapham	Wright J	Holland	Armstrong*	Stewart!	Scowcroft	**subs:** Naylor/Reuser/Brown
Martyn	Harte	Mills	Radebe	Ferdinand	Matteo	Bowyer	Dacourt*	Batty	Viduka	Keane^ — Bakke/Smith

Town seem a little jaded after two cup exits. Bowyer's low cross is diverted into his own net by Venus and Keane lashes in from close range. Venus' free-kick reduces the arrears. Both managers agree Stewart is unlucky to be sent off for a challenge on Harte, who tumbles theatrically.

26 — A 10/2 **ARSENAL** — 38,011 · Pos 6 · Pt 40 · **0-1** · L · H-T 0-0
Henry 67. Ref: R Harris

Wright R	Venus	Croft"	Clapham	Magilton	Holland	Reuser*	Stewart	Scowcroft	**subs:** Brown/Naylor
Seaman	Dixon	Cole	Adams	Stepanovs	Grimandi	Pires	Lauren*	Parlour	Bergkamp — Wiltord*, Henry/Ljungberg

Arsenal's fifth successive clean sheet and Town's fifth loss in a row. Wright is busy and makes a series of fine saves until Henry finishes off a move engineered by Wiltord and Bergkamp. Town's best opportunity sees Stewart stumble over the ball after a low cross from the right flank.

27 — H 24/2 **EVERTON** — 22,220 · Pos 5 · Pt 43 · **2-0** · W · H-T 0-0
Holland 82, Armstrong 84. Ref: G Poll

Wright R	Wilnis*	Croft"	Clapham	McGreal	Venus*	Wright J	Magilton"	Holland	Burchill	**subs:** Armst'ng/Reuser/**Abidallah**
Gerrard	Weir	Nyarko!	Ball	Jeffers*	Naysmith	Gravesen	Abel Xavier	Tal^	Campbell	Jevons/McLeod

Kachloul turns down a move from Southampton, but Mark Burchill joins on loan from Celtic. On a bright debut, his fresh legs help Town wear down Walter Smith's men. Nyarko sees red for two bookable fouls. Holland fires Burchill's cross in and Armstrong heads in from close range.

28 — H 4/3 **BRADFORD C** — 21,820 · Pos 3 · Pt 46 · **3-1** · W · H-T 0-1
Reuser 59, 72, Burchill 75 / Carbone 27. Ref: A D'Urso

Wright R	Wilnis	Bramble	Clapham	McGreal	Wright J"	Reuser	Magilton"	Holland	Burchill	**subs:** Armst'g/Clapham/Abidallah
Walsh	O'Brien	Wetherall	Molenaar	Myers	Locke*	McCall	Hopkin	Jess	Ward	Carbone — Halle

Carbone fires in a great drive after a free-kick to give Jim Jeffries' strugglers a surprise lead. After half-time Reuser curls exquisite goals past Walsh, the first after cutting in from the left, the second direct from a free-kick. Heidarsson's header from a corner is deflected in by Burchill.

29 — A 10/3 **ASTON VILLA** — 28,216 · Pos 3 · Pt 46 · **1-2** · L · H-T 1-0
Armstrong 30 / Joachim 53, 71. Ref: R Styles

Wright R	Wilnis	**Makin**	Heidars'n	McGreal	Clapham*	Wright J^	Holland	Armstrong	Scowcroft	**subs:** Magilton/Burchill
James	Southgate	Staunton	Alpay	Hendrie	Taylor	Stone	Ginola*	Merson	Dublin	Joachim — Barry

Mercurial Ginola returns after a long absence and grabs the limelight, overshadowing the likes of £1.25 million Town debutant Chris Makin. Southgate blasts the ball against Armstrong and Town go ahead and are well on top, but Joachim's classy finishes turn the game on its head.

30 — A 17/3 **WEST HAM** — 26,046 · Pos 3 · Pt 49 · **1-0** · W · H-T 0-0
Reuser 60. Ref: M Dean

Wright R	Wilnis	Makin	Heidarsson	McGreal	Clapham*	Wright J	Holland	Armstrong	Stewart^	**subs:** Clapham/Burchill
Hislop	Song	Pearce S	Schemmel*	Carrick	Cole^	Winterburn	Kanoute	Lampard	Di Canio	Todorov/Moncur

Looking solid and smooth, Town win it on the hour with Reuser's superb shot direct from a free-kick. Stuart Pearce is the only real threat from Harry Redknapp's side, but his fierce shots are twice acrobatically saved by Wright. Bright young prospect Cole is overshadowed by Magilton.

31 — A 2/4 **SOUTHAMPTON** — 15,244 · Pos 3 · Pt 52 · **3-0** · W · H-T 1-0
Stewart 32, 68, 70p. Ref: A Wiley

Wright R	Bramble	Makin	Heidarsson	McGreal	Wright J	Clapham	Holland	Reuser*	Scowcroft*	Stewart*	**subs:** Armstrong/Venus/Burchill
Jones	El Khalej	Lundekvam	Richards	Bridge	Tessem	Oakley	Marsden^	Petrescu*	Beattie	Pahars"	Dodd/Le Tissier/Rosler

Stewart ends his goal 'drought' with a super hat-trick in front of England boss Eriksson. Home fans seem more preoccupied by the recent exit of boss Hoddle to Spurs. A close-range goal is followed by a neat header after Heidarsson's fine run and the third is a coolly-chipped penalty.

No	H/A	Date	Opponent	Att			Pos	Result		HT	FT	Scorers		Referee
32	H	10/4	LIVERPOOL	23,405	5	3	D	53	1-1	0-0	Armstrong 77	Heskey 46	Ref: S Dunn
33	H	14/4	NEWCASTLE	24,028	14	3	W	56	1-0	0-0	Stewart 76p		Ref: M Dean
34	A	16/4	MIDDLESBROUGH	34,294	17	3	W	59	2-1	0-1	Armstrong 46, 60	Windass 39	Ref: S Bennett
35	H	21/4	COVENTRY	24,612	18	3	W	62	2-0	1-0	Reuser 20, Wright J 56		Ref: G Barber
36	A	30/4	CHARLTON	20,043	8	4	L	62	1-2	1-1	Reuser 20	Svensson 12, Rufus 57	Ref: R Styles
37	H	7/5	MANCHESTER C	25,004	18	4	W	65	2-1	0-0	Holland 78, Reuser 85	Goater 74	Ref: S Lodge
38	A	19/5	DERBY	33,239	17	5	D	66	1-1	0-1	Carbonari 46(og)	Christie 36	Ref: G Poll

Home Average 22,532
Away 31,626

32. LIVERPOOL (H) 10/4
Wright R, Bramble^, Makin, Heidarsson, McGreal, Wright J*, Magilton, Holland, Reuser, Armstrong, Stewart, Scowcroft/Wilnis
Westerveld, Carragher, Hyypia, Babbel, Vignal, Gerrard, Biscan^, Ziege*, Murphy, Berger, Heskey, Hamman/McAllister
The fight for a Champions League place hots up. Part of the new South Stand is opened to increase ground capacity. Heskey gets free to poke the Reds ahead, but Armstrong steals in to convert Makin's deep cross. Alan Ferguson wins the Premiership Groundsman of the Year award.

33. NEWCASTLE (H) 14/4
Wright R, Wilnis*, Makin, Heidarsson, McGreal, Wright J*, Magilton, Holland, Reuser", Armstrong, Stewart, Venus/Scowcroft/Clapham
Given, Barton, O'Brien, Hughes, Quinn, Solano !, Acuna, Lee*, Speed, Cort, Amoebi^, Gallagher/Lua Lua
Bobby Robson gets a huge ovation on his first competitive return as a manager. Unlucky Cort has a goal ruled out but later allows Heidarsson a free header which is handled on the line by Solano. The Peruvian is red-carded and Stewart clips home the spot-kick to win back third place.

34. MIDDLESBROUGH (A) 16/4
Wright R, Bramble, Makin, Heidarsson, Venus, Wright J, Magilton, Holland, Reuser*, Armstrong^, Stewart*, Clapham/Naylor/Burchill
Schwarzer, Ehiogu, Gavin, Vickers*, Gordon, Ince, Okon, Karembeu^, Boksic, Windass", Ricard, Mustoe/Stamp/Marinelli
Windass's clinical strike for Terry Venables' side knocks Town out of their stride. Fifteen seconds after the re-start, 'Boro 'reject' Armstrong drives a shot past Schwarzer. He misses other opportunities, but snatches the winner when he loses his marker and flicks home a Stewart cross.

35. COVENTRY (H) 21/4
Branaghan, Bramble, Makin, Heidarsson, McGreal, Wright J*, Magilton, Holland, Reuser*, Armstrong, Stewart", Clapham/Naylor
Kirkland, Quinn^, Shaw, Breen, Hall, Eustace, Telfer, Carsley", Bellamy, Hartson, Bothroyd" Zuniga/Elworthy/Williams
Three points will ensure top six, meaning Euro football next term. City are in form also and need the points to avoid the drop. R Wright is hurt in the warm-up so Branaghan steps in. J Wright's cross is guided in by Reuser. Slack defending allows J Wright to fire home a fine 25-yarder.

36. CHARLTON (A) 30/4
Wright R, Bramble, Makin, Heidarsson, McGreal, Wright J, Magilton, Holland, Reuser*, Armstrong, Stewart*, Burchill
Ilic, Fish, Powell, Todd, Rufus, Jensen^, Parker", Robinson, Kinsella, Bartlett, Svensson* Stuart/Lisbie/Konchesky
Robinson's cross is thundered home by the head of late stand-in Svensson. Reuser levels with a wickedly curling cross-shot, which threads its way into the net. Town look the better side and create more chances, but Rufus nips ahead of Wright to jab the winner. Reuser also hits the bar.

37. MANCHESTER C (H) 7/5
Wright R, Bramble, Makin, Heidars'n* McGreal, Wright J*, Magilton, Holland, Reuser, Armstrong, Scowcroft, Clapham/Naylor
Nash, Charvet, Dunne, Howey, Granville, Whitley, Wiekens, Grant^, Tiatto, Wanchope, Dickov* Kennedy/Goater"/Prior
Town must win to keep alive third-place hopes, while City will be relegated if they lose. A tense night bursts into life when Goater squeezes City ahead and is injured in the process. The joy is extinguished as Holland fires into the corner and Reuser dives to head in Armstrong's cross.

38. DERBY (A) 19/5
Wright R, Bramble, Makin", Heidarsson, Carbonari, Wright J*, Magilton, Holland, Reuser, Armstrong, Stewart^, Scowcroft/Naylor/Wilnis
Poom, Riggott*, Carbonari, Higginboth' Mawene, Eranio" Delap, Kinkladze, Boertien, Christie, Gudjons'n^ Jackson/Evatt/Bolder
A Champions League place is still within Town's reach, but Christie sidesteps Wright to convert a Kinkladze pass. Stewart limps off, but his replacement Naylor has a shot deflected home off Carbonari. Results elsewhere keep Town fifth, which means UEFA Cup action next season.

FA CARLING PREM (CUP-TIES) Manager: George Burley SEASON 2000-01

Worthington Cup	Att	F-A	H-T	Scorers, Times, and Referees	SQUAD NUMBERS IN USE	subs used
2:1 A MILLWALL 19/9	11 L 8,068 2:13	0:2	0:1	Ifill 37, Cahill 80 Ref: R Styles	Wright R / Croft* / Clapham / Scales / Heidarsson / McGreal / Magilton / Reuser^ / Wright J / Johnson" / Scowcroft	Wilnis/Holland/Stewart
					Warner / Lawrence / Dolan / Nethercott / Ryan / Cahill / Livermore / Kinet' / Harris / Ifill" / Braniff'	Reid/Odunsi/Tyne

Ray Harford takes temporary control of Millwall after the sacking of Keith Stevens and Alan McLeary. Town fail to deal with a free-kick and Ifill drills home a neat goal. Town have plenty of possession but lack bite. Australian Cahill seals victory by squeezing his shot past Wright.

Worthington Cup	Att	F-A	H-T	Scorers, Times, and Referees	SQUAD NUMBERS IN USE	subs used
2:2 H MILLWALL 26/9	11 W 13,008 2:8	5:0 aet	0:0	Johnson 74, 115, Bramble 87, [Holland 91, Magilton 105] Ref: A Hall (Town win 5-2 on aggregate)	Wright R / Wilnis* / Clapham / McGreal / Heidars'n" / Bramble / Magilton / Holland / Reuser / Johnson / Scowcroft"	Wright J/Naylor/**Karic**
					Warner / Lawrence / Ryan / Cahill / Nethercott / Dolan ! / Hill" / Livermore / Harris* / Reid ! / Braniff'	Dyche/Odunsi

Dolan is sent off for hauling down Reuser, but Magilton's spot-kick is saved. Then Reid is unluckily red-carded after a collision and the goals begin to flow. Johnson's power header is the launch-pad. Two extra-time injuries reduce Lions to seven men, but the ref insists one stays on!

Worthington Cup	Att	F-A	H-T	Scorers, Times, and Referees	SQUAD NUMBERS IN USE	subs used
3 A ARSENAL 1/11	5 W 26,105 2	2:1	1:1	Clapham 2, Scowcroft 89, Stepanovs 45, Ref: J Winter	Wright R / Wilnis / Clapham / McGreal / Heidarsson / Bramble / Holland / Stewart* / Johnson / Wright J / Scowcroft^	Reuser"/**Karic**
					Taylor / Vivas / Upson / Stepanovs / Weston" / Cole / Volz^ / Vernazza / Pennant* / Barrett / Witord	Mendez/Wreh/Canoville

Gunners boss Arsene Wenger shows his priorities by naming a much-weakened side. Clapham catches them cold as he fires home from a tight angle. Latvian debutant Stepanovs heads the leveller. Scowcroft wins it with some neat finishing after Upson blocks Johnson at the near post.

Worthington Cup	Att	F-A	H-T	Scorers, Times, and Referees	SQUAD NUMBERS IN USE	subs used
4 H COVENTRY 28/11	3 W 19,563 17	2:1	1:0	Bramble 6, Johnson 65, Bellamy 53p, Ref: P Durkin	Branagan / Wilnis / Clapham / Bramble / Heidarsson / Scales / Holland* / Reuser^ / Johnson / Scowcroft / Wright J	Croft/Stewart
					Kirkland / Quinn / Breen / Konjic / Williams / Thompson / Telfer / Eustace / Bellamy / Aloisi / Chippo*	Hadji

Bramble catches Chippo in possession and fires past Kirkland. City level out of the blue when Chippo races on to Kirkland's huge kick and is brought down by Wilnis, for Bellamy to convert the spot-kick. Stewart's volleyed pass sees Johnson race through to fire a shot under Kirkland.

Worthington Cup	Att	F-A	H-T	Scorers, Times, and Referees	SQUAD NUMBERS IN USE	subs used
QF A MANCHESTER C 19/12	3 W 31,252 18	2:1	0:1	Holland 60, Venus 109, Goater 10, Ref: G Poll (After extra time)	Wright R / Wilnis / Clapham / McGreal / Heidars'n" / Venus / Holland / Magilton / Reuser^ / Scowcroft" / Johnson^	Croft / Wright J/Reuser/Bramble
					Weaver / Haaland / Tiatto" / Morrison" / Prior / Wr't-Phillips / Whitley / Wiekens / Horlock^ / Wanchope / Goater	Kennedy/Granville/Bishop

A waterlogged pitch saw the first attempt abandoned after 20 minutes at 1-1. City take the lead as Goater fires in from 15 yards. Holland levels after a Weaver fumble. In extra-time Venus surges forward and finishes expertly when clean through. Bramble clears off the line at the death.

Worthington Cup	Att	F-A	H-T	Scorers, Times, and Referees	SQUAD NUMBERS IN USE	subs used
SF 1 H BIRMINGHAM 9/1	4 W 21,684 1:7	1:0	1:0	Stewart 45p, Ref: C Wilkes	Wright R / Wilnis / Clapham* / Bramble / Heidarsson / Venus / Holland / Magilton / Stewart / Wright J / Reuser	Reuser
					Bennett / Jenkins / Purse / Johnson M / Grainger / Eaden* / Sonner / O'Connor / Hughes / Adebola" / Ndlovu^	Marcelo/Lazaridis/Horsfield

On his 29th birthday, ex-Town man Sonner is jeered throughout and suffers a highly debatable penalty decision when Magilton's fierce cross hits him. Stewart converts the kick and also misses a good chance, screwing Wilnis' cross wide. Hreidarsson hits a post from Venus' free-kick.

Worthington Cup	Att	F-A	H-T	Scorers, Times, and Referees	SQUAD NUMBERS IN USE	subs used
SF 2 A BIRMINGHAM 31/1	5 L 28,624 1:5	1:4 aet	0:1	Scowcroft 57 [Johnson 117], Grainger 43, Horsfield 56, 103, Ref: J Winter (Town lose 2-4 on aggregate)	Wright R / Croft^ / Clapham / Venus / Heidarsson / Clapham / Wright J / Holland / Magilton* / Stewart / Naylor*	Scowcroft/Reuser/**Karic**
					Bennett / Gill / Purse / Johnson M / Grainger / Eaden^ / O'Connor / Sonner / Lazaridis^ / Horsfield / Adebola^	John'n A/Hughes/Burrows

Town look unhappy on a dreadful pitch against muscular opponents. Sub Scowcroft pulls them level on aggregate from Clapham's cross, but City reach their first major final in 38 years as Horsfield gets through to net, and A.Johnson then makes the most of a freak bounce in the mud.

FA Cup

FA Cup	Att	F-A	H-T	Scorers, Times, and Referees	SQUAD NUMBERS IN USE	subs used
3 A MORECAMBE 6/1	4 W 5,923 NL	3:0	1:0	Stewart 14, Armst'g 65, Wright J 75, Ref: U Rennie	Wright R / Wilnis / Croft / Bramble / Heidarsson / Wright J / Holland / Reuser^ / Scowcroft* / Stewart / Armstrong	Magilton/Clapham/Logan
					Smith / Fensome / Lyons" / McKearney / Hardiker / Walters / Thompson / Drummond / Quayle* / Norman / Black^	Rigoglioso/Eastw'd/McGuire

As expected, the Conference part-timers put up a great fight, but Stewart's neat and confident finish sets Town on their way. The odd anxious moment is survived before Wilnis' cross is headed firmly in by Armstrong. Jim Harvey's Shrimps are finished off by Wright's clever volley.

FA Cup	Att	F-A	H-T	Scorers, Times, and Referees	SQUAD NUMBERS IN USE	subs used
4 A SUNDERLAND 27/1	5 L 33,626 2	0:1	0:1	Dichio 23, Ref: S Bennett	Wright R / Wilnis / McGreal / Bramble^ / Heidarsson / Venus* / Holland / Magilton / Stewart / Armstrong" / Wright J	Clapham/Naylor/Scowcroft
					Sorensen / Gray^ / Williams / Craddock / Vaga / Hutchison / McCann / Rae / Schwarz / Phillips* / Dichio	Kilbane/Makin

After seven successive scoring games, Stewart fails to equal the 40-year-old club record. Hutchison's first-time cross goes over Bramble and Dichio stoops to head home. Town miss several chances before the break, but Peter Reid's men rarely look in danger later and Town bow out.

League Table

		P	W	D	L	F	A	W	D	L	F	A	Pts
			Home					**Away**					
1	Manchester U	38	15	2	2	49	12	9	6	4	30	19	80
2	Arsenal	38	15	3	1	45	13	5	7	7	18	25	70
3	Liverpool	38	13	4	2	40	14	7	5	7	31	25	69
4	Leeds	38	11	3	5	36	21	9	5	5	28	22	68
5	IPSWICH	38	11	5	3	31	15	9	1	9	26	27	66
6	Chelsea	38	13	3	3	44	20	4	7	8	24	25	61
7	Sunderland	38	9	7	3	24	16	6	5	8	22	25	57
8	Aston Villa	38	8	8	3	27	20	5	7	7	19	23	54
9	Charlton	38	11	5	3	31	19	5	5	11	19	38	52
10	Southampton	38	11	2	6	27	22	3	8	8	13	26	52
11	Newcastle	38	10	4	5	26	17	4	5	10	18	33	51
12	Tottenham	38	11	6	2	31	16	2	4	13	16	38	49
13	Leicester	38	10	4	5	28	23	4	2	13	11	28	48
14	Middlesbro	38	4	7	8	18	23	5	8	6	26	21	42
15	West Ham	38	6	6	7	24	20	4	6	9	21	30	42
16	Everton	38	6	8	5	29	27	5	1	13	16	32	42
17	Derby	38	8	7	4	23	24	2	5	12	14	35	42
18	Manchester C	38	4	3	12	20	31	4	7	8	21	34	34
19	Coventry	38	4	7	8	14	23	4	3	12	22	40	34
20	Bradford C	38	4	7	8	20	29	1	4	14	10	41	26
		760	184	101	95	587	405	95	101	184	405	587	1039

Odds & ends

Double wins: (6) Manchester C, Everton, Bradford C, Coventry, Southampton, Middlesbrough.

Double losses: (1) Aston Villa.

Won from behind: (6) Leeds (a), South'pton (h), Bradford C, C (h), Middlesbro (a), Man C (h & a, WC).

Lost from in front: (5) Tottenham (a), Newcastle (a), Sunderland (a), Chelsea (a), Aston Villa (a).

High spots: Confounding (nearly) everyone by finishing 5th. Qualifying for Europen football for the first time since 1982. George Burley winning the Carling and LMA Manager of the Year awards. Magnificent victories away to Leeds and Liverpool. Marcus Stewart's clinical finishing. Early collapse of a 'relegation countdown' feature in a Norwich newspaper! Burley's successful excursions into the transfer market.

Low spots: Five successive defeats in January-February. Losing matches after leading in five away games. Luc Nilis' dreadful injury during the Aston Villa home game. The Worthington Cup semi-final defeat at Birmingham.

Player of the Year: Marcus Stewart.

Ever-presents: (1) Matt Holland.

Hat-tricks: (1) Marcus Stewart (v Southampton).

Opposing hat-tricks: (0).

Leading scorer: (21) Marcus Stewart.

Appearances & Goals

	Appearances						Goals			
	Lge	Sub	LC	Sub	FAC	Sub	Lge	LC	FAC	Tot
Abidallah, Nabil		2								
Armstrong, Alun	15	6			2		7	1		9
Bramble, Titus	23	3	4	1	2		1	2		3
Branagan, Keith	2		1							
Brown, Wayne		4								
Burchill, Mark	2	5					1			1
Clapham, Jamie	28		7		7	2	2	1		3
Croft, Gary	6	2	3	1	1					
Holland, Matt	38		6	1	2		3			5
Heidarsson, Hermann	35	1	7		2		1			1
Johnson, David	6	8	4					3		3
Karic, Amir				3						
Makin, Chris	10									
Magilton, Jim	32	1	6		1	1	1	1		2
McGreal, John	25	3	5		1	1	1			1
Naylor, Richard	5	8	2	1		1	1			2
Reuser, Martijn	13	13	3	4		1	6			6
Scales, John	2	2								
Scowcroft, James	22	12	5	2	1	1	4	2		6
Stewart, Marcus	33	1	3	2	2		19	1	1	21
Venus, Mark	23	2	3		2		3	1		4
Wilnis, Fabian	27	2	5	1	2		2			2
Wright, Jermaine	35	2	5	2	2		2		1	2
Wright, Richard	36		6		2					
(own-goals)							3			2
24 players used	418	82	77	18	22	6	57	13	3	73

LIST OF SUBSCRIBERS

VOTES FOR THE MOST POPULAR IPSWICH PLAYER 1971-2001

Subscriber	Vote
Michael Allen	Kevin Beattie
Chris Austin	Kevin Beattie
Mark Avery	Kevin Beattie
Peter Baker	Alan Brazil
Paul Barker	Mauricio Taricco
Veronica & Michael Barley	John Wark
D R Barnard	Kevin Beattie
Gerry Barrack	Kevin Beattie
Mary E Barton	Arnold Muhren
Jonathan A Beatton	Paul Mariner
Brian Stephen Bell	Mick Mills
Alan Benedick	Colin Viljoen
Mark Bergdahl	John Wark
Roy Bergdahl	Mick Mills
Alex Berry	Alex Mathie
Pat Boon	Ray Crawford
John Booth	Arnold Muhren
Nicholas Braley	Arnold Muhren
Ben Brown	Eric Gates
D Bulmer	George Burley
David Burgess	John Wark
Barrie Catchpole	Arnold Muhren
Duncan Catchpole	John Wark
Reginald Catchpole	Kevin Beattie
Roger Catchpole	Kevin Beattie
Ron Cheek	Kevin Beattie
John Chubb	John Wark
R P Clements	Frans Thijssen
G Cocksedge	Paul Mariner
Graham Cole	Kevin Beattie
Stephen Cook	Kevin Beattie
Neville Cooper	Marcus Stewart
Ray Cooper	Terry Butcher
Wayne Corder	Dalian Atkinson
John Cresswell	Ray Crawford
Dorothy E Cross	Mick Mills
Steve Cross	John Wark
Andy Dalziel	Arnold Muhren
Guy Dawson	Roy Bailey
Chris Deal	Kevin Beattie
Barry W Dines & Sons	Arnold Muhren
Stephen Doe	John Wark
Elizabeth Edwards	Kevin Beattie
Mr E Fairweather	Kevin Beattie
Martin Farrell	Matt Holland
Mark Farrow	Kevin Beattie
Jane Fayers	John Wark
Alec Fayers	Mick Mills
Keith Ferry	John Wark
Lee Forsdyke	Terry Butcher
Joanna Foster	Paul Mariner
Shaun Friend	'The team that took us back up'
Michael Grimes	Kevin Beattie
David Groom	John Wark
Christopher Hadgraft	Matt Holland
L C Hadgraft	Matt Holland
Miss Carole Hale	John Wark
Denise Hammond	Terry Butcher
Colin Handley	Paul Mariner
Gary Hannam	Mick Mills
Arild Sorknes Hansen	John Wark
Jens Walter Hansen	Terry Butcher
Jill and John Hardy	Kevin Beattie
Paul Hart	Kevin Beattie
Valerie Hartley	Titus Bramble
Karl Harvey	Martijn Reuser
Carl Hastings	Allan Hunter
Paul Hedger	Paul Mariner
Lars Johan Heindal	Kevin Beattie
Gerald C Hogg	Ray Crawford
John S Hogg	Ray Crawford
Dr David Iain Holmes	Ray Crawford
Adrian Hubbard	Paul Mariner
Kevin Huckfield	Paul Mariner

VOTES FOR THE MOST POPULAR IPSWICH PLAYER 1971-2001

LIST OF SUBSCRIBERS

Subscriber	Vote
Steve Hunter	Allan Hunter
Mark Gordon Jackson	Kevin Beattie
Mark Jarman	Kevin Beattie
David E Johnson	Ray Crawford
Trevor Johnson	Kevin Beattie
Andrew Kaye	Paul Mariner
Matt Keates	Clive Woods
Paul Keeble	Roger Osborne
John Kelly	Arnold Muhren
P Kent	Kevin Beattie
John Kolodziej	Kevin Beattie
John Ledger	Kevin Beattie
Jane E & Chris T Lyford	John Wark
Ian and Averil Lockwood	Arnold Muhren
Carl and Alison Mann	Kevin Beattie
Julian and Lucy Mann	Mauricio Taricco
Andrew McNabb	John Wark
Afroze Miah	Arnold Muhren
Brian Mills	Matt Holland
Ralph Morris	Arnold Muhren
David Hilary Mountcastle	Kevin Beattie
Nigel Richard Nunn	Kevin Beattie
Michael Oakley	Kevin Beattie
Carl Parrish	Eric Gates
Stephen Peck	Marcus Stewart

Subscriber	Vote
Robert Porter	Arnold Muhren
Miss Teresa Elaine Pyke	Matt Holland
Wayne Rice	John Wark
Laurie J Ritchie	Kevin Beattie
Paul David Rose	Kevin Beattie
Alasdair Ross	Laurie Sivell
Wilf Ruffles	Paul Mariner
Mr. R Sarda	Terry Butcher
Keith A Savage	Kevin Beattie
Desmond Say	Kevin Beattie
Peter Shawler	John Wark
Richard Sinnett	
Oriel Simpson	Matt Holland
Peter Simpson	Alan Brazil
Andrew Skinner	Martijn Reuser
A V Skinner M B E	John Wark
Jamie Smith	John Wark
Steve Sopp	Kevin Beattie
Malcolm Stafford & Daughters	Arnold Muhren
Richard Stocken	
Andreas Sunde	Martijn Reuser
Martin Talbot	Frans Thijssen
Ian Taylor	John Wark
James Peter Taylor	Matt Holland
Rebecca Clare Taylor	Matt Holland

Subscriber	Vote
Jane Tew	Russell Osman
Owen Thomas	Marcus Stewart
Adrian Topple	John Wark
Richard Townsend	Paul Mariner
Eric A Tyler	Kevin Beattie
Ben Vulliamy	Kieron Dyer
Daniel Vulliamy	Danny Hegan
Russell Walker	Kevin Beattie
Chris Walne (Felixstowe)	Allan Hunter
Fred Warner	Kevin Beattie
Andrew Warren	John Wark
Brian E Whatling	Arnold Muhren
Terry Robert White	Paul Mariner
Richard Woodhouse	Mick Mills

Most popular Ipswich player 1971-2001
(27 different players received votes)

1st	Kevin Beattie
2nd	John Wark
3rd	Arnold Muhren
4th	Paul Mariner
5th	Matt Holland

George Burley, the man who guided Ipswich Town back to the Premiership

Happy days